ISBN 978-0-428-76867-6
PIBN 11306596

# White Pine
# Red Pine
# Jack Pine
# Spruce
# Lumber
# and Lath

**UNION LUMBER COMPANY LIMITED**
701 DOMINION BANK BUILDING
TORONTO            CANADA

# *Awake Ye!*

### for the

### Darkness

### of

### 1921

### Fades

### and

### A New Day

### of

### Hope and Promise

### Dawns.

# BUY
# BRITISH COLUMBIA
# Red Cedar Shingles

The life of a British Columbia Red Cedar Shingle Roof can almost be gauged by the life of the nail with which the shingle is nailed in place. Judging from available data, the average life of the ordinary steel wire nail, which has been in such common use, is only from seven to twelve years. Some wire nails will last longer, depending upon the condition of exposure, climate and similar features, but considering our climate as a whole, at the end of from seven to twelve years a large percentage of wire nails will have rusted either completely through or so extensively that the first strong wind will complete the work. The shingles that have been held in position by such nails are then free to work down, permitting rains or melting snows to leak through and damage the interior of the structure. Examination will disclose that the fibre of the shingle itself is still in perfect condition, and a leaky roof, in the majority of occasions is due entirely to the use of faulty nails, but the average home owner, placed at such inconvenience, will not stop to reason this out and the poor wooden shingle comes in for more unjust abuse.

There are several kinds of nails which experience has proven will give lasting satisfaction, and the wise dealer will advise his customers of these satisfactory nails. A pure zinc shingle nail meets all the demands of durability required. Its principal drawback is its high cost and a slight tendency to bend under careless driving. Galvanized wire nails theoretically are rust proof, and if the galvanized coating is properly applied, and of sufficient thickness, such a nail will last as long as the shingle it holds in place. The life of this shingle roof, properly applied with these nails then is from 40 to 50 years. Pure iron nails, or the old cut or wrought nails are ideal but difficult to secure. Copper nails also constitute a perfect shingle nail.

## Better Times Ahead!

L ET us forget the past and set our faces to the future, instilled with the renewed confidence the New Year brings.

Better times are ahead. A little while and we shall be out of the mist and onto the calmer waters of more healthy, normal business.

Then it will be those who saw and prepared who will benefit most.

In this respect we believe we can be of valuable service. Our stocks are large and varied, and our prices are right.

Just let us show you what we can do to help you get your share of the 1922 business.

### G. A. GRIER & SONS LIMITED

Montreal           Toronto
1112 Notre Dame St., W.      22 Royal Bank Chambers, 454 King St. W.

*We have no connection with or interest in any
other firm bearing a name similar to ours.*

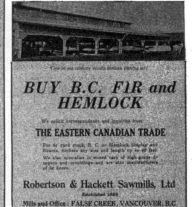

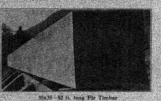

# Inter Insurance

in the past 15 years has been the means of reducing other Fire Insurance rates about 50% and all the propaganda of competitors has only served to remind lumbermen of its great value.

*Licensed in Canada and legal everywhere.*

# Manufacturing Wood Workers Underwriters

LEE BLAKEMORE, INC., (Atty. in Fact)

## CHICAGO, ILL.

**/ounded 1880**

*The National Lumber Journal for Forty Years*

Issued on the 1st and 15th of every month by

**HUGH C. MACLEAN PUBLICATIONS, Limited**

THOS. S. YOUNG, Managing Director

HEAD OFFICE - - - - 347 Adelaide Street, West, TORONTO
Proprietors and Publishers also of Electrical News, Contract Record,
Canadian Woodworker and Footwear in Canada.

| | |
|---|---|
| VANCOUVER - - - - - - - | Winch Building |
| MONTREAL - - - - - | 119 Board of Trade Bldg. |
| WINNIPEG - - - - - | Electric Railway Chambers |
| NEW YORK - - - - - | 296 Broadway |
| CHICAGO - - - - | Room 803, 63 E. Adams St. |
| LONDON, ENG. - - - - | 16 Regent Street, S.W. |

TERMS OF SUBSCRIPTION

Canada, United States and Great Britain, $3.00 per year, in advance; other
foreign countries embraced in the General Postal Union, $4.00.
Single copies, 30 cents.

Authorized by the Postmaster-General for Canada, for transmission as
second-class matter.

Vol. 42                           Toronto, January 1, 1922                           No. 1

## What Will This Year Bring Forth?

With the advent of the New Year the attention of the average lumberman naturally turns to what will take place during the coming twelve months. There are various views expressed regarding the outlook, but few would attempt to make any definite forecast.

The questions asked are—is 1922 to be an export year? Are prices likely to go higher? Will there be a shortage of stock if a normal demand sets in? What will be the proportionate cut this season as compared with last? Will industrial activity be resumed? Is the process of deflation and liquidation at an end, etc.? If one could answer these, there would be little necessity of taking thought of the morrow. It is much easier, however, to propound questions than to answer them satisfactorily. Of course, the speculative is always interesting. We know what has taken place ,but regarding what may come to pass, is an altogether different proposition.

The whole situation regarding the hardwood and softwood fields was ably outlined recently in practical addresses delivered before the Wholesale Lumber Dealers' Association in Toronto. Mr. A. E. Clark made two or three important points when he said that the trade must have better prices, but he also felt that the situation was such that betterment in price was fraught with danger because of the apparently close at hand shortage in the hardwood industry, which might possibly lead to a runaway market similar to that of 1919-20.

In reviewing the softwood situation, Mr. A. C. Manbert declared that a change was here and ventured the assertion that no man could produce lumber to-day and sell it at present prices. He declared that now is the time to have a little courage to marshall all the facts that we know, and to develop new ideas of value, he added that they could be developed by the gradual affirmations of men like lumbermen based upon their experience.

Regarding the market situation, there is a wide difference of opinion, and financiers, statisticians, business experts and merchandising authorities do not by any means agree. They all believe that there will be good business for many lines this year. Just what lines will reap the benefit and how soon the improvement will come, they cannot say. Others declare that the corner has not yet been turned and that the turn will take place in 1922. No hard and fast answer can be given to the question, how the lumber business or any other business will be during this year. Much will depend on the business itself. The theory has also been laid down that the industry that was the first to be hit will be the first to recover and the one that was the last to be hit will be the last to recover.

Speaking before a recent gathering in Montreal, Mr. Roger W. Babson, head of the Babson Statistical Organization, declared that the wholesaler and the manufacturer were the first to be struck and would be the first to come back. They had taken their losses they had left on their books properly and would have a fairly good year in 1922. Unfortunately the retailer was not hit as early, and many would have something to learn before good business returns to them.

In wholesale lines 25 per cent. of goods were back to pre-war prices and another 25 per cent. within 20 per cent. of the pre-war price. When it came to the retailer, this did not hold true.

Referring particularly to the lumber business, there has been a disposition in some quarters, during the past year, to blame the manufacturer for comparative inactivity in trade. The manufacturer in turn has passed the censure on to the wholesaler and the wholesaler has intimated that it was the retailer, who was still hanging out for long values. The retailers blamed labor and labor blamed contractors and contractors blamed the loan societies and the people with money to invest. Thus the "vicious circle" went its rounds with nobody willing to assume full responsibility and everyone trying to lay the cause for stagnation at the door of the other fellow, who was only too willing to carry it a block and deposit it at the porchway or entrance of those farther down the street.

Summing up the whole situation, it may be said that so far as the correspondents of the "Canada Lumberman" in Halifax, Quebec. Montreal and Vancouver, can descry the future, 1922 should be a pretty fair year for export. The pound Sterling is becoming stabilized, ocean freight rates are likely to be reduced to a further point, the situation abroad is clearing up, labor troubles are disappearing, and while no records may be broken, exports are likely to be much heavier both east and west than they were during the past year.

In regard to domestic demand and requisitions from the United States, it is as yet too early to speak. There is a radical alteration in the attitude and approach of the buyer. A feeling of optimism is prevalent, and while there has been a few ups and downs and flurries and set-backs, the trend of opinion is in the right direction. It is believed that the domestic demand will develop steadily within the next few months.

Stocks of lumber in the retail yards are known to be light. Factories that use wood have also permitted their reserve supplies to decline to a low level. Wholesalers have not been buying ahead of requirements, at least, not until within the last few months. These facts, coupled with a shortage of stocks in certain lines of wood, particulary in the higher grades, may create a condition which has in it all the elements making for a rapid advance in prices when buying becomes anything like normal.

Producers would prefer not to see another runaway market; in fact no one desires it, and they are advising buyers to get into the game now so that they may govern their manufacturing operations before the real requirements for consumption arrive. Unless this is done, and if a revival of buying comes in with a rush, it will be almost impossible to control prices within normal and reasonable mounds.

There is no regulating of prices in the lumber arena outside of the old economic condition of supply and demand. The business is individualistic in character and wide open so far as competition is concerned: Each operator has to play a lone hand. There is no large consolidation of interests. At recent trade meetings, pleas have been put forth for a greater measure of co-operation and mutual confidence. It is declared that the manufacturer, wholesaler and retailer should have a better understanding of one another's problems and interests to establish harmonious relations that will be a benefit to all. No one branch of the industry is greater than the united whole, and no one branch can successfully function separate and apart from the others. Working together on a common basis, with the interest of the industry alone at stake, better results can be obtained with less friction and, at the same time, the consumer can be better and more economically served.

W. S. Dickason, Kansas City, Mo., ably summed up the situation in a stirring address before the National Retail Lumber Dealers' Association in Chicago, when he said,—"What we ask the manufacturers is only what we are willing to grant them, that is, that we be given the opportunity to present our side of the question when they propose any changes that may effect our business and our interests be given the protection they are entitled to." Speaking of the recent market situation he said,—"About a year ago there was a lot of unjust criticism of retail prices by some manufacturers and some threatened to publish manufacturers' prices in an endeavor to show that the retail dealer was blocking progress and a revival of building. The retail dealer had nothing to fear, but the criticism was hasty and without a semblance of justification, for inquiry developed the fact that not only had retail prices of lumber declined faster than the prices of any other staple commodity, but they had declined in ratio to reductions made by manufacturers.

"The retail dealer bore the burden of this decline and I will make the statement that the manufacturer did not lose one dollar of money actually invested in stock at that time, manufactured from the stump to the car. His stocks were sold for more than the cost of production or replacement for months after we started down the toboggan. His loss was failure to realize on the profits he had anticipated but the retail dealer's loss was actual and immediate. In a short time his

stock could be replaced for 50 per cent. of what he paid for it in good hard dollars. He sold much of it for 50 per cent. of what it cost and had to bear the cost of handling besides; and still lumber was rolling in to his yard bought at peak prices. The manufacturers manifested a great deal more distress about the decline than did the retail dealer who took his medicine as he paid the advances. At a time when prices of all commodities are being criticised justly and unjustly, it is right and natural that the manufacturer should be interested in having his product delivered to the consumer at the lowest price possible, but he has no right to ask the distributor to do more than his share that he may avert criticism.

The retail dealer is not responsible for the wide fluctuations in the market; it is the law of supply and demand that is responsible for high prices. The same law is responsible for low prices and it is unjust to attempt to place the responsibility on the retail dealer. Let no one attempt to shirk his responsibility nor place the burden of his acts upon another's shoulders. All we ask is a square deal—this we demand, nothing more or less.

I could cite many other instances, but these are sufficient. What is the answer? Recognition by each that our interests are mutual and one can not succeed without the other; that our responsibility is to the public and the public looks to us for a square deal; co-operation that begets confidence in one another; respect for one another; thoughtful consideration of one another's interests; regard for contract and a spirit of fairness for all.

## Permanency Needed in Forestry Policies

It is significant that the subject of a permanent and practical forestry will be the principal subject of discussion at the annual meeting of the Woodlands section of the Pulp and Paper Association to be held in Montreal in January, and that the question has been before other associated interests in the co-operation of our natural resources.

The idea is that this policy should be adopted by the Provincial Governments of Quebec, Ontario, and the Maritime Provinces. Through its Forestry Department the Federal Government is carrying out definite work in the West in the forest reserves and on the prairies. The great burden of such a policy as suggested would fall upon the Provincial Governments in the East, as they control the Crown lands within their boundaries, and as the bulk of the forest wealth is situated there. A beginning has been made in some directions, notably in the Province of Quebec, but is desired that the work should be extended and co-ordinated.

A policy of the nature indicated would no doubt include additional facilities for training forest engineers and a survey of forest resources, concerning which our knowledge is admittedly inadequate. Estimates have been made of the extent of Canadian forests, but they are far from complete. Such information would not only be of value to the lumber trade as showing how we stand in the matter of forest wealth, but would be useful as a basis for reforestation work by the various provinces.

Mr. Edward Beck, in his pamphlet on methods and conditions in Europe, points out that the forest regulations in Scandinavia are enforced through the medium of the provinces, and that the private owners and the state co-operate in perpetuating the forests and in obtaining a maximum annual yield of production. Conditions in Canada, of course, differ in many respects from those in Scandinavia, but it should not be beyond the wit of man to devise a plan by which the provinces, the private owners, and the licencees of Crown lands could co-operate in makers of reforestation and regulations designed to increase the yield of forest lands.

A permanent policy on these lines will involve a much larger expenditure than is now called for, and this would probably be the most formidable objection to be overcome. There are those who do not believe in spending large amounts on what they characterize as forestry fads—men who hold the view that Nature will do all that is necessary in the way of reforestation, and that therefore the authorities will be wasting money by entering upon an extensive programme of replanting. It will also take a lot of hard talking to persuade provincial treasurers to give-up a considerable portion of the revenue now derived from Crown lands.

## The Cutting of Christmas Trees Defended

For many years it has been the custom to have a Christmas tree in Canadian homes. For this purpose young growths of spruce and balsam have served as the pedestals for decorative purposes.

It has often been asked, are Canadians wantonly destroying their forests by making use of the ever-popular Christmas tree? Dr. Howe, Dean of the Faculty of Forestry at Toronto University, says no, and

on this point recently gave an opinion of interest in which he said, "there is a general misconception on this point. Forestry is a business, and the forester must look for profits for himself or his employer. If he can get from ten to twenty cents for fir trees ten feet high he is doing a good and legitimate business.

"This year more balsam than spruce is sold for Christmas trees," he continued. "Spruce is going out of the market, and that means that balsam is easier to get. There may be 2,000 young balsams ten feet high to an acre in the natural forest. When those trees are ready for pulpwood there will be not more than a hundred left. All the rest have been killed in the struggle for existence.

"If these trees, that are going to die anyway, can be sold at a profit, that is a good business to know, and he does know, what trees will be in the race at the end.

"A large number of these Christmas trees come from pastures where they are weeds. Therefore it is a great boon to the farmer to get paid for clearing these trees from his land.

"Although an enormous number of young trees are used at Christmas time their use for this purpose will never seriously interfere with the pulpwood and timber supplies.

"I like to emphasize with all my strength that the object of a forester is not to protect trees from being cut. There would be no foresters employed in this country or in any other country if there were no lumbering operations. It is the forester's business to produce wood, and if he can make money in cutting and selling trees three inches in diameter he is doing perfectly legitimate business.

"The guiding principle in forestry is to see that wood production is continuous for all time; to see that areas that have been cut over shall come up again to commercial trees; that areas that have been burned over shall be regenerated with commercial trees; and that waste lands and areas unfit for agriculture shall be made to bear commercial trees."

---

### Getting Fun Out of Your Business

The happiest man in the world is the one who is doing what he's always wanted to do and making it pay.

There are all sorts of reasons for carrying on a business, but the best reason is, because you like it.

Fun is a good deal a matter of habit, and of point of view.

And if you get into the way of finding your joy in life in the game of business you will discover as much joy there as you would if you gave yourself up entirely to golf.

It is as interesting to make tack hammers and sell overalls as it is to play pinochle or polo, if you look at it that way.

The fact is, Business is Self-expression.

And that is all any kind of fun is, from leap frog to baseball.

A child is happy when he stretches his legs, expands his lungs and sharpens his wits playing hide and seek. And a merchant is happy when he plays the great game of buying and selling, because it interests him, while hide and seek does not.

For in all business is a dash of adventure. We have to take chances. There are no sure things, outside of the pages of stock-jobbing literature and Monte Carlo.

Every deal is an adventure. Business men are always standing in the doubtful ridges of the battle.

Which makes it as interesting as poker.

And, take it by and large, it's a fair game, and, played honestly, both sides stand to win.

Business is the most wholesome occupation in which a healthy man can engage, and has in it more resources of enjoyment.

Because the business man is the Servant of the people.

He is not merely feathering his own nest, he is not grafting, but he is doing something for the people they want done.

And the man who best Serves is the man who has the best excuse for living.

As a rule, business men are the soundest-minded, least egotistic, least given to bunk and humbug, and altogether the most wholesome and cheerful kind of folks I have ever met, and I have mixed around some with kings, nobles, artists, poets and priests.

If there is going to be any jury on the Day of Judgment, I hope it will be made up of men who worked hard all their lives. Such a jury would come nearer handing out even justice than any other sort of jury.—Dr. Frank Crane.

# Everything Set and Ready For Big Gathering

## Fourteenth Annual Convention of Canadian Lumbermen's Association to be Held in Toronto January 11 and 12.  Will be Most Representative and Important Ever Held

Preparations are now practically complete for the fourteenth annual meeting of the Canadian Lumbermen's Association which will be held at the King Edward Hotel, Toronto, on Wednesday and Thursday January 11th and 12th.  Before another edition of the "Canada Lumberman" reaches its readers, the convention will have passed into history, and every indication points to the forthcoming sederunt of the great national body being the biggest in attendance and entertaining in features of any that has ever taken place in the record of this institution.

In previous issues the "Canada Lumberman" has drawn attention to the inception and upbuild of this aggressive aggregation of lumbermen, and the officers who have guided its destinies.  At first, progress was slow and of an uphill character, but of late years the growth has been steady and most encouraging.

The retiring directors this year are: W. E. Bigwood, Toronto; Gordon C. Edwards, Ottawa; A. E. Clark, Toronto; W. M. Ross, Ottawa; W. Gerard Power, Quebec; Alex. MacLaurin, Montreal and Angus McLean, Bathurst.  All of these are eligible for re-election.

It is understood that steps will be taken at the forthcoming gathering to make possible the election of a director from the United States, as the membership of the Canadian Lumbermen's Association is international in character.  Quite a large number of firms, who do business in Canada or have branch offices or mills in the Dominion, are members of the C.L.A.  The election of an American director might be termed, as Premier Drury of Ontario, would say, "a broadening-out process."

### Local Committees are Hard at it

The local committees in Toronto, who have been working diligently for the success of the gathering, have been headed by A. E. Clark, vice-president of the Canadian Lumbermen's Association, who has been busy in season and out of season getting everything in shape.  Those associated with him for the reception and entertainment of the visitors are, W. E. Bigwood, A. E. Eckardt, Duncan McLaren, W. C. Laidlaw and G. E. Spragge.

The various sub-committees are as follows:

Ladies' Committee—Mrs. A. E. Clark, Mrs. W. E. Bigwood, Mrs. A. C. Manbert, Mrs. A. E. Eckardt, Mrs. G. E. Spragge, Mrs. W. J. Lovering, Mrs. D. C. Johnstone and Mrs. W. B. Maclean.

Finance—A. C. Manbert (Chairman), W. F. Oliver, A. K. Johnston, C. G. Anderson.

Reception Committee—W. E. Bigwood (Chairman), H. J. Terry, Alex. Gordon, W. C. Gall, W. J. Lovering.

Theatre Committee—A. E. Eckardt (Chairman), A. N. Dudley, C. A. Wesley, Maurice Welsh.

Committee on Supper-Dance—D. McLaren, D. C. Johnston, Frank H. Harris, and also the members of the Ladies' Committee.

Committee on Motors and Motor Tours—W. C. Laidlaw (Chairman), Frank A. Kent, J. B. Jarvis, Alex. Read, J. A. McBean.

Luncheon Committee—G. E. Spragge (Chairman), L. D. Barclay, K. M. Brown, F. H. Horning, W. B. MacLean.

Publicity Committee—A. E. Clark (Chairman), E. C. Parsons, H J. McDermid, G. B. VanBlaricom.

As a recent announcement of Secretary Frank Hawkins, of Ottawa, states the business features will surpass in importance, interest and value those of any previous convention, while the visiting delegates will be properly entertained when not at work.  The hotel management have promised that nothing shall be lacking that will make for the comfort and convenience of the guests.  All visitors are invited to bring their ladies as ample provision is being made for their entertainment.

### The Luncheon and Annual Banquet

At the luncheon, which will be held at noon on Thursday January 12th, at the King Edward Hotel, A. R. Whittemore, of Toronto, manager of McLean's Building Reports, will give a short, snappy address on the building and construction situation of the past year, and outline what is looming up during 1922.  Mr. Whittemore is a forceful speaker, who will make his facts stand out, and he will have something to say relating to structural operations which are so closely allied with the prosperity and expansion of the lumber trade.

The annual banquet of the association will be held in the evening of the second day, Thursday January 12th.  An effort is being made to have Hon. W. L. Mackenzie King, the new Premier of Canada, speak, if his many engagements will permit, but in case he is not able to be present, some representative of the new cabinet will be on hand to deliver the chief address of the evening.

There is not a great deal more to be said except that it is confidently expected there will be a large representation from the west, and particularly British Columbia.  The lumbermen of the east are desirous of meeting more of those from the Pacific coast, and as several national problems are to be taken up, a co-ordination of interests is desirable in connection with such vital questions as freight rates, anti-shingle legislation and other live issues.  Unity and solidity are particularly desirable, so that when the lumbermen go before the Railway Commission of Canada, or the federal parliament, they will present a strong front and have the support of the industry in every part of Canada, on any issue that may arise.

J. A. Coderre, of the Forest Products Laboratories, McGill University, Montreal, will be present during the convention and deliver an address on "Shingles," with particular reference to the treatment of the same to make them fire-resistant.

Among other features of the convention will be the visit of John

## SOME FORMER PRESIDENTS OF THE ASSOCIATION

Gordon C. Edwards,  Ottawa

Hon. George Gordon,  North Bay

Alex. MacLaurin,  Montreal

W. E. Bigwood,  Toronto

W. McLure, of Memphis, Tenn., president of the National Wholesale Lumber Dealers' Association, and Horace P. Taylor, of Buffalo, N.Y., president of the National Hardwood Lumber Association. Both these gentlemen will be accompanied by their wives, and it is expected that a number of other American guests will also be present.

The program will probably be carried out as follows, with slight variations which may be made at the last moment:

On Wednesday Janurray 11th the delegates will assemble and the convention will open, when the address of President McLachlin will be delivered. The reports of the executive committee and the transportation committee will be presented, and also the appointment made of a committee on resolutions.

The afternoon session will open at 2 o'clock and continue till 5.

### Supper-Dance in New Ball Room

In the evening there will be a supper-dance in the new ball room on the top floor of the new King Edward Hotel. Every arrangement will be made for an enjoyable function, and for those who do not trip the light fantastic, there will be other amusements, so that there will be no excuse for absence on the part of any visitor or his lady friend.

W. Gerard Power, Quebec P.Q.
Former President of C. L. A.

On Thursday January 12th, there will be another business session in the forenoon and at 12.30, a men's luncheon tendered the visitors by the lumbermen of Toronto. A. R. Whittemore, of Toronto, will be the speaker and will talk particularly on the building situation and the structural and industrial outlook for the coming year.

In the afternoon the business of the association will be wound up by the election of officers for 1922 and seven new directors for a three-year term.

The annual banquet will be held in the evening. This will be an outstanding social event, and it is hoped to have Hon. W. L. Mackenzie King, Premier of Canada, address the gathering.

### The Entertainment of the Ladies

Before the closing, one word must be said regarding the entertainment of the ladies. A special committee is at work.

On the afternoon of the first day, January 11th, there will be a theatre party for the ladies, and in the evening the fair sex will attend the supper-dance. It is expected that Thursday morning, January 12th, will be spent by the majority of the gentle sex, in shopping and visiting the departmental stores. At noon the wives and daughters of the visiting delegates will be entertained to a special ladies' luncheon at the King Edward, which will be followed by a bridge party or a motor drive in the afternoon, depending upon the weather.

In the evening the ladies will be the guests at the banquet and will, no doubt, thoroughly enjoy the proceedings. The banquet has always been the outstanding social adjunct of the convention.

---

### Mr. Scofield Again to the Front

Something distinctly new in the annals of the building trade is the "Built-Your-Own-Home" campaign conducted by the Windsor Lumber Company, Limited. Although the campaign is being carried out quietly, it is a leaven that is slowly but surely working in the minds of the public, and it seems destined to gain a host of followers within the near future, says the Border Cities "Star" of Windsor, Ont.

"When you go into a store to order a suit," says J. C. Scofield,

president and general manager of the company, "you do not ask what this and that material will cost a yard, or what each detail entering into that suit is going to cost. You simply ask the price of a certain suit made up in a particular material and in a particular style. This is the new fashion in buying houses. The purpose of the campaign is to get the public accustomed to ordering their houses as they order their suits, not figuring the cost of the lumber, lath, shingles, paint and all the other details separately, but obtaining a quotation on a home built in a certain way.

"This is a service that we are giving our clients, and to this end we have books of plans and illustrations of many different types of homes to choose from.

"You have been planning on building a home for years. You have worked out every detail in your own mind. You hope your ideas can be worked up into something presentable, but since you have never had the advantage of an architectural education, you have not the faintest idea in the world as to what your dream house is going to look like. When the various units are put together they may be produce a monstrosity instead of a beautiful home.

### Miniature Home Before You

"Suppose that after you have evolved all of these ideas, you could sit down some evening and have a miniature home brought before you—the home that you have dreamed out—the place that you had decided would fit every one of your requirements.

"This miniature is an exact model, built to scale—every detail exactly as you planned it. The windows are accurately placed, the porches are built, the chimney is where it belongs, and the home is even painted as you had thought that you would like to have it painted.

"The model is fastened to the center of a platform or tray, and even the landscape is worked out. Miniature trees are properly placed in order to show off the house to good advantage, and the sidewalks are in place. Flower beds are decorating the green lawn, and vines are on the house.

"You place the tray on the dining room table, and for hours you study your future home. You look at it from the north, south, east and west. You study it from the front and rear, and after you have done all this, you know exactly how your future home is going to look.

"This is what we have done, and, in addition, can furnish blue prints, and if necessary can supply a contractor who can give you an estimate as to its cost, all of which is a part of our building proposition, which we believe is due for the Border Cities.

"Anyone interested can see this model now on exhibition at our office and any information desired will be gladly given by any one of our employees in connection with the building department.

"Anyone not caring for the particular lay-out as shown in this model might be interested in knowing that we have in addition several plan books showing various designs that are both instructive and interesting to anyone contemplating a future home."

Mr. Scofield is optimistic as to the amount of building in the coming year, and in order to give its customers better service his company will establish a builders' section in connection with its business.

### General Paragraphs of Interest

Alliston, Ont., wants the Chestnut Canoe Co., of Fredericton, N.B., whose plant was burned down recently, to locate in that town. A decision will, however, not be reached for some time yet.

G. R. Wightman, of the Wightman Lumber Company, Montreal, returned from a visit to the Maritime Provinces. He states that some of the companies have put in larger camps than was originally contemplated.

The Monarch Tractors, Limited, with a capital stock of $2,000,000 and headquarters in Brantford, have been granted a charter to take over as a going concern the business now carried on by Monarch Tractors, Limited.

James Buchanan, of the J. Buchanan Lumber Company, Montreal, returned lately to business after three weeks' illness. On his doctor's advice he will spend the winter in the South, returning to Montreal in the spring.

H. P. Rowles, representing The Duncan Lumber Co., Vancouver, who has been spending several months in the east, left recently on a business trip to the west. Mr. Rowles will return to Toronto in a short while.

The Ontario Government has opened up a permanent lumber camp on the Algoma Central Railway, about 150 miles from Sault Ste. Marie, Ont. S. W. Butt, superintendent of bridge construction for Sudbury North, has charge of the camp. It is understood that the government will take out 250,000 feet of timber this year, and portable mills are being installed.

# Ottawa Now Ready to Welcome the Retailers

## Splendid Entertainment Arranged for the Visitors from All Over Ontario Who Will Gather in the Capital City at the Chateau Laurier on January 18 and 19

5: E. M. Barrett, Ottawa
President of O.R.L.D.A.

The fifth annual convention of the Ontario Retail Lumber Dealers' Association will be held at the Chateau Laurier, Ottawa, on Wednesday and Thursday January 18th and 19th. The members of the lumber industry in Ottawa are making every preparation for the entertainment of a large and representative gathering from every part of the province.

This will be the first time that the annual session of the provincial body has convened east of Toronto, and it is expected that those from Western Ontario will rally in goodly numbers and make it a point to be present. There is no doubt that the yardmen from the east will be in attendance at the gathering in full force.

Every preparation has been made for the welcome and entertainment of the guests, and many important matters are to come up for consideration. The proceedings will be profitable and pleasant. For several years the retail lumbermen of Ontario have always been present at the convention in other parts of Ontario, and they are naturally looking forward to a large assembly in the capital city on Wednesday and Thursday Jnuary 18th and 19th. The "boys" from Southwestern Ontario have engaged a special car and they will fill it too.

The "Chateau Laurier" is a magnificent hotel with every modern appointment. It is one of the most delightful retreats in Canada, and Ottawa, the chief law-making centre of the Dominion, never looks more-varied and attractive than in its winter garb.

There will be nothing dull or lifeless about the convention, and among the chief measures to come up for discussion will be the progress on the proposed new mechanics' lien act, a plan book for the association, the suggested midsummer outing to the head of the Great Lakes and various questions on legislation, transportation, trade relations, insurance, etc.

Allen M. Stewart, of Winnipeg, secretary of the Western Retail Lumber Dealers' Mutual Fire Insurance Corporation, will be present and give a timely and interesting address. His remarks will be well worth hearing. Other pleasing features are a theatre party on the evening of Wednesday January 18th, while the annual banquet will take place on Thursday January 19th, at which there will be some outstanding speakers.

E. M. Barrett, of Ottawa, who is president of the Ontario Retail Lumber Dealers' Association, has issued a strong invitation to the members of the retail fraternity throughout Ontario to come to Ottawa on January 18th and 19th. His message is as follows:

### The Agenda of the Gathering

An outline of the program follows. It is worth while cutting out and posting in the hat in order that no detail may be overlooked:

**Wednesday, January 18th**

Morning:

10 O'clock—Registration and meeting of directors.

Afternoon:

2 O'clock—Opening Session.
Reading of Minutes.
President's Address
Secretary's Report.
Election of Officers.
Treasurer's Report.
Report of Committee on Insurance.

Evening:

8 O'clock—Theatre Party.

**Thursday, January 19th**

Morning:

10 O'clock—Report of Committee on Legislation and Transportation.
Report of Committee on Trade Relations.
Report of Committee on Resolutions.

Afternoon:

2 O'clock—Discussion and voting upon Resolutions.
New Business.

Evening:

8 O'clock—Banquet at Chateau Laurier.

### A GREAT GET-TOGETHER OCCASION

Editor, "Canada Lumberman":

On behalf of the Ontario Retail Lumber Dealers I wish to thank you for the opportunity offered in your letter of recent date, to send a message to your readers and the members of the Ontario Retail Lumber Dealers' Association, regarding our annual convention.

This is our fifth annual convention and is the most important yet held. Every member should endeavor to be on hand. Matters will be discussed which will be of a great deal of interest and value to the trade.

There has been a big reduction in prices and the majority of us have had a lean year, but business is improving, more permits are being issued and the architects' offices are congested with proposed work. We need co-operation more to-day than ever and our association offers to the trade a "get-together gathering," for an exchange of ideas that will greatly benefit all who attend.

Our proposed lien law will be up for discussion and as this will be the only opportunity the association will have to place their views before the directors, it is important that every member attend.

Your insurance committee are arranging to bring from Winnipeg, Mr. Allen M. Stewart, secretary of the Western Retail Lumber Dealers' Mutual Fire Insurance Corporation. Mr. Stewart will have an interesting message and one that should prove profitable.

Ottawa members are endeavoring to entertain you in their usual manner.

The convention, as already noted, will be at the Chateau Laurier, one of the m°st pa²atia¹ hotels in the Dominion of Canada. The convention will afford you an opportunity to see the capital of Canada. Our location, as you know, is one very much to be desired. The Ottawa River is frozen and all roads lead North.

Wishing you and your readers a happy and prosperous New year.

Sincerely yours,
ERNEST M. BARRETT,
Pres. Ontario Retail Lumber
Ottawa, Dec. 27, 1921. Dealers' Association.

### Mr. Reid Is Enjoying the Sunny South

John B. Reid, of Toronto, Honorary President of the Ontario Retail Lumber Dealers' Association, who, with Mrs. Reid, is spending the winter months at St. Petersburg, Florida, in a letter to the "Canada Lumberman," says: "The weather is great here, summer every day. I am on the bowling green every morning and expect to start fishing soon. This is the greatest place to live in that I ever struck. Nothing to do but eat and sleep and no worry whatever. I hope the boys of the Ontario Retail Lumber Dealers' Association will have a splendid convention at Ottawa. The lumber business is good here, as they are building a lot of houses, but they are all constructed of Georgia pine. Building here is carried on twelve months in the year. Kind regards to all my friends in the trade."

## Widely Known in Lumber Arena

W. H. Stubbs, Kitchener, Ont.

W. H. Stubbs, Canadian manager of The J. M. Card Lumber Co., manufacturers of hardwood lumber, Chattanooga, Tenn., which firm recently joined the Wholesale Lumber Dealers' Association, Toronto, is widely known to the lumber trade in the east.

Mr. Stubbs entered the lumber and veneer line in 1901 as salesman for Maley, Thompson & Moffitt, who at that time had their headquarters in Ohio. He opened up a Canadian trade for the firm and covered the territory between Windsor and Montreal along with the state of New York. Later he went to New York City and launched a branch business for the same organization at 32nd St. & East River, remaining there for some time. His next position was as Canadian representative for J. S. Williams & Sons, of New York.

Some thirteen years ago Mr. Stubbs became connected with the J. M. Card Lumber Co., of Chattanooga, Tenn., to represent them in Canada and establish a veneer business for the company. He was successful from the beginning as it was not long after that the firm began furnishing all the different kinds of veneer known to the veneer business to a large number in western Ontario. Trade developed to such an extent that it was necessary to establish a Canadian warehouse which is located in Kitchener, where a large stock is carried and a good service given.

## Senator Edwards Left Large Estate

The late Senator W. C. Edwards, of Ottawa, who was one of Canada's prominent lumbermen and mill owners, left an estate valued at $1,992,000. The entire estate, of which more than $1,000,000 is in Victory bonds, is divided among the members of his family and that of his widow. Mrs. Edwards is given a substantial life annuity. The Senator explained in his will that, owing to the large amount of succession duties which would be levied against his estate, and which he understood were utilised by the Government largely for the benefit of various charitable, benevolent institutions, he made no bequest to any charities, "such as I otherwise would have done," as his statement concludes. It is estimated that the Province of Ontario will obtain about 20 per cent. of the estate, or nearly $400,000.

## Winnipeg Wholesaler Goes to Vancouver

Wm. H. Hoover, one of Winnipeg's best known and most popular lumber wholesalers, left that city recently to take over, temporarily, the position of manager for Vancouver office of the H. S. Galbraith Company, Ltd.

Mr. Hoover has been connected with the Winnipeg office of the Galbraith Company in the capacity of secretary-treasurer and sales manager for the past four years, and has a wide acquaintance with all branches of the lumber trade in the prairie provinces.

The Galbraith Company have for some time been extensively cultivating the eastern market for British Columbia lumber, and during his stay in Vancouver Mr. Hoover will devote much of his energy to still further extending the eastern connections of the firm. Western business will be handled as heretofore from Winnipeg.

## Will Forest Laboratories Go to Ottawa?

The removal of the Forest Products Laboratories from Montreal to Ottawa is under consideration, but has not been decided finally, says a recent despatch from Ottawa. It is proposed to establish in the Capital a research institute and, if the Montreal staff is transferred, the idea will be consolidation.

Difficulties, it is stated, have been encountered in directing the laboratories from Ottawa, among them being the fact that as soon as a member of the staff displays special proficiency, he is snapped up by Montreal commercial firms. The new government will have the final decision as to what is to be done about it.

The Forests Products Laboratories have been in existence since 1913, and have been working in close co-operation with McGill University, Montreal, which has provided the house on University street

in that city in which they are situated and permits the use, free of charge, of its testing laboratory in the engineering building and other laboratories and equipment in its science departments.

Reports indicating that it was the intention of the government to remove the Forest Products Laboratories to Ottawa have been current for the past eight months, it was stated at McGill. No definite instructions to that effect have been issued by the government, but the matter has been considered, and it is understood certain departments at Ottawa are in favor of the move.

Such action has always been opposed by the authorities of McGill, who claim that there is greater likelihood of research work of benefit to the province being carried on if the laboratories are left here, than if they are transferred to Ottawa, where there is danger that they may become routine departmental laboratories rather than purely scientific.

## Western Lumbermen Will Meet in Winnipeg

The thirty-first annual convention of the Western Retail Lumbermen's Association will be held in this city at the Fort Garry Hotel, Winnipeg, Jan. 25, 26 and 27. Secretary Fred. W. Ritter has prepared a comprehensive program. Among the foremost problems that will be tackled is one relating to costs in the retail lumber industry. It is believed that the time has come when a uniform cost system should be adopted for the members of the association. The Western Retail Lumbermen's Association is of the opinion that there is not the least doubt but that if the lumber dealers knew their costs as they should be known, a great many of the lumber yards in the country to-day, instead of shewing a profit, would actually be shewing a loss.

## Mr. McKillop Elected in West Elgin

Hugh C. McKillop was recently elected a Member of Parliament for West Elgin. He has for the past year been Warden of the county and has always taken an active interest in its progress and prosperity.

Mr. McKillop, who ran in the Conservative interest, is a 100 per cent. Canadian. He was born in West Lorne, Ont., where he now resides, 46 years ago. His parents were pioneer residents in Elgin County, coming originally from Scotland.

Mr. McKillop's father many years ago established a sawmill and lumber business in West Lorne, which is still thriving under the McKillop direction, the newly-elected M.P. being a member of the firm of brothers who operate the plant. In addition, Mr. McKillop is extensively engaged in agriculture, owning a large cattle farm. He is a genial, jolly man of rather large proportions, and has numerous friends throughout the county, and in 1907 married Miss Norma Sherk, daughter of Mr. J. C. Sherk, formerly of Aylmer. He is the proud father of two sturdy sons.

## Gropp Bros'. Sawmill Wiped Out

The sawmill, crating mill and warehouse of Gropp Bros., Penetanguishene, Ont., was destroyed by fire recently. The blaze originated from some unknown cause. The loss is about $25,000, partly covered by insurance. There was a high wind blowing at the time, which made it difficult to keep the fire from the lumber yards, but fortunately the flames were confined to the buildings. Many friends of the firm will regret to learn of their loss and hope that they may see their way clear to undertake rebuilding operations in the near future.

## New Course in Lumber Salesmanship

The New York State College of Forestry at Syracuse University believing that more efficient and complete utilization of the products of forests is practicing as good forestry as replanting cut-over areas, leaving seed trees to reforest areas that are being lumbered, protection from forest fires, etc., and that lumber salesmanship is a phase of lumbering seriously needed by this great industry, recently offered such a course to students specializing in lumbering and wood utilisation. This is the first course of its kind in forestry schools.

Among the students are a large number of sons of lumbermen. Many of these young men have already signified their intention of going into the lumber business through the medium of salesmanship. After taking the course in theoretical and practical lumber at the school, a number of large and representative logging and manufacturing operations are visited in the northeast and south and then a course from four months to a year is given on the sorting tables on the lumber piles and about the shipping docks or lumber mills, learning the business first hand. As a result of this course in the school of "Hard Knocks" as well as a course in the theory of the business, it is believed the boys should make good lumber salesmen.

# Southwestern Retailers all Going to Ottawa

## Rousing Meeting Held at London Endorses Midsummer Trip up Great Lakes and Extends Invitation to O. R. L. D. A. to Meet in Windsor Next Year

J. T. Wallace, London, Chairman of S.W.O.R.L.D.A.

The lumber retailers of southwestern Ontario will travel by special C.P.R. car to Ottawa, to attend the big provincial convention in the capital city on Wednesday and Thursday January 18th and 19th.

The dealers also have decided to invite the O.R.L.D.A. to meet in Windsor in 1923, and also propose that the retailers of the province should have a real holiday next June by taking one of the Northern Navigation Company's boats at Detroit or Sarnia and enjoy a week's sail up the Great Lakes to Duluth.

Bright and helpful in every respect was the special meeting held in the Builders' Exchange Rooms, London, on December 21st, of the South Western Ontario Retail Lumber Dealers' Association. There was a splendid attendance and many matters of interest were discussed, including the proposed plan book for the Association, the forthcoming provincial convention at Ottawa, the annual midsummer trip for next year, the Mechanics' Lien law, advertising, trade ethics, building outlook and collections.

John T. Wallace, president, presided and the first matter taken up was the proposed plan book. Secretary Boultbee, of the Ontario Retail Lumber Dealers, Association, explained that getting out such a book would involve considerable expense and that some progress had been made. To obtain the detailed drawings, have the plates made and the book printed and bound in good shape, would entail a heavy outlay, and advertisements would likely be obtained to offset the expense. It was hoped, if the plan book was issued, that the association would break about even on the transaction.

Mr. Boultbee announced that the members of the association could obtain from the service department of the Western Lumbermen's Association, Winnipeg, their book of plans for houses, barns, etc., at fifteen cents each, that floor plans and elevations would be sent for any building therein for $1.75, and for the same amount a bill of materials could be obtained. It was explained, however, that while many services were being offered the O.R.L.D.A., yet general plans were not suitable as each locality demanded a special type of line.

### Plan Service Helps Building

J. C. Scofield, Windsor, thought that the business of lumbermen could be greatly increased if they were in a position to give prospective builders some outline of what the finished structure would look like, together with bill of materials, survey of quantities, etc., so that the approximate cost might be arrived at. He believed that such a movement would aid greatly in a Build-Your-Own-Home campaign. A book of plans and illustrations of different types of houses to choose from was rendering helpful, practical service, which was what counted to-day.

B. F. Clarke, of Glencoe, also spoke along similar lines. There was nothing like giving prospective builders an idea of what they had in their minds as it stimulated them to go ahead in their undertakings. He thought that the retail lumber dealers did not advertise enough. He had been looking through a London paper on his way in that morning and found only one or two firms using very small space. He believed that the dealer in forest products should encourage building and do something in the way of display announcements in the press.

Mr. Scofield said that he did not think an advertisement of a retailer, stating that he handled lumber, shingles, lath, posts, etc., was of any particular benefit. A lumber merchant, when he had something to say, should come out and say definitely. The best results he had ever had from an advertisement was when he put in an advt. last summer, entitled "Build Now," showing that $350.00 a year ago would buy only 1,000 feet of oak flooring, and for the same money

to-day ther could be purchased in addition 1,000 feet of bill stuff, 1,000 feet of sheathing, 1,000 feet of cove siding, 1,000 XXX shingles, 1,000 lath, two outside door frames and doors and five window frames and sash complete. This declaration had aroused the interest of the public who were firmly convinced that lumber was coming down. This advt. showed that it had.

A further discussion along these lines showed that the retail lumber dealer was not active enough in his locality in giving the public information through the printed word. It was felt that a cumulative advt. to the effect that lumber prices had struck rock bottom and that now is the time to build and nothing was to be gained by deferring action, might prove most effective.

### Progress on Mechanics' Lien Act

Another matter which came up for discussion during the day was the Mechanics' Lien act, and it is expected that a new bill will be presented at the forthcoming session of the legislature. Secretary Boultbee told of the progress that has been made and how opposition was being offered by certain interests. He felt, however, that if the retail lumbermen got busy with their respective local representatives in parliament and showed them the uselessness and inadequacy of the present act, they could arouse their support on behalf of the proposed measure, which has been explained from time to time in the columns of the "Canada Lumberman," and reference to which will be found on another page of this issue.

Another matter, which stirred up enthusiasm, was the forthcoming convention to be held at Ottawa on January 18th and 19th. After a thorough discussion, during which Mr. Scofield stated that the railways would place a special car at the disposal of the western Ontario lumbermen, it was moved by Mr. Scofield and seconded by C. H. Belton that the members of the South Western Ontario Retail Lumber Dealers' Association travel in a body by the C.P.R. to the capital city. A canvass was made of those present at the meeting and the majority declared that they would be only too pleased to attend. It is confidently expected that fully twenty-five or thirty members of the South Western Association will go to Ottawa.

### Windsor Wants Big Convention

In this connection another important matter loomed up when it was moved by George N. Kernohan and seconded by Chas. Hubbell, that the South Western Retail Lumber Dealers' Association invite the Ontario Association to hold its 1923 meeting in Windsor. That city is completing a fine palatial hotel which represents the last word in entertainment and accommodation and will be in a splendid position to take care of 200 or 300 delegates.

Trade ethics were discussed at length and the threatened action of a manufacturing firm supplying both retail lumbermen and contractors in the same town came in for a certain amount of criticism. It was alleged by the manufacturer that the lumbermen were taking contracts to do certain work in competition with the contractors. This was denied by those present who pointed out that the manufacturing firm in question allowed private individuals to go to its plant and take away certain material at practically the same figure which the retail lumbermen could obtain it. The secretary was instructed to look into this matter and see if some arrangement could not be definitely arrived at whereby the retail lumbermen would be fully protested by the company, who, it is alleged, has "offended." A resolution was passed that the association was opposed to the concern selling direct to contractors or consumers, but that it should sell through the retail lumber dealer and that the latter had a right to quote his own price on the product.

### Summer Trip up Great Lakes

G. B. Van Blaricom, editor of the "Canada Lumberman," was asked by the president to say a few words, and congratulated the South Western Ontario Association upon the representative and lively character of its gatherings. He conveyed greetings from John B. Reid, Toronto, honorary president of the O.R.L.D.A, who is spending the winter months at St. Petersburg, Florida. Mr. Reid stated in a letter that he hoped Mr. Scofield, of Windsor, would be elected president of the provincial association for 1923 and that the Great Lakes trip would be boomed as an ideal summer outing. Mr. Reid has long been a strong advocate of having a pleasant, restful week's sail upon the water,

during which the members could be accompanied by their wives and daughters.

This brought up the question of when the event should take place, and it was felt that the last week in June would be most suitable. The members of the party and their wives would board the boat at Windsor or Sarnia and travel up through the St. Mary's River and Soo Canal to Port Arthur and Fort William, and thence on to Duluth where large sawmills are located. J. C. Scofield, Chester H. Belton, D. J. McPherson and others spoke of the delightful character of such a voyage and said that its association could not be surpassed. The Northern Navigation Co. always looked well after its patrons and the lumbermen would have special attention. It was decided that the matter of a jaunt up the Great Lakes should be brought up and discussed at the Ottawa meeting.

### Outlook is Growing Brighter

Some informal discussion took place regarding business conditions, the trend of prices and the outlook for next year. While the dealers stated that the past few months had been rather quiet and that they had not been doing much buying, it was declared that stocks were low

and the bottom had been reached in price recessions. The outlook for next year was regarded more hopefully than it had been for some time.

The London dealers entertained the visitors to a splendid dinner at Wong's Cafe, and a vote of thanks was moved by Chas. Hubbell and seconded by D. J. McPherson, to the London men for their hospitality. John T. Wallace replied on behalf of the local members stating it was always a pleasure to have the boys meet in the Forest City and concluded the proceedings by wishing everyone the compliments of the season.

Among those present at the gathering were: John T. Wallace, London, president of the S.W.O.R.L.D.A.; D. J. McPherson, Alvinston; C. H. Belton, Sarnia; E. C. Russell, Walkerville; M. Noxell, Komoka; W. H. Longfield, Mount Brydges; A. J. Clatworthy, Granton; W. J. Taylor, Ridgetown; George H. Belton, London; Chas. Hubbell, Thamesville; B. F. Clarke, secretary-treasurer, Glencoe; J. C. Scofield, Windsor; C. S. Hadley, Chatham; M. R. Bogart, Chatham; T C. Warwick, Blenheim; A. R. Sanders, St. Thomas; A. McPherson, Glencoe; Geo. N. Kernohan, London; H. Boultbee, Toronto, secretary of the O.R.L.D.A., and G. B. Van Blaricom, editor "Canada Lumberman."

# Orangeville District Holds Annual Meeting

## Business During Past Year has been Fair—Necessity of Careful Buying and Watching Credits Emphasized—Old Officers Re-elected— Building Prospects

The annual meeting of District No. 6 of the Ontario Retail Lumber Dealers' Association was held in Orangeville on December 9th, when the dealers from that section of the province renewed their acquaintances and exchanged news and views on general conditions.

Among the topics considered at the round table conference were rural credits, the building outlook, the trend of prices and demand for lumber during the coming year, the competition of catalogue or mail order houses, the value of the local service rendered by the retail lumberman and more effective and convincing advertising in the weekly newspapers. The meeting was a most profitable and instructive one, and resulted in the re-election of the old officers, J. A. Matthews as chairman and J. B. Mackenzie as secretary, who were accorded a hearty vote of thanks for their services.

J. A. Matthews, Orangeville, chairman, opened the proceedings in a short address reviewing the subjects that he thought would be of interest to the members and requested that all join in and give their views and experiences on each question.

J. B. Mackenzie, Georgetown, started a discussion on future trade prospects. He said that certain kinds of building were at a standstill in his district and several houses were vacant in the town. This was due, he believed, to the housing commission scheme, which did not help matters much in Georgetown. On the contrary many dwellings were left on the hands of the commission, owing to the would-be owners going too deeply in debt. A fair farm business was being done, but mostly along modest lines.

E. W. McCulloch, Brampton, said that up to a week ago he had been rushed on small repair jobs, but no building of large proportions was being done in his district. The farm trade was fair, and collections were hard to make.

N. J. Howes, Harriston, reported two or three prospects for building, but he expected nothing big would be started until the spring. A good repair trade was being done in his vicinity, but farmers refused in many cases to pay cash, and in some instances requested long credit.

### Too Much Credit Granted

An interesting incident was related by Mr. Howes of a farmer who ordered some lumber from him and asked for credit on the plea that he had also to buy corn. Mr. Howes said that by giving the farmer credit he was putting the money into the pocket of the corn merchant. After a lengthy argument Mr. Howes received half the amount of the bill from the yeoman, the rest to be paid in January. He learned later that the self-same customer had paid cash for his corn and that he also had some more money in the bank. This was an example of the business which the retail lumber dealer was expected to carry on with the farmers. "It is impossible, of course, to do an entirely cash lumber business in the rural districts," continued Mr. Howes, "and, while there are many cases where credit is advisable and has to be granted, it is a wise plan to size up your man well before extending it too readily."

W. G. Gorvett, Arthur, said that with the exception of one fair-sized building prospect, business was not brisk in his town and dis-

trict. A period of critical merchandising was at hand, he thought, and careful placing of credit was essential. He also related some difficulties he had in obtaining his money from the farmers. "However," he concluded, "in many cases I knew they had the cash and I did some plain talking and generally managed to get a fair payment."

The mail order problem, which always comes in for considerable comment by the rural merchants, was freely discussed and many pointers derived from the different experiences.

Mr. Mackenzie, in explanation regarding the popularity of the mail order catalogue, showed how an article, which was not in great demand, was featured frequently by catalogue concerns at a low

J. A. Matthews, Orangeville Ont. Re-elected
Chairman of District No. 6

figure. The remaining articles, which were in common demand, were extremely high in price. The public, seeing one low price in big print, often failed to investigate other quotations.

A suggestion was made by one of the members that the advertising of the retail lumber dealer should be so constructed as to educate the public to see the short-sightedness in buying from outside, and set forth in an attractive manner the helpful service which was available at the plant of the local dealer. The suggestion was well received and will no doubt be employed to advantage.

Among those at the gathering were: J. A. Matthews, Orangeville, chairman; J. B. Mackenzie, Georgetown, secretary; W. G. Gorvett, Arthur; E. W. McCulloch, Brampton; N. J. Howes, Harriston; Mr. Dixon, Grand Valley, and others.

# Montreal Lumber Association Holds Annual

### Chairman Grier Says Members of the Trade Are Looking Forward to 1922 With Confidence—Believes That Corner Has Been Turned—New Officers Elected

The annual meeting of the Montreal Lumber Association was held recently at the Board of Trade Rooms, Montreal, with a representative attendance. George W. Grier, chairman, presided, and in his annual address reviewed a number of matters which had come up for consideration during the past year. He stated that the industry had come through probably the most strenuous and difficult year of its history and is to-day in a position to discover exactly how it stands in regard to market conditions.

Mr. Grier remarked that at this period a year ago lumbermen were in the dark, facing a deflation of market prices, the extent of which they had no means of determining. This deflation was in some lines a great deal more than many members of the trade expected. To-day lumber prices had reached a somewhat more stable basis. It would not be unduly prophetic to say that the next move would in all likelihood be in an upward direction, especially on some lines on which the market is short at the present time.

Mr. Grier said that the lumbermen were looking forward to 1922 with confidence, although they did not expect anything in the nature of a boom. Continuing, he referred to the sales tax, general increase in freight rate, carload weights, car demurrage rates and other topics.

#### Several Trade Matters Reviewed

On the subject of the sales tax Mr. Grier said:

The Western lumber interests early in the year made representation to the authorities at Ottawa to change the sales tax regulations, so that the Canadian lumber manufacturer would be compelled to absorb the total amount of the sales tax. The members of this association were asked to join in this representation. After thoroughly discussing this question, this Association petitioned the Canadian Lumber Association to call a meeting of their Executive Committee and consult with the lumber interests of the entire Dominion regarding the "sales tax or such amendments thereto, or substitute therefor, as would bear equitably on every branch of the lumber business in Canada." It also placed itself on record as being of the opinion that it would be inexpedient for any section of the lumber trade to demand a change in the present regulations until this meeting had taken place.

On May 9 the Minister of Finance delivered his Budget speech in which he outlined several new features of the sales tax, the application of which as regards lumber was somewhat changed. It provided that a tax of 3 per cent. be imposed, levied and collected on deliveries by the Canadian manufacturer of lumber, but that there would not be any further excise tax payable on resale. The manufacturers interpreted this to mean that they had the right to collect said tax from the wholesaler, and were upheld by the Customs Department, who ruled that lumber manufacturers might treat the sales tax as part of the cost of the goods, or might charge for same on invoices to their customers; in short, that the question of charging the sales tax was, in so far as the wholesaler was concerned, one of contract. Finally, on June 4 amendments were passed, whereby a sales tax of 2 per cent. was imposed on sales and deliveries by Canadian manufacturers and 3 per cent. on all importations, no further tax being payable on resale.

Weighing of Carload Freight Traffic—This question was referred to in last year's report. The board ruled in October of this year that general order No. 288 represents the final and definite expression of the board's judgment on the matters involved in the hearing, and that

George W. Grier, Retiring President

the order was drawn after the whole matter had been given detailed consideration. It is likely the question will have to be gone into again, and the Board of Railway Commissioners requested to grant a further hearing.

Lumber to and from Quebec Central Ry. Stations—The rates on lumber to and from stations on the Quebec Central Ry. are considered excessive by the trade. This question was taken up with the Canadian Pacific Railway, and it is hoped an equitable basis will be reached at an early date. Failing a satisfactory settlement with the railways, this question will be referred to the Railway Commission.

General Increase in Freight Rates.—This matter is also referred

D. H. McLennan Newly-elected
President

S. F. Rutherford, Newly-elected
Vice-President

W. K. Grafftey Newly-elected
Treasurer

J. P. MacLaurin, Elected Director  W. A. Filion, Elected Director  Arthur H. Campbell, Elected Director  W. T. Mason, Elected Director

to last year's report. In accordance with the board's general order No. 308, under which rates were increased 40 per cent. east of Fort William and 35 per cent. west of Fort William, a reduction of 35 per cent east and 30 per cent. west of Fort William was made January last. The board's general order No. 351 covers a further reduction of 10 per cent. both east and west, effective December 1. The whole question of lumber rates east of Fort William is now before the Railway Commission for consideration.

Car Demurrage Rates—In May last the Canadian Manufacturers' Association, the Toronto Board of Trade, the Canadian Lumbermen's Association and other organizations applied to the Board of Railway Commissioners for the restoration of the former normal rate of demurrage of $1.00 per car per day. The Board of Trade Transportation Bureau, acting for the hay, grain, lumber and other shipping interests in Montreal opposed the application and recommended instead that the following scale be approved—$1.00 per day for the first three days after free time and an advance of $1.00 on the previous day's charge for each succeeding day, until a charge of $5.00 per day was reached, which figure should be the charge for all subsequent days delay. After the hearing in Ottawa on June 21 the Board of Railway Commissioners on November 23 issued order No. 439, providing for the following demurrage charges after the expiration of the usual free time, the same to become effective December 5:

For the first day, or fraction thereof, of delay, $1.00; for the second day, or fraction thereof, of delay, $1.00; for the third and each succeeding day, or fraction thereof, $5.00.

After the consideration of some other matters, officers were elected for the coming year as follows:

President, D. H. McLennan, of the McLennan Lumber Co.
Vice-President, S. F. Rutherford, of Wm. Rutherford & Sons.
Treasurer, W. K. Grafftey, of the Montreal Lumber Co.
Directors—W. T. Mason, of Mason, Gordon & Co.; Arthur H. Campbell, of Campbell, MacLaurin Lumber Co.; J. P. MacLaurin, of the St. Maurice Lumber Co., and W. A. Filion, of E. H. Lemay & Co.

## Here Is an Outlet for Your Lumber

Opportunities in the lumber business are opening up every day. All kinds of enquiries and propositions, good, bad and indifferent are being received, and there is no dearth of bonanzas.

One of the most unique that has been presented to Toronto firms during the past fortnight was that of a New York concern which sent a plausible plea for business, and in order to establish its identity and creditability, furnished a report from a well-known mercantile agency. Here are the documents which are presented in exactly the maner in which they were typewritten:

Please advise us the lowest Prices,f.o.b.Mill You will Contract the sale of Your lumber,Mill cut,bY log run or bY grades, for (12) mths(one Year)with the refusal of it for thr ee(3)Years.

Give about the percentof (%)of each kind of timber You have to cut from,and total feet of stumpage, approximatelY. Give CaPacitY(Band or Circular )of Mill, DrY. Kiln, and Planer. Send stock list of lumbr You have readY to ship, and Prices You will take for it f.o.b.Mill bY grades or bY log run, if it avarages log run,having all grdes in it.

On terms of NintY(90%)Prr cent of agr eed Price,S/D attached to B/L through the Banks, balance 10% when un-

loaded and checked,as to quanitY & etc bY a Licensed Lumber Inspector. Quote Prices on R.R.Ties, Piling etc. Give R.R.& water Fr eight rate to N.Y.C.

Awaiting Your kind favor, we r emai n.
Yours respectfullY,
P.S. See enclosed copY of report to Mercantile AgencY.

### Letter to Mercantile Agency

We heard You sent a man to see us a few daYs ago, which happened while we were out at the Noon hour, business Men PraYer meeting at———Church,which has been going on for about FiftY(50)Years,having a new leader most everY daY, Preacher or Evangelist from different Parts of the City,U.S. and the world, which makes them wonderful and verY interesting meetings. "Putting God First," in our dailY business life.

We have recentlY opened up a wholesale Land & Lumber Co.business, soliciting Contracts of purchase of the out of Saw-Mills,buYing & selling lumber (and to Colonize lands) on terms of NintY(90%)per cent of agreed prices, S/D to B/L f.o.b.Mill, baiance when unloaded and checked bY Licensed lumber Inspector, as to quantitY and grades officiallY.

Our Capitol is limited, but bY having Contract of sale of lumber to be paid on similar terms we buY it, there will be no trouble about us meeting all of our obligations.

We came to New YorkCity on promise of a partY to take or handle $2,500,000.worth of 6% first mortgage Bonds on 50,-000 acres of Colonization lands, having on it about 400,000,000 ft. of hardwood timber, worth manY times more than the Bonds, after all expenses of manufacturing and freight to N.Y.C. But he proved to be a fake, wanting us to deposit in Bank $10,000.subject to his order, for him to go see propertY, which expense we were willing to paY,if he would give guarantee, that he would take the Bonds, if propertY proved to be as represented.

So false representations and failure to complY with agreements bY others has put us out for the present in our expectations. We trulY beleive in "Putting God First,"& " Golden Rules," "Therefore all things,whatsoever Ye would that men should do to You, do Ye even so to them Matt.7: 12, for this the law and the ptofets,". (PraY for us,for we trust that we have a good conscience in all things wiliing to live honestlY Heb.13:18.

MY son(30 Years)twe(2)daughters and mYself(a widower) are the onlY ones in the CompanY, which expect, to Charter, later, so as not to conflict.with other organizations, we maY be instrumental in effecting on basis, that we propose to place ½ to ¾ of the Bonds of a Mill plant,and timber land proposition, to anY other partY cashing or get cashed ¼ to ½ of the 6% first mortgage Bonds, and buY and operate the proposition.

Treating You will kindlY make a report on us in accordance with the above, we remain.
Yours respectfully,

Robert Murray, of Huntsville, Ont., has been appointed a deputy national inspector to serve in the Toronto district of the National Hardwood Lumber Dealers' Association.

# Wholesale Dealers Have Fine Time at School

### Yuletide Meeting Held at the Albany Club, Toronto, Was Most Enjoyable Occasion — Mr. Jennings Spoke on Humor and Mr. Maus Announces He Has Formed New Company

It is usual at the December gathering of the Wholesale Lumber Dealers' Association to dispose of the more serious affairs of business and have a rollicking, animated session, and this year proved to be no exception to the rule. The long rows of tables were attractively decorated with holly and mistletoe and nearly fifty dispensers and producers of wood products gathered around the festive board. A. E. Eckardt, chairman, presided, and after a short business session the proceedings were taken charge of by D. C. Johnston, who is a past master in the art of making things "go."

It was announced that the J. M. Card Lumber Co., of Chattanooga, Tenn., of which W. H. Stubbs, of Kitchener, is the Canadian manager, has joined the association.

For the transportation committee, Roy Halliday reported on the recent new ruling by the Dominion Railway Commission regarding demurrage charges. This ruling places a charge of $1.00 a day for the first day over the forty-eight hours allowed, $1.00 for the second day and $5.00 for each succeeding day. The former charge has been $1.00 for the first day, $2.00 for the second day, $3.00 for the third, etc.

It was moved by Mr. Halliday, seconded by Mr. A. E. Clark, "that this association goes on record as being opposed to the demurrage rates, made effective under the board's general order No. 349, as being too drastic, and further, as they are not in accordance with the evidence produced at the board's meeting in July, the consensus of opinion was that the demurrage rates should be $1.00 per day for the first three days, then a 'graduated scale of $2.00, $3.00, $4.00 and $5.00 after that period. Furthermore, we think that the order should be rescinded, as only two of the commissioners, outside of the chairman, have concurred in this ruling."

This was carried unanimously and copies will be sent to the Dominion Railway Commission, the Canadian Manufacturers' Association and Canadian Lumbermen's Association.

### Mr. Maus Forms New Company

A short address was given by C. O. Maus, of South Bend, Ind., in which he referred to the fact that less hardwood lumber was being manufactured now in the south than at any time during the past five years. The long rainy season and the shutting down of so many mills had made many loggers desist in their operations and secure other positions, and now an effort was being made to break in new men, but not with any great success. Dry lumber stocks were very scarce and there had been a considerable raise in the prices for gum, oak and hardwoods. Wholesalers in the north had also bought up large quantities of lumber in the south, for which they had offered an attractive price, providing the seller would allow it to remain in the yard a few months. Business on the whole had greatly improved during the past few weeks, and the outlook was most hopeful. Mr. Maus advised the lumbermen not to cut prices, but to hold out strongly for a fair figure. Slashing values did not result in sales and only made buyers more determined to hang back. They should also seek when disposing of their better grades to include No. 1 and 2 common; otherwise their stocks would be top-heavy at the lower ends.

Mr. Maus, who is well-known in the Canadian trade in which he has been calling for the past ten years as a representative of the Hyde Lumber Co., announced that he had concluded his services with that organization in order to go into business for himself under the name of the Chas. O. Maus Lumber Co., with headquarters at South Bend, Ind. He stated that he had a Canadian partner in his enterprise in the person of A. E. Clark, of Toronto, who was so widely known in hardwood circles in both the United States and Canada. Mr. Maus, who will sell Canadian hardwoods in the western states, was accorded a hearty applause for his interesting address.

### Mr. Jenning Told Some Good Ones

John Jennings, of Jennings & Clute, solicitors for the Ontario Retail Lumber Dealers' Association, was introduced and gave a breezy talk on "Wit and Humor." It was one of the most entertaining and facetitious speeches made before the gathering in a long while. Mr. Jennings disclaimed that he had any gift in the line of humor, but he had not uttered half a dozen sentences before he had the members roaring with laughter. He told story after story illustrative of the various national types of humor, such as the Scotch, English, Irish, American, Canadian and Hebrew. He also regaled his hearers with many droll anecdotes relating to the bench and bar, all of which were bright and refreshing.

### School Days—Breaking the Rules

The gathering was then turned into a school and the lumbermen became pupils. D. C. Johnston was the appointed teacher and propounded various questions which each pupil had to stand up, place his hands behind his back and answer to the satisfaction of the domineering instructor and Mr. Jennings.

These questions veered from the grave to the gay, including all subjects from philosophy to femininity. Many pupils did not have their lessons prepared and were fined for ignorance, inattention, impudence, indolence or other "offences." Each was called by his first name and had to be as meek and humble as a child toward the revered and stern dominie.

### Preparations for C.L.A. Convention

After school was out, A. E. Clark, vice-president of the Canadian Lumbermen's Association, told of the preparations that were being made for entertaining the visitors on the occasion of the annual convention in Toronto on Wednesday and Thursday, January 11th and 12th. He stated that preparations were proceeding splendidly and that the forthcoming meeting should be the most successful and representative in the history of the association. It behooved all lumbermen to join heartily in the efforts to make the stay of the representatives of the industry pleasant and profitable. Arrangements were being effected for the entertainment of the ladies and all lumbermen were invited to have their better halves attend the luncheon and the banquet, as well as the other festivities. They hoped to have Premier King as chief speaker at the banquet on January 12th.

During the evening many fines were levied for various misdemeanors on the part of the lumbermen, and it is understood that a sum amounting to about $50.00 was collected, which was sent to the "Toronto Star's" Christmas fund for bringing good cheer to the children in many Toronto families who are not favored with too much of this world's requisites.

### Mr. Stalker Launches Out for Himself

Douglas A. Stalker, who recently launched in the wholesale lumber business in Sherbrooke, Que., is a young man who has many friends in the industry.

After leaving college he started in the lumber game with Williamson & Crombie, of Kingsbury, Que., which is his home town, at the age of sixteen. He became much interested in the work and paid attention to all the details and numerous operations of logging, scaling, grading, shipping, etc. In 1919 he took a position with the Fletcher Pulp & Lumber Co., of Sherbrooke, working his way up from scaler to head scaler, yard superintendent and inspector, and last spring he was put on the sales staff, where he worked until they sold out their dressing and retail yard to the Bissell Irwin Lumber Co., when Mr. Stalker decided to go into business for himself. He is specializing in hemlock, spruce, white pine, red pine, lath, shingles, B. C. fir and also crating stock.

Mr. Stalker reports that he has done exceptionally well since starting off his own bat, and is looking forward to a satisfactory year in 1922.

### Many Forestry Meetings in Montreal

As usual, a number of meetings connected with forestry interests will be held in Montreal during the week of January 23. The Province of Quebec Limit Holders' Association will meet in the Windsor Hotel on Wednesday, January 25, while meetings of the Quebec Forest Protective Association, Limited, St. Maurice Fire Protective Association, Limited, and Southern St. Lawrence Fire Protective Association, Limited, will be held on the same day and at the same place. The annual meeting of the Woodlands Section of the Pulp and Paper Association is fixed for Thursday, January 26, and the annual meeting of the parent association on the following day.

# New Mechanics' Lien Act Again in Committee

### Financial Interests Suggest Certain Changes in the Proposed Measure—The Position of Owner Explained as Well as That of Mortgagee—Good Progress

A sitting of the Special Legislative Committee on the proposed new Mechanics' and Wage-Earners' Lien Act, was held on December 13th at the Parliament Buildings, Toronto, when the representatives from mortgage, loan and trust companies were heard. Some opposition was offered to the proposed measure on various grounds, and certain changes suggested.

It will be remembered that at a previous sitting of the committee representatives from the Ontario Retail Lumber Dealers' Association, the Builders' Supply men and other bodies, who favor a new measure, were given a favorable hearing. It is likely a new act will be introduced at the forthcoming session of the legislature, and, in the meantime, another sitting of the committee, of which W. E. N. Sinclair is chairman, will be held.

The principle of the proposed legislation, which is patterned after the Ohio Lien Act, is the extension of absolute protection to those supplying material or labor in the erection of buildings. The existing act in Ontario, which is generally recognized as ancient, weak and inadequate, provides for a 20 per cent. hold-back of the contract amount by the owner until assurance is given that all claims for labor or material have been met by the contractor.

The bill before the special committee places upon the owner and upon the mortgagee, responsibility for the payment of all accounts to the amount of the contract. It is on this point that some criticism has been offered by the trust companies and others. The special legislative committee appointed B. N. Davis, its counsel, to visit Ohio and Michigan to enquire into the working of the lien laws in those states, and report at its next sitting.

In the meantime it is only fair to say that good progress has so far been made with measure, and retail lumbermen are requested to interview the local members of the Ontario Legislature in their respective centres, calling attention to the measure and urging that it be given support.

One of the chief advantages of the new act as pointed out by John Jennings of Toronto, solicitor for the Ontario Retail Lumber Dealers' Association, is as follows:

#### Some Features of the Proposed Act

As between the owner and the immediate contractor, there is no need for any lien registration. The owner is liable on his contract, and all the owner's assets are made available to answer his obligation. It is sub-contractors, mechanics and wage-earners, and building supply men, who require the protection of a Lien Act. Bill 114, with the suggested amendments, provides that when the general contractor desires to obtain payment from the owner, he shall give to the owner an affidavit, duly sworn, setting forth the names of all wage-earners, sub-contractors and material men to whom anything is owing. Nothing need be said about those who have been paid. Anyone supplying labor or material for a building may, in the most informal manner by letter, advise the owner that he is doing so, and such informal notice will obligate the owner to see that the person giving the notice is paid. In practice, therefore, the general contractor desiring to draw money, completes his affidavit in the printed form (it is proposed, for convenience, that such affidavits may be sworn before any architect), presents his affidavit to the owner, the owner looks to see if he has any notices from persons not referred to in the affidavit, and then issues his cheques to the unpaid wage-earners and supply men, and the balance of the amount then payable is handed over to the general contractor.

#### The Owner Protects Himself

At present, the owner requires a statutory declaration or affidavit from the contractor, but having obtained it, he gets no legal protection thereby. The present bill, while it lays upon the owner the obligation to see that his contract money goes to pay labor and material, absolutely protects him, i. e., it relieves him from any liability to any person who has not filed with the owner an informal notice, or who is not referred to in the general contractor's affidavit. The owner, therefore, is in a much better position than he now is and can advance money with greater freedom and with greater security.

It will be seen, therefore, that because the owner is bound to provide for payment of wage-earners and material men as the work progresses, the necessity for recording a lien against the title of the property will rarely arise. Provision, however, is made for recording liens in a manner somewhat similar to the present, but a longer time is given for so doing, in order that there may be a greater opportunity for adjustment. There is no doubt that a great deal of money will be saved in law costs, and embarrassing delays will be avoided, both to the wage-earners and material men.

#### The Position of the Mortgagee

It is not the intention of the supporters of the bill to alter the position of the mortgagees, either under what has been known as "prior mortgages," or under mortgages in respect to building loans, except possibly in one respect. The position of prior mortgages will remain exactly as it is now; the position of mortgages making building mortgage must assume some duty to see that the money advanced by him is used for the payment of labor and material entering into the construction of the building with respect to which the loan is made. When an advance on a building loan is asked for, the mortgagee, if he desires, may issue the cheque direct to the sub-contractors, wage-earners and supply men; or he may take the certificate of the owner as to the amount owing on these accounts and that the mortgage advance will be used for the payment of these accounts. The building mortgagee is conceded priority over lien-holders to the extent of the actual advances made by him under the mortgage in either of the two ways just set forth.

### Sudden Death of Peter McGibbon

Peter R. McGibbon, M.P., who was re-elected in the Liberal interests on December 6th for the county of Argenteuil, Que., died on Dec. 18th at his home in Lachute, Que. It appears that Mr. McGibbon was watching a fire which destroyed a building near the town,

The late Peter R. McGibbon, M.P., Lachute, Que.

and, while so doing, contracted a cold which developed seriously and resulted in his death. He had represented Argenteuil in the House of Commons since 1917.

Mr. McGibbon was engaged in the lumber business and was widely and favorably known. He was born in Argenteuil County in 1854 and was educated at the Lachute Academy. He is survived by his wife, two sons and three daughters.

Mr. McGibbon was a man of considerable wealth and enjoyed the esteem and confidence of his fellow members, not only in the federal parliament, but also in the lumber business.

Damage to the extent of $60,000 was done recently to the McCarter Shingle Mills Plant, Victoria, B.C.

# The Purpose and Plan of Forestry Work

*By C. D. HOWE, Dean of Faculty of Forestry, University of Toronto

Dr. C. D. Howe, Toronto.

As I understand it, the primary object of forestry is the production of wood of a certain quantity and of a certain quality under certain given climatic and soil conditions. The material which we call wood is a certain chemical substance produced in large quantities only by certain types of plants which we call trees. If the chief object of a forester is the production of wood, then it goes without saying, that he must understand how wood is produced in nature, that is, he must understand the physiological relationships of trees; how they manufacture their food, how they digest h ir food, how they assimilate the digested food and transform it into wood. Now, we know that certain things external to the tree influence its wood production. These are particularly the climate and the soil. In order to produce the largest quantity of the most desirable quality of wood, the forester must understand how trees are influenced in their growth by the climatic and soil factors, that is, he must understand the biological relationships of trees.

While a forester must understand the life relationships of individual trees, I believe that, in order to be successful in his work of producing wood, he must acquire a broader conception of forest life. He deals not with single trees alone, but with tree aggregates, with tree communities. These tree communities, like communities of humans, have their mutual relationships, their dependencies, and their interdependencies And like other living communities, they have their stratifications, their laws of reproduction, development and decay; their laws of progression and of retrogression. By this I mean to say that in order to do his best work, a forester must have the broader vision which regards the forest as an entity, an organism with its own peculiar structures and its own peculiar functions; an organism which has its period of birth, of infancy; its juvenile period, its adolescent period, its period of maturity and decay.

I have already elaborated this idea of the structure and function of a forest in my lectures which many of you have heard, but let me again outline the matter in a broad way. "It takes all kinds of people to make a world," and it takes all kinds of plants to make a forest. The reformer or the politician will fail, if he recognizes only one class in human society, so the forester will fail who sees only and thinks only about the pines and spruces, or whatever the commercial class may be in his woodlands.

In the forest the differentiation of the social structure is just as pronounced as in the city of Toronto. There are the meek and lowly in the forest; even those who live in the dark places beneath the soil cover. There is the great middle class of ordinary every day trees. They make up the bulk of the forest and give it stability and character. And then there are the few dominants, the aristocrats, who stand head and shoulders above their associates. They indicate what might be accomplished in the forest world if living conditions were equally good for all To state the case more specifically there is greater or less number of vertical layers of vegetation in every forest: a moss layer, an herbaceous layer, a layer of shrubs or seedlings, a layer of saplings, a layer of suppressed trees, of co-dominant and of dominant trees. This is called vertical zonation, and it results from the fact that there is a difference in life conditions at the ground and at various heights above the ground in a forest, This leads to a differentiation in the structure of the forest, just as there is a differentiation in the structure of a tree itself. The conditions in a forest also vary in a lateral direction. The soil may vary from place to place; here sand and there clay. In one place the soil may be so thin that trees cannot row; in another place the soil may be damper than the average and a stand of different trees result, or there may have been a windfall and conditions

*Address Delivered Before The Foresters' Club, Toronto.

are changed so that another kind of tree comes in. These horizontal differences result in alteration in the structure of the forest.

## The Functions of Individual Trees

Now, a forest regarded as an organism not only has structures, but it has functions of its own apart from the functions of individual trees. The first of these is reproduction, which consists in the production of seeds and their germination. When the seeds have germinated they must establish themselves on the area. Whether or not the seedlings will live depends upon the natural vigor of the seedlings, the amount of food material stored in the seed, the length and vigor of growth of the roots, the ability to endure drying-out conditions. When seedlings have succeeded in establishing themselves, they at once come into competition with seedlings of their own kind or those of other trees, and as you know this competition continues throughout life. We do not know, by experimental evidence at least, why some succeed and others fail, but we do know that the slaughter is terrific. I have seen Douglas fir seedlings at the rate of 500,000 to the acre, and Western hemlock at the rate of 3,000,000 to the acre; yet, when these trees reach maturity scarcely a hundred will be left upon the acre. The ordinary coniferous tree requires about four square feet of soil when 20 years old, and 150 square feet when 100 years old. There is neither room, food nor light enough for them all. The fit survive and the weaklings die. As a rule, 95 per cent. of the trees in a forest sacrifice themselves that others may live. Competition then is one of the normal functions of a forest.

Another function is succession. By this is meant that the composition of the forest is constantly changing until it finds itself in equilibrium with the factors of soil and climate which have brought it into being. The familiar illustration of this is the birch and poplar on the burned areas. They control the ground for 20 or 30 years, then if there is reproduction of the original forest, it in turn gains its former control. Vegetation through its influence on light and soil conditions is constantly making conditions less favorable to its own kind and more favorable to another kind. This results in succession, one of the most pronounced functions of vegetation and nowhere more pronounced than in the forest, to those who have the eyes to see.

## Should Look Ahead for a Century

As I have just said, succession ends in a forest in equilibrium with the factors of its environment, that is with its climatic and soil conditions. We call such a forest a climax forest, and we regard it as stationary. This conception is perhaps satisfactory if we look ahead only 100 years, and as foresters we should look ahead that far. But freeing ourselves from this cramped vision, we can look still farther ahead and say there is nothing fixed and stable in nature and, therefore, in the strict sense of the word, there is no stationary type of forest. In the first place, there would always be minor fluctuations, due to openings from natural causes, such as windfalls, lightning, and consequent changes in the light relations. There would also be wider fluctuations due to biological causes. For example, a light-demanding species such as the pines cannot control an area for more than one generation. The white pine in central Ontario cannot be considered as a climax type, especially when in pure stand. It cannot reproduce itself beneath its own shade; therefore, it must give way in the end to a shade-enduring species, such, perhaps, as the balsam in the northern portions of its range in Ontario.

Coming back to our conception of a forest as a community with its own particular activities, we note another fact of general application, and that is, that a forest community reacts upon its environment, qualitatively and perhaps quantitatively, as does a community of human beings. The human community reacts upon its environment by clearing the forest, tilling the fields, building houses, harnessing the power of boiling and falling water and the lighting in the skies. The forest does things just as wonderful. The forest harnesses the energy from the sun; it solidifies the carbon of the air; it adds a very dilute solution of mineral salts and transforms them into wood. It is the function of the forester to regulate and direct the growth-energy of the forest.

Just as in human community the individuals react upon each other so in a forest community. No tree can live surrounded by other trees and be the same tree that it would if it were living alone in the open. This leads to a change in the form of a tree, and it is the function of a forester to fashion that tree into the form which best serves his

purpose. The forest community reacts upon its local climate; the temperature, the humidity and the precipitation are not quite the same as in the open. The forest community reacts upon the water regime, the storage and the drainage of waters.

### Reaction of Forest Upon the soil

Of greatest importance to the forester who is to direct and regulate wood production, is the reaction of the forest community upon the soil conditions. The forest is the great restorer of the soil. You know the vegetative cycle and you know how the forest keeps that cycle unbroken. A larger percentage of its contents comes from the air than in the case of the field crops, the trees being chiefly solidified sunshine. Not only the material taken from the soil, bu the additional material taken from the air, decays upon the soil and thus the soil is enriched year after year, generation after generation. The soil is the cemetery of the ages. In order to have something living there, something must be dying there. The forest quite literally lives on the bones of its ancestors.

The character of the forest to-day depends upon the successive generations that have gone before. The accumulated vegetable matter in the soil increases its waterholding content, and thus replenishes and regulates one of the most necessary and most variable factors in plant life. You know, the decaying vegetable matter in the soil is dark colored and so readily absorbs heat; it is mostly carbon, and carbon when once warmed is one of the best conservators of heat. Therefore, soils containing large quantities of humus are warmer than otherwise.

You see, the forest community reacts upon the soil by making it constantly richer in food materials, richer in moisture, richer in heat, at least more uniform in heat relations. You see what this means: A progressive change in the adaptability of the soil for various trees. This is one of the chief factors at the basis of the succession which we have already noted. You must have this conceptiaon before you can wisely direct and regulate wood production.

The forest community reacts upon the light conditions, so that they are different from those in any other community. And here also we find progressive changes, varying with the age of the community and usually improving as the community grows older. At each age class, if we put them 20 years or so apart, there are different light values beneath the forest. This gives the opportunity for the various species requiring different degrees of light-exposure to come in This is another chief factor in succession leading to gradual changes in the forest complex.

### How Nature of Vegetation Changes

Pure stands of light-demanding species cannot maintain themselves in competition with shade-endurers. When by the natural processes of elimination and decay the crown cover has been broken sufficiently to give overhead light to the forest floor, a condition in which light-demanders might establish themselves, the ground is too densely shaded by an advanced growth of shade-endurers. When they in turn have reached the dominant crown class, they have the next crop of their own species already established beneath them. So the rotation may go on generation after generation. The only way a pure stand of intolerants can be re-established on the area is by some catastrophe such as windfall, insects or fire completely removing the crown cover. Then the struggle between tolerants and intolerants will begin all over again.

Thus we see, when light values change in the forest there is a disturbance of equilibrium and the nature of the vegetation changes. Here again you must understand the significance of these progressive changes in light values, if you would successfully direct and regulate the growth-energy resulting in wood production in the forest.

I trust by this time you see the point I am trying to emphasize; that in your work as foresters you are dealing with an individual, an organism whose development you can fashion and guide into the lines which you desire and your desire is for the largest quantity of the best quality of wood, adapted for some particular purpose. Nature has no economic sense. Your function is to improve upon nature as expressed in the forest and guide her into economic channels, just as the farmer has improved upon nature in his work and compelled her to serve his economic purposes. Where would we be to-day if the farmer had allowed nature to have her own way? Why, we would have no No. 1 wheat, no dent corn, no northern spy apples, no jersey cows. Having produced these things the farmer still has to control nature or otherwise his wheat fields would be full of tares, his corn covered with smut, his apples filled with worms, and the jersey cows filled with tuberculosis.

### Canada Has Billion Acres of Forest

So as time goes on you will be more and more concerned in controlling the destructive forces in the forest, above all the fire demon and then the fungus and insect pests.

We have in Canada around 1,900,000 square miles of soil covered with forests, That is over a billion acres. A billion acres of forest, that is a wonderful heritage. Let us see how we have treated this great free gift of nature. When we examine this matter our pride is touched at once for we come right up against a fact that involves our obligations of citizenship and this fact is that we have allowed from two thirds to three fourths of our great forest heritage to be destroyed by fire within the past 75 years. Forest fires have destroyed the saw logs on more than 1,000,000 square miles of good Canadian territory.

A million square miles in 75 years burned; total forested area hardly twice that amount. It is only a problem of simple arithmetic to realize what that means for our forests, if these ravages continue. That isn't all. It takes nearly 5 years to produce a stick of spruce pulpwood and nearly twice that length of time to produce a 12-inch spruce sawlog, under the average growing conditions in the forest. Suppose the destruction by forest fires goes on at its present rate, then make another simple arithemetical calculation from the above statement, and you will realize what may become of our spruce pulpwood and spruce sawlog supplies, even within the period when you are still active foresters.

> I wish I could make you all missionaries to preach forest fire protection from the housetops, or better perhaps from soap boxes on the street corners because we will never accomplish adequate fire protection until public opinion is aroused on the subject to a greater extent than it has ever been done yet. You must help in educating the people to realize that every acre of forest land burned means a lost job for some one; you must help to educate the fool with his match out of the forest; you must help the railway corporations, especially the people's railways, to realise that burned forests mean reduced revenues; you must help educate the settler in the north country to realize that the lumberman's right to his purchased timber is equal to his own right in his puchased soil. Unless you help in accomplishing these things you will have been remiss in duty to your country and remiss in obligations to your profession.

There is still another, and more serious, aspect of our present forest fire situation, and that is the prevalence of repeated fires on the same area. There are undoubtedly many situations where one burning under proper control after the logging operations would improve the conditions from the standpoint of the next crop. It would accelerate regeneration both in time and in growth; it would remove many disease-spreading agencies and it would do away with the most dangerous fire hazard by the destruction of the slash. But the repeated burning of the same area is the great destroyer of future forests. The first fire may not destroy all the seed trees, but the second fire usually finishes the job besides killing the young growth that may have followed the first fire. When both seed trees and the young growth have been killed there are no means by which nature unaided can re-establish the commercial species. After a few fires, the area becomes a man-made desert so far as the valuable pulpwood and timber trees are concerned. Thousands of acres of thrifty young growth are being transferred every year from the potential forest class to the desert class through the agency of the repeated fire. If we systematically kill the young growth of our commercial species, what can we expect of the future?

Fire protection is the most important problem in forestry policy to-day; in fact, it is one of the most important economic problems facing Canada at the present time. It transcends the tariff question in its importance in relation to the future prosperity of the country, yet I doubt if you will hear it mentioned in any political speech during the present campaign.

### The Advances in Fire Protection

I wish I had the power to use words that would sear your souls with the importance of forest fire protection. We have made great advances in this respect in the past few years, thanks to the untiring efforts of the Canadian Forestry Association and to various forest fire-fighting organizations throughout the country. Members of our own staff deserve much credit for their part in it, but even at that the present conditions cannot be allowed to continue if we are to keep our forests continuously productive and our lumber industries prosperous, industries that increase our national wealth by a half billion dollars a year.

Forest protection will be your most important work for the next few years, but you will help solve other problems, all interesting and stimulating. You occupy a favored position in forestry. The men who have gone before you have been preparing the way for you. Their

duties have been largely administrative. Now the price of lumber and the condition of markets are such that things can be done in certain forest localities that could not be done before. We are now on the threshold of intelligent management of our forests, the practice of forestry in the technical meaning of the word assuming, of course, that the present business depression is only temporary. You are to take part in the remoulding and recreating of the forest organism, in guiding and directing nature's growth-energy to an extent impossible to your predecessors in the profession. As soon as you attempt to direct nature's forces in the forest you will at once come up against problems that will put a serious strain upon your gray matter. Suppose you are placed in a white pine forest. You know that white pine has contributed more to the wealth of the eastern provinces than any other forest tree, but it is gradually passing out of the forest, even on areas that have not been seriously burned. The present logging methods create conditions unfavorable to the re-establishment of white pine forests. It is a very valuable tree because its wood is useful for many purposes and it grows quite rapidly. It would be good business to perpetuate it in the forest without resorting to expensive planting. How is it to be done? We don't know. That is one of the problems some of you must solve.

Let us turn to the former pineries that have been burned. Some of them, as you know, have abundant regeneration, fine young stands of white pine of great promise, while an adjacent area burned at the same time is in the possession of poplar or birch with little or no pine. Why? We don't know. We may guess, but we really don't know. Some of you or your successors will solve the problem. A monument may be erected in Queen's Park some day to the man who devises a cutting method that will ensure an adequate natural regeneration of white pine in our forests, this in spite of the fact that he won't need such a monument. The gratitude of generations of lumbermen will be his monument, as well as the white pine forests he will leave behind, for they will go on long after there bronze or marble in Queen's Park

### The Depletion of Pulpwood Lands

Suppose you were placed in a pulpwood forest. You know the story of the cut-over pulpwood lands, how the spruce, undoubtedly furnishing the best wood for all round pulp and paper purposes of any tree in our forests, is being gradually crowded out by inferior species. It will be your problem through your knowledge of its biological relations, its seedbed requirements, its light requirements, its soil requirements to reinstate the spruce to its former position in the forest. The pulp and paper industry adds around $100,000,000 to our national wealth each year, besides distributing amout $30,000,000 in wages. The principal source of supply is spruce, yet the commercial supply is fast disappearing. It is going the same way white pine has gone in our forest. The man who can devise a logging method, fair to the operator and fair to the people, the owners of the land, that will ensure the establishment of successive crops of spruce may also have a monument erected to his memory.

It may be that you will be called upon to help recreate forests by artificial methods on areas where the possibility of natural regeneration has been destroyed by abuse or mismanagement. There are close to a half million acres of waste lands in Old Ontario that could be very profitably brought into tree-bearing again by artificial reforestation. These areas are very near local markets, and so will be reforested first, but when that is done there would still remain a half million acres of old pineries in central Ontario, areas that in the past have borne 10,000, perhaps, 20,000 feet of pine per acre, that have been burned and reburned until all the young pine growth has been destroyed. The pine forest will have to be recreated by artificial planting if it ever exists again on those areas. In the not distant future, generally speaking, products from planted forests will contribute to the supply of local markets, and some of you will have the satisfaction of creating those forests.

### The Economic Life of the Nation

So I might go on outlining your problems in the forests north of the prairies, on the East Slope of the Rocky Mountains and in British Columbia. They are fundamentally the same everywhere. The creation of a forest by guiding and directing tree growth energy for the purposes of continuous public service, in order that industries which touch the economic life of the nation in almost every phase may be always maintained in a prosperous condition. What would it mean to Canada if all our twelve hundred million acres of absolute forest soil were fully stocked with commercial trees, adequately protected from fire and managed for continuous production? What would the resources from such forests mean in terms of reduced taxation, in furnishing the financial aid in the building of highways, the endowment of schools and universities, the founding of hospitals and libraries? You see, you are to be important factors in the effort to lead your own country into the path of its higher destiny. Unless you have this vision and faith in the ultimate success of that vision, you will have failed in the duty of your profession and in the obligations of citizenship.

# Pulpwood Logging in the Abitibi District

By CHAS. G. LEVIE, Manager St. Regis Paper Co., Limited, Oscalanea, Que.

On the Canadian National Railway, between La Tuque, Que., and Cochrane, Ont., lies one of the largest pulpwood forests in the province of Quebec. This district is generally known as the Abitibi district, named after lake Abitibi, which has an area of 640 square miles.

The chief industries of this district are paper, sulphite, groundwood mills and pulpwood. Agriculture is developed as the wood is taken off the land. Owing to the country being not opened up sufficiently, the crops suffer more or less from early fall and late spring frosts, but this is becoming less year by year.

Considerable land is unfit for cultivation, due to the bogs, swamps and muskegs that predominate, but within a few years, as the timber is removed, this land will possibly be reclaimed. Employment is, however, furnished several thousand men converting the timber growing on these places, into pulpwood. Owing to the density of the bush, and the nature of the soil, the trees do not grow to a very large size, hence there is very little manufactured into lumber, although there are a few sawmills.

The different kind of trees that grow, are black spruce, balsam fir, white birch, and jack-pine in the sandy regions. The quality of the wood is very good, very little rot being found, and as for pulpwood, the spruce and balsam fir cannot be excelled. The trees are more or less scrubby, short in length, two and three, twelve feet logs generally being the average per tree.

The system of logging employed, is that usually in the month of March, when travelling in the bush is good, the woods' boss, with a few assistants, generally cruises the timber that is proposed to be cut during the following fall and winter. This timber is then blocked out into several sections, each section representing a "job" for which contracts are made later. In September, when the leaves are off the trees, these "jobs" or sections are shown over to prospective contractors or jobbers, who again travel them before signing the contract.

After the contract has been signed for the cutting of all pulpwood on the job or section contracted for, no time is lost by the jobber in starting work. He immediately goes into the woods with his crew, teams, logging and cooking outfits, and starts the construction of his camps. A set of three camps is generally put up, viz.: a cooking camp, hovel and sleep camp. The size of the camps vary according to the number of men and horses employed.

The jobber then blazes out his main roads and forks, which his men cut out and clear, bunching the timber in small piles. After the roads are cut, the jobber then divides his "job" into smaller sections, which he subs to his men at a price per cord. Three men generally form a crew, two choppers and one swamper. The jobber does the piling and hauling of the logs, paying his teamsters and other help by the month.

The logs are cut in lengths of 12 or 16 feet long, and in the early fall, the wood which is close to the shores of the river and lakes, is usually "snaked" or chained out in places where the ground is dry; otherwise, this wood is left until later, when the ground is frozen. The timber that is away from the shores is generally piled on convenient skidways, to be taken out when there is sufficient snow for the sleighs. The wood is then piled on skidways along the shore, and when the ice is sufficiently strong, the logs are piled on the ice.

In the spring, the company send their river-drivers, who place a boom around all these loose logs, after which they roll the logs piled on the lakeshore into pocket booms. These booms are then towed to the mill, with an alligator or warping tug, and stored in the mill boom until they are put through the barkers. The logs on the creeks and rivers are floated down into the main lake, where they are driven into a storage boom, and later towed to the mill boom.

### Mr. Wilson Passes Another Milestone

Many friends in the pulp and paper and lumber arena extended congratulations to Percy Bateman Wilson, of Sault Ste Marie, president of the Canadian Pulp & Paper Association, who on December 20, celebrated his 55th birthday.

Mr. Wilson, who is vice-president of the Spanish River Pulp & Paper Mills, was born in England in 1866, and, after serving with several representative firms in the Old Country in a financial and

P. B. Wilson, Sault Ste. Marie, Ont.

accounting capacity, came to Canada just nine years ago. He was secretary and director of the Forest Mills of British Columbia, Limited, Revelstoke, B.C., for two years and in 1914 joined the Spanish River Pulp & Paper Co., at Sault Ste. Marie as comptroller and director. The next year he was made vice-president of the Fort William Paper Co., a director of the North American Securities Co. and other organizations.

Last January at the annual meeting of the Canadian Pulp & Paper Association, held in Montreal, Mr Wilson was made head of that organization, a position which he has filled with credit to himself and honor to this great representative body.

### Death of Mr. James Crawford

James Crawford, general manager of the Blue River Lumber Co., Limited, Blue River, P.Q., passed away recently. A few days before his death he contracted a severe cold, which later developed into congestion of the lungs.

Mr. Crawford was born in Frampton, Que., in 1854, where he spent his boyhood days, and after leaving home, secured his first position with Stetson, Cutler & Co., in Van Buren, Maine, with which firm he was associated for many years. In 1898 he became American customs officer at Van Buren, the duties of which position he ably and faithfully discharged for nineteen years. In 1917 he resigned as customs officer and took up his residence in Blue River, where he entered the firm of the Blue River Lumber Co. as one of its leading shareholders and general manager.

The funeral service was held in Blue River, after which the remains were taken to Van Buren for interment. Many beautiful floral offerings were received, evincing the esteem in which the late Mr. Crawford was held. He leaves three sons, James, Fred and Charles, and one daughter, Nora, to mourn his death. Mrs. Crawford, who was Miss Elizabeth Lapointe, of St. Leonard's, N.B., predeceased her husband in 1913.

The passing of Mr. Crawford removes a lumberman who was widely known and highly thought of in the community. He possessed a high sense of honor and justice and rich and poor were always welcomed by him in times of distress, and many found in Mr. Crawford a cheerful giver, counsellor and friend.

### Was Widely Known in Lumber Circles

Wm. H. Parker died recently in his 87th year at the Laurentian Club, Lac la Peche, Que., after an illness of two months. He was well-known among the lovers of outdoor sports and was a exceptionally fond of fishing and hunting. He usually spent his winters as a guest at the Windsor Hotel, Montreal. Mr. Parker's father was a wealthy and successful timber operator, who came to Montreal about

seventy years ago from New Hampshire, and made a successful entrance into the then little developed business of this province, building several large sawmills at Charlemagne and Louisville, above Three Rivers. He died, leaving a substantial fortune, which was inherited by his son, the late Wm. H. Parker. The latter married Miss Mary Tyler, daughter of one of the pioneer lumber merchants of Lower Canada, who predeceased him in 1891. The late Mr. Parker was an ardent sportsman and was one of the first to exploit Caledonia Springs, now controlled by the C. P. R., where he built a race track and where one of the first races for the Queen's Plate was won many years ago.

### Death of Another Veteran Lumberman

David S. Sherk, a widely-known lumberman, died recently in his 82nd year at Ridgeway, Ont. The cause of his passing was apoplexy. He leaves to mourn his death his wife, four sons and two daughters. Four sons and one daughter predeceased him. Mr. Sherk entered the lumber business at Gilmour, Ont., about thirty years ago and conducted operations under his own name for about sixteen years. He then took into the business two of his sons, running it as D. S. Sherk & Sons, the firm consisting of D. S. Sherk, Frank M. Sherk and E. Bruce Sherk. In 1904 he retired from the lumber business and the firm was changed to Sherk Bros., being conducted by Frank M. and W. Scott Sherk. The late Mr. Sherk was of United Empire Loyalist stock, his grandfather having come to Welland County about 1800. He was in politics a staunch Conservative and served both in county and township affairs on many occasions. He was also receiver of wrecks along the shore of Lake Erie for quite a number of years.

### Passing of Halton County Lumberman

Murray Crawford, a prominent lumberman of Halton county, died recently at his home in Campbellville, Ont. He was born in Halton county in 1860, and had lived in that district all his life. He was the president of Murray Crawford, Limited, which company was incorporated some time ago, and has been identified with the lumber business for over two-score years. He is survived by his wife, three sons and two daughters. The passing of Mr. Crawford will be regretted by a large circle of friends and business associates, among whom he was held in high esteem.

### Eastern Lumberman Wins Seat in Commons

George B. Jones was one of the lumbermen returned in the recent federal election for King's County, N.B., in the Conservative interests. Mr. Jones, who resides at Apohaqui, is the founder of the large mercantile busines carried on by Jones Bros., who have been engaged in logging and manufacturing lumber for the past twenty-four years. They cut from 5,000,000 to 7,000,000 feet annually of spruce, pine, hemlock and hardwood. All the limits of the firm are freehold as there are no Crown Lands around Apohaqui.

Mr. Jones is a director of the Bayside Lumber Co., Bayside, Halifax County, N.S., and has always taken a lively interest in every-

George B. Jones, M. P., Apohaqui, N. B.

thing pertaining to the lumber industry. He was first chosen to represent King's County in the New Brunswick Legislature in 1908 and was successful in the subsequent elections of 1912, 1917 and 1920.

Mr. Jones, who states that he has always been a loyal and consistent supporter of the Conservative party, was born in 1866

# Keeping Tab on Stock in Retail Yard

## System by Which Yardman Can Tell at Glance Just What he Has on Hand—The Plan Outlined

### By Walter Warren, Toronto

There are comparatively few retail lumber yards that can tell at a glance just what their stock consists of, and this in spite of the fact, that it is more profitable to operate a perpetual stock keeping system than not to keep one.

Let me outline our own method of keeping track of our stock, together with some of the advantages gained. Our yard is laid out in streets, or alleys, each one named or numbered. The front foundations are divided into spaces of 4 feet, 4 inches, and each space is numbered similar to street numbering, odd on one side and even on the other. The lumber piles are all 4 feet wide or multiples of 4 feet, the extra 4 inches giving piling space. This method applies not only to the yard piles, but also to the sheds, and to everything wherever it is stored.

The material is segregated as much as possible. At all corners of the streets or the roads the number or the name appears in prominent letters, or figures, printed on metal plates of black with white lettering.

The pile numbers are all marked in the same way and each pile also bears a black plate giving a full description of the material and the date piled, which is also lettered in white.

All stocks of lumber are then recorded in a stock book alphabetically arranged, giving the road, the pile number, a full description and the quantities. This work is done by one man, the stock book being brought up to date every Saturday. This book is kept in triplicate, one copy being for the use of the stockkeeper, the second for the local yard, while the third is used by the head office, so that any department can tell at a glance just what the stock consists of.

The old fashioned method, very much in vogue, is that of going out to take stock upon receipt of the customer's enquiry. The result

| Path | Year | Road | Pile | Size * Description | K.D. | 1" Quarter | Cut | Waste | Oak | Page |
|---|---|---|---|---|---|---|---|---|---|---|
| 4 | 21 | 14 | 16 | 1" 10" Under 1x2 Qtr.W.O. | | 3666 | | | | |
| 10 | 20 | 14 | 14 | 1" " " | | 1462 | | | | |
| | | | | | | | | | | |
| 10 | 20 | 13 | 19 | 1" 1 1/2 1x2 Qtr.W.O. | | 680 | | | | |
| 4 | 21 | 14 | 1 | 1" " " | | 2352 | | | | |
| | | | | | | | | | | |
| 11 | 21 | 14 | 48 | 1" 12" Under Qm. | | 2268 | | | | |
| 11 | 21 | 14 | 47 | 1" " " " | | 2880 | | | | |
| 4 | 21 | 55 | 1 | 1" " " " | K.D. | 2000 | | | | |
| 10 | 21 | 14 | 37 | 1" " " " | | 2740 | | | | |
| | | | | | | | | | | |
| 4 | 21 | 16 | 88 | 1" 7/16 1x2 Qtr.W.O. | | 3072 | | | | |
| 4 | 21 | 16 | 66 | 1" " " " | | 1680 | | | | |
| 4 | 21 | 16 | 84 | 1" " " " | | 3040 | | | | |
| 4 | 21 | 16 | 80 | 1" " " " | | | | | | |
| 4 | 21 | 33 | 9 | 1" 7/16 " " | K.D. | 4860 | | | | |
| | | | | | | | | | | |
| 4 | 21 | 58 | 2 | 1" Thin Qtr. White Oak | | 783 | | | | |
| 6 | 21 | 13 | 63 | 1" Wormy 7/16 Qm.W.O. | | 414 | | | | |

*A sample sheet from the stock book*

is that quite frequently, after a lapse of some hours when the information and quotation is handed to the customer, the lumber dealer finds himself in the unenviable position of being informed that order has been placed with one of his aggressive competitors.

Another advantage to be gained by a perpetual stock is that of knowing at all times the status of the stock.

That the stock should be kept in order daily is of the utmost importance. To do this the stockkeeper consults the daily charge sheets, making those deductions from his inventory and, as each carload of lumber is unloaded and placed in the respective piles; it is at once placed on the inventory and duly recorded.

My contention is that in keeping track of stock in this way the office has perfect control, and can direct the use of the oldest piles. The plan also speeds up and makes the work of the sales force easy, enabling them to effect a quick sale, sometimes without further competition, whereas the hesitating and obsolete method of having to investigate the stock frequently drives away a customer to a competitor.

We also find that it speeds up very materially our shipping department. In fact, the cost of stock keeping can be considered in the light of an investment, and it pays a dividend of several hundred per cent. per annum. It keeps undesirable and slow moving stock always before us, and by this means, assist in early sales.

I submit a sample of our stock sheets, which I hope may be found of interest to the readers of the "Canada Lumberman." We find that this method is particularly valuable in keeping a plentiful supply of material on hand for our factory needs, and it is essential that an adequate supply of kiln dried lumber should be provided for at all times.

## New Brunswick Log Scale Falls Short

In reference to the announced stumpage dues passed by the New Brunswick Government, the River Valley Lumber Co. of Oromocto, N.B., says that their action in granting a reduction on the trees damaged, or rather destroyed, by the budworm, is in our opinion nothing more than a joke, as it cannot under existing conditions offer any inducement to manufacturers. The budworm injured trees are for the greater part fir, which after being allowed to stand two or more years, after actually dead, have now reached a point where they are, generally speaking, worthless. The lumber manufacturers have for the past number of years been getting quite enough refuse from the ordinary run of logs which are supposed to be sound. This budworm eaten, grub eaten, woodpecker riddled growth which they offer a reduction on can class as nothing but REFUSE. Where is the inducement?

If the request made by the lumbermen of the province had been granted in its entirety we certainly believe it would have had a very marked effect on this season's operations. In our opinion, the season is now too advanced to do anything which will tend to increase or contribute to larger operations in the bush for 1921-22.

The present authorized log scale comes far short of doing justice to the lumber manufacturer on logs from 5 to 8 in. diameter. We are herewith enclosing you a sheet comparing the present authorized with that which the log scale from 5 to 7 in. will actually produce and after you have compared the two we think you will certainly agree that there is a marked difference, particularly when you realize that over 50% of the logs now manufactured are below the 8 in. diameter at top. If the manufacturers are to be dealt nearly fair with, then the Scale Rule must be corrected or he will be forced out of business.

### Small Logs

| | Present | | | | Amended | | |
|---|---|---|---|---|---|---|---|
| Length | Diameter Inches | | | Length | Diameter Inches | | |
| Feet | 5 | 6 | 7 | Feet | 5 | 6 | 7 |
| 10 | 10 | 15 | 20 | 10 | 9 | 12 | 18 |
| 12 | 12 | 18 | 24 | 12 | 11 | 15 | 21 |
| 14 | 14 | 21 | 28 | 14 | 12 | 17 | 25 |
| 16 | 16 | 24 | 32 | 16 | 14 | 20 | 28 |
| 18 | 18 | 27 | 36 | 18 | 16 | 22 | 30 |
| 20 | 20 | 30 | 40 | 20 | 17 | 25 | 33 |
| 22 | 22 | 33 | 44 | 22 | 19 | 27 | 36 |
| 24 | 24 | 36 | 48 | 24 | 21 | 30 | 40 |

The Westminster Mill Co. of New Westminster, B.C., has just closed one of the biggest timber deals of recent years by buying from Alex. McLaren, of Buckingham, Quebec, some 32,000 acres of timber at Cultus Lake, near Chilliwack, for a price in the neighborhood of $600,000. The Westminster Mill Co. is owned by Messrs. G. W. Beach, C. J. Culter, and associates. These timber limits have been in the possession of the McLaren family for 32 years, since the days of the North Pacific Lumber Company's mill at Barnet.

A federal charter has been granted to the Rimouski Lumber & Lath Co., Limited, with a capital stock of $300,000 and headquarters in Rimouski. The company is empowered to carry on the business of lumbering in all its branches and to manufacture and deal in wood and timber of all kinds and to establish mills for the production of mechanical pulp, sulphite pulp, sulphate pulp, carboard, etc.

A leading lumberman, who recently returned from the South, says that practically every manufacturer down there has a fear of what they term a runaway market, for they know that if there is a sudden demand for lumber on account of the shortage, values are likely to go out of all proportion to what they should be. It is stated that if lumber buyers would only place their orders for their legitimate requirements now, and buy gradually, there would be no upheaval in the market. Lumber manufacturers are doing their best to keep stocks of dry hardwoods on hand, but with the rainy season upon them and very few available logs, it is a rather difficult proposition. It is said that one big company recently sent out a letter to all southern manufacturers, urging them to cut up every log available in order to get a bigger stock on hand, and thus offset any tendency towards runaway quotations, which all view somewhat apprehensively.

## Live Pacific Coast Representatives

Elliot & Elliot, who have established offices in the Bartlett Building, Windsor, Ont., and are the selling agents for representative British Columbia sawmills, have built up, during the past year, a splendid connection in Ontario west of Toronto and particularly in the Niagara peninsula. The Elliot boys were born in Listowel, Ont. W. R. went west twelve years ago and acquired a practical knowledge in the sash and door line. His brother, J. E., came later to Vancouver and gained a similar experience, which qualifies both members of the firm to render splendid service to the retail lumber yards and woodworking interests.

W. R. Elliot, Windsor, Ont.       J. E. Elliot, Windsor, Ont.

Elliot & Elliot represent the Apex Lumber Co, and the Pacific Box Co., of Vancouver, and handle timbers, lumber, shingles and lath, as well as box shooks, heading, staves, etc.

The firm announce that they are not jobbers but representatives of west coast manufacturers and wholesalers, and it is their intention during the coming season to handle considerable quantities of Mountain stocks in western pine and spruce.

Elliot & Elliot say that during 1922 they intend to broaden their connections. They believe that this year will see a decided improvement in the lumber trade generally, and are making their plans accordingly. In going over their territory they find practically every yard with a limited amount of stock, and it is their opinion that there may soon be an advance in prices on account of many firms not covering their requirements for another season. Yardmen have hesitated to do this earlier on account of stocktaking, endeavoring to keep their inventories as low as possible.

Elliot & Elliot do not anticipate a runaway market, such as was experienced a couple of years ago, but they do believe that the West Coast manufacturers especially, will be in a position to get a reasonable price for their stock by reason of the volume of business offering.

### Pulp Timber Will Pay Pulp Royalty

Several important amendments are contained in the bill to amend the Forest Act, introduced by Hon. T. D. Pattullo, Minister of Lands. Power is taken to dispose of timber, either by public auction or public tender. Hitherto the mode of disposal has been entirely by public tender.

Certain old leases, which carried a low rental and a low royalty, and which have not been changed into perpetual licenses, will be given until March 31, 1922, to exchange leases for licenses upon payment of one dollar per acre, and will thereafter pay the present license fees and royalties.

It is made clear that a pulp license stands exactly in the same position as an ordinary timber license in case of failure to pay the prescribed fees.

An extension of time is granted for survey of unsurveyed licenses. On account of both surveys and back fees being required this year, it is felt that both falling at once is unduly heavy and extension of time is being given for survey.

As the Forest Act stands at present, pulpwood is not specifically defined. To make the matter perfectly clear and simple of operation, pulpwood is defined and provision is made that all timber from pulp licenses used for pulp purposes will pay pulp royalty, while all timber put through the sawmill will pay sawmill royalty.

Power is given to the Lieutenant-Governor in Council to declare as pulpwood timber all that below the standard of utilization for sawmill purposes, and this class of timber will then come under pulpwood royalty. The advantage of this section is that it will result in clean cutting, as it will enable the operator to cut a lot of small timber that is now left uncut. This will result in much larger revenue to the government and will reduce the fire hazard. Provision is made to bring all the scaling service into the civil service.

## W. J. MacBeth Joins Silent Majority

The death took place in Toronto on December 24 of William J. MacBeth, a widely-known lumberman, who passed away at the home of his son, Dr. W. L. C. MacBeth, 160 Jameson Avenue, from an attack of pneumonia. The late Mr. MacBeth has not been enjoying the best of health for some time. A little over a year ago his wife died, and during the war he lost a son, Robert E. MacBeth, who was a member of the Royal Air Force, and was killed in an aeroplane accident overseas. Mr. MacBeth, who was in his sixty-fourth year, was a son of the late John MacBeth, who for many years ran a sawmill at Gilford, in Simcoe county. In association with his brother, Charles G. MacBeth (who for many years has been identified with the R. Laidlaw Lumber Co., Toronto), he operated a mill under the name of MacBeth Bros. & Co. at Craighurst, Simcoe county, until the limits were all cut off. The brothers then came to Toronto and established a retail lumber business in Parkdale for some years. In 1892, Charles G. Macbeth joined the R. Laidlaw Lumber Co., and William J. became connected with the A. R. Williams Machinery Co., having charge of their lumber interests. His next position was as sales manager of the J. D. Shier Lumber Co. of Bracebridge, after which he joined the Parry Sound Lumber Co. of Parry Sound in a similar capacity, and was with that organization until it went out of business. Since then he was engaged in a wholesale lumber business on his own account in Toronto. Mr. MacBeth was always deeply interested in the affairs of lumbermen's bodies, and attended the last annual convention of the Canadian Lumbermen's Association in Ottawa. He was a member of the Masonic Order and also of Parkdale Presbyterian Church. He leaves to mourn his departure two daughters, Mrs. F. A. Gaby and Mrs. G. C. MacLaren, of Toronto, and three sons, John and Benjamin, of the law firm of MacBeth & MacBeth, and Dr. W. L. C. MacBeth.

## Quebec Looks for Stronger Export Business

Though the advices received by the Quebec lumber trade from their European agents, do not indicate any sign of improvement in the United Kingdom market, there is a ring of a new spirit of optimism in the letters in consequence of the European confidence in a happy termination of the Washington Conference and the sanguine belief of a settlement of the Irish difficulty, which is calculated to bring peace and contentment to the British Empire and give Lloyd George an opportunity to apply his talents in the settlement of economic conditions of Central Europe; this, together with the hope that the United States will take serious cognizance of the report made to this government, from the special committee delegated by the United States Chamber of Commerce to proceed to and investigate economic conditions resultant of the war in Europe.

This phase of the situation has been carefully studied by the banking interests of Canada and the United States, and by the same export interests in the United Kingdom. This is the beginning of a spirit of optimism that is bound to spread, and within 1922 bring about a reaction in commerce and industry which will rejuvenate construction and result to the benefit of the Canadian timber and sawn lumber trade. The general feeling in business circles, shared by the Quebec lumber interests, is that the ultimate success of the Washington Conference will cause the United States to take part in the economic settlements of the world.

The Quebec firm of W. & J. Sharples, Ltd., shipped to the United Kingdom, including shipments via the port of Montreal to the United Kingdom, 4,542,688 feet of timber and deals B.M., and from the company's mills to the United States 3,479,234 feet.

Price Bros. shipped from the port of Quebec to the United Kingdom 3,970,000 feet, and from Quebec to the United States 6,970,000 feet, and from the firm's mills to the United States 22,793,000 feet, making a total shipment of 33,793,000 feet.

The firm of Dobell, Beckett & Co. shipped from the port of Quebec 1,245,675 feet, B.M., spruce deals, and 176,241 cubic feet of lumber. The latter included 3,663, c. ft. of oak, 54,928 c. ft. elm, 107,447 c. ft. waney pine timber, and 10,203 c. ft. of waney birch timber.

The Louise Lumber Co. shipped from the port of Quebec to Ireland by the steamers "Ramore Head" and "Lord Antrim," 400 standards of deals, and toward the end of the season received orders for treble that quantity, but were unable to ship from the port of Quebec to meet the latter demand for want of cargo space.

## Breezy Jottings From Far and Near

The many friends of J. L. MacFarlane, of the Canadian General Lumber Co., Toronto, will regret to learn that he is confined to his house by illness and hope that he may be soon restored to good health.

Allan McPherson, of McPherson & Clarke, retail lumber dealers, Glencoe, Ont., has been re-elected reeve of Glencoe for the coming year. His many friends will congratulate him on the renewal of confidence in his services on behalf of the municipality for another term.

A federal charter has been granted to the Dominion Wood Specialties, with a capital stock of $50,000, and headquarters in Montreal. The company is empowered to manufacture and deal in lumber, wood and wood products of all kinds, and all articles of which wood forms a part. Among the incorporators are John F. Forman, Ernest Lindelius, Montreal, and Chas. H. Ancrum, of Westmount.

The death took place recently in Toronto of David G. B. Ross at the age of seventy-eight years. He was an employee of the Department of Lands and Forests at the Parliament Buildings for over sixty years, retiring only a short time ago. He is survived by his wife, one son and two daughters.

M. A. Grainger, of Vancouver, B.C., president of the Canadian Society of Forest Engineers, was in Toronto recently attending the Forestry Section of the American Association for the Advancement of Science. Mr. Grainger is the man who drafted the Forest Act of British Columbia, which is regarded as a model for similar legislation throughout Canada.

A federal charter has been granted the Laidlaw-Belton Lumber Co., with headquarters in Sarnia, Ont., with a capital stock of $200,000, to acquire the assets, property and good-will of the partnership carried on by George H. Belton, Chester H. Belton, Robert Laidlaw and Walter C. Laidlaw, under the name of the R. Laidlaw Lumber Co., in the city of Sarnia, to take over its business as a going concern on January 1st and to continue the same. The incorporators are George H. Belton, of London; Chester H. Belton, of Sarnia; Robert Laidlaw, R. A. Laidlaw and Walter C. Laidlaw.

The S.S. Robert Dollar, flagship of the Canadian Robert Dollar fleet, plying from Vancouver to all parts of the world, sailed recently on her second trip around the world under the guiding hand of Captain Kerr, the popular master of the vessel. In her holds was one of the largest cargoes ever shipped from this port, consisting of nearly 2,000,000 feet of lumber and 3,000 tons of general. Half of the lumber will be unshipped in China and the rest will go to Calcutta and Yokohama.

The George H. Belton Lumber Co., with a capital stock of $100,000, and headquarters in London, has been federally incorporated, to acquire the assets, property and good-will of the partnership carried on by George H. Belton, Robert Laidlaw and Walter C. Laidlaw, under the name of the George H. Belton Lumber Co., of London, and to take over this business as a going concern on January 1st. The incorporators of the new company are George H. Belton, London; Chester H. Belton, Sarnia; Robert Laidlaw, R. A. Laidlaw and Walter C. Laidlaw, of Toronto.

Logging is more active, owing to reduced stocks and firmer prices. The improvement noticeable in the demand for lumber is evidenced by the fact that at Vancouver, early in November, the export orders on hand were sufficient to keep the mills fully occupied until the end of the year, beyond which time the operators are unwilling to make contracts, apparently for fear of a rising market. Exports of lumber from British Columbia for the first nine months of this year amounted to 106,000,000 feet, of which Japan took 65,000,000 feet. The latter country, according to trade advices, is likely to provide a large and permanent market for certain classes and sizes of lumber, in manufacturing which a residue of yard stock is left to be disposed of locally. China has also recently come on the market for Canadian lumber.

## Safeguarding Forest Wealth of Canada

The American Association for the Advancement of Science recently held its seventy-fourth meeting in Toronto and attracted many scientists of world-wide reputation. One of the most important questions taken up was forestry.

Ellwood Wilson, chief forester of the Laurentide Co., Grand Mere, Que., delivered a rousing talk. He said that hydroplanes were employed in his work to scout for fires, inspect logging operations, make maps and estimates of timber areas. The two greatest needs in Canada to-day in the management of the all-important forest resources are, according to Mr. Wilson, their protection from fire and an estimate of their extent and amount. This would have taken years of work, but with aircraft it can be completed in a comparatively short time.

Mr. Wilson cited as an example the work done by the Air Board for the Ontario Government at English River this past season. Those who had the experience with aircraft feel that a new era has dawned in the proper management of Canada's forests based on the knowledge gained from the air.

T. W. Dwight, of the Dominion Forest Service, Ottawa, spoke before the Canadian Society of Forest Engineers and the Society of American Foresters. His remarks were on timber administration in the Dominion Forest Service.

Progress in sound forestry practice can be secured only as it is supported by educated public opinion and the advance of technical knowledge; and the work of informing the public and the securing of technical information is an important function of the Dominion Forest Service. This work falls into the main lines of stocktaking of the forests; securing of statistics as to the manufacture and consumption of forest products; the improvement of utilization methods through the work of the forest products laboratories of Canada, and of research into silvicultural problems by means of forest experiment stations.

The work of administering the timber on Dominion national forests was described in detail. In brief, the time is to provide from year to year as much fuel and building timber as possible for the settlers on the agricultural lands surrounding the reserved, and at the same time to increase the stock of the better classes of timber till the area has reached its rate of production.

A paper full of helpful experiences was read by G. H. Prince, of Fredericton, provincial forester of New Brunswick.

To make possible the adoption of improved methods of management in the future a complete classification of the Crown lands is being made. Over 4,000,000 acres have already been classified as to nature of the soil, amounts of timber by size and species per unit of area, with complete forest maps to various scales showing the location of the topography and timber. The survey is being made on a four per cent. basis and is the most comprehensive of its kind ever undertaken in America.

To prescribe the best cutting method for stands of slow-growing spruce, which does not reach the regulation cutting limit, and upon which special cutting permits are granted, an area of one square mile has been reserved and logged experimentally under different cutting methods on a scale sufficiently large to form under intensive study conclusive results in a few years. Co-operation is maintained with the Dominion Government and lumber companies in this work, and it is expected that more experimental preserves will be established in other forest types for the purpose of improving cutting methods now in force.

## Several Timber Sales Made in Ontario

Several timber sales have taken place in Ontario since the first of October under the auspices of the Department of Lands and Forests:

There were sold on December 10th, berth No. 1, southwest quarter, township of Pardo, district of Sudbury, 9½ square miles, to the Mageau Lumber Co., of Field, whose tender was the highest. The price paid was $16.15 per M feet, b.m., for the red and white pine timber; 25c each for railway ties; all in addition to Crown dues.

Lot 4, concession 5 and lot 4, concession 6, township of Lyman, district of Nipissing, consisting of 1 square mile, was recently sold to the Canadian Timber Co., Limited, Toronto. The price paid was $8.10 per M feet, b.m., for red and white pine; 30c each for railway ties; all in addition to Crown dues.

Lots 7 to 20, inclusive, concession 1, lots S pts. 7 to 19, inclusive, concession 2, Fowler township, district of Thunder Bay, consisting of 9½ acres, were sold during the latter part of November to James T. Greer, Port Arthur, the price paid being $8.00 per M feet, b.m., for pine; $8.50 per M feet, b.m., for spruce; $5.00 per M feet, b.m., for poplar; $6.00 per M feet, b.m., for other timber; 20c each for railway ties; 50c per cord for spruce pulpwood; 25c per cord for other pulpwood; all in addition to Crown dues.

The tender of the Indian Lake Lumber Co., of Osaquan, Ont. (per D. L. Mather, of Winnipeg), was recently accepted for berth W.R., 4-A, district of Kenora, consisting of 53½ square miles. The price paid was $7.50 per M feet, b.m., for pine timber; $6.85 per M feet, b.m., for spruce and poplar; $5.40 per M feet, b.m., for other timber; 5c each for railway ties; 75c per cord for spruce pulpwood; 50c per cord for other pulpwood; 10c per cord for fuelwood; all in addition to dues.

Another sale made in November was to A. G. Murray of Fort Frances, consisting of 6½ square miles, an area lying east of Stokes Bay and south of Pipestone River, running into Rainy Lake. The bids received by the Government were $10.00 per M feet for white and Nor. way pine; $8.00 per M feet for jack pine; $8.00 per M feet for spruce; $5.00 per M feet for poplar; 6c each for railway ties; $2.00 per cord for spruce pulpwood; 35c per cord for other pulpwood; 25c per cord for fuelwood; all in addition to Crown dues.

# CURRENT LUMBER PRICES—WHOLESALE

## TORONTO

(In Car Load Lots, F.O.B. cars Toronto)

### White Pine

| | | |
|---|---|---|
| 1 x 4/7 Good Strips | $110.00 | $115.00 |
| 1¼ & 1½ x 4/7 Good Strips | 120.00 | 125.00 |
| 1 x 8 and up Good Sides | 150.00 | 160.00 |
| 2 x 4/7 Good Strips | 130.00 | 140.00 |
| 1¼ & 1½ x 8 and wider Good Sides | 185.00 | 190.00 |
| 2 x 8 and wider Good Sides | 190.00 | 200.00 |
| 1 in. No. 1, 2 and 3 Cuts | 85.00 | 90.00 |
| 5/4 and 6/4 No. 1, 2 and 3 Cuts | 100.00 | 105.00 |
| 2 in. No. 1, 2 and 3 Cuts | 105.00 | 110.00 |
| 1 x 4 and 5 Mill Run | 52.00 | 55.00 |
| 1 x 6 Mill Run | 53.00 | 56.00 |
| 1 x 7, 9 and 11 Mill Run | 53.00 | 56.00 |
| 1 x 8 Mill Run | 55.00 | 58.00 |
| 1 x 10 Mill Run | 60.00 | 62.00 |
| 1 x 12 Mill Run | 62.00 | 63.00 |
| 5/4 and 6/4 x 5 and up Mill Run | 58.00 | 60.00 |
| 2 x 4 Mill Run | 52.00 | 53.00 |
| 2 x 6 Mill Run | 53.00 | 56.00 |
| 2 x 8 Mill Run | 55.00 | 58.00 |
| 2 x 10 Mill Run | 58.00 | 62.00 |
| 2 x 12 Mill Run | 60.00 | 64.00 |
| 1 in. Mill Run Shorts | 43.00 | 45.00 |
| 1 x 4 and up 6/16 No. 1 Mill Culls | 30.00 | 32.00 |
| 1 x 10 and up 6/16 No. 1 Mill Culls | 34.00 | 36.00 |
| 1 x 12 and up 6/16 No. 1 Mill Culls | 35.00 | 37.00 |
| 1 x 4 and up 6/16 No. 2 Mill Culls | 23.00 | 25.00 |
| 1 x 10 x 12 6/16 No. 2 Mill Culls | 26.00 | 30.00 |
| 1 x 4 and up 6/16 No. 3 Mill Culls | 15.00 | 20.00 |

### Red Pine

(In Car Load Lots, F.O.B. Toronto)

| | | |
|---|---|---|
| 1 x 4 and 5 Mill Run | $42.00 | $44.00 |
| 1 x 6 Mill Run | 43.00 | 45.00 |
| 1 x 8 Mill Run | 45.00 | 47.00 |
| 1 x 10 Mill Run | 48.00 | 50.00 |
| 2 x 4 Mill Run | 42.00 | 44.00 |
| 2 x 6 Mill Run | 43.00 | 45.00 |
| 2 x 8 Mill Run | 43.00 | 45.00 |
| 2 x 10 Mill Run | 46.00 | 48.00 |
| 2 x 12 Mill Run | 48.00 | 50.00 |
| 1 in. Clear and Clear Face | 70.00 | 72.00 |
| 2 in Clear and Clear Face | 70.00 | 72.00 |

### Spruce

| | | |
|---|---|---|
| 1 x 4 Mill Run | 37.00 | 39.00 |
| 1 x 6 Mill Run | 39.00 | 41.00 |
| 1 x 8 Mill Run | 41.00 | 43.00 |
| 1 x 10 Mill Run | 46.00 | 48.00 |
| 1 x 12 Mill Run Spruce | 50.00 | 52.00 |
| Mill Culls | 28.00 | 30.00 |

### Hemlock (M R)

(In Car Load Lots, F.O.B. Toronto)

| | | |
|---|---|---|
| 1 x 4 and 5 in. x 9 to 16 ft | $29.00 | $30.00 |
| 1 x 6 in. x 9 to 16 ft | 33.00 | 35.00 |
| 1 x 8 in. x 9 to 16 ft | 34.00 | 36.00 |
| 1 x 10 and 12 in. x 9 to 16 ft | 35.00 | 37.00 |
| 1 x 7, 9 and 11 in. x 9 to 16 ft | 33.00 | 34.00 |
| 2 x 4 to 12 in., 10 to 16 ft | 34.00 | 35.00 |
| 2 x 4 to 12 in., 18 ft | 37.00 | 39.00 |
| 2 x 4 to 12 in., 20 ft | 40.00 | 42.00 |
| 1 in. No. 2, 6 ft. to 16 ft | 26.00 | 28.00 |

### Fir Flooring

(In Car Load Lots, F.O.B. Toronto)

| | | |
|---|---|---|
| Fir flooring, 1 x 3 and 4", No. 1 and 2 Edge Grain | | $73.00 |
| Fir flooring, 1 x 3 and 4", No. 1 and 2 Flat Grain | | 48.00 |

(Depending upon Widths)

| | | |
|---|---|---|
| 1 x 4 to 12 No. 1 and 2 Clear Fir, Rough | $69.00 | 77.00 |
| 1¼ x 4 to 12 No. 1 and 2 Clear Fir, Rough | 77.00 | 81.00 |
| 2 x 4 to 12 No. 1 and 2 Clear Fir, Rough | 70.00 | 77.00 |
| 3 & 4 x 4 to 12 No. 1 & 2 Clear Fir, Rough | | 84.00 |
| 1 x 5 and 6 Fir Casing | | 73.00 |
| 1 x 8 and 10 Fir Base | | 77.00 |
| 1¼ and 1½ 8, 10 and 12" E.G. Stepping | | 90.00 |
| 1¼ and 1½, 8, 10 and 12" F.G. Stepping | | 80.00 |
| 1 x 4 to 12 Clear Fir, D4S | | 70.00 |
| 1¼ and 1½ x 4 to 12, Clear Fir, D4S | | 72.00 |
| XX Shingles, 6 butts to 2", per M | | 3.00 |
| XXX Shingles, 6 butts to 2", per M | | 5.00 |
| XXXXX Shingles, 5 butts to 2", per M | | 6.00 |

### Lath

(F.O.B. Mill)

| | |
|---|---|
| No. 1 White Pine | $11.00 |
| No. 2 White Pine | 10.00 |
| No. 3 White Pine | 8.00 |
| Mill Run White Pine, 32 in. | 5.00 |
| Merchantable Spruce Lath, 4 ft | 7.00 |

## TORONTO HARDWOOD PRICES

The prices given below are for car loads f.o.b. Toronto, from wholesalers to retailers, and are based on a good percentage of long lengths and good widths, without any wide stock having been sorted out.

The prices quoted on imported woods include American exchange.

### Ash, White

(Dry weight 3800 lbs. per M. ft.)

| | 1s & 2s | No. 1 Com. | No. 2 Com. |
|---|---|---|---|
| 1" | $110.00 | $ 60.00 | $ 45.00 |
| 1¼ and 1½" | 115.00 | 65.00 | 50.00 |
| 2" | 120.00 | 70.00 | 50.00 |
| 2½ and 3" | 135.00 | 95.00 | 60.00 |
| 4" | 145.00 | 105.00 | 65.00 |

### Ash, Brown

| | | | |
|---|---|---|---|
| 1" | $110.00 | $ 55.00 | $ 40.00 |
| 1¼ and 1½" | 120.00 | 65.00 | 45.00 |
| 2" | 130.00 | 70.00 | 55.00 |
| 2½ and 3" | 145.00 | 80.00 | 65.00 |
| 4" | 165.00 | 95.00 | 75.00 |

### Birch

(Dry weight 4000 lbs. per M. ft.)

| | 1s & 2s | No. 1 Com. | No. 2 Com. |
|---|---|---|---|
| 4/4 | $ 90.00 | $ 55.00 | $ 30.00 |
| 5/ and 6/4 | 90.00 | 55.00 | 30.00 |
| 8/4 | 100.00 | 65.00 | 40.00 |
| 10/4 and 12/4 | 105.00 | 70.00 | 50.00 |
| 16/4 | 110.00 | 80.00 | 50.00 |

### Basswood

(Dry weight 2500 lbs. per M. ft.)

| | 1s & 2s | No. 1 Com. | No. 2 Com. |
|---|---|---|---|
| 4/4 | $ 85.00 | 55.00 | 30.00 |
| 5/4 and 6/4 | 90.00 | 65.00 | 35.00 |
| 8/4 | 95.00 | 70.00 | 40.00 |

### Chestnut

(Dry weight 2800 lbs. per M. ft.)

| | 1s & 2s | No. 1 Com. | Sound Wormy |
|---|---|---|---|
| 1" | $140.00 | 80.00 | 40.00 |
| 1¼" to 1½" | 145.00 | 85.00 | 43.00 |
| 2" | 150.00 | 90.00 | 43.00 |

### Maple, Hard

(Dry weight 4200 lbs. per M. ft.)

| | 1s & 2s | No. 1 Com. | No. 2 Com. |
|---|---|---|---|
| 4/4 | $ 80.00 | $ 55.00 | $ 25.00 |
| 5/4 and 6/4 | 85.00 | 55.00 | 30.00 |
| 8/4 | 90.00 | 60.00 | 35.00 |
| 12/4 | 95.00 | 70.00 | 40.00 |
| 16/4 | 105.00 | 85.00 | 40.00 |

### Elm, Soft

(Dry weight 3100 lbs. per M. ft.)

| | 1s & 2s | No. 1 Com. | No. 2 Com. |
|---|---|---|---|
| 4/4 | $ 85.00 | $ 55.00 | $ 30.00 |
| 6/4 and 8/4 | 90.00 | 65.00 | 35.00 |
| 12/4 | 95.00 | 70.00 | 40.00 |

### Gum, Red

(Dry weight 3300 lbs. per M. ft.)

| | Plain 1s & 2s | Plain No. 1 Com. | Quartered 1s & 2s | Quartered No. 1 Com. |
|---|---|---|---|---|
| 1" | $125.00 | $ 78.00 | $133.00 | $ 83.00 |
| 1¼" | 135.00 | 83.00 | 148.00 | 88.00 |
| 1½" | 135.00 | 83.00 | 148.00 | 88.00 |
| 2" | 145.00 | 93.00 | 158.00 | 103.00 |

Figured Gum, $10 per M. extra, in both plain and quartered.

### Gum, Sap

| | 1s&2s | No. 1 Com. |
|---|---|---|
| 1" | $ 68.00 | $ 48.00 |
| 1¼" and 1½" | 73.00 | 53.00 |
| 2" | 83.00 | 63.00 |

### Hickory

(Dry weight 4500 lbs. per M. ft.

| | 1s&2s | No. 1 Com. |
|---|---|---|
| 1" | $130.00 | $ 65.00 |
| 1¼" | 155.00 | 70.00 |
| 1½" | 155.00 | 70.00 |
| 2" | 160.00 | 75.00 |

### Plain White and Red Oak

(Plain sawed. Dry weight 4000 lbs. per M. ft.)

| | 1s&2s | No. 1 Com. |
|---|---|---|
| 4/4 | $135.00 | $ 75.00 |
| 5/4 and 6/4 | 140.00 | 80.00 |
| 8/4 | 145.00 | 85.00 |
| 10/4 | 155.00 | 90.00 |
| 12/4 | 150.00 | 90.00 |
| 16/4 | 155.00 | 95.00 |

### White Oak, Quarter Cut

(Dry weight 4000 lbs. per M. ft.)

| | 1s&2s | No. 1 Com. |
|---|---|---|
| 4/4 | $160.00 | $ 95.00 |
| 5/4 and 6/4 | 170.00 | 105.00 |
| 8/4 | 190.00 | 115.00 |

### Quarter Cut Red Oak

| | 1s&2s | No. 1 Com. |
|---|---|---|
| 4/4 | $145.00 | $ 75.00 |
| 5/4 and 6/4 | 160.00 | 90.00 |
| 8/4 | 165.00 | 95.00 |

### Beech

The quantity of beech produced in Ontario is not large and is generally sold on a log run basis, the locality governing the prices. At present the prevailing quotation on log run, mill culls out, delivered in Toronto, is $35.00 to $40.00.

---

## OTTAWA

Manufacturers' Prices

### Pine

| | | |
|---|---|---|
| Good sidings: | | |
| 1 in. x 7 in. and up | | $140.00 |
| 1¼ in. and 1½ in., 8 in. and up. | | 165.00 |
| 2 in. x 7 in. and up | | 165.00 |
| No. 2 cuts 2 x 8 in. and up | | 80.00 |
| Good strips: | | |
| 1 in. | $100.00 | $105.00 |
| 1¼ in. and 1½ in. | | 120.00 |
| 2 in. | | 125.00 |
| Good shorts: | | |
| 1 in. x 7 in. and up | | 110.00 |
| 1 in. 4 in. to 6 in. | 85.00 | 90.00 |
| 1¼ in. and 1½ in. | | 110.00 |
| 2 in. | | 125.00 |
| 7 in. to 9 in. A sidings | 54.00 | 56.00 |
| No. 1 dressing sidings | 82.00 | 85.00 |
| No. 1 dressing strips | | 78.00 |
| No. 1 dressing shorts | 68.00 | 73.00 |
| 1 in. x 4 in. s.c. strips | 56.00 | 58.00 |
| 1 in. x 5 in. s.c. strips | 56.00 | 58.00 |
| 1 in. x 6 in. s.c. strips | 63.00 | 65.00 |
| 1 in. x 7 in. s.c. strips | 63.00 | 64.00 |
| 1 in. x 8 in. s.c. strips, 12 to 16 ft. | 63.00 | 66.00 |
| 1 in. x 10 in. M.R. | 65.00 | 70.00 |
| S.C. sidings, 1½ and 2 in. | 63.00 | 67.00 |
| S.C. strips, 1 in. | | 64.00 |
| 1¼, 1½ and 2 in. | 57.00 | 58.00 |
| S.C. shorts, 1 x 4 to 6 in. | 48.00 | 50.00 |
| S.C. and bet., shorts. 1 x 5 | | 48.00 |
| S.C. and bet., shorts, 1 x 6 | | 50.00 |
| S.C. Shorts, 6'-11', 1" x 10" | 52.00 | 54.00 |
| Box boards: | | |
| 1 in. x 4 in. and up, 6 ft.-11 ft. | | 45.00 |
| 1 in. x 3 in. and up, 12 ft.-16 ft. | 50.00 | 53.00 |
| Mill culls, strips and sidings, 1 in. x 4 in. and up, 12 ft. and up | 43.00 | 45.00 |
| Mill cull shorts, 1 in. x 4 in. and up, 6 ft. to 11 ft. | 34.00 | 36.00 |
| O. culls r and w p | 24.00 | 28.00 |

### Red Pine, Log Run

| | | |
|---|---|---|
| Mill culls out, 1 in. | 34.00 | 48.00 |
| Mill culls out, 1¼ in. | 34.00 | 48.00 |
| Mill culls out, 1½ in. | 35.00 | 47.00 |
| Mill culls out, 2 in. | 35.00 | 47.00 |
| Mill Culls, white pine, 1 in. x 7 in. and up | 38.00 | 40.00 |

### Mill Run Spruce

| | | |
|---|---|---|
| 1 in. x 4 in. and up, 6 ft.-11 ft. | | 25.00 |
| 1 in. x 4 in. and up, 12 ft.-16 ft. | 32.00 | 34.00 |
| 1" x 9"-10" and up, 12 ft.-16 ft. | 38.00 | 40.00 |
| 1¼" x 7, 8 and 9" up, 12 ft.-16 ft. | | 35.00 |
| 1¼ x 10 and up, 12 ft.-16 ft. | 38.00 | 42.00 |
| 1½" x 12" x 12" and up, 12'-16' | | 42.00 |
| Spruce, 1 in. clear fine dressing and B | | 55.00 |
| Hemlock, 1 in. cull | | 20.00 |
| Hemlock, 1 in. log run | 24.00 | 26.00 |
| Hemlock, 2 x 4, 6, 8, 10 12/16 ft. | | 28.00 |
| Tamarac | 25.00 | 28.00 |
| Basswood, log run, dead culls out | 45.00 | 50.00 |
| Basswood, log run, mill culls out. | 50.00 | 54.00 |
| Birch, log run | 45.00 | 50.00 |
| Soft Elm, common and better, 1, 1½, 2 in. | 58.00 | 68.00 |
| Ash, black, log run | 62.00 | 65.00 |
| 1 x 10 No. 1 barn | 57.00 | 62.00 |
| 1 x 10 No. 2 barn | 51.00 | 56.00 |
| 1 x 8 and 9 No. 2 barn | 47.00 | 52.00 |

# CURRENT LUMBER PRICES—WHOLESALE

**Lath per M.:**

| | | |
|---|---|---|
| No. 1 White Pine, 1¼ in. x 4 ft. | | 8.00 |
| No. 2 White Pine | | 6.00 |
| Mill run White Pine | 10.00 | 10.50 |
| Spruce, mill run, 1½ in. | | 6.00 |
| Red Pine, mill run | | 6.00 |
| Hemlock, mill run | | 5.50 |

**White Cedar Shingles**

| | | |
|---|---|---|
| XXXX, 18 in. | 9.00 | 10.00 |
| Clear butt, 18 in. | 6.00 | 7.00 |
| 18 in. XX | | 5.00 |

## QUEBEC

**White Pine**
(At Quebec)

| | Cts. Per Cubic Ft. | |
|---|---|---|
| First class Ottawa wany, 18 in. average according to lineal | 100 | 110 |
| 19 in. and up average | 110 | 120 |

**Spruce Deals**
(At Mill)

| | | |
|---|---|---|
| 3 in. unsorted, Quebec, 4 in. to 6 in. wide | $ 20.00 | $ 25.00 |
| 3 in. unsorted, Quebec, 7 in. to 8 in. wide | 26.00 | 28.00 |
| 3 in. unsorted, Quebec, 9 in. wide | 30.00 | 35.00 |

**Oak**
(At Quebec)

| | Cts. Per Cubic Ft. | |
|---|---|---|
| According to average and quality, 55 ft. cube | 125 | 130 |

**Elm**
(At Quebec)

| | | |
|---|---|---|
| According to average and quality, 40 to 45 ft. cube | 100 | 120 |
| According to average and quality, 30 to 35 ft. | 90 | 100 |

**Export Birch Planks**
(At Mill)

| | | |
|---|---|---|
| 1 to 4 in. thick, per M. ft. | $ 30.00 | $ 35.00 |

## ST. JOHN, N.B.

(From Yards and Mills)
**Rough Lumber**
Retail Prices per M. Sq. Ft.

| | | |
|---|---|---|
| 2x3, 2x4, 3x3, 3x4, Rgh Merch Spr | $32.00 | |
| 2x3, 2x4, 3x3, 3x4, Dressed 1 edge | 33.00 | |
| 2x3, 2x4, 3x3, 3x4, Dressed 4 sides | 33.00 | |
| 2x6, 2x7, 3x5, 4x4, 4x6, all rough | 34.00 | |
| 2x8, 3x7, 5x5, 6x6 | 37.00 | $ 40.00 |
| 2x9, 3x8, 6x8, 7x7 | 37.00 | 40.00 |
| 2x10, 3x9 | 45.00 | |
| 2x12, 3x10, 3x12, 8x8 and up | 45.00 | |
| Merch. Spr. Bds., Rough, 1x3-4 & 5 | 30.00 | |
| Merch. Spr. Bds., Rough, 1x6 | 34.00 | |
| Merch. Spr. Bds., Rough, 1x7 & up | 40.00 | |
| Refuse Bds., Deals & Setgs. | 20.00 | 23.00 |

Above random lengths up to 18-0 long.
Lengths 19-0 and up $5.00 extra per M.
For planing Merch. and Refuse Bds. add $2.00 per M. to above prices.
Laths, $7.00.

**Shingles**

| | Per M. |
|---|---|
| Cedar, Extras | $6.25 |
| " Clears | 5.50 |
| " 2nd Clears | 4.50 |
| " Extra No. 1 | 2.90 |
| Spruce | 4.50 |

## SARNIA, ONT.

**Pine, Common and Better**

| | |
|---|---|
| 1 x 6 and 8 in. | $105.00 |
| 1 in., 8 in. and up wide | 125.00 |
| 1¼ and 1½ in. and up wide | 175.00 |
| 2 in. and up wide | 175.00 |

**Cuts and Better**

| | |
|---|---|
| 4/4 x 8 and up No. 1 and better | 120.00 |
| 5/4 and 6/4 and up No. 1 and better | 145.00 |
| 8/4 and 8 and up No. 1 and better | 145.00 |

**No. 1 Cuts**

| | |
|---|---|
| 1 in., 8 in. and up wide | 110.00 |
| 1¼ in., 8 in. and up wide | 120.00 |
| 1½ in., 8 in. and up wide | 120.00 |
| 2 in., 8 in. and up wide | 125.00 |
| 2½ in. and 3 in., 8 in. and up wide | 170.00 |
| 4 in., 8 in. and up wide | 180.00 |

**No. 1 Barn**

| | | |
|---|---|---|
| 1 in., 10 to 16 ft. long | $ 70.00 | $ 85.00 |
| 1¼, 1½ and 2 in., 10/16 ft. | 75.00 | 90.00 |
| 2½ to 3 in., 10/16 ft. | 80.00 | 95.00 |

**No. 2 Barn**

| | | |
|---|---|---|
| 1 in., 10 to 16 ft. long | 68.00 | 77.00 |
| 1¼, 1½ and 2 in., 10/16 ft. | 68.00 | 80.00 |
| 2½, 1½ and 3 in. | 78.00 | 90.00 |

**No. 3 Barn**

| | | |
|---|---|---|
| 1 in., 10 to 16 ft. long | 55.00 | 62.00 |
| 1¼, 1½ and 2 in., 10/16 ft. | 59.00 | 63.00 |

**Box**

| | | |
|---|---|---|
| 1 in., 1¼ and 1½ in., 10/16 ft. | 40.00 | 42.00 |

**Mill Culls**

| | |
|---|---|
| Mill Run Culls— | |
| 1 in., 4 in. and up wide, 6/16 ft. | 30.00 |
| 1¼, 1½ and 2 in. | 31.00 |

## WINNIPEG

**No. 1 Spruce**

| Dimension | S.1.S. and 1.E. 10 ft. | 12 ft. | 14 ft. | 16 ft. |
|---|---|---|---|---|
| 2 x 4 | $31 | $30 | $30 | $31 |
| 2 x 6 | 32 | 30 | 30 | 31 |
| 2 x 8 | 33 | 31 | 31 | 32 |
| 2 x 10 | 34 | 32 | 32 | 33 |
| 2 x 12 | 35 | 33 | 33 | 34 |

For 2 inches, rough, add 50 cents.
For S1E only, add 50 cents.
For S1S and 2E, S4S or D&M, add $3.00.
For timbers larger than 8 x 8, add 50c. for each additional 2 inches each way.
For lengths longer than 20 ft., add $1.00 for each additional two feet.
For selected common, add $5.00.
For No. 2 Dimension, $3.00 less than No. 1.
For 1 x 2 and 2 x 2, $2 more than 2 x 4 No. 1.
For Tamarac, open.

## BUFFALO and TONAWANDA

**White Pine**
Wholesale Selling Price

| | |
|---|---|
| Uppers, 4/4 | $225.00 |
| Uppers, 5/4 to 8/4 | 225.00 |
| Uppers, 10/4 to 12/4 | 250.00 |
| Selects, 4/4 | 200.00 |
| Selects, 5/4 to 8/4 | 200.00 |
| Selects, 10/4 to 12/4 | 225.00 |
| Fine Common, 4/4 | 155.00 |
| Fine Common, 5/4 | 160.00 |
| Fine Common, 6/4 | 160.00 |
| Fine Common, 8/4 | 160.00 |
| No. 1 Cuts, 4/4 | 115.00 |
| No. 1 Cuts, 5/4 | 130.00 |
| No. 1 Cuts, 6/4 | 130.00 |
| No. 1 Cuts, 8/4 | 140.00 |
| No. 2 Cuts, 4/4 | 70.00 |
| No. 2 Cuts, 5/4 | 100.00 |
| No. 2 Cuts, 6/4 | 105.00 |
| No. 2 Cuts, 8/4 | 110.00 |
| No. 3 Cuts, 5/4 | 60.00 |
| No. 3 Cuts, 6/4 | 65.00 |
| No. 3 Cuts, 8/4 | 67.00 |
| Dressing, 4/4 | 95.00 |
| Dressing 4/4 x 10 | 98.00 |
| Dressing, 4/4 x 12 | 110.00 |
| No. 1 Moulding, 5/4 | 150.00 |
| No. 1 Moulding, 6/4 | 150.00 |
| No. 1 Moulding, 8/4 | 155.00 |
| No. 2 Moulding, 5/4 | 125.00 |
| No. 2 Moulding, 6/4 | 125.00 |
| No. 2 Moulding, 8/4 | 130.00 |
| No. 1 Barn, 1 x 12 | 90.00 |
| No. 1 Barn, 1 x 6 and 8 | 76.00 |
| No. 1 Barn, 1 x 10 | 80.00 |
| No. 2 Barn, 1 x 6 and 8 | 62.00 |
| No. 2 Barn, 1 x 10 | 63.00 |
| No. 2 Barn, 1 x 12 | 75.00 |
| No. 3 Barn, 1 x 6 and 8 | 40.00 |
| No. 3 Barn, 1 x 10 | 42.00 |
| No. 3 Barn, 1 x 12 | 45.00 |
| Box, 1 x 6 and 8 | 36.00 |
| Box, 1 x 10 | 38.00 |
| Box, 1 x 12 | 39.00 |
| Box, 1 x 13 and up | 40.00 |

## BUFFALO

The following quotations on hardwoods represent the jobber buying price at Buffalo and Tonawanda.

| | 1s & 2s | No. 1 Com. | No. 2 Com. |
|---|---|---|---|
| **Maple** | | | |
| 1 in. | $ 80.00 | $ 45.00 | $ 30.00 |
| 5/4 to 8/4 | 85.00 | 50.00 | 30.00 |
| 10/4 to 4 in. | 90.00 | 55.00 | 30.00 |
| **Sap Birch** | | | |
| 1 in. | 90.00 | 48.00 | 30.00 |
| 5/4 and up | 100.00 | 53.00 | 30.00 |
| **Soft Elm** | | | |
| 1 in. | 70.00 | 45.00 | 30.00 |
| 5/4 to 2 in. | 75.00 | 50.00 | 30.00 |
| **Red Birch** | | | |
| 1 in. | 120.00 | 75.00 | |
| 5/4 and up | 125.00 | 80.00 | |
| **Basswood** | | | |
| 1 in. | 70.00 | 45.00 | 30.00 |
| 5/4 to 2 in. | 80.00 | 55.00 | 35.00 |
| **Plain Oak** | | | |
| 1 in. | 95.00 | 55.00 | 35.00 |
| 5/4 to 2 in. | 105.00 | 65.00 | 40.00 |
| **Ash** | | | |
| 1 in. | 85.00 | 50.00 | 30.00 |
| 5/4 to 2 in. | 95.00 | 55.00 | 30.00 |
| 10/4 and up | 110.00 | 70.00 | 30.00 |

## BOSTON

Quotations given below are for highest grades of Michigan and Canadian White Pine and Eastern Canadian Spruce as required in the New England market in car loads.

| | |
|---|---|
| White Pine Uppers, 1 in. | |
| White Pine Uppers, 1¼, 1½, 2 in. | |
| White Pine Uppers, 2½, 3 in. | |
| White Pine Uppers, 4 in. | |
| Selects, 1 in. | $170.00 |
| Selects, 1¼, 2 in. | 180.00 |
| Selects, 2½, 3 in. | |
| Selects, 4 in. | |

Prices nominal

| | |
|---|---|
| Fine Common, 1 in., 30%, 12 in. and up | 150.00 |
| Fine Common, 1 x 8 and up | 150.00 |
| Fine Common, 1¼ to 2 in. | 160.00 |
| Fine Common, 2½ and 3 in. | 180.00 |
| Fine Common, 4 in. | 195.00 |
| 1 in. Shaky Clear | 85.00 |
| 1¼ in. to 2 in. Shaky Clear | 90.00 |
| 1 in. No. 2 Dressing | 95.00 |
| 1¼ in. to 2 in. No. 2 Dressing | 95.00 |
| No. 1 Cuts, 1 in. | 110.00 |
| No. 1 Cuts, 1¼ to 2 in. | 130.00 |
| No. 1 Cuts, 2½ and 3 in. | 160.00 |
| No. 2 Cuts, 1 in. | 80.00 |
| No. 2 Cuts, 1¼ to 2 in. | 92.00 |
| Barn Boards, No. 1, 1 x 12 | 91.00 |
| Barn Boards, No. 1, 1 x 10 | 87.00 |
| Barn Boards, No. 1, 1 x 8 | 84.50 |
| Barn Boards, No. 2, 1 x 12 | 75.00 |
| Barn Boards, No. 2, 1 x 8 | 71.00 |
| Barn Boards, No. 2, 1 x 10 | 71.00 |
| Barn Boards, No. 3, 1 x 12 | 55.00 |
| Barn Boards, No. 3, 1 x 10 | 53.00 |
| Barn Boards, No. 3, 1 x 8 | 52.00 |

**No. 1 Clear**

| | | |
|---|---|---|
| Can. Spruce, No. 1 and clear, 1 x 4 to 9" | | $ 75.00 |
| Can. Spruce, 1 x 10 in. | | 78.00 |
| Can. Spruce, No. 1, 1 x 4 to 7 in. | | 72.00 |
| Can. Spruce, No. 1, 1 x 8 and 9 in. | | 74.00 |
| Can. Spruce, No. 1, 1 x 10 in. | | 76.00 |
| Can. Spruce, No. 2, 1 x 4 and 5 in. | | 36.00 |
| Can. Spruce, No. 2, 1 x 6 and 7 in. | | 37.00 |
| Can. Spruce, No. 2, 1 x 8 and 9 in. | | 39.00 |
| Can. Spruce, No. 2, 1 x 10 in. | | 42.00 |
| Can. Spruce, No. 2, 1 x 12 in. | | 45.00 |
| Spruce, 12 in. dimension | | 49.00 |
| Spruce, 10 in. dimension | | 48.00 |
| Spruce, 9 in. dimension | | 46.00 |
| Spruce, 8 in. dimension | | 45.00 |
| 2 x 10 in. random lengths, 8 ft. and up | | 41.00 |
| 2 x 12 in., random lengths | | 45.00 |
| 2 x 3, 2 x 4, 2 x 5, 2 x 6, 2 x 7 | | 32.00 |
| 3 x 4 and 4 x 4 in. | | 33.00 |
| 2 x 9 | | 39.00 |
| All other random lengths, 7 in. and under, 8 ft. and up | 32.00 | 36.00 |
| 5 in. and up merchantable boards, 8 ft. and up, D 1s | 31.00 | 35.00 |
| 1 x 2 | | 32.00 |
| 1 x 3 | | 32.00 |
| 1⅝ in. Spruce Lath | | 8.50 |
| 1½ in. Spruce Lath | | 7.50 |

**New Brunswick Cedar Shingles**

| | |
|---|---|
| Extras | 5.50 |
| Clears | 4.50 |
| Second Clear | 3.50 |
| Clear Whites | 2.75 |

Second Hand Machinery & Equipment Wanted & For Sale

# Quick Action Section

Special Lots Of Lumber— —Positions Wanted & Vacant

## Lumber Wanted

### Hard Maple and Birch Wanted

A limited quantity of 4/4 and 8/4 dry stock No. 2 Common and Better. For further particulars apply Box. 704 Canada Lumberman, Toronto. 22-1

### Lath Wanted

Especially White Pine and Hemlock. Write us what you have with prices.
BREWSTER LOUD LUMBER CO.,
508-509 Lincoln Building,
DETROIT, MICH.
24-3

### Lumber Wanted

We are in the market for a block of Hemlock, Spruce and White Pine. Send us lists giving quantities. Box 755 Canada Lumberman, Toronto. 1

### Wanted

1 inch, 1½ inch and two inch cull Oak. Must be low price. Box 751 Canada Lumberman Toronto, Ont. 1

### Wanted—Hardwood Dimension

5 Cars 1 x 1 42 & 48" Clr Maple, Beech Birch Dry
3 " 1¼ x 1¼. 42" Clr Maple Beech Birch Dry
1 " 1 x 1¼ to 4½ 20-24" Long, Maple Beech Birch Dry
Box 748 Canada Lumberman, Toronto. 1-2

## Lumber For Sale

### Hardwood Lumber

400/500 M feet Birch, Maple, Basswood and Ash; sawed 4.5.6.8. and 10/4, 75% Birch. Bargain for immediate sale—Also lath.
EAST CLIFTON PULP & LUMBER CO,
Cookshire, Que. 23-3

### Timber For Sale

3,000 acres Crown Right Virgin Timber in Ontario. Birch, Hemlock, some White Pine, Basswood, Elm. Warren Ross Lumber Co., Jamestown, N.Y. 6-t.f.

### Timber for Sale

Approximately 30 acres of elm and soft maple timber (Land reserved) situated about eight miles from Galt, on the County Road Box 724. Canada Lumberman, Toronto 23

## Sale of Timber to Close an Estate

South East Quarter of Township of PROUDFOOT containing twenty-three and a quarter square miles, and known as Berth No. 2. Containing the following timber as cruised by one of the most reliable timber cruisers in Ontario:-

| | |
|---|---|
| BIRCH | 10,050,000 ft. |
| MAPLE | 4,000,000 ft. |
| HEMLOCK | 2,000,000 ft. |
| ELM | 100,000 ft. |
| PINE | 100,000 ft. |
| CEDAR poles 25' up 50' | 5,000 |
| SPRUCE & BALSAM Cordwood | 5,000 cords |
| HARDWOOD CORDWOOD first-class | 80,000 cords |

PRICE ........ $20,184.00
Favorable terms can be arranged:-
F. C. Clarkson, Assignee,
E. R. C. Clarkson & Son,
TORONTO.
24-3

PUBLISHER'S NOTICE

Advertisements other than "Employment Wanted" or "Employees Wanted" will be inserted in this department at the rate of 25 cents per agate line (14 agate lines make one inch). $3.50 per inch, each insertion, payable in advance. Space measured from rule to rule. When four or more consecutive insertions of the same advertisement are ordered a discount of 25 per cent. will be allowed.

Advertisements of "Wanted Employment" will be inserted at the rate of one cent a word, net. Cash must accompany order. If Canada Lumberman box number is used, enclose ten cents extra for postage in forwarding replies. Minimum charge 25 cents.

Advertisements of "Wanted Employees" will be inserted at the rate of two cents a word, net. Cash must accompany the order. Minimum charge 50 cents.

Advertisements must be received not later than the 10th and 20th of each month to insure insertion in the subsequent issue.

## Machinery For Sale

### For Sale

Three Lima Locomotives—good condition, now at Flanders, Ont.
Shevlin Clarke Co. Ltd.,
Fort Frances, Ont
23-2

### Second-Hand Carriage for Sale

Have good three head block Mowry carriage 36" opening complete with V and Flat track, good frictional set works. Have no room to store it and will give any party a good bargain for a quick sale. Apply to P. Payette Co., Penetang, Ont. 24-1

### Used Equipment

We have all kinds of machinery, boilers, engines, motors, and air compressors, etc., for quarries, lumber and pulp mills and mines. Let us have your inquiries. Montreal Agents American Saw Mill Machinery Co.,
Barrie Engineering Co., Ltd.,
208a St. Nicholas Bldg.,
23-4 Montreal.

### For Sale

2 Factory Refuse Hogs,
1 Sawmill Refuse Hog,
1 Shingle Machine,
1 Band Resaw Grinder,
1 Lath Machine,
1 Jack Ladder Haul-up Chain, Bullwheel and Sprockets,
1 7" Steam Feed,
Several pieces of Link and Bar Slush Chain.
Apply; The C. Beck Mfg. Co., Ltd.,
Penetanguishene, Ont.
1-2

### 500 H.P. Geary Boiler

Double drums each 48" x 24'-6" long.
Shells 5/8" thick-double rivetted.
Double butt longitudinal seams.
237-4" B. and W. cap tubes—20 ft. long
Complete with stop, safety and blow off valves and with water column front and cyclone shaking and dumping grates.
Ontario Inspection for 200 pounds.
Inspection point:—Toronto,
Box 714 Canada Lumberman, Toronto, Ont.
23-2

## Good Values
### Subject to Prior Sale

Band Resaw, Connell & Dengler, 54 and 60"
Band Rip Saw, Fay & Egan, No. 202, chain feed.
Circular Saw Mill, Hoosier Pony.
Circular Resaw, 44".
E. B. Hayes Dowell Gluer and Driver.
E. B. Hayes Dowell Rod Machine.
E. B. Hayes Standard Power Door Clamp.
Jointers, 8 and 24".
Matcher and Sizer, 30" x 12" American.
Matcher, Hardwood Berlin No. 89.
Matcher, 14 x 6 Glen Coe.
Matcher, Hardwood American, No. 229.
Moulder, Hermance 10" wide open side.
Moulder, Woods No. 2 light inside.
Moulder, C. B. Rogers, 6" outside.
Moulder, Berlin 10" No. 118, inside.
200 prs. Moulding Knives ground to shape.
Planer, Whitney 24" single cabinet.
Planer, Berlin 30 x 6 No. 182, Double.
WOODWORKING MACHINERY CO.,
OF BUFFALO
54 Mechanic St., Buffalo, N.Y.
21-E01-TF

### Wickes Gang

GANG: No. 12 Wickes Gang, 40" sash, 15" stroke, steam binder rolls, front and back in two sections, feed and oscillation combined, 1908 model, and has been in use for five years. We furnish with this gang 11 rolls for cants and stock, one filing machine, and 4 sets of saws.
THE PEMBROKE LUMBER CO.,
1t.f. Pembroke, Ont.

### Engines, Boilers, etc., for Sale

One "Williams" Upright Engine 6" x 6"
One Upright Engine 5" x 6"
Six Return tubular boilers of following dimensions:-
One "Butterfield" 72" x 14' - 3¼" tube - ⅜" shell.
One "Polson" 64" x 14' - 3¼" tube - ½" shell
One "Doty" 60" x 15' - 4" tube - ½" shell
One "Doty" 60" x 14½' - 4" tube - ½" shell
One "Doty" 60" x 15' -4" tube - ½" shell
One "Inglis" 60" x 16' - 3" tube - ½" shell
One double acting "Northey" Fire pump, 6" suction, 5" discharge, 14" steam cylinder, 8" water cylinder, 18" stroke, Capacity 450 gallons per minute.
One "Northey" feed pump 6 x 4 x 7" stroke, Capacity 60 gallons per minute.
One brass Mill steam whistle.
For further particulars apply The Conger Lumber Co Limited., Parry Sound. Ontario.
24 T.f.

## Second Hand Machinery

We have over $250,000 worth of used machinery of all kinds for sale. Suitable for mines, quarries, railroads, pulp and lumber mills, etc.

Everything carefully overhauled at our shops before shipped.

Send us your inquiries.
R. T. GILMAN & CO.,
19tf. Montreal.

## Machinery Wanted

### Wanted

a second hand Band Mill, Carriage, and Steam feed—in good condition. Border Lumber Co., Fort Frances, Ont. 1

### Wanted

Planer & Matcher, must be in good condition. State age, price and maker. Box 750 Canada Lumberman Toronto, Ont. 1-2

### Wanted

1 Planing Mill Exhauster about 40" left hand, bottom horizontal discharge.
The Freeman & Giffin Co., Ltd.,
Isaac's Harbor, N.S.
1

## Situations Wanted

An expert Band Saw Filer, twenty years experience in all kinds of Eastern timber and foreign woods. Ten years on the big mills of the Pacific coast. Work guaranteed second to none. Am open for a position. Best references. Box 756 Canada Lumberman, Toronto. 1-3

EXPERIENCED STENOGRAPHER wants position with Lumber Company in Montreal. Can furnish best references. Salary moderate. Box 719 Canada Lumberman. Toronto. 24

POSITION WANTED: As manager for a good responsible Lumber Co., 36 years experience in Lumbering. Box 729 Canada Lumberman. Toronto. 1-4

PRACTICAL saw-mill man, with good knowledge woods work both Eastern & Western Canada, last two years works manager for London firm of Importers, & Manuf. of Lumber, Boxes, Shooks, best connections. Wide knowledge of shook manufacture, Swedish Ground-off saws etc. Open for engagement, or a business proposition. Box 744 Canada Lumberman, Toronto. 1

Steady young Scotchman, married, wishes position as bookkeeper, stenographer etc., in lumber company's office. Has had almost twenty years' experience. Six years financial training, ten years lumber and pulp companies' offices. Prefer Southern Ontario but would go anywhere in Ontario. Salary $100/125.00 to commence, or could arrange salary to suit. Apply Box 746 Canada Lumberman, Toronto. 1

Wanted position as Mill Superintendent. Eight years experience as Mill Superintendent fifteen years as sawyer. Can furnish best references. Box 747 Canada Lumberman, Toronto. 1-3

Wanted Position as superintendent or foreman of planing mill or woodworking factory. Have had over 12 years experience in interior fittings, sash, doors, hardwood flooring, box-making, estimating and detail drawing. Expert on production and first-class references. Will guarantee results. Box 752 Canada Lumberman, Toronto. 1-4

WANT position as Buyer, Manager Branch Sales Office or Sales Manager, large Mill or Wholesale interests. Long experience handling Pacific Coast, B. C. Mountain, Northern Spruce and Pine stocks, also Poles Piling Posts etc., some bush and mill experience. Good Salesman, large connection Prairie Provinces. Locate anywhere. Post Office Box 1681—Winnipeg, Man. 24-1

WANTED POSITION: for 1922 as head filer in good large Band Mill. Expert in every detail. Satisfaction guaranteed. Apply Box 730 Canada Lumberman, Toronto. 1-4

Young lady desires responsible position with lumber firm in Montreal. Seven years' experience all branches office routine five years with lumber company. Box 749 Canada Lumberman, Toronto. 1

Young man, twenty-two, with initiative, ability, integrity and five years' experience in Millwork and Lumber offices, desires position. Can handle correspondence, sales and orders etc. Only positions with progressive firms in a town considered. All correspondence treated confidentially. Excellent credentials. Box 748 Canada Lumberman, Toronto. 1

## Situations Vacant

Established lumber firm has opening for experienced traveller covering Ontario soft woods. State salary, experience, age etc. Applications treated confidentially. Box 754 Canada Lumberman, Toronto. 1-2

WANTED Young man with lumbering experience as traveller for soft woods in Ontario. State age, experience etc., in first letter. Box 758 Canada Lumberman, Toronto. 1-2

### Hardwood Salesman Wanted

to represent in Canada a high-class firm on a salary and expenses basis. Must be well acquainted with lumber buyers and be a producer. Apply in confidence to Box 742 Canada Lumberman, Toronto. 1

## Sale of Timber

TENDERS will be received by the undersigned up to and including Monday, the 16th day of January, 1922, for the right to cut the timber on two small areas of Rainy River District, being part of Timber Berths G. 23 and N. 7.

Further information may be obtained upon application to the undersigned, or to Mr. J. A. Alexander, Acting Crown Timber Agent, Fort Frances, Ontario.

Beniah Bowman,
Minister of Lands and Forests.
Toronto, December 21st 1921. 1

## Sale of Timber

TENDERS will be received by the undersigned up to and including Saturday the 31st day of December next for the right to cut the timber on the East-half of Sheraton Township in the District of Temiskaming.

For conditions of sale and other information, apply to the undersigned or to Dalton Spence, Crown Timber Agent Cochrane, Ontario.

Beniah Bowman,
Minister of Lands and Forests.
Toronto, November, 3nd, 1921.
N.B.—No unauthorized publication of this notice will be paid for. 22-24

### Business Interests

#### Heavy Fire Losers

Canada closed the year 1920 with a fire loss of approximately $27,400,00, equal to $3.42 per capita on an eight million population, or $17.10 per family—a new record, and one worthy of much thought.

An analysis of this fire loss discloses certain facts which are not creditable to the business life of the country, and which account, in part, for our high cost of protection in Canada, as compared with Europe. One-half of the

fire waste was due to 72 fires, practically all in commercial property. Fires causing damage of $10,000 and over numbered 301, and these again were largely in business property.

A question which every business man should study is, "Why these fires?"

Are we more interested in what we earn than in the means by which we earn it?

Are we so intently watching sales that we cannot devote sufficient attention to the plants which make the sales possible?

True, the average business man carries insurance, but this is charged up to cost of production, and the people pay the insurance. Is it fair to the public, however, to increase unnecessarily the cost of living through neglect or careless living through neglect or carelessness in eliminating fire dangers. Section five of the Criminal Code as amended says: "Every one is guilty of an indictable offence, and liable to two years imprisonment, who by negligence causes any fire which occasions loss of life or loss of property." The rigid enforcement of this section would probably do more to reduce the fire waste than any other influence which might be brought to bear.

### Interest in Forest Tree Planting

Items are constantly going the rounds of the Canadian press setting forth various plans for replanting the forests of this continent. Some have found a solution in letting the squirrels and bluejays reforest cut-over tracts by their habit of secreting nuts and tree seeds in the ground where later on, if the animals or birds have forgotten about them, they will begin to grow. A more ambitious scheme is the enrolment of twenty thousand boys in a society the members of which are pledged to plant so many trees per year. It is naively asserted that a boy can plant and care for five acres of trees without interfering either with his school work, or his doing the "chores." While these schemes show a considerable lack of knowledge both of trees and boys not to speak of squirrels, they are nevertheless important in that they show that the public is waking up to the need of doing something to reforest denuded areas, where the soil is not fit for agriculture, but is suited for growing trees. The greatest power in securing reforestation is public opinion, and from the amount of discussion now going on it is evident that that power is being enlisted in this work.

### Canadian Forest Tree Seeds

During the season of 1920; the work of collecting the cones of

coniferous trees for reforestation purposes went on in practically all the provinces. The work was, perhaps, most vigorously pressed in the West where the Dominion Forestry Branch collects seed for its own forest nurseries and for the Forestry Commission of Great Britain, but, to a greater or less extent, it was done in all the provinces, either by government or private individuals. This is a hopeful sign in regard to forest conservation.

# Review of Current Trade Conditions

### St. John Says English Market is Steadier

As far as the lumber industry at St. John is concerned there has been no change during the last two weeks. The English market, certainly, is steadier, but no buying has taken place during the last week, and while this has caused for the time being a stagnation, it is no more than to be expected as the holiday season is upon us. Winter has also set in, and what work is started is either held up until spring or going along at a very slow pace. This condition will, no doubt, continue throughout the next month until after stock-taking and purchasers find out what they need, so it is simply mark time for the next few weeks. It is useless to try to force sales because the buyer will either cause one to sell ridiculously low, and kick at every carload, so it is far better to wait until later before offering any stocks.

Little manufacturing is being carried on, both by stationary and portable mills, and very little logging, so that when the winter's work is summed up it will be much less than was anticipated some time ago, and certainly, it will be a year, at least, before any new developments on sawing and logging take place. In the meantime the old stocks will be absorbed and there will be no new stock behind it. The outcome will certainly be higher prices and very little to draw from.

No weakness in price has taken place in the demand for Irish deals. The only thing which has stopped shipment is no space by ships until after the first of the year. Possibly by that time better prices will be obtained for 7, 8, 9 and 11 x 3, which are very scarce, and held on the hands of a very few. Freights have not reduced and liners to Great Britain are still asking 100 shillings. Unless these freights are deducted shippers and boats are certainly going to suffer. It seems the steamship people are acting unwisely, simply cutting the throats of the eastern lumbermen and their own as well. It appears utterly useless to tell them the real facts, as they refuse to believe them, it matters not how truthfully put before them. The steamship interests and not the shippers will eventually suffer the most. Last year they waited until near spring before cutting freights in two. When they did, the market was gone and lost, and the lumbermen, who could have sold all winter, could not give their lumber away. Possibly the ocean transportation people believe in trying this procedure again this winter. If they do they will certainly lose out entirely. If they would work with the shippers, making at least a 25 shilling per standard reduction, they would benefit by the results.

American market conditions are bad and very little will, probably, be done in this market until early March, or if prices remain no higher meagre quantities will be shipped. Laths have, like all other lumber products, gone broke and fallen to $7.50 per M in New York, with few buyers, but the price will surely go higher as there are practically few laths to be had to-day.

Local factory conditions are fair, with a fairly good retail trade, and prices locally are not weaker than three months ago.

### Montreal Looks for Better Sales and Prices

Business in Montreal has been dull during the last two weeks, not an unusual thing during the holiday period, when men's minds were centred on other considerations besides commercial transactions. Besides that, inventories are being made up, and there is no disposition to add to the stocks at this time. Occasionally a wholesaler is to be found who reports that trade is satisfactory in volume, although the margin of profit is small.

Most men are looking forward not only to a subtantial revival in the matter of sales, but also in better prices. It looks as if we are at the end of the cutting in prices, which induced a pessimistic feeling in the market, and resulted in substantial losses. The more general feeling of confidence is based on a belief in a general trade improvement and on an extended building programme. Certainly, so far as Montreal is concerned, there is need for thousands of additional houses. From the general trade point the signs of the times are distinctly favorable. It looks as if the questions of world-wide importance, affecting industry in every country, are in a fair way of being settled, and that we may look forward with confidence to a return of conditions which will make for a general revival of business.

As against this feeling must be set the opinion of some wholesalers that 1922 will see a still lower range of values, particularly in pine. In their view pine has not been reduced in line with other

grades of lumber, and that the demand will not be stimulated until lower prices obtain.

The pulpwood situation has not improved. Very few sales are being made, and prices keep on a low level. Rough wood has been sold at point of shipment for $6.75 per cord; peeled at $11, and rossed at $13. Both Canadian and American concerns have very extensive stocks, and until these are partially used up very little business is expected.

It is reported that the Associated Importers, of London, England, who bought the British Government stocks in Canada, proposed to ship a portion of these to the Old Country. Mr. S. G. Denman, the representative of the Timber Department of the Board of Trade, London, states that no tonnage has been chartered, and he has no information which leads him to believe that the stocks will be shipped to the other side.

The official figures of the exports from Montreal during the past season. As anticipated, the figures are not encouraging. The total was 39,272,000, a decrease of 70,083,497 as compared with 1920. This is the second lowest record in the history of the port, the lowest being 30,805,921 in 1917, when shipments were restricted to 10 per cent. of the shipping space available. Exports were very slack during the first part of the season, and only reopened to a better U. K. market near the close of navigation. In one or two cases firms who have been exporters for years only sent a single shipment.

### Ottawa Looks for Better and Brighter Times

Better business, better days, happier times and smoother ways, beckon on the Ottawa valley lumber manufacturer and the lumber trade in general, on the inception of the important year 1922. Underlying factors of the trade during the month of December continued to show slow though steady movement toward the general concentration point of—t-r-a-d-e.

The outlook for better business in 1922, is considerably brighter than for a similar period in 1921. A year ago members of the trade, after the depression set in, in the latter part of 1920, fostered their hopes on the assumption, that good contracts would be available, there would be as much ready money, and the need for houses would force people to build.

Some of the trade forgot, unfortunately for themselves, to consider the fight that must come between capital and labor to bring down building costs. The battle came, resulted for months in a stagnation of business, while contractors and unions kept at loggerheads. The settlement came too late to cause the average prospective home builder to figure on taking a chance. Briefly, many put off their operations until "next year" which happens to be 1922.

One of the best features of the market during the closing month of 1921 was the upkeep of pine prices. Spruce quotations sagged a little and the price of lath went down. The drop in spruce, however, it was confidently expected, would be made up before next spring.

Forecasts of a heavy depression in building covering the past year were not justified as for the first eleven months of 1921 a decrease of a little over half a million dollars took place at Ottawa. Eleven months in 1921 showed the estimated cost of building as being $2,660,940 as compared with $3,312,472 for a corresponding period in 1920.

The decrease perhaps does not properly reflect the trend of building operations as the prices of both labor and materials have come down during the interval.

The demand for lumber was on the whole slow owing to the season of the year. Inquiries from the United States remained fairly good. The labor situation was most satisfactory from the standpoint of men available. In connection with woodworkers it was stated that a ten per cent. reduction in wages would be put into force sometime early this year.

Indications that trade is picking up was shown by the receipt of new orders for doors. James Davidson's Sons, in addition to previous orders, received a new order during December for two carloads, part of which are for Europe and the remainder for South Africa.

### Ontario and the East

There are no particularly new features in connection with the general market situation as December is always a quiet month in the trade and all travellers are now off the road and will not go out until the second or third week in January. It is not expected that business

View of Mills in Sarnia.

# BUY THE BEST

Retailers and woodworking establishments who like to get A1 NORWAY and WHITE PINE LUMBER always buy their stocks from us because we can ship them on quick notice. It pays to have the goods, but it pays better to "deliver" them.

We also make a specialty of heavy timbers cut to order any length up to 60 feet from Pine or B. C. Fir.

*"Rush Orders Rushed"*

# Cleveland-Sarnia Sawmills Co., Limited
### SARNIA, ONTARIO

B. P. Bole, Pres.    F. H. Goff, Vice-Pres.    E. C. Barrs, Gen. Mgr.    W. A. Saurwein, Ass't. Mgr.

will open with a rush as the cold weather has had a somewhat unsettling effect upon building and building plans. Everything, however, points to 1922 as likely to be a year in which greater activity will be manifested in all lines of industry, and lumber, instead of sagging in price as it has during the past year, will, at least, be firmer in tone, and that there will be a stronger demand and livelier impetus to the situation.

Logging operations are being conducted on a larger scale than they have for some little time and this is regarded as a pretty good indication that things are not going to be so doubtful or uninteresting as predicted a few weeks ago.

Actual business during the past two or three months has perhaps not shown any heavy gain in the lumber line, but there is more optimism displaying itself with regard to the future. In hardwoods, the past season's cut of several firms has been sold and some buying developed on the part of the furniture manufacturers who sought moderate quantities of birch. Decreasing supplies on hand are indicated by their inquiries and there are signs that a number of New York furniture plants, who neglected birch, while gumwood was relatively cheap, are anxious to get back to the Canadian market for hardwoods. The requisitions from automobile concerns have, owing to the quietness of that trade, been very limited during the past few months.

It is expected that the whole outlook of the lumber trade from every standpoint, both local, international and foreign, will be discussed in its various phases at the annual meeting of the Canadian lumbermen, which will be held in Toronto on January 11th and 12th. There will be representatives from every province present, and in the symposium of opinions and interchange of thought, much valuable data can, no doubt, be obtained.

So far as the general wage situation is concerned, eastern lumber dealers are expected to buy steadily, though conservatively, during the spring months. Railroads and car builders are in the market in a moderate way.

Summed up, the situation has been quiet for the past few months, but possessing an undertone of considerable optimism that is tending to sustain prices and a volume of current business that is thoroughly in keeping with the season. Hemlock is in pretty fair demand. Several cuts have been disposed of recently at a figure considerably higher than that which prevailed a couple of months ago. The lath market is quiet and shingles are moving slowly.

### Demand For Railway Ties Falls Off

There has been quite a slump in the demand for railway ties, and it is announced that practically all the leading transportation lines in Canada are covered so far as their requirements for the coming year are concerned. One company some time ago advertised for tenders for 7,500,000 ties, and purchased only a million and a half, while another road asked for 8,000,000 and bought only 2,000,000.

There has been a drop of about 25 to 30 per cent. on the average in the prices paid, and large contracting firms strongly advise that before private parties or other concerns go ahead and take out ties it would be well for them to have a contract.

There was an over-production of ties in 1920-1921 owing to the drop in the price of lumber and the fact that many hardwood producers turned their logs into ties, which commanding a pretty fair price. The result has been that of late the price of ties has come down in sympathy with other forest products, and it is announced that the Grand Trunk Railway is practically all filled up for 1922, so far as tie requirements are concerned, and is in splendid shape.

The Canadian Tie & Lumber Co., of Toronto, which handled between 2,000,000 and 3,000,000 ties last year, report that business is rather quiet at the present time and that the outlook is likely to be much better a year from now than at this juncture, owing to the reasons already stated. There is practically no demand for No. 2 ties at all. It is stated that all the producers would be well advised to have hard and fast contracts before going ahead and taking out any large output. The majority of ties taken out in Eastern Canada during the last year were sawn ties, about one-fifth of which were cedar, the remainder being tamarac, jack-pine, birch, beech, maple and oak.

### Timber Market in Manchester District

Canadian Trade Commissioner J. E. Ray, in writing the Department of Trade and Commerce, Ottawa, says: A diversity of opinion exists among timber importers interviewed regarding the trend of the timber trade this winter. Many firms appear to content themselves with the holding of their present stocks until such times as the atmosphere becomes clearer. The instability of prices and the meagre demand have created a spirit of caution among importers. A consignment of Canadian timber is due in the port of Manchester, but it cannot be said that business is active, or that the immediate future exhibits any sign of increased demand for building and structural woods. In the current issue of The Timber Trades Journal there appears an article, in the course of which the writer predicts a coming shortage of timber. His prediction is founded on an examination of conditions in Finland and Scandinavia, from which countries so much of the British imports is drawn. Apparently, the log-get from Finland this winter will not be more than 80 per cent. of the normal, and the production of sawn goods in Sweden will not be more than 20 to 25 per cent. of the average. In 1922, says the writer, there will probably be a smaller supply from Finland, and from Sweden a very great reduction. For 1923 "the prospects are in favor of almost normal quantities from Finland, and of a very big diminution indeed from Sweden. Assuming that the general trade revival is of slow growth—and this is now almost the unanimous opinion—experts state that a real wood famine may be expected in 1923 led up to by a shortage next year."

### Fighting the Insect Pest at Chicoutimi

Price Bros., Limited, of Quebec, have set an example in regard to the study and control of the insect plague in forest tree resources, which is well worthy of all timber limit holders. This representative Canadian lumber firm, who are also extensive manufacturers of pulp and paper, with vast forest holdings, have of late been paying serious attention to the insect part, which has caused more destruction in the last two decades than forest fires.

Having noticed the presence of the black beetle, attacking and destroying the balsam trees in their Chicoutimi limits, Price Bros. communicated with the Entomological Division of the Department of Agriculture, Ottawa, with the result that Dr. F. C. Craighead recently arrived from Ottawa, on his way to Chicoutimi, to take control of the beetles, wich are attacking and destroying the balsam trees. These beetles generally follow in the wake of the budworm and make their way inside the bark destroying the trees.

Sir Wm. Price, president of Price Bros., Limited, is a man of action and not likely to stand idle and see the firm's rich forest resources destroyed by insects, is science can cope and combat successfully with the situation. With the permission of the government but at the expense of the firm, he has Dr. Craighead on the job with his scientific knowledge. The doctor is confident of getting control of the pest.

The insect pest and its destruction of forest trees has become enormous and, within the past twenty years, has destroyed over a billion dollars of property. In the United States, the federal and state governments are giving the greatest possible attention to the science of entomology to stamp out the insect pest which is causing incalculable ravage in American forests. H. S. Peerson, entomologist for the State of Maine, in a recent interview, said it was long recognized that forest insects did far more damage yearly than fire in the United States. He stated that a conservative estimate made by the United States Department of Agriculture, places the yearly losses at $300,-000,000, and that this damage is largely concentrated in Maine and in the Western States whose great areas are covered by the so-called pure stands of timber. In the States where the stands consist largely of mixed species, the damage is greatly minimized.

Maine has been the Mecca for insects, due to the relatively few species of trees found in the forests throughout the greater part of this state. The spruce budworm is undoubtedly the most serious insect pest in Maine, in spite of the fact that it comes periodically. At the present time it is estimated that 30 per cent. of the mature spruce and 70 per cent. of the mature fir throughout that state has been killed, and the last infection of the budworm destroyed approximately $70,000,000 worth of mature fir and spruce.

These are serious conditions for the Canadian federal and provincial governments to ponder over as well as the Canadian limit holders and the lumber interests of the country in general, and it is to be hoped that some method of economic control applicable to forest protection can be evolved before the Canadian forests be further destroyed by this insect pest, as well as for the protection of the areas of reproduction in spruce and other trees. The report of Dr. Craighead is being awaited with interest as to the result of his work in the control of the beetle in the Chicoutimi district.

### Vanishing Timber Supply of Uncle Sam

"The outstanding points in our present serious situation as to timber supply are the disappearance of three-fifths of the virgin forests of the country, a present drain upon our remaining forests over four times their yearly production of wood and the accumulation of enormous areas of denuded and idle forest lands," says W. B. Greeley, chief forester of the United States, in his annual report to the Secretary of Agriculture at Washington. "The past year," according to the report, "has been notable for general discussion of the forestry situation in both its national and local aspects and the consideration of remedies."

## Pulpwood Market is Improving Slightly

There has been some improvement in the pulpwood situation of late and certain firms are entering into contracts a little more freely than formerly. The Thompson & Heyland Lumber Co., of Toronto, have already contracted for 22,000 cords for the coming year, and possibly will handle about 30,000 cords, all told, which will surpass last year's activities.

Of course, the offerings are much larger than any firm can accept and settlers are not going ahead and taking out wood on speculation as they did a year or two ago. They desire to have contracts before they start cutting.

The prices of pulpwood are generally from 33 to 50 per cent. lower than a year and a half ago. Peeled spruce, south of North Bay, Ont., is bringing $11.00 to $14.00, f.o.b. cars, according to freight rates, and north of North Bay, $8.00 to $9.00. Some rough spruce is being bought south of North Bay from $7.50 to $8.50 per cord, while the figure in the extreme north is $5.00 to $6.00 per cord. Quite a large quantity of poplar is being bought, the figure being from $5.00 to $8.00 per cord, according to location and freight rates.

If the paper mills get as busy as present signs indicate, a number may have to enter the market for pulpwood before the season of 1922 is over.

## Dryden Company Holds Annual Meeting

The annual meeting of the Dryden Pulp & Paper Co., Dryden, Ont., was held in Montreal recently. The balance sheet presented showed considerable strength throughout, although operating deficits of last year amounted to $321,720, which includes timber depletion and inventory written off around $166,000. No provision has been made for depreciation but $109,573 has been charged against operations in respect to maintenance and repairs.

The assets side of the balance sheet, as at September 30, shows total assets at $6,873,424. Total active assets stand at $1,508,553, against which are accounts payable of $48,907, indicting net working capital of $1,459,646. Active assets include cash, $41,445; special deposit for plant expenditure, $416,610; cash and demand loans, $481,116; total receipts, $91,959; and inventories, $477,423. Real estate, plant, etc., is given as $5,353,503. There is outstanding the first lien notes of $386,000 mortgage debenture stock of $1,100,000; note redemption reserves, $2,167; and depletion reserve, $24,246. Capital stock stands at $3,125,000, and capital surplus $2,508,825.

## Will Develop Big Industry

P. T. Reid, president of the Reid-Newfoundland Co., has extensive plans under way for the development of the natural resources of Newfoundland, for the immediate employment of two thousand men. Mr. Reid recently returned from a visit to Great Britain and says that while there he entered into a contract with the Armstrong-Whitworth Co., Limited, to develop the resources of the Humber River Valley. It is said that paper mills would be established twice the size of the large Harmsworth plant at Grand Falls, which supplies newsprint to the Northcliffe papers in London, and has a daily capacity of 1,000 tons. It is learned that there will be an expenditure of $7,000,000 within two years and that other industries will be launched in addition to the paper and pulp mills.

## Pulpwood Cut Is Small This Winter

It is announced that the Spanish River Pulp & Paper Mills intend taking out considerably more pulpwood during the coming winter than they originally intended. This is due to the low cost of production. It is doubtful if pulpwood logging will ever be conducted at a less figure than it is to-day. Wages in the camps are running around $1.00 a day There is a surplus of labor of all kinds and men are more efficient than at any period since the war. Settlers and farmers are, however, cutting very little wood, as they claim that present prices are not sufficiently high to pay them for their efforts. Then again, there is a limited call from the contractors for their product and much more wood is being offered all buyers than they can possibly accept. Most contractors are chary about committments, and have no desire

to speculate or indulge in "futures." In their purchasing they are largely governed by the requisitions they have in hand from the mills.

## Need of Ice-Breaker Service for Shipping

The importance of having adequate ice-Breaker service on the St. Lawrence river so far as the pulpwood industry is concerned, is reflected in the fact that there were difficulties with the clearance of two vessels on the Saguenay, which had been scheduled to load. This means that there would have been half a million dollars' worth of exports out of Quebec had there been available, in the closing days of the season, a powerful ice-breaker for service around the mouth of, and on the Saguenay. A. M. Irvine, a director of Becker & Company of America, Montreal, said that this season Fifteen vessels have been cleared with pulpwood cargoes for European and United States ports from the Saguenay; but owing to lack of ice-breaker service, two vessels over and above the number bound for the Saguenay were involved with ice difficulties.

Mr. Irvine added that if an ice-breaker could have been at the disposal of shipping in the lower St. Lawrence for the closing days of this season, that Canada would have benefited to the extent of a million or more dollars' worth of exports this season.

## Forestry Engineers Elect New Officers

The first annual meeting of the Provincial Forestry Engineers Association, chartered at the last session of the Quebec Legislature, recently elected new officers and members and discussed timber cutting and forestry resources inventory. Officers elected were: President, Omer Lussier, Montreal; vice-president, R. De Carteret; secretary-treasurer, Hector Baillarge; councillors, Ellwood Wilson, manager Laurentide Pulp and Paper Co.; Henry Sorgius, manager of the St. Maurice Forest Protective Association; G. C. Piche, chief of the Provincial Forestry Service; Borrome, Guerin, George Maheux. Fifteen new members were admitted.

## New Paper Mill For Port Arthur

The new book paper mill of the Provincial Paper Mills, Limited, will be begun at Port Arthur in the near future. The building will be 900 feet long and will be capable of accommodating two machines. For some time past work on the rock excavation has been proceeding satisfactorily under the direction of the Port Arthur Construction Co. The Port Arthur city council has granted a fixed assessment of $500,000 on the mill for a period of ten years. The total expenditure on the buildings and plant will be $1,000,000, and it is expected that the industry will be in operation early in the fall of 1923. The Provincial Paper Mills have operated a sulphite pulp plant of 50 tons capacity at Port Arthur for some years.

The Belgo Export Co., Limited, with a capital stock of $49,000 and headquarters in Montreal, have been granted a federal charter to import, export, buy, sell and deal in paper of all kinds, logs, lumber, timber, pulp and pulpwood.

The new newsprint mill of the International Paper Co., which is located at Three Rivers, Que., will be started in February. The initial production will be 100 tons a day, and if the market warrants it, the plant will be doubled, the output being at the rate of 60,000 tons a year. The opening of this mill will make the capacity of the Canadian newsprint mills well over 1,000,000 tons a year.

T. S. Woollings & Co. of Connaught Station, Ont., are cutting more timber for their rossing plant, an illustration and description of which appeared in the last issue of the "Canada Lumberman." The company are also taking out 170,000 ties and 300,000 feet, b.m., of switch timber. The company have just completed a two-drum rossing mill with a capacity of 200 cords in ten hours. They ran about one month last fall and found the mill worked nicely. In addition, they have purchased about 40,000 cords on the mainline of the T. & N.O. Railway from settlers. The company have offices at Englehart, Porquois Junction and Cochrane.

# EDGINGS

The Millar Lumber Co., North Battleford, Sask., has been incorporated with a capital stock of $25,000.

J. J. Crowe Co., Limited, have taken over the lumber yard at Sandy Lake, Man., formerly operated by D. Mytruk.

Lumber & Contracting Co., Limited, Young, Sask., has recently been granted a charter. The capital stock is $20,000.

R. S. Plant, of the Toronto office of the Vancouver Lumber Co., left recently to spend the holidays with relatives and friends in Vancouver.

The Virginia Lumber Company's mill at Coombs, thirty miles from Nanaimo, B.C., was destroyed by fire recently. The loss is about $70,000.

Douglas A. Stalker has embarked in the wholesale lumber business in Sherbrooke, Que., and has opened offices at 40A Wellington St., in that city.

The National Hardwood Lumber Association of Chicago, in its official bulletin announce that application for membership had been received from George Kersley, Montreal, and Samuel Ouelette, Mont Laurier, Que.

The annual meeting of the Canadian Pulp & Paper Association will be held at the Ritz-Carlton Hotel, Montreal, on January 27th. The meetings of the different sections will be held on the Wednesday and Thursday previous.

Fibre Boxes, Limited, of Toronto, have been granted a federal charter with a capital stock of $250,000. The company will take over the business and property of Fibre Boxes, Limited, of Toronto, which has been operating under a provincial charter.

Brigadier-General J. B. White, D.S.O., of the Riordon Company, was present at the reception given by the Canadian Club, Montreal, to Marshall Foch. General White was also one of the guests at a private dinner tendered to Marshall Foch by Brig.-General C. J. Armstrong, C.B., C.M.G., and the other officers of M.D.4.

A charter has been granted to the F. G. Phippen Lumber Co., with headquarters in Toronto, and a capital stock of $40,000, to carry on business of saw and timber merchants and to deal in lumber and building supplies. Among the incorporators of the company are Frederick G. Phippen, Edward V. T. Phippen and Albert J. Phippen, builders, all of Toronto.

Amos J. Colston died recently in Montreal in his 73rd year. For a long time he was a prominent figure in business circles in Quebec and was at one time manager of the firm of Price Bros., but withdrew to go into the real estate business on his own account. He is survived by one son, his wife passing away last spring, and his only daughter a few years ago.

Andrew Merritt Bennett, an old and esteemed resident of Walkerton, Ont., died recently, after a brief illness. Mr. Bennett was born in the town of Thorold 87 years ago, and for many years was engaged in lumbering and farming at Walsingham Centre. Later he lived in Kingsville. Twenty-eight years ago Mr. Bennett came to the border and for a number of years was assessor for Walkerville.

Douglas fir will now be used instead of Oregon pine by the British Admiralty in dealing with timber orders, as a result of action taken by F. C. Wade, agent-general for British Columbia in London, England. Director Navy Contracts O. R. Jenkins reports that a recent fir timber contract for the British Navy was awarded a contractor who undertook that the material should come from British Columbia.

The large sawmill building of A. McFaul & Bros. at Lachute, Que., which had not been in use for a number of years, was recently destroyed by fire. The mill was dismantled of its machinery, excepting the lath department, some time ago. The loss to the proprietors is a rather heavy one, as it includes nearly a score of sets of logging sleighs, which were stored in the building and only partially covered by insurance.

The question of the definition of the boundary between Canada and Newfoundland in the Labrador Peninsula is now before the Privy Council. According to Mr. F. C. Berteau, who was collector of customs for Newfoundland for the whole of Labrador north of Red Bay, the dispute is due, among other reasons, to the establishment of lumber mills at the bottom of the Hamilton Inlet by W. C. Edwards and the Benjamin Company.

Mr. Dunbar, of the Hendun Lumber Co., Haileybury, says they are getting out about as many logs as last season at Barber's Bay, which will be about 3,000,000 feet. Labor is plentiful and considerably

cheaper, while supplies are a little lower than a year ago. The weather conditions so far have not been favorable. Colder weather was needed earlier in the season to freeze up the swamps, which were early in December covered with snow.

The plant of the Abitibi Power & Paper Co. at Iroquois Falls, Ont., is very busy at present and is running to capacity on newsprint. Recently shipments of the product of the mill have been made from Iroquois Falls to New York and Chicago within forty-eight hours, which is a remarkable record. From the standing tree to the printed sheets selling on the streets of the great cities, the operation and transportation has been reduced to a question of a few hours.

There has been organized in connection with the Brompton Pulp & Paper Co., East Angus, Que., an organization known as the Good Fellow Club, which meets twice a month. The object of the club is to discuss topics of vital interest to each one connected with the organization. At the inaugural meeting an instructive address was given by J. A. Bothwell, general manager of the company, who spoke on co-operation. He emphasized the necessity of team work in the industry, especially in the times we are now passing through.

The revenue from the Lands and Forests Department in Ontario during the last fiscal year was $4,090,482, which is a gratifying gain over the previous year of over $1,000,000. The earnings of the department in 1920 were $2,911,047 and for 1919 were $2,221,000. The increase is due to a larger cut during the past season, while the dues on pulpwood went up 100 per cent, and the dues on other woods about 20 per cent A better business system has also been introduced into the department, according to Hon. Beniah Bowman, Minister of Lands and Forests.

A bill providing for the branding of boom chains has been introduced in the B.C. Legislature by Hon. P. D. Pattullo, Minister of Lands. This is in line with a request from the Loggers' Association who claim that in the past they have experienced much difficulty in segregating their chains once the booms are brought down from the timber limits and separated at Vancouver, Victoria and New Westminster. The bill provides for a register of boom chain brands to be kept by the Forest branch. A penalty is imposed for branding chains with other than a registered brand and for mutilating or defacing brands.

Nathan H. Stevens, one of the most prominent business men of Chatham, Ont., died recently in his 80th year. In 1867 he purchased a general store in Blenheim, Ont., and afterwards acquired an interest in a planing mill. In 1880 he moved to Chatham, where he became prominently identified with the flour milling business. He built the Kent mills, the first roller flour mills in Canada. In 1900 the business was incorporated under the name of the Canada Flour Mills, Limited, of which Mr. Stevens was president. He was also president of the Blonde Lumber Co., Chatham, and vice-president of the Sutherland-Innes Co., Chatham, for several years, as well as other organizations.

Twelve third-year students in the Faculty of Forestry, Toronto University, recently left to spend some days in the lumber camps, where they will study logging operations at first-hand. Half of the students went to camps in the Ottawa Valley and the other half to shanties in the Parry Sound district. The students are required to bring back with them detailed information on logging, and to write practical essays on the result of their study and observation. These essays of third-year or graduate students have appeared from time to time in the "Canada Lumberman" and have always aroused much interest. It shows that the majority of the boys are alert, energetic and thoughtful.

The Temiskaming & Northern Ontario Railway will be extended to Tin Can Portage, seventy miles north of Cochrane. The Ontario Government is now calling for tenders for the work. The successful contractors will be required to complete the first forty miles from Cochrane to the Abitibi River at the end of 1922, and the whole line by the end of 1923. The cost is expected to be $3,000,000. Chairman Lee, of the T. & N. O. Railway Commission, says that the new line will open up one of the finest timber countries in the north and will make great quantities of pulpwood available. There are also unlimited water-powers, particularly at Tin Can Portage, where it is said 200,000 h.p. can be easily produced.

G. T. Clarkson, of Toronto, who is the receiver for the Mattagami Pulp & Paper Co., Limited, whose plant is at Smooth Rock Falls, has forwarded a statement to the bondholders, debenture holders, creditors and shareholders of the firm. The plant has been operated for some time and the progress made to date has been fairly satisfactory, having regard to conditions which have been obtained and in particular to the low market price of pulp. Mr. Clarkson says it has been found that a number of economies in operating can be effected, and these are being put into force as soon as conditions permit. When completed it is expected that if any improvement in the price of pulp shall take place the operations will yield a satisfactory return.

## ALPHABETICAL INDEX TO ADVERTISERS

# DISSTON
## NEWS FOR LUMBERMEN

| Published now and then. | HENRY DISSTON & SONS, LTD., Toronto, Canada. | January, 1922. |

## Let Us Send You the Crucible

THE House of Disston publishes a monthly magazine. Did you know that? This magazine, "The Crucible", is published monthly,—a magazine for lumbermen.

It contains stories of successful lumbermen in all parts of the country. It carries write-ups of interesting operations. It often has an article on some special phase of saw sharpening or repairing. There is a page of jokes which is the equal of any;

We will send you this magazine, free of charge—if you would care for it. All you have to do is ask for it. Drop us a postcard with your name and address on it and say, "Please put my name on the Crucible Mailing list". Do it today, you'll like it.

---

## Speed!

Some Facts About Disston High Grade Cross-Cut Saws.

MOST all Cross-cut saws look alike when they are finished. But they do not all cut alike when they are in use.

More than "looks" are required in a cross-cut saw to do good work. It is what goes into the saw when it is being made that determines its cutting and wearing qualities.

And the famous Disston-made

Steel, Disston expert workmanship and experience, developed through 81 years experience as leaders in the saw making industry, are the things that go into Disston Cross-cut saws and make them popular everywhere.

The following are reports of two performances of Disston Cross-cuts.

On Sept. 8th, 1920 in Herkimer County, New York, two men using a Disston 6 foot High-Grade Cross-Cut Saw cut through a Hard Black Ash log 14" in diameter in just 12 seconds.

## Things Not to Do in Operating a Saw

THE following is a list of "Don'ts" for the saw operator that are taken from the "Disston Lumberman's Handbook". Many readers have told us that a list of this kind was a time-saver for them and we print it here, in the hope that it will be of value.

DON'T USE:—
Insufficient power to maintain regular speed.
Too thin a saw for the class of work required.
Too few or too many teeth for the amount of feed carried.
Weak or imperfect collars.
Collars not large enough in diameter.
Ill-fitting mandrel and pin holes.
Uneven setting and filing.
Points of teeth filed with a "lead"; not square across.
Too little set for proper clearance.
Too much pitch or hook of teeth.
Irregular and shallow gullets.
A saw out of round and consequently out of balance.
A sprung mandrel, or allow lost motion in mandrel boxes.
A carriage track neither level nor straight.
A carriage not properly aligned with saw.
A journal which heats.
Guide-pins too tight or not properly adjusted.
Teeth which have backs too high for clearance.
Any saw too long without sharpening.

Near Stevens Point, Wisconsin, on September 19th, 1920 two men using a Disston High-Grade Cross-cut Saw cut through a Grey Elm log 18½" in diameter in 15 seconds.

We do not hold up these two examples of fast cutting as records. They are just two instances that we know of and may not be record accomplishments.

But they do illustrate what our statement that the combination of the famous Disston-made Steel, Disston manufacturing methods,

Photograph of end of log.

the latest improvements in cross-cut saw design, and Disston workmanship mean to users of cross-cut saws.

## One of the Reasons for Disston Quality

ON the same day, August 23, 1844, two boy babies were born. Their homes were less than a square apart.
One of these boys was Hamilton Disston, son of Henry Disston, founder of the House of Disston;

same time. These men have had Disston quality impressed on them from childhood, until it has become their creed. These are the men who add stability to the works and maintain the high standard set by the founder.

These four brothers — Harry, Charles, William and George Kinkead — have aggregated 125 years of service for the house of Disston.

and the other was Robert H. Kinkead. In 1859 the fifteen-year-old "Bobbie" Kinkead started to work for Disston. He remained with the firm fifty-four consecutive years. At the time of his death, eight years ago, he was foreman of the trowel department.

Four of Mr. Kinkead's sons also selected Disston's as a desirable place to learn and ply their trade. They grew to manhood in the firm's employ. Steady, efficient, and congenial—these brothers have aggregated 125 years of service for Disston. They are:—

| | | |
|---|---|---|
| William, Foreman of Band Saw Hammer Department | 40 | years |
| Harry, Barrel Saw Department | 14 | " |
| Charles, Hand Saw Blocking Department | 35 | " |
| George, Smither in Band Saw Hammer Department | 34 | " |
| Aggregate | 125 | " |
| Average | 31¼ | " |

When Henry Disston was asked how he made such fine saws, he answered, "Good Steel and honest work".

While "honest work" covers almost every element entering the manufactured product, other than the raw material, yet it may be well to emphasize the element of skill; the inherent skill of men following in the work of their fathers and their grandfathers; skill developed by proper training and application; skill reduced to a science by many years of practical experience

There is probably no other firm in the country that can boast of a larger number of long-term, skilled employees than the House of Disston. The Kinkead family is only one of many who have chosen the Disston Works as a desirable place to work. As many as four generations of the same family have been on the payroll at the

# CANADA LUMBERMAN BUYERS' DIRECTORY

The following regulations apply to all advertisers:—Eighth page, every issue, three headings;
quarter page, six headings; half page, twelve headings; full page, twenty-four headings

**ALLIGATORS**
Payette Company, P.
West, Peachy & Sons

**BABBITT METAL**
Canada Metal Company
General Supply Co. of Canada, Ltd.

**BALE TIES**
Canada Metal Co.
Laidlaw Bale Tie Company

**BAND MILLS**
Hamilton Company, William
Waterous Engine Works Company
Yates Machine Company, P. B.

**BAND RESAWS**
Mershon & Company, W. B.

**BARKERS**
Bertrand, F. X., La Compagnie Manu-
factiere.
Smith Foundry & Machine Co.

**BEARING METAL**
Canada Metal Co.
Beveridge Supply Co., Ltd.

**BEDSTEADS (STEEL)**
Simmons Limited

**BELT DRESSING**
Dominion Belting Co.
General Supply of Canada, Ltd.

**BELTING**
Canadian Consolidated Rubber Co.
Dominion Belting Co.
General Supply Company
Goodhue & Co., J. L.
Gutta Percha & Rubber Company
D. K. McLaren, Limited
McLaren Belting Company, J. C.
Sumner & Co.
York Belting Co.

**BELTING (Transmission)**
Sumner & Co.

**BLOWERS**
B. F. Sturtevant Co. of Canada, Ltd.
Toronto Blower Company

**BOILERS**
Engineering & Machine Works of
Canada
Hamilton Company, William
Waterous Engine Works Company

**BOILER PRESERVATIVE**
Beveridge Supply Company
Shell-Bar, Boice Supply Co. Ltd.

**BOX MACHINERY**
Yates Machine Company, P. B.

**CABLE CONVEYORS**
Engineering & Machine Works of
Canada.
Hamilton Company, Wm.
Waterous Engine Works Company

**CAMP SUPPLIES**
Davies Company, William
Dr. Bell Veterinary Wonder Co.
Hay, A. H. M.
Johnson, A. H.
Swift Canadian Co.
Turner & Sons, J. J.
Woods Manufacturing Company. Ltd.

**CANT HOOKS**
General Supply Co. of Canada, Ltd.
Pink Company, Thomas

**CEDAR**
Bury & Co., Robt.
Cameron Lumber Co.
Canadian Western Lumber Company
Chesbro, R. G.

Dry Wood Lumber Co.
Edgecumbe-Newham Company
Fesserton Timber Company
Muir & Kirkpatrick
Rose, McLaurin, Limited
Terry & Gordon
Thurston-Flavelle Lumber Company
Vancouver Lumber Company
Victoria Lumber & Mfg. Co.

**CHAINS**
Canadian Link-Belt Company, Ltd.
General Supply Co. of Canada, Ltd.
Engineering & Machine Works of
Canada
Hamilton Company, William
Pink & Co., Thomas
Waterous Engine Works Company

**CLOTHING**
Woods Mfg. Company

**CONVEYOR MACHINERY**
Canadian Link-Belt Company, Ltd.
General Supply Co. of Canada, Ltd.
Hamilton Company, Wm.
Hopkins & Co., Ltd., F. H.
Mathews Gravity Carrier Company.
Waterous Engine Works Company

**CORDAGE**
Consumers Cordage Company

**CORDWOOD**
McClung, McLellan & Berry

**COUPLING (Shaft)**
Engineering & Machine Works of
Canada

**CRANES**
Hopkins & Co., Ltd., F. H.
Canadian Link-Belt Company

**CUTTER HEADS**
Shimer Cutter Head Company

**CYPRESS**
Wistar, Underhill & Nixon

**DERRICKS AND DERRICK
FITTINGS**
Hopkins & Co., Ltd., F. H.

**DOORS**
Brompton Lumber & Mfg. Co.
Canadian Western Lumber Co.
Mason, Gordon & Co.
Midland Woodworkers
Midland Wood Products, Ltd.
Terry & Gordon

**DRAG SAWS**
Gerlach Company, Peter
Hamilton Company. William

**DRYERS**
Coe Manufacturing Company
Proctor & Schwartz Inc.
B. F. Sturtevant Co. of Canada, Ltd.

**DUST COLLECTORS**
B. F. Sturtevant Co. of Canada, Ltd.
Toronto Blower Company

**EDGERS**
Hamilton Company, Ltd., William
Green Company, G. Walter
Long Mfg. Company, E.
Payette Company, P.
Waterous Engine Works Company

**ELEVATING AND CONVEYING
MACHINERY**
Canadian Belt-Link Company, Ltd.
Engineering & Machine Works of
Canada
Hamilton Company, William
Waterous Engine Works Company

**ENGINES**
Robt. Bell Engine & Thresher Co.
Engineering & Machine Works of
Canada
Hamilton Company, William

Payette Company, P.
Waterous Engine Works Company

**EXCELSIOR MACHINERY**
Elmira Machinery & Transmission
Company

**EXHAUST FANS**
B. F. Sturtevant Co. of Canada, Ltd.
Toronto Blower Company

**EXHAUST SYSTEMS**
B. F. Sturtevant Co. of Canada, Ltd.
Toronto Blower Company

**FILES**
Diston & Sons, Henry
Simonds Canada Saw Company

**FIR**
Apex Lumber Co.
Associated Mills, Limited
Bainbridge Lumber Company
Cameron Lumber Co.
Canadian Western Lumber Co.
Canfield, F.
Chesbro, R. G.
Dry Wood Lumber Co.
Edgecumbe-Newham Company
Fesserton Timber Company
Grier & Sons, Ltd., G. A.
Heeney, Percy E.
Knox Brothers
Likely, Ltd., Joseph A.
Mason, Gordon & Co.
Robertson & Hacket Sawmills
Rose, McLaurin, Limited
Terry & Gordon
Timberland Lumber Company
Timms, Phillips & Co.
Underhill Lumber Co.
Vancouver Lumber Company
Vanderhoof Lumber Co.
Victoria Lumber & Mfg. Co.

**FIRE BRICK**
Beveridge Supply Co., Ltd.
Elk Fire Brick Company of Canada
Shell-Bar, Boice Supply Co. Ltd.

**FIRE FIGHTING APPARATUS**
Waterous Engine Works Company

**FITTINGS**
Crane Limited

**FLOORING**
Cameron Lumber Co.
Chesbro, R. G.
Long-Bell Lumber Company

**GEARS (Cut)**
Smart-Turner Machine Co.

**GRAVITY LUMBER CARRIER**
Mathews Gravity Carrier Co.

**GRINDING WHEELS**
Canadian Hart Products Ltd.

**GUARDS (Machinery and Window)**
Canada Wire & Iron Goods Co.

**HARDWOODS**
Anderson Lumber Company, C. G.
Anderson Shreiner & Mawson
Atlantic Lumber Company
Barrett, Wm.
Bartram & Ball
Bury & Co., Robt.
Cameron & Co.
Edwards & Co., W. C.
Fesserton Timber Co.
Gillespie, James
Gloucester Lumber & Trading Co.
Grier & Son, G. A.
Hart, Hamilton & Jackson.
Heeney, Percy E.

Knox Brothers
Mason & Co., Geo.
McDonagh Lumber Co.
McLennan Lumber Company
McLung, McLellan & Berry
Musgrave & Co.
Pedwell Hardwood Lumber Co.
W. & J. Sharples.
Spencer, Limited, C. A.
Strong, G. M.
Summers, James R.
Tennessee Lumber & Coal Co.
Webster & Brother, James

**HARDWOOD FLOORING**
Brompton Lumber & Mfg. Co.
Grier & Son, G. A.

**HARNESS**
Beal Leather Co., R. M.
Carson & Company, Hugh

**HEMLOCK**
Anderson Lumber Company. C. G
Anderson, Shreiner & Mawson
Bartram & Ball
Beck Lumber Co.
Bethune Pulp & Lumber Co.
Bourgouin, H.
Canadian General Lumber Company
Edwards & Company, W. C.
Fesserton Timber Co.
Grier & Sons, Ltd., G. A.
Hart, Hamilton & Jackson
Hocken Lumber Company
Mason, Gordon & Co.
McCormack & Stewart
McDonagh Lumber Co.
McGibbon Lumber Co.
Robertson & Hacket Sawmills
Spanish River Lumber Co.
Spencer, Limited, C. A.
Tennessee Lumber & Coal Co.
Terry & Gordon
Vancouver Lumber Co.
Vanderhoof Lumber Co.

**HOISTING AND HAULING
ENGINES**
General Supply Co. of Canada, Ltd.
Hopkins & Co., Ltd., F. H.

**HOSE**
General Supply Co. of Canada, Ltd.
Gutta Percha & Rubber Company

**INSURANCE**
Rankin Benedict Underwriting Co
Hardy & Co., E. D.
Lee, Blakemore Inc.
Lumbermen's Underwriting Alliance

**INTERIOR FINISH**
Cameron Lumber Co.
Canadian Western Lumber Co.
Canfield, F. L.
Eagle Lumber Company
Mason, Gordon & Co.
Rose, McLaurin, Limited
Terry & Gordon

**KILN DRIED LUMBER**
Bury & Co., Robt.

**KNIVES**
Disston & Sons, Henry
Simonds Canada Saw Company
Waterous Engine Works Company

**LARCH**
Otis Staples Lumber Co.

**LATH**
Anderson, Shreiner & Mawson
Apex Lumber Co.
Austin & Nicholson
Beck Lumber Co.
Brennen & Sons, F. W.
Cameron Lumber Co.
Canadian General Lumber Company
Carew Lumber Co., John
Chaleurs Bay Mills
Dupuis, Limited, J. P.

Eagle Lumber Company
Foley Lumber Company
Fraser Bryson Lumber Co.. Ltd.
Gloucester Lumber & Trading Co.
Grier & Sons, Ltd., G. A.
Harris Tie & Timber Company, Ltd.
Larkin Co., C. A.
Mason & Co., Geo.
McLennan Lumber Company
Miller, W. H. Co.
Musgrave & Company
New Ontario Colonization Company
Otis Staples Lumber Company
Power Lumber Co.
Price Bros. & Company
Shevlin-Clarke Co.
Spencer, Limited, C. A.
Terry & Gordon
U. G. G. Sawmills. Limited
Union Lumber Company
Victoria Harbor Lumber Company

**LATH BOLTERS**

General Supply Co. of Canada, Ltd.
Hamilton Company, Wm.
Payette & Company, F.

**LOCOMOTIVES**

Engineering & Machine Works of
 Canada
General Supply Co. of Canada, Ltd.
Hopkins & Co., Ltd., F. H.
Climax Manufacturing Company
Montreal Locomotive Works

**LATH TWINE**

Consumers' Cordage Company

**LINK-BELT**

Canadian Link-Belt Company
Mathews Gravity Carrier Company.
Hamilton Company, Wm.
Williams Machinery Co., A. R., Van-
 couver

**LOCOMOTIVE CRANES**

Canadian Link-Belt Company, Ltd.
Hopkins & Co. ,Ltd., F. H.

**LOGGING ENGINES**

Engineering & Machine Works of
 Canada
Hopkins & Co., Ltd., F. H.

**LOG HAULER**

Engineering & Machine Works of
 Canada
Green Company. G. Walter
Hopkins & Co., Ltd., F. H.
Payette Company, F.

**LOGGING MACHINERY AND
EQUIPMENT**

General Supply Co. of Canada, Ltd.
Hamilton Company, William
Hopkins & Co., Ltd., F. H.
Payette Company, P.
Waterous Engine Works ,Company
West, Peachey & Sons

**LUMBER EXPORTS**

Fletcher Corporation

**LUMBER TRUCKS**

Hamilton Company, Wm.
Waterous Engine Works Company

**LUMBERMEN'S BOATS**

Adams Engine Company
West, Peachey & Sons

**LUMBERMEN'S CLOTHING**

Kitchen Overall & Shirt Co.
Woods Manufacturing Company, Ltd.

**MATTRESSES**

Simmons Limited

**METAL REFINERS**

Canada Metal Company

**OAK**

Long-Bell Lumber Company

**OAKUM**

Stratford Oakum Co., Geo.

**PACKING**

Beveridge Supply Company
Consumers' Cordage Co.
Gutta Percha & Rubber Company

**PANELS**

Bury & Co., Robt.

**PAPER**

Beveridge Supply Co., Ltd.
Price Bros. & Co.

**PINE**

Anderson Lumber Company, C. G.
Anderson, Shreiner & Mawson
Atlantic Lumber Co.
Austin & Nicholson
Barratt, William
Beck Lumber Co.
Cameron & Co.
Cameron Lumber Co.
Canadian General Lumber Company
Canadian Western Lumber Co.
Canfield, P. L.
Chesbro, R. G.
Cleveland-Sarnia Sawmills Company
Cox, Long & Company
Dudley, Arthur N.
Eagle Lumber Company
Edwards & Co., W. C.
Excelsior Lumber Company
Fesserton Timber Company
Fraser Bryson Lumber Co., Ltd.
Gillies Bros, Limited
Gloucester Lumber & Trading Co.
Gordon & Co., George
Goodday & Company, H. R.
Grier & Sons, Ltd., G. A.
Harris Tie & Timber Company, Ltd.
Hart, Hamilton & Jackson
Hettler Lumber Company, Herman H.

Hocken Lumber Company
Julien, Roch
Lay & Haight.
Lloyd, W. Y.
Loggie Co., W. S.
Long-Bell Lumber Company
Mason, Gordon & Co.
Mason & Co., Geo.
McCormack & Stewart
McFadden & Malloy
McLennan Lumber Company
Mickle Lumber Co.
Montreal Lumber Company
Muir & Kirkpatrick
Musgrave & Co.
Northern Lumber Mills.
Otis Staples Lumber Co.
Parry Sound Lumber Company
Rolland Lumber Co.
W. & J. Sharples.
Shevlin-Clarke Co.
Spanish River Lumber Co.
Spencer, Limited, C. A.
Strong, G. M.
Summers, James R.
Tennessee Lumber & Coal Co.
Terry & Gordon
Union Lumber Company
Victoria Harbor Lumber Co.
Watson & Todd, Limited
Wuichet, Louis

**PLANING MILL EXHAUSTERS**

Toronto Blower Co.

**PLANING MILL MACHINERY**

Mershon & Co., W. B.
B. F. Sturtevant Co. of Canada, Ltd.
Toronto Blower. Co.
Yates Machine Company, P. B.

**PORK PACKERS**

Davies Company, William

**5 THINGS TO LOOK FOR**

in a BELT

SOLID LEATHER

UNIFORM THICKNESS

STRENGTH

FLEXIBILITY

**D. K. McLAREN**
Limited

Head Office and Factory
351 St. James St., Montreal

TORONTO
194 King St. West

VANCOUVER
34 Cordova St. West

ST. JOHN, N. B.
90 Germain Street

**POSTS AND POLES**
Anderson, Shreiner & Mawson
Auger & Company
Canadian Tie & Lumber Co.
Dupuis, Limited, J. P.
Eagle Lumber Company
Harris Tie & Timber Co., Ltd.
Long-Bell Lumber Co.
Mason, Gordon & Co.
McLennan Lumber Company
Terry & Gordon

**PULLEYS AND SHAFTING**
Canadian Link-Belt Company
General Supply Co. of Canada, Ltd.
Green Company, G. Walter
Engineering & Machine Works of Canada
Hamilton Company, William

**PULP MILL MACHINERY**
Canadian Link-Belt Company, Ltd.
Engineering & Machine Works of Canada
Hamilton Company, William
Payette Company, P.
Waterous Engine Works Company

**PULPWOOD**
Bethune Pulp & Lumber Co.
British & Foreign Agencies
D'Auteuil Lumber Co.
Price Bros. & Co.
Scott, Draper & Co.

**PUMPS**
General Supply Co. of Canada, Ltd.
Engineering & Machine Works of Canada
Hamilton Co., William
Hopkins & Co. ,Ltd., F. H.
Smart-Turner Machine Company
Waterous Engine Works Company

**RAILS**
Gartshore, John J.
Hopkins & Co. ,Ltd., F. H.

**ROOFINGS**
(Rubber, Plastic and Liquid)
Beveridge Supply Company

**ROPE**
Consumers' Cordage Co.

**RUBBER GOODS**
Dunlop Tire & Rubber Goods Co.
Gutta Percha & Rubber Company

**SASH**
Brompton Lumber & Mfg. Co.
Midland Woodworkers
Midland Wood Products, Ltd.

**SAWS**
Atkins & Company, E. C.
Disston & Sons, Henry
General Supply Co. of Canada, Ltd.
Gerlach Company, Peter
Green Company, G. Walter
Hoe & Company, R.
Radcliff Saw Mfg. Co.,
Shurly Co., Ltd., T. F.
Shurly-Dietrich Company
Simonds Canada Saw Company

**SAW MILL LINK-BELT**
Canadian Link-Belt Company

**SAW MILL MACHINERY**
Canadian Link-Belt Company, Ltd.
General Supply Co. of Canada, Ltd.
G. Walter Green Co., Ltd.
Hamilton Company, William
La Compagnie Manufacture, F. X. Bertrand
Long Manufacturing Company, E.
Mershon & Company, W. B.
Parry Sound Lumber Company
Payette Company, P.
Waterous Engine Works Company
Yates Machine Co., P. B.

**SAW SHARPENERS**
Hamilton Company, William
Waterous Engine Works Company

**SAW SLASHERS**
Hamilton Company, Wm.
Payette Company, P.
Waterous Engine Works Company

**SHINGLES**
Apex Lumber Co.
Associated Mills, Limited
Brennen & Sons, P. W.
Cameron Lumber Co.
Campbell-MacLaurin Lumber Co.
Canadian Western Lumber Co.
Carew Lumber Co., John
Chaleurs Bay Mills
Cheabro, R. G.
Coast & Mountain Lumber Co.
D'Auteuil Lumber Co.
Dry Wood Lumber Co.
Eagle Lumber Company
Edgecumbe-Newham Company
Federal Lumber Company
Fraser, Limited
Gillespie, James
Gloucester Lumber & Trading Co.
Grier & Sons, Limited, G. A.
Hartia Tie & Timber Company, Ltd.
Heaps & Sons
Heeney, Percy E.
Mason, Gordon & Co.
McLennan Lumber Company
Miller Company, Ltd., W. H.
Musgrave & Co.
Reynolds Company, Limited
Rose, McLaurin, Limited
Terry & Gordon
Timms, Phillips & Co.
Vancouver Lumber Company
Vanderhoof Lumber Co.

**SHINGLE & LATH MACHINERY**
Green Company, C. Walter
Hamilton Company, William
Long Manufacturing Company, E.
Payette Company, P.

**SILENT CHAIN DRIVES**
Canadian Link-Belt Company, Ltd.

**SLEEPING EQUIPMENT**
Simmons Limited

**SLEEPING ROBES**
Woods Mfg. Company, Ltd.

**SMOKESTACKS**
Hamilton Company, Wm.
Waterous Engine Works Company

**SNOW PLOWS**
Pink Company, Thomas

**SOLDERS**
Canada Metal Co.

**SOUTHERN YELLOW PINE**
Mickle Lumber Co., H. L.

**SPARK ARRESTORS**
Waterous Engine Works Company

**SPRUCE**
Anderson, Shreiner & Mawson
Barrett, Wm.
Bartram & Ball
Cameron Lumber Co.
Campbell, McLaurin Lumber Co.
Canadian Western Lumber Co.
Chesbro, R. G.
Cox, Long & Co.
Dudley, Arthur N.
Edgecumbe-Newham Company
Fraser, Limited
Fraser-Bryson Lumber Company

Gillies Brothers
Gloucester Lumber & Trading Co.
Goodday & Company, H. R.
Grier & Sons, Ltd., G. A.
Harris Lumber Co., Frank H.
Hart, Hamilton & Jackson
Hocken Lumber Company
Julien, Roch
Larkin Co., C. A.
Lay & Haight
Lloyd, W. Y.
Loggie Co., W. S.
Mason, Gordon & Co.
McCormack & Stewart
McDonagh Lumber Co.
McLennan Lumber Company
Muir & Kirkpatrick
Musgrave & Co.
New Ontario Colonization Company
Northern Lumber Mills.
Power Lumber Co.
Price Bros. & Co.
Rolland Lumber Co.
Rose, McLaurin, Limited
W. & J. Sharples.
Spencer, Limited, C. A.
Strong, G. M.
Terry & Gordon
U. G. G. Sawmills. Limited
Vanderhoof Lumber Co.

**STEAM SHOVELS**
Hopkins & Co., Ltd., F. H.

**STEEL CHAIN**
Canadian Link-Belt Company, Ltd.
Hopkins & Co. ,Ltd., F. H.
Waterous Engine Works Company

**STEAM PLANT ACCESSORIES**
Waterous Engine Works Company

**STEEL BARRELS**
Smart-Turner Machine Co.

**STEEL DRUMS**
Smart-Turner Machine Co.

**TARPAULINS**
Turner & Sons, J. J.
Woods Manufacturing Company, Ltd.

**TANKS**
Hopkins & Co., Ltd., F. H.

**TENTS**
Turner & Sons, J. J.
Woods Mfg. Company

**TIES**
Austin & Nicholson
Bethune Pulp & Lumber Co.
Carew Lumber Co., John
Canadian Tie & Lumber Co.
Chaleurs Bay Mills
D'Auteuil Lumber Co.
Gloucester Lumber & Trading Co. Ltd.
Harris Tie & Timber Company, Ltd.
McLennan Lumber Company
Miller, W. H.
Price Bros. & Co.
Scott, Draper & Co.
Terry & Gordon

**TIMBER BROKERS**
Bradley, R. R.
Cant & Kemp
Farnworth & Jardine
Wright, Graham & Co.

**TIMBER CRUISERS AND ESTIMATORS**
Savage & Bartlett.
Sewall, James W.

**TIMBER LANDS**
Department of Lands & Forests, Ont.

**TOWING MACHINES**
Corbet Foundry & Machine Co.
Payette Company, P.
West, Peachey & Sons

**TRACTORS**
Hopkins & Company, Ltd., F. H.
Monarch Tractors

**TRANSMISSION MACHINERY**
Canadian Link-Belt Company, Ltd.
Engineering & Machine Works of Canada
General Supply Co. of Canada, Ltd.
Grand Rapids Vapor Kiln
Hamilton Company, William
Waterous Engine Works Company

**TURBINES**
Engineering & Machine Works of Canada
Hamilton Company, William
B. F. Sturtevant Co. of Canada, Ltd.

**VALVES**
Crane Limited

**VAPOR KILNS**
Grand Rapids Vapor Kiln
B. F. Sturtevant Co. of Canada, Ltd.

**VENEERS**
Bury & Co., Robt.

**VENEER DRYERS**
Coe Manufacturing Company
Proctor & Schwartz Inc.
B. F. Sturtevant Co. of Canada, Ltd.

**VENEER MACHINERY**
Coe Machinery Company
Proctor & Schwartz Inc.

**VETERINARY REMEDIES**
Dr. Bell Veterinary Wonder Co.
Johnson, A. H.

**WARPING TUGS**
West, Peachey & Sons

**WATER WHEELS**
Engineering & Machine Works of Canada
Hamilton Company, William

**WELDING**
Barton Electric Welding Co.
St. John Welders & Engineers

**WIRE**
Canada Metal Co.
Laidlaw Bale Tie Company
Canada Wire & Iron Goods Co.

**WIRE CLOTH**
Canada Wire & Iron Goods Co.

**WIRE ROPE**
Canada Wire & Iron Goods Co.
Hopkins & Co., Ltd., F. H.
Dominion Wire Rope Co.
Greening Wire Co., B.

**WOODWORKING MACHINERY**
General Supply Co. of Canada, Ltd.
Long Manufacturing Company, E.
Mershon & Company, W. B.
Waterous Engine Works Company
Yates Machine Company, P. B.

**WOOD PRESERVATIVES**
Beveridge Supply Company

**WOOD PULP**
Austin & Nicholson
New Ontario Colonization Co.
Power Lumber Co.

## LUMBERMEN'S EQUIPMENT

## Heavy Duty Gang Edger

This Machine has many features that commend themselves to the mill owner. Here is just one. The frame is cast in one piece— and it is of such massive design as to absorb all the strains and shocks to which the machine can be subjected. Of the others we shall be pleased to send full particulars. Will you write us for them?

# The E. Long Manufacturing Co., Limited

### Orillia

### Canada

Vol. 42        Toronto, January 15, 1922        No. 2

# Canada Lumberman

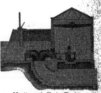

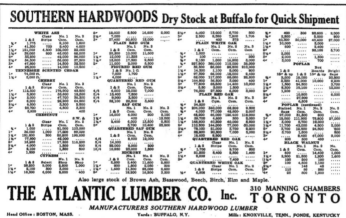

# White Pine
## Red Pine
## Jack Pine
## Spruce
## Lumber
## and Lath

**UNION LUMBER COMPANY LIMITED**
701 DOMINION BANK BUILDING
TORONTO          CANADA

# Well Bought is Half Sold!

*"The tumult and the shouting dies The Captains and the Kings depart"*

## 'ts over !

The greatest Convention of the Canadian Lumbermen's Association.

Splendid affair! Everybody satisfied!

### Now
### to work, and make
### 1922
### "a good 'un!"

We're ready.
Best assorted Stock ever.
Graded (not guessed at).

## SERVICE? YES !

*What* you want,
*When* you want it,
That's all.

Selah !

# Canadian General Lumber Co.
Limited

# FOREST PRODUCTS

TORONTO OFFICE :— 712-20 Bank of Hamilton Building
Montreal Office :—203 McGill Bldg.
Mills : Byng Inlet, Ont.

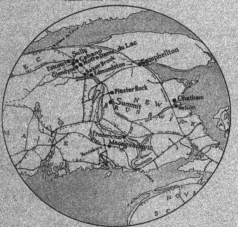

# Arkansas Soft Pine
## Satin-like Interior Trim
### Soft, close-grained, light-weight common lumber

# The South's Finest
# Lumber *for all 'round*
*yard stock*

### Makes permanent customers of casual buyers — thousands of dealers know it; more thousands can prove it with a trial car.

*Write* { The Mills for quotations
The Bureau for literature, sales aids, samples

All stock bearing the Arkansas Soft Pine registered trade-mark
is manufactured and sold exclusively by the following companies:

ARKANSAS LAND & LUMBER COMPANY
MALVERN, ARKANSAS

ARKANSAS LUMBER COMPANY
WARREN, ARKANSAS

COTTON BELT LUMBER COMPANY
BEARDEN, ARKANSAS

CROSSETT LUMBER COMPANY
CROSSETT, ARKANSAS

EAGLE LUMBER COMPANY
EAGLE MILLS, ARKANSAS

EDGAR LUMBER COMPANY
WESSON, ARKANSAS

FREEMAN-SMITH LUMBER COMPANY
MILLVILLE, ARKANSAS

FORDYCE LUMBER COMPANY
FORDYCE, ARKANSAS

GATES LUMBER COMPANY
WILMAR, ARKANSAS

OZAN-GRAYSONIA LUMBER COMPANY
PRESCOTT, ARKANSAS

SOUTHERN LUMBER COMPANY
WARREN, ARKANSAS

STOUT LUMBER COMPANY
THORNTON, ARKANSAS

WISCONSIN AND ARKANSAS
LUMBER COMPANY
MALVERN, ARKANSAS

Composing the

## Arkansas Soft Pine Bureau
### Little Rock, Arkansas

# BUY
## BRITISH COLUMBIA
# Red Cedar Shingles

The life of a British Columbia Red Cedar Shingle Roof can almost be gauged by the life of the nail with which the shingle is nailed in place. Judging from available data, the average life of the ordinary steel wire nail, which has been in such common use, is only from seven to twelve years. Some wire nails will last longer, depending upon the condition of exposure, climate and similar features, but considering our climate as a whole, at the end of from seven to twelve years a large percentage of wire nails will have rusted either completely through or so extensively that the first strong wind will complete the work. The shingles that have been held in position by such nails are then free to work down, permitting rains or melting snows to leak through and damage the interior of the structure. Examination will disclose that the fibre of the shingle itself is still in perfect condition, and a leaky roof, in the majority of occasions is due entirely to the use of faulty nails, but the average home owner, placed at such inconvenience, will not stop to reason this out and the poor wooden shingle comes in for more unjust abuse.

There are several kinds of nails which experience has proven will give lasting satisfaction, and the wise dealer will advise his customers of these satisfactory nails. A pure zinc shingle nail meets all the demands of durability required. Its principal drawback is its high cost and a slight tendency to bend under careless driving. Galvanized wire nails theoretically are rust proof, and if the galvanized coating is properly applied, and of sufficient thickness, such a nail will last as long as the shingle it holds in place. The life of this shingle roof, properly applied with these nails then is from 40 to 50 years. Pure iron nails, or the old cut or wrought nails are ideal but difficult to secure. Copper nails also constitute a perfect shingle nail.

| | |
|---|---|
| **Timms Phillips & Co., Ltd.**<br>Yorkshire Bldg., Vancouver<br>Manufacturers and Wholesalers<br>**Red Cedar Shingles**<br>3x-5x- Perfections, Royals, Imperials<br>**Red Cedar Bevel Siding** | **Vancouver Lumber Co., Ltd.**<br>Manufacturers<br>**XXX—XXXXX CEDAR SHINGLES**<br>(Rite Grade Inspected)<br>Head Office.    Eastern Sales Office<br>**Vancouver, B.C.**    **Toronto, Ont.** |
| **Westminster Mill Co.**<br>LIMITED<br>New Westminster, B.C.<br>**Red Cedar Shingles**<br>**Cedar Bevel Siding** | **Dominion Timber Products Ltd.**<br>Vancouver Block<br>Vancouver<br>Largest Manufacturers of<br>**Perfection Shingles**<br>in Canada |
| **Underhill Lumber Co., Ltd.**<br>Dominion Bldg., Vancouver<br>**RED CEDAR SHINGLES**<br>3x-5x- Perfection and Eurekas<br>**CEDAR BEVEL SIDING**<br>**CEDAR BUNGALOW SIDING** | **Shull Lumber & Shingle Co.**<br>Limited<br>New Westminster B. C.<br>Trade Mark<br>**RED BAND SHINGLES**<br>**XXX XXXXX Stars Clears**<br>From Mill to You |
| **If you want a market for B. C. Red Cedar Shingles put an advertisement on this page.** | **Kootenay Shingle Co. Ltd.**<br>Salmo, B C.<br>**Red Cedar Shingles**<br>xxx and xx.<br>Packed by the thousand |

# British Columbia Lumber
# Red Cedar Shingles

**In these days of broken
stocks and limited sup-
ply, you need a rea
definite service in your
requirements.**

*Are you getting it?*

## Timms Phillips & Co., Ltd.
### Vancouver, B. C.

TORONTO OFFICE: Canada Permanent Bldg.
Phone Adel. 6490
MONTREAL OFFICE: 2  Marconi Bldg.
Phone M

# Canada Lumberman

Founded 1880

*The National Lumber Journal for Forty Years*

Issued on the 1st and 15th of every month by

### HUGH C. MACLEAN PUBLICATIONS, Limited

THOS. S. YOUNG, Managing Director

HEAD OFFICE  - - - -  347 Adelaide Street, West, TORONTO

Proprietors and Publishers also of Electrical News, Contract Record,
Canadian Woodworker and Footwear in Canada.

| | | |
|---|---|---|
| VANCOUVER | - - - - | Winch Building |
| MONTREAL | - - - - | 119 Board of Trade Bldg. |
| WINNIPEG | - - - - | Electric Railway Chambers |
| NEW YORK | - - - - | 296 Broadway |
| CHICAGO | - - - - | Room 803, 63 E. Adams St. |
| LONDON, ENG. | - - - - | 16 Regent Street, S.W. |

### TERMS OF SUBSCRIPTION

Canada, United States and Great Britain, $3.00 per year, in advance; other
foreign countries embraced in the General Postal Union, $4.00.
Single copies, 20 cents.

Authorized by the Postmaster-General for Canada, for transmission as
second-class matter.

| Vol. 42 | Toronto, January 15, 1922 | No. 2 |
|---|---|---|

## Getting Ready for an Active Year

It would appear as if 1922 is going to be a pretty fair year in the lumber business and all industrial undertakings are likely to share in the renewal of activity. Many periodicals have been issuing annual reviews or survey numbers in which leading exponents of all lines of enterprise have been given their views with respect to present and prospective conditions. Without scarcely an exception a hopeful view is taken of the future.

No one is wildly enthusiastic about a sudden return to the abnormal and fictitious state of affairs which characterized the first few months of 1920. No sane, level-headed man desires a repetition of the conditions which then prevailed for the re-action has been severe and prolonged. These relapses, whether in ordinary illness or business recovery are most uncertain in their outcome and debilitating in their tendencies.

To-day uncertainty is giving place to 'confidence,' and co-operation is manifested on many sides, and only a few who have not yet learned their lesson, desire to see a runaway market or any of the features which permeated the situation two years ago.

There is every evidence that the demand for lumber products is broadening, and the great need at present is a standardized and stabilized business. However, there is no use bolstering up an artificial state of affairs. One cannot raise himself by the pull-straps on his boots, and in many quarters there is a cautious attitude. Collections are also reported to be rather difficult. Farmers are not buying as yet in large quantities due to the low price of their product.

Industrial trade has been pent up for months but of late weeks there has been something of a change. Factory users of lumber have come into the market and others are making inquiries. The railroads have also commenced to buy and will require a lot of lumber.

Those who are looking for further decreases in lumber prices will, have to have another think coming to them. Production costs are now at rock bottom and the only lowering in sight is a probable cut in wages around the mills in the spring from 10 to 15%. This ,however, will not make very material difference in the original outlay for lumber which, owing to the gradual depletion of the timber resources of the country, is getting more expensive to drive manufacture and distribute.

The outlook respecting the whole situation is presented in the annual reports of the president and committees of the Canadian Lumbermen's Association, which are presented in another column of this paper and speak with considerable assurance regarding the future and the need of a cool head, steady hand and calm disposition.

If wages in the building trade come down, no doubt there will be more house construction during the coming year than has been in a long period. There is great need yet for dwelling accommodation,

and although regret has been expressed on many sides that rents show no tendency to decrease, it may be stated that the present high figure is likely to continue until more houses are available.

In a recent address delivered before the Southern Pine Manufacturers in Memphis, Chas. S. Keith, president of the Central Coal & Coke Co., of Kansas City, Mo., who is one of the best industrial authorities, unhesitatingly declared that 1922 should be a prosperous year. He quoted many figures illustrative of his contentions, showing that the nation's lumber production capacity had diminished while the country's requirements for production had pyramided.

Analyzing the situation from the viewpoint of the manufacturer he pointed out that there was no surplus stock at any of the producing districts, while the amount in the retail lumber yards was less than half of their normal requirements. He then went somewhat into detail: The volume of trade coming from various sources now equalled or exceeded production. The prospective demand from the cities, the industries and the railroads, alone promised to tax the producing capacity. There was no reason to expect that the great agricultural districts would refrain from buying building material but if they contributed one half of last year's patronage it would compel the retail lumbermen of this district to buy double what they did in 1921. "Prices of forest products have declined to a point where lumber is being sold at less than the cost of production. Just as soon as this prospective demand begins to materialize prices will substantially advance."

## What About the Building Outlook?

The question is being asked in many circles "How will business turn in 1922?" There are many opinions regarding activity and expansion on the one hand or continued quietness on the other hand, but it is generally conceded that much will depend upon the building situation.

During the year just closed there was spent on construction contracts in Canada over $240,000,000, compared with $255,605,000 in 1920, being a decrease of 6.05.% In December 1921, $19,000,000 was spent on new buildings, making the second largest December total on record, being exceeded only once and that in December 1912 when $31,125,000 was expended.

It is stated that the pressure for housing accommodation is almost as urgent now as at the close of the war. In Great Britain it is estimated that there are over a 1,000,000 houses required, and in the United States the estimate runs from 2,000,000 to 3,000,000, while in Canada it is quite safe to say that, at least, 300,000 dwellings are needed. Whether this want will be supplied or not, depends very much on the attitude of the building trades and their willingness to take a cut in wages.

It is believed that material of all kinds is now down to bed-rock prices, and it largely rests with labor whether many new homes and other structures will be built. It is unhesitatingly declared by those who have given close study to the situation that labor must realize that longer hours and honest work is the only remedy for present conditions. Already there are some ominous signs in the shape of strikes and a persistent refusal to take a cut in wages.

In a recent review by the Chamber of Commerce of the United States, it was stated that three factors enter largely into the problem of building during the coming months,—the high price of material, high price of labor and the question of obtaining funds for construction. It is declared that the prices of material are the more favorable of the three factors, and it is only here and there that there is any apparent difficulty. The matter of too high-priced labor does not stack up well as that of material, but it is hoped as spring advances, a more reasonable attitude and keen appreciation of the situation will be witnessed by labor, and the long period of idleness on the part of many trades, come to an end.

One problem arising is the necessity and availability of money. In regard to this there are differences of opinion. The usual stories are heard about cash being hard to get, of collections being slow, impossible to raise funds, etc., but at the same time, there seems to be a gradual trend toward solving this question by reason of the high interest rates which have prevailed on bonds, mortgages and other securities, showing some decrease.

The foregoing observations are given as a result of an examination into present conditions, and no attempt is made to forecast the future. The most dangerous role to play at the present juncture is that of a prophet. No honor is coming to him either at home or abroad. The main thing just now is a spirit of courage, confidence and co-operation.

As pointed out, few factors will tend to hasten the return to better times than the building industry. Things used in the erection of dwelling houses call upon practically all industries of the country for their products, and a general and far-reaching construction programme in Canada during 1922 is the best possible harbinger of a return to a more prosperous period.

# How Live Yardman May Speed Up His Deliveries

### The Economical Service and Facilities Afforded by Motor Truck—Practical Advice on its Upkeep and Maintenance—Some Timely Suggestions

The lumber retailer must be ever awake to speed up his delivery problems, and to do this, must use motor trucks for some part of his delivery.

This method of delivery presents no terrors to those who realize that when they add a truck to their equipment, they are adding a piece of machinery as valuable as any they may possess within their mill. Realizing this, they do not look for returns beyond a reasonable amount of increased delivery of their stock.

Many yards introduce a light truck for the reason that they believe that in a cheap investment there is not the amount of capital involved, and if delivery by truck does not come up to their expectations, they can very easily scrap their purchase and not be at any considerable loss. This viewpoint is wrong and decidedly so.

As many of us can affirm, the cheap machine never proved as efficient or returned to us the profits as have the machines which we purchased knowing that they were designed to perform their work under conditions which were daily arising. Briefly, we cannot hope to run flooring on a machine which one day we use to turn out mouldings and the next set up for a run of hardwood flooring. We may turn out the stock after a fashion, but we cannot hope to compete against the retailer whose equipment consists of machines designed to do the various types of work at a speed and finish required to obtain us repeat orders for our product.

#### Choosing the Proper Truck

Since we have learned the lesson from experiences of having to be continually on the alert in the introduction of newest types of machinery, even so must we be awake to the necessity of using the most modern methods to make our delivery.

The fundamental principle to be acquired in the purchase of a motor truck is permanency of organization by the manufacturer of the truck. The company behind the motor truck must be one sufficiently sound financially to be able to supply us during the five, ten or more years we are using their product, with repairs and replacement of worn-out parts. Unless they are in a position to guarantee their existence during the life-time of their product, we will not be well advised to contemplate the purchase of their product.

Briefly, the purchase of a motor truck can be summed up as follows: Buy first of all a permanency of manufacture, then a distributing agency equally as sound and then buy their product, for no matter the condition of the latter, it will be well and quickly serviced.

These few remarks are given with the idea of driving home the fact that to-day, as in every line of industry, the manufacture of motor trucks is gradually narrowing to the control of a few stable firms whose product can be relied upon to give a maximum of delivery at a minimum of expenditure.

In considering the delivery of lumber from retail yards by trucks, it can be quickly summed up into two classes—those operating a single truck or two and those operating fleets. Those whose delivery depends on a few trucks at most must watch them closely in order that they are always in a condition to be in service and must plan the loads so that there is no loss of time in loading or delivering the load at the job. This class of retailer has, as a rule, no service plant of his own and must depend upon his driver to attend to all road trouble or upon the firm from whom he buys to service his truck; consequently he cannot allow long delays due to having to lay up the truck for repairs.

He must watch his routing so that the driver is allowed sufficient time to care for his truck. As an example, I would mention of one yard which I know of where the driver is allowed a certain time each day for attending to the proper lubrication of his truck and to tighten up any part which has become slack, and as a consequence of this practice, the truck to-day is in as good condition as when its owner purchased it some years ago, and his actual delivery time is not impaired in the least; yet near this yard is another whose truck, much younger in point of service, is very often laid up because the driver has not been allowed sufficient time to properly adjust loose bolts or make certain that the truck is in condition to do the day's work.

The first retailer spends a certain amount of money each day in having his truck cared for and is reaping a return many times his investment in having no expensive repair accounts or delays due to neglect. His stock of lumber is being moved continually and new

customers are being added to his books because they know that they can depend upon receiving their orders when promised. On the other hand the second retailer has suffered many serious set-backs because of his lack of caring for his motor truck and many of his customers are giving their business to other yards.

To obtain satisfaction from truck delivery, we must first of all know that our equipment is in a condition to meet the requirements, and then we must make due provision for loading and unloading, and possibly the quickest and best method of doing this is by having our truck body equipped with a roller at the back with which the load can be rolled off the truck. This enables the driver to make much more rapid delivery than by having to handle each individual piece on the load.

Having generally spoken of motor trucks, let us go back over some features which are necessary to the successful operation of trucks and from the retail lumberman's viewpoint he requires loading space and a minimum of operating expense.

He can obtain practically all the length of body he requires by the purchase of a long wheel base truck, others buy a trailer. This will be very necessary for the delivery of timbers much longer than usual, but unless a yard specializes in long timbers, one does not need a trailer as part of his motor equipment as the two wheels of a wagon will answer very well.

Then, too, he must buy a truck of capacity great enough to prove economical both from a delivery and also load-carrying standpoints.

Possibly a two-ton long wheel base truck will be his most satisfactory unit as his cost of operation will be approximately fifteen cents per mile exclusive of driver and other charges which should be written against the truck each day, as example, license and interest charges. Yet with this cost of operating, he will be able to handle, not only loads equal to the truck's capacity, but also can draw as much more if his equipment includes trailers.

#### The Detail of Truck Manufacture

Having decided upon the capacity he will require, he must look for some necessary features to be found in trucks of reputable manufacture and very necessary to the economical operation of motor trucks.

First he will require to have a detailed investigation of the type of steel used in the chassis or frame, then the type of springs, and having found these two points to his satisfaction, namely, that they are designed to be both flexible and possess the maximum of elasticity consistent with good manufacture, he can turn his attention to the motor and other parts of the truck. Vital as motor transmission and rear axle may seem, they do not decide entirely the fate of a motor truck, for a truck is primarily a load-carrying unit defined best as a development of power, a conversion of the same and an application of that power to cause the load to be propelled along the road, and we must have our units designed to carry our load easily and with as little strain as possible, and having done so, we then must design our three next chief items of motor truck construction to function with a balance and co-operation found only in a proper understanding of the power developed in the motor and transmitted through the transmission to the rear axle and then to the road by means of a perfect balance of engine speed and gear ratios.

A terrific engine speed and low gear reduction cannot hope to become a factor in giving a minimum of operating costs, and a truck possessing a long life, nor can a low-speeded engine with high gear reductions accomplish that for which we purchase our truck, namely, long, life, economical operation and low maintenance.

We must balance the revolutions per minute of our motor and the reductions of our transmission and rear axle to give a proper application of power at a minimum cost of operation.

Having found our load carrying units to our satisfaction, and our power plant transmission and rear axle balances properly, we can then look for some component principles of manufacture necessary to efficient operation. First, we should have our truck equipped with radius rods which permit of the rear axle and springs being completely equipped to do their part in carrying the load without having to receive the road shocks which would be given to them but for the presence of the radius rods.

Then our lubrication should be efficient and accessible and possibly the best type is the Alemite system by which the grease is forced under pressure to the bearings.

# Lumbermen Hold the Greatest Session Ever

### Record Attendance at Gathering in Toronto—Aggressive Action Against High Freight Rates—A.E. Clark Elected President—Next Assembly in Montreal

 Remarkable for attendance, enthusiasm and interest, the fourteenth annual convention of the Canadian Lumbermen's Association was held at the King Edward Hotel, Toronto, on January 11th and 12th. Every feature of the great gathering, whether of a business or social character, left nothing to be desired, and the proceedings were marked by harmony, sincerity and goodwill. The lumbermen of Toronto excelled themselves as hosts and were much gratified at the appreciation expressed by the visitors regarding the warm welcome that attended their stay in Toronto.

The officers elected for the coming year are energetic members who have done valiant service for the organization. Some of the outstanding business of the gathering was the unanimous decision to carry on the agitation in favor of lower freight rates; the extension of the directorate to include representation from the United States; the matter of seeking an adjustment of ocean transportation charges and deciding to watch the anti-wooden shingle campaign.

Many tributes were paid to R. L. Sargant, traffic manager of the Association, for his vigorous work on behalf of the members, individually and collectively. It was agreed that the new department was "making good" in every respect; in fact, a large portion of the session was devoted to traffic matters, so keenly do the lumbermen feel that, in the matter of carrying rates both by land and by water, an injustice is being done the industry, and that business in the old country now going to Scandinavian countries, should properly come to Canada. Many other items came up for consideration, and a reference to these will be found on the pages that follow.

### The New Men at the Helm

The officers elected for the coming year were :—

President, A. E. Clark (Edward Clark & Sons), Toronto;

First Vice-President, J. Fraser Gregory, (Murray & Gregory), St. John, N. B.;

Second Vice-President, Angus McLean, (The Bathurst Co). Bathurst, N. B.;

Secretary, Frank Hawkins, Ottawa;

Treasurer, R. G. Cameron, Ottawa.

Directors for the coming three years—for Ontario, A. E. Clark, Toronto; W. E. Bigwood, Toronto; Gordon C. Edwards, Ottawa; for Quebec, W. Gerard Power, Quebec City; for Maritime Provinces, Angus McLean, Bathurst, N. B.; United States directors,—Spencer Kellogg, Utica, N. Y., and R. E. Stocking, New York City.

The executive elected, G. E. Spragge, of the Victoria Harbor Lumber Co., Toronto, to fill out the unexpired term (one year) of the late James G. Cane, as a director of the Association.

It was decided, on the invitation of the Montreal members, that the next gathering would be held in that city. It was stated that the Mount Royal Hotel, now in course of construction, would be completed by the end of 1922 and that the 1923 gathering of the C. L. A. would, probably, be the first large convention held within its walls.

The newly-elected executive at a special sitting passed votes of thanks and appreciation to A. R. Whittemore, manager of MacLean Building Reports, Toronto, for his admirable address at the luncheon; the members of the different local committees; the management of the hotel; the various speakers of the day; the trade press and daily newspapers for their reports.

The directors decided that an extensive campaign should be carried on for membership, and every director pledged himself to bring in as many new members as possible. It is expected that the roster will soon show over the 200 mark.

The appointment of the executive committee and the transportation committee was left in the hands of the new president. The personnel of these bodies will be announced as soon as the selections are made.

### President Ably Reviews Year's Work

The first item of business at the opening of the convention was the presentation of the annual address from the President of the Association, Dan McLachlin, of Arnprior, Ont. His report is as follows:

This is the 14th annual meeting and we are really a husky youngster. In spite of the period of war deflation which has been so painful a memory to us all, we stand today as an Association stronger than ever. Our membership is now 181 as compared with 173 a year ago, and what is equally important, we are recognized as really the

official body of the lumber trade of Canada by all government departments who, by virtue of their duties, come in contact,—I almost said conflict,— with the lumber world. And in passing, may I take this opportunity of expressing to the officials our appreciation of the courtesy with which we have been received and the serious consideration that has been given to our views and our requests. We do not always get what we want, but we get a cordial reception and are usually victorious.

The year through which we have just passed, has marked a more unsettled state than the five years of war. The horrors of war are over the aftermath of war, in the period which I hope and believe is ended, resulted in a trade condition which is best described as chaos.

The fall in values, the dislocation of trade and the stagnation of industry combined to discourage both building and the box trade; and the railways, which are the largest consumers did not buy at all. But sunrise follows night as surely as night comes and I feel that the overdue dawn is near and that it will come,—not with the boom of a false prosperity,—but with a steadily increasing normal trade that means continued prosperity to us, our employees and all that numerous retinue who combined make the lumber trade one of the key industries of the Dominion.

Statistics are dry things but we must claim honor where honor is due, and the last report of the census bureau places our industry high in order of merit, with 3410 log product establishments, representing $231,000,000 of invested capital and a pay roll of over $60,000,000 divided among 60,000 men; and a product for the year 1919 valued at $222,000,000.

In producing exports that hold up the credit of Canada, both for value and quality, the lumber trade does its full share.

The report of the Honorary Treasurer, the activities of the various committees and your transportation department will be submitted to you for consideration. I ask your earnest attention to these reports, as they represent hard and conscientious work on your behalf.

I regret to record that we have lost during the year the late Senator Edwards, the late James G. Cane, Sir D. C. Cameron and Joseph Oliver, all members who greatly aided this Association.

In conclusion, may I sincerely thank officers, members and staff for that wise counsel and able assistance to which the success of our association is entirely due.

### Secretary Gives General Survey of Things

Frank Hawkins, of Ottawa, Secretary of the Association presents the following encouraging report:—

Your secretary in an endeavor to take a general survey of conditions in Canada, with of course particular reference to the lumber industry, has arrived no doubt at the same point where perhaps all of you have already arrived. The upward swing of general business conditions though it may be slow, has without doubt set in. The worst is over and business must be prepared to meet conditions calling for readjustment almost at a moment's notice. Advantage must be taken of any and every opportunity which has the appearance of making for increased business activity.

It would be a tragedy if wild speculation got the upper hand, but, with the financial institutions still keeping a tight rein on anything which appears to be of a speculative character or in the nature of luxuries, things must right themselves more and more every day as we pass along. Everybody should encourage a sane enthusiasm after suffering from the doldrums which business and business men have experienced for so many months. In this regard Association work should be taken advantage of at every point, but do not imagine that any association can serve you or the best interests of the country without individual earnest co-operation. This problem is as much yours today as it ever was, and your Association will be no bigger than the individual member cares to make it.

We have the Association and you have the power to use it. Co-operation in this direction can accomplish much; without it, little or nothing. The Special Committees' reports, that is the Executive and Transportation Committees will speak for themselves, and no reference need be made to your secretary to the work which has been performed during the year by these two committees. Your secretary presumes to urge upon each individual member the realization of his responsibilities to his fellow members.

If you ask me for something really practical along this line I

J. Fraser Gregory, St. John, N. B.
Newly-elected first vice-president C.L.A.

Angus McLean, Bathurst, N. B.
Re-elected second vice-president C.L.A.

W. Gerard Power, Quebec, Que.
Re-elected director of C.L.A.

Gordon C. Edwards, Ottawa, Ont.
Re-elected director of C.L.A.

would ask how many members have discussed with firms who are not members of the Association the advisability of joining up at this time. In the envelopes which you each received on registering at our booth, a blank form of application was included and you were asked to find out from your neighbor sitting next to you whether or not he is a member. If he is not it is up to you to do a little propaganda work and get him to sign the application. If he is already a member urge upon him to co-operate in every way possible and don't let it stop at this but do the same thing yourself.

Your secretary wonders how many members are making use for instance, of the Association Crest. There are not many, and everyone ought to be proud to advertise the fact that he is a member of this Association. The electrotypes of the crest can be supplied for $1.00 a piece, mounted on solid metal, if we get orders in sufficient quantities

Remember we have passed through the periods of prosperity, liquidation and stagnation and are now entering on the fourth cycle revival. All the prominent public economists agree in this.

In closing, your secretary wishes to testify to the loyalty and efficiency of the staff, and desires to acknowledge the many evidences of your confidence, esteem and helpfulness and is only anxious that the office of your Association should turn out its full quota of work every working day in the year.

## Executive Committee Presents Report

The report of the Executive Committee of the Canadian Lumbermen's Association was, at the recent convention in Toronto, read by secretary Frank Hawkins. Several matters were mentioned in the last report which were again brought forward. Speaking of the sales tax, the report said:—

It will be remembered that a resolution was introduced into the Dominion Parliament by the Minister of Finance making certain changes in the Sales Tax regulations effective May 10th, 1921. The precise details have been given to our members in circular form from time to time as changes were made. The only point of which special mention may be made is in connection with the regulation providing that the Sales Tax was to be paid by the manufacturer and in billing out lumber to his customers he must show not less than 1½ per cent thereon which must be paid by the manufacturer. In this way the manufacturer can absorb one half of one per cent. When the regulation was first promulgated it was entirely optional, that is it was a matter between the seller and buyer, as to whether the Sales Tax was to be handed on to the wholesaler or not.

### Conditions and Wages of Labor

Relating to labor, the Executive Committee reported that, while there had undoubtedly been considerable done in the way of wage adjustments, they had not yet reached the point where Canada can hope to compete with the other nations of the world. A comparison of wages was furnished, taking three typical industries,—iron, steel, leather manufacturing and textile. The statement showed that the wages per hour paid out in these industries in Canada were much higher for both skilled and unskilled labor than what were paid in Britain, France or Germany.

It was declared that in the iron and steel industry the wages for skilled labor in Canada ran from 60 to 65 cents an hour and for unskilled 30 to 35 cents; in leather manufacturing, skilled 50 to 65 cents an hour; unskilled 30 to 40 cents an hour; in textiles, skilled 35 to 65 cents an hour, unskilled 30 to 40 cents an hour. In Britain, France and Germany the wages in these trades are much lower.

It was also shown that wages in the lumber industry in Canada, as compared with the United States are generally higher, and an interesting table was presented.

### What Men Around Sawmills Get

Common labor in Ontario has been paid 40 cents an hour during the past season. In British Columbia 35 cents an hour; California 35 cents; Florida 18 to 24 cents; Louisiana 17 cents; Minnesota 35 cents; Pacific Northwest 40 to 45 cents.

Sawyer, in Ontario 92 cents an hour; in British Columbia $1.00; California 90 cents; Florida 70 cents; Louisiana 85 cents; Minnesota 90 cents; Pacific Northwest 98 cents.

Planer Grader, in Ontario 47 cents an hour; British Columbia 40 cents; California 42 cents; Florida 37 cents; Louisiana 37 cents; Minnesota 42 cents; Pacific Northwest 37 cents.

Planer Feeder, in Ontario 45 cents an hour; British Columbia 42 cents; California 40 cents; Florida 22 cents; Louisiana 20 cents; Minnesota 35 cents; Pacific Northwest 40 to 45 cents.

It was also pointed out that the average wages paid for common labor in 1920 was,—Canada $4.82 per day; United States $3.88 per day; in 1921,—Canada $3.37 per day; United States $2.86 per day.

The report next touched upon the exports of wood and wood products from Canada for the three years ending March 31st 1919, 1920 and 1921, and were as follows :—

| | | | |
|---|---|---|---|
| To United Kingdom ... | $10,026,687 | $ 37,090,150 | $ 32,728,353 |
| United States ...... | 88,509,036 | 102,965,457 | 143,248,244 |
| Other countries .... | 7,762,045 | 10,001,600 | 15,540,365 |
| | $106,297,738 | $150,057,207 | $191,516,962 |

It need hardly be said that the export of lumber from Canada is one of the prime factors in the total export trade of the Dominion and undoubtedly has a very important place to play in the future as regards restoring the rate of exchange on the Canadian dollar. To this extent the export trade of the country affects every person in the Dominion and is entitled to enthusiastic co-operation and support.

A. C. Manbert, of Toronto, during the year was appointed a representative of the Canadian Lumbermen's Association, to act on the Ontario Provincial Employment Service Council. Secretary Hawkins, it was stated, also attended the third annual meeting of the Employment Service of Canada, held in Ottawa in September last.

### Proposed Anti-Shingle Legislation

We referred to this matter a year ago in connection with a statement prepared by Mr. J. B. Laidlaw, Manager of the Norwich Union Fire Insurance Co., of Toronto, before the Ontario Fire Prevention League and our efforts put forth at that time in opposition to resolution adopted by the Ontario Fire Prevention League at that meeting urging the Provincial Government to pass a law prohibiting the use of wooden shingles within the Province either on new buildings or for repairs to old buildings situated within fifty feet of each other.

A meeting of the Dominion Fire Prevention Association was held in Ottawa on the 29th and 30th of Sept. 1921 and Mr. Laidlaw again appeared before that body and urged practically what he previously

put forward in Toronto at the annual meeting of the Ontario Fire prevention League. Your officers found that Mr. Laidlaw gained his experience and got his information largely from the National Fire Protection Association, 87 Milk St., Boston, Mass., and amongst the most glaring examples of the alleged culpability of the wooden shingle is the so-called Nashville conflagration which took place March 22nd, 1916. A careful and unbiased judgment of the special report on the Nashville conflagration fails to show that the wooden shingle was responsible for the spread of that fire. Indeed throughout the report there are many conflicting statements and there are also some remarkable evidences of a keen desire to conceal the real reasons by laying the blame on the wooden shingle. We quote from the report as follows:

"The building of origin, a small, one storey, iron clad structure, used as a planing mill. The fire started about 11.47 a.m., and when the Fire Department arrived the flames had passed through the entire length of the buildings and were going across a 60 foot street igniting frame dwellings 100 feet east. A 44 mile gale was blowing at the time which increased to 51 miles per hour by 12.30 p.m., and by 12.20, that is 33 minutes after the fire started 33 frame dwellings, only 18 of which were covered with shingle roofs, had been destroyed and the claim is made that the Fire Dept. had the fire under control up to this time." There does not appear to have been any attempt on the part of the Fire Dept. to play the hose on buildings in the wake of the fire and it was not until, so is is claimed, burning shingles were carried across an 1800 foot clear space and started fire in another section, that a general alarm was turned in and that Companies No. 5, 6, 7 and 8 responded: Companies No. 1, 2, 3, 4, 9 and 10 having responded to the first alarm turned its attention to keeping the fire directed in a certain, comparatively speaking, narrow lane by playing on both sides of the path, followed by the fire. We have this remarkable prejudiced statement:—"The origin of the fire in the second zone was due to shingle roofed buildings in both zones though the spread of the fire cannot be contributed to that of exposure from one building to another as the freaks of the wind in places carried the fire around frame buildings and ignited brick buildings beyond". Several cases were noted where frame buildings were not damaged and brick buildings less than 5 feet away were destroyed. And again: "In certain portions of the fire zone the intensity of the heat was so great that many buildings were seen to burst into flames all over at practically the same instant. Burning grass was also responsible for many buildings igniting, both in and out of the fire zone".

"The fire consumed:—

| | |
|---|---:|
| Frame buildings with shingle roofs | 159 |
| Frame buildings with fire resisting roofs | 180 |
| Brick buildings with shingle roofs | 1 |
| Brick buildings with fire resisting roofs | 79 |
| Frame stable, garages and out houses | 229 |

Taking into account the further facts—That frame houses in the southern cities in many cases are built with open foundations; that the roof boards on same are not close fitting; that there had been a period of extreme drought; that the fire originated in a metal clad ,one storey building; that there was a 44 mile gale blowing at the time which increased to 51 miles within an hour; and that when the fire started in the second zone and an attempt was made to call out the reserve of the Fire Dept. owing to the fact that wires were down there was a considerable delay before the general alarm could be turned in. It is apparent that the wooden shingle was only a very small contribu-

tor to this terrible loss, not as much as the fire resisting roofed buildings, and it is as unfair as it is untruthful to place the responsibility of that conflagration at the door of the wooden shingle.

### Still Spreading Inaccurate Reports

Mr. Laidlaw is still continuing to spread inaccurate statements, as is evidenced by an article which appeared in The Chronicle of Montreal, dated Nov. 25th, 1921, entitled, "The Menace of the Shingle Roof" by John B. Laidlaw in an annual report of the Ontario Fire Prevention League, from which we cull the following:—

Any kind of roof is a safer roof than one of wooden shingles. Other roofs may burn but they will not ignite from sparks and will not furnish flying brands". Mr. Laidlaw should have the decency to state the perils of the other kinds of roofs. A roof which is stated to be fire proof and is relied upon by the owner of the building to that extent is far more of a menace than a shingle roof, which under given conditions and to quote a very strong argument of our opponents "if the bombardment is long enough", shingle roofs will burn. Again we quote, "It is no hardship upon any class of citizen to compel him to co-operate in public safety". We do not think that the lumbermen are behind Mr. Laidlaw or any of his followers in regard to matters of citizenship or of public safety.

Again we quote, "Wooden shingles are the direct cause of conflagration in the United States and Canada where building conditions are similar". An unbiased judgment based on the evidence produced by Mr. Laidlaw does not prove anything of the kind.

A further statement in this report says that wooden shingles are really dear in the long run because they are very short lived and require constant repairing and that they are often made from the refuse or otherwise waste of the saw mill and the short ends of logs which would otherwise have to be wasted.

### Mistaken Charges Have Been Laid

It has been shown repeatedly that the actual loss by fire owing to sparks on roofs is somewhat about 2.36 per cent. and from exposure including conflagrations, 22.51 per cent., making 24.87 per cent. in all, but as has been said it is not fair or honest to charge the conflagration loss to wooden shingles. Another point—of the total fire loss in canada in 1919, which was approximately $24,000,000 this loss was caused by approximately 17,000 fires, which would of course include the loss from sparks on roofs exposure including conflagrations, and all other causes, but it is a remarkable fact that almost 50 per cent of the total loss was occasioned by 51 fires, in which it is safe to say there was not one shingle on any roof. This reduces the loss to all other causes outside of the 51 fires to approximately $12,000,000 spread over 16,949 fires approximately. Taking this $12,000,000 loss and the percentage of loss from sparks on roofs we have the total loss which may be charged against sparks on roofs of all kinds including shingles, amounting to the sum of $238,200 a year. This is all that can legitimately be charged against sparks on roofs of all kinds, so that there must be some other reason why this senseless onslaught against wooden shingles has been inaugurated. It will be noticed that Mr. Laidlaw and Mr. George F. Lewis, the Deputy Fire Marshall of the Province of Ontario, apparently stand alone as the champions for the elimination of the wooden shingles.

### Output of Shingles in Dominion

The production of shingles in Canada during 1919, which are the latest figures available, are as follows:—

W. B. Snowball, Chatham, N. B.
One of the live wires of the gathering

H. J. Terry, Toronto, Ont.
Who taught "the boys how to warble"

W. E. Bigwood, Toronto, Ont.
Re-elected director of C.L.A.

G. E. Spragge, Toronto, Ont.
Appointed new director of C.L.A.

Total manufactured .................... 2,915,149,000
Total exported ........................ 1,881,195,000
Leaving for domestic consumption ....... 1,033,954,000

Whilst for the time being hope has been abandoned of getting a bill through the Provincial Legislature prohibiting the use of wood shingles, our opponents are now endeavoring to incorporate their ideas into the Building Codes and therein will lie the danger. After full discussion of this matter we urge the adoption of a resolution covering this entire question.

The National Lumber Manufacturers' Association through their Publicity Director, Mr. Edward P. Allan, have designed a fire resistive frame construction to which your careful attention is drawn.

Housing conditions still remain critical. We understand there is a shortage of 1,300,000 houses in the United States; and notwithstanding the fact that shipment of southern woods are largely in excess of production they continue to be considerably below normal. For the month of September southern pine production amounted to about 82 per cent. of normal, shipments to about 91 per cent of normal, stocks about 93 per cent. of normal whilst orders were 6 per cent. over normal. These conditions indicate a better movement of lumber, and it is to be hoped that the lumber is being moved at prices which will enable both manufacturer and wholesaler to make a living profit. All indications point to business having started on the upward swing. The estimated cost of building work as indicated by building permits in thirty-five Canadian cities for October 1920 amounted to $9,025,725. In October 1921 the figures are $8,431,113.

To show roughly the position of Canada in world-wide affairs it is stated that Canada's production of natural resources is approximately as follows:— Asbestos, 88 per cent., Nickle, 85 per cent., Pulpwood, 32 per cent., Lumber, 20 per cent., Cured Fish, 20 per cent., Oats, 18 per cent., Potatoes, 15 per cent., Wheat, 11½ per cent., Barley, 11 per cent.

In gold production Canada stands 4th, in silver, 3rd, in wheat, 3rd, in barley, 4th, in oats, 2nd.

In recent months your Association has been communicated with in an endeavor to find markets for various lines of lumber products and also have received inquiries for lumber supplies. It may be a matter of consideration for the Association at this time whether or not it would be advisable to organize a branch of our work in this direction. The report was adopted.

## High Freight Rates Call for Redress

In moving the adoption of the report of the Transportation Committee, A. E. Clark, of Toronto, called attention to the good work done by Mr. Sargant, traffic manager of the Association, since his appointment in May last. While several large firms might have traffic managers to look after their own transportation matters, yet claims against the roads could be not handled successfully by individuals. It was only by working in conjunction and consideration with others that attention could be secured and all such matters should be co-ordinated. They should be brought up in some concrete form and presented, which would help to clarify the situation in many cases.

Mr. Clark expressed the opinion that the traffic department of the C. L. A. had made good. Mr. Sargant has been fighting a number of questions in connection with the freight tariff on lumber. The lumber situation today is in what might be described as a chaotic condition and one of the principal corrective measures is a reduction on the lumber freight tariff.

"It is the purpose of this Association," added Mr. Clark, "to bring this to an issue. The increases have been in greater proportion than the reductions and lumbermen are not getting justice from the roads. We have been fortunate at last in getting an acknowledgment from Hon. F. B. Carvell, of the Dominion Railway Board in which he has agreed to give the lumbermen a special hearing. This hearing will take place in Ottawa some time early in February. It is up to the Canadian Lumbermen's Association to put any matters that they desire to be brought up, into the hands of the traffic department of the Association as soon as possible. The railways claim that the lumber situation as far as the roads are concerned is no different from that of any other interests. While the lumbermen have no brief for any other interests, most of our product is delivered on private sidings and no terminals are used. We use a poorer class of equipment than others do, and therefore, our case should be a special one."

In conclusion, the speaker said that the railway situation was one at present of great difficulty and responsibility especially, but he contended that the arrangement with their employees was not a good one and too many men were employed to do certain kinds of work. Lumbermen in their own operations were making use of economy and the

railways should do the same. "We want your support in fighting our case before the Railway Commission.".

### Some Comparisons of Freight Charges

W. B. Snowball, of Chatham, N. B. seconded the motion for the adoption of the report. There had, he said, been a great increase in freight rates and the lumbermen of the Maritime provinces realized that it had been abnormal.

The lumbermen of the Pacific Coast have been given greater reductions than those of the East. He said that the freight rate from Chatham, N. B. to Toronto in December 1916 was 21 cents. This was raised on March 15, 1918 to 24 cents and again boosted to 27 cents on August 12, 1918. On September 13, 1920, it went up to 38 cents, on December 1, 1921, it was reduced to 35 cents. Between December, 1916 and September, 1920 the increase had been 67 per cent. It now stands at, 65 per cent increase.

Reverting to the position of lumber from Vancouver to Toronto, Mr. Snowball said that in 1915 the rate was 67 cents,—on September 16, 1920, it had jumped to $1.05 and on January 1, 1921, had dropped to $1.03½. On April 1, 1921, there had been a drop to 90 cents and in December last to 88½ cents where it now stands, making the increase 32 per cent over the rate prevailing in 1915. There was nothing to justify an increase, as it now stood, of 65 per cent from the Maritime provinces to Toronto and only 32 per cent from the Pacific Coast.

"We in the East," he declared, "deserve similar treatment. We have no quarrel with the West but, by the handicap which they enjoy, we in the East are debarred from this market and western stuff is coming in and getting the preference in the matter of carriage charges.

Touching on freight rates, Mr. Snowball said that they were 200 to 300 per cent above pre-war times. The lumbermen of the Maritime provinces were large shippers to the British Isles, and Canadian steamship lines appeared to be in league with the other shipping interests or federation in holding up rates. If there was a proper reduction, maritime province producers could get a fair share of the lumber business on the English market but, as it stood now, with the freight rates from Norway, Sweden and Finland ranging at about 55 to 60 shillings, supplies in the forest products line were being obtained from Baltic countries, whereas before the war the charges for transportation were about the same from Canada as from the countries mentioned. Canadian Steamships should be run in the interest of the

R. L. Sargant, Ottawa, Ont.
Traffic Manager of C. L. A.

Dominion but they had not been and instead, the trade of the Motherland had gone to other countries. Why could not Canadian lumbermen get a similar rate? The present time from Canada is 100 shillings per standard. So far as freight rates on ocean are concerned, he thought the C. L. A. as an Association should go before the proper authorities and see that justice was obtained.

### How St. John Shippers are Handicapped

J. Fraser Gregory, of St. John, N. B. said the freight rate now was 100 shillings and it seemed impossible to have it broken. He fully endorsed all that Mr. Snowball had said in regard to heavy charges which were even now 300 per cent higher than before the war.

He thought that pressure should be brought to bear on the Canadian merchant marine to have the rates lessened in the interest of

Canadian trade. The traffic department of the Association should take the matter up. Lumber was being shipped from other countries to Britain which should have gone from Canada but, at present, the rates were prohibitive of competition.

Mr. Gregory moved, seconded by Hon. John B. Burchill, of South Nelson, B. C. —That existing rates of freight being an increase of 300 per cent over previous rates asked by the steamship companies under their conference rate, are unreasonably high and out of all proportion of the readjustment, that the trade should expect in view of the general readjustment of conditions. This motion was carried unanimously.

### Will Give Lumbermen Special Hearing

R. L. Sargant, traffic manager of the C. L. A., told of some of the difficulties he had experienced in getting matters before the Railway Commission and how many important items had been side tracked by the Board. In August last a formal application had been made by the C. L. A. for a restoration of the rates on lumber in effect prior to Sept. 13, 1920. If the Board had carried out its premise of making a reduction, it would have gone ahead and done it. Mr. Sargant read a letter which he had received from Hon. Mr. Carvell stating that a hearing would be accorded the lumbermen at a special sitting of the Board to be held in Ottawa early next month but the reply had been very late in coming to hand.

In regard to the forthcoming sitting of the Board in Halifax and St. John, Mr. Gregory said that it was the original intention to take up only arbitraries or differentials from the Port of St. John, when a general case in such matters would be presented. He understood, however, that Mr. Carvell had intimated that the Board would hear from any interests showing how the present railway rates have affected their business.

Mr. Gregory then presented the following which, he said, would come before the Board from his firm.

Memorandum as to Railway freight rates to St. John, N. B. for export, as it effects Murray and Gregory, Limited, at their Lake Frontier Mill and the Port of St. John, as compared with Portland, Maine. In the published tariffs of the Quebec Central Railways, the export rate to Portland, Maine is 26 cents. To St. John, N. B. the rate is 31½ cents. Murray & Gregory applied to the C. P. R. to see if they could not get the rate to St. John made the same as to Portland, Maine, i. e. 26 cents. The Quebec Central came back saying that they would make the rates equal to both ports, by raising the Portland, Maine, rate from 26 cents to 31½ cents,— Rather an unusual proceeding at such a time as this. At the present time, the freight rate on lumber from Montreal to St. John is 26 cents. The distance is 589 miles. From Montreal to St. John the rate is 23 cents and from Quebec to St. John 26 cents.

### Portland has Quite an Advantage

Murray & Gregory's mill is situated at Lake Frontier, the end of the Chaudiere branch of the Quebec Central Railway. The distance from their mill to St. John is 456 miles and the quoted rate 31½ cents. It is made up as follows:—

Rate from Lake Frontier To Megantic—13 cents—distance 149 miles. (this is the local rate charged by the Quebec Central Railway)

Rate from Megantic to St. John—18 cents—distance 307 miles. (including terminal charges which amount to about 5 cents)

As you will note, the Quebec Central Railway charges 13 cents for a haul of 149 miles, while the Canadian Pacific charges 18 cents, which includes terminals of about 5 cents, for a haul of 307 miles. We do not think that the C. P. R. charge is unfair but we claim the Quebec Central charge is altogether too high. We would be satisfied at this time with a rate equal to Ottawa.—i. e. 26 cents, although we are 140 miles shorter haul to St. John than Ottawa.

It is the desire of all good Canadians that export to foreign countries should be through Canadian Ports and any advantage possible should be given to a Canadian port in preference to Portland, Maine, whereas at the present, Portland has an advantage of 6½ cents, and after the 17th of this month, although the charge will be the same, the bulk of the business will go to Portland, by reason of it being a shorter haul and better shipping facilities.

### Will Get After Ocean Freight

Mr. Snowball suggested that Mr. Sargant, traffic manager of the C. L. A., should be allowed to come to St. John to assist the New Brunswick Lumbermen's Association in the presentation of their claims for redress before the Board at its sittings in that city. This was agreed to. Hon. Mr. Burchill suggested the appointment of a committee from the C. L. A. to confer with Mr. Sargant in the matter of ocean freight rates and moved, seconded by Leonard O'Brien, of South Nelson, N. B. that the committee be composed of Messrs, W. B. Snowball, of Chatham, Rufus E. Dickie, of Stewiacke, N. S. and W. E. Golding of St. John. This was carried.

## *The C.L.A. Becomes International in Its Scope*

President McLachlin brought up the matter of an amendment to the constitution, enabling the Association to have directors from the United States, as a large number of firms across the border belong to the C. L. A. The national lumber bodies of America have paid a compliment to Canada in electing Canadian directors on their boards and he thought this should be reciprocated. The number would be elected on the basis of membership of the C. L. A. from across the border.

Mr. A. E. Clark said that, for many years, a number of United States firms, some of whom carried on milling or logging operations in Canada but had offices in cities across the border, had belonged to the C. L. A. These men had rendered the Association valuable service in many lines and the extension of the directorate to make such members eligible, was one which should, in his opinion, be supported. They would assist materially in the affairs of the Association.

It was then moved by W. T. Mason, of Montreal, and seconded by A. C. Manbert, of Toronto, and unanimously carried—

Whereas, at the 11th Annual Meeting of the Canadian Lumbermen's Association, held at St. John, N. B., February 5th and 6th, 1919, directors were elected for the first time—seven directors to serve one year, seven directors to serve two years and seven directors to serve three years, based upon the pro rata according to membership in the provinces of Ontario, Quebec and British Columbia after providing for directors to be elected, irrespective of the membership, as follows: New Brunswick—one director, Manitoba and Saskatchewan—one director: and

### The New Directors for Next Three Years

Whereas, since that time considerable changes have taken place in the membership from the various provinces and also including the United States of America, be it therefore resolved.—That the elective directorship in this Association be continued to consist of twenty-one members, as at present, seven directors retiring each year consecutively, but the representation to be on a pro rata basis according to the number of members in each province and also including the number of members, of the Association in the United States.

The directors, whose term of office, expired this year were W. E.

Bigwood, Toronto; Gordon C. Edwards, Ottawa; A. E. Clark, Toronto; W. M. Ross, Ottawa; W. Gerard Power, Quebec; Alex. MacLaurin, Montreal and Angus McLean, Bathurst. All of these are eligible for re-election.

Ballots were distributed and three directors were elected from Ontario, one from Quebec, one from New Brunswick and two from the United States. (the latter in accordance with the amendment to the constitution)

The result of the election was as follows:—

Ontario—A. E. Clark, Toronto, (re-elected) W. E. Bigwood, Toronto, (re-elected) Gordon C. Edwards, Ottawa. (re-elected)

Quebec—W. Gerard Power, Quebec city. (re-elected)

New Brunswick—Angus McLean, Bathurst. (re-elected)

United States—Spencer Kellogg, of Charles C. Kellogg & Sons Co. Utica, N. Y. and R. E. Stocking, of Power, Moir & Stocking Inc. 1302 Flatiron Building, New York city, formerly with Wm. Whitmer & Sons, Inc. New York.

Both Messrs Kellogg and Stocking are widely known in Canada and have for many years taken an active interest in the proceedings of the C. L. A.

During the afternoon of the first day of the proceedings, an interesting and instructive address was delivered by H. R. Poussette, Director of the Commercial Intelligence Service, Ottawa. He told of the work that the Service is doing in the extension of Canadian trade and commerce and how employees were trained in the department for the important duties which they carry on.

This was followed by an excellent exhibition of moving pictures under the direction of D.S. Cole, of Ottawa, who is Mr. Poussette's assistant. He dealt with the subject of proper packing of articles that are exported, and furnished a number of views of careless and insecure packing, showing how boxes should be made and of what material. The advantage of goods shipped arriving in good condition was clearly depicted.

The work of the Commercial Intelligence Department and the subject of "Packing" will be given a more extended reference in a later edition of the "Canada Lumberman".

# Prosperity Coming—Now Go Out And Meet It

### General Building Activity Will Show Substantial Increase During Present Year Which Will be One of Recuperation—Some Comparative Costs

*By A. R. Whittemore, Toronto, Manager MacLean Building Reports

The construction industry in the principal countries of the world is, with the exception of agriculture, greater than any other industry, when the yearly volume, expressed in money, is taken into consideration, and it is the greatest of all when expressed in terms of labor employment. It is computed that for the successful operation and carrying on of structural activities there are required the products of over 3,000 industries. It is estimated that this industry in Canada represents a value of $7,700,000,000 or 27 per cent of the national wealth. Fully 1,100,000 persons, either as workers or as members of workers' families, are estimated as deriving their living from this field, either directly or through manufacturing and mining products used in the construction industry.

This is a growing country; it requires in connection with that normal growth a correspondingly normal growth of building. If we go back to the year 1910 and trace the increase up to 1914, this normal increase is quite clearly defined. The line marked XY on the chart, graphically illustrates this point. This chart is developed by using the monthly averages and their increases up to the war, and theoretically continuing the increase up to the present. Since the growth of the country has continued fairly consistently year by year, such a chart cannot be said to be unreasonable or to distort the situation to any extent.

**Volume Based on 1913 Costs**

This chart shows a very great falling off in building of all kinds during the war—a greater falling off in actual volume of work than is indicated by the money totals of work let—because, as we know, the costs of building increased over that period quite substantially. The black line on the chart shows the value of construction contracts awarded, based on 1913 construction costs, with subsequent price inflation eliminated. These figures cover the small and rural districts as well as the large cities. In order to arrive at this curve, 1913 was taken as a normal base. In 1914 and 1915 costs dropped, and then in 1916 and 1917 the cost began to rise, as compared with the volume, until 1920, when the actual cost of construction work was 165 per cent more than what it would have cost at 1913 prices.

The dotted line on the chart shows the total value of construction contracts awarded in Canada during the past eleven years with their values placed at the current costs of the respective years.

**Volume of Depressed Building in Canada**

The shaded area on the chart between the estimated normal increase straight line and the black line indicating volume of quantity, gives a fair idea of the shortage of construction work in Canada and is the strongest possible way of indicating the real situation. The difference between the normal requirements of the country up to date and the buildings of all kinds provided, shows a great cumulat-

• Address delivered at luncheon tendered the Canadian Lumbermen's Association in Toronto.

ive volume of work unquestionably held back and actually required to bring the situation to normal. What we beleive to be a fair estimate of what this means to the industry (and we think that, while it may be based on more or less theoretical conditions, it is nevertheless reasonable) is that this country is short of buildings and public works at the present day, including dwellings and works of all kinds, amounting to the staggering total of one and one quarter billion dollars. If this represents the demand for building in Canada, it promises great activity in this industry, with resulting advantages to the whole country. No industry that we know of is as well fortified by a large reserve of deferred work that must be taken in hand sooner or later.

At the meeting of the Associated General Contractors of America, held in Washington last September, the statement was made that building is the key to employment. It was shown that for every 200 people employ-

**A. R. Whittemore, Toronto**

ed in construction 500 to 700 are set to work in basic industries, such as lumber, cement, manufacturing, mining, transportation, etc.

**Review of Building in 1921**

Contracts awarded for construction in Canada in 1921 fell but little short of the previous year in value. The total amount for the year was $240,133,300 against $255,605,500 in 1920, $190,028,300 in 1919 and $99,842,100 in 1918. The most sweeping changes for the year took place in the increase in residential building and public works construction, and the decrease in the industrial as compared with the previous year. Residential building amounted to $76,655,400 against $54,891,100 in 1920. Business building was practically unchanged and constituted the largest group at $84,721,700 against $86,073,200. Industrial was $16,503,700 compared with $64,625,900. Public works construction was $62,252,500 against $50,015,300. During 1921 contracts were awarded for 16,283 residences, 3,224 business buildings, 241 industrial buildings and 1,136 public works.

Returns for December were $19,118,500, being the second largest December total on record, being exceeded only once and that in

the boom time of December 1912 with a total of $31,125,528.

For the year 1921, Ontario led all the provinces with a total of $113,855,000, Quebec next with $61,337,500; the western provinces third with $55,651,900 and the Maritimes last with $9,228,900. Both Ontario and Quebec showed moderate gains, the West a substantial falling off, and the Maritimes a severe slump. If price recessions in materials and labor costs are taken into consideration, the volume of new construction in 1921 was many millions greater than the 1920 total.

**Largest Housebuilding Year on Record**

Building in the cities found Toronto in first place with a total of $23,878,240, Montreal next with $21,381,273, York Township next with $8,101,100, Winnipeg fourth with $5,580,400, and Hamilton, Quebec, Vancouver, Ottawa, London, Halifax, Regina, Calgary and Edmonton next in the order named. 1921 was the largest housebuilding year on record in Canada. However, despite this, a very real shortage still exists. Last year, for instance, 16,000 houses were built, but 110,000 couples were married. There were 117,000 immigrants who would require at least 20,000 homes. Add to this the additional thousands who are doubled up with friends or relatives, and it is easy to see why Canada requires at least 165,000 more homes.

The significance of these facts is comprehended when we realize that as soon as the wheels of industry are turning again, and the factories already built are working at normal capacity, there will be a shortage of homes far greater than Canada has ever known before. The small moderate-price dwelling is decidedly in the ascendancy.

**Will Not Return to 1913 Levels**

We hear a great deal of loose talk about lumber costs. Some people imagine that prices will return to the levels of a decade ago. It is our opinion that this can never come to pass. On what grounds do we base this statement? Simply by taking cognizance of what has happened in the United States and what is happening in Canada.

The original forests of the United States are estimated to have covered 822 million acres and to have contained 5,200 billion board feet of timber. Over two-thirds of this area has been culled, cut-over, or burned. There are left to-day about 137 million acres of virgin timber, 112 million acres of culled and second-growth timber large enough for sawing, 133 million acres are partially stocked with smaller growth, and 81 million acres of devasted and practically waste land. There are 463 million acres of forest land of all sorts which contain about 2,214 billion feet of timber of merchantable size. Three-fifths of the timber originally in the United States is gone.

The cutting and loss of merchantable timber consume about 56 billion board feet yearly. About 40 billion feet of this amount is cut from the virgin forests still left, the rest from second growth. They are even cutting

into pulpwood, acid wood, and fuel 14 billion cubic feet per year of material too small for sawing. All told they are taking about 26 billion cubic feet of material out of their forests every year and growing about 6 billion feet in them. They are cutting more of every class of timber than they are growing. They are even using up the trees too small for the sawmill but upon which their future lumber supply depends three and one-half times as fast as they are being produced.

In Canada there is no actual increment two-thirds of the original timber inheritance. Our area of merchantable timber now covers 400 to 500 million acres. About 100,000 square miles have been cut for lumber and pulp compared with nearly 1,000,000 square miles sacrificed to fire.

The frontiers of our timber land are being pushed farther and farther back. Every year our forests are being depleted at an appalling rate through lack of conservation, reforestation, and fire protection. This, coupled with a progressive increase in the distance timber must be hauled to the market, can mean nothing but gradually mounting costs.

**What Lack of Protection is Doing**

The forest area of Germany is equal to the timber limits in the Ottawa Valley and in toal area, about 25 million acres, would represent only a fraction of the timber area of the single province of Quebec. However, the German forests have been worked for the last two centuries on the principle of sustained yield, the idea being that the forest

itself should represent a capital stock of timber from which each year only the interest or natural increment should be made. This increment alone provided the Germans in 1913 with a timber cut of over 5 billion board feet which was considerably more than the cut of the Dominion of Canada in an average year. Between the continental forestry systems and that of Canada there is this difference. That while the Europeans remove each year an enormous quantity of timber which is sold at their seaports for a price closely approximating that of Canada, the cut represents only the natural growth.

In Canada, there is no actual increment in the forests east of the Rocky Mountains. Forest fires and insect attacks, particularly the spruce bud worm trouble, annually remove from our capital stock many times the quantity of timber taken out by the lumber and pulp and paper interests. In recent years the devastations of forest insects have greatyl outmatched the damage done by fire. The actual menace to the Canadian forest, therefore, is not the lumberman's axe, but the purely destructive forces of forest fires and insect depredation.

Nearly 80 per cent of the habitable area

of Canada is of non-agriculture character and adapted only to the production of timber crops. Unless kept under such production continuously, it represents idle land. There is therefore, no conflict whatever between the growing of timber and the extension of our farm area, as timber growing requires only the soil unless for farm purposes.

The problem of forest perpetuation is a scientific one, and while our Canadian conditions differ essentially from those of Europe nevertheless the same general forestry principles under Government leadership must be applied to this country before there will be any surety that the timber resources are placed on a self-perpetuating basis.

**Comparative Lumber Costs**

The index number of 14 lines of lumber compiled by the Department of Labor indicate that present prices are 80.3 per cent more than in 1913. The peak was reached in May 1920, when prices were 195.8 per cent over 1913 levels. Present costs are 38.9 per cent less than peak prices.

Comparative wholesale prices obtained last week show some remarkable reductions as compared with the high prices of 1920. On 7 lines of hemlock the peak price was f22 per cent over 1914, but is now only 45 per cent. 14 lines of pine showed a high price 171 per cent over 1914 but are now 119 per cent. 4 lines of spruce were 135 per cent over 1913 but have now declined to 13 per cent over 1913.

Current prices of certain lumber commodities bring forward the fact that to-day's producing cost and selling prices are so close together as to retard production. The present situation is such that the small margin of profit in production of some of these articles has so reduced output that should purchasing be increased to any extent, the shortages developing would be apt to produce again the dangerous runaway market. Such a condition would be most undesirable.

**Building Material Costs**

In May 1920 the wholesale price of 48 building materials reached a peak price of 184 per cent above 1913, whereas the average for the year was 165 per cent above the pre-war. In December, 1921, material costs had receded to a point 93 per cent above 1913, or about 50 per cent below the peak.

While prices are still much above prewar levels, the decline from the peak has been fairly radical. During the past building year they have remained relatively stable and with the prospect of general business activity increasing, the probabilities are that they will go but little below present levels until the edge is taken off demand by a year of fairly active building.

Building activity has been greatest in those sections wherein wages have liquidated most or where some other contributing factor has made building more attractive, relatively than in other sections. We expect this movement already underway in some sections, to spread rather generally, and believe that by next spring, the level of such wages will be considerably reduced. The present scale of building wages for the country as a whole is less than 10 per cent below the peak of 1920. There is no doubt at all that this condition has contributed most largely towards deferring activity. This year a real effort should be made to provide work for the building trades as soon as winter breaks. During recent years there has been so much jockeying over wages and hours of labor that several weeks or months of good spring weather have been lost. Let us hope that employers and employees will come to an agreement this year before the end of March.

**The Outlook for 1922**

All told we think that 1922 should see a substantial increase in general building activity. The country has passed through the worst stages of depression, and is now on the upgrade. Indications are multiplying that general industry is advancing slowly but surely. The fact that construction activity is holding up at an unusually high level through the winter months, taken with other known factors that are likely to effect the rate of activity next year, gives promise to an unusually good year for construction in 1922.

With the progress of credit liquidation and the rise in bond prices, and the lower cost of building, mortgage money will probably be in easier supply and at lower rates, and there is a fair probability of lower freight rates in building materials. While over the longer trend it is almost certain that a year or two of active building will bring construction values downward, the present unfilled need indicates no such trend for 1922.

The present prospect is that spring will furnish an unusual opportunity for profit to the builder. Interest rates, wages, and material prices will all presumably be relatively low. Both 1922 and 1923 will probably be years of more than normal building activity, but the prospects are that the man who builds this year will stand a much better chance of making a profitable return than will the man who postpones construction work until 1923.

1921 was a year of liquidation. 1922 will be a year of recuperation. We are not in a period of "hard times coming." We are in a period of "soft times going." Prosperity is coming—it's time to go out and meet it.

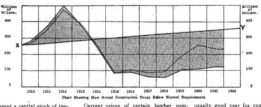

Chart Showing How Actual Construction Drops Below Normal Requirements.

# Vigorous Defence of Wooden Shingle

### Secretary Lamar, of Vancouver, Speaks of High Quality of Product and Conveys Greetings

Fred H. Lamar, of Vancouver, secretary of the Shingle Manufacturers' Association of B. C., was given a cordial welcome. He gave a splendid talk on the wooden shingle as an excellent roofing material, and told of the progress that had been made in its quality, extended use and production. Mr. Lamar bore greetings from the Pacific Coast province. The lumbermen from British Columbia had thought they were carrying all the burdens of the entire lumber trade, but, after listening to the discussions at the convention here, he found that they had not all the problems on their hands out there, although they seemed to be bearing the whole load.

He felt that the attacks levelled against the wooden shingle were not warranted. There were on the roofs of certain houses erected fifteen or twenty years ago, shingles which are poor and rotten but, instead of the assaults being directed against these, the whole product had to bear the brunt. Cheap, flat grain shingles used and sold two decades ago, did not begin to compare with the high grade, edge grain wooden shingle now turned out. In the old days the manufacturer would take a log and endeavor to produce the largest number of shingles from it without any regard to grade or thickness. The shingle manufacturers had gone to work and studied the problem, which had led to the production of the present edge grain shingle, which made a roof covering that could be used for years and years and give satisfaction. Of all the fires started directly from sparks on the roofs it was stated by Mr. Lamar that during the last five years, statistics showed less than three per cent were chargeable to the wooden shingle.

The B. C. manufacturers had recently decided to enter upon a campaign of wide publicity, and would advocate the proper shingles for the proper roof and enlist the support of the retail dealers. They believed that flat grain shingles should not be used except on side walls, and it would be, through the co-operation and goodwill of the eastern lumber dealers, that the sale and popularity of British Columbia shingles could be expanded. Mr. Lamar felt that there had not been the co-operation between the eastern and western lumbermen that there should have been. They were too widely separated by distance, perhaps, to get in close touch, and he had come to the convention to thank the Canadian Lumbermen's Association for the strong fight it had put up against the attacks being made on the use of the wooden shingle. He believed that the C. L. A. was, as a body, fighting the battle for the Pacific Coast manufacturers. The West had to depend on the retail lumber dealers in the east, and also the manufacturers, to resist these attacks.

Mr. Lamar then went into a detailed explanation of the cost of manufacture, and said from a M. ft. log the average output obtained was 9000 XXX shingles, No. 1, and about 1000 of No. 2. In XXXXX shingles the output was about 8000 of No. 1 and about 1000 of No.2, commonly known as the "droopings." The most popular selling shingle in the east was the XXX.

He produced several diagrams showing that the swelling in ordinary, flat-grained shingles is 104% greater than those cut in an opposite direction. Shingles that were not cut parallel were apt to warp or distortion occur when shrinking or swelling takes place due to moisture or other atmospheric changes. In 100% edge-grained shingles all the forces were parallel to the edge and also to the face of the shingle; hence no warping, curling or cupping of the shingle when swelling or shrinkage occurs.

Mr. Lamar showed a circle, containing various sectors which set forth some timely data. Freight rates and raw material represented 75 per cent of the cost of the shingles or finished product per M; laid down in Toronto. On a M shingles shipped from Vancouver to Toronto weighing 180 pounds, the freight rate at the present carrying charge of $1.02½ per 100 pounds amounted to $1.85 or 32 per cent of the delivered price.

The cedar timber at $20 base price for logs used in turning out the shingles, represents—$2.53 per M or 43 per cent of the delivered price. Thus raw material and freight rates made up 75 per cent of the cost per M in the East.

General milling expenses ran 32 cents per M or 5½ per cent. This included saws, oil and grease, belting, shingle straps, bands and nails, general mill repairs, etc.

Overhead and general expenses ran 40 cents per M or 7 per cent. This included insurance, depreciation, selling expenses, taxes, Workmen's Compensation, H. O. expense etc.

General labor, (outside of sawing and packing) cost 44 cents per M or 7½ per cent. This includes cut-off sawers, filers, knee bolts, kiln tenderers, roustabouts, car loaders, etc.

Sawing and packing cost 29 cents per M or 5 per cent of the delivered price, making up the one hundred per cent or the figure received for the goods laid down in Toronto.

In explanation of cutting, Mr. Lamar said that from the centre portion of small logs flat grain shingles were made and the edge grain were obtained from the outer portion.

In answer to a question, Mr. Lamar said that kiln drying, if properly done, improved the efficiency of the shingle. They were kiln dried at 180 degrees for about eight days. Concluding he declared that if thick edge grain shingles were used on roofs and properly laid with the right kind of nails—and nothing was more important than proper nails,—a covering would be secured that would last for forty years.

### The Part That Lumber Plays

J. Grove Smith, of Ottawa, Dominion Fire Commissioner, gave one of the most acceptable addresses of the session on "The Part Lumber Plays." Years ago lumbermen may have mined the forests, culled the trees and left a trail of fire-inviting slash and reckless waste, yet such practices had long since been discarded by operators. In recent years lumbermen had taken a new stand and are enthusiastically looking for the conservation of the natural wooded wealth of the country. They were much interested in the preservation and perpetuation of the forests.

Mr. Smith said that although fire may wipe out a large area of timber resources, nature reclothed the area, but when buildings and

homes are destroyed, the loss is one in an entirely different sense in that it is a loss that in itself can never be regained.

During the last four years the fire losses in Canada amounted to $118,463,500. and the number of fires exceeded 67,000. The amount paid to insurance companies each year for protection was $48,000,000, and all this was a tremendous handicap. The fire losses in Great Britain last year were $36,000,000. with her 50,000,000 of population, while in Canada with less than 6,000,000, the loss was $31,400,-000. It is said the insurance companies paid the loss. It was not them at all; it was the people.

Mr. Smith pointed out that all lumber was insured, and practically all other commodities, and it might be enquired to what extent lumber is responsible for this tremendous loss. Lumber had been assigned a prominent place in causes of destruction, and the question often arose,—whether the material is to blame for fires, or the method of using it? No material is entirely fire-resistant. It is only comparatively fireproof, whether it be brick, stone or cement. The loss to-day on so-called "fireproof" buildings is often greater than those of mill construction. A large dimension structure with no hollow spaces, 3-inch flooring, if properly protected by an automatic sprinkler system, was, in his opinion, safer from fire than a modern fireproof building with no sprinkler system. Large dimension timber, added Mr. Smith, is not generally subject to destruction as much as iron, steel and concrete. Economy still came into the whole question of building materials. He thought that lumber could be safely used in all structures of a domestic and industrial character, although he would not favor its employment in the erection of public institutions.

Three factors enter into the consideration of the construction of all buildings—cost, safety and endurance. He did not consider endurance itself as the main factor: Safety was of prime importance. The menace from fire is not so much from the frame building as it is in the method of its construction. A large proportion of the fire losses in Canada were due to poor construction and not necessarily to materials.

Reverting to the proposed anti-shingle legislation Mr. Smith said that the whole question is now being taken into serious consideration by the Dominion Fire Prevention Association, who had appointed a committee, composed of three non-professional gentlemen, to conduct an exhaustive investigation into the comparative inflammability of all roof-covering materials. The great difficulty is not in the shingles employed to-day, as much more has become known about their quality and use during the last four of five years Properly-laid shingles of good quality did not create as much concern regarding fire as those shingles which are curled, split and cheap. The manufacturers were doing a good work in seeing that their product is properly graded, sorted and classified

After all is said and done, while wood itself may be inflammable, it might be added that no material is fire-resistant. The danger lies in the wrong use of wooden shingles. They had their legitimate place in construction, and the whole question of fire hazard harks back to proper methods. Poor workmanship was responsible for the vast majority of the charges laid against lumber and shingles as to their inflammability.

# Noon-Day Luncheon Much Enjoyed

### Guests Spent Pleasant Time Around Festive Board and Listened to Program of Interest

The noon day luncheon tendered the visiting lumbermen by the wholesalers and manufacturers of Toronto, in the ball room of the King Edward Hotel on Thursday, January 12th was attended by about 300 persons. They heard an edifying and logical address on the promising building situation and encouraging industrial outlook by A. R. Whittemore, manager of MacLean Building Reports. A full report of his remarks appears in another column of the "Canada Lumberman." A. E. Clark, chairman of the local committee of arrangements, presided at the gathering and was assisted by G. E. Spragge, chairman of the luncheon committee.

While the menu was being partaken of several choruses were sung, the company around the festive board being led by H. J. Terry, who proved himself a pastmaster in the art of inciting "the boys" to warble. Several, who preferred eating to singing, were promptly "yanked up" and commanded either to sing a ditty all alone or recite a suitable poem. Among those, who paid the penalty for not displaying 100% vocal efficiency were A. E. Clark, W. B. Snowball, W. G. Power and others. Mr. Snowball said that he had left his musical talent at home but he recited the following poem which made a great hit in view of the large number of American visitors present: —

Sing a song of six pence, a bottle full of Rye.
Four and twenty Yanks, Oh! so very dry.
When the Rye was opened, the Yanks began to sing:
"To H —— with the Stars and Stripes,
God save the King."

Three boys, who have come under the aegis of the Rotary Club, and possess marked ability in certain lines, demonstrated what they can do. These prodigies are what is known as "the under privileged boys." The Rotary Club is doing much to cultivate the special gifts and bring out all the latent talent they possess. There was a marvellous boy whistler, a colored boy singer and a juvenile violinist, all around ten years of age. They were given what political writers would call a "vociferous reception."

After the address of Mr. Whittemore, Dan. McLachlin, president of the Association, expressed appreciation of the hospitality of the Toronto lumbermen in taking such good care of the visitors and providing so abundantly for all their needs.

This was heartily seconded by Gordon C. Edwards, of Ottawa, and all the visiting lumbermen rose en masse and gave three rousing cheers for their hosts. F. H. Lamar, of Vanvouver, "the man from the West," also added his quota of praise for what the Toronto trade had done toward making their stay happy and memorable.

C. V. Haerem has entered into partnership with E. E. House who has been with him over fifteen years, and the style of the firm will be C. V. Haerem & Co., with offices at 4 Chorlton St., Manchester, England.

## Lumbermen's Banquet Was Most Enjoyable

Marked by delightful and novel features and animated by verve and co-operation never previously witnessed in the annals of Canadian lumberdom, the fourteenth annual banquet of the Canadian Lumbermen's Association held in the spacious and artistic ball room of the King Edward hotel on Thursday, January 12 was both the crowning and concluding event in the proceedings of the convention. This outstanding social function, which has become historic, attracted an attendance of about five hundred ladies and gentlemen, who thoroughly enjoyed the occasion and will long remember its congenial associations. The tables were admirably arranged and the menu was satisfying in every respect.

The speaker of the evening was Captain, the Rev. W. A. Cameron, who delivered a stirring oration on Canada. He held his hearers spell bound by his flights of eloquence and related many humorous stories which were received with every manifestation of pleasure. The banquet was also of an international character as greetings were conveyed by Horace F. Taylor, of, Buffalo, N.Y., President of the National Hardwood Lumber Association and by W. W. Schupner of New York City, Secretary of the National Wholesale Lumber Dealers Association. One of the newly elected American directors of the Canadian Lumbermen's Association, Spencer Kellogg, of Utica, N.Y. also added a few words of fraternal relationship from the forest products men across the line.

A feature par excellence was the coronation and investiture of A. E. Clark as president, a laurel wreath being placed upon his brow by Mrs. McLachlin wife of the retiring President, while Mrs. Clark was similarly honored by Mr. McLachlin, when relinquishing his office. The dedicatory ode was composed and read by A. C. Manbert, of Toronto, and was a model of wit, wisdom and philosophy.

Mayor Maguire also graced the gathering by his presence and delivered what Chairman MacLachlin said would be a "sixty second welcome." His Worship extended cordial greetings from the city of Toronto to such a representative and responsible body as the lumbermen, who stood for great interests and the development of Canada. He was not aware of the character of the business that had been transacted at their session but understood that aggressive action had been taken in the matter of that terrible handicap to the revival of industry—the high freight rates—which are working to the great disadvantage of all the cities of the Dominion. Mayor Maguire said that he was pleased to see the ladies present and referred with appreciation to the noble work they had done during the war. The great struggle had taught us that we could not live to ourselves but must work for the benefit and welfare of others.

Prior to the toasts H. J. Terry led the singing and kept all in a jolly mood by his apt remarks and pertinent comments on the brand of vocalism offered by some of the well known banqueters, threatening them with dire punishment if they did not exercise their natural talent to the utmost. To employ a colloquialism, Mr. Terry was "the right man in the right place."

### Greetings from National Associations

"Sister Associations" was first responded to by President Taylor of the National Hardwood Lumber Association, who warmly thanked his Canadian brethren for their hospitality, and conveyed heartiest greetings. He also paid a tribute to President-elect A. E. Clark, whose work and worth was recognized across the line in connection with American lumber bodies, on which he had served. The ladies also came in for an ardent tribute. On entering the hall, Mr. Taylor said he had been impressed with the horizontal dimensions of some of the Canadian lumbermen. He thought that he had discovered the secret in perusing the constitution of the C. L. A. for there he read that this was an "organization for lumbermen extending from Coast to Coast." No wonder that so many of them were rotund, well fed and jovial in appearance. (laughter) This was a history making period, and there were many problems to solve. Perhaps we were inclined to forget some of the lessons of the war, thrift, unselfishness and thoroughness, but on these points he would not dwell. No better investment could be made by any lumberman than in becoming a member of the C. L. A. Such organizations were needed today as never before in helping fellow lumbermen and only by co-operation and unity could many perplexing problems be unfolded. Speaking of the N. H. L. Association, it sought to make universal rules and regulations for the inspection of hardwood lumber, not only in definition but in application. A large measure of success had been met with and the Association would soon celebrate its 25th anniversary. It was helping to solve international questions in the lumber interests and to eliminate sectionalism, and had in Canada 70 members. Mr.

Taylor in conclusion said that he hoped 1922 would bring good fortune to all the members of the Canadian Lumbermen's Association and that they would pay the largest income tax they ever had.

### Lumbermen's Contributions to the Province

Hon. Beniah Bowman, Minister of Lands and Forests for Ontario, spoke of the importance of the lumber industry which employed a large amount of labor. Lumbermen contributed largely to the revenue of the province and during the past year had paid into the treasury of Ontario four millions of dollars. He wished the Association every success and prosperity.

W. W. Schupner, of New York, regretted the absence of President McClure of Memphis, who had fully expected to be present. He believed that the National Wholesale Lumber Dealers Association, of which he was Secretary, had been the first to introduce the presence of ladies at the annual banquet and he was pleased to see that the Canadian Association had copied their example. The N. W. L. D. Association embraced in its membership some forty Canadians and two of them, Dan McLachlin and A. E. Clark, were valued members of the Board of Trustees. The Canadian Association had magnanimously reciprocated by the election of two American directors at the meeting just held. Of the forty-two members of the National Wholesale Lumber Dealers Association, who had attended this convention, twenty-one were from Canada and the same number from across the line He invited as many as possible to come to the annual gathering of the association which he represented. It would be held in Washington on March 22 and 23. Mr. Schupner assured them all of a sincere welcome.

### The Greatness and Future of Canada

Captain W. A. Cameron, who was the chief speaker was heartily greeted and, after some pleasantries at the expense of the lumbermen, took as his subject "Canada." He spoke of its birth, expansion and high ideals; the great work done by the pioneers of the country and their splendid faith and vision. Canadians were beginning to think in Canadian terms, perspective and conceptions and bring to accomplishment Canadian ideals and aspirations. Of Canada as an integral part of the British Empire, of the birth of sister Dominions like Australia, New Zealand and South Africa and lastly the Irish Free State, he painted a graphic verbal picture. He made a strong plea for more tolerance, breadth of view and thought. He sketched the magnificent future that was dawning and recounted the glories and traditions of the past. For the uprooting of prejudices of every nature and for a bigness and broadness that would ensure days bright with promise and capable of achieving the highest hopes and ambitions, he made a strong plea. Captain Cameron closed with a glowing peroration and rarely has any speaker ever aroused an audience more in patriotic persuasiveness and influence. President McLachlin thanked him for his splendid effort.

The finale was the reading of a poem paying tribute to the newly elected president of the Association, A. E. Clark, of Toronto, by A. C. Manbert who, amid many happy references, said that " now is the night of our discontent made glorious by this son of York." A laurel wreath was placed upon the head of the newly appointed presiding officer, amid ringing cheers from the banqueters, by Mrs. McLachlin and Mrs. Clark was escorted to the front and was similarly decorated. The installation ceremony was unique and impressive but, was not without its humorous touches.

Mr. Clark said that he had been placed in a rather difficult position, being accorded so much honor and responsibility. He made a plea for the co-operation of his fellow directors in aiding him in the great task and was sure he would have the hearty assistance of the old officers in carrying out the policy of the association and continuing its progress. The past year had been the most successful in its history and the work would, he hoped, under his direction be conducted aggressively and earnestly for the benefit and welfare of the lumber industry.

### Pledges of Fidelity and Friendship

Greetings and pledges of support were then made by W. B. Snowball on behalf of New Brunswick, W. Gerard Power for Quebec, Walter M. Ross for the Ottawa Valley lumbermen, Ed. Letherby for the Ontario interests, and Fred H. Lamar, of Vancouver, who invited the Association to meet in the West in the near future where he assured them of a breezy welcome. Spencer Kellogg spoke for the American members.

Tributes were also paid by the speakers to the unbounded hospitality of the Toronto lumbermen, whose kindness and generosity would never be forgotten.

Messrs. Snowball, Power, Ross, Letherby and Lamar, then wended their way to the head table and saluting President Clark, renewed their vows of fidelity and extended their hand in token of their troth. The vast concourse then rose and sang Auld Lang Syne, followed by the National Anthem. The fourteenth annual banquet of the Canadian Lumbermen's Association was over, "happy to meet, sorry to part, happy to meet again."

# The New President is "Birch King of Canada".

## Some Interesting Information Regarding A. E. Clark, of Toronto, Who Will Guide Destinies of Canadian Lumbermen's Association for Coming Year

A. E. Clark, Toronto
Who now heads the C. L. A.

Alfred Edward Clark, of Toronto, the newly elected president of the Canadian Lumbermen's Association, although of English extraction, came, as he says, within two days of being a thoroughly-seasoned, directly descended Irishman. Time decreed that he should be born on March 19th in 1880 instead of, on St. Patrick's Day. However, he has managed to get along in spite of this handicap and attain the highest position in the gift of the Canadian lumber interests.

Mr. Clark is vice-president and managing-director of Edward Clark & Sons, Limited, Toronto, one of the largest wholesalers and distributors of hardwood lumber in Canada. The subject of this reference first saw the light of day in the village of Brigden, Lambton County, where his father, Edward Clark, was for many years engaged in sawmill and timber operations, taking out considerable quantities of oak, elm and hickory for ship work and bending stock. Considerable of the output of the mill was despatched to Marine City, Mich., and Sarnia, where it was used in the building of vessels.

Mr. Clark, Sr., loves to recall associations of the trade of forty and fifty years ago, when he took out white oak sills for the construction of the locks on the old Welland Canal. These sills were among the finest specimen of timber ever sawn in Western Ontario, being 24 x 24 inches and 36 feet in length.

Previous to moving to Lambton County, the Clark family lived in Dundas, where they cleared a bush farm and supplied bridge timber, ties and other material to the railway then being built from Hamilton to Caledonia and other points in Southwestern Ontario.

Alfred Edward Clark, the eldest son of Edward Clark, attended the public school at Brigden and continued his studies at the Strathroy Collegiate Institute. During the summer he assisted his father in the sawmill and worked in the bush, driving teams, skidding logs and doing everything that a tall, healthy auburn haired lad could perform. Blocks of timber were bought from the neighboring farmers and the operations of Mr. Clark Sr. extended over a considerable area.

After completing his studies in Strathroy, Alfred Clark taught school for one year at Kerwood in Middlesex County, and during the time that he was away from home, his father sold his sawmill at Brigden and removed to Hamilton where he engaged in the wholesale lumber line.

Alfred became connected with the firm, which was known as Edward Clark & Son, and continued to do business in the Ambitious City until 1907 when a removal was made to Toronto. It was then that Dr. R. L. Clark, who had graduated in medicine from Toronto University, joined the firm with which he was indentified until his death on July 12th 1913. In the latter year Edward Clark & Sons had become a federally incorporated company, with Edward Clark as president, Dr. R. L. Clark, as vice-president and A. E. Clark as secretary-treasurer and managing director. On the death of R. L. Clark, A. E. Clark was made vice-president and managing-director, and W. A. Walker became secretary-treasurer.

Several subsidiary companies were organized in connection with the hardwood operations of the firm. In 1907 the Ballantyne Lumber Co. was formed. This concern owned some forty-two square miles of limits and there was also the Trout Creek Logging Co. which built a railway in order to get the timber to the mill, and the operating end was carried on by the Dominion Wood & Lumber Co. at Trout Creek, Ont., who manufactured, not only lumber, but also wood alcohol, acetate of lime and charcoal. These enterprises were all disposed of a few years ago, and in 1917 a controlling interest was obtained by the firm in the Jones-Webster Corporation, with mills at

Wenlock, Vermont, and a sales office in Boston. The corporation controlled about 80,000 acres of hardwood and was engaged extensively in the production of lumber until 1919 when Edward Clark & Sons disposed of their holdings in the business. Since then they have been confining themselves largely to Canadian hardwoods, specializing in birch.

"Alf." Clark as he is popularly known, is often called the "Birch King of Canada." He has always been actively interested in anything pertaining to the welfare and progress of lumberman or lumbering activities. He was one of the organizers and chairman for two years of the Wholesale Lumber Dealers' Association Inc., Toronto, and for a number of years has been a director of the Canadian Lumbermen's Association. At the last convention in Ottawa he was made first vice-president of that body, and at the recent one in Toronto he was elevated to the presidency.

The new president of the Canadian Lumbermen's Association is also widely known across the border, being a trustee of the National Wholesale Lumber Dealers' Association, New York, and a former director and member of the Rules Committee of the National Hardwood Lumber Association, Chicago. He is a member of the Ontario Club, the Rotary Club, the Scarboro Golf & Country Club, and the Deer Park Golf & Country Club, at Grimsby.

Mr. Clark, who resides at 15 Edgar Ave., Toronto, has an attractive cottage at Grimsby, where he spends several weeks very pleasantly each summer. He is as stated, thoroughly familiar with lumbering in all its phases and when he first became connected with the firm was on the inspection staff quite a while, after which he spent some years on the road, and even to-day he does considerable travelling. He has always given liberally of his time and talent to further anything that would be of advantage to lumbermen.

### Greetings from National Hardwood

Frank F. Fish, of Chicago, secretary of the National Hardwood Lumber Association, was welcomed by president McLachlin. Mr. Fish said he was no stranger to many of those present. The Association, which he had the honor to represent, had 71 members in Canada, 46 of whom were in Ontario.

The object and work of the N. H. L. A. was to establish and maintain uniform rules for the measurement and inspection of hardwood lumber. Grading had not been reduced to an exact science and still must be left largely to the individual judgment of the inspectors The Association now had five licensed inspectors in Canada. Its progress in the Dominion had been brought about in a great measure by the close co-operation of the manufacturers and distributors of lumber.

### Mr. Miller for the Rules Committee

A meeting of the hardwood lumber dealers and manufacturers was held at the King Edward hotel, Toronto, on January 13 at which there were over thirty representatives in attendance. Frank F. Fish, of Chicago, addressed the gathering and said that at present there was no representative from Canada on the inspection and rules committee of the N. H. L. A. It was decided by those present that John J. Miller, a member of the Anderson Miller Lumber Co., Toronto, who was for several years chief inspector in Ontario, should be recommended for a place on the committee.

The convention was a record-breaker in many respects. All the officers were on the job from start to finish.

The delegation from the Maritime Provinces was very satisfactory considering the great distance the members had to travel. Montreal will be the Mecca of the convention next year. The visitors from that city say it will be the greatest ever.

Dan. McLachlin paid a warm tribute to the work of the Canadian Forest Prducts Laboratories, Montreal, and the service rendered in the research and technical branches. The Laboratories offered courteous co-operation to lumbermen in the solution of any problems encountered in the use of wood. Expert advice on the causes and prevention of decay in timber could also be given.

# Those Who Attended the Great Gathering

The delegates to the fourteenth convention of the Canadian Lumbermen's Association in Toronto, who registered at the Secretary's booth, were:

Appleby, B.G., W. Malcolm Mackay, New York, N.Y.
Anderson, C. G., C. G. Anderson Lumber Co., Toronto, Ont.
Allen, R. A. R., Allen Lumber Co., Mill Bridge, Ont.
Allen, Chas., The Charles Allen Co., Rochester, N.Y.
Adams, George C., Duquesne Lumber Co., Philadelphia, Pa.
Baker, F. C., Devon Lumber Co., Sherbrooke, Que.
Beatty, W. R., Colonial Lumber Co., Pembroke, Ont.
Black, John, J. R. Booth, Ottawa, Ont.
Belton, Chester H., Laidlaw Belton Lumber Co., Sarnia, Ont.
Beck, W. F., C. Beck Mfg. Co., Penetang, Ont.
Booth, J. Fred, J. R. Booth, Ottawa, Ont.
Bruce, Frederick J., Homan & Puddington, Inc., New York, N.Y.
Benson, F. M., Rierdon Co., Montreal, Que.
Brady, H. J., Jr., Brady Bros., Buffalo, N.Y.
Bock, J. S., Eagle Lumber Co., Montreal, Que.
Burchill, J. P., George Burchill & Sons, South Nelson, N.B.
Black, Robson, Canadian Forestry Association, Ottawa, Ont.
Brown, K. M., Vancouver Lumber Co., Toronto, Ont.
Brankley, J. W., Miramichi Lumber Co., Chatham, N.B.
Bigwood, W. E., Graves, Bigwood & Co., Byng Inlet, Ont.
Bain. B., George Gordon Co., Cache Bay, Ont.
Bartram, J. C., Ottawa, Ont.
Blair, R. P., Blair Bros., Montreal, Que.
Cole, Douglas S., Commercial Intelligence Service, Ottawa, Ont.
Brenner, E. R., Watson & Todd, Ottawa, Ont.
Blackburn, R. L., Hawkesbury Lumber Co., Ottawa, Ont.
Bartlett, C., Strong Lumber Co., Orillia, Ont.
Barre, E. C., Cleveland-Sarnia Sawmills, Sarnia, Ont.
Barrett, Wm., Memphis Land & Lumber Co., Toronto, Ont.
Cleveland, Frederick, Albany, N.Y.
Cameron, G. O., Mickle, Dyment & Son, Barrie, Ont.
Cole, Douglas S., Commercial Intelligence Service, Ottawa, Ont.
Craig, A. C., Firstbrook Bros., Toronto, Ont.
Chesbro, R. J., Toronto, Ont.
Courtenay, F. L., Muir & Kirkpatrick, Toronto, Ont.
Carter, W. J., Fesserton Timber Co., Toronto, Ont.
Coderre, J. A., Forest Products Laboratory, Montreal.
Cameron, R. G., Cameron & Co., Ottawa, Ont.
Cummings, R. B., New Ontario Colonization Co., Buffalo, N.Y.
Carney, Chas. N., Hope Lumber Co., Thessalon, Ont.
Crombie, A. C., W. M. Crombie Co., Inc., New York, N.Y.
Carr, Wm. P., A. S. McKibbee & Son, Albany, N.Y.
Carswell, J. H., J. R. Carswell, Renfrew, Ont.
Clark, A. E., Edward Clark & Sons, Toronto.
Currie, D. H., Rat Portage Lumber Co., Stackpool, Ont.
Cooper, A. F., Standard Chemical Co., Longford Mills, Ont.
Christie, L. F., Marshay Lumber Co., Sudbury, Ont.
Dadson, A. T., Montreal Lumber Co., Toronto.
Dunlop, E. A., Pembroke Lumber Co., Pembroke, Ont.
Donovan, James, C. G. Anderson Lumber Co., Toronto, Ont.
Dinsmore, R. G., Bethune Pulp & Lumber Co., Huntsville, Ont.
Dudley, Arthur N., Toronto.
Davidson, G. P., James Davidson's Sons, Ottawa, Ont.
Davis, A. M., McAuliffe-Davis Lumber Co., Ottawa, Ont.
Dwight, T. W., Dominion Forestry Branch, Ottawa, Ont.
Dickie, Rufus E., Stewiacke, N.S.
Edwards, Gordon C., W. C. Edwards Co., Ottawa, Ont.
Elgie, R. B., Elgie & Jarvis Lumber Co., Toronto, Ont.
Eckardt, A. E., R. Laidlaw Lumber Co., Toronto, Ont.
Edgecomb, A. E., Fassett Lumber Co., Philadelphia, Pa.
Earing, D. D., Gillies Bros., Braeside, Ont.
Fairchild, R. E., Mixer & Co., Buffalo, N.Y.
French, Guy M., Rideau Lumber Co., Ottawa, Ont.
Fillon, W. A., E. H. Lemay, Montreal, Que.
Fenderson, C. L., A. C. Dutton, Jacquet River, N.B.
Fish, Frank F., National Hardwood Lumber Association, Chicago, Ill.
Fleming, C. A., Harris Tie & Lumber Co., Ottawa, Ont.
Fergus, H. S., G. A. Grier & Sons, Toronto.
Grafftey, W. A., Montreal Lumber Co., Montreal, Que.
Gillies, J. S., Gillies Bros., Arnprior, Ont.
Grabowsky, J. W., Grabowsky & McGee, Thessalon, Ont.
Golding, W. E., George McKean & Co., St. John, N.B.
Gall, A. J., Gall Lumber Co., Toronto, Ont.
Grier, Geo. W., G. A. Grier & Sons, Montreal, Que.
Garlock, Wm., Garlock Machinery Co., Toronto, Ont.
Grafftey, George A., Montreal, Que.
Grier, A. E., G. A. Grier & Sons, Montreal, Que.
Gordon, A. C., Mickle, Dyment & Son, Barrie, Ont.
Gillies, John H., Gillies Bros., Braeside, Ont.
Gregory, J. Fraser, Murray & Gregory, St. John, N.B.
Gordon, A. E., Terry & Gordon, Toronto, Ont.
Graham, W. E., Ottawa, Ont.
Gray, George F., New York, N.Y.
Goodman, Chas. A., Sawyer-Goodman Co., Marinette, Wis.
Hales, S. J., John B. Smith & Sons, Toronto, Ont.
Heeney Percy E., Kitchener, Ont.
Hunter, W. L., Northern Timber Co., Pembroke, Ont.
Hocken, Norman C., Hocken Lumber Co., Toronto, Ont.
Hill, C. C., Rankin-Benedict Co., Kansas City, Mo.
Hitchcock, H. C., Sawyer-Goodman Co., Marinette, Wis.
Haws, J. R., James R Summers, Toronto, Ont.

Harris, R. C., Russell Harris Lumber Co., Toronto, Ont.
Halliday, Roy, R. Laidlaw Lumber Co., Toronto, Ont.
Hardy, E. D., Caandian Lumber Insurance Exchange, Ottawa, Ont.
Howa, Joseph, Ottawa, Ont.
Hubbard, H. P., E. C. Atkins & Co., Hamilton, Ont.
Hurlbut, S. A., A. Sherman Lumber Co., Syracuse, N.Y.
Hall, John, Wm. Ritter Lumber Co., Columbus, Ohio.
Harry, Robert E., Rideau Lumber Co., Ottawa, Ont.
Hawkins, Frank, Secretary, Canadian Lumbermen's Association, Ottawa, Ont.
Harris, Frank H., Frank H. Harris Lumber Co., Toronto, Ont.
Herschemiller, J. F., Fulburn, Inc., Buffalo, N.Y.
Hutcheson, R. J., Muskoka Wood Mfg. Co., Huntsville, Ont.
Horning, F. H., C. Beck Mfg. Co., Penetang, Ont.
Holt, George H., Holt Timber Co., Chicago, Ill.
Johnson, A. K., J. P. Johnson & Son, Toronto, Ont.
Johnson, Chas., Mowbray-Robinson Co., Rochester, N.Y.
Joyce, H. D., Montreal Que.
Jullen, R., Quebec, Que.
Kriechbaum, A. R., "Lumber," New York, N.Y.
Kellogg, Spencer, Chas. C. Kellogg & Sons Co., Utica, N.Y.
Kinsella, M. P., R. Laidlaw Lumber Co., Buffalo, N.Y.
Kent, Frank, Seaman, Kent Co., Toronto, Ont.
Klaas, Alfred, Holt Timber Co., Ononto, Wis.
King, Wm. R., Mickle, Dyment & Son, Barrie, Ont.
Kinnon, George, Toronto, Ont.
Kennedy, C. E., C. E. Kennedy, Inc., New York, N.Y.
Kynoch, W., Forest Products Laboratories, Montreal, Que.
Larkin, H. W., Larkin Lumber Co., Toronto, Ont.
Laidlaw, W. C., R. Laidlaw Lumber Co., Toronto, Ont.
Laidlaw, R. A., R. Laidlaw Lumber Co., Toronto, Ont.
Linehan, Joseph J., Mowbray-Robinson Co., Cincinnati, Ohio.
Loud, Brewster, Brewster Loud Lumber Co., Detroit, Mich.
Large, Hamilton R., Smith, Fassett & Co., North Tonawanda, N.Y.
Leak, H. A., Leak & Co., Toronto, Ont.
Letherby, E., Chew Bros., Midland, Ont.
Luby, John, Robert Cox & Co., Ottawa, Ont.
Lamont, A. B., C. G. Anderson Co., Toronto, Ont.
Littleton, J. E., R. Laidlaw Lumber Co., Toronto, Ont.
Lovering, W. J., Toronto, Ont.
Lapreas, W. J., C. B. Kennedy, Inc., New York, N.Y.
Lamar, Fred. H., B. C. Shingle Manufacturers' Association, Vancouver, B.C.
Mallett, O., Painchaud & Miquelon, Hebert Station, Que.
Miller, J. J., C. G. Anderson Lumber Co., Toronto, Ont.
Manbert, A. C., Canadian General Lumber Co., Toronto, Ont.
Mageau, Z., Magure Lumber Co., Sturgeon Falls, Ont.
Muir, J. K., Muir & Kirkpatrick, Toronto, Ont.
Morrison, A. C., Price Bros., Quebec, Que.
Mason, Wm. Thos., Mason, Gordon & Co., Montreal, Que.
McLean, Hugh, The Bathurst Co., Buffalo, N.Y.
McBean, John A., McBean & Verrall Co., Toronto, Ont.
McLean, Angus, The Bathurst Co., Bathurst, N.B.
McCabe, C. W., Campbell-MacLaurin Lumber Co., Montreal, Que.
MacLaurin, J. P., St. Maurice Paper Co., Montreal, Que.
McDermid, H. G., Union Lumber Co., Toronto, Ont.
McDonagh, Roderick, McDonagh Lumber Co., Toronto, Ont.
McFadden, J. J., McFadden & Malloy, Sprague, Ont.
McNally, Frank S., A. Sherman Lumber Co., Potsdam, N.Y.
McDonald, Chas., C. A. Larkin Co., Toronto, Ont.
McGoldrick, P. J., Power Lumber Co., St. Pacome, Que.
McLennan, D. H., McLennan Lumber Co., Montreal, Que.
Maclean, W. B., Conger Lumber Co., Toronto, Ont.
McLachlin, Dan., McLachlin Bros., Arnprior, Ont.
McLaren, Duncan, Union Lumber Co., Toronto, Ont.
Nadeau, Chas. H., Port Daniel, Que.
Napier, W. F., Shives Lumber Co., Campbellton, N.B.
O'Brien, J. Leonard, O'Brien, Limited, South Nelson, N.B.
Power, W. Gerard, W. & J. Sharples, Quebec, Que.
Paterson, T. A., Mickle, Dyment & Son, Toronto, Ont.
Plunkett, H. J., Plunkett, Webster Lumber Co., New York, N.Y.
Painchaud, Arthur, Painchaud & Miquelon, Hebert Station, Que.
Paynes, W. G., Campbell, Welsh & Paynes, Toronto, Ont.
Pratt, D. S., Fratt & Shanacy Midland, Ont.
Pedwell, E. R., Pedwell Lumber Co., Toronto, Ont.
Pickard, F. D., Panuke Pulp & Power Co., Windsor, N.S.
Priest, W. H., Dalhousie Lumber Co., Dalhousie, N.B.
Poussette, E. R., Commercial Intelligence Service, Ottawa, Ont.
Page, O. Cardinal & Page, Montreal, Que.
Paxton, G. A., Firtsbrook Bros. Toronto, Ont.
Patenaude, Eng., Nominingue, Que.
Quarterman, O. C. "American Lumberman," Chicago, Ill.
Raymond, M. T., Spanish River Lumber Co., Toronto, Ont.
Richards, W. S., Richards Mfg. Co., Campbellton, N.B.
Rhynas, O. W., Mickle, Dyment & Son, Brantford, Ont.
Russell, Wm., James Richardson Co., Matane, Que.
Ross, Walter M., J. R. Booth, Ottawa, Ont.
Ross, Hugh A., Rose, McLaurin, Toronto, Ont.
Roth, A. H., C. A. Kennedy, Inc., New York, N.Y.
Read, A. F., Read Bros., Toronto, Ont.
Read, C. F., Jr., Daventry Lumber Co., Ottawa, Ont.
Ray, Col. W. J., Price Bros. & Co., Quebec, Que.
Smith, Robert, John B. Smith & Sons, Toronto, Ont.
Smith, W. J., John B. Smith & Sons, Toronto, Ont.
Snowball, W. B., J. B. Snowball Co., Chatham, N.B.
Safford, E. B., Jr., A. Sherman Lumber Co., Potsdam N.Y.
Stuart, J. T., Pembroke Shook Mills, Pembroke, Ont.

Scarlett G. A., Union Lumber Co., Toronto, Ont.
Summers, James R., Toronto, Ont.
Stewart, W. J., Union Lumber Co., Toronto, Ont.
Shreiner, W. C., Anderson, Shreiner & Mawson, Toronto, Ont.
Schupner, W. W., Secy., National Whol. Lumber Dealers' Assn., New York.
Stearns, F. H., F. H. Stearns Co., Montreal, Que.
Slater, J. W., Hocken Lumber Co., Toronto, Ont.
Stocking, R. E., Power, Moir & Stocking, Inc., New York, N.Y.
Story, W. F. T., Story Lumber Co., Montreal, Que.
Staniforth, S. J., Fassett Lumber Co., Fassett, Que.
Sherman, John, Hawkesbury Lumber Co., Hawkesbury, Ont.
Smith, A. R., Clark & Smith, Weston, Ont.
Shearer, James G., James Shearer Co., Montreal, Que.
Strong, G. M., Montreal, Que.
Shanacy, H., Pratt & Shanacy, Midland, Ont.
Sisson, Walter C., A. Sherman Lumber Co., Potsdam, N.Y.
Story, John A., Story Lumber Co., Ottawa, Ont.
Smith, J. Grove, Dominion Fire Commissioner, Ottawa, Ont.

Treat, S. J., "New York Lumber Trade Journal," New York.
Taylor, Horace F., President, National Hardwood Lumber Assn., Buffalo, N.Y.
Taylor, Gardner W., R. T. Jones Lumber Co., Inc., New York, N.Y.
Thompson, F. M., Robert Bury & Co., Toronto, Ont.
Thibert, D., Mageau Lumber Co., Field, Ont.
Terry, H. G., Terry & Gordon, Toronto, Ont.
Thompson, S. C., Riordon Co., Ottawa, Ont.
VanBlaricom, G. B., "Canada Lumberman," Toronto, Ont.
Wilmot, A. G, Otis Staples Lumber Co., Toronto, Ont.
Williams, R. R., Williams Lumber Co., Ottawa, Ont.
Welsh, Maurice, Campbell, Welsh & Paynes, Toronto, Ont.
Walker, E. H., H. H. Hettler Lumber Co., Midland, Ont.
Wentworth, Wm. H., James W. Sewall Co., Old Town, Maine.
Westley, C. A., G. A. Grier & Sons, Toronto, Ont.
White J. R., Riordon Co., Montreal, Que.
Webster, A. G., George Webster & Sons, Swanton, Vt.
Young, A. J., Young Lumber Co., North Bay, Ont.
Youmans, W. R., Gayoso Lumber Co., Memphis, Tenn.

# Lady Delegates Had One Round of Pleasure

The social features of the convention were bright and interesting. The local ladies' committee, which was composed of Mesdames A. E. Clark, A. C. Manbert, W. E. Bigwood, D. M. McLaren, G. C. Spragge, W. C. Wilkinson, D. C. Johnston, W. J. Lovering and W. B. MacLean, were ably assisted by the other committees, including the reception, theatre, dance, motor, etc. A. E. Clark was chairman of the local executive and G. E. Spragge of the luncheon committee, Walter C. Laidlaw of the motor committee, A. C. Manbert, finance committee; D. McLaren, dance committee, W. E. Bigwood, reception, A. E. Eckardt, theatre.

While their husbands were attending the business session, the ladies were well looked after, and on the afternoon of the first day there was an enjoyable theatre party at the Princess, where the musical comedy, "Two Little Girls in Blue," was well received. This was followed by a supper-dance in the evening in the new ball room of the King Edward Hotel, at which about 200 people were present. Romanelli's orchestra of 10 pieces furnished splendid music and every detail of the assembly was marked by much interest. Supper was served at 11.30 o'clock in the Pompeian room.

On the second day of the convention there was a ladies' luncheon at 1 p.m., tendered by the Toronto ladies' committee, and at the conclusion of this event, the members were taken for a motor drive around Toronto, visiting the art gallery, provincial museum and other points of interest. In the evening the members of the fair sex were present in large numbers at the annual banquet.

The hospitality of the Toronto lumbermen and their wives will long be remembered and the delegates will always recall with pleasure their associations at the 1922 conclave in the Queen City.

The visiting ladies at the convention were:—

Mrs. Armand Burwash, Arnprior, Ont.
Mrs. W. F. Beck, Penetang, Ont.
Mrs. G. A. Beck, Penetang, Ont.
Mrs. H. G. Bartlett, Orillia, Ont.
Mrs. Robson Black, Ottawa, Ont.
Mrs. J. W. Brankley, Chatham, N.B.
Mrs. F. C. Baker, Sherbrooke, Que.
Mrs. G. O. Cameron, Barrie, Ont.
Mrs. A. F. Cooper, Longford Mills, Ont.
Mrs. J. H. Carswell, Renfrew, Ont.
Mrs. E. S. Crocker, Chatham, N.B.
Mrs. C. B. Dake, Muskegon, Mich.
Mrs. A. E. Dunlop, Pembroke, Ont.
Mrs. G. P. Davidson, Ottawa, Ont.
Mrs. A. M. Davis, Ottawa, Ont.
Mrs. C. L. Fenderson, Jacquet River, N.B.
Mrs. J. S. Gillies, Braeside, Ont.
Mrs. Geo. Gordon, North Bay, Ont.
Miss Gordon, North Bay, Ont.
Mrs. Frank Rawkins, Ottawa, Ont.
Mrs. J. F. Hirschmiller, Buffalo, N.Y.
Miss Veryl Herron, Tionaga, Ont.
Mrs. Lennox Irving, Renfrew, Ont.
Mrs. J. E. Keenan, Owen Sound, Ont.
Mrs. W. R. King, Barrie, Ont.
Mrs. J. Lewis, Chatham, N.B.
Mrs. E. Letherby, Midland, Ont.

Mrs. McLaurin, Stackpool, Ont.
Mrs. Dan. McLachlin, Arnprior, Ont.
Mrs. J. J. McFadden, Blind River, Ont.
Miss Mary McFadden, Blind River, Ont.
Miss Laura McFadden, Blind River, Ont.
Mrs. F. S. McNally, Potsdam, N.Y.
Mrs. D. H. McLennan, Montreal, Que.
Mrs. W. T. Mason, Montreal, Que.
Mrs. J. P. MacLaurin, Montreal, Que.
Mrs. W. F. Napier, Campbellton, N.B.
Mrs. W. Gerard Power, Quebec, Que.
Mrs. D. S. Pratt, Midland, Ont.
Mrs. W. M. Ross, Ottawa, Ont.
Mrs. Chas. E. Read, Jr., Ottawa, Ont.
Mrs. A. J. Smith, Montreal, Que.
Mrs. H. Shanacy, Midland, Ont.
Mrs. G. M. Strong, Montreal, Que.
Mrs. John Sherman, Hawkesbury, Ont.
Mrs. R. L. Sargant, Ottawa, Ont.
Mrs. W. B. Snowball, Chatham, N.B.
Mrs. S. M. Wedd, Sherbrooke, Que.
Mrs. E. W. Walker, Midland, Ont.
Mrs. J. B. White, Montreal, Que.
Mrs. W. H. Wentworth, Arnprior, Ont.
Mrs. A. G. Wilmot, Wycliffe, B.C.

## Some Lumbermen Recently Honored by the People

Zotique Mageau, M.L.A., Sturgeon Falls.
Once more occupies Mayor's chair.

Hugh C. McKillop, M.P., West Lorne, Ont. Recently elected M.P. for West Elgin.

K. J. Shirton, Deseville, Ont. Re-elected Mayor of that progressive town.

# Transportation Report Covers Many Matters

It will be remembered that at the last convention of the Canadian Lumbermen's Association, held in Ottawa, one of the most progressive steps taken was that of forming a Transportation Department. It was felt that such a branch was urgent in view of increasing freight rates, dissatisfaction in shipments, delays, overcharges by the railway companies etc. R. L. Sargant, a traffic man of wide experience, was, in May last appointed head of the new department and has done effective work.

A. E. Clark, chairman of the Transportation Committee, in his introductory remarks to the report, said that a short time was necessary to acquire tariff data and necessary lumber information, and then, after Mr. Sargant's appointment, an appeal was made to the Board of Railway Commissioners for a hearing on lumber rates, which appeal was sidetracked by the Board. Mr. Clark added, "We are still hammering at the Board who display a manifest reluctance to face the weight of evidence we have accumulated and proof of the necessity for decidedly lower rates on building materials, and particularly lumber." Concluding, Mr. Clark said, "The minor accomplishments of the Transportation Department are set out in detail. The value of the department is fully established and we face with confidence the coming year, secure in the knowledge that we have an able exponent to combat any attempts of the railways to add to our troubles or evade any of their responsibilities.

The remainder of the Transportation Department's report was read by R. L. Sargant, traffic manager for the Canadian Lumbermen's Association. He first called attention to several matters which came before the last annual meeting of the Association and which might come under the head of "Transportation Department's Unfinished Business."

The first of these subjects related to Tariff No. 14 regarding the allowance of 500 to 1,000 lbs. on all cars December 1st to April 30th for variation in the tariff of a car owing to absorption of moisture, and an accumulation of ice, snow, etc. This had been left out of the above-mentioned tariff, and the attention of the Canadian Lumbermen's Association was directed to it at its last meeting, and the subject was discussed.

It was stated in a quotation from a report by Chief Commissioner Carvell, Mr. Sargant said, that lumber and other rough forest products would also receive a minimum allowance of 500 pounds, when loaded in box cars, against the present absolute allowance of 500 pounds, making a total minimum of 1,000 pounds, as against the present maximum of 1,000 pounds.

Upon the formation of your traffic department this matter was taken up with the Board of Railway Commissioners, and it was pointed out to them that we believe there is a very serious discrepancy between the wording and intention of that portion of the late Commissioner Goodeve's judgment and the Board's order No. 283 of February 24th 1920 on this subject. In communicating with the Board we quoted a portion of Commissioner Goodeve's judgment, and also the Board's order, explaining that to our mind it was certainly the intention of the late Commissioner Goodeve that a distinct allowance should be made from the track scale weights on certain classes of traffic to cover absorption of moisture, etc., that the allowance for bark when loaded in box cars should be 1 per cent of the lading of the car, minimum 500 pounds, and the same for open cars. Lumber and other rough forest products the allowance to be 1 per cent of the lading of the car with a minimum of 500 pounds when in box cars, and when loaded on flat or gondola cars an additional 500 pounds making a total minimum of 1,000 pounds. We further stated "That inasmuch as that portion of the Board's Order No. 283 giving reference to allowance for foreign matter not part of the lading, such as snow, ice, etc, in or on cars at the time of weighing is at variance with that portion of the late Commissioner Goodeve's judgment on the subject, we would appreciate an expression of opinion from the Board as to whether the Board's Order No. 283 is correct in view of the late Commissioner Goodeve's judgment. If the judgment is correct, and we do not see how it could be considered otherwise, we presume the Board will issue the necessary instructions to the carriers, whereby they will be obliged to reissue their tariffs in order to comply with the judgment on this matter."

The Board rather side-stepped the issue and replied that that portion of Canadian Freight Association tariff No. 14 covering this matter was exactly the same as the wording of that portion of the Board's order on the subject. We replied that in our opinion this hardly settled the matter as we firmly believed that the late Commissioner Goodeve had not any mistaken ideas as to the meaning of the two terms "Tolerance" and "Allowance," and we believed that

Commissioner Goodeve apparently found that their provisions in the tariff for an estimated allowance by the weighman for foreign matter, refuse, etc., not part of the lading of the car was somewhat inadequate and capable of discrimination on the part of weighmen in favor of, or adverse to, different shippers or consignees, and therefore, in order to obviate these conditions he (Commissioner Goodeve) apparently decided that he would recommend the adoption of the U. S. "Tolerance" of 1 per cent if the lading of the car, minimum 500 lbs., or 1,000 lbs., according to the traffic, as a definite "Allowance" in all cases where foreign matter, refuse, etc. was present instead of leaving it to the discretion or indiscretion of an individual weighman.

"A reply received from the Dominion Railway Board was not at all satisfactory," says Mr. Sargant, "and does not close the matter so far as we are concerned; in fact, it has only whetted our appetite for a definite show-down, and it is the intention to ask the Board to reopen the subject for hearing after a full discussion by the Association in open meeting."

Mr. Sargant then dealt with the increase in export rates which became effective August 20th, 1921 and had the effect of augmenting rates on lumber for export from Atlantic ports. As it was felt that the carriers should not be permitted to put these increased rates into effect until such time as the general application of the Canadian carriers for an increase in freight had been dealt with. Representation to this effect was made to the Board of Railway Commissioners with the result that the effective date of these tariffs was postponed indefinitely.

### Prepayment of Freight Charges

After referring to the prepayment of freight charges and other matters, Mr. Sargant said:—

A regulation was issued by the Canadian Railways effective March 1st, 1921, directing their agents not to accept prepayment of charges from shippers on freight traffic from Canada to the United States except traffic on which the freight classification or tariffs required prepayment. This regulation brought about a storm of protest and the matter was placed before the Board of Railway Commissioners, who after hearing and investigating the complaint decided that for want of jurisdiction of the subject matter thereof, the complaint made by the shippers be dismissed. The Railways were, however instructed to find a satisfactory solution of the matter but it was not until January 11th, 1921, that a written statement was furnished the Board by the Railway Association of Canada, which was the result of extended negotiations between the Railway Association and the various Boards of Trade and trade organizations, the scheme suggested by the Railways was adopted, and was covered by the Board's General Order No. 326 of January 14, 1921.

After dealing with several other matters, the report says:—

Now that the exchange between Canada and the United States is beginning to improve and we trust that conditions in this respect which prevail at the present writing will continue to improve, if they do, we may in the not far distant future endeavor to prevail upon the Board of Railway Commissioners to repeal their legislation providing for a surcharge on freight charges paid in Canada on shipments moving between points in Canada and the United States. This is a matter which will be taken up just as soon as we are reasonably sure that the exchange situation between the two countries has righted itself or has reached what might be considered a normal basis.

This concludes the Transportation subjects discussed at the last annual meeting with the exception of, "Ocean Transportation." It is within the realm of possibility that ocean rates may drop, more especially if there is not some sign of an increase in the export trade of the country within a short time. It is to be expected that someone will break away from the agreed rates, but unless the country is in no position to materially increase its export trade no one is going to benefit very much by an ocean rate war. There is also a possibility that there may be an agreed reduction in ocean freight rates but if this reduction takes place, it would not come into effect until the spring of 1922.

### The Change in Demurrage Charges

In regard to demurrage rates made effective by the Railway Board's general order No. 349, several changes were made to the effect that $1.00 a day should be the rate for the first day over the forty-eight hours allowed; $1.00 for the second day and $5.00 for each succeeding day. The former charge has been $1.00 for the first day, $2.00 for the second, $3.00 for the third, etc.

"There is no change, "continued Mr. Sargant," in the free time for loading, unloading, etc.

(Continued in next issue).

# Canadian Forestry Association is Growing

## Convention in Toronto Elects Dan McLachlin as President and Robson Black as Manager—Premier Drury Tells What Ontario is Doing in Timber Conservation

The annual convention of the Canadian Forestry Association was held at the King Edward Hotel, Toronto, on January 10th. There was a large and representative attendance and much interest was taken in the proceedings. Several prominent lumbermen were present. C. E. E. Ussher, of Montreal, president of the Association, presided, and one of the important matters was the appointment of secretary Robson Black as manager of the Association.

The new president is Dan McLachlin, of Arnprior, Ont., late president of the Canadian Lumbermen's Association. The other officers elected were,—vice-president, R. H. Campbell, of Ottawa, (chief of the forestry service of Canada); manager and secretary, Robson Black, Ottawa; assistant-secretary, G. Gerald Blyth, Ottawa; treasurer, Miss M. Robinson, Ottawa.

Directors,— (ex-officio), Wm. Little, Thos. Southworth, C. E. E. Ussher, Hon. W. A. Charlton, F. C. Whitman, Lieut.-Col. J. B. Miller, Col. J. S. Dennis. Elected directors: Ontario—Gordon C. Edwards, Clyde Leavitt, R. H. Campbell, Dr. B. E. Fernow, C. J. Booth, E. J. Zavitz, W. C. Cain, Percy B. Wilson, T. W. Dwight, J. A. Gilles, J. W. Black, W. E. Bigwood, Cyril T. Young, Hon. Geo. Gordon, Dr. A. C. Rutherford. Quebec—David Champoux, Alex. McLaurin, Monseignor Roy, G. C. Piche, Sir Wm. Price, Brig.-Gen. J. B. White, Geo. Chahoon, Jr., Ellwood Wilson, R. O. Sweezey, Sir Lomer Gouin. New Brunswick—G. H. Prince, Angus McLean, W. E. Golding. Nova Scotia—Hon. N. C. Curry, F. J. D. Barnjum. British Columbia—Hon. H. Bostock, Hon. A. C. Flumerfelt, R. D. Prettie, P. Z. Caverhill, Chas. D. McNab, H. R. MacMillan. Alberta—Wm. Pearce, G. P. Marnoch, Wm. Brownlee, attorney-general. Saskatchewan—G. H. Auld, Hon. W. R. Motherwell. Manitoba—John W. Dafoe, Ed. Fitzgerald, G. W. Allan, K. C.

### Progress of Forestry in Ontario

The treasurer's report showed an increase of $9,418 over 1920. The income in 1920 was $38,418, while last year it reached $47,836.

The secretary's report showed that the organization has grown in membership from 2,900 in 1914 to 13,000 in 1921. The growth from 1920 to 1921 was 500. Note was also made of the fact that these increases were made while many organizations throughout the United States were reporting financial difficulties and decreased membership.

An admirable address was delivered by Hon. E. C. Drury, Premier of Ontario on what the province is doing and intends to do in the way of conservation and reforestation. He said that Ontario's virgin pine forests were unpleasantly nearing their end and added,—"Fully 350,000,000 feet of pine are cut each year, a hundred million more than is replaced by natural growth. At this rate in 35 years the virgin forests will be finished. The remedy is to grow trees, so as to replace wastage.

"Trees grow and can be replaced like a crop of corn. To administer our forest wealth wisely is not to hold large areas untouched,

but to take stock of our resources and to replace wastage by new growth."

The premier pointed out that the problem of the forest had hitherto not been sufficiently considered. People were just wakening up to the fact.

A proper survey of the forest situation was now being made. In Ontario it would be completed and then would be the time to take such vigorous action as was needed.

Farm woodlands were important, particularly as a source of fuel. The coal resources of Canada were not inexhaustible, and to-day often inferior coal was mined because of the difficulty of getting the best kinds.

Mr. Drury suggested that the association get in touch with the farm organizations, to influence their opinion with regard to farm woodlands.

The premier pointed out the advantages, besides that of fuel, that were derived from farm woodlands.

"Why cannot towns and countries purchase woodland areas or vacant areas and plant trees if necessary?" asked Mr. Drury. This is done in many parts of Europe."

Simcoe county had led the way in this respect. Simcoe bought 1,000 acres of land and next year the department was going to undertake the work of planting this area.

A new forestry station had been started last year in Prince Edward county and other places should do the same thing.

In many districts forest fires had laid waste the land, and it could not reforest itself. In such areas this condition should be taken care of. A scheme to plant several square miles a year in such areas was under consideration.

The matter was not as difficult and costly as had been anticipated. It was estimated that, if 10,000 acres a year were planted, sufficient trees would come on to supply in fifty years fifty million feet a year more than the present annual cut. This would cost annually about $200,000.

It was ridiculous that so many years had been allowed to pass without anything being done.

### Other Features of the Convention

In an interesting paper on "A Canadian Observer in Scandinavia," Mr. Edward Beck, manager Canadian Pulp and Paper Association, Montreal, called attention to the widespread knowledge and understanding among the people of all classes in Scandinavia as to the economic value and the social importance of the great source of natural wealth of the forests.

Mr. Archibald Mitchell, who has charge of the tree-planting campaign in the West, gave an account of his work, and Mr. Arthur H. Richardson of the Ontario Forestry Branch, gave an interesting lantern lecture on the reafforestation of the waste lands of the province.

Dan McLachlin, Arnprior, Ont.
New President, Canadian Forestry Ass'n.

Robson Black, Ottawa, Ont.
Manager and Secretary of the C. F. A.

Hon. E. C. Drury, Premier of Toronto.
Who delivered stirring address on forestry

Edward Beck, Montreal, Que.
Who spoke on forestry conditions abroad

## Mr. Maus Launches New Company

Charles O. Maus, South Bend, Ind.

Chas. O. Maus, who is widely known in the lumber ranks in Montreal, Toronto and throughout Eastern Ontario, has gone into business for himself in South Bend Ind., under the style of The Charles O. Maus Lumber Co. He has had twenty-two years' experience in the lumber line and was in the manufacturing end for four years, during which period he was the travelling buyer and looked after the cuts of three mills for a large Philadelphia concern, now out of business.

From 1903 to 1913 Mr. Maus sold lumber on salary and commission for several reliable concerns, and in the latter year connected up with the Hyde Lumber Co., South Bend Ind., which he successfully represented until the end of 1921, calling upon the buying trade in Ontario, Ohio, Michigan, Pennsylvania and New York states.

Mr. Maus, who is an energetic and optimistic representative of the lumber industry, has made a large number of friends who wish him every success in his new venture.

The Charles O. Maus Lumber Co. will handle the output of several mills in the South who manufacture southern gums, oak, elm, ash, tupelo and cypress. In addition to these woods, the company has made a contract with Edward Clark & Sons, Limited, of Toronto, to handle all their production, principally birch maple and basswood, to the trade in the United States. The headquarters of the Charles O. Maus Lumber Co. will be in South Bend, Ind.

### Expansion of Progressive Eastern Firm

Messrs. Flemming & Gibson, of Juniper, N. B. recently acquired the lands and mills owned by the Michael Welch Estate on the head waters of the Miramichi. The deal takes in the freehold lands of the Welch Estate, twenty one square miles of leased N. B. Crown Lands, together with all the mills, equipment, buildings, logging camps, etc., now owned by the heirs of the late Michael Welch. The late purchase gives Flemming & Gibson, Limited, four sawmills in all, situated on the Upper Miramichi waters, with an annual manufacturing capacity 10,000,000 feet of softwood lumber and about the same quantity of lath.

Flemming & Gibson contemplate additional improvements to their sawmills during the coming summer in order to take care of the increased available raw material.

The deal with the Welch Company was closed by Hon. J. K. Flemming, former premier of New Brunswick and now president and general manager of Flemming & Gibson, Limited, and Mr. Guy Welch, representing the Welch estate.

Flemming & Gibson, Limited, have their yards pretty well cleaned out and are now operating three sawmills all engaged in turning out spruce and fir lumber with most of the product deing shipped to United States markets.

### Has Founded Mission For Lumberjacks

Rev. John Antle, J. P., founder and superintendent of the Columbia Coast Mission, was in Toronto recently and related some of the features of the work in his immense mission district, which embraces upwards of 10,000 square miles of territory.

His mission field, which takes in the north-eastern corner of Vancouver Island and a big portion of the mainland opposite, is practically the centre of the lumber district of British Columbia. When he first visited the district, 17 years ago, he went in a sixteen-foot sailboat, which he himself built in spare moments while conducting the work of Holy Trinity Church in Vancouver. He found there were some 4,000 men working in the logging and mining camps, that they had to go from 50 to 250 miles every time a doctor was needed and that no regular religious services of any kind were being held.

The great necessity for ready medical assistance can be gleaned from the fact that Mr. Antle stated last night that a man is killed practically every day in the lumber camps because the work is so precarious.

"I look upon the lumbering business in British Columbia as the most dangerous calling in Canada. The accidents are more frequent and the injuries more dangerous," he asserted. He said the gigantic size of the trees and the fact that there is now a system by which the huge logs are partly dragged through the forest on high overhead wires added to the hazards of the work.

### Quebec Will Explore More Limits

G. C. Piche, provincial forester for Quebec, addressing a joint meeting of the Canadian Society of Forest Engineers and the Society of American Foresters in Toronto, recently, said that a thorough exploration would be made of the country surrounding the north of the St. Lawrence, the Bay of Ungava and Hudson Bay. These reconaissances will enable the government better to protect the country and also to put rapidly into use various units for pulp and power development.

K. G. Woodward declared that the woodlots, in which is one-sixth of the standing timber of the United States would play an increasing important role in the future because the timber is the more accessible, the most easily protected, and the most easily managed. "Farm leaders," he said, "don't understand the woodlot, and they think of forestry as a low-rate investment for the benefit of their children. Better woodlot management will come as the result of better education.

"Foresters are overlooking an important point in not emphasizing more strongly, the fact that regulation of the cut, whether voluntary or mandatory, is an intergral part of forestry, and is just as essential as protection or silviculture for the continuity of the forest and woodusing industries and other industries dependant on them," was the opinion of Samuel F. Dana, Forest Commissioner of Maine.

Dr. C. D. Howe read a paper sent in by John Sutherland from Scotland, which gave an account of the remarkable success of various species of American and Canadian trees that had, at various times from 1830 on, been planted in Scotland. These included the Douglas fir, Grand fir, Noble fir, Norway spruce, Sitka spruce, white spruce, giant cedar, Western hemlock, white pine and larch.

### Passing of Mr Alfred W. Parkin

Alfred W. Parkin, one of the oldest and most respected residents of Lindsay, Ont., died recently in his eighty-fifth year. He was one of the pioneers in the community and president of the Digby Lumber Co., Limited.

In all his relations in life Mr. Parkin was a man who was fair and honest in his dealings, and in lumber circles with which he was so long associated, was held in high esteem. He had been in poor health for some time past. His wife predeceased him five years ago. A family of three sons and three daughters are left to mourn his departure.

### Lumberman Again Mayor of Sturgeon Falls

Zotique Mageau, who is head of the Mageau Lumber Co., Field, Ont., has been re-elected Mayor of Sturgeon Falls by acclamation. This makes his tenth year of service in the civic chair since 1900.

Mr. Mageau is a member for Sturgeon Falls in the Ontario legislature. He was first elected as a Liberal in 1911 and re-elected at the general elections in 1914 and 1919. He is an active member of the Canadian Lumbermen's Association and has always taken a lively interest in the affairs of that progressive body.

## Mr. Oliver Joins the Silent Majority

Joseph Oliver, president of the Oliver Lumber Co., Toronto, passed away on January 9th after a long illness. He had been ailing for several weeks. Mr. Oliver was a widely known and highly esteemed citizen of Toronto where he had resided practically all his life. Throughout his career he was engaged in forest products pursuits, his first job being in the carpentering line. Many years ago he founded the Oliver Lumber Co., wholesale lumber dealers, and associated with him in the business his two sons, Ormsby and Frank Oliver.

Mr. Oliver devoted a large part of his time to public life and rendered useful, effective service. He was a former Mayor of Toronto, former President of the Commercial Travellers' Mutual Benefit Society, former President and life member of the Canadian National Exhibition Association, and Grand Sire of the Sovereign Grand Lodge of Oddfellows in America which is the highest position that can be attained in the order. Only twice has this distinction been conferred upon a Canadian, and the meeting of the Sovereign Grand Lodge in Toronto last fall was a tribute to the worth and leadership of the late Grand Sire.

The late Joseph Oliver, Toronto

Mr. Oliver was in his 70th year and leaves a widow, two sons and two daughters. He belonged to many other fraternal organizations besides the Oddfellows, and was one of the first public ownership exponents. Mr. Oliver was a Liberal in politics and his candidature was often sought by party supporters.

The funeral, which took place on January 10th, was one of the largest ever seen in Toronto, being under the auspices of the Grand Lodge of Oddfellows. The body lay in state in St. Andrews Presbyterian Church, of which the late Mr. Oliver was a member, and was viewed by hundreds of people. The civic authorities, Knights Templar, Patriarchs Militant and other bodies attended, as well as many lumberman from Toronto and throughout the province.

## Wholesale Lumber Firm Hold Reunion

The annual reunion and dinner of the staff of Terry & Gordon, Limited, Toronto, was held at the King Edward Hotel recently. All the outside members of the organization were present except A. E. Richards, of Vancouver, B. C.

After justice had been done to the many good things provided, H. J. Terry, the president of the company, extended hearty greetings to all present. Short addresses were given by A. E. Gordon, vice-president, who spoke of conditions in the Northern woods; A. E. Cates, secretary-treasurer of the company who furnished an interesting financial statement, and A. S. Nicholson, managing-director, who talked briefly on organization and co-operation. C. E. Harris, transportation manager of the firm, presided at the piano and rendered a number of excellent selections. Among others who spoke were J. E. Green, of Montreal, Eastern Canada manager; and Earle C. Hall, of Philadelphia, New York and Pennsylvania representative. A flashlight photo was taken of the gathering and afterwards an enjoyable dance took place.

Two or three days previous to the annual dinner, the male members of the staff visited Penetang and Midland where the large stocks of white pine, spruce and hemlock bought by the firm, were inspected and found to be in splendid condition.

## Trade Balance Now Runs in Right Direction

The summary of the trade of Canada for November, shows that as represented in dollars, imports for consumption were valued at $641,271,434, as against $98,671,116 in November 1920, and $97,718,270 in November 1919. The imports from the United Kingdom were $9,600,854 as against $14,834,258 in November 1920. Those from the United States show a still greater falling off, being $44,699,509 as against $74,328,841 in November 1920. The total imports for the twelve months ending November 1921, were $825,226,585 as against $1,345,592,300 for the corresponding period of 1920.

The exports of Canadian produce for the month were valued at $86,533,862 compared with $147,508,002 in November 1920. The exports to the United Kingdom again show an increase, being $37,640,148 as against $29,100,524 in November 1920. Exports to the

United States, however, are lower, $30,854,939 as against $63,894,790. The total exports for the twelve months ending November,1921, show a falling off of about 25 per cent, as compared with the similar period of 1920, being 865,256,914,922. The month's returns show a favourable balance of trade of $22,262,428; the returns for the twelve months' period show a favourable balance of $40,453,397.

## Forest Flourished Five Centuries Ago

Actual photographs of the stumps and shattered trunks of a forest that flourished five centuries ago were shown lately with a most interesting lecture in Toronto by Professor Wm. S. Cooper of the University of Minnesota, on "The Interglacial Forests of Glacier Bay, Alaska."

When Captain Vancouver explored this region a century and a half ago the bay was filled almost to its mouth by a single huge glacier. But since then the ice has retreated steadily and the salt water has followed it a distance of 60 miles.

In the course of this retreat the ice has brought to light the remains of a large forest which must have covered the shores of the bay over 500 years ago. But being buried in gravel and silt and then covered by a great sheet of ice the roots and stumps of these trees have been preserved till today, and since the final retreat of the ice the sediments are being steadily washed away, continually uncovering fresh traces of the forest for the study of scientists.

## Fewer Accidents Reported to the Board

There were 45,191 accidents reported to the Ontario Workmen's Compensation Board in 1921, as against 54,851 in 1920, a decrease of 9,660. The fatal accidents decreased from 452 to 386. The daily average was 151 accidents reported in 1921, as against 183 in 1920.

The compensation awarded during 1921 amounted to $5,526,519.60, as against $7,076,439.59 during 1920, a decrease of $1,549,919.99. The high figures for 1920 were partly owing to the retroactive increase in death pensions under the amendments of that year.

The amount paid by the Board for medical aid during 1921 was $662,793.89, as against $703,705,66 in 1920. This made the total benefits awarded during 1921 $6,189,313.49, as against a total of $7,780,145.25 in 1920.

The average daily number of cheques issued by the Board during the year was 485, and the benefits awarded averaged $20,631 per day.

## The Natural Resources of Canada

Attention is now being directed towards the country's natural resources as never before, since it is generally recognized that only by a more widespread utilization of Canada's undeveloped lands, mines, forests, water-powers and fisheries can present day economic problems be solved.

The Natural Resources Intelligence Branch of the Department of the Interior has published a map showing the leading natural resources of each province.

In the Prairie Provinces the prospective settler or investor may obtain adequate returns on capital and labour in either grain growing, mixed farming or ranching, while in British Columbia timbering, fishing, fruit-growing and mining are among the leading industries.

In addition to information on natural resources, the map shows all railways and trade routes. An interesting and valuable feature is a series of comparative diagrams illustrating the production and exports of the various provinces. A copy of the map may be obtained free of charge upon application to the Natural Resources Intelligence Branch, Department of the Interior, Ottawa.

## Alberta Hopes for Wood Pulp Industry

A thorough investigation into the possibilities of a wood pulp industry in Alberta is to be made under the direction of the advisory scientific research council. The matter was dealt with at a meeting of the council, at which it was decided to go on with the work as soon as necessary arrangements can be made.

Great stretches of spruce and poplar timber all over the north country and in the neighborhood of the western foothills will be turned to some profitable account if these enquiries prove as successful as now expected. The opinions of some expert pulp and timber men have already been secured, and their belief in general is that this province has the makings of a big industry that has not yet been touched. Experiments are to be made at the university laboratories in Edmonton to see whether this belief is well founded or not.

D. Aitcheson & Co., retail lumber dealers, Main St. West, Hamilton, are erecting a handsome and commodious new office.

## Lumbermen's Section Holds Annual

W. J. Lovering, Toronto
Re-elected Chairman of Section

At the annual meeting of the Lumbermen's Section of the Toronto Board of Trade, held on January 6th in the office of the Chairman, W. J. Lovering, there was a representative attendance.

This body of lumbermen, which is composed of wholesale and retail dealers, is the parent of the present flourishing organizations in Toronto and throughout the province, including the Lumbermen's Credit Bureaus.

The Lumbermen's Section is naturally proud of its progeny, and although there was not a great deal of work carried out during 1921, it was felt that the usefulness of the section was by no means past. It represents the cohesion and centralization of the lumber interests as a whole, and being affiliated with such a representative and influential body as the Board of Trade, effective work can be done if need be, in legislative traffic and other matters of vital import.

Chairman Lovering gave a short review of conditions during the past year and H. Boultbee, secretary-treasurer, presented a satisfactory financial report. It was suggested that some arrangement might be come to with the Board of Trade Luncheon Club whereby a special table might be reserved each day for the lumbermen members. They would sit at this table and "talk shop" to their hearts' content. Any visiting lumbermen coming to Toronto could also be taken to the Board of Trade and there around the festive board he would meet a large number of those handling forest products pursuit.

A committee consisting of R. G. Chesbro, (chairman), J. B. Jarvis and G. B. Van Blaricom, "Canada Lumberman," was appointed to interview the secretary of the Board of Trade with the object of securing, if possible, the practical working out of the proposition.

The election of officers for the coming year, with one or two exceptions, resulted in the former occupants being returned.

Chairman—W. J. Lovering; vice-chairman, T. A. Paterson; secretary-treasurer, H. Boultbee; executive committee, A. E. Clarke, W. C. Gall, J. B. Jarvis, C. G. Anderson, Sam. McBride.

The following nominations were made:—

Representative to Council of Board of Trade,—Hugh Munro; representative to Board of Arbitration, J. B. Jarvis; representative on Canadian National Exhibition Association, Sam. McBride.

## Getting on the Trail of New Business

"Recently," says a correspondent, "I had the pleasure of calling upon a live, service rendering lumber merchant in an Eastern city—a man who gives timely helps and business-like suggestions to prospective builders. This firm renders valuable help on building problems through its novel window displays, newspapers advertising and attractive service room, and contractors actually endeavor to be friendly in order to get in on a share of the business, which comes to the lumber firm through their publicity and practical building helps.

"How is business?" I asked.

"Pretty fair," the junior member of the firm said, "but we don't expect to be very busy before spring.

"I see your father is making good use of his service department."

"Yes sir," he answered. "Dad has two men working on plans and designs all the time, and can furnish his customers with complete layouts for every kind of home."

"Does your father have much trouble with the contractors and builders?"

"No. He is on good terms with the majority of them."

"I suppose he finds it to his benefit to be on good terms with the builders."

The young man laughed.

"Dad doesn't let the contractors get ahead of him on new business. On the contrary, the builders are glad to call on him and get a line on who's going to build or make extensive repairs."

"But how does your father get a line on the new business before the contractors?"

"I suppose I shouldn't be telling too much of the inside workings of the business, but I'll tell you something about it now."

Pulling open one of the drawers of his father's desk, the youth produced a small leather-bound book.

"This is the firm's money maker," he explained.

"Dad doesn't wait until the notice appears in the paper of prospects intending to build, but goes a little farther and looks for signs that might mean the building of a home. Here's the last entry dated yesterday. I'll read it to you. 'James Worth, retiring farmer, R. R. No. 7, selling farm and stock. His son, Albert, is living in town.' As soon as father sees these little notices in the newspaper he jots them down and sends literature and bright illustrations accompanied with a series of home plans," explained the young lumberman. "More than likely this old couple, of whom I just quoted from the book, are fairly well fixed and are looking for a comfortable home near their son. Whoever offers them service stands the best chance of getting the business, if they decide to build."

"Your father merely sells the materials, he doesn't do any building?"

"No. He doesn't do any big building, but he sells the materials direct to the consumer and has no trouble about commissions, because he digs up the business and the contracters are only too glad to make friendly calls and be put on the trail, after father has supplied the customer direct with the plans and made arrangements to supply the materials."

At this moment the father entered the office, having finished with the customers and I had a long talk with the progressive retailer. He told me more about his plans of getting after business and how it paid him to get out among the people and take an interest in public affairs. It certainly made me feel good to run into a bright spot like this town proved to be.

## Ontario Retail Lumbermen at Ottawa

The fifth annual convention of the Ontario Retail Lumber Dealers' Association will be held at the Chateau Laurier, Ottawa, on January 18th and 19th. It is expected that there will be a very large and representative attendance from all parts of the province. An outline of the proceedings appeared in the last edition of the "Canada Lumberman," and a full report of the gathering will be published in the February 1st issue.

Among those who will address the assembly are F. H. Lamar, of Vancouver, secretary of the Shingle Association of British Columbia, who will present some facts showing conclusively that the B. C. red cedar shingle is not the fire menace which certain exponents of anti-shingle legislation would lead the public to believe. Mr. Lamar was formerly secretary of the Western Retail Lumbermen's Association of Winnipeg, which will hold its annual convention in that city on January 25th to 27th.

## Busy Lumbering Operations in Haliburton

The John Carew Lumber Co., Limited, of Lindsay, Ont., say that lumbering in the Haliburton District is about the same as elsewhere. Very little lumber is being sold just now although the retail yards have practically nothing in stock.

The John Carew Co. have one camp of 50 men and two camps of 35 each, beside five or six jobbers. Last season they had to leave the whole output of one camp in the bush owing to there not being enough snow, and it was only recently that they got at the hauling. At the present time they have twelve teams at work, and it will take some three weeks to land this cut.

Owing to the favorable weather conditions at the present time, the company are operating in the bush very extensively and will take out a bigger stock than they will require for next season.

The company consider the outlook for 1922 to be very favorable as there has been little buying done for a year now. The retail yards that used to carry a fair stock, are practically working from hand to mouth.

W. W. Hill, 15 Nickle Ave., Mount Dennis, Ont., is erecting a small woodworking shop. He proposes to manufacture a patent combination child's crib and store and office fixtures. For the present he has put in a combination Elliott woodworker, and in the near future proposes adding a band saw, shaper and planer.

James W. Elliott, president of the Elliott Lumber Co., New Toronto, passed away recently. The late Mr. Elliott was well known in the industry, and the funeral, which took place on December 26th, was largely attended. The remains were taken to Port Elgin, Ont., for interment.

S. P. W. Cooke, has rejoined the sales staff of Mason, Gordon & Company, Montreal. He will cover the Ontario territory, with headquarters in Toronto.

W. Norman Fox of Toronto, has taken a position as accountant in the offices of Edward Clark & Sons, wholesale lumber dealers, Toronto, succeeding Wm. A. Walker, who recently resigned.

E. M. Ball, wholesale lumberman has removed to 605 McGill Building, McGill Street, Montreal.

# Eastern Forest Engineers Convene in Quebec

### First Convention Held Recently Takes Progressive Steps—Live Officers Elected and Enterprising Program Mapped Out—Efficiency of Aeroplane Service

The first convention of the Association of Forest Engineers of the Province of Quebec, composing a membership of eighty forest engineers, was convened recently in Quebec City. This association of Quebec forest enginers was organized in the early part of 1920 with the Hon. Mr. Mercier, Minister of Lands and Forests, to co-operate with the department on all matters connected with the protection and technical work in relation to Quebec forest lauds, the interest of limit holders, etc., in cutting logs and lumber in general in the province.

At the inception and organization of the association last year, an Advisory Board was elected to draft and submit by-laws for approval at the first annual convention just closed.

The election of officers took place with the following result:- President, Mr. Omer Loussier, of Quebec; vice-president, Mr. Decarteret, of The Brown Corporation; secretary-treasurer, V. Ballarge, of Department of Lands and Forests. Council:- G. C. Piche, Chief Superintendent of Provincial Forestry, Ellwood Wilson, Laurentide Co.; Henry Sorguis, St. Maurice Forest Protective Association; B Guerin, Southerin, St. Lawrence Protective Association, and G. Maheux, Provincial Entomologist.

The by-laws drafted were submitted, and approved, and a technical outline of policy for inventory and working plan of forests was submitted by the Advisory Board, and discussed between forestry experts of the Department, and the forest engineers connected with Quebec lumber interests regarding forest subjects, which were finally approved and ordered sent to the Committee on Standardization for consideration, with the understanding that the conclusions of this committee would be printed and copies of same mailed to the engineers of all Quebec lumber firms.

Mr. Piche was asked by Mr. Ellwood Wilson, of the Laurentide Co., if it was the intention of the Department to bring in legislation in connection with the suggestions discussed and sent to the Committee on Standardization. The chief Entomologist, of the Department of Lands and Forests, replied that it was the wish of the Department to co-operate and assist the Association and work in harmony with ideals for the advancement of the forest interests.

In reply to another question, Mr. Piche said after May 1st, the time alloted by the Order-in-Council in September last, giving privileges in cutting logs this winter, that the law which prevailed prior to September last, in regard to logging and stumpage dues, would again govern forest operations.

### Aeropalne Service Described

Mr. G. C. Piche referred to the Forestry Convention at Toronto, saying that Mr. Ellwood Wilson read a paper at the convention regarding his company's experience with an aeroplane service for forest surveying and air photography, and he requested Mr. Wilson to favor the meeting with a talk on the essentials of his paper.

Mr. Wilson complied in a short talk and in reference to the value of the aeroplane for survey work in the forests, said the method was was a decided advancement over previous ones. He delated on the forest engineer to get results, in estimates and information as to, areas and their assets in timber stands. Mr. Wilson pointed out that, after three years' experience with aeroplanes in forestry work, he would say they were decidedly useful for vertical work in connection with forestry.

Speaking of the values of photography taken in the air, Mr. Wilson asserted that they were far superior to maps and plans, and so perfect in an educational sense that, when photographs of lumber property and lakes were shown to the management of lumber firms, they could realize the location and extent of the areas. He also said that the trees could even be distinguished to such an extent, so as one could name the various species. Another thing he referred to in order to show the value of photography taken in the air, was in the purchase of a lot or even of limits which enabled the forest engineer to know the value of the properties and advise his firm whether to buy or not.

In answer to a question Mr. Wilson said aeroplanes could be operated in winter as well as in summer, but owing to the white ground caused by the snow the photographs were not so accurate, and futhermore the green leaves on the trees and the various shades were a great help in summer to the perfection of the photographs.

P. Z. Caverhill, chief forester of the Department of Lands, British Columbia, who was in attendance at the convention, was introduced by Supt. Price. He said British Columbia had its wealth of forest resources like Quebec, but difference in growth and in specimens of trees. He had, however, attended the convention of Quebec forest engineers to gain information. The speaker took a deep inteest in the remarks made by Mr. Wilson in support of the aeroplane for forest survey and photography in the air, and would say that British Columbia had the same results from aeroplane experiments, Mr. Caverhill referred to an occasion of a big windstorm which swept over the British Columbia province, and the destruction of 300,000,000 feet of timber, and how the aeroplane with the photographic expert had been sent into the air and gave an almost exact report of the area destroyed.

### Getting Accurate Estimate of Timber

Mr. Nesbitt, forest engineer in the employ of Price Bros., Limited, gave a short talk on the aeroplane service for his company. He told of the work he is now carrying on for his company in connection with their vast timber limits and the use of aeroplanes, three in number. He submitted a number of photographs taken in the air in demonstration of the efficiency of forest engineering with the aid of the aeroplane, which was enabling Price Bros., to obtain an accurate estimate of their limit holdings, their values, and the various specimen of trees.

Alphonse Landry, in charge of the government airdrome at Roberval, in the Lake St. John district, also spoke of the efficiency of the aeroplane in the interest of forest engineering, now being utilized by the Quebec Lands and Forest Department, for the survey of virgin forest Crown Lands in the Lake St. John district and the northern timberland of the province. He exhibited photographs taken in the air to demonstrate the values of photography from the aeroplane in forest survey work.

Mr. Wilson requested to know if the Quebec government was suggesting the adoption of the cubic foot instead of the board measure foot for all future lumber operations.

Mr. Piche, superintendent of forestry for the Lands and Forests Department, replied that that cubic foot measurement was only being suggested for adoption in connection with forest engineer technical work, and would in no way interfere with lumber firms' operations.

The committee on resolutions referred the suggestions adopted at the convention in regard to technical work in connection with forest engineering, to the Standardization Committee, which will meet at the end of next February or beginning of March.

### The Demand for Christmas Trees Grows

During the past holiday season, Harold D. Joyce of Montreal, who is well known to the lumber trade, was instrumental in having shipped to the Montreal market a large number of Christmas trees. The past two years there has been a much greater sale for these trees in Canadian cities than ever before, which fact is probably accounted for by the post-war celebrating along with the increased population of the bigger centres. The business however, as a commercial enterprise, so far as Montreal is concerned, has not been gone into to any large extent. Practically the only competition in furnishing these trees is the near-by farmer, whose object it is, in many cases, to clear pasture land and make a few dollars, rather than to supply a good tree. On the other hand Christmas trees are shipped from within fifty miles of Montreal to as far distant cities as New York and even Philadelphia, which is on a .49 rate of freight.

This Christmas tree Trade calls for a uniformly round balsam, 6 ft. 8 ft. 10 ft. or 12 ft. in height, bundled together. A 36 ft. flat car, on which they are usually shipped will carry 1,000 to 1,200 trees. Mr. Joyce says that this business if properly handled, can be run on a profitable cash basis. It is estimated that in Montreal alone during the past holiday season, 35,000 to 40,000 trees were sold.

# CURRENT LUMBER PRICES — WHOLESALE

## TORONTO

(In Car Load Lots, F.O.B. cars Toronto)

**White Pine**

| | | |
|---|---|---|
| 1 x 4/7 Good Strips | $110.00 | $115.00 |
| 1¼ & 1½ x 4/7 Good Strips | 120.00 | 125.00 |
| 1 x 8 and up Good Sides | 150.00 | 160.00 |
| 2 x 4/7 Good Strips | 130.00 | 140.00 |
| 1¼ & 1½ x 8 and wider Good Sides | 185.00 | 190.00 |
| 2 x 8 and wider Good Sides | 190.00 | 200.00 |
| 1 in. No. 1, 2 and 3 Cuts | 85.00 | 90.00 |
| 5/4 and 6/4 No. 1, 2 and 3 Cuts | 100.00 | 105.00 |
| 2 in. No. 1, 2 and 3 Cuts | 105.00 | 110.00 |
| 1 x 4 and 5 Mill Run | 52.00 | 55.00 |
| 1 x 6 Mill Run | 53.00 | 56.00 |
| 1 x 7, 9 and 11 Mill Run | 53.00 | 56.00 |
| 1 x 8 Mill Run | 55.00 | 58.00 |
| 1 x 10 Mill Run | 60.00 | 62.00 |
| 1 x 12 Mill Run | 62.00 | 63.00 |
| 5/4 and 6/4 x 5 and up Mill Run | 58.00 | 60.00 |
| 2 x 4 Mill Run | 52.00 | 53.00 |
| 2 x 6 Mill Run | 53.00 | 56.00 |
| 2 x 8 Mill Run | 55.00 | 58.00 |
| 2 x 10 Mill Run | 58.00 | 62.00 |
| 2 x 12 Mill Run | 60.00 | 64.00 |
| 1 in. Mill Run Shorts | 43.00 | 45.00 |
| 1 x 4 and up 6/16 No. 1 Mill Culls | 30.00 | 32.00 |
| 1 x 10 and up 6/16 No. 1 Mill Culls | 34.00 | 36.00 |
| 1 x 12 and up 6/16 No. 1 Mill Culls | 35.00 | 37.00 |
| 1 x 4 and up 6/16 No. 2 Mill Culls | 23.00 | 25.00 |
| 1 x 10 x 12 6/16 No. 2 Mill Culls | 26.00 | 30.00 |
| 1 x 4 and up 6/16 No. 3 Mill Culls | 15.00 | 20.00 |

**Red Pine**

(In Car Load Lots, F.O.B. Toronto)

| | | |
|---|---|---|
| 1 x 4 and 5 Mill Run | $42.00 | $44.00 |
| 1 x 6 Mill Run | 43.00 | 45.00 |
| 1 x 8 Mill Run | 45.00 | 47.00 |
| 1 x 10 Mill Run | 48.00 | 50.00 |
| 2 x 4 Mill Run | 42.00 | 44.00 |
| 2 x 6 Mill Run | 43.00 | 45.00 |
| 2 x 8 Mill Run | 43.00 | 45.00 |
| 2 x 10 Mill Run | 46.00 | 48.00 |
| 2 x 12 Mill Run | 48.00 | 50.00 |
| 1 in. Clear and Clear Face | 70.00 | 72.00 |
| 2 in Clear and Clear Face | 70.00 | 72.00 |

**Spruce**

| | | |
|---|---|---|
| 1 x 4 Mill Run | 37.00 | 39.00 |
| 1 x 6 Mill Run | 39.00 | 41.00 |
| 1 x 8 Mill Run | 41.00 | 43.00 |
| 1 x 10 Mill Run | 46.00 | 48.00 |
| 1 x 12 Mill Run Spruce | 50.00 | 52.00 |
| Mill Culls | 28.00 | 30.00 |

**Hemlock (M R)**

(In Car Load Lots, F.O.B. Toronto)

| | | |
|---|---|---|
| 1 x 4 and 5 in. x 9 to 16 ft | $29.00 | $30.00 |
| 1 x 6 in. x 9 to 16 ft | 33.00 | 35.00 |
| 1 x 8 in. x 9 to 16 ft | 34.00 | 36.00 |
| 1 x 10 and 12 in. x 9 to 16 ft | 35.00 | 37.00 |
| 1 x 7, 9 and 11 in. x 9 to 16 ft | 33.00 | 34.00 |
| 2 x 4 to 12 in., 10 to 16 ft | 34.00 | 35.00 |
| 2 x 4 to 12 in., 18 ft | 37.00 | 39.00 |
| 2 x 4 to 12 in., 20 ft | 40.00 | 42.00 |
| 1 in. No. 2, 6 ft. to 16 ft | 26.00 | 28.00 |

**Fir Flooring**

(In Car Load Lots, F.O.B. Toronto)

| | | |
|---|---|---|
| Fir flooring, 1 x 3 and 4", No. 1 and 2 Edge Grain | | $73.00 |
| Fir flooring, 1 x 3 and 4", No. 1 and 2 Flat Grain | | 48.00 |

(Depending upon Widths)

| | | |
|---|---|---|
| 1 x 4 to 12 No. 1 and 2 Clear Fir, Rough | $69.00 | 77.00 |
| 1¼ x 4 to 12 No. 1 and 2 Clear Fir, Rough | 77.00 | 81.00 |
| 2 x 4 to 12 No. 1 and 2 Clear Fir, Rough | 70.00 | 77.00 |
| 3 & 4 x 4 to 12 No. 1 & 2 Clear Fir, Rough | | 84.00 |
| 1 x 5 and 6 Fir Casing | | 73.00 |
| 1 x 8 and 10 Fir Base | | 77.00 |
| 1¼ and 1½ 8, 10 and 12" E.G. Stepping | | 90.00 |
| 1¼ and 1½, 8, 10 and 12 " F.G. Stepping | | 80.00 |
| 1 x 4 to 12 Clear Fir, D4S | | 70.00 |
| 1¼ and 1½ x 4 to 12, Clear Fir, D4S | | 72.00 |
| XX Shingles, 6 butts to 2", per M | | 3.00 |
| XXX Shingles, 6 butts to 2", per M | | 4.90 |
| XXXXX Shingles, 5 butts to 2", per M | | 5.40 |

**Lath**

(F.O.B. Mill)

| | |
|---|---|
| No. 1 White Pine | $11.00 |
| No. 2 White Pine | 10.00 |
| No. 3 White Pine | 8.00 |
| Mill Run White Pine, 32 in | 5.00 |
| Merchantable Spruce Lath, 4 ft | 7.00 |

## TORONTO HARDWOOD PRICES

The prices given below are for car loads f.o.b. Toronto, from wholesalers to retailers, and are based on a good percentage of long lengths and good widths, without any wide stock having been sorted out.

The prices quoted on imported woods include American exchange.

**Ash, White**

(Dry weight 3800 lbs. per M. ft.)

| | 1s & 2s | No. 1 Com. | No. 2 Com. |
|---|---|---|---|
| 1" | $110.00 | $ 60.00 | $ 45.00 |
| 1¼ and 1½" | 115.00 | 65.00 | 50.00 |
| 2" | 120.00 | 70.00 | 50.00 |
| 2½ and 3" | 135.00 | 95.00 | 60.00 |
| 4" | 145.00 | 105.00 | 65.00 |

**Ash, Brown**

| | | | |
|---|---|---|---|
| 1" | $110.00 | $ 55.00 | $ 40.00 |
| 1¼ and 1½" | 120.00 | 65.00 | 45.00 |
| 2" | 130.00 | 70.00 | 55.00 |
| 2½ and 3" | 145.00 | 80.00 | 65.00 |
| 4" | 165.00 | 95.00 | 75.00 |

**Birch**

(Dry weight 4000 lbs. per M. ft.)

| | 1s & 2s | No. 1 Com. | No. 2 Com. |
|---|---|---|---|
| 4/4 | $ 90.00 | $ 55.00 | $ 30.00 |
| 5/ and 6/4 | 90.00 | 55.00 | 30.00 |
| 8/4 | 100.00 | 65.00 | 40.00 |
| 10/4 and 12/4 | 105.00 | 70.00 | 50.00 |
| 16/4 | 110.00 | 80.00 | 50.00 |

**Basswood**

(Dry weight 2500 lbs. per M. ft.)

| | 1s & 2s | No. 1 Com. | No. 2 Com. |
|---|---|---|---|
| 4/4 | $ 85.00 | 55.00 | 30.00 |
| 5/4 and 6/4 | 90.00 | 65.00 | 35.00 |
| 8/4 | 95.00 | 70.00 | 40.00 |

**Chestnut**

(Dry weight 2800 lbs. per M. ft.)

| | 1s & 2s | No. 1 Com. | Sound Wormy |
|---|---|---|---|
| 1" | $130.00 | $ 80.00 | $ 40.00 |
| 1¼" to 1½" | 135.00 | 85.00 | 43.00 |
| 2" | 145.00 | 90.00 | 43.00 |

**Maple, Hard**

(Dry weight 4200 lbs. per M. ft.)

| | 1s & 2s | No. 1 Com. | No. 2 Com. |
|---|---|---|---|
| 4/4 | $ 80.00 | $ 55.00 | $ 25.00 |
| 5/4 and 6/4 | 85.00 | 55.00 | 30.00 |
| 8/4 | 90.00 | 60.00 | 35.00 |
| 12/4 | 95.00 | 70.00 | 40.00 |
| 16/4 | 105.00 | 85.00 | 40.00 |

**Elm, Soft**

(Dry weight 3100 lbs. per M. ft.)

| | 1s & 2s | No. 1 Com. | No. 2 Com. |
|---|---|---|---|
| 4/4 | $ 85.00 | $ 55.00 | $ 30.00 |
| 6/4 and 8/4 | 90.00 | 65.00 | 35.00 |
| 12/4 | 95.00 | 70.00 | 40.00 |

**Gum, Red**

(Dry weight 3300 lbs. per M. ft.)

| | Plain 1s & 2s | Plain No. 1 Com. | Quartered 1s & 2s | Quartered No. 1 Com. |
|---|---|---|---|---|
| 1" | $125.00 | $ 73.00 | $133.00 | $ 83.00 |
| 1¼" | 135.00 | 75.00 | 148.00 | 88.00 |
| 1½" | 135.00 | 75.00 | 148.00 | 88.00 |
| 2" | 145.00 | 95.00 | 158.00 | 103.00 |

Figured Gum, $10 per M. extra, in both plain and quartered.

**Gum, Sap**

| | 1s&2s | No. 1 Com. |
|---|---|---|
| 1" | $ 60.00 | $ 43.00 |
| 1¼" and 1½" | 65.00 | 48.00 |
| 2" | 70.00 | 55.00 |

**Hickory**

(Dry weight 4500 lbs. per M. ft.

| | 1s&2s | No. 1 Com. |
|---|---|---|
| 1" | $130.00 | $ 65.00 |
| 1¼" | 155.00 | 70.00 |
| 1½" | 155.00 | 70.00 |
| 2" | 160.00 | 75.00 |

**Plain White and Red Oak**

(Plain sawed. Dry weight 4000 lbs. per M. ft.)

| | 1s&2s | No. 1 Com. |
|---|---|---|
| 4/4 | $130.00 | $ 75.00 |
| 5/4 and 6/4 | 135.00 | 80.00 |
| 8/4 | 140.00 | 85.00 |
| 10/4 | 150.00 | 90.00 |
| 12/4 | 150.00 | 90.00 |
| 16/4 | 155.00 | 95.00 |

**White Oak, Quarter Cut**

(Dry weight 4000 lbs. per M. ft.)

| | 1s&2s | No. 1 Com. |
|---|---|---|
| 4/4 | $160.00 | $ 95.00 |
| 5/4 and 6/4 | 170.00 | 105.00 |
| 8/4 | 190.00 | 115.00 |

**Quarter Cut Red Oak**

| | 1s&2s | No. 1 Com. |
|---|---|---|
| 4/4 | $145.00 | $ 80.00 |
| 5/4 and 6/4 | 160.00 | 90.00 |
| 8/4 | 165.00 | 95.00 |

**Beech**

The quantity of beech produced in Ontario is not large and is generally sold on a log run basis, the locality governing the prices. At present the prevailing quotation on log run, mill culls out, delivered in Toronto, is $35.00 to $40.00.

## OTTAWA

Manufacturers' Prices

**Pine**

| | | |
|---|---|---|
| Good sidings: | | |
| 1 in. x 7 in. and up | | $140.00 |
| 1¼ in. and 1½ in., 8 in. and up. | | 165.00 |
| 2 in. x 7 in. and up | | 165.00 |
| No. 2 cuts 2 x 8 in. and up | | 80.00 |
| Good strips: | | |
| 1 in. | $100.00 | $105.00 |
| 1¼ in. and 1½ in. | | 120.00 |
| 2 in. | | 125.00 |
| Good shorts: | | |
| 1 in. x 7 in and up | | 110.00 |
| 1 in. 4 in. to 6 in. | 85.00 | 90.00 |
| 1¼ in. and 1½ in. | | 110.00 |
| 2 in. | | 125.00 |
| 7 in. to 9 in. A sidings | 54.00 | 56.00 |
| No. 1 dressing sidings | 82.00 | 85.00 |
| No. 1 dressing strips | | 78.00 |
| No. 1 dressing shorts | 68.00 | 73.00 |
| 1 in. x 4 in. s.c. strips | 56.00 | 58.00 |
| 1 in. x 5 in. s.c. strips | 56.00 | 58.00 |
| 1 in. x 6 in. s.c. strips | 63.00 | 65.00 |
| 1 in. x 7 in. s.c. strips | 63.00 | 64.00 |
| 1 in. x 8 in. s.c. strips, 12 to 16 ft. | 63.00 | 66.00 |
| 1 in. x 10 in. M.R. | 65.00 | 70.00 |
| S.C. sidings, 1½ and 2 in. | 63.00 | 67.00 |
| S.C. strips, 1 in. | | 64.00 |
| 1¼, 1½ and 2 in. | 57.00 | 58.00 |
| S.C. shorts, 1 x 4 to 6 in. | 48.00 | 50.00 |
| S.C. and bet., shorts. 1 x 5 | | 48.00 |
| S.C. and bet., shorts, 1 x 6 | | 50.00 |
| S.C. Shorts, 6'-11', 1" x 10" | 52.00 | 54.00 |
| Box boards: | | |
| 1 in. x 4 in. and up, 6 ft.-11 ft. | | 45.00 |
| 1 in. x 3 in. and up, 12 ft.-16 ft. | 50.00 | 53.00 |
| Mill culls, strips and sidings, 1 in. x 4 in. and up, 12 ft. and up | 43.00 | 45.00 |
| Mill cull shorts, 1 in. x 4 in. and up, 6 ft. to 11 ft. | 34.00 | 36.00 |
| O. culls r and w p | 24.00 | 28.00 |

**Red Pine, Log Run**

| | | |
|---|---|---|
| Mill culls out, 1 in. | 34.00 | 48.00 |
| Mill culls out, 1¼ in. | 34.00 | 48.00 |
| Mill culls out, 1½ in. | 35.00 | 47.00 |
| Mill culls out, 2 in. | 35.00 | 47.00 |
| Mill Culls, white pine, 1 in. x 7 in. and up | | 35.00 |

**Mill Run Spruce**

| | | |
|---|---|---|
| 1 in. x 4 in. and up, 6 ft.-11 ft. | | 25.00 |
| 1 in. x 4 in. and up, 12 ft.-16 ft. | 32.00 | 34.00 |
| 1" x 9"-10" and up, 12 ft.-16 ft. | 38.00 | 40.00 |
| 1¼" x 7, 8 and 9" up, 12 ft.-16 ft. | | 35.00 |
| 1¼ x 10 and up, 12 ft.-16 ft. | 38.00 | 42.00 |
| 1½" x 12" x 12" and up, 12'-16' | | 42.00 |
| Spruce, 1 in. clear fine dressing and B | | 55.00 |
| Hemlock, 1 in. cull | | 20.00 |
| Hemlock, 1 in. log run | 24.00 | 26.00 |
| Hemlock, 2 x 4, 6, 8, 10 12/16 ft. | | 28.00 |
| Tamarac | 25.00 | 28.00 |
| Basswood, log run, dead culls out | 45.00 | 50.00 |
| Basswood, log run, mill culls out. | 50.00 | 54.00 |
| Birch, log run | 45.00 | 50.00 |
| Soft Elm, common and better, 1, 1½, 2 in. | 58.00 | 68.00 |
| Ash, black, log run | 62.00 | 65.00 |
| 1 x 10 No. 1 barn | 57.00 | 62.00 |
| 1 x 10 No. 2 barn | 51.00 | 56.00 |
| 1 x 8 and 9 No. 2 barn | 47.00 | 52.00 |

# CURRENT LUMBER PRICES—WHOLESALE

**Lath per M.:**

| | | |
|---|---|---|
| No. 1 White Pine, 1¼ in. x 4 ft. | | 8.00 |
| No. 2 White Pine | | 6.00 |
| Mill run White Pine | | 7.00 |
| Spruce, mill run, 1½ in. | | 6.00 |
| Red Pine, mill run | | 6.00 |
| Hemlock, mill run | | 5.50 |
| **White Cedar Shingles** | | |
| XXXX, 18 in. | 9.00 | 10.00 |
| Clear butt, 18 in. | 6.00 | 7.00 |
| 18 in. XX | | 5.00 |

## QUEBEC

**White Pine**
(At Quebec)

| | Cts. Per Cubic Ft. | |
|---|---|---|
| First class Ottawa wancy, 18 in. average according to lineal | 100 | 110 |
| 19 in. and up average | 110 | 120 |

**Spruce Deals**
(At Mill)

| | | |
|---|---|---|
| 3 in. unsorted, Quebec, 4 in. to 6 in. wide | $ 20.00 | $ 25.00 |
| 3 in. unsorted, Quebec, 7 in. to 8 in. wide | 26.00 | 28.00 |
| 3 in. unsorted, Quebec, 9 in. wide | 30.00 | 35.00 |

**Oak**
(At Quebec)

| | Cts. Per Cubic Ft. | |
|---|---|---|
| According to average and quality, 55 ft. cube | 125 | 130 |

**Elm**
(At Quebec)

| | | |
|---|---|---|
| According to average and quality, 40 to 45 ft. cube | 100 | 120 |
| According to average and quality, 30 to 35 ft. | 90 | 100 |

**Export Birch Planks**
(At Mill)

| | | |
|---|---|---|
| 1 to 4 in. thick, per M. ft. | $ 30.00 | $ 35.00 |

## ST. JOHN, N.B.

(From Yards and Mills)

**Rough Lumber**

Retail Prices per M. Sq. Ft.

| | | |
|---|---|---|
| 2x3, 2x4, 3x3, 3x4, Rgh Merch Spr | $32.00 | |
| 2x3, 2x4, 3x3, 3x4, Dressed 1 edge | 33.00 | |
| 2x3, 2x4, 3x3, 3x4, Dressed 4 sides | 33.00 | |
| 2x6, 2x7, 3x5, 4x4, 4x6, all rough | 34.00 | |
| 2x8, 3x7, 5x5, 6x6 | 37.00 | $ 40.00 |
| 2x9, 3x8, 6x8, 7x7 | 37.00 | 40.00 |
| 2x10, 3x9 | 45.00 | |
| 2x12, 3x10, 3x12, 8x8 and up | 45.00 | |
| Merch. Spr. Bds., Rough, 1x3-4 & 5 | 30.00 | |
| Merch. Spr. Bds., Rough, 1x6 | 34.00 | |
| Merch. Spr. Bds., Rough, 1x7 & up | 40.00 | |
| Refuse Bds., Deals & Setgs. | 20.00 | 23.00 |

Above random lengths up to 18-0 long.
Lengths 19-0 and up $5.00 extra per M.
For planing Merch. and Refuse Bds. add $2.00 per M. to above prices.
Laths, $7.00.

**Shingles**

| | Per M. |
|---|---|
| Cedar, Extras | $6.25 |
| " Clears | 5.50 |
| " 2nd Clears | 4.50 |
| " Extra No. 1 | 2.90 |
| Spruce | 4.50 |

## SARNIA, ONT.

**Pine, Common and Better**

| | |
|---|---|
| 1 x 6 and 8 in. | $105.00 |
| 1 in., 8 in. and up wide | 125.00 |
| 1¼ and 1½ in. and up wide | 175.00 |
| 2 in. and up wide | 175.00 |
| **Cuts and Better** | |
| 4/4 x 8 and up No. 1 and better | 120.00 |
| 5/4 and 6/4 and up No. 1 and better | 145.00 |
| 8/4 and 8 and up No. 1 and better | 145.00 |
| **No. 1 Cuts** | |
| 1 in., 8 in. and up wide | 110.00 |
| 1¼ in., 8 in. and up wide | 120.00 |
| 1½ in., 8 in. and up wide | 120.00 |
| 2 in., 8 in. and up wide | 125.00 |
| 2½ in. and 3 in., 8 in. and up wide | 170.00 |
| 4 in., 8 in. and up wide | 180.00 |

**No. 1 Barn**

| | | |
|---|---|---|
| 1 in., 10 to 16 ft. long | $ 70.00 | $ 85.00 |
| 1¼, 1½ and 2 in., 10/16 ft. | 75.00 | 90.00 |
| 2½ to 3 in., 10/16 ft. | 80.00 | 95.00 |
| **No. 2 Barn** | | |
| 1 in., 10 to 16 ft. long | 68.00 | 77.00 |
| 1¼, 1½ and 2 in., 10/16 ft. | 68.00 | 80.00 |
| 2½, 1½ and 3 in. | 78.00 | 90.00 |
| **No. 3 Barn** | | |
| 1 in., 10 to 16 ft. long | 55.00 | 62.00 |
| 1¼, 1½ and 2 in., 10/16 ft. | 59.00 | 63.00 |
| **Box** | | |
| 1 in., 1¼ and 1½ in., 10/16 ft. | 40.00 | 42.00 |
| **Mill Culls** | | |
| Mill Run Culls— | | |
| 1 in., 4 in. and up wide, 6/16 ft. | | 30.00 |
| 1¼, 1½ and 2 in. | | 31.00 |

## WINNIPEG

**No. 1 Spruce**

| Dimension | S.1.S. and 1.E. 10 ft. | 12 ft. | 14 ft. | 16 ft. |
|---|---|---|---|---|
| 2 x 4 | $30 | $29 | $29 | $30 |
| 2 x 6 | 31 | 29 | 29 | 30 |
| 2 x 8 | 32 | 30 | 30 | 31 |
| 2 x 10 | 33 | 31 | 31 | 32 |
| 2 x 12 | 34 | 32 | 32 | 33 |

For 2 inches, rough, add 50 cents.
For S1E only, add 50 cents.
For S1S and 2E, S4S or D&M, add $3.00.
For timbers larger than 8 x 8, add 50c. for each additional 2 inches each way.
For lengths longer than 20 ft., add $1.00 for each additional two feet.
For selected common, add $5.00.
For No. 2 Dimension, $3.00 less than No. 1.
For 1 x 2 and 2 x 2, $2 more than 2 x 4 No. 1.
For Tamarac, open.

## BUFFALO and TONAWANDA

**White Pine**
Wholesale Selling Price

| | |
|---|---|
| Uppers, 4/4 | $225.00 |
| Uppers, 5/4 to 8/4 | 225.00 |
| Uppers, 10/4 to 12/4 | 250.00 |
| Selects, 4/4 | 200.00 |
| Selects, 5/4 to 8/4 | 200.00 |
| Selects, 10/4 to 12/4 | 225.00 |
| Fine Common, 4/4 | 155.00 |
| Fine Common, 5/4 | 160.00 |
| Fine Common, 6/4 | 160.00 |
| Fine Common, 8/4 | 160.00 |
| No. 1 Cuts, 4/4 | 115.00 |
| No. 1 Cuts, 5/4 | 130.00 |
| No. 1 Cuts, 6/4 | 130.00 |
| No. 1 Cuts, 8/4 | 140.00 |
| No. 2 Cuts, 4/4 | 70.00 |
| No. 2 Cuts, 5/4 | 100.00 |
| No. 2 Cuts, 6/4 | 105.00 |
| No. 2 Cuts, 8/4 | 110.00 |
| No. 3 Cuts, 5/4 | 60.00 |
| No. 3 Cuts, 6/4 | 65.00 |
| No. 3 Cuts, 8/4 | 67.00 |
| Dressing, 4/4 | 95.00 |
| Dressing 4/4 x 10 | 98.00 |
| Dressing, 4/4 x 12 | 110.00 |
| No. 1 Moulding, 5/4 | 150.00 |
| No. 1 Moulding, 6/4 | 150.00 |
| No. 1 Moulding, 8/4 | 155.00 |
| No. 2 Moulding, 5/4 | 125.00 |
| No. 2 Moulding, 6/4 | 125.00 |
| No. 2 Moulding, 8/4 | 130.00 |
| No. 1 Barn, 1 x 12 | 90.00 |
| No. 1 Barn, 1 x 6 and 8 | 76.00 |
| No. 1 Barn, 1 x 10 | 80.00 |
| No. 2 Barn, 1 x 6 and 8 | 62.00 |
| No. 2 Barn, 1 x 10 | 63.00 |
| No. 2 Barn, 1 x 12 | 75.00 |
| No. 3 Barn, 1 x 6 and 8 | 42.00 |
| No. 3 Barn, 1 x 10 | 44.00 |
| No. 3 Barn, 1 x 12 | 47.00 |
| Box, 1 x 6 and 8 | 36.00 |
| Box, 1 x 10 | 38.00 |
| Box, 1 x 12 | 39.00 |
| Box, 1 x 13 and up | 40.00 |

## BUFFALO

The following quotations on hardwoods represent the jobber buying price at Buffalo and Tonawanda.

**Maple**

| | 1s & 2s | No. 1 Com. | No. 2 Com. |
|---|---|---|---|
| 1 in. | $ 80.00 | $ 45.00 | $ 30.00 |
| 5/4 to 8/4 | 85.00 | 50.00 | 30.00 |
| 10/4 to 4 in. | 90.00 | 55.00 | 30.00 |
| **Sap Birch** | | | |
| 1 in. | 90.00 | 48.00 | 30.00 |
| 5/4 and up | 100.00 | 53.00 | 30.00 |
| **Soft Elm** | | | |
| 1 in. | 70.00 | 45.00 | 30.00 |
| 5/4 to 2 in. | 75.00 | 50.00 | 30.00 |
| **Red Birch** | | | |
| 1 in. | 120.00 | 75.00 | |
| 5/4 and up | 125.00 | 80.00 | |
| **Basswood** | | | |
| 1 in. | 70.00 | 45.00 | 30.00 |
| 5/4 to 2 in. | 80.00 | 55.00 | 35.00 |
| **Plain Oak** | | | |
| 1 in. | 95.00 | 55.00 | 35.00 |
| 5/4 to 2 in. | 105.00 | 65.00 | 40.00 |
| **Ash** | | | |
| 1 in. | 85.00 | 50.00 | 30.00 |
| 5/4 to 2 in. | 95.00 | 55.00 | 30.00 |
| 10/4 and up | 110.00 | 70.00 | 30.00 |

## BOSTON

Quotations given below are for highest grades of Michigan and Canadian White Pine and Eastern Canadian Spruce as required in the New England market in car loads.

| | | |
|---|---|---|
| White Pine Uppers, 1 in. | | |
| White Pine Uppers, 1¼, 1½, 2 in. | | |
| White Pine Uppers, 2½, 3 in. | | |
| White Pine Uppers, 4 in. | | |
| Selects, 1 in. | | $170.00 |
| Selects, 1¼, 2 in. | | 180.00 |
| Selects, 2½, 3 in. | | |
| Selects, 4 in. | | |
| Prices nominal | | |
| Fine Common, 1 in., 30%, 12 in. and up | | 150.00 |
| Fine Common, 1 x 8 and up | | 150.00 |
| Fine Common, 1¼ to 2 in. | $160.00 | 170.00 |
| Fine Common, 2½ and 3 in. | | 180.00 |
| Fine Common, 4 in. | | 195.00 |
| 1 in. Shaky Clear | | 85.00 |
| 1¼ in. to 2 in. Shaky Clear | | 90.00 |
| 1 in. No. 2 Dressing | | 95.00 |
| 1¼ in. to 2 in. No. 2 Dressing | | 95.00 |
| No. 1 Cuts, 1 in. | | 110.00 |
| No. 1 Cuts, 1¼ to 2 in. | | 130.00 |
| No. 1 Cuts, 2½ and 3 in. | | 160.00 |
| No. 2 Cuts, 1 in. | | 80.00 |
| No. 2 Cuts, 1¼ to 2 in. | | 102.00 |
| Barn Boards, No. 1, 1 x 12 | | 91.00 |
| Barn Boards, No. 1, 1 x 10 | | 87.00 |
| Barn Boards, No. 1, 1 x 8 | | 84.50 |
| Barn Boards, No. 2, 1 x 12 | | 75.00 |
| Barn Boards, No. 2, 1 x 8 | | 71.00 |
| Barn Boards, No. 2, 1 x 10 | | 71.00 |
| Barn Boards, No. 3, 1 x 12 | | 55.00 |
| Barn Boards, No. 3, 1 x 10 | | 53.00 |
| Barn Boards, No. 3, 1 x 8 | | 52.00 |
| **No. 1 Clear** | | |
| Can. Spruce, No. 1 and clear, 1 x 4 to 9" | | $ 75.00 |
| Can. Spruce, 1 x 10 in. | | 78.00 |
| Can. Spruce, No. 1, 1 x 4 to 7 in. | | 72.00 |
| Can. Spruce, No. 1, 1 x 8 and 9 in. | | 74.00 |
| Can. Spruce, No. 1, 1 x 10 in. | | 76.00 |
| Can. Spruce, No. 2, 1 x 4 and 5 in. | | 36.00 |
| Can. Spruce, No. 2, 1 x 6 and 7 in. | | 37.00 |
| Can. Spruce, No. 2, 1 x 8 and 9 in. | | 39.00 |
| Can. Spruce, No. 2, 1 x 10 in. | | 42.00 |
| Can. Spruce, No. 2, 1 x 12 in. | | 45.00 |
| Spruce, 12 in. dimension | | 49.00 |
| Spruce, 10 in. dimension | | 48.00 |
| Spruce, 9 in. dimension | | 46.00 |
| Spruce, 8 in. dimension | | 45.00 |
| 2 x 10 in. random lengths, 8 ft. and up | | 41.00 |
| 2 x 12 in., random lengths | | 45.00 |
| 2 x 3, 2 x 4, 2 x 5, 2 x 6, 2 x 7 | | 32.00 |
| 3 x 4 and 4 x 4 in. | | 33.00 |
| 2 x 9 | | 39.00 |
| All other random lengths, 7 in. and under, 8 ft. and up | 32.00 | 36.00 |
| 5 in. and up merchantable boards, 8 ft. and up, D 1s | 31.00 | 35.00 |
| 1 x 2 | | 32.00 |
| 1 x 3 | | 32.00 |
| 1⅝ in. Spruce Lath | | 8.50 |
| 1½ in. Spruce Lath | | 7.50 |
| **New Brunswick Cedar Shingles** | | |
| Extras | | 5.50 |
| Clears | | 4.50 |
| Second Clear | | 3.50 |
| Clear Whites | | 2.75 |

Second Hand Machinery & Equipment Wanted & For Sale

# Quick Action Section

Special Lots Of Lumber— —Positions Wanted & Vacant

## Lumber Wanted

### Hard Maple and Birch Wanted

A limited quantity of 4/4 and 8/4 dry stock No 2 Common and Better. For further particulars apply Box 761 Canada Lumberman, Toronto, Can. 2-5

### "Hemlock Wanted"

We are in the market for a few blocks of Mill Run or No. 1 and No. 2 Hemlock.
THE ELGIE & JARVIS LUMBER CO., LIMITED 18 Toronto St., Toronto, Ont. 2

### Lath Wanted

Especially White Pine and Hemlock. Write us what you have with prices.
BREWSTER LOUD LUMBER CO.,
508-509 Lincoln Building,
DETROIT, MICH. 24-3

### Logs Wanted

to saw in transit, at G.T.R. siding Oro, on main line between Toronto and North Bay. Satisfaction guaranteed. Prices on application.
T. R. Crawford, Oro Station, Ont. 2-5

### Wanted

To contract for one hundred thousand feet of Rock Elm plank for delivery next summer and fall. Quote price to St. Mary's Wood Specialty Co. Ltd., St. Mary's, Ont. 2

### We Will Buy

A block of Hemlock, Spruce, Red or White Pine that is sawn or will be sawn before the 15th of March. Box 770 Canada Lumberman, Toronto. 2 T.f.

### Wanted—Hardwood Dimension

5 Cars 1 x 1 42 & 48" Clr Maple, Beech Birch Dry
3 " 1¼ x 1¼ 42" Clr Maple Beech Birch Dry
1 " 1 x 1¼ to 4½ 20-24" Long, Maple Beech Birch Dry
Box 748 Canada Lumberman, Toronto. 1-2

## Lumber For Sale

### For Sale

3 M. ft. well seasoned red oak. Box 760 Canada Lumberman, Toronto. 2

### For Sale

10,000,000 feet of Quebec Spruce Lumber, 100,000 cords of pulpwood and 500 cars of Standard No. 1 Spruce and Fir Lath, apply to The Canadian Forest Corporation, 140 St. Peter Street, Quebec, Que.

### For Sale

At Blind River, Ontario, Pine and Spruce Lath, also some Cedar and Hemlock Lath. Grades, four foot mill run, 32" mill run, and four foot No. 3.
F. P. Potvin,
Blind River, Ont. 2-T.f.

### For Sale

125 M. ft 1" Maple
85 M. ft 1" Birch
75 M. ft 1" Beech
15 M. ft 1" Elm

All No. 3 Common and Better. Last winter's cut. Dry and ready to ship from Stanstead on Boston and Maine Railway.
W. A. Hadley,
Stanstead, Que.

PUBLISHER'S NOTICE

Advertisements other than "Employment Wanted" or "Employees Wanted" will be inserted in this department at the rate of 25 cents per agate line (14 agate lines make one inch). $3.50 per inch, each insertion, payable in advance. Space measured from rule to rule. When four or more consecutive insertions of the same advertisement are ordered a discount of 25 per cent. will be allowed.

Advertisements of "Wanted Employment" will be inserted at the rate of one cent a word, net. Cash must accompany order. If Canada Lumberman box number is used, enclose ten cents extra for postage in forwarding replies. Minimum charge 25 cents.

Advertisements of "Wanted Employees" will be inserted at the rate of two cents a word, net. Cash must accompany the order. Minimum charge 50 cents.

Advertisements must be received not later than the 10th and 20th of each month to insure insertion in the subsequent issue.

### For Sale.

8 M. 2 in Hemlock
3 M. 1 in Hemlock
4 M. 2 in Spruce
3 M. 1 in Spruce
6 M. 1 in Basswood
3 M. 1 in Butternut
36 M. 1 in Ash
18 M. 1 in Maple
18 M. 1 in Elm
100 Cords Hardwood Slabs and Edgings
150 Cords Softwood Slabs and Edgings
175 Cords Hemlock & Spruce Squares from 6 x 6 by 12, 10 to 16 ft. long.
Apply to L. H. Martine,
Bury, Quebec. 2

### Hardwood Lumber

400/500 M feet Birch, Maple, Basswood and Ash; sawed 4.5.6.8. and 10/4. 75% Birch. Bargain for immediate sale—Also lath.
EAST CLIFTON PULP & LUMBER CO.
Cookshire, Que. 23-2

### Timber for Quick Sale

$6,000 will buy six square miles covered by Ontario timber license, one and a half million feet white red, green and standing Pine within two miles of shipping point.
S. S. Herrmann,
Worthington, Ont. 2

### Sale of Timber to Close an Estate

South East Quarter of Township of PROUDFOOT containing twenty-three and a quarter square miles, and known as Berth No. 2. Containing the following timber as cruised by one of the most reliable timber cruisers in Ontario:-

| | | |
|---|---|---|
| BIRCH | 10,950,000 | ft. |
| MAPLE | 4,000,000 | ft. |
| HEMLOCK | 2,000,000 | ft. |
| ELM | 100,000 | ft. |
| PINE | 100,000 | ft. |
| CEDAR poles 25' up 50' | 5,000 | |
| SPRUCE & BALSAM Cordwood | 5,000 | cords |
| HARDWOOD CORDWOOD first-class | 80,000 | corde |

PRICE ........ $26,184.00
Favorable terms can be arranged:-
F. C. Clarkson, Assignee,
E. R. C. Clarkson & Son,
TORONTO. 24-3

## Machinery For Sale

### Chain for Sale

We have the following second hand conveyor chain for sale. This chain is in first class condition, having only been used about six weeks, is well oiled and free from rust.
000 ft. No. 103 Chain at .44 cts. per foot
350 ft. No. 103 K-1 Attachments at .68 cts per foot
240 ft. No. 88 chain at .30 cts. per foot
8 ft. No. 88 F-2 Attachments at .54 cts. per foot
200 ft. No. 77 Chain at .20 cts. per foot
13 ft. No. 77 F-2 Attachments at .44 cts per foot
also sprockets, etc. for driving same.
Canadian Wirebound Boxes Limited,
1000 Gerrard St. E., Toronto, Ont. 2

### Used Equipment

We have all kinds of machinery, boilers, engines, motors, and air compressors, etc., for quarries, lumber and pulp mills and mines. Let us have your inquiries. Montreal Agents American Saw Mill Machinery Co.,
Barrie Engineering Co., Ltd.,
208a St. Nicholas Bldg.,
23-4 Montreal.

### Wickes Gang

GANG: No. 12 Wickes Gang, 40" sash, 18" stroke, steam binder rolls, front and back in two sections, feed and oscillation combined, 1908 model, and has been in use for five years. We furnish with this gang 11 rolls for cants and stock, one filing machine, and 4 sets of saws.
THE PEMBROKE LUMBER CO.,
t.f. Pembroke, Ont.

### For Sale

2 Factory Refuse Hogs,
1 Sawmill Refuse Hog,
1 Shingle Machine,
1 Band Resaw Grinder,
1 Lath Machine,
1 Jack Ladder Haul-up Chain, Bullwheel and Sprockets,
1 7" Steam Feed,
Several pieces of Link and Bar Slush Chain.
Apply; The C. Beck Mfg. Co., Ltd.,
Penetanguishene, Ont. 1-2

### 500 H.P. Geary Boiler

Double drums each 48" x 24'-6" long.
Shells 5/8" thick-double rivetted.
Double butt longitudinal seams.
237-4" B. and W. cap tubes—20 ft. long
Complete with stop, safety and blow off valves and with water column front and cyclone shaking and dumping grates.
Ontario Inspection for 200 pounds.
Inspection point:—Toronto,
Box 714 Canada Lumberman, Toronto, Ont. 23-2

### Engines, Boilers, etc., for Sale

One "Williams" Upright Engine 6" x 6"
One Upright Engine 5" x 6"
Six Return tubular boilers of following dimensions:-
One "Butterfield" 72" x 14' - 3¼" tube - ⅜" shell.
One "Polson" 64" x 14' - 3¼" tube - ½" shell
One "Doty" 60" x 15' - 4" tube - ¼" shell
One "Doty" 60" x 14½" - 4" tube - ½" shell
One "Doty" 60" x 15' -4" tube - ½" shell
One "Inglis" 60" x 16' - 3" tube - ½" shell
One double acting "Northey" Fire pump, 6" suction, 5" discharge, 14" steam cylinder, 8" water cylinder, 13" stroke, Capacity 450 gallons per minute.
One "Northey" feed pump 6 x 4 x 7" stroke, Capacity 60 gallons per minute.
One brass Mill steam whistle.
For further particulars apply The Conger Lumber Co Limited., Parry Sound, Ontario. 24 T.f.

### Second Hand Machinery

We have over $250,000 worth of used machinery of all kinds for sale. Suitable for mines, quarries, railroads, pulp and lumber mills, etc.
Everything carefully overhauled at our shops before shipped.
Send us your inquiries.
R. T. GILMAN & CO.,
19tf Montreal.

### For Sale

Three Lima Locomotives—good condition, now at Flanders, Ont.
Shevlin Clarke Co. Ltd.,
Fort Frances, Ont
23-2

## Machinery Wanted

### Wanted

Planer &Matcher, must be in good condition. State age, price and maker. Box 780 Canada Lumberman Toronto, Ont. 1-2

## Situations Wanted

An expert Band Saw Filer, twenty years experience in all kinds of Eastern timber and foreign woods. Ten years on the big mills of the Pacific coast. Work guaranteed second to none. Am open for a position. Best references. Box 756 Canada Lumberman, Toronto. 1-3

Can you use the services of a young married man, 35 years of age who has been on the executive of a large woodenware manufacturing concern for the past ten years. Has plenty of initiative and would consider salary as a secondary consideration if given an opportunity to grow up with an established concern. Excellent references. Box 769 Canada Lumberman, Toronto. 2

Millwright foreman wants position in a sawmill, capacity one hundred thousand feet a day. Can furnish best of references. Box 768 Canada Lumberman, Toronto, 2

Position wanted by expert saw hammerer and filer repairing saws for the coming season. Will do the work in your mill and guarantee satisfaction at reasonable rates. Box 773 Canada Lumberman, Toronto. 2-3

POSITION WANTED; As manager for a good responsible Lumber Co., 36 years experience in Lumbering. Box 729 Canada Lumberman. Toronto. 1-4

Young man, twenty-six, good connections in Quebec Province, wants position as buyer for Toronto or American lumber firm. Box 771 Canada Lumberman, Toronto. 2

Want position as bandsaw filer, double cut preferred. Worked for the same company last four seasons. A1 references. Box 759 Canada Lumberman, Toronto. 2

Wanted: Position as hand sawyer, left or right hand. Can furnish best references. Box 764 Canada Lumberman, Toronto. 2

Wanted position as Mill Superintendent. Eight years experience as Mill Superintendent fifteen years as sawyer. Can furnish best references. Box 747 Canada Lumberman, Toronto. 1-3

Wanted Position as superintendent or foreman of planing mill or woodworking factory. Have had over 12 years experience in interior fittings, sash, doors, hardwood flooring, boxmaking, estimating and detail drawing. Expert on production and first-class references. Will guarantee results. Box 752 Canada Lumberman, Toronto. 1-4

WANTED POSITION; for 1922 as head filer in good large Band Mill. Expert in every detail. Satisfaction guaranteed. Apply Box 750 Canada Lumberman, Toronto. 1-4

Young man, twenty-two, with initiative, ability, integrity and five years' experience in Millwork and Lumber offices, desires position. Can handle correspondence, sales and orders etc. Only positions with progressive firms in a town considered. All correspondence treated confidentially. Excellent credentials. Box 743 Canada Lumberman, Toronto. 1

## Situations Vacant

Established lumber firm has opening for experienced traveller covering Ontario soft woods. State salary, experience, age etc. Applications treated confidentially. Box 784 Canada Lumberman, Toronto. 1-2

LUMBER SALESMAN—Required by Toronto wholesale firm, must be experienced salesman. Apply, giving references, age and salary, required. Applications confidential. Box 464, Canada Lumberman, Toronto. 21tf

WANTED Young man with lumbering experience as traveller for soft woods in Ontario. State age, experience etc. in first letter. Box 755 Canada Lumberman, Toronto. 1-3

### Salesman

of saw-mill and woodworking machinery wanted. Applicant must speak both languages fluently, be sober and know mill machinery by practice. State previous employment and salary wanted. Apply Box 706 Canada Lumberman, Toronto. 22

## Business Chances

### For Sale Cheap

Water power factory or mill site in thriving community on North shore of Lake Huron. White Pine Lumber Company, Blind River, Ont. 2-5

### Wanted

To arrange with Mill which has facilities for supplying timbers for barns in Hemlock or Spruce in large quantities. Box 777 Canada Lumberman, Toronto. 2-5

### Planing Mill

Wanted to purchase all or part interest in small planing mill in Central Ontario. Must be in a locality where there is a demand for building material, especially house material. Replies treated confidential. State full particulars to Box 774 Canada Lumberman, Toronto. 2

### Portable Sawmill Service

First class work done quickly and efficiently in Quebec and Ontario. Reasonable charges based on acre of order, location, etc. Inquiries or orders must be sent in two weeks before mill is desired. Shingle and lath mills also. Birch and Beech wanted 6/4 to 10/4 or logs. Apply J. R. Spendlove, Katevale, Que. 2 T.f.

### Are You Manufacturing Some Special Wood Article ?

We have a Woodworking Plant, 200 Horse Water Power, up to date Dry Kilns, capacity 60 M. ft., situated about 100 miles from Montreal in Province of Quebec. Ideal labor conditions, plenty hardwood lumber for years—cheap. Want to get in touch with parties now manufacturing some special wood article who would consider establishing in Quebec with view of organizing company. We have the plant—have you the business and capital? Address Box 702 Canada Lumberman, Toronto, Ont. 2-5

## Miscellaneous

### Wanted

To contract with party owning a large sawmill to saw twenty million of spruce a year would make long term contract. Will deliver logs to mill. Address S. A. Mundy, 9 College Street, Toronto, Ont. 28-3

### For Sale

500 gross of (2 x 12) Bright Wood Screws in original 60 gross packages—in first class condition; also a quantity of Sash Pins, different lengths, say 1,000 pounds, also a number of 12 inch Hollow Columns 8 ft. long, complete with bases and caps, (bright and new) and will accept for any of these lines very reasonable prices. Chas. H. Vanduzen, Brantford, Ont. 2

## Tugs for Sale

Kirkwood Steamship Line 14 Place Royale, Montreal. 1-2

### Making Prairie Homesteads Comfortable

One of the lines of work in which the people of Western Canada show the keenest interest is that of planting shelter-belts across prairie farms and around the homestead buildings and garden. The Dominion Forest Nursery Station at Indian Head has been distributing trees, free, for planting on prairie farms since 1901. In the early years only a few hundred thousand trees per annum were distributed, but for the last four or five years it has averaged well up to five millions per year and is likely to exceed that in the near future. As it takes a year to grow the seedlings or cuttings, it is necessary that applications be made a year in advance, but this is not a loss of time because it enables the farmer to prepare the ground to receive the trees; and thorough cultivation is the secret of successful tree growing on the prairie. Mr. Norman M. Ross, Superintendent of the Indian Head Forest Nursery Station, reports an even greater interest in the subject this season than in previous years.

### Definiteness Needed in Forest Contracts

The more general appreciation by government forestry branches of the advantage of administering our timber lands along lines of scientific forestry practice should be an incentive to foresters to promote the adoption of more specific terms than heretofore customary in descriptions of forest or timber. In the past, no little confusion has resulted in different interpretations being placed upon the nomenclature adopted in forest legislation; it would, therefore, be of advantage that a standard terminology be followed. A matter under discussion at present is as to whether licenses issued but a few years ago, in which a condtion appeared reserving "pine," included jack pine or only white and red pine. More recent forest legislation included a classification of "spruce and other soft woods." "Soft woods" is, of course, a very indefinite term, and may mean anything. With the high prices of all kinds of timber this broad classification has become a very live problem, one in which both the public and the timber trade are intensely interested.

The "pine" controversy has demonstrated that while a certain designation may seem sufficiently specific to define what is present conditions the use later of a certain timber species for some industrial purpose may render the term ambiguous. For instance, with the increasing use of jack pine for pulpwood purposes, a pulpwood concession which contained a restriction reserving "pine" would very largely reduce the amount of pulpwood available, if the interpretation of "pine" were to include jack pine.

To overcome what may at any time become an acute situation more definite names should be applied to timber species. Undoubtedly, the most satisfactory terminology to be used in legislation would be the recognized botanical names, since common names are too often varied by local conditions.

# Review of Current Trade Conditions

### Ottawa Looks for Better Business in Near Future

The Ottawa lumber market so far as general trading was concerned experienced one of the quietest periods in its history, during the first two weeks of 1922. The entrance on the new year was not as auspicious as it might have been. Early January, however, bore promise of a most imporant year, if factors underlying the trade can be taken as a criterion.

From what the correspondent of the "Canada Lumberman" can gather, there are more reasons than one for 1922 being an important year in the lumbering industry, and signs show indications for increased sales and trading before 1922 is out.

There is a new cabinet, which before it gets through will in all probability enact or support certain lines of policy that, in the end, will have a bearing on the lumbering industry. What is contemplated or deemed as an advisable measure has not yet even been spoken of in print, but there was speculation tending toward the belief that there was "something in the wind."

The improvement in the value of the British pound sterling and the price of the Canadian dollar in the United States, was viewed in a variety of manners, and should the £ come back to its pre war valuation the export trade would be relieved of much of its present difficulties and larger woods cut and better business would ensure. Also, there was the strong possibility of the Canadian dollar getting close to pre war rates in the American market, which it was believed by some would put the trade back to a par basis as far as sales were concerned.

Another important factor is the prospect of a greater era of building this year than last. The value per job counting in materials and labor may or may not be as large, but it seems assured that there will be more individual undertakings.

What the price of the various grades of lumber for the next twelve months will be could not be determined, but the general opinion was that the law of supply and demand was coming back and that a competitive market would result. A slim woods cut this winter with the prospect of a big demand for stock next April or May, some believed would send lumber prices higher.

During the early part of the month many rumors sprang up as to the future of the Ottawa plant of the Gatineau Company, Limited, which, before the Riordon merger, was known as the W. C. Edwards' Sussex Street mill. Some viewed the closing down or almost complete cessation of work in its box, and sash and door factory, as an intimation that the company would not conduct sawing operations at Ottawa this year. No woods activities have so far been undertaken for the supply of logs to this mill. Another report is to the effect that the Gilmour-Hughson mill, Hull, Que., and the Rockland mill of the W. C. Edwards Company would operate. Mr. J. C. Thompson, General Manager of the Gatineau Company, declined to make any statement as to the future of the Ottawa plant.

A decrease in the wages to be paid to general factory and woodworking plant hands, after April first, is also receiving the attention of some operators, notably James Davidsons' Sons. The plant did not close down as usual for its annual factory repairs but will run to around the end of the month when, it is the intention to shut down for a month on account of shortage of orders. On re-opening, it is planned to put a wage reduction running from ten to fifteen per cent into effect.

James Davidsons' Sons will get on their biggest woods cut in the history of the business, it being estimated in early January that their log cut would be two million feet. About 85 per cent of the cut is white pine, and the remainder, spruce, basswood and cedar.

Rail transportation remained good as did also the supply of woods and factory labor. Lath and shingle remained slow.

### Montreal Business Continues in Fair Volume

Considering the period of the year, business in the Montreal lumber market is of fair volume. Prices are generally on the same level, although in certain lines of spruce there is an inclination to slightly harder quotations. Probably the most encouraging feature is the general feeling that 1922 will witness a steady market—nothing in the way of a sensational demand and advance, but a good volume of orders both for industrial and building purposes.

The year has opened with the assignment of a local woodworking firm—nothing very serious, but an unpleasant reminder to some wholesalers that the effect of last year's bad season may yet be felt.

According to a manufacturer in the Abitibi district, the stocks here total about 100,000,000 feet.

Advices received from the West Coast are to the effect that many mills and camps are closed down because of unprecedented cold weather. Some of the creeks are frozen solid to the bottom. The mills on the Fraser River have stopped operations. This condition has naturally interfered with business with the East.

It will be seen from the following figures that Montreal building in the past year was fairly active. The permits for December totalled $554,938, a decrease of $117,962. The total for 1921 was $21,381,273 an increase of $7,313,664 over 1920.

Prospects for 1922 may be described as good. In 1921 building costs, so far as skilled labor was concerned, did not come down very much, but it is expected that there will be a further decline when the season opens.

The demand for houses is still great, and there is an inclination for people to build their own houses, thanks to the facilities given by building societies. What ean be accomplished, when a council is willing to co-operate by securing a government loan, is demonstrated at St. Lambert, on the south shore of the St. Lawrence, where dozens of dwellings have been erected. The council was sympathetic, and loaned to individuals and societies.

The pulp industry is slow, with prices, except for bleached, on a basis showing little or no profit. Foreign competition in the American market is very keen. The condition of the pulpwood market may be seen from the exports during November, when the total was 49,476 cords valued at $614,974. Compared with 137,090 cords valued at $1,948,241 in November of 1920. The exports to the U. S. during the eight months of the fiscal year totalled 518,067 cords, of a value of $6,749,433, as against 915,336 cords of a value of $11,504,496 in the corresponding period of 1920.

---

### Ontario and the East

Although it is a little early yet to speak with any degree of assurance, many wholesalers, who have been interviewed, report that trade is opening up well and more inquiries are being received than for some considerable time. This indicates a healthy omen for spring business. Activity will not, however, manifest itself to any pronounced degree until well into February or March when the majority of building plans are completed and the construction situation is looked into thoroughly by architects, contractors and others in regard to cost of material, wages, etc. In the meantime all buying is cautious and retailers and others have just completed their inventories and are getting things squared away for the coming season.

So far as Ontario is concerned, there has been too much snow in the woods. The ice was formed in most districts before the snow came, and hauling the logs on the ice roads to the banks for skidding or out on the lakes has been conducted under favorable conditions. One leading lumberman stated recently that he had never known a better state of affairs to prevail so far as bush activities are concerned. He estimated that the cut of hardwoods in Ontario would not be more than 50% of last winter but thought that in certain districts the softwood take-out would run as high as 60 and even 70%. One company in Northern Ontario has had 1000 men engaged in its camps—not that all the logs felled will be converted into lumber during the coming season, but the manufacturer is desirous of having some in reserve.

The export situation is looking a little brighter, the pound sterling strengthening in value, and industrial conditions in the Old Land becoming more settled, with a firmer business outlook.

In softwoods, hemlock is pretty firm in price, and is none too plentiful. Those who have stocks on hand are convinced that there is going to be an advance before many weeks. A number of mill stocks have been sold recently and this is a good indication of the growing strength of the market. In white pine, stocks are not over heavy. True, there has been a super-abundance of mill culls for some time but No. 1 culls are now pretty well cleaned up, and as soon as the box factories start running to anything like capacity, No.2 culls will also disappear. White pine in some of the better grades is rather scarce. There is very little improvement in spruce which continues to be a rather weak wood on the market.

In hardwoods there is a fair domestic demand for birch and maple in furniture factories, piano firms and hardwood flooring plants, the latter having bought several cars recently. The one problem is a surplus of No. 2 and 3 common and a shortage of firsts and seconds

View of Mills in Sarnia.

# BUY THE BEST

Retailers and woodworking establishments who like to get A1 NORWAY and WHITE PINE LUMBER always buy their stocks from us because we can ship them on quick notice. It pays to have the goods, but it pays better to "deliver" them.

We also make a specialty of heavy timbers cut to order any length up to 60 feet from Pine or B. C. Fir.

*"Rush Orders Rushed"*

# Cleveland-Sarnia Sawmills Co., Limited
## SARNIA, ONTARIO

B. P. BOLE, Pres.    F. H. GOFF, Vice-Pres.    E. C. BARRE, Gen. Mgr.    W. A. SAURWEIN, Ass't. Mgr.

and selects. Those who have a fairly good supply of the better grades of hardwood, are holding out unless they get their price.

There is less disposition now to dicker over quotations and it is the firm belief that lumber has certainly touched bottom. There are so many manifestations of this that reiteration of the statement seems unnecessary. Most buyers are just now feeling their way out and taking a survey of the requirements.

In B. C. forests products the movement is rather quiet. There is very little call for timbers but there may be an improvement in this direction before spring, especially if certain large projects, now talked of, get under way. The shingle market is quiet at the season but it is probable several cars will be disposed of during the next two months for spring delivery. Shingles have been a little easier in price during late weeks due to lower freight charges.

There was recently an advance of $5.00 in rough clear fir but other prices have remained stationary. Car material has been ordered quite freely in both fir and hemlock owing to the extensive repair work going on. Clear red cedar is high in price and scarce owing to heavy shipments from the Coast to Japan. There have also been purchases of cedar bevel and bungalow siding by American buyers which have restricted the available quantity for the East. The quietest item, so far as the demand for B. C. products is concerned, consists of common boards and shiplap. The mixed carload trade was quiet during December.

That the outlook is considered propitious by B. C. mills is evidenced by the fact that some are increasing their sales force in Toronto and Montreal while others are looking around for more aggressive representation.

## Better Things in Store For Coming Year, Says St. John

The condition of the market at St. John N. B. is at the moment disappointing, it is being practically stagnant, as no sales of any consequence are being put through at the moment. Buyers and sellers alike sitting down awaiting a chance. No one seems able to point to a future which will foretell better or worse prices.

As a forecast, the writer feels that there are better things in store for the coming year just entered. The American market to-day, while dormant, will not sleep forever. Many inquiries are coming to hand from this market, making no quotations, but asking for the same from the manufacturers, who so far see little use in quoting for profitable prices seem impossible in this market for the moment.

Some rotary portable sawn stocks are being sold from the nearby interior at low prices, leaving only about $20.00 per M. to the shipper. There is of course, only a limited quantity of these stocks as very few mills are operating on these small tracts this winter. Operations are largely on wood lots where leases are expiring and unless the timber is cut, the owner will lose out entirely. Operating costs bring the total, including stumpage, up about to the price being paid so there is really no profit only saving of the amount invested in the stumpage, and sometimes not even that.

The English market is still dead, only a limited amount of shipments having gone forward. Prices are not as good as two weeks ago, and exchange has somewhat weakened, so taking it all around, this market is disappointing. Only limited amounts of 7 inches and up deals are on hand, and reproduction will be meagre in 1922. No doubt there will be three months of uncertainty in values with perhaps, spurts in price, but it certainly looks as if we had reached the lowest production and the bottom of the prices, with a very light demand and everything at low water mark; so it must be upward from now on, and, when spring opens, we should have greatly improved conditions, as far as confidence is concerned. It will take some time for operators, buyers and sellers alike, to pay up all outstanding paper and obligations of all kinds, but as this liquidation goes on, renewed activity will take place, building will be started and, by midsummer, conditions should show a great improvement.

What is needed is close supervision of business, watching each and every move and saving in all departments where possible, with rigid attention to reduction in costs of manufacturing. When this has been accomplished, we shall be well on the road to profitable business.

## How Eastern Men View Prospects in Lumber

What has 1922 in store for the lumber trade? Shall we experience a still further fall in prices, or a buoyant market, or a fair volume of business with prices moving within a narrow range? Although the trade has passed through a perplexing period, and the worst is over, yet the situation is not clarified to the extent that many will venture a hard and fast opinion as to the course of the market.

In the course of an interview with Montreal wholesalers, the representative of the "Canada Lumberman" found that the views as to business this year are in the main, divided into two classes—those who believe that business will be good, and that prices will remain at the present level or slightly advance—and those who think that the market will go still lower. Few are sanguine enough to suggest that the demand will be so urgent as to force quotations up to a very high point, although in some lines there may be a decided improvement.

The wholesalers who believe that we may expect a steady market base their opinion upon the reports from Canadian points, Great Britain, and the United States, nearly all of which look for improved general conditions during the current year. That improvement will be gradual, the the business being built upon prices which are more nearly stabilized. In addition to this general condition, which, of course, affects the lumber trade, there are two or three special conditions which are local in their application. Thus yards have not by any means large stocks; there is evidence of a coming revival in building; more enquiries are being received; and above all, there is a decidedly more cheerful tone in the market.

With regard to pulpwood, those who deal in that commodity frankly state there is little hope of a revival for some months—not in fact, until the American and Canadian mills have consumed part of their heavy stocks.

### Keen Competition in Export Market

The export position is not by any means clear. While there is every reason to think that the U. K. market will improve, it must not be forgotten that keen competition is likely to continue. It is understood that freight rates will be reduced to 80 shillings a standard—and this will help some. Canadian exporters are hopeful of a considerably better season than the one which is over, and certainly the total could be easily passed.

A manufacturer and wholesaler expressed the opinion that mill prices are almost certain to advance. "At the present time few manufacturers are making a profit. This condition cannot continue, and if we are to stay in business we must get more for our products. The fact that the cut this year will be restricted to evidence that there has no been much money in the game. Wholesalers will of course have to put up their prices in a corresponding ratio."

A wholesaler and exporter is of the opinion that spruce prices will advance slighty until the 1921—22 cut comes on to the market, when he looks for a fall in values.

I base my opinion on the belief that the demand for the first part of the year will be sufficient to keep prices fairly steady and to advance certain lines, but when the new stock is available, quotations will recede. It is argued that prices must rise during the year to meet the cost of production—but as a matter of fact, the cost of production has little to do with the price to be obtained. The demand rules the price the wholesaler obtains and consequently the price he is willing to give the manufacturer. As to pine, the Ottawa Valley manufacturers, as I see it, will have to reduce their prices owing to competition. They have held their stocks very firmly, but this cannot continue, and if they want to do business the mills will have to lower their prices.

### Price Cutting has Nearly Disappeared

The representative of a large firm of wholesalers stated that his experience led him to a pretty confident feeling that business would considerably improve. For one thing there was generally a more optimistic attitude, price cutting had nearly all disappeared, enquiries were more numerous, and should general business conditions brighten up even slightly, users of lumber would have to come more freely into the market.

The head of another wholesale firm remarked that while it is yet too early to give a decided opinion, there were indications that 1922 would be a better year than 1921. He could not see how manufacturers could reduce their prices—and he certainly did not look for cheaper lumber.

According to another wholesaler, prices are not sufficiently low, partienlarly of pine to attract American buyers. Several representatives of American firms who had been visiting various Canadian points expressed the opinion that unless the mills lowered their prices business which had ordinarily come to Canada would go elsewhere. Other woods would be substituted for Canadian lumber. Once this trade was lost it would be difficult to divert it again to Canada. The mills must face the fact that it was better to retain that trade even at a loss than to allow it to go into other channels.

An exporter declared that there was reason to expect a revival in trade. He was convinced that conditions in the U. K. would improve on the settlement of the outstanding political questions, which would inspire confidence.

K.J. Shirton, of the Wm. Shirton Co., who was recently re-elected Mayor of Dunnville, Ont. says that he believes the outlook for business for the coming year is good although things are now rather quiet. The cross-arm department of his company suffered quite a slump from 1920, but the firm are hopeful for a larger trade in 1922 than during the past year. "Taking it all in all, we are inclined to be quite optimistic regarding the coming months." concluded Mr. Shirton.

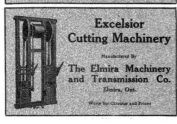
### Mr. Thuerck Operating in the North

W. C. Thuerck, of Haileybury, Ont., who has been engaged for some time in the lumber business on his own behalf, spent a few days in Toronto recently. Mr. Thuerck was formerly associated with Terry & Gordon, Limited, Toronto. He is having taken out and sawn this season about a million and a half feet of timber; some 60% jack pine and 40% spruce. Mr. Thuerck reports that logging conditions in the north have been very good and the weather favorable. The cut of pulpwood, however, is small owing to the low prices received and the indifferent demand. Mr. Thuerck intends in the near future to open up an office in Haileybury where he is well and widely known.

### Big Contract for Cross Ties Awarded

The Temiskaming & Northern Ontario Railway is extending the line from Cochrane to Tin Can Portage, some 75 miles north. Contracts have been placed for 115,000 ties, a large proportion of them being of jack pine with a percentage of cedar and other woods.

The contract has been awarded to the Harris Tie & Timber Co., of Ottawa, R. S. Potter Lumber Co., of Matheson, and Patrick Mc-Cool, of North Bay, to be delivered during the coming season. The greater portion of these ties will be used on the addition to the road, but a number will be employed for replacing those on the line south of Cochrane. Sixty percent of the ties are to be 7 inches thick and forty percent 6 inches. It is understood that the price paid is only about half of what cross ties were commanding a year ago, the demand from he railways having fallen off considerably.

### The Growth was a Little Too Swift

In the last issue of the "Cauada Lumberman" there appeared a report of an interesting and instructive address delivered by Dr. C. D. Howe, dean of the Faculty of Forestry, University of Toronto, on "The Purpose and Plan of Forestry Work." On the second page of the article, a typographical error made Dr. Howe say that it takes nearly five years to produce a stick of spruce pulpwood and nearly twice that length of time to produce a 12-inch spruce sawlog. The paragraph should have read— "It takes nearly seventyfive years to," etc.

The mistake was, of course, manifest to anyone acquainted with the comparatively slow growth of coniferous trees, but it is advisable that a correction should be made in order that no one may labor under a misapprehension as to the time required for our young spruce forests to develop in Canada. They certainly do not bloom over night.

### National Association to Move Offices

On February 1st, the offices of the National Wholesale Lumber Dealers' Association will be moved from 66 Broadwak to the Liggett Bldg., 41 East Forty-Second St. New York City Headquarters have been maintained at "66" for over twenty-one years and during that time the Manhattan Life Bldg. has really become a landmark in the lumber industry. However, for some years the drift of the metropolitan lumber section has been up town and inasmuch as the facilities at 66 Broadway have proven inadequate to meet with the growing needs of the membership, Secretary W. W. Schupner states that the larger and lighter space in the Liggett Bldg. will permit the Association to more efficiently cater to the membership.

### Annual Meeting of Woodlands Section

That pulpwood cut and shipped by bona fide settlers should be carried free of charge to the mill by the Canadian National Railways and the T. & N. O., which are both government-owned lines, is the substance of a memorial which has been sent to Primier King at Ottawa by leading residents in the district of Haileybury, Ont.

It is reported that the condition of some settlers is very serious owing to the lack of sale of this product of theirland. High freight rates are said to be the principal cause of the present situation, and at a recent meeting of the Temiskaming Liberal Executive it was declared many settlers might be compelled to leave their holdings if some relief is not found.

The government is being urged to take steps toward providing a market for pulpwood. Newcomers to the farming lands in the Haileybury district must depend almost entirely on the sale of pulpwood for their living.

The close of 1921 marked the passing of another milestone of progress for the Long-Bell Lumber Company. The authorized capital stock of the company was increased to $25,000,000 at a meeting of the stockholders. The increase was made to decrease the company's surplus account. Heretofore the company has had paid-up capital stock of $9,000,000.

# EDGINGS

The plant of the McCarter Shingle Co., Victoria, B. C. was recently damaged by fire to the extent of $60,000.

L. D. Todd, of Buffalo, representing Edward Hines Lumber Co., of Chicago, spent a few days in Toronto recently on business.

W. V. Lloyd, wholesale lumber dealer, Toronto, who was laid up for some time with illness, is able to be at his office again.

Edward Clark, president of Edward Clark & Sons, Toronto, left recently on a visit to Louisiana and Florida where he will spend the winter months.

J. E. Gardiner, who is a member of the firm of P. W. Gardiner & Son, door manufacturers, Galt, Ont., has been re-elected alderman in that city for 1922.

A. D. F. Campbell, of A. F. Campbell & Son, retail lumber dealers, Arnprior, Ont., was re-elected by acclamation a member of the council of that town for 1922.

W. N. Belair, of the Schuster Co., retail lumber dealers, Belleville, Ont., was at the recent elections re-elected by acclamation as Separate School Trustee for Ketcheson ward.

F. R. Anglin, of S. Anglin & Co., retail lumber dealers, Kingston, was elected a school trustee at the recent Municipal Elections in the Limestone City. Mr. Anglin defeated Mrs. Enoch Godwin.

P. Z. Caverhill, of Victoria, B. C., chief forester for British Columbia, was a recent visitor to Toronto and called upon a number of friends in the industry.

W. H. Connor, formerly a lumber merchant of Dundas, Ont., recently died in Toronto following a brief illness. More recently he had engaged in the tobacco business and was a great enthusiast of all out-door sports.

Frank J. Carew, of the John Carew Lumber Co., Lindsay, Ont., was in the recent municipal elections returned as one of the town fathers. Mr. Carew has spent several years in the council and has rendered the municipality good service.

A provincial charter has been granted to the Demers Lumber Co., Limited, with a capital stock of $49,000, and headquarters at Saint-Agapit, Lotbiniere County, Que. The company in empowered to carry on a general lumber business in all its branches.

The building permits in the city of Toronto during 1921 amounted to $23,877,609, as compared with $25,784,732, in 1920, a deficit for the year of $1,907,123. The total number of permits issued in 1921 was 8,797 as compared with 10,645 in 1920.

J. L. Lachance, Limited, Quebec, P. Q. were recently incorporated under provincial charter to manufacture and deal in all kinds of building supplies. Capital $100,000. Among the incorporations are J. L. Lachance and J. A. Cardinal, both of Quebec City.

At the annual meeting of the Toronto Kiwanis Club, held recently, Fred H. Bigwood, of the Canadian General Lumber Co., Toronto, was elected first vice-president. Mr. Bigwood has been an active worker of the organization for a number of years.

L. D. Barclay, of Toronto, manager of the eastern sales office of the Canadian Western Lumber Co., Fraser Mills, B. C., returned recently from a holiday trip to the coast. He also spent some time visiting relatives in Edmonton.

J. A. Laberge, of the Laberge Lumber Co., Sudbury, Ont., who ably filled the position of Mayor of Sudbury during the last two years, has retired from municipal life and will now devote all his time to the rapidly developing business of his firm.

N. W. Trimble, owner of a sawmill and a tract of land near Hillman, five miles from Leamington, Ont., was instantly killed by a falling tree. Mr. Trimble was cutting down a tree when another tree leaning against the one which he was chopping, fell on him.

K. J. Shirton, retail lumber dealer, Dunnville, Ont., has been re-elected mayor of that progressive town for the coming year. During the past year he rendered the municipality faithful and efficient service.

The Welsh Lumber Company, Limited, Toronto, has been incorporated to acquire the firm of Welsh Bros. and to conduct a wholesale and retail lumber business. Capital $40,000. Among the incorporators are J. M. Welsh and W. F. Welsh, both of Toronto.

Chartered Timber Lands, Mines, Limited, Toronto, was recently incorporated to deal in timber lands and mining properties. Capital $50,000. G. T. Graham, broker, and A. R. Kenny, lumberman, both of Toronto are among the incorporators.

All records for wood cutting were broken recently at the farm of H. Sayers, near Milton, Ont., when D. McPhedran and W. E. Britton

and son cut sixty cords of 16-inch hardwood in six hours with a circular saw outfit. This is at the rate of 240 cords r day.

J. T. Payette, of P. Payette Co., Penetanguishene, Ont., was re-elected mayor of that progressive town in the recent municipal contest. Mr. Payette had strong opposition but came off a victor. He has long taken an active interest in the welfare and advancement of Penetanguishene.

White & Sullivan Lumber Co., Limited, Toronto, was recently granted a provincial charter to take over the business conducted by Ernest White and to carry on a wholesale and retail lumber business. Capital $50,000. T. N. Phelan and E. A. Richardson, both of Toronto, are two of the incorporators.

Daniel McLeod, well known resident of Vancouver and one of the original organizers and recent president of the False Creek Lumber Co., passed away in Vancouver recently from pneumonia. Mr. McLeod sold out his interest in the business about two years ago when he retired.

Gropp Bros., of Penetanguishene, Ont., whose saw and planing mill were recently burned, say they have not decided as yet whether or not they will rebuild the sawmill. It is likely, however, that they will go ahead with the construction of a planing mill in the spring.

R. Murray, of Huntsville, Ont., was recently added to the inspection staff of the National Hardwood Lumber Association, Toronto. This force has grown considerably of late years and now consists of Messrs: H. F. Holton, H. H. Hastings, J. A. Cadenhead and Robert Murray. The work is also becoming increasingly important and extended in its scope.

The Fesserton Timber Co., of Toronto, are taking out in the Temiskaming District about 5,000,000 feet of spruce, which will be cut in the new sawmill of the company at Krugersdorf, some twelve miles north of Englehart, Ont. The mill was completed last year and is modernly equipped, having a sawing capacity of about 40,000 feet a day.

The office of the Sturgeon Lake Lumber Company, at Prince Albert, Sask., was entered by burglars during the Christmas Holidays but the thieves did not succeed in securing any booty. A valiant attempt had been made to open the safe in the office but without success and no doubt as a mark of their disappointment and disproval the yeggmen set fire to the office buildings. Damage from this cause is estimated to be about $1,000.

Douglas fir will now be used instead of Oregon pine by the British Admiralty in dealing with timber orders, as a result of action taken by F. C. Wade, agent general in London, Premier Oliver announced recently. Director Navy Contracts O. R. Jenkins reports that a recent fir timber contract for the British navy was awarded a contractor who undertook that the material should come from British Columbia.

The Appellate Division at Osgoode Hall, Toronto, recently reduced the judgment of $11,707. which the Russell Timber Co., of Port Arthur, obtained some time ago against the Pulpwood Company, to $3,443. The tug "Whalen," leased by the Pulpwood Company, towed the raft, consisting of 4,110 cords of wood, across Lake Superior. The Russell Timber Co., owned 2,510 cords of wood in the raft. During a severe storm, 39% of the raft was lost and the action and appeal to proportion the loss, resulted as already stated.

The proposed Provincial Association of Builders' Exchanges is making good progress in the province of Quebec. The new association will press for various changes in the laws of the province, one of the most important changes asked for, being the act which makes builder and architect jointly responsible for the safety of any building they erect. This, it is claimed, is an unfair advantage to the foreign contractor who can easily assume all these liabilities, knowing that he will be outside the jurisdiction of the Quebec courts after the contract is concluded.

Due to an improvement in the situation confronting the British Columbia lumbering industry, the quantity of logs exported out of the province of British Columbia has fallen off considerably and any surplus is being absorbed by the local market. At present the supply of logs does not exceed the demand and the latter is expected to steadily increase. Most of the exported logs go to the United States and Japan, to the former country in boom form, while Japanese orders are filled by cutting the logs into short lengths and transporting them on freight steamers. The bulk of the exported logs is cut from crown granted limits, the rest, if intended to go outside the Dominion, coming within the jurisdiction of a board constituted by the Provincial Government, which decides whether the export permits should be issued. The policy is to prevent as much as possible the export of raw material and so assist in the building up of British Columbia industries.

## ALPHABETICAL INDEX TO ADVERTISERS

## TIE CUTTING

where you have from ten to twenty-five horse-power is most easily and efficiently done with a

### Fisher & Davis No. 1 Mill

You will appreciate its accuracy in sawing and the complete absence of those annoying and expensive breakdowns that characterize the cheap mill.

If you are interested in the highest class of Saw Mill Machinery, it will pay you to write to us.

## Fisher & Davis Mfg. Company
935 N. Main St.　　　　　　　　　　　St. Louis, Mo.

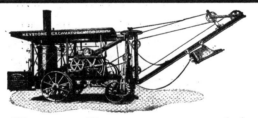

## Subscribers' Information Form

Many letters reach us from subscribers enquiring where a certain machine,
a certain kind of lumber or veneer, or some other class of goods, can be obtained. We can usually supply the information. We want to be of service to our
subscribers in this way, and we desire to encourage requests for such information. Make use of this form for the purpose.

"CANADA LUMBERMAN"            Date.......................................... 19....
345 Adelaide Street West, Toronto

Please tell us where we can procure .................................................................................

.......................................................................................................................................

.......................................................................................................................................

.......................................................................................................................................

Name ...........................................................................

Address ...........................................................................

## The nearest approach to absolute reliability in belting performance

Dominion Friction Surface Belting is the result of the combined experience of all our rubber factories. It is the finished product of the finest materials put together with all the skill of the belt-maker's art.

The in-built strength and pulley gripping power of Dominion Friction Surface Belting make it the most dependable and economical for all drives. Every Dominion Friction Surface Belt installed means so much power conserved and so much more freedom from troubles due to stretch and slip.

It will cost you nothing to have one of our belt experts study your belting problems and submit recommendations for your approval. Phone or wire our nearest Service Branch.

## Dominion Rubber System
### Service Branches

Our Dominion Hose, Packing and Industrial Rubber Goods are of the same High Standard as Dominion Friction Surface Belting

| | | |
|---|---|---|
| Halifax | London | Regina |
| St. John | Windsor | Saskatoon |
| Quebec | Kitchener | Edmonton |
| Montreal | North Bay | Calgary |
| Ottawa | Fort William | Lethbridge |
| Toronto | Winnipeg | Vancouver |
| Hamilton | Brandon | Victoria |

### DOMINION RUBBER SYSTEM PRODUCTS

| Belting | Hose | Packing | Miscellaneous |
|---|---|---|---|

---

# FIRE BRICK
## AND CLAY

We make several brands of fire brick by every known process of manufacture from a selection of various high grade Pennsylvania clays. This enables us to furnish the best for your boilers, dutch ovens, refuse burners, kilns, etc.

We specialize in fire brick for power plants and if you will advise us whether your boilers are hand fired or stoker fired and kind of fuel used we can then give you the proper brick for your work.

We carry a large stock of our different brands in various sizes and shapes in our Hamilton warehouse which enables us to ship at once.

**We manufacture the following well-known brands:**

### "Elkco Special," "Elk Steel," "St. Marys," "Keystone" and "M.D. Elk"
Write for copy of our catalogue.

## Elk Fire Brick Co. of Canada, Ltd.
HIGH GRADE FIRE BRICK and CLAY

### Sun Life Bldg., Hamilton, Canada
Representatives for Maritime Provinces:
RHODES, CURRY COMPANY, Ltd., Head Office, AMHERST, N.S.
Branches at Sydney and New Glasgow, N. S.

---

## SOUND - CLEAN - RELIABLE

STEEL
GRAY - IRON
MALLEABLE IRON

# Wm. Kennedy & Sons
LIMITED
## OWEN SOUND

Prompt Deliveries --- Quality Guaranteed

8 Silver Street, Cobalt
901 Royal Bank Bldg., Toronto
504 University Street, Montreal

# THE LINN LOGGING TRACTOR

The Linn Logging Tractor designed exclusively for Winter Log Hauling in the North Country. Was developed and perfected in actual logging operations in the Adirondack Woods. 90% of the Logging Tractors in use in the North Woods are Linn Tractors.

The Linn Logging Tractor is equipped with a body for loading—which enables toting over summer Portage roads—up steep grades—and over country where it would be impossible to haul a trailer.

Will haul 50 cords of Spruce (4000 lbs per cord) per trip, over branch roads and main roads and on to the ice at the landing—hauling speed on the level is 6½ miles per hour. Does not require sanding on down grades.

Will of itself hold 75 tons on a 25% down grade.

Will reduce horse haulage costs by more than half.

Will operate with absolute safety over lakes and rivers where ice has a minimum thickness of 14 inches.

Is the only Tractor built having the flexible Lag-bed (track) so absolutely essential to successful north country winter and summer haulage.

Seeing is believing. If you are interested, for next season's haulage—won't you go with us this season to the nearest operation, and see a Linn Tractor doing possibly more than we claim for it—under our own winter conditions—in our own country.

--Logging Department--

## MUSSENS LIMITED

Dubrule Building                    MONTREAL

## Fletcher Corporation Limited

Sherbrooke, Que.

*Manufacturers, Wholesalers and Exporters of the*

## Finest Grades of Hard and Softwood Lumber.

Mills and Timberlands Lowelltown, Me.

*Sole Agents for Europe:*

### W. N. Hillas & Co, Ltd.
HULL · · ENGLAND

*TO CANADIAN EXPORTERS:*

Our agents are in daily touch with all the buyers in the United Kingdom. Send us your lists with full particulars. Our agents assume the delcredere risk on buyers.

---

## Give Your Coal Department A Chance

Are you watching developments in the coal business closely?

Are you familiar with the different brands and grades of coal being sold in Western Canada?

Are you in a position to advise your customers as to the best methods of storing, handling and burning coal?

Each issue of the WESTERN CANADA COAL REVIEW contains valuable information, hints and suggestions of a practical nature which will be of great assistance to you.

*Only $2.00 per year.*

### Western Canada Coal Review

302 Travellers' Building
WINNIPEG, MANITOBA

---

# Alligator Brand Harness

THIS IS AN 1922 ALLIGATOR YEAR

## LUMBERMEN!

When you think of Harness Think of Lamontagne

Let us send you further information

*Lamontagne Limited.*

338 Notre Dame St. W., MONTREAL

52 Crown Street, QUEBEC.

110 Princess Street, WINNIPEG.

*Slow Speed Low Power*  *Planing-Mill Exhausters*

# A Proven Success in many Plants throughout the Dominion

There's nothing new or experimental about the Sturtevant System of dust collecting and conveying. It is an established success.

Since 1866 this system has been used in the leading woodworking plants and sawmills of America, and for many years has been used throughout the Dominion. Its influence on

the health of the employees and the production of the plant, together with the elimination of the fire hazard, is well known.

Today the B. F. Sturtevant Company are manufacturing and installing dust collecting and conveying systems of every description in greater numbers than ever before.

There is a Sturtevant Systems that will exactly fill your needs—can you afford to operate without it?

*Let us send you full information.*

# CANADA LUMBERMAN BUYERS' DIRECTORY

The following regulations apply to all advertisers:—Eighth page, every issue, three headings; quarter page, six headings; half page, twelve headings; full page, twenty-four headings

**ALLIGATORS**
Payette Company, P.
West, Peachy & Sons

**BABBITT METAL**
Canada Metal Company
General Supply Co. of Canada, Ltd.

**BALE TIES**
Canada Metal Co.
Laidlaw Bale Tie Company

**BAND MILLS**
Hamilton Company, William
Waterous Engine Works Company
Yates Machine Company, P. B.

**BAND SAW BLADES**
Simmonds Mfg., Co.

**BAND RESAWS**
Mershon & Company, W. B.

**BARKERS**
Bertrand, F. X., La Compagnie Manufactiere.
Smith Foundry & Machine Co.

**BEARING METAL**
Canada Metal Co.
Beveridge Supply Co., Ltd.

**BEDSTEADS (STEEL)**
Simmons Limited

**BELT DRESSING**
Dominion Belting Co.
General Supply of Canada, Ltd.

**BELTING**
Canadian Consolidated Rubber Co.
Dominion Belting Co.
General Supply Company
Goodhue & Co., J. L.
Gutta Percha & Rubber Company
D. K. McLaren, Limited
McLaren Belting Company, J. C.
Sumner & Co.
York Belting Co.

**BELTING (Transmission)**
Sumner & Co.

**BLOWERS**
Reed & Co., Geo. W.
B. F. Sturtevant Co. of Canada, Ltd.
Toronto Blower Company

**BOILERS**
Engineering & Machine Works of Canada
Hamilton Company, William
Waterous Engine Works Company

**BOILER PRESERVATIVE**
Beveridge Supply Company
Shell-Bar, Boice Supply Co. Ltd.

**BOA MACHINERY**
Yates Machine Company, P. B.

**CABLE CONVEYORS**
Engineering & Machine Works of Canada.
Hamilton Company, Wm.
Waterous Engine Works Company

**CAMP SUPPLIES**
Davies Company, William
Dr. Bell Veterinary Wonder Co.
Johnson, A. H.
Swift Canadian Co.
Turner & Sons, J. J.
Woods Manufacturing Company. Ltd.

**CANT HOOKS**
General Supply Co. of Canada, Ltd.
Pink Company, Thomas

**CEDAR**
Bury & Co., Robt.
Cameron Lumber Co.
Canadian Western Lumber Company
Chesbro, R. G.

**Dry Wood Lumber Co.**
Fesserton Timber Company
Muir & Kitkpatrick
Rose, McLaurin, Limited
Terry & Gordon
Thurston-Flavelle Lumber Company
Vancouver Lumber Company
Victoria Lumber & Mfg. Co.

**CHAINS**
Canadian Link-Belt Company, Ltd.
General Supply Co. of Canada, Ltd.
Engineering & Machine Works of Canada
Hamilton Company, William
Pink & Co., Thomas
Waterous Engine Works Company

**CLOTHING**
Woods Mfg. Company

**CONVEYOR MACHINERY**
Canadian Link-Belt Company. Ltd.
General Supply Co. of Canada, Ltd.
Hamilton Company, Wm.
Hopkins & Co., Ltd., F. H.
Mathews Gravity Carrier Company.
Waterous Engine Works Company

**CORDAGE**
Consumers Cordage Company

**CORDWOOD**
McClung, McLellan & Berry

**COUPLING (Shaft)**
Enginering & Machine Works of Canada

**CRANES**
Hopkins, & Co., Ltd., F. H.
Canadian Link-Belt Company

**CUTTER HEADS**
Shimer Cutter Head Company

**CYPRESS**
Wistar, Underhill & Nixon

**DERRICKS AND DERRICK FITTINGS**
Hopkins & Co., Ltd., F. H.

**DOORS**
Brompton Lumber & Mfg. Co.
Canadian Western Lumber Co.
Mason, Gordon & Co.
Midland Woodworkers
Midland Wood Products, Ltd.
Terry & Gordon

**DRAG SAWS**
Gerlach Company, Peter
Hamilton Company. William

**DRYERS**
Coe Manufacturing Company
Proctor & Schwartz Inc.
B. F. Sturtevant Co. of Canada, Ltd.

**DUST COLLECTORS**
Reed & Co., Geo. W.
B. F. Sturtevant Co. of Canada, Ltd.
Toronto Blower Company

**EDGERS**
Hamilton Company, Ltd., William
Green Company, G. Walter
Long Mfg. Company, E.
Payette Company, P.
Waterous Engine Works Company

**ELEVATING AND CONVEYING MACHINERY**
Canadian Belt-Link Company, Ltd.
Engineering & Machine Works of Canada
Hamilton Company, William
Waterous Engine Works Company

**ENGINES**
Robt. Bell Engine & Thresher Co.
Engineering & Machine Works of Canada
Hamilton Company, William

**Payette Company, P.**
Waterous Engine Works Company

**EXCELSIOR MACHINERY**
Elmira Machinery & Transmission Company

**EXHAUST FANS**
B. F. Sturtevant Co. of Canada, Ltd.
Toronto Blower Company

**EXHAUST SYSTEMS**
Reed & Co., Geo. W.
B. F. Sturtevant Co. of Canada, Ltd.
Toronto Blower Company

**FIBRE BOARD**
Manley Chew

**FILES**
Diaston & Sons, Henry
Simonds Canada Saw Company

**FIR**
Apex lumber Co.
Associated Mills, Limited
Bainbridge Lumber Company
Cameron Lumber Co.
Canadian Western Lumber Co.
Canfield, P. L.
Chesbro, R. G.
Dry Wood Lumber Co.
Fesserton Timber Co.
Grier & Sons, Ltd., G. A.
Heeney, Percy E.
Knox Brothers
Mason, Gordon & Co.
Robertson & Hacket Sawmills
Rose, McLaurin, Limited
Terry & Gordon
Timberland Lumber Company
Timms, Phillips & Co.
Underhill Lumber Co.
Vancouver Lumber Company
Vanderhoof Lumber Co.
Victoria Lumber & Mfg. Co.

**FIRE BRICK**
Beveridge Supply Co., Ltd.
Elk Fire Brick Company of Canada
Shell-Bar, Boice Supply Co. Ltd.

**FIRE FIGHTING APPARATUS**
Waterous Engine Works Company

**FITTINGS**
Crane Limited

**FLOORING**
Cameron Lumber Co.
Chesbro, R. G.
Long-Bell Lumber Company

**GEARS (Cut)**
Smart-Turner Machine Co.

**GRAVITY LUMBER CARRIER**
Mathews Gravity Carrier. Co.

**GRINDING WHEELS**
Canadian Hart Products Ltd.

**GUARDS (Machinery and Window)**
Canada Wire & Iron Goods Co.

**HARDWOODS**
Anderson Lumber Company, C. G.
Anderson Shreiner & Mawson
Atlantic Lumber Company
Barrett, Wm.
Bury & Co., Robt.
Cameron & Co
Edwards & Co., W. C.
Fesserton Timber Co.
Gillespie, James
Gloucester Lumber & Trading Co.
Grier & Son, G. A.
Hart, Hamilton & Jackson
Heeney, Percy E.

**Knox Brothers**
Mason & Co., Geo.
McDonagh Lumber Co.
McLennan Lumber Company
McLung, McLellan & Berry
Pedwell Hardwood Lumber Co.
W. & J. Sharples.
Spencer, Limited, C. A.
Strong, G. M.
Summers, James R.
Webster & Brother, James

**HARDWOOD FLOORING**
Brompton Lumber & Mfg. Co.
Grier & Son, G. A.

**HARNESS**
Beal Leather Co., R. M.
Carson & Company, Hugh

**HEMLOCK**
Anderson Lumber Company, C. G.
Anderson, Shreiner & Mawson
Bartrum & Balt
Beck Lumber Co.
Bourgouin, H.
Canadian General Lumber Company
Edwards & Company, W. C.
Fesserton Timber Co.
Grier & Sons, Ltd., G. A.
Hart, Hamilton & Jackson
Hocken Lumber Company
Mason, Gordon & Co
McCormack Lumber Co.
McJonagh Lumber Co.
Robertson & Hacket Sawmills
Spanish River Lumber Co.
Spencer, Limited, C. A.
Terry & Gordon
Vancouver Lumber Co.
Vanderhoof Lumber Co.

**HOISTING AND HAULING ENGINES**
General Supply Co. of Canada, Ltd
Hopkins & Co., Ltd., F. H.

**HOSE**
General Supply Co. of Canada, Ltd.
Gutta Percha & Rubber Company

**INSURANCE**
Burns Underwriting Co.
Hardy & Co., E. D.
Lea, Blakemore Inc.
Lumbermen's Underwriting Alliance
Rankin Benedict Underwriting, Co

**INTERIOR FINISH**
Cameron Lumber Co.
Canadian Western Lumber Co.
Canfield, P. L.
Eagle Lumber Company
Mason, Gordon & Co.
Rose, McLaurin, Limited
Terry & Gordon

**KILN DRIED LUMBER**
Bury & Co., Robt.

**KNIVES**
Diaston & Sons, Henry
Simonds Canada Saw Company
Waterous Engine Works Company

**LARCH**
Otis Staples Lumber Co.

**LATH**
Anderson, Shreiner & Mawson
Apex Lumber Co.
Austin & Nicholson
Beck Lumber Co.
Brennen & Sons, F. W.
Cameron Lumber Co.
Canadian General Lumber Company
Carew Lumber Co., John
Chaleurs Bay. Mills
Dupuis, Limited, J. P.

Eagle Lumber Company
Foley Lumber Company
Fraser Bryson Lumber Co., Ltd.
Gloucester Lumber & Grading Co.
Grier & Sons, Ltd., G. A.
Harris Tie & Timber Company, Ltd
Larkin Co., C. A.
Mason & Co., Geo.
McLennan Lumber Company
Miller, W. H. Co.
New Ontario Colonization Company
Otis Staples Lumber Company
Power Lumber Co.
Price Bros. & Company
Shevlin-Clarke Co.
Spencer, Limited, C. A
Terry & Gordon
U. G. G. Sawmills, Limited
Union Lumber Company
Victoria Harbor Lumber Company

**LATH BOLTERS**

General Supply Co. of Canada, Ltd.
Hamilton Company, Wm.
Payette & Company, P.

**LOCOMOTIVES**

Engineering & Machine Works of
Canada
General Supply Co. of Canada, Ltd.
Hopkins & Co., Ltd., F. H.
Climax Manufacturing Company
Montreal Locomotive Works

**LATH TWINE**

Consumers' Cordage Company

**LINK-BELT**

Canadian Link-Belt Company
Mathews Gravity Carrier Company.
Hamilton Company, Wm.

**LOCOMOTIVE CRANES**

Canadian Link-Belt Company, Ltd.
Hopkins & Co. ,Ltd., F. H.

**LOGGING ENGINES**

Engineering & Machine Works of
Canada
Hopkins & Co., Ltd., F. H.

**LOG HAULER**

Engineering & Machine Works of
Canada
Green Company, G. Walter
Holt Manufacturing Co.
Hopkins & Co., Ltd., F. H.
Payette Company, P.

**LOGGING MACHINERY AND
EQUIPMENT**

General Supply Co. of Canada, Ltd.
Hamilton Company, William
Holt Manufacturing Co.
Hopkins & Co., Ltd., F. H.
Payette Company, P.
Waterous Engine Works Company
West, Peachey & Sons

**LUMBER EXPORTS**

Fletcher Corporation

**LUMBER TRUCKS**

Hamilton Company, Wm.
Waterous Engine Works Company

**LUMBERMEN'S BOATS**

Adams Engine Company
West, Peachey & Sons

**LUMBERMEN'S CLOTHING**

Kitchen Overall & Shirt Co.
Woods Manufacturing Company, Ltd.

**MATTRESSES**

Simmons Limited

**METAL REFINERS**

Canada Metal Company

**OAK**

Long-Bell Lumber Company

**PACKING**

Beveridge Supply Company
Consumers' Cordage Co.
Gutta Percha & Rubber Company

**PANELS**

Bury & Co., Robt.

**PAPER**

Beveridge Supply Co., Ltd.
Price Bros. & Co.

**PINE**

Anderson Lumber Company, C. G.
Anderson, Shreiner & Mawson
Atlantic Lumber Co.
Austin & Nicholson
Barratt, William
Beck Lumber Co.
Cameron & Co.
Cameron Lumber Co.
Canadian General Lumber Company
Canadian Western Lumber Co.
Canfield, P. L.
Chesbro, R. G.
Cleveland-Sarnia Sawmills Company
Cox, Long & Company
Dudley, Arthur N.
Eagle Lumber Company
Edwards & Co., W. C.
Excelsior Lumber Company
Fesserton Timber Company
Fraser Bryson Lumber Co., Ltd.
Gillies Bros, Limited
Gloucester Lumber & Trading Co.
Gordon & Co., George
Goodday & Company, H. R.
Grier & Sons, Ltd., G. A.
Harris Tie & Timber Company, Ltd.
Hart, Hamilton & Jackson
Hettler Lumber Company, Herman H.

Hocken Lumber Company
Julien, Roch
Lay & Haight.
Lloyd, W. Y.
Loggie Co., W. S.
Long-Bell Lumber Company
Mason, Gordon & Co.
Mason & Co., Geo.
McCormack Lumber Co.
McFadden & Malloy
McLennan Lumber Company
Montreal Lumber Company
Muir & Kirkpatrick
Northern Lumber Mills.
Otis Staples Lumber Co.
Parry Sound Lumber Company
Rolland Lumber Co.
W. & J. Sharples.
Shevlin-Clarke Co.
Spanish River Lumber Co.
Spencer, Limited, C. A.
Strong, G. M.
Summers, James R.
Terry & Gordon
Union Lumber Company
Victoria Harbor Lumber Co.
Watson & Todd, Limited
Wuichet, Louis

**PLANING MILL EXHAUSTERS**

Toronto Blower Co.

**PLANING MILL MACHINERY**

Mershon & Co., W. B.
B. F. Sturtevant Co. of Canada, Ltd.
Toronto Blower Co.
Yates Machine Company, P. B.

**PORK PACKERS**

Davies Company, William

# YATES

## Horizontal and Slab Band Resaw

The above machine is our H-6 Horizontal and Slab Band Resaw, a machine adapted for handling split logs. With this machine it is possible to get every inch of good lumber from your logs, also an ideal machine for following the Band Mill and resawing slabs or timbers into accurately cut boards. Maximum capacity 32 inches wide 14 inches thick; Will handle stock at the rate of 150 and 225 feet per minute. You can run two different widths and two different thicknesses of stock through this machine at one time. Send for your copy of circular and in your own interests make a thorough investigation of this machine before your busy season starts.

## P.B.Yates Machine Co.Ltd.

### Hamilton     Canada

**POSTS AND POLES**
Anderson, Shreiner & Mawson
Auger & Company
Canadian Tie & Lumber Co.
Dupuis, Limited, J. P.
Eagle Lumber Company
Harris Tie & Timber Co., Ltd.
Long-Bell Lumber Co.
Mason, Gordon & Co.
McLennan Lumber Company
Terry & Gordon

**PULLEYS AND SHAFTING**
Canadian Link-Belt Company
General Supply Co. of Canada, Ltd.
Green Company, G. Walter
Engineering & Machine Works of
   Canada
Hamilton Company, William

**PULP MILL MACHINERY**
Canadian Link-Belt Company, Ltd.
Engineering & Machine Works of
   Canada
Hamilton Company, William
Payette Company, P.
Waterous Engine Works Company

**PULPWOOD**
Bethune Pulp & Lumber Co.
British & Foreign Agencies
D'Auteuil Lumber Co.
Price Bros. & Co.
Scott, Draper & Co.

**PUMPS**
General Supply Co. of Canada, Ltd.
Engineering & Machine Works of
   Canada
Hamilton Co., William
Hopkins & Co. ,Ltd., F. H.
Smart-Turner Machine Company
Waterous Engine Works Company

**RAILS**
Gartshore, John J.
Hopkins & Co. ,Ltd., F. H.

**ROOFINGS**
(Rubber, Plastic and Liquid)
Beveridge Supply Company
Reed & Co., Geo. W.

**ROPE**
Consumers' Cordage Co.

**RUBBER GOODS**
Dunlop Tire & Rubber Goods Co.
Gutta Percha & Rubber Company

**SASH**
Brompton Lumber & Mfg. Co.
Midland Woodworkers
Midland Wood Products, Ltd.

**SAWS**
Atkins & Company, E. C.
Disston & Sons, Henry
General Supply Co. of Canada, Ltd.
Gerlach Company, Peter
Green Company, G. Walter
Hoe & Company, R.
Radcliff Saw Mfg. Co.,
Shurly Co.. Ltd., T. F.
Shurly-Dietrich Company
Simonds Canada Saw Company

**SAW MILL LINK-BELT**
Canadian Link-Belt Company

**SAW MILL MACHINERY**
Canadian Link-Belt Company, Ltd.
General Supply Co. of Canada, Ltd.
G. Walter Green Co., Ltd.
Hamilton Company, William
La Compagnie Manufacture, F. X.
   Bertrand
Long Manufacturing Company, E.
Mershon & Company, W. B.
Parry Sound Lumber Company
Payette Company, P.
Waterous Engine Works Company
Yates Machine Co., P. B.

**SAW SHARPENERS**
Hamilton Company, William
Waterous Engine Works Company

**SAW SLASHERS**
Hamilton Company, Wm.
Payette Company, P.
Waterous Engine Works Company

**SHINGLES**
Apex Lumber Co.
Associated Mills, Limited
Brennen & Sons, F. W.
Cameron Lumber Co.
Campbell-MacLaurin Lumber Co.
Canadian Western Lumber Co.
Carew Lumber Co., John
Chaleurs Bay Mills
Chesbro, R. G.
Coast & Mountain Lumber Co.
D'Auteuil Lumber Co.
Dry Wood Lumber Co.
Eagle Lumber Company
Federal Lumber Company
Fraser, Limited
Gillespie, James
Gloucester Lumber & Trading Co.
Grier & Sons, Limited, G. A.
Harris Tie & Timber Company, Ltd.
Heaps & Sons
Heeney, Percy E.
Mason, Gordon & Co.
McLennan Lumber Company
Miller Company, Ltd., W. H.
Reynolds Company, Limited
Rose, McLaurin, Limited
Terry & Gordon
Timms, Philips & Co.
Vancouver Lumber Company
Vanderhoof Lumber Co.

**SHINGLE & LATH MACHINERY**
Green Company, C. Walter
Hamilton Company, William
Long Manufacturing Company, E.
Payette Company, P.

**SILENT CHAIN DRIVES**
Canadian Link-Belt Company, Ltd.

**SLEEPING EQUIPMENT**
Simmons Limited

**SLEEPING ROBES**
Woods Mfg. Company, Ltd.

**SMOKESTACKS**
Hamilton Company, Wm.
Reed & Co., Geo. W.
Waterous Engine Works Company

**SNOW PLOWS**
Pink Company, Thomas

**SOLDERS**
Canada Metal Co.

**SPARK ARRESTORS**
Reed & Co., Geo. W.
Waterous Engine Works Company

**SPRUCE**
Anderson, Shreiner & Mawson
Barrett, Wm.
Cameron Lumber Co.
Campbell, McLaurin Lumber Co.
Canadian Western Lumber Co.
Chesbro, R. G.
Cox, Long & Co.
Dudley, Arthur N.
Fraser, Limited
Fraser-Bryson Lumber Company
Gillies Brothers

Gloucester Lumber & Trading Co.
Goodday & Company, H. R.
Grier & Sons, Ltd., G. A.
Harris Lumber Co., Frank H.
Hart, Hamilton & Jackson
Hocken Lumber Company
Julien, Roch
Larkin Co., C. A.
Lay & Haight
Lloyd, W. Y.
Loggie Co., W. S.
Mason, Gordon & Co.
McCormack Lumber Co.
McDonagh Lumber Co.
McLennan Lumber Company
Muir & Kirkpatrick
New Ontario Colonization Company
Northern Lumber Mills.
Power Lumber Co.
Price Bros. & Co.
Rolland Lumber Co.
Rose, McLaurin, Limited
W. & J. Sharples.
Spencer, Limited, C. A.
Strong, G. M.
Terry & Gordon
U. G. G. Sawmills, Limited
Vanderhoof Lumber Co.

**STEAM SHOVELS**
Hopkins & Co., Ltd., F. H.

**STEEL CHAIN**
Canadian Link-Belt Company, Ltd.
Hopkins & Co. ,Ltd., F. H.
Waterous Engine Works Company

**STEAM PLANT ACCESSORIES**
Waterous Engine Works Company

**STEEL BARRELS**
Smart-Turner Machine Co.

**STEEL DRUMS**
Smart-Turner Machine Co.

**TARPAULINS**
Turner & Sons, J. J.
Woods Manufacturing Company, Ltd

**TANKS**
Hopkins & Co., Ltd., F. H.

**TENTS**
Turner & Sons, J. J.
Woods Mfg. Company

**TIES**
Austin & Nicholson
Carew Lumber Co., John
Canadian Tie & Lumber Co.
Chaleurs Bay Mills
D'Auteuil Lumber Co.
Gloucester Lumber & Trading Co.
Harris Tie & Timber Company. Ltd.
McLennan Lumber Company
Miller, W. H. Co.
Price Bros. & Co.
Scott, Draper & Co.
Terry & Gordon

**TIMBER BROKERS**
Bradley, R. R.
Cant & Kemp
Farnworth & Jardine
Wright, Graham & Co.

**TIMBER CRUISERS AND
ESTIMATORS**
Savage & Bartlett.
Sewall, James W.

**TIMBER LANDS**
Department of Lands & Forests, Ont.

**TOWING MACHINES**
Corbet Foundry & Machine Co.
Payette Company, P.
West, Peachy & Sons

**TRACTORS**
Holt Manufacturing Co.
Hopkins & Company, Ltd., F. H.
Monarch Tractors

**TRANSMISSION MACHINERY**
Canadian Link-Belt Company, Ltd.
Engineering & Machine Works of
   Canada
General Supply Co. of Canada, Ltd.
Grand Rapids Vapor Kiln
Hamilton Company, Wm.
Waterous Engine Works Company

**TURBINES**
Engineering & Machine Works of
   Canada
Hamilton Company, William
B. F. Sturtevant Co. of Canada, Ltd.

**VALVES**
Crane Limited

**VAPOR KILNS**
Grand Rapids Vapor Kiln
B. F. Sturtevant Co. of Canada, Ltd.

**VENEERS**
Bury & Co., Robt.

**VENEER DRYERS**
Coe Manufacturing Company
Proctor & Schwartz Inc.
B. F. Sturtevant Co. of Canada, Ltd.

**VENEER MACHINERY**
Coe Machinery Company
Proctor & Schwartz Inc.

**VETERINARY REMEDIES**
Dr. Bell Veterinary Wonder Co.
Johnson, A. H.

**WARPING TUGS**
West, Peachey & Sons

**WATER WHEELS**
Engineering & Machine Works of
   Canada
Hamilton Company, William

**WELDING**
Barton Electric Welding Co.
St. John Welders & Engineers

**WIRE**
Canada Metal Co.
Laidlaw Bale Tie Company
Canada Wire & Iron Goods Co.

**WIRE CLOTH**
Canada Wire & Iron Goods Co.

**WIRE ROPE**
Canada Wire & Iron Goods Co.
Hopkins & Co. ,Ltd., F. H.
Dominion Wire Rope Co.
Greening Wire Co., B.

**WOODWORKING MACHINERY**
General Supply Co. of Canada, Ltd.
Long Manufacturing Company, E.
Mershon & Company, W. B.
Waterous Engine Works Company
Yates Machine Company, P. B.

**WOOD PRESERVATIVES**
Beveridge Supply Company

**WOOD PULP**
Austin & Nicholson
New Ontario Colonization Co.
Power Lumber Co.

# For Modern Mills-*the Band Resaw*

The Horizontal Band Resaw is the one outstanding machine of modern sawmill practice. Its greatest feature, perhaps is its adaptability to all classes of work. It can be used in a tie mill for producing lumber from the slabs that are left when a small log is cut into a tie. It can be used in the ordinary lumber mill for working up the slabs that are produced in the ordinary course of manufacture. And it can be used in a mill, cutting very small logs which can be split on the head rig and worked up into lumber on the resaw.

## The E. Long Manufacturing Co., Limited

### Orillia                    Canada

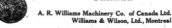

Robert Hamilton & Co., Vancouver
Gormans, Limited
   Calgary and Edmonton

A. R. Williams Machinery Co. of Canada Ltd.
Williams & Wilson, Ltd., Montreal

# A Super Re-Saw

For years we have recognized the limits of the horizontal re-saw, such as the excessive space taken up in the mill—the necessity of raising or lowering the bed, or the saw blade itself in order to change the thickness of cuts—the difficulty of separating the slab from the lumber at the rear of the machine, and the advisability of having every slab inspected by the sawyer before being passed through the machine. But until recently we have never been able to perfect a vertical re-saw which would meet in every way the high standard of excellence which every machine bearing the name of WATEROUS must possess.

We are at last however, able to offer to the Sawmill Men of Canada, a machine that not only overcomes the above limits, but one which combines all the advantages of the horizontal and vertical re-saws.

Here is a machine which will positively cut

straight slabs and half logs regardless of irregularities in material. The bed consists of four fluted rolls which are adjustable and which raise the face of the planer table.

There are two press rolls. The first swings on a vertical shaft in a frame which presses firmly against the feed rolls, bent so the saw in a streamlined saw into a roll. These two rolls are so arranged as to automatically take care of all variations in the size and shape of the slabs. The swinging arm roller mounts any slabs immediately and the pressure of the oscillating cylinder aligns the slabs against the first two feed rolls, swinging the tail of the slab immediately into line at the same cut, this taking place as soon as the saw enters the cut.

This arrangement prevents the usual thickness of slab at each end that we encounter in all re-saws carrying the single press rolls and feed rolls.

# Waterous
### BRANTFORD, ONTARIO, CANADA

Molson's Bank Bldg., Vancouver, B.C.                    Winnipeg, Manitoba.

Vol. 42          Toronto, February 1, 1922          No. 3

# Canada Lumberman

# White Pine
# Red Pine
# Jack Pine
# Spruce
# Lumber
# and Lath

**UNION LUMBER COMPANY LIMITED**
701 DOMINION BANK BUILDING
TORONTO          CANADA

# CONFIDENCE—
## The Basis
# of All Business

DOWN through the ages, from the days of the early Phoenician traders to modern times, fair dealing has been the firm foundation on which every successful business has been built. The mutual confidence of buyer and seller, the knowledge that each will carry out his side of the transaction, has welded a world in commerce.

Ever since we have been in business we have jealously guarded our good name, striving always to maintain our reputation for Service and Quality. That our business has grown steadily through good times and bad, is proof positive that we have endeavoured to fill every order to the satisfaction of the buyer.

When you want lumber, remember that we are always ready to give you the Quality and Service you have a right to expect.

## TERRY AND GORDON
### LIMITED
### CANADIAN FOREST PRODUCTS
HEAD OFFICE
TORONTO
BRANCH
MONTREAL
EUROPEAN AGENTS
BRANCH
VANCOUVER
SPENCER LOCK & Co., LONDON, ENG.

# Well Bought is Half Sold!

*"The tumult and the shouting dies*
*The Captains and the Kings depart"*

## 'ts over !

The greatest Convention of the Canadian Lumbermen's Association.

Splendid affair! Everybody satisfied!

### Now
### to work, and make
### 1922
### *"a good 'un!"*

We're ready.
Best assorted Stock ever.
Graded (not guessed at).

## SERVICE? YES!

*What* you want,
*When* you want it,
That's all.

·Selah !

# Canadian General Lumber Co.
Limited

# FOREST PRODUCTS

TORONTO  OFFICE :—  712-20  Bank  of  Hamilton  Building
Montreal Office :—203 McGill Bldg.
Mills : Byng Inlet, Ont.

---

# FRASER COMPANIES, Limited

Bleached Sulphite Pulp Mill.    Saw Mills (all Band Saw Mills).    Shingle Mill

### HERE THEY ARE ON THE MAP

## Mills and Railway Connections

| Saw and Shingle Mills | Railway Connections | Saw and Shingle Mills | Railway Connections |
|---|---|---|---|
| Cabano, Que. | Temiscouata Ry. | Baker Brook, N.B. | C.N.Ry., Temiscouata Ry. |
| Notre Dame du Lac, Que. | Temiscouata Ry. | Blaster Rock, N.B. | C.P.R. |
| Glendyne, Que. | C. N. Ry. | Summit, N. B. | C. N. R. |
| Estcourt, Que. | C. N. Ry. | Fredericton, N. B. | C.P.Ry and C.N.Ry. |
| Sully, N. B. | C. N. Ry. | Nelson, N. B. | C. N. Ry. |
| Edmundston, N. B. C.P.R., C.N.R. and Temiscouata Ry. | | Campbellton, N. B. | C. N. Ry. |
| Magaguadavic, N.B. | C. P. R | | |

Bleached Sulphite Mill, Edmundston, N. B. .....Railway Connection, C.P.R., C.N.R. and Temiscouata Ry.
Sulphite Mill, Chatham, N. B. .............Railway Connection, C. N. R.

Bleached Sulphite.    Rough and Dressed Spruce.    White Cedar Shingles.    Railway Ties
Piano Sounding Board Stock a Specialty.

## Selling and Purchasing Offices :--    EDMUNDSTON, N. B.

# British Columbia Lumber
# Red Cedar Shingles

In these days of broken
stocks and limited sup-
ply, you need a real
definite service in your
requirements.

*Are you getting it?*

## Timms Phillips & Co., Ltd.
### Vancouver, B. C.

TORONTO OFFICE: Canada Permanent Bldg.
Phone Adel. 6490
MONTREAL OFFICE: 23 Marconi Bldg.
Phone M 2909

## Ask the Man Who Has Used it

The proof of the value of wood is in the service obtained therefrom.

Lumber dealers and their customers are getting to like BRITISH COLUMBIA WESTERN HEMLOCK better the more they deal in it or use it.

It is not a hardwood but is possessed of a grain that is externally beautiful. It takes a high polish, is free from pitch and "shakes" and possesses great strength.

Don't wait until all your competitors have established a reputation for handling BRITISH COLUMBIA WESTERN HEMLOCK.

We'll be glad to send you BRITISH COLUMBIA WESTERN HEMLOCK in mixed carloads along with our other BIG CHIEF Brand Specialties, British Columbia Red Cedar Shingles, and Cedar and Fir lumber in all sizes known to high-class manufacture.

## VANCOUVER LUMBER CO., LIMITED, Vancouver, B.C.

Branch Sales Offices at Toronto, Ont., Winnipeg, Man., Chicago, Ill

# BUY
## BRITISH COLUMBIA
# Red Cedar Shingles

The life of a British Columbia Red Cedar Shingle Roof can almost be gauged by the life of the nail with which the shingle is nailed in place. Judging from available data, the average life of the ordinary steel wire nail, which has been in such common use, is only from seven to twelve years. Some wire nails will last longer, depending upon the condition of exposure, climate and similar features, but considering our climate as a whole, at the end of from seven to twelve years a large percentage of wire nails will have rusted either completely through or so extensively that the first strong wind will complete the work. The shingles that have been held in position by such nails are then free to work down, permitting rains or melting snows to leak through and damage the interior of the structure. Examination will disclose that the fibre of the shingle itself is still in perfect condition, and a leaky roof, in the majority of occasions is due entirely to the use of faulty nails, but the average home owner, placed at such inconvenience, will not stop to reason this out and the poor wooden shingle comes in for more unjust abuse.

There are several kinds of nails which experience has proven will give lasting satisfaction, and the wise dealer will advise his customers of these satisfactory nails. A pure zinc shingle nail meets all the demands of durability required. Its principal drawback is its high cost and a slight tendency to bend under careless driving. Galvanized wire nails theoretically are rust proof, and if the galvanized coating is properly applied, and of sufficient thickness, such a nail will last as long as the shingle it holds in place. The life of this shingle roof, properly applied with these nails then is from 40 to 50 years. Pure iron nails, or the old cut or wrought nails are ideal but difficult to secure. Copper nails also constitute a perfect shingle nail.

| | |
|---|---|
| **Timms Phillips & Co., Ltd.**<br>Yorkshire Bldg., Vancouver<br>Manufacturers and Wholesalers<br>**Red Cedar Shingles**<br>3x-8x- Perfections, Royals, Imperials<br>**Red Cedar Bevel Siding** | **Vancouver Lumber Co., Ltd.**<br>Manufacturers<br>**XXX—XXXXX CEDAR SHINGLES**<br>(Rite Grade Inspected)<br>Head Office, Eastern Sales Office<br>Vancouver, B.C. Toronto, Ont. |
| **Westminster Mill Co.**<br>LIMITED<br>New Westminster, B.C.<br>**Red Cedar Shingles**<br>**Cedar Bevel Siding** | **Dominion Timber Products Ltd.**<br>Vancouver Block<br>Vancouver<br>Largest Manufacturers of<br>**Perfection Shingles**<br>in Canada |
| **Underhill Lumber Co., Ltd.**<br>Dominion Bldg., Vancouver<br>**RED CEDAR SHINGLES**<br>3x-5x- Perfection and Eurekas<br>**CEDAR BEVEL SIDING**<br>**CEDAR BUNGALOW SIDING** | **Shull Lumber & Shingle Co.**<br>Limited<br>New Westminster B. C.<br>Trade Mark<br>**·RED BAND SHINGLES**<br>XXX XXXXX Stars Clears<br>From Mill to You |
| If you want a market for B. C. Red Cedar Shingles put an advertisement on this page. | **Kootenay Shingle Co. Ltd.**<br>Salmo, B. C.<br>Red Cedar Shingles<br>xxx and xx.<br>Packed by the thousand |

# Canada Lumberman

/ounded 1880

### The National Lumber Journal for Forty Years

Issued on the 1st and 15th of every month by

## HUGH C. MACLEAN PUBLICATIONS, Limited

THOS. S. YOUNG, Managing Director

HEAD OFFICE  - - - -  347 Adelaide Street, West, TORONTO

Proprietors and Publishers also of Electrical News, Contract Record,
Canadian Woodworker and Footwear in Canada.

| | |
|---|---|
| VANCOUVER - - - - - - | Winch Building |
| MONTREAL - - - | 119 Board of Trade Bldg. |
| WINNIPEG - - - - | 302 Travellers' Bldg. |
| NEW YORK - - - - - | 296 Broadway |
| CHICAGO - - - | Room 803, 63 E. Adams St. |
| LONDON, ENG. - - - | 16 Regent Street, S.W. |

### TERMS OF SUBSCRIPTION

Canada, United States and Great Britain, $3.00 per year, in advance; other
foreign countries embraced in the General Postal Union, $4.00.

Single copies, 20 cents.

Authorized by the Postmaster-General for Canada, for transmission as
second-class matter.

| | | |
|---|---|---|
| Vol. 42 | Toronto, February 1, 1922 | No. 3 |

## Getting Good Out of Conventions

January has been a month of conventions and get-together occasions in the Canadian lumber trade. The organization activities are not confined to any one special branch but the spirit of co-operation permeates the manufacturing, wholesale and retail ranks. By an interchange of visits, by a broadening out in purpose and ideals, each section of the trade has come to realize that it cannot stand alone, that it is an integral part, and only, by unity of effort and harmonious dealings, can business be brought out of the slough in which it has been for some time past, and based upon a more active plane with a bigger outlook and more encouraging fundamental features.

Those men who are devoting their time to association interests are not inspired by any selfish or sordid spirit. They are broad-minded and progressive and doing all in their power to help the other fellow to higher and better things. Sometimes the other fellow is too blind, prejudiced or biased to recognize what is being undertaken on his behalf. He is quite willing to share in any benefits and claim a part of all the advantages without rendering any service himself or paying a small membership fee to aid in carrying on the good work.

Ingratitude on the part of many is the penalty of pioneers in any important movement and leaders in any great cause are often decried. No institution or organization rises to 100% efficiency, as long as there are differences in men and disposition, there will be the individual who is of suspicious nature, thinking that others are out to "do him" or are acting from purely mercenary motives. Such a being moves around in a circle which leads nowhere, and never gets a loftier perspective than that bounded by self-interest and narrow thoughts.

The man, who goes to a convention and rubs shoulders with his fellow-men, who takes part in the discussion and seeks to carry away as many ideas and pointers as possible, will always get out of any great organization something really worth while,—something that will count and enable him to be a better and more vigilant member of the community, a more public-spirited citizen, a more efficient merchant, a kindlier neighbor and a more tolerant tradesman. He will realize that life consists not altogether in getting, but in giving. His view will become larger than that of the almighty dollar, and he will recognize that the highest achievement is in genuine service or doing a good turn to the other fellow. He seeks in his pathway through life to scatter brightness and sunshine and feels that his mission is a worthy one. No man can serve a community in a more public-spirited and uplifting way than the dealer in forest products; he plays no small part in carrying forward the home-building campaign which aa it strengthens and develops, marks the welfare, prosperity and happiness of every centre. The retail lumberman is engaged today in a vocation that is eminently worth while, encouraging and optimistic.

## Best Wishes for the New President

J. C. Scofield, who is president and managing-director of the Windsor Lumber Co., Windsor, Ont., is being heartily congratulated on his elevation to the presidency of the Ontario Retail Lumber Dealers' Association.

He is an ardent advocate of organization and has been an untiring worker in building up the O. R. L. D. A. to its present high status. He has served on a number of committees, and has been active in season and out of season in doing everything possible to increase the prestige and usefulness of the body which he now has the distinction to lead.

Mr. Scofield is one of the live wire and really aggressive retail lumbermen of Ontario. He is a thorough believer in advertising and in all modern facilities for doing business. He has inaugurated a number of campaigns which have resulted in increasing greatly the sale of interior and exterior trim among home owners, and at the same time created a desire in the public mind to possess their own domiciles in the Border Cities.

Under the direction of Mr. Scofield, the Ontario Retail Lumber Dealers' Association should have a prosperous and pleasant year. The next convention will be held in the Border Cities in 1923 which is a tribute to the new president, the same as the recent gathering in Ottawa was to the retiring president, E. M. Barrett, who also filled the chair with credit to himself and honor to his associates.

## Mr. Lamar Messenger of Good Cheer

The visit of Fred. H. Lamar, of Vancouver, secretary-manager of the Shingle Manufacturers' Association of British Columbia, to the East, and his breezy and instructive talks before the Canadian Lumbermen's Association at its meeting in Toronto, and the Ontario Retail Lumber Dealers' Association in Ottawa, will long be remembered.

Mr. Lamar bore greetings from the West and at once placed himself in accord with those whom he had the pleasure of meeting either individually or collectively. He paid a graceful tribute to the retailers of Ontario as the logical distributors of B. C. shingles, and gave much timely information regarding their manufacture, quality, distribution and use.

Mr. Lamar's addresses were well received. He proved to be an alert and genial representative, one in whose hands the future interests of the shingle manufacturers of the coast will be ably looked after. He has had a long experience in connection with association and secretarial work and has always made a success of anything that he has undertaken.

On returning to the West, Mr. Lamar carries with him the best wishes of the many friends that he met during his altogether too brief stay in the East.

---

## Getting Customer and Holding His Trade

y "Optimist"

It is one thing to procure a customer or patron and another to hold his patronage.

We are too self-satisfied with our former achievements and living upon our past reputation, which is a sure sign of deterioration.

Are we 100 per cent efficient?—absolutely no—we talk of advertising as a medium whereby to procure business. Let us advertise by the simple method of satisfying each and every customer, giving them a square deal, courteous treatment, quick deliveries, making every order a special...If this course is followed rigidly no other advertising will be necessary.

We are taking too much time to execute an order, in some cases twice the length of time required. This applies to mill, yard, warehouse, and factory.

If a patron requires a small order of sash, doors, or other factory work at a day's notice and his request is possible we should comply, assuming of course that he does not make it a general rule.

It is the individual and firm that can render extraordinary service that gathers up the good things.

There is a lack of co-operation between our different departments which is costing money and interfering with service. Another noticeable weakness is in the indifferent way in which we hand out information to our customers. We seem to forget that it is a matter of very grave importance to him when his goods will be delivered. We make promises to him and forget or neglect to see that they are executed. No matter what the cause of non-fulfilment may be, if we fail to execute we have lied to him and consequently dropped in his estimation.

# Ontario Lumber Retailers in Big Convention

### The Annual Gathering Marked by Much Interest and Enthusiasm—Important Trade Topics Discussed at Ottawa—Windsor Gets the Next Meeting

J. C. Scofield, Windsor, Ont.
New President of O.R.L.D.A.

Successful in every detail, harmonious in action, and enthusiastic in outlook, was the fifth annual convention of the Ontario Retail Lumber Dealers' Association held in Ottawa on January 18th and 19th. The attendance was representative of all parts of the province, there being a large delegation from the Niagara Peninsula, South Western Ontario and other points. The discussions were interesting, the reports instructive and the associations inspiring. The Ottawa lumber fraternity left nothing undone to make the assembly outstanding and memorable. The Chateau Laurier was an admirable rendezvous, and in addition to the many retailers present, a number of manufacturers and wholesalers looked in upon the sessions from time to time.

It was decided to hold the next annual convention in Windsor, Ont., where a fine, large hotel is being completed. It is probable that the gathering will be a three-day affair as the Detroit lumber dealers are anxious to join with those of the Border Cities in entertaining the Ontario yardmen.

J. C. Scofield, of Windsor, the new president of the association, has long been a live wire and will put plenty of pep into the organization. He will be ably assisted by the new vice-president, K. J. Shirton, who has been active in promoting the O. R. L. D. A. ever since its inception, and is chairman of the Niagara Peninsula District. Mr. Scofield was nominated by J. T. Wallace, of London, and seconded by B. F. Clarke. He in turn nominated E. M. Barrett as president for another term but the latter gracefully retired.

For vice-president there were three names put forward, those of G. W. Boake, of Toronto, W. M. Tupling, of Orillia, and K. J. Shirton, of Dunnville. Mr. Shirton who is also Mayor of Dunnville, was the winner but the contest was a close one.

### The Officers for Coming Year

The complete list of officers and directors for the coming year are:—

President,—J. C. Scofield, Windsor Lumber Co., Ltd., Windsor.
Vice-president,—K. J. Shirton, William Shirton Lumber Co., Dunnville.
Secretary-treasurer,—H. Boultbee, Toronto.
Directors:—
Eastern District,—F. B. Van Dusen, Brockville; G. P. Davidson, Ottawa.
Central District,—W. M. Tupling, Orillia; W. C. Irvin, Toronto.
Western District,—Thomas Patterson, Hamilton; J. T. Grantham, Brantford.
Southern District,—E. R. Sanders, St. Thomas; J. T. Wallace London.
Northern District,—F. E. Hollingsworth, Sault Ste. Marie; D. H. Andress, Sudbury.
In addition to the foregoing, each chairman of the other districts, such as Niagara Peninsula, Georgetown, etc., as they are elected, become members of the executive as well as the immediate past president.

### Midsummer Jaunt up Great Lakes

It was also decided to hold a midsummer outing up the Great Lakes to Duluth. The trip will take place during the last week in June and the members will be accompanied by their wives and families.

A letter was read by president Barrett from John B. Reid, of Toronto, honorary president of the O. R. L. D. A., who is spending the winter months in St. Petersburg, Florida. Mr. Reid conveyed

greetings to his many friends in the organization and said he was with them in spirit if not in person. He put in a word or two for the proposed outing up the Great Lakes. The suggestion was well received and later when the Resolutions Committee presented its report, the question was definitely settled without any opposition. To Duluth by the Northern Navigation Company's steamers from Windsor and Sarnia will the retailers of the province sail during the coming summer.

Many other important matters were discussed at the session such as; the organization of a Mutual Fire Insurance Association among the members; the necessity of reducing the present freight rates and backing up the efforts of other public bodies in this direction; the extension of the stop-over privilege for dressing, grading and kiln drying from thirty days to twelve months; the correction of the present demurrage charges; the inviting of ladies to the convention; the progress made on the proposed new Mechanics' Lien Act; the opposition to the anti-shingle legislation; the formation of more local associations; the extension of the membership and the use of the plan book of the Western Retail Lumber Dealers' Association, etc. These and other topics were taken up and the discussion is covered fully in another page of the "Canada Lumberman."

### Social and Other Features

In a general review of the gathering, it may be stated that on the afternoon of the first day a visit was paid to the new Parliament Buildings and under competent guides a tour through the Commons Chambers, Senate Chamber, Hall of Fame, Restaurant, Library and other departments of the Nepean sandstone building, was enjoyed. In the evening there was a theatre party to Loew's, while others attended the winter fair stock show or went to see the hockey match. A few enjoyed a game of curling and, perhaps, others of the retail lumbermen went across the river to Hull, but on this point it is not possible to speak with any degree of certitude as no register was kept. The banquet on the evening of January 19th closed a highly successful and remarkable convention.

A. G. Rose, who is acting secretary-treasurer of the Ottawa Lumbermen's Credit Bureau, was also the secretary of the local committee of arrangements and saw that everybody was well looked after. Mr. Rose has been taking up the work temporarily of H. A. L. Swan, former secretary-treasurer of the Bureau, who has gone to Nashville, Tenn., to reside. The absence of Mr. Swan is much regretted and many friends will wish him every success in his new sphere of activity.

## President Barrett on Trade Conditions

E. M. Barrett of Ottawa, President of the Association, presented the following comprehensive report:—

"Gentlemen of the Ontario Retail Lumber Dealers' Association, on behalf of the Ottawa members I welcome you to Ottawa. It is our wish that your visit may be a pleasant and profitable one.

Trade conditions during the past year have not been up to expectations and competition has been so keen that the margin of profit has almost disappeared. There are several reasons for this. Firstly during the war and for nearly two years after its closing, we went through an era of trade expansion and unheard of period of financial and credit inflations. All business men realized that a readjustment of this condition was imperative before we could get down to normal. This trade expansion was partly due to a reaction from years of saving and sacrifice during the war and, when the Armistice was signed, people began to spend as never before and the demands upon industry became so insistent that a trade boom without a parallel followed.

This boom like all others was accompanied by the evils of over-expansion. Company promoters and gold brick artists were organizing all kinds of fake companies, such as oil, mining and doubtful commercial propositions; the public as usual being shorn almost over night during the year 1920. Conditions changed and what looked like a real boom developed into a boomerang; people stopped spending. The demand for reduction in prices became general. The agri-

E. J. Shirliff, Dunnville, Ont.
New Vice-President O.R.L.D.A.

H. Boultbee, Toronto, Ont.
Secy.-Treas. O.R.L.D.A.

F. B. Van Dusen, Brockville, Ont.
Director O.R.L.D.A.

G. P. Davidson, Ottawa, Ont.
Director O.R.L.D.A.

cultural community suffered severely, the prices of agricultural products dropping away below pre-war standards. Uncertain demand and fluctuating prices of raw materials forced manufacturers to close their factories; unemployment became general; banks and loan companies began to withdraw credits and call in loans.

At present conditions are slowly improving. The big problem to-day is one of convincing the public that we have reached the bottom and the only way we can accomplish this is to work and get our prices down. The lumber trade is doing its part, but unfortunately labor and a great many other staple industries are not making the effort which they should to approach pre-war standards.

It is not my intention to take up much of your time discussing this as our secretary, Mr. Boultbee, will give you a report in detail and I am, therefore, going to comment briefly on our activities during the past year.

## Mechanics' Lien Act

During the year we have made good progress with this. Our solicitor, Mr. Jennings, prepared a bill and had it submitted to the Government through Mr. W. F. N. Sinclair, M.P.P. This bill received two readings and was then submitted to a committee of the house. This committee has met twice and we were represented by Mr. Jennings of Toronto, Mr. Lucas, of Columbus, Ohio, and a large deputation of our Toronto members. We have impressed the Government with the fact that the present act is obsolete and they are at present preparing a new act. We believe they will incorporate the best features of our draft bill.

## New Sales Tax Bill

On May 19th, 1921, the new Sales Tax came into effect. It was the opinion that this act would remove all misunderstanding and that we would know exactly where we stood. The act itself is very clear and the Department's original rulings which followed confirmed our first impression. The mill or operator who cuts the logs into lumber, lath, or shingles is required to pay sale tax at the rate of 2 per cent upon the sale price of such article.

A dealer purchasing lumber rough or dressed from a manufacturer who converted such goods directly from the logs and charged 2 per cent tax thereon is not required to pay a further tax when reselling such articles. When we got these rulings we thought we would have no further trouble but the officials appointed to carry out the terms of the act are giving contrary rulings and also classifying contractors as manufacturers. I believe the only satisfactory way to handle this tax is for the Department to levy a tax on the manufacturers large enough to cover their requirements, and that this tax should stop there and the manufacturer should absorb the amount the same as any other item of cost.

## Association Plan Book

From the investigation that we have made we have come to the conclusion that for an Association as small as ours this is going to be an expensive proposition, and we are not prepared to recommend it unless we get a guarantee from each member of sufficient to cover cost of production.

## Anti-Shingle Legislation

During the year we have had to contend with the usual Anti-Shingle Legislation instigated by interested parties working through the Fire Prevention League. This organization is controlled absolutely by the paint-using people. At nearly every convention of the As-

sociation they out number all other representatives. As a distributor I have no objection to those people selling their products, but I firmly believe that in any case, the product should be sold on its merits and not through favorable legislation which they lobby through parliament. Of course, lumber distributors stock patent roofings but we do general merchants, hardware dealers and others. We should, therefore, insist on cedar shingles (a product which only lumber men handle) getting a square deal.

## Traffic Department

During the year I received several bulletins from the Traffic Department of Ohio and Illinois associations. These I have forwarded to our Secretary, but we are differently located to Illinois and Ohio. They have a large population and a great many roads and many short hauls, whereas we have a small population, only two main railways and a large portion of our business is through traffic from either West or East. I am, therefore, of the opinion that it will not pay us to establish a traffic department.

## Mutual Fire Insurance

During the year I have been corresponding with Mr. Alan M. Stewart, of the Western Retail Lumbermen's Mutual Fire Insurance Company. Under date of October the 10th, Mr. Stewart wrote me as follows:

"I might say that we formed a Mutual Fire Insurance Company sixteen years ago. At the time of forming the same, our basis rate with Board Companies was $2.50 to $3.00. Since then the Board Companies have come down from time to time, and their basis rate now is 75 cents."

"For the first three years of our existence, our basis rate was 72 cents, and in that time we built up a reserve of $8,500 odd. The next two years our basis rate was 54 cents per $100, and we brought our reserve up to $20,500 odd. The next three years our basis rate was 48 cents per $100 and we brought our reserve to $40,500 odd. We then insured down as low as 36 cents, bringing our reserve to $41,000. In 1915-16-17, our losses were higher, and we went back to our 48 cent rate, bringing our reserve to $45,000 odd. In 1918 our rate was 36 cents per $100, 1919, 12 cents, and 1920, 15 cents and our reserve now stands at $55,500 odd and our total insurance is over $6,000,000 so you can see that we have done a perfectly safe and conservative business, and have made the insurance to our members very cheap. When we started, our limit was $3,000; this was increased to $5,000 and then to $7,000, and last year to $10,000."

## Favors Mutual Fire Insurance

Now, gentlemen, this information has been passed on to our committee on insurance and no doubt they will have a recommendation for you. Personally, I believe the time has arrived when we should extend our activities and I believe that we should take immediate steps to form a Lumbermen's Mutual Fire Insurance Corporation. In addition to the benefits that we would derive from our own underwriting we could place our total insurance through this bureau and the commissions which they would collect would eventually make a handsome reserve.

Now gentlemen, we have been organized for four years and while we have accomplished a lot I believe the need for co-operating is greater to-day than ever; when you consider the problems we have solved the credit information we have secured and passed on to our members, the disputes we have been able to settle by arbitration, the

manner in which we have been able to protect our members from unfair competition. This, gentlemen, during the year has been a big question. The secretary's report will show numerous cases where mushroom wholesalers and even a few manufacturers adopted the practice of selling to farmers' clubs, contractors and individuals. The dealer who felt this competition always reported particulars to our Secretary with the result that in the majority of cases he was able to correspond with the parties and get favorable results.

Now consider for a moment what we accomplished through our negotiations with the Department of Inland Revenue and the dollars we saved our members by giving them prompt, first-hand information, in regard to the manner in which the new act worked and the amount of tax you had to pay. Another benefit that your Association claims a share of credit for is the reduction in the price of cement. The secretary will show the steps we took to bring this matter to the attention of the Canada Cement Co., and the results that followed. We believe our suggestions were of value to the company when they were considering the reduction of the price.

**The Friendly Spirit of Co-operation**

Before concluding this part of my address, I must draw your attention to the friendly spirit of co-operation that exists between ourselves, the wholesaler and the manufacturer. Our interests are identical and our organizations are bringing us closer together and assist us to understand each other better.

It is claimed by men in position to judge that the building industry gives more employment and a greater variety of employment than any other industry. It is, therefore, very necessary for building to proceed, so as to furnish suitable living accommodations and employment to the huge army of men that are walking our streets looking for work.

One of our greatest handicaps to-day is unfair valuation of buildings by loaning companies and individuals. They, at present, are only advancing 40 to 45 per cent. This is retarding building, even more than the present high cost of labour and making it impossible

for contractors and others to proceed. I believe we should petition the Government to try and induce it to start a campaign amongst the loan companies and individuals to be more generous in placing loans. It would even be preferable for the Government to guarantee loans to the extent of 75 per cent of the value of the property. This would be the means of starting a legitimate building boom that would greatly relieve present unemployment.

**The Annual Midsummer Outing**

Now, gentlemen, an association such as ours should not spend all the time working. We must have a little diversion and occasionally get away from business. Our midsummer outings give us this opportunity. During 1920 our trip to North Bay and vicinity was brought to a very successful close by a couple of days' fishing at the Alabama Hotel on the French River. Then again this year our trip to Byng Inlet was thoroughly enjoyed by everyone taking part. The arrangements which our host, Mr. Bigwood, made were very generous and of the best. The Model Camp on John Haystead's Island, the generous furnishing of blankets, boats, launches, etc., was very much appreciated, but when our party arrived at the dining scow we felt like the Queen of Sheba when she saw Solomon in his glory. The thanks of our Association should be tendered to the good fellows who entertained us. Now for this summer make it a trip to the wilds where we can forget starched collars and business.

By your fruits you shall know them; our fruits are many and the benefits derived also are many. If our Association was only instrumental in bringing a lot of good fellows together and getting them better acquainted it would justify its existence, but it has done much more. It is ours, yours and mine. We have spent time and money to organize and bring it to the present, it has made good. It is, therefore, our duty, yours, and mine to work for it and make it more useful and a greater benefit in the future.

In conclusion I wish to again express my very deep appreciation for the honor which you have bestowed on me at your last annual meeting when you elected me your president.

# *Secretary Reviews Busy Year in The Association*

H. Boultbee, of Toronto, Secretary of the Ontario Retail Lumber Dealers' Association, presented a long report covering many matters of interest, giving a complete review of what had come up during the year and the action that had been taken by the executive. He said that the most fitting subject with which to start was a reference to the midsummer outing which was held last August to Byng Inlet, Ont. There the fifty-two retailers, who took in the jaunt, were entertained for three days by Graves, Bigwood & Co., and spent a most delightful time in fishing, motor-boating, canoeing, etc. The members of the party were well looked after by their hosts and had a delightful experience sleeping in tents and living close to nature.

In regard to the proposed outing for the coming year, Mr. Boultbee stated that Mr. J. C. Scofield, of Windsor, vice-president of the Association, had commenced as far back as August 1921, to consider a good programme for the midsummer trip of the present year. He had suggested that the members should hold their outing on board one of the Northern Navigation Company's steamers running up from Sarnia to Duluth and return. The cost might be greater than on previous picnics but meeting under such circumstances would undoubtedly prove to be most interesting and enjoyable.

**The Sales Tax Regulations**

On May 10th, 1921, new sales tax regulations came into effect. Our Association got into touch as early as possible with the Department at Ottawa so as to obtain information regarding the effect of the changes, upon retail lumber dealers. It was some weeks before the Department was able to give us definite information for the guidance of our members. At the earliest possible moment this was obtained and mailed by circular to our members, as well as being published in the Monthly Bulletin.

In connection with the new sales tax, our Association has been of definite and practical value to the whole retail trade in Eastern Canada. The regulations effective from May 10th, imposed a tax of 2 per cent upon lumber sold by a manufacturer, after which, the regulations say, "there is no further tax upon resale." One would think that this phrase was about as clear as any phrase in the English language could be. Nevertheless, wholesale lumber dealers in Western Canada have interpreted the new sales tax in such a manner as to justify them in charging a tax upon their invoices to retailers. We advised all our members that the new sales tax regulations would not require them to pay a tax upon lumber when pur-

chased from a wholesaler, but that if they purchased lumber from a manufacturer they must pay a tax of at least 1½ per cent, or 2 per cent if the manufacturer does not absorb one half of 1 per cent. We made the matter as clear as possible to our members and urged them all to adopt a policy of refusing to pay any sales tax to a wholesaler.

It was very important that our members should be advised of this situation promptly and distinctly, because the Pacific Coast Shippers' Association had obtained a statement from the Commissioner of Taxation advising them that "wholesalers CAN charge on their invoices the sales tax paid to manufacturers". The Pacific Coast Shippers' Association advised its members to add the tax to their invoices and all Western wholesalers who had customers in Eastern Canada attempted to charge them the tax. Our members took a practically unanimous stand by refusing to pay. The result is, that in Eastern Canada, retail lumber dealers are following the exact wording of the regulations and are not paying a sales tax to wholesalers whereas in Western Canada retail lumber dealers are being charged the sales tax by wholesalers and are paying it. The joker in connection with this whole matter is the statement made by the Commissioner of Taxation to the Pacific Coast Shippers' Association to the effect that they "CAN charge on their invoices the sales tax paid to manufacturers." No one contradicts them on this point. They CAN charge the tax, but the Government does not say it will back them up in collecting it. Not only CAN the wholesalers charge the tax on their invoices but if they want to they can charge 50 per cent of a sales tax, but their chances of collecting it, whether 2 per cent or 50 per cent are not good, nor do we imagine that having collected it they would pay it over to the Government.

**Association Showed its Usefulness**

In connection with the sales tax a very important situation developed about the middle of July in which our Association again was fortunate enough to be of definite and practical value to its members. A representative of the Department of Customs and Inland Revenue commenced visiting some of our members' offices in Eastern Ontario about midsummer and examined their books of accounts. In several cases he advised our members that they should have collected and paid a tax to the Government on all material sold to contractors. This was a distinct contradiction of the regulations upon which our members had been working throughout

W. M. Tepling, Orillia, Ont.
Director O.R.L.D.A.

W. C. Irvin, Toronto, Ont.
Director O.R.L.D.A.

Thomas Patterson, Hamilton, Ont.
Director O.R.L.D.A.

A. R. Sanders, St. Thomas, Ont.
Director O.R.L.D.A.

the twelve months previous to May 10th, 1921. We had been advised by the Commissioner of Taxation that any material sold by a retail lumber dealer in exactly the same condition as when purchased by him was not subject to a tax, even though sold to a contractor. The official who called upon some of our members last summer assessed heavy amounts against them, amounting to $500.00 and in one case about $700.00.

The situation looked very serious. If it was allowed to pass without complaint on our part it meant that every one of our members would probably be called upon to pay large additional sums which they could not obtain from the customers to whom the goods had been sold without tax. We took the matter up with the Department. We wrote them as vigorous a letter as we could. We quoted the regulations and instructions we had obtained from the Commissioner of Taxation. At first our correspondence brought very little result. The Department seemed disposed to misunderstand our letter, but after several letters we finally received a letter which we think cleared up the situation.

The letter was under date of Sept. 22nd, and said "a bona-fide retail lumber dealer operating a planing mill, if his retail trade is segregated from the mill, may apply to the Department for refund in respect of sales tax which he paid upon goods resold by him in the same condition as when purchased, provided that satisfactory evidence is forthcoming that the lumber in question had previously borne the maximum rate of sales tax at the time of its being purchased by the retailer". Those of our members who had already been assessed were advised of this and we believe that in the few cases in which they made payment they were able to obtain a refund. In other cases the Department's claim against them was settled accordingly.

### Value Secured from Organization

No doubt it sometimes occurs to a few retail lumber dealers to ask a question as to what value they get out of membership in The Ontario Retail Lumber Dealers' Association. To any of these doubtful ones we would reply by asking another question. Let us leave aside for the moment every other consideration except the final one and narrow it down to a consideration of this sales tax matter. Let each retail lumber dealer in Ontario figure out how much lumber he has bought from wholesalers since May 10th, 1921, when the new sales tax regulations went into effect. Then let him figure out 1½ per cent on the total cost of his year's purchases from wholesalers. Had the retail lumber dealers in Ontario not been organized, the western wholesalers and probably the Eastern ones would have collected from them a sales tax of 1½ per cent on all their purchases since May 10th, 1921. Balance this off against the amount paid for membership in our Association and we venture to say that there will be a large amount to the credit of our organization, which has been saved to every dealer. This is an unquestionable fact, because, we know that wholesalers are collecting this tax in other parts of Canada contrary to the expressed terms of the sales tax regulations.

### Standard Order Form

At our annual meeting last year a resolution was carried approving the standard order form that had been submitted by a Special Committee, and instructing the Secretary to have it printed and to furnish copies to those members who desired to place orders for it at cost. This was done and orders for the form were received

from about fifteen members of the Association. After the members had been using the order form for a few months the Secretary wrote to them asking for a report upon the way in which it was being received. The replies sent in were practically all of the same kind, reporting that no difficulty had been experienced in placing orders upon these forms and that they believed the form would be of value to the trade. One member reported to the opposite effect, but apparently had not made a serious attempt to use the form, after having it criticized by the first wholesaler to whom he submitted it. Having adopted this form and having proved that it can be successfully used, it is advisable now that our Association should take some steps towards having it more generally used by the members.

### Mechanics' Lien Act

We are able this year to report more progress in connection with this important matter. We have not, by any means, come to the end of our campaign for a modern Mechanics' Lien Act, but we have, at last, convinced the Government and the other interested parties, including mortgage companies, contractors, architects, and the labour element, that the present Mechanics' Lien Act gives very little protection to any one and is an unnecessary burden to the building trade. These various interests have all admitted before a Special Committee of the Ontario Legislature, that a new Act is necessary.

At the last session of the Legislature our members will recall that we submitted a Bill through Mr. W. E. N. Sinclair, M. P. P., which was given a second reading and referred to a Special Committee. The purpose of submitting this Bill was to get the matter definitely before the House so that a Committee could be appointed. We are endeavouring to include in this Bill everything that our members have submitted to us as important. We modelled the Bill very largely upon an Act that has been in force in the State of Ohio for eight years past, and which has given complete satisfaction to all parties concerned. Its main principle is that the owner shall be considered responsible for the payment of all material and labour bills, to the extent of a full 100 per cent of the contract price, and that he can protect himself by securing, from the main contractor, an affidavit showing what material and labour bills have not been paid when the contractor asks for a draw. Material men and labourers who fear that the contractor's affidavit may not contain their names and claims, are expressly permitted by our Bill to notify the owner informally. With such notices and the contractor's affidavit the owner will see that the unpaid bills are paid, and then he is free to give to the contractor any surplus then payable.

There are other important features in our Bill, but this is the main principle. It extends the responsibility of the owner from 15 and 20 per cent to a full 100 per cent of the contract price and furnishes him with means of protecting himself, if he makes payments to the contractor in accordance with the requirements of the Act. This principle is so fair, that we believe we have impressed the Special Committee of the Legislature with the reasonableness of our point of view. We feel sure that our members can count upon a new Bill being submitted at the next Session of the Legislature, and we are optimistic enough to think that it will be sponsored by the Government and will contain many of the features that our Association desires. It still remains for us, however, to convince the Members of Parliament that our Bill is a good one, and should be passed. Our members are strongly urged not to allow any oppor-

tunity to pass by in this connection, and to bring home to their local Members of Parliament as clearly as possible the great necessity for a new Act, and the fairness of the Act that we have proposed.

### Credit Information

Our Association has not developed anything at all definite in the nature of a credit bureau for the use of all its members. Local credit bureaus are, however, being established and operated with success in Toronto, Ottawa, Niagara Peninsula and by our Branch No. 7, which usually holds its meetings at Stratford. The plan of operation in connection with all of these credit bureaus is that members exchange through their local Secretary, information regarding the credit standing of their customers. The protection thus secured is of inestimable value. This matter is referred to in the hope that other branches or groups of dealers in Ontario may decide to work out a similar service.

There have been several cases during the past year in which our members have asked us for information regarding the financial standing of parties with whom they have been considering the advisability of opening up business. We have been able in each case to furnish information and in some important cases this information has saved our members considerable money and trouble.

### Association Plan Book

In accordance with a resolution carried at our last Annual meeting your President and Secretary have been devoting considerable time to an investigation of the best manner in which to furnish our members with a book of house plans, barn plans, etc. The matter is an important one and at the same time a difficult one, in connection with which to arrive at a conclusion as to the best method for working it out. We have communicated during the year with publishers of a number of plan books in Canada and the United States. We have received copies of their plan books and offers to co-operate with us in furnishing them to our members. While all of these plan books were interesting, we did not feel that any of them would fill the bill definitely and permanently for the members of our Association. We have therefore fallen back upon a proposal to originate a plan book of our own. Investigations that we made at Toronto indicated that we might not find hearty co-operation from the architects if we were getting out such a book. Fortunately, however, our President was able to get into touch with a firm of architects in Ottawa who will probably be able to furnish us with their services in the preparation of plans, bills of material, etc., for such a book at a reasonable cost.

### The Wooden Shingle Situation

Reference to this subject was made in the Secretary's last annual report. At that time we were facing a serious campaign on the part of some Insurance enthusiasts and the manufacturers of patent roofings, who were endeavoring to have the Ontario Legislature pass an Act eliminating the use of the wooden shingle. The opposition which we presented to this campaign was fortunately successful, as we learned early in July that the Ontario Fire Prevention League had decided to drop its campaign, as it had come to the conclusion that the public would not stand for it.

There has been only one other development in connection with this matter during the past year. On Sept. 29th, and 30th, the third Annual Convention of the Dominion Fire Prevention Association was held in Ottawa. It was attended by advocates of the Anti-Wooden Shingle Movement, including representatives of patent and metal shingles and the executive of the Fire Chief's Association. Mr. J. B. Laidlaw, General Manager of the Norwich Union Fire Insurance Company, of Toronto, who brought the matter up a year previous, again submitted it at this meeting. The Secretary of the Canadian Lumbermen's Association and the Secretary of the Canadian Forestry Association were both in attendance and presented strong arguments against the adoption of any Anti-Wooden Shingle Resolution.

The Secretary of the Canadian Lumbermen's Association submitted a substitute resolution, which was carried, and which gives the Wooden Shingle Industry a fair chance of success in this campaign. The resolution as carried states that it is expedient that an impartial committee should be appointed to examine, test and report upon various kinds of roof coverings sold in Canada. The result of carrying this resolution is that the wooden shingle remains on the map for the time being, and the lumber industry has sufficient time to plan a vigorous campaign to defeat the aims of the advocates of the Anti-Wooden Shingle Legislation. This is a subject which will be a fitting one for our Association to discuss in detail with a view to the adoption of a definite line of policy.

### Traffic Department

This matter has only come up during the year upon one occasion, in correspondence with our President, who, after receiving information from the Illinois Association as to the operation of their Traffic Department suggested that we might again bring the matter up at our annual meeting. It seems to your Secretary that the establishing of a Traffic Department by our Association is not a practical proposition with our limited membership. Take for instance the case of the Illinois Association, whose figures were submitted to our President. During the month of July they collected for their members traffic claims amounting to $182.00. During August they collected $375.00. During September they collected $177.00. For the three months their total collections were $734.00, making a monthly average of $244.00. Suppose the Association were to receive 25 per cent for its services, that would make $61.00 per month income to the Association. This would not go far towards paying the salary and expenses of an expert traffic man. Even supposing the Association received 50 per cent of the collections, the total income of the Association would be $122.00 per month. The Association certainly could not make a Traffic Department self-supporting on such a basis. Possibly the Illinois Association has a man giving only part time to this work. In Ontario we would not have anything like the number of claims that the Association in Illinois will have and for these reasons it has not seemed to your Secretary that under present conditions a Traffic Department can be created with any reasonable prospect of success. This is a subject, however, which should not be passed by on the mere suggestion of your Secretary, as it may be possible for us, after discussing the matter, to devise a means of securing the desired results.

### Arbitration Proceedings

Two matters calling for Arbitration were submitted to the Association during the year. In each case the Arbitration Committee considered all the documents submitted. In accordance with the request of the parties interested, the documents were also considered by the Arbitration Committee of the Wholesale Lumber Dealers' Association. It was not found necessary to hold joint meetings of the two Committees. Each Committee tendered its own decision. In one case the decision was in favor of the retail dealer. In the other case the Wholesalers decided against the retailers and the retailers gave a decision placing the responsibility equally upon both parties. The result was reported to the parties interested and the wholesaler agreed to accept the decision that was least favorable to him—that of the Retail Committee. This decision suggested that the amount in dispute be divided in half and we understand that the retailer sent his check to the wholesaler accordingly.

### Mutual Fire Insurance

There has been at each of our Annual Meetings, and some of our local district and branch meetings, a discussion of the possibility of organizing among our members an Association for handling their Fire Insurance on a Mutual Basis. We have not taken any definite steps in this direction, as our members have never passed a resolution directing that this should be done. Nevertheless, the subject is one that is dear to the hearts of many of our members and it has again been submitted to us this year. Our President, Mr. Barrett, has been in communication with Mr. Alan M. Stewart, Manager of the Retail Lumbermen's Mutual Fire Insurance Company, of Winnipeg, and has obtained some interesting facts regarding the Insurance work of the Western Retail Lumbermen's Association, under whom the Retail Lumbermen's Mutual Fire Insurance Company is operated. Mr. Barrett has suggested that we should have Mr. Stewart with us at this annual meeting, and that our Committee on Insurance should go carefully into the whole subject. This has been submitted to the Chairman of our Committee on Insurance,— Mr. Walter C. Laidlaw, who will deal with the matter in his annual report.

### Income Tax Forms

Early in June we received blank Income Tax Return Forms from the Inspector of Taxation, with instructions to fill them out in duplicate and return them. The form called for a list of purchases during the past year and for a great deal of information regarding such purchases. It would have involved a very large amount of work and expense for any firm to fill in these forms. We submitted immediate objection as vigorously as we could to the Department, and we received on June 29th, instructions from the Department to withhold the completion of these forms for the time being. Fortunately we have not received any further advice from the Department on this subject.

### The Price of Cement

Early last summer your Secretary received a letter from a wholesale lumber dealer in Montreal, drawing your attention to the fact that the price of cement, in his opinion, was far higher than it should be. He gave figures indicating that since the highest price had been reached, as a result of the war there had been little or no decline, and he asked our Association whether we could bring any

influence to bear upon the Canada Cement Company, who practically control the output of cement in Canada. We gave this matter considerable thought and finally upon instructions of your President we wrote a letter to Mr. F. P. Jones, General Manager of the Canada Cement Company, Limited. We published our letter in the Monthly Bulletin. We made out as strong a case as we could for a reduction in price. Mr. Jones favored us with a very diplomatic reply in which he endeavored to justify his company's price policy. We published his reply. In a subsequent letter he advised us that the company had now found it possible to make a reduction of 25 cents per barrel. It may have been only a coincidence that this reduction followed so closely upon the correspondence we had with Mr. Jones. Some of our own members, however, who handle cement and are closely in touch with the Canada Cement Company have assured us that our efforts in this connection were largely responsible for the reduction in price. We have received a similar assurance from the Montreal wholesaler who first submitted the matter to us.

### Programme for Our Convention

It has been suggested by one of our energetic members from Windsor, Mr. J. C. Scofield, that at the present convention and at future conventions the election of Officers for the ensuing year should be given an early place on the programme. Mr. Scofield's idea is that this is one of the most important matters of the many that we have to deal with, and that an early election will enable the Directors to hold a good meeting, during the convention. Our President agrees with Mr. Scofield in this regard and accordingly the election of Officers has been set down as an early item in our programme this year.

In view of the many important matters that are dealt with annually by our Association and particularly in view of the fact that the present year is likely to be a very busy one with retail lumber dealers, it is important that we should arrange during this year to bring into the Association a far greater membership than we have had in the past. As Secretary of the Association, I would like to ask every member whether he had his money's worth during the past year, and put it up to him as a business proposition that he owes to the Secretary and to the Directors considerably more effort than he has given in the past, towards increasing the membership of the Association and towards widening its field of usefulness. To my mind,

this is the most important matter that our Association has to consider.

During the year 1921 our Association shows only slight growth. Practically speaking our membership during 1921 was the same as during 1920. We finished the year with a total of 182 members. Out of a possible membership of 430 dealers in Ontario we should at least have 250 active members in our Association. The Secretary has done everything he could in the way of attending meetings and writing to prospects with a view to increasing the membership. There is no doubt that a considerable increase in our membership could be made without a great deal of effort, if the individual members of the Association would assume the duty of canvassing every retail lumber dealer they can who is not already a member.

### Membership of the Association

We have already reached a sufficient strength to demonstrate to the rest of the lumber trade that we are well organized and are a powerful unit wherever our mutual interests are concerned; but the influence which we have thus obtained will be greatly increased if during 1922 we are able to increase our membership to somewhere in the neighborhood of 250 if not more. This matter should be taken into consideration at the present meeting with a view to preparing a practical plan for obtaining this end. While on the subject of membership, the Secretary would like to impress upon all dealers who have already joined the Association, the importance of maintaining their membership from year to year and the equally great importance of paying their annual fees as early in the year as possible. Every year we have obtained a fair number of new members, but these have been offset to a considerable extent by old members who have failed to pay their fees. Somewhere in the neighborhood of a dozen members each year have not joined in the succeeding year and it has required much correspondence on the part of the Secretary to collect the fees during the latter months of the year from those who have not realized the importance of paying up promptly at the beginning of the year.

The variety of ways in which an Association such as ours, can be of service to its members, is great. Your Secretary's report covers a wide range of subjects. It does not begin to cover all the subjects that are dealt with in his daily correspondence.

The balance of the Secretary's report dealt largely with matters of trade ethics.

# Insurance Committee Emphasizes "Safety First" Work

The report of the Insurance Committee was read by the chairman, Walter C. Laidlaw, and was as folows:

The functions of the Insurance Committee cover two departments—Fire Insurance and Workmen's Compensation Insurance. A few years ago Fire Insurance was the only subject of interest. In those days the cost of Workmen's Compensation was so small it was not a serious item. To-day, under the operation of our Workmen's Compensation Act in Ontario, the cost has increased until it is a very serious item in the cost of handling lumber. This report will deal briefly with the two subjects.

### Fire Insurance

Under the heading of Fire Insurance your committee has very little to report. A considerable volume of Retail Lumber Insurance is being carried by various Mutual Companies at fair rates. The suggestion has been considered from time to time of forming an Ontario Lumber Mutual Fire Insurance Company. Your committee has not considered this matter seriously owing to the facilities now afforded us by other Mutual Companies. Your secretary, however, has been in communication with the Winnipeg office of the Western Retail Association who are operating a Mutual Lumber Fire Insurance Company for the benefit of retail lumber yards and you may have a report on this subject from him.

### Workmen's Compensation Insurance

The report for 1920 of the Workmen's Compensation Board of Ontario was issued on December 9th, 1921. The report for 1921 will not be available for some time. You will be interested in a brief summary of the Income and Expenditure for Class No. 4 which includes Planing Mills, Sash and Door Factories and Retail Lumber Yards.

The Total Income for the year 1920 amounted to $302,299. The expenditure divides itself into the amounts actually paid and the amounts estimated as follows.—

| 1. Compensation Paid | $85,555. |
| 2. Medical Aid | 26,204. |
| 3. Paid Safety Associations | 2,673. |
| 4. Administration | 3,965. |

Actually paid ........... $118,397.
5. Transferred for Pensions ................. 67,168.

| 6. Reserve for Disaster | 1,967. |
| 7. Compensation Deferred | 6,760. |
| 8. Compensation Estimated for Continuing Disabilities | 39,280. |
| 9. Compensation Estimated for Outstanding Accidents | 39,753. |
| 10. Compensation Estimated for Medical Aid | 12,969. |

Estimated ............ $167,706.

Total Charged as Expenditure ....286,303.
Provisional Balance ....... ....$15,996.

Total Income ...... ....... $302,299.
You will see from the above that the Board have been careful in setting up reserve funds and estimating future contingencies. There has been a good deal of criticism of the operation of this Act and it may be that the Legislature will be asked for a change in its working conditions. This, however, would come under the jurisdiction of the Legislation Committee.

### Eliminating the Cost of Accidents

The Insurance Committee has to deal with the condition as it is. The Act is in operation and is costing a lot of money. How can we reduce the cost? The only answer is by reducing accidents.

Under the terms of the Act the employers in group 4 were organized as the Wood Workers Accident Prevention Association and inspectors call regularly at each of your plants to endeavour to assist you in any possible way to eliminate the cost of accidents. The first duty of the inspector is to examine the physical hazards and to suggest to you mechanical safeguards where needed. These men are experienced in their work. They are working in your interest and you are asked to give them every consideration and endeavor to follow up any suggestions they may make in order to make your plant safe.

Over two-thirds of accidents that occur may be classed as due to pure carelessness. This can only be overcome by educational work among the men themselves. It must begin at the top and be passed on by you men, to your foremen and through them to your employees. The importance of "safety first" must be emphasized. Get the men interested in preventing accidents and in checking the man who is habitually careless. In some large plants in Ontario it is now the

F. E. Hollingsworth, Sault Ste Marie, Director O.R.L.D.A.     D. H. Andress, Sudbury, Ont. Director O.R.L.D.A.     J. T. Wallace, London, Ont. Director O.R.L.D.A.     E. M. Barrett, Ottawa, Ont. Retiring President, O.R.L.D.A.

practice to examine a man physically and mentally before hiring him, with a view to finding out whether he is safe. If the examination shows that he is likely to be an accident case, he is not hired. When a man has more than one accident he is at once dismissed. In this way this plant is endeavoring to get rid of the careless man.

### The Cause of Many Claims

Infection and blood poison is the cause of a great many claims. It is important that your men be compelled to come to the office and have any cut or scratch properly disinfected and bandaged at the time so as to prevent blood poison from setting in. If this rule were carefully followed a great many claims would be avoided.

It is astonishing, but true, that a great many men are satisfied to stay at home and collect two-thirds of their pay without working, as long as they can. It is also true that, in many cases, the doctors are willing to allow the men to do this. Each employer should have a talk with the doctors who look after his case and try to get them to chase the men back to work when they are fit for it and avoid this pernicious habit of loafing at the expense of the funds of the Board. The Board realize that it is our money that is being paid out and they feel that it is our duty as individual employers to check up any loafing of this character by our own employees. You are, therefore, recommended to have someone call regularly on any man who is off by reason of an accident and make reports to you as to his condition. If each of us follows this suggestion we will materially reduce the cost of accident insurance.

The report was adopted.

## What the Various Districts are Doing

One of the features of the session was the reports from the chairmen of the different districts.

C. R. Robertson, of Ottawa, Ont., stated the Eastern District had carried on and held weekly meetings and good work had been done by the Credit Bureau in furnishing information regarding the financial responsibility of contractors and others. Matters of interest pertaining to the trade were talked over at the regular gatherings and any grievances were brought up and thrashed out on the spot. Thus an understanding was reached and good feeling prevailed throughout the trade in Ottawa. Before the organization of the Eastern District and the Ottawa Retail Credit Bureau, every man was out with a knife to get business at any price, with little or no consideration for the other fellow. He believed that every member was well satisfied that he got his money's worth in connection with the district service.

T. H. Hancock, of Toronto, Ont., reporting for the Central District, said that monthly meetings were held and trade matters discussed. He regretted to find there were some scalpers cutting into the trade at certain periods of the year, and would like to see some remedy to stop the evil. He thought it would be better if the trade in Toronto held weekly meetings. They had been able to carry on and hoped they would always do so.

Frederick Taylor, of Hamilton, Ont., for the Western District, stated that regular meetings had been held with good results. There were two or three retailers outside the Association who seemed to take a special delight in cutting prices. Business had been rather

slow during the past year and an effort had been made to bring the outsiders in line. He believed that the Association of the Western District was a benefit to everyone and was giving satisfaction.

J. T. Wallace, of London, Ont., declared that the South Western Retail Lumber Dealers' Association was a fairly lively body and several successful meetings had been held. Trade had been fair in the cities but in the smaller districts business had not been so good. We have, said Mr. Wallace, our troubles the same as the others, but there is a good spirit among the members and we look forward to the coming year with confidence so far as our district is concerned.

F. E. Hollingsworth, of Sault Ste. Marie, Ont., representing the Northern District, spoke briefly concerning its activities.

K. J. Shirton, of Dunnville, Ont., chairman of the newly-organized Niagara Peninsula District, said that the territory covered by that body was too large and the train connection was not good for meeting at any central place. He had already taken up the matter with the Central Association with the idea of dividing the Niagara District and making it two,—an eastern and western division. He thought with smaller districts and more frequent meetings, better results would be achieved. "I was present," declared Mr. Shirton, "five years ago when the Ontario Association was started with just 22 members. To-day the membership is 186, and we have a good bank balance."

J. B. Mackenzie, of Georgetown, Ont., reporting on behalf of District No. 6, said that his territory was somewhat unique in that there was no town of more than 5,000 in the area which included some 12 lumber dealers. Two of them had recently sold out. All the towns were so widely situated that the dealers did not conflict in any way. Mr. Mackenzie paid a tribute to the fine gentlemanly qualities of the members in his district and said such men were an acquisition to any organization.

George S. Zimmerman, of Tavistock, Ont., chairman of the Stratford District, said that their district had got off to a good start but had been somewhat affected by the depression. He felt that retail lumber dealers were not careful enough in watching the statements in the press, and often allowed misleading information regarding trend of prices, etc., to pass unchallenged; for instance, it had been stated in one of the Stratford papers by a certain resident that there was a difference of $40.00 on white pine between Tavistock prices and those of Stratford. This remark had been allowed to go without contradiction although one price referred to mill run lumber and the other to entirely clear boards. He believed that needed readjustments had taken place in the price list of retail dealers and that the trade had come through the recent depression better than others.

W. M. Tupling, of Orillia, Ont., was the energetic chairman of the committee on Resolutions.

B. F. Clarke, of Glencoe, Ont., presented a very brief report on the Legislation and Transportation Committee, and W. C. Irvin on behalf of the Committee on Arbitration and Trade Relations. Mr. Clarke said that nothing very important had come up in connection with legislation and transportation except the new Mechanics' Lien Act, which had been fully outlined in the secretary's report.

H. P. Rowles, sales manager of the Duncan Lumber Co., Vancouver, B. C. returned recently from a business trip to the Coast, and has opened an office at Room 22, 6 King St. West, Toronto.

# "Ten Minute Talks" on Vital Retail Problems

### New Feature Introduced in Lumber Dealers' Convention Received with Appreciation—Every Day Propositions Presented in Heart-to-Heart Manner by Aggressive Yardmen

One of the features of the Ontario Retail Lumber Dealers' Association convention at Ottawa, was a number of ten minute talks on practical topics by representative lumber merchants who were allowed to choose their own subjects.

F. B. Van Dusen, of Brockville, opened the proceedings with an able address on "co-operation". There was need in his opinion for greater co-operation not only between manufacturers, wholesalers and retailers, but the latter should co-operate more with their customers. The dealers desired grades on lumber from manufacturers so that they might know what they were going to get. They should know what kind of a mill run board they were likely to receive for at present no two were alike. Some little places got the low grade boards which they could not use. Generally speaking the small dealer did not wish a black knotted board, although he could use a red knotted one. In grading mill run and dressing there should be a clearer definition and distinction. Then again, certain wholesalers sent out men on the road as lumber salesmen who did not know what they were talking about and, in making this statement, Mr. Van Dusen said he cast no reflection on salesmen for whom he had the highest respect. His firm some time ago had bought a car load of spruce in which there had been shipped five hundred feet of tamarack. Eventually the mistake had been corrected, although at first, a wire had been received that no tamarack had been sent out in the lot.

There was too much "passing the buck" all along the line in the lumber industry. He believed that the great bulk of retailers of lumber were honest men. They should co-operate more with one another, and not send out printed price lists of building materials giving misleading information as to the grades of the material quoted and showing prices, apparently lower than those of local dealers, and lower also than would be charged by the retailer in catering to his own customers. In New York state they called such a practice "poaching". Customers often came to the yard and asked for so much lumber, not saying what kind or what they wanted to do with it? It was the duty of the retailer to find out and give him real service by pointing out, after ascertaining the use, whether a higher or lower grade would answer the purpose desired, and thus they would be co-operating with customers more closely. Very often a dealer could save a patron money by giving him something that would meet his requirements for less money. The dealer should, Mr. Van Dusen added, be ready to resent any unjust criticism of his own business. Too many incorrect statements were printed in the press regarding the lumber trade, which were allowed to pass unanswered. He referred particularly to observations regarding the fire hazard of wooden shingles. The retailer was the logical customer and distributor of the wooden shingle. Recent returns had shown that only two per cent of the total losses caused by fires, were ignited by wooden shingles while ten per cent of the losses were caused by careless handling of matches. The dealer, said Mr. Van Dusen in conclusion, should devote time to fighting untruthful statements. He would thus be helping himself and others coming after him.

### Meeting Competition from Catalogue Houses

"Meeting Competition from Catalogue Houses" was dealt with by J. B. Mackenzie of Georgetown, Ont. He admitted these concerns putting out ready-cut houses and other supplies in the building line did some really clever advertising but the local dealer should meet such competition by equally clever advertising on his part. They featured a certain style of door not in much demand, in large type, a size 2 x 6 foot, while on the ordinary, standard doors such as 2 ft. 8 inch by 6 ft. 8 inch, the prices of catalogue houses were often dearer than those of the local yardman. The mail order firms also advertised hard wood flooring, in an attractive way at so much per lineal or running foot instead of by the thousand feet and their price, when figured out on the ordinary basis was higher. Nearly all dealers assenabled their own door and window frames and cut their own studding and could give as good or even better prices than the ready-cut house concerns. Mr. Mackenzie emphasized the necessity of using house plans wherever possible. An attractive picture captured attention and went a long way toward creating a sale for the materials in home construction. He laid great stress on pictures or plans to offset mail order trade. While it was possibly too costly a scheme for the Association to produce a regular plan book at the present time with detail drawings and bill of materials, he felt that they all should do something in this direction individually. "We can compete,'" he added "with all outside competition if we make effective use of house and barn plans. We must devote more attention to advertising in the press and in issuing general publicity matter."

### The Collection of Accounts

K. J. Shirton, of Dunnville, spoke on the "Collection of Accounts." While many dealers had a sign up in their offices stating that their terms were cash he felt he was safe in saying that not ten per cent. of them found it feasible to adhere to this regulation, particularly in regard to contractors and farmers who were reputable in every way. The outcome, however, was when a business was not all cash, that credit crept in and the dealer was up against the problem to discriminate between the good and the bad. If he was not careful he would get some accounts on his books that could not be collected. It all required a study of local conditions. Accounts could be divided into three sections—good accounts, slow (or doubtful), and bad, although there was, strictly speaking, no proper use of the latter term for there was often no collection of bad accounts and it was necessary to avoid this class. There were frequently good people who were sometimes slow in settling. After rendering the account he found that a good plan was to make a personal appeal to them explaining that it required a large amount of capital in the lumber line to carry stock and that it was essential to have money or something equally tangible in the way of security to finance the business. He found this method successful. Very often the customer would say that he could not pay just then but he was expecting money in by such and such a time and then he would pay. Mr. Shirton stated that he frequently requested a cheque for about the time that the customer expected to get in the cash and, if there was still hesitancy on the part of the customer he would ask that the cheque be given and post-dated—say fifteen days. Very seldom did he come back without a settlement in the way of a cheque or an interest bearing note, which could be negotiated in the bank and was a substantiation of the account. There could then be no room for dispute. If slow accounts were not looked after they were apt to get down to doubtful. In the latter case it was advisable to get a lien on the building if possible but, if the time for placing a lien had gone past, it was advisable to search the registry office and see if the customer had any property. Often collections could be made by getting a judgment against the party who was lagging too long. Mr. Shirton advised all to watch their collections carefully during these trying days and remarked that he had only roughly outlined methods in use in small towns and much that had been said by him might not apply to city lumber merchants who had their own special way of dealing with these matters.

### Local Branch Work and Proper Cost Systems

G. S. Zimmerman, of Tavistock, dealt with local branch work and costs systems. He found that very few dealers had a proper cost system. Formerly, he based his costs on manufacturing but this had been changed by him to the actual selling or sales. Too often where the costs for Workmen's Compensation, Insurance, Interest Depreciation, etc., averaged and spread out over twelve months and, when the year was concluded, the result was disappointing and misleading. Instead of averaging costs at so much a month they should be charged up regularly and the exact amount of the outlay known. He believed that one of the reasons why retailers started to cut prices was because they did not konw the cost of what they were selling. Formerly his cost system had been based on manufacturing but he had altered this, as stated, to the cost of actual selling. If everything was charged month by month as things went along, the retailer would be the gainer in the end and be able to show his fellow man wherein he had made mistakes.

There were many cost systems but it was not advisable to have one too cumbersome or unwieldy. All costs for compensation, insurance, bad debts, depreciation, etc., should be put against the actual sales that had been made for the month. Mr. Zimmerman said he kept a job record for every piece of work that came in or was turned out in the factory. Each lumber pile was given a number, the quantity of feet that it contained, the price paid for the stock, etc., and the record also showed the time spent on each job in the plant, number of hours, rate of wages, material used, etc. "In case of dispute or alleged overcharge, a customer if you do not have such a record will go away dissatisfied but with the facts before him, there can be no room left for doubt", added the speaker.

Asked if he recorded the percentage of cost on each thousand

feet of lumber or on the basis of dollars and cents, Mr. Zimmerman replied on the latter basis—not feetage. He took the actual cost of the lumber delivered in his yard, plus the cost of the work, percentage of overhead gauged from each month's records, etc. He knew his actual sales and costs each month and how much he had made by this plan.

A general discussion took place at this point in regard to the average wages paid for bench work and general labor. The figures paid for bench work ranged all the way from 40 to 60 cents an hour, machine work 45 to 65 cents and for general labor from 30 to 45 cents, according to the population of the cities or towns.

### Service Rooms Pay Handsomely

The next topic taken up was in regard to the sale and distribution of hardwood flooring. A. R. Sanders of St. Thomas, T. H. Hancock of Toronto, Frank Kent, Toronto and others took part and talked over matters regarding the protection of the retail lumberman who carried stock, etc. The practice, in a few centres, of dealers giving a discount to floor layers, home building associations, etc., was

A. G. Rose, Ottawa, Ont.
Local Secretary who was Kept Busy

Frank Kent, Toronto, Ont.
Who Spoke on Service Rooms.

deprecated. There should be, it was declared by one speaker, no discrimination but co-operation on the part of all retailers, and discounts should be given by manufacturers only to legitimate retail lumbermen. If certain rebates were granted there would be no confidence on the part of the public in reference to flooring prices.

Mr. Kent spoke of service rooms and remarked that they were big dividend payers. To-day, he regarded them as a real necessity in connection with the retail lumber yard. A service room marked an advance in merchandising methods on the part of the retail lumberman, and the installation of such a convenience was certainly a good business promoter. More attention was being paid to this feature of service than ever. Mr. Kent said that his own company in Toronto had fitted up a service room in Toronto and would be glad to have any retailer call at any time and inspect it. Dealers were obtaining good results from artistic, attractive service rooms, showing doors, mouldings, finish, trim, flooring, built-in features, breakfast nooks, etc., which afforded practical and helpful ideas. Some lumber merchants were even installing plate glass fronts in their service apartment in order to arrest the attention and interest of the public.

### Moving Pictures of Shingle Industry

During the afternoon of the second day of the convention, a series of moving pictures in connection with the manufacture of British Columbia red cedar shingles proved to be interesting and instructive. The machine was operated by Mr. Shaw of the military department of the Y. M. C. A., and the speaker was Fred H. Lamar, Secretary-Manager of the British Columbia Shingle Manufacturers' Association. He dealt with the subject of shingle production from manufacturing, sales, and other standpoints and refuted several aspersions regarding the fire hazard of this widely known roof covering. An outline of what Mr. Lamar said, has already appeared in the columns of the "Canada Lumberman" in connection with the report of the proceedings of the Canadian Lumbermen's Association. Mr. Lamar said that about eighty per cent of the output of B. C. shingle mills went to the United States. The Fordney tariff bill aimed at placing a duty of fifty cents per thousand on shingles. The Association, which he represented, was about to enter upon an extensive advertising campaign, which would provide dealer helps and other publicity matter,

emphasizing the need of using galvanized or zinc coated nails and handling thick, vertical grain shingles, which would last if properly laid, at least, forty years. He recognized that the retail dealer was helping greatly the Association in its battles and their good will and co-operation was much appreciated. The policy of the B. C. Association was to restrict the sales of shingles to regularly constituted trade channels.

L. L. Brown, of Toronto, B. C. Lumber Commissioner for the East, told of the plans which he had in view of engaging larger display rooms in Toronto, which would be finished and furnished in different B. C. woods, affording a splendid object lesson on their uses, merits, adaptability, etc. He also spoke of the quality of well manufactured, edge grain, B. C. shingles, employing proper nails for laying, etc. .

President-elect Scofield tendered Mr. Lamar a hearty vote of thanks on behalf of the O. R. L. D. A., for his timely and edifying address.

### Freight Rates and Stop-Over Privileges

Among other matters discussed during the afternoon were the questions of mutual fire insurance, the excessive freight rates on lumber, plan book service, the stop-over privilege and demurrage charges. The result of the debate on these matters is embodied in the resolutions which will be found in another column of the "Canada Lumberman".

President Barrett in referring to the excellent paper from A. M. Stewart of Winnipeg, expressed gratitude for the detailed information given in reference to mutual fire insurance. He favored the establishment of such a service in connection with the O. R. L. D. A., which would add prestige to the Ontario organization of retailers and result in giving real service to its members. It would, in his opinion, be taking a step in the right direction. Mr. Barrett also thought an Association plan book would be well worth considering even if the initial cost was high.

In regard to freight rates, F. B. Van Dusen, of Brockville, spoke of the necessity of immediate reduction in the high charges of carrying raw material which, in the end, the consumer had to bear. He thought that railway employees should be willing to accept lower wages and said that ordinary gate keepers were getting more money from the roads than skilled labor in the planing mill. He felt the abuse of high freights and big wages of railway employees would soon be corrected.

R. J. Hutcheson of the Muskoka Wood Mfg. Co., Huntsville, said that the thirty days' stop-over privileges for dressing, grading and kiln drying was not enough as the material in many cases could not be got ready for reshipment. American roads allowed twelve months and Canadian lines should afford the same concession. While the privilege in the past may have been abused by a few all should not be made to suffer in consequence. In regard to demurrage charges on cars, the rate had been formerly 1, 2, 3, 4 and 5 dollars. It was now 1 and 1 and 5 dollars for each succeeding day over the 48 hours allowance. Cars often arrived in bunches and could not be unloaded within the time allotted, with the result that heavy demurrage charges had to be paid. He had had thirteen cars dumped on him at once.

In regard to claims for overcharges, after the car was delivered and the original freight bill paid, these claims should not be put in months after and a settlement called for. There should be a time limit for such claims.

L. H. Richards, of Sarnia, also spoke along similar lines. On lumber shipments from the west the freight was often more than the actual value of the lumber. He concurred in all that Mr. Hutcheson had said in regard to the time allowed for stop-over service and demurrage charges. He advised all dealers to check carefully their freight bills and told of a clerical error that had been made by one railway line in billing: It had taken his firm two months to get back the amount while in another instance an application had been made eighteen months after, for an undercharge.

Mr. Hutcheson thought that on the stop-over privilege, so far as sorting stuff was concerned, there should be allowed by the railway companies at least six months, and on reshipments the allowance should be up to 90 per cent of the inweight instead of 70 per cent as at present, in order to secure the carload rate. At one time when many cars had been dumped on him, he had been compelled to pay over $1000 demurrage owing to the scarcity of labor, etc.

Messrs. Tupling, of Orillia, Naylor, of Essex, and others took part in the discussion which ended in the adoption of resolutions regarding freight rates, demurrage, etc. These will be found in another column of the "Canada Lumberman."

# Business of Convention in Concrete Form

## Resolutions Adopted by O.R.L.D.A. Deal With Freight Rates, Stop-Over Privilege, Demurrage, Midsummer Outing, Mutual Fire Insurance, Plan Book and Trade Ethics

The following resolutions were adopted at the recent annual meeting of the Ontario Retail Lumber Dealers' Association in Ottawa.

### Mechanics' Lien Act

Moved by Mr. Cluff, seconded by Mr. Wallace,—That the work done by the Legislation Committee in connection with the Mechanics' Lien Act be approved, and that the same Committee continue their efforts to have a new Act passed.—Carried.

### Anti-Shingle Campaign

Moved by Mr. Richards, seconded by Mr. Savage,—That the Legislation Committee be instructed to take whatever steps they consider necessary in order to oppose any proposed Anti-Shingle Legislation.—Carried.

### Forest Preservation

Moved by Mr. Wallace, seconded by Mr. Clarke,—That this Association commend the Government of Ontario for its efforts to preserve the forest wealth of the Province, and would recommend that all members of our association should join the Canadian Forestry Association.—Carried.

### Workmen's Compensation

Moved by Mr. Rhyans, seconded by Mr. Cummings,— That a memorandum be sent to the Ontario Government opposing anything in the nature of increased compensation to workmen under the Workmen's Compensation Act, and that the Government be asked to appoint an the Board a representative from the employers, and that a copy of this resolution be sent to the Canadian Manufacturers Association.— Carried.

### Patronizing Bulletin Advertisers

Moved by Mr. Tupling, seconded by Mr. Mackenzie. —That our Association appreciates very highly the support of the Wholesalers who advertise in the Monthly Bulletin, and urges all members to give these advertisers a preference when placing their orders, everything else being equal.— Carried.

### Local Associations

Moved by Mr. Cummings, seconded by Mr. Shirton.— That dealers in districts where no local organizations have as yet been formed be urged to recognize the importance of establishing such branches as soon as possible. Further, that where existing local branches find that their territory is too large, that we recommend that the territory be subdivided.— Carried.

### Thanks to the Ottawa Trade

Moved by Mr. Cluff, seconded by Mr. Wallace,—That this Association extend its very warm thanks to the Ottawa Trade for their generous hospitality and entertainment of the visiting retailers.—Carried.

### Annual Meeting

Moved by Mr. Van Dusen, seconded by Mr. Wallace.— That our next annual meeting of the Association be held at Windsor at a date to be fixed by the incoming directors.

Further, that this association feels that the expenses incurred in the way of entertainment, etc., by the local dealers of the towns or cities where our Annual Conventions are held, are too much to accept of them, and that hereafter the expense in connection with the Annual Convention and entertainment at that time may be borne by the association up to the extent of $5. per member in attendance.—Carried.

### Standard Order Forms

Moved by Mr. Shirton, seconded by Mr. Rhynas.—That the Standard Order Form prepared by the Trade Relations Committee has proved quite satisfactory, that we urge upon our members the advantage to them of using same.—Carried.

### Association Plan Book

Moved by Mr. Clarke, seconded by Mr. Rhynas,—That the work done by the president and secretary in connection with the plan book, be approved, and that this committee recommend that this Association use the Western Retail Lumber Dealers' plan book and service.—Carried.

### Thanks to Mr. Stewart

Moved by Mr. Cummings, seconded by Mr. Wallace,— That the secretary of our Association be instructed to write Mr. A. M. Stewart, of Winnipeg, expressing to him our appreciation of the detailed information he has given us in regard to Mutual Fire Insurance.—Carried.

### Neat and Useful Souvenir

Moved by Mr. Watt, seconded by Mr. Tupling,—That our secretary convey to Terry & Gordon, Limited, of Toronto, our appreciation of the neat and useful souvenir they have so generously given our members.—Carried.

### Mutual Fire Insurance

Moved by Mr. Barrett, seconded by Mr. Cummings,— That our Committee on Insurance be requested to investigate and report through our Monthly Bulletin upon the feasibility of organizing a mutual insurance association among our members or upon the placing of our members insurance through our secretary as an insurance broker, and in placing the commissions thereon to the credit of the association; or if possible, a combination of these two suggestions in the most acceptable form; and that the President, if he considerss it necessary, shall have power to add to the members of the committee.— Carried.

### Midsummer Outing up the Lakes

Moved by Mr. Richards, seconded by Mr. Rhynas,—That the directors of the association be instructed to arrange for a midsummer outing for the present year. This was carried, and it was decided that the trip should take place during the last week in June, up the Great Lakes to Duluth and return, starting at either Windsor or Sarnia. The outing was endorsed strongly by Mr. Richards, Mr. Scofield and others who praised highly the service of the Northern Navigation Co. and spoke of the beauties of the many points that would be visited. It was intimated that the individual cost of the outing by the steamer, if the excursion took place during the last week in June, would be about $55.00, including meals and berths. No certain number will have to be guaranteed and the wives and daughters of the retail lumbermen will accompany them on this occasion. At Duluth it is expected that a number of sawmills will be inspected.

### Three Days Convention

Moved by Mr. Rhynas, seconded by Mr. Cummings,— That this meeting consider the advisability of holding a three days convention next year in order that we may have ample time to more thoroughly take up matters of interest. The matter was finally left to the new Board of Directors.—Carried.

### Freight Rates

Moved by Mr. Van Dusen, seconded by Mr. Richards.— That this association feels that much of the present business depression is caused by the present high freight rates, the rates in some cases adding so much to the delivered cost of the commodity as to restrict the trade, that we feel that the present rates on building commodities are so high they retard the building of much needed houses, and that the secretary of our association be authorized to communicate with the Canadian Lumbermen's Association expressing to them our desire to co-operate with them in every possible way, in order to bring this matter to the attention of the proper authorities as forcibly as thought proper, and that a copy of this resolution be sent to the C. L. A.; the C. M. A.; Minister of Railways; Minister of Trade and Commerce and the Board of Railway

### Stop Over

Moved by Mr. Van Dusen, seconded by Mr. Richards,— That this association feels that the present limit of thirty days of the stop-over privilege now allowed by the Railway Companies for dressing, grading and kiln drying, etc., is not of

sufficient duration to permit the proper use of this privilege, and that the secretary take this matter up with the C. L. A., in order that both associations may make a joint plea that this stop-over period be extended to twelve months, instead of thirty days.—Carried.

### Demurrage

Moved by Mr. Van Dusen, Seconded by Mr. Richards,—That this association feels that the recent change in the demurrage rates was, under present conditions, not at all warranted, and that the secretary of our association co-operate with the C. L. A. in order that this matter may be corrected.—Carried.

### Past Presidents

Moved by Mr. Mackenzie, seconded by Mr. Cluff,—That the immediate past president of the association be ex-officio a member of the Board of Directors.—Carried.

### Trade Ethics

Moved by Mr. Van Dusen, seconded by Mr. Cluff,—That the members of this association do not approve of the practise of some retail lumber dealers who send out to nearby towns printed price list of building material giving misleading information as to the grades of material quoted, and showing prices that are apparently lower than the local dealers in those towns can sell at, or at which the said firms would sell customers in their home towns.—Carried.

### Ladies at the Convention

Moved by Mr. Van Dusen, seconded by Mr. Watt,—That the members of this association recognizing the help and encouragement given to us in our business by our wives and sweethearts, hereby ask them to attend future conventions, and sit with us at our annual banquet.—Carried.

### Membership

Moved by Mr. Shirton, seconded by Mr. Cluff,—That the association be a Committee of the Whole on Membership.—Carried.

Moved by Mr. Van Dusen, seconded by Mr. Kent,—That this meeting consider the advisability of admitting Farmers' Clubs as members of our association, be referred to the Executive Committee for further consideration.—Carried.

## The Delegates Who "Came, Saw and Conquered"

The retailers who registered for the Convention in Ottawa were as follows:—

Anglin,F. R., S. Anglin & Co., Kingston, Ont.
Armstrong, W. J., McAuliffe Davis Lumber Co., Ottawa.
Barrett, E. M., Barrett Bros., Ottawa.
Barrett, G. T., Barrett Bros., Ottawa.
Bernard, J. A., Seaman, Kent Co., Toronto.
Boake, G. Wilf., The Boake Mfg. Co., Ltd., Toronto.
Boultbee, H., Secretary, O. R. L. D. A., Toronto.
Bond, John S., The Buyer's Door & Mfg. Co., Toronto.
Bowden, H. V., Bowden Lumber Co., Toronto.
Bradley, C., Barrett Bros., Ottawa.
Burton, F. R., Consumers Lumber Co., Ltd., Hamilton.
Bissell, D., Barrett Bros., Ottawa.
Campbell, John. D., Cornwall.
Clarke, B. F., McPherson & Clarke, Glencoe.
Cluff, J. J., N. Cluff & Sons, Seaforth.
Copeland, A. H. M., R. Laidlaw Lumber Co., Toronto.
Copeland, J. D., R. Laidlaw Lumber Co., Toronto.
Coyles, G. W., W. C. Edwards & Co., Ottawa.
Cummings, Fred. J., Kingston Road Lumber Co., Toronto.
Cummings, M. N., Westboro.
Davidson, E. Keith., James Davidson's Sons, Ottawa.
Davidson, G. F., James Davidson's Sons, Ottawa.
Davis, M. E., McAuliffe Davis Lumber Co., Ottawa.
Dagneau, Leo, The C & J Hadley Co., Limited, Chatham.
Doty, C. F., Davis & Doty, Oakville.
Dryden, R. G., Toronto.
Edwards, D., Kemp, Gatineau Co., Ottawa.
Elliott, J. E., Apex Lumber Co., Windsor.
Emery, W. B., Marlatt & Armstrong Co., Ltd., Oakville.
Flack, A. D., Barrett Bros., Ottawa.
Fletcher, J. A., Fletcher Lumber Co., Ltd., Windsor.
Free, James., Mimico.
Gillespie, P., James Davidson's Sons, Ottawa.
Grantham, Carter., John T. Grantham, Brantford.
Grimes, Allan., McAuliffe Davis Lumber Co., Ottawa.
Hadley, W. A., S. Hadley Lumber Co., Chatham.
Hale, Allan, Kernohan Lumber Co., Ltd., London.
Hancock, T. H., T. H. Hancock, Limited, Toronto.
Heise, O. M., The Seaman, Kent Co., Toronto.
Henderson, L., James Davidson's Sons, Ottawa.
Herath, S., Essex Development Co., Limited, Ojibway.
Herdman, J., Barrett Bros., Ottawa.
Hollingsworth, F. E., Corrigan Lumber & Mill Co., Sault Ste Marie.
Irvin, John C., Irvin Lumber Co., Toronto.
Irvin, W. C., Irvin Lumber Co.,Toronto.
James, John., James Davidson's Sons, Ottawa.
Kent, Frank., Seaman, Kent Co., Toronto.
Kernohan, Geo. N., Kernohan Lumber Co., London.
Keily, J. R., M. N. Cummings, Westboro.

Light, J., Robert Light, Napanee.
Ludlam, H. S., Ludlam, Ainslee Lumber Co., Leamington.
Mason, E. P. Woodroffe.
Megloughlin, W. B., McAuliffe Davis Lumber co., Ottawa.
Merrill, W. C., James Davidson's Sons, Ottawa.
Morrison, H. L., Barrett Bros., Ottawa.
McAuliffe, David., McAuliffe Davis, Ottawa.
McDermid, A. L., A. L. McDermid & Co., Apple Hill.
Mackenzie, J. B., Georgetown.
McKenzie, Thos. E., Seaman, Kent Co., Toronto.
McMaster, R. D., McMaster Lumber Co., Ltd., Kemptville.
Naylor, J. L., The Naylor-Osborne Co., Essex.
Osborne, A. W., The Naylor-Osborne Co., Ltd., Sandwich.
Paterson, T. A., Mickle, Dyment & Son, Toronto.
Piggott, F. G., P. G. Piggott LumberCo., Chatham.
Poisson, E. C., Ford.
Pounder, E., Pounder Bros., Stratford.
Press, R. J., Alliance Lumber Co., Hamilton.
Pushman, Jas. H., W. C. Edwards & Co., Ottawa.
Rastall, R. A. W., Rastall Lumber Co., Toronto.
Ressor, F. A., Locust Hill.
Richards, L. H., Laidlaw Belton Co., Sarnia.
Rhynas, O. W., Mickle, Dyment & Son, Brantford.
Rhynas, Phillip., Mickle, Dyment & Son, Brantford.
Robertson, C. R., Gatineau Co., Limited, Ottawa.
Rodgers, J. H., Ball Planing Mill Co., Limited, Barrie.
Sanders, A. R., Sanders & Bell, Limited, St. Thomas.
Savage, W. E. S., Mimico.
Scofield, J. C., Windsor Lumber Co., Limited, Windsor.
Shirton, K. J., The Wm. Shirton Co., Ltd., Dunnville.
Sinclair, S. M., Nicholson Lumber Co., Burlington.
Taylor, Fred., D. Aitchison & Co., Hamilton.
Taylor, W. J., Watson & Taylor, Ridgetown.
Terry, George., Barrett Bros., Ottawa.
Thompson, S. C., Gatineau Co., Ltd., Ottawa.
Thomson, W. H., Thomson Bros., Port Credit.
Tubman, Reid., M. C. Neate Lumber Co., Ottawa.
Tupling, W. M., J. R. Eaton & Sons, Ltd., Orillia.
Van Dusen, F. B., Brockville Lumber Co., Brockville.
Van Dusen, H. F., Brockville Lumber Co., Brockville.
Van Blaricom, G. B., "Canada Lumberman," Toronto.
Wallace, John T., Dyment, Baker Lumber Co., London.
Walsh, Robt. J., Renfrew Planing Mills, Renfrew.
Warwick, T. C., Blenheim.
Watt, Allan., The Watt Milling Co., Toronto.
Wiggins, Mr., James Davidson's Sons, Ottawa.
Williams, Gordon. T., C. Williams Co., Ltd., Toronto.
Williamson, F. S., Wm. Williamson, Toronto.
Wilson, Edward E., J. E. Eilson Planing Mills, Ottawa.
Wilson, George., McAuliffe Davis Lumber Co., Ottawa.
Wilson, W. F., James E. Wilson & Sons Ltd., Ottawa.
Zimmerman, Geo. S., Zimmerman Bros., Tavistock.

# How Western Mutual Insurance Concern Expands

### Factors Which Have Contributed to Development—Story of Its Inception and the Way Its Financial Affairs Have Been Managed—Other Points of Interest

*By A. M. STEWART, Winnipeg
Secretary, Western Retail Lumber Dealers' Mutual Fire Insurance Corporation

It is indeed a disappointment to me not being able to attend your Annual Convention, and place before you personally, the history of our Insurance Company, and give you any help towards forming a similar company amongst your members, but unfortunately our annual meeting coming on so close and the extra amount of work in the office, which always comes at this time of year, prevents me from being with you, and so I will give you to the best of my ability a short history of our company and how we have been able to make such a successful showing at the end of 17 years. This I know at the best will be of poor satisfaction to you, however, it may be of some little use in the way of information, and should you at any time want anything further, you have only to call on me and I shall be very pleased to give you all the assistance I can.

## Story of Steady Expansion

Our company started in 1905. At that time the Board companies were charging a basis rate of $2.50 and $3.00 per $100. and though our Association put before them facts and figures regarding losses in retail lumber yards, they absolutely refused to reduce their rate, but oddly enough just as soon as we got our Charter and started to do business they cut their rate in half, viz., to $1.50 per $100. However, having launched out we decided to go on with our venture and met with the following results:—

| | Ins. in Force. | Fire Loss. | Basis Rate. Cents | Reserve. |
|---|---|---|---|---|
| 1905...... | $370,790.00 | Nil | 72 | |
| 1906 | 635,790.00 | $3,899.62 | 72 | 63,810.52 |
| 1907 | 851,690.00 | 655.80 | 72 | 8,519.46 |
| 1908 | 1,457,225.00 | 3,063.56 | 54 | 11,730.90 |
| 1909 | 1,634,700.00 | 1,686.55 | 54 | 20,450.29 |
| 1910 | 2,148,985.00 | 3,774.54 | 48 | 27,026.74 |
| 1911 | 2,353,060.00 | 5,838.38 | 48 | 33,092.34 |
| 1912 | 2,189,840.00 | 9,876.14 | 48 | 34,630.34 |
| 1913 | 2,079,295.00 | 5,188.48 | 42 | 38,538.45 |
| 1914 | 2,355,565.00 | 5,886.06 | 36 | 41,078.12 |
| 1915 | 3,016,775.00 | 14,436.41 | 48 | 41,065.36 |
| 1916 | 3,728,925.00 | 11,965.15 | 48 | 43,103.60 |
| 1917 | 3,074,175.00 | 14,393.82 | 48 | 45,474.63 |
| 1918 | 3,764,420.00 | 7,580.63 | 36 | 53,121.05 |
| 1919 | 4,181,905.00 | 3,617.58 | 12 | 55,083.03 |
| 1920 | 4,703,181.00 | 8,395.77 | 15 | 55,483.09 |
| 1921 | 6,328,480.00 | 19,774.23 | 30 | 55,696.03 |

You will see by the figures I have given you that notwithstanding the absurdly low rates we were able to give our members up to 1918, we were able to accumulate a handsome reserve, in fact, our Directors considered it a sufficient reserve for our needs and since that date we have carried our members as nearly at actual cost as it is possible to figure.

As our method of carrying on our company is slightly different from most Mutual companies, I will endeavor to explain it in as concise a manner as possible.

1st.—We do not take Premium Notes, but a cash Guarantee Deposit.

2nd.—At the end of the year we figure our losses and expenses and then assess our members so much per cent of the Guarantee Premium Deposit so as to cover the same and in the early history of our company to create a reserve.

3rd.—We invest our Guarantee Premium Deposit and Reserve to the best possible advantage (of course in selected and liquid investments) thereby making our interest practically pay our expenses.

Our method of setting the rate for our Guarantee Premium Deposit is as follows:—

The rate for straight insurance on an isolated risk, (i. e. one with no exposures within 50 feet and no mill plant or steam plant within 150 feet) is $1.00 per $100, or for 80% co-insurance 75 cents per $100. Should there be exposures we add for them practically the same as the Board Companies, except that we only charge for exposures within 50 feet.

This Guarantee Premium Deposit is paid in cash at the time of taking out a policy and remains to the credit of the policy as long as

it is in force, and should the policy be cancelled, is returned, less the carrying charges, from the date of the last assessment.

Example.—A has a $5,000 policy on an isolated risk. Pays $50.00—at the time of taking out the same; at the end of the year you find that to meet your losses and expenses etc., you have to assess him 50%, he then pays you $25.00, which is what his insurance costs him plus interest on his $50.00. Should he cancel say in six months of the second year you would charge him $12.50 for the six months and return him the balance of his Guarantee Premium Deposit viz., $12.50. In event of anyone refusing to pay an assessment our by-laws provide for the cancellation of the policy and loss of the Guarantee Premium Deposit. Our Insurance Act provides that at no time can anyone be assessed for a greater amount than his deposit, and I think the Ontario Act is the same.

This I think covers fairly well our method of carrying on our insurance and I think you will agree with me that it has proved a very safe and profitable business for our members. At first we met with all kinds of obstacles from rival companies, but through the loyalty of our members, we overcame them and are now considered a standing factor in the insurance line. Most companies only canvas lumbermen for insurance they want over and above our line taking it for granted that anyone would take our company first.

Our company at the start were very conservative only carrying $3,000 on any one risk and then selecting their risks most carefully, not taking any in any towns, nor any with any mill or wood working plant in connection, or with such a plant near the risk. Gradually we expanded and took risks and gradually raised our limit, first to $5,000, then to $7,000 and now we carry $10,000, but in no event with a mill or woodworking plant. Probably we were favored by conditions, starting in when the country was new. We would generally have only two risks in a small place and as a rule one was at one end of the town and the other at the other end, and in the event of a fire our loss would generally only be in one of the risks. Of course, these conditions are changing, several of the small places have extended and so our risks are getting surrounded by other hazards.

Another great factor in the success of the company of course is the moral hazard, and I think I am perfectly justified in saying that there is no higher moral hazard than that of the lumberman, in fact we can prove it by the fact that in our existence we have only had four or five cases where a fire started in our risk, almost all our fires started from outside exposures, those that have started on our own risks being caused by coal gas explosion and overheated stoves in offices and in none of those cases has the loss amounted to more than a few hundred dollars.

## Success Would Depend on Yards

Of course, I am not familiar with the lay out of your risks, but from the information I have gathered I take it that they differ very materially from ours. First, I judge that a large percentage of your yards are large ones in large towns and carry heavy stocks. Secondly, that a large percentage have woodworking plants in connection. Such being the case, I hardly know what to say as to the possibilities of making a success of your company such as ours. If you had enough absolutely retail yards with no woodworking in connection, to start your company, and carry it on until such a time as you got fairly strong, well and good, as everyone knows the critical time of a Mutual company is at the start and if you glance over the table I read of our company, you can see by our fire losses how fortunate we were during our infancy.

Again it would largely depend on the number of yards you could get in. When we started we had some 400 members to draw from and now we have 1,200 or more and still we have not got them all by any means. I am afraid I have done very little justice to the subject, but my endeavour has been to explain things as simply as possible without wearying you, but, at the same time, it makes me regret even more than ever, not being able to be at your convention in person as I am sure I could then put things more lucidly to you. However, I can do no more than assure you that if you do start a company, I wish you every success and again reiterate that I shall at all times be most happy to give you all the assistance in my power.

*Paper read before the Ontario Retail Lumber Dealers' Association at Ottawa.

# Coming Year Should Be Good One

### Retail Lumberman Reviews the Outlook for 1922 — Says All Sholud Get Down to Hard Work

An interesting address was delivered by W. M. Tupling, of Orillia, on "The Outlook for 1922," and in the course of his interesting remarks, he said:—The lumber industry as a whole faces a much better year in 1922 than in 1921. Some one once asked the question,—'How far can a dog run into the woods?' Various answers were made but one bright individual replied that he could only run in half way, after that he would be coming out. Evidences are multiplying in that our dog has passed the half-way mark and that he is now coming out of the woods.

The retail lumber dealer was the first to be deflated. He was deflated suddenly and severely but the agony is over that much sooner. He has taken low prices but he has moved his stock and kept his plant going. We have not said that the bottom has yet been reached but we do say that we are eighteen months nearer bottom than when we stood on the dizzy heights in July 1920.

We believe that there is a fair volume of residential building under way and that the demand for lumber products from our factories will be good. With more homes we will have an increased demand for more schools, churches, stores, banks and factories.

Transportation is one of the big items of costs on building commodities. We have recently had one reduction in freight rates and can reasonably look forward to another this year. The readjustment in labor costs is progressing but is by no means complete. However, time and competition will work this out. The Peace Conference which has not yet completed its work will help our export trade, and eventually reduce burdensome taxation, thus furnishing increased funds for development purposes. The foreign exchange rates are gradually receding to a lower level. This is bound again to help us.

Some one has stated that the farmer has gone on a buying strike. This is not true. The farmer has always bought up to the capacity of his income and he will continue to buy up to the capacity of his income but he has not bought as much during the past year as he would have liked to buy, but must, however, buy more in the coming years.

There is every evidence that the consuming industries such as furniture, automobiles and box business, will require a fair amount of lumber. On the whole the demand for lumber and lumber products will be much better in 1922 than in 1921.

In closing, let me say that the volume of business this year will not be excessive but there will be a fair business. Competition will be keen and if you are to get your share, you must get out and fight for it. Take off your coat and roll up your sleeves and get down to hard work. You must keep your eye on the ball and put more pep into the game. Steady work and large production form the only basis of real prosperity. Prosperity is surely coming with the Ontario retail lumber dealers in the lead.

## Local Committee Left Nothing Undone

The members of the local committee deserve great credit for the way in which every event, both social and business, was carried out. The visiting retailers were certainly given a warm welcome and complimented the Ottawa fraternity highly on their hospitality and splendid entertainment.

The members of the Ottawa committee were:—E. M. Barrett, (chairman), G. P. Davidson, A. G. Rose, G. R. Robertson, A. Mayno Davis, S. C. Thompson, Wm. B. Megloughlin, M. Davis, M. N. Cummings and others.

## Some Timely Light on Causes of Fires

L. L. Brown, of Toronto, B. C. Lumber Commissioner for the East recently received the following letter from J. Grove Smith, Dominion Fire Commissioner, Ottawa, in regard to the causes of fires and the attacks that have been made on the wooden shingle as a fire menace.

Following your last visit to Ottawa, I attempted to obtain from our records, and also from the records of various fire chiefs, particulars of fires that could justifiably be attributed to shingle roofs. I regret to say that I have found the result very unsatisfactory, for while it is possible to determine with a fair degree of accuracy the amount of loss occasioned by fires that spread from the buidings in which they originate, it is quite impossible to differentiate between the exposure loss chargeable to wooden shingles and that arising from other structural characteristics. I may add that it is the concensus of opinion of fire chiefs that wooden shingles constitute a serious menace and, in a general way, they hold the opinion that many fires spread from wooden shingle roof

coverings. They are not, however, able to give any exact data respecting the number of fires or the amount of loss that has occured within a stated period from this cause, and I am therefore unable to compile the information which you desire to obtain.

### Seventy Percent of Frame Construction

During the four years 1918 to 1921, both inclusive, fire losses in Canada amounted to approximately $118,563,400. The number of fires reported was 74,263 and 2.9 percent of these fires spread from the building in which they originated. The loss so occasioned amounted to 12.4 percent of the total loss. Of the spreading fires, approximately 72 percent started in frame buildings and 65 percent occurred in small towns. Villages and rural communities where there are no building restrictions. Presumably the majority of these fires originated in buildings roofed with wooden shingles, but whether the shingles were a vital factor in the spread of the fires is not recorded.

In this connection, it is interesting to note that about 70 percent of all the buildings in Canada are of frame construction and that a still greater percentage of buildings are at present roofed with wooden shingles. From the foregoing facts I do not think that any reliable argument can be deduced either for or against wooden shingles, nor do I think that one would be justified in making an authoritative statement without a complete record of individual fires showing the exact circumstances in each case. During the present year I will endeavor to obtain more exhaustive information but the difficulties are very great. For instance, in the frequently stated cause of "sparks on roof" the actual origin may in many cases be traced to defective chimneys. That does not, of course, overcome the argument that if roofs were of incombustible material these fires would not occur. On the other hand, it is equally true that if the chimneys were not defective, the roofs would not be subjected to the danger of ignition. It is a case of using the particular argument that best supports one's views.

### Wooden Shingles Do Not Enter Into It

Relative to your further enquiry, I am able to state that the losses in Toronto and Montreal, respectively, for the years 1919, 1920 and 1921 were as follows:—

| Year | Montreal | Toronto |
|---|---|---|
| 1919 | $1,584,881 | $1,156,995 |
| 1920 | 4,961,639 | 2,121,185 |
| 1921 | 3,000,586 | 918,150 |
| Total | 9,547,106 | 4,196,330 |

I do not think that you would be safe in drawing from these figures the deduction to which you make reference in your letter. As I have repeatedly pointed out, the larger proportion of the total loss in all important cities and towns is occasioned by fires in mercantile and manufacturing buildings.

Wooden shingle roofs anl wooden construction in general does not enter into the question. In numerous cases we suffer most extensively from fires in semi-fireproof buildings where the contents are of high value. The only remedy for this condition is the more adequate protection of such buildings and their content. As a matter of irrefutable fact it cannot be too strongly stated that a building of ordinary construction equipped with automatic sprinkler protection is a far better fire risk than a fireproof building lacking such protection. By effectively presenting that viewpoint to the public, you will measurably assist in reducing Canada's scandalous fire loss.

### Will Electrify Western Sawmill

Thurston, Flavelle, Limited, Port Moody, B. C., have started to electrify their sawmill at a cost of $60,000. The work includes the supplying of a 1000 Kilowatt generator and individual motors and independent control for each machine in the entire plant. The 1000 Kilowatt generator will be steam driven from present engines, direct connected. The individual drive motors will be installed later after some changes are made in the mill machinery.

E. B. Salyerds, Preston, Ont., whose hockey stick and brush factory was recently destroyed by fire, has taken over the plant formerly occupied by the Canada Machinery Corporation, and will put in the equipment necessary to carry on the manufacture of his line. Mr. Salyerds has secured a lease of this building and will resume manufacturing operations at the earliest date possible.

# Fitting Finale Was Annual Banquet

### Social Gathering at Chateau Laurier was an Outstanding One in Humor, Oratory and Fellowship

The banquet tendered the visiting retail lumbermen by the trade of Ottawa was one of the most enjoyable in the local annals of the industry. There were over two hundred guests assembled in the artistic dining room of the Chateau Laurier, the menu was inviting, the decorations attractive and the company congenial. The speeches were of an unusually high order of merit and everything passed off with great eclat. The function was a fitting termination of the two days' successful convention and sparkled with wit and good fellowship. During the evening local talent contributed a number of most acceptable selections and Fred H. Lamar, of Vancouver, popularly known as the "shingle man," gave a stirring song, which earned a hearty encore. E. M. Barrett, of Ottawa, the retiring President of The Association ably presided, and the chief speaker was Hon. Martin Burrell, former Minister of Agriculture for Canada.

After the toast of "The King" had been loyally honored, Mayor Frank Plant of the capital city extended a warm welcome to the visitors and extolled the beauties of Ottawa. He also paid a tribute to Mr. Barrett as a splendid citizen.

S. C. Thompson, of Ottawa, proposed the toast of "The Trade"

In the heart of Canada's capital, showing on the right the Chateau Laurier, where the O.R.L.D.A. convention was held

and the first to reply was President-elect J. C. Scofield, of Windsor, who thanked the members for the honor conferred on him and referred to the cordiality with which they had been received in Ottawa. He invited all those present to come to Windsor next year where the convention would be held. Mr. Scofield stressed three points in his brief remarks to the retail lumbermen which were—to put more punch into their business during the coming year; to do more advertising and to believe in their own towns.

A. E. Clark, of Toronto, the new President of the Canadian Lumbermen's Association, responded on behalf of the wholesalers. The wholesale trade was an important and influential integral part of the lumber industry. Of the benefits of association and getting together, he spoke in convincing terms. When home building started it inaugurated a period of prosperity and the lumber industry should do all in its power to encourage the erection of more homes for the people. The situation regarding freights must be adjusted in the interest of the industry. The situation must be faced and faced now, even if adjustments meant strikes and labor troubles.

W. B. Snowball, of Chatham, N. B. struck a high note of optimism in his speech, which was well received. He humorously added that the manufacturer kept the wholesaler and retailer going by bearing the major share of their burdens.

Lumber activities employed a large number of the men in varied operations and when once the industry was humming again, unemployment would largely be a thing of the past. If the lumber business improved, conditions throughout the country would follow its upward trend. Mr. Snowball sincerely hoped a better day was dawning for all those engaged in the forest products line and emphasized the necessity of faith, courage, optimism and co-operation.

Gordon C. Edwards, of Ottawa, proposed the toast of "Our Country". He congratulated the Ontario Retail Lumber Dealers' Association on the success of its convention and stated that, as the first President of the Canadian Lumbermen's Association, he knew what an uphill fight an organization of the kind had. Mr. Edwards paid a tribute to Hon. Martin Burrell.

The latter proved to be a speaker of unusual brilliancy and versatility. He strongly declared that a noble service was being done the country by the much maligned and slandered public man. Many people stated they did not enter the public arena because they either did not wish to take part in the petty squabbles which they claimed characterized the public man or that they had no time to "mess" in affairs of that kind. Mr. Burrell said that he realized that the first duty of man was to make a living, yet the fact remained that in the prosecution of one's own affairs solely, one enjoyed all the privileges obtained through legislation while one shirked the responsibilities which attached to a citizen of the country.

One of the reasons for the present corruption of politics, if it could be so termed, was that very able men left affairs of state to a number of men who bedeviled the situation. At the same time the situation was hopeful, not only in Canada but in the world, when one reminded one's self that people today were living in a generation which witnessed the settlement of Ireland's age-long feud and the momentous conference at Washington relative to disarmament.

F. B. Van Dusen, of Brockville, in moving a vote of thanks to Hon. Mr. Burrell and to the Ottawa lumbermen said that the lumber industry had suffered great losses during the past year. The note of confidence struck by the speakers and by the convention would make them all go home encouraged to boost for better times.

The seconder of the resolution was President-elect Scofield. Chairman Barrett suitably acknowledged the sentiments expressed by the speakers and added that anything, which the trade in the capital city had done to entertain or instruct the visitors, was, indeed, a work of pleasure and satisfaction. The happy gathering broke up with the singing of the National Anthem.

## General News and Jottings of the Trade

W. H. Harris of the Frank H. Harris Lumber Co., Toronto, left recently on an extended business trip to the company's mills at Meridian and Lake, Miss.

A. B. Lamont of the C. G. Anderson Lumber Co., Toronto, has been confined to his home during the past few weeks with illness but is steadily improving.

John Carew, of Lindsay, Ont., who is president of the John Carew Lumber Co., has been elected president for the coming year of the Lindsay Central Fair Board.

C. W. Wilkinson and D. C. Johnston of the Union Lumber Co., Toronto, who recently took a four weeks' business trip to Jamaica and Cuba, have returned home. They had an enjoyable outing.

J. R. Booth, Limited, of Ottawa, a corporation incorporated under the laws of the Dominion, has taken out a license in mortmain to acquire and hold land in Ontario to the value of $1,100,000, necessary for its actual use and occupation, or to carry on its undertaking.

Hall Bros., wholesale lumber dealers, Toronto, are operating a heavy portable mill at Marlbank, Ont., and cutting about fifteen thousand feet a day of maple and basswood, which is being hauled to the railway track for shipment. The firm report that winter operating conditions in Hastings county so far have been ideal.

D. A. Webster, of Boston, eastern representative of Ed. Clark & Sons, Toronto, and Charles O. Maus of the Charles O. Maus Lumber Co., South Bend, Ind., who represents Ed. Clark and Sons in Illinois, Michigan, Indiana and Ohio, were in Toronto on business recently and report that there has been a noticeable improvement in the hardwood lumber trade since the first of the year.

Arthur B. Cowan, Galt, Ont., recently passed away at his home in that city, in his 75th year. The late Mr. Cowan was well known in the woodworking machinery field, having been actively connected with Cowan & Co., of Galt, Limited, from its inception until he retired four years ago. He was known by woodworkers from coast to coast, having travelled for 40 years. Mr. Cowan is survived by two brothers, William and James, and one sister, Miss Margaret Cowan.

L. L. Brown, B. C. Lumber Commissioner for the East, who has had offices and display rooms at No. 1 Adelaide St. East, Toronto, has moved to larger premises at 51 Yonge St., where an elaborate showroom will be fitted up and exhibits made of various kinds of B. C. forest products along with furniture manufactured from the same stock. The new quarters of the B. C. Lumber Commissioner are centrally located, spacious and attractive. When completed they will be a striking advertisement for all the lines of Coast and Mountain woods that are handled in Ontario and the East.

## Canadian Association's New Committees

### Active Campaign to be Conducted by the C. L. A. to Increase Membership in Various Provinces

At a recent conference of the President of the Canadian Lumbermen's Association and the Executive officers held in the head office of the C. L. A. in Ottawa, several important matters were attended to such as the appointment of committees for the coming year.

The personnel of all the subsidiary bodies is now complete, and it is expected that the committees on membership will get to work and bring in several recruits. The prospects are that the roll of the C. L. A. will shortly top the 200 mark.

A resolution of condolence was passed in regard to the death of Joseph Oliver, and a copy has been forwarded to W. F. Oliver, of the Oliver Lumber Co., Toronto. The resolution was that the directors and members of the Canadian Lumbermen's Association mourn the death of their late respected member and friend, Joseph Oliver, and extend to the relatives of the deceased heartfelt sympathy in their bereavement.

The complete list of officers, directors and committees of the Canadian Lumbermen's Association for 1922 is as follows:—

President—A. E. Clark, Edward Clark & Sons, Ltd., Toronto.

Vice-Presidents—J. Fraser Gregory, Murray & Gregory, Ltd., St. John, N. B., Angus McLean, Bathurst Co., Ltd., Bathurst, N. B.

Directors—To Serve Three Years—A. E. Clark, Edward Clark & Sons, Ltd., Toronto, Gordon C. Edwards, W. C. Edwards & Co., Ltd., Ottawa, W. E. Bigwood, Graves, Bigwood & Co., Toronto. W. Gerard Power, W. & J. Sharples, Ltd., Quebec, P. Q., Angus McLean, Bathurst Company, Ltd., Bathurst, N. B., Spencer Kellogg, Chas. C. Kellogg & Sons Co., Utica, N. Y., R. E. Stocking, Power, Moir & Stocking, New York, N. Y.

To Serve Two Years—Dan McLachlin, McLachlin Bros., Ltd., Arnprior, Ont., E. R. Bremner, Watson & Todd, Ltd., Ottawa, David Champoux, Chaleurs Bay Mills, Restigouche, P. Q., Geo. W. Grier, G. A. Grier & Sons, Ltd., Montreal, Brig. Gen. J. B. White, Riordon Company, Ltd., Montreal, J. Fraser Gregory, Murray & Gregory, Ltd., St. John, N. B., E. C. Knight, Vancouver Lumber Company, Ltd., Vancouver, B. C.

To Serve One Year—G. E. Spragge, Victoria Harbor Lumber Co., Ltd., Toronto, W. J. Bell, Spanish River Lumber Co., Ltd., Sudbury, Ont., Duncan McLaren, Union Lumber Co., Ltd., Toronto, Sir William Price, K. B., Price Bros. & Co., Ltd., Quebec, P. Q., Arthur H. Campbell, Campbell, MacLaurin Lumber Co., Ltd., Montreal, W. B. Snowball, J. B. Snowball Co. Ltd., Chatham, N. B., Rufus E. Dickio, Stewiacke, N. S.

Director at large—R. G. Cameron, Cameron & Co., Ltd., Ottawa.

### Executive Committee

A. E. Clark, (Chairman) Edward Clark & Sons, Ltd., Toronto, W. E. Bigwood, Graves, Bigwood & Co., Toronto, G. E. Spragge, Victoria Harbor Lumber Co., Ltd., Toronto, E. R. Bremner, Watson & Todd. Ltd., Ottawa, Dan McLachlin, McLachlin Bros., Arnprior, W. Gerard Power, W. & J. Sharples, Ltd., Quebec, Brig. Gen. J. B. White, Riordon Co., Ltd., Montreal, J. Fraser Gregory, Murray & Gregory, Ltd., St. John, N. B., Angus McLean, Bathurst Company, Ltd., Bathurst, N. B.

### Transportation Committee

E. R. Bremner, (Chairman), Watson & Todd, Ltd., Ottawa, E. C. Barre, Cleveland, Sarnia Saw Mills Co., Ltd., Sarnia, Ont., Duke C. Johnson, Union Lumber Co., Ltd., Toronto, A. O. Anderson, Jas. MacLaren Co., Ltd., Buckingham, P. Q., P. J. McGoldrick, Power Lumber Co., Ltd., St. Pacome, P. Q., W. E. Golding, Geo. McKean & Co., St. John, N. B., Rufus E. Dickie, Stewiacke, N. S., Frederick Cleveland, 78 State St., Albany, N. Y.

### Membership Campaign Committee

Montreal District—W. A. Filion, E. H. Lemay, Montreal, P. Q., (Chairman), J. S. Bock, Eagle Lumber Co., Ltd., Montreal, Arthur H. Campbell, Campbell, MacLaurin Lumber Co., Ltd., Montreal, Wm. Thos. Mason, Mason, Gordon & Co., Montreal.

Quebec—W. Gerard Power, (Chairman), W. & J. Sharples, Ltd., Quebec, P. Q., David Champoux, Chaleurs Bay Mills, Restigouche, P. Q., F. C. Baker, The Devon Lumber Co., Ltd., Sherbrooks, P. Q.

Ontario—Northern & Georgian Bay Territory—W. E. Bigwood, (Chairman), Graves, Bigwood & Co., Toronto, J. J. McFadden, McFadden & Malloy, Blind River, Ont., W. R. King, Mickle, Dyment & Sons, Barrie, Ont., E. Letherby, Chew Bros., Midland, Ont., D. McLeod, Keewatin Lumber Co., Kenora, Ont.

Ottawa Valley—Dan McLachlin, (Chairman), McLachlin Bros., Ltd., Arnprior, Ont., W. R. Beatty, Colonial Lumber Co., Ltd., Pembroke, Ont., P. C. Walker, Shepard & Morse Lumber Co., (Canada), Ltd., Ottawa, A. Mayno Davis, McAuliffe-Davis Lumber Co., Ltd., Ottawa, Grant Davidson, Jas. Davdson's Sons, Ottawa.

Southern and Central Territory—A. C. Manbert, (Chairman),

Canadian General Lumber Co., Ltd., Toronto, W. F. Oliver, Oliver Lumber Co., of Toronto, Ltd., Toronto, Frank H. Harris, Frank H. Harris Lumber Co., Ltd., Toronto, (A representative of the Cleveland-Sarnia Saw Mills Co., Ltd., Sarnia, Ont., to be appointed by the Chairman), C. G. Anderson, C. G. Anderson Lumber Co., Ltd., Toronto, Percy E. Heeney, Kitchener, Ont.

New Brunswick—Angus McLean, (Chairman), Bathurst Co., Ltd., Bathurst, N. B., W. F. Napier, Shives Lumber Co. Ltd., Campbellton, N. B., J. W. Brankley, Miramichi Lumber Co., Chatham, N. B. W. B. Snowball, J. B. Snowball, Co., Ltd., Chatham, N. B., Leonard O'Brien, O'Brien, Ltd., South Nelson, N. B.

Nova Scotia—Rufus E. Dickie, (Chairman), Stewiacke, N. S., T. D. Pickard, Panoke Pulp & Power Co., Ltd., Windsor, N. S., B. H. Dunfield, Dunfield & Co., Ltd., Halifax, N. S.

The Chairmen of the above Committees have power to add to their numbers. Changes of this character should be promptly reported to the Secretary at Ottawa.

### Committee to Pass on Applications

E. R. Bremner, Watson & Todd, Ltd., Ottawa, Ont., R. G. Cameron, Cameron & Co., Ltd., Ottawa, Ont., Gordon C. Edwards, W. C. Edwards & Co., Ltd., Ottawa, Ont., W. M. Ross, J. R. Booth, Ltd., Ottawa, Ont.

### Provincial Regulations

Committee for the purpose of dealing with provincial government regulations or proposed legislation with particular reference to the use of rivers, lakes and streams, camp regulations, workmen's compensation, etc., etc.;—

Dan McLachlin, (Chairman), McLachlin Bros., Ltd., Arnprior, Ont., W. E. Bigwood, Graves, Bigwood & Co., Toronto, John Black, J. R. Booth, Ltd., Ottawa, John S. Gillies, Gillies Bros., Ltd., Braeside, Ont., Duncan McLaren, Union Lumber Co., Ltd., Toronto.

In other provinces where local questions of a similar nature to the above require settlement small active committees can be appointed as the necessity arises, on notification being given to the Secretary at Ottawa.

## National Wholesalers Will Meet in Washington

The annual convention of the National Wholesale Lumber Dealers' Association, will be held in the New Willard Hotel, Washington, D. C., on March 22nd and 23rd. The committee in charge of the annual meeting arrangements has been appointed, and a member of that committee is Dan. McLachlin, of Arnprior, Ont. It is reported that membership is at present 550.

In regard to transportation, an elaborate comparison of freight rates from numerous shipping points to many destinations will shortly be distributed to members in order to show in a practical manner existing higher freight costs as compared with former rates. It will thus be recognized that assuming every other operating cost to be reduced to a pre-war level, higher transportation charges necessitate an advance of several dollars per M on lumber sold on a delivered basis. The table will also show the comparisons on an enlightening basis.

J. G. Levie, of W. & J. Sharples, Limited, Quebec, P.Q., left recently on an extended business trip to London, England.

L. J. Baltes and his son, Frank Baltes, of North Tonawanda, N. Y., were in Toronto recently, calling upon the members of the lumber industry.

# Why Not Give Honest Work a Fair Trial

For one, I am plumb sick of all this talk about "Capital and Labor," "The Great Unwashed Proletariat," "Is the Binet Test a Cure for Falling Hair?" "Does the Eigh-hour Day Unfit a Man for Toddling?" and "Knee Skirts as a Stimulant in Place of Alcohol."

It strikes me that what this world needs right now is a damcite fewer reformers and a damcite more performers.

We are so busy talking efficiencies that we only have time left to produce deficiencies; we discuss industrial relations so much that we fail to practice industry.

We need less advice about how to do things—and a heluva lot less device for not doing them.

We need less argument and more action, less "welfare" and more work, less give and more get.

I knew a man who had rheumatism and moved around entirely on his knees for four years, during which time he cleared thick beach and maple timber from forty acres of heavy land, besides carrying on the work of a pioneer farm.

He was aided and abetted in this crime against the four-hour day by an energetic and thrifty wife and numerous growing children.

He lived to eat a dozen simon-pure buckwheat flapjacks as trimmings for a breakfast of solid food every morning until he was well past eighty. His average working day was around seventeen hours.

He wasn't particularly remarkable in his generation.

It was a generation that never got fogged on the fundamentals. It knew that to eat bread, a man had to raise wheat. If he failed to raise wheat and the neighbors couldn't help him (generally they couldn't in those days), he stood an excellent chance of acquiring starvation title to a 6 x 2 plot of ground.

The men of that day didn't give much of a tinkersdam about the relations of owner and worker or whether employers kept a chiropodist for every ten employees.

Those men, as do all of us, lived and loved and smiled and suffered and, when their time came, died—but through it all until the end, they WORKED. And they made America the greatest producing country in the world.

The almost elemental proposition in nature is that man must work to live—"in the sweat of his face shall he eat bread." The trouble to-day is that most of us want to eat only cake and three-inch porterhouses, without sweating—beg pardon, perspiring one single, little perspire.

Everyone has the "gimmes."

Two colored boys, one tall and one short, were standing down at the St. Louis Union Station the other day. The tall one produced from his pocket, paper, tobacco and match, rolled a cigarette and lit it.

The short boy watched him and finally said, "Say, boy, gimme a slip."

The smoking negro fished in his pocket and handed over the paper.

"O'mon, boy, gimme some tobacco," begged the little fellow.

He got it, along with a corner-eyed look, and proceeded to make his cigarette. That finished and in his mouth, he looked again at the taller negro.

"Now, gimme a match, won't yuh?" he asked finally.

The tall negro slowly produced the match and passed it. As he did so, he spoke for the first time.

"Say, boy, where at you git that thar moufful o' gimmes, anyhow?" he queried.

The universal request is "gimme an easy job and gimme more money and gimme everything the other fellow has—and then gimme butter on it!"

It is sickening! The only things any of us should ask for are a little less government and a lot more grit—and HEALTH. We can hustle for all else we are entitled to.

The only persons whose positions are secure are the dead ones—and most folks don't want security at the price of death.

Here is what ails us—we are plain, shiftless, good-for-nothing, lazy. We try to get wages without work—ease without expenditure of energy. We attempt to dictate the value of our efforts, rather than accept the market price for the products of those efforts.

And it can't be done.

The law of compensation has never been repealed—and perpetual motion is still a chimera. We can't get something for nothing or lift ourselves by our boot-straps. And if we all turn preachers where will the congregation come from?

It is time for us to quit living in to-morrow and begin living in TO-DAY. To-day is the only day in which we ever will accomplish anything.

We should quit dreaming about what we will do when success strikes us or the millenium overtakes us—and start planning how to give more real service and better value for every dollar we receive to-day.

The world is facing some big problems, we are told.

Most of these problems depend upon readjustment from war conditions and the mental attitude of the last few years.

Readjustment will be here when all of us know that we are getting a dollar's worth for every dollar that we spend. And that, again, is predicated upon each of us giving a dollar's worth for every dollar that we get.

This means greater output at lower cost—more economical production, which will permit more equitable prices and restore normal demand.

In other words, it means honest work and useful service.

By way of the solution of the problem of economical production, let every individual in this country—every individual in your business and our business—let you and I—try this:

Get right down in harness on the particular job that is ours or the first job that comes to hand, be it sweeping a floor or directing a bank, and do it in the very best and the very quickest way that we can discover—and let the other fellow go and do similarly.

If we do that I'm thinking it will be mighty short time until we have no need to worry about prices or profiteers, leagues of nations or fool notions, unions or uniforms.

If all of us will try to be satisfied with our job and our joys, our food and our Ford, our faith and our friends—AND WILL WORK LIKELL AND SMILE, quite probably most of the world's problems will solve themselves, without special legislation by congress or by appointment of additional government commissions.

And should conditions not be pleasing after we have given that plan a fair test, there is still time for us to go to the Fiji Islands and launder fig leaves, join the Utopia being operated by Messrs. Lenine, Trotzky et al, or become prohibition enforcement agents.

But for prosperity's sake and all our sakes, let's give honest work a trial first.—The Dart.

# CURRENT LUMBER PRICES—WHOLESALE

## TORONTO

(In Car Load Lots, F.O.B. cars Toronto)

### White Pine

| | | |
|---|---|---|
| 1 x 4/7 Good Strips | $110.00 | $115.00 |
| 1¼ & 1½ x 4/7 Good Strips | 120.00 | 125.00 |
| 1 x 8 and up Good Sides | 150.00 | 160.00 |
| 2 x 4/7 Good Strips | 130.00 | 140.00 |
| 1¼ & 1½ x 8 and wider Good Sides | 185.00 | 190.00 |
| 2 x 8 and wider Good Sides | 190.00 | 200.00 |
| 1 in. No. 1, 2 and 3 Cuts | 85.00 | 90.00 |
| 5/4 and 6/4 No. 1, 2 and 3 Cuts | 100.00 | 105.00 |
| 2 in. No. 1, 2 and 3 Cuts | 105.00 | 110.00 |
| 1 x 4 and 5 Mill Run | 52.00 | 55.00 |
| 1 x 6 Mill Run | 53.00 | 56.00 |
| 1 x 7, 9 and 11 Mill Run | 53.00 | 56.00 |
| 1 x 8 Mill Run | 55.00 | 58.00 |
| 1 x 10 Mill Run | 60.00 | 62.00 |
| 1 x 12 Mill Run | 65.00 | 70.00 |
| 5/4 and 6/4 x 5 and up Mill Run | 58.00 | 60.00 |
| 2 x 4 Mill Run | 52.00 | 53.00 |
| 2 x 6 Mill Run | 53.00 | 56.00 |
| 2 x 8 Mill Run | 55.00 | 58.00 |
| 2 x 10 Mill Run | 58.00 | 62.00 |
| 2 x 12 Mill Run | 60.00 | 64.00 |
| 1 in. Mill Run Shorts | 43.00 | 45.00 |
| 1 x 4 and up 6/16 No. 1 Mill Culls | 30.00 | 32.00 |
| 1 x 10 and up 6/16 No. 1 Mill Culls | 34.00 | 36.00 |
| 1 x 12 and up 6/16 No. 1 Mill Culls | 35.00 | 37.00 |
| 1 x 4 and up 6/16 No. 2 Mill Culls | 23.00 | 25.00 |
| 1 x 10 x 12 6/16 No. 2 Mill Culls | 26.00 | 30.00 |
| 1 x 4 and up 6/16 No. 3 Mill Culls | 15.00 | 20.00 |

### Red Pine

(In Car Load Lots, F.O.B. Toronto)

| | | |
|---|---|---|
| 1 x 4 and 5 Mill Run | $41.00 | $43.00 |
| 1 x 6 Mill Run | 42.00 | 44.00 |
| 1 x 8 Mill Run | 44.00 | 46.00 |
| 1 x 10 Mill Run | 47.00 | 49.00 |
| 2 x 4 Mill Run | 41.00 | 43.00 |
| 2 x 6 Mill Run | 42.00 | 44.00 |
| 2 x 8 Mill Run | 42.00 | 44.00 |
| 2 x 10 Mill Run | 45.00 | 47.00 |
| 2 x 12 Mill Run | 47.00 | 49.00 |
| 1 in. Clear and Clear Face | 69.00 | 71.00 |
| 2 in. Clear and Clear Face | 69.00 | 71.00 |

### Spruce

| | | |
|---|---|---|
| 1 x 4 Mill Run | 37.00 | 39.00 |
| 1 x 6 Mill Run | 39.00 | 41.00 |
| 1 x 8 Mill Run | 41.00 | 43.00 |
| 1 x 10 Mill Run | 46.00 | 48.00 |
| 1 x 12 Mill Run Spruce | 50.00 | 52.00 |
| Mill Culls | 28.00 | 30.00 |

### Hemlock (M R)

(In Car Load Lots, F.O.B. Toronto)

| | | |
|---|---|---|
| 1 x 4 and 5 in. x 9 to 16 ft. | $29.00 | $30.00 |
| 1 x 6 in. x 9 to 16 ft. | 33.00 | 35.00 |
| 1 x 8 in. x 9 to 16 ft. | 34.00 | 36.00 |
| 1 x 10 and 12 in. x 9 to 16 ft. | 35.00 | 37.00 |
| 1 x 7, 9 and 11 in. x 9 to 16 ft. | 33.00 | 34.00 |
| 2 x 4 to 12 in., 10 to 16 ft. | 34.00 | 35.00 |
| 2 x 4 to 12 in., 18 ft. | 37.00 | 39.00 |
| 2 x 4 to 12 in., 20 ft. | 40.00 | 42.00 |
| 1 in. No. 2, 6 ft. to 16 ft. | 26.00 | 28.00 |

### Fir Flooring

(In Car Load Lots, F.O.B. Toronto)

| | | |
|---|---|---|
| Fir flooring, 1 x 3 and 4", No. 1 and 2 Edge Grain | | $73.00 |
| Fir flooring, 1 x 3 and 4", No. 1 and 2 Flat Grain | | 48.00 |

(Depending upon Widths)

| | | |
|---|---|---|
| 1 x 4 to 12 No. 1 and 2 Clear Fir, Rough | $69.00 | 77.00 |
| 1¼ x 4 to 12 No. 1 and 2 Clear Fir, Rough | 77.00 | 81.00 |
| 2 x 4 to 12 No. 1 and 2 Clear Fir, Rough | 70.00 | 77.00 |
| 3 & 4 x 4 to 12 No. 1 & 2 Clear Fir, Rough | | 84.00 |
| 1 x 5 and 6 Fir Casing | | 73.00 |
| 1 x 8 and 10 Fir Base | | 77.00 |
| 1¼ and 1½ 8, 10 and 12" E.G. Stepping | | 90.00 |
| 1¼ and 1½, 8, 10 and 12" F.G. Stepping | | 80.00 |
| 1 x 4 to 12 Clear Fir, D4S | | 70.00 |
| 1¼ and 1½ x 4 to 12, Clear Fir, D4S | | 72.00 |
| XX Shingles, 6 butts to 2", per M | | 3.00 |
| XXX Shingles, 6 butts to 2", per M | | 4.90 |
| XXXXX Shingles, 5 butts to 2", per M | | 5.40 |

### Lath

(F.O.B. Mill)

| | |
|---|---|
| No. 1 White Pine | $11.00 |
| No. 2 White Pine | 10.00 |
| No. 3 White Pine | 8.00 |
| Mill Run White Pine, 32 in. | 6.00 |
| Merchantable Spruce Lath, 4 ft. | 7.00 |

## TORONTO HARDWOOD PRICES

The prices given below are for car loads f.o.b. Toronto, from wholesalers to retailers, and are based on a good percentage of long lengths and good widths, without any wide stock having been sorted out.

The prices quoted on imported woods are payable in U. S. funds.

### Ash, White

(Dry weight 3800 lbs. per M. ft.)

| | 1s & 2s | No. 1 Com. | No. 2 Com. |
|---|---|---|---|
| 1" | $110.00 | $ 60.00 | $ 45.00 |
| 1¼ and 1½" | 115.00 | 65.00 | 50.00 |
| 2" | 120.00 | 70.00 | 50.00 |
| 2½ and 3" | 135.00 | 95.00 | 60.00 |
| 4" | 145.00 | 105.00 | 65.00 |

### Ash, Brown

| | | | |
|---|---|---|---|
| 1" | $110.00 | $ 55.00 | $ 40.00 |
| 1¼ and 1½" | 120.00 | 65.00 | 45.00 |
| 2" | 130.00 | 70.00 | 55.00 |
| 2½ and 3" | 145.00 | 80.00 | 65.00 |
| 4" | 165.00 | 95.00 | 75.00 |

### Birch

(Dry weight 4000 lbs. per M. ft.)

| | 1s & 2s | Sels. | No. 1 Com. | No. 2 Com. |
|---|---|---|---|---|
| 4/4 | $105.00 | $ 80.00 | $ 50.00 | $ 35.00 |
| 5/4 | 105.00 | 80.00 | 55.00 | 38.00 |
| 6/4 | 110.00 | 85.00 | 60.00 | 45.00 |
| 8/4 | 120.00 | 90.00 | 65.00 | 50.00 |
| 12/4 | 130.00 | 100.00 | 70.00 | 55.00 |
| 16/4 | 140.00 | 110.00 | 80.00 | 60.00 |

### Basswood

(Dry weight 2500 lbs. per M. ft.)

| | 1s & 2s | No. 1 Com. | No. 2 Com. |
|---|---|---|---|
| 4/4 | $ 80.00 | $ 50.00 | $ 25.00 |
| 5/4 and 6/4 | 85.00 | 60.00 | 30.00 |
| 8/4 | 90.00 | 65.00 | 35.00 |

### Chestnut

(Dry weight 2800 lbs. per M. ft.)

| | 1s & 2s | No. 1 Com. | Sound Wormy |
|---|---|---|---|
| 1" | $130.00 | $ 80.00 | $ 40.00 |
| 1¼" to 1½" | 135.00 | 85.00 | 43.00 |
| 2" | 145.00 | 90.00 | 43.00 |

### Maple, Hard

(Dry weight 4200 lbs. per M. ft.)

| | F.A.S. | Sels. | No. 1 Com. | No. 2 Com. |
|---|---|---|---|---|
| 4/4 | $ 85.00 | $ 65.00 | $ 50.00 | $ 33.00 |
| 5/4 | 90.00 | 70.00 | 55.00 | 38.00 |
| 6/4 | 95.00 | 75.00 | 60.00 | 45.00 |
| 8/4 | 100.00 | 80.00 | 65.00 | 50.00 |
| 12/4 | 120.00 | 100.00 | 80.00 | 60.00 |
| 16/4 | 140.00 | 120.00 | 90.00 | 65.00 |

### Elm, Soft

(Dry weight 3100 lbs. per M. ft.)

| | 1s & 2s | No. 1 Com. | No. 2 Com. |
|---|---|---|---|
| 4/4 | $ 80.00 | $ 45.00 | $ 25.00 |
| 6/4 and 8/4 | 85.00 | 55.00 | 30.00 |
| 12/4 | 90.00 | 60.00 | 35.00 |

### Gum, Red

(Dry weight 3300 lbs. per M. ft.)

| | —Plain— | | —Quartered— | |
|---|---|---|---|---|
| | 1s & 2s | No. 1 Com. | 1s & 2s | No. 1 Com. |
| 1" | $125.00 | $ 73.00 | $133.00 | $ 83.00 |
| 1¼" | 135.00 | 75.00 | 148.00 | 88.00 |
| 1½" | 135.00 | 75.00 | 148.00 | 88.00 |
| 2" | 145.00 | 95.00 | 158.00 | 103.00 |

Figured Gum, $10 per M. extra, in both plain and quartered.

### Gum, Sap

| | 1s&2s | No. 1 Com. |
|---|---|---|
| 1" | $ 58.00 | $ 40.00 |
| 1¼" and 1½" | 62.00 | 44.00 |
| 2" | 67.00 | 50.00 |

### Hickory

(Dry weight 4500 lbs. per M. ft.

| | 1s&2s | No. 1 Com. |
|---|---|---|
| 1" | $120.00 | $ 60.00 |
| 1¼" | 145.00 | 65.00 |
| 1½" | 145.00 | 65.00 |
| 2" | 150.00 | 70.00 |

### Plain White and Red Oak

(Plain sawed. Dry weight 4000 lbs. per M. ft.)

| | 1s&2s | No. 1 Com. |
|---|---|---|
| 4/4 | $120.00 | $ 75.00 |
| 5/4 and 6/4 | 130.00 | 80.00 |
| 8/4 | 135.00 | 85.00 |
| 10/4 | 145.00 | 90.00 |
| 12/4 | 145.00 | 90.00 |
| 16/4 | 150.00 | 95.00 |

### White Oak, Quarter Cut

(Dry weight 4000 lbs. per M. ft.)

| | 1s&2s | No. 1 Com. |
|---|---|---|
| 4/4 | $160.00 | $ 90.00 |
| 5/4 and 6/4 | 170.00 | 95.00 |
| 8/4 | 190.00 | 105.00 |

### Quarter Cut Red Oak

| | 1s&2s | No. 1 Com. |
|---|---|---|
| 4/4 | $145.00 | $ 80.00 |
| 5/4 and 6/4 | 160.00 | 90.00 |
| 8/4 | 165.00 | 95.00 |

### Beech

The quantity of beech produced in Ontario is not large and is generally sold on a log run basis, the locality governing the prices. At present the prevailing quotation on log run, mill culls out, delivered in Toronto, is $35.00 to $40.00.

## OTTAWA

Manufacturers' Prices

### Pine

| | | |
|---|---|---|
| Good sidings: | | |
| 1 in. x 7 in. and up | | $140.00 |
| 1¼ in. and 1½ in., 8 in. and up. | | 165.00 |
| 2 in. x 7 in. and up | | 165.00 |
| No. 2 cuts 2 x 8 in. and up | | 80.00 |
| Good strips: | | |
| 1 in. | $100.00 | $105.00 |
| 1¼ in. and 1½ in. | | 120.00 |
| 2 in. | | 125.00 |
| Good shorts: | | |
| 1 in. x 7 in. and up | | 110.00 |
| 1 in. 4 in. to 6 in. | 85.00 | 90.00 |
| 1¼ in. and 1½ in. | | 110.00 |
| 2 in. | | 125.00 |
| 7 in. to 9 in. A sidings | 54.00 | 56.00 |
| No. 1 dressing sidings | 82.00 | 85.00 |
| No. 1 dressing strips | | 78.00 |
| No. 1 dressing shorts | 68.00 | 73.00 |
| 1 in. x 4 in. s.c. strips | 56.00 | 58.00 |
| 1 in. x 5 in. s.c. strips | 56.00 | 58.00 |
| 1 in. x 6 in. s.c. strips | 63.00 | 65.00 |
| 1 in. x 7 in. s.c. strips | 63.00 | 64.00 |
| 1 in. x 8 in. s.c. strips, 12 to 16 ft. | 63.00 | 66.00 |
| 1 in. x 10 in. M.R. | 65.00 | 70.00 |
| S.C. sidings, 1½ and 2 in. | 63.00 | 67.00 |
| S.C. strips, 1 in. | | 64.00 |
| 1¼, 1½ and 2 in. | 57.00 | 58.00 |
| S.C. shorts, 1 x 4 to 6 in. | 48.00 | 50.00 |
| S.C. and bet., shorts. 1 x 5 | | 48.00 |
| S.C. and bet., shorts, 1 x 6 | | 50.00 |
| S.C. Shorts, 6'-11', 1" x 10" | 52.00 | 54.00 |
| Box boards: | | |
| 1 in. x 4 in. and up, 6 ft.-11 ft. | | 45.00 |
| 1 in. x 3 in. and up, 12 ft.-16 ft. | 50.00 | 53.00 |
| Mill culls, strips and sidings, 1 in. x 4 in. and up, 12 ft. and up | 43.00 | 45.00 |
| Mill cull shorts, 1 in. x 4 in. and up, 6 ft. to 11 ft. | 34.00 | 36.00 |
| O. culls r and w p | 24.00 | 28.00 |

### Red Pine, Log Run

| | | |
|---|---|---|
| Mill culls out, 1 in. | 34.00 | 48.00 |
| Mill culls out, 1¼ in. | 34.00 | 48.00 |
| Mill culls out, 1½ in. | 35.00 | 47.00 |
| Mill culls out, 2 in. | 35.00 | 47.00 |
| Mill Culls, white pine, 1 in. x 7 in. and up | | 35.00 |

### Mill Run Spruce

| | | |
|---|---|---|
| 1 in. x 4 in. and up, 6 ft.-11 ft. | | 25.00 |
| 1 in. x 4 in. and up, 12 ft.-16 ft. | 32.00 | 34.00 |
| 1" x 9"-10" and up, 12 ft.-16 ft. | 38.00 | 40.00 |
| 1¼" x 7, 8 and 9" up, 12 ft.-16 ft. | | 35.00 |
| 1¼ x 10 and up, 12 ft.-16 ft. | 38.00 | 42.00 |
| 1½" x 12" x 12" and up, 12'-16' | | 42.00 |
| Spruce, 1 in. clear fine dressing and B | | 55.00 |
| Hemlock, 1 in. cull | | 20.00 |
| Hemlock, 1 in. log run | 24.00 | 26.00 |
| Hemlock, 2 x 4, 6, 8, 10 12/16 ft. | | 28.00 |
| Tamarac | 25.00 | 28.00 |
| Basswood, log run, dead culls out | 45.00 | 50.00 |
| Basswood, log run, mill culls out. | 50.00 | 54.00 |
| Birch, log run | 45.00 | 50.00 |
| Soft Elm, common and better, 1, 1½, 2 in. | 58.00 | 68.00 |
| Ash, black, log run | 62.00 | 65.00 |
| 1 x 10 No. 1 barn | 57.00 | 62.00 |
| 1 x 10 No. 2 barn | 51.00 | 56.00 |
| 1 x 8 and 9 No. 2 barn | 47.00 | 52.00 |

# CURRENT LUMBER PRICES—WHOLESALE

**Lath per M.:**

| | | |
|---|---|---|
| No. 1 White Pine, 1¼ in. x 4 ft. | | 8.00 |
| No. 2 White Pine | | 6.00 |
| Mill run White Pine | | 7.00 |
| Spruce, mill run, 1½ in. | | 6.00 |
| Red Pine, mill run | | 6.00 |
| Hemlock, mill run | | 5.50 |

**White Cedar Shingles**

| | | |
|---|---|---|
| XXXX, 18 in. | 9.00 | 10.00 |
| Clear butt, 18 in. | 6.00 | 7.00 |
| 18 in. XX | | 5.00 |

## QUEBEC

**White Pine**

(At Quebec)

| | Cts. Per Cubic Ft. | |
|---|---|---|
| First class Ottawa wancy, 18 in. Average according to lineal | 100 | 110 |
| 19 in. and up average | 110 | 120 |

**Spruce Deals**

(At Mill)

| | | |
|---|---|---|
| 3 in. unsorted, Quebec, 4 in. to 6 in. wide | $ 20.00 | $ 25.00 |
| 3 in. unsorted, Quebec, 7 in. to 8 in. wide | 26.00 | 28.00 |
| 3 in. unsorted, Quebec, 9 in. wide | 30.00 | 35.00 |

**Oak**

(At Quebec)

| | Cts. Per Cubic Ft. | |
|---|---|---|
| According to average and quality, 55 ft. cube | 125 | 130 |

**Elm**

(At Quebec)

| | | |
|---|---|---|
| According to average and quality, 40 to 45 ft. cube | 100 | 120 |
| According to average and quality, 30 to 35 ft. | 90 | 100 |

**Export Birch Planks**

(At Mill)

| | | |
|---|---|---|
| 1 to 4 in. thick, per M. ft. | $ 30.00 | $ 35.00 |

## ST. JOHN, N.B.

(From Yards and Mills)

**Rough Lumber**

Retail Prices per M. Sq. Ft.

| | | |
|---|---|---|
| 2x3, 2x4, 3x3, 3x4, Rgh Merch Spr | $32.00 | |
| 2x3, 2x4, 3x3, 3x4, Dressed 1 edge | 33.00 | |
| 2x3, 2x4, 3x3, 3x4, Dressed 4 sides | 33.00 | |
| 2x6, 2x7, 3x5, 4x4, 4x6, all rough | 34.00 | |
| 2x8, 3x7, 5x5, 6x6 | 37.00 | $ 40.00 |
| 2x9, 3x8, 6x8, 7x7 | 37.00 | 40.00 |
| 2x10, 3x9 | 45.00 | |
| 2x12, 3x10, 3x12, 8x8 and up | 45.00 | |
| Merch. Spr. Bds., Rough, 1x3-4 & 5 | 30.00 | |
| Merch. Spr. Bds., Rough, 1x6 | 34.00 | |
| Merch. Spr. Bds., Rough, 1x7 & up | 40.00 | |
| Refuse Bds., Deals & Setgs. | 20.00 | 23.00 |

Above random lengths up to 18-0 long.
Lengths 19-0 and up $5.00 extra per M.
For planing Merch. and Refuse Bds. add $2.00 per M. to above prices.
Laths, $7.00.

**Shingles**

| | Per M. |
|---|---|
| Cedar, Extras | $6.25 |
| " Clears | 5.50 |
| " 2nd Clears | 4.50 |
| " Extra No. 1 | 2.90 |
| Spruce | 4.50 |

## SARNIA, ONT.

**Pine, Common and Better**

| | |
|---|---|
| 1 x 6 and 8 in. | $105.00 |
| 1 in., 8 in. and up wide | 125.00 |
| 1¼ and 1½ in. and up wide | 175.00 |
| 2 in. and up wide | 175.00 |

**Cuts and Better**

| | |
|---|---|
| 4/4 x 8 and up No. 1 and better | 120.00 |
| 5/4 and 6/4 and up No. 1 and better | 145.00 |
| 8/4 and 8 and up No. 1 and better | 145.00 |

**No. 1 Cuts**

| | |
|---|---|
| 1 in., 8 in. and up wide | 110.00 |
| 1¼ in., 8 in. and up wide | 120.00 |
| 1½ in., 8 in. and up wide | 120.00 |
| 2 in., 8 in. and up wide | 125.00 |
| 2½ in. and 3 in., 8 in. and up wide | 170.00 |
| 4 in., 8 in. and up wide | 180.00 |

**No. 1 Barn**

| | | |
|---|---|---|
| 1 in., 10 to 16 ft. long | $ 70.00 | $ 85.00 |
| 1¼, 1½ and 2 in., 10/16 ft. | 75.00 | 90.00 |
| 2½ to 3 in., 10/16 ft. | 80.00 | 95.00 |

**No. 2 Barn**

| | | |
|---|---|---|
| 1 in., 10 to 16 ft. long | 68.00 | 77.00 |
| 1¼, 1½ and 2 in., 10/16 ft. | 68.00 | 80.00 |
| 2½, 1½ and 3 in. | 78.00 | 90.00 |

**No. 3 Barn**

| | | |
|---|---|---|
| 1 in., 10 to 16 ft. long | 55.00 | 62.00 |
| 1¼, 1½ and 2 in., 10/16 ft. | 59.00 | 63.00 |

**Box**

| | | |
|---|---|---|
| 1 in., 1¼ and 1½ in., 10/16 ft. | 40.00 | 42.00 |

**Mill Culls**

| | |
|---|---|
| Mill Run Culls— | |
| 1 in., 4 in. and up wide, 6/16 ft. | 30.00 |
| 1¼, 1½ and 2 in. | 31.00 |

## WINNIPEG

**No. 1 Spruce**

| Dimension | S.1.S. and 1.E. 10 ft. | 12 ft. | 14 ft. | 16 ft. |
|---|---|---|---|---|
| 2 x 4 | $30 | $29 | $29 | $30 |
| 2 x 6 | 31 | 29 | 29 | 30 |
| 2 x 8 | 32 | 30 | 30 | 31 |
| 2 x 10 | 33 | 31 | 31 | 32 |
| 2 x 12 | 34 | 32 | 32 | 33 |

For 2 inches, rough, add 50 cents.
For S1E only, add 50 cents.
For S1S and 2E, S4S or D&M, add $3.00.
For timbers larger than 8 x 8, add 50c. for each additional 2 inches each way.
For lengths longer than 20 ft., add $1.00 for each additional two feet.
For selected common, add $5.00.
For No. 2 Dimension, $3.00 less than No. 1.
For 1 x 2 and 2 x 2, $2 more than 2 x 4 No. 1.
For Tamarac, open.

## BUFFALO and TONAWANDA

**White Pine**

Wholesale Selling Price

| | |
|---|---|
| Uppers, 4/4 | $225.00 |
| Uppers, 5/4 to 8/4 | 225.00 |
| Uppers, 10/4 to 12/4 | 250.00 |
| Selects, 4/4 | 200.00 |
| Selects, 5/4 to 8/4 | 200.00 |
| Selects, 10/4 to 12/4 | 225.00 |
| Fine Common, 4/4 | 155.00 |
| Fine Common, 5/4 | 160.00 |
| Fine Common, 6/4 | 160.00 |
| Fine Common, 8/4 | 160.00 |
| No. 1 Cuts, 4/4 | 115.00 |
| No. 1 Cuts, 5/4 | 130.00 |
| No. 1 Cuts, 6/4 | 135.00 |
| No. 1 Cuts, 8/4 | 140.00 |
| No. 2 Cuts, 4/4 | 70.00 |
| No. 2 Cuts, 5/4 | 100.00 |
| No. 2 Cuts, 6/4 | 105.00 |
| No. 2 Cuts, 8/4 | 110.00 |
| No. 3 Cuts, 5/4 | 60.00 |
| No. 3 Cuts, 6/4 | 65.00 |
| No. 3 Cuts, 8/4 | 67.00 |
| Dressing, 4/4 | 95.00 |
| Dressing 4/4 x 10 | 98.00 |
| Dressing, 4/4 x 12 | 110.00 |
| No. 1 Moulding, 5/4 | 150.00 |
| No. 1 Moulding, 6/4 | 150.00 |
| No. 1 Moulding, 8/4 | 155.00 |
| No. 2 Moulding, 5/4 | 125.00 |
| No. 2 Moulding, 6/4 | 125.00 |
| No. 2 Moulding, 8/4 | 130.00 |
| No. 1 Barn, 1 x 12 | 90.00 |
| No. 1 Barn, 1 x 6 and 8 | 76.00 |
| No. 1 Barn, 1 x 10 | 80.00 |
| No. 2 Barn, 1 x 6 and 8 | 62.00 |
| No. 2 Barn, 1 x 10 | 68.00 |
| No. 2 Barn, 1 x 12 | 75.00 |
| No. 3 Barn, 1 x 6 and 8 | 42.00 |
| No. 3 Barn, 1 x 10 | 44.00 |
| No. 3 Barn, 1 x 12 | 47.00 |
| Box, 1 x 6 and 8 | 36.00 |
| Box, 1 x 10 | 38.00 |
| Box, 1 x 12 | 39.00 |
| Box, 1 x 13 and up | 40.00 |

## BUFFALO

The following quotations on hardwoods represent the jobber buying price at Buffalo and Tonawanda.

**Maple**

| | 1s & 2s | No. 1 Com. | No. 2 Com. |
|---|---|---|---|
| 1 in. | $ 80.00 | $ 45.00 | $ 30.00 |
| 5/4 to 8/4 | 85.00 | 50.00 | 30.00 |
| 10/4 to 4 in. | 90.00 | 55.00 | 30.00 |

**Sap Birch**

| | | | |
|---|---|---|---|
| 1 in. | 90.00 | 48.00 | 30.00 |
| 5/4 and up | 100.00 | 53.00 | 30.00 |

**Soft Elm**

| | | | |
|---|---|---|---|
| 1 in. | 70.00 | 45.00 | 30.00 |
| 5/4 to 2 in. | 75.00 | 50.00 | 30.00 |

**Red Birch**

| | | | |
|---|---|---|---|
| 1 in. | 120.00 | 75.00 | |
| 5/4 and up | 125.00 | 80.00 | |

**Basswood**

| | | | |
|---|---|---|---|
| 1 in. | 70.00 | 45.00 | 30.00 |
| 5/4 to 2 in. | 80.00 | 55.00 | 35.00 |

**Plain Oak**

| | | | |
|---|---|---|---|
| 1 in. | 95.00 | 55.00 | 35.00 |
| 5/4 to 2 in. | 105.00 | 65.00 | 40.00 |

**Ash**

| | | | |
|---|---|---|---|
| 1 in. | 85.00 | 50.00 | 30.00 |
| 5/4 to 2 in. | 95.00 | 55.00 | 30.00 |
| 10/4 and up | 110.00 | 70.00 | 30.00 |

## BOSTON

Quotations given below are for highest grades of Michigan and Canadian White Pine and Eastern Canadian Spruce as required in the New England market in car loads.

| | | |
|---|---|---|
| White Pine Uppers, 1 in. | | |
| White Pine Uppers, 1¼, 1½, 2 in. | | |
| White Pine Uppers, 2½, 3 in. | | |
| White Pine Uppers, 4 in. | | |
| Selects, 1 in. | | $190.00 |
| Selects, 1¼, 2 in. | | 200.00 |
| Selects, 2½, 3 in. | | |
| Selects, 4 in. | | |

Prices nominal

| | | |
|---|---|---|
| Fine Common, 1 in., 30%, 12 in. and up. | | 150.00 |
| Fine Common, 1 x 8 and up | | 150.00 |
| Fine Common, 1¼ to 2 in. | $160.00 | 170.00 |
| Fine Common, 2½ and 3 in. | | 180.00 |
| Fine Common, 4 in. | | 195.00 |
| 1 in. Shaky Clear | | 100.00 |
| 1¼ in. to 2 in. Shaky Clear | | 110.00 |
| 1 in. No. 2 Dressing | | 95.00 |
| 1¼ in. to 2 in. No. 2 Dressing | | 95.00 |
| No. 1 Cuts, 1 in. | | 110.00 |
| No. 1 Cuts, 1¼ to 2 in. | | 140.00 |
| No. 1 Cuts, 2½ to 3 in. | | 180.00 |
| No. 2 Cuts, 1 in. | | 80.00 |
| No. 2 Cuts, 1¼ to 2 in. | | 110.00 |
| Barn Boards, No. 1, 1 x 12 | | 91.00 |
| Barn Boards, No. 1, 1 x 10 | | 87.00 |
| Barn Boards, No. 1, 1 x 8 | | 84.50 |
| Barn Boards, No. 2, 1 x 12 | | 75.00 |
| Barn Boards, No. 2, 1 x 8 | | 67.00 |
| Barn Boards, No. 2, 1 x 10 | | 68.00 |
| Barn Boards, No. 3, 1 x 12 | | 55.00 |
| Barn Boards, No. 3, 1 x 10 | | 53.00 |
| Barn Boards, No. 3, 1 x 8 | | 52.00 |

**No. 1 Clear**

| | | |
|---|---|---|
| Can. Spruce, No. 1 and clear, 1 x 4 to 9" | | $ 75.00 |
| Can. Spruce, 1 x 10 in. | | 78.00 |
| Can. Spruce, No. 1, 1 x 4 to 7 in. | | 72.00 |
| Can. Spruce, No. 1, 1 x 8 and 9 in. | | 74.00 |
| Can. Spruce, No. 1, 1 x 10 in. | | 76.00 |
| Can. Spruce, No. 2, 1 x 4 and 5 in. | | 36.00 |
| Can. Spruce, No. 2, 1 x 6 and 7 in. | | 37.00 |
| Can. Spruce, No. 2, 1 x 8 and 9 in. | | 39.00 |
| Can. Spruce, No. 2, 1 x 10 in. | | 42.00 |
| Can. Spruce, No. 2, 1 x 12 in. | | 45.00 |
| Spruce, 12 in. dimension | | 49.00 |
| Spruce, 10 in. dimension | | 48.00 |
| Spruce, 9 in. dimension | | 46.00 |
| Spruce, 8 in. dimension | | 45.00 |
| 2 x 10 in. random lengths, 8 ft. and up | | 41.00 |
| 2 x 12 in., random lengths | | 45.00 |
| 2 x 3, 2 x 4, 2 x 5, 2 x 6, 2 x 7 | | 32.00 |
| 3 x 4 and 4 x 4 in. | | 33.00 |
| 2 x 9 | | 39.00 |
| All other random lengths, 7 in. and under, 8 ft. and up | 32.00 | 36.00 |
| 5 in. and up merchantable boards, 8 ft. and up, D 1s | 31.00 | 35.00 |
| 1 x 2 | | 32.00 |
| 1 x 3 | | 32.00 |
| 1⅝ in. Spruce Lath | | 8.50 |
| 1½ in. Spruce Lath | | 7.50 |

**New Brunswick Cedar Shingles**

| | |
|---|---|
| Extras | 5.50 |
| Clears | 4.50 |
| Second Clear | 3.50 |
| Clear Whites | 2.75 |

Second Hand Machinery & Equipment Wanted & For Sale

# Quick Action Section

Special Lots Of Lumber— —Positions Wanted & Vacant

## Lumber Wanted

### Hard Maple Wanted

Carload lots 1¼" x 6" x 10' 1sts, and 2nds, dry.
1¼" x 2½" x 40" clear dry equal number of.
Carload lots 1" x 3½" x 40" pieces each size in each car. Box 782, Canada Lumberman, Toronto. 3-5

### Hard Maple and Birch Wanted

A limited quantity of 4/4 and 8/4 dry stock No. 2 Common and Better. For further particulars apply Box 761 Canada Lumberman, Toronto, Can. 2-5

### Hardwood Wanted

Several cars 1" also some 2" No 3 Common, Maple Birch etc. State dryness and quote best prices.
Huntington & Finke Co., Buffalo, N.Y. 3-4

### Lath Wanted

Several cars 3/8" x 1½" x 4' No. 1 Hemlock. State when cut and quote best price.
Huntington & Finke Co., Buffalo, N.Y. 3-4

### Lath Wanted

Especially White Pine and Hemlock. Write us what you have with prices.
BREWSTER LOUD LUMBER CO.,
508-509 Lincoln Building,
DETROIT, MICH.
24-3

### Logs Wanted

to saw in transit, at G.T.R. siding Oro, on main line between Toronto and North Bay. Satisfaction guaranteed. Prices on application.
T. R. Crawford, Oro Station, Ont. 2-5

### Wanted

1 Carload of good White Pine Slabs.
James Scouler, Forest, Ont. 3

### Wanted

To contract a large quantity of 5/8" x 4" and 5" log run spruce with mill culls out. Address H. V. Berry, Fort Plain, N.Y. 3-6

### We Want to Buy

3 million Hemlock
2 million Jack Pine
1 million White Pine
5 million Lath
Send us your list.
Thompson & Heyland Lumber Co., Ltd.,
Stair Building, Toronto, Ont.
3

### We Will Buy

A block of Hemlock, Spruce, Red or White Pine that is sawn or will be sawn before the 15th of March. Box 770 Canada Lumberman, Toronto. 2 T.f.

## Lumber For Sale

### For Sale

10,000,000 feet of Quebec Spruce Lumber, 100,000 cords of pulpwood and 500 cars of Standard No. 1 Spruce and Fir Lath, apply to The Canadian Forest Corporation, 140 St. Peter Street, Quebec, Que.

### For Sale

At Blind River, Ontario, Pine and Spruce Lath, also some Cedar and Hemlock Lath, Grades, four foot mill run, 32" mill run, and four foot No. 3.
F. P. Potvin,
Blind River, Ont.
2-T.f.

### PUBLISHER'S NOTICE

Advertisements other than "Employment Wanted" or "Employees Wanted" will be inserted in this department at the rate of 25 cents per agate line (14 agate lines make one inch). $3.50 per inch, each insertion, payable in advance. Space measured from rule to rule. When four or more consecutive insertions of the same advertisement are ordered a discount of 25 per cent. will be allowed.

Advertisements of "Wanted Employment" will be inserted at the rate of one cent a word, net. Cash must accompany order. If Canada Lumberman box number is used, enclose ten cents extra for postage in forwarding replies. Minimum charge 25 cents.

Advertisements of "Wanted Employees" will be inserted at the rate of two cents a word, net. Cash must accompany the order. Minimum charge 50 cents.

Advertisements must be received not later than the 10th and 20th of each month to insure insertion in the subsequent issue.

### For Sale

125 M. ft 1" Maple
85 M. ft 1" Birch
75 M. ft. 1" Beech
15 M. ft 1" Elm

All No. 3 Common and Better. Last winter's cut. Dry and ready to ship from Stanstead on Boston and Maine Railway.
W. A. Hadley,
Stanstead, Que.

### Lumber for Sale

Crating Spruce—
About 200,000 of 5/8" Common Sound Spruce, also 1 2 & 3" Culls Spruce.
J. P. Abel-Fortin, Limited,
879 Desjardins Ave.,
Maisonneuve, Montreal. 3

## Sale of Timber
### to
### Close an Estate

South East Quarter of Township of PROUDFOOT containing twenty-three and a quarter square miles, and known as Berth No. 2. Containing the following timber as cruised by one of the most reliable timber cruisers in Ontario:-

| | | |
|---|---|---|
| BIRCH .................... | 10,950,000 | ft. |
| MAPLE .................... | 4,000,000 | ft. |
| HEMLOCK .................. | 2,000,000 | ft. |
| ELM ...................... | 100,000 | ft. |
| PINE ..................... | 100,000 | ft. |
| CEDAR poles 25' up 50' .... | 5,000 | |
| SPRUCE & BALSAM Cordwood | 5,000 | cords |
| HARDWOOD CORDWOOD first-class | 80,000 | cords |

PRICE .................... $26,184.00
Favorable terms can be arranged:-
F. C. Clarkson, Assignee,
E. R. C. Clarkson & Son,
TORONTO.
24-3

## Machinery For Sale

### For Sale

10" Steam feed 36' long complete with valves. Apply Bishop Lumber Company, Nesterville, Ont. 3-4

### For Sale

Edger with front table, Filar & Stowel make four saws, width of edger 54", in A1 mechanical condition. Apply Bishop Lumber Company, Nesterville, Ont. 3-4

### For Sale

Cross Compound Corliss Engine 18"-32" x 42" (Polson Iron Works) used 6 years. Bargain for cash. Must be moved. J. L. Neilson & Co., Winnipeg, Man. 3-4

### Used Equipment

We have all kinds of machinery, boilers, engines, motors, and air compressors, etc., for quarries, lumber and pulp mills and mines. Let us have your inquiries. Montreal Agents American Saw Mill Machinery Co.,
Barrie Engineering Co., Ltd.,
208a St. Nicholas Bldg.,
23-4 Montreal.

### For Sale En-Bloc

Complete Saw Mill equipment, including one Four Block Hamilton Carriage. One pair heavy twin engines, feed complete and steam nigger. One three block E. Long Carriage with eight inch gun shot feed and steam nigger. One heavy three saw edger, W. Hamilton, make. Three 75 H.P. Boilers complete with dutch ovens and stacks. One 90 H.P. engine and fly-wheel complete. One lath and shingle mill. Complete filing equipment. One refuse burner. Shafting pulleys, transmission, etc., complete. Apply Box 788 Canada Lumberman, Toronto. 3-8

### For Sale

2 Factory Refuse Hogs,
1 Sawmill Refuse Hog,
1 Shingle Machine,
1 Band Resaw Grinder,
1 Lath Machine,
1 Jack Ladder Haul-up Chain, Bullwheel and Sprockets,
1 7" Steam Feed,
Several pieces of Link and Bar Slush Chain.

Apply: The C. Beck Mfg. Co., Ltd.,
Penetanguishene, Ont.
1-2

### Wickes Gang

GANG: No. 12 Wickes Gang, 40" sash, 15" stroke, steam binder rolls, front and back in two sections, feed and oscillation combined, 1908 model, and has been in use for five years. We furnish with this gang 11 rolls for cants and stock, one filing machine, and 4 sets of saws.
THE PEMBROKE LUMBER CO.,
1t.f. Pembroke, Ont.

## Second Hand Machinery

We have over $250,000 worth of used machinery of all kinds for sale. Suitable for mines, quarries, railroads, pulp and lumber mills, etc.

Everything carefully overhauled at our shops before shipped.

Send us your inquiries.
R. T. GILMAN & CO.,
19tf Montreal

## Good Values
### Subject to Prior Sale

Band Resaw, Connell & Dengler, 54 and 60"
Band Rip Saw, Yates No. 281
Circular Saw Mill, Hoosier Pony
Circular Resaw, 44"
E. B. Hayes Dowell Gluer and Driver
E. B. Hayes Dowell Rod Machine
E. B. Hayes Standard Power Door Clamp
Jointers 12, 16 and 24"
Matcher and Sizer, 30" x 12" American
Matcher, Hardwood Berlin No. 89
Matcher, 14 x 6, S. A. Woods
Matcher, Hardwood, American No. 229
Moulder, Hermance 10", wide open side
Moulder, Woods No. 2 light inside
Moulder, C. B. Rogers, 6" outside
Moulder, Berlin 10" No. 118, inside
Moulders, American 4" and 10"
Planers, all sizes, single and double
Sanders, Columbia 42", 48" and 60"
Saw, mitre, double and Maddox
Saws, Variety, several makes.

Woodworking Machinery Company of Buffalo,
54 Mechanic St.,
Buffalo, N.Y.
3-E.o.I.-T.f.

### Chain for Sale

We have the following second hand conveyor chain for sale. This chain is in first class condition, having only been used about six weeks, is well oiled and free from rust.
600 ft. No. 103 Chain at .44 cts. per foot
350 ft. No. 103 K-1 Attachments at .68 cts per foot
240 ft. No. 88 chain at .30 cts. per foot
8 ft. No. 88 F-2 Attachments at .84 cts. per foot
290 ft. No. 77 Chain at .20 cts. per foot
13 ft. No. 77 F-2 Attachments at .44 cts. per foot
also sprockets, etc. for driving same.
Canadian Wirebound Boxes Limited,
1000 Gerrard St. E., Toronto, Ont.
2

### Engines, Boilers, etc., for Sale

One "Williams" Upright Engine 6" x 6"
One Upright Engine 5" x 6"
Six Return tubular boilers of following dimensions:-
One "Butterfield" 72" x 14' - 3¼" tube - ½" shell.
One "Polson" 64" x 14' - 3¼" tube - ½" shell
One "Doty" 60" x 15' - 4" tube - ½" shell
One "Doty" 60" x 14½" - 4" tube - ½" shell
One "Doty" 60" x 15' - 4" tube - ½" shell
One "Inglis" 60" x 16' - 3" tube - ½" shell
One double acting "Northey" Fire pump, 6" suction, 5" discharge, 14" steam cylinder, 8" water cylinder, 13" stroke, Capacity 450 gallons per minute.
One "Northey" feed pump 6 x 4 x 7" stroke, Capacity 60 gallons per minute.
One brass Mill steam whistle.
For further particulars apply The Conger Lumber Co Limited., Parry Sound, Ontario.
24 T.f.

## Situations Wanted

An expert Band Saw Filer, twenty years experience in all kinds of Eastern timber and foreign woods. Ten years on the big mills of the Pacific coast. Work guaranteed second to none. Am open for a position. Best references. Box 756 Canada Lumberman, Toronto. 1-3

Position Wanted as Band Saw Filer for season 1922. Experienced and can give good references. Box 780 Canada Lumberman, Toronto. 3

POSITION WANTED: As manager for a good responsible Lumber Co., 36 years experience in Lumbering. Box 729 Canada Lumberman, Toronto. 1-4

Position wanted by expert saw hammerer and filer repairing saws for the coming season. Will do the work in your mill and guarantee satisfaction at reasonable rates. Box 773 Canada Lumberman, Toronto. 2-3

Wanted position as Mill Superintendent. Eight years experience as Mill Superintendent fifteen years as sawyer. Can furnish best references. Box 747 Canada Lumberman, Toronto. 1-3

Wanted Position as superintendent or foreman of planing mill or woodworking factory. Have had over 12 years experience in interior fittings, sash, doors, hardwood flooring, box-making, estimating and detail drawing. Expert on production and first-class references. Will guarantee results. Box 752 Canada Lumberman, Toronto. 1-4

WANTED POSITION: for 1922 as head filer in good large Band Mill. Expert in every detail. Satisfaction guaranteed. Apply Box 730 Canada Lumberman, Toronto. 1-4

Young man, with initiative, ability, integrity and five years' experience Millwork and Lumber offices desires position. Can handle correspondence, sales and orders, etc. Only positions with progressive firms in a town considered. All correspondence treated confidential. Excellent references. Box 779 Canada Lumberman, Toronto. 3

### Forestry Department at B. C. University

An important recent development in forestry is the inauguration of a Department of Forestry in the Faculty of Science, University of British Columbia, under Prof. H. R. Christie. A five-year course will be given, during the first two years of which the instruction will consist of general arts and science subjects, as in the courses in chemical, mechanical, mining and civil engineering. During the last three years the student will specialize in for-estry, this being definitely recognized as a branch of the engineering profession. Prof. Christie was for a number of years in the British Columbia Forest Branch, also with the Canadian Engineers in France. He is a graduate of the Faculty of Forestry, University of Toronto. The establishment of the new School of Forestry at Vancouver should mean much in the future development of forestry work in the western provinces, particularly British Columbia, which has had to bring her forestry experts from outside the province. The existence of progressive forest faculties is largely responsible for the progress of the forestry movement in Canada.

### Forests and Water Power

We are just as callous and indifferent over the destruction of our natural resources. People seem to lose sight of the fact that the wiping out of large forest areas by fire also means the obliteration to a large extent, of our water power so that the permanency and utilization of this great asset is also jeopardized; threatening not only the development of our industries, but also transportation facilities and the thousand and one other necessaries of life which modern ingenuity has provided for our comfort, entertainment, and pleasure.—Deputy Fire Marshal Lewis, Ont.

### British Statesmen and Forestry

Great Britain, which was aroused during the war to the need of adequate timber supplies within the Empire, is determined not to permit things to drop back into the old rut. First she called an Empire Forestry conference, at which Canada was represented, and took stock of the situation; next, she entered upon a definite planting programme in the British Isles, calling upon Canada, through the Dominion Forestry Branch, to secure about a ton and a half of tree seed per annum for this purpose; and lastly, to keep up the work and give people information on this most important subject, she has established an Empire Forestry Association with headquarters in London, which will link up the work of Dominion-Lovat expressed it "pool the resources of their knowledge." It is expected that conventions will be held in different parts of the Empire and that Canada will be one of the first Dominions to be thus honoured.

### New Forests For Old

Field work on the Petawawa experiment station and other stations carried on by the Forestry Branch of the Department of the Interior ceased about the middle of December, and the officers have returned to Ottawa to make a record of the work of the field season. Just as the farm experiment stations have aided agriculture by discovering new methods of growing plants and indicating the best varities, so the forest experiment stations are assisting forestry and lumbering by studying and putting on record the best methods of harvesting handling cut-over or burned areas in order to get a new crop started second most important natural resource and whatever assists in the development and utilization of this great resource is of importance to every Canadian.

### Trees for the Prairies

A feature of the work of the Dominion Forestry Branch, which increases in importance from year to year, is the supplying, free of charge, of tree seedlings and cuttings for planting windbreaks on prairie farms. For the last few years about five millions of seedlings and cuttings have been sent out annually, under the direction of the Superintendent of the Dominion Forest Nursery Station at Indian Head, Saskatchewan, and it is expected the number shipped in the coming spring will show an increase. The species of trees sent out, and which do well on the prairies, are Manitoba maple, Russian poplar, willow, green ash, and caragana. The last named is really a large shrub, an importance called Siberian pea, which has proved very valuable for hedges and wind-breaks on the prairies.

### Identification of Woods in Canada

As competition in manufacturing and merchandising increases between country and country, Canadians need to have all the assistance science can give them. In the case of forest products this is provided by the Forest Products Laboratories of the Department of the Interior. The Labor-identifying woods of all kinds and do this without charge for any citizen of Canada. This service has been much utilized by Canadian manufacturers and others in the past year and the number of examinations made is constantly increasing. Inquiries may be addressed to the Superintendent, 700 University St., Montreal.

### France Restores Her Forests

Many of the forests of France were badly shot to pieces in the war and others were cut down to provide war material. The people of France in the years since the rapidly getting the forests back into shape to again grow timber. In addition to salvaging damaged timber, the work involved removal of barbed wire entanglements, filling in trenches and mine craters, discovery and removal of unexploded shells, and the re-opening of roads. In the case of these forests it will take at least seventy-five years to restore them to the state of productiveness they were in when war broke out.

### First Thing In The Morning

# Review of Current Trade Conditions

## Montreal Market is Rather Unsettled

Business in Montreal is only moderate; some firms report a scarcity of orders and others state that trade is satisfactory. It is agreed, however, that prices are not too good. Buyers are still looking for bargains, and a very small sum makes all the difference between a sale and its loss. Some wholesalers, however, are taking up a much stiffer attitude, and are refusing to accept offers which, in their view, are quite out of line with values.

The market has not yet settled down to a basis which can be called stable. While there is a general belief that the volume of business will show considerable increase, there is a certain amount of difference as to whether prices will advance. There are those who incline to the belief that spruce will go lower, but this is not the idea of the majority of wholesalers.

According to some, stock bought at high prices is still being liquidated, and this naturally affects certain lines.

Stocks in local yards are very low, and there is a disinclination to purchase, some retailers being under the impression that quotations will show further declines. Collections, too, are poor.

While it is yet too early to say anything definite as to building, there is a belief that when the spring opens up there will be considerable activity. Most contractors think that this will be in the direction of house construction, and that the present buildings for industrial purposes will fill all demands. If this activity materializes, prices for lumber will probably slightly advance, but there is not likely to be any appreciable rise.

A fair amount of business is passing in B. C. products, with prices keeping firm in most grades.

There is little doing in pulpwood. The pulp market is slow, and is not likely to pick up for at least another month.

The St. Maurice Paper Company, Limited, is now using a Linn gasoline logging tractor in its woods operations north of Lake Archambault, P. Q. The company tried the experiment last season, but found it advisable to purchase an improved type of machine, which is giving good results so far. Lumber companies in the province of Quebec have not been extensive users of this form of logging equipment, although there are lumbermen who think that it will not be many years before tractors will be widely employed, and that they will prove more economical than horses.

## St. John Reports Conditions Quiet

Locally conditions in the lumber trade are quiet, probably more so than at any time during the last year. It is now between seasons and, together with the unusual quietness of the other trades, there is practically no business being done in St. John, N. B. The factories are short of orders and men are being laid off at the different plants as the maufacturers do not feel like piling up any further stocks of building material.

The American spruce market while not improving in price is showing a larger volume of enquiries, many of the buyers evidently thinking that prices will go no lower. The offers being made to-day for cargoes running strong in 2 by 4 and 2 by 8 are not over $30, Boston, less commission and discount. Some trading is being done, but on a very limited scale as this would not leave much over $20, f. o. b. St. John and sellers are refusing to sell special cargoes at any price. Some country sawn random is being purchased at about $19, on cars shipping point, but it is very narrow sized. This kind of stock, of course has its effect upon the market and if there is very much of it manufactured this winter it will continue to show its evil effects for some time.

No dimension mills are sawing anywhere in the province and very few dimension logs are being cut for market, so it looks now as if there will be a shortage of dimension stock. This will certainly have a tendency to draw from the random stocks later on in the year. Another condition which has arisen in the winter sawing is that of large logs being sawn into 7 by 3 and up for the Irish market which leaves only a small quantity of 2 by 8 offering.

The British market is wakening, but only a few small sales are being made to Ireland at around $33 to $34 f.o.b., St. John, for parcel cargoes of 7 by 3 and up, 50 per cent being 9 by 3 and up. Later on it is hoped that freights will be reduced so as to allow shipments to net something. 90 shillings still pertains to Irish ports and 100 shillings to British ports. The steamship companies are trying in every way to hold their prices no matter what other lines of business are being pinched or starved and all endeavours to make the steamship people look at present rates in a reasonable manner seem to be without avail. Freights, both ocean and land, are holding back trade and doing more to starve the country and cause unemployment than any other condition which prevails to-day. It is hoped that some English buying will take place before long and many are optimistic about this trade.

What little logging is being done is progressing well and cuts are well out of the woods to the streams. Men are working more efficiently than for years past and logs are being produced for considerable less money; in some cases for one half of the price paid a year ago.

The lath market is improving to some extent, largely for New York trade during the last week, $8 being paid for round wood lath from the province. Many mills are idle having stopped making lath when prices fell. The pulpwood market still continues dead, the best offer for wood being around $7.50 per cord for peeled fir and spruce, f. o. b. cars.

## Ontario and the East

The past month has been one of conventions and gatherings of various sorts, as well as inventory-taking, and it is not possible as yet to get a proper perspective of business conditions for 1922. In the aggregate, however, there has been considerable business during the past few weeks, although there is a disposition on the part of the retailers to delay placing orders until some time next month or early in March.

Hardwoods are in better demand and particularly birch. Auto mobile concerns are now entering the market, and one leading Toronto concern report a record sale during the past month. Furniture factories are also getting busy, and as stocks with them are low, they are doing more buying than for some time past.

Hemlock is firm and white pine is holding its own. The representatives for Coast mills say that the mixed carload trade is very good and that there is a disposition evidenced by some dealers to buy a little more freely, particularly if they are offered a bargain in boards, shiplap, rough clears, V-Joint, etc.

It is too early as yet to speak regarding the building outlook, but a general survey of the field seems to indicate that prospects are bright, particularly in the line of house construction. At gatherings of the lumber, construction and building trades during the past month, the opinion was freely expressed that better times were in store, and while there might not be any decided impetus to the lumber business this year, it would be one of steady recuperation and recovery.

Operations in the bush have been hampered in Northern Ontario to some extent by an unusually heavy fall of snow; in fact the depth of the beautiful is greater than in any corresponding month for some years past. However, up to the 1st of January conditions were ideal, and on the average there may be little cause for complaint. The cut is going to be much smaller than last year and the estimates which have been given in these columns from time to time, stand so far unchanged.

It is believed by lumberman that if freight rates were substantially reduced,—and the prospects of it are growing brighter every day,—there would be a much freer exchange of forest produces, an incentive to building and other lines of activity. In the meantime, as spring approaches it is expected that business will show an appreciable increase in all kinds of lumber and that prices will be well maintained. If anything like buying movement develops along certain grades, there may be a scarcity of stock.

In order to get a comprehensive view of the whole situation, it would be well for the average reader to look over the remarks made at recent lumber conventions by representative authorites of the trade. It will be found that they all take a fairly hopeful view of the future and think the corner has been turned.

Recent advices received from Boston are to the effect that prices for good pine are rather difficult to quote. Dry stock is very scarce and although the demand is small, it is fast using up all that is being offered. A few mills have advanced good pine siding considerably lately and it is said by some that this will react on them later as it will curtail business and cause the use of substitutes such as sugar pine, redwood, etc.

According to advices received from Winnipeg the lumber industry on the prairies is now down to a cash basis, but with little business in sight. At the annual meeting of the Western lumbermen in Win-

nipeg recently, the matter of credit and prices was the chief subject of discussion. The tendency is toward higher prices and cash between the mill, the retailer and the consumer. If there is building on the prairies this summer it can be taken for granted it will be at higher figures, probably fifteen per cent., unless there is a reduction in freights to overcome the necessary advance of the mill men, the trade claims. More money is in sight for building from mortgage companies at eight per cent. on a seventy-five per cent. valuation of construction cost. Mortgage company managers report a considerable number of applications, but most of them are for renewals.

## Eastern Conditions in Lumber Line
### By "Onlooker"

For about five years a world's war was on. The whole economic system of the universe was disorganized. The wealth and manhood of all nations were engaged in a mighty struggle of waste and devastation. The enormous sum represented will have to be made up and this can only be done by the strictest thrift and economy. Some progress along this line has been made, but immediate and greater energy will be required to save the situation. The older countries of Europe are having a supreme struggle to meet their interest indebtedness; the payment of their war debt will have to be postponed for future generations. Taxation will be heavy and will continue so for some years. The burden will be such that some of the countries are likely to go into immediate bankruptcy as they are not in a position to finance their immediate needs.

In Canada, however, a more hopeful and brighter feeling prevails. Our country is new, with great, rich and undeveloped resources. The great fertile plains of the West are bidding welcome to newcomers and it is therefore probable that this year and the years following will see a great exodus of people from the older European countries to this section of our fair Dominion and their wants and their needs will have to be supplied. Canada will likely benefit more than any other country in the world on account of being new and undeveloped.

However, one cannot look for a speedy recovery. It will be gradual and almost unnoticed. There will be periods of alternate rise and fall in the price of commodities and it will be some time before conditions anywhere stable are reached. Discontent is seated on the throne. Discontent swayed the last election and will likely be in evidence in many ways during this year. The tendency to get costs down will meet with much opposition from labor, so much so that many strikes will likely occur; in fact we have two of them on our hands in this city to-day----the plasterers and the sheet metal workers have walked out. Almost from the outbreak of the war labor was in the ascendancy. Labor dictates not only its wages but also its hours of work, and until such times as there is an awakening from these conditions, trouble with labor will be in evidence. Labor must realize that longer hours and honest work are the only remedy for its present conditions.

There is a great need for buildings throughout the world: in Great Britain it is estimated that there is over a million houses required; in the United States the estimate runs from two to three million, and in Canada it is quite safe to say that at least two to three hundred thousand are needed. The question is, how are we going to build them? Is the money available? The loan companies are demanding higher rates of interest and have also lowered the percentage usually loaned. They are not giving more than from 30 to 35 per cent of the cost. It looks as though construction will have to depend more on private funds although when good bonds, safe and secure and paying from 6 to 6½ per cent, are on the market, private funds are liable to go in that direction.

## Building Costs Will Trend to Increase

At the recent convention of the Canadian Association of Building and Construction Industries held in Hamilton, Ont., a report presented on present and prospective conditions in the trade said:—"This conference realizes that the future horizon is clouded and that prophecies in these days are dangerous. It also realizes that the national prosperity cannot remain much longer in the present state of stagnation; further, that as soon as business from a national standpoint commences to move, just so soon will building work start to move.

In the construction industry there exists a scarcity of mechanics, which scarcity will be accentuated when work becomes plentiful, and which condition will undoubtedly be accompanied by the usual drop in efficiency. At the same time it is realized that certain of the basic materials are at the present at an artificially low level; and for all the above reasons building costs will tend to increase. On the other hand, there still remain many centres where reasonable reductions in wages have not been put into effect, and there still remain many major

materials the prices of which have not undergone proper deflation, both of which factors will, when righted, tend to decrease prices.

## Company Temporarily Closes Canadian Office

The Bennett Lumber Company, Limited, Montreal, have suspended operations in Canada until such time as conditions in the export lumber trade indicate improvement. In the opinion of the directors, next season's exports will not be very large, and they believe that any Canadian business can be transacted from their head office, 297-302 Dashwood House, 9 New Broad St., London, E. C. Mr. J. I. Bennett, the president, has been in England several months, and Mr. S. Bick, the vice-president, sailed on January 25th from New York. He stated that the suspension of operations was only temporary, due to business conditions, and to the fact that the presence of Mr. Bennett and himself were required in England in connection with business. Mr. Bick, whose family remains on this side, expects to return in about six months' time.

## Popular Young Lumberman Becomes Benedict

Wm. J. Stirrett, son of John Stirrett, Port Arthur, Ont., was united in marriage recently to Miss Myrtle Mary Hatch, eldest daughter of Mr. and Mrs. J. W. Hatch, of Mount Forest, Ont. The ceremony was performed by the Rev. A. J. Loveday. After spending their honeymoon in Toronto and Buffalo, Mr. Stirrett and bride have taken up their residence in Maudslay Court, Port Arthur. Many friends will wish them every success and prosperity. The bridegroom is a director of the newly-organized firm of John Stirrrett & Sons, Limited, Port Arthur, who are wholesale and retail dealers in forest products.

## Lower Rates on Lumber Called For

Claiming that the present excessive freight rates are hampering the movement of lumber and greatly increasing the cost of this commodity to the consumer, the Rocky Mountain Lumber Manufacturers' Association, at the first session of the annual convention in Calgary recently, passed a resolution urging the transportation companies of Canada to co-operate in stimulating a revival of trade and industry by restoring lumber freight rates to at least the level of those in effect prior to September, 1920.

## Furniture Factories Report Good Business

At the recent annual furniture exhibition held in Kitchener, Ont., the attendance of buyers surpassed all previous records. Purchasers came from all parts of the Dominion. Most of the manufacturers who made displays, reported splendid orders which would keep their plants busy for months to come. A banquet was tendered by the exhibitors to the visitors, in the Dominion Rubber System club rooms.

## Call for Reduction in Freight Rates

The Lumber and Shingle Manufacturers' Association of British Columbia, recently adopted a resolution against the present exorbitant freight rates, and urged that rates which were in effect before September, 1920, be immediately restored.

Present freight rates constitute 60 per cent of the total cost to retail dealers in the Prairie Provinces, says the resolution, while the Ontario and Quebec freight charges swallow up 70 per cent of the price to retailers.

The shingle manufacturers of British Columbia have formed a $600,000 corporation known as the British Columbia Consolidated Shingle Manufacturers, Limited. Foreign as well as local markets will be supplied. The headquarters of the company will be at Vancouver.

## Lordly Maple now Threatened by Pest?

Is the maple tree and its by-products to become the latest sacrifice made to the insect world?

The question was raised recently by a paper before the Economic Entomologists of the American Association for the Advancement of Science by Prof. Glenn W. Herrick of Ithaca, New York. Many owners of maple groves in that State, Mr. Herrick said, were becoming alarmed over the prospects of the destruction of their trees by a small moth, the Maple Case-Borer.

This pest, he went on, was a new one, as it had ravaged New York State some sixty years ago. Its caterpillars appeared in thousands, riddling the leaves so that they dropped from the trees, which, if badly infested, lost their foliage and died. This moth, he said, had done much already toward the decline of the maple industry in that State.

### High Honor for Western Legislator

Hon. J. H. King, who will be the new Minister of Public Works in the Liberal cabinet at Ottawa, is well-known in the lumber and medical arenas. - He is a son of Senator G. G. King of Chipman, N. B., and a brother of G. Herbert King, M. L. A. for Queen's County, N. B., who is identified with his father in the King Lumber Co., at Chipman. Dr. King has also a brother, M. B. King, who is a member of the King-Farris Lumber Co., Newton, B. C.

Dr. King has been Minister of Public Works in British Columbia, and comes from a family engaged for many years in lumbering and timbering operations. He is a graduate in medicine of McGill University and for a number of years practised his profession in St. John.

Hon. (Dr.) J. H. King, Victoria, B.C.

Going to British Columbia in 1898, he located in Cranbrook where he was president of the King Lumber Mills which were burned in 1919 and dismantled.

Hon. Dr. King was born in 1872 and represented Cranbrook in the B. C. legislature from 1903 to 1909. He was an unsuccessful candidate in Kootenay for the House of Commons in 1911 but was returned as a member of the B. C. legislature in 1916, and on the formation of the new government was appointed Minister of Public Works. Dr. King in 1919 attended the western congress of medicine and surgery, in Budapest, Hungary, and on that occasion was presented to the Austrian court. He was also one of the original founders and governors of the American College of Surgeons in Chicago. Dr. King has taken several post-graduate courses in medicine at the leading universities of London, Paris, Vienna and other European cities.

### Brompton Company Had Very Good Year

The annual statement of the Brompton Pulp & Paper Co. of East Angus, Que., which has just been issued, show that the earnings during the past year, like those of most other concerns, decreased considerably. After deducting expenses, insurance and income tax, the earnings are set at $1,097,784. as against $1,853,988.

Francis N. McCrea, M. P. for Sherbrooke, Que., is president of the company and J. A. Bothwell, general manager. The latter is now recovering from a rather severe illness which has confined him to the house for some time.

Deductions for depreciation, bond interest and preferred dividends left a balance of $498,010., which is equal to a return of slightly over 7% on the common stock of the company. This compares with 9.57% a year ago and 9.86% for 1919. Inventories have been written down heavily and are now set at $3,130,931. as against $2,476,604. last year, and from these is deducted $944,964. to allow for the shrinkage in values.

The report of the directors points out that in May 1920 the issue of $2,500,000. 8% convertible sinking fund bonds was made to reimburse the company in part for the amount spent on plant and property, and that improvement in sales and in the company's financial position made it possible to restrict the issue to $1,750,000., at which figure it now stands.

The Brompton Pulp & Paper Co. are making extensive preparations to cut pulp wood this year. Its present supply will carry it into 1923, but in the meantime advantage is being taken of the low rates at which wood can be taken out and stored for the future.

### Alleges Canadian Lobby Against Lumber Duty

Charges that "a Canadian lobby" in Washington has been conducting an "insidious propaganda" against any duty on lumber and shingles were made recently before the Senate Finance Committee by Robert B. Allen of Seattle, Wash., representing the West Coast Lumber Manufacturers' Association.

Mr. Allen said he had been informed that Canadian shinglemakers had been assessed a total of $47,000 to defray expenses of the tariff fight. He added that he had seen no evidence of the use of this money until he saw the "propaganda" from Washington.

Mr. Allen informed the committee he considered this "propaganda" was "as insidious even as that produced in Germany before the war." Much of it, he charged, had been put out under the name of the Western Pine Manufacturers' Association, but that this association had disclaimed any responsibility for it.

We confidently assert that

# Golden Spruce

has no superior among mountain woods.

This may seem a tall statement, but our long list of steady customers bears it out.

Try GOLDEN AIR-DRIED SPRUCE for your requirements in Boards, Shiplap, Shelving, Flooring and Siding. Our GRADES are DEPENDABLE and SERVICE THE BEST OBTAINABLE.

OUR SPECIALTIES—1¼ x 6 Well Curbing and 6" No. 3 Siding and Flooring

We also manufacture Fir and Cedar.
Spruce, Fir and Cedar Lath.

And, don't forget that our stock always comes to you bright, clean, and newly milled, being run through the planing mill at time of shipment.

With a daily ten-hour cutting capacity of 200,000 feet, and a stock of 10 to 20 million feet at all times, we are in position to give prompt shipment. Urgent orders given special attention.

Send Your Enquiries to

## Columbia River Lumber Co., Ltd., Golden, B. C.

affiliated with and represented jointly by salesmen of

## Canadian Western Lumber Co., Ltd., Fraser Mills, B. C.

Eastern Sales Office—TORONTO—L. D. Barclay, E. C. Parsons and C. J. Brooks

| ALBERTA | MANITOBA | SASKATCHEWAN |
|---------|----------|--------------|
| T. R. Griffith | Hugh Cameron and D. T. McDowall | Chas. R. Skene |

## More Facts About Traffic Topics

By R. L. SARGANT, Ottawa
Transportation Manager of Canadian Lumbermen's Association

Checking freight bills is a matter of interest to most of you and particularly to those members who have not facilities in their own office for checking the freight charges which they pay. We would therefore like to place before the members of this Association the following plan which if adopted may be the means of saving some of you considerable money. The plan is this:—the members to send in to the Transportation Department each month their paid freight bills together with the original or a copy of the bill of lading covering the car referred to by the freight bill. These bills will be thoroughly checked and returned to you together with the bill of lading, with a memo in duplicate attached to any expense bill upon which an overcharge has been discovered. The memo will explain exactly how the overcharge is arrived at and you will then be in a position to enter your claim with the Carrier. If this plan is adopted it is suggested that the Transportation Department will undertake to do this work for a time without extra charge to the members, at least until such time as we have proved that the arrangement is one which would be of material benefit to any of the members. It is therefore only by co-operating with us and sending in your expense bills that we can prove whether or not the arrangement is worth while and we trust that you will give the matter your careful consideration. If the arrangement proves to be satisfactory the matter of adopting some specific charge for doing this work and possibly handling the overcharge claims through this office to an ultimate conclusion will be considered.

### Handling Claims For Overcharges

During May of last year, in fact shortly after the formation of your Transportation Department, we asked the members to let us have any old claims which still remained open and we would do what we could arrange for an amicable settlement of them. Not many of the members availed themselves of this opportunity; in fact we only received in all about five old claims. We have been able to arrange settlements of these claims with the exception of one small loss and damage claim which is still pending but which we hope to have settled very shortly. We have received letters from some members covering most recent transactions and upon checking the charges in connection with these shipments we found that there is in a great many cases overcharges, some of them small amounts and others for larger amounts. These papers have been returned to the members with an explanation as to how the overcharge was arrived at and advising them the name of the Carriers' official with whom the claim should be filed. We have also asked that we should be advised if the overcharge claim is not settled within from two to three months time when we would take the matter up and endeavor to arrange for settlement without further delay.

### Always Glad to Get Inquiries

We have received some inquiries as to the correctness of certain switching charges which the Carriers have made at inter-switching points and we have also received inquiries in connection with the surcharge on freight charges covering shipments to points in the United States, also the war tax on freight charges on shipments from the United States to Canada, all of which apparently have been answered to the satisfaction of the inquirer. We are always very glad to receive these inquiries as it shows that the members are taking an interest in their Transportation Department and feel that it can be of some service to them in all matters affecting transportation.

Rates are quoted and new rates arranged where no through rates previously existed. We have received inquiries and have quoted the members of the Association, since the formation of the Transportation Dept., 271 rates and in most cases have also given routings. The majority of the rates quoted were to points in the United States. We have had requests for rates where no through rates were previously provided and have been successful in arranging with the Carriers for the publication of through rates from six different points in Canada to a large number of destinations in Canada and to the United States. This has particular reference to rates from points on the Canadian National Railways but also includes one or two points on the C. P. R. and Grand Trunk.

When on this subject we would like to point out that the Canadian National Railways are at the present time working on a basis of through rates from points on the Canadian National west of Cochrane and Sudbury including the Algoma Central and Hudson Ry., and also Algoma Eastern Railway to territory in the United States, and also from Canadian National stations east, that is all Canadian Government Ry., to points on the Long Island Railroad and also to destinations in what is known as Central Freight Association territory west of the Buffalo-Pittsburg line and as far west as Chicago and south.

west as far as East St. Louis. The Canadian National have for some time been endeavoring to arrange a basis of through rates to points on the New York, New Haven and Hartford Ry., but have not as yet been able to come to any satisfactory agreement with the New Haven Railroad, inasmuch as the latter appears to want their local rate or nearly that from their junction points.

### Arranging for Car Supply

It is just possible that during the coming year some members may experience difficulty in obtaining a satisfactory supply of cars to meet their requirements. Just at present of course we realize that orders are not any too plentiful and for this reason the car supply is fairly normal, but if business should pick up cars might not be so easily obtained. Therefore, if you have any difficulty at any time in obtaining what cars you require, and if you will communicate with this Department either by phone, wire or letter we should be only too glad to do what we can with the Carriers towards relieving the situation.

### Application for Rates Restoration

Mr. Sargant concludes his report by a reference to the application for a restoration of rates in lumber in effect prior to September 13th, 1920, and on which he says:— Inasmuch as we have not yet received definite reply to our application to the Board of Railway Commissioners on this subject it has been deemed advisable to make a separate report on it and one which will include whatever transpires on the subject up to the time of the general meeting.

It is to be regretted that more of the members of the Association have not availed themselves of the services of the Transportation Department, as outside of general matters affecting the lumber industry as a whole there must be certain difficulties and questions which arise from time to time, which cause a certain amount of annoyance and trouble, and perhaps expense. If matters of this nature were referred to us it would not only give us an opportunity to serve you but it might be the means of offsetting similar difficulties which other members might experience at any time. We cannot be expected to know what your troubles are unless you give us something to work on, so please remember that this is your Transportation Department, and whether or not you have a Traffic Department in connection with your individual business there must at times be some matters which could very well be taken up with us to your individual advantage, or the advantage of the Association as a whole.

The report was adopted.

### Trade Paragraphs in Short Shape

P. Manning Lumber Co., Edmonton, Alta., was recently incorporated.

W. W. Avey, Norwich, Ont. is contemplating the erection of a planing mill at an approximate cost of $10,000.

The Reid Mfg. Co., lumber dealers of Bury, Que., recently registered. The firm is composed of Peter Reid and Henry E. Reid.

The Newfoundland Government has negotiated with the Armstrong Whitworth Co., of England, and Reid-Newfoundland Railway Co. with regard to the project to create a waterproof development totalling 235,000 h. p., on the west coast of Newfoundland. This would be utilized for the establishment of a paper mill with a daily capacity of 400 tons of newsprint.

The Westminster Shook Mill, Lulu Island, New Westminster, B. C., is producing finished box material at the rate of 35,000 to 40,000 feet per day, or about 1,000,000 feet per month. The bulk of this product is going to the East Indian market. The officials of this company are the same as those of the B. C. Manufacturing Co., though the two organizations are carried on as distinct operations. J. H. McDonald is the manager, R. L. Cluff, president, and P. J. McMurphy, secretary.

A provincial charter has been granted to P. W. Gardiner & Son, Limited, Galt, Ont., to carry on business as dealers and manufacturers of all kinds of lumber and its products, to conduct activities as builders and contractors and to acquire the assets and goodwill of the partnership firm of P. W. Gardiner & Son, now carried on in Galt. The capital stock of the new company is $500,000. and among the incorporators are Peter W. Gardiner, James E. Gardiner, Gladstone W. Gardiner and Harold M. Gardiner.

Prominent eastern lumbermen are connected with the Bridge River Timber & Manufacturing Company, which has 19,000 acres of limits in the Lillooet district, British Columbia, and which is floating a stock issue in Montreal, preparatory to erecting a plant. Charles B. Graddon, Montreal, president of the Graddon Lumber Company, is president of the new company; Herbert Greer, Montreal, a director of the Log Supply Company, vice-president; the directors being M. J. McNeill, Montreal, president McNeill Lumber Company; W. H. Sharpe, lumberman of Ottawa; M. H. Levine, Montreal, vice-president Loew's Theatre; Spencer Rogers, secretary-treasurer, and Patrick Donnelly, Vancouver.

## Mr. Ellis Doing Good Work in New Zealand

L. M. Ellis, Auckland, N. Z.
Director of Forestry

L. McIntosh Ellis, director of forestry for New Zealand, has sent the "Canada Lumberman" a copy of the annual report of the forest service for the year ending March 31st 1921. Mr. Ellis, who is a former Toronto boy, says that they have got away to a fairly good start, and he hopes that they will be able to continue the progress that has been made during the years to come.

In a general review of the advancement made, Mr. Ellis in his annual report says:—

New Zealand is now in the third "forestry boom," the first one dating back to the year 1874, when the self-same symptoms and fears of timber famine were expressed as are being voiced at the present time . The positions are parallel, but with the important difference that to-day the Parliament, Press, and people are beginning to appreciate the meaning of timber conservation and national forestry. This growing interest has found expression during the year in a definite forest policy, the creation of an administrative instrument, the Forest Service, and the additional dedication to technical management of forest and woodlands which now bring the total up to 6,800,000 acres.

The year under review may be considered as the year of stocking, of orientation, and of study of the conditions and problems incident to a sound and businesslike administration, and of the procedure and modus operandi necessary to forest-management. The year ending March 31, 1922, will be known as the year of establishment and of application, whilst the year ending March 31, 1923, may be known as the year of fruition and results.

During 1920—21, a study was made of the quantity and distribution of the indigenous forests of the State; of afforestation activities; of New Zealand methods of forest administration and exportation of timber; of the silvical and ecological problems attendant on the regrowth of the indigenous forests, and of many other factors incident to timber and timber use.

The period April to August was spent by the writer in studying forest milling and industrial wood consumption throughout the Dominion. In September a comprehensive survey traversing the whole field of forestry and forest activities was prepared and presented to the Minister in Charge of Forestry. After a deliberate consideration of the report a plan of administration was approved and steps were taken to bring into being the State Forest Service.

The central management and administrative control of the service briefly consists of the Director of Forestry (assisted by the Chief Inspector) and the Secretary, with offices at Wellington.

## Fungi Plays Havoc with Wood Pulp

"Enormous losses are suffered annually by the paper industry during the necessary periods of storage of wood pulp due to deterioration caused by fungi," declared Mr. C. Audrey Richards, member of the Mycological Section of the Botanical Society of America in addressing the members of the American Association for the Advancement of Science in Toronto. Eighty-nine species of fungi have been isolated from wood pulp. A large number of these fungi have been studied in relation to the actual loss they occasioned in pulp. Forty-two of the fungi isolated are capable of producing damage.

Among the 106 chemicals which were sprayed on pulp, to test their efficiency in preserving it, sodium fluoride, borax, boric acid, sodium dinitrophenolate and sodium dichromate were found most effective.

## How Pine Timbered Areas Have Been Depleted

Declaring that pine timber areas in Ontario had been so depleted that natual regrowth on cut-over areas will not supply the needs of the future, E. J. Zavitz, Provincial Forester for Ontario, in speaking at a joint session of the Canadian Society of Forest Engineers and the Society of American Foresters, said that Ontario had taken steps to initiate a comprehensive reforestation program.

Mr. Zavitz placed a large part of the blame for depletion of the pine forests on fire. "In less than a half century," he said, "we have used up the larger part of our virgin supplies of timber. Only 20

years' supply of virgin pine remains. Originally there were 30 million acres of pine lands in Ontario. Possibilities of natural replacement had been destroyed on half this enormous area, chiefly by fire.

"From studies made in various parts of our original pineries," continued the speaker, "it is shewn that natual regroth cannot supply our future needs. A survey of the conditions in the region from which our raw material is obtained has awakened the Government to the necessity of providing for reforestation in the cut-over districts. Plans are now under way to establish forest stations in the cut-over pineries. Forest nurseries will be established and a comprehensive planting program initiated. It is expected that a forest planting scheme will be developed which will produce a new growth equalling at least the present annual cut of pine.

## Airplane Service for Forestry Purposes

Thomas Hall, president of the Canadian Services, Montreal, is head of a new company which has been organized to take over the entire flying plant and equipment of the Laurentide Air Service, Grand Mere, Que. During the coming season the new company will take over the air cruising work of the St. Maurice Valley with Headquarters at Lac La Tortue, Que.

The principal work of the fleet of aircraft handled by the new company will consist of aerial photography, to decide the value and potential worth of timber limits, re-placing the old time timber cruisers, aerial fire patrol and reconnaisance and transportation.

It is planned that photographic mosaics of large forest areas in the St. Maurice district shall be taken, just as was done by the flying craft over the enemy lines during the war. In addition it is planned that an effective fire patrol shall be established, with telephone connections and other methods to prevent forest fires from getting out of hand.

## Hon. Mr. Low Gets Cabinet Distinction

Hon. T. A. Low, who has been made a member of the new Liberal cabinet at Ottawa, without portfolio, is well known in political lines, which he entered some thirteen years ago, when he was elected to the House of Commons for South Renfrew. He was returned in 1911 but retired in 1912, remaining in private life until the recent campaign.

Mr. Low is well known in the lumber arena, having been a lumber merchant and manufacturer for many years and owning extensive limits. He was born in the city of Quebec, but has lived for the greater part of his life in Pembroke, where he carries on business as a lumber merchant and manufacturer, being connected with a large number of industries.

## It Will Pay to Grow Pulpwood

"It will not be difficult to demonstrate to the paper manufacturer that he can afford to grow trees for pulpwood, when he is paying $30 per cord for peeled wood," said Dr. Hugh P. Baker, Secretary of the American Pulp & Paper Association, before the Yale Forest Club at New Haven.

"It is my belief that we are passing out of the sentimental stage in forestry, and that in the next five years we are going to see the beginning of a real economic development in forestry. That is, the time has come when it is going to pay in dollars and cents to grow trees. In another, as business becomes better, and our industries come back to reasonable production, we are going to come again to the condition which faced us a year ago, that wood for our industries will cost us more that it costs to grow it . When we can demonstrate to the paper manufacturer, for instance, that he can afford to grow pulpwood, we are going to see the same sensible turning to forestry that we have seen in the turn to better banking methods and better methods of manufacture."

## Will Explore More Pulpwood Areas

"Forest engineers will explore the country surrounding the north shore of the St. Lawrence, the Bay of Ungava and Hudson Bay," G. C. Piche, Provincial Forester for Quebec,declared recently.

"The Government intends to build various forest stations which will serve as bases for these explorations, and it is expected that these reconnaissances will enable the Government better to protect the country and also to put rapidly into use various units for pulp and power development.

"Quebec has six million acres of timber lands in private ownership, forty-five million acres under license for timber and pulpwood purposes."

The Government, Mr. Piche continued, aimed to work in co-operation with the private owners by helping them in fire protection and reforestation. The limit holders in Quebec have already done a great deal in the way of forest surveys, fire protection, conservative lumbering and reforestation.

# EDGINGS

The B. C. Red Shingle Company, Limited, Vancouver, B. C., was recently incorporated with a capital of $200,000.

Egypt is back in the market again, and B.C. mills are at present cutting on a 2,000,000-foot railway tie order, to be shipped to Port Soudan.  The ties are not to be creosoted.

McCarter Bros., Rock Bay, Victoria, B.C., whose shingle plant was destroyed by fire recently are making preparations for the erection of a shingle factory at a cost of $5,000.

J. D. McArthur & Co., who recently purchased extensive timber limits on Mud Creek, intends erecting a sawmill of 60,000 feet daily capacity near Prince George, B. C.

U. E. Germain has resigned the position of managing director of the Brompton Lumber and Manufacturing Company, Limited, Bromptonville, P. Q.

J. H. McDonald, manager of the B. C. Manufacturing Co., Limited, New Westminster, B. C., managed to secure several large orders for boxes recently while on a business trip to Eastern Canada.

The Fairbank Lumber & Coal Co., Fairbank, Ont., are building a two-storey planing mill, 50 x 60 feet, and are in the market for the necessary machinery and equipment.

A new sash and door factory and planing mill has been completed recently by R. Truax, Son & Co., Walkerton, Ont.  The building, which includes a warehouse and general offices, is 310 x60 feet, and is of brick construction.

Thomas George Wiggins, aged 45, engaged in lumbering operations at Venosta, in the Gatineau Valley, was found dead, sitting in an arm chair in his shack on Friday last.  Death ensued from natural causes.

Oak River Lumber Company, Montreal, was recently organized to manufacture and deal in all kinds of forest products.  Capital $75,000.  Among the incorporators are J. A. Gagne and L. S. St. Laurent, both of Quebec City.

When the boiler exploded recently in the lath mill of Walsh & Fleming at Foreston, N. B., G. H. Dutcher of Newcastle and H. Dingee, of Foreston lost their lives.  The mill was razed to the ground and several employees were hurt by falling material.

The McMaster Lumber Co., Limited, of Kemptville, Ont., who operate a retail lumber yard in that town and also a sawmill at Hallville, in Dundas County, recently opened another retail yard in Prescott, Ont., where a representative stock of lumber is being carried.

The timber berth which is at the junction of the Coquihalla River and the Kettle Valley Railway in British Columbia, known as berth No. 596, has been sold to the Nicola Pine Mills of Merritt, for $8,052.

W. W. Hill, 15 Nickle Ave., Mount Dennis, Ont., is erecting a small woodworking shop.  He proposes to manufacture a patent combination child's crib and store and office fixtures.  For the present he has put in a combination Elliott woodworker, and in the near future proposes adding a band saw, shaper and planer.

Guelph Lumber Co., Guelph, Ont., have been granted a federal charter to take over the Guelph Lumber Co., and to manufacture and deal in forest products.  Capital $40,000.  Among the incorporators are W. C. Laidlaw, A. E. Eckardt, R. Laidlaw, J. Harrison and R. A. Laidlaw.

George H. Belton, of the George H. Belton Lumber Co., London, Ont., accompanied by his wife and daughter, intends leaving this month on an extended holiday trip to the Mediterranean, France, Italy, Great Britain and other European countries.  They will be absent several weeks.

Snow in the Temiskaming district is reported to be the deepest in years.  It has lately interfered with logging operations, while in some districts the depth is four feet.  While this is not unusual later on in the winter, it is rarely that such a vast amount of the beautiful has fallen early in January.

One of the largest timber limit deals in British Columbia in a number of years was transacted in Victoria recently when Alex. McLaren of Buckingham, P. Q. sold his interests in the Callus Lake timber limits, near Chilliwack, to Beach and Coulter, owners of the Westminster Mill Co., New Westminster, B. C.

The forest revenue for the province of Quebec shows a gratifying gain according to a report of Hon. H. Mercier, Minister of Lands and

Forests. The revenue from all sources in the department was $3,567,-588., which is the heaviest total since confederation. In 1910 the total revenue from the forests was only $900,000.

James E. Wilson & Sons, Limited, Ottawa, Ont., were recently incorporated with federal charter to take over the business of James Edward Wilson, and to carry on a general timber business, manufacturing and dealing in lumber, timber and pulpwood. Capital $150,-000. Two of the incorporators are J. E. Wilson and J. A. Wilson, both of Ottawa.

Another indication of better times ahead is evinced in advices from British Columbia, which state that the Whalen Pulp & Paper Company has started its third mill in the manufacture of sulphite pulp. The company is fairly well fixed for orders from the eastern states and the Orient. President T. W. McGarry is now in British Columbia in connection with the company's affairs.

The stock, plant and equipment of the St. Thomas Boxes, Limited, St. Thomas, Ont., have been purchased and taken over by a company of local men formed for the purpose, viz., W. H. Street, manager of the plant since its establishment; F. W. Sutherland, of the Sutherland Press, Limited; James Sutherland, real estate agent. George H. Fiske of Toronto was the former owner of the plant.

The Kinnon Lumber Co., with head office in Toronto and a capital stock of $25,000, has been granted a charter. Among the incorporators are George Kinnon, of Toronto, who was for many years with the Wm. Laking Lumber Co.; Gerald D. Martin, of Burk's Falls, and John P. Waters, of Kent, Ont. The company is empowered to carry on business as wholesale and retail merchants and maufacturers of lumber and wood products of all kinds.

Grant, Smith & Co., and McDonnell, Limited, Vancouver, B. C. have succeeded in securing the contract for the extension of the T & N O Railway, in Northern Ontario. The new road will extend 70 miles and must be completed within two years. The approximate cost is estimated at $3,500,000. Valuable pulpwood forests and other rich timber lands will be made accessible by the extension which are now commercially valueless owing to their isolated position.

In his annual report on Colonization in Quebec, the Hon. J. E. Perrault refers to the stoppage of the lumber business in the Abitibi region, and expresses the belief that the settlers will turn their attention more to cultivation. British Columbia mills expect to get considerable business this year from the Great Northern Railroad, which is reported to be contemplating the expenditure of $10,000,000 in the Northwest.

Walter C. Cain, Deputy Minister of Lands and Forests for Ontario, has been added to the directorate of the Canadian Forestry Association for the Province of Ontario. Sir Lomer Gouin, Minister of Justice for Canada and a director of the Laurentide Co., was made a director for Quebec. At the recent annual meeting in Toronto, G. H. Auld, Deputy Minister of Agriculture for Saskatchewan, and Hon. W. H. Motherwell, the new federal Minister of Agriculture were made directors for Saskatchewan.

Sir Frederick Becker, London, Eng., was the recipient of a knighthood recently. He is widely known in Canada by his interest in Canadian pulpwood and pulp mills. He is a large stockholder in the Ha Ha Bay Sulphite Co., Sissiboo Pulp & Paper Co., of Nova Scotia, Clyde River Pulp Co., Nova Scotia, as well as the Chicoutimi Pulp Co., and the St. Lawrence Pulp & Lumber Co. Becker & Co. have offices or agencies in nearly every country in the world, including banches at Halifax and Montreal.

A provincial charter has been granted to the Tionaga Lumber Co. with a capital stock of $500,000. The company is empowered to carry on lumbering, sawmilling, logging and timber-growing in all its activities. The mills of the company are located at Tionage on the Canadian National Railway, west of Cochrane, and four camps are being conducted at the present time. Among those who are associated with the company are Col. L. T. Martin, of Ottawa; Capt J. P. Gillies, of Blind River, and Major R. B. Herron, of Toronto.

Discussion of the best means of protecting forest areas and other topics of interest to fire rangers came up at the annual gathering of the forest rangers of the Vancouver district which was held recently. Maj. L. R. Andrews, district forester, gave a short address on the filing methods in use in the forester's office in Vancouver. Maj. C. S. Cowan, head of the department's operations branch, gave a paper on forest protection. Most of the damage to forests, he said, is caused by loggers, but the actual number of fires caused by loggers is less than those caused by campers. E. R. Robson, of Bloedel, Stewart & Welch, logging operators, detailed how logging costs were worked out so that a company could be assured a fair profit on its output. W. R. Flumerfelt dealt with the subject of educating the public in forest protection, and suggested among other things that well painted and permanent signs be erected in public places. "The Forest Protection Problem in British Columbia" was the name of a paper read by R. V. Stewart and which was the subject of much discussion.

# ALPHABETICAL INDEX TO ADVERTISERS

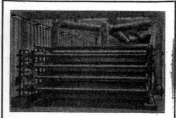

# THE LINN LOGGING TRACTOR

The Linn Logging Tractor designed exclusively for Winter Log Hauling in the North Country. Was developed and perfected in actual logging operations in the Adirondack Woods. 90% of the Logging Tractors in use in the North Woods are Linn Tractors.

The Linn Logging Tractor is equipped with a body for loading—which enables toting over summer Portage roads—up steep grades—and over country where it would be impossible to haul a trailer.

Will haul 50 cords of Spruce (4000 lbs per cord) per trip, over branch roads and main roads and on to the ice at the landing—hauling speed on the level is 6½ miles per hour. Does not require sanding on down grades. Will of itself hold 75 tons on a 25% down grade.

Will reduce horse haulage costs by more than half.

Will operate with absolute safety over lakes and rivers where ice has a minimum thickness of 14 inches.

Is the only Tractor built having the flexible Lag-bed (track) so absolutely essential to successful north country winter and summer haulage.

Seeing is believing. If you are interested, for next season's haulage—won't you go with us this season to the nearest operation, and see a Linn Tractor doing possibly more than we claim for it—under our own winter conditions—in our own country.

### —Logging Department—

# MUSSENS LIMITED

Dubrule Building        MONTREAL

# CANADA LUMBERMAN BUYERS' DIRECTORY

The following regulations apply to all advertisers:—Eighth page, every issue, three headings;
quarter page, six headings; half page, twelve headings; full page, twenty-four headings

**ALLIGATORS**
Payette Company, P.
West, Peachy & Sons

**BABBITT METAL**
Canada Metal Company
General Supply Co. of Canada, Ltd.

**BALE TIES**
Canada Metal Co.
Laidlaw Bale Tie Company

**BAND MILLS**
Hamilton Company, William
Waterous Engine Works Company
Yates Machine Company, P. B.

**BAND SAW BLADES**
Simonds Mfg., Co.

**BAND RESAWS**
Mershon & Company, W. B.

**BARKERS**
Bertrand, F. X., La Compagnie Manu-
facture.
Smith Foundry & Machine Co.

**BEARING METAL**
Canada Metal Co.
Beveridge Supply Co., Ltd.

**BEDSTEADS (STEEL)**
Simmons Limited

**BELT DRESSING**
Dominion Belting Co.
General Supply Co. of Canada, Ltd.

**BELTING**
Canadian Consolidated Rubber Co.
Dominion Belting Co.
General Supply Company
Goodhue & Co., J. L.
Gutta Percha & Rubber Company
D. K. McLaren, Limited
McLaren Belting Company, J. C.
York Belting Co.

**BLOWERS**
Reed & Co., Geo. W.
B. F. Sturtevant Co. of Canada, Ltd.
Toronto Blower Company

**BOILERS**
Engineering & Machine Works of
Canada
Hamilton Company, William
Waterous Engine Works Company

**BOILER PRESERVATIVE**
Beveridge Supply Company
Shell-Bar, Boice Supply Co. Ltd.

**BOX MACHINERY**
Yates Machine Company, P. B.

**CABLE CONVEYORS**
Engineering & Machine Works of
Canada.
Hamilton Company, Wm.
Waterous Engine Works Company

**CAMP SUPPLIES**
Davies Company, William
Dr. Bell Veterinary Wonder Co.
Johnson, A. H.
Swift Canadian Co.
Turner & Sons, J. J.
Woods Manufacturing Company, Ltd.

**CANT HOOKS**
General Supply Co. of Canada, Ltd.
Pink Company, Thomas

**CEDAR**
Bury & Co., Robt.
Cameron Lumber Co.
Canadian Western Lumber Company
Chesbro, R. G.

Dry Wood Lumber Co.
Fesserton Timber Company
Muir & Kirkpatrick
Rose, McLaurin, Limited
Terry & Gordon
Thurston-Flavelle Lumber Company
Vancouver Lumber Company
Victoria Lumber & Mfg. Co.

**CHAINS**
Canadian Link-Belt Company, Ltd.
General Supply Co. of Canada, Ltd.
Engineering & Machine Works of
Canada
Hamilton Company, William
Pink & Co., Thomas
Waterous Engine Works Company

**CLOTHING**
Woods Mfg. Company

**CONVEYOR MACHINERY**
Canadian Link-Belt Company. Ltd.
General Supply Co. of Canada, Ltd.
Hamilton Company, William
Hopkins & Co., Ltd., F. H.
Waterous Engine Works Company

**CORDAGE**
Consumers Cordage Company

**CORDWOOD**
McClung, McLellan & Berry

**COUPLING (Shaft)**
Engineering & Machine Works of
Canada

**CRANES**
Hopkins & Co., Ltd., F. H.
Canadian Link-Belt Company

**CUTTER HEADS**
Shimer Cutter Head Company

**CYPRESS**
Wistar, Underhill & Nixon

**DERRICKS AND DERRICK
FITTINGS**
Hopkins & Co., Ltd., F. H.

**DOORS**
Brompton Lumber & Mfg. Co.
Canadian Western Lumber Co.
Mason, Gordon & Co.
Midland Wood Products, Ltd.
Terry & Gordon

**DRAG SAWS**
Gerlach Company, Peter
Hamilton Company, William

**DRYERS**
Coe Manufacturing Company
B. F. Sturtevant Co. of Canada, Ltd.

**DUST COLLECTORS**
Reed & Co., Geo. W.
B. F. Sturtevant Co. of Canada, Ltd.
Toronto Blower Company

**EDGERS**
Hamilton Company, Ltd., William
Green Company, G. Walter
Long Mfg. Company, E.
Payette Company, P.
Waterous Engine Works Company

**ELEVATING AND CONVEYING
MACHINERY**
Canadian Belt-Link Company, Ltd.
Engineering & Machine Works of
Canada
Hamilton Company, William
Waterous Engine Works Company

**ENGINES**
Engineering & Machine Works of
Canada
Hamilton Company, William

Payette Company, P.
Waterous Engine Works Company

**EXCELSIOR MACHINERY**
Elmira Machinery & Transmission
Company

**EXHAUST FANS**
B. F. Sturtevant Co. of Canada, Ltd.
Toronto Blower Company

**EXHAUST SYSTEMS**
Reed & Co., Geo. W.
B. F. Sturtevant Co. of Canada, Ltd.
Toronto Blower Company

**FIBRE BOARD**
Manley Chew

**FILES**
Disston & Sons, Henry
Simonds Canada Saw Company

**FIR**
Apex Lumber Co.
Associated Mills, Limited
Bainbridge Lumber Company
Cameron Lumber Co.
Canadian Western Lumber Co.
Canfield, P. L.
Chesbro, R. G.
Dry Wood Lumber Co.
Fesserton Timber Co.
Grier & Sons, Ltd., G. A.
Heeney, Percy E.
Knox Brothers
Mason, Gordon & Co.
Robertson & Hacket Sawmills
Rose, McLaurin, Limited
Terry & Gordon
Timberland Lumber Company
Timms, Phillips & Co.
Underhill Lumber Co.
Vancouver Lumber Company
Vanderhoof Lumber Co.
Victoria Lumber & Mfg. Co.

**FIRE BRICK**
Beveridge Supply Co., Ltd.
Elk Fire Brick Company of Canada
Shell-Bar, Boice Supply Co. Ltd.

**FIRE FIGHTING APPARATUS**
Waterous Engine Works Company

**FITTINGS**
Crane Limited

**FLOORING**
Cameron Lumber Co.
Chesbro, R. G.
Long-Bell Lumber Company

**GEARS (Cut)**
Smart-Turner Machine Co.

**GRINDING WHEELS**
Canadian Hart Products Ltd.

**GUARDS (Machinery and Window)**
Canada Wire & Iron Goods Co.

**HARDWOODS**
Anderson Lumber Company, C. G.
Anderson, Shreiner & Mawson
Atlantic Lumber Company
Barrett, Wm.
Bury & Co., Robt.
Cameron & Co.
Edwards & Co., W. C.
Fesserton Timber Co.
Gillespie, James
Gloucester Lumber & Trading Co.
Grier & Son, G. A.
Hart, Hamilton & Jackson
Heeney, Percy E.

Knox Brothers
Mason & Co., Geo.
McDonagh Lumber Co.
McLennan Lumber Company.
McLung, McLellan & Berry
Pedwell Hardwood Lumber Co.
W. & J. Sharples
Spencer, Limited, C. A.
Strong, G. M.
Summers, James R.
Webster & Brother, James

**HARDWOOD FLOORING**
Brompton Lumber & Mfg. Co.
Grier & Son, G. A.

**HARNESS**
Beal Leather Co., R. M.

**HEMLOCK**
Anderson Lumber Company. C. G
Anderson, Shreiner & Mawson
Bartram & Ball
Beck Lumber Co.
Bourgouin, H.
Canadian General Lumber Company
Edwards & Company, W. C.
Fesserton Timber Co.
Grier & Sons, Ltd., G. A.
Hart, Hamilton & Jackson
Hocken Lumber Company
Mason. Gordon & Co.
McCormack Lumber Co.
McDonagh Lumber Co.
Robertson & Hacket Sawmills
Spanish River Lumber Co.
Spencer, Limited, C. A.
Terry & Gordon
Vancouver Lumber Co.
Vanderhoof Lumber Co.

**HOISTING AND HAULING
ENGINES**
General Supply Co. of Canada, Ltd.
Hopkins & Co., Ltd., F. H.

**HOSE**
General Supply Co. of Canada, Ltd.
Gutta Percha & Rubber Company

**INSURANCE**
Barton & Ellis Co.
Burns Underwriting Co.
Hardy & Co., E. B.
Lumbermen's Underwriting Alliance
Rankin Benedict Underwriting Co

**INTERIOR FINISH**
Cameron Lumber Co.
Canadian Western Lumber Co.
Canfield, P. L.
Eagle Lumber Company
Mason, Gordon & Co.
Rose, McLaurin, Limited
Terry & Gordon

**KILN DRIED LUMBER**
Bury & Co., Robt.

**KNIVES**
Disston & Sons, Henry
Simonds Canada Saw Company
Waterous Engine Works Company

**LARCH**
Otis Staples Lumber Co.

**LATH**
Anderson, Shreiner & Mawson
Apex Lumber Co.
Austin & Nicholson
Beck Lumber Co.
Brennen & Sons, F. W.
Cameron Lumber Co.
Canadian General Lumber Compan
Carew Lumber Co., John
Chaleurs Bay Mills
Dupuis, Limited, J. P.

Eagle Lumber Company
Foley Lumber Company
Fraser Bryson Lumber Co., Ltd.
Gloucester Lumber & Grading Co.
Grier & Sons, Ltd., G. A.
Harris Tie & Timber Company, Ltd.
Larkin Co., C. A.
Mason & Co., Geo.
McLennan Lumber Company
Miller, W. H. Co.
New Ontario Colonization Company
Otis Staples Lumber Company
Power Lumber Co.
Price Bros. & Company
Shevlin-Clarke Co.
Spencer, Limited, C. A.
Terry & Gordon
U. G. G. Sawmills, Limited
Union Lumber Company
Victoria Harbor Lumber Company

**LATH BOLTERS**

General Supply Co. of Canada, Ltd.
Hamilton Company, Wm.
Payette & Company, P.

**LOCOMOTIVES**

Engineering & Machine Works of
Canada
General Supply Co. of Canada, Ltd.
Hopkins & Co., Ltd., F. H.
Climax Manufacturing Company
Montreal Locomotive Works

**LATH TWINE**

Consumers' Cordage Company

**LINK-BELT**

Canadian Link-Belt Company
Mathews Gravity Carrier Company.
Hamilton Company, Wm.

**LOCOMOTIVE CRANES**

Canadian Link-Belt Company, Ltd.
Hopkins & Co. ,Ltd., F. H.

**LOGGING ENGINES**

Engineering & Machine Works of
Canada
Hopkins & Co., Ltd., F. H.
Mussens Ltd.

**LOG HAULER**

Engineering & Machine Works of
Canada
Green Company, G. Walter
Holt Manufacturing Co.
Hopkins & Co., Ltd., F. H.
Payette Company, P.

**LOGGING MACHINERY AND
EQUIPMENT**

General Supply Co. of Canada, Ltd.
Hamilton Company, William
Holt Manufacturing Co.
Hopkins & Co., Ltd., F. H.
Payette Company, P.
Waterous Engine Works Company
West, Peachey & Sons
Mussens Ltd.

**LUMBER EXPORTS**

Fletcher Corporation

**LUMBER TRUCKS**

Hamilton Company, Wm.
Waterous Engine Works Company

**LUMBERMEN'S BOATS**

Adams Engine Company
Gidley Boat Co.
West, Peachey & Sons

**LUMBERMEN'S CLOTHING**

Kitchen Overall & Shirt Co.
Woods Manufacturing Company, Ltd.

**MATTRESSES**

Simmons Limited

**METAL REFINERS**

Canada Metal Company

**OAK**

Long-Bell Lumber Company

**PACKING**

Beveridge Supply Company
Consumers' Cordage Co.
Gutta Percha & Rubber Company

**PANELS**

Bury & Co., Robt.

**PAPER**

Beveridge Supply Co., Ltd.
Price Bros. & Co.

**PINE**

Anderson Lumber Company, C. G.
Anderson, Shreiner & Mawson
Atlantic Lumber Co.
Austin & Nicholson
Barratt, William
Beck Lumber Co.
Cameron & Co.
Cameron Lumber Co.
Canadian General Lumber Company
Canadian Western Lumber Co.
Canfield, P. L.
Chesbro, R. G.
Cleveland-Sarnia Sawmills Company
Cox, Long & Company
Dudley, Arthur N.
Eagle Lumber Company
Edwards & Co., W. C.
Excelsior Lumber Company
Fesserton Timber Company
Fraser Bryson Lumber Co., Ltd.
Gillies Bros, Limited
Gloucester Lumber & Trading Co.
Gordon & Co., George
Goodday & Company, H. R.
Grier & Sons, Ltd., G. A.
Harris Tie & Timber Company, Ltd.
Hart, Hamilton & Jackson
Hettler Lumber Company, Herman H.

Hocken Lumber Company
Julien, Roch
Lay & Haight
Lloyd, W. Y.
Loggie Co., W. S.
Long-Bell Lumber Company
Mason, Gordon & Co.
Mason & Co., Geo.
McCormack Lumber Co.
McFadden & Malloy
McLennan Lumber Company
Montreal Lumber Company
Muir & Kirkpatrick
Northern Lumber Mills
Otis Staples Lumber Co.
Parry Sound Lumber Company
Pigeon River Lumber Co., Ltd.
Rolland Lumber Co.
W. & J. Sharples.
Shevlin-Clarke Co.
Spanish River Lumber Co.
Spencer, Limited, C. A.
Strong, G. M.
Summers, James R.
Terry & Gordon
Union Lumber Company
Victoria Harbor Lumber Co.
Watson & Todd, Limited
Wuichet, Louis

**PLANING MILL EXHAUSTERS**

Toronto Blower Co.

**PLANING MILL MACHINERY**

Mershon & Co., W. B.
B. F. Sturtevant Co. of ,Canada, Ltd
Toronto Blower Co.
Yates Machine Company, P. B.

**PORK PACKERS**

Davies Company, William

# Beardmore Extra Quality Waterproof Cement Leather Belting

## For the Wet Place

Tell us your belting troubles and we can help you.

## The General Supply Company of Canada, Limited

OTTAWA · MONTREAL · TORONTO · NORTH BAY · MONCTON · WINNIPEG · VANCOUVER

*Large stocks available for immediate shipment*

---

# Rubber Goods
## FOR LUMBERMEN

**Belting** Our long experience in the making of Rubber Belts enables us to specialize on this line. "P.M.S.," "Special Drive" and "Lion" are our leading brands for power transmission.

**Packings** "Redstone" High Pressure Sheet Packing has proved by test that it will outlast any other similar packing on the market. We make Spiral and Ring Packings, etc., that are equally reliable.

**Hose** for Steam, Water, etc., in various grades, made especially to give satisfactory and economical service under different conditions.

**Fire Hose** One or more of our twenty brands of Fire Hose will be found, not only in the best equipped Factories, Mills, etc., but in almost every Fire Department in the Dominion.

## Gutta Percha & Rubber, Limited

TORONTO · HALIFAX · MONTREAL · OTTAWA · FORT WILLIAM · WINNIPEG · REGINA · SASKATOON
EDMONTON · CALGARY · LETHBRIDGE · VANCOUVER · VICTORIA

**POSTS AND POLES**

Anderson, Shreiner & Mawson
Auger & Company
Canadian Tie & Lumber Co.
Dupuis, Limited, J. P.
Eagle Lumber Company
Harris Tie & Timber Co., Ltd.
Long-Bell Lumber Co.
Mason, Gordon & Co.
McLennan Lumber Company
Terry & Gordon

**PULLEYS AND SHAFTING**

Canadian Link-Belt Company
General Supply Co. of Canada, Ltd.
Green Company. G. Walter
Engineering & Machine Works of
  Canada
Hamilton Company, William

**PULP MILL MACHINERY**

Canadian Link-Belt Company, Ltd.
Engineering & Machine Works of
  Canada
Hamilton Company. William
Payette Company, P.
Waterous Engine Works Company

**PULPWOOD**

Bethune Pulp & Lumber Co.
British & Foreign Agencies
D'Auteuil Lumber Co.
Price Bros. & Co.
Scott, Draper & Co.

**PUMPS**

General Supply Co. of Canada, Ltd.
Engineering & Machine Works of
  Canada
Hamilton Co., William
Hopkins & Co., Ltd., F. H.
Smart-Turner Machine Company
Waterous Engine Works Company

**RAILS**

Gartshore, John J.
Hopkins & Co. ,Ltd., F. H.

**ROOFINGS**

(Rubber, Plastic and Liquid)
Beveridge Supply Company
Reed & Co., Geo. W.

**ROPE**

Consumers' Cordage Co.

**RUBBER GOODS**

Dunlop Tire & Rubber Goods Co.
Gutta Percha & Rubber Company

**SASH**

Brompton Lumber & Mfg. Co.
Midland Woodworkers
Midland Wood Products, Ltd.

**SAWS**

Atkins & Company, E. C.
Disston & Sons, Henry
General Supply Co. of Canada, Ltd.
Gerlach Company, Peter
Green Company, G. Walter
Hoe & Company, R.
Radcliff Saw Mfg. Co.,
Shurly Co. Ltd., T. F.
Shurly-Dietrich Company
Simonds Canada Saw Company

**SAW MILL LINK-BELT**

Canadian Link-Belt Company

**SAW MILL MACHINERY**

Canadian Link-Belt Company, Ltd.
General Supply Co. of Canada, Ltd.
G. Walter Green Co., Ltd.
Hamilton Company, William
La Compagnie Manufacture, F. X.
  Bertrand
Long Manufacturing Company, E.
Mershon & Company, W. B.
Parry Sound Lumber Company
Payette Company, P.
Waterous Engine Works Company
Yates Machine Co., P. B.

**SAW SHARPENERS**

Hamilton Company, William
Waterous Engine Works Company

**SAW SLASHERS**

Hamilton Company, Wm.
Payette Company, P.
Waterous Engine Works Company

**SHINGLES**

Apex Lumber Co.
Associated Mills, Limited
Brennen & Sons, F. W.
Cameron Lumber Co.
Campbell-MacLaurin Lumber Co.
Canadian Western Lumber Co.
Carew Lumber Co., John
Chaleurs Bay Mills
Chesbro, R. G.
D'Auteuil Lumber Co.
Dry Wood Lumber Co.
Eagle Lumber Company
Federal Lumber Company
Fraser, Limited
Gillespie, James
Gloucester Lumber & Trading Co.
Grier & Sons, Limited, G. A.
Harris Tie & Timber Company, Ltd.
Heaps & Sons
Heeney, Percy E.
Mason, Gordon & Co.
McLennan Lumber Company
Miller Company, Ltd., W. H.
Reynolds Company, Limited
Rose, McLaurin, Limited
Terry & Gordon
Timms, Phillips & Co.
Vancouver Lumber Company
Vanderhoof Lumber Co.

**SHINGLE & LATH MACHINERY**

Green Company, C. Walter
Hamilton Company, William
Long Manufacturing Company, E.
Payette Company, P.

**SILENT CHAIN DRIVES**

Canadian Link-Belt Company, Ltd.

**SLEEPING EQUIPMENT**

Simmons Limited

**SLEEPING ROBES**

Woods Mfg. Company, Ltd.

**SMOKESTACKS**

Hamilton Company, Wm.
Reed & Co., Geo. W.
Waterous Engine Works Company

**SNOW PLOWS**

Pink Company, Thomas

**SOLDERS**

Canada Metal Co.

**SPARK ARRESTORS**

Reed & Co., Geo. W.
Waterous Engine Works Company

**SPRUCE**

Anderson, Shreiner & Mawson
Barrett, Wm.
Cameron Lumber Co.
Campbell, McLaurin Lumber Cd.
Canadian Western Lumber Co.
Chesbro, R. G.
Cox, Long & Co.
Dudley, Arthur N.
Fraser, Limited
Fraser-Bryson Lumber Company
Gillies Brothers

Gloucester Lumber & Trading Co.
Goodday & Company, H. R.
Grier & Sons, Ltd., G. A.
Harris Lumber Co., Frank H.
Hart, Hamilton & Jackson
Hocken Lumber Company
Julien, Roch
Larkin Co., C. A.
Lay & Height
Lloyd, W. Y.
Loggie Co., W. S.
Mason, Gordon & Co.
McCormack Lumber Co.
McDonagh Lumber Co.
McLennan Lumber Company
Muir & Kirkpatrick
New Ontario Colonization Company
Northern Lumber Mills.
Pigeon River Lumber Co.
Power Lumber Co.
Price Bros. & Co.
Rolland Lumber Co.
Rose, McLaurin, Limited
W. & J. Sharples.
Spencer, Limited, C. A.
Strong, G. M.
Terry & Gordon
U. G. G. Sawmills, Limited
Vanderhoof Lumber Co.

**STEAM SHOVELS**

Hopkins & Co., Ltd., F. H.

**STEEL CHAIN**

Canadian Link-Belt Company, Ltd.
Hopkins & Co. ,Ltd., F. H.
Waterous Engine Works Company

**STEAM PLANT ACCESSORIES**

Waterous Engine Works Company

**STEEL BARRELS**

Smart-Turner Machine Co.

**STEEL DRUMS**

Smart-Turner Machine Co.

**TARPAULINS**

Turner & Sons, J. J.
Woods Manufacturing Company, Ltd.

**TANKS**

Hopkins & Co., Ltd., F. H.

**TENTS**

Turner & Sons, J. J.
Woods Mfg. Company

**TIES**

Austin & Nicholson
Carew Lumber Co., John
Canadian Tie & Lumber Co.
Chaleurs Bay Mills
D'Auteuil Lumber Co.
Gloucester Lumber & Trading Co.
Harris Tie & Timber Company, Ltd.
McLennan Lumber Company
Miller, W. H. Co.
Price Bros. & Co.
Scott, Draper & Co.
Terry & Gordon

**TIMBER BROKERS**

Bradley, R. R.
Cant & Kemp
Farnworth & Jardine
Wright, Graham & Co.

**TIMBER CRUISERS AND
ESTIMATORS**

Savage & Bartlett.
Sewall, James W.

**TIMBER LANDS**

Department of Lands & Forests, Ont.

**TOWING MACHINES**

Corbet Foundry & Machine Co.
Payette Company, P.
West, Peachy & Sons

**TRACTORS**

Holt Manufacturing Co.
Hopkins & Company, Ltd., F. H.
Monarch Tractors
Mussens Ltd.

**TRANSMISSION MACHINERY**

Canadian Link-Belt Company, Ltd.
Engineering & Machine Works of
  Canada
General Supply Co. of Canada, Ltd.
Grand Rapids Vapor Kiln
Hamilton Company, Wm.
Waterous Engine Works Company

**TURBINES**

Engineering & Machine Works of
  Canada
Hamilton Company, William
B. F. Sturtevant Co. of Canada, Ltd.

**VALVES**

Crane Limited

**VAPOR KILNS**

Grand Rapids Vapor Kiln
B. F. Sturtevant Co. of Canada, Ltd.

**VENEERS**

Bury & Co., Robt.

**VENEER DRYERS**

Coe Manufacturing Company
B. F. Sturtevant Co. of Canada, Ltd.

**VENEER MACHINERY**

Coe Machinery Company

**VETERINARY REMEDIES**

Dr. Bell Veterinary Wonder Co.
Johnson, A. H.

**WARPING TUGS**

West, Peachey & Sons

**WATER WHEELS**

Engineering & Machine Works of
  Canada
Hamilton Company, William

**WELDING**

St. John Welders & Engineers

**WIRE**

Canada Metal Co.
Laidlaw Bale Tie Company
Canada Wire & Iron Goods Co.

**WIRE CLOTH**

Canada Wire & Iron Goods Co.

**WIRE ROPE**

Canada Wire & Iron Goods Co.
Hopkins & Co. ,Ltd., F. H.
Dominion Wire Rope Co.
Greening Wire Co., B.

**WOODWORKING MACHINERY**

General Supply Co. of Canada, Ltd.
Long Manufacturing Company, E.
Mershon & Company, W. B.
Waterous Engine Works Company
Yates Machine Company, P. B.

**WOOD PRESERVATIVES**

Beveridge Supply Company

**WOOD PULP**

Austin & Nicholson
New Ontario Colonization Co.
Power Lumber Co.

# Subscribers' Information Form

Many letters reach us from subscribers enquiring where a certain machine, a certain kind of lumber or veneer, or some other class of goods, can be obtained. We can usually supply the information. We want to be of service to our subscribers in this way, and we desire to encourage requests for such information. Make use of this form for the purpose.

"CANADA LUMBERMAN"            Date........................................19......
347 Adelaide Street West, Toronto

Please tell us where we can procure.......................................................................
..........................................................................................................
..........................................................................................................
..........................................................................................................

Name ...........................................................

Address ...........................................................

## The Stationary Cylinder Steam Nigger

### Saves Time, Labor, and Money

This Stationary Cylinder, Steam Nigger effects a big saving where logs have formerly been handled by hand, or by the old type oscillating nigger.

It occupies less space, there being no horizontal bar to come in the way of feed ropes, conveyors, etc.

Possessing all the good qualities of the oscillating type, it has many new features that give precedence over all others.

*Write to-day for full particulars.*

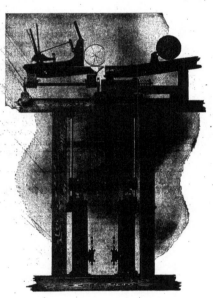

# The E. Long Manufacturing Co., Limited
## Orillia          CANADA

Robt. Hamilton & Co., Vancouver          A. R. Williams Machinery Co., of Winnipeg, Ltd.
Gorman, Clancy & Grindley Ltd. Calgary & Edmonton          Williams & Wilson Ltd., Montreal

# A Super Re-Saw

For years we have recognized the faults of the horizontal re-saw, such as the excessive space taken up in the mill—the necessity of raising or lowering the belt, or the saw blade itself in order to change the thickness of cut—the difficulty of separating the slab from the lumber at the rear of the machine, and the advisability of having every slab inspected by the sawyer before being passed through the machine. But until recently we have never been able to perfect a vertical re-saw which would meet in every way the high standard of excellence which every machine bearing the name of WATEROUS must possess.

We are at last, however, able to offer to the Sawmill Men of Canada, a machine that not only overcomes the above faults, but one which combines all the advantages of the horizontal and vertical re-saws.

Here is a machine which will positively cut straight slabs and half logs regardless of irregularities in material. The bed consists of four fluted rolls which are adjustable and which take the place of the planed table.

There are two press rolls. The first swings on a vertical shaft in a frame which presses firmly against the feed rolls, bent to the saw in a stream actuated saw tooth roll. These two rolls are so arranged as to automatically take care of all variations in the size and shape of the slabs. The swinging arm roller mounts any slabs immediately and the pressure of the oscillating cylinder aligns the slab against the first two feed rolls, swinging the tail of the slab immediately in the line of the saw cut, this taking place before the saw enters the cut.

This arrangement prevents the usual thick or thin or scooped ends that are so common in all re-saws carrying the single press rolls and feed rolls.

# Waterous
## BRANTFORD, ONTARIO, CANADA

Molson's Bank Bldg., Vancouver, B. C.                    Winnipeg, Manitoba.

ol. 42      Toronto, February 15, 1922      No. 4

# Canada Lumberman

*Founded 1880*

# MacLean's Patent Receder

Difficulty is often experienced in operating sawmill carriages in the endeavour to obtain evenly sawn lumber, which trouble is often attributed to the saws not running true, or to incorrect work on the part of the setter, when possibly neither of these are at fault, but is caused from lost motion in some of the various connections in the mechanism of the set works or in the offsetting device of the taper movement of the head blocks.

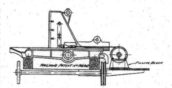

After considerable experimenting **MacLean's Patent Receder** was eventually produced which is so simple and yet so completely satisfactory it should be applied to every sawmill carriage. It has been in successful operation for two years with most satisfactory results.

The device is particularly to be recommended where steam setters are in use on account of the strain and wear produced on the working parts of the carriage, causing lost motion to develop very rapidly on these parts, but is equally effective for either steam or hand-set, as there are different styles of the appliance for steam and hand-set works and can be applied to any make of carriage with very little expense.

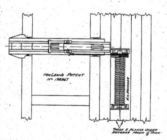

For lighter set works that are not powerful enough to set against the tension of the spring of this device as shown, an alternative device can be supplied which is also covered by this patent. The spring causes no strain on the set works but effectively prevents any slack motion in the rack and pinion or taper movement. The spring in this case is attached one end to the end of the rack and the other end to the head block knee. **These devices are covered by Patent 198967, and have given most satisfactory results wherever installed.**

*Prices and all information gladly given upon request.*

# William Hamilton Co., Limited

Agents: J. L. Neilson & Company, Winnipeg, Man.  PETERBORO, ONTARIO

# Geo. Gordon & Co.

**Limited**

CACHE BAY - ONTARIO

We Manufacture

# PINE

## Lumber, Timber and Lath

If in a hurry for high quality Pine, properly graded, Rough or Dressed, send us your next order.

---

## COX, LONG & COMPANY, LIMITED

### 433 Coristine Building, MONTREAL, Canada.

Are the Authorized Agents for the

## Associated Importers, Limited

of London, England

Owners of the

# British Government Lumber Stocks in the Quebec and Lower Port Districts

to whom all enquiries for any of these goods must be sent

*COLONIAL PAPERS PLEASE COPY*

# White Pine
# Red Pine
# Jack Pine
# Spruce
# Lumber
# and Lath

## UNION LUMBER COMPANY LIMITED
701 DOMINION BANK BUILDING
TORONTO          CANADA

## The Spanish River Lumber Co. Limited

**LUMBER MANUFACTURERS**     **CUTLER, ONTARIO**

WHITE PINE,
   NORWAY PINE,
      HEMLOCK

Shipments
   by Rail
     or Water

---

*Manufacturers
and Wholesalers of*

# LUMBER and LATH

## WHITE PINE——NORWAY PINE

## Shevlin-Clarke Company Limited

### FORT FRANCES, ONTARIO

# Common Sense *in* Business

SUCCESSFUL business is the result of common sense—plain, solid, old fashioned "horse sense" —the fruit of knowledge and experience.

Common sense is stability. It adapts itself to changing conditions of the market; but it does not seek the cyclone cellar for every April shower. It has confidence in itself and inspires it in others. It respects competition but does not fear it.

Common sense is sincerity. It is plain spoken and straight forward. It deals fairly and up-rightly. It is just, but generous. It is genuine.

Common sense seeks knowledge—it considers no detail too small for conscientious attention. It is cautious but does not hesitate to step out of line and take the lead. It has pride without vanity. It does not boast emptily; neither does it fail to let the world know of its existence.

There is no secret about common sense and no one person or group of persons has a monopoly on it. It is free to all who stop to seek it out.

Many years ago, our business was founded on a common-sense basis. Through all our business life we have stuck to our principles. To you who buy lumber—remember that we are always ready to serve you to your satisfaction.

## TERRY AND GORDON
### LIMITED
## CANADIAN FOREST PRODUCTS

HEAD OFFICE
**TORONTO**

BRANCH
**MONTREAL**
EUROPEAN AGENTS
**VANCOUVER**
BRANCH

SPENCER LOCK *&* Co., LONDON. ENG.

## "Well Bought is Half Sold!"

### Why buy
## "A Pig in a Poke?"

### Why buy
### Dressing when you want Common

—or—

### Box when you want Dressing?

---

### Buy what you want to use!

### Byng Inlet Stock is graded for use.

### What you want!
### When you want it!

---

## Canadian General Lumber Co.
Limited

# FOREST PRODUCTS

TORONTO OFFICE:— 712-20 Bank of Hamilton Building

Montreal Office:—203 McGill Bldg.

Mills : Byng Inlet, Ont.

---

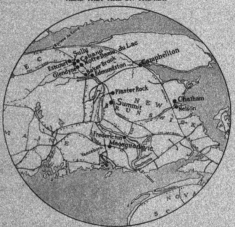

# Symbol of the South's Finest in Satin-like Interior Trim
### and
## Soft, easily workable, non-splitting common lumber

A woodwork and framing material for homes of the better sort, which appeals to lumber dealers and planing mills who consistently stock *the best* for particular, exacting trade

*Write the Mills direct, for prices, and the Bureau for informative literature, house plans and sales aids*

ARKANSAS LUMBER COMPANY
WARREN, ARKANSAS

COTTON BELT LUMBER COMPANY
BEARDEN, ARKANSAS

CROSSETT LUMBER COMPANY
CROSSETT, ARKANSAS

EAGLE LUMBER COMPANY
EAGLE MILLS, ARKANSAS

EDGAR LUMBER COMPANY
WESSON, ARKANSAS

FORDYCE LUMBER COMPANY
FORDYCE, ARKANSAS

FREEMAN-SMITH LUMBER COMPANY
MILLVILLE, ARKANSAS

GATES LUMBER COMPANY
WILMAR, ARKANSAS

OZAN-GRAYSONIA LUMBER COMPANY
PRESCOTT, ARKANSAS

SOUTHERN LUMBER COMPANY
WARREN, ARKANSAS

STOUT LUMBER COMPANY
THORNTON, ARKANSAS

UNION SAW MILL COMPANY
HUTTIG, ARKANSAS
*Sales Office: Boatmen's Bank Building  St. Louis, Mo.*

WISCONSIN AND ARKANSAS
LUMBER COMPANY
MALVERN, ARKANSAS

*Composing the*

# ARKANSAS SOFT PINE BUREAU
### LITTLE ROCK, ARKANSAS

# BUY
## BRITISH COLUMBIA
# Red Cedar Shingles

The life of a British Columbia Red Cedar Shingle Roof can almost be gauged by the life of the nail with which the shingle is nailed in place. Judging from available data, the average life of the ordinary steel wire nail, which has been in such common use, is only from seven to twelve years. Some wire nails will last longer, depending upon the condition of exposure, climate and similar features, but considering our climate as a whole, at the end of from seven to twelve years a large percentage of wire nails will have rusted either completely through or so extensively that the first strong wind will complete the work. The shingles that have been held in position by such nails are then free to work down, permitting rains or melting snows to leak through and damage the interior of the structure. Examination will disclose that the fibre of the shingle itself is still in perfect condition, and a leaky roof, in the majority of occasions is due entirely to the use of faulty nails, but the average home owner, placed at such inconvenience, will not stop to reason this out and the poor wooden shingle comes in for more unjust abuse.

There are several kinds of nails which experience has proven will give lasting satisfaction, and the wise dealer will advise his customers of these satisfactory nails. A pure zinc shingle nail meets all the demands of durability required. Its principal drawback is its high cost and a slight tendency to bend under careless driving. Galvanized wire nails theoretically are rust proof, and if the galvanized coating is properly applied, and of sufficient thickness, such a nail will last as long as the shingle it holds in place. The life of this shingle roof, properly applied with these nails then is from 40 to 80 years. Pure iron nails, or the old cut or wrought nails are ideal but difficult to secure. Copper nails also constitute a perfect shingle nail.

| | |
|---|---|
| **Timms Phillips & Co., Ltd.**<br>Yorkshire Bldg., Vancouver<br>Manufacturers and Wholesalers<br>**Red Cedar Shingles**<br>5x-5x- Perfections, Royals, Imperials<br>**Red Cedar Bevel Siding** | **Vancouver Lumber Co., Ltd.**<br>Manufacturers<br>**XXX—XXXXX CEDAR**<br>**SHINGLES**<br>(Rite Grade Inspected)<br>Head Office,    Eastern Sales Office<br>Vancouver, B.C.    Toronto, Ont. |
| **Westminster Mill Co.**<br>LIMITED<br>New Westminster, B.C.<br>**Red Cedar Shingles**<br>**Cedar Bevel Siding** | **Dominion Timber Products Ltd.**<br>Vancouver Block<br>Vancouver<br>Largest Manufacturers of<br>**Perfection Shingles**<br>in Canada |
| **Underhill Lumber Co., Ltd.**<br>Dominion Bldg., Vancouver<br>**RED CEDAR SHINGLES**<br>5x-5x- Perfection and Eurekas<br>**CEDAR BEVEL SIDING**<br>**CEDAR BUNGALOW SIDING** | **Shull Lumber & Shingle Co.**<br>Limited<br>New Westminster B. C.<br>Trade Mark<br>**RED BAND SHINGLES**<br>XXX  XXXXX  Stars Clears<br>From Mill to You |
| **If you want a market for B. C. Red Cedar Shingles put an advertisement on this page.** | **Kootenay Shingle Co. Ltd.**<br>Salmo, B. C.<br>**Red Cedar Shingles**<br>xxx and xx.<br>Packed by the thousand |

# British Columbia Lumber
# Red Cedar Shingles

In these days of broken stocks and limited supply, you need a real definite service in your requirements.

*Are you getting it?*

## Timms Phillips & Co., Ltd.
### Vancouver, B. C.

TORONTO OFFICE: Canada Permanent Bldg.
Phone Adel. 6490
MONTREAL OFFICE: 23 Marconi Bldg.
Phone M 2999

# Canada Lumberman
### *Founded 1880*

*The National Lumber Journal for Forty Years*

Issued on the 1st and 15th of every month by

**HUGH C. MACLEAN PUBLICATIONS, Limited**

THOS. S. YOUNG, Managing Director

HEAD OFFICE  -  -  -  -  347 Adelaide Street, West, TORONTO

Proprietors and Publishers also of Electrical News, Contract Record, Canadian Woodworker and Footwear in Canada.

| | | |
|---|---|---|
| VANCOUVER | -  -  -  -  -  - | Winch Building |
| MONTREAL | -  -  -  - | 119 Board of Trade Bldg. |
| WINNIPEG | -  -  - | 302 Travellers' Bldg. |
| NEW YORK | -  -  -  - | 296 Broadway |
| CHICAGO | -  -  - | Room 803, 63 E. Adams St. |
| LONDON, ENG. | -  -  - | 16 Regent Street, S.W. |

TERMS OF SUBSCRIPTION

Canada, United States and Great Britain, $3.00 per year, in advance; other foreign countries embraced in the General Postal Union, $4.00.

Single copies, 20 cents.

Authorized by the Postmaster-General for Canada, for transmission as second-class matter.

| Vol. 42 | Toronto, February 15, 1922 | No. 4 |
|---|---|---|

## Better Lumbermen and Better Service

Service in the retail yard, a proper cost system, the efficient taking of inventories, the advantage of a service room or what might be properly called a sample room, the convenience of plans—books—all these and many other features have been emphasized from time to time in the "Canada Lumberman."

Travellers, in visiting the retail yards, know that methods are as yet slip-shod, and comparatively few dealers have a system whereby they know where they are at, all the time. Many, however, are learning all the while, and are putting up attractive offices, with spaces for exhibiting interior and exterior trim, hardwood flooring, ceiling, doors, and all other accessories of the modern home. Then, too, the walls are being decorated with plans of up-to-date dwellings giving prospective home-builders some idea of what a completed project looks like.

The facilities of service rooms will be discussed from time to time in the "Canadian Lumberman" and illustrations presented of the most progressive enterprises in this line.

When it comes to knowing how to keep stock, few better systems have been devised than that which appeared from the pen of W. Warren. It was published on page 53 of the January 1st edition. By this plan the yardman can tell at a glance just what stock he has on hand, where, how disposed of, etc.

One of the leading representatives in south western Ontario has a complete record of each day's sales so that on any day of the year he can tell how many cedar posts, how many thousand shingles, how many 2 x 4 and 2 x 8 in hemlock; how much in the way of white pine strips, edge grain fir stepping, etc., he has disposed of. He tabulates this data at the close of each month and thus has a record of what kind of woods, grades, widths and thicknesses are moving most freely. Before him there is a comprehensive summary setting forth that, in certain months, certain stock was turned even more rapidly and abundantly than at other periods. The dealer can thus gauge his buying accordingly and stock up at the proper time, allowing the material to run low when there is no particular movement on. This enables him to do a splendid business on the lowest possible stock, which is an economic argument, for he knows what certain seasons are best for cedar posts, others for shingles and still others for hemlock, and, perhaps, there is a special time when white pine is in most urgent demand.

Speaking the other day to a wholesaler who spent many years in the retail lumber yard, he said that he took a special delight in keeping everything up to the mark. By going over the piles he knew just exactly how much was in hand of the various sizes and grades; in fact, he spent two or three hours in the yard every two weeks to get this information which he carefully tabulated. Coming back to his desk he found the firm was low on No. 1, 2 and 3 white pine cuts or clear and clear face, or 2 x 4, 2 x 8, 2 x 10 in hemlock, or shy in XXX shingles. He would immediately see that orders were placed to replenish their requirements. To do a regular, active business and satisfy ordinary requirements, a certain number of thousand feet

in each line has to be kept, whether flooring, ceiling, casing, dase, dimension, etc. He made it his business to see that no trade was lost through inability to fill the customary demands from day to day. Then a record was kept of all millwork, showing the time it was promised to be through the factory, the day on which delivery would be made and other data. This was, indeed, a decisive factor in keeping production up to the mark and securing the confidence of patrons by prompt deliveries, in maintaining service, living up to promises and giving satisfaction.

There are many other pointers in connection with retail yard management that tend to increase efficiency and help to place things on a smooth-running basis. In the common parlance of the day, a little more jazz and pep are sadly needed by some dispensers of forest products. The dealer today must get away from the old idea that lumber is lumber and that a yard is just a yard. He must catch the vision of better merchandizing methods, more expert service, clear and valuable advice, and show that he is doing his part, in no unimportant sense to encourage the building of homes which are the bulwark and backbone of a nation. In the own-your-home campaigns, the retail lumber merchant has a real mission, and if he will only seriously consider the role he is enacting, he would get a loftier conception of his calling and believe more truly in his business. He can do his share, in developing and fostering public spirit by catering unreservedly and whole-heartedly to the home instinct and the domestic desire that exists in the breast of every sane, normal minded individual of possessing the roof that covers his or her head.

## Vital Factors in Great Industry

Much blame for deforested conditions is thrown at our lumbermen. It is not the purpose of this reference to hold a brief for any mistakes of the lumbermen. It is rather an attempt to point out the true underlying cause of ruthless forest exploitation, placing the blame where it honestly belongs, to the end that an adequate solution of the very serious problem of forest restoration may be found.

Lumbermen did not create the enormous demand for their wares. This demand originated in the God-given impulse within mankind for progress and development. The lumbermen have been the instrument through which the demand has been supplied. They have been the experts in the conversion of trees into lumber shapes for building the homes which fill the land and make it bloom; for the construction of railroads and bridges, ships and piers to transport all necessary supplies, and to distribute to their various markets the produce of farm and factory.

The lumbermen supplied the raw materials for manufacturing furniture, farm implements, vehicles, boxes, crates, paper pulp, musical instruments, toys and all other articles made from wood. They have built their rail and tram roads, their flumes and sled roads into the wild and inaccessible places from our loftiest mountain tops to the lowest swamps. They have bridged the canyons and hurled steel cables from tail to spar and made the huge logs yield to irresistible force. By the application of powerful and wonderfully designed machinery they have gathered the raw products of the forest, converted them into usable shapes, and distributed them to our local marts for further fabrication. Their spirit of adventure, courage, hardihood, hazardous risks for large capital, able management and skill have never been exceeded in any line of endeavor by any race of men. The countries of the world have sent their agents to them for instruction in the harvesting of forest crops.

He has succeeded most in the lumber industry who has been able to supply best and at lowest cost what the consuming public has demanded. Keen competition and hazardous risks of large investments have threatened him with financial ruin and many there have been who failed. Mere self-preservation has been the restraining force keeping th woods operator from conducting selection cuttings, from leaving seed trees, from providing adequate protection against forest fires and from carrying on all methods advocated for the public interest and for future generations.

Such measures necessitate scattered logging over extensive areas and could have been adopted only at increased costs all along the line. One operator could not incur such expenses unless all operators would do the same. One operator could not increase the price of his product in order to cover such increased costs unless his competitor would do likewise. Every purchaser of lumber has sought the cheapest market. What purchaser ever stopped to inquire as to whether the price he was about to pay for his lumber would justify the manufacturer in taking steps to insure a new crop of trees on the cut-over area? If the operators made any attempt to unite for the purpose of increasing their selling price they received a quick call. That they were between an upper and nether millstone in this matter is perfectly clear.

The point which should be appreciated is that the cost of growing timber as a crop has never been included as a factor in determining

the selling price of lumber. To what extent the cost of growing timber should govern the cost of lumber in the future is a mooted question. But that the country must have future forests, and that we all must pay in some way or other for the growing of them, is beyond dispute.

## Eastern Exporters and European Trade

Nothing is more difficult these days than to write from study and conscientious observation an accurate trade letter. Reviewing conditions as one sees them, in a spirit of optimism, which in a measure of philosophical judgment, does not exist. This especially refers to the European situation in the lumber trade as well as all other lines of business. A careful, horoscopic review of the existing state of affairs does not permit a prognostication of any change in the near future, but rather the sounding of a note of worry against any forcing of business with extended credits to buyers in European markets without a careful inquiry in advance as to the status of their assets and liabilities. z .........

But before discussing the conditions in European markets, it is apropos to make reference to the markets of Canada and the United States which can be alluded to in an encouraging spirit in so far as they apply to the lumber trade. In the city and district of Quebec and, from information gained from the whole of Canada the lumber trade is destined to meet with a change for the better during the coming spring and summer. The same policy, now prevailing in the ranks of labor denoting a reduction in wage earnings, is having the effect of encouraging investors to place their money in building construction with the prospect of greater structural activity in Canada during 1922 than in any year within the past ten. The postponement of large public works, as well as housing propositions, on account of the high cost of labor and material is apparently over, and work will be proceeded with to meet the compulsory demand of business expansion and the dearth of living quarters.

The increase in the price of lumber shows there is already an awakening demand in Canada. This also applies to the United States, which should benefit the lumber industry of Canada, and produce business which will tide the trade over until things become more settled in Europe.

Quebec lumber merchants engaged in the European export trade, when interviewed regarding the United Kingdom market, all give the same answer. They have not up to the present received any encouraging advices from the agents, and do not look for any news until the end of March or the month of April.

Reverting to European conditions, the barometer and the banking chart forecasting future events, based on assumption of action and inaction applying to economics and business relations, can be judged by the strength in foreign exchanges, which during the past two months, made many feel that the situation abroad was getting better. Various rumors were current that new plans of adjustment were being arranged, which would suddenly change conditions for the better as a forerunner to good business in European countries. The plans did not materialize and it is now an admitted fact in financial circles, that the majority of European bankers are extremely nervous over the situation as they see it. They realize that their business is in a position which if not handled carefully and with proper judgment, may result in a general financial panic . They have no hope for sudden prosperity but on the contrary, are battling with all their strength to avert the greatest crisis in European history. The closing of the Italian Bank de Scouti, is but the rumbling of a threatening upheaval. Therefore, the trade selling goods abroad should take every precaution to keep in close touch with their customers and make sure that they cover their commitments in order that they may not suffer by a drop in exchange.

No one can tell what is likely to happen. A perspective panic may be averted and an adjustment brought about in a general manner. Some economic plan absolutely necessary may be devised to ease the stress during this critical period. But it is evident that a further slump is inevitable, as European business has not as yet had such a house-cleaning as the United States and Canada. Prices have fallen somewhat but there has not been such liquidation as has taken place in Canadian and American quotations.

The most critical part of the readjustment will be experienced when deflation in government finances really begins. The process of inflation necessarily has an end. In the case of Germany, Austria, Poland and other central European nations, it has nearly been reached. On the other hand, any appreciation in the value of money, means a drop in commodity prices with consequent distress to business. Hence Europe is not only confronted with the problem of reconstructing its money but preventing a general crisis in business during the process. This is clearly apparent by the feverish anxiety displayed over the matter of the proposed Genoa economic conference. It also explains the difficulty of writing an optimistic trade letter by the Quebec correspondent of the "Canada Lumberman.".

Percy E. Thomas, son of L. C. Thomas, secretary of the Vancouver Lumber Co., Vancouver, recently arrived in Toronto and has become a member of the selling staff of the company, being associated with K. M. Brown, eastern sales manager, who lately returned from a flying business trip to the Coast. Mr. Brown speaks in hopeful terms of the outlook of the industry in British Columbia during the coming season.

---

## LOADING LUMBER LONG AGO

If I'd got to choose alone
One of all the freights I've known—
All my cargoes live and dead,
Bacon pigs and pigs of lead,
Cattle, copra, rice, and rails,
Pilgrims, coolies, nitrates, nails,
Lima beans and China tea—
What do you think my pick would be?

If I'd got to name the best—
Take just one and leave the rest
Out of all the ports I've known—
Coral beaches white as bone,
All the hot lands and the cold,
Nights of stars and moons like gold,
Tropics smells and Spanish wine,
Whispering palm and singing pine,
All the isles of all the sea—
Where do you think I want to be?

Loading lumber long ago
In a ship I used to know,
With the bow-ports open wide
In her stained and rusted side,
And the saws a-screaming shrill
At the Steveston lumber mill,
Where the Fraser floods and flows
Green and cold with melting snows,

And the tow-boats' wailing din,
As the booms come crawling in,
Fills the echoing creeks with sound,
And there's sawdust all around,
Deep and soft like drifted snow;
Nowhere much a man can go,
Nothing much to see or do,
Moldiest burg you ever knew.

But I'd give the years between—
All I've done and all I've seen,
All the fooling and the fun,
All the chances lost and won,
All the good times and the bad,
All the memories sweet and sad,
Far and near, by shore and sea,
I would give them all to be
Loading lumber years ago
With the lads I used to know—
Loading lumber all days long
Stacks of scented deals among—
Till the screaming saws were still
And the rose-red sunset died
From the mountain and the tide,
Till the darkness brought the stars
And the wind's song in the spars
Of that ship I used to know—
Loading lumber, long ago.

—C. F. S., in Punch.

# Wholesale Dealers Review Work of Past Year

### Encouraging Reports Presented and New Officers Elected for Coming Twelve Months—H. J. Terry is New Presiding Officer—Splendid Meeting Held

H. J. Terry, Toronto,
Newly Elected Chairman W.L.D.A.

The period of depression and "comparative stagnation through which the lumber trade has passed during the past twelve or eighteen months, found no visible evidence in the enthusiasm and success which characterized the annual meeting of the Wholesale Lumber Dealers' Association, Inc., held at the Albany Club, Toronto, on Friday January 27th. There was a representative attendence and the reports from the different committees and the secretary-treasurer were satisfactory and encouraging A. E. Eckardt, who has been the energetic presiding officer during the past year, was in the chair.

For the coming year several new members will be on the Board of Directors. H. J. Terry, of Terry & Gordon, Limited, was unanimously elected chairman, and under his direction another year of interest and advancement is assured. The following are the new officers of the Association:—

Chairman,—H. J. Terry.

Board of Directors:—D. C. Johnston, (re-elected); J. B. Jarvis; Hugh A. Rose; Kenneth M. Brown and Alex. C. Gordon.

Secretary-treasurer,— H. Boultbee.

The firms which the new directors represent are,— Union Lumber Co., Elgie & Jarvis Lumber Co., Rose, McLaurin, Limited, Vancouver Lumber Co., and Mickle, Dyment & Son.

Another matter of importance, which came up, was the expediency of changing the date of the meeting from the third Friday in each month to the fourth Monday. As a number of important events occur on Friday night and as travellers, who are specially invited to attend the sittings, return from their weekly trips on that afternoon, it was thought advisable to change, at least temporarily, from the third Friday to the fourth Monday. This, it was felt, will be an interesting experiment and, in case the new arrangement does not work out as satisfactorily as expected, from an attendance standpoint, the old order of things may be reverted to later.

### No Reason to Open Up Matter

Secretary Boultbee read a letter from A. D. Cartwright of Ottawa, secretary of the Board of Railway Commissioners for Canada, regarding car service demurrage which was as follows:—

"Referring to your letter of the 20th inst., I am directed to inform you that the Board has on its file considerable correspondence of a similar nature at present, and particularly in connection with the application of the Canadian Manufacturers' Association in this regard, and correspondents have been reminded of the fact that there are usually two sides to every case; that every phase of this case was represented to the Board both by the Canadian Manufacturers' Association, business men and railway companies, and that the Board decided, after mature consideration what in their judgment was a proper solution of the disputed point, and so far as what has been adduced up to date, sees no reason why the matter should be reopened.

### Retiring Chairman Reviews Conditions.

The retiring chairman, Mr. Eckardt, in a short review of conditions, referred to the growth and harmony of the organization since its inception four years ago. The present membership was fourty-two whereas, at the start, there had been only seventeen firms. He thanked all for their kindness and assistance to him during his term of office, and said that the great cementing force of the association was the Credit Bureau, which, he ventured to state had saved them their membership fees two or three times over The Credit Bureau of the retailers now charged those desiring to join an initiation fee of one hundred dollars. Conditions in the lumber industry during the past year had not been what they would like to see them although they had looked forward to it with hopes and aspirations which had been more or less shaken.

Mr. Eckardt said when lumbermen had taken off their inventories at the end of 1920, they had not taken them low enough, and, at the close of last year, the balance sheet had not shown up very well. Lumber had not been affected as much as some other commodities. The average deflation on all commodities was, he said, about 33% White pine had deflated around 40% and hardwoods generally about 60%. Brick had deflated about 5%, cement 12% radiators and boilers 38%, hardware 25 to 30%, and plumbing 30%. The labor of the plumber, however, was still rewarded at the same high wages. Raw sugar—wholesale—had gone down since 1920 from 25 to about 2 cents per lb. While it was thought that lumber had been hard hit, other lines had also been struck a blow. The past year has shown a greater number of commercial and industrial failures than the preceding six years, and the reverses during December had been very heavy. It was necessary for lumbermen to be watchful in guarding their interests during the coming year.

In closing, Mr. Eckardt thanked all the members for the support they had extended to him and referred to the interesting character of the meetings. They had been addressed by representative speakers in allied lines, and he felt the wholesalers had all been benefited. The retiring chairman bespoke for the incoming occupant the support of every member.

### Different Committees Report on Work

The reports from the chairman of the different standing committees were then presented.

For the Finance Committee, W. J. Lovering said his work had been easy and that the accounts had been audited and found correct.

A. E. Cates for the Insurance Committee said that one of the matters which had come up during the past year was a bill to levy a 15% tax on unlicensed companies doing business in Canada. Owing to opposition the measure had been withdrawn but might come up again. Mr. Cates said that it would be a good idea for each company to ask the Insurance people with whom they do business, to go out and check up the risks. The losses in insurance during the past year had been heavy and lumbermen were advised by the speaker to be careful in placing their risks and to see that they were properly protected.

J. P. Johnson, on behalf of the Membership Committee, reported that the roll now embraced 42 names.

Alex. C. Gordon, for the Arbitration and Inspection Committee, said that, owing to the pleasant relations which had existed between the wholesaler and retailer during the past year, his committee had little to do. They had had very few complaints and less kicks than usual, which showed that the wholesalers gave the retailers a fair deal when they sold them anything. The Arbitration Committee had not been called upon to adjust a single case.

L. D. Barclay, reported for the Entertainment Committee and spoke of the successful dance held last spring. The Committee hoped that the new chairman would put on a similar function.

### Mr. Clark Reviews Traffic Troubles

A. E. Clark, for the Transportation Committee, first thanked the members for their able assistance during the recent C. L. A. convention which event was a huge success. Several matters in regard to transportation had come up from time to time, including the present freight rates, stop-over privilege and demurrage. The members of the committee were not satisfied with the present excessive carrying charges and were still fighting for a decrease. A special hearing will be given to the lumber interests on March 7, the sitting taking place at Ottawa. All firms, who had any data to present, should get it ready and place in the hands of the Transportation Committee to strengthen the contention of the lumbermen that the existing carrying charges are altogether out of reason. Incongruities in rates or other specific points affecting through our local tariffs should be forwarded to Mr. Sargent, traffic manager of the C. L. A. That official had been down east assisting the railway men in the Maritime Provinces in the battle for reasonable rates, especially on the Quebec Central.

Milling in transit was another matter that had come before the committee. The hardwood flooring manufacturers had been requested to get together and outline their requirements so far as the stop-over privilege is concerned, in order, to get something definite before the Railway Commission.

In regard to demurrage, it was understood that the rates to be named by the new order issued by the Railway Board would be, after

A. E. Eckardt,
Retiring Chairman W.L.D.A.

D. C. Johnston,
Re-elected Director W.L.D.A.

Alex. C. Gordon,
Elected Director W.L.D.A.

the 48 hours' allowance, $1.00 for the third day, $2.00 for the fourth; $3.00 for the fifth; $4.00 for the sixth and $5.00 for each day thereafter. When the recent order came out, it was found that the charge after the 48 hours' allowance was $1.00 for the third and fourth days and $5.00 demurrage for each succeeding day. This naturally created surprise and the matter should be pressed by the lumbermen until a new order is made. This application should be presented in spite of the reason which had been read from the Secretary of the Railway Board, A. D. Cartwright, to the effect that the judgment of the Board, was a proper solution of the disputed point and that no reason had been adduced as to why the matter should be reopened.

In regard to weighing allowances, while the Association had tried to get these definitely fixed, Mr. Clark said the western men had beaten out the eastern and secured the following concessions:— On box cars a weighing allowance of 500 lbs. from the original weights; on flat cars from May 1st to November 30, 500 lbs.; from December 1st to April 30th, 1000 lbs., and in addition 500 lbs. allowance for stakes.

Eastern manufacturers would have to waken up and get their own from the railways, declared Mr. Clark.

The Transportation Department of the Wholesale Lumber Dealers' Association could collect data and thus save a lot of work from falling on the traffic manager of the C. L. A., who had his hands full with so many problems. The speaker thought men should be appointed on the committee with some knowledge of transportation problems who would be able to look at things fairly and squarely. The lumber-

men had never had proper recognition from a railway standpoint, but if an aggressive committee was appointed, Mr. Clark believed they could put over whatever they went after.

### What Legislature Committee Did

Mr. Manbert, reporting for the Legislature Committee, said that any report which he might present would be a repetition of what the members had already heard. The committee had dealt with all matters that had arisen. The chief one that had come to the attention of the Legislative Committee was the sales tax. This measure naturally did not satisfy all the branches of the industry. The idea of such a tax was accepted as a theory or peculiar opportunity, but when it came to the application of it, many did not feel the same way about it and viewed the levy in quite a different light. Several were impatient with the sales tax which exists, and varying views were heard upon it. All were realizing that while the wholesaler was paying it so far as lumber was concerned, in reality it was passed on to the consumer.

In agreeable times the market swings from a buyer's to a seller's and trade forces these sales taxes. They are not felt then because all are making money and, to some degree, the pinch is minimized. All taxes, however, came out of industry.

Commenting further upon the necessity and wisdom of the sales tax, Mr. Manbert said there had appeared little idea of retrenchment, in government expenditures, but he hoped some housecleaning would be brought about by the new administration in the way of economy.

Hugh A. Rose,
Elected Director W.L.D.A.

J. B. Jarvis,
Elected Director W.L.D.A.

K. M. Brown,
Elected Director W.L.D.A.

# Wanton Waste of Canadian Timber Must Cease

### The Urgency of Situation and Force of Public Opinion Will Compel Federal Government to Take Action in Conserving Pulpwood of the Dominion

By FRANK J. D. BARNJUM

Frank J. D. Barnjum,
Annapolis Royal, N.S.

It has been recently brought to my attention that some foreign buyers of Canadian wood, who are trying to camouflage their own operations, are making the statement that my efforts to conserve Canadian wood for Canadian industries are not an unselfish campaign, as an embargo on wood being shipped out of the country would materially increase the value of lands which they claim I own in the United States.

I do not own an acre of land in the United States or a dollar's worth of property of any nature in that country. Even my own relatives who have small land holdings in Maine have sold a small supply of wood for their own mill, so that they are in the same boat with other pulp and paper manufacturers in the United States.

If I had any selfish motives I would not be advocating an embargo on fee land wood, as my holdings are all fee land in Nova Scotia, and if it is worth more to the settler and farmer to be free to ship his wood to the United States, the same argument would apply to my holdings as well.

I have become so thoroughly imbued wih the critical situation that is facing this continent with regard to its wood and timber supply that I am withdrawing from business as rapidly as possible so as to be in a position to devote my whole time to what I consider is the most important problem facing Canada, namely, the conservation of her wood supply.

It has been frequently stated that the bud worm has passed over New Brunswick and departed, but from a recent cruise on quite a large area in that province it was discovered that thirty five per cent of the soft wood trees were defoliated by this pest the past summer.

An owner of some 250,000 acres of land in Maine advised me last week that after a careful cruise of his lands the investigators found the fir was all dead, and from 48 to 52 per cent of the spruce as well.

I have seen another recent report on a large area in Northern Maine which shows 64% spruce and fir dead.

The whole situation looks very serious to me. It would seem as if man and insect were fighting for control of the earth as, without trees, human life could not exist.

#### Logging Slash Threatens Destruction of Forests

The time is approaching when we shall be forced, for the very preservation of our lives, to burn all logging slash and debris left in the woods. This slash has been very aptly termed by Dr. J. M. Swaine, "The garbage of the forest." It is just as much a menace to our tree growth as a breeding place for insect life which threatens the destruction of our forests as the garbage of a city is to human life, with the added danger from the enormously increased fire risk. If all land owners are required to burn their slash, it will be no hardship as everyone will be on the same basis and the cost will simply be passed along or added to the sale price of the product, whether it be pulp wood or lumber. As this is one of the most effective measures in prolonging the life of our forests, no one should object to its adoption. The Canadian pulp and paper companies should:—

1st.—Reduce the cut on their own lands as near one-half as possible.

2nd.—Insist on an embargo export tax of not less than $10.00 per cord on fee land wood, so as to save for the mills of Canada the large amount of wood that is now being shipped out of the country, and

with the immense amount of capital invested in Canada in the pulp and paper industry this is imperative.

3rd.—Insist on more and better fire protection.

4th.—Insist on the burning of all slash.

5th.—Insist on the utilization of every inch of the tree that is cut down.

6th.—Improve present wasteful logging methods.

7th.—Insist on reforestation on a large scale.

The most serious question to consider in this connection is what we are to do for a wood supply for our mills between the time of the exhaustion of our present stand, some fifteen years hence, and the time when the seedlings we are about to plant come to maturity, some forty years hence.

Very few writers figure on the enormous increase in consumption of all kinds of wood that is going on on this continent through increase in population. This increased consumption, together with the enormous destruction caused through fire, bugs, wind, and waste in every logging operation, is usually overlooked in computing the duration of our present wood supply. They simply take the estimated stand, which is always very wide of the facts, and then compare this with the annual cut, which is always much larger than is reported, leaving out of consideration entirely the very much larger elements, namely, increase in consumption and the tremendous loss through waste. Even the annual shipments of Christmas trees from the State of Maine increased in twelve years from 500 to 1,750,000 trees. I merely cite this as an example of the enormous increase in consumption in only one small branch of the wood-using industries.

In this connection I should like to call attention to Bulletin No. 835, entitled "Wood for the Nation," written by Colonel W. B. Greeley, Chief Forester of the United States, and published by the U. S. Department of Agriculture, which is one of the best written and most comprehensive articles that has come to my notice. This Bulletin should be read by every one who takes any interest in forestry.

There should be no further expansion of the pulp and paper industry in the East, from the standpoint that there is not the raw material to feed them. Any new mills that are built in the East will simply be taking the raw material away from the mills which are already operating and which have very large captial investments and upon which whole towns and cities are depending for their existence. This year we shall, of course, see the same high prices, proportionately, for wood that obtained a year ago, and personally I have always felt that high prices for pulp wood and paper are the only salvation of the situation, as high prices are the only thing that will reduce waste and prolong the life of our wood supply and the life of the pulp and paper mills.

#### High Prices Most Practical Conservation Measure

Just so long as low prices for wood and paper continue this enormous waste will go on. High prices are the most practical conservation measure we can have. The higher the value the greater the conservation; so in my efforts to arouse the public to our critical condition with regard to our wood supply I am simply working not only in the best interests of the pulp and paper mills but for the good of the whole continent as well.

The price for pulp wood for the future will have to be much higher than in the past in order to compensate the land owner for the cost of slash burning, increased fire protection, reforestation, continual increase in length of haul and increasing scarcity in the supply.

The one consolation the timberland owner has with regard to the loss he has suffered through the ravages of the bud worm is the fact that what he has left will be worth four times as much per cord or thousand on account of the great reduction in the remaining supply. This is, of course, only from the mercenary standpoint, and the said question remains as to what our children are to do for wood, as we are even now using up their heritage. Every time we cut one of these small, half grown trees, of which our operations are largely made up to-day, we are simply robbing our own children. In fact, it is worse than robbery as it is a menace to their lives.

I have heard the remark made that we are still cutting, in spite of the prediction made thirty years ago that timber would be exhausted in the east by the present time.

My answer to this is that the prediction made at that time has

proved absolutely correct as what was called timber in those days is gone forever. I sold my first stumpage at that time and the operator would only cut a mark of logs that would run four to the thousand or two hundred and fifty board feet per tree, while we are cutting mere poles to-day running down as small as forty trees to the thousand board feet and which at that time would have been considered worthless. So we must not derive any comfort from the fact that we are still cutting trees, but rather the reverse, when we look at the size of the poles in our river drives and the amount of three and four inch pulp wood seen at our railway sidings.

### Ignorance Regarding Timber Resources

There seems to be so much ignorance with regard to our timber resources that I shall here merely state a few well known and acknowledged facts, and then everyone, whether he be an expert or a layman, can figure out whether we need any further information before we come to a realization of the alarming condition that is facing us with regard to the future of our wood supply.

In the first place, the word timber is a misnomer as applied to our wood growth east of the Rockies to-day; for our timber is practically a thing of the past, and we are down now largely to a pulp wood proposition.

Take the State of Maine, for instance. A few years ago this was called the Pine Tree State, while to-day the pine is gone. It next became the great spruce lumber producer. To-day the saw mills of the mighty Penobscot and Kennebec Rivers are little more than a memory; while here in Nova Scotia it is very difficult to fill an order for lumber calling for even 5% of 12 inch stock.

In addition to the loss from cutting, fire and wind, very few are yet fully aware of the tremendous loss we have suffered the past three or fours years through the spruce bud worm and its resultant pests or followers. It is perfectly safe to state that Maine has lost through dead and still dying timber 50% of her spruce and fir stand. The same figure will apply to New Brunswick. The loss in Quebec has been set by competent authorities at 75,000,000 cords. Nova Scotia has practically escaped this pest. Owing to the small amount of fir or balsam in this Province, it has been unable to gain a foothold here. This scourge, having swept over the eastern country, is now working west through Ontario, as well as along the north shore of the St. Lawrence and in the Lake St. John district, and is doing a vast amount of damage in these sections.

### All Know What Situation Is

Some writers have advocated that we should take a census of our timber supplies, but we already know, without any further information, for all practical purposes, just what the situation really is. All we need is to take the figures we now have and use a little intelligence.

The United States is cutting more than half of the entire amount of timber that is consumed in the whole world, and is using 95% of this at home.

In the United States to-day there remains only 137,000,000 acres of virgin timber, quite a proportion of which is in inaccessible locations and is of indifferent quality. The cut-over and partly burned land amounts to some 250,000,000 acres, making a total of only 387,000,000 acres of forested and partly denuded land.

The loss by fire alone in the United States during the past five years amounts to over 56,000,000 acres, or more than 11,000,000 acres per year. This is from fire alone to which must be added the depletion from cutting, wind and insects, which means at least an additional annual shrinkage of 15,000,000 acres or a total destruction in the United States of not less than 26,000,000 acres per annum.

With regard to loss from wind, the United States, in just one storm last January, lost from this cause some 7,000,000,000 feet of timber, equal to 14,000,000 cords. In addition to the damage by these gales, we have the continuous loss that is going on all the time in the woods from wind which, if it amounts to only three trees per acre, more than offsets any annual growth, and the harder our lands are cut, the greater this loss from wind will be.

### Enormous Waste as Compared With Amount Actually Used

The situation in Canada is equally alarming, for while our annual cut is very much less than in the United States, our standing supply is also very much smaller, and our destruction from fire, wind and bugs is proportionately larger. As a matter of fact, the entire supply remaining in Canada to-day would not last the United States over six and one-half years. In British Columbia alone 665,000,000,000 feet of timber have been burned, while on the Transcontinental Railroad between La Tuque and Cochrane 20,000,000 cords have been destroyed by fire as against considerably less than 1,000,000 cords which have been cut and hauled out on the same railroad. This shows the enormous waste as compared with the amount that is actually cut.

When we consider all the above facts, it is ridiculous for anyone to suggest that some hardship might accrue to the farmer if he were to be deprived of an open market for his pulpwood in the United States. All I can say to this is that every day the farmer allows his wood to stand and grow he is making money very much faster than he possibly can by cutting it now, as it is increasing faster in value than anything else in which he can possibly invest; and I cannot urge the farmer too strongly to let his trees grow, even to the point of borrowing money if necessary.

In addition, he must remember that every cord of wood he ships out of the country shortens the life of one of our greatest industries, namely, pulp, paper and lumber; and he is thereby destroying his home market for his produce by the premature closing down of our home industries through the exhaustion of their wood supply. Finally, by reducing the cut one-half, which would produce a shortage rather than a surplus, as at present, the farmer's income would be just as large because the price of wood would automatically double and instead of practically giving his stumpage away which he is doing at present, he would then be obtaining a fair stumpage return as well as an operating profit, and at the same time be conserving our timber supply. I am not cutting a tree on my own land and shall not do so while I remain in business, just so long as I can buy a cord of wood at any price.

In any event, the Government of a country must, of course, always consider the greatest good to the greatest number, and when one figures the number of employees and dependents upon our great pulp and paper industry, as compared with the comparatively few who may be shippers of wood to a foreign country, who might be temporarily inconvenienced to their ultimate benefit, there can be no possible question as to what the Government's action should be.

### Conserve Canadian Wood for Canadian Mills

I am positive, now, that the whole truth is apparent, that the urgency of the situation and the force of public opinion will compel the Government to take action to conserve Canadian wood for Canadian mills, and that in the future no Government can stand that does not provide adequate protection for Canadian wood-using industries. These industries are in a class by themselves, as every industry and every individual in Canada is dependent upon the preservation of our wood supply.

The subject of an embargo or export duty on pulpwood is not a question of what Canada might like to do. It is an absolute necessity for the protection of her own mills. It is a situation where she must retain what small wood supply she has left or close down prematurely one of her own most important industries in order to ship the wood out of the country to supply the mills of the United States. Therefore, any suggestion of retaliation by the United States is unthinkable and could not be seriously considered. It must not be forgotten that small as the supply of standing timber in the United States now is, it is still four times as large as the Canadian stand. The wood supply is unlike any other commodity, as it takes from 50 to 150 years to raise a new crop of trees.

## Jobber Fined for Having Unsanitary Camps

It is not often that one hears of a prosecution being entered in Ontario against a lumberman for unsanitary camps. The accommodation of late years has been greatly improved and there have been few complaints made to the Health Inspectors; in fact, the advances made in feeding and lodging men have been most marked and what protests have come to the attention of the provincial authorities have been mainly from jobbers or small operators, and not from any of the larger companies.

Inspector Mckee, of the Ontario Provincial Board of Health, recently launched a test prosecution against W. J. Carriere, a jobber operating near Gogama, charged with maintaining unsanitary camps. The case was heard in the Sudbury police court and the defendant was fined $25.00 and costs on each of two separate accounts and given two weeks to make such alterations as would place his camps in a condition conforming with the Act. The prosecution is the result of an investigation following complaints received by the department.

Despite the plea of guilty, Magistrate Brodie deemed the taking of evidence most essential and it revealed a miserable state of affairs at the Carriere camps. Sleeping accommodation for the men was inadequate and overcrowded, toilet accommodation not in accordance with the act, while a stable drained into a creek which further down the stream supplied drinking water for other camps.

James Vincent, of Fesserton, Ont., passed away recently in his 68th year. Previous to his very sudden death he had never been ill a day. For a quarter of a century he was foreman of the yard of the Fesserton Timber Co., at Fesserton, and was widely known in lumber circles. J. W. Jacobson, of the Atlantic Lumber Co., Toronto, is a son-in-law of the late Mr. Vincent.

# Gradual Loosening of Hampering Conditions

## How British Columbia Views Existing Situation and Outlook in the Lumber Arena—Export Trade Showed Big Increase Last Year Over Previous Twelve Months

### By HENRY C. COPELAND, VANCOUVER STAFF.

A considerable degree of uncertainty as to the export market has developed during the past three or four weeks. The demand for Japanese squares has fallen to a low point and many of the exporters in this class of trade profess to be at a loss as to the cause.

Nevertheless, one of the largest factors in this particular line states that the slackening is due simply to the congestion in the Japanese ports. The squares and logs have to be taken into the interior to the mills for resawing and manufacturing. The storage capacity of the ports is small, the cars on the Japanese railroads are short, only twenty feet long, with the result that the facilities for handling are soon absorbed.

There seems to be a firm opinion that the best outlook for new markets for British Columbia lumber is to be found in the Atlantic seaboard trade for reshipment throughout the east and as far west as the points where the freight rates equalize. With 500,000,000 feet going to those points and California from Oregon and Washington in 1921 and only some 20,000,000 from British Columbia it would appear that that market would offer the most attractions to the export trade.

The demand from California is fair and doubtless will come up to 1921, unless the citrus crops have been almost totally destroyed by frost. Eight and nine years ago the frosts practically stopped things in California for several months. Since then, however, the industrial development has been so great, with that of the moving picture industry, that there is little likelihood of there being any effects other than locally.

During the past month the steamship freight rate has been weak and falling. The rate of $14.50 has replaced that of $16.50 on Jap squares to common Oriental ports. There has even gone forward one distress shipment of 400,000 feet of baby squares that was taken at $7.50.

Many operators in the export trade feel that the lack of activity in the Japanese line is due to this freight rate situation. Buying in this line is usually at a standstill in January and the delay may be prolonged, even into March, as the Japanese are not likely to overlook any influence by which they can bear the market. It has gone out over the coast that they are predicting a rate of $12.50 on squares before April 1st.

The best opinion seems to be that this market for 1922 will fully equal that of 1921. Japan has asked for samples of fir, hemlock and cedar, as a preliminary to placing orders for 4,000,000 of ties for the Japanese government railways.

Out of a total scale of 1,700,000,000 feet of lumber produced in British Columbia in 1921, there was exported to foreign countries as water-borne freight 188,733,299 feet. Those figures constitute eleven per cent of the total. Five years ago the total export of British Columbia was only four per cent of the total.

The destination of these exports may be interesting, they were as follows:—

| | |
|---|---:|
| Australia | 27,275,928 |
| China | 41,944,011 |
| Egypt | 8,566,400 |
| Fiji Islands | 447,344 |
| Indian and Straits | 8,429,403 |
| Japan | 52,447,160 |
| New Zealand | 4,553,603 |
| South Africa | 2,931,969 |
| South Sea Islands | 494,078 |
| South America, east coast | 33,096 |
| South America, west coast | 1,284,730 |
| United Kingdom and Continent | 13,592,562 |
| West Indies | 20,668 |
| Atlantic Coast | 5,431,054 |
| Hawaii | 1,055,580 |
| Philippine Islands | 103,225 |
| San Francisco Bay | 2,320,819 |
| San Pedro Bay (Los Angeles) | 10,003,586 |
| California (unclassified) | 7,798,084 |
| | 188,733,299 |

With 89 per cent of the total British Columbia cut to be absorbed in the domestic markets the conditions of those outlets will continue to be of much the greatest importance. As long as such is the condition the question of freight tariffs will be also of the utmost importance. The situation has become so acute regarding this matter that all the organizations of lumbermen, shingle-men and loggers have passed drastic resolutions demanding a heavy downward revision of the freight rates on lumber, particularly as affecting the prairie points. It is claimed that the transportation charges on lumber to those points amount to 60 to 70 per cent of the price of the lumber, with the result that the industry is stifled.

### As the Prairie Market Appears

While the reports as to business conditions in the prairie country are very depressing, there are views expressed by competent authorities that give a brighter side. One of the best known operators in this Province states it as his personal knowledge that the prairie yards are down to the piling sticks. One line of yards that cut stocks to the limit for the 1920 inventory, in the 1921 inventory showed less than 20 per cent of the 1920.

Another line yard concern that normally buys fifty cars the last four months of the year did not buy a single car of lumber but shipped from yard to yard to make sorts for their orders. In the larger towns there will undoubtedly be considerable activity, particularly if immigration moves freely, in order to do any business it will be necessary to do a very satisfactory amount of buying. So our authority believes that 1922 on the markets will be at least as good as 1921.

### As the East Looks from the West

Regardless of the high freight differential and adverse business conditions, several of the large mills are finding a very satisfactory outlet in the eastern Canada market. Some have added to their eastern sales-force in order that they may take better care of the trade offered.

Some specifications have been received for sorts in the rough. A few inquiries have been received for log-run taking up to No.1. Most of the orders are, however, for the regular "quarter scant" specification. As the eastern business of several large B. C. concerns has shown a handsome yearly increase during the past five years and the opening 1922 orders are coming in better than before the outlook of those concerns is quite optimistic.

### From the Loggers

The market on fir logs is fairly steady at $12.00-$17.00-$24.00 and is being obtained. However, the weather conditions have been such that there is a real shortage of logs in the Vancouver market. Some booms are coming in but the No. 2's and No. 3's predominate. As the specifications for foreign orders call heavily for No. 1's the general tendency of the market is upwards.

Cedar logs, 10 per cent and upwards No. 1, are strong at $20.00 and $22.00. This figure is, however, likely the peak of the cedar market and it would seem due for a falling off to a more normal figure.

The general expectation among the trade at large in Vancouver, B. C., seems to be that things will move along about as they are now with a gradual loosening up of hampering conditions until the year will end with a considerable improvement over 1921. Wages in other lines of building materials will likely seek a normal level, freight-rates will probably take a decided drop and with world conditions gradually straightening out, the entire fabric of the timber industries will become stabilized and bettered.

Col. J. Lightbody, D. S. O., timber broker, late of Glasgow, Scotland, widely known in Eastern Canada and the United States, has become a member of the McElroy Lumber Co., Limited, of Victoria, B. C. The McElroy Lumber Co. announce that their own connections and that of Col. Lightbody, they are in a position to take care of a larger volume than ever. They are the selling agents for four lumber and one shingle mill. The members of the McElroy Lumber Co. are,—G. H. Walton, D. A. Matthews and Col. J. Lightbody.

## Mr. Todd Now Located in Toronto

J. T. Todd, sales manager of the Adams River Lumber Co., Limited, Chase, B. C., recently arrived in Toronto and intends opening an office in the interest of his firm, who specialize in fir, cedar, spruce and pine, the mill having an output of about 150,000 feet a day.

Mr. Todd has already called upon a number of members of the trade and has met with an encouraging reception. He has been engaged in the lumber line for several years, having spent about five years in the Puget Sound district. He was for some time with the St. Paul and Tacoma Lumber Co., Tacoma, Wash., and later with the Anacortes Lumber & Box Co., Anacortes, Wash. In 1918 Mr. Todd joined the Adams River Lumber Co. He has sold forest products in all the western provinces where he is widely known, and in coming east, carries with him the best wishes of many friends.

Mr. Todd will also represent the Associated Mills of Vancouver, the daily capacity of which is about 500,000 feet, and also the Edgecumbe-Newham Co., of Vancouver, whose shingle output is 500,000 a day.

The Adams River Lumber Co., in opening up an eastern branch and placing Mr. Todd in charge believe they have taken a step in the right direction. It will enable them to furnish better service, more prompt deliveries and facilitate a better understanding and appreciation of the needs of their customers in Ontario, Quebec and the maritime provinces.

## Nicola Pine Mills Opens Eastern Office

J. E. Jones, sales manager of the Nicola Pine Mills, Limited, of Merritt, B. C., is now in Toronto, and intends opening an office in the interests of his firm, whose plant has a daily capacity of 250,000 feet, and is now running night and day. He came to Canada some ten or eleven years ago from the "right little, tight little isle" across the sea and first joined the Campbell River Lumber Co., of White Rock, B. C. He then became identified with the Nicola Pine Mills, and has had charge of their sales for the past year and a half. The company are the largest distributors of western white pine, and the mills have been producing successfully since 1910. A couple of years ago they were burned to the ground but the new plant was set going

## Will Government Cancel Pulpwood Concessions?

With reference to the request by the Ontario government that the Great Lakes Paper Co., Fort William, Ont., show reason why it should not have its pulpwood concessions on the Pic and Black Sturgeon rivers cancelled, it is considered likely, should the Ontario government's requirements in the matter not be met with, that legislation will be introduced.

It appears that the original agreement in 1917 called for certain things to be done within a year, but that in 1918 an extension was granted until power would be available. The question has arisen as to whether the company was bound to take Hydro power. It is stated the understanding was that power would be given at cost, and the company is said to have the view that they cannot afford to pay what the Hydro commission says is cost.

In litigation the company has already been successful and apparently the government is met with the contention that the agreement does not call for construction of the mills until one year after power has been made available.

## Lumber Freight Rate Hearing at Ottawa

R. L. Sargant, traffic manager of the Canadian Lumbermen's Association, Ottawa, spent a few days recently down in the Maritime Provinces. A hearing was given the lumbermen by the Board of Railway Commissioners at St. John, on January 19th in regard to through rates on forest products to and from points on the Quebec Central.

The Canadian Pacific representatives at the hearing objected and claimed that they had not been previously notified of the intention of the Canadian Lumbermen's Association to bring this matter before the Board at that sitting. The Canadian Lumbermen's Association admitted this but stated as they had had considerable correspondence with the Canadian Pacific Railway on the subject and they did not appear to be very anxious to take any definite action in the matter. As one of the members of the Association (Murray & Gregory, Limited, of St. John,) was vitally interested in the rates on lumber from points on the Quebec Central Railway, it was deemed advisable to bring the proposition before the Board at the sitting in St. John.

The Board decided to hear the lumbermen and the case was presented. The chief commissioner made the statement that he did not see any good reason why the railways and the complainants could not get together and come to some agreement on this question. He stated that he would give the Railway Companies two weeks in

Spencer Kellogg, Utica, N.Y.          R. R. Stocking, New York, N.Y.
Who Were Elected Directors from the United States on the Executive of the Canadian Lumbermen's Association

which to make some effort toward a satisfactory settlement. It is understood this is now under way and may result in an amicable arrangement.

Mr. Sargant states that the Board of Railway Commissioners have intimated that they would be willing to hear the application of the Canadian Lumbermen's Association for a reduction in the rates on lumber at a special sitting to be held in Ottawa, Tuesday, March 7th. The members of the Transportation Committee have been notified and it is expected that a strong case will be presented by the Association. The C.L.A. is asking that the carrying charges be reduced to what they were prior to September 1920.

The coming sitting is a most important one to lumbermen and the lumber interest, and it is expected that there will be a large representation of the industry at the sitting.

## Death of Veteran Ontario Lumberman

James Carswell, in his day one of the most extensive lumber operators in the Ottawa Valley, died recently at his home in Renfrew, Ont. after a long illness, due to weakness and old age. He was born in Pakenham, 84 years ago, but lived in Renfrew since 1866. For years he was engaged in mercantile business in the town, besides lumbering, and was also an extensive land owner at the time of his death. He is survived by his wife, three sons and three daughters.

## Work on Plan for Timber Cutting

A delegation of representatives of the big lumber companies throughout Quebec, headed by Sir William Price, waited on the Prime Minister and the Minister of Lands and Forests recently to discuss with them and with G. C. Piche, Chief of the Forestry Department, the best system for the future cutting of timber. As a result of the discussion the companies were asked to make a complete inventory of the forests leased to them and work out a plan which could be followed in the cutting of timber.

## Gale Does Big Damage Down East

Considerable damage was done by a recent gale in the forests in various parts of New Brunswick, particularly in the central portion and head waters of the St. John River. A wind velocity of sixty miles an hour was registered. Many trees were broken down by the gale. Budworm-damaged timber suffered heavily, being weakened so much that it could not stand the force of the wind. Both hardwood and coniferous suffered in the storm which was one of the worst in years.

## Quebec Limit Holders in Annual Meeting

At the annual meeting of the Province of Quebec Limit Holders' Association, held at the Windsor Hotel, Montreal, on January 25, Mr. W. G. Power was elected president and Mr. A. Price Vice-President.

It was decided to appoint a committee, to act jointly with a committee of the Woodlands section of the Pulp and Paper Association, on questions effecting forest conservation, stumpage, etc. The necessity of getting into closer touch with the Provincial Government was urged, especially in relation to proposed changes affecting the members of the Association. This co-operation would be of mutual benefit to the government and the association.

# Live Topics at Forest Protective Association

### Everything Discussed from Forest Pests to Aviation—Committee on Logging Methods May Appoint Competent Man to Act in Advisory Capacity to Anyone Requiring Such Service

The subjects discussed at the annual conference of the Quebec Forest Protective Association, held at the Windsor Hotel on January 25, covered a wide range—from forest pests to aviation.

The opening paper was on "The Possibilities of Preventing Losses from the Spruce Budworm" by Dr. F. C. Craighead, Division of Forest Insects, Ottawa. He pointed out that in Quebec 50 per cent of the merchantable balsam had been killed and three years' increment lost on spruce. The seriousness of this position had not been realized. They might expect another outbreak in the future, judging by history, possibly in 30 to 50 years, but further outbreaks could be rendered less potent and the losses reduced to a minimum by preventive measures. Aims in the future management of the forests should be the encouraging of types least susceptible to the budworm, utilization of hardwoods to develop the hardwood type, utilization of conifers before they were over mature, and better adaptation of type to soil.

Dr. Craighead discussed these recommendations as applied to cut-over lands, the remaining virgin forests, and future planting. He stated that the virgin forests had suffered the greatest injury during the present attack. The new growth of white spruce furnished the most suitable food for the development of the budworm larvae. They matured sooner than on balsam and grew to a larger size. Planting policies should aim to produce a variety of condition and not to chance all on a single throw. Plant the various species of conifers, especially those affected by the budworm, mix them thoroughly over the area, and experiment with mixed stands of rapid-growing hardwoods. The adaptation of the tree to the soil was one of the most important features to be recommended. Balsam and red and white spruce should only be grown on the best forest soils. On poorer soils other conifers, not subject to budworm attack, such as jack pine or black spruce, should be grown.

### Permits for Persons Entering Forests

Mr. R. P. Kernan, of the Donnacona Paper Company, in a paper advocating a system of permits for entering lumber limits, pointed out the enormous loss by fire, due to carelessness and negligence. In order to prevent such fires, it was proposed to introduce a system under which some control could be exercised over every person entering the forest, which might take the form of permits, which would state the destination, duration of occupation and perhaps the object of the trip, and would also give the name and address of the person obtaining the permit. No charge would be made. Mr. Kernan admitted that such a system might be regarded as undue interference with personal liberty, but he claimed that such interference was justifiable in the light of the appalling losses by forest fires. A permit system would be welcomed by those who are interested in protecting the forests.

After discussing plans for issuing permits and the legal aspect of the subject, Mr. Kernan declared the practical certainty of the lack of legal right of the limit holders to enforce a permit system, and the grave doubt of even the statutory right of the Government to carry it into effect, made it imperative that, before taking any steps toward carrying out the plan, Parliament should enact a statute giving the Lieutenant-Governor-in-Council full authority to enact and put into effect any regulations necessary to establish the proposed permit system. The best method perhaps of issuing the permits, would be through the fire guardians and inspectors of the Crown, forest protective associations, officials of the various hunting and fishing clubs and officials of the Crown, who at the present time were authorized to issue hunting and fishing permits. Clerks and foremen of the operating companies could issue permits to the workmen at the time of hiring them; these permits could be revoked when the men were paid off.

Probably a term of imprisonment would be the only penalty attached to infringement of the regulations, but if it were practical, a power to deny a person, for a term of years, the right to have a permit might be an excellent one.

Mr. W. G. Power suggested that the matter should be taken up with the Government, with a view of securing legal authority for a system, which could be later extended.

Mr. Dan. McLachlin remarked that it might be a good thing for the rangers to have the right to question people, and on the absence of satisfactory answers, to turn them back.

Mr. Piche stated that the Provincial Government was considering drastic measures to prevent forest fires which last year destroyed about 200 square miles.

Mr. Creesman, of the Waygagamack Pulp & Paper Company, described the company's system under which every man going into the woods received a badge, for which he was charged $5.00, returnable when he was discharged. He suggested a system by which permits could be issued from central depots.

### Railroads and Prevention of Fires

In a paper on "The Railroads and Forest Protection against Fire," Avila Bedard, assistant chief of the Forest Service of the Province of Quebec, described the part played by the railroads in preventing fires, stating that the companies had willingly complied with the legislation affecting them. The companies had an interest in the conservation of forests, as in 1919 the tonnage of forest products transported was one-sixth of the total tonnage, and further the railways were dependent on the forest for an important part of their raw material.

R. H. Nisbet, forester in charge of the Aviation Department of Price Bros. & Co., Quebec, read a paper on the work of that department, outlining the difficulties of aviation as applied to aerial photography. Mosaic pictures, he said, had certain advantages, but there were drawbacks which made him favor the map form for aerial surveys, particularly in view of the fact that the map was more easily read by woods operators. Mr. Nisbet summed up the work which could be done by aviators and deprecated the too sweeping claims made for their work. This could stand on its merits, and would be gradually developed. In fire-fighting the aeroplane must be subsidiary to the ground organization, without efficiency in which the aeroplane, in the majority of cases, must fail. Flying was costly but it must not be overlooked that a great deal of work could be accomplished in a short time.

### Logging Methods and Equipment

Mr. Ellwood Wilson submitted the report of the Committee on Logging Methods and Equipment. He stated that, during last summer, a questionnaire was sent to the members of the section, asking for answers to two main questions. Was the time ripe to establish a central experimental station where machinery could be tested on a small scale, or should work be assigned to different companies? The result was that nobody was inclined to spend money on the project. The proposals did not meet with a favorable reception, and the committee decided to change the procedure with a view to securing results. The proposal was to appoint a secretary for the section—a man with mechanical or civil engineering experience, who would, in addition to the secretarial work, act in an advisory capacity to any member requiring advice on logging methods. He would visit the various plants and limits and secure data, which would be reported to the Association. The committee were of the opinion that this would be a beginning for practical work, which would be of benefit to the industry as a whole.

It was decided to recommend the executive council of the Association to appoint a secretary, and in the alternative for authority for the section to appoint a secretary, the expense to be met by assessment on the members of the section. It was understood that the new council of the section would give due consideration to the fact that in making the assessment, some members of the section were lumbermen and not interested in the pulp and paper problems.

### Tractors for Hauling Logs

G. E. Vose, general manager and treasurer of the Lombard Traction Engine Company, outlined the advantages of tractors in woods and other operations, stating that his company had 23 tractors at work in Eastern Canada. He gave figures showing the saving of tractors as compared with horse haulage, adding that experiments were being made with a view to using tractors from the point of cutting the trees to the termination of the required hauling. Mr. Vose's figures related to both steam and gasoline tractors.

At the afternoon session, Messrs. W. G. Power and Dan. McLachlin spoke on "Is Canada Making Progress in Forestry and Logging Methods?" Mr. Power's speech was a brief review of old and new conditions in the province of Quebec. In introducing the speakers, Mr. DeCarteret pointed out that woods operations and forest management must provide a profit in the immediate future or in a period not too far remote. It was well to make plans for the next generation, but the life of any commercial enterprise was dependent upon its annual business.

**Lumber Must Suit the Market**

Mr. Power remarked that the first logging operations in the province of Quebec were for white pine, operators having in view getting out the best lumber for square planks. As time went on a market was found for boards and sawmills were constructed. For many years spruce had no value for the operators, but as pine became more difficult to obtain, the operators started to cut spruce logs, all logs having to be 12 inches and up at the top. Conditions changed, and with the opening up of the U. S. market, and the difficulty of getting wide lumber increased, narrower widths came into use. When he commenced in the lumber business 9 inches at the top was in vogue. The prohibition of the export of pulpwood from Crown lands also made a change in methods. Gradually lumbermen reached a basis where they could use smaller sizes, especially for the American market. Mr. Power insisted that, in order to ensure the ready sale of lumber, it must be made in such a manner as to suit the market, having regard to the fact that Quebec had to compete with other manufacturers. Any improvement in logging methods should be of such a character that the cost was within a reasonable limit. Mr. Power also dealt with slash-burning and suggested that the province should have a definite policy.

Mr. Dan. McLachlin gave a time analysis of the operations at two-camps at Black River and Kipawa. The results in percentages were,—shanty, 16.94; cutting and rolling 45.84; skidding 8.51; main roads 33.02. The production was 3½ logs per man per day. He had under consideration using a light railway, such as was used overseas, but found the cost prohibitive.

Mr. R. P. Kernan, in reporting on a proposal for the establishment of a Government school for forest rangers in Quebec, stated that the replies of members to a circular were to the effect that the time was not ripe. It was a question of finance.

Mr. Piche suggested that the matter should be taken up with the Government, as the premier was favorable to the idea. The question was left to the new council.

**New Officers of the Section**

The following officers for 1922 were elected:—Chairman, Mr. R. P. Kernan, Donnacona Paper Co., Quebec; Vice-chairman, Mr. B. F. Avery, Spanish River Pulp & Paper Mills, Limited, Sault Ste. Marie. Council:—Messrs. S. L. De Carteret, Brown Corporation, Quebec; T. F. Kenny, James McLaren Company, Buckingham, P. Q., and Ellwood Wilson, Laurentide Company, Grand Mere, Que.

The proceedings concluded with motion pictures,—"The Romance of Paper," which included pictures of Linn tractors at work. Mr. J. S. Innes, of Mussens Limited, Montreal, and S. H. Sisson, of the A. Sherman Lumber Co., Potsdam, N. Y., gave some details of the working of the tractors, six in number.

The daily cost of each tractor was $43.6 or 71 cents a cord of pulpwood. The tractors hauled in 38 days 24000 cords of 16 ft. pulpwood for a distance of 12 miles. Each tractor made two round trips, a total of 48 miles per day.

# "Sauce for the Goose is Sauce for the Gander"

There will always be the careless and the indifferent; those who give too little consideration to the value of what they possess. Such persons will frequently find a multitude of faults in others for neglect and inattention, oversight and shiftlessness, being in a position to see the mote in their brother's eye but not the beam in their own.

It would be interesting to have tabulated the aggregate amount of damage done annually to farm machinery and implements in Canada through such equipment being left out in the open air to brave the wind, rain, frost, sun and snow. An implement shed or store house may cost some money but it will more than repay itself within a few years.

Herein lies an opportunity for the aggressive retail lumberman to get busy and present a few facts to rural residents respecting what the housing of machinery really means. It has been stated that the depreciation of $2000 worth of machinery, if left unhoused, is $500 per year, whereas if housed the depreciation is only $200; thus the actual loss due to exposure is $300, which is no small item in these days of low-priced farm produce and livestock.

The accompanying illustration may be amusing, but at the same time it depicts a lesson. It appeared in "Judge," the comic periodical, and shows how a farmer will leave his hayrake and cultivator out in the open but yet he would stand aghast—stark stiff—if he sauntered toward the house on a rainy day and found that his spouse had left her sewing machine, costing much less than the average farm implement, outdoors to endure the elements. He would read her a lecture on thrift and accuse her of all kinds of extravagance, yet, at the same time, he is more reprehensible for the course he has pursued in neglecting to shelter his own equipment.

Some interesting literature has been issued on the care and maintenance of machinery, and a recent pamphlet was published, showing a cartoon with the pertinent query "Why not the sewing machine too?"

Reverting to the depreciation and the loss of practically $1.00 a day on $2000 worth of machinery between the properly housed and unhoused implements, it is pointed out that, leaving out Sundays and holidays, there are approximately three hundred working days in a year. An implement shed will, therefore, earn for the man who erects it, $1.00 per day. A saving of $300.00 invested each year in 6 per cent securities and allowed to accumulate for twenty years, would amount to a little over $11,600.

Where, it is asked, can a farmer obtain a better investment for his money in the light of these facts, than putting up an implement shed and building it now while lumber is down in price and labor is cheap?

There is no need to enlarge further upon the economy, wisdom, foresight and sound common sense evidenced by the farmer in the erection of implement sheds, and herein lies a fruitful source of exploitation and development by the enterprising retail lumberman.

Recently an agriculture publication presented this interesting fact—the average depreciation of well-housed machinery is not more than 10 per cent a year; some specialists estimate it as ranging from 3 to 12 per cent according to the character and intricacy of the ma-

*Reprinted by courtesy of "Judge"*

How "hubby" received a rude awakening

chine. The rate of depreciation on unhoused machinery will run well over twice this amount; in fact it will average fully 25 per cent a year. This makes exposure responsible for, at least 15 per cent depreciation.

Enough said. Get busy Mr. Retail Lumberman in extending your trade in the surrounding country.

Morin Freres, Cap de la Madeline, Que., retail lumber dealers, had their yards and buildings completely destroyed by fire last month. The firm are now rebuilding and doing business from a temporarily erected office on the old site.

Creation of two new provincial parks by the British Columbia Government has been announced by Hon. T. D. Pattullo, Minister of Lands. One of these parks is the Mount Assiniboine Park, near Banff, and the other, the Kokanee Park, at the head of the Kootenay and Slocan Lakes.

## Mr. Miller Appointed on Rules Committee

John J. Miller, of Toronto, who is a member of Anderson-Miller Lumber Co., has been appointed a member of the Inspection Rules Committee of the National Hardwood Lumber Association by President Horace F. Taylor, of Buffalo. Mr. Miller was for several years on the inspecting staff of the N.H.L.A.

The National Hardwood Lumber Association is now in its twenty-fifth year and was organized to establish, maintain and apply uniform rules over the measurement and inspection of hardwood lumber. Any manufacturer of or wholesale dealer in hardwood lumber in good standing is eligible for membership. It is understood there is only one class of membership and everyone joining pays $50.00, initiation fee, with annual fees thereafter of $50.00.

When an agreement exists between buyer and seller to be covered by national inspection, the report of the national inspection is final, but if either party is dissatisfied with the report, the inspection

**John J. Miller, Toronto,**
Who is new Canadian representative on N.H.L.A. inspection rules

may be demanded whether the one demanding the same is a member of the Association or not, is one of the conditions provided the stock is intact. Commenting upon this phase of the matter, the National Hardwood Lumber Association says:—

"Upon application for the re-inspection of a block of lumber for which a certificate has been regularly issued by a National Inspector, the chief inspector shall proceed as promptly as possible to reinspect the lumber in person, or by a deputy, other than the inspector making the original inspection. If the re-inspection results in a difference in favor of the party complaining, of more than four per cent in money value from the original inspection, the party complaining may receive the amount of such difference directly from this Association by sending to the Secretary an itemized statement showing in details the items and amounts as shown on the original certificate and the re-inspection certificate. No claim on re-inspection will be paid until prices placed on off grade items are approved by the Executive Committee. If the difference does not exceed four per cent, the party demanding the re-inspection shall pay all expenses connected therewith.

"The above rule and guarantee does not apply on certificates issued on lumber loaded green; nor on lumber inspected and piled down at point of shipment and reinspected at destination.

"The Association reserves the right to decline official re-inspection on lumber in leaky cars or delayed beyond a reasonable period in transit. The Association assumes no liability on account of demurrage. All applications for re-inspection shall be made within ten days from receipt of lumber at destination, provided the original inspection was made at point of shipment; or within ten days from date of original inspection, if same is made at destination."

The National Hardwood Lumber Association now maintains five inspectors in Canada, four being located in Toronto and one in Montreal. The present membership of the Association in the Dominion is 71, Ontario having 46.

The foregoing information in regard to the activities of the National Hardwood Lumber Association, whose headquarters are in the McCormick Building, Chicago, Frank F. Fish, secretary-treasurer, in response to requests from several readers of the "Canada Lumberman."

Frank Adolph, of the Adolph Lumber Co., Baynes Lake, B. C. was a recent caller on the trade in Toronto.

## Everybody Profits by Home Building

"Few things tend to hasten the return to better times more than the building industry:" "Things used in the building of dwelling houses call upon virtually all of the industries of the country for their products. A general and far-reaching construction program in this country in 1922 is the best possible harbinger of a return to more prosperous conditions."

There is in truth no more reliable barometer of public confidence and general business conditions than the building industry, according to Dr. Wilson Compton, Manager of the National Lumber Manufacturers Association, who is, perhaps, the most authoritative spokesman for the building industry in America. "Everybody profits when a new house is built." says Dr. Compton. "It furnishes business for the real estate man, it immediately exerts a stabilizing influence upon neighborhood land values. Every new home means employment for workmen and business for the brick, stone, lumber, hardware and paint dealers, reflecting back to manufacturers and the railroads. It means selling furniture, draperies, wall paper, kitchen utensils and baby buggies. It means more business for the daily newspapers, the banks and the department stores. The home supports the churches and schools and the great public utilities that make modern life a luxury. So that, it is no mere figure of speach to say, building calls upon virtually all the industries of the country for their products.

## Canadian Match Co. is Now Operating

The Canadian Match Co., Limited, Pembroke, Ont., which was granted incorporation with a capital of $1,000,000 last November has started a large sales force to work throughout the provinces. The new company has been operating its plant at Pembroke, steadily, since last fall but the product was not placed on the market until a sufficient supply of manufactured matches was on hand, ready to meet the initial demand. It has now a large supply of the goods ready to meet the expected business. So far the production has been confined to one brand, known as the "Maple Leaf" match, put up in large and small boxes, but the company will produce also a "strike-on-box" or safety match, which will be known as the "red-top."

Sir Alexander Maguire was chosen president of the new company and A. G. Woodruff, who came to Pembroke from Savannah, Ga., is Vice-President and in charge of the plant. B. Chandler Snead of New York is Secretary. Among the directors are a number of prominent English and Canadian capitalists. The new industry at Pembroke is employing a large staff of workers and will also create a market for large quantities of soft wood. Mr. Woodruff, the Vice-President and General Manager is making his home in Pembroke. He has had long experience in the match business and was in charge of the Diamond Match Co.'s largest plants in Savannah, Georgia.

When Maguire, Paterson & Palmer(Canada) Ltd., Pembroke, Ont., splint manufacturers, incorporated a year ago it was rumored that they would embark in the match manufacturing branch, but new plans were made and the Canadian Match Co., Limited, a distinct enterprise, was formed, representing the Diamond Match Co., interests in the United States, Bryant & May of England and Maguire, Paterson Palmer, Limited, the three largest match manufacturing firms in the world.

## Whitewood in Strong Demand in Great Britain

Whatever may be said about the demand for redwood next year, says the British Timber Trades Journal, there is no doubt that whitewood is firmer than ever, and we should not be surprised if, before long, higher prices were being paid for whitewood than for redwood. We have already heard of buyers who, not able to secure suitable specifications in redwood, have had to be content with whitewood at the same figures. So far, the business has gone very largely to the Finns. The Dutch, French and Scotch firms have all purchased heavily, and a big proportion of the early deliveries has already been sold. Whitewood, indeed, instead of being a drug, has proved of the greatest value, and no sooner does a suitable specification come over than offers are immediately made for the goods. Whitewood from Bohemia has met with a fair sale, but the quality of the wood is generally poor. The Canadian shippers are eagerly looking forward to good prices for their over-lying spruce, and when values have advanced a little farther, negotiations with Canada will undoubtedly be seriously undertaken. At the present time there is a difference of £2 to £3 per standard between the buyers' and sellers' idas, but with a keen inquiry this difference should soon be bridged.

The Canadian National Lumber Co. has been formed with head office at 515 Temple Building, Toronto. The head of the company is Martin Kehoe, of Atherley, Ont., who owns ten square miles of timber in Parry Island, in the Parry Sound district. Mr. Kehoe will take out quite a large quantity of switch ties, cross ties, poles, etc.

## New Director is Live Lumberman

John T. Grantham, Brantford, On.

John T. Grantham, Brantford, Ont., who was recently elected a director of the Ontario Retail Lumber Dealers' Association, is a live wire in the business and his son, Carter Grantham, is associated with him. The factory, yard and office of the firm are at 23 Water St., Brantford, in that rapidly-growing portion of the city commonly known as "Eagle Place". Until a few years ago Mr. Grantham carried on an extensive contracting business. Then he laid in a small stock of lumber principally for his own use, and from this broadened out into operating a planing mill. Gradually various lines were added until now the firm can supply everything for building from cellar to the roof. Mr. Grantham has always been a believer in timely and effective advertising, and around his well-kept yards the name of the firm appears in large lett' ers. Many novelties have been distributed through the mails and at rural fairs setting forth the fact that the business of John T. Grant' ham is that of supply builders with everything from foundation to ridgeboard. Mr. Grantham makes some doors, sash and frames in his own plant but not to any great extent, for he purchases standard sizes in all these lines which he states, he can handle more advantageously. He says that he never makes anything that some other fellow can produce just as good in quality and cheaper than he can. He realizes that firms turning out quantity production of standard goods are in a position to give better service and quotations than one who operates to a limited capacity. He, therefore, believes in stocking all ordinary requirements rather than making them himself.

## Pacific Province Had Very Fair Year

In spite of falling prices and a quiet home market. complete returns from the Forest Branch of the Minister of Lands for Brit' ish Columbia show that the timber industry enjoyed a fairly active year.

Hon. Mr. Pattullo, Minister of Lands, said that there was a drop of only 12½ per cent, and it must be remembered that 1920 was a record year, and the industry exerting every effort had in' creased production. During 1921 1,750,000,000 feet b. m., of all grades were scaled and reported to the Forest Branch, as compared with 2,046,000,000 feet, during 1920. The previous high scale was 1,761,000,000 feet of slightly less than 1921.

Mr. Pattullo remarked that timber industries during 1920 had been one of the biggest factors in industrial life in providing work and markets. Considerable credit was due to those who in spite of adverse conditions, kept their logging camps and mills open and achieved for the province such a record.

## New Lumber Company Opens Offices

The Kinnon Lumber Co., Limited, has been incorporated and have opened up offices at Room 12, 454 King St. West, Toronto, in the Royal Bank Building. The company has a yard at the foot of Spadina Ave.

Mr. George Kinnon, who was for many years associated with the Wm. Laking Lumber Co. and latterly has been in business on his own behalf, has associated with him John P. Waters of Toronto, who is well-known to the lumber industry in Ontario, and G. D. Martin of Burk's Falls. The new company which will specialize in Canadian and imported hardwoods, have absorbed the business carried on by George Kinnon, and expect to do a nice trade during the coming year.

## High Freight Rates Scored on all Sides

The present heavy freight charges are being attacked on all sides. Lumbermen in the east, west, north and south have voiced the unanimous expression of disapproval against the exorbitant tolls.

This all-important topic was thoroughly considered at the annual meeting of the Canadian Lumbermen's Association in Toronto, and the recent convention of the Ontario Retail Lumber Dealers in Ottawa. The Western Retail Lumbermen's Association at Winnipeg,

also brought up the matter, and the Lumber and Shingle Manufac' turers of British Columbia have joined in the chorus of protest At their annual meeting held recently in Vancouver, the present excessive freight rates were severely criticized, and a resolution was passed in which the lumbermen declared that the present carrying charges were prohibitive and were the principal reason for the stag' nation of the lumber industry in British Columbia.

Present freight charges constitute 60 per cent. of the total cost to dealers in Alberta, Saskatchewan and Manitoba, says the resolu' tion, while the Ontario and Quebec freight charges swallow up 70 per cent. of the price of retailers. In an effort to reduce the cost of construction, says the resolution, manufacturers have lowered selling prices until today they are 60 per cent. below prices prevailing in September 1920. Wages have been reduced by an average of 40 per cent., it is declared.

## Airplanes for Manitoba Forest Patrol

Manitoba will have a fleet of five airplanes next summer, two or three of which will be able to carry at least 10 passengers, to patrol the forest areas and perform various other duties for the dominion government officers in the province. Several machines are being erected and overhauled, while two large F-3 seaplanes were expected early in spring from British Columbia. Duties of the air fleet, besides patroling forest regions to detect fires, will include the conveying of officials who will pay treaty money to the Indians in the northlands, and the rendering of assistance in the government reclamation survey of the Carrot River district.

## Shingle Producers in Big Corporation

Shingle manufacturers of British Columbia have formed a $600,000 corporation known as the British Columbia Consolidated Shingle Manufacturers, Limited. Foreign as well as local markets will be supplied. Headquarters of the company will be in Vancouver.

One of the features of this corporation is that a maximum limit of 10 per cent. a year is placed on the cash dividends the directors can pay to stockholders. Arrangements are made, however whereby extra profits above the 10 per cent. will be paid to shareholders in the form of extra shares instead of cash.

## Death of Mr. Henry Marsh

Henry Herbert Marsh, of Grimsby, Ont., died in the Hamilton General Hospital on January 27th, in his 54th year. Mr. Marsh had been suffering for some time previous to going to the hospital and his demise followed an operation. He was born in Winona, being the eldest son of Daniel Marsh. After leaving school, he worked for many years in his father's planing mill at Grimsby Park and also assisted in the construction of many buildings put up by his father. He was a member for twelve years of the town council of Grimsby, being reeve last year, and was in a great measure responsible for much of the progress and prosperity of the town. Mr. Marsh leaves to mourn his death, his widow, one son and three daughters, as well as his father and several brothers and sisters.

## Brunette Sawmills Suffer Big Loss

Fire did heavy damage, recently, to the Brunette Sawmills at Sapperton, B. C. The sawmill and planing mill were completely destroyed. By attacking the conflagration from both land and water the sheds and the lumber piles were saved. The box factory had a narrow escape, but was not seriously damaged.

The night watchman first detected the flames near the boiler room and turned in the alarm. The blaze was well under way then and herculean efforts prevented it from spreading to the little town of Sapperton. The flames were almost beyond control when the first streams of water were plied, being fanned by a strong wind from the river.

## Will Do the Cutting—Not Selling

Writing to the "Canada Lumberman," a rural manufacturing dealer in lumber, lath and shingles, who does business in Western Ontario; says,—"The rise in the price of lumber is not much excuse or agreement to continue at the present time. I do not intend to take out a manufacturer's license this year as there is very little timber to buy in this locality. If I sold only $5.00 worth of timber in a month I would have to go to town and send 10 cents sales tax to the Govern' ment and pay 25 or 50 cents to some other person to sign an affidavit. If I buy standing timber and hire men to cut it, the Workmen's Com' pensation Board calls for about five per cent. of the wages paid. The farmers seem able to avoid all this expense. In future I intend to do customs sawing only and let farmers sell the lumber.

# Some New Thoughts on Retail Service

### Certain Practices Which Should be "Canned" by Yardman if He Wishes to Develop Trade

By W. Warren, Toronto

I am much interested in an article appearing recently in the "Canada Lumberman", under the heading: "What Constitutes Real Service." The word service, when applied to many businesses, is a misnomer and only too often a shield for cant, or dishonest transactions. "He profits most who serves best."

There is nothing in heaven or earth as wonderful as service. The happiest people in the world are those having something useful to do. One has made a genuine discovery when he has grasped the fact that joy is a thing that is linked fast with service.

This service idea that is permeating the world is the most potent and vital idea of the present day. Real genuine service is the only foundation on which to build a lasting business. It is the only thing able to bring us constant, recurring profitable patronage.

Courtesy and honorable dealings coupled with scientific knowledge are the principal ingredients which help to make efficient service.

Let us now run over some of the points requisite for our own peculiar needs in the lumber industry. To be in a position to render service we must be equipped and thoroughly organized. Each member of the organization must be expert and conversant with his share of the burden. To be in possession of such men we must first train them and having trained them, we must appreciate them, giving them credit for work well performed and encouragement for bigger and better achievement.

We cannot give efficient up-to-date service with obsolete equipment; the entire machine must be modern; a chain is as strong as its weakest link. Therefore, if the selling force is strong and the mill and the factory equipment weak, the former loses its power and the back pressure applied by the weaker sections brings it down to the level of the latter.

#### First Seen in Taking of Order

Service is first applied in the taking of an order. A large percentage of buyers of lumber and millwork do not know what they want, and are, therefore, at the mercy of the salesman. In cases of this kind it is our privilege to advise them as to the grades and kinds of material best suited for their needs and if possible effect a saving for the customer, although it may reduce the amount of the sale. This is service and salesmanship and, although the size of the order may be reduced, it has made a friend, and will bring recurring patronage. This friend and patron will advertise for us, in such a way to give results that no other form of publicity can accomplish.

Having arrived at this stage another equally important matter must be taken up namely: That of delivery. Many of our inexperienced customers view the lumber and woodworking business, generally, on a par with a hardware business, and think that we have only to turn to our shelves and send out the article forthwith. Most orders do contain a big percentage of stock run or standard material and there is no occasion for any delay in the delivery of same. Regarding the special orders such as detail moulding, sash, doors, frames, stairs panelling, veneered work, etc., we cannot be too careful in advising the buyer as to the length of time required to complete the work. Every day, salesmen are making absurd promises of early delivery, which they know cannot be fulfilled, simply to clinch an order. Consequently they and their houses are being branded as deceivers and brought into disrepute. What is the effect? The job is sometimes turned out in an incomplete state in an endeavour to pull up, sometimes at an enormous cost, owing to dislocations in its hurried trip through the mill or factory. The final result is a dissatisfied patron and a lost confidence, whereas the reverse would land the next order with a preference. A salesman who continues to sell in this way should be relieved of his duties; he is a misfit, a bill of expense, and of no commercial value.

Misrepresentation of grade is another despicable practice. To sell one class of material and ship something else is an act that will assuredly bring about chaos and dissatisfaction. If the goods shippd fall short of the customer's understanding, then we have lost a patron. If they exceed his expectation, then we have retained a patron and added, at least one more to our list. There is no advertising as effective as a satisfied customer.

There are many customers who do not ask for an estimate; they simply place themselves in our hands and trust us. Do we take un-

due advantage of these trusting customers, or do we give them the best that we can offer both in regard to price and goods?

Then regarding stocks, we cannot give service unless we have an adequate supply of all standard lines always on hand. It is our duty as well as our privilege to anticipate the customer's requirements and to be prepared for any exacting demands that he may advance. Too often we expect the buyer to be satisfied with anything we may have to offer and then wonder why he passes us by on the next occasion.

Quality is an important factor in the question of service. This applies in a greater sense in regard to factory products than to yard and mill. Do we give to our customer all that he is entitled to, or do we strip our work giving it to him in an incomplete form; in short, do we give him what he understood he should receive and what our own conscience tells us we should give him.

The summing up of service is, I think just this: Have an up-to-date supply of material on hand; an up-to-date sales force; an up-to-date manufacturing plant; an up-to-date shipping department, all honestly and honorably operated and I venture the opinion that results will be satisfactory.

#### New Departure in Saw Swages

E. C. Atkins & Co., of Indianapolis has always controlled the patents and manufactured the Pribnow Swage Shaper and now they are the sole manufacturers of it and the Pribnow Swage. They have put on the market a new roller-bearing swage which will be exceedingly interesting to the filer.

The roller-bearing feature embodied in the New Atkins Pribnow Swage for heavy duty work as shown in the sectional engraving has greatly increased the efficiency of the Swage.

The friction on the die is greatly reduced, which permits the die to act with great precision, thus producing the strongest possible working corner and with much less energy than is required to operate any other swage.

The roller-bearing as shown in the accompanying cut is placed between the eccentric die bushing and the swage block. As the die revolves forward under pressure the rollers (HSI) travel with the die-bearing. The cage (HS) is loosely mounted so as to travel with the rollers and hold them in place. The rollers travel forward more under pressure than they do on the reverse stroke of the die lever; so all the rollers come under pressure simultaneously, which insures

an even wear on all the rollers and also eliminates the head drag of the die bearings in the swage block which means long life to the die bearing and the swage block.

The swage die (WI has four working corners running from end to end. The die is mounted in a pair of eccentric bushings (WWI) above centre, so that the working edges in use has a perfect clearance and with no dead drag over the finished part of the tooth, thus allowing the die to swage clear through and produce a strong working corner with the least waste of steel.

It is a well known fact that a large die, while it puts up the strongest working corner, is hard to operate and especially when a large sleeve revolving with the die is used. This obstacle is entirely overcome by the roller-bearing.

The roller-bearing as shown in the cut in the efficiency of the swage nor does it weaken the swage block but it adds to the efficiency of the swage and it is claimed the saving effected in the wear of the Saw is of great importance.

---

Word has been received in the east of the death of Robert McMann, of the wholesale and retail lumber firm of Silliker & McMann, Halifax. He passed away from heart failure while on a business trip to Bridgewater, N.S. Mr. McMann who had not been in good health for some time was one of the brightest and most progressive lumbermen in the Maritime Provinces, and his passing is deeply regretted.

# Selling Price Should Be Based on Cost List

## Necessity for Uniform and Efficient System Applicable with Certain Modifications to all Plants Emphasized at Representative Gathering—Visit of Mr. Flint

An important gathering was held at the King Edward Hotel, Toronto, recently, consisting of representative woodworkers, to consider millwork costs and allied problems. There was a good attendance and much interest was taken in the proceedings.

The occasion was made all the more interesting by reason of the presence of W. P. Flint, of Chicago, secretary of the Millwork Cost Bureau. E. R. Eaton, of J. R. Eaton & Sons, Orillia, Ont., who is a Canadian director of the Millwork Cost Bureau, was responsible for the assembly and Walter C. Laidlaw of Toronto occupied the chair.

Mr. Flint, in his remarks, explained the aims and objects of the Millwork Cost Bureau, which is a co-operative body of sash, door and millwork manufacturers, organized to promote cost knowledge. Some eight years ago the idea originated when a dozen manufacturers in the woodwork line in the Middle States came together and engaged cost accountants to make a detailed study of cost work in each plant, and to agree upon a uniform and efficient system which would be applicable, with certain modifications, to all plants. Other woodworkers wanting to come in on these cost studies, the scheme was enlarged and the Millwork Cost Information Bureau, now known as the Millwork Cost Bureau, formed. Since then the membership has grown until it now embraces, 500 woodworkers in the United States and Canada.

The cost data issued by this organization is the composite average costs based on figures submitted by the 500 members. Cost exhibits, covering various classes of special millwork, are submitted by members. These are assembled, analyzed, the times studied and an average composite figure issued. Mr. Flint claimed that these composite costs were more representative than actual cost studies made in any one plant, and as such provided a better foundation on which to base prices.

The reason for this is that the cost of any job will be found to vary almost from day to day in each plant. One week the men will take so much time to do a certain piece of work. The next week they might do it in half the time or might take longer. Estimates based on such varying cost factors are of doubtful value. While estimates and prices based on the average costs taken from 500 plants are applied on a known standard.

### The Application of Overhead

There are many ways of applying overhead. Some add a percentage on lumber; others on labor, while still others on labor, plus material. Percentage is not the most equitable or the most accurate way to apply overhead. The machine may be operated by a 60 cent man one day and a 40 cent man the next. The actual overhead is the same in each case but the charge varies because it is applied as a percentage on the per-man hour rate. It costs practically as much to handle 1000 feet of oak as the same quantity of hemlock, yet if the overhead is applied as a comparison on value, the charge will be nearly three times as much in one case as in the other.

A better way is to divide the overhead. On lumber add a fixed charge per M feet to the f.o.b. price. If the material goes through the kiln, add a fixed kiln-drying charge per M. This gives the lumber cost at the factory door. In the plant add a fixed burden charge not percent, per man hour. This charge will vary for machine and cabinet men. Then for commercial burden add a percentage on the factory cost which really amounts to a fixed charge per dollar. Thus we have three definite units for applying burden,—unit per M feet, unit per man hour and unit per dollar on factory cost.

It has been found in studying the figures submitted by the members of the Millwork Cost Bureau that the average burdens are $5.30 per M for yard burden, $6.00 per M, kiln burden, 57 cents per hour machine burden and 34 cents an hour, bench burden, while the commercial burden averages 20 per cent on factory cost. The average wage paid is 60 cents per hour for machine labor and 66 cents per hour for bench labor, average set-up for sticker work, $1.32 net.

### Basing Prices on Standard Lists

Mr. Flint emphasized the value of basing prices and estimates on standard lists. A woodworker hires an estimator and hopes against hope that he has secured a man with almost supernatural knowledge so that he is enabled to estimate or guess not too high

so as not to lose the business, neither too low so that money will not be lost on the order. It is out of the question to expect one man to be able to keep in close touch with labor and material fluctuations on all classes of work. The better way is to have certain standard lists and for the manager to fix the price by instructing the estimator to add or subtract a certain percentage from the prices shown. These lists would be based on a definite cost factor. By figuring costs and then adding a profit, competition may be met in an intelligent manner, as if the business is considered desirable, the amount a person may cut before reaching the cost line, is definitely known.

Why should a woodworker hire an estimator and then gamble by backing him with his profits and even with his capital? It appears to be far more logical to establish certain known costs and then base the selling price on these figures and tell the estimator that these are the prices at which he must figure the material or the items in the various jobs. In this way the person with the most at stake is fixing the prices, not the estimator, who has little or nothing to lose.

The estimating course which is conducted in connection with the work of the Bureau, was described by Mr. Flint. This is a service to members, who may enrol a number of their employees. The work consists of a study of plans, the taking off of quantities and the application and use of Cost Book A and the universal price book. The student is given a thorough training in the taking off of material, in drawing up specifications and making out estimates as well as in the application of the Cost Book A, which is in reality a basic cost list for special millwork details.

In the general discussion which followed Mr. Flint's talk, the comparative cost estimates which have been appearing in recent issues of the "Canadian Woodworker," were used to show the lack of uniformity which exists as to the idea of cost and to the necessity for woodworkers giving greater attention to this end of their business. All present displayed a lively interest in the work of the Bureau and in the points outlined by Mr. Flint, and a number intimated their intention of becoming members.

### Toronto Lumberman Honored in the South

It is difficult to keep a good man down—or out of a job. J. B. Reid, of Toronto, Honorary President of the Ontario Retail Lumber Dealers Association, went to St Petersburg, Florida, three months ago to spend the winter and finds himself in office. A Canadian Club has just been formed in that city and Mr. Reid has been elected Vice President of the organization. He writes that he is bowling every morning and having a good time generally. Building is very brisk in St Petersburg and there is considerable house construction going on. Although the population of St. Petersburg is only 25,000 there are four hundred real estate agents there and values in property are climbing all the time, many Northern tourists purchasing lots for the erection of winter homes.

### Larger Quarters for B. C. Commission

L. L. Brown, B. C. Lumber Commissioner, whose permanent quarters are now located at 51 Yonge St., in the Commercial Travellers' Building, has a ground-floor space of over 1600 square feet. The lighting facilities are excellent and there will be fitted up in the building, a dining room, living room and sleeping apartment in which B. C. woods will be used to good effect. Furniture created from the different western woods and finished in a variety of styles, will lend a home-like appearance to the environs and afford visitors a practical demonstration of the merits, uses and adaptability of the forest products of the Pacific Coast provinces.

It is the intention of Mr. Brown to carry samples of all the different kinds of lumber, interior and exterior trim, etc., that are sold in the East, along with samples of grades, widths and thicknesses; in fact the showrooms of the B. C. Lumber Commissioner will contain a complete representation of everything that the eastern consumer, wholesaler or manufacturer would like to know. The western manufacturers have united whole-heartedly with Mr. Brown in preparing such an instructive and varied exhibit. It will be several weeks before all the interior arrangements are carried out owing to the great amount of detail work in hand.

# Worst Fire Season Encountered in Many Years

Frank I. Ritchie, Three Rivers, P.Q.

The annual meetings of the St. Maurice Forest Protective Association and the Southern St. Lawrence Forest Protective Association were held at the Windsor Hotel, Montreal, on January 25th.

At the meeting of the first named, Mr. F. I. Ritchie was elected President, and Mr. J. P. MacLaurin, Vice-President, with the following directors:— Messrs. F. Faure, F. I. Ritchie, Ellwood Wilson, J. M. Dalton, J. P. MacLaurin, Robert F. Grant and S. L. de Carteret.

The report of Mr. F. Faure, the retiring president, referred to the past season as the worst on record, as far as fires were concerned. In view of the large number of fires set by sportsman, nonmembers of organized clubs, Mr. Faure suggested that representations be made to the Provincial Government to have the fire laws amended, making it compulsory for every person entering the woods during the season of the year when there is a fire hazard, to carry permits issued by patrolmen. The cost of fire fighting during the past season was great. However, the cost of all operations of the Association including the fire fighting, did not exceed one cent per acre of the area patrolled.

In his report, M. H. Sorgius, the manager, added that the fire cost was more than the last ten years added together. Several fires burned for a period of over two months. The number of fires along the railroad was greatly reduced owing to the railway officials taking a more serious view of fire protection. There was no doubt that several fires were purposely set so as to give employment, but unfortunately, the Association could not discover the offenders. Several fires were caused by log drivers, jobbers, explorers, dam keepers,etc., all employees of members. During the past few years there had been a great improvement made in the precautions taken to prevent and fight fires caused by employees but there was still room for improvement. There was an indifference among some of the logging foremen, but this could be remedied by continuing to educate them as to the value of the forest.

### Had Trying Year With Fires

Like the St. Maurice Association, the Southern St. Lawrence Association reported a very trying year in connection with fires, Mr. D. C. T. Atkinson, the President, stating that the conditions were probably unequalled during the past fifteen years. Mr. J. D. Brule, the Manager of the Eastern division, reported a total area of 52,331 acres of forest land devastated by fire during 1921, of which 45,534 acres pertained to members and 6,797 acres to settlers. The losses on member's holdings were nearly 250% larger than those of last year, whilst on the other hand the losses on private lands (settlers' lands) were 250% less than last year. This showed that settlers were giving much more attention to their fires than ever before.

Mr. C. B. Guerin, Manager of the Western division stated that although more fires occurred in his district, the area affected was 60% less than in 1920. Regarding slash he expressed the opinion that the settlers should do the work in the summer instead of the spring, which would reduce the fire hazard.

The following officers were elected: Hon. President Mr. W. G. Power, President, Mr. D. C. T. Atkinson; Vice-President Western Division, Mr. S. L. De Carteret; Vice-President, Eastern Division, Mr. D. Champoux. Directors: Western Division, Messrs. R. B. Adams, W. G. Power, H. M. Wilson, A. Fraser, F. G. Quincy, E. L. Woods, E. A. Rockett, F. G. Moss, Eastern division: Angus McLean, W. Vetie, W. Russell, E. S. Holloway, H. Calhoun, G. C. Scott, F. M. Anderson, R. S. P Smyth.

# Woodlands Men Hear Bright Talk on Logging Methods

G. C. Piche, Quebec, P.Q.

This year's meeting of the Woodlands section of the Canadian Pulp and Paper Association, held on January 26, at the Windsor Hotel, Montreal, extended over two sessions. Mr. S. L. de Carteret presided.

At the first session, Mr. G. C. Piche, chief forester of the Province of Quebec,read a paper on "Observations on Practical Forestry n Sweden," the result of a trip he made last year. The paper dealt in a comprehensive way with conditions and methods in that country. Mr. Piche expressing admiration for many of the practices carried out there. It was, he said, interesting to note the forester had complete charge of the lumbering operations. The utilization of the trees aimed to be as conservative as practical. The stumps were very low, not more than half a foot in height.

The Swedish foresters took great pain in carrying their operations in every district and sub-district, so as to remove as quickly as possible all the over mature stands as well as trees which might be damaged by fire, insects or fungi. He was surprised to see how few trees were affected by insects or by fungi. The explanation was found in the fact that dead trees, as well as straggling trees, which are regular hosts for parasites, were always removed in the course of the operation, instead of being left behind. The Swedes were very thorough in their fire prevention methods, everyone co-operating to prevent fires.—As to precautions taken to avoid the brushing of logs in the passing of falls and rapids, the Swedes did not hesitate to make a long sluice to float logs where there was danger of their suffering breakage at the ends.

Furthermore, they were not afraid of making logs as long as possible, whereas, in Canada operators stuck to the small sizes as the average length of the logs made on the Crown lands in Canada was about twelve foot, the overlength of six inches, represented as much as 5% of the total cut. In other words, every year, fifty million feet of good lumber was wasted during the driving operations. In sorting logs, care was taken so that logs of the same diameter could be sawn at the same time. They even divided them into half inch classes, that was to say logs of say 5½ inches in diameter would be brought at the same time to the conveyor of the saw mill, and directed to the same gang saw. They claimed that in this manner they do not need to readjust the width of the saws as in Canadian mills. They had made careful studies of the output which could could be realized by various methods of sawing and with logs of every size. They fixed up their saws once for all, and when they were through with the logs of one diameter class, they started the operations for another group of logs. The machinery was well made, very solid, and though the general handling of the logs and boards was not made as fast as in Canadian mills, their sawing was certainly A-1. The pieces were edged, carefully, but not immediately trimmed to the standart length; they were sent to the loading piles, and it was only when they were ready to be shipped that they were trimmed to the desired lengths.

If Canada, concluded Mr. Piche, was to compete successfully with, Sweden, our people must protect the forest, eliminate fires make a thorough inventory of our resources and reclaim all waste lands by judicious plantations. The Government and lumbermen must co-operate in forestry matters. Lumbering operations must be carried on more economically by cutting out waste in the forests and keeping the forests clean. The programme was ambitious, but it could be carried out.

R. C. Farrow, who has offices in the Dominion Bank Building, Vancouver, has been appointed western representative of the Larkin Lumber Co., wholesale lumber dealers, Toronto.

Joseph Kaake, lumberman and farmer, who resided near Clarksburg, Ont., died recently. He was working near his barn at the time when he suffered a stroke and fell unconscious in the snow where he was found by his daughter. Mr. Kaake who was sixty years of age, passed away shortly after.

# Pulp and Paper Men in Annual Session

### George M. McKee, Donnacona, Que., is New President —Retiring Secretary Dawe Highly Honored

George M. McKee, Donnacona, P.Q.

Geo. M. McKee, general manager of Donnacona Paper Company, Quebec, is the new president of the Canadian Pulp and Paper Association, with H. F. E. Kent vice-president of the Kinleith Paper Company, Toronto, vice-president. The appointments were made at the annual meeting held at the Ritz Carlton Hotel, Montreal, on January 27.

In his retiring presidential address Percy B. Wilson referred to the difficulties of the past year. He stated that a falling market and a decreasing demand almost at the outset of the year found the industry with high-priced inventories, excessive labor costs, abnormal transportation charges and burdensome taxation to contend with. Liquidation of such of these items as it had been within their power to bring about had necessarily been slow. As to the others, they had been powerless to secure readjustment which the circumstances called for and which must follow before the industry was once more upon a firm foundation. A very considerable contributing cause of the present difficulties resulted from the attitude taken by the different price-fixing authorities in Canada and the United States which, from 1917 to 1920, undertook, under government authority, to regulate the conditions under which they were permitted to carry on business. The fact demonstrated once more the fallacy of arbitrary interference with the recognized and established laws of trade. The outlook had distinctly improved, and they could look forward to the future with confidence. The present high freight rates on pulp and other materials were detrimental to the industry, especially in view of trans-Atlantic ocean rates enjoyed by European competitors.

The reports of the various sections were adopted. These dealt with the difficulties of the past year and prospects to the current 12 months.

Ellwood Wilson requested the executive council to consider an application by the Woodlands section for the appointment of a secretary pointing out that the supply of wood was fundamental in the existance of the industry, and that a trained engineer as secretary of the section would be of advantage to the members. Mr. Wilson, went on to discuss the relations of members of the industry with the governments of Ontario and Quebec. He remarked that there was a divergence of aim between the members of the Association and lumbermen. The latter were seeking immediate profits, whereas the pulp and paper industry took a longer view of the situation. When it came to representations to Governments on the question of legislation, the representation was largely in the hands of lumbermen. It was, as believed absolutely necessary, if the association desired to take care of the Woodlands end of the industry, that legislative bodies should have the attention of the members. It was useless to complain after legislation had been passed. He had recently interviewed the Ontario and Quebec Governments on the subject of closer relations, and found Hon. Mr. Bowman responsive to the idea. Mr. Wilson suggested the appointment of advisory committees for both provinces, with representatives of the Lumbermen's Association and the pulp and paper interests. Such committees could consult with the Government as occasion demanded. The Woodlands section had been asked to meet with representatives of the Quebec Limits Holders' Association to go into the question. It was essential that the members of any committee should be men of standing.

It was decided to refer both questions raised by Mr. Wilson to the executive council.

### Mr. Dawe Given Gold Watch

A. L. Dawe, who recently resigned as secretary, was presented with a gold watch, many compliments being paid Mr. Dawe for his tact and services during the five years he was secretary.

At the luncheon which followed, Hon. H. Mercier, Minister of Lands and Forests, outlined the policy of the Quebec Government, in the matter of reforestation. It was intended, he said to commence the work very soon, and asked for the co-operation of the private owner. The Government hoped to plant a tree for every one that was cut; and legislation would be introduced to encourage individual effort. Mr. Mercier also hinted of possible legislation to stop the evasion of the law prohibiting the export of pulpwood from Crown lands, as evasion carried out by sending pulpwood into the States via other provinces.

### Great Storm Levelled Many Trees

James Ludgate, of Pakesley, Ont., manager of the Schroeder Mills & Timber Co., in a recent communication to the "Canada Lumberman", says they had a very severe storm in that section during the latter part of December. Many of the larger trees with stiffer boles were stripped bare of limbs. This was particularly noticeable in the birch and elm. The more slender trees were bent right over until their tops touched the ground. They were frozen there and are still in that position Mr. Ludgate says the storm did not affect the pine very much nor any of the evergreens, the birch and elm being the principle sufferers. Fortunately the storm was confined, it did not create much havoc except for more than ten miles north south of Pakesley, but it went thirty to forty miles west.

The Schroeder Mill & Timber Co. have 24,000,000 feet of logs this year, half of which they will be offering for sale at the mouth of the French River and Key Harbor on the Georgian Bay. During the early week in February they were watering 15,000 to 20,000 pieces every day and expected to have to continue this all through the month to get the timber out. The company have several two-trip hauls in connection with their work.

### Wholesale Lumber Firm Changes Name

J. L. McCormack, of Hamilton, Ont., who since the death of his partner, Roy Stewart, which took place about a year ago, has been conducting the business of McCormack & Stewart, has secured entire control and changed the name of the organization to the McCormack Lumber Co. The offices are still maintained in the Bank of Toronto Building, Hamilton, and the McCormack Lumber Co. will continue to specialize in jack pine, spruce, hemlock, white pine, shingles, lath and cedar posts. Mr McCormack reports that the outlook for business is improving and looks for trade generally to pick up within the next few weeks. Wilbur Stewart, a brother of the late Roy Stewart, is travelling for the firm and meeting with good success on the road.

### Heavy Snow Falls Retarding Log Hauling

Recent advices received from Northern Ontario state that the pulpwood situation has not changed very much during the past month. Prices remain about the same for dry and peeled wood but are strengthening for rough, unpeeled spruce owing to the Temiskaming Pulp & Paper Co., of Haileybury, entering the field for about 10,000 cords of rough wood for their pulp plant at Dixon Creek, which is nearing completion.

The hauling of pulpwood, ties and lumber was retarded during January due to the deep snow and continued storms. Not one week passed without it being necessary to plough out the roads two to four times. The last few days of the month were, however, ideal for drawing. When the snow was deep, the weather was mild. The roads are packed down in good shape and now have a good bottom. The snow is, however, so deep on both sides of the road that a very little snow will tie things up unless a mild spell of weather came first.

There will be very little more lumber or pulpwood cut in the Haileybury district for the remainder of the season owing to the heavy fall which from Latchford to Englehart is about three feet and north of there averages at least one foot more.

A lumberman from Haileybury, in conversation with the "Canada Lumberman" the other day regarding output, said:—

"The production of lumber from Latchford to Englehart will not exceed 3,000,000 feet and over two-thirds of this will be required for the northern market. This is being manufactured as follows, about 200,000 feet around Cobalt, about 300,000 feet at Haileybury, about 500,000 feet at New Liskeard; Uno Park about 400,000 feet, the Elk Lake branch about 1,200,000 feet, and the Charlton branch 400,000 feet. This does not include logs taken out for summer sawing.

"Toronto wholesalers have been showing an interest in this market for the past few days, but very little stock has been sold except for immediate delivery.

"Everything points to a very good year up here in the building line, especially at Englehart, Cochrane and Kirkland Lake, and the general opinion of the manufacturers is that prices will be at least $4.00 per thousand higher by the middle of April."

## Selling Flooring Over the Counter

### Centrally Located Store in Hamilton Kept Busy Taking Orders From Citizens Far and Near

An innovation in the way of retailing hardwood flooring, interior trim, etc., was inaugurated in Hamilton, Ont., nearly a year ago by the Consumers' Lumber Co., of that city, who in conjunction with the Seaman, Kent Co., Limited, Toronto, manufacturers of hardwood flooring, decided to rent a ground-floor store centrally located at 109 King St. West, and carry samples and generally develop business by giving a service affording facilities that are quite unusual in disposing of wood products. Fred C. Watson, of the Consumers' Lumber Co., was placed in charge of the new establishment, with a competent lady assistant.

The front of the establishment is painted yellow, and in the window are displayed samples of "Beaver Brand" flooring, along with different panels. In the store there are various panels, resting on easels, which serve to acquaint all customers with the different grades of flooring, the kinds shown being clear maple, clear birch, clear plain oak, clear quarter cut and clear beech, while on the reverse side are representations of the same kind of material in No. 1 grade. Estimates are cheerfully given for furnishing the material or for both furnishing and laying hardwood floors in any house, apartment, block, warehouse, etc..

Of particular interest to private citizens is this retail shop. There come over the phone each day many questions regarding the price and product handled. These are followed up personally by Mr. Watson, who not only takes measurements but gives advice and estimates of what the work will cost either in single rooms or for a house complete. In the telephone inquiries received or by personal calls, prices on any line of lumber required for building purposes are cheerfully given.

In the store there is stocked and sold, waxes, fillers, varnishes, shellac, kleen floor and other lines so much in demand.

It may be said that all the flooring is disposed of in Hamilton by face measure, and workmen charge 15 cents per square foot for laying tongue and groove flooring and 20 cents for square edge flooring. Of recent months one of the leading lines sold has been ¾ plain red oak. There is also a good call for birch and maple.

Many old houses in the city are being modernized and relaid with hardwood floorings, and in this respect the store at 109 King St. West has served a very useful purpose. The idea was largely experimental at first but the Consumers' Lumber co., say that the results have been so satisfactory that they may extend the service and carry more representative lines in the way of interior and exterior trim, doors, panels, etc. At present, there is in the office a beaver board partition, showing a French window with three-piece plate rail, chair rail, steps, built-up newel post, hand-rail, balastrade, etc. These are all in chestnut, which appears to be leading just now in the interior finish of moderately priced dwellings.

There was shown in the window during the Christmas holidays a miniature church built of lath. This structure was lighted up and attracted considerable attention. It was a perfect model of one of the sacred edifices which is being built in the Ambitious City, and was the handicraft of M. B. Zimmerman, of the Consumers' Lumber Co. From the display of this model at a public gathering no less than $500 was raised toward the building fund. Naturally, the presence of the miniature structure called attention to the home-building requisites handled by the Consumers' Lumber Co., and the Seaman, Kent Co., at 109 King St. West.

The idea behind this service store for retailing hardwood flooring and interior trim appears to be a good one, and it will, no doubt, be developed in the future along wider lines. The day may come when lumber will, figuratively speaking, be sold over the counter; at least there may be stores opened up in central localities by retail lumber dealers where facilities will be afforded, not only for the examination of the goods which the ordinary user of wood requires and likes to see and examine, but prices, estimates and other information that is usually desired on such an occasion, may be furnish on the spot.

### Will Look After Legislation More Keenly

From the statement made by Mr. Ellwood Wilson at the annual meeting of the Canadian Pulp & Paper Association, it is evident that members of the Woodlands section are awaking to the importance of watching legislation, thus following the example of the Canadian Lumbermen's Association, which has made a point of closely following measures affecting the lumber industry and of acting promptly. The members of the Woodlands Section, which include lumbermen, have hitherto devoted their chief attention to other matters, but it is now the intention to look after legislation more keenly.

The Section is particularly interested in such questions as stump-age dues, forest protection, and re-afforestation, and as the Quebec Government intend to bring in bills dealing with the two last named subjects affecting the interest of pulp and paper companies and also of lumbermen, there is an opportunity for co-operation with the Government, which has shown its willingness to work with the two industries. Indeed, in a speech at the luncheon of the Pulp and Paper Association, Hon. H. Mercier, Minister of Lands and Forests, declared that it was not only advisable but necessary that the leaders in the lumber and pulp industries of the Province should confer with his department when any vital changes or improvements were contemplated. For that reason, he was glad that the Association contemplated making provision through a committee for such pouparlers. The Quebec Government has shown that it is alive to the paramount value of the industries, which provide substantial revenues and also give employment for thousands of men in all parts of the Province. As to the Ontario Government, Mr. Bowman assured Mr. Wilson that he welcomes the co-operation of the proposed advisory committees.

The idea is to get into closer touch with the Governments of Quebec and Ontario, to cement the relations with the departments, and to secure the aid of the Lumbermen's Association and the Province of Quebec Limit-Holders Association through representation on the advisory committees. As owners of immense limits, members of the Woodlands Section will thus be in a better position to scrutinize legislation which adversely affects theis interests. It is no use complaining after Acts of Parliament have been passed, the time to act is when the measures are proposed or introduced. The advisory committees will provide the necessary means for action and will also form representative bodies which can be consulted by the Governments as occasion demands.

### Mr. Scully Enters Upon New Duties

C. J. Scully, who for the last eleven years has been mill superintendent in the Pembroke Lumber Co., Pembroke, Ont., has joined the sales staff of the Waterous Engine Works Co., Limiter, Brantford, Ont., and will look after the territory formerly covered by A. J.

C. J. Scully, Pembroke, Ont.

Wallace, from Pembroke, North Bay, Sault Ste Marie, Cochrane and as far west as Port Arthur.

Mr. Scully has gained a wide experience in the sawmilling business, having been in the employ of the "Clergue Syndicate" at Sault Ste. Marie, for four years, where he was in charge of the "cutting-up process" in the sulphite and sawing departments. From the Soo he went to the St. Anthony Lumber Co., at Whitney, Ont., and for ten years was employed as sawyer and millwright. Then he was with the Golden Lake Lumber Co., where he remained for a period of two years. His next post was as mill superintendent of the Pembroke Lumber Co.

Mr. Scully has made a wide circle of friends in the industry and, possesses a thorough knowledge of sawmill equipment.

### Many Logs Lost on Journey to Mills

In the Timber Inquiry conducted in Ontario, some interesting facts were brought out with respect to the logs that are sunk in the streams on their way to the mills in Northern Ontario. It was stated by Col. Thomas Gibson, of the Spanish River Pulp & Paper Co., that an allowance of 10% was made for sinkage. In one year the Spanish River Co., had to write off 30,000 cords of pulpwood for which it had paid. He admitted that a number of the logs might be hauled out of the rivers when the water is low, but a good many, on which Crown dues had been paid, were never recovered by the companies.

One of the many novel displays of building materials at the annual convention of the Western Retail Lumbermen's Association.

# Better Business is Keynote of 1922 Convention of Western Retail Lumbermen's Association

With more than 400 lumbermen from all sections of the prairie provinces in attendance, the thirty-first annual convention of the Western Retail Lumbermen's Association opened on Jan. 25th in Winnipeg, under favorable conditions. No sign of the reported pessimistic feeling was in evidence, to the contrary every man present was filled with a determination to make a special bid for business during 1922, even if conditions generally were not as favorable as they might be.

The general opinion among the delegates was that this annual parliament of the retail lumber dealers of the West was bigger and better than ever from every point of view. President, Theo. A. Sparks and Secretary Fred Ritter received a flood of sincere congratulations upon the quality of the program.

The addresses were well calculated in their subject to inspire the delegates to put forth their best efforts this year, while in the belief that all work and no play is not good for any man, the business sessions were made short and snappy and an excellent program of entertainment provided for the visitor.

President Theo. Sparks, in his annual address, dealt fully and frankly with the situation as it really is. Among many interesting subjects the president spoke on the practical topic of "Credits and Collections and the cost of Doing Business," in which he said in part; "Unquestionably the next few years will see many changes in ours as well as in other businesses as a direct result of the survival of the fittest, which will apply as it has never done before during the life of the industry. As to whether your business is absorbed by others by virtue of necessity, or even suffers a worse fate, is going to depend largely upon your exact knowledge possessed of it, and the more careful analysis being made of cost of conducting it, with the consequent stoppage of waste in its operation.

"In closing the president made a strong appeal to the Association.

Some of the new directorate of the Western Retail Lumbermen's Association. Front Row—D. Sutherland, Camrose, Alta.; W. F. Dutton, Winnipeg, Man. (President); R. Shaw, High River, Alta., (vice-president); Fred. W. Ritter, secretary-treasurer. Back Row—A. J. Malsted, Domremy, Sask.; R. Fletcher, Hanna, Alta.

"There is another matter which I hesitate to mention, in view of the loyal support given your Association in the past, by the Prairie Lumber Dealers, namely the necessity for their continued support in the year we are just entering. The centralizing influence of your Association is to my mind, of far greater importance at the present time than ever before. While I have every confidence in the members of the industry maintaining that support, I feel it would be a positive calamity to ourselves in the face of restricted business, if the membership were not maintained, through any false desire to economize."

Secretary Fred W. Ritter in submitting his annual report unfolded many encouraging subjects. In opening, he said; "Even in the face of unexpected, disappointing and most peculiar conditions, we have carried on stronger and with more determination than ever, with the result that during the past year the association has gained twenty new members and has a financial statement which no one will be ashamed to own.

Mr. Ritter reviewed the year's business and reported on the different enterprises of the association and their progress; the building department and its importance; the association training course; the 1922 plan book and its preparation; advertising cut book; and other social and business activities.

### Instructive Addresses Delivered

Many interesting addresses were delivered during the course of the convention by visitors and members, which were received with much appreciation. Roy G. Roberts, Credit Manager, Monarch Lumber Co., gave the conclusions that the Association Committee on Credits and Collections had arrived at:

(1) That, though the country is more heavily indebted than at any time heretofore, a uniform credit policy is required to serve the interests of the country.

(2) That absolute cash trading should be adopted from November 1st to March 1st in each year as same would not prejudice the interests of the communities and would facilitate collections.

(3) That, as the figures obtained by the Association prove the average outstanding per yard is $16,000.00 and that the estimate turnover per yard during 1921 was not more that $16,000.00 a restricted credit policy must be adopted.

(4) That uniform regulations are essential to the best interests of the trade in order to eliminate destructive competition in the matter of credit.

(5) That the use of financial statements is absolutely necessary in order that the lumber yard manager may be in receipt of sufficient knowledge of the facts to exercise good judgment in the extension of credit.

Parsons Simpkins, of Salt Lake City, Utah, gave two snappy addresses on "Better Organization of Business—Why? and "Toward Morning— A Business Outlook."

Andrew E. Hay, General Sales Manager, Pratt & Lambert manufacturers of varnishes, Bridgeburg, Ont., gave an edifying talk on "The Art of Selling."

A. K. Leitch, president of the Mountain Lumber Manufacturers Association reviewed the activities of the past year and told of the resolutions his Association had endorsed, among which, was the resolve to combat the high freight rates.

### Lower Freight Rates Advocated

The most important resolution passed by the delegates at the annual convention of the Western Retail Lumbermen's Association was that urging lower freight rates on all farm products, lumber and coal. The resolution follows:

(1) Whereas the farmers and general public of the Western Provinces are suffering depressed conditions, aggravated by heavy cost of marketing everything produced or raised on the farms and the high cost of bringing in all of the commodities required to carry on farming, and

(2) Whereas the price of commodities produced or raised in the Prairie Provinces are down to pre-war prices,and

(3) Whereas the present excessive freight rates are hampering the revival of business and creating unemployment, and

(4) Whereas lower freight rates on farm products, lumber and coal are most essential to relieve the depressed and stifled conditions of the farming industry, and

(5) Whereas the freight rates on lumber are 50 per cent higher than pre-war rates while the prices of all commodities raised in the Prairie Provinces are down to pre-war prices.

Wherefore be it resolved that the Western Retail Lumbermen's Association in convention assembled request and urge that the railway companies of Canada be required to reduce freight tariffs on all farm products and coal, and restore lumber freight rates to at least those in effect prior to September 1920.—Further be it resolved that copies of this resolution be forwarded to the Railway Companies, Hon. McKenzie King, Hon. T. A. Crerar, Hon. Arthur Meighan and the chairman of the Railway Commission.

What is classed as the best program yet originated for the entertainment of the delegates was a feature of the 31st Annual convention. Much credit is due to Fred Ritter whose intiring efforts had much to do with the fund of pleasure visiting lumbermen had while in Winnipeg.

The crowning achievement was the party and ball at the Fort Garry Hotel on the Thursday evening under the auspices of the wholesale lumbermen's Association, the planing mill operators, and the W. R. L. A. A record attendance was noted, and more than 800 guests being present. Immediately after supper, paper caps, streamers, horns, rattles, etc., were distributed to the dancers, which added much to the jollity of the evening. It has been the custom of the lumbermen to stage a Ball at each annual convention, but this year surpassed all others, both for attendance and brilliancy.

"Just ordinary routine business was transacted at the annual meeting of the Retail Lumbermen's Mutual Fire Insurance Company." stated the secretary, Allan Stewart.

Mr. Stewart says that the company had a very good year, more than $1,630,000 of additional insurance having been written during 1921.

The only change in the officials of the company being that G. F. Robertson was appointed to the directorate.

**Officers For 1922**

The election of officers for 1922 were as follows:—

President; W. P. Dutton, Winnipeg: Vice-President; R. Skov, High River, Alta. Directors:— R. Fletcher, Hanna, Alta; J. A. Sutherland,Camrose, Alta.; F. E. Sine,; Calgary. Alta.; H. G. Molstad, Domremy, Sask.; A. G. Sanborn, Avonlea, Sask.; J. Rutley, Regina, Sask.; Donald Kanantz, Winnipeg; J. H. McKaig, Portage la Prairie, Man.; L. Northrop, Winnipeg.

In accepting office President Dutton paid high tribute to the sterling qualities of the retiring president, Theodore A. Sparks, who had well and faithfully served the association through two of the most trying and strenuous years of its history.

---

# LAST MINUTE NEWS OF THE TRADE

## American Lumber Congress in April

Many delegates have been appointed and others are now being appointed by state, regional and national organizations of manufacturers, retailers and wholesalers, to attend the Fourth American Lumber Congress in Chicago, April 6 and 7.

A tentative general outline of matters to be considered by the Lumber Congress has been prepared by Mr. Wilson Compton and sent to a number of individuals and organizations for further suggestions. In a general way it is contemplated that the Lumber Congress shall consider:—

First, matters relating to publicity, national and local advertising, building codes and trade extension;

Second, matters relating to terms and conditions of sale and arbitration of disputes;

Third, lumber grades and sizes; inspection;

Fourth, recommendation for permanent organization of the American Lumber Congress.

---

## Mr. McRae Buys Mill at Whitney

J. S. M. McRae, of Barry's Bay, Ont., was in Toronto recently calling upon the trade. He is a well-known young lumberman in the Ottawa Valley district and for several years operated a sawmill at Madawaska. Recently he purchased the mill of Mickle, Dyment & Son, located just outside of Whitney, and will put it in operation this spring. It is equipped with two double-cut band saws, a resaw, lath department and all other accessories of an up-to-date plant with a productive capacity of about 75,000 feet a day.

Mr. McRae has two camps of his own, and two jobbers working for him this season and will take out a considerable larger quantity of timber than a year ago. He anticipates his cut during 1922 will be about 3,000,000 feet of hemlock, 2,500,000 feet of spruce and 500,000

feet of pine. He owns 130 square miles of timber limits, and believes that the coming year will witness a great improvement in business.

## How Fire Eats up Growing Timber

Declaring that fire had destroyed ten trees in Canada for every one felled by the woodman's axe, Robson Black, manager of the Canadian Forestry Association, urged upon the members of the Rotary Club in Ottawa the necessity for adequate fire protection throughout the Dominion. It was a question, he said, which should take precedence over all others that agitated politicians generally.

Stressing the value of the timber resources of the country Mr. Black declared that 80 per cent of the habitable area of Canada was timber land. Referring again to the forest fire evil he declared that one fire in Ontario last year had destroyed enough white pine to keep a certain well-known mill supplied for 56 years.

## Mr. Barnjum is Encouraging Forestry

In order to encourage reforestation in Nova Scotia, Mr. Frank J. D. Barnjum of Annapolis Royal, N. S., is offering a cash bonus of $2.00 per acre to the farmers of Nova Scotia for every acre of spruce or pine seedlings planted by them on their farms during the coming spring, no one farmer to be paid a bonus on more than 100 acres, so as to distribute the plantings as widely as possible over the Province. The location and method of planting must be approved by the Government Forester of Nova Scotia, if one is appointed, otherwise by Mr. Barnjum's forester, to insure satisfactory results.

A new lath mill has been started in Preston, Ont., by Harold Burke. Mr. Burke says his plant will turn out sufficient lath to supply the building trade of Waterloo County.

J. J. Vance, Cottam, Ont., is erecting a sawmill at a cost of $10,000. The building to be one-storey, 45 x 65 feet, and of frame construction.

---

# WHOLESALERS APPOINT STANDING COMMITTEES

At the first regular meeting of the newly elected Board of Directors of the Wholesale Lumber Dealers' Association, Inc. held on February 7th, at which the new chairman, H. J. Terry, presided, the following committees were elected for the year:

Admission and Membership:—A. C. Gordon (Chairman); R. B. Elgie and A. N. Dudley.

Attendance:—K. M. Brown (Chairman); G. Fleming and T. N. Phillips.

Audit and Finance:—A. E. Gordon, (Chairman); J. L. MacFarlane and Alex. Read.

Bureau of Information.—H. G. McDermid (Chairman); A. Leak and J. P. Johnson.

Fire and Marine Insurance:—W. C. Laidlaw (Chairman); J. B.

Jarvis and A. E. Cates.

Inspection:—W. E. Bigwood. (Chairman) (Ontario Pine), A. S. Nicholson (General and B. C.), John McBean (Hardwoods).

Legislation:—A. C. Manbert (Chairman), A. E. Eckardt, and W. C. Gall.

Transportation:—A .E. Clark (Chairman), R. Halliday and C. E. Harris.

Trade Relations:—Alfred Read, (Chairman); C. G. Anderson and H. W. Larkin.

Terms of Sale:—Hugh A. Rose (Chairman); W. J. Lovering and F. H. Horning.

Entertainment:—L. D. Barclay (Chairman); D. C. Johnston and K. M. Brown.

# CURRENT LUMBER PRICES—WHOLESALE

## TORONTO

(In Car Load Lots, F.O.B. cars Toronto)

**White Pine**

| | | |
|---|---|---|
| 1 x 4/7 Good Strips | $100.00 | $110.00 |
| 1¼ & 1½ x 4/7 Good Strips | 120.00 | 125.00 |
| 1 x 8 and up Good Sides | 150.00 | 160.00 |
| 2 x 4/7 Good Strips | 130.00 | 140.00 |
| 1¼ & 1½ x 8 and wider Good Sides | 185.00 | 190.00 |
| 2 x 8 and wider Good Sides | 190.00 | 200.00 |
| 1 in. No. 1, 2 and 3 Cuts | 75.00 | 80.00 |
| 5/4 and 6/4 No. 1, 2 and 3 Cuts | 95.00 | 100.00 |
| 2 in. No. 1, 2 and 3 Cuts | 105.00 | 110.00 |
| 1 x 4 and 5 Mill Run | 52.00 | 55.00 |
| 1 x 6 Mill Run | 53.00 | 56.00 |
| 1 x 7, 9 and 11 Mill Run | 53.00 | 56.00 |
| 1 x 8 Mill Run | 55.00 | 58.00 |
| 1 x 10 Mill Run | 60.00 | 62.00 |
| 1 x 12 Mill Run | 65.00 | 70.00 |
| 5/4 and 6/4 x 5 and up Mill Run | 58.00 | 60.00 |
| 2 x 4 Mill Run | 52.00 | 53.00 |
| 2 x 6 Mill Run | 53.00 | 56.00 |
| 2 x 8 Mill Run | 55.00 | 58.00 |
| 2 x 10 Mill Run | 58.00 | 62.00 |
| 2 x 12 Mill Run | 60.00 | 64.00 |
| 1 in. Mill Run Shorts | 43.00 | 45.00 |
| 1 x 4 and up 6/16 No. 1 Mill Culls | 30.00 | 32.00 |
| 1 x 10 and up 6/16 No. 1 Mill Culls | 34.00 | 36.00 |
| 1 x 12 and up 6/16 No. 1 Mill Culls | 35.00 | 37.00 |
| 1 x 4 and up 6/16 No. 2 Mill Culls | 23.00 | 25.00 |
| 1 x 10 x 12 6/16 No. 2 Mill Culls | 26.00 | 28.00 |
| 1 x 4 and up 6/16 No. 3 Mill Culls | 15.00 | 20.00 |

**Red Pine**

(In Car Load Lots, F.O.B. Toronto)

| | | |
|---|---|---|
| 1 x 4 and 5 Mill Run | $35.00 | $36.00 |
| 1 x 6 Mill Run | 38.00 | 40.00 |
| 1 x 8 Mill Run | 40.00 | 42.00 |
| 1 x 10 Mill Run | 42.00 | 44.00 |
| 2 x 4 Mill Run | 38.00 | 40.00 |
| 2 x 6 Mill Run | 40.00 | 42.00 |
| 2 x 8 Mill Run | 41.00 | 43.00 |
| 2 x 10 Mill Run | 44.00 | 47.00 |
| 2 x 12 Mill Run | 49.00 | 50.00 |
| 1 in. Clear and Clear Face | 69.00 | 71.00 |
| 2 in. Clear and Clear Face | 69.00 | 71.00 |

**Spruce**

| | | |
|---|---|---|
| 1 x 4 Mill Run | 35.00 | 36.00 |
| 1 x 6 Mill Run | 36.00 | 37.00 |
| 1 x 8 Mill Run | 38.00 | 40.00 |
| 1 x 10 Mill Run | 45.00 | 47.00 |
| 1 x 12 Mill Run Spruce | 48.00 | 50.00 |
| Mill Culls | 25.00 | 27.00 |

**Hemlock (M R)**

(In Car Load Lots, F.O.B. Toronto).

| | | |
|---|---|---|
| 1 x 4 and 5 in. x 9 to 16 ft | $26.00 | $27.00 |
| 1 x 6 in. x 9 to 16 ft | 33.00 | 35.00 |
| 1 x 8 in. x 9 to 16 ft | 34.00 | 36.00 |
| 1 x 10 and 12 in. x 9 to 16 ft | 35.00 | 37.00 |
| 1 x 7, 9 and 11 in. x 9 to 16 ft | 33.00 | 35.00 |
| 2 x 4 to 12 in., 18 ft | 37.00 | 39.00 |
| 2 x 4 to 12 in., 20 ft | 40.00 | 42.00 |
| 1 in. No. 2, 6 ft. to 16 ft | 23.00 | 25.00 |

**Fir Flooring**

(In Car Load Lots, F.O.B. Toronto)

| | | |
|---|---|---|
| Fir flooring, 1 x 3 and 4", No. 1 and 2 Edge Grain | | $73.00 |
| Fir flooring, 1 x 3 and 4", No. 1 and 2 Flat Grain | | 48.00 |
| (Depending upon Widths) | | |
| 1 x 4 to 12 No. 1 and 2 Clear Fir, Rough | $69.00 | 77.00 |
| 1¼ x 4 to 12 No. 1 and 2 Clear Fir, Rough | 77.00 | 81.00 |
| 2 x 4 to 12 No. 1 and 2 Clear Fir, Rough | 70.00 | 77.00 |
| 3 & 4 x 4 to 12 No. 1 & 2 Clear Fir, Rough | | 84.00 |
| 1 x 8 and 10 Fir Base | | 78.50 |
| 1¼ and 1½ 8, 10 and 12" E.G. Stepping | | 90.00 |
| 1¼ and 1½, 8, 10 and 12" F.G. Stepping | | 80.00 |
| 1 x 4 to 12 Clear Fir, D4S | | 72.50 |
| 1¼ and 1½ x 4 to 12, Clear Fir, D4S | | 75.25 |
| XX Shingles, 6 butts to 2", per M | | 3.00 |
| XXX Shingles, 6 butts to 2", per M | | 5.15 |
| XXXXX Shingles, 5 butts to 2", per M | | 6.10 |

**Lath**

(F.O.B. Mill)

| | |
|---|---|
| No. 1 White Pine | $11.00 |
| No. 2 White Pine | 10.00 |
| No. 3 White Pine | 8.00 |
| Mill Run White Pine, 32 in | 5.00 |
| Merchantable Spruce Lath, 4 ft | 6.50 |

## TORONTO HARDWOOD PRICES

The prices given below are for car loads f.o.b. Toronto, from wholesalers to retailers, and are based on a good percentage of long lengths and good widths, without any wide stock having been sorted out.

The prices quoted on imported woods are payable in U. S. funds.

**Ash, White**

(Dry weight 3800 lbs. per M. ft.)

| | 1s & 2s | No. 1 Com. | No. 2 Com. |
|---|---|---|---|
| 1" | $ 95.00 | $ 55.00 | $ 40.00 |
| 1¼ and 1½" | 100.00 | 60.00 | 40.00 |
| 2" | 105.00 | 65.00 | 50.00 |
| 2½ and 3" | 125.00 | 80.00 | 55.00 |
| 4" | 140.00 | 95.00 | 60.00 |

**Ash, Brown**

| | | | |
|---|---|---|---|
| 1" | $ 95.00 | $ 55.00 | $ 40.00 |
| 1¼ and 1½" | 100.00 | 60.00 | 40.00 |
| 2" | 105.00 | 65.00 | 50.00 |
| 2½ and 3" | 125.00 | 80.00 | 55.00 |
| 4" | 140.00 | 95.00 | 60.00 |

**Birch**

(Dry weight 4000 lbs. per M. ft.)

| | 1s & 2s | Sels. | No. 1 Com. | No. 2 Com. |
|---|---|---|---|---|
| 4/4 | $ 95.00 | $ 70.00 | $ 60.00 | $ 30.00 |
| 5/4 | 100.00 | 75.00 | 65.00 | 35.00 |
| 6/4 | 100.00 | 75.00 | 65.00 | 35.00 |
| 8/4 | 110.00 | 80.00 | 70.00 | 40.00 |
| 12/4 | 115.00 | 85.00 | 75.00 | 45.00 |
| 16/4 | 120.00 | 90.00 | 80.00 | 45.00 |

**Basswood**

(Dry weight 2500 lbs. per M. ft.)

| | 1s & 2s | No. 1 Com. | No. 2 Com. |
|---|---|---|---|
| 4/4 | $ 80.00 | $ 50.00 | $ 25.00 |
| 5/4 and 6/4 | 85.00 | 60.00 | 30.00 |
| 8/4 | 90.00 | 65.00 | 35.00 |

**Chestnut**

(Dry weight 2800 lbs. per M. ft.)

| | 1s & 2s | No. 1 Com. | Sound Wormy |
|---|---|---|---|
| 1" | $130.00 | $ 80.00 | $ 40.00 |
| 1¼" to 1½" | 135.00 | 85.00 | 43.00 |
| 2" | 145.00 | 90.00 | 43.00 |

**Maple, Hard**

(Dry weight 4200 lbs. per M. ft.)

| | F.A.S. | Sels. | No. 1 Com. | No. 2 Com. |
|---|---|---|---|---|
| 4/4 | $ 85.00 | $ 65.00 | $ 50.00 | $ 33.00 |
| 5/4 | 90.00 | 70.00 | 55.00 | 38.00 |
| 6/4 | 95.00 | 75.00 | 60.00 | 45.00 |
| 8/4 | 100.00 | 80.00 | 65.00 | 50.00 |
| 12/4 | 120.00 | 100.00 | 80.00 | 60.00 |
| 16/4 | 140.00 | 120.00 | 90.00 | 65.00 |

**Elm, Soft**

(Dry weight 3100 lbs. per M. ft.)

| | 1s & 2s | No. 1 Com. | No. 2 Com. |
|---|---|---|---|
| 4/4 | $ 75.00 | $ 50.00 | $ 25.00 |
| 6/4 and 8/4 | 80.00 | 60.00 | 30.00 |
| 12/4 | 96.00 | 70.00 | 35.00 |

**Gum, Red**

(Dry weight 3300 lbs. per M. ft.)

| | Plain 1s & 2s | Plain No. 1 Com. | Quartered 1s & 2s | Quartered No. 1 Com. |
|---|---|---|---|---|
| 1" | $125.00 | $ 73.00 | $133.00 | $ 83.00 |
| 1¼" | 135.00 | 75.00 | 148.00 | 88.00 |
| 1½" | 135.00 | 75.00 | 148.00 | 88.00 |
| 2" | 145.00 | 95.00 | 158.00 | 103.00 |

Figured Gum, $10 per M. extra, in both plain and quartered.

**Gum, Sap**

| | 1s&2s | No. 1 Com. |
|---|---|---|
| 1" | $ 58.00 | $ 40.00 |
| 1¼" and 1½" | 62.00 | 44.00 |
| 2" | 67.00 | 50.00 |

**Hickory**

(Dry weight 4500 lbs. per M. ft.

| | 1s&2s | No. 1 Com. |
|---|---|---|
| 1" | $120.00 | $ 60.00 |
| 1¼" | 145.00 | 65.00 |
| 1½" | 145.00 | 65.00 |
| 2" | 150.00 | 70.00 |

**Plain White and Red Oak**

(Plain sawed. Dry weight 4000 lbs. per M. ft.)

| | 1s&2s | No. 1 Com. |
|---|---|---|
| 4/4 | $120.00 | $ 75.00 |
| 5/4 and 6/4 | 130.00 | 80.00 |
| 8/4 | 135.00 | 85.00 |
| 10/4 | 145.00 | 90.00 |
| 12/4 | 145.00 | 90.00 |
| 16/4 | 150.00 | 95.00 |

**White Oak, Quarter Cut**

(Dry weight 4000 lbs. per M. ft.)

| | 1s&2s | No. 1 Com. |
|---|---|---|
| 4/4 | $160.00 | $ 90.00 |
| 5/4 and 6/4 | 170.00 | 95.00 |
| 8/4 | 190.00 | 105.00 |

**Quarter Cut Red Oak**

| | 1s&2s | No. 1 Com. |
|---|---|---|
| 4/4 | $145.00 | $ 80.00 |
| 5/4 and 6/4 | 160.00 | 90.00 |
| 8/4 | 165.00 | 95.00 |

**Beech**

The quantity of beech produced in Ontario is not large and is generally sold on a log run basis, the locality governing the prices. At present the prevailing quotation on log run, mill culls out, delivered in Toronto, is $35.00 to $40.00.

## OTTAWA

Manufacturers' Prices

**Pine**

| | | |
|---|---|---|
| Good sidings: | | |
| 1 in. x 7 in. and up | | $140.00 |
| 1¼ in. and 1½ in., 8 in. and up. | | 165.00 |
| 2 in. x 7 in. and up | | 165.00 |
| No. 2 cuts 2 x 8 in. and up | | 80.00 |
| Good strips: | | |
| 1 in. | $100.00 | $105.00 |
| 1¼ in. and 1½ in. | | 120.00 |
| 2 in. | | 125.00 |
| Good shorts: | | |
| 1 in. x 7 in. and up | | 110.00 |
| 1 in. 4 in. to 6 in. | 85.00 | 90.00 |
| 1¼ in. and 1½ in. | | 110.00 |
| 2 in. | | 125.00 |
| 7 in. to 9 in. A sidings | 54.00 | 56.00 |
| No. 1 dressing sidings | 82.00 | 85.00 |
| No. 1 dressing strips | | 78.00 |
| No. 1 dressing shorts | 68.00 | 73.00 |
| 1 in. x 4 in. s.c. strips | 56.00 | 58.00 |
| 1 in. x 5 in. s.c. strips | 56.00 | 58.00 |
| 1 in. x 6 in. s.c. strips | 63.00 | 65.00 |
| 1 in. x 7 in. s.c. strips | 63.00 | 64.00 |
| 1 in. x 8 in. s.c. strips, 12 to 16 ft. | 63.00 | 66.00 |
| 1 in. x 10 in. M.R. | 65.00 | 70.00 |
| S.C. sidings, 1½ and 2 in. | 63.00 | 67.00 |
| S.C. strips, 1 in. | | 64.00 |
| 1¼, 1½ and 2 in. | 57.00 | 58.00 |
| S.C. shorts, 1 x 4 to 6 in. | 48.00 | 50.00 |
| S.C. and bet., shorts. 1 x 5 | | 48.00 |
| S.C. and bet., shorts, 1 x 6 | | 50.00 |
| S.C. Shorts, 6'-11', 1" x 10" | 52.00 | 54.00 |
| Box boards: | | |
| 1 in. x 4 in. and up, 6 ft.-11 ft. | | 45.00 |
| 1 in. x 8 in. and up, 12 ft.-16 ft. | 50.00 | 53.00 |
| Mill culls, strips and sidings, 1 in. x 4 in. and up, 12 ft. and up | 43.00 | 45.00 |
| Mill cull shorts, 1 in. x 4 in. and up, 6 ft. to 11 ft. | 34.00 | 36.00 |
| O. culls r and w p | 24.00 | 28.00 |

**Red Pine, Log Run**

| | | |
|---|---|---|
| Mill culls out, 1 in. | 34.00 | 48.00 |
| Mill culls out, 1¼ in. | 34.00 | 48.00 |
| Mill culls out, 1½ in. | 35.00 | 47.00 |
| Mill culls out, 2 in. | 35.00 | 47.00 |
| Mill Culls, white pine, 1 in. x 7 in. and up | | 35.00 |

**Mill Run Spruce**

| | | |
|---|---|---|
| 1 in. x 4 in. and up, 6 ft.-11 ft. | | 25.00 |
| 1 in. x 4 in. and up, 12 ft.-16 ft. | 32.00 | 34.00 |
| 1" x 9"-10" and up, 12 ft.-16 ft. | 38.00 | 40.00 |
| 1¼" x 7, 8 and 9" up, 12 ft.-16 ft. | | 35.00 |
| 1¼ x 10 and up, 12 ft.-16 ft. | 38.00 | 42.00 |
| 1½" x 12" x 12" and up, 12'-16' | | 42.00 |
| Spruce, 1 in. clear fine dressing and B | | 55.00 |
| Hemlock, 1 in. cull | | 20.00 |
| Hemlock, 1 in. log run | 24.00 | 26.00 |
| Hemlock, 2 x 4, 6, 8, 10 12/16 ft. | | 28.00 |
| Tamarac | 25.00 | 28.00 |
| Basswood, log run, dead culls out | 45.00 | 50.00 |
| Basswood, log run, mill culls out. | 50.00 | 54.00 |
| Birch, log run | 45.00 | 50.00 |
| Soft Elm, common and better, 1, 1½, 2 in. | 58.00 | 68.00 |
| Ash, black, log run | 62.00 | 65.00 |
| 1 x 10 No. 1 barn | 57.00 | 62.00 |
| 1 x 10 No. 2 barn | 51.00 | 56.00 |
| 1 x 8 and 9 No. 2 barn | 47.00 | 52.00 |

# CURRENT LUMBER PRICES—WHOLESALE

**Lath per M.:**

| | | |
|---|---|---|
| No. 1 White Pine, 1¼ in. x 4 ft. . | | 8.00 |
| No. 2 White Pine | | 6.00 |
| Mill run White Pine | | 7.00 |
| Spruce, mill run, 1½ in. | | 6.00 |
| Red Pine, mill run | | 6.00 |
| Hemlock, mill run | | 5.50 |
| **White Cedar Shingles** | | |
| XXXX, 18 in. | 9.00 | 10.00 |
| Clear butt, 18 in. | 6.00 | 7.00 |
| 18 in. XX | | 5.00 |

## QUEBEC

**White Pine**
(At Quebec)

| | Cts. Per Cubic Ft. | |
|---|---|---|
| First class Ottawa wancy, 18 in. average according to lineal.... | 100 | 110 |
| 19 in. and up average | 110 | 120 |

**Spruce Deals**
(At Mill)

| | | |
|---|---|---|
| 3 in. unsorted, Quebec, 4 in. to 6 in. wide | $ 20.00 | $ 25.00 |
| 3 in. unsorted, Quebec, 7 in. to 8 in. wide | 26.00 | 28.00 |
| 3 in. unsorted, Quebec, 9 in. wide | 30.00 | 35.00 |

**Oak**
(At Quebec)

| | Cts. Per Cubic Ft. | |
|---|---|---|
| According to average and quality, 55 ft. cube | 125 | 130 |

**Elm**
(At Quebec)

| | | |
|---|---|---|
| According to average and quality, 40 to 45 ft. cube | 100 | 120 |
| According to average and quality, 30 to 35 ft. | 90 | 100 |

**Export Birch Planks**
(At Mill)

| | | |
|---|---|---|
| 1 to 4 in. thick, per M. ft. | $ 30.00 | $ 35.00 |

## ST. JOHN, N.B.

(From Yards and Mills)

**Rough Lumber**

Retail Prices per M. Sq. Ft.

| | | |
|---|---|---|
| 2x3, 2x4, 3x3, 3x4, Rgh Merch Spr | $32.00 | |
| 2x3, 2x4, 3x3, 3x4, Dressed 1 edge | 33.00 | |
| 2x3, 2x4, 3x3, 3x4, Dressed 4 sides | 33.00 | |
| 2x6, 2x7, 3x5, 4x4, 4x6, all rough. | 34.00 | |
| 2x8, 3x7, 5x5, 6x6 | 37.00 | $ 40.00 |
| 2x9, 3x8, 6x8, 7x7 | 37.00 | 40.00 |
| 2x10, 3x9 | 45.00 | |
| 2x12, 3x10, 3x12, 8x8 and up | 45.00 | |
| Merch. Spr. Bds., Rough, 1x3-4 & 5 | 30.00 | |
| Merch. Spr. Bds., Rough, 1x6 | 34.00 | |
| Merch. Spr. Bds., Rough, 1x7 & up | 40.00 | |
| Refuse Bds., Deals & Setgs. | 20.00 | 23.00 |

Above random lengths up to 18-0 long.
Lengths 19-0 and up $5.00 extra per M.
For planing Merch. and Refuse Bds. add $2.00 per M. to above prices.
Laths, $7.00.

**Shingles**

| | Per M. |
|---|---|
| Cedar, Extras | $6.25 |
| " Clears | 5.50 |
| " 2nd Clears | 4.50 |
| " Extra No. 1 | 2.90 |
| Spruce | 4.50 |

## SARNIA, ONT.

**Pine, Common and Better**

| | |
|---|---|
| 1 x 6 and 8 in. | $105.00 |
| 1 in., 8 in. and up wide | 125.00 |
| 1¼ and 1½ in. and up wide | 175.00 |
| 2 in. and up wide | 175.00 |
| **Cuts and Better** | |
| 4/4 x 8 and up No. 1 and better | 120.00 |
| 5/4 and 6/4 and up No. 1 and better | 145.00 |
| 8/4 and 8 and up No. 1 and better | 145.00 |
| **No. 1 Cuts** | |
| 1 in., 8 in. and up wide | 110.00 |
| 1¼ in., 8 in. and up wide | 120.00 |
| 1½ in., 8 in. and up wide | 120.00 |
| 2 in., 8 in. and up wide | 125.00 |
| 2½ in. and 3 in., 8 in. and up wide | 170.00 |
| 4 in., 8 in. and up wide | 180.00 |

| | | |
|---|---|---|
| **No. 1 Barn** | | |
| 1 in., 10 to 16 ft. long | $ 70.00 | $ 85.00 |
| 1¼, 1½ and 2 in., 10/16 ft. | 75.00 | 90.00 |
| 2½ to 3 in., 10/16 ft. | 80.00 | 95.00 |
| **No. 2 Barn** | | |
| 1 in., 10 to 16 ft. long | 68.00 | 77.00 |
| 1¼, 1½ and 2 in., 10/16 ft. | 68.00 | 80.00 |
| 2½, 1½ and 3 in. | 78.00 | 90.00 |
| **No. 3 Barn** | | |
| 1 in., 10 to 16 ft. long | 55.00 | 62.00 |
| 1¼, 1½ and 2 in., 10/16 ft. | 59.00 | 63.00 |
| **Box** | | |
| 1 in., 1¼ and 1½ in., 10/16 ft. | 40.00 | 42.00 |
| **Mill Culls** | | |
| Mill Run Culls— | | |
| 1 in., 4 in. and up wide, 6/16 ft. | | 30.00 |
| 1¼, 1½ and 2 in. | | 31.00 |

## WINNIPEG

**No. 1 Spruce**

| Dimension | S.1.S. and 1.E. 10 ft. | 12 ft. | 14 ft. | 16 ft. |
|---|---|---|---|---|
| 2 x 4 | $30 | $29 | $29 | $30 |
| 2 x 6 | 31 | 29 | 29 | 30 |
| 2 x 8 | 32 | 30 | 30 | 31 |
| 2 x 10 | 33 | 31 | 31 | 32 |
| 2 x 12 | 34 | 32 | 32 | 33 |

For 2 inches, rough, add 50 cents.
For S1E only, add 50 cents.
For S1S and 2E, S4S or D&M, add $3.00.
For timbers larger than 8 x 8, add 50c. for each additional 2 inches each way.
For lengths longer than 20 ft., add $1.00 for each additional two feet.
For selected common, add $5.00.
For No. 2 Dimension, $3.00 less than No. 1.
For 1 x 2 and 2 x 2, $2 more than 2 x 4 No. 1.
For Tamarac, open.

## BUFFALO and TONAWANDA

**White Pine**
Wholesale Selling Price

| | |
|---|---|
| Uppers, 4/4 | $225.00 |
| Uppers, 5/4 to 8/4 | 225.00 |
| Uppers, 10/4 to 12/4 | 250.00 |
| Selects, 4/4 | 200.00 |
| Selects, 5/4 to 8/4 | 200.00 |
| Selects, 10/4 to 12/4 | 225.00 |
| Fine Common, 4/4 | 155.00 |
| Fine Common, 5/4 | 160.00 |
| Fine Common, 6/4 | 160.00 |
| Fine Common, 8/4 | 160.00 |
| No. 1 Cuts, 4/4 | 115.00 |
| No. 1 Cuts, 5/4 | 130.00 |
| No. 1 Cuts, 6/4 | 135.00 |
| No. 1 Cuts, 8/4 | 140.00 |
| No. 2 Cuts, 4/4 | 70.00 |
| No. 2 Cuts, 5/4 | 100.00 |
| No. 2 Cuts, 6/4 | 105.00 |
| No. 2 Cuts, 8/4 | 110.00 |
| No. 3 Cuts, 5/4 | 60.00 |
| No. 3 Cuts, 6/4 | 65.00 |
| No. 3 Cuts, 8/4 | 67.00 |
| Dressing, 4/4 | 95.00 |
| Dressing 4/4 x 10 | 98.00 |
| Dressing, 4/4 x 12 | 110.00 |
| No. 1 Moulding, 5/4 | 150.00 |
| No. 1 Moulding, 6/4 | 150.00 |
| No. 1 Moulding, 8/4 | 155.00 |
| No. 2 Moulding, 5/4 | 125.00 |
| No. 2 Moulding, 6/4 | 125.00 |
| No. 2 Moulding, 8/4 | 130.00 |
| No. 1 Barn, 1 x 12 | 90.00 |
| No. 1 Barn, 1 x 6 and 8 | 76.00 |
| No. 1 Barn, 1 x 10 | 80.00 |
| No. 2 Barn, 1 x 6 and 8 | 62.00 |
| No. 2 Barn, 1 x 10 | 63.00 |
| No. 2 Barn, 1 x 12 | 75.00 |
| No. 3 Barn, 1 x 6 and 8 | 42.00 |
| No. 3 Barn, 1 x 10 | 44.00 |
| No. 3 Barn, 1 x 12 | 47.00 |
| Box, 1 x 6 and 8 | 36.00 |
| Box, 1 x 10 | 38.00 |
| Box, 1 x 12 | 39.00 |
| Box, 1 x 13 and up | 40.00 |

## BUFFALO

The following quotations on hardwoods represent the jobber buying price at Buffalo and Tonawanda.

| **Maple** | 1s & 2s | No. 1 Com. | No. 2 Com. |
|---|---|---|---|
| 1 in. | $ 80.00 | $ 45.00 | $ 30.00 |
| 5/4 to 8/4 | 85.00 | 50.00 | 30.00 |
| 10/4 to 4 in. | 90.00 | 55.00 | 30.00 |
| **Sap Birch** | | | |
| 1 in. | 90.00 | 48.00 | 30.00 |
| 5/4 and up | 100.00 | 53.00 | 30.00 |
| **Soft Elm** | | | |
| 1 in. | 70.00 | 45.00 | 30.00 |
| 5/4 to 2 in. | 75.00 | 50.00 | 30.00 |
| **Red Birch** | | | |
| 1 in. | 120.00 | 75.00 | |
| 5/4 and up | 125.00 | 80.00 | |
| **Basswood** | | | |
| 1 in. | 70.00 | 45.00 | 30.00 |
| 5/4 to 2 in. | 80.00 | 55.00 | 35.00 |
| **Plain Oak** | | | |
| 1 in. | 95.00 | 55.00 | 35.00 |
| 5/4 to 2 in. | 105.00 | 65.00 | 40.00 |
| **Ash** | | | |
| 1 in. | 85.00 | 50.00 | 30.00 |
| 5/4 to 2 in. | 95.00 | 55.00 | 30.00 |
| 10/4 and up | 110.00 | 70.00 | 30.00 |

## BOSTON

Quotations given below are for highest grades of Michigan and Canadian White Pine and Eastern Canadian Spruce as required in the New England market in car loads.

| | | |
|---|---|---|
| White Pine Uppers, 1 in. | | |
| White Pine Uppers, 1¼, 1½, 2 in. | | |
| White Pine Uppers, 2½, 3 in. | | |
| White Pine Uppers, 4 in. | | |
| Selects, 1 in. | | $190.00 |
| Selects, 1¼, 2 in. | | 200.00 |
| Selects, 2½, 3 in. | | |
| Selects, 4 in. | | |
| Prices nominal | | |
| Fine Common, 1 in., 30%, 12 in. and up. | | 150.00 |
| Fine Common, 1 x 8 and up | | 150.00 |
| Fine Common, 1¼ to 2 in. | $160.00 | 170.00 |
| Fine Common, 2½ and 3 in. | | 180.00 |
| Fine Common, 4 in. | | 195.00 |
| 1 in. Shaky Clear | | 100.00 |
| 1¼ in. to 2 in. Shaky Clear | | 110.00 |
| 1 in. No. 2 Dressing | | 95.00 |
| 1¼ in. to 2 in. No. 2 Dressing | | 95.00 |
| No. 1 Cuts, 1 in. | | 110.00 |
| No. 1 Cuts, 1¼ to 2 in. | | 140.00 |
| No. 1 Cuts, 2½ to 3 in. | | 180.00 |
| No. 2 Cuts, 1 in. | | 80.00 |
| No. 2 Cuts, 1¼ to 2 in. | | 110.00 |
| Barn Boards, No. 1, 1 x 12 | | 91.00 |
| Barn Boards, No. 1, 1 x 10 | | 87.00 |
| Barn Boards, No. 1, 1 x 8 | | 84.50 |
| Barn Boards, No. 2, 1 x 12 | | 75.00 |
| Barn Boards, No. 2, 1 x 8 | | 67.00 |
| Barn Boards, No. 2, 1 x 10 | | 68.00 |
| Barn Boards, No. 3, 1 x 12 | | 55.00 |
| Barn Boards, No. 3, 1 x 10 | | 53.00 |
| Barn Boards, No. 3, 1 x 8 | | 52.00 |
| **No. 1 Clear** | | |
| Can. Spruce, No. 1 and clear, 1 x 4 to 9" | | $ 75.00 |
| Can. Spruce, 1 x 10 in. | | 78.00 |
| Can. Spruce, No. 1, 1 x 4 to 7 in. | | 72.00 |
| Can. Spruce, No. 1, 1 x 8 and 9 in. | | 74.00 |
| Can. Spruce, No. 1, 1 x 10 in. | | 76.00 |
| Can. Spruce, No. 2, 1 x 4 and 5 in. | | 36.00 |
| Can. Spruce, No. 2, 1 x 6 and 7 in. | | 37.00 |
| Can. Spruce, No. 2, 1 x 8 and 9 in. | | 39.00 |
| Can. Spruce, No. 2, 1 x 10 in. | | 42.00 |
| Can. Spruce, No. 2, 1 x 12 in. | | 45.00 |
| Spruce, 12 in. dimension | | 49.00 |
| Spruce, 10 in. dimension | | 48.00 |
| Spruce, 9 in. dimension | | 46.00 |
| Spruce, 8 in. dimension | | 45.00 |
| 2 x 10 in. random lengths, 8 ft. and up | | 41.00 |
| 2 x 12 in., random lengths | | 45.00 |
| 2 x 3, 2 x 4, 2 x 5, 2 x 6, 2 x 7 | | 32.00 |
| 3 x 4 and 4 x 4 in. | | 33.00 |
| 2 x 9 | | 39.00 |
| All other random lengths, 7 in. and under, 8 ft. and up | 32.00 | 36.00 |
| 5 in. and up merchantable boards, 8 ft. and up, D 1s | 31.00 | 35.00 |
| 1 x 2 | | 32.00 |
| 1 x 3 | | 32.00 |
| 1⅝ in. Spruce Lath | | 8.50 |
| 1½ in. Spruce Lath | | 7.50 |
| **New Brunswick Cedar Shingles** | | |
| Extras | | 5.50 |
| Clears | | 4.50 |
| Second Clear | | 3.50 |
| Clear Whites | | 2.75 |

Second Hand Machinery & Equipment Wanted & For Sale

# Quick Action Section

Special Lots Of Lumber—Positions Wanted & Vacant

## Lumber Wanted

### Lath Wanted

Several cars 3/8" x 1½" x 4' No. 1 Hemlock. State when cut and quote best price.
Huntington & Finke Co., Buffalo, N.Y. 3-4

### Wanted

To contract a large quantity of 5/8" x 4" and 5" log run spruce with mill culls out. Address H. V. Berry, Fort Plain, N.Y. 3-6

### Wanted

Sawdust and Baled or Loose. Shavings. Pine or Hardwood. Quote f.o.b. mill and describe. Apply Box 780 Canada Lumberman, Toronto. 4-6

### Hard Maple Wanted

A number of cars each of 1", 1-1/8" and 1¼" dry; quote lowest price, stating grade and shipping point. Box 805 Canada Lumberman, Toronto. 4-7

### We Will Buy

A block of Hemlock, Spruce, Red or White Pine that is sawn or will be sawn before the 15th of March. Box 770 Canada Lumberman, Toronto. 2 T.f.

### Hard Maple and Birch Wanted

A limited quantity of 4/4 and 8/4 dry stock No. 2 Common and Better. For further particulars apply Box 761 Canada Lumberman, Toronto, Can. 2-5

### Logs Wanted

to saw in transit, at G.T.R. siding Oro, on main line between Toronto and North Bay. Satisfaction guaranteed. Prices on application.
T. R. Crawford, Oro Station, Ont. 2-5

### Hardwood Wanted

Several cars 1" also some 2" No. 3 Common, Maple Birch etc. State dryness and quote best prices.
Huntington & Finke Co., Buffalo, N.Y. 3-4

### Hard Maple Wanted

Carload lots 1¼" x 6 x 10'—1sts and 2nds, dry.
Carload lots (1¼" x 2½" x 49", 1" x 3½" x 49" clear, dry, equal number of pieces each size in each car.
Box 782 Canada Lumberman, Toronto. 3-7

## Lumber For Sale

### For Sale

At Blind River, Ontario, Pine and Spruce Lath, also some Cedar and Hemlock Lath. Grades, four foot mill run, 32" mill run, and four foot No. 3.
P. P. Potvin,
Blind River, Ont.
2-T.f.

## Machinery For Sale

### Saw Mill Machinery for Sale

Including Engine, Boilers, Edger, Shafting, Solid Iron Pulleys, Gears etc. Attractive prices for immediate sale. Box 790 Canada Lumberman, Toronto. 4-7

### PUBLISHER'S NOTICE

Advertisements other than "Employment Wanted" or "Employees Wanted" will be inserted in this department at the rate of 25 cents per agate line (14 agate lines make one inch). $3.50 per inch, each insertion, payable in advance. Space measured from rule to rule. When four or more consecutive insertions of the same advertisement are ordered a discount of 25 per cent. will be allowed.

Advertisements of "Wanted Employment" will be inserted at the rate of one cent a word, net. Cash must accompany order. If Canada Lumberman box number is used, enclose ten cents extra for postage in forwarding replies. Minimum charge 25 cents.

Advertisements of "Wanted Employees" will be inserted at the rate of two cents a word, net. Cash must accompany the order. Minimum charge 50 cents.

Advertisements must be received not later than the 10th and 20th of each month to insure insertion in the subsequent issue.

### For Sale

10" Steam feed 36' long complete with valves. Apply Bishop Lumber Company, Nesterville, Ont. 3-4

### For Sale

Edger with front table, Filar & Stowel make four saws, width of edger 54", in A1 mechanical condition. Apply Bishop Lumber Company, Nesterville, Ont. 3-4

### For Sale

Cross Compound Corliss Engine 18"-32" x 42" (Polson Iron Works) used 6 years. Bargain for cash. Must be moved. J. L. Neilson & Co., Winnipeg, Man. 3-4

### Used Equipment

We have all kinds of machinery, boilers, engines, motors, and air compressors, etc., for quarries, lumber and pulp mills and mines. Let us have your inquiries. Montreal Agents American Saw Mill Machinery Co.,
Barrie Engineering Co., Ltd.,
298a St. Nicholas Bldg.,
23-4 Montreal.

### Wickes Gang

GANG: No. 12 Wickes Gang, 40" sash, 18" stroke, steam binder rolls, front and back in two sections, feed and oscillation combined, 1908 model, and has been in use for five years. We furnish with this gang 11 rolls for cants and stock, one filing machine, and 4 sets of saws.
THE PEMBROKE LUMBER CO.,
1t.f. Pembroke, Ont.

### Used Equipment and Supplies for Sale

Boom Chains, Anchors, Hand & Steam Winches, Lumber Trucks of various gauges, Small Rails, Pipe Pulleys, Shafting, Bearings, Marine Engines & Boilers, Mill Machinery. Enquiries and personal visits solicited. Ask for our Printed Lists published periodically. Why buy new articles when good reliable used ones can be purchased at attractive prices? QUEBEC MACHINERY & SUPPLY CO., LTD., 19 CANOTERIE HILL QUEBEC, QUE. 4

### For Sale

Band Resaw, 54" Berlin with 3—5½"saws, $1000.00
Box-Board Printer, one-color, Con. & Deng. 19" x 44" $400.00
Box-Board Squeezer, 40" x 48" Mereen-oper Late type, Chain feed $800.00
Box-Board Squeezer, 40" x 40" Mereen-Johnson automatic $700 00
Corrugated Fastener Driver, Doig 2-head $475.00
Equalizer, Berlin No. 229 automatic, Cap. up to 6' 6" long $675.00
Lock-Corner Cutter, Morgan No. 8 double end, $600 00
Lock-Corner Setting-Up machine, Morgan No. 2, $400.00
Nailing machines, all styles, Morgan & Doig, State your wants.
Sander, double-disc, 48" Fischer, all iron $235.00
Screw Driving Machines, Reynolds No. 2 $250.00 Each. (2).
Surfacer, single, 24" x 6" J. A. Fay & Co. Sectional Roll, $350.00
Surfacer, double, 30" x 7" Whitney, Sectional roll, $1150.00.
Chas. N. Braun Machinery
4-7 Fort Wayne, Indiana.

### For Sale En-Bloc

Complete Saw Mill equipment, including one Four Block Hamilton Carriage. One pair heavy twin engines, feed complete and steam nigger. One three block E. Long Carriage with eight inch gun shot feed and steam nigger. One heavy three saw edger, W. Hamilton, make. Three 75 H.P. Boilers complete with dutch ovens and stacks. One 90 H.P. engine and fly-wheel complete. One lath and shingle mill. Complete filing equipment. One refuse burner. Shafting pulleys, transmission, etc., complete. Apply Box 783 Canada Lumberman, Toronto. 3-8

### Second Hand Machinery

We have over $250,000 worth of used machinery of all kinds for sale. Suitable for mines, quarries, railroads, pulp and lumber mills, etc.
Everything carefully overhauled at our shops before shipped.
Send us your inquiries.
R. T. GILMAN & CO.,
19tf Montreal.

### Engines, Boilers, etc., for Sale

One "Williams" Upright Engine 6" x 6"
One Upright Engine 5" x 6"
Six Return tubular boilers of following dimensions:-
One "Butterfield" 72" x 14' - 3¼" tube - ¾" shell.
One "Polson" 64" x 14' - 3¼" tube - ½" shell
One "Doty" 60" x 15' - 4" tube - ¼" shell
One "Doty" 60" x 14½" - 4" tube - ½"shell
One "Doty" 60" x 15' - 4" tube - ½" shell
One "Inglis" 60" x 16' - 3" tube - ½" shell
One double acting "Northey" Fire pump, 6" suction, 5" discharge, 14" steam cylinder, 8" water cylinder, 13" stroke, Capacity 450 gallons per minute.
One "Northey" feed pump 6 x 4 x 7" stroke, Capacity 60 gallons per minute.
One brass Mill steam whistle.
For further particulars apply The Conger Lumber Co Limited., Parry Sound. Ontario. 24 T.f.

## Machinery Wanted

### Wanted

Right Hand carriage for Mill 30 M. capacity. Must be in good condition. Box 806 Canada Lumberman, Toronto. 4-7

## Situations Wanted

Want positon as bandsaw filer, double cut preferred. Worked for the same company last four seasons. A1 references. Box 759 Canada Lumberman, Toronto. 4-7

Aggressive Young Man with ability, integrity and five years' experience Lumber and Woodworking offices, desires permanent position with progressive concern in a town. Am adaptable to any phase of work. Replies treated confidential. Excellent references. Box 800 Canada Lumberman, Toronto. 4

Want Position as Band Saw Filer, accustomed to handling big jobs, 20 years' experience, good references. Box 786 Canada Lumberman, Toronto. 4

POSITION WANTED: As manager for a good responsible Lumber Co., 36 years experience in Lumbering. Box 729 Canada Lumberman, Toronto. 1-7

Wanted position as Mill Superintendent. Eight years experience as Mill Superintendent fifteen years as sawyer. Can furnish best references. Box 747 Canada Lumberman, Toronto. 1-3

WANTED POSITION: for 1922 as head filer in good large Band Mill. Expert in every detail. Satisfaction guaranteed. Apply Box 780 Canada Lumberman, Toronto. 1-4

Accountant and General office man, with ten years experience in all branches of the Lumber Trade, seeks re-engagement. Accustomed to payrolls, orders, costing, Correspondence and can operate typewriter. First-class references. Box No. 801, Canada Lumberman, Toronto. 4-5

Wanted Position as superintendent or foreman of planing mill or woodworking factory. Have had over 12 years experience in interior fittings, sash, doors, hardwood flooring, boxmaking, estimating and detail drawing. Expert on production and first-class references. Will guarantee results. Box 752 Canada Lumberman, Toronto. 1-4

Young Scotchman married, abstainer, wishes permanent progressive position as bookkeeper, stenographer and general office man. Have two years assistant bookkeeper and stenographer had following experience: Six years banking pher, London, England; eight years lumber office experience. Willing to go anywhere. Salary $100/$125. Apply Box 799 Canada Lumberman, Toronto. 4-5

## Situations Vacant

Wanted competent man to take complete control of retail lumber yard and planing mill. Must understand all angles of the retail business and estimating. Apply to Box 797 Canada Lumberman, Toronto. 4

Wanted, First class double cut band sawyer for right hand mill, long season, must be a good grader on white pine, references required, good wages to the right man. Box 792 Canada Lumberman, Toronto. 4

LUMBER SALESMAN—Required by Toronto wholesale firm, must be experienced salesman. Apply, giving references, age and salary required. Applications confidential. Box 656, Canada Lumberman, Toronto. 21tf

## Business Chances

### For Sale

1000 acres of timber, portable mill 1000 capacity. Snap for quick sale. Apply Box 4 Orrville, Ontario. 4

### Would Exchange up to $13,000 Mortgages

for lumber at current prices.
York Wrecking Co.,
4-5 2 Hallawell Ave., Toronto.

### Sawmill Service in Toronto

We are equipped to cut logs, timber, etc. at reasonable price.
York Wrecking Co.,
4-5 2 Hallawell Ave., Toronto.

### For Sale Cheap

Water power factory or mill site in thriving community on North shore of Lake Huron. White Pine Lumber Company, Blind River, Ont. 2-5

## Why Is Forestry

There is a good deal in the press these days about the necessity for forest conservation and wise utilization, and people may be led to ask: Why should Canadians bother their heads about forestry? The answer is very simple. Canada, like every other country in the world, has a large proportion of land that is not good for agriculture but which will grow timber. In some countries it is with great difficulty that these non-agricultural areas are got to grow trees, and even then the timber is of inferior quality. In Canada, on the contrary, the land, if given a chance, readily bears a new crop of trees, and when grown these trees provide the finest structural timbers in the world. How much of Canada is of this character is not yet definitely known but a conservative estimate places it at sixty per cent of the country. The reason why Canadian statesmen and leaders in all walks of life are urging forestry is that if citizens sit still and allow these non-agricultural over, then these immense areas will become deserts, whereas if kept growing timber they will provide a permanent and increasing revenue. This is the "Why" of forestry.

## Quick Growing Trees

Many of the species which can be used on the prairies are very rapid growers, for example, cottonwood, willow, Russian poplar, and Manitoba maple. It is safe to say that wood large enough for fuel can be grown from any of these trees within sixty years. After that time a plantation will increase in value and productiveness year by year and will prove one of the best investments on the farm.—Norman M. Ross, Indian Head Forest Nursery Station.

## Hamilton Wholesaler Gave Talk on Lumber

An interesting address was delivered before the Purchasing Agents' Association, of Hamilton, Ont., recently by Guy H. Long, president of the Long Lumber Co. The gathering was held at the Royal Connaught Hotel, Hamilton. Mr. Long spoke of the progress and development of the lumber business from the early days down to the present, and said he first became interested in lumber while selling groceries for Gillard & Co. in the north country. He impressed upon his hearers the fact that different locations and climates had great influence on the growth of trees and that purchasing agents should buy from the districts that produce the most suitable wood for their particular requirements.

## The Benefits of Forest Cover

The benefit of a forest-covering of watersheds as a stabilizer of stream flow is often claimed by advocates of reforestation, without any very convincing argument in favor of the claim being offered. Investigation of effect of forest upon stream flow has been carried on in Europe, however, notably at Zurich, Switzerland, where observations extending over 18 years were made of two small watersheds, one wholly, and the other one-third, forested.

On a proportional basis, the total annual stream discharge was approximately equal on the two watersheds. In short, heavy rainfalls the maximum run-off per second in the forested watershed was only one-third to one-half that on the lightly forested watershed, and the total flood stage discharge usually one-half. Although, as a result of very long, heavy rains, the run-off was the same after the forest soil had become saturated, the forest cover appreciably stabilized the stream flow and reduced the extremes of both high and low water. The forest cover was also beneficial in preventing landslides, which were common on steep, unforested slopes during heavy rains, and in preventing erosion, which greatly increased flood damage throughout the entire course of the streams.

## New Members Are Coming in Rapidly

The membership of the Canadian Lumbermen's Association is growing rapidly. Committees have been appointed in various sections of the Dominion to increase the number of firms that should belong to this progressive, national lumber body. During the past two or three weeks no less than twenty new members have "signed up." Among the list is as follows:—

R. A. R. Allen, R. A. R. Allen Lumber Co., Mill Bridge, Ont.
W. A. Cockburn, North Bay, Ont.
S. C. Thompson, Gatineau Company, Ltd., Ottawa, Ont.
Frank H. Harris, Frank H. Harris Lumber Co., Toronto, Ont.
Percy E. Heeney, Kitchener, Ont.
H. A. Leak, Leak & Co., Ltd., Toronto, Ont.
R. McDonagh, McDonagh Lumber Co., Toronto, Ont.
J. A. Fraser, Pine Lake Lumber Co., Ltd., Pickerel, Ont.
Frank Kent, The Seaman, Kent Co., Ltd., Toronto, Ont.
Geo. A. Grafftey, Montreal, Que.
Harold D. Joyce, Montreal, Que.
H. F. McClung, Sherbrooke, Que.
E. C. Plant, E. C. Plant Lumber Co., Ltd., Montreal, Que.
A. F. Cooper, Standart Chemical Co., Ltd., Montreal, Que.
T. D. Pickard, Panuke Pulp & Power Co., Ltd., Windsor, N. S.
A. C. Crombie, W. H. Crombie Co., Inc., New York, N. Y.
Frederick J. Bruce, Homan & Puddington, Inc., New York, N. Y.
H. J. Hymans, H. J. Hymans, Inc., New York, N. Y.
R. E. Stocking, Power, Moir & Stocking, New York, N. Y.

Lieut. Col. A. E. Kenny, formerly of Ottawa, who is head of the Big Bear Lumber Co., Toronto, has removed his offices from the Manning Arcade to 208 Excelsior Life Building. Col. Kenny has had many years' experience in the lumber line in the Ottawa Valley and served several years overseas. His company is handling all kinds of forest products.

J. E. Michaud of Edmunston, N. B., reviewing the lumber situation with a correspondent of the "Canada Lumberman" recently said the outlook in Madawaska is looking more favorable. There are quite a large number of men in the woods and conditions are expected to keep on improving. Regarding the cutting of burnt over lumber, he said, a large quantity would be taken out this winter and saved, which would otherwise be lost to the province and the licensees. This, he attributed largely to the action of the government in cutting down the stumpage rate.

# Review of Current Trade Conditions

## Montreal Market is Showing an Improvement

The Montreal market has improved. Whether the condition is in the nature of a mere flurry or is indictive of an upward movement, remains to be seen, but it is certain that in some directions business has picked up and prices are firmer. Some stocks are still in the process of liquidation, and can be bought cheaply, but these are the exceptions and wholesalers are declining to sell at the cut rate quotations which so often marked transactions in 1921. The general feeling is distinctly better.

Local retailers are not yet in the market to buy to any extent; they will only buy for immediate needs. This attitude is, in a measure, due to a belief that freights will soon come down, and they do not wish to hold stocks for which current rates have to be paid. They may be right, or they may, according to the views of some wholesalers have to pay appreciably higher prices for stocks in two months.

There has been a large increase in the number of inquiries from across the border, and orders are also on the up-grade. The representatives of several U. S. wholesale firms have passed through Montreal on their way to the Maritime Provinces with a view to purchasing lumber. Without exception, they were optimistic as to the immediate future, and one representative expressed a belief that the spring would witness a runaway market.

Wholesalers report that the mills are asking stiffer prices for the new cut of spruce. The lath market is firmer, with an improved demand. B. C. stocks are in fair demand, with upper stock prices being maintained. According to a manufacturer with limits in eastern Quebec, any number of men can be hired for the woods for $30, a month. The opinion that Montreal will see a large increase in building, as soon as the season opens, is more pronounced. The permits for January totalled $216,460, a decrease of $86,795; the smaller number of repairs is responsible for the decline.

The demand for pulpwood shows no improvement. The dullness which has characterized this department is illustrated by the exports to the U. S. during December last. They then totalled 46,379 cords of a value of $480,160, compared with 172,024 cords and $2,621,061. in December of the previous year. For the nine months of the fiscal year, the total was 564,446 cords and $7,229,593, as against1,087,360 cords and $14,125,577.

## Ontario and the East

There is not much change in the general market situation as it it too early yet for business to open up to any great extent. Many retail lumbermen are showing a greater disposition to purchase than for some time past, and some are looking forward to a good season in the building trade. If the present plans materialize, house construction should proceed on a large scale in the bigger cities and good-sized towns.

In the hardwood line come many inquires for birch and maple, but the upper grades are rather scarce and there is a wide margin in prices, depending upon the stock held, where located or how badly the enquirer needs certain thicknesses and grades. The disposition of those who have stock on hand is to hang on, knowing that the trend of values is upwards and the cut of hardwoods this season is much smaller than last. It is felt that values have struck bottom and with the opening up of industrial activity and the low stocks in the hands of many manufacturers, there is going to be a greater movement than some anticipate.

In softwoods hemlock is firm in price and in very good demand, while white pine is holding its own. Red pine is not so strong and the demand for jack pine is limited. Spruce is still inactive and slow to move.

Many wholesalers are quite jubilant over the number of cars they have sold during the past month, and look for a return to normalcy at an early date. There are, however, uncertain features yet regarding the future, and just when prosperity is going to return, as soon as some predict, is doubtful. At present there seems to be a ceratin amount of business that is being deliberately withheld from the market, and doubts will come to the surface within the next few weeks. Many are adopting the "watchful, waiting" attitude, and as soon as they feel assured that the corner has been rounded, they are going to come into the market and buy quite freely.

The cut in the bush this year when all the returns are in, may be larger than at first reported. Conditions in logging were hampered during January to a large extent by severe storms and deep snow, but the present month has been favorable and different companies

report that men are very efficient and the logs are being hauled out on the ice without serious delay.

The demand for B. C. forest products is fairly active and during the past few days many mixed carloads have been sold while the railways have been buying some material for siding and running boards. There has been another advance of $5.00 on rough clear fir and eastern representatives now say that Coast mills are unable to compete against B & Better southern pine, which is still coming in in scattered, quantities.

It is difficult, some wholesalers say, to dispose of the 1 x 4's and 5's in hemlock owing to competition of 1 x 8, 1 x 10 and 1 x 12 in western fir. There is still some Michigan hemlock arriving on the Ontario market.

That the east is being more and more looked upon as a growing market, is evidenced by the fact that large companies in British Columbia are opening up offices in the east and increasing their sales forces. During the past year, at least, a dozen, new firms have become directly represented, while others, have added to the ranks of their salesmen so that the western representatives now look upon the east as their great consuming field and a constantly developing outlook.

The stocks of many retail lumbermen are low and they are quite willing to buy but, a large proportion are naturally hesitating as they do not know how trade is going to open up in their respective towns. Farmers are still diffident in talking or thinking about construction owing to the low price of live stock and rural produce, and many retailers do a growing business in the country round about. If there is no activity in certain pastoral sections, it has a resultant effect on the trade of the yardman. Most dealers, however, are on the lookout for anything that looks attractive in price, and special offerings are eagerly snapped up.

The one factor that may increase building this year is the lowering of costs. Prices of many materials have dropped, and while there has not been a corresponding fall in wages, labor efficiency is greater. Building costs are, of course, much above prewar levels, but it is doubtful if either wages or material will ever get down to the 1914 figures. The standard of those days is one institution that is numbered among the things of the past and should be a forgotten experience. Everything else seems to be moving fairly well and on the whole the trade is optimistic.

The total projects in Canada reported during the past month as contemplated showed a very decided gain over those for December. The figures indicate a gain of 60 per cent. in January compared with December. The increase at this period of the year is encouraging, and for the time at least bears out predictions as to the growth of building activity. Contemplated building for January totaled $22,391,600 compared with $13,997,800 in December. Construction contracts awarded in the Dominion during the same month totaled $8,392,500 compared with $8,947,500 in January a year ago.

During 1922, residential building will undoubtedly be active at approximately the present levels of cost. There will also be much better activity along the lines of railroad and public utility rehabilitation. In industrial construction little can be expected at least until we have seen several months of decidedly more active business than that of present levels. Extensive road building programs of the Provincial Governments promises more active public construction work than during 1921.

## Ottawa Reports Little Change in Situation

Conditions in the Ottawa lumber market during the closing period of January and the first part of this month showed very little change. Business was very quiet and orders were few and far between. Inquiries increased but they did not in the most cases result in orders being placed, the majority of them desiring to know if certain stocks were to be had.

Despite the slow market, the members of the trade held a hopeful outlook and expected that business would soon begin to pick up. Prices continued to hold firm despite the lack of normal trading, and it was expected that present levels would be maintained for the next month or six weeks.

Woods operations with the majority of the companies were reported to be progressing favorably. Grant Davidson of James Davidson's Sons, which is getting out 12,000,000, feet this season states that good headway is being made by the camp end.

Business with the sash and door factories continued dull and the sash and door department of the Gatineau Company, Limited, closed

down. All of the Ottawa plant of this company ceased operation with the exception of the retail yard and the planing mill. It is not known whether the departments now closed will be re-opened.

The outlook toward building did not materially brighten during January when only about a dozen permits for small undertakings were taken out at the city hall. It is expected, however, that as the spring progresses that building will increase considerably and there are several in Ottawa, who predict that if labor costs are anywhere near the pre-war scale that Ottawa will experience one of the biggest building booms of years.

The annual report of the Ottawa Public School Board showed that $530,735 had been expended last year for land and buildings and $9,856 for furniture. The estimates for new building by the Board this year have not yet been struck, but it is expected that they will be greater that in 1921.

## Lumber Business Picks Up in East

From present indications the lumber industry in the Maritime Provinces is beginning to recover after one of the most depressing periods on record. While there is no indication of a boom the trend of the tide seems to be toward a resumption of normal conditions and as a result crews are in the woods getting out much larger cuts than originally intended. There is a small movement of lumber overseas, but not as large as the operators would like. They still have large quantities of lumber piled on every available space and this is one of the biggest obstacles to be overcome before mills can be operated on full time.

The St. John Lumber Company is finding a marked increase in the demand for lumber and is now operating its mills at Van Buren night and day. John A. Morrison of Fredericton, who is an operator for the company on the Upper St. John, was recently instructed to double the amount of his contract. He has a large crew of men in the woods and they are making satisfactory progress. Wages this year in the woods are about one third less than they were last year.

A large lumber deal was recently put through in Nova Scotia by A. J. Sollows of Hampton and St. John interests. These men purchased an area of over 2,000 acres of timber land from the owners in Yarmouth County. This big tract of land lies in the counties of Digby, Yarmouth and Queens and includes some large and thickly studded areas of hemlock, pine and spruce. It is said the new owners will operate, but no definite announcement has as yet been forthcoming.

A meeting of the New Brunswick Lumbermen's Association was held in St. John recently, F. C. Beatteay of Stetson, Cutler & Co. Ltd., presiding. Several matters of routine business were disposed of and the prospects for the coming season discussed.

Stephen L. Moore of Grand Bay N. B., is rebuilding his saw mill near Westfield which was burned last summer. He has installed a large Leonard locomotive boiler of special construction. The plant is expected to be ready for operation in the near future.

## Blister Rust Attacks White Pine in B.C.

With regard to reports that blister rust has attacked the white pine forests of British Columbia, A. W. McCallum, pathologist in forest tree diseases, prepared the following memorandum.

"Early in the present century large quantities of white pine nursery stock was imported from Europe for planting purposes on account of the low prices at which such stock could be secured. In this manner blister rust was brought to this continent.

"Since its advent in America, it has become widely distributed in the New England states while in Canada it is present in southern Ontario and southern Quebec, not having as yet reached the important white pine areas. Since the occurrence of this rust in eastern America there has always been the expectation and fear that it would reach the west, where fiveleaved pines form a very important part of the timber land. Here it should be made clear that this rust attacks only those pines which have their needles in fascicles of five, and further that it is a heteroecious rust, i.e., to complete its life cycle it must pass a portion of its existance upon some other plant.

For some years the authorities in both western Canada and in the western states have been on the lookout for this disease, but only last autumn was it discovered in British Columbia. Investigations carried on by the provincial plant pathologist showed that it was present at several points in the Fraser Valley and also on Vancouver Island.

"As yet there is no information available which would indicate how the fungus was brought to the west. In British Columbia white pine is a tree of minor importance Douglas fir, spruce, cedar and hemlock all exceeding it in value because of the greater abundance of these species. In the western states, however, there are two five-leaved species, which are extremely valuable.

"On Dec. 19 and 20 of last year an international blister rust conference was held at Portland, Oregon, to decide upon measures to be adopted in combating this disease.

## Re-roofing Over the Old Roof

Reroofing over the old roof, regardless of what the old or new roofs may be, is basically wrong, notwithstanding suggestions to the contrary. The "easiest way" perhaps reduces the first cost of laying a new roof, but is not the best and cheapest over a period of years. If you have tried it, you know, says R. S. Whiting, Sec'y of the Shingle Branch, West Coast Lumbermen's Association.

Take an old shingle roof for example, where some of the shingles have worked loose and the roof has become leaky because of improper nails, too few nails, or low grade shingles not suitable for roofing: Often, particularly in cases of roofing old buildings not intended for permanent use, careful renailing of the old shingles and the replacement of a few shingles, will result in making the roof tight, and renew its life for several years. Often the "easiest way" is followed, and some form of paper roofing rolled out right over the shingles, and nailed to them. This does not make a good tight roof for several reasons, and can be considered no more than a makeshift at best.

Roll roofing requires a smooth, solid, flat surface as a base upon which to be laid. Therefore, to lay it over a shingle roof is not practical, and beside this roll roofing cannot be nailed properly and securely to shingles without great danger of puncturing the paper full of holes, and cannot be stepped upon after being laid without great danger of puncturing more holes with the impressions of each step. The contents of many storage buildings have been ruined because of leaky roll roofings caused by punctures from heel prints. Water seeps through and cannot flow off the under layer, as in the case of a shingle roof.

Remove the old shingle roof, if it has outlived its usefulness. Avoid dirt in this process by catching the falling shingles in tarpaulin or canvas sheets, by which they may be easily carried away. Roll roofing, in order to retain its vitality, must not become dry or be ventilated. It therefore must be laid on solid sheathing, and as a guard against being ripped off or blown away, must be well cemented to the sheathing.

Many times roll roofings applied over shingles have been burnt off by falling sparks, leaving the old shingles intact. This is evidence again of the fire resistive qualities of the shingles. Even more often will be seen roll roofing wholly or partially torn from a roof by the elements, on account of laying this roofing over shingles which do not form a sufficiently secure foundation.

It is equally unsatisfactory to attempt to lay asphalt shingles over old shingle roofs for the same reason, partlcularly so because of the uneven surfaces, and because the ventilation and heat dries them up and permits them to loosen, allowing them to blow away or pull out

Slate or asbestos roofings may hold temporarily in place by reason of their own weight, when laid over shingles, but unless the shingles were originally laid over solid sheathing, no other roofing material will hold for any length of time, when applied over them, because sufficient holding surface cannot be secured.

Shingles should be laid on open sheathing, the same spaced 5 in., 5½ in. and 7½ in. on center, depending on their length, whether they be 16 in., 18 in. or 24 in. In order to secure regular nailing points at proper intervals. No other roofing is applied in this manner. This is the approved way to lay shingles because the more ventilation a shingle roof has, the longer it will last. Do not lay a new shingle roof over an old roof of any description, and do not lay any kind of a roof over a shingle roof.

Use a good shingle, with the right nail, over the proper kind of sheathing, as it should be laid, and you will not have to consider laying a new roof of any description for decades.

When the time arrives that a new roof is required, remove the old shingles. They have served their purpose, then apply new shingles right over the old sheathing. It will make the best and cheapest roof. Be consistent in all things. Use good shingles properly laid with the right nails and you are using good judgment.

A charter has been granted to the Hamilton Home Builders' Limited, Hamilton, Ont., with a capital stock of $500,000.

## Mayor Payette Captures Golf Trophy

J. T. Payette,
Penetanguishene, Ont.

J. T. Payette, Mayor of Penetanguishene and head of the firm of P. Payette Co., which is well known to the lumbering and woodworking industries throughout Canada, has recently won the big silver trophy given by the Midland and Penetang Golf Club for the amateur golf championship for the Midland and Penetang Golf Club of 1921. D. S. Pratt, of Midland, was the contender in the finals, the score being 92-103.

Speaking of business instead of golf, Mr. Payette says his firm intends to equip its shop with the most modern machines, including brand new lathes, large power steam hammers, big pipe machines, etc. Recently the company received a letter of commendation from Mr. R. Pemberton, the Government Marine inspector at Ottawa, regarding a large job done on the "Canadian Logger," which vessel is taking a cargo from Midland down to Montreal. Mr. Pemberton adds that the "Canadian Logger" is the best-finished of any of the lake type that has been built for the Dominion Government. Unfortunately its construction was held up through some engine trouble, which was made good by the Payette Company.

Mr. Pemberton thinks that a great deal of praise is coming to the Payette firm, as the work of casting a new liner is more than some of the larger shops in Canada care to take on. This liner is cast of gun metal in one piece, almost nine feet long, one inch thick and fourteen inches outside diameter. The most difficult part was the shrinking on, and everything turned out so successfully that the representative had no doubt that the Payette firm could again undertake the same sort of job. Mr. Pemberton lauded the Payette firm for the way that the work was carried out. In his opinion it is equally as good as the liner which was damaged and was supplied by an expert company specializing exclusively in these things. The casting weighs about two thousand pounds. The mixture to make a good gun metal casting is very intricate and it takes a moulder of great experience to make a successful casting.

### Port Arthur Will Have Busy Year

The industrial outlook in Port Arthur is regarded as exceptionally bright. The ratepayers recently carried a by-law by a vote of ten to one, ratifying an agreement made by the Port Arthur City Council and the Provincial Paper Mills, Limited, of Toronto, whereby the Company agrees, in return for a fixed assessment of $500,000 for a period of ten years, on the new paper mill which is being erected and other minor concessions, to go ahead with the construction of the plant, which will cost about a million and a half dollars and employ some five hundred hands. It is expected that the new industry will be in operation early in the fall of 1923.

Word received from Port Arthur states that it is believed the manufacture of the big paper machine which will be installed at a cost of some $600,000, will be carried out at the Port Arthur shipyards which have recently been fitted up for that work, thus giving employment to a large force of men for several months. The shipyards were also awarded a contract recently for a 10,000 ton freighter, which will mean work for some eight hundred men for nearly a year.

### News and Jottings of Interest

Ray B. Maxson has become associated with the Charles O. Maus Lumber Co., of South Bend, Ind., which was recently formed. Mr. Maxson was for 16 years connected with the Studebaker Corporation of South Bend, and was for a considerable period purchaser of all the lumber that they used. He will occupy the position of manager of the Chas. O. Maus Co., and brings to bear on his new duties a wide experience and much insight into the forest products line. Mr. Maxson will also look after the buying while Mr. Maus will be in charge of the selling end.

The C. A. Larkin Co., Toronto, has recently added several men to its selling staff. Chas. McDonald, late manager of the Allen Lumber Co., Kingston, Ont., has been appointed city representative, while Donald McNeil, formerly of Latchford, Ont., and Ernest Kay, of Toronto, are covering Ontario in the interests of the firm. The C. A.

Larkin Co., is specializing in Ontario softwoods and B. C. forest products.

Lumber and shingles are being steadily shipped from the port of Vancouver to the Atlantic Coast via the Panama Canal. Orders in 250,000-foot lots are being received on an average of one a week. Boston is becoming a good market for British Columbia lumber and nearly every vessel sailing from here for the east coast, if calling at Boston, carries lumber and shingles for that port.

### Did This Ever Happen to You?

You know the kind of orders. They are small and often take the big, slow, but powerful delivery truck away out of its way—perhaps many miles. The heavy truck is a paying proposition, but when made to deliver a hurry-up order for a couple of bags of cement, or a few hundred feet of white pine strips, it's slow and expensive.

In a western Ontario city there are three old established builders' supply merchants. The owners themselves are all members of the old school who do not believe in "these here new fangled ideas." But one of them has a son, a junior partner, who is noted for doing things just a pace or two ahead of the other fellow.

Now this urban community has some twelve or fifteen thousand people and is surrounded by a particularly rich fruit growing country. The fruit farms are smaller than the average size of farms, and the district is the centre of a comparatively thickly populated countryside.

The merchants, consequently, have seen the necessity of establishing a delivery service to the suburban farms, and within a five-mile radius a reliable mercantile delivery service has been found profitable by the majority of the business men.

But one day a complaint was received by the junior partner of one of the lumber firms regarding the delivery of some cement. This order was placed over the phone by a farmer customer who needed four bags in a big hurry. So the material was taken along with a big load of barn material on the powerful, but slow, lumber truck. From the time the truck left the yard until the cement was delivered nearly four hours had elapsed.

The next day when the complaint was made the young man went to his father and said:

"Dad, we're losing business."

"How's that?" asked the father.

"We have a complaint this morning from Lucas, on the third concession, about that cement we sent him yesterday," answered the son.

"What's the matter with the cement?" asked the father.

"Oh, the cement's all right, but he didn't get it till four hours after he ordered it," returned the younger man.

"Four hours, eh! Little longer than I thought, but still that's not bad considering. You know we're not delivering groceries, Billy, it takes time to deliver building materials."

"Yes, I know, dad, but we're slow when it comes to despatching small hurry-up orders. We've got to get another light truck for small stuff."

"We don't have enough hurry-up orders to make another truck pay. Another thing, I'm through with paying out cold cash before it's made," returned the father.

"If nothing is ever up to us, we will never get up to anything, it's up to us to make that truck pay; if we let complaints go by like this one we received this morning, and not try to give better service, even for so small an order, our customers will go where they can receive quick service when they decide to do some extensive building," explained the young partner.

"Yes, there's some truth in that, Billy," said the father, "but how are you going to make this thing pay?"

The young man was ready with his answer:

"First we have to get a light truck and then we've got to advertise our quick service. We've got to tell them how they can order small materials such as cement, builders' supplies and small orders of wood materials, over the phone and receive them in double quick time. This will boost our small sales away up and save the expensive running of the big truck."

"We can make our delivery service as fast and reliable, both around town and within the five-mile radius as any of the feed supply merchants," concluded the young man.

So they started out with one light service truck. To-day the company is keeping two busy, delivering materials that are wanted in a hurry. The trucks are all painted alike. The firm name and the different lines carried are displayed on the side of the cab, and in attractive letters are the words: "Ask us for quick service."

"E. C. Atkins & Co., of Hamilton, Ont., have made substantial reduction in the price of their STERLING QUALITY Saws, both in the territories covered by their Eastern travellers, and in British Columbia. In Vancouver, they have a very complete shop, and a large stock, at 109 Powell Street."

# Wire at Our Expense

## —for Quotations on Mixed Cars

Fir Finish S4S

V. G. Fir Flooring

Cedar Bevel Siding

Cedar Bungalow Siding

B. C. Red Cedar Shingles

We specialize in these four items. They are a natural product of a superior quality which has made British Columbia famous in the world's lumber markets. We can serve you promptly and intelligently to our mutual profit. Try us.

# Underhill Lumber
### Company Ltd.
### VANCOUVER
## British Columbia

# PINE SHOP

Mill stocks getting low.

We still have a fair stock, thoroughly air-dried and ready for immediate shipment.

Or a mixed car of

### Shop - Clears - Commons

### The Otis Staples Lumber Co., Ltd.
Wycliffe,                              B. C.

All Eastern inquiries handled direct at our Eastern Service Office—

**1311 Bank of Hamilton Bldg. TORONTO**

Phone Main 4708.          A. E. Wilmot, Manager

R. T. Grant, manager of the St. Maurice Lumber Co., Thre
Rivers, P. Q., has been appointed a member of the local Harbor board

John Eastman, of the Forest Lumber Co., Hamilton, left recent
ly to spend a few weeks in the sunny South.

Nelson Clarke of Clarke & Smith, Weston, Ont., visited Britisl
Columbia during January to study coast conditions first hand.

Edward Norton, of Toronto, has joined the selling staff of R
G. Chesbro, and will cover Toronto and part of Ontario.

G. E. Sprague, of the Victoria Harbor Lumber Co., Toronto
and Mrs. Sprague, who have been spending the past few weeks ii
Bermuda, have returned home.

G. T. McLaurin, Montreal, is suffering from an injury to his kne
caused by a fall on the ice.  He has sufficiently recovered to be agaii
at business.

Mills Bros. shingle mill at Langley Prairie, B. C., was recentl
destroyed by fire.  The loss was partially covered by insuranc
Construction on a new mill has begun.

A. G. Couch, lecturer, for the Canadian Forestry Association i
touring the province of New Brunswick lecturing, and illustratin
by slides and films, the conservation and protection of the forest

J. R. Carter, of the Fesserton Timber Co., Toronto, who wa
recently operated upon for appendicitis, is, his many friends will b
pleased to learn, making good progress towards recovery.

The sawmill and planing mill of the Brunette Sawmills, Limi
ted, Sapperton, B. C., was recently damaged by fire.  The loss i
estimated to run several hundred dollars.

There was a log-sawing contest held recently at Moraviantown
Kent County, Ont.  It was the second match this winter and ther
was some fast sawing.  The quickest time was 16 seconds for
13-inch hard maple log.

E. D. Warner, until lately with the Associated Mills, Limite
of Vancouver, who had his office at 26 Adelaide St. West, Toronto
has taken a responsible position with the Kingston Road Lumber Co
Toronto and entered upon his new duties.

J. E. Lancaster Construction Co., Ltd., Montreal, have bee
granted a provincial charter to manufacture and deal in lumber an
other building materials.  Capital $50,000.  Two fo the incorpora
tors are W. J. Hyndman and G. R. Tooke, both of Montreal.

The annual meeting of the New Brunswick Lumbermen's Asso
ciation will be held on Tuesday March 14th.  This was decided upor
at a meeting of the executive a few days ago in St. John at whic
matters of general routine were taken up.

J. B. Mackenzie, retail lumber dealer of Georgetown, Ont., ha
been re-elected chairman of the Board of Education of that progres
sive centre.  Mr. Mackenzie was last year chairman of the Board o
which he is now serving his third term.

Joseph Connelly died recently at Kirkwood, N. B., aged 75 year:
He was a well-known lumberman and farmer and is survived by hi
wife and three children.  Mr. Connelly was a highly-respected res
dent and his illness was of comparatively short duration.

M. M. Gilbert, late of Winnipeg, recently arrived in Toront
and has taken charge of the office of Terry & Gordon, Limited, suc
ceeding A. E. Cates, who is now devoting his time exclusively to th
sales organization of the firm.

The office of the National Wholesale Lumber Dealers' Associa
tion has been removed from 66 Broadway, New York, to the Ligge
Building, 41 East 42nd St., New York, where larger quarters are a
the disposal of the staff.

Mitchell & Wilson, Limited, Gananoque, Ont., were recentl
granted a provincial charter with a capital of $200,000, to manufac
ture and deal in lumber and other building materials.  D. A. Mi
chel and R. M. Richardson, both of Gananoque are two of the inco
porators.

The residence of Mr. Mitchell, Sr. father of the junior partne
of the retail lumber firm of Wills & Mitchell, St. Catharines, Ont
was recently destroyed by fire at Stamford, in Welland County.  Th
loss on the house and contents amounted to $20,000., and was onl
partially covered by insurance.

Mrs. M. B. King and Miss Allison King, who are the wife an
daughter of M. B. King, president of the King-Ferris Lumber Co

Limited, of Vancouver, were in Toronto recently and were the guests of Mr. A. G. Wilmot, of the Otis-Staples Lumber Co., and Mrs. Wilmot.

Rimouski Lumber & Lath Co., Ltd., Montreal, has been incorporated with federal charter to manufacture and deal in logs, lumber, pulpwood and by-products. Capital $1,000,000. Among the incorporators are W. J. White, K. C. and P. A. Badeaux, both of Montreal.

William M. Sullivan, Limited, of Nelson, N. B., has recently been granted a provincial charter. The head of the company is William M. Sullivan, lumber merchant, of Red Bank, N. B. and the organization is empowered to buy, sell and deal in all kinds of goods as well as manufacture lumber, timber and pulp wood and all kinds of paper and pulp.

The Sussex St. plant of the Gatineau Co., Ottawa, formerly the property of W. C. Edwards & Co., which has been almost inactive for some months, has, it is understood, closed down entirely. The industry has been doing very little work for some time and reduced its operations nearly to the cessation point about Christmas, when some forty employees were allowed to go.

The town of Wiarton, Ont., some time ago went into the wood business establishing a municipal wood yard and lost several hundred dollars through the enterprise. The mayor of the town said the chief thing was to get out of this line of business, and, generally speaking, the council agreed with him. Many contracts were not worth the paper they were written on and considerable wood was stolen.

The depression of the lumber business in New Brunswick has been so marked during the past year that there has been a considerable falling off in provincial revenue. The decline in the annual income from stumpage on lumber cut upon Crown Lands amounts to more than half a million dollars. Various means are being considered by the provincial administration regarding new sources of revenue and among the schemes propounded is that of a land tax.

Thurston & Flavelle Ltd., Port Moody, B. C. are contracting for the electrification of their sawmill and plant buildings at a cost of $60,000. A 1,000 Kilowatt generator and individual motors and independent control for each machine in entire mill will be installed and also a 1,000 Kilowatt generator to be steam driven from the present engines direct connected. Individual drive motors will be installed later after some changes are made in the mill machinery.

The Forest Exhibit car of the Canadian Forestry Association recently paid a visit to Montreal and the beauty of the forests is revealed by colored transparancies, effectively lighted. The car is equipped with models showing the ravage of forest devastation by fire, and also by models showing the effects by fire on forest fertility. The car lately concluded a 1,900 mile tour from Winnipeg to Halifax and is in charge of Gerald Blythe, assistant secretary of the Canadian Forestry Association.

M. B. Zimmerman, B. L. Harper and Daniel Webster, who have for some years been associated with the Long Lumber Co. and the Consumers' Lumber Co., of Hamilton, have, it is understood, decided to form a company and enter the wholesale lumber business. Next month they will open up an office in the Ambitious City Mr. Zimmerman was manager of the Consumers' Lumber Co's yards and factory for several years. Mr Harper was city traveller and Mr. Webster accountant for the Long Lumber Co.

At the recent meeting of the Rocky Mountain Lumbermen's Association, held at Calgary, the question of the grading and sorting of lumber and the problem of standardization were the principal subjects under discussion. It was planned to adopt and use the grading rules now in use by the Western Pine Manufacturers' Association. Nothing was done in regard to standardization, but it is understood an effort will be made to co-operate with the lumber manufacturers with a view to standardization throughout the country.

The protection of the Seymour watershed is a live issue in Vancouver. Approximately 4000 acres of timberland located in the heart of the civic water operations on Seymour Creek, are held by Elmer Todd, counsellor for the Union National Bank of Seattle, who offered the property to Vancouver for $175,000. He said that the bank wants to get the money it has tied up in these lands, and that if Vancouver fails to buy the timber logging operations will be commenced.

An application for summary judgment in the case of O'Brien Limited, vs Alex. Voye, at Frederick, N. B., resulted in counter affidavits being submitted by the defence and a resultant order which will put the case on for trial. O'Brien Limited, who are a well-known lumber firm at South Nelson, N. B., claim that Voye, a resident of Frederiction, who is a pulpwood buyer, purchased wood to the value of $3,500. from them and that he had since refused to accept delivery of the same.

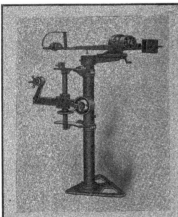

## ALPHABETICAL INDEX TO ADVERTISERS

START WITH ANY NUMBER OF UNITS—EXPAND AS ADDITIONAL SLEEPING ACCOMMODATIONS ARE REQUIRED

# Simmons Steel Bunk Units

### For Industrial, Lumber and Railroad Construction Camps

Every employer of labor knows something of the problem of sanitary sleeping quarters for the men in the field.

They appreciate the importance of sound, restful sleep, for the workers; realize the part *such sleep* plays in promoting efficiency and in lessening the dangers of sickness and disease. The *value* of standardized Steel Bunk Units of this character, therefore becomes

many times greater than their small cost. Where sleeping accommodations must be provided for vast armies of industrial workers, Simmons Sanitary Steel Bunks become a very necessary part of the Camp Equipment.

These Bunks may be ordered in any quantity, Single or Double Deck Units,—all of standardized construction, easily taken down, moved or stored, and practically indestructible.

Write today for full information regarding our sanitary, comfortable and serviceable standardized Steel Bunk Units. Complete data, specifications and illustrations of all styles, furnished promptly upon request

SIMMONS LIMITED
Executive Offices, Montreal
MONTREAL    TORONTO    WINNIPEG    CALGARY    VANCOUVER

# SIMMONS BEDS
### *Built for Sleep*

The "High-Efficiency" Belt
For the Lumbering Industry

# Dunlop "Gibraltar" RedSpecial

A Better Belt for the work.

A Belt adapted to the conditions.

A Belt that will reduce Belting overhead to rock-bottom.

The Dunlop Belt Service Department will tell you why you can save money by its adoption.

## Dunlop Tire & Rubber Goods Co., Limited

Head Office & Factories: Toronto      Branches in the Leading Cities

# THE LINN LOGGING TRACTOR

### Designed and developed for winter log hauling, in the North Woods

To fulfill all requirements of the Northern Logger a tractor must:—

Haul heavy trains of sleighs **down steep sandhills** and around sharp curves.

Haul with **absolute safety** over **lakes** and **rivers**, where the ice is sometimes not thicker than fourteen inches.

Haul heavy trains over main hauls over all encountered grades—to landings.

Have carrying capacity **on itself**, so that it can be used for supply haulage over Portage roads.

Must have a **fast high speed** so that return trips to rollways may be rapid.

Must be foolproof and easily operated and controlled.

All these requirements are fulfilled **only**, by The **Linn Logging Tractor**.

Ask the operator who uses Linn.

*—Logging Department—*

## MUSSENS LIMITED

**Dubrule Building**           MONTREAL

# LINK-BELT
## CHAINS

EVERY modern facility is employed by our skilled chain makers to produce Link-Belt quality chains.

To the user this means long life, durability (freedom from annoying breakdowns,) in his chains—whether in elevating, conveying or power transmission. That is why many experienced users always specify Link-Belt Chains.

And remember this:—The wheels play an equally important part in the satisfactory operation of every chain drive—every elevator or conveyor. Therefore, money paid for well fitting sprocket wheels yields large returns. Link-Belt Sprockets are made to fit Link-Belt Chains.

### CANADIAN
### LINK-BELT COMPANY, LTD.

TORONTO—Wellington and Peter Streets
MONTREAL—10 St. Michaels Lane

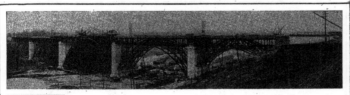

# Building and Engineering

Every week we come to tell you of contemplated construction in every province in the Dominion. Every week, since 1886; we have told how great engineering feats have been performed—the material used and the machinery employed. Besides interesting technical reading, we supply you with advance information on lumber requirements for every contemplated structure.

### Contract Record
#### ⟶ Engineering Review

349 West Adelaide Street, Toronto

*Is this not worth Three Dollars a year to you?*

# HIGH HUMIDITY DRY KILN——

### THE MODERN FAN KILN DELIVERS
a constant and uniform circulation of automatically humidified air with automatic temperature control.

### AND YOU GET
quick drying of green stock—greater holding capacity per unit—lower freight charges—quick shipping facilities.

### PREPARE NOW
to meet 1922's demands for dry lumber—the prices are at rock bottom—over 30 units sold in December.

### "THE KILN WITH THE CIRCULATION YOU CAN UNDERSTAND"
Have you written for a copy of our new dry kiln catalog.

## B. F. STURTEVANT COMPANY of CANADA, LTD.
HEAD OFFICE AND WORKS: GALT, ONTARIO
Sales Offices: TORONTO and MONTREAL

—Territorial Representatives—
Empire Engineering & Supply Co., Edmonton, Alberta — Fryer-Barker Co., Vancouver, B. C. — Kipp-Kelly Ltd., Winnipeg, Man.

# CANADA LUMBERMAN BUYERS' DIRECTORY

The following regulations apply to all advertisers:—Eighth page, every issue, three headings; quarter page, six headings; half page, twelve headings; full page, twenty-four headings

**ALLIGATORS**
Payette Company, P.
West, Peachy & Sons

**BABBITT METAL**
Canada Metal Co.
General Supply Co. of Canada, Ltd.

**BALE TIES**
Canada Metal Co.
Laidlaw Bale Tie Company

**BAND MILLS**
Hamilton Company, William
Waterous Engine Works Company
Yates Machine Company, P. B.

**BAND SAW BLADES**
Simonds Mfg. Co.

**BAND RESAWS**
Mershon & Company, W. B.

**BARKERS**
Bertrand, F. X., La Compagnie Manufactiere.
Smith Foundry & Machine Co.

**BEARING METAL**
Canada Metal Co.
Beveridge Supply Co., Ltd.

**BEDSTEADS (STEEL)**
Simmons Limited

**BELT DRESSING**
Dominion Belting Co.
General Supply of Canada, Ltd.

**BELTING**
Canadian Consolidated Rubber Co.
Dominion Belting Co.
General Supply Company
Goodhue & Co., J. L.
Gutta Percha & Rubber Company
D. K. McLaren, Limited
McLaren Belting Company, J. C.
York Belting Co.

**BLOWERS**
Reed & Co., Geo. W.
B. F. Sturtevant Co. of Canada, Ltd.
Toronto Blower Company

**BOILERS**
Engineering & Machine Works of Canada
Hamilton Company, William
Waterous Engine Works Company

**BOILER PRESERVATIVE**
Beveridge Supply Company
Shell-Bar, Boice Supply Co. Ltd.

**BOX MACHINERY**
Yates Machine Company, P. B.

**CABLE CONVEYORS**
Engineering & Machine Works of Canada.
Hamilton Company, Wm.
Waterous Engine Works Company

**CAMP SUPPLIES**
Davies Company, William
Dr. Bell Veterinary Wonder Co.
Johnson, A. H.
Swift Canadian Co.
Turner & Sons, J. J.
Woods Manufacturing Company. Ltd.

**CANT HOOKS**
General Supply Co. of Canada, Ltd.
Pink Company, Thomas

**CEDAR**
Bury & Co., Robt.
Cameron Lumber Co.
Canadian Western Lumber Company
Chesbro, R. G.

Dry Wood Lumber Co.
Fesserton Timber Company
Muir & Kitkpatrick
Rose, McLaurin, Limited
Terry & Gordon
Thurston-Flavelle Lumber Company
Vancouver Lumber Company
Victoria Lumber & Mfg. Co.

**CHAINS**
Canadian Link-Belt Company, Ltd.
General Supply of Canada, Ltd.
Engineering & Machine Works of Canada
Hamilton Company, William
Pink & Co., Thomas
Waterous Engine Works Company

**CLOTHING**
Woods Mfg. Company

**CONVEYOR MACHINERY**
Canadian Link-Belt Company, Ltd.
General Supply Co. of Canada, Ltd.
Hamilton Company, Wm.
Hopkins & Co., Ltd., F. H.
Waterous Engine Works Company

**CORDAGE**
Consumers Cordage Company

**CORDWOOD**
McClung, McLellan & Berry

**COUPLING (Shaft)**
Engineering & Machine Works of Canada

**CRANES**
Hopkins, & Co., Ltd., F. H.
Canadian Link-Belt Company

**CUTTER HEADS**
Shimer Cutter Head Company

**CYPRESS**
Wistar, Underhill & Nixon

**DERRICKS AND DERRICK FITTINGS**
Hopkins & Co., Ltd., F. H.

**DOORS**
Brompton Lumber & Mfg. Co.
Canadian Western Lumber Co.
Mason, Gordon & Co.
Midland Wood Products, Ltd.
Terry & Gordon

**DRAG SAWS**
Gerlach Company, Peter
Hamilton Company, William

**DRYERS**
Coe Manufacturing Company
B. F. Sturtevant Co. of Canada, Ltd.

**DUST COLLECTORS**
Reed & Co., Geo. W.
B. F. Sturtevant Co. of Canada, Ltd.
Toronto Blower Company

**EDGERS**
Hamilton Company, Ltd., William
Green Company, G. Walter
Long Mfg. Company, E.
Payette Company, P.
Waterous Engine Works Company

**ELEVATING AND CONVEYING MACHINERY**
Canadian Belt-Link Company, Ltd.
Engineering & Machine Works of Canada
Hamilton Company, William
Waterous Engine Works Company

**ENGINES**
Engineering & Machine Works of Canada
Hamilton Company, William

Payette Company, P.
Waterous Engine Works Company

**EXCELSIOR MACHINERY**
Elmira Machinery & Transmission Company

**EXHAUST FANS**
B. F. Sturtevant Co. of Canada, Ltd.
Toronto Blower Company

**EXHAUST SYSTEMS**
Reed & Co., Geo. W.
B. F. Sturtevant Co. of Canada, Ltd.
Toronto Blower Company

**FIBRE BOARD**
Manley Chew

**FILES**
Disston & Sons, Henry
Simonds Canada Saw Company

**FIR**
Apex lumber Co.
Associated Mills, Limited
Bainbridge Lumber Company
Cameron Lumber Co.
Canadian Western Lumber Co.
Canfield, P. L.
Chesbro, R. G.
Dry Wood Lumber Co.
Fesserton Timber Co.
Grier & Sons, Ltd., G. A.
Heeney, Percy E.
Knox Brothers
Mason, Gordon & Co.
Robertson & Hacket Sawmills
Rose, McLaurin, Limited
Terry & Gordon
Timberland Lumber Company
Timms, Phillips & Co.
Underhill Lumber Co.
Vancouver Lumber Company
Vanderhoof Lumber Co.
Victoria Lumber & Mfg. Co.

**FIRE BRICK**
Beveridge Supply Co., Ltd.
Elk Fire Brick Company of Canada
Shell-Bar, Boice Supply Co. Ltd.

**FIRE FIGHTING APPARATUS**
Waterous Engine Works Company

**FITTINGS**
Crane Limited

**FLOORING**
Cameron Lumber Co.
Chesbro, R. G.
Long-Bell Lumber Company

**GEARS (Cut)**
Smart-Turner Machine Co.

**GRINDING WHEELS**
Canadian Hart Products Ltd.

**GUARDS (Machinery and Window)**
Canada Wire & Iron Goods Co.

**HARDWOODS**
Anderson Lumber Company, C. G.
Anderson Shreiner & Mawson
Atlantic Lumber Company
Barrett, Wm.
Bury & Co., Robt.
Cameron & Co.
Edwards & Co., W. C.
Fesserton Timber Co.
Gillespie, James
Gloucester Lumber & Trading Co.
Grier & Son, G. A.
Hart, Hamilton & Jackson
Heeney, Percy E.

Knox-Brothers
Mason & Co., Geo.
McDonagh Lumber Co.
McLennan Lumber Company
McLung, McLellan & Berry
Pedwell Hardwood Lumber Co.
W. & J. Sharples.
Spencer, Limited, C. A.
Strong, G. M.
Summers, James R.
Webster & Brother, James

**HARDWOOD FLOORING**
Brompton Lumber & Mfg. Co.
Grier & Son, G. A.

**HARNESS**
Beal Leather Co., R. M.

**HEMLOCK**
Anderson Lumber Company, C. G
Anderson, Shreiner & Mawson
Bartram & Ball
Beck Lumber Co.
Bourgouin, H.
Canadian General Lumber Company
Edwards & Company, W. C.
Fesserton Timber Co.
Grier & Sons, Ltd., G. A.
Hart, Hamilton & Jackson
Hocken Lumber Company
Mason, Gordon & Co.
McCormack Lumber Co.
McDonagh Lumber Co.
Robertson & Hacket Sawmills
Spanish River Lumber Co.
Spencer, Limited, C. A.
Stalker, Douglas A.
Terry & Gordon
Vancouver Lumber Co.
Vanderhoof Lumber Co.

**HOISTING AND HAULING ENGINES**
General Supply Co. of Canada, Ltd.
Hopkins & Co., Ltd., F. H.

**HOSE**
General Supply Co. of Canada, Ltd.
Gutta Percha & Rubber Company

**INSURANCE**
Barton & Ellis Co.
Burns Underwriting Co.
Hardy & Co., E. M.
Lumbermen's Underwriting Alliance
Rankin Benedict Underwriting Co.

**INTERIOR FINISH**
Cameron Lumber Co.
Canadian Western Lumber Co.
Canfield, P. L.
Eagle Lumber Company
Mason, Gordon & Co.
Rose, McLaurin, Limited
Terry & Gordon

**KILN-DRIED LUMBER**
Bury & Co., Robt.

**KNIVES**
Disston & Sons, Henry
Simonds Canada Saw Company
Waterous Engine Works Company

**LARCH**
Otis Staples Lumber Co.

**LATH**
Anderson, Shreiner & Mawson
Apex Lumber Co.
Austin & Nicholson
Beck Lumber Co.
Brennen & Sons, F. W.
Cameron Lumber Co.
Gloucester Lumber & Trading Company
Carew Lumber Co., John
Chaleurs Bay Mills
Dupuis, Limited, J. P.

Eagle Lumber Company
Foley Lumber Company
Fraser Bryson Lumber Co., Ltd.
Gloucester Lumber & Grading Co.
Grier & Sons, Ltd., G. A.
Harris Tie & Timber Company, Ltd.
Larkin Co., C. A.
Mason & Co., Geo.
McLennan Lumber Company
Miller, W. H. Co.
New Ontario Colonization Company
Otis Staples Lumber Company
Power Lumber Co.
Price Bros. & Company
Shevlin-Clarke Co.
Spencer, Limited, C. A.
Terry & Gordon
U. G. G. Sawmills. Limited
Union Lumber Company
Victoria Harbor Lumber Company

**LATH BOLTERS**

General Supply Co. of Canada, Ltd
Hamilton Company, Wm.
Payette & Company, P.

**LOCOMOTIVES**

Engineering & Machine Works of
  Canada
General Supply Co. of Canada, Ltd.
Hopkins & Co., Ltd., F. H.
Climax Manufacturing Company
Montreal Locomotive Works

**LATH TWINE**

Consumers' Cordage Company

**LINK-BELT**

Canadian Link-Belt Company
Mathews Gravity Carrier Company.
Hamilton Company, Wm.

**LOCOMOTIVE CRANES**

Canadian Link-Belt Company, Ltd.
Hopkins & Co. ,Ltd., F. H.

**LOGGING ENGINES**

Engineering & Machine Works of
  Canada
Hopkins & Co., Ltd., F. H.
Mussens Ltd.

**LOG HAULER**

Engineering & Machine Works of
  Canada
Green Company. G. Walter
Holt Manufacturing Co.
Hopkins & Co., Ltd., F. H.
Payette Company, P.

**LOGGING MACHINERY AND
EQUIPMENT**

General Supply Co. of Canada, Ltd.
Hamilton Company, William
Holt Manufacturing Co.
Hopkins & Co., Ltd., F. H.
Payette Company, P.
Waterous Engine Works Company
West, Peachey & Sons
Mussens Ltd.

**LUMBER EXPORTS**

Fletcher Corporation

**LUMBER TRUCKS**

Hamilton Company, Wm.
Waterous Engine Works Company

**LUMBERMEN'S BOATS**

Adams Engine Company
Gidley Boat Co.
West, Peachey & Sons

**LUMBERMEN'S CLOTHING**

Kitchen Overall & Shirt Co.
Woods Manufacturing Company, Ltd.

**MATTRESSES**

Simmons Limited

**METAL REFINERS**

Canada Metal Company

**OAK**

Long-Bell Lumber Company

**PACKING**

Beveridge Supply Company
Consumers' Cordage Co.
Gutta Percha & Rubber Company

**PANELS**

Bury & Co., Robt.

**PAPER**

Beveridge Supply Co., Ltd.
Price Bros. & Co.

**PINE**

Anderson Lumber Company, C. G.
Anderson, Shreiner & Mawson
Atlantic Lumber Co.
Austin & Nicholson
Barratt, William
Beck Lumber Co.
Cameron & Co.
Cameron Lumber Co.
Canadian General Lumber Company
Canadian Western Lumber Co.
Canfield, P. L.
Chesbro, R. G.
Cleveland-Sarnia Sawmills Company
Cox, Long & Company
Dudley, Arthur N.
Eagle Lumber Company
Edwards & Co.. W. C.
Excelsior Lumber Company
Fesserton Timber Company
Fraser Bryson Lumber Co., Ltd.
Gillies Bros, Limited
Gloucester Lumber & Trading Co.
Gordon & Co., George
Gooday & Company, H. R.
Grier & Sons, Ltd., G. A.
Harris Tie & Timber Company, Ltd.
Hart, Hamilton & Jackson
Hettler Lumber Company, Herman H.

Hocken Lumber Company
Julien, Rech
Lay & Haight
Lloyd, W. Y.
Loggie Co., W. S.
Long-Bell Lumber Company
Mason, Gordon & Co.
Mason & Co., Geo.
McCormack Lumber Co.
McFadden & Malloy
McLennan Lumber Company
Montreal Lumber Company
Muir & Kirkpatrick
Northern Lumber Mills.
Otis Staples Lumber Co.
Parry Sound Lumber Company
Pigeon River Lumber Co., Ltd.
Rolland Lumber Co.
W. & J. Sharples.
Shevlin-Clarke Co.
Spanish River Lumber Co.
Spencer, Limited. C. A.
Stalker, Douglas A.
Strong, G. M.
Summers, James R.
Terry & Gordon
Union Lumber Company
Victoria Harbor Lumber Co.
Watson & Todd, Limited

**PLANING MILL EXHAUSTERS**

Toronto Blower Co.

**PLANING MILL MACHINERY**

Mershon & Co., W. B.
B. F. Sturtevant Co. of Canada, Ltd.
Toronto Blower Co.
Yates Machine Company, P. B.

**PORK PACKERS**

Davies Company, William

**POSTS AND POLES**
Anderson, Shreiner & Mawson
Auger & Company
Canadian Tie & Lumber Co.
Dupuis, Limited, J. P.
Eagle Lumber Company
Harris Tie & Timber Co., Ltd.
Long-Bell Lumber Co.
Mason, Gordon & Co.
McLennan Lumber Company
Terry & Gordon

**PULLEYS AND SHAFTING**
Canadian Link-Belt Company
General Supply Co. of Canada, Ltd.
Green Company. G. Walter
Engineering & Machine Works of
   Canada
Hamilton Company, William

**PULP MILL MACHINERY**
Canadian Link-Belt Company, Ltd.
Engineering & Machine Works of
   Canada
Hamilton Company, William
Payette Company, P.
Waterous Engine Works Company

**PULPWOOD**
Bethune Pulp & Lumber Co.
British & Foreign Agencies
D'Auteuil Lumber Co.
Price Bros. & Co.
Scott, Draper & Co.

**PUMPS**
General Supply Co. of Canada, Ltd.
Engineering & Machine Works of
   Canada
Hamilton Co., William
Hopkins & Co. ,Ltd., F. H.
Smart-Turner Machine Company
Waterous Engine Works Company

**RAILS**
Gartshore, John J.
Hopkins & Co. ,Ltd., F. H.

**ROOFINGS**
(Rubber, Plastic and Liquid)
Beveridge Supply Company
Reed & Co., Geo. W.

**ROPE**
Consumers' Cordage Co.

**RUBBER GOODS**
Dunlop Tire & Rubber Goods Co.
Gutta Percha & Rubber Company

**SASH**
Brompton Lumber & Mfg. Co.
Midland Woodworkers
Midland Wood Products, Ltd.

**SAWS**
Atkins & Company, E. C.
Disston & Sons, Henry
General Supply Co. of Canada, Ltd.
Gerlach Company, Peter
Green Company, G. Walter
Hoe & Company, R.
Radcliff Saw Mfg. Co.,
Shurly Co., Ltd., T. F.
Shurly-Dietrich Company
Simonds Canada Saw Company

**SAW GRINDERS**
Smith Foundry Co.

**SAW MILL LINK-BELT**
Canadian Link-Belt Company

**SAW MILL MACHINERY**
Canadian Link-Belt Company, Ltd.
General Supply Co. of Canada, Ltd.
G. Walter Green Co., Ltd.
Hamilton Company, William
La Compagnie Manufacture, F. X.
   Bertrand
Long Manufacturing Company, E.
Mershon & Company, W. B.
Parry Sound Lumber Company
Payette Company, P.
Waterous Engine Works Company
Yates Machine Co., P. B.

**SAW SHARPENERS**
Hamilton Company, William
Waterous Engine Works Company

**SAW SLASHERS**
Hamilton Company, Wm.
Payette Company, P.
Waterous Engine Works Company

**SHINGLES**
Apex Lumber Co.
Associated Mills, Limited
Brennen & Sons, F. W.
Cameron Lumber Co.
Campbell-MacLaurin Lumber Co.
Canadian Western Lumber Co.
Carew Lumber Co., John
Chaleurs Bay Mills
Chesbro, R. G.
D'Auteuil Lumber Co.
Dry Wood Lumber Co.
Eagle Lumber Company
Federal Lumber Company
Fraser, Limited
Gillespie, James
Gloucester Lumber & Trading Co.
Grier & Sons, Limited, G. A.
Harris Tie & Timber Company, Ltd.
Heaps & Sons
Heeney, Percy E.
Mason, Gordon & Co.
McLennan Lumber Company
Miller Company, Ltd., W. H.
Reynolds Company, Limited
Rose, McLaurin, Limited
Stalker, Douglas A.
Terry & Gordon
Timms, Phillips & Co.
Vancouver Lumber Company
Vanderhoof Lumber Co.

**SHINGLE & LATH MACHINERY**
Green Company, C. Walter
Hamilton Company, William
Long Manufacturing Company, E.
Payette Company, P.

**SILENT CHAIN DRIVES**
Canadian Link-Belt Company, Ltd.

**SLEEPING EQUIPMENT**
Simmons Limited

**SLEEPING ROBES**
Woods Mfg. Company, Ltd.

**SMOKESTACKS**
Hamilton Company, Wm.
Reed & Co., Geo. W.
Waterous Engine Works Company

**SNOW PLOWS**
Pink Company, Thomas

**SOLDERS**
Canada Metal Co.

**SPARK ARRESTORS**
Reed & Co., Geo. W.
Waterous Engine Works Company

**SPRUCE**
Anderson, Shreiner & Mawson
Barrett, Wm.
Cameron Lumber Co.
Campbell, McLaurin Lumber Co.
Canadian Western Lumber Co.
Chesbro, R. G.
Cox, Long & Co.
Dudley, Arthur N.
Fraser, Limited
Fraser-Bryson Lumber Company
Gillies Brothers

Gloucester Lumber & Trading Co.
Goodday & Company, H. R.
Grier & Sons, Ltd., G. A.
Harris Lumber Co., Frank H.
Hart, Hamilton & Jackson
Hocken Lumber Company
Julien, Roch
Larkin Co., C. A.
Lay & Haight
Lloyd, W. Y.
Loggie Co., W. S.
Mason, Gordon & Co.
McCormack Lumber Co.
McDonagh Lumber Co.
McLennan Lumber Company
Muir & Kirkpatrick
New Ontario Colonization Company
Northern Lumber Mills
Pigeon River Lumber Co.
Power Lumber Co.
Price Bros. & Co.
Rolland Lumber Co.
Rose, McLaurin, Limited
W. & J. Sharpless.
Spencer, Limited, C. A.
Strong, G. M.
Terry & Gordon
U. G. G. Sawmills. Limited
Vanderhoof Lumber Co.

**STEAM SHOVELS**
Hopkins & Co., Ltd., F. H.

**STEEL CHAIN**
Canadian Link-Belt Company, Ltd.
Hopkins & Co. ,Ltd., F. H.
Waterous Engine Works Company

**STEAM PLANT ACCESSORIES**
Waterous Engine Works Company

**STEEL BARRELS**
Smart-Turner Machine Co.

**STEEL DRUMS**
Smart-Turner Machine Co.

**TARPAULINS**
Turner & Sons, J. J.
Woods Manufacturing Company, Ltd.

**TANKS**
Hopkins & Co., Ltd., F. H.

**TENTS**
Turner & Sons, J. J.
Woods Mfg. Company

**TIES**
Austin & Nicholson
Carew Lumber Co., John
Canadian Tie & Lumber Co.
Chaleurs Bay Mills
D'Auteuil Lumber Co.
Gloucester Lumber & Trading Co.
Harris Tie & Timber Company. Ltd.
McLennan Lumber Company
Miller, W. H. Co.
Price Bros. & Co.
Scott, Draper & Co.
Terry & Gordon

**TIMBER BROKERS**
Bradley, R. R.
Cant & Kemp
Farnworth & Jardine
Wright, Graham & Co.

**TIMBER CRUISERS AND
ESTIMATORS**
Savage & Bartlett.
Sewall, James W.

**TIMBER LANDS**
Department of Lands & Forests, Ont.

**TOWING MACHINES**
Corbet Foundry & Machine Co.
Payette Company, P.
West, Peachy & Sons

**TRACTORS**
Holt Manufacturing Company
Hopkins & Company; Ltd., F. H.
Monarch Tractors
Mussens Ltd.

**TRANSMISSION MACHINERY**
Canadian Link-Belt Company, Ltd.
Engineering & Machine Works of
   Canada
General Supply Co. of Canada, Ltd.
Grand Rapids Vapor Kiln
Hamilton Company, Wm.
Waterous Engine Works Company

**TURBINES**
Engineering & Machine Works of
   Canada
Hamilton Company, William
B. F. Sturtevant Co. of Canada, Ltd.

**VALVES**
Crane Limited

**VAPOR KILNS**
Grand Rapids Vapor Kiln
B. F. Sturtevant Co. of Canada, Ltd.

**VENEERS**
Bury & Co., Robt.

**VENEER DRYERS**
Coe Manufacturing Company
B. F. Sturtevant Co. of Canada, Ltd.

**VENEER MACHINERY**
Coe Machinery Company

**VETERINARY REMEDIES**
Dr. Bell Veterinary Wonder Co.
Johnson, A. H.

**WARPING TUGS**
West, Peachy & Sons

**WATER WHEELS**
Engineering & Machine Works of
   Canada
Hamilton Company, William

**WELDING**
St. John Welders & Engineers

**WIRE**
Canada Metal Co.
Laidlaw Bale Tie Company
Canada Wire & Iron Goods Co.

**WIRE CLOTH**
Canada Wire & Iron Goods Co.

**WIRE ROPE**
Canada Wire & Iron Goods Co.
Hopkins & Co. ,Ltd., F. H.
Dominion Wire Rope Co.
Greening Wire Co., B.

**WOODWORKING MACHINERY**
General Supply Co. of Canada, Ltd.
Long Manufacturing Company, E.
Mershon & Company, W. B.
Waterous Engine Works Company
Yates Machine Company, P. B.

**WOOD PRESERVATIVES**
Beveridge Supply Company

**WOOD PULP**
Austin & Nicholson
New Ontario Colonization Co
Power Lumber Co.

# YATES

## TYPE A 4
# PLANER - MATCHER

The A 4 is another of the Yates-line of Planers and Matchers, and a medium priced machine. It does not give as fast a feed as some of our other types, but will give feeds from 50 to 200 feet per minute. Can be equipped with or without profiling attachment. Bottom head can be lowered in an instant to do single surfacing.

*Our Planer and Matcher booklet describes this machine fully, setting forth its outstanding features. Send for your copy.*

### P. B. Yates Machine Co. Ltd.
#### Hamilton        Canada

Eastern Sales Office
M. E. CASEY CO. LIMITED
263 St. James Street,        Montreal, Quebec

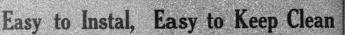

# A Super Re-Saw

For years we have recognized the faults of the horizontal re-saw, such as the excessive space taken up in the mill—the necessity of raising or lowering the bed, or the saw blade itself, in order to change the thickness of cut—the difficulty of separating the slab from the lumber at the rear of the machine, and the advisability of having every slab inspected by the sawyer before being passed through the machine. But until recently we have never been able to perfect a vertical re-saw which would meet in every way the high standard of excellence which every machine bearing the name of WATEROUS must possess.

We are at last, however, able to offer to the sawmill Men of Canada, a machine that not only overcomes the above faults, but one which combines all the advantages of the horizontal and vertical re-saws.

Here is a machine which will positively cut

straight slabs and half-logs regardless of irregularities of material. The bed consists of four fluted rolls which are adjustable and which take the place of the planed table.

There are two press rolls. The first swings on a vertical shaft in a frame which presses firmly against the feed rolls, bent to the saw in a stream actuated saw tooth roll. These two rolls are so arranged as to automatically take care of all variations in the size and shape of the slabs. The swinging arm roller mounts any slab immediately and the pressure of the oscillating cylinder aligns the slab against the next two feed rolls swinging the tail of the slab immediately in the line of the saw cut, this taking place before the saw enters the cut.

This arrangement prevents the usual thick or thin or stepped ends that are so common in all re-saws carrying the single press rolls and feed rolls.

# Waterous
### BRANTFORD, ONTARIO, CANADA

Molson's Bank Bldg., Vancouver, B. C.                    Winnipeg, Manitoba.

Vol. 42                    Toronto, March 1, 1922                    No. 5

# Canada Lumberman

*founded 1880*

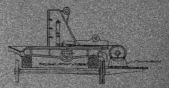
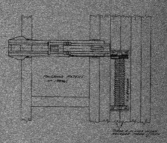

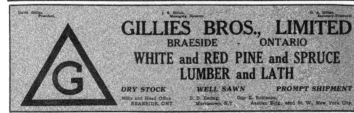

# Geo. Gordon & Co.

### Limited

#### CACHE BAY - ONTARIO

We Manufacture

# PINE

## Lumber, Timber and Lath

If in a hurry for high quality Pine, properly graded, Rough or Dressed, send us your next order.

## COX, LONG & COMPANY, LIMITED

### 433 Coristine Building, MONTREAL, Canada.

Are the Authorized Agents for the

## Associated Importers, Limited

of London, England

Owners of the

# British Government Lumber Stocks in the Quebec and Lower Port Districts

to whom all enquiries for any of these goods must be sent

*COLONIAL PAPERS PLEASE COPY*

# White Pine
# Red Pine
# Jack Pine
# Spruce
# Lumber
## and Lath

**UNION LUMBER COMPANY LIMITED**
701 DOMINION BANK BUILDING
TORONTO                CANADA

# MR. DEALER

## Is Your Yard
## Stocked AND Ready
### FOR
## Spring Requirements?

## We are ready to supply your wants
### FROM
## ONTARIO - QUEBEC - BRITISH COLUMBIA

## TERRY AND GORDON
### LIMITED
## CANADIAN FOREST PRODUCTS
HEAD OFFICE
BRANCH **TORONTO** BRANCH
MONTREAL EUROPEAN AGENTS VANCOUVER
SPENCER LOCK & Co., LONDON, ENG.

---

# LUMBER
## ─Wanted─
## Mill-cuts in

# W. Pine
# Hemlock
# Birch
# Elm
# Maple

## C. G. Anderson Lumber Company, Limited

**Manufacturers and Strictly Wholesale Dealers in Lumber**

SALES OFFICE

## 705 Excelsior Life Building
## Toronto

---

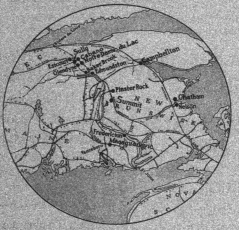

DOUGLAS FIR
LUMBER
RED CEDAR
SHINGLES

## The Question of Supply

During the past two months our mill
connections have been handicapped
by unusual weather conditions, but
we are glad to state that we are now
in a position to give our usual prompt service in your requirements.

### Timms Phillips & Co., Ltd.
Vancouver, B. C.

TORONTO OFFICE: Canada Permanent Bldg.
Phone Adel. 6490
MONTREAL OFFICE: 23 Marconi Bldg.
Phone M 2999

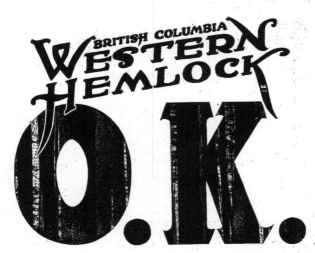

## Ask the Man Who Has Used it

The proof of the value of wood is in the service obtained therefrom.

Lumber dealers and their customers are getting to like BRITISH COLUMBIA WESTERN HEMLOCK better the more they deal in it or use it.

It is not a hardwood but is possessed of a grain that is externally beautiful. It takes a high polish, is free from pitch and "shakes" and possesses great strength.

Don't wait until all your competitors have established a reputation for handling BRITISH COLUMBIA WESTERN HEMLOCK.

We'll be glad to send you BRITISH COLUMBIA WESTERN HEMLOCK in mixed carloads along with our other BIG CHIEF Brand Specialties, British Columbia Red Cedar Shingles, and Cedar and Fir lumber in all sizes known to high-class manufacture.

## VANCOUVER LUMBER CO., LIMITED, Vancouver, B.C.

Branch Sales Offices at Toronto, Ont., Winnipeg, Man., Chicago, Ill

# BUY
## BRITISH COLUMBIA
# Red Cedar Shingles

The life of a British Columbia Red Cedar Shingle Roof can almost be gauged by the life of the nail with which the shingle is nailed in place. Judging from available data, the average life of the ordinary steel wire nail, which has been in such common use, is only from seven to twelve years. Some wire nails will last longer, depending upon the condition of exposure, climate and similar features, but considering our climate as a whole, at the end of from seven to twelve years a large percentage of wire nails will have rusted either completely through or so extensively that the first strong wind will complete the work. The shingles that have been held in position by such nails are then free to work down, permitting rains or melting snows to leak through and damage the interior of the structure. Examination will disclose that the fibre of the shingle itself is still in perfect condition, and a leaky roof, in the majority of occasions is due entirely to the use of faulty nails, but the average home owner, placed at such inconvenience, will not stop to reason this out and the poor wooden shingle comes in for more unjust abuse.

There are several kinds of nails which experience has proven will give lasting satisfaction, and the wise dealer will advise his customers of these satisfactory nails. A pure zinc shingle nail meets all the demands of durability required. Its principal drawback is its high cost and a slight tendency to bend under careless driving. Galvanised wire nails theoretically are rust proof, and if the galvanized coating is properly applied, and of sufficient thickness, such a nail will last as long as the shingle it holds in place. The life of this shingle roof, properly applied with these nails then is from 40 to 50 years. Pure iron nails, or the old cut or wrought nails are ideal but difficult to secure. Copper nails also constitute a perfect shingle nail.

| | |
|---|---|
| **Timms Phillips & Co., Ltd.**<br>Yorkshire Bldg., Vancouver<br>Manufacturers and Wholesalers<br>**Red Cedar Shingles**<br>5x-8x Perfections, Royals, Imperials<br>**Red Cedar Bevel Siding** | **Vancouver Lumber Co., Ltd.**<br>Manufacturers<br>**XXX—XXXXX CEDAR SHINGLES**<br>(Rite Grade Inspected)<br>Head Office    Eastern Sales Office<br>Vancouver, B.C.    Toronto, Ont. |
| **Westminster Mill Co.**<br>LIMITED<br>New Westminster, B.C.<br>**Red Cedar Shingles**<br>**Cedar Bevel Siding** | **Dominion Timber Products Ltd.**<br>Vancouver Block<br>Vancouver<br>Largest Manufacturers of<br>**Perfection Shingles**<br>in Canada |
| **Underhill Lumber Co., Ltd.**<br>Dominion Bldg., Vancouver<br>**RED CEDAR SHINGLES**<br>5x-8x Perfection and Eureka<br>**CEDAR BEVEL SIDING**<br>**CEDAR BUNGALOW SIDING** | **Shull Lumber & Shingle Co**<br>Limited<br>New Westminster, B.C.<br>Trade Mark<br>**RED BAND SHINGLES**<br>XXX XXXXX Stars Clears<br>From Mill to You |
| If you want a market for B. C. Red Cedar Shingles put an advertisement on this page. | **Kootenay Shingle Co. Ltd.**<br>Salmo, B. C.<br>**Red Cedar Shingles**<br>xxx and xx.<br>Packed by the thousand |

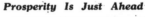

Excerpts from a booklet by
The H. K. Ferguson Co., Engineers and Builders

# Advertising and Construction

An actual and definite relation between the two

The past twenty-five years, marked by the ever-increasing application of the force called advertising to a wider and wider range of business problems, have, of course, built up a growing fund of general information with regard to the effects of advertising.

We have all recently seen the publication of figures indicating that 84% of all business failures in 1920 were of concerns which failed to advertise. An analysis of the factory-construction records of my own company shows that 83¾% of our customers are advertisers.

Stated differently, the figures indicate that the manufacturer who advertises is five times as likely to stay in business as his non-advertising competitor, and is five times as likely to need more factory space which he will probably buy in two and one-half times the quantity required by the non-advertiser.

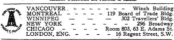

**Canada Lumberman**

founded 1880

*The National Lumber Journal for Forty Years*

Issued on the 1st and 15th of every month by

HUGH C. MACLEAN PUBLICATIONS, Limited

THOS. S. YOUNG, Managing Director

HEAD OFFICE - - - - 347 Adelaide Street, West, TORONTO

Proprietors and Publishers also of Electrical News, Contract Record, Canadian Woodworker and Footwear in Canada.

VANCOUVER - - - - - - Winch Building
MONTREAL - - - - - 119 Board of Trade Bldg.
WINNIPEG - - - - - 302 Travellers' Bldg.
NEW YORK - - - - - - 296 Broadway
CHICAGO - - - - - Room 803, 63 E. Adams St.
LONDON, ENG. - - - - 16 Regent Street, S.W.

TERMS OF SUBSCRIPTION

Canada, United States and Great Britain, $3.00 per year, in advance; other foreign countries embraced in the General Postal Union, $4.00.

Single copies, 20 cents.

Authorized by the Postmaster-General for Canada, for transmission as second-class matter.

Vol. 42                 Toronto, March 1, 1922                 No. 5

## Pushing Repair Work is Good Business

While there may be building activity in the cities and larger towns this season, it is predicted that in most of the rural sections trade will be quiet.

Owing to the low prices of farm produce and live stock, many yeomen seem pessimistic or discouraged, declaring they will not spend anything until values ascend, and they are assured of a good crop; in fact in rural ranks there are apparently quite a number of blue ruin apostles. Record prices were realized by the farmer for his goods during the war, and it is difficult for him to become reconciled with the present low figure set upon his wheat, hogs, cattle, etc.

While the farmer may not see his way clear to undertake new buildings or fences it is false economy overlooking his present ones in the way of repairs. An old aphorism is "A stitch in time saves nine," and no truer epigram was ever uttered. It is a short-sighted policy and blind injustice to neglect keeping what he possesses in good order, for once a structure starts on the road to ruin, disintegration rapidly takes place.

The retail lumberman has here a splendid opportunity to come in live, vital contact with his customers. He should take drives out around the surrounding country and see whose barns, sheds and houses need attention. Then, either by personal call or timely literature, he should get in touch with the owners. The retailer can do much to stir up interest in repairs and carry on an effective publicity campaign under attractive captions such as "Make those repairs now;" "Don't neglect that roof until it is too late;" "Get busy before the spring rush sets in." "The longer the delay, the greater the cost." He should drive home the point that many repairs and alterations can be carried out when weather permits. The proper time for the farmer to conduct such operations is between his busy seasons. Here is where the retail lumberman can show that he has a little initiative and foresight by exercising good judgment and common sense.

The repair business is one that should not be neglected. It makes for expansion of trade and establishes new friends, because where a customer goes to procure his material for overhauling his buildings, there he will likely proceed for supplies when he starts new construction. The local lumber merchant, who comes in active touch with those, who, while they may not build now, yet may later launch out, has double the chance of catering to their requirements.

Repairs and replacements should always be made promptly. It is hard to instil this doctrine into the minds of some persons, particularly those in an agricultural community, who are professedly procrastinators, in the matter of attending to things when they ought to be done. This does not apply, of course, to all classes of farmers, but some, especially those on rented places, are notoriously shiftless. A little tact and diplomacy will have to be shown, by the retail lumberman in getting after these persons, who keep putting off repairs, but the leaven of education bears fruit, and in time the cumulative results will prove satisfactory.

A few boards, a bunch or two of shingles, some cedar posts and a bundle of lath, may seem scarcely worth bothering with, but it is the attention to these details that strengthens connection with one's trade and paves the way for larger items and enduring business relationships.

Many firms advertise "No job too small, no order too little to receive our prompt and careful attention." This is the right spirit, and upon little things vast undertakings are reared. It will be remembered that the nimble 5 cent and 10 cent piece has built up one of the greatest chain of department stores in America and also resulted in the erection of the Woolworth Building in New York, the world's most stupendous structure. An old Scotch proverb says "Many mickles mak a muckle," and small orders in the aggregate mount up more rapidly than would appear on the surface.

By boosting repairs and looking after the minor wants of the farmer, the retail lumberman is building one of the greatest assets that he can possess, viz., the goodwill of his customers. At the same time he is playing an important part in keeping alive the spirit for order, beauty and neatness in the neighborhood in which he does business. It should be his object to serve in a wider sense than that of merely selling so many boards for a specified amount. He is a community builder and should be a little bigger than his business. He who can see beyond the mere taking in of so much cash, who establishes for himself a name and a standing that are worth while, continues to function while others sit around and shout hard times, just because they have not caught the proper vision of service and co-operation.

## Why Should Retail Lumbermen Give Discount?

Money is made in various ways and in different vocations. Some people are born wealthy, others accumulate a fortune and a few others work the graft game and get by with it too. There are higher callings, however, than being a mere promoter, a divvy-up man, a fellow who has to have a secret rebate or who views everything in life from a mercenary motive.

The question arises among those of meagre mind. "How much is there in it for me?" Some fellows never want to render a service unless they can get something out of it. Like the dining room waiter, the bell boy and the pullman porter, they always have the hand-out in view. It is the same way with a few contractors in nearly every centre who do business with the retail lumberman. Unless he grants them a certain discount or commission on their business they openly assert they will place their purchases elsewhere. Sometimes an invertebrate individual yields to this threat.

This is a somewhat sordid side of the great lumber problems of to-day but one worthy of attention. In very few towns in the East, do the retail lumbermen grant a discount to contractors. They find that they can do business without it. Once the door is opened to this practice there is no end to the abuse which widens, until confidence in the whole fabric of the industry is undermined and, in the end, there are apt to be many bickerings and heart-burnings. There are, in every centre, of course, contracting carpenters and contractors who want to bleed the retail lumberman. They imagine they should have a 5% or 10% discount off list prices on all business placed; yet many of these self-same contractors and local carpenters are put in touch with most profitable jobs and secure a lot of valuable contracts by pointers or advice received from the lumber dealer.

In order to get a proper view of many problems, it is necessary to approach them from the reverse side, or in other words, instead of being on the outside looking in, why not enter and take a gaze outwards?

Whoever heard of a contractor giving a retail lumber dealer 5 or 10% on the contract price of a job simply because the retail dealer had given him a pointer or furnished him with a list of prospects; yet the latter proposition is just as feasible and sensible from many standpoints as the former.

The only ground on which a contractor often makes a claim for a special discount is that he is performing a service for his customer by buying materials. The ordinary citizen is not familiar with what he requires when it comes to construction and, therefore, depends upon the contractor who may think that he is entitled to some consideration for the extra labor involved. Perhaps this is true, but why should the retail lumber dealer be made the victim? The contractor is acting as a purchasing agent for his client, and it is the client who should pay. If the former wants to make an extra 10%, let him do so out of the man from whom he has received the contract and not from the lumber dealer whose prices are low enough, and has to carry stocks and invest a large amount of money in the way of yard, plant and equipment. He has also to run great market fluctuations in these days of drastic depression, and if there is any profit to be made, the lumber dealer is the one entitled to it and not the contractor who travels on much safer ground. His outlay con-

sists principally in tools and equipment, and is not nearly as heavy as that of the ordinary materials men.

From interviews with representative retailers in various cities of Canada, it is almost unanimously declared that it is not necessary any rebate should be granted the contractor. The stamp of men, who are looking for any concessions from the retail lumberman are not, generally speaking, worth having on the lists of patrons. The trouble with too many incompetent individuals, is that they want to "cash in" on propositions "both going and coming." Some unscrupulous contractors have been known to exact an extra percentage from the owner and then get a similar gratuity from the lumberman. In this respect he resembles the servant trying to satisfy two masters, but it cannot be done openly and above board. If a contractor or builder cannot make a legitimate profit on his own operations, there is something radically wrong with his mental make-up or business acumen.

There are other sides to this question,—"Should the contractor have a special discount?" The bulk of opinion outside of the ethical aspect altogether, is that each trade should stand on its own bottom. There is no reason why, the retail lumberman, who has enough to bear during this period of keen competition, uncertain outlook and industrial inactivity, should be made "the goat" of any organization or individual with whom he does business. The lumber dealer, who will not face the issue straightforwardly is unworthy of being engaged in a fair, stand-up fight in which service, efficiency and honor play the part rather than intrigue, secrecy and double-dealing.

---

### Personality as a Factor in Business

Much has been said about service in lumber merchandising; in fact the subject has possibly been written about and talked about until it is threadbare.

Another feature which might receive attention is that on personality in business. Personality, plus service, makes a strong combination. There is no doubt that, other things being equal, in the way of stock, price and delivery, many a man selling lumber to-day gets a preference in orders, through the genial, obliging, helpful and friendly qualities which he possesses. It is the same, too, in connection with the retail business of the dealer in smaller towns. Where he is able to greet his customers by name or to remember a caller, he is in a much more fortunate position than the fellow who has to spar around for an opening to find out the identity of a visitor every time one enters. Most persons like to be remembered, and not be asked on every occasion "name please." "where will we send this to?" etc. Some retailers will recall the name of a customer months after, even although the person, may have come into the office only once or twice, while other men will make three or four calls and frequently more before the merchant is able to "label them."

The retail lumberman who makes some effort to recollect the name of his customers, to know their addresses, to preserve a correct mailing list and see that certain literature goes out at different periods of the year, is going a long way to establish a relationship that is bound to count for the future.

The distributor of forest products knows what personality means. It is not necessary to give it any definite, detailed description. All he has to do is to think over the wholesalers or manufacturers with whom he does business, and apart altogether from the character of their stock, grading, service, etc., there are certain firms with whom he likes to trade much better than with others. It is the same, too, in connection with the visit of salesmen. There are always a few who are particularly welcome and are given more than an ordinarily cordial reception, whether the dealer desires to buy, or not. Other fellows come in and pass the time of day, exchange a few generalities or inquiries and move out again without leaving any lasting impression or pleasant memories. There is nothing offensive about them; they do not seem to find favor with their customers or, use a colloquial expression "catch on" or "fit in."

Personality is something hard to explain. There is no doubt that many lumbermen are gifted with a pleasing, cheerful, optimistic nature. By that is not meant hot-air artists or the bull-shooters, but those who take the sane, common-sense view of life, who show that they have tact and judgment, are able to think of someone outside of themselves, and possess an interest in that which is beyond the immediate signing of an order. Personality, is a silent, potent intangible element in business success and expansion which, while many-sided is, after all, comprehensive and may be cultivated to an unusual degree. Personality is like good-will, something that cannot be fathomed in the ordinary artificialities and insencerities of life.

### Practical Results in Lumbering Activities

Although the papers read at the annual meeting of the Woodlands Section of the Canadian Pulp & Paper Association and the Province of Quebec Forest Protective Association, reported in the last issue of the "Canada Lumberman" dealt chiefly with forestry subjects, they had a more or less direct bearing on matters which are of interest to lumbermen, especially those engaged in the manufacturing end. Naturally, the main interest of the pulp and paper companies is in pulp-wood and its products, but several are manufacturers of lumber and in that respect their problems are those of other limit-holders and mill men. Such questions as fire protection, stumpage dues and logging methods and improvements are common to all, and so far as the Province of Quebec is concerned, there is a distinct tendency for the pulp and paper companies to co-operate with lumbermen on subjects which affect them both.

In the past, there probably has been an inclination on the part of forestry engineers to indulge too much in theory—they have not fully grasped what may be described as the commercial side of the lumber trade. Theories have sometimes an unfortunate habit of not working out in practice and the idealists, say for example, on the subject of re-afforestation, do not always consider the practical aspect. On the other hand, some lumbermen are inclined to disregard questions which have no direct bearing on the business end of lumbering. The middle course would appear to be the right one—the application of such forestry measures as experience shows will make for the permanency of our forest resources and the expansion of our domestic and foreign lumber trade. The discussion at the meetings of such associations are of value in that they tend to bring the practical men in contact with the theorists and thus develop ideas and methods which are of importance to the industry.

In connection with the technical side of the lumber and pulp trades, the action of the Governors of McGill University is of interest. They have decided to establish the Mrs. E. B. Eddy Chair of Industrial Research. Mrs. Eddy left a sum for the founding of chairs at the University, and in view of the fact that the Eddy family have been connected with the forest products of Canada, in the lumber and other departments for many years, it was decided that the holders of the professorship must give special attention to chemistry connected with wood products. It will be recollected that the Forest Products Laboratories already form a part of McGill University, and no doubt the new chair of industrial research will be associated with the work of the Laboratories.

---

### Sign Posts in Successful Lumber Career

One of the outstanding retail lumbermen in America is Julius Seidel, president of the Julius Seidel Lumber Co., of St. Louis, Mo. He recently celebrated his 40th anniversary in business and had a reunion of his leading employees, many of whom have been associated with him for years. It is on occasions such as these, especially when a gentleman of Mr. Seidel's influence, perspicacity and analytical mind, turns over the events of his career, that some strong points in present-day conditions are brought out; for instance, when he started in the lumber line 40 years ago 90% of the lumber used in St. Louis was white pine, which was floated down the Mississippi in rafts. The cost of transporting this was 90 cents per M feet. To-day the transportation charge from southern production centres is $8.00 per M.

Mr. Seidel stressed the point of thrift in connection with the development of any young man's character and manhood. He said this lesson had been impressed upon him by his father, and it was by the exercise of thrift that he had been enabled to go into business in 1903 on his own capital—and not that of other people.

It is interesting to harken to the advice of one who knows what he is talking about and personally has achieved signal success. Such counsel is much more timely and pertinent than that of a mere dreamer or theorist, hence the following points from this widely-known St. Louis lumberman will be read with interest.

Do not forget that contentment should be your aim while filling your life's work. Be satisfied to do your best and happy that you have done the work well. My mother's maxim to her children, "that if we had done our best we had only done our duty," is well applied. Do your work thoroughly—for the love of it and aim to be a master of the art rather than a second, third or fourth-rater.

Character must be within you, and ability added in your field will illumine your future. Be honest and true to yourself and always to your co-worker, be they your employee, customer, associate or seller. Life is, indeed, what you make it and while I have been diligent and constantly at it, I admit that I get much pleasure out of my daily work—really more than I can express.

# Lumbermen Should Adopt Code of Trade Ethics

### Forceful Talk by Mr. Littlefield, Outlining Great Movement Sweeping Influential Business Circles in Establishing Standard Practices— Science of Human Duty

Under the new regime and characterized by enthusiasm, the first regular meeting of the Wholesale Lumber Dealers' Association, Inc., was held on February 20th in the banquet room of the King Edward Hotel, Toronto. There was a representative attendance and the proceedings were intresting from start to finish. F. H. Littlefield, general-manager of the Canadian Oil Companies, Limited, Toronto, gave a splendid address on "Business Ethics," in which he pointed out the force of this great movement and urged the lumbermen to join the procession, by adopting a code of established practices.

H. J. Terry presided and under his direction everything went off smoothly and satisfactory. Among those present was George H. Holt, of the Holt Timber Co., Chicago.

It was decided that at the monthly meeting, which will be held on Monday March 20th, the retailers of Toronto will be the guests of the wholesalers.

#### Railway Rates Hearing at Ottawa

Several interesting reports were presented from the committees: H. G. McDermid, for the Bureau of Information, urged more promptness and co-operation in this department.

Roy Halliday, reporting for the Transportation Department, stated that the railway men would receive a hearing on March 7th before the Railway Board in Ottawa, and certain information had been asked for by the Transportation Manager of the Canadian Lumbermen's Association, and it was hoped that it would be forwarded. Mr. Terry said that unless the lumbermen made a strong and effective showing before the Board, they would not get decreased freight rates. He believed that if they struck a united blow at the present time, they would make good headway.

Reporting for the Attendance Committee, K. M. Brown stated the Association desired to have a full representation at each meeting if it was going to accomplish anything definite during 1922. He urged all if they liked the meetings and were interested, to pass along the information and help to get all the members out.

In reference to the March meeting, which will be addressed by Douglas Malloch, of Chicago, the lumberman poet, there will be a musical programme, and it was decided that a complimentary ticket would be sent by the Wholesalers' Association to each of the 33 retail lumber firms in the city, asking that one representative be present. It is expected that this gathering will be an outstanding one in the wholesale and retail trade of Toronto. Mr. Brown explained the financial arrangements.

It was moved by W. W. Carter and seconded by H. G. McDermid, that the Association invite Mr. Malloch for the next meeting in March. This was carried.

#### Matter of Sales Tax Deferred

It was expected that there would be an important discussion of the sales tax which may come up at the forthcoming session of Parliament. Owing to the absence of Mr. Manbert, chairman of the Legislative Committee, a short reference from that body was read by Secretary Horace Boulbee. It said that the Legislative Committee are of the opinion that nothing should be done without further information. They believed that lumber had been specially favored in so far as there is one tax only and is different, therefore, from other manufacturers, who are obliged to collect 1½% and the wholesaler 1½%. They were of the opinion that it is not altogether from reasons economic that the tax is placed where it is, political conditions having a great effect upon the Ministers when placing the tax. On motion of H. G. McDermid and Alex. C. Gordon, the matter of taking further action in regard to the sales tax, was left in the hands of the members of the Legislative Committee until they got some further opinions.

"Business Ethics" was the subject ably and convincingly dealt with by F. H. Littlefield, who was introduced by Chairman Terry. Mr. Littlefield said that trade or business ethics was a matter which various organizations were considering to-day. It was a most vital question, and many representative bodies were striving to reach some ultimate goal. Three questions should be considered in writing a code of ethics. These were,—"Is it worth while to adopt such a code?" and "Does our business demand the adoption of one?" "If

we feel it is worth while, then what kind does the lumber business demand, and what influence will the adoption of it have on the lumber business in our community?" The speaker said he wished to take three texts,—one from an English, another from an American and a third from a Canadian writer. Lord Bacon had said that "men's thoughts are made according to their inclinations," while an American had remarked that "as a man thinketh so he is." Nellie McClung, the widely-known Canadian novelist, in one of her books, said "that humanity can do anything it wants to do, and whoever declares that things can't be done for the betterment of the race, insults the Creator of us all."

#### The Science of Human Duty

"Whether or not what we choose to do is a success, rests largely with ourselves," declared Mr. Littlefield. Webster defined ethics as the science of human duty, while the commandments and laws given to Moses on Mount Sinai were the greatest ever known and the basis of all civilized law to-day. Socrates emphasized the principle of men doing right because it is right, not because it is convenient or expeditious. Do the right thing because it is right and not from any advantage which might be gained

"Honesty is the best policy" had been one of the mottos which the speaker said he had learned at a school. The teacher had driven home the fact that acting upon the principle that honesty should be carried out only for policy's sake, was not honesty at all. It had as a boy taken him some time to get that idea into his head. Plato, Socrates and Pythagoras, who lived before the Christian era, were right in many of their teachings, and laid down as good a code of ethics as could be compiled by us in this generation.

The question arises,—Is it possible to adopt a code of ethics based upon the golden rule, applicable to all lines of human endeavor? It is possible to have an ethical union. Some said that business is an organization solely for profit; yet was it not a fact that the basis of all profitable business is service to your fellow-man. No man can make a success of his business unless his thought is of service to the public and giving a square deal to all, and the more service you give to others, the bigger and better you will build your business. He firmly believed that this is true.

There is too much misunderstanding of the term "ethics" and the principles employed, and to many, the word is visionary in meaning. To use the term "ethics" does not mean we are drifting into Bolshevism, Socialism or some other untried theories. It does mean that we are acting on what Webster described as "the science of human duty," which simply implies that the interpretation of the term is a square deal for all, and that it is possible to have a written code of ethics in every organization.

#### Cause of Business and Public Service

Mr. Littlefield referred to the code of ethics of the Canadian National Newspapers and Periodicals Association. Among the standards of practice of that body was that the members should dedicate their best efforts to the cause of business and public service, and to this end shall pledge themselves; to work for truth and honesty in all departments and to decline any advertising which has a tendency to mislead and, to co-operate with all organizations and individuals engaged in creative advertising work; to avoid unfair competition and to determine what is the highest and largest function in the field which they serve, and then to strive in every legitimate way to promote that function. The American Engravers' Association also adopted a code of ethics and standards of practice. That justice and fair dealing should characterize all their transactions, was one of the leading principles, while striving for quality of service and skill rather than that of lowering prices, was another of its objects.

In adopting a code of ethics by any organization, Mr. Littlefield said the thoughts of service should be uppermost in the mind, the relationship of employer with employee, relationship to other organizations with which we do business, and the relationship to customers and others connected with the welfare and progress of the institution. He thought that a code of ethics could be adopted by the Lumbermen's Association in which the principles he enunciated could be carried out. To-day the thought of all business men and organizations was not primarily that of financial success, but

rather was it a movement along right lines, a square deal and efficient service, thus bringing about the teaching which is called the "brotherhood of man." This had evidently taken root in the lumber organization, and found its expression in the fact that as members they met together and discussed matters of mutual interest and trade topics. This was one of the encouraging signs of the times.

### Some Suggestions for Trade Code

Mr Littlefield spoke of the adoption of a code of correct practices for the lumbermen which would band them together as nothing else could and demonstrate that they had faith in themselves and in one another. He offered the following suggestions:—

A statement covering the personal character rules of conduct for the craftsman himself, or the executive officer, if it be a corporation.

Rules of conduct governing the relation of the employer with the employee, (the observation of which may be the only known antidote for social unrest).

Rules of conduct governing the craftsman's relations with those from whom he makes purchases.

Rules of conduct governing the craftsman's relations with his fellow craftsmen.

Rules of conduct governing the craftsman's relations with professional men whose professions are interlocked with the craft; such as physicians, engineers, architects, etc.

Rules of conduct respecting the craftsman's relations with the public, presumbly his patrons, both clients and purchasers.

The underlying principles of these rules is Service, flanked with truth and honesty.

Rules of conduct cover ng the making and executing of contracts with special reference to specifications. (This is included as a special heading not only because of its importance but to avoid splitting the topic in its phases under four or five headings.)

A statement of certain well-known violations of the code of correct practices, with strong discouragement of such practices. In brief,—a statement of the DON'TS of business conduct.

Concluding the speaker said—the adoption of a code of business ethics will make you one of the great army in a movement that is sweeping the world, organizing not a league of nations or cities or communities, but a league of men who are pledged to a square deal for themselves, their competitors their employes and their customers. I want to say that if the commercial life of the world had been based on the ideas and ideals of a square deal for the last one hundred years there would have been no war with Germany. Among the various organizations who are adopting a code of trade ethics, and correct practices, you will find the biggest and brainiest men and, when this new order of things prevails, we are going to look out upon a condition of affairs in which strife will be eliminated—not altogether perhaps—but a step will have been taken in the right direction. I would recommend your organization to give this matter due consideration and that his matter due consideration and had met with considerable success. I hope you may see your way clear to adopt a code of business ethics, that will give to the world those high principles for which such a body as the wholesale lumber dealers should stand.

### National Wholesalers Will Meet in Washington

Plans are rapidly developing for the thirtieth Annual Convention of the National Wholesale Lumber Dealers' Association to be,

held at the New Willard Hotel, Washington, D. C., Wednesday and Thursday, March 22nd and 23rd. Addresses of a purely perfunctory nature will be eliminated. The committee reports will be pointed and brief, plenty of time being permitted for discussions of problems of direct Association interest, such as credits, collections, arbitration, transportation, etc..

The Annual Banquet will be held on Thursday evening, March 23rd, the principal speaker being the Hon. George Wharton Pepper, the newly appointed Senator from Pennsylvania. In addition a distinguished speaker will come from Canada. As usual with the National Association, the ladies will participate with the men in the Banquet and listen to the after dinner speaking. Among the honorary guests will be Vice-president and Mrs. Calvin Coolidge, Secretary of the Treasury Mellon, and others. A Dinner Dance will be given on Wednesday evening, March 22. The President of the United States, Warren G. Harding, would like to have made his plans to be one of the Banquet speakers, but this being out of the question, he has invited the members of the Association, their guests and accompanying ladies, to meet him in the East Room of the White House during the convention.

### Mr. Joyce Starts Business for Himself

Harold D. Joyce, who for the past seven years was eastern representative of the Union Lumber Co., of Toronto, in both a buying and selling capacity, has gone into the wholesale lumber business on his own behalf. Mr. Joyce's office is at present at 262 Hampton Ave., Montreal, but in a few weeks he will take up his quarters in the new Canada Cement Building, in the commercial metropolis.

Mr. Joyce has had a wide insight in buying and selling, and also gained experience in yard work and office routine in the lumber line. He is specializing in Quebec forest products and in Ontario pine.

Mr. Joyce is widely known in Quebec and the Maritime Provinces and is an energetic and well liked lumberman. He is of the opinion that from now on the industry may look for a gradual improvement in trade without anything sensational in the way of market conditions. "These are," he says, "undoubtedly the days when salesmanship counts for the most and an expenditure of energy will be required to bring results. A keen eye will be needed to watch credits which for the next month in particular will warrant careful attention."

### Using Jack-Pine for Paper Making

That it is quite feasible to use jack pine in the manufacture of newsprint, was the contention of Maurice Neilson of the Belgian Industrial Company, Limited, Shawinigan Falls, Que., in a paper read by him before the technical section of the Canadian Pulp and Paper Association, at its annual meeting held recently in Montreal. Mr. Neilson stated that his company had been carrying on extensive experiments with jack pine, under both the sulphite and ground-wood processes, and had met with considerable success.

The point was brought out in discussion that available spruce forests were being rapidly depleted, and that the consequence was longer hauls, more expensive wood and a higher-priced wood at the mill. Jack pine, on the other hand, is plentiful, cheap, and attains commercial size forty years earlier than spruce.

Making "Ship Knees" in Nova Scotia Woods Shops

Scene in Yarmouth County where the axemen are carefully felling a tree, taking a portion of the curved root, which forms the bow of the boat.

# How Canada Trains Young Men for the Extension of Export Trade

*By H. R. Poussette, Ottawa, Director of Commercial Intelligence Service

I am particularly pleased to be present at the convention of the Canadian Lumbermen's Association as, owing to your splendid organization and the fact that lumbering is one of the basic industries of this country, I feel that it is a meeting of considerable importance. It is perhaps because you are so efficiently organized and so many of your members have been engaged in export trade for such a long period of time that I feel that we are not able in the Commercial Intelligence Service to be of so much use to you as perhaps the producers of other classes of commodities. In spite of this, I have little doubt that you will find from time to time that we can be of service to you, and particularly to some of those lumber firms who may be opening out new markets. In fact, I know from my correspondence that this is the case, although perhaps it applies more to operators on the Coast than to Eastern Canada. However, time will show to what degree you will find it to your interest to make use of the Commercial Intelligence Service. But, whatever may be your sources of information, and whatever the ramifications of your several organizations, you may rest assured that it will be very gratifying to us to find at any time that we can be of service to the members of this organization.

I am in hopes that the Service may continue to improve in efficiency, and I feel confident that this will prove to be the case owing to the system which we now have of securing recruits for it and also for training our young officers. In the old days Trade Commissioners were appointed directly from private life and more, often than not through the system of political patronage. Some of these appointments were satisfactory, some were indifferent and some were practically useless, but happily, however, the last have been weeded out. In those days the appointee to an office usually made a short tour of a part of Canada, and departed for his post with but a hazy idea of his duties.

### The Curriculum of the Department

Today, the successful candidate enters the Department for a year or more intensive training. He has to go through a regular course in my office, remaining so long with one division of it and so long with another. He spends a certain amount of time with the Secretary, to make himself familiar with the correspondence which passes through the Secretary's office, which acts as a sort of clearing house for the branch. Then he has a turn of duty in the office of the Chief of the Foreign Tariffs Division where he learns something of foreign tariffs. Of course, tariffs are pretty well a life study but all we aim to do is to direct the mind of the junior to the subject of tariffs which is necessary when he comes to having an office of his own. He has also to put in a month or more under the watchful eye of the Editor of the "Commercial Intelligence Journal." He has an opportunity in that office to see how the reports of the various Trade Commissioners are edited and by this means he is able to see just what constitutes a useful interesting report. He learns here that while a report may be very interesting it is not entirely useful unless it contains exactly the kind of information that is required by Canadian exporters. I feel sure that the training in the office of the Editor of the "Commercial Intelligence Journal" will prove very valuable to the young officer later on in his career when he has to compile reports himself for publication.

### Meeting Manufacturers and Gaining Knowledge

In addition to the training just mentioned, he has to make a tour of the Trade Enquiry Division, of the Records Branch and the office of the Chief Accountant. Besides this, Junior Trade Commissioners are given odd jobs to do on which they have to make reports. Finally, they make a tour of the country to meet as many manufacturers as possible and to gain a good practical knowledge of the Dominion and its resources before they go abroad as Assistant Trade Commissioners to be attached to an experienced Trade Commissioner for further training and experience. After this, if considered suitable for promotion the Assistant Trade Commissioner is given an office as a vacancy occurs. From the time a Junior Trade Commissioner enters the service until he goes abroad as an Assist-

*Address delivered before the Canadian Lumbermen's Association in Toronto.

ant Trade Commissioner he is under constant observation and all of his reports and most of his correspondence is scrutinized. We do not do this in order to find fault but for the good of our young officers so that, before they leave the office, if they have any weaknesses we may discover them in order that they may be corrected. That this is appreciated by the Juniors rather than resented is proved by the fine spirit which prevails in our office.

Compare the present system with the old. Formerly a man went out to a foreign country, possibly not suited for the job and with little idea of his duties. Today these young men will go out with a knowledge of what is expected of them and they should thus be able to jump in and perform valuable work from the beginning. Indeed, I may say that some of them have done very excellent work, or are doing very excellent work before going abroad, as the records of my office will show.

It is of course easy to make comparisons and today we have the advantage of years of experience and the knowledge gained from mistakes made. There were many difficulties to overcome in the early days when the Canadian Commercial Intelligence Service or the Trade Commissioner Service as it was then known, was the only one of its kind in the world for it is the pioneer in the work it is performing. If it is the equal of any other today,—as we hope and believe it is,—it is largely due to the foresight, enthusiasm and zeal displayed by Mr. O'Hara, the present Deputy Minister of Trade and Commerce, who nursed it along from babyhood and to whom largely belongs the credit for its present efficiency.

### Paying Greater Attention to Packing

I spoke about jobs performed by the Junior Trade Commissioners. I have with me one of the gentlemen who in addition to his other work has been working on one of these odd jobs. This is Mr. Cole, a Junior Trade Commissioner. I have been much interested in the question of packing for many years and have at various times urged that greater attention should be paid to it and that an attempt should be made to carry out experiments with a view to arriving at as near perfection in the design of packages as possible. I was never able to do more than allude to this subject in my report, but shortly after taking over my present office determined to see if something could not be done to give effect to my earlier ideas. With this in view I detailed Mr. Cole, who is a B. Sc. of McGill, shortly after he joined us last fall, to make as an exhaustive a study as he could of the art of packing. He and I went so far as to pay a visit last November to Harrison, New Jersey, in order that we might see working for ourselves a Hazard machine that we learned had been installed by the Edison Lamp Works for the purpose of carrying on experiments in packing. Mr. Cole also visited the works of a firm of box manufacturers who have installed a machine for the same purpose.

The Edison people told us that formerly they had suffered very grievously from damage to their packages, but owing to the exhaustive experiments which they had conducted with their Hazard machine they had been able to reduce these to an extremely small figure. With its help they had been able to design a container which for a minimum of weight and size possessed a maximum of strength. We also learned that no less than eight box manufacturers from the U. S. A. had installed these machines and were prepared to furnish the necessary data to design cases for their customers either for domestic or foreign trade which would have a maximum of efficiency.

There seems to be no doubt that American manufacturers. having made a start with improving their methods of packing and with a result, I am very confident, that will be highly satisfactory and profitable to them. It may be that someone will ask if they are taking too much trouble over their packing. It may be advanced that the difference between fair packing and the very best is not sufficient to warrant all these pains. But so far as my experience goes,—I have no hesitation in saying that the trouble is not too great.

### Many Complaints on Improper Sealing

If we are to build up a large and profitable export trade,—and everyone admits that the country needs it,— no trouble is too great to arrive at that end. If a thing is worth doing it is worth doing well. It is not sufficient to produce a first-class article, and Canada can

formed before the goods can be placed in the hands of foreign buyers, produce commodities that are second to no others in any part of the world. There are a number of other operations that must be per- and one of these is packing. I have found faults in packing to be a fruitful source of complaint. Picture to yourself an importer who receives a consignment of goods that have been so carelessly packed that part of them have been pilfered en route or damaged so as to render them unsaleable. He may require the goods immediately but, even if not, he is probably subjected to loss and one can be very sure it would rouse in his mind an irritation that may be difficult to allay.

**Details That Require Attention**

Packing, marking, preparation of documents, correspondence, etc.,—these are all details which require minute attention and which make for success or failure. It was close attention to detail that made the German exporters so successful before the war. It is attention to detail, that makes for success in all the big operations of the world, whether it be war or trade, and, if we are to build up a successful trade and a fine name, we must pay more attention to these details. We have no right to neglect any factor that will make for success. If an exporter by his carelessness brings himself into disrepute with foreign merchants he cannot help but also to some extent bring the whole body of Canadian exporters into disrepute, and this especially

applies in the present day when our foreign trade is still in a com- paratively young state.

It may be of interest to you gentlemen to hear that one of the most complimentary things I ever heard said, was said of a Canadian lumbering firm, and what is more, I heard this expressed in almost identical terms in two distinct quarters of the globe. The importers to whom I refer, one on the East coast of Africa, the other on the West coast of South America, said that when their orders were ac- cepted by this particular Canadian mill, they had no fears whatever but that they would be executed exactly according to specifications. One of them stated that it was easily worth an extra 5% in price to secure their supplies from such people, as dealings with them involved neither loss nor disputes. I was proud to hear such praise and it seemed to me to be a fine reward for all the pains and trouble that must have been extended to build up a name and to earn such unsolicited encomiums. What was the result? This Canadian mill could not begin to cope with the demands made upon it. Alas, that the man who by his energy and his probity and his enterprise built up a fine business is no more, but, in my judgment and in yours too, I am sure, the words of those foreign importers constitute the finest requiem that a merchant can hope to have, for they testify to the attainment of success in the very fullest acceptions of the word.

# Progress in Fire Retardent Treatment of Canadian Woods

*By J. H. Coderre, Montreal
Wood Preservation Specialist, Forest Products Laboratories of Canada

Wood in its natural state is a very good construction material, but did you ever stop to think how much better it would be if it did not burn? Do you realize that many substitutes which are used today in the place of wood, would never have been born if wood was fire- proof? And that some would soon lose favor if wood could be ef- fectively treated against fire. Do you realize that year after year more objections, some serious and some childish, are being rais- ed against its use as a construction material especially in congested centres.

It is your duty to see that the childish objections are removed. As to the serious objections, you have at your disposal the Forest Products Laboratories, who are prepared to do everything in their power to help you in their solution. One of the serious objections raised is that wood is combustible, and there is no doubt that if by fireproofing treatment, wood could be made properly resistant to fire, it would become an almost ideal material of construction.

This will become evident if we consider the amount of protec- tion given by a modern so-called fire-proof building, put up at an almost prohibitive cost. This prevents a too easy starting of a fire, but once let the fire get properly started and the whole building, al- though fire-proof in itself, will soon be a mass of ruins, on account of its combustible contents and the collapse of its structure. This is unhappily common knowledge and does not need demonstration. It is also certain that even in the face of these facts, fire-proofed wood is not extensively used. Many objections may be raised against the use of the best known fire-proofing agents on account of their high cost, their solubility in water, their corrosive action on metals, their effect on the strength of wood and on paint and varnishes.

These defects may be minimized but are none the less very real, but present methods of treatment can undoubtedly be improved upon by study and research, and the public must be shown the possibilities and properties of properly fire-proofed wood. To realize these two essentials to the successful development of the use of fire-proofed wood, it is necessary to work on a sound basis.

This implies first a clear definition of fire-proofed wood and the laying down of the properties desired of an ideal fire-proofing agent.

I will not attempt to go into the theory of the combustion of wood, but for our present needs, I will divide the combustion of wood into two general phases:

The ignition of wood with production of flames;
Its ultimate destruction by fire.

The fireproofing of combustible materials does not aim to pre- vent their ultimate destruction by fire, but to prevent or render difficult their ignition with production of flames, thus retarding the spreading of fire.

**Desired Qualities in Ideal Fire Retardent**

Properly fire-proofed wood may then be defined as a material that will be destroyed if exposed to the action of fire but that will not ignite and communicate fire by the production of flames. From

*Address delivered before Canadian Lumbermen's Association in Toronto.

the above it may be seen that the term "Fireproofing of Wood" is very misleading and will consequently be replaced hereafter by the term "Rendering Wood Fire Retardant" as this appears to be better appropriated to the nature of the results secured. I do not intend to deal with he theory of rendering wood fire retardant, but I will proceed immediately to the consideration of the qualities desired of an ideal fire retardent for wood.

It must be relatively cheap but this does not mean that the wood after treatment must necessarily be cheaper than other inferior pro- ducts, but the added cost must be justified by the higher value of the product improved by treatment.

It must be reasonably effective at low concentrations. and this is closely related to the low cost of the treated pro- duct.

It must be insoluble in water so as to remain effective if the treated wood is exposed to atmospheric conditions.

It must not be volatile under ordinary atmospheric con- ditions of heat.

After the ultimate restruction of the wood, it must pre- vent the formation of a glowing coal that might be carried away by the wind or otherwise, and be the cause of the start- ing of another fire.

It must not be corrosive to metals coming into contact with it such as nails, hinges, etc.

It must not have any detrimental action to paint and varnishes.

Its application must be easy and relatively inexpensive.

It was with the above as a basis that the Division of Wood Pre- servation of the Forest Products Laboratories of Canada recently undertook an experimental investigation on the fire retardent treat- ment of wood, at the request of the Canadian Lumbermen's Associa- tion.

**Making Study of Various Treatments**

As is usual in investigations of this nature, the first step was a study of the existing methods to ascertain if any of the treatments proposed could be used effectively. This led first to the rejection of all existing superficial processes as providing insufficient protection, and of all the numerous soluble salts recommended as fire retardents such as ammonium phosphate, ammonium sulphate, sodium phos- phates, aluminium sulphate etc., as the rain water would soon wash these chemicals from wood exposed to atmospheric conditions and leave it without protection. After a complete survey of all available data on the subject, the most promising method was found to be a double impression with borax and zinc chloride, giving an insoluble precipitate of zinc borate in the wood.

This treatment presented some difficulties as the precipitate will not be formed if the borax solution is acid. Before treating, it was therefore necessary to test it for acidity and to neutralize it; The borax solution also rapidly became adulterated in use, making it difficult to employ the same solution several times without trouble. This is a very serious objection, as the frequent renewing of the solu-

tion of borax would render its use prohibitive on account of costs. The results obtained with this treatment were rather disappointing and while a certain amount of protection was indicated, it was not judged sufficient. While there may be some very simple reasons for our nonsuccess with this treatment, it was decided to try some other insoluble salts before looking into the possible causes of the relatively poor results secured with the zinc borate treatment.

### Insoluble Compound Ammonium Salts

After further unsuccessful attempts along this line, a new departure was made, the basis of the work being the trial of insoluble compound ammonium salts. The first of these salts to be tried was a calcium ammonium phosphate, the precipitate being obtained by a double treatment using first a solution of ammonium phosphate and second one of calcium chloride. The results secured with this treatment appeared to be superior to any obtained so far

While it will be necessary to carry out a considerable amount of experimental work with this salt before coming to definite con-

J. H. Coderre Montreal,
In charge of wood preservation, Forests Products Laboratories of Canada

clusions, the success obtained so far appears to justify the belief that it may be made a commercial possibility.

But a treatment of this nature, involving a double injection and drying of the wood, would be practical only if used by the consumer or possibly the dealer and these are serious objections to a double treatment. The only process that appears practical for the manufacturer is one that could be called a one movement process, that is one that could be applied by the injection of one single solution, the insoluble salt being precipitated during the drying out process.

The salts that offer a better chance of success are those which, while being insoluble in water are soluble in a solution of ammonium hydroxide and when the solvent disappears be evaporation during the subsequent drying of the wood, reprecipitation takes place and a salt insoluble in water remains in the wood.

### Properties When Exposed to Fire

It was found that promising results could be secured with a treatment precipitating zinc ammonium phosphate in the wood after the evaporation of the excess of ammonia. Test pieces treated with this salt appeared to have the following properties when exposed to fire.

They were very difficult to ignite, and there was no spreading of fire beyond the portions in immediate contact with the flame.

There were no signs of glowing coal after the destruction of the wood by fire.

The protection given to the wood by this treatment will presumably be permanent as the salt precipitated is neither soluble in water nor volatile at ordinary atmospheric temperatures.

This treatment which at first may appear non-commercial is nevertheless of a very promising nature. All the chemicals used are relatively cheap, it is a one movement process, and it appears to be effective. We therefore believe that its possibilities should be thoroughly investigated.

The points to be determined appear to be the following:
What is the real value of the substance as a fire retardant agent.

What is the minimum concentration necessary to give a sufficient amount of protection against fire?

Could this treatment be applied to green wood if it is

steamed and a vacuum drawn prior to injection with the preservative?

What would be the cost of such a treatment if used commercially?

But to do this, more experimental work is necessary. We believe that the results secured in the short time we have devoted to this work offer a reasonable ground for expectation that the problem of rendering wood fire retardant may be solved in the near future.

In order that this may be accomplished, co-operation between the lumber producers and consumers and the investigators is necessary, and if we work together in this connection I feel that we shall come to a satisfactory solution of the problem and that any increase in cost will be more than justified by the increased value of the treated product.

## Hardwood Prices For Six Years

W. W. Dings, of the Garetson-Greason Lumber Co., St. Louis, Mo., has compiled the prices f. o. b. St. Louis on a few standard items of southern hardwoods for December covering the years 1916 to 1921, inclusive, as follows:

|  | 1916 | 1917 | 1918 | 1919 | 1920 | 1921 |
|---|---|---|---|---|---|---|
| plain oak 1-in 1st & 2nd | $51.00 | $57.00 | $64.50 | $141.50 | $122.00 | $116.00 |
| 1-in No.1 common plain oak | 32.00 | 34.50 | 42.50 | 99.50 | 83.00 | 52.00 |
| 1-in No.2 common plain oak | 21.50 | 24.50 | 30.50 | 66.50 | 43.00 | 26.00 |
| 1-in 1st & 2nd Qtd. white oak | 76.00 | 84.50 | 97.50 | 266.50 | 193.00 | 134.00 |
| 1-in No.1 common Qtd. white oak | 46.00 | 46.50 | 62.50 | 176.50 | 122.00 | 63.00 |
| 1-in No.2 common Qtd. white oak | 26.00 | 30.50 | 34.50 | 106.30 | 68.00 | 46.00 |
| 1-in 1st & 2nd red gum | 33.00 | 46.50 | 48.50 | 129.00 | 117.00 | 102.00 |
| 1-in No.1 common red gum | 25.00 | 36.50 | 37.50 | 102.00 | 87.00 | 50.00 |
| 1-in 1st & 2nd sap gum | 26.00 | 32.00 | 36.50 | 72.00 | 61.00 | 44.00 |
| 1-in No.1 common sap gum | 20.50 | 27.50 | 31.00 | 58.00 | 46.00 | 28.00 |
| 1-in No.2 common sap gum | 17.50 | 22.00 | 27.00 | 37.00 | 31.00 | 23.00 |
| 1-in Log run soft maple | 27.50 | 31.50 | 34.00 | 57.50 | 50.00 | 37.00 |

The advance in prices for December, 1919, over the same month of 1918 was caused by shortage of stocks at the mills coupled with demand and increased cost of production. Mill stocks are generally short at the present time, and many large operators are closed down. If production remains below normal and demand for hardwood lumber increases, who knows where prices will go in 1922.

## Report English Demaud as Improving

Among the recent callers on the lumber trade in Quebec City, were O. N. Shepard, of Shepard & Morse Co., Boston, and R. E. Stocking, of Power, Moir & Stocking, New York, who on his return to the latter city said: "The demand from England has shown some improvement in recent weeks. A normal amount of Canadian stock suitable for this market is lacking. There is a lot of 3-inch lumber cut for the English market but it is not readily saleable, although 3 x 9 and 3 x 11 inch are very scarce.

Pulpwood men, lumbermen and others of Ontario, are making a strong effort to have the present freight rates reduced, and a special hearing will be granted them by the Board of Railway Commissioners in Ottawa in the near future. It is said there are large amounts of pulp and lumber ready for shipment from the north but the owners will not send it to market until a lower rate makes it advisable to do so. Buyers, it is said, are also reluctant to encourage the shipments.

## Responsible Post for Quebec Lumberman

W. Gerard Power, Que, P.Q.

W. Gerard Power, who is president of the Quebec export timber and lumber firm of W. & J. Sharples, Limited, and of the St. Pacome Lumber Co., etc., and also of the Quebec Timber Limits Association, and a director of the Canadian Lumbermen's Association, has been appointed by the federal government as president of the Quebec Harbor Commission in place of the late Major General Sir David Watson resigned. The appointment of Mr. Power to this important position by the federal government or, rather by the large-hearted, broadminded Minister of Marine and Fisheries, Hon. Ernest Lapointe, has met with general approval, especially by the shipping interests and commercial community of Quebec.

The personality and genial characteristics of Mr. Power, are too well known to readers of the "Canada Lumberman" to need a sketch of his career, already so well established in the business life of the Dominion for a man of his years, not yet 40 and a true chip off the block. His father was the late William Power, M. P., who in his lifetime was one of Quebec's best-known lumbermen and respected citizens, and the successor to the late Hon. John Sharples, as president of the firm of W. & J. Sharples.

The newly-appointed president of the Quebec Harbor Commission has a difficult task in front of him, which, however, he is easily capable of overcoming, should he be accorded the support the important office calls for, by the government. His predecessor, the late Sir David Watson, was an exceptionally capable man of business, and during his short term of office, propounded many questions for the port of Quebec, the development of its natural and national resources, but was handicapped by outside influence, the same influence which Mr. Power will have to contend with if he is not backed by the federal government, says the Quebec correspondent of the "Canada Lumberman." This in no respect has reference to the expending of public monies, for it is a notorious fact that the federal treasury when taken over by the present administration, was found empty. It does, however, refer to the dissatisfaction a certain transportation oligarchy in various cities of Canada created during the war and continued ever since in their selfish interests, to the detriment of Canadian trade and commerce and the welfare of Canada and the Canadian people in general.

One of the causes of complaint is the non-operation of the Transcontinental Railway for the purpose for which it was built, especially in the movement of western Canadian grain over this railway for shipment to European countries through the port of Quebec in the summer season of navigation and through the Maritime ports of St. John, N. B. and Halifax, N. S., during the winter season of navigation instead of being routed over United States railroads to United States ports for shipment. The advantages offering by the transportation of grain over the Transcontinental Railway in grades and distance, would permit of lower freight rates and save the western Canadian farmers at least 12 cents per bushel on their grain shipments, besides keeping the money expended in American railroad transportation in Canada.

The occasion does not offer your Quebec correspondent to enter into detail by statistical argument on this important subject. It is only to point out that, if the Transcontinental Railway was operated for the purpose it was built, it would eventually prove a valuable asset to the country, to the western farmers and the national as well as natural parts of Canada, and, at the same time, give the port of Quebec its fair share in shipment, which would keep the Harbor Commission grain elevators busy and help to rejuvinate ocean shipping at the port of Quebec that would result in its being sought for development to become the greatest inland port in the world.

The newly-appointed president of the Quebec Harbor Commission is a live wire in business acumen and activities, and no doubt will give his attention to these matters, but, in order that he may meet with success, the government will have to come to his assistance with its moral support, dissolve trade and commercial oligarchies who have had the country's transportation by the throat since the outbreak of the war in 1914, and give the port of Quebec, the fair play it has been deprived of by studied discrimination for years past.

## The New Chairman is Very Aggressive

The new chairman of the Wholesale Lumber Dealers' Association, Inc. Toronto, is H. J. Terry, who is widely known in the forest products arena. "Jeff" Terry as he is generally hailed by his friends, is the second son of the late Edward Terry who for forty years conducted a builders' supply business in Toronto. Some twenty odd years ago H. J. Terry found himself in London, Ont., "out of luck" but was fortunate in meeting at the railway station a gentleman that he had known for a long period in the person of C. A. Larkin of Toronto, who was then, as now, engaged prominently in the lumber business. Under the leadership of Mr. Larkin, Mr. Terry went on the road as travelling salesman which he followed until 1909, when the firm of Muir and Terry was launched. In 1911 Albert E Gordon, salesmanager of the Ontario Lumber Co., Limited, joined the firm which was known as Muir, Terry and Gordon. Upon Mr. Muir's retiring a few years later, the name was changed to Terry & Gordon, which in 1920 was incorporated under the title of Terry & Gordon, Limited.

Mr. Terry has always taken a deep interest in organization work of various kinds and particularly in connection with the lumber interests. He is one of the original promoters of the Wholesale Lumber Dealers' Association, Inc.; is sergeant-at-arms of the Toronto Rotary Club, a member of the High Park Lawn Bowling Club, a director of the Parkdale Canoe Club, Limited, a member of Parkdale Lodge, A. F. & A. M., and also Toronto Lodge of Perfection, A. & A. S. R. He is keenly interested in boys' work, the more so because he remembers his own experience as a lad. Actively engaged in this department of Parkdale Methodist church, he is also a director of the National Boys' Life Council, Toronto. Mr. Terry has made a success of the lumber business, and following the line of worthy chairmen who have preceded him, the Wholesale Lumber Dealers' Association should during 1922 have one of its most successful and prosperous years.

### Does Business Just Happen?
By V. T.

In the good old days of a year or two back when we were all so busy that we were dodging the business that was humbly offered to us—business that came without particular effort on our part—most people became imbued with the idea that it required no vast amount of energy, no initiative nor active effort, to acquire business.... Just happened.

This idea has been jarred loose from our system during the economic upheavals of the last two years. We are face to face today with the realization that, in the general average of things, nothing really worth while just happens.

Some time necessarily elapsed before we really absorbed this truth. We had to become adjusted to a new perspective. We had gorged somewhat at the feast and lay dormant from the physical inertia and mental apathy which follows. We were loath to believe that once again it required real ENERGY to turn the wheels of industry.

We know now that there will be no Business Utopia. We know for all time that it takes vision, courage and PEP to CREATE business and we know further that if we are to get real business today or in the future it must be created. Do you then fully appreciate the responsibility of the marketing channels under present economic conditions? Do you realize that thousands of men, citizens of this country, are engaged in the producing ends of industry and that their employment to a large degree depends upon those engaged in the marketing of their products? It is our work to induce the public to buy by showing them conclusively that HOMES are the most enduring of all civilizing influence and that the lumber entering into their construction is full value today. Therefore, if we are not thinking CREATIVELY if we are not putting the maximum amount of PRODUCTIVE EFFORT into our business today, we are shirking our duty when the welfare and progress of the whole country is at stake.

We saw the "Big Chief" a while back. He was hitting the trail again under a full head of steam and with a full coat of warpaint. He volunteered the information that in addition to making his name synonymous with VALUE he would this year add SERVICE. As the Chief speaks only rarely, we are going to watch his actions with interest.

# Practical Plan to Replenish Forests of Ontario

R. C. Strickland of Lakefield, Ont., who is well known in the lumber industry, recently sent an important letter to Hon. E. C. Drury, Premier of Ontario, in regard to replenishing the depleted pine limits of Ontario and showing how a practical method of protecting the second growth can be carried out. The communication to the Premier was as follows:—

Having spent most of a long life in the forests of this province, for the last 25 years, I have lived in hopes that some practical step would be taken towards reforestation or as I should say protecting the second growth in the old pineries in the counties of Victoria, Peterborough, Hastings and Renfrew. There has been considerable agitation and discussion on the subject every year, but alas, nothing practical in my mind has been accomplished. The restoration of the forest wealth of this province is the most prominent question before you today and I trust that from fifty years experience and a sincere interest in the future prosperity of my native province, you will pardon me if I presume to lay before you, in my estimation, the only practical course to pursue towards reforestation:

1st. Your Government to select from each of the above counties in the pineries, twenty-five thousand acres of Crown lands and set them aside as forest and game reserves.

2nd. Management. A head forester should be appointed with supreme power (even magisterial power if necessary) over each reserve, and three or four assistants, and a large log dwelling for their accommodation in a central locality on each reserve.

3rd. Their Duties. Throughout all these reserves there will be found creeks that were formerly widened out into beaver ponds that, full of water, were a great protection against fire spreading. The beaver dams that formed these ponds having rotted away, and the pounds dried up and became hay meadows, this hay dying down yearly, becomes a very dangerous element in the midst of the reserve, for lightning striking one of the dead tamarac or spruce in these hay meadows immediately causes a small prairie fire during dry weather.

The head forester would have to employ his men either to cut this hay yearly or to renew the dams so as to fill these meadows with water, the latter preferable, as it would in a few years so increase

fur-bearing animals that their value in the market would more than pay the wages of hirde help.

Another duty would be wherever a bare spot was found on the reserve, to sew white clover or other grasses that would be food for deer or game birds.

Hired help could cut all the beaver hay on meadows not flooded, for which there is always a profitable market.

4th. Revenue. (a) Marketing surplus fur-bearing pelts. (b) Special licenses every three years to sportsmen. (c) Profit on hay cut each year. (d) Pasturing farmers' stock on the reserves, which I think advisable, as this course (from practical experience) is rather more beneficial to the forest than a detriment.

5th. Location, County Peterboro. Beg to suggest the section in the townships of North and South Burleigh, north of the east end of Stoney Lake, between Eels and Jack's Creeks, as I estimate there are growing to- day in this area over one million young pine, spruce and hemlock trees from one to eight inches in diameter. These trees having an average growth of 25 years, showing that time advance over seeding.

6th. Location in the other countries. If my suggestions meet with your approval, three practical wood rangers could be appointed to suggest reserves for your approval in the other counties.

7th. If the above suggestions were adopted by your Government as a test and proved successful at the end of five years, new reserves in these counties could be selected.

All the timber licenses covering the old pineries in these counties ought to be cancelled, as 25 per cent. of the logs cut under these licenses are seven inches and under in diameter and from which the Government receives no revenues, and it always seems to me a great farce to talk about reforestation while second growth timber of the Government.

Believing that you feel that reforestation is one of the most serious questions facing the province. I don't hesitate in submitting for your consideration what I believe to be the most practical plan towards accomplishing that end.

# Quebec Awakens to Need of More Conservation

The Quebec Government Lands and Forest Department is fully awake to the value of the protection, not only from fire and insect ravages, but through waste in the cutting of logs.

The total area of forest land in the province of Quebec is now 450,337,761 acres, or 703,653 square miles. This does not include the Ungava territory annexed to the province in 1912, which practically doubles the surface. The lakes and water surfaces are estimated at 15,964 square miles. According to the last census taken in 1911, the properties belonging to private individuals, and communities, covered at that time 15,613,267 acres, giving the Crown control in old Quebec of 209,585,249 acres, making a grand total of 434,724,394.

Omitting Ungava and a portion of the Labrador upland, which are said to contain an appreciable area of commercial timber value, it is figured that the merchantable forests of the province of Quebec are capable of producing saw logs, pulpwood, etc., from over 130,000,000 acres, divided into the following classes:—Private forests 6,000,000 acres; forest lots under location ticket; forests based as timber limits 44,500,000 acres; township forest reserves, 200,000, and vacant lands 78,000,000 acres. The private lands are managed on the principles of forestry, and the same may be said of the forests belonging to settlers. It is only upon the Crown Lands (timber limits and township reserves) that the Forest Service of the province exercises its influences in the direction and supervision of the cutting of trees and their utilization.

The private lands come from the old seigniors and farms sold to settlers by the Government and land subsidies to railways. The greatest part of these forests lie in the central valley of the St. Lawrence and is divided into farm properties seldom exceeding in acreage 50 on the average. Every year the Government sells to settlers lots 300 acres of land, which are usually well timbered under certain

conditions in a special contract in regard to residence, clearances, etc., which if the settler complies with, entitles him to ownership by letters patent, but if it is found that the land has been sought after and exploited for speculation in the timber, the land reverts to the Crown lands or the timber limit holders, from which they may have been taken. The progress made in the pulp and paper industry caused many speculators to apply to the Government for settlers' location tickets, who simply went on the land to cut the spruce , balsam and fir, and sell it to the pulp and paper purchasing interests. It was some time before the Quebec Government realized what was going on, but when it did, no time was lost in taking energetic steps to stop this source of plunder of the public domain, and the lots taken from the limit holdings.

### Reforestation Goes on Apace.

It was only recently in the year 1889 that efforts were advanced to reclaim waste lands in the province of Quebec. The first experiment was made at Aka in that year under the direction of Father Lefebvre, who succeeded in reforesting eighteen acres of shifting sands. This plantation consisted mainly of white pine and spruce wildstock, but it has grown so well that many of the trees have at the present day a diameter of 9 to 13 inches and a height from 45 to 70 feet. These dimensions would have been greater had a judicious thinning been made occasionally. Several private parties followed this example and devoted their attention to the introduction and planting of foreign trees which took root, developed and to-day can be seen at the seigniorial residence of the Joly family in the county of Lotbiniere, a beautiful grove of black walnut.

In 1908 the Quebec Government established a provincial nursery of forest trees at Berthierville, with the object of raising, not only indigenous trees for the reforestation of waste lands and plantations in the forest area, with the view of increasing this product.

ivity, but also of foreign species and systematic study of all trees growing in this latitude. At the present time this nursery has a stock of, approximately, four million plants, and has already shipped more than 3,500,000 trees. As a result of experiments, 300· acres of shifting sands have been reclaimed, partly by planting and partly by sewing of beach-grass.

In the vicinity of Berthier the same work is in progress, and planting stock distributed to different provincial colleges for the education in forestry of the pupils, and the demand for plants from private land owners are becoming very large. The limit holders are following the example and beginning to plant, the Laurentide Company having done considerable work in this connection, and it is the hope of the forestry branch of the Lands and Forests Department of the province, with the aid of its corps of forest engineers and schools of forestry, now in operation, to see a spirit engendered in the province of Quebec for reforestation before many years, that will put Quebec in a class with Sweden and Finland.

### Movement Will Gain in Magnitude.

The Minister of the Department of Lands and Forests, and Mr. Piche, chief forester, believe that the movement will go on increasing until it reaches a magnitude looked forward to by the minister who is determined by way of encouragement and ultimate success that the Government will keep pace with the demand.

The students of the Quebec Forest School proceed to Berthierville every spring to assist in the shipping of the material and in the work of seeding, transplanting, etc. The work being carried on under the auspices of the Quebec Government to educate and further the ends of reforestation, includes the establishment of forest school nurseries and the creation of scholastic societies to propagate reforestation and carry on plantation in every village of the province, not only this planting of forest trees, but also shade trees, as is done in European countries, and the creation of commercial forests or city forests are under consideration.

The plantation of roadways in co-operation with the Department of Public Roads, will be inaugurated this coming spring, when 25,000 trees will be planted along the public highways. The plantation of all waste lands of the province, covers 3,000,000 miles, and should private owners wish to do their share, the Government will provide the material at a moderate price.

The plantation of timber limits in order to reforest the burned ones, and introduction of better species, is estimated to cover 4,000,000 acres. These projects are now under government consideration and it is expected that an agreement will soon be made with the limit holders as to conditions under which the work will be proceeded with.

The Department is introducing foreign stock, European larch, Norway spruce and Scotch pine. Owing to the great facilities of obtaining good and fresh seed, and the good growth made by these trees, the Government prefers to limit the use of the foreign trees for the creation of parks and aboretums, until they show their thoroughly acclimated. Some fifty foreign species are under observation now at the Berthierville nursery.

### Loggers Now Live in Fine Style

Henry Ford has revolutionized the system of conducting logging camps at Iron Mountain, Michigan.

When Ford started lumber production, besides carrying on operations in a progressive manner, he gave consideration to the accommodation and the comforts of men in his lumber camps at Sidnaw and Ontonagon.

The men now enjoy all the comforts of a real home. In the good old days, the men slept in dirty bunks with straw for mattresses, ate food that was good, bad and sometimes worse, were paid low wages, and were forced to read by lamplight, providing they bought their own reading matter.

Now it's different. The buildings are equipped with electric lights, reading room, dining tables and writing desks. Each man has his own bed, not a bunk, equipped with a mattress, comforter, sheets, blankets and pillows.

And last, but not least, there are bath rooms. Now every man takes a bath at least once a week and has a complete change of clean clothing to put on. In the old days, many a lumberjack would go to the woods in the fall and not take a bath until the camp broke up in the spring.

### Court Holds That Notes Were Valid

The Court of Review, Montreal, has confirmed a judgment of the Superior Court holding La Compagnie des Entreprises Publiques, Ltee, responsible to Paul Galibert for payment of $20,100, on notes signed on behalf of the company by Horace Dussault, as president after his presidency had expired. As the company Etienne Dussault of Quebec, the defendants, contracted to supply Achille Gagnon of

Arthabaska with lumber to a value of $30,000. The contract with Gagnon and a number of promissory notes relating to the contract were signed by Horace Dussault as president of the company. These notes were discounted by Gagnon with Paul Galibert, of Montreal and were duly honoured with the exception of those at issue in the present action. The Court held the notes were validly signed in virtue of a tacit mandate held by Horace Dussault and that if the mandate had been extinguished when the company changed its name to the Compagnie des Enterprises Publiques, Ltee the defendants were still bound towards third parties for acts of its mandatory performed within the power of the mandate, by reason of the fact that its intended extinction was not made known to the third party, in this instance, Paul Galibert.

### New Plant at Guelph Will Start Soon

Robert Stewart, Limited, of Guelph, Ont., who are completing a new wood-working plant in that city, expect to have it in operation about the middle of March. The building has a frontage of 100 feet by 154 feet deep, is two storeys high and is erected of solid brick. It is served by both C. P. R. and G. T. R. switches. The first floor is of 6 inch concrete and the second is 2 x 6 laminated flooring laid on edge covered with 1-inch maple flooring. The factory has a 3-ton power elevator, 8 feet wide and 18 feet long, and also one 2-ton electric elevator.

On account of the contour of the land, Robert Stewart Limited, are enabled to drive their trucks from the ground level into the rear end of the upstairs of the factory. Downstairs is served with five doors, 10 x 10 on either side, half glass, worked on pulleys by which means they are able to raise the same to the upper floor.

The company have installed a 175 h.p. Goldie & McCulloch Corliss engine, and will specialize in stock millwork. All kinds of highgrade interior finish doors, columns, flooring, hardwood, and other panelling, stair work and sash, will be turned out. The equipment is most modern in every respect.

The firm also carry a large stock of timbers and their downstairs machinery is specially heavy in order to take care of the resawing and dressing of this material.

### Ontario Association Appoints Standing Committees

J. C. Scofield, of Windsor, president of the Ontario Retail Lumber Dealers' Association, has appointed the following standing committees for that organization for the coming year:—

Insurance and Workmen's Compensation:—W. C. Laidlaw, of Toronto, chairman; A. M. Davis, Ottawa; W. M. Tupling, Orillia; W. C. Irvin, Toronto; W. A. Hadley, Chatham.

Legislation and Transportation:—B. F. Clarke, Glencoe, chairman; K. J. Shirton, Dunnville, E. M. Barrett, Ottawa, T. H. Hancock, Toronto; F. B. Van Dusen, Brockville; George S. Zimmerman, Tavistock.

Membership Committee:—Eastern District,—E. M. Barrett and A. G. Rose, Ottawa.

Western District,—T. A. Paterson, Toronto; E. I. Gill, Toronto.

Western District,—J. B. Mackenzie, Georgetown; A. Henderson, Cheltenham; H. Crosthwaite, Hamilton; R. J. Press, Hamilton; K. J. Shirton, Dunnville; O. W. Rice, Welland; E. K. Kalbfleisch, Stratford; G. S. Zimmerman, Tavistock.

Southern District,—B. F. Clarke, Glencoe; J. T. Wallace, London.

Northern District,—F. E. Hollingsworth, Sault Ste Marie; D. H. Andreas, Sudbury.

In connection with the midsummer outing up the Great Lakes to Duluth and return, to be held during the last week in June, L. H. Richards, of Sarnia, has been appointed chairman. He will constitute the committee along with the president and the secretary of each of the various sections. Another member of the committee has been appointed in the person of J. B. Reid, of Toronto; honorary president of the O. R. L. D. A., who has been a booster for this trip; in fact are enthusiastic endorsers of the excursion which the trade will take Mr. Reid and Mr. Richards, in conjunction with President Scofield this year and say that it will be the best in the history of the Association.

### Says There is no Lumber in Yards

John Willman, manager of the Kleanza Company, Limited, owners of a lumber mill and extensive timber limits at Usk, B. C., who was in Vancouver, recently, states that there is no lumber in the yards on the prairies, and all the mills between Vancouver and Edmonton will be working in the spring or early summer.

Some are already getting out logs and others will soon be busy. Mr. Willman's company has a contract to get out 150,000 ties for the Canadian National Railways, and orders for bridge timbers for the prairies. Already he has a big gang of men working on this at Usk.

# Retailer Should Have Fine Service Facilities
### Department Should be Most Active and Practical Among His Sales Aids—
### Equipment Should Consist of Plan, Books, Drawings
### and Illustrated Literature

The organization of a service department and its composition vary so greatly, according to the territory to be served and other peculiarly local conditions, that it would be best to give merely the general principles and list some of the services actually in use by progressive dealers, says the "Gulf Coast Lumberman."

The service department is the most active and practical of the retail lumber merchant's sales aids; the stronger proof you can give of the desirability of your product, the more ways for using it you can suggest, the more fully you can clarify the conflicting desires and solve the doubts or enlighten the ignorance of your prospect, the easier you can make it for him to buy—the more easily can you sell him.

So then, the object of the service department is to provide not only answers for your prospect's questions and solutions for his dilemmas, but also information that will anticipate possible sales arguments and thus smooth the trade path.

In the article under "Equipment Courtesy" it was pointed out that to provide such service was a proper business courtesy—and herewith are presented and discussed the items of that service.

In the first place you should have in your files one complete set of all of the "dealer helps" provided by the several associations or individual makers of the goods you handle.

The best procedure is to have a case or shelf where these can be safely kept—and this file should be kept intact for office use alone. Experience will soon show which items you will need for distribution and these can be secured in proper quantities.

A plan book system of some kind, of course. Indeed this might well be considered the foundation of your "Service Department." Some dealers—a growing number indeed—have several of these systems—and out of the number on the market to-day you should have little difficulty in making a choice.

The aim of your efforts is to sell the building—and that means by which the entire building is visualized to the prospect is surely the fundamental sales force. The size and the extent of the plan book system will depend to a certain degree on the size of your business—but let it certainly be, to paraphrase the words of Polonius, "Costly as purse can stand."

Many of the line yard companies and some of the larger single yards have installed more or less elaborate architectural departments and these are proving of great value.

The Federal Government issues many documents of interest, and you can select from the published list quite a number that will apply to your business.

Many of the State institutions and departments, agricultural colleges, experiment stations, etc., issue reports and pamphlets that will help you solve many a vexing question put by a prospect.

A contractor's table, fitted with paper, pencils, rules and estimating tables will help pave the way to amicable relations.

Samples of your materials should occupy a prominent place. These should be clearly labeled with full information and kept clean and attractively presented. Visitors will examine them with more interest than you may think.

Samples of builders hardware and paints and color cards will assist your prospect to make up his mind while illustrations and photographs of built-in features will often "turn the trick" in the sale of the home.

The foregoing represent a small list of some of the items of your service department and this can be easily added to as the need arises.

An important detail is to know what you have. You should read each document and study each sample until you are thoroughly familiar with it and know how it can be of use to you.

Then you should so file these items that you can lay your hands on any one without any annoying search. This is very important for a sale has often been lost because the dealer made a statement and failed to find the documentary proof, leaving the prospect either cold or actually disbelieving and antagonistic.

Working in intimate relations with the service department is, of course, the prospect chart—indeed there is no distinct line of demarcation between any of your business departments—each is but a cog in the one machine.

We have specialized on the material side of the service department in this article because the personal side of your business has already been sufficiently emphasized in previous articles, and we judged it unnecessary to argue that the value of this as well as all other departments depends entirely on the personal attention to its functioning.

The service department, on its material side, in the larger establishments, has been extended into a bureau of information, from which data is secured for the purchasing, advertising and sales departments, as well as being used directly in actual customer-contact.

In some offices, a set of filing boxes is used, with appropriate titles, such as silos—implement sheds—barns, garages—pergolas—play rooms —hardwood floors—wall board—heating—lighting—fire places—wall beds—sewerage—and other allied subjects.

Herein are filed all sorts of booklets, clippings, pictures, etc., and it is but a moment's work to have under your hand a quantity of valuable data on the particular subject under discussion.

There are such a multitude of questions that arise during the planning of a building that it would be commercially impossible to hold all the necessary information in mind; but those questions must be answered and the method suggested will be found the easiest and most practical.

Then, a reputation of having this information, in authentic form and readily accessible, will have a powerful influence in establishing confidence in your knowledge of your business and will also be a strong factor in spreading that reputation and this will naturally have a good effect on your prospective business.

As a goal towards which to work in establishing the service department aim to have on hand such information that you will never have to say: "I don't know"

A new labor-saving device, recently tested in New York, for felling trees. The machine does the work of eighteen men, in that it requires exactly one-eighteenth of the time to cut the trunk of a tree that would be necessary by human hands.

## Colonel Mackie Engaged in Worthy Work

Col. H. J. Mackie, former member of Parliament for North Renfrew, is now president of the Save-the-Children Fund in Ottawa, and has charge of the distribution for the starving little ones in Russia.

Recently the Ottawa Government endorsed the formation of a Canadian committee of the Save-the-Children Fund, which has been taken up in Great Britain and the United States. This organization is officially recognized by the federal authorities and through

Col. H. J. Mackie, Ottawa, Ont.

it the generosity of Canada will express itself by direct means. Sir George Burn, of Ottawa, is treasurer of the Fund.

Recently Col. Mackie received a letter from a woman living in the Niagara Peninsula, stating she had been so touched by the appeal on behalf of the starving children in Russia that she sent her diamond ring which, she said, was all that she could spare. Within eight days sufficient food was recently shipped from St. John to feed 20,000 Russian children for a month.

Col. Mackie who was for many years a widely-known lumberman was born and brought up in Pembroke and has many friends in the forest product industry.

## Death of Mr. James E. Marrett

The death of James E. Marrett, President of the Marrett Lumber Company, of Portland, Maine, occurred at the Falmouth Hotel, Portland, Maine, on February 8th.

Mr. Marrett was well and favorably known in the lumber trade not only in the United States and Canada, but in England and South America. For many years he was General Sales Manager and Treasurer of the Chaleurs Bay Mills, of Restigouche, Que., and the product of this company was sold and shipped to the Argentine Republic.

The late Mr. Marrett was sixty-seven years of age at the time of his death and was always known to be a man of charming personality and fine ability. He was a Democrat in politics and was always interested in civic affairs of Portland which was the city of his birth. He was a member of the Old Colony Club of Portland and Montreal, the Cumberland Club, the Country Club and Motor Boat Club of Portland, also a member of the Cadets, Veteran Association and United States Consul for the Republic of Uruguay.

Mr. Marrett is survived by his wife and three daughters.

## Northern Lumberman Looks for Better Things

A large lumber operator in the Sudbury district in conversation with the "Canada Lumberman," recently stated that logs would be produced considerably cheaper this winter than last. "We were paying," he said, "from $70.00 to 80.00 in the fall of 1920, and this season our wage bill runs from $26.00 to $32.00 per man. It cost us last season from $1.10 to $1.20 per day to board the men, and so far as I can gather figures at this particular period, the expenditure now is about 80 to 90 cents a man.

"During the last six weeks, although the snow has been deep, sleigh-hauling conditions have been good, and we are getting most of our pieces out on the ice with more expedition than previously.

"The prospects for the coming season look very good. I do not expect a return to solid, substantial prosperity but am looking for a strengthening of conditions. Stocks of white pine are not large and some firms are now down to green lumber, and it will be July before the new cut comes on the market. During the past eighteen months the situation has been very trying, but we are slowly emerging from the grievous experience, and with confidence and co-operation, should be able to surmount all difficulties.

"I regret to say that some employees seem inclined to look upon employers of labor as if they were responsible for the state of affairs that has been brought about as an aftermath of the world-wide war upheaval and unrest, evidently overlooking the fact that, in many instances, we have been sweating blood to keep our organizations together and carry on at a heavy loss, producing lumber without any visible outlet or demand for our product.

"To my mind, there will be no sudden return to prosperity but conditions will be better than they have been during the past few months, although it may be quite a while yet before we have fully rounded the corner and are on the upgrade."

## Operating Logging Railway in Eastern Canada

In Eastern Canada there are not many logging railways in operation. Before constructing such a transportation line, the amount of timber to be moved, the distance and the nature of the country are the three principal elements to be considered. Then again, the equipment employed is a vital factor in installing a logging operation, and this also needs to be planned in relation to the conditions already outlined.

Among the firms in Ontario and Quebec, who operate logging railways, are Dennis-Canadian Co., of Whitney, the Fassett Lumber Co., of Fassett, Que., and J. R. Booth, Limited, at Madawaska, Ont.

There is no doubt that the logging railway is the only practical method of logging hardwoods situated at a considerable distance from the point of manufacture. The chief difficulty, however, in and around many places is the small amount of timber per acre and the broken and rocky surface which makes it impossible to put the road where you sometimes want to run it, and the smaller amount of timber coming out over the track after it is installed. Those who have installed logging railways, are of the opinion that where the conditions are right, the method of haulage is very satisfactory unless the comparatively new-developed plan of using tractors comes more universally to the front.

The Dennis-Canadian Co. built their logging railway nine miles away and have ten miles of standard gauge track laid with 56 lb. rails; a geared locomotive and steam log loader that moves from one log car to the other, and with this equipment the firm are bringing out 24 carloads of logs per day.

The Fassett Lumber Co. make use of a considerable length of track in Eastern Canada, while J. R. Booth has, at Madawaska, about 15 miles of railway from Whitney, an operation which is different from that of the Fassett and Dennis-Canadian Co. in that the firm take the regular flat cars of the Grand Trunk Railway, and load them and bring them out to the main line for shipment of the logs to Ottawa.

## Toronto Wholesalers Will Entertain Retailers

The chairmen of the various standing committees and the newly-elected directors of the Wholesale Lumber Dealers' Association Inc., were called together on February 13, by the newly-elected chairman, H. J. Terry, and a dinner was held at the King Edward Hotel, Toronto. Among those present were,—A. C. Gordon, H. G. McDermid, A. C. Manbert, W. E. Bigwood, A. E. Clark, Hugh A. Rose, L. D. Barclay, J. B. Jarvis, D. C. Johnston, H. Boultbee, and H. J. Terry.

Various matters were discussed relating to future meetings and making each monthly session outstanding. It was decided that the wholesale and retail trade should come closer together, and on Monday March 20th the wholesalers will entertain the retailers of Toronto to a banquet at the King Edward Hotel.

## Lumber Exports From British Columbia

Off-shore shipments of lumber during the year 1921 from the mainland of British Columbia amounted to 164,000,000 feet. Shipments to China and Japan accounted for 93,000,000 feet; Australia and New Zealand, 27,000,000; United Kingdom, 9,000,000; other places 21,500,000. In addition 700,000 bundles of shingles were shipped to United States Atlantic ports, while 24,600 tons of box shooks went to Australia and Singapore.

## Prominent Midland Lumberman Weds

Manley Chew, M. P., the widely-known lumberman of Midland, Ont., was married recently in Toronto, by Rev. R. J. D. Simpson, to Miss Marjorie Byrne, youngest daughter of Mrs. A. Byrne, of Midland. Many friends are extending congratulations.

Mr. Chew is a son of the late George Chew, of Midland, and has been actively engaged in the lumbering line for over a quarter of a century. He has always taken a prominent part in the advancement of his native town and represented the constituency of East Simcoe

Manley Chew, M.P. Midland, Ont

in the federal parliament for one term. He was defeated at the next election but was returned again in the Liberal interests November last by a handsome majority.

Mr. Chew is the proprietor of that progressive industry Fibre Board, Limited which is in operation at Penetanguishene. About a year and a half ago he sold out his extensive lumber plant, limits and camps to G. Mason & Co., of Manchester, England, but retains his interest in the firm of Chew Bros., Midland, which partnership is composed of Mr. Chew and Mr. Ed, Letherby.

## Eastern Hardwood Firm is Kept Busy

The Annapolis Hardwood Co., Limited was organized in 1920 and is now conducting a flourishing industry at Annapolis Royal, N. S. Applewood specially processed for the purpose of manufacturing hand-saw handles, was the first production. The firm also began selling hardwood lumber across the border and this led it into another venture, that of making hardwood flooring. Up-to-date dry kilns of the humidity type and morerm machiners were installed, and the new enterprise has proved most successful. During the first year of operation over a million and a half feet of lumber were consumed, while this year it is expected that the two million mark will be reached.

The product of the company is known as "Scotia" hardwood flooring. It is being handled by discriminating dealers throughout Nova Scotia and New Brunswick and as far west as Montreal. Shipments have also been made to the Eastern States and Newfoundland.

## Lumbermen on Insurance Deputation

A deputation of lumbermen and others waited upon the attorney-general of Ontario recently in connection with the proposed insurance bill which is to be brought down at the present session, definitely granting licenses to insurance organizations and defining more clearly whether federal or provincial regulations shall govern these bodies. The lumbermen represented the reciprocal and inter-insurance companies and laid certain matters before Hon. Mr. Raney for his consideration.

## Western Mills Faced Winter Weather

Writing to the "Canada Lumberman" a wholesale dealer in Vancouver says that December, January and part of February were rather severe winter months for British Columbia, and it greatly affected lumber production. First there was the season of heavy rains in the fall, causing flood conditions that interfered with logging and in towing logs to Vancouver. This was followed by a freeze-up in late December that was not really broken until the middle of February. The mills were not prepared for such a visitation and many—especially those away from Vancouver—had to shut down. As only about sixty per cent of the mills were running anyway, this further shut-down made it very difficult to get orders filled.

Continuing, he says, "Moreover the export trade has offered more remuneration to those plants which we could get in on than has the domestic trade, so when we bring along our little orders at the low prices offered by the prairie and further east, the millman says "nothing doing." Of course, the big handicap is the excessive freight rate. When you realize that between 60 and 70% of what the Ontario dealers pay for their B. C. lumber, goes for freight alone, can you wonder at the millman squirming at having to take what is left, but even at that our shipments to Eastern Canada are increasing each year."

## Western Deliveries Have Been Rather Slow

Some eastern representatives of western lumber mills state that shipments are a little slow at present due to a number of the mills having been shut down in British Columbia, while others were inoperative for a considerable time owing to ice in the log ponds, the weather having been exceptionally cold for several weeks. There is a little better movement in timbers and some inquiries for dimension, but as a rule the retailer is as yet ordering only mixed cars for sorting up.

There is a tendency for certain prices to increase, particularly in B. C. fir, base and casing, edge and flat grain stepping, and dressed clears. The manufacturers say they must get more money for their product as they cannot sell at the present low values. Demand is expected to strengthen considerably within the next three or four weeks.

## Veteran Senator Celebrates Golden Wedding

Hon. Valentine Ratz and Mrs. Ratz, of New Hamburg, Ont., recently celebrated the golden anniversary of their marriage and received the congratulations of a host of friends. Many children and grandchildren brought their greetings to the bride and groom of 50 years ago.

Hon. Valentine Ratz
New Hamburg, Ont

Senator Ratz entered political life in 1896, when he was elected to the House of Commons. He was defeated in 1900 and again elected in 1904. He declined nomination in 1908 and was summoned to the Senate in 1909.

Mr. Ratz is a Liberal in politics and for many years was engaged in the lumber business, being president of the South River Lumber Co. He was born at St. Jacobs, Waterloo County, Ont., on November 12th 1848 and was married in 1872 to Miss Mary Yager of New Hamburg.

Walter Mason, of Mason, Gordon and Company, Montreal, has returned from a trip to the Maritime Provinces.

### Using Airplanes in Forest Protection

By a co-operative arrangement between the Air Board of Canada and the Dominion and Provincial forest services, airplanes are being tested this season in five provinces in the work of forest surveying and forest protection. The provinces in which airplanes are operating are: Quebec, Ontario, Manitoba, Alberta and British Columbia. The use of machines of different types, tested under different conditions, will by the end of this season give an immense amount of information in regard to the usefulness of airplanes for this work. The offices of the Air Board, the Dominion Forestry Branch, and the different provincial forestry departments are following the results of this season's operations with close interest, and will be guided by them in laying out future work.

### Personal Items of Interest

J. A. Laferte, wholesale lumber-dealer, has removed to 97 St. James Street, Montreal.

Louis Rolland, wholesale lumber dealer and exporter, Montreal, in on a business visit to England.

H C. Foy, of H. R. Goodday & Co., Quebec, and J. Burstall, of J. Burstall & Co., Quebec, are now in England.

Fred W Wigg, of J. & D. A. Harquail Co., Limited, Campbellton, N. B., was in Toronto recently calling upon the lumber trade.

D. L. O'Gorman, representing the Brewster Loud Lumber Co., Detroit, Mich., was in Toronto recently, calling upon the trade.

C. W. Wilkinson, of the Union Lumber Co., Toronto and Mrs. Wilkinson, left recently on a holiday trip to Cuba.

J. L. Campbell, of Campbell Welsh & Paynes, Toronto, who was ill for three weeks with bronchitis, is able to be at his desk once more.

Guy Tombs has succeeded P. D. Gordon, of Mason, Gordon & Co., as chairman of the Committee of Management of the Transportation Bureau, Montreal Board of Trade.

C. H. Lightbourne, who spent several weeks in Canada in the interests of the Associated Importers, Limited, of London, England, purchasers of the Canadian stocks of the British Government, has returned to England. He disposed of several million feet of lumber to Canadian firms.

W. Gerard Power, of W. & J. Sharples, Limited, Quebec, spent a few days in Montreal, visiting one of his sons, who was suffering from pneumonia, but who is now, on the road to recovery.

Fred. W. Plant, manager of the Hespeler yard of the Robert Stewart Co., Limited, Guelph, Ont., for some months past, has rejoined the selling force of Frank H. Harris Lumber Co., Toronto, and will cover Ontario in the interests of the firm.

J. L. MacFarlane, of the Canadian General Lumber Co., Toronto, who has been confined to his home with illness for a considerable period, and was operated upon at Grace Hospital recently, is making good progress toward recovery.

### New Method Used for Preserving Wood

A new method for the preserving of wood has recently been employed in Germany and is known as the "Cobra Process." The method is executed by the use of a hypodermic needle injecting a mixture of five parts pulverized copper sulphate and a saturated solution of calcium chloride. The needle has an oval section and is mechanically driven into the tree to a depth of three inches. This is done while the tree is yet in the bush and the mixture flows through the natural tissues and mixes with the sap. The process is also claimed to be a good preventative of rot in wooden piles, posts, telegraph poles, etc.

The Abitibi Power and Paper Company, Iroquois Falls, Ont., has just scored a record as far as production goes, the seven machines in their mill at Iroquois Falls turning out an average of over 449 tons of paper per day for a whole week. The individual daily record was 456 tons. The record was made under difficulties owing to coal and wood supplies being tied up by snowstorms and it is confidently expected that this record can be eclipsed.

The Annual General Meeting of the Wayagamack Pulp and Paper Company, Limited was held at the head office of the Company, Three Rivers, Que., recently. The following were elected directors: Norman J. Dowes, G. H. Duggan, Hugh Mackay, K.C.; Alex. Maclaren, Sir William Price, James Pyke, C. R. Whitehead. At a subsequent meeting of the Directors, Mr. C. R. Whitehead was elected President, and Mr. James W. Pyke, vice-president.

## Cost of British Columbia Red Cedar Shingles
### And Various Substitute Roofings at Toronto --- Jan. 1922.

| | B.C. Red Cedar XXX 4% Exposure | B.C. Red Cedar XXXX 5"Exposure | B.C. Red Cedar 5 Perfections 6½ Exposure | B.C. Red Cedar 2x Royals 7½ Exposure | Asphalt Slate Shingles | Asphalt Roll 1 Ply | Asphalt Roll 2 Ply | Asphalt Roll 3 Ply |
|---|---|---|---|---|---|---|---|---|
| Rafters and Sheathing | 6.80 | 6.80 | 6.80 | 6.80 | 6.80 | 6.80 | 6.80 | 6.80 |
| Roof Covering | 5.20 | 6.00 | 7.00 | 8.50 | 7.00 | 2.50 | 2.90 | 3.30 |
| Nails | .40 | .40 | .40 | .35 | .47 | | | |
| Applying Sheathing | 1.00 | 1.00 | 1.00 | 1.00 | 1.00 | 1.00 | 1.00 | 1.00 |
| Applying Covering | 3.25 | 3.25 | 3.00 | 2.75 | 3.25 | 1.00 | 1.00 | 1.00 |
| Total Cost per Square Laid | 16.65 | 17.45 | 18.20 | 19.40 | 18.25 | 11.30 | 11.70 | 12.10 |
| Estimated Life | 30 Years | 30 Years | 40 Years | 45 Years | 10 Years | 5 Years | 10 Years | 15 Years |
| Cost per Sq're per year | $0.55 | $0.50 | $0.46 | $0.43 | $1.85 | $2.29 | $1.19 | $0.82 |

Cost chart of British Columbia Red Cedar Shingles prepared and displayed by Fred. H. Lamar, of Vancouver, Secretary of the B. C. Shingle Manufacturers' Association, at the annual meeting of the Ontario Retail Lumber Dealers' Association held recently in Ottawa.

## Pulpwood Market Shows But Little Change

So far as the pulpwood of Northern Ontario is concerned, several companies are buying a moderate supply at present. Owing to the low prices prevailing, there was not nearly the quantity of wood cut by settlers during the past season that there was a couple of years ago. On the Canadian National east and west of Cochrane, however, are large quantities alongside the tracks. It has not been moved for several reasons, owing to the fact that the mills are pretty well supplied, and the present freight rates are too heavy. A great deal of the wood has bark upon it and most mills now will not purchase anything except the peeled product.

A recent report says that between LaReine and Nottawa, Que., on the Canadian National Railway, a distance of 112 miles, there are 120,000 cords, a large proportion of which is sold. Practically all this wood is unpeeled. An effort was being made to have the railways grant an "emergency rate" for a fixed period in order that a great deal of the wood up north might be moved. Some mills are taking a quantity of pulpwood, but buying is by no means extensive.

There are practically no changes in prices. Peeled spruce and balsam south of North Bay is selling at around $12.00, and poplar at $8.00 f.o.b. cars. North of North Bay, which town is about 225 miles from Toronto, the figures are lower owing to the higher freight rates, spruce bringing about $9.00 and poplar $6.00 to $7.00.

One Ontario firm has this year contracted for 40,000 cords of pulpwood which will be delivered to various mills in the Niagara district, Wisconsin, Pennsylvania and Michigan.

## Decay of Wood Pulp Can be Prevented

Forty-eight pulp mills in the United States are reported to have a stock of over 2,200,000 cords of pulpwood in storage. Investigations by the Forest Products Laboratory, at Madison, Wis., have revealed the fact that losses from decay amounting to at least 10 per cent. of the weight of the wood may be expected in these mills under the prevailing storage conditions. A 10 per cent. loss, at a cost conservatively estimated at $15 per cord, would amount to a total of $3,300,000 due to shrinkage from decay at these mills. At least half of this loss could be prevented if proper methods of handling the wood were followed. Methods of keeping the wood yards sanitary have been suggested by the Laboratory, but convincing demonstrations are needed to bring the pulp and paper industry to realize its losses, and persistent education of mill operators is required to bring about the adoption of known preventative measures.

By far the greatest amount of pulp deterioration is found in stored groundwood. Groundwood pulp is generally stored, owing to large seasonal fluctuations in the hydraulic power used in its manufacture. Furthermore, it is usually stored in the form of wet or hydraulic pressed laps, which are more subject to decay than the machine-dried chemical pulps.

Several antiseptics have been demonstrated by the Forest Products Laboratory as effective in preventing the spread of infection in pulps, if applied at the time of manufacture. The Laboratory should have men available to assist the pulp mills to install and operate the facilities for applying these antiseptics, and to help the mills develop safe storage conditions for their future stocks of pulp wood.

## Groundwood Pulp Plant at Port Arthur Sold

The estate of the Kaministiquia Pulp & Paper Co., of Port Arthur, Ont., was sold by public auction on February 20th. The purchaser was George T. Berkey, vice-president and general-manager of the Consolidated Waterpower & Paper Co., of Wisconsin Rapids, Wisconsin.

The plant of the Kaministiquia Company, which has been idle for several months, has a capacity of thirty tons a day of groundwood pulp and is situated of sixteen acres of property owned by Port Arthur and held under a 99-year lease from the corporation. It is said that the mill and equipment which was completed a year ago, cost nearly half a million dollars. It was run for less than three

months when it had to close owing to financial difficulties. U. M. Waite, of Port Arthur, was the president and general-manager of the company.

The Consolidated Company, which has just acquired possession through Mr. Berkey, is a strong one financially, and it is said will reopen the mill at once. The groudwood mill is of reinforced concrete construction throughout and is well equipped. The wood room has equipment for slashing and barking of forty tons of wood in ten hours and the boiler house has a capacity of 220 h.p.

## Canadian Pulp Favorably Regarded in France

Hercule Barre, Canadian Government trade commissioner to France, reports that stagnation prevails in the several European timber markets, mainly attributed to the widespread dullness of trade This in conjunction with a tendency of the dealers to overstock in the past, in anticipation of the abnormal demands forecasted for industrial needs, railroad improvements and re-construction of the devasted areas, and finally the shutting off of advances by the banks, has lead to a decided slump in timber prices in France.

Similar conditions have brought about a surprising reversal in the condition of pulp trade in France. In 1919 the paper manufacturers were in desperate straits for their supply of raw material but on account of the slump it would not be difficult to place a small lot of 100 tons. The reversal is due to the diminished demand following the general reduction in business activity which in turn has resulted in the ability of the French mills to supply the requirements now.

While present conditions are considered quite exceptional, it will require, nevertheless, a pronounced revival of trade to induce a renewal of importation to any extent. When it does come, the Canadian product should make an excellent showing as it has come to be regarded with much favor on the French market, and on even terms will be preferred to the Scandinavian product.

## Whalen Company Develops Export Trade

Hon. T. W. McGarry, President of the Whalen Pulp & Paper Mills, Ltd., who spent several weeks inspecting the company's properties and plants in British Columbia, returned lately to Toronto. He says that all mills were operating at capacity—three pulp mills, two sawmills and three shingle mills, and a ready market was found for the company's products. At the present time the production of pulp runs to 5,000 tons a month, all of which is shipped out. Mr. McGarry stated that his company was shipping direct from the mills to New York by steamer, by way of the Panama Canal, and direct to Japan from Vancouver. The Company, he said, was operating full blast in all departments, and he regarded the outlook as highly encouraging.

Mr McGarry said that unusual weather conditions had been experienced in British Columbia this winter. The cold had been more severe than for many years, and there has been a continuous covering of snow on the ground. The severe cold and the lack of rainfall. he said, had combined to deplete the water supply of the Province, with the result that many mills had been forced to shut down for an indefinite period. His own company, he said, had been affected in some degrees by the lessened water supplies, but not to the extent that the mills had to be shut down. This situation was now being relieved by the annual winter rains which were just beginning when he left.

## Big Pulp Plant Will be Erected

Mayor Edmaston, of Fort William, returned from Toronto, and stated that the application to cancel the Sturgeon River and Pic limits had been withdrawn, and the Great Lakes Pulp and Paper Company would spend two million dollars on a paper mill at Fort William within three years, their time being extended for a year. Premier Drury assured the Mayor that power from Nipigon would be delivered at Fort William at the same price as at any point served by the Hydro plant, and intimated that steps would be taken to ensure that the price of power would be reasonable.

# CURRENT LUMBER PRICES—WHOLESALE

## TORONTO

(In Car Load Lots, F.O.B. cars Toronto)

### White Pine

| | | |
|---|---|---|
| 1 x 4/7 Good Strips | $100.00 | $110.00 |
| 1¼ & 1½ x 4/7 Good Strips | 120.00 | 125.00 |
| 1 x 8 and up Good Sides | 150.00 | 160.00 |
| 2 x 4/7 Good Strips | 130.00 | 140.00 |
| 1¼ & 1½ x 8 and wider Good Sides | 185.00 | 190.00 |
| 2 x 8 and wider Good Sides | 190.00 | 200.00 |
| 1 in. No. 1, 2 and 3 Cuts | 75.00 | 80.00 |
| 5/4 and 6/4 No. 1, 2 and 3 Cuts | 95.00 | 100.00 |
| 2 in. No. 1, 2 and 3 Cuts | 105.00 | 110.00 |
| 1 x 4 and 5 Mill Run | 52.00 | 55.00 |
| 1 x 6 Mill Run | 53.00 | 56.00 |
| 1 x 7, 9 and 11 Mill Run | 53.00 | 56.00 |
| 1 x 8 Mill Run | 55.00 | 58.00 |
| 1 x 10 Mill Run | 60.00 | 62.00 |
| 1 x 12 Mill Run | 65.00 | 70.00 |
| 5/4 and 6/4 x 5 and up Mill Run | 58.00 | 60.00 |
| 2 x 4 Mill Run | 52.00 | 53.00 |
| 2 x 6 Mill Run | 53.00 | 56.00 |
| 2 x 8 Mill Run | 55.00 | 58.00 |
| 2 x 10 Mill Run | 58.00 | 62.00 |
| 2 x 12 Mill Run | 60.00 | 64.00 |
| 1 in. Mill Run Shorts | 43.00 | 45.00 |
| 1 x 4 and up 6/16 No. 1 Mill Culls | 32.00 | 34.00 |
| 1 x 10 and up 6/16 No. 1 Mill Culls | 36.00 | 38.00 |
| 1 x 12 and up 6/16 No. 1 Mill Culls | 37.00 | 39.00 |
| 1 x 4 and up 6/16 No. 2 Mill Culls | 25.00 | 27.00 |
| 1 x 10 x 12 6/16 No. 2 Mill Culls | 28.00 | 30.00 |
| 1 x 4 and up 6/16 No. 3 Mill Culls | 17.00 | 22.00 |

### Red Pine

(In Car Load Lots, F.O.B. Toronto)

| | | |
|---|---|---|
| 1 x 4 and 5 Mill Run | $35.00 | $36.00 |
| 1 x 6 Mill Run | 38.00 | 40.00 |
| 1 x 8 Mill Run | 40.00 | 42.00 |
| 1 x 10 Mill Run | 42.00 | 44.00 |
| 2 x 4 Mill Run | 38.00 | 40.00 |
| 2 x 6 Mill Run | 40.00 | 42.00 |
| 2 x 8 Mill Run | 41.00 | 43.00 |
| 2 x 10 Mill Run | 44.00 | 47.00 |
| 2 x 12 Mill Run | 49.00 | 50.00 |
| 1 in. Clear and Clear Face | 69.00 | 71.00 |
| 2 in. Clear and Clear Face | 69.00 | 71.00 |

### Spruce

| | | |
|---|---|---|
| 1 x 4 Mill Run | 35.00 | 36.00 |
| 1 x 6 Mill Run | 36.00 | 37.00 |
| 1 x 8 Mill Run | 38.00 | 40.00 |
| 1 x 10 Mill Run | 45.00 | 47.00 |
| 1 x 12 Mill Run Spruce | 48.00 | 50.00 |
| Mill Culls | 25.00 | 27.00 |

### Hemlock (M R)

(In Car Load Lots, F.O.B. Toronto)

| | | |
|---|---|---|
| 1 x 4 and 5 in. x 9 to 16 ft | $26.00 | $27.00 |
| 1 x 6 in. x 9 to 16 ft | 33.00 | 35.00 |
| 1 x 8 in. x 9 to 16 ft | 34.00 | 36.00 |
| 1 x 10 and 12 in. x 9 to 16 ft | 35.00 | 37.00 |
| 1 x 7, 9 and 11 in. x 9 to 16 ft | 33.00 | 35.00 |
| 2 x 4 to 12 in., 18 ft | 37 00 | 39.00 |
| 2 x 4 to 12 in., 20 ft | 40.00 | 42.00 |
| 1 in. No. 2, 6 ft. to 16 ft | 23.00 | 25.00 |

### Fir Flooring

(In Car Load Lots, F.O.B. Toronto)

| | | |
|---|---|---|
| Fir flooring, 1 x 3 and 4", No. 1 and 2 Edge Grain | | $73.00 |
| Fir flooring, 1 x 3 and 4", No. 1 and 2 Flat Grain | | 48.00 |
| (Depending upon Widths) | | |
| 1 x 4 to 12 No. 1 and 2 Clear Fir, Rough | | 77.00 |
| 1¼ x 4 to 12 No. 1 and 2 Clear Fir, Rough | | 81.00 |
| 2 x 4 to 12 No. 1 and 2 Clear Fir, Rough | | 77.00 |
| 3 & 4 x 4 to 12 No. 1 & 2 Clear Fir, Rough | | 84.00 |
| 1 x 4, 5 and 6 in. Fir Casing | $73.00 | 80.00 |
| 1 x 8 and 10 Fir Base | 78.00 | 86.00 |
| 1¼ and 1½ 8, 10 and 12 in. E.G. Stepping | 90.00 | 95.00 |
| 1¼ and 1½ 8, 10 and 12 in. F.G. Stepping | 80.00 | 85.00 |
| 1 x 4 to 12 Clear Fir, D4S | 72.50 | 79.50 |
| 1¼ and 1½ x 4 to 12 Clear Fir, D4S | 75.25 | 82.25 |
| XX Shingles, 6 butts to 2", per M | | 3.20 |
| XXX Shingles, 6 butts to 2", per M | | 5.25 |
| XXXXX Shingles, 5 butts to 2", per M | | 6.10 |

### Lath

(F.O.B. Mill)

| | |
|---|---|
| No. 1 White Pine | $11.00 |
| No. 2 White Pine | 10.00 |
| No. 3 White Pine | 8.00 |
| Mill Run White Pine, 32 in. | 5.00 |
| Merchantable Spruce Lath, 4 ft. | 6.50 |

## TORONTO HARDWOOD PRICES

The prices given below are for car loads f.o.b. Toronto, from wholesalers to retailers, and are based on a good percentage of long lengths and good widths, without any wide stock having been sorted out.

The prices quoted on imported woods are payable in U. S. funds.

### Ash, White

(Dry weight 3800 lbs. per M. ft.)

| | 1s & 2s | No. 1 Com. | No. 2 Com. |
|---|---|---|---|
| 1" | $100.00 | $ 60.00 | $ 40.00 |
| 1¼ and 1½" | 105.00 | 65.00 | 40.00 |
| 2" | 110.00 | 70.00 | 50.00 |
| 2½ and 3" | 125.00 | 80.00 | 55.00 |
| 4" | 140.00 | 95.00 | 60.00 |

### Ash, Brown

| | | | |
|---|---|---|---|
| 1" | $ 95.00 | $ 55.00 | $ 40.00 |
| 1¼ and 1½" | 100.00 | 60.00 | 40.00 |
| 2" | 105.00 | 65.00 | 50.00 |
| 2½ and 3" | 125.00 | 80.00 | 55.00 |
| 4" | 140.00 | 95.00 | 60.00 |

### Birch

(Dry weight 4000 lbs. per M. ft.)

| | 1s & 2s | Sels. | No. 1 Com. | No. 2 Com. |
|---|---|---|---|---|
| 4/4 | $105.00 | $ 80.00 | $ 50.00 | $ 32.00 |
| 5/4 | 110.00 | 85.00 | 55.00 | 35.00 |
| 6/4 | 115.00 | 90.00 | 60.00 | 38.00 |
| 8/4 | 120.00 | 100.00 | 65.00 | 42.00 |
| 12/4 | 125.00 | 105.00 | 70.00 | 50.00 |
| 16/4 | 130.00 | 110.00 | 80.00 | 55.00 |

### Basswood

(Dry weight 2500 lbs. per M. ft.)

| | 1s & 2s | No. 1 Com. | No. 2 Com. |
|---|---|---|---|
| 4/4 | $ 80.00 | $ 50.00 | $ 25.00 |
| 5/4 and 6/4 | 85.00 | 60.00 | 30.00 |
| 8/4 | 90.00 | 65.00 | 35.00 |

### Chestnut

(Dry weight 2800 lbs. per M. ft.)

| | 1s & 2s | No. 1 Com. | Sound Wormy |
|---|---|---|---|
| 1" | $130.00 | $ 80.00 | $ 40.00 |
| 1¼" to 1½" | 135.00 | 85.00 | 43.00 |
| 2" | 145.00 | 90.00 | 43.00 |

### Maple, Hard

(Dry weight 4200 lbs. per M. ft.)

| | F.A.S. | Sels. | No. 1 Com. | No. 2 Com. |
|---|---|---|---|---|
| 4/4 | $ 80.00 | $ 65.00 | $ 45.00 | $ 33.00 |
| 5/4 | 80.00 | 65.00 | 45.00 | 38.00 |
| 6/4 | 85.00 | 70.00 | 50.00 | 45.00 |
| 8/4 | 95.00 | 75.00 | 60.00 | 50.00 |
| 12/4 | 100.00 | 75.00 | 65.00 | 60.00 |
| 16/4 | 120.00 | 100.00 | 70.00 | 65.00 |

### Elm, Soft

(Dry weight 3100 lbs. per M. ft.)

| | 1s & 2s | No. 1 Com. | No. 2 Com. |
|---|---|---|---|
| 4/4 | $ 75.00 | $ 50.00 | $ 25.00 |
| 6/4 and 8/4 | 80.00 | 60.00 | 30.00 |
| 12/4 | 96.00 | 70.00 | 35.00 |

### Gum, Red

(Dry weight 3300 lbs. per M. ft.)

| | Plain 1s & 2s | Plain No. 1 Com. | Quartered 1s & 2s | Quartered No. 1 Com. |
|---|---|---|---|---|
| 1" | $120.00 | $ 70.00 | $133.00 | $ 83.00 |
| 1¼" | 120.00 | 70.00 | 148.00 | 88.00 |
| 1½" | 130.00 | 75.00 | 148.00 | 88.00 |
| 2" | 135.00 | 95.00 | 158.00 | 103.00 |

Figured Gum, $10 per M. extra, in both plain and quartered.

### Gum, Sap

| | 1s&2s | No. 1 Com. |
|---|---|---|
| 1" | $ 55.00 | $ 40.00 |
| 1¼" and 1½" | 60.00 | 44.00 |
| 2" | 65.00 | 50.00 |

### Hickory

(Dry weight 4500 lbs. per M. ft.

| | 1s&2s | No. 1 Com. |
|---|---|---|
| 1" | $120.00 | $ 60.00 |
| 1¼" | 145.00 | 65.00 |
| 1½" | 145.00 | 65.00 |
| 2" | 150.00 | 70.00 |

### Plain White and Red Oak

(Plain sawed. Dry weight 4000 lbs. per M. ft.)

| | 1s&2s | No. 1 Com. |
|---|---|---|
| 4/4 | $120.00 | $ 75.00 |
| 5/4 and 6/4 | 130.00 | 80.00 |
| 8/4 | 135.00 | 85.00 |
| 10/4 | 145.00 | 90.00 |
| 12/4 | 145.00 | 90.00 |
| 16/4 | 150.00 | 95.00 |

### White Oak, Quarter Cut

(Dry weight 4000 lbs. per M. ft.)

| | 1s&2s | No. 1 Com. |
|---|---|---|
| 4/4 | $160.00 | $ 90.00 |
| 5/4 and 6/4 | 170.00 | 95.00 |
| 8/4 | 190.00 | 105.00 |

### Quarter Cut Red Oak

| | 1s&2s | No. 1 Com. |
|---|---|---|
| 4/4 | $145.00 | $ 80.00 |
| 5/4 and 6/4 | 160.00 | 90.00 |
| 8/4 | 165.00 | 95.00 |

### Beech

The quantity of beech produced in Ontario is not large and is generally sold on a log run basis, the locality governing the prices. At present the prevailing quotation on log run, mill culls out, delivered in Toronto, is $35.00 to $40.00.

## OTTAWA

Manufacturers' Prices

### Pine

| | | |
|---|---|---|
| Good sidings: | | |
| 1 in. x 7 in. and up | | $140.00 |
| 1¼ in. and 1½ in., 8 in. and up. | | 165.00 |
| 2 in. x 7 in. and up | | 165.00 |
| No. 2 cuts 2 x 8 in. and up | | 80.00 |
| Good strips: | | |
| 1 in. | $100.00 | $105.00 |
| 1¼ in. and 1½ in. | | 120.00 |
| 2 in. | | 125.00 |
| Good shorts: | | |
| 1 in. x 7 in. and up | | 110.00 |
| 1 in. 4 in. to 6 in. | 85.00 | 90.00 |
| 1¼ in. and 1½ in. | | 110.00 |
| 2 in. | | 125.00 |
| 7 in. to 9 in. A sidings | 54.00 | 56.00 |
| No. 1 dressing sidings | 82.00 | 85.00 |
| No. 1 dressing strips | - | 78.00 |
| No. 1 dressing shorts | 68.00 | 73.00 |
| 1 in. x 4 in. s.c. strips | 56.00 | 58.00 |
| 1 in. x 5 in. s.c. strips | 56.00 | 58.00 |
| 1 in. x 6 in. s.c. strips | 63.00 | 65.00 |
| 1 in. x 7 in. s.c. strips | 63.00 | 64.00 |
| 1 in. x 8 in. s.c. strips, 12 to 16 ft | 63.00 | 66.00 |
| 1 in. x 10 in. M.R. | 65.00 | 70.00 |
| S.C. sidings, 1½ and 2 in. | 63.00 | 67.00 |
| S.C. strips, 1 in. | | 64.00 |
| 1¼, 1½ and 2 in. | 57.00 | 58.00 |
| S.C. shorts, 1 x 4 to 6 in. | 48.00 | 50.00 |
| S.C. and bet., shorts. 1 x 5 | | 48.00 |
| S.C. and bet., shorts, 1 x 6 | | 50.00 |
| S.C. Shorts, 6'-11', 1" x 10" | 52.00 | 54.00 |
| Box boards: | | |
| 1 in. x 4 in. and up, 6 ft.-11 ft. | | 45.00 |
| 1 in. x 3 in. and up, 12 ft.-16 ft. | 50.00 | 53.00 |
| Mill culls, strips and sidings, 1 in. x 4 in. and up, 12 ft. and up | 43.00 | 45.00 |
| Mill cull shorts, 1 in. x 4 in. and up, 6 ft. to 11 ft. | 34.00 | 36.00 |
| O. culls r and w p | 24.00 | 28.00 |

### Red Pine, Log Run

| | | |
|---|---|---|
| Mill culls out, 1 in. | 34.00 | 48.00 |
| Mill culls out, 1¼ in. | 34.00 | 48.00 |
| Mill culls out, 1½ in. | 35.00 | 47.00 |
| Mill culls out, 2 in. | 35.00 | 47.00 |
| Mill Culls, white pine, 1 in. x 7 in. and up | | 35.00 |

### Mill Run Spruce

| | | |
|---|---|---|
| 1 in. x 4 in. and up, 6 ft.-11 ft. | | 25.00 |
| 1 in. x 4 in. and up, 12 ft.-16 ft. | 32.00 | 34.00 |
| 1" x 9"-10" and up, 12 ft.-16 ft. | 38.00 | 40.00 |
| 1¼" x 7, 8 and 9" up, 12 ft.-16 ft. | | 53.00 |
| 1¼ x 10 and up, 12 ft.-16 ft. | 38.00 | 42.00 |
| 1½" x 12" x 12" and up, 12'-16'. | | 42.00 |
| Spruce, 1 in. clear fine dressing and B | | 55.00 |
| Hemlock, 1 in. cull | | 20.00 |
| Hemlock, 1 in. log run | 24.00 | 26.00 |
| Hemlock, 2 x 4, 6, 8, 10 12/16 ft. | | 28.00 |
| Tamarac | 25.00 | 28.00 |
| Basswood, log run, dead culls out | 45.00 | 50.00 |
| Basswood, log run, mill culls out. | 50.00 | 54.00 |
| Birch, log run | 45.00 | 50.00 |
| Soft Elm, common and better, 1, 1½, 2 in. | 58.00 | 68.00 |
| Ash, black, log run | 62.00 | 65.00 |
| 1 x 10 No. 1 barn | 57.00 | 62.00 |
| 1 x 10 No. 2 barn | 51.00 | 56.00 |
| 1 x 8 and 9 No. 2 barn | 47.00 | 52.00 |

# CURRENT LUMBER PRICES—WHOLESALE

**Lath per M.:**

| | | |
|---|---|---|
| No. 1 White Pine, 1¼ in. x 4 ft. | | 8.[illegible] |
| No. 2 White Pine | | 6.[illegible] |
| Mill run White Pine | | 7.00 |
| Spruce, mill run, 1½ in. | | 6.00 |
| Red Pine, mill run | | 6.00 |
| Hemlock, mill run | | 5.50 |
| **White Cedar Shingles** | | |
| XXXX, 18 in. | 9.00 | 10.00 |
| Clear butt, 18 in. | 6.00 | 7.00 |
| 18 in. XX | | 5.00 |

## QUEBEC

**White Pine**
(At Quebec)

| | Cts. Per Cubic Ft. | |
|---|---|---|
| First class Ottawa wancy, 18 in. average according to lineal | 100 | 110 |
| 19 in. and up average | 110 | 120 |

**Spruce Deals**
(At Mill)

| | | |
|---|---|---|
| 3 in. unsorted, Quebec, 4 in. to 6 in. wide | $ 20.00 | $ 25.00 |
| 3 in. unsorted, Quebec, 7 in. to 8 in. wide | 26.00 | 28.00 |
| 3 in. unsorted, Quebec, 9 in. wide | 30.00 | 35.00 |

**Oak**
(At Quebec)

| | Cts. Per Cubic Ft. | |
|---|---|---|
| According to average and quality, 55 ft. cube | 125 | 130 |

**Elm**
(At Quebec)

| | | |
|---|---|---|
| According to average and quality, 40 to 45 ft. cube | 100 | 120 |
| According to average and quality, 30 to 35 ft. | 90 | 100 |

**Export Birch Planks**
(At Mill)

| | | |
|---|---|---|
| 1 to 4 in. thick, per M. ft. | $ 30.00 | $ 35.00 |

## ST. JOHN, N.B.

(From Yards and Mills)

**Rough Lumber**

| | | |
|---|---|---|
| 2x3, 2x4, 3x3, 3x4. Rgh Merch Spr | $30.00 | |
| 2x3, 2x4, 3x3, 3x4, Dressed 1 edge | 31.00 | |
| 2x3, 2x4, 3x3, 3x4, Dressed 4 sides | 31.00 | |
| 2x6, 2x7, 3x5, 4x4, 4x6, all rough. | 30.00 | |
| 2x6, 2x7, 3x5, 4x4, 4x6, all rough. | 34.00 | |
| 2x8, 3x7, 5x5, 6x6 | 37.00 | $ 40.00 |
| 2x9, 3x8, 6x8, 7x7 | 37.00 | 40.00 |
| 2x10, 3x9 | 45.00 | |
| 2x12, 3x10, 3x12, 8x8 and up | 45.00 | |
| Merch. Spr. Bds., Rough, 1x3-4 & 5 | 30.00 | |
| Merch. Spr. Bds., Rough, 1x6 | 34.00 | |
| Merch. Spr. Bds., Rough, 1x7 & up | 40.00 | |
| Refuse Bds., Deals and Setgs. | 18.00 | 20.00 |

Above random lengths up to 18-0 long.
Lengths 19-0 and up $5.00 extra per M.
For planing Merch. and Refuse Bds. add $2.00 per M. to above prices.
Laths, $7.00.

**Shingles**

| | Per M. |
|---|---|
| Cedar, Extras | $6.00 |
| Cedar, Clears | 5.25 |
| Cedar, 2nd Clears | 4.25 |
| Cedar, Extra No. 1 | 2.90 |
| Spruce | 4.50 |

## SARNIA, ONT.

**Pine, Common and Better**

| | |
|---|---|
| 1 x 6 and 8 in. | $110.00 |
| 1 in., 8 in. and up wide | 130.00 |
| 1¼ and 1½ in. and up wide | 180.00 |
| 2 in. and up wide | 180.00 |
| **Cuts and Better** | |
| 4/4 x 8 and up No. 1 and better | 123.00 |
| 5/4 and 6/4 and up No. 1 and better | 150.00 |
| 8/4 and 8 and up No. 1 and better | 150.00 |
| **No. 1 Cuts** | |
| 1 in.. 8 in. and up wide | 110.00 |
| 1¼ in., 8 in. and up wide | 125.00 |
| 1½ in., 8 in. and up wide | 125.00 |
| 2 in., 8 in. and up wide | 130.00 |
| 2½ in. and 3 in., 8 in. and up wide | 175.00 |
| 4 in., 8 in. and up wide | 185.00 |

**No. 1 Barn**

| | | |
|---|---|---|
| 1 in., 10 to 16 ft. long | $ 75.00 | $ 85.00 |
| 1¼, 1½ and 2 in., 10/16 ft. | 80.00 | 85.00 |
| 2½ to 3 in., 10/16 ft. | 85.00 | 100.00 |
| **No. 2 Barn** | | |
| 1 in., 10 to 16 ft. long | 65.00 | 75.00 |
| 1¼, 1½ and 2 in., 10/16 ft. | | 66.00 |
| 2½, 1½ and 3 in. | | 85.00 |
| **No. 3 Barn** | | |
| 1 in., 10 to 16 ft. long | 48.00 | 55.00 |
| 1¼, 1½ and 2 in., 10/16 ft. | 50.00 | 56.00 |
| **Box** | | |
| 1 in., 1¼ and 1½ in., 10/16 ft. | 33.00 | 35.00 |
| **Mill Culls** | | |
| Mill Run Culls— | | |
| 1 in., 4 in. and up wide, 6/16 ft. | | 27.00 |
| 1¼, 1½ and 2 in. | | 28.00 |

## WINNIPEG

**No. 1 Spruce**

| Dimension | S.1.S. and 1.E. 10 ft. | 12 ft. | 14 ft. | 16 ft. |
|---|---|---|---|---|
| 2 x 4 | $30 | $29 | $29 | $30 |
| 2 x 6 | 31 | 29 | 29 | 30 |
| 2 x 8 | 32 | 30 | 30 | 31 |
| 2 x 10 | 33 | 31 | 31 | 32 |
| 2 x 12 | 34 | 32 | 32 | 33 |

For 2 inches, rough, add 50 cents.
For S1E only, add 50 cents.
For S1S and 2E, S4S or D&M, add $3.00.
For timbers larger than 8 x 8, add 50c. for each additional 2 inches each way.
For lengths longer than 20 ft., add $1.00 for each additional two feet.
For selected common, add $5.00.
For No. 2 Dimension, $3.00 less than No. 1.
For 1 x 2 and 2 x 2, $2 more than 2 x 4 No. 1.
For Tamarac, open.

## BUFFALO and TONAWANDA

**White Pine**
Wholesale Selling Price

| | |
|---|---|
| Uppers, 4/4 | $225.00 |
| Uppers, 5/4 to 8/4 | 225.00 |
| Uppers, 10/4 to 12/4 | 250.00 |
| Selects, 4/4 | 200.00 |
| Selects, 5/4 to 8/4 | 200.00 |
| Selects, 10/4 to 12/4 | 225.00 |
| Fine Common, 4/4 | 155.00 |
| Fine Common, 5/4 | 160.00 |
| Fine Common, 6/4 | 160.00 |
| Fine Common, 8/4 | 160.00 |
| No. 1 Cuts, 4/4 | 115.00 |
| No. 1 Cuts, 5/4 | 130.00 |
| No. 1 Cuts, 6/4 | 135.00 |
| No. 1 Cuts, 8/4 | 140.00 |
| No. 2 Cuts, 4/4 | 70.00 |
| No. 2 Cuts, 5/4 | 100.00 |
| No. 2 Cuts, 6/4 | 105.00 |
| No. 2 Cuts, 8/4 | 110.00 |
| No. 3 Cuts, 5/4 | 60.00 |
| No. 3 Cuts, 6/4 | 65.00 |
| No. 3 Cuts, 8/4 | 67.00 |
| Dressing, 4/4 | 95.00 |
| Dressing 4/4 x 10 | 98.00 |
| Dressing, 4/4 x 12 | 110.00 |
| No. 1 Moulding, 5/4 | 150.00 |
| No. 1 Moulding, 6/4 | 150.00 |
| No. 1 Moulding, 8/4 | 155.00 |
| No. 2 Moulding, 5/4 | 125.00 |
| No. 2 Moulding, 6/4 | 125.00 |
| No. 2 Moulding, 8/4 | 130.00 |
| No. 1 Barn, 1 x 12 | 90.00 |
| No. 1 Barn, 1 x 6 and 8 | 76.00 |
| No. 1 Barn, 1 x 10 | 80.00 |
| No. 2 Barn, 1 x 6 and 8 | 62.00 |
| No. 2 Barn, 1 x 10 | 63.00 |
| No. 2 Barn, 1 x 12 | 75.00 |
| No. 3 Barn, 1 x 6 and 8 | 42.00 |
| No. 3 Barn, 1 x 10 | 44.00 |
| No. 3 Barn, 1 x 12 | 47.00 |
| Box, 1 x 6 and 8 | 36.00 |
| Box, 1 x 10 | 38.00 |
| Box, 1 x 12 | 39.00 |
| Box, 1 x 13 and up | 40.00 |

## BUFFALO

The following quotations on hardwoods represent the jobber buying price at Buffalo and Tonawanda.

| | 1s & 2s | No. 1 Com. | No. 2 Com. |
|---|---|---|---|
| **Maple** | | | |
| 1 in. | $ 80.00 | $ 45.00 | $ 30.00 |
| 5/4 to 8/4 | 85.00 | 50.00 | 30.00 |
| 10/4 to 4 in. | 90.00 | 55.00 | 30.00 |
| **Sap Birch** | | | |
| 1 in. | 90.00 | 48.00 | 30.00 |
| 5/4 and up | 100.00 | 53.00 | 30.00 |
| **Soft Elm** | | | |
| 1 in. | 70.00 | 45.00 | 30.00 |
| 5/4 to 2 in. | 75.00 | 50.00 | 30.00 |
| **Red Birch** | | | |
| 1 in. | 120.00 | 75.00 | |
| 5/4 and up | 125.00 | 80.00 | |
| **Basswood** | | | |
| 1 in. | 70.00 | 45.00 | 30.00 |
| 5/4 to 2 in. | 80.00 | 55.00 | 35.00 |
| **Plain Oak** | | | |
| 1 in. | 95.00 | 55.00 | 35.00 |
| 5/4 to 2 in. | 105.00 | 65.00 | 40.00 |
| **Ash** | | | |
| 1 in. | 85.00 | 50.00 | 30.00 |
| 5/4 to 2 in. | 95.00 | 55.00 | 30.00 |
| 10/4 and up | 110.00 | 70.00 | 30.00 |

## BOSTON

Quotations given below are for highest grades of Michigan and Canadian White Pine and Eastern Canadian Spruce as required in the New England market in car loads.

| | | |
|---|---|---|
| White Pine Uppers, 1 in. | | |
| White Pine Uppers, 1¼, 1½, 2 in. | | |
| White Pine Uppers, 2½, 3 in. | | |
| White Pine Uppers, 4 in. | | |
| Selects, 1 in. | | $190.00 |
| Selects, 1¼, 2 in. | | 200.00 |
| Selects, 2½, 3 in. | | |
| Selects, 4 in. | | |
| **Prices nominal** | | |
| Fine Common, 1 in., 30%, 12 in. and up. | | 165.00 |
| Fine Common, 1 x 8 and up | | 165.00 |
| Fine Common, 1¼ to 2 in. | $165.00 | 170.00 |
| Fine Common, 2½ and 3 in. | | 180.00 |
| Fine Common, 4 in. | | 195.00 |
| 1 in. Shaky Clear | | 100.00 |
| 1¼ in. to 2 in. Shaky Clear | | 110.00 |
| 1 in. No. 2 Dressing | | 95.00 |
| 1¼ in. to 2 in. No. 2 Dressing | | 95.00 |
| No. 1 Cuts, 1 in. | | 110.00 |
| No. 1 Cuts, 1¼ to 2 in. | | 140.00 |
| No. 1 Cuts, 2½ to 3 in. | | 180.00 |
| No. 2 Cuts, 1 in. | | 80.00 |
| No. 2 Cuts, 1¼ to 2 in. | | 110.00 |
| Barn Boards, No. 1, 1 x 12 | | 91.00 |
| Barn Boards, No. 1, 1 x 10 | | 87.00 |
| Barn Boards, No. 1, 1 x 8 | | 84.50 |
| Barn Boards, No. 2, 1 x 12 | | 75.00 |
| Barn Boards, No. 2, 1 x 8 | | 67.00 |
| Barn Boards, No. 2 1 x 10 | | 68.00 |
| Barn Boards, No. 3, 1 x 12 | | 55.00 |
| Barn Boards, No. 3, 1 x 10 | | 53.00 |
| Barn Boards, No. 3, 1 x 8 | | 52.00 |
| **No. 1 Clear** | | |
| Can. Spruce, No. 1 and clear, 1 x 4 to 9" | | $ 75.00 |
| Can. Spruce, 1 x 10 in. | | 78.00 |
| Can. Spruce, No. 1, 1 x 4 to 7 in. | | 72.00 |
| Can. Spruce, No. 1, 1 x 8 and 9 in. | | 74.00 |
| Can. Spruce, No. 1, 1 x 10 in. | | 76.00 |
| Can. Spruce, No. 2, 1 x 4 and 5 in. | | 36.00 |
| Can. Spruce, No. 2, 1 x 6 and 7 in. | | 37.00 |
| Can. Spruce, No. 2, 1 x 8 and 9 in. | | 39.00 |
| Can. Spruce, No. 2, 1 x 10 in. | | 42.00 |
| Can. Spruce, No. 2, 1 x 12 in. | | 45.00 |
| Spruce, 12 in. dimension | | 46.00 |
| Spruce, 10 in. dimension | | 44.00 |
| Spruce, 9 in. dimension | | 43.00 |
| Spruce, 8 in. dimension | | 42.00 |
| 2 x 10 in. random lengths, 8 ft. and up | | 41.00 |
| 2 x 12 in. random lengths | | 42.00 |
| 2 x 3, 2 x 4, 2 x 5, 2 x 6, 2 x 7 | | 32.00 |
| 3 x 4 and 4 x 4 in. | | 33.00 |
| 2 x 9 | | 39.00 |
| All other random lengths, 7 in. and under, 8 ft. and up | 32.00 | 36.00 |
| 5 in. and up merchantable boards, 8 ft. and up, D 1s | 33.00 | 32.00 |
| 1 x 2 | | 32.00 |
| 1 x 3 | | 30.00 |
| 1⅝ in. Spruce Lath | | 8.50 |
| 1½ in. Spruce Lath | | 7.50 |
| **New Brunswick Cedar Shingles** | | |
| Extras | | 5.50 |
| Clears | | 4.50 |
| Second Clear | 3.50 | 3.75 |
| Clear Whites | 2.75 | 3.00 |

# Quick Action Section

Young man wants position with a good reliable Lumber Company. 10 years experience in both Wholesale and Retail. For past 8 years have been, and still am employed as Manager, but am desirous of making a change. Box 810 Canada Lumberman, Toronto.

Returned soldier—married, wishes steady position with Lumber Company in Ontario operating saw and planing mill as oiler, second engineer, fireman, dogger or setter, have third class Stationary Certificate. Can give good references. Box 814 Canada Lumberman, Toronto.

Aggressive Young Man with ability, integrity and five years' experience Lumber and Woodworking offices, desires permanent position with progressive concern in a town. Am adaptable to any phase of work. Replies treated confidential. Excellent references. Box 809 Canada Lumberman, Toronto.

Accountant and General office man, with ten years experience in all branches of the Lumber Trade, seeks re-engagement. Accustomed to payrolls, orders, costing, Correspondence and can operate typewriter. First-class references. Box No. 801, Canada Lumberman, Toronto.

Position Wanted as Lumber Inspector and Scaler, by young Russian, four years experience on Rough and Dressed lumber, can handle yard work and Shipping, has good connection with the Saw Mill. Single, can go anywhere. First Class Canadian references. Apply Box 813, Canada Lumberman, Toronto, Ont.

Young Scotchman married, abstainer, wishes permanent progressive position as bookkeeper, stenographer and general office man. Have had following experience: Six years banking two years assistant bookkeeper and stenographer, London, England; eight years lumber office experience. Willing to go anywhere. Salary $100/$125. Apply Box 799 Canada Lumberman, Toronto.

## B. C. Lumber Buyer

Is open for appointment as British Columbia representative of Eastern Canada house. At present employed. Have large experience in buying and selling. Well known among Coast mills and to trade generally. Good references. Box - 820 "Canada Lumberman" Toronto.

## Situations Vacant

An opening in retail lumber office for high class salesman who can estimate accurately, handle customers and telephone. Apply in own handwriting, enclosing Copy of references. Box 880 Canada Lumberman, Toronto.

## Business Chances

### For Sale

1000 acres of timber, portable mill 10,000 capacity. Snap for quick sale. Apply Box 4 Orrville, Ontario.

### Would Exchange up to $13,000 Mortgages

for lumber at current prices.
York Wrecking Co.,
4-5          8 Hallowell Ave., Toronto.

### Sawmill Service in Toronto

We are equipped to cut logs, timber, etc. at reasonable price.
York Wrecking Co.,
4-5          8 Hallowell Ave., Toronto.

### For Sale Cheap

Water power factory or mill site in thriving community on North shore of Lake Huron. White Pine Lumber Company, Blind River, Ont.                                       3-5

### Wanted

To arrange with Mill which has facilities for supplying timbers for barns in Hemlock or Spruce in large quantities. Box 772 Canada Lumberman, Toronto.          3-5

### Timber Lands for Sale

In Nova Scotia about 80 miles east of Halifax 10,000 acres well timbered, containing Pine, Spruce, Hemlock, Birch, Maple, etc. in virgin state. Box 797 Canada Lumberman, Toronto.

### For Sale

Woodworking factory well equipped with all machinery—water power, also 86 H.P. engine, in good central locality, province of Quebec, easy terms, apply to "UNIVERSAL TRADING COMPANY" 294 St. Catherine St. East, Montreal.                              5

### For Sale

Sawmill at Excelsior, West Bay with stock 350,000 ft. of first class Birch, Elm, Ash and Maple in logs, plenty of good timber in surrounding country, good location. Address, H. L. Corbiere, Box 237 Little Current Ont.

## "British Columbia Saw Mill and Limits for Sale

100,000,000" Standing Timber—Fir, Cedar, Spruce and Pine with first class Saw Mill for sale in central southern part of British Columbia. Cash or Terms Apply Box No. 817 Canada Lumberman, Toronto.          5

### Portable Sawmill Service¦

First class work done quickly and efficiently in Quebec and Ontario. Reasonable charges based on size of order, location, etc. Inquiries or orders must be sent in ten weeks before mill is desired. Shingle and lath mills also. Birch and Beech wanted 6/4 to 12/4 or logs. Apply J. K. Spendlove, Katevale, Que.
2 T.f.

### Are You Manufacturing Some ⭐ Special Wood Article ?

We have a Woodworking Plant, 100 Horse Water Power, up to date Dry Kilns, capacity 60 M. ft., situated about 100 miles from Montreal in Province of Quebec. Ideal labor conditions, plenty hardwood lumber for years, cheap. Want to get in touch with parties now manufacturing some special wood article who would consider establishing in Quebec with a view of organizing company. We have the plant—have you the business and capital? Address Box 762 Canada Lumberman, Toronto, Ont.

## "To Canadian Lumber Manufacturers"

Highly-rated wholesale and retail Western New York Lumber Corporation handling large volume of Canadian Stocks, buying extensive yard and factory stock of Canadian White Pine, Spruce, etc. a large common stock interest at present held by stock holder who wishes to retire from active business through age. The assets of this corporation are around a half million with unlimited credit. This offer has as its object a selling arrangement through close connection or alliance with a large mill and which offers large mutual profit possibilities. Box 824 Canada Lumberman, Toronto.
3—T f.

## Miscellaneous

### Wanted

One Lath Binder and Trimmer. Also several carloads of white pine. Box 815 Canada Lumberman, Toronto.          5

### Getting Business is Great Sport

Because getting business is about the finest sport in the world, the merchant—so called —who never has gone on a hunt for trade has missed the joy of discovery, and if he has not "invented" a business-getting idea he has not known the joy of an Edison.

There are but two kinds of persons in the world—inventors and imitators; and even the inventors sometimes copy, while too often copiers are never anything else. When an unenterprising community is discovered by one of these real business inventors, who is called to it by opportunities that are unnoticed by merchants already on the ground, there is trouble ahead for the latter. Not infrequently this generator of ideas is a lumberman, who sets up shop where there are already enough dealers. This new comer knows better than to expect success without earning it, and about the last thing he would attempt would be to follow the trails and methods of other dealers in his community. He attacks the buyers' strongholds from other vantage points, comes at them from other angles and makes his advances in different ways.

## MacLean Building Reports
### Limited

MacLean Building Reports will give you accurate, advance information on every building and engineering contract of consequence in the Dominion.

These Reports are issued daily and reach subscribers in ample time to bid on the work or submit prices for the machinery, equipment, materials or supplies required.

Hundreds of firms are deriving much financial benefit from the use of MacLean Building Reports. Tell us what territory you cover and put it up to us to show how we can help you get more business. Be sure to write to-day for rates and free sample reports.

### MacLean Building Reports, Ltd.

345 Adelaide St. W. - TORONTO
119 Board of Trade Bldg. - MONTREAL
348 Main St. - WINNIPEG
212 Winch Bldg. - VANCOUVER

# Review of Current Trade Conditions

### Considerable Stocks are Being Moved at St. John

No improvement in price of lumber both in the English and American market has taken place at St. John, N. B., during the last fortnight. Demand has been fair and considerable stocks are being moved, largely from portable and stationary mills in the interior of the country. Most of the sales made of narrow random have been made at prices which are only netting about $20.00 per M on cars.

The most of the stock being shipped to American points is going to New York state where little better prices are being obtained, largely in the Long Island district, but as the rate of freight from this section of the country is excessive, it reduces the price to only about $2.00 per M over Boston. Cargoes for future summer delivery are being sold for narrow specification at around $31.80 to $32.00 delivered Sound points. All these prices prohibit any profit and cannot keep up indefinitely even on present reduced logging costs, as it leaves the operator nothing for stumpage. This condition would not apply where there are lengthy drives or high stumpage, as in cases like this the present price received would mean a loss around $10.00 per M.

The English market shows no improvement but a further weakening. Freights have not reduced and present prices are prohibitive of any further shipments. It certainly means that if present conditions keep up, the manufacturer of good stocks of deals will do very little shipping. The winter of 1922—23 should see a strong demand for good deals of broad average widths and good lengths at prices which will be far in excess of the present prices offered. Freights will, no doubt, then be less and demand greater with general conditions world-wide much improved.

The present condition of the trade is stagnant and will remain so for a short time, but we shall soon pass to the period of a (buying and demand) revival of trade when prices should improve to some extent.

Certainly in as far as stocks being replaced is concerned logging has been carried on very conservatively, and in Maine, New Hampshire and Vermont only 135,000,000 feet of logs and lumber are being produced for 1922. This is the smallest cut made in years; also in New Brunswick when everything is summed up there is only one-third the usual cut being taken out.

Granted that there is a considerable quantity of old stocks, how much of it is fit for commercial purposes. Probably not over 50%. The balance is culls and much of it not fit to lift out of the pile. Should a fair demand for lumber take place, it will not be long before a tremendous inroad is made upon the stocks, and by early fall heavy buying will, no doubt, take place and prices will advance.

In the meantime, no doubt limited shipments will keep up. Probably buying will take place in small quantities as, no doubt, for a few months business of all kinds will be upon a limited basis. Trading will be in fair volume but from day to day as speculation even within reason will not be favorably looked upon by the lenders of cash.

The mills at St. John are yet idle and will continue so until April, when if labor can be procured at a reasonable price and under good working conditions, the plants will start, but under no other conditions, as there is no bright outlook to warrant paying any high wage.

Freights, ocean wide, continue to remain at 100 shillings for Great Britain. The steamship companies refuse to reduce their price on tonnage. Taken altogether, the freight rates are over one-third the price of the lumber.

Laths are much firmer than two weeks ago and to-day are selling at about $6.50 on cars St. John with only limited offerings.

### Quebec Exporters Adopt Conservative Attitude

Though the month of March is now here the period of the year when the lumber and timber trade barometer generally gives indication as to the business expected in regard to spring and summer shipments of Canadian wood to the market of the United Kingdom, no premonition has yet been given as to the certainty of conditions. Farnworth & Jardine's annual timber circular does not afford any indication of the business outlook for 1922. It refers to a note of caution contained in the 1921 January circular. The note of caution given has been fully justified, and in a review of last year's business, says that 1921 was, perhaps, the most difficult ever experienced in the timber trade. The year opened with a depressed and uncertain market, which continued almost throughout. Prices

steadily declined with the result that buying was carried out from hand to mouth, whilst holders of stocks were faced with serious losses and great difficulties in realizing. The difficulties were accentuated by trouble in the labor world. The coal mines' stoppage seriously affected all industry, causing dislocation in practically all branches of business.

Canadian spruce was one of the most difficult markets, Stocks at the commencement were full, and holders, in order to liquidate offered large quantities by public auction, mostly "without reserve," which had the effect of materially lowering prices for spot goods, and thereby making sales for forward delivery increasingly difficult.

Helped by advantageous exchange rates, Finnish and Riga, etc., whites were offering at comparatively cheap prices and commanded attention on the west coast to the detriment of the Canadian product.

The money shortage was acute, but during the year the bank rate was lowered from 7 per cent to 5 per cent, thus relieving the tension in no small degree.

The future is, however, still obscure, and many difficulties have to be surmounted, but the feeling generally is that the worst has passed and with renewed confidence, the position should slowly recover.

Quebec export timber and lumber houses in constant touch with the United Kingdom agencies, are not too sanguine over new business in the United Kingdom for 1922. They gather from reports that it will take another year to sail in safe waters, as the spirit of readjustment is not as yet proceeding with confidence on account of the exchange and unrest in the European political atmosphere. There are yet many dark clouds to roll by and until these commence to move and show a clearer sky, the moneyed interests and, in consequence, industrial interests and markets dealing in raw material for construction, will remain dormant.

In the meantime there is every appearance that the more adventurous leaders in the cause of adjustment and promotion of construction, will endeavor to force the issue. This phase of the situation is being closely watched by the Quebec exporters, who have already begun to realize that they may expect during the coming season of navigation in the St. Lawrence, orders, and has made them keep in continual touch with their European agencies. The banks carrying their accounts, advise the utmost caution for another year at least.

Even in the United States all branches of business are feeling and complaining of the low pressure in the markets, and it is a well-known fact that some of the largest business interests in the American Republic have been obliged to draw upon bonded interests to prop the reserves of their commercial interests, which, in itself, is a worry to the Canadian timber and lumber trade, to wait one more year before taking risks which might involve them in difficulties.

This opinion is not advanced in a spirit of pessimism. It is from a review of the situation as it presents itself to the vision of the student in economics, continually sizing up conditions through a telescopic visualization of political aspects still existing from the great war.

### Ontario and the East

The situation characterizing the general lumber market is somewhat complex in character and there is no denying that business is slower in opening up than was looked for at the beginning of the year. Those who are in closest touch with affairs say that it will be well into March before it is definitely known what the spring demand is going to be and what proportion the anticipated house building boom will assume.

There are many predictions and counter-predictions, some looking for an almost instantaneous return to normalcy while others,—and these are in the vast majority,—maintain that, while there will be more business going than last year, every order will involve a contest. As one leading wholesaler expressed it the other day, the day has gone by when a lumberman can sit in his office and do business by mail or over the telephone. He has to get out and dig for anything that he gathers in and dig hard. It is largely a question of price, grade and service, and it takes some convincing talk to close sales. There is little or no speculative buying, and factories and other large users are disposed to hold back until things assume a more definite aspect.

Some rural retailers declare that prosperity will not return in

View of Mills in Sarnia.

# BUY THE BEST

Retailers and woodworking establishments who like to get A1 NORWAY and WHITE PINE LUMBER always buy their stocks from us because we can ship them on quick notice. It pays to have the goods, but it pays better to "deliver" them.

We also make a specialty of heavy timbers cut to order any length up to 60 feet from Pine or B. C. Fir.

*"Rush Orders Rushed"*

# Cleveland-Sarnia Sawmills Co., Limited

### SARNIA, ONTARIO

B. P. Bole, Pres.   F. H. Gove, Vice-Pres.   E. C. Barre, Gen. Mgr.   W. A. Saurwein, Ass't. Mgr.

their towns until another crop is harvested. The farmers are desirous of being assured of a respectable yield from their broad acres before launching out in expenditures of any character. In the meantime, recession is their watchword.

As each week goes by, however, there are more encouraging features and a larger number of inquiries. Collections are slowly improving and business is getting down to a more stable, scientific basis. Money is easing and this gives rise to a more cheerful sentiment in several communities. Continued strength of foreign exchange is evidence of an improvement in the national situation which will sooner or later find corresponding action in the domestic situation. Wheat has begun to take an advance and provisions have gone up somewhat which is an encouraging sign.

In the continued broadening of commercial activity, improvement may be slow and the volume of business may not come up to expectation, but it is believed that the hardwoods in the upper grades have reached their level although there may be fluctuations in the lower ends of which there is a super-abundance. A leading Toronto hardwood firm stated this week that in their opinion the situation in Eastern Canada was getting better. The liquidation process had been followed along carefully and there was now very little stock of the choice ends for sale in sections of which the market was more stable.

A tender spot to-day in the whole situation is a surplus of low-grade lumber, more particularly in 1 inch. On the whole a fair year's business is looked for, but nothing of a record character, presupposing of course that prices are maintained on a reasonable basis, and there is no sudden demand made upon the markets as holdings are not nearly as large as last year. Flooring manufacturers are among the largest consumers of hardwood just now. The amount of hardwood taken out during the past winter has shown a considerable falling off, but on the whole prices of flooring are holding their own, with a few revisions here and there. One leading flooring manufacturer reports that shipments since the first of the year have been considerably ahead of the corresponding period of 1921, but regarding the future will make no predictions as much depends upon the building situation.

In softwoods, hemlock continues fairly firm with quite a few inquiries and prices unchanged. White pine is looking better all the while and there is a fair movement of stock across the border. Mill culls are still rather dull. Several small stocks of jack pine and red pine in Northern Ontario have been bought up during the past week which is a hopeful sign. White pine lath as a whole are scarce and prices are stiff, and it is the disposition of those who have any, to hang on until the demand becomes even more active with spring structural activities.

In B. C. materials a fair number of mixed carloads are being sold. Red cedar shingles are in fairly active requisition, and it is expected from this out the demand will increase. Prices have been strengthening somewhat. That the eastern field is being looked upon more and more as an outlet for western woods, is evidenced by the fact that larger numbers of B. C. mills are opening up offices in Toronto and Montreal. Since the prairie trade has gone flat, coast stocks of fir, hemlock, cedar and pine have been offered in larger quantities.

There is, perhaps, a disposition on the part of eastern men to hang back on their purchases until after March 7th when a special sitting of the Dominion Railway Board will be held in Ottawa. The forest product interests will present their case for hearing in an effort to have the present excessive carrying charges reduced. It has been felt all along that there are many incongruities in rates, not to speak of the abnormal advances of recent years, which require adjusting. Strong evidence will be presented by the Transportation Department of the Canadian Lumbermen's Association for some relief in the existing situation in the hope that lower levies may stimulate business and allow a freer movement of wood materials.

The situation in regard to freight rates is being watched with interest. All over the continent an agitation for a decrease is going on, and its cumulative effects should make something give way. Eastern lumber dealers also say that if ocean freight rates would show any evidence of a decline, the export trade would correspondingly increase. As it is now, very little spruce or other material is going forward overseas.

One lumberman said recently that the manufacturer who cannot now make a profit at the present price levels must re-arrange his costs, and that now was no time for retailers to tell the public that prices were going higher. Stocks of dry lumber of certain kinds and grades are getting scarce and may not be obtainable in the desired widths and thicknesses later on. He added that while sales may not reach the maximum volume this year, there will be considerably more bought than there was last.

## Canadian Spruce May Soon be Wanted Abroad

During the greater part of 1921 the British timber market was over shadowed by the possibility of big shipments of spruce from Canada at a time when the arrival of these would have had a bad effect on current prices, which were already on a very low basis. The wood, however, did not come over because of the ruinous prices prevailing, but in 1922 the case is different. The banks will scarcely help the exporters to hold their stocks any longer, and whatever the market prices are British importers anticipate heavy shipments during the coming season.

Fortunately for the Canadian shippers and the British importers, there is good promise of prices much in excess of those current during last year, and the stocks will therefore find a free market in Great Britain and possibly in some Continental countries. In this connection the attitude adopted by the Swedish and Finnish shippers is a factor. Their argument is that a scarcity of timber will force up values, and many importers are being impressed by the statistics

The sweep of the storm king near Pakesley, Ont., showing how slender trees were bent right over by the weight of the snow until their tops touched the ground

putforward. The Canadian position, however, has to be reckoned with. Much of the Canadian spruce at present available for export may be of poor quality, but its arrival will serve many useful purposes, and as such will be welcomed by the British market.

Meanwhile the most striking feature of the timber trade at the moment is the growing firmness of practically all the markets—soft wood and hard wood, spot or to arrive. So far as the spot market is concerned, the explanation mainly lies in the fact that stocks are comparatively low and the regular importing season is over from Canada and from many of the North European ports. Should the demand improve in the slightest—and hopes are entertained that this is imminent—there is barely sufficient stock of some woods—Canadian spruce, for example—to see the winter through. Hence prices for goods ex quay are stiffening. Some holders, indeed, are not too anxious to sell in bulk, preferring to spend their sales over antended period.

## Lumber Outlook in East Gets Brighter

From various sections of the Maritime Provinces come the encouraging reports that lumbering conditions are showing a steady improvement and that the cut will exceed the first estimate decided on. These conditions prevail not only on crown lands, but also on private holdings.

For some time it was evident that the depression was slowly, but surely lifting and, in fear of under estimating the demands, new preparations were made in event of the anticipated improvement of the market.

On crown lands alone it is estimated that one hundred million feet will be cut. This is considerably smaller than in former years when conditions were normal, but it is considerably more than was expected last autumn when it looked as if there would be no logging operations in the provinces.

One cheerful factor is the fact that conditions for operating were never better. There has been considerable snow but it has not been heavy enough to interfere with yarding, and has been ideal for general working etc.

There is still one thing that is tending to retard progress in the lumber industry and that is pulpwood and freight rates. They are so high that business is being practically stifled. If a reduction would be forthcoming it is generally conceded that there would be a marked revival, and at the present time there is nothing more desired in the Maritime Provinces.

"The manufacturers in New Brunswick and Nova Scotia generally are taking a more confident view. The frantic desire to sell,

so common a short time ago, is disappearing rapidly and is not likely soon to return if only a fair proportion of all that is being said about the shortage in the log cut is true. There are people who believe that the next error of the Canadian producers will be too much rather than too little faith and hope.

From Salsbury N. B. comes the glad tidings that small lumber operators in that locality are actively engaged following a lull earlier in the season. The mills of Colpitts Bros. and C. A. Brown, Company are in full operation, the latter working on laths. On the North river district Eben Lewis and J. J. O'Sullivan are operating portable mills.

A meeting of creditors of the United Lumber Company, with head office in the city of Fredericton, and doing business in various parts of the Maritime Provinces, was held recently in Fredericton. At this meeting a decision was reached to make an assignment with the Eastern Trust Company of St. John, as the assignee and trustee in bankruptcy.

A mill, owned by Willard P. Miller at Newcastle Creek, Queens County, N. B., was recently destroyed by fire, in addition to a large cut of lumber, which fell prey to the flames. The machinery was new and the loss is heavy.

A shingle shed of the Fort Kent Mill Company, on the St. John river, was recently destroyed by fire and a large quantity of goods and a freight car burned. The loss was estimated at $8,000.

## The English Timber Market Still Doubtful

In an interview with the Quebec correspondent of the "Canada Lumberman," Mr. W. G. Power said the advices so far received from the United Kingdom are not very encouraging, nevertheless he was hopeful for a change for the better in the early summer.

Discussing the general outlook, he quoted from the written opinions of the trade in England who maintain that without question the month of January 1922 has proved in many respects a disappointing month. That there was one outstanding exception — the settlement of the Irish question; but then in European politics there was the disappointment in the Cannes Conference, and now the want of harmonious agreement over the proposed Genoa Conference, which has brought us no nearer the solution of the many difficult problems which are hampering improvements in the timber trade.

Consumption during January was little if any, better than it was in December, and so far as can be learned, the same applies to the past month of February. In the f. o. b. and c. i. f. markets, business has fallen off, and stockholders have found their orders to be for smaller quantities than ever.

"But, said Mr. Power," with all these disappointments the trade in the United Kingdom is much more hopeful. In the meantime the trade is prepared to meet the situation, convinced that the worst cannot be as bad as the condition in 1921. The determination evidently is to wait patiently for the spring, and in the meantime refuse to speculate, which is a warning sounded by the well-informed heads of the trade in England to the shippers in this country, who announce that when consumption improves they, as importers, will purchase, but not before.

There are signs that the trade will have a reaction for the better in March and April, and though hopeful in this respect, importers are fixed in their resolution not to anticipate any improvement, but to be content with the purchases they have made and close at prices which should be perfectly safe.

The results of the London auction in the last week of January reflect the general position of the trade. The auction was dull and prices reported as being about maintained, but only with difficulty. In some instances lower figures were recorded, among them being the price for 3 x 9, Quebec spruce £26, 10s - £4 less than at the previous sale. On the other hand sizes, such as 2 x 4, 2 x 5, 2½ x 7, etc. in good Swedish or Finnish went satisfactorily. The spruce results looked far worse than they really were. As we are informed, much of the spruce offered was not only poor in quality and manufacture, but badly discolored and not worth more than it brought. It is said that the auction is likely to do some good in Canada when the prices are known. It will enlighten shippers and moderate their extravagant views which many exporters are debating about the ability of English firms to give higher figures free on board.

News to hand is that at a meeting of the Associated Importers held in London at the latter part of January, that favorable arrangements had been made with the British Board of Trade regarding the balance of stocks unsold that are likely to strengthen British importers in their determination not to give way at present to the views of the Swedish and Finnish shippers. The Associated Importers are now anxious to clear up their business and to realize as speedily as possible their remaining stocks. It is said that the company has been relieved of its stocks of spruce in Canada and has now only to place the wood which is already in Great Britain, but even to do this

in the present state of trade and of the money market, it will be necessary to accept prices considerably below the current rates, and there will be many bargains to be had during the next few months. To purchase these, instead of sinking money in comparatively clear Swedish productions, will be the object of nearly all the large firms, and if the Association is able to make extensive contracts, the market will be affected. The spruce trade could not be conducted on a satisfactory scale as long as the heavy stocks of the Associated Importers over-balance the position, and until these are finally disposed of, no steady business can be looked for in Canada.

The conditions in the British timber trade during the month of January were very similar. A disinclination to speculate has been reported as noticeable in all quarters, but on the other hand firms who failed to take advantage of the early buying last autumn, have been holding up their most urgent requirements at the higher prices.

The discrepancy between the relative height of spot prices and current f. o. b. quotations, continue to be very striking, which is the main reason why f. o. b. purchasing power is not more active. As the market stands at present, there is no indication that the difficult position can yet be ameliorated. It is said that stockholders in England are finding it difficult to make satisfactory progress at current figures, and whenever they attempted to obtain higher prices, they choke off the demand. As the total stocks in Great Britian are comparatively small, a rise in the prices would undoubtedly take place were the demand to increase. At present the trade in the United Kingdom reports a small stock generally speaking, a small demand and a steady market as all they can for the present hope for.

## Breezy Paragraphs of Timber Trade

The Knight Mfg. & Lumber Co., Limited, Meaford, Ont., plan on engaging in the manufacture of door on a more extensive scale. To this end the following equipment has been added:—Power door clamp; roller table cut-off saw; glue jointer; 15 spindle boring machine; two new presses; 44-inch glue spreader and a 12-inch glue spreader. Both the latter machines are run by small motors. In addition to having a new line of fir doors, they propose to go after the veneer door business more strongly.

Replying to a recent inquiry as to the state the lumber business and the prospects for the coming season, a leading dealer in Halifax recently said that conditions might be a great deal worse. As for shipping, he said they were sadly handicapped. "If we had good facilities on the Dartmouth side," he added, "and I think we can have it the Railway Company is willing, then look out for a boom in the lumber business in Halifax. We have the lumber, we have the railway, and now give us the shipping facilities, and we will do the rest."

The Cranbrook Sash & Door Co., Limited, Cranbrook, B. C., have completed their main factory building and the machinery is now being installed. The building itself is two storeys, 112 x 60 feet. The boiler room, dry kiln and lumber sheds are yet to be built, but the whole unit is expected to be in operation some time in March. The output will consist principally of sash and doors, the capacity of the plant being 500 sash and 200 doors per day. H. A. McCallum is the general-manager, with W. P. Attridge, secretary-treasurer, J. H. Spence, vice-president, and Joseph Woodman, director. From 40 to 60 men will be employed. They expect to make an addition next year in the shape of a box factory to cater to the demand for fruit and butter boxes.

Hon. C. W. Robinson, Minister of Lands and Mines for New Brunswick, recently presided at a meeting of the Forest Advisory Board of New Brunswick. It is understood there will be some reductions in rate of pay and also it will be recommended that the staff may be reduced. Mr. Robinson says that all material has been prepared for the government. Regarding the proposal to introduce the Quebec scale and the Quebec method of fire protection in New Brunswick, the New Brunswick Lumbermen's Association provided this information for the use of the department. The representatives of the lumbermen on the Forest Advisory Board are Archie Fraser Fredericton, N.B. and J. W. Brankley of Chatham, N.B.

From both Crown lands and private lands in New Brunswick, comes reports that the logging yield this season will be larger than at first estimated. New operations were started some time ago in various parts of the province, the evident expectations being that the lumber market will show an improvement. 100,000,000 feet is the estimate of the cut on the Crown lands of New Brunswick during the present season. This total is, of course, what was expected last autumn. Operating conditions have been very favorable. There has not been too much snow and yarding has been carried on without difficulty. With a substantial reduction in freight rates, it is believed that considerable impetus will be given the industry.

New heavy duty band mill being installed in the plant of Poupore Lumber Co., at Gogama, Ont

## Northern Mill Adding to Its Equipment

The Poupore Lumber Co. are increasing the output of their saw-mill at Gogama, Ont., and are installing one of the new heavy duty band mills which is now being produced by the E. Long Mfg. Co. of Orillia, Ont.

The foregoing illustration gives an excellent idea of the appearance of this new heavy duty band mill. This machine was commenced before the war which caused it to be laid aside temporarily, but in 1919 work was resumed and the heavy duty band mill has been the subject of much study and continuous experiment since that time.

The E. Long Mfg. Co. state that the mill is equipped with every device that has proved a success when applied to this class of machine, including steam cylinder for operating the upper saw guide, with adjustable control to prevent violent action, and Dake engine for raising and lowering the upper wheel.

## The Heroism of Humane Lumberjack

From Port Arthur comes word that a lumberjack, as yet not known, recently, plunged in the ice-cold waters of Lake Larson in order to save his horses. The man is an employee of the New Ontario Construction Co. and was crossing the ice with a load of 106 logs when the outfit broke through. The logs floated but the horses and heavily-chained sleigh were drawn down. It is stated that at the risk of his life the lumberjack plunged into 15 feet of water, and after a hard, numbing struggle, rescued his team.

Col. J. A. Little, of Port Arthur, who is head of the New Ontario Construction Co., received word of the teamster's action, and will place on record appreciation of his deed in risking his life to save those of his dumb animals.

After the horses broke through, the teamster, leaping upon his load, removed his heavy mackinaw and plunged in headfirst, grappled his way to the sunken sleigh, reached the chain fastening, unhooked it and rose to the surface, clinging to the harness of the horses. Scrambling up on the ice edge again, the teamster supported the heads of the horses above the water and called for help. With his soaked garments rapidly freezing in the below-zero temperature, he clung to the equines until assistance came.

The plant of the Mattagami Pulp and Paper Company, at Smooth Rock Falls, Ont., which has a daily capacity of 150 tons of sulphite fibre, has been closed since the first of the year but will resume operation as soon as the conditions of the market warrant it. The company has just completed the erection of a large addition to its wood room, the extension being 150 x 75 ft., one-storey high, of steel, tile and concrete construction. Two American drum barkers have been added, each being 28 feet long and of 10 feet diameter. There is ample space for two more barkers which may be installed later. The company has a large supply of pulpwood on hand.

## High Honor for Ontario Lumberman

R. H. Spencer, Trenton, Ont

At the meeting of the Grand Chapter of Canada, Royal Arch Masons. which was held recently in Hamilton, R. E. Comp, R. H. Spencer, of Trenton, Ont., was elected Grand Z, the highest office in the gift of the gathering. Mr. Spencer has always been a leading light in Masonry and his record in the craft has been one of advancement and devotion to duty. A member of Trent Lodge No. 38 he made his first acquaintance with the craft nearly thirty years ago. He is also a member of St. Mark's Chapter No. 26, R. A. M., Trenton, and has held various subordinate positions until he has now reached the top. Mr. Spencer also belongs to King Baldwin Perceptory No. 6, Knights Templar, Belleville, and Ramesis Temple Mystic Shriners, Toronto.

Mr. Spencer is equally well known in the lumber arena, particularly in the eastern part of Ontario. He has been associated with Gill & Fortune, lumber merchants, of Trenton, ever since they bought out Gilmour & Co., some seventeen or eighteen years ago, and has full charge of their accounting. Before that he was with the Gilmour organization for a number of years and also with the Central Ontario Railway.

Mr. Spencer has served the citizens of Trenton in various public capacities being an alderman for several years and also secretary-treasurer of the Board of Education.

## Keeping Ends of Lumber From Checking

Regarding the use of reliable mixtures for painting the ends of lumber to keep it from checking, a subscriber writing to the "Canada Lumberman", says, that any coating that will tend to retard the rate of air-drying from the ends, will tend to prevent checking. It is the rapid drying of the ends that causes the check. The harder and greener the wood, the more effective the coating must be. Paint is easy to handle and apply but is not very effective, and the same observation may be made with reference to white or red lead. Rosin lamp black is not so convenient to handle but is very effective in checking and end-drying. This mixture is made by melting rosin (60 parts) and stirring in lamp black (1 part). This mixture must be applied hot either by brushing or dipping the ends.

In addition to the materials suggested in the foregoing for coating the ends of the stock, it is said that a mixture of whitewash and glue makes a coating that will last a year or more and will tend to prevent excessive drying at the ends. This mixture is made by adding a quart of good glue and 3 lbs. of salt to a barrel of whitewash.

Another method for overcoming this trouble is to place the piling sticks at the very end of the pile; a slight overhang is even better. The weight of the pile acts as a clamp and keeps the stock from checking. If the sticks are allowed to protrude, they will shade the ends from the sun and will also carry off the rain, thus reducing end straining. This is a simple method and one that should be adopted in all piling.

## Business in Montreal Has Firmer Tone

Business in Montreal is fair, with a good tone generally prevailing. Many inquiries are to hand, and some satisfactory orders have been placed, although here and there wholesalers assert that competition is still very active and that in certain instances the prices obtained leave little or no margin. At the same time there is as a rule, a disinclination to cut values, particularly in spruce, to a basis which involves losses.

A wholesaler of long experience states that he never saw the retail yards in such low condition as regards stocks. The owners are out of the market for the present, in the hope that prices will drop, but if the ideas of the majority of the wholesalers are correct there is little chance of a pronounced downward movement. Some are of opinion that there may be a little recession, while others assert that the movement will be upwards.

The demand for birch has broadened, with values inclined to harden. Sellers especially those with stocks of the better grades, are not in a hurry to sell believing that quotations will improve.

Lath continues to be a good market, the mills asking a slightly higher price.

The trade in B. C. forest products is moderate, although the recent advance on rough clear fir is likely to restrict business. The chief demand is for mixed carloads. Very little is doing in timbers.

Many inquiries have been received from U. S. firms, but the difference in buyers' and sellers' quotations makes it difficult to close orders.

The pulpwood market is slightly better. All grades of pulp are slow of sale. In this connection the U. S. Government have ordered the Customs officers to stop shipments of pulp from Canadian mills going into the States pending an inquiry under the Anti-dumping Law.

While it is difficult to say anything definite as to building prospects the indications are favorable for a good season. The question of wages will soon be brought up again, but the contractors have let it be known that they will oppose any increase this year, believing that an addition to the cost of building will restrict operations. The projects this season include a ten storey office building, a hospital and some schools. The Province of Quebec Builders' Association, which has just been formed, will devote some attention to the Lien Law, which is almost a dead letter as far as the priviledges of suppliers of material are concerned, but which has been taken advantage of by some owners of property to the detriment of lumber and other firms. It is held that the law needs revision.

## Mr. Burke Opens Office in Toronto

J. B. Burke, late of Ottawa, recently arrived in Toronto and has opened up an office at 314 Manning Chambers, Toronto, which will henceforth be his headquarters. He represents the Allen-Stoltze Lumber Co., of Vancouver, who are specialists in all kinds of B. C. forest products and particularly shingles and timbers.

Mr. Burke comes of a family long identified with the lumber industry of the Ottawa Valley. His father, the late J. R. Burke, was for many years superintendent of bush operations for W. C. Edwards & Co. After leaving school, J .B. Bukre gained his first acquaintance in the wood goods line with the same firm starting in as tally boy and culler and serving in various other capacities. Later he joined the McAuliffe-Davis Lumber Co. and was assistant manager of one of their retail yards in the capital city.

During the war he was a shipper for the Imperial Munitions Board and later started selling B. C. forest materials. In the last three years Mr .Burke has built up an excellent connection in the East and is now devoting his time solely to the Allen-Stoltze Lumber Co., looking after their interests in Ontario, Quebec and the Maritime Provinces.

## Creating Wider Demand For Matches

The problems of marketing a new Canadian match in the Dominion, were briefly outlined and future plans touched on for creating an everwidening demand for "Maple Leaf" matches from coast to coast, at a luncheon held lately in Montreal, to launch the new Canadian industry organized under the direction of the Canadian Match Company, Limited. F. Manning, in charge of the organization of the company presided, and the guests included G. G. Cummings, who will direct the field work, J. O. Pratt, in charge of the Montreal office, and the entire sales and office staff of the Quebec sales division.

"The new company's factory at Pembroke is the most modern match factory in the world," said Mr. Manning, "equipped with the latest type of match-making and packing machinery. It is also filling a pressing need in providing employment, the speaker continued. Work in placing "Maple Leaf" matches on sale in all the provinces will be undertaken immediately.

## Some Things are in Strange Contrast

According to a press despatch from Fort Frances the Department of Public Works for Ontario has sent out instructions to officials in that district authorizing the payment of not more than twenty dollars per thousand board measure for bridge and culvert timber and lumber required this season. This represents the Government idea of fair value for manufactured lumber in the district, and offers a strange contrast to the Government's claim of $25 per thousand feet for timber on the stump one thousand and fifty miles from the mill, and Mr. Justice Logie's judgment of $17.60 plus $2.50 dues in the Shevlin-Clarke case. Small millmen and the citizens generally are very indignant.

## Conditions in St. John Remain About the Same

The past few weeks have not seen very much, if any, change in the lumber market at St. John. Locally business is quiet and the factories are doing comparatively very little. The weather, of course, has been very stormy and with all other conditions against any building, it certainly causes a comparative quiet over all the trade.

Prices locally are weaker for ordinary house frames which can be purchased and delivered on the job at from $28.00 to $30.00 for Merch. scantling and for joists from $32.00 to $35.00 per M. Cull lumber is also weaker at around $18.00 delivered to works.

The English market does not show any action in as far as buying is concerned from this side, but trade and general conditions in England continue to improve. There is so much narrow and low-grade government stocks being offered that it keeps the market in an uproar all the time. Any good, well-sawn, well-kept stocks seem to be treated on the same basis as the poor material, and buyers are evidently picking up a great deal of good stock at low prices; scantling selling at £150-0 per standard and good rotary sawn broad deals at £16 to £17 per standard.

The Irish market continues to send out enquiries but prices are about 10 shillings to £1 per standard less than a month ago. All buyers seem to be purchasing very small parcels at these low prices, claiming they can purchase from the Finns and Swedes at prices which will be much less. Just what will happen in this market, remains to be seen, but certainly the next few months will see a great change in the price of broad Irish deals. It will certainly be upwards, for each month these broad deals are becoming scarcer and the logs being produced this winter will not make but very few of such deals. Taken all around, the English and Irish markets have reached rock bottom and when demand improves, prices will ascend.

The American market is not any weaker. Demand is becoming heavier and by spring we shall see a slight advance in this market. At the present time Canadian rotary cut 1 inch and over is leaving from $18.00 to $20.00 on cars St. John shipping points. Lath are firm at around $6.00 on cars St. John.

Freights continue very stiff with no reduction being put into effect at this writing, the rate being 100 shillings to London and Liverpool and Manchester, and 90 shillings to Belfast, Ireland.

Logging is being carried on in good style and men are working more efficiently that for a number of years. Logs are being produced very much cheaper than a year ago, but the quality is limited. The lumber is being largely shipped as sawn, taking the market price and a profitable business in some sections is reported.

## The Broadening Experience of Life

"I never knew how dear lumber was until I bought some boards the other day from a retailer to build a fence," humorously remarked a leading wholesale dealer in a recent letter to one of his friends.

It is sometimes good policy for a man to execute a right-about-face movement; to take a step across the street, as it were, and have a square uninterrupted look at himself. If he can for a time detach his own individuality, personality and inclinations, he will, doubtless, get a new conception of himself, his privileges, limitations and responsibilities. Meditation and experiment often change the tenor of a fellow's whole course and career—broaden him out and present new angles of usefulness and service.

However, this is a long way from the lumber business, but leads up to the observations of a lumber merchant who says, I am a retailer and, while I know a good deal about the grades of lumber, prices, etc., I got a wider view of myself and a larger vision of my business during the past summer by deciding to build a new home in the outskirts of the city where I reside. This enabled me to look at the lumber trade from the standpoint of an amateur contractor or builder or architect or whatever you want to call me. Of course, I did not let it be known that I was in the lumber line which was comparatively easy to conceal, the location being several miles from my own place. I wanted to gain some pointers which I could put to profitable employment and equip myself for rendering better service to customers. I was my own contractor on the house, drew the plans and got out the specifications and ordered the material, through one of my workmen, I took two weeks' holidays which I spent actually working on the structure with the carpenters that I had engaged. After that in the early morning I ran the job and often got home in the evening before the men left. All of this meant a decided saving in costs. I made some mistakes which cost me real money, but even then I am considerably ahead of a contract basis.

I know which is a point which should be emphasized,—what quality of material has gone into that building, and I was also benefited in seeing the stuff that I am handling every day being actually used in construction. One may help to manufacture a piece of mat-

erial in the plant or sell it in the yard and be familiar with it to a certain extent, but it greatly assists you to know just how that board is finally used. There is a lot for all of us to learn about the lumber business, and I believe that the man who puts up his own house, will discover a few things in connection with the merchandising of lumber that may be of value and service to him in the days that are to come.

It has often been said that a traveller, who has had retail experience, is a much better man in any line than one who has not, for he can see propositions from the viewpoints of production and distribution. He appreciates the difficulties of the average retailer better than if his insight in merely confined to salesmanship. Thus I

Walter C. Cain, Toronto,
Newly-elected Deputy Minister of Lands and
Forests for Ontario

maintain that a lumber retailer who has erected a house or two for himself can work more sympathetically and co-operatively with contractors, farmers and others, for he possesses a keener recognition of their wants and a more extensive knowledge of what household-ing entails in the way of plans, specifications, materials, etc.

## An Artistic Booklet on Thatch Roofs

One of the most attractive and artistic booklets issued is that of "Thatch Roofs," which was recently issued by the Creo-Dipt Co., Inc., North Tonawanda, N. Y., who are producers of Creo-Dipt Stained Shingles. The book is admirably illustrated with every conceivable style of residence and architecture, showing the neat and effective structures topped with this class of stained shingle. The houses illustrated have an expression of individuality with the character of the design standing out prominently.

It is announced that thatched Creo-Dipt shingles are made possible by an ingenious method of sawing the shingle, butts in special patch patterns so that the workmen can, by following printed instructions and working drawings, lay each course of shingles out of the monotonous horizontal in long, irregular ways, varying the width of exposed surface of every course from 1 to 5 inches, avoiding uniformity to produce the wavy thatched effect.

## Fast Feed Planer & Matcher Book

An illustrated 92-page book on Fast Feed Planers and Matchers has been issued by the S. A. Woods Machine Co., Boston, Mass

W. A. McGregor, 73 years of age, died suddenly from heart trouble recently at his home in Toronto. He was born in Maine, and came to Canada at the age of 13. He later went to Muskoka, where he was engaged in the lumber business for a number of years. Retiring four years ago, he came to Toronto, where he resided until his death. Surviving are his wife, four sons and two daughters.

Patrick Murphy, who was for many years confidential advisor to the firm of W. & J. Sharples, Limited, Quebec, Que., died recently at his home, 8 Fleury St., in that city. The members of the entire staff of W. & J. Sharples, Limited, and also the members of the operating staff of the Power Lumber Co., at St. Pacome, Que., were present in a body, as well as many representatives in other walks of life, to pay their last respects to a revered member of the community.

# EDGINGS

Baker & Redden, Windsor, N. S., are contemplating the erection of a sash and door factory.

William Vicars, Port Arthur, Ont., founder of the Vicars-Shear, Lumber Co., died recently in his 81st year.

E. W. Beckett, Crown Timber Agent, New Westminster, B. C., has been superannuated after a long period of service.

Edward Clark, of Edward Clark & Sons, Limited, Toronto, returned recently after spending several weeks in Louisiana.

Capt. G. T. Reid, of Reid & Co., retail lumber dealers, Toronto, and Mrs. Reid recently spent a pleasant holiday at Algonquin Park.

W. W. Avey, Norwich, Ont., contemplates a planing mill to cost $10,000. A by-law was carried recently granting a fixed assessment on this property.

Andrew Stark, late of the C. G. Anderson Lumber Co., Toronto, has joined the selling staff of Elgie & Jarvis Lumber Co., and entered upon his new duties.

The planing mill and sash and door factory of J. Hanbury & Co., Limited, Vancouver, B. C., which shut down for repairs, has been re-opened with a full force.

A. E. Gordon, of Terry & Gordon, Limited, is on an extended business trip to the Coast and before his return to Toronto, will spend a few weeks in California.

The Thompson & Heyland Lumber Co., who have offices in the Stair Building, Toronto, have recently enlarged their quarters and now have double their former floor space.

The St. Mary's Wood Specialty Co., Limited, St. Mary's, Ont., are in the market for 100,000 feet of rock elm logs, also for quantities of white ash, hickory and second growth maple.

The Pontiac Lumber & Pulp Co., whose pulp mills was destroyed by fire over a year ago at Makamick, Abitibi County, Que., intends rebuilding. Eugene Rouleau is the manager of the company.

A charter has been granted the Jackson Cabinet Co., Limited, to manufacture, buy and deal in wares of all kinds. The head office of the company is in Durham, Ont., and the capital stock is $100,000.

The Western Lumber & Lath Co., Limited, of Vancouver, B. C., of which J. R. B. Wilson is manager, will soon commence work on a new sawmill. It will be 40 x 60 and will be built by day labor.

The machine shops of the Comox Logging Company at headquarters, near Courtenay, B. C., were almost totally destroyed by fire recently. The shops were equipped with machinery, valued at about $50,000.

J. S. Deschamps, lumber manufacturer, of Rossland, B. C., spent a few days in Toronto and Montreal recently calling upon his friends in the trade. Mr. Deschamps is a well-known producer of pine, cedar and spruce lumber.

The Wallace Shipbuilding Co., North Vancouver, B. C., were the successful tenderers for repairs and alterations to the "Admiral Farragut." This contract was secured in the face of keen competition from American yards.

Edward Penniwell, manager of Beaver Board factory, Thorold, Ont., while walking towards the factory recently on the Thorold road was shot in the leg by an unknown source. Mr. Penniwell is convalescing at his home in Buffalo.

The order for doors for the new Prince Edward Hotel at Windsor, Ont., which is to cost $1,000,000, has been given to the McLean Lumber Co., while Schultz Bros. & Co., Limited, of Brantford, have, been given the order for the casings.

Wm. F. Foley, of North Battleford, Sask., a well-known lumberman of the West, has arrived in Toronto and is spending some time with his brother M. C. Foley, of the Foley Lumber Co. The latter is just recovering from a serious illness.

Chas. Hill, of Truro, N. S., is carrying on extensive logging activities during the present winter at Bass River in Colchester County. He has 10,000 acres of pine timberland in that locality and his entire cut for the season will be shipped to the United States.

H. R. Christie, who was formerly connected with the British Columbia Department of Forestry and served overseas with the Canadian Engineers during the war, has been appointed to an important position on the staff of the Faculty of Forestry, Toronto University.

The North West Lumber Co., have started a shipment of over

18,000,000 feet of logs from their logging camp at Whitewater, 177 miles north of Edmonton on the E. D. & B. C. Railway. The entire consignment will be delivered to the company's mill at the Dunvegan yards Edmonton.

John McArthur of Aldborough township passed away recently at the age of eighty. He conducted a saw mill in Rodney for many years under the name of McLaren and McArthur, and was one of the best known men in Southern Ontario. He is survived by two sisters and one brother.

Frank L. Adolph, of the Adolph Lumber Co., Baynes Lake, B. C, who recently arrived in Toronto, intends opening an eastern office in the city. He is well-known to the trade in the East and his firm are manufacturers of pine, fir and larch lumber and lath, specializing particularly in western soft pine.

Trans-Canada Lumber Co., Limited, Montreal, Que.. have been granted a federal charter with a capital of $200,000 to conduct a general lumber business, manufacturing and dealing in all kinds of forest products. Two of the incorporators are J. W. Cook, K. C. and A. A. Magee, both of Montreal.

Clarence C. Jackson, has joined the selling staff of Edward Clark & Sons, Limited, Toronto. Mr. Jackson is well-known in hardwood lumber circles, having spent ten years with the Trout Creek Lumber Co., at Powassan, Ont., and during the last four years was engaged with Hart & McDonagh Lumber Co., Toronto.

The Border Lumber Co., Limited, with headquarters at Fort Frances, and a capital stock of $200,000.. is an organization which was recently granted a charter to manufacture and deal in all kinds of wood products, pulpwood, etc., and to operate sawmills. Among the incorporators of the company is Hugh A. Tibbetts, of Fort Frances, Ont.

The Hanbury Mfg. Co., Limited, Brantford, Ont., have again put their plant into operation and are manufacturing boxes of all kinds, crates, shooks, cross arms and open sash. A considerable amount of new machinery has been installed and the plant is now up to date in every respect. At the present time about twenty hands are being employed.

A. E. Clark, of Toronto, president of the Canadian Lumbermen's Association, was in South Bend, Ind.. on February 20th, and delivered an address before the South Bend Hardwood Club, on the hardwood lumber situation in Canada and the outlook. He spoke hopefully of business conditions during the coming year and was given a cordial reception.

The Ontario Iron & Lumber Co., Limited. of Sault Ste Marie, Ont., with a capital stock of $1,000,000., has been incorporated to manage mines and mineral lands, and to buy, sell and deal in limits, logs, lumber, etc., as well as operate sawmills. Among the incorporators of the company are Albert A. Pickering, James M. McNeil and John A. McPhail, all of Sault Ste Marie.

Requests were also made that any members, who had any information regarding discrepancies in railway rates to certain shipping points, should hand the same into the secretary who will forward the information to the transportation manager of the C. L. A. at Ottawa so that the data may be available for presentation at the special hearing before the Railway Commission on March 7th.

Colin C. Tyrer, of Colin C. Tyrer Co., Limited. of Halifax. N. S., spent a few days recently in New York city, and while there he was most of his time with the W. A. Webster Co., by whom he is represented in New York. Mr. Tyrer is one of the largest shippers of Canadian woods, shipping from 30,000,000 to 40,000,000 feet annually, exporting to England, the West Indies and other countries.

It is understood that the Timber Commission, which has been enquiring into the demonstration of the timber and pulpwood resources of the province of Ontario for the past two years, has cost the provincial government between 30,000,000 to $200,000. Up to the present $130,000. has been recovered in back dues and other deferred payments as a result of its activities, and it is said that the financial benefits have not yet been fully realized.

A chair to be known as the "Mrs. E. B. Eddy Chair of Industrial Chemistry," has been founded at McGill University. This was made possible through the bequest in the will of the late Mrs. Eddy. According to the plans for the new chair. the holders of the professorship will devote special attention to wood chemistry as the Eddy family has been concerned largely with forest products in Canada both in the lumbering and manufacturing ends of the industry. The development of the lumber and pulp and paper industries and the necessity for greater conservation of Canadian forest resources, has increased the demand in this field for men trained.

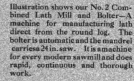

## ALPHABETICAL INDEX TO ADVERTISERS

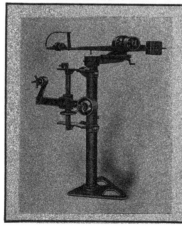

LINN TRACTOR HAULING 82 CORDS OF MIXED SPRUCE AND HEMLOCK

# THE LINN LOGGING TRACTOR

## Designed and developed for winter log hauling, in the North Woods

To fulfill all requirements of the Northern Logger a tractor must:—
Haul heavy trains of sleighs **down steep sandhills** and around sharp curves.
Haul with **absolute safety** over **lakes** and **rivers**, where the ice is sometimes not thicker than fourteen inches.
Haul heavy trains over main hauls over all encountered grades—to landings.
Have carrying capacity **on itself**, so that it can be used for supply haulage over Portage roads.
Must have a **fast high speed** so that return trips to rollways may be rapid.
Must be foolproof and easily operated and controlled.
All these requirements are fulfilled **only**, by The Linn **Logging Tractor**.
Ask the operator who uses Linn.

*—Logging Department—*

## MUSSENS LIMITED

**Dubrule Building**          MONTREAL

# CANADA LUMBERMAN BUYERS' DIRECTORY

The following regulations apply to all advertisers:—Eighth page, every issue, three headings;
quarter page, six headings; half page, twelve headings; full page, twenty-four headings

**ALLIGATORS**
Payette Company, P.
West, Peachy & Sons

**BABBITT METAL**
Canada Metal Company
General Supply Co. of Canada, Ltd.

**BALE TIES**
Canada Metal Co.
Laidlaw Bale Tie Company

**BAND MILLS**
Hamilton Company, William
Waterous Engine Works Company
Yates Machine Company, P. B.

**BAND SAW BLADES**
Simonds Mfg. Co.

**BAND RESAWS**
Mershon & Company, W. B.

**BARKERS**
Bertrand, F. X., La Compagnie Manufactiere.
Smith Foundry & Machine Co.

**BEARING METAL**
Canada Metal Co.
Beveridge Supply Co., Ltd.

**BEDSTEADS (STEEL)**
Simmons Limited

**BELT DRESSING**
Dominion Belting Co.
General Supply of Canada, Ltd.

**BELTING**
Canadian Consolidated Rubber Co.
Dominion Belting Co.
General Supply Company
Goodhue & Co., J. L.
Gutta Percha & Rubber Company
D. K. McLaren, Limited
McLaren Belting Company, J. C.
York Belting Co.

**BLOWERS**
Reed & Co., Geo. W.
B. F. Sturtevant Co. of Canada, Ltd.
Toronto Blower Company

**BOILERS**
Engineering & Machine Works of Canada
Hamilton Company, William
Waterous Engine Works Company

**BOILER PRESERVATIVE**
Beveridge Supply Company
Shell-Bar, Boice Supply Co. Ltd.

**BOX MACHINERY**
Yates Machine Company, P. B.

**CABLE CONVEYORS**
Engineering & Machine Works of Canada.
Hamilton Company, Wm.
Waterous Engine Works Company

**CAMP SUPPLIES**
Davies Company, William
Dr. Bell Veterinary Wonder Co.
Johnson, A. H.
Turner & Sons, J. J.
Woods Manufacturing Company. Ltd.

**CANT HOOKS**
General Supply Co. of Canada, Ltd.
Pink Company, Thomas

**CEDAR**
Bury & Co., Robt.
Cameron Lumber Co.
Canadian Western Lumber Company
Chesbro, R. G.

Dry Wood Lumber Co.
Fesserton Timber Company
McElroy Lumber Co., Ltd.
Muir & Kitkpatrick
Rose, McLaurin, Limited
Terry & Gordon
Thurston-Flavelle Lumber Company
Vancouver Lumber Company
Victoria Lumber & Mfg. Co.

**CHAINS**
Canadian Link-Belt Company, Ltd.
General Supply Co. of Canada, Ltd.
Engineering & Machine Works of Canada.
Hamilton Company, William
Pink & Co., Thomas
Waterous Engine Works Company

**CLOTHING**
Woods Mfg. Company

**CONVEYOR MACHINERY**
Canadian Link-Belt Company, Ltd.
General Supply Co. of Canada, Ltd.
Hamilton Company, Wm.
Hopkins & Co., Ltd., F. H.
Waterous Engine Works Company

**CORDWOOD**
McClung, McLellan & Berry

**COUPLING (Shaft)**
Engineering & Machine Works of Canada

**CRANES**
Hopkins, & Co., Ltd., F. H.
Canadian Link-Belt Company

**CUTTER HEADS**
Shimer Cutter Head Company

**CYPRESS**
Wistar, Underhill & Nixon

**DERRICKS AND DERRICK FITTINGS**
Hopkins & Co., Ltd., F. H.

**DOORS**
Canadian Western Lumber Co.
Gardiner, P. W. & Son
Mason, Gordon & Co.
Midland Wood Products, Ltd
Terry & Gordon

**DRAG SAWS**
Gerlach Company, Peter
Hamilton Company, William

**DRYERS**
Coe Manufacturing Company
B. F. Sturtevant Co. of Canada, Ltd.

**DUST COLLECTORS**
Reed & Co., Geo. W.
B. F. Sturtevant Co. of Canada, Ltd.
Toronto Blower Company

**EDGERS**
Hamilton Company, Ltd., William
Green Company, G. Walter
Long Mfg. Company, E.
Payette Company, P.
Waterous Engine. Works Company

**ELEVATING AND CONVEYING MACHINERY**
Canadian Belt-Link Company, Ltd.
Engineering & Machine Works of Canada
Hamilton Company, William
Waterous Engine Works Company

**ENGINES**
Engineering & Machine Works of Canada
Hamilton Company, William

Payette Company, P.
Waterous Engine Works Company

**EXCELSIOR MACHINERY**
Elmira Machinery & Transmission Company

**EXHAUST FANS**
B. F. Sturtevant Co. of Canada, Ltd.
Toronto Blower Company

**EXHAUST SYSTEMS**
Reed & Co., Geo. W.
B. F. Sturtevant Co. of Canada, Ltd.
Toronto Blower Company

**FIBRE BOARD**
Manley Chew

**FILES**
Diaston & Sons, Henry
Simonds Canada Saw Company

**FIR**
Apex Lumber Co.
Associated Mills, Limited
Bainbridge Lumber Company
Cameron Lumber Co.
Canadian Western Lumber Co.
Canfield, P. L.
Chesbro, R. G.
Dry Wood Lumber Co.
Fesserton Timber Co.
Grier & Sons, Ltd., G. A.
Heeney, Percy E.
Knox Brothers
Mason, Gordon & Co.
McElroy Lumber Co., Ltd.
Robertson & Hacket Sawmills
Rose, McLaurin, Limited
Terry & Gordon
Timberland Lumber Company
Timms, Phillips & Co.
Underhill Lumber Co.
Vancouver Lumber Company
Vanderhoof Lumber Co.
Victoria Lumber & Mfg. Co.

**FIRE BRICK**
Beveridge Supply Co., Ltd.
Elk Fire Brick Company of Canada
Shell-Bar, Boice Supply Co. Ltd.

**FIRE FIGHTING APPARATUS**
Waterous Engine Works Company

**FITTINGS**
Crane Limited

**FLOORING**
Cameron Lumber Co.
Chesbro, R. G.
Long-Bell Lumber Company

**GEARS (Cut)**
Smart-Turner Machine Co.

**GUARDS (Machinery and Window)**
Canada Wire & Iron Goods Co.

**HARDWOODS**
Anderson Lumber Company, C. G.
Anderson Shreiner & Mawson
Atlantic Lumber Company
Barrett, Wm.
Bury & Co., Robt.
Cameron & Co.
Edwards & Co. W. C.
Fassett Lumber Co., Ltd.
Fesserton Timber Co.
Gillespie, James
Gloucester Lumber & Trading Co.
Grier & Son, G. A.
Hart, Hamilton & Jackson
Heeney, Percy E.

Knox Brothers
Mason & Co., Geo.
McDonagh Lumber Co.
McLennan Lumber Company
McLung, McLellan & Berry
Pedwell Hardwood Lumber Co.
W. & J. Sharples.
Spencer, Limited, C. A.
Strong, G. M.
Summers, James R.
Webster & Brother, James

**HARDWOOD FLOORING**
Grier & Son, G. A.

**HARNESS**
Beal Leather Co., R. M.

**HEMLOCK**
Anderson Lumber Company, C. G
Anderson, Shreiner & Mawson
Bartram & Ball
Beck Lumber Co.
Bourgouin, H.
Canadian General Lumber Company
Edwards & Company, W. C.
Fesserton Timber Co.
Grier & Sons, Ltd., G. A.
Hart, Hamilton & Jackson
Hocken Lumber Company
Mason, Gordon & Co.
McCormack Lumber Co.
McDonagh Lumber Co.
McElroy Lumber Co., Ltd.
Robertson & Hacket Sawmills
Spanish River Lumber Co.
Spencer, Limited, C. A.
Stalker, Douglas A.
Terry & Gordon
Vancouver Lumber Co.
Vanderhoof Lumber Co.

**HOISTING AND HAULING ENGINES**
General Supply Co. of Canada, Ltd.
Hopkins & Co., Ltd., F. H.

**HOSE**
General Supply Co. of Canada, Ltd.
Gutta Percha & Rubber Company

**INSURANCE**
Barton & Ellis Co.
Burns Underwriting Co.
Hardy & Co., E. D.
Lumbermen's Underwriting Alliance
Rankin Benedict Underwriting Co

**INTERIOR FINISH**
Cameron Lumber Co.
Canadian Western Lumber Co.
Canfield, P. L.
Eagle Lumber Company
Mason, Gordon & Co.
Rose, McLaurin, Limited
Terry & Gordon

**KILN DRIED LUMBER**
Bury & Co., Robt.

**KNIVES**
Diaston & Sons, Henry
Simonds Canada Saw Company
Waterous Engine Works Company

**LARCH**
Otis Staples Lumber Co.

**LATH**
Anderson, Shreiner & Mawson
Apex Lumber Co.
Austin & Nicholson
Beck Lumber Co.
Brennen & Sons, F. W.
Cameron Lumber Co.
Canadian General Lumber Company
Carew Lumber Co., John
Chaleurs Bay Mills
Dupuis, Limited, J. P.

# DISSTON
## NEWS FOR LUMBERMEN

| Published now and then | HENRY DISSTON & SONS, LTD., Toronto, Canada. | March, 1922. |

## They Say—

IN our office there is a correspondence file which we call our "inspiration file." Here we keep letters that are written to us by users of Disston Saws, Tools, and Files. The following sentences are from a few of the letters taken at random from this collection:

"I use a Disston Saw that my father bought in 1887 and used to build the first house in Whitewood, S.D."—"I have two of your saws that I have used approximately 4500 working days. I have filed them down to less than ¼ inch at the point, but the temper is the same as when new."—"I sent to Europe for the best saw they could get, and when it came back it had 'Henry Disston & Sons' on the blade. Then I laughed."—"I have one of your cross-cut saws which has been in almost constant service since 1860, and it is today a perfect tool."—"I have one of your saws that is older than I am—46 years. My father had it before me. It is a good tool yet."—"The saws you made for us are giving great satisfaction, cutting more and better lumber than any other saws we have used."

It is indeed an inspiration to us, who are working to maintain and increase the reputation of the House of Disston for superior quality and workmanship, to know that our products are giving such unusual satisfaction to users in every part of the world.

## Walt Masonry

A sawyer hot was bawling—"Who taught you how to file? You surely missed your calling by ten quarters of a mile. Your saws run hot, they snake a lot, the teeth are split they do not fit. And when those blades begin to rattle I think of some enormous battle. You think you are a 'filer' great but I can say you are a fake." The filer first was much surprised, but soon became quite dignified, and roared in tones that terrified. "You saw up knees, instead of trees. You think a log is made of cheese the way that carriage hits the breeze. The carriage riders cling like death and half the time they have no breath. They bow their backs and bend their knees and hang on like fermented fleas. You must be full of Jack Ass Brandy; a sober man would be more handy. Those saws were made for cutting logs instead of spikes and guides and dogs. If, we don't soon a sawyer get this old saw mill will be to let.

—Disston Crucible

## Where Quality Tells

AN average log band saw, traveling from 9,000 to 10,000 feet per minute, makes more than 300 revolutions per minute.

Have you ever stopped to consider the great strain put in such use, and the wonderful quality of steel required to withstand that strain.

If the saw is making 300 revolutions

## Disston Saw-Makers For 256 Years

WHEN one considers that there is no trade which requires more skill and personal judgement than saw-making, the old saying, "that it takes seven years to make a saw-maker," seems well founded. Even after seven years of careful training and practical experience, there frequently arise problems and conditions which only skill and mature judgment can master. In the Arnold families we have

ranges from 11 years to 53 years—an average of 28½ years.

The Arnold family is only one of the many Disston families and only a few of the hundreds of Disston mechanics who have from ten to sixty years to their credit at the saw-making trade. Visitors who have been through the plant were impressed with the many grey-haired men in every department, and also with the intense interest these men take in their work.

Three Brothers—John George, and James Arnold, and Their Sons Have Been Disston Saw-Makers for an Aggregate of 256 Years

nine men who have plied the saw-making trade for the House of Disston more than twice the exception of the youngest Arnold, and he has passed his eleventh year at the trade. (One of the Arnold men was not present when above picture was made.)

The length of service of these men

These men started in youth to make saws and have worked at their trade, honestly, and intelligently ever since, and they always strive with jealous care, as do also the younger saw-makers, to maintain the quality and workmanship which has made Disston Saws the standard of the industry for the past 81 years.

per minute, that means that every part of the saw must completely change its shape 300 times every minute—14 times a second! The saw goes over the top wheel and it conforms to a half-circle, comes down the cutting side, is straightened out, goes under the lower wheel and conforms to a half-circle in the opposite direction to the first, comes up and is straightened out—and so on, the complete bending process 14 times every second!

If you pick up a piece of metal and wish to break it, you bend it—first one way and then the other —just as a band saw is bent when in operation.

Consider that, in a saw, this bending goes on, 14 times a second, day and day out for 'months—and the quality and strength of the steel is not injured!

It is for reasons such as these that we speak so often of the quality of Disston-made Steel—because quality is surely required.

## A List of What Disston Makes
### And in these Saws, Tools and Files is that quality found in
### "The Saw Most Carpenters Use"

Back Saws
Band Saws for Wood and Metal
Bevels

Buck Saws
Butcher Saws and Blades
Circular Saws for Wood, Metal, and Slate
Compass Saws
Cross-cut Saws and Tools
Cylinder Saws
Drag Saw Blades
Files and Rasps
Grooving Saws
Gauges—Carpenters' Marking, etc.
Hack Saw Blades
Hack Saw Frames
Hand, Panel, and Rip Saws
Hedge Shears
Ice Saws
Inserted Tooth Circular Saws
Keyhole Saws
Kitchen Saws
Knives—Cane, Corn, Hedge
Knives—Circular for Cork, Cloth, Leather, Paper, etc
Knives—Machine
Levels—Carpenters' and Masons'
Machetes
Mandrels
Milling Saws for Metal
Mitre-box Saws
Mitre Rods
One-man Cross-cut Saws
Plumbs and Levels
Plumbers' Saws
Pruning Saws
Re-saws
Saw Gummers
Saw-sets
Saw Screws
Screw Drivers
Screw-slotting Saws
Segment Saws
Shingle Saws
Slate Saws—Circular
Squares—Try and Mitre
Stave Saws
Sugar Beet Knives
Swages
Tools for Repairing Saws
Tool Steel
Trowels—Brick, Plastering, Pointing, etc.
Veneering Saws
Webs—Turning and Fellos

## A Magazine You Should Read

THERE is a magazine, different from all others, published especially for lumbermen. It will be sent free of charge to you if you would like it.

It contains stories, of timber-land and operations in other countries. There are stories about fires, about filers and sawyers, about big mills and little mills. There are articles on the care of saws—articles prepared by experts from our factory. There is always a page of rattling good jokes.

This little magazine, The Disston Crucible, is widely known and quoted. It is mailed to over sixteen thousand persons, and we have received enough

compliments from them to feel that you would like it and find some valuable information in it. If you would care to receive the Crucible please fill out and mail the attached coupon.

Eagle Lumber Company
Fassett Lumber Co., Ltd.
Foley Lumber Company
Fraser Bryson Lumber Co., Ltd.
Gloucester Lumber & Grading Co.
Grier & Sons, Ltd., G. A.
Harris Tie & Timber Company, Ltd.
Larkin & Co., C. A.
Mason & Co., Geo.
McLennan Lumber Company
Miller, W. H. Co.
New Ontario Colonization Company
Otis Staples Lumber Company
Power Lumber Co.
Price Bros. & Company
Shevlin-Clarke Co.
Spencer, Limited, C. A.
Terry & Gordon
U. G. G. Sawmills. Limited
Union Lumber Company
Victoria Harbor Lumber Company

**LATH BOLTERS**

General Supply Co. of Canada, Ltd.
Hamilton Company, Wm.
Payette & Company, P.

**LOCOMOTIVES**

Engineering & Machine Works of Canada
General Supply Co. of Canada, Ltd.
Hopkins & Co., Ltd., F. H.
Climax Manufacturing Company
Montreal Locomotive Works

**LINK-BELT**

Canadian Link-Belt Company
Hamilton Company, Wm.

**LOCOMOTIVE CRANES**

Canadian Link-Belt Company, Ltd.
Hopkins & Co. ,Ltd., F. H.

**LOGGING ENGINES**

Engineering & Machine Works of Canada
Hopkins & Co., Ltd., F. H.
Mussens Ltd.

**LOG HAULER**

Engineering & Machine Works of Canada
Green Company, G. Walter
Holt Manufacturing Co.
Hopkins & Co., Ltd., F. H.
Payette Company, P.

**LOGGING MACHINERY AND EQUIPMENT**

General Supply Co. of Canada, Ltd.
Hamilton Company, William
Holt Manufacturing Co.
Hopkins & Co., Ltd., F. H.
Payette Company, P.
Waterous Engine Works Company
West, Peachey & Sons
Mussens Ltd.

**LUMBER EXPORTS**

Fletcher Corporation

**LUMBER TRUCKS**

Hamilton Company, Wm.
Waterous Engine Works Company

**LUMBERMEN'S BOATS**

Adams Engine Company
Gidley Boat Co.
West, Peachey & Sons

**LUMBERMEN'S CLOTHING**

Kitchen, Overall & Shirt Co.

**MATTRESSES**

Simmons Limited

**METAL REFINERS**

Canada Metal Company

**OAK**

Long-Bell Lumber Company

**PACKING**

Beveridge Supply Company
Gutta Percha & Rubber Company

**PANELS**

Bury & Co., Robt.

**PAPER**

Beveridge Supply Co., Ltd.
Price Bros. & Co.

**PINE**

Anderson Lumber Company, C. G.
Anderson, Shreiner & Mawson
Atlantic Lumber Co.
Austin & Nicholson
Barratt, William
Beck Lumber Co.
Cameron & Co.
Cameron Lumber Co.
Canadian General Lumber Company
Canadian Western Lumber Co.
Canfield, P. L.
Cheabro, R. G.
Cleveland-Sarnia Sawmills Company
Cox, Long & Company
Dudley, Arthur N.
Eagle Lumber Company
Edwards & Co. W. C.
Excelsior Lumber Company
Fesserton Timber Company
Fraser Bryson Lumber Co., Ltd.
Gillies Bros, Limited
Gloucester Lumber & Trading Co.
Gordon & Co., George
Goodday & Company, H. R.
Grier & Sons, Ltd., G. A.
Harris Tie & Timber Company, Ltd.
Hart, Hamilton & Jackson
Hettler Lumber Company, Herman H.
Hocken Lumber Company
Julien, Roch
Lay & Haight
Lloyd, W. Y.
Loggie Cp., W. S.

**LONG-BELL Lumber Company**
Mason, Gordon & Co.
Mason & Co., Gee.
McCormack Lumber Co.
McFadden & Malley
McLennan Lumber Company
Montreal Lumber Company
Muir & Kirkpatrick
Northern Lumber Mills.
Otis Staples Lumber Co.
Parry Sound Lumber Company
Pigeon River Lumber Co., Ltd.
Rolland Lumber Co.
W. & J. Sharples.
Shevlin-Clarke Co.
Spanish River Lumber Co.
Spencer, Limited, C. A.
Stalker, Douglas A.
Streng, G. M.
Summers, James R.
Terry & Gordon
Union Lumber Company
Victoria Harbor Lumber Co.
Watson & Todd, Limited

**PLANING MILL EXHAUSTERS**

Toronto Blower Co.

**PLANING MILL MACHINERY**

Merahon & Co., W. B.
B. F. Sturtevant Co. of Canada, Ltd.
Toronto Blower Co.
Yates Machine Company, P. B.

**PORK PACKERS**

Davies Company, William

**POSTS AND POLES**

Anderson, Shreiner & Mawson
Canadian Tie & Lumber Co.
Dupuis, Limited, J. P.
Eagle Lumber Company

# IMPERIAL GENUINE
## BABBITT METAL

### FOR THE GREATEST RESPONSIBILITY
### THE BEST THAT MONEY CAN BUY
(Contains No Lead)

### Harris Heavy Pressure
BEARING METAL
For All General Machinery Bearings

## The CANADA METAL CO., Limited
Hamilton   Montreal   TORONTO   Winnipeg   Vancouver

# Put your problem up to us

We are specialists in building locomotives. We build all types and sizes, also all kinds of repair parts for locomotives and tenders.

Our experience puts us in a position to give you expert advice as to what particular type and size of locomotive is best suited to your needs.

*Put Your Locomotive Problem up to us.*

## Montreal Locomotive Works
Limited
Dominion Express Building.   Montreal, Canada

Harris Tie & Timber Co., Ltd.
Long-Bell Lumber Co.
Mason, Gordon & Co.
McLennan Lumber Company
Terry & Gordon

**POST GRINDERS**

Smith Foundry Co.

**PULLEYS AND SHAFTING**

Canadian Link-Belt Company
General Supply Co. of Canada, Ltd.
Green Company. G. Walter
Engineering & Machine Works of Canada
Hamilton Company, William

**PULP MILL MACHINERY**

Canadian Link-Belt Company, Ltd.
Engineering & Machine Works of Canada
Hamilton Company, William
Payette Company, P.
Waterous Engine Works Company

**PULPWOOD**

British & Foreign Agencies
D'Auteuil Lumber Co.
Price Bros. & Co.
Scott, Draper & Co.

**PUMPS**

General Supply Co. of Canada, Ltd.
Engineering & Machine Works of Canada
Hamilton Co., William
Hopkins & Co., Ltd., F. H.
Smart-Turner Machine Company
Waterous Engine Works Company

**RAILS**

Gartshore, John J.
Hopkins & Co., Ltd., F. H.

**ROOFINGS**

(Rubber, Plastic and Liquid)
Beveridge Supply Company
Reed & Co., Geo. W.

**RUBBER GOODS**

Dunlop Tire & Rubber Goods Co.
Gutta Percha & Rubber Company

**SASH**

Midland Woodworkers
Midland Wood Products, Ltd.

**SAWS**

Atkins & Company, E. C.
Disston & Sons, Henry
General Supply Co. of Canada, Ltd.
Gerlach Company, Peter
Green Company, G. Walter
Hoe & Company, R.
Radcliff Saw Mfg. Co.,
Shurly Co., Ltd., T. F.
Shurly-Dietrich Company
Simonds Canada Saw Company

**SAW GRINDERS**

Smith Foundry Co.

**SAW MILL LINK-BELT**

Canadian Link-Belt Company

**SAW MILL MACHINERY**

Canadian Link-Belt Company, Ltd.
General Supply Co. of Canada, Ltd.
G. Walter Green Co., Ltd.
Hamilton Company, William
La Compagnie Manufacture, F. X. Bertrand
Long Manufacturing Company, E.
Mershon & Company, W. B.
Parry Sound Lumber Company
Payette Company, P.
Waterous Engine Works Company
Yates Machine Co., P. B.

**SAW SHARPENERS**

Hamilton Company, William
Waterous Engine Works Company

**SAW SLASHERS**

Hamilton Company, Wm.
Payette Company, P.
Waterous Engine Works Company

**SHINGLES**

Apex Lumber Co.
Associated Mills, Limited
Brennen & Sons, F. W.
Cameron Lumber Co.
Campbell-MacLaurin Lumber Co.
Canadian Western Lumber Co.
Carew Lumber Co., John
Chaleurs Bay Mills
Chesbro, R. G.
D'Auteuil Lumber Co.
Dry Wood Lumber Co.
Eagle Lumber Company
Fraser, Companies Limited
Gillespie, James
Gloucester Lumber & Trading Co.
Grier & Sons, Limited, G. A.
Harris Tie & Timber Company, Ltd.
Heaps & Sons
Heeney, Percy E.
Mason, Gordon & Co.
McLennan Lumber Company
Miller Company, Ltd., W. H.
Rose, McLaurin, Lim'ted
Stalker, Douglas A.
Terry & Gordon
Timms, Phillips & Co.
Vancouver Lumber Company
Vanderhoof Lumber Co.

**SHINGLE & LATH MACHINERY**

Green Company, C. Walter
Hamilton Company, William
Long Manufacturing Company, E.
Payette Company, P.
Smith Foundry Co.

**SILENT CHAIN DRIVES**

Canadian, Link-Belt Company, Ltd.

**SLEEPING EQUIPMENT**

Simmons Limited

**SLEEPING ROBES**

Woods Mfg. Company, Ltd.

**SMOKESTACKS**

Hamilton Company, Wm.
Reed & Co., Geo. W.
Waterous Engine Works Company

**SNOW PLOWS**

Pink Company, Thomas

**SOLDERS**

Canada Metal Co.

**SPARK ARRESTORS**

Reed & Co., Geo. W.
Waterous Engine Works Company

**SPRUCE**

Anderson, Shreiner & Mawson
Barrett, Wm.
Cameron Lumber Co.
Campbell, McLaurin Lumber Co.
Canadian Western Lumber Co.
Chesbro, R. G.
Cox, Long & Co.
Dudley, Arthur N.
Fassett Lumber Co., Ltd.
Fraser, Companies Limited
Fraser-Bryson Lumber Company
Gillies Brothers
Gloucester Lumber & Trading Co.
Goodday & Company, H. R.

Grier & Sons, Ltd., G. A.
Harris Lumber Co., Frank H.
Hart, Hamilton & Jackson
Hocken Lumber Company
Julien, Roch
Larkin Co., C. A.
Lay & Haight.
Lloyd, W. Y.
Loggie Co., W. S.
Mason, Gordon & Co.
McDonagh Lumber Co.
McElroy Lumber Co., Ltd.
McLennan Lumber Company
Muir & Kirkpatrick
New Ontario Colonization Company
Northern Lumber Mills.
Pigeon River Lumber Co.
Power Lumber Co.
Price Bros. & Co.
Rolland Lumber Co.
Rose, McLaurin, Limited
W. & J. Sharples.
Spencer, Limited, C. A.
Strong, G. M.
Terry & Gordon
U. G. G. Sawmills. Limited
Vanderhoof Lumber Co.

**STEAM SHOVELS**

Hopkins & Co., Ltd., F. H.

**STEEL CHAIN**

Canadian Link-Belt Company, Ltd.
Hopkins & Co., Ltd., F. H.
Waterous Engine Works Company

**STEAM PLANT ACCESSORIES**

Waterous Engine Works Company

**STEEL BARRELS**

Smart-Turner Machine Co.

**STEEL DRUMS**

Smart-Turner Machine Co.

**TARPAULINS**

Turner & Sons, J. J.
Woods Manufacturing Company, Ltd.

**TANKS**

Hopkins & Co., Ltd., F. H.

**TENTS**

Turner & Sons, J. J.
Woods Mfg. Company

**TIES**

Austin & Nicholson
Carew Lumber Co., John
Canadian Tie & Lumber Co.
Chaleurs Bay Mills
D'Auteuil Lumber Co.
Gloucester Lumber & Trading Co.
Harris Tie & Timber Company, Ltd.
McLennan Lumber Company
Miller, W. H. Co.
Price Bros. & Co.
Scott, Draper & Co.
Terry & Gordon

**TIMBER BROKERS**

Bradley, R. R.
Cant & Kemp
Farnworth & Jardine
Wright, Graham & Co.

**TIMBER CRUISERS AND ESTIMATORS**

Savage & Bartlett.
Sewall, James W.

**TIMBER LANDS**

Department of Lands & Forests, Ont.

**TOWING MACHINES**

Corbet Foundry & Machine Co.
Payette Company, P.
West, Peachy & Sons

**TRACTORS**

Holt Manufacturing Co.
Hopkins & Company, Ltd., F. H.
Mussens Ltd.

**TRANSMISSION MACHINERY**

Canadian Link-Belt Company, Ltd.
Engineering & Machine Works of Canada
General Supply Co. of Canada, Ltd.
Grand Rapids Vapor Kiln
Hamilton Company, Wm.
Waterous Engine Works Company

**TURBINES**

Engineering & Machine Works of Canada
Hamilton Company, William
B. F. Sturtevant Co. of Canada, Ltd.

**VALVES**

Crane Limited

**VAPOR KILNS**

Grand Rapids Vapor Kiln
B. F. Sturtevant Co. of Canada, Ltd.

**VENEERS**

Bury & Co., Robt.

**VENEER DRYERS**

Coe Manufacturing Company
B. F. Sturtevant Co. of Canada, Ltd.

**VENEER MACHINERY**

Coe Machinery Company

**VETERINARY REMEDIES**

Dr. Bell Veterinary Wonder Co.
Johnson, A. H.

**WARPING TUGS**

West, Peachy & Sons

**WATER WHEELS**

Engineering & Machine Works of Canada
Hamilton Company, William

**WIRE**

Canada Metal Co.
Laidlaw Bale Tie Company
Canada Wire & Iron Goods Co.

**WIRE CLOTH**

Canada Wire & Iron Goods Co.

**WIRE ROPE**

Canada Wire & Iron Goods Co.
Hopkins & Co., Ltd., F. H.
Dominion Wire Rope Co.
Greening Wire Co., B.

**WOODWORKING MACHINERY**

General Supply Co. of Canada, Ltd.
Long Manufacturing Company, E.
Mershon & Company, W. B.
Waterous Engine Works Company
Yates Machine Company, P. B.

**WOOD PRESERVATIVES**

Beveridge Supply Company

**WOOD PULP**

Austin & Nicholson
New Ontario Colonization Co
Power Lumber Co.

# Efficiency in Belt Performance

The one thing you want to feel certain about in your Belt Purchases these days—when so much depends on the ability to lower costs and maintain quality—is efficiency in Belt Performance.

That "efficiency" has been built into

### DUNLOP
#### "GIBRALTAR REDSPECIAL"

through years of belt-making experience for every possible use to which a Transmission Belt could be put.

When you buy this Belt your interests are safeguarded from the very first moment it is installed.

That satisfaction alone is worth considerable, although you don't have to pay one cent more for this proven Belt than one you are doubtful about.

## Dunlop Tire & Rubber Goods Co., Limited

Head Office and Factories: TORONTO          Branches in the Leading Cities

# LUMBERMEN'S      EQUIPMENT

The thin saw kerf of the LONG resaw gets the maximum amount of lumber out of each log and as the feed is uniform and constant the human element is not as apparant as in the operation of the head rig.

In addition to this our machines are so constructed that short pieces can readily be sawn, and profit-able lumber produced from slabs that would otherwise be wasted.

Get in touch with us now for full information and prices. Perhaps there is a LONG resaw in operation in your locality. If so we shall be pleased to tell you, that you may see it under actual working conditions.

# The E. Long Manufacturing Co., Limited
## Orillia        CANADA

Robt. Hamilton & Co., Vancouver
Gorman, Clancy & Grindley Ltd., Calgary & Edmonton

A. R. Williams Machinery Co., of Winnipeg, Ltd.
Williams & Wilson Ltd., Montreal

Vol. 42        Toronto, March 15, 1922        No. 6

# Canada Lumberman

*Founded 1880*

# C. A. LARKIN COMPANY

### 630 CONFEDERATION LIFE BUILDING
## TORONTO, CANADA

OUR CONNECTION with the Wholesale Lumber Trade in Toronto dates back to the year 1892; during this lengthy period we have always endeavored to give our customers the best possible values combined with good and efficient service. That we have succeeded in this effort is evident from the marked appreciation and confidence we enjoy with the trade throughout Ontario. By continued prompt and efficient service and honorable dealing we shall do our utmost to maintain the confidence and good will of the trade.

## Routes of our Travelling Representatives

MR. C. McDONALD calls on the trade in Toronto and Hamilton.

MR. E. CAY covers the Niagara District, and west to London, St. Thomas and Windsor and the district south of these points.

MR. D. McNEIL takes the territory east of Toronto and west on Grand Trunk to Stratford and Sarnia, and the district north of this line.

We have a good line of stock in
### WHITE PINE
### SPRUCE
### JACK PINE
### HEMLOCK
### and LATH

*We solicit your enquiries*          **Telephone, Main 465**

# White Pine
# Red Pine
# Jack Pine
# Spruce
# Lumber
# and Lath

## UNION LUMBER COMPANY LIMITED
### 701 DOMINION BANK BUILDING
### TORONTO          CANADA

*"Well bought is half sold!"*

# Forest Products

## Canadian General Lumber Co., Ltd.
### Bank of Hamilton Bldg.
### Toronto
Montreal Office        603 McGill Building

*We have "the best!"*

# Statistics *and* Progress

STATISTICS—the history of the past by which we guage the trend of the future —conclusively show that general conditions are on the up-grade and gathering momentum. In the lumber business, a man need not be an optimist to believe that 1922 will be a vastly better year than 1921.

Building reports for the last three months of 1921 show an increase of nearly 25% over the same period of 1920. With mounting bond prices and easier money, this improvement should become more marked each month.

This progress means more business for every lumber dealer. Are you ready with adequate stocks to meet the demand? We are prepared to supply your wants from Ontario, Quebec or British Columbia. "Service and Quality" is the keynote of our business.

## TERRY AND GORDON
### LIMITED
## CANADIAN FOREST PRODUCTS
#### HEAD OFFICE
#### TORONTO
BRANCH — MONTREAL    EUROPEAN AGENTS    VANCOUVER — BRANCH

SPENCER LOCK & Co., LONDON, ENG.

Ontario Representatives for
THE BRITISH COLUMBIA MILLS TIMBER AND TRADING CO., VANCOUVER, B. C.

The Plant of

# CHEW BROS.

MIDLAND, ONT.

*Manufacturers of*

## White Pine, Red Pine and Spruce Lumber, Lath and Pickets

For 1922 we shall have some of the finest White and Red
Pine also Hemlock, we have taken out of the North
Country—first raft of which should arrive at
our mill about the middle of May

*We solicit inquiries which will receive prompt and careful attention*

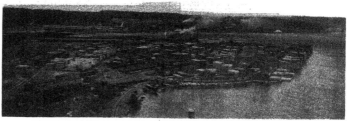

Panoramic view of the mill property of Chew Bros., Midland, Ont., taken from the elevator and showing the extensive yards.

# SAVE ONTARIO'S FORESTS

FORESTS of Ontario are the basis for a very large part of the prosperity of Ontario's people.

The lumber industry of Ontario in camps and mills alone gives employment to 17,000 men, with a pay roll of $12,000,000, and an invested capital of $45,000,000. Ontario employs one-third of Canada's lumbermen and produces one-quarter of Canada's total annual cut.

The sash and door and planing mills of Ontario, which depend on the 800 lumber mills and the log making industry for their raw materials, employ 4000 persons with a total wage roll of $3,000,000 per year

## They're Yours!

Pulp and paper mills employ 8,000 persons, and pay $7,000,000 in wages with over $90,000,000 invested.

In addition, there is the railway tie industry, wood distillation industry, cooperage industry, and many others. These are the foundation industries for all that immense number of other industries which use their products, so that if you trace it down, directly or indirectly, every citizen of Ontario is affected.

This is why your co-operation is needed to help prevent fire and save Ontario's forests.

*Remember, every stick of timber, little or big, wasted and burned by forest fire — that greatest of all menaces to the forest and wood-working industries—is a direct loss to YOU.*

Issued by

## Hon. Beniah Bowman
Minister of Lands and Forests

# QUALITY LUMBER

Pine
Spruce
Hemlock
Hardwoods
B. C. Lumber
and Timber

*Established 1871*

# G. A. GRIER & SONS
## LIMITED

MONTREAL
1112 Notre Dame St. W.

TORONTO
22 Royal Bank Chambers, 454 King St. W.

*We have no connection with or interest in any other firm bearing a name similar to ours.*

# BUY
## BRITISH COLUMBIA
# Red Cedar Shingles

The life of a British Columbia Red Cedar Shingle Roof can almost be gauged by the life of the nail with which the shingle is nailed in place. Judging from available data, the average life of the ordinary steel wire nail, which has been in such common use, is only from seven to twelve years. Some wire nails will last longer, depending upon the condition of exposure, climate and similar features, but considering our climate as a whole, at the end of from seven to twelve years a large percentage of wire nails will have rusted either completely through or so extensively that the first strong wind will complete the work. The shingles that have been held in position by such nails are then free to work down, permitting rains or melting snows to leak through and damage the interior of the structure. Examination will disclose that the fibre of the shingle itself is still in perfect condition, and a leaky roof, in the majority of occasions is due entirely to the use of faulty nails, but the average home owner, placed at such inconvenience, will not stop to reason this out and the poor wooden shingle comes in for more unjust abuse.

There are several kinds of nails which experience has proven will give lasting satisfaction, and the wise dealer will advise his customers of these satisfactory nails. A pure zinc shingle nail meets all the demands of durability required. Its principal drawback is its high cost and a slight tendency to bend under careless driving. Galvanized wire nails theoretically are rust proof, and if the galvanized coating is properly applied, and of sufficient thickness, such a nail will last as long as the shingle it holds in place. The life of this shingle roof, properly applied with these nails then is from 40 to 50 years. Pure iron nails, or the old cut or wrought nails are ideal but difficult to secure. Copper nails also constitute a perfect shingle nail.

## The Question of Supply

During the past two months our mill
connections have been handicapped
by unusual weather conditions, but
we are glad to state that we are now
in a position to give our usual prompt
service in your requirements.

**Timms Phillips & Co., Ltd.**
Vancouver, B. C.

TORONTO OFFICE: Canada Permanent Bldg.
Phone Adel. 6490
MONTREAL OFFICE: 23 Marconi Bldg.
Phone M 2999

# GEORGE MASON & COMPANY

### (Successors to Manley Chew)

"The
Largest Mill in
Midland"

———producing———

# PINE  MAPLE
# BEECH  BASSWOOD
# LUMBER  LATH

Our 1922 Cut of Pine
estimated to produce
30,000,000 feet is
available for
purchase
en
bloc

Are You Interested?

Mills at Midland, Ont., Thunder Bay, Ont.      Head Office:—Midland, Ont.

# THE GREAT NATIONAL LUMBER JOURNAL

Pioneer and Leader
in the Industry

Recognized Authority
for Forty Years

Vol. 42      Toronto, March 15, 1922      No. 6

## How Leading Lumber Operators "Size Up"
## General Conditions in the Industry

It is easy to look back over the road we have travelled, but to peer any distance in the future is not so simple a task, as the journey ahead may be full of dangerous curves, sharp declines or rocky steeps.

In the lumber industry it is always interesting to review the past in the hope that a proper understanding of it may afford us some conception of what the future holds in store. It is true that the days, which are gone cannot be recalled, but, in examining the record, it will be noticed that, in the lumber line especially, there has been a gradual improvement and growing confidence since October of last year.

True, the process of readjustment has been tardy and the market at times spotty. Some weeks would be particularly good and others would be disappointing in results; nevertheless, it is generally conceded that conditions in the forest products arena are now headed in the right direction; that the costs of manufacture are reduced to about as low a point as they can be, and values of the finished product are not expected to sag any more. Of course, as long as trade has its ebbs and flows, its period of abnormal prosperity, acute depression and gradual recovery, there will be widely varying opinions as to production, prices, costs and distribution.

The Statistical Number of the "Canada Lumberman" is always looked forward to with much interest as it endeavors to present in an instructive and impartial manner, reliable data and authoritative views concerning the past year's operations, and to furnish indices of what leading lumbermen in the various provinces of the Dominion have to say concerning the future.

### Symposium of Trade Opinions

Many questions have been submitted to representative manufacturing firms, covering such points as—was the volume of trade in 1921 greater or less than in 1920? How did profits compare with those of 1920? How did prices compare; how do stocks line up with those of a year ago? What peculiar conditions characterized the trade with the United States, and how does your log output this winter compare with last winter? What, in your opinion, is the trade outlook for 1922, etc?

Many good friends of the "Canada Lumberman" have forwarded interesting comments on the cost of production, price prospects, the future of the market, etc. It is manifestly impossible to publish all these replies, but an effort has been made to correlate them in many respects and furnish in concrete form some firsthand particulars concerning what producers in various parts of the Dominion feel, think and say.

The estimates of the volume of trade in 1921 as compared with 1920 vary from 40 to 60%, with the preponderance of opinion declaring that it was about 50%. So far as their profits are concerned these are reported, in practically every instance, to be less than in 1920, which, of course, was a boom year and characterized by an annual demand and runaway prices, especially during the first six months; in fact a number of firms say they operated at a loss in 1921 and no net profit can be inscribed on the pages of their ledgers. This is, however, a feature in which the members of the industry are not particularly interested as, with comparatively few exceptions, be the reader a wholesaler, manufacturer or retailer, he has had some trouble in making ends dovetail during the past twelve months, many being caught with heavy stocks, most of it bought at high prices, and having to

dispose of it, in numerous instances, at far less than he paid. However, this is not a blue ruin story or a lugubrious reference to things that are past. It is simply presenting a plain statement in a frank and effective way, and it is only fair to add there are only a very limited number of pessimists in the lumber world today.

So far as prices are concerned, of course, these were naturally much lower in 1921, the deflation varying according to different localities and the amount of stock with which wholesalers and manufacturers were caught, the local building situation, crop returns, the industrial inactivity in the district, and various other factors. However, as a general rule, it is estimated that on box and better, so far as white pine is concerned, the decrease was on the average about 25%, while culls were 50% off and hemlock reputed to be from 43 to 50% below the peak prices of 1920. Hardwoods generally deflated from 50 to 60%.

Respecting the trade outlook for 1922, this is on the whole regarded as favorable, although quite a few express some doubt about there being any very decided change in the situation for some months yet. They maintain that, while there may be more business going, it will be ardently competed for, and service and quality will be the basis of sales, rather than price-cutting, of which during the past twelve months there has been quite an orgy. Some slashed quotations because of necessity, others because of financial pressure, overproduction, retiring from business, etc. and there are still some who never sold commodities at regular price. However, this element is fast disappearing.

But to get back to trade conditions, sweeping observations and glittering generalities may be soothing and satisfying, but the average man wants to get down to "brass tacks." From the province of Ontario 100 representatives mill owners have been kind enough to furnish their views on trade, profits, prices, stocks, log output and business outlook. As to whether trade was greater or less in 1921 than in the year previous, 70 say that it was less, 14 that it was greater and 16 the same.

### How Profits and Prices Compared

Regarding profits, only 5 but of 100 declare that they were greater last year than in 1920; 85 say that it was less and 10 the same.

As to how prices for 1921 compared with those of 1920, only one has the temerity

---

to believe that they were greater, 96 declare that they were far less in many instances, and 3 say they got about the same for their stocks.

Concerning how stocks compare with a year ago, 44 lumbermen of Ontario declare they are greater than in the corresponding period last year, 36 say they are less and 20 report the same as a year ago.

In the log output, it is instructive to note that only 11 report their cut in the bush will be larger than a year ago; 69 say it will be less and 20 reply "about the same."

Touching upon the trade outlook for 1922, 65 regard it as "fair," 20 as "good" or "encouraging" and 15 as doubtful." This is a summmary of how 100 representative manufacturers view the present and future in the lumber line.

Travelling further east to Quebec and the Maritime Provinces, expressions of opinion from 90 representative mill owners furnish the following symposium:—10 declare the volume of trade was greater in 1921 than in the year previous; 75 say it was less and 5 report about the same. With only one exception, all manufacturers report that profits were far below those of the previous 12 months, and with the same unanimity they affirm that prices greatly decreased on every kind of lumber they turn out.

On the question of stocks, there is an almost equal division of opinion. 29 declare they are now greater than they were a year ago; 33 that they are less and 28 about the same.

It is declared by 62 manufacturers that their log output of the past winter will be less than in 1920-1921; 19 state that it will be about the same and only 9 report that it will be greater.

Touching upon trade outlook, 11 believe that it will be "good;" 63 view it in the light of "fair" and 16 "doubtful" or "slow."

### The Ups and Downs of Trade

It will thus be seen from the questionnaire submitted by the "Canada Lumberman" to leading exponents of the industry, that there is a greater divergence of views when everything is considered in the aggregate except that, with practically one accord, they voice the opinion that profits were less and also prices, which facts are patent to anyone who has had anything to do with the lumber industry.

One leading firm, which handles about 30,000,000 feet a year and has kept careful tab on the prices it has received during the past nine years, furnishes a comparative statement that is of real interest. It shows that the lowest prices received for lumber were in 1914, the year in which the great world war started and that there was a gradual increase in values until 1920 was reached, when they climbed in several cases from 40 to 70%. The figures for last year show that values shrunk rapidly. In some districts there was practically no market for stock at all while export trade declined perceptibly.

It is always interesting to present the views of the other fellow, and here are a few "snap shots" taken at random from different sections of the country.

A northern Ontario producer says until all trades accept less wages and more money is available for mortgages and labor, and costs relative to transportation decrease in basic industries like iron, steel and others and we can again meet foreign quotations at a profit, the lumbermen may carry on but very few will have anything to substantially show in the way of net earnings.

Another northern dealer says,—"We did not operate during 1921. We have 75% of the output of 1920 on hand but it will be moving in the spring. In the loss caused by the extraordinary expense of operation during the winter of 1920, and the drop in prices during 1921, we are like other small operators."

A central Ontario firm writes,—"We have received more inquiries in the last few weeks than in the previous six months, and look for advances in hemlock and hardwood during the next three months. Wages have declined markedly. A year ago they were $50. to $60., and to-day around $26. per month. There was not much logging done in this section, but some small lots of timber have been taken out by farmers and others."

From a Hastings county operator comes the following,—"I am pleased to say that for the last two months trade has picked up considerably and prices are about as they were in 1919. I look for 1922 to be a fair year in the lumber business."

"We are not cutting this winter, so cannot say how the cost of logging compares with a year ago, but we are taking out pulpwood at half the cost of 1920—1921," remarks a lumberman in the North Bay district.

### Lower Freight Rates Necessary

Speaking of pulpwood activities, another firm along the T. & N. O. Railway say,— "We deal chiefly in pulpwood. Our cut of lumber last year was small. A lower freight rate would stimulate trade considerably. Our total pulpwood turn-over this season will be 15,000 cords. In our opinion, pulpwood will be in good demand in northern Ontario toward the end of the coming summer. Numerous buyers from the United States are in the country at present."

From the Magnetewan district one man writes,—"The local trade here was fair. Do not think the outlook for 1922 is any better. Don't expect to ship half our stock this coming season."

Another dealer not many miles away says that trade is encouraging and good business in sight for spring.

Another opines,—"I think there will be a fair demand for lumber in the spring but do not expect a very big advance in price."

From North Bay comes word that the 1922 cut will cost 30% less than that of 1921. "The market is opening up well with more inquiries in the last thirty days for hardwood than in the six months previous. The hardwood cut for 1922 will not be 50% of what it was in 1921."

In the same section another operator declares,—"We look for a small advance on low-grade lumber, hemlock and spruce. We think the better grades of white pine will remain firm and that with lower sawing costs, together with much reduced logging outlay, lumbermen should make a fair profit during the coming year. Our logging bill does not exceed 40% of last year's."

From Bracebridge comes word from one millman that there is going to be a shortage

Champion Wood Choppers of the World

Messrs. Jackson and MacQueen, of Australia, who have established the fastest record in the world at tree chopping. The photograph shows these felling oaks and poplars on the estate of the Marquis of Salisbury, at Hatfield, England. Some of the trees were over one hundred feet high and six feet in girth. They were cut down to have than three minutes each and logs sawn in fifteen seconds.

# "A Long Pull and a Strong Pull"

The past year was a trying one in the lumber industry owing to industrial inactivity, falling prices and diminished demand both at home and abroad. Many stocks of high-priced lumber were carried on which a loss had to be taken by manufacturers and wholesalers as the cost of replacement could not be realized. As the holders of this high-priced material endeavored to move it, they realized how thoroughly all branches of trade and manufacture were demoralized.

About September signs of considerable improvement set in. A better feeling was evidenced, confidence began to reassert itself and the outlook brightened. While the volume of trade did not perceptibly increase, still prices were firmer, there was less bickering regarding quotations and it was felt that the values, so long receding had touched rock bottom.

What the trade particularly desires to-day is a reasonable profit and a stabilized situation. The corner has been turned and things now appear headed in the right direction, although they are a long way from being normal. The cut during the present winter will be only about half of what it was last season, and lumbermen desire that there shall be no runaway market or the fictitious conditions which characterized the trade in the early part of 1920 when things ran riot and all sense of values were shattered. The reaction has been great and longer than many expected, but apparently the worst is now over. Brighter days are in store, although no one expects that 1922 will be a boom year. It should, however, prove to be one of larger volume and sounder values than that which has just closed.

Although one does not care to figure in the role of a prophet, it is believed that we cannot look for a speedy recovery. On the other hand it will be gradual and perhaps unnoticed. There will be periods of alternate rise and fall in the price of commodities, and it may be for some time yet before conditions anywhere stable are reached. Much depends upon the attitude of labor and its willingness to share in the responsibility and readjustment.

Until such times as the various trades awaken and realize that they must do their bit in the way of longer hours and efficient work, the building revival, which is so urgently needed, may be delayed.

It is believed that the liquidation of prices in structural materials is about over, and after many months of the decreasing price levels and diminishing requisitions, owing to industrial and other conditions, it is hoped that 1922 will witness a satisfactory solution of many of the problems and difficulties which we in the lumber business have had to face and overcome during 1921.

As pointed out, few things will tend to hasten the return to better times than the building industry. Things used in the erection of dwelling houses call upon practically all industries of the country for their products, and a general and far-reaching construction programme in Canada during 1922 is the best possible harbinger of a return to more prosperous times.

---

of hemlock and hardwood, and prices may go up in these two lines before the next stocks are dry and ready for shipment.

"Our volume of trade in 1921 was less than 1920, and 1921 showed no profits at all. Prices for the entire year of 1921 averaged in the neighborhood of 30% less than in 1920, but the decrease during the latter portion of the year was much greater. Our stocks at the close of 1921 were slightly greater than 1920. Trade with the United States was much less in volume and receipts than the preceding year showed. It is our present expectation that our log output this winter will be about 50% less than last. We are hopeful that the lumber trade will show a gradual improvement beginning in the early Spring," concludes a big producer in the district of Kenora.

A firm in the Parry Sound district say "We are bound to lose money on our 1921 cut for this reason as wages and supplies were so high in the fall of 1920 in this district. We appear to be getting back to normal times once more and are looking forward to better conditions this coming season.

From Pakesley is wafted the advice that logging is 40% lower than last year; that the trade outlook is fair while the log output will be 30, per cent greater.

In Algoma district one lumberman says "The cost of logging is only about 50 per cent of last year. The market shows more activity and prices low."

A Huntsville operator remarks—"The cost of production will be one-third less than that of a year ago and 50 per cent higher than pre-war costs. The market will be higher than for 1921."

Another producer in the same locality adds "In operating costs, wages are down but there is not a great deal of business in provisions and horse feed. Men are working better, however, and staying on the job. Market conditions seem to be improving, especially for the better grades. Demand for low end lumber is fair."

A dozen opinions taken at random from trade outlooks, contain the following:—

"We look for an improvement during the latter half of the year." "We expect a nice healthy business." "Trade prospects none too good." "Good," "Better," Improvement erratic but greater than in 1921," "Brighter," "Fair," "Seems to be looking up," "Better," "Can be worse," "Dull," "Should be fair," "Too early to state;" "Expect to see upper ends hold up; lower ends still slack in price." "Doubtful," "Should be better;" "Demand promises good as prices are very low with cost of production in 1921." And thus the diversity of views holds sway.

A Matheson manufacturer says that he did not take out any saw logs last year but cut some 15000 cords of spruce pulpwood. He adds,—"We are not taking out any saw log timber this winter but are cutting 30,000 railway ties for the James Bay extension of the T. & N. O. Railway. We look for pulpwood business to pick up."

"We operated a new mill part of last season, hence our cut shows an increase," reports an old-established Algoma concern. "The operating costs reached the peak during the logging season of 1920-21. They have dropped this year but are still 25 per cent above normal pre-war times. The efficiency of the men is improving but it is not up to what it was before the war."

Around Haileybury it is reported that the cost of logs this year will be lower and the cost of sawing and piling about the same as last year. There is likely to be a fairly steady demand with prices about the same as they are now.

A Fort Frances firm believes that the lower cost of production is mainly due to a reduction in prices of supplies and woods. From the fall of 1920-21 the market dropped considerably but the present trend is upward.

A Parry Sound sawmiller says, "We think if lumber stays at present prices and wages remain the same, it will give the lumberman a fair chance to operate at a profit, more so than when wages ran from $80 to $100 a month and board. The lumbermen could not sell their stock, even at the big prices, and make money.

Here is a Muskoka district opinion of interest,—"1921 stock cost considerably less than that of 1920 to produce. Present market values are too low to make much margin on the same. We have nearly all of 1921 stock unsold and one-third of 1920 on hand, which was sold a year ago."

In the Sudbury district one manufacturer asserts, "Present market price for spruce and jack pine is less than the cost of production. We are making a fair profit on white pine."

So many firms and wholesalers insist on buying nothing but No. 1 common and better that they have cleaned out a lot of the best stocks in our district and left so much of No. 2 and 3 common on the millmen's hands that a lot of us are not going to operate till the wholesaler gets in a position where he will take No. 2 common and better in our hardwoods. We notice from some of the inquiries that they are now asking for No.2 common and better. We cannot see but that trade is going to be much ahead of last year," declares a central Ontario hardwood producer.

A Frontenac county lumberman observes "We believe that market conditions are shaping so that we will find a great shortage, and prices will advance beyond a reasonable price. 60 per cent of our output is hardwood."

A Halton county company say, "Owing to very little snow, we had to truck the greater part of our logs to the mill, thereby increasing the production costs very materially. Our stuff was also slower in getting on the market with the result that we had to take a lower price. This year our stock of logs is all in the yard and the woods are cleaned up so that costs should be a lot below those of last year."

# Log Production in New Brunswick Greatly Restricted This Season Owing to Limited Demand

Buctouche, N. B.—There is a light cut for next summer but the stock on hand will have to be moved so there will be no shortage in our estimation. As to probable prices, this depends on what dumping the British Admiralty and capital does. Lumber can be produced and manufactured for about 50% of 1920 prices.

Another firm says,—We have all faith in the United States market, holding if lumbermen hold together and do not try to force the market, as an overstocked market has no stimulating effect on prices.

Hillsboro, N. B.—Our usual cut of lumber is about 1,000,000 feet annually. On account of the cost of operation being so high in in 1921, we made no cut. The prospects not looking good for 1922, we also made no cut. The cost of cutting and delivering on cars this year is $12.00 per M compared with $18.00 in 1921.

In 1921 we had, on account of the poor prospects of sale, almost stopped our lumber operations and only cut 400,000 feet, which we have on hand. We are now cutting 400,000 feet costing at the mill about $14.00 as compared with $20,000 in 1921 for logs. Our usual cut when prices are fair is about 3,000,000 feet annually.

Jacquet River, N. B.—Owing to the general depression and the attitude taken by the New Brunswick Government in regard to stumpage, there is very little lumber being cut this winter, consequently the supply of labor is greater than the demand, with the result that the prevailing wages are $1.00 per day and board in the woods. With this condition, our costs this winter will not exceed one half of what they were last winter. Our opinion is that demand will be fair this summer, with prices steadier, but not higher, and, considering production costs, the operator will be able to make a little money on the logs he takes out this winter.

Dalhousie, N. B.—The cost of production will be considerably less than the previous year—at least 50% less. We believe that for the first half of the year, at least, the market will be unsettled and low —until a large part of the stock on hand and pressing for sale have been consumed or placed in strong hands.

Chatham, N. B.—Very little being done in the woods in this province and the few rotary mills that are winter sawing are selling stock at what they can get for it, so that this will be largely out of the way by the time the larger mills start sawing.

The lumber on hand here will sell at a loss. 1922 should see business on a firmer footing.

South Nelson, N. B.,— A comparatively small part of stocks held here were moved during 1921, and this at a heavy loss. Stocks are heavy here, both manufactured and round. A large portion of the former is held by the British Government, and until that is out of the way, we do not look for normal or satisfactory business. The cut of logs generally in this district this season will be very light.

Operations in the wood in this district this winter are of a restricted character. The cost of production has been reduced somewhat by a reduction in wages, but the cost of feeds and some kinds of provisions still keeps high. Markets are still dull. We are getting more enquiries but prices are low,—much too low—in view of the fact that our stocks have cost us high. The British Admiralty still hold large stocks here, which if disposed of, would tend greatly to improve the situation.

Doaktown, N. B.,—We are cutting 450,000 feet spoolwood this winter which did not have the slump other lumber products had, so

that the profit from this source is better than in 1921 owing to decreased cost of raw material and manufacture. Although Crown Land stumpage is a little high, greatly reduced labor rates and cost of supplies made it possible for us to get logs to our mill at a safe figure for 1922 cutting. We look for labor 30% under 1921 or 50% of 1920 rates. The market during 1921 showed a gradual decline, but strengthened a little after 1922. Freight rates to U. S. A. points appear to be beyond all reason.

Juniper, N. B.—Production cost is much reduced with exception of transportation charges. We figure $13.00 to pay transportation and bokerage charges whereas in 1914 we figured $6.00. This applies to shipments based on Boston rate of freight.

Blissfield, N. B.,—We think the market looks better than it did at this time last year, but log prices lower.

Charlo Station, N. B.,—The cost of production is much less this year, but owing to large stock of both logs and sawn lumber on hand, it will take two years to work off the expensive stock.

Campbellton, N. B.,—Our cut was considerably smaller than last season and the volume of trade was only about 40% of what it was in 1920. There were no profits on wood goods during 1921 and prices were about 30% less. In regard to trade conditions with the United States, we may say that how low a price you quoted buyers would come back and wanted to know if you would not take less. The output in this district this winter will be only about 2,500,000 feet as compared with 23,809,000 feet of a year ago. We cannot see much better business in 1922 than in 1921. The log costs we would say are about 10% less last winter than they were a year ago, and the cost of sawing andd shipping about 22½%.

Bristol, N. B.,—The situation here was bad in 1920 owing to the absence of cars to carry away the material that had been contracted for. Stocks held over until 1921 were sold at half the original price. The lumbermen in this district were able to come through last year better than was expected by holding over their 1920 cut of logs and sawing them cheaper in 1921 than they would have the year previous, and also by reducing them to lath for which there was an active demand.

Fredericton, N. B.—We believe trade generally will improve. The market was dead most of the year, stocks lower than a year ago and there was a drop in prices of from $15. to $20. per M. We, certainly, did not make any money in our business last year.

Redmonville, N. B.,—We have cut no lumber during the last two years. The stumpage is $5.00 per M feet, and we could only get about $7.00 per M feet. We only have a small block of ground. Probably it will be better for the mills next summer.

St. John, N. B.,—Prices were from 30 to 40% below those of 1920. Stocks are not so heavy. There was a fair trade in the United States but at poor prices. Our log output this winter will only be about half of what it was last year. In our opinion the trade prospect for 1922 is rather slow but sure of improvement.

Another manufacturer states,—"Outlook is fair but prices will stabilize. The cut this winter is only 25% of what it was last winter and on our shipments to the United States we received both low prices and a number of "kicks." There was a drop of about 50% in quotations on lumber when the whole is considered, and our own cut was several million feet less than it was in 1920."

# Quebec Operators Report That Costs Have Taken Big Tumble During Last Few Months

St. Tite, Que.—We believe that the market will be much better in the spring than it is at present.

Shawinigan Falls, Que.,—The cost of production is coming down. There seems to be an increasing demand with prices about stationary or possibly a little higher during the early part of the summer.

Montreal, Que.,—As the mills have logs in the streams to run during next season, over-production will continue and prices may go low next fall. The outlook is, however, steadily improving and confidence is reasserting itself. The export trade will be good, if as advices coming to hand are that general industrial cons are improv-

ing and a business revival cannot be delayed. The corner has evidently been turned and the unemployment problem, acute as it was, is being gradually solved. The political British outlook is , however, far from being a fixety and just how it will affect trade remains to be seen.

Morin Heights, Que.,—We are of the opinion that we will be obliged to accept prices considerably below cost for our 1920 and 1921 cut of lumber, much of which is still in our yards.

Port Daniel East, Que.,—Costs of production this season are much lower; wages in fact lower than they should be to allow the

bushmen and millmen a fair living. The cut in this section will be 50% of normal.

Chandler, Que.,—Conditions are so uncertain that the best is to stand on the fence watching whatever may come, but there seems to be some slight improvements in sight.

Amos, Que.,—Last winter logs cost us $17.70 f.o.b. camps. This winter some camps cost is $7.00 per M feet, Quebec log scale. We lost 40% on the scale of our lumber last year on what we did sell. We don't know what we will get this year yet. Our idea is prices will be about the same as last year, but with a better demand, and not quite so hard on the inspections. In our district last winter 200,000 cords of pulpwood and about 60,000,000 feet of lumber were cut. This winter there will be at the most about 10,000 cords of pulpwood and about 10,000,000 feet of lumber. In 1920 we got for lumber about $39. per M feet, f. o. b. cars, Amos. In 1921 the most we got was $20. per M on cars. Some points of shipment it cost us about $30. f. o. b. cars. We expect United States business will be good in 1922.

Magog, Que.,—The cost of logging here is about 50% of last winter; labor more efficient, but the cost of logging tools, harness and hay is practically the same as in 1920-21. Lumber cannot be produced for less than the market price of today, and this leaves a very small profit.

Restigouche, Que.,—The price is much lower, stocks much larger and very few sales in 1921 characterized the market here last season along with falling demand and few requisitions. The log output this winter will only be about 50% of last year. We look for more demand but at lower prices.

Sherbrooke, Que.,—The horoscope is brighter and stocks are about the same as last year. As to profits, there were none. Prices on the whole were much lower that in 1921.

Bury, Que.,—Prices lower, profits much smaller, volume of trade less, log output about half and prospects fair are the outstanding features of the lumber situation here.

New Richmond, Que.,—Our volume of trade was 65% less than in 1920, and we operated at a heavy loss. Prices realized were only about 40% of those in the previous year. Stocks here are very much heavier than a year ago. Our log output will only be 65% of 1921 which was a reduced cut.

St. Pacome, Que.,—Our cut was several millions less than last year and the volume fell off considerably, while profits were a minus quantity. Stocks are about the same as those of twelve months ago and our log output will be slightly over last winter. It is impossible to tell the market outlook.

Matane, Que.,— The lumber outlook is not encouraging to date and the log output here will be about 25% less than last winter. The stocks are heavier and prices have dropped about 40%. We operated with a deficit last season.

# Nova Scotia Lumbermen Believe Stocks Will Be Low This Fall If Business Ii Normal

Sydney, N. S.,—Production costs have been reduced and labor is more efficient. The outlook is fair. Much will depend on the general building situation and regarding that it is too early to make any definite forecasts.

Newville, N. S.,—As to profits in 1920, there was no such animal. The prices dropped on the average about 15%. Stocks are about 75% less than a year ago. The log production here will be the same as last winter and prospect of business in 1922 is fairly good for ordered stock.

Liverpool, N. S.,—Labor costs are about 40% less than a year ago. Feed for men and animals considerably less on the whole. Some items, such as hay, molasses, sugar and flour still too high. The high cost of transportation is still the biggest handicap we are up against. The price of lumber has been forced down below average production costs and production is greatly curtailed. The stock of lumber in the hands of retailers in United States are evidently greatly depleted. Anything like normal demand must cause higher prices, as only the best situated mills, with low production costs can now afford to operate.

Bear River, N. S.,—we do not look for a boom but regard the future hopefully. Prices are too low. Quantity cut will not be more than 20 to 25% of an average cut,—leaving very little for export as building on a comparatively large scale in United States will absorb practically all the lumber cut in this province.

Halifax, N. S.,—Trade was comparatively quiet during the year and the log cut in the province this winter has been only from 25 to 40% of what it was a year ago. We look for a better demand from the United States as the building prospects are brightening all the while. Nova Scotia lumbermen generally feel that the worst of the depression is over and during 1920 considerable lumber changed hands below the cost of replacement. The export business was very dull, wooden shipbuilding was almost at a standstill and shipping generally at a low ebb. We do not want another runaway market like that of 1920 as the reaction is too great. Carrying charges both by rail and boat must come down as they are far too high at present.

About December of last year the Nova Scotia lumbermen were optimistic and had hopes that 1922 would see prices gradually work back to a remunerative basis. The English market held out the promise of a steady market and prices, and we were expecting to sell what little hardwood and spruce deals we were getting out over there. However, about a month ago, our hopes were very much shattered, when almost over night the English market dropped approximately £5 per standard on both spruce and hardwood. This drop made that market prohibitive, except for small special orders which can yet be obtained for special stuff at lower prices.

The American market from the Nova Scotian standpoint, is not satisfactory. The prices that can be obtained there are almost too low to allow any profit, over and above operating cost and stumpage. I presume the Americans will say that the prices they are paying are high enough, which may be true, but we are penalized by high rail freight rates. The New Brunswick shippers are more fortunate on account of being handier the market than we are.

Regarding production costs, would say that I think what lumber is going out this winter will be handled cheaper than it will any winter in the future. Woodmen's wages are down to pre-war rates, and board is also pretty well down. There is only a small cut being taken out in Nova Scotia this winter, and I do not think the whole cut will amount to over 15 per cent of normal. The most of this new cut has been sold and is being shipped as fast as it is being produced. This will leave only a very small quantity of the new to market. The quantity of old lumber in Nova Scotia is small, so under ordinary circumstances we would expect prices to improve during the year, but as world conditions, etc., keep interfering with markets and prices, one man's guess is about as good as another as to what will be their course.

There is one thing, however, that we feel quite certain about, and that is that you will be able to put all the lumber in your hat, that will be left in Nova Scotia at the end of this year.

The Nova Scotia lumbermen are as a rule, a very optimistic class of men, and it takes a lot to discourage them, but the experience of the last two years is teaching them to be cautious about future cutting.

Should these few rambling remarks be of any use to you, you may publish them. It is sometimes a fact, however, that when one cannot say something good about a situation, it is better to leave it unsaid. It seems to me that this applies to the lumber situation as we see it.

Freight rates are slowly killing our business. This applies not only to rail rates, but to water rates as well. Our Government is a party to a combine which is holding trans Atlantic rates, at least, 35S per standard too high. Comparing the trans Atlantic rates today with the Baltic rates, we should not be paying over 60S or 65S to the British Isles. Further, we have it on unassailable authority, that Upper Canadian shippers are securing rates at 80S per standard as against the 100S which we have to pay. This is decidedly unfair in more ways than one. To begin with, the Upper Canadian lumber is worth considerable more than ours at point of shipment, even considering the extra rail haul, and I think I am safe in saying that their production costs are not very much higher than ours this year.

# "Our Lumber is Now Sold at Less Than Cost"

## Mill Price Will not be Lower Than at Present—Decline in Mountain Product Quotations Over Thirty Per Cent—How Business in East Has Developed

### By A. K. Leitch
#### President of Mountain Manufacturers' Association of British Columbia

A brief review of conditions during the past year would doubtless be of interest. The year 1921 was a most unfortunate one in the lumber industry in fact during the past 18 months or so the lumber industry has gone through a period of falling prices and inactive demand the worst it has experienced for years past. The deflation of lumber prices which was well underway during the later part of 1920 continued throughout the year just closed, the average return during the year droping about $10.00 per thousand being a decline of over 30%.

We recently concluded a very successful meeting at Calgary where many questions of importance were discussed and acted upon. Probably the most important matter dealt with was that of revising our system of grading and sorting lumber. After going thoroughly into the question it was decided that more uniform grades applicable to all markets could be obtained by adopting and using the grading and finished sizes now in use by the Western Pine Manufacturers Association. To establish efficiently the new grades and launch the same on a proper footing our association has arranged to establish a mill inspection service and, as a result of the same, we hope to effect an improvement over the old methods and feel that this will go a long way towards minimising complaints.

While the question of grading rules was being discussed that of standardization of sizes was also considered. The need of more uniformity in the finished sizes of lumber must be apparent to all engaged in the industry and an effort will be made to secure the co-operation of manufacturers and dealers in lumber throughout Canada to attain this end.

We feel that anything we can do towards standardizing finished sizes of lumber would tend to eliminate waste and thereby lower the cost of production at the mills and, at the same time effect a great saving in expense and trouble to the retail dealer through doing away with the necessity of carrying in stock so many different sizes of lumber.

### Present Freight Rates are Excessive

Another question taken up at our meetng was that of lumber freight rates. The question of freight rates is probably the most important one before the public at the present time and, after very careful considering of this subject, the following resolution was passed.

Whereas, the present freight rates are seriously hampering the movement of lumber and greatly increasing cost of lumber to the consumer, thereby discouraging the consumption of same:

And whereas, the present freight rates are out of all proportion to the mill value of common lumber representing approximately 75 per cent. of the mill value on shipments of lumber from the mountain district to prairie points and over 125 per cent. of same on shipments to Eastern Canada:

And whereas, unemployment is rife throughout Canada extending to railroad employees in common with other industrial activity.

And whereas, in the opinioin of this meeting lower freight rates on lumber are most essential to create a revival of trade and industry throughout this country:

And, therefore, be it resolved that the Mountain Lumber Manufacturers' Association in general meeting assembled do hereby urge the transportation companies of Canada to co-operate in stimulating a revival of trade and industry by restoring lumber freight rates at least to the level of rates in effect prior to September 1920.

Copies of this resolution were given to the press and were forwarded to all railways interested. We realize that the railway companies have their own troubles during this period of readjustment, yet it is only right they should bear their share of the deflation which has taken and is continuing to take place in other lines of industry.

### Outlook Difficult to Forecast

As to the future it is exceedingly difficult if not impossible for anyone to predict with any degree of accuracy just what the year 1922 holds for the lumber industry. We do know that a year of deflation is behind us and that we are, at least, a year nearer to more stabilized conditions in all lines of business. There has been no overproduction of lumber during the past year as sales from the principal producing centres have been in excess of the curtailed production. In the Mountain District production during 1921 amounted to approximately 200,000,000 ft. being some 85,000,000 less than for the previous year. Our shipments were about on a par with the production so that there is no material changes in the amount of stock on hand as compared with one year ago.

It might interest you to know that our volume of business with Eastern Canada during the past year amounted to 35,000,000 ft., being an increase of 30% over the previous year. Sales on the prairie market amounted to 54% of the whole, a great contrast to the % formly absorbed by this market. In 1917 the three provinces purchased over 91% of the total shipments from the mountain mills so that during the past 4 years shipments to the prairie market have declined over 37%. We do not hope for much improvement in demand from the prairie provinces during the first six months of this year, but present indications lead us to believe that there are excellent prospects to greatly increase our business in United States and Eastern Canadian markets. A great deal of educational work in the interests of our products has been done in these markets particularly that of Eastern Canada during the past few years and we are now beginning to reap the benefits of this work. We do not anticipate that the mill price of lumber will be any lower than it is at the present time. Lumber is now being sold at less than the cost of production or replacement value, and it should be quite apparent to any one that this condition can not continue indefinitely.

### Looks for no Lower Prices

The cost of production has been decreased by lower wages and some reduction in the cost of supplies but a great many conditions, which enter into the cost of producing lumber and over which the manufacturer has no control, make it impossible for production costs to stabilize at a level much lower than at present.

Some of the conditions are:—

First,—the present high taxes unknown a few years ago are with us to stay.

Second,—the supply of raw material is each year getting further away for transportation facilities and more inaccessible.

Third,—the increased labor cost the result of a higher standard of living among labor generally.

One of the most vital problems at the present time is that of collections and credits. It would seem to me that, while collections must be pressed strongly, that they should not be pressed to the point where they will drive the settler off the land. To my mind, the great need of the country at the present time is to try and give the settler a chance to come back. Credits should be arranged to sufficient extent to allow of the putting in and taking off of crop, but the old idea of indiscriminate credits for expansion should be discontinued.

It seems to be the opinion of a great many leading public men of the day that the only real salvation of our problems is more population of the right kind. I heartily endorse any sane and energetic campaign by the government, or any public body in the country, that has for its object the bringing into the country more and more of the right class of people as settlers.

M. S. Caine, of the Foreman Lumber Co., Prince Rupert, B. C., is logging 1,000,000 feet of white spruce this season and intends erecting a mill next month to convert the logs into lumber. The timber limits of Mr. Caine are located near Foreman, B. C.

# Lumbermen Declare Greatest Retarding Factor of Return to Business Prosperity is High Cost of Transportation

From all parts of Eastern Canada lumbermen gathered in Ottawa on March 7th and presented a strong case before the Railway Commission of Canada in an application to have the carrying charges on lumber restored to what they were prior to the increase that went into effect on September 13th 1920 or, in other words, to have a reduction of 25%.

The case was ably prepared and introduced by R. L. Sargant, of Ottawa, traffic manager of the Canadian Lumbermen's Association, who had collected many interesting statistics on the increase in carrying charges. He contended that the lumbermen were perfectly justified in their application in asking for the reduction as the ratio of operating expenses had been steadily decreasing. If the lumber industry got some relief it would result in more business for the carriers as well as the lumbermen, and have a beneficial effect in turnover, transportation, building operations, etc. Although an application was made to the Board in August last for an order to restore rail rates on lumber to what were prior to September 1920, matters have been delayed for one reason or another until the recent sitting in Ottawa.

Mr. Sargant was given strong support in the presentation of the case by A. E. Clark, of Toronto, who spoke on behalf of the Canadian Lumbermen's Association, W. B. Snowball, of Chatham, N. B., who appeared for the New Brunswick lumbermen, A. C. Manbert, of Toronto, appearing on behalf of the Wholesale Lumber Dealers' Association, Rufus E. Dickie, of Stewiacke, N. S., in the interest of the operators in that province, and J. Fraser Gregory, of St. John, who spoke for the exporters of New Brunswick, and others.

As to whether action will be taken on the application of the lumbermen remains to be seen as naturally the outcome will not be made known for some time. The Board has taken the matter into its consideration and the request for lower freight rates is being opposed by the transportation companies.

The lumbermen who were present during the proceedings in the Dominion Railway Board room were,—A. E. Clark, Toronto; President of the Canadian Lumbermen's Association, Daniel McLachlin, Arnprior; Rufus E. Dickie, Stewiacke, N. S.; Gordon C. Edwards, Ottawa; J. B. Allan (Cox & Co.) Ottawa, Ont.; Louis Bolduc (Louise Lumber Co.) Quebec; A. C. Manbert (Canadian General Lumber Co.) Toronto; D. H. McLennan, Montreal, Que.; Arthur H. Campbell, Montreal, W. T. Mason (Mason, Gordon & Co.) Montreal; J. W. Brankley, president of the New Brunswick Lumbermen's Association, Chatham, N. B.; W. B. Snowball, Chatham, N. B.; J. Fraser Gregory, first vice-president of the Canadian Lumbermen's Association) St. John, N. B.; Hugh A Rose, (Rose McLaurin, Limited) Toronto, Ont.; D. C. Johnston, (Union Lumber Co.) Toronto; Roy Halliday (R. Laidlaw Lumber Co.) Toronto; C. E. Harris (Terry & Gordon Limited) Toronto; A. O. Anderson, (James MacLaren Co., Limited) Buckingham, Que.; P. C. Walker (Shepard & Morse Lumber Co.) Ottawa, Ont.; Grant P. Davidson, Ottawa.; P. J. McGoldrick (Power Lumber Co.) St. Pacome, Que.; W. A. Filion, (E. H. Lemay) Montreal; S. L. Thompson, (Gatineau Co., Limited)Ottawa; J. C. Bartram, Ottawa, Ont.; R. E. Harry, (Rideau Lumber Co.) Ottawa; E. M. Barrett (Barrett Bros.) Ottawa, (former president of the Ontario Retail Lumber Dealers' Association, who represented that body,) G. E. McFarlane, (E. B. Eddy Co.) Hull, Que; Frank Hawkins, secretary, Canadian Lumbermen's Association, Ottawa, Ont.; R. G. Cameron, Ottawa, G. B. VanBlaricom "Canada Lumberman" Toronto, and others.

Those present represented the following bodies who united in their efforts to have the carrying charges reduced,—Canadian Lumbermen's Association, Montreal Lumber Association, New Brunswick Lumbermen's Association, Wholesale Lumber Dealers' Association, and Ontario Retail Lumber Dealers' Association.

Among the railway men sitting inside the circle were,—W. B. Lanigan, freight traffic manager, C. P. R., Montreal; Frank J. Watson, general traffic agent, G. T. R., Montreal; Allistair Fraser, general solicitor C. N. R., Toronto; W. C. Chisholm, solicitor, G. T. R., Montreal. Stewart Brown, Traffic Manager, C.M.A., Toronto; J. K. Smith, Traffic Manager, Montreal Board of Trade; George P. Ruickbie, Traffic Manager, Canadian Pulp & Paper Association, Montreal; R. L. Sargant, Traffic Manager, Canadian Lumbermen's

Association; E. P. Flintoft, Montreal assistant general counsel C. P. R.; J. Clark Reilly, Ottawa executive secretary of the Association of Canadian Building & Construction Industries, and others.

## Mr. Clark Opens Up Argument

A. E. Clark, of Toronto president of the C. L. A. was the first speaker on behalf of the lumber interests, all branches of which he said, were united in the matter of a reduction in the carrying charges of forest products.

Continuing he said "I believe I may state without fear of contradiction, that one of the greatest retarding features of the return to business prosperity is the excessive cost of transportation on basic commodities. Up to a year and a half ago we were enjoying an almost unprecedented period of prosperity in our trade. During those prosperous years the railway companies approached the Railway Commission at various times and secured material advances in rates amounting in all in this eastern territory to something approximating an average of about one hundred per cent. on lumber rates. We at the time opposed the method of flat percentage advances as being the wrong method of handling this matter and also maintained that the advanced rates were excessive. The reason advanced by the railways at the time these various requests were made was to meet the mounting costs of labor and materials and that they were entitled to share in a measure of the country's prosperity.

"Unfortunately for us all that period of activity and prosperous business has come to an end and commodity prices have suffered serious deflation. In our business we have had to suffer heavy losses by these depreciations and our only method of meeting the situation has been to reduce our prices to the lower levels, reorganize our business, seek new agreements with our employees and reduce our costs to the lowest minimum in producing our goods. Were the railway companies to put an equal amount of energy into the reorganization of their internal affairs, that they have put into maintaining and endeavoring to increase their carrying charges to us, I do not think we should have found it necessary to appear before this Board to-day.

"We recognize the fact that certain of our transportation systems are not on a paying basis but that matter lies entirely in the hands of their management. We suggest that a little house-cleaning on their part as most of us have had to do, and releasing the strangle hold they have on us, would help. Reduced rates on basic commodities would soon create a volume of traffic which would get railway equipment back into action and make this machinery of the companies earn something on its heavy investments.

## What Lumber Revival Would Do

"Revival of the lumber producing and construction industries would restore activity to many allied industries and soon create employment for thousands of unemployed. Canada at present is sadly in need of homes. The prices of raw material, such as lumber, are now very close to pre-war levels, but the cost of getting these materials to the centres where they are most needed and consumed is excessive. The timber we now have to manufacture is of a much inferior character to that of earlier years and consequently produces a much greater percentage of low-grade stock which, with the present excessive rates, cannot be marketed at any distance from its point of production. This has, of course, led to a curtailment of production. A mill producing lumber at any considerable distance from seaboard is barred from any export markets as the inland freight is about equal to the ocean carriage.

"The business of manufacturing lumber cannot be localized. We must cut the trees where they grow, neither can we ask our customers to move their factories to the sources of timber supply nor our friends to go up to the woods and build their homes. Rate construction should take these matters into consideration.

"Even prior to the increases lately granted in freight rates we maintain that the charges paid for lumber transportation were excessive. We use principally the cull rolling stock of the railways. We require little terminal facility since both our loading and receiving are largely done on private sidings. Our goods are not perishable and are very seldom claimed against for either shortage or breakage.

"R. L. Sargant, traffic manager of the Canadian Lumbermen's Association, has presented the detailed data on our brief for reduced rates, I hope that you may see wherein it is the duty of the railway companies to assume their share of reorganization of business activities," concluded Mr. Clark.

Mr. Boys—"Have not the dull times in building been brought about by the high rate for money?"

Mr. Clark—"I believe that has had something to do with it but that is not wholly the situation."

Mr. Carvell—"Has anybody figured out what the increased freight rates are on materials used in a house costing, say, $5,000, in any city or town?"

Mr. Clark said that many elements entered into the construction and lumber was only one of the basic commodities in housebuilding.

Mr. Carvell—"If the building situation were not abnormal would the question of freight rates prove a deterrent?"

Mr. Clark—"The demand is now unfavorable and the greater percentage of lumber entering into the ordinary house is low-grade stock which cannot stand a high freight rate. One of our main troubles is there is no localization of the industry. We have to take the product to our customers as we cannot bring them to the mills. We must market all our product each season before we know whether we lose or win."

### Mr. Snowball Recites Many Facts

W. B. Snowball of Chatham, N. B., said the lumbermen felt this was one of the most important matters that could be dealt with in the readjustment of conditions in Canada to-day. He spoke of the far-flung nature of the lumber industry and how many were so vitally concerned in the application for a reduction of the present high freight rates that they travelled hundreds of miles to lay the matter before the Board. The question was one which deserved grave consideration at the hands of the Commission.

"We are," continued Mr. Snowball, "not here in any personal or selfish interest but as patriotic Canadians who feel that something must be done to get us back into more favorable trade conditions and make our country a fit place to live in. We have had nothing but stagnation in the lumber line in New Brunswick during the past year. Mills, which had been in operation for forty-two years in the Maritime Provinces, have been closed down for the first time in their history. The cost of production has also been brought down but the stumpage dues have been increased. In 1914 they were $1.50 per M, but they have advanced from time to time until they reached $5.00 per M in 1919. These dues were a fixed charge. The high price of lumber in 1920 was brought about by the scarcity of the stock and the anxiety of the people to buy. Naturally the cost of producing lumber then went up through the increase in stumpage, wages etc. Since then, however, there has been a radical change and to-day the lumber business was in a very flat state."

Speaking of his own activities, Mr. Snowball said that from 1913 to 1916 the freight rate from Chatham, N. B., to Montreal was 15 cents or $4.50 per M feet on spruce lumber. In 1920 this had been raised to 28½ or $8.55 per M feet. Buyers of lumber had a radical change and to-day the lumber business was in a very flat state. Mr. Snowball expressed the view that the reason railway employees had not accept further reductions in wages was because they were determined to stand back until the railways gave the public some consideration in the matter of reduced carrying charges.

### The Cheapness of Water Haul

Touching upon water communication and its cheapness compared with the present exalted levies of the railways, Mr. Snowball said the "Gaspe Trader" had made three trips during the past season from the Miramichi to Montreal carrying large loads of lumber each time and was in competition with the railroads. The latter could have got the business if they had made a material reduction in cost, but although he had drawn the attention of the management to the situation, nothing had been done. He believed that if rail rates do not come down, water competition would be much keener in the future. Its chief difficulty was that it was limited to a few weeks in the summer, but he believed the railways could obtain much more business if the 40% increase which had been put on to carrying charges in 1920 was all taken off.

The speaker touched upon the importation of laths from the United States into Canada. This had during the morning session been referred to by Mr. Carvell, who enquired why lath in the Maritime Provinces went to Boston and other U. S. cities, when lath from across the border entered Canada. The Chairman was told by Mr. Sargent one of the reasons was that the cheapness of labor in the South.

Mr. Snowball had something to add to this. He declared that apart altogether from the cheaper labor of the south, one reason why lath was imported in the Windsor and Sarnia districts of Ontario was owing to the low freight rate and because there was a scarcity at certain centres due to mills not operating. The carrying charges

to Windsor, Ont., from New Brunswick points were 38 cents, and where railway rates were lowest there the business would go.

In regard to the production of lath down East, he said that they were being sold to-day for $5.00 f. o. b. mill. There was no money in the manufacture at this figure. The lath wood was bought for $5.00 or $6.00 per cord, delivered at the mill and from a cord only 1,850 to 1,950 pieces of lath could be obtained. The cost of the labor for converting this wood into lath, two men being required, would be $2.50 each, and to sell the product at $5.00 per M, left no profit.

### Is the Outlook Getting Better?

Next Mr. Snowball had an interesting exchange of views with the Chairman of the Board. The Chatham lumber manufacturer said that the condition of the lumber trade was the most critical since he had been in business and that dated back to 1882. There was never a period, he added, when he could not sell at a price a quantity of lumber.

Mr. Carvell—"I am not prepared to accept that statement in its entirety. Is it not true that the lumber trade was never as flourishing as a year and a half ago when the boom was on. Did not the bottom start to drop out of the business before the increase in freight rates went into effect or become a factor in the situation and is not the business a little better during the last five or six months?"

Mr. Campbell, Montreal,—"The volume may be better but the price is worse.

Mr. Carvell—"You can sell some lumber to-day whereas you could not do it when the bottom fell out. The question arises, what part has freight rates played in the situation? Is it not true that although the rates were decreased 15% some time ago there was an absolute dulness in the market.

Mr. Snowball went on to tell of the increases in the rates in the East as compared with those in the West. He said on B. C. shipments of lumber to Toronto the rate in 1915 was 67 cents, on September 16th 1920 it jumped to $1.05 and on January 1st 1921 had fallen to $1.03½. In April of the same year, the figure came down to 90 cents and in December last to 88½ cents, where it now stands, making the increase 32% over the rate prevailing in 1915. On shipments from Chatham, N. B., to Toronto, Mr. Snowball declared that between December 1916 and December 1920 the increase had been 65%. Why only 32% increase on lumber shipments from the West against a 65% jump on those from the East? He submitted that the operators in the East deserved equal treatment to those in the West. They had no quarrel with western producers by any means, but the freight handicap with which they were met debarred Maritime Province manufacturers from coming in and competing for business on an even basis. He contended that the lumbermen in the Maritime Provinces had faced enormous obstacles in this respect compared with B. C. producers. He hoped the Board would see its way clear to decrease the carrying tolls on the basic industries of Canada among which lumber was one of the most important. Labor had done its share in order to bring the price of lumber down and had shown its willingness to co-operate in every respect.

### The Interests of the Wholesaler

A. C. Manbert, of Toronto, former Chairman of the Wholesale Lumber Dealers' Association, spoke on behalf of that body. He said that he could subscribe to all that had been set forth by Mr. Clark and Mr. Snowball. The lumbermen approached this matter of freight rates in no contentious spirit as it was mutual in character and related to the commerce and business of the country. The lumbermen and railways could not exist one without the other. Trade was languishing at present, prices have gone down and other changes in costs had been made. The lumbermen were trying to get adjustment on all operating conditions in the industry but were met with the one factor in the situation, the question of railway rates, which were arbitrary and fixed, hence they were appealing to the Board for relief. The only way they had in settling the question was to get back to conditions which had escaped the abnormal relationships of recent times. The major fact was that this was a broad, economic question and we had to get back to the situation which was generally referred to as normal. Lumber was a basic commodity—one of the key industries—and there was every endeavor being made on the part of its exponents to hasten a return to what was called reasonable times.

Mr. Carvell asked Mr. Manbert what would be the increase in the sale of lumber if the Board reduced the freight rates twenty-five per cent?

Mr. Manbert replied that, of course, it would be impossible for him to act definitely, but such action would be in line with the experience and accomplishments of lumber in other avenues and to that extent, benefit the industry. The mind of man ran back intuitively and instinctively to conditions that he called stable. "Lumber is a basic commodity as I have already stated, and we are part of the key industries that are essential to the prosperity and development of Canada. When out of joint the great basic products do

The new forty-ton ground wood pulp plant of the Temiskaming Pulp and Paper Company, near Haileybury, Ont., which will soon start operations

not flow freely into the fields of conversion and use and thus we have what is known as "hard times." If this integer or factor of excessive freight rates on lumber is swept away, we get the freest access to raw materials and hence competition and we, therefore, appeal to the Railway Board to give consideration to the purely contemplative situation as it affects our industry," continued Mr. Manbert.

Commissioner Boys asked if there were any other elements beside freight rates entering into the matter.

### Other Elements in Situation

Mr. Manbert replied that the lumberman had reduced woods wages one half and saw logging supplies had gone down to about the same extent. Milling costs had been lessened about twenty five per cent. In Ontario the wages of labor around the mills had come down from four and four and a half dollars per day to three dollars. The Crown dues in Ontario on pine had been increased from one dollar and a half to two dollars and a half and, in addition to this, there are stumpage charges. Prices were down on the finished product he would say, so far as their own product was concerned, about fifty per cent.

Mr. Carvell—You say that your production costs have come down as far as possible and that the freight rates on lumber from Byng Inlet—your mill location to Toronto—are now sixteen and one half cents whereas they were formerly nine cents on the haul. This would make a difference of about one seventy five or two dollars per thousand feet on lumber. Does this interfere with the sale of your product.

Mr. Manbert—That is one of the elements which enter into it. You know the old story Mr. Chairman, about the inch on the end of a man's nose. We have chased the laborer until he cannot live today, we have driven our salesmen nearly crazy, the banks are pressing us to the limit and now we come to the railways to help us out.

Rufus E. Dickie who spoke for the lumbermen of Nova Scotia said that the previous speakers had covered the ground. "We are somewhat out of the way in the extreme east and have had to get our product down to the lowest milling costs, which are not now more than fifteen to twenty five per cent over what they were before the war." He added, all the limits in Nova Scotia were privately owned. Many bush lots had been bought up during the peak prices when lumber was selling freely. When the slump came this wood had all been cut into lumber and much of this material was on their hands and the lumbermen had to pocket the loss and get whatever they could. "We have got to the bottom in cutting production costs," added Mr. Dickie "and cannot market our lumber up this way owing to the high freight rates."

Commissioner Boys—If we cut the cost of transportation would you be able to find any market for lumber?

Mr. Clark—We are not asking for a reduction to put money into our pockets but as a means of moving the lumber to our customers. If we keep it in our yards we are losing money on it for it is depreciating in value. We want to send the dry lumber out and to start over again.

Mr. Boys—How will this affect the railways?

Mr. Clark—We believe that it will increase their business as well as our own.

### Mr. Gregory Drives Home Some Points

J. Fraser Gregory, of St. John, N. B., was another of the speakers on behalf of a reduction in freight rates. He referred to the fact that the carrying charges on lumber were the same, whether the product consisted of upper or lower ends. Culls had to bear as heavy a transportation toll as first quality spruce. To fix the rate of freight on the value of the product carried might not be a bad scheme after all. Ocean freight rates which still stood at 100 shillings per Standard, were far too high and had resulted in stagnation of export business, in the forest products line. In addition to this, the exporters in the Maritime Provinces had to take their product to a seaport for overseas shipment and the high cost of hauling lumber by rail was one of the deterrent factors in the business of the lumbermen down East. The rail haul and exorbitant ocean freight levies made the marketing of the stock practically prohibitive.

Mr. Gregory asked the Commissioners to remember that the lumber business was different from any other activities in that it required a year or more for the operator to turn over his money. The logs had to be cut in the bush and brought down to the mill and sawn, the stock piled in the yard and dried for a long time before it could be shipped out. The price of boards in the mill yards had been cut to the bone and it must be remembered that the lumber cut this season would have to stay on stick many months before it could be sold. Mr. Gregory said that his firm and many others had not yet cut up all their high-priced logs into planks and deals. He himself had six and a half million feet of logs in pond which had cost him $36.00 per M.

Mr. Carvell here said that a private corporation or company could take advantage of the market at any time and make money when business was good but a public utility like a railway was controlled and could not do so, not being a free lance.

Mr. Gregory continuing, spoke of further difficulties the lumbermen had to face at the present time and said that prices on some lines were practically back to the 1914 figures or earlier.

Mr. Carvell—I understand from the representations made here to-day that the lumber business was never in a worse condition than it is now. What have you to say to the duty of this Board in asking a public utility to come to the rescue of the industry if it entails a loss. How far do you think we should go?

### Labor is Playing the Game Fairly

Mr. Gregory replied that it was not for the lumbermen to say as the decision remained with the Board, but when commodities began to move at a lower rate of freight, the tendency had always been to increase business. Mr. Gregory added that the "peak pay for labor in the mill yard in 1920 was $5.00 per day. Last year it was $4.00 and this year the wages would be $3.00 per day which the men are willing to accept. Some of my men have said 'Mr. Gregory, we are going to do our best to help you out of the hole, and if we see anyone around the yards loafing, we are going to tell you about it.' The attitude of labor at the present time is very fair. Labor is playing its part in the readjustment of conditions," concluded Mr. Gregory.

Mr. Clark—The lumber market to-day is not nearly the same as in normal times and the better grades are being used to the exclusion of the lower. There is also a comparatively small amount of the lumber produced that there is in ordinary years. If there was anything like a normal market I believe there would soon be a scarcity in some kinds of wood.

In further discussion regarding the export situation and the rates prevailing over lines of transportation in the United States, it was stated that in some instances these were lower than those in Canada. Mr. Carvell pointed out that the jurisdiction of the Board extended only over Canadian lines. They had no power in fixing rates over roads outside of the Dominion.

### Railway Men Have Their Innings

W. B. Lanigan, of the C. P. R., Montreal, when asked by the Board what he had to say on behalf of the railways, declared that the lumber business was in the same condition as the common carriers in that they were all feeling the effects of the present stag-

nation. The railway companies' experience had not been different from that of the others and they could not afford any further reduction in rates.

Any increase of business which it had been predicted would result from a lowering of the freight tariff, would only result in a greater loss to the roads if the charges were below those of to-day. He furnished examples in several instances, showing that in hauling cars of lumber from one point to another his road was losing money. In this computation were not included such items as overhead expenses, movement of empty cars, superintendents, etc.—only the actual physical expense of handling. The C. P. R. had its labor costs down to as low a point as they could at the present time and were reducing the other elements to as low a figure as possible.

On a car of lumber shipped, say, from Blind River, Ont. to Montreal, a distance of 547 miles, the car tare would be 35,000 lbs. and the minimum contents of the car 40,000 lbs. The actual revenue on this rate of 24½ cents per 100 lbs. showed a profit of less than $5.00, on this haul not taking into consideration the items already referred to. "Our operating ratio last year," said Mr. Lanigan, "was 17 per cent."

Mr. Clark asked Mr. Lanigan when the C. P. R. started loading its cars of lumber to 40,000 lbs. The average carload was on the basis of 60,000 lbs. Mr. Lanigan—"Well add 50 per cent to the figures I have given you and the result is proportionately the same." Continuing, he said that on a car of lumber shipped from Three Rivers to Toronto, the revenue was $90.00 and the physical cost $81.02—not much profit there.

After furnishing other figures relative to cost of hauling from several other points and showing the small amount earned, Mr. Lanigan said that on a car of lumber 50,000 lbs. minimum haul from Vancouver to Toronto the actual revenue under the present rate per 100 lbs. was $442.50, and the cost was $447.10; or from Vancouver to Montreal the revenue on a car of lumber was $450.00 for freight and the cost of handling was $489.60. Mr. Lanigan inquired, "if you make any advances or reductions, how is the expense going to be met when we are carrying lumber at practically cost to-day?"

Mr. Sargent—Reduce your costs.

Mr. Lanigan rather sarcastically observed—"We will leave that sir to your superior intelligence and judgment."

Mr. Clark—"I submit in spite of the sarcasm of Mr. Lanigan that his figures do not show a loss on hauling lumber in the East. We would like to know how many cars of lumber that his road has carried at the minimum of 40,000 lbs. His figures should be based on 60,000 lbs. to the car.

### Freight Rates Magnified Too Much

Frank W. Watson for the Grand Trunk Railway, declared that the Board should not segregate lumber from other commodities. What observations or references Mr. Sargent had made in his report in regard to the cost of carrying lumber were applicable to commodities in all other lines. The Railways were not sure of any big increase in business if freights were reduced. The trouble was that, in considering the readjustment of industrial conditions and relations, the influence of freight rates on the situation was greatly magnified and other deterrents of business were minimized.

Mr. Watson declared that a brick manufacturer had applied to him some time ago for a certain reduction in carrying charges. When asked what would be the difference in cost on the brick used in building a $25,000 house if the rates were lowered—he had later volunteered the information that it would be only about $50.00, a very small item indeed. Mr. Watson pointed out that was an example of the way freight charges were being held up as a barrier to expansion and revival of industry. There were many other elements to take into consideration. The trend of his argument was that freight rates were being made "the goat," although Mr. Watson did not use this term.

A. Fraser, for the Canadian National Railway, said he had nothing to add to what had been said by Mr. Lanigan and Mr. Watson. The whole question resolved itself into what was a fair and reasonable rate on lumber.

### Will Give the Matter Consideration

This concluded the argument on both sides and Chairman Carvell expressed his appreciation of the way the arguments for a readjustment of freight rates had been presented by the lumbermen and discussed by the railway representatives. With a smile he remarked, Gentlemen we will give the matter consideration. You surely do not expect us to decide today." The hearing which had lasted four hours, was over.

# The Long Lumber Lane May Have Sudden Turn

### By "Prospector"

Each week lumbermen all over the country are looking for an improvement in both demand and price, and being of a hopeful mind, they never lose courage, but month after month goes on and any change that comes, seems to be for less demand and weaker prices, until to-day the demand for lumber as a whole is down as low as it can possibly be, along with prices which are real gift prices. If prices drop any more there won't be any price at all, and all the consumer will have to do is pay the cartage and haul the lumber away.

The real condition to-day of the lumber trade is no demand and no price. The bottom has been reached, and a solid foundation will be steadily placed so that, in a few months, when demand becomes general, prices will react upwards to a level where a possible profit may be expected. No manufacturer can continue in business for any extreme length of time under the present conditions. As a matter of fact they have about reached the end of the road, and, unless conditions change, lumber manufacturers must pass out of business. This condition applies to many commodities, so that a shift can be expected at any time and that for the better.

Both the American and English markets remain extremely dead. The only market now buying a limited amount of good bright, well-sawn deals of broad widths and long average length is Ireland. Even the prices netted are low, 3 x 5 leaving about $22.00, 7 and 8 x 3 $26.00, 9 x 3 $34.00, 11 x 3 $40.00 on wharves St. John. As space on the Irish boats from St. John has been well taken up, very few furl their sales can be effected. Liverpool and Manchester are not taking any deals, only old government stock which is on hand at the docks is being marketed at extreme low prices, some sales of scantling being made at around $12.00 per M.

The stocks belonging to the Government in New Brunswick are being sold around $16.00 for some lots at the shipping centres, and no doubt more sales will be made in the near future until all this stock is out of the road, and consumed by the yards. This feeling of uncertainty will continue for the brokers and manufacturers are always in fear that it will some day be entirely dumped on the market and cause a panic in price and demand. Slowly but surely this stock will be worked off and in a few months it will surely disappear.

Demand for lumber will be slow in some centres while in others it will have a good call. Prices for some time to come will be moderate. Money as yet in Canada is not being offered for mortgages, only a limited amount and at high rates. This will be a factor which will cause a slow reaction in building. Many flats are needed, but money at mortgage is the only remedy with which to purchase goods of any kind. Banks in Canada cannot loan on mortgage, so that money for building must come from loan or trust companies or individuals, and as yet there does not seem to be any disposition on their part to loosen up. Confidence is slowly being felt in trade in general, and with elections in several countries cleaned up, in the next few months trade shall revive.

The mills at St. John, to a limited number may begin operations in April on a reduced wage scale, providing that employees wish to accept; otherwise the plants will remain closed.

Prices for random New Brunswick stock in the American market leave only about $19.00 per M on cars, which is certainly unprofitable business.

Two years ago lumber was selling for 2 x 3, 2 x 4 to 2 x 6 at $44.00 to $45.00, on cars, St. John. To-day the same lumber is impossible to trade for ahead at $18.00 per M, while boards 2 x 8 and up was selling at $50.00 to $55.00 on cars St. John, all with exchange of 15 per cent added. To-day exchange is around 2 per cent, so that one can see the enormous drop which has taken place. Stumpage has not been reduced to any extent. Wages are only 40 per cent less, supplies not over 30 per cent less, in some cases not that much, so contrast the difference and one can guess the results.

# The Record of British Columbia Lumber Production in Statistical Shape

### By H. C. Copeland, Vancouver

H. .C. Copeland, Vancouver, B.C.

In considering the figures relative to the timber industry they may mean much or little according to the interpretation put on them. For instance an able engineering authority of British Columbia estimates that the total stand of timber in the province is 350 billion feet; also that, by growth, the stand is increasing at the rate of six billion feet a year. It would therefore appear that, with the cut around two billion feet, the forests were actually exceeding by growth the amount of the cut.

Let us now consider the views of another engineer. He asks "Out of this 350 billion feet, how much is of the quality and kind and as easily accessible as the timber now being cut." He answers his own question by saying "Likely not more than 100 billion feet." That being the case, and as it takes some hundreds of years to grow the kind of timber we are now cutting, we can begin to see danger ahead. In other words, if the people of this province are to have timber a hundred years from now we must replace what we are taking and not depend upon annual increase by growth.

It is a well known fact that, under the conditions of the war and the pre-reconstruction period, the timber industry has been followed by abnormal conditions, yet some valuable conclusions can be arrived at by the consideration of statistics of the last five years.

| | Tot. in B. F. | Value | Export in B. F. |
|---|---|---|---|
| 1914 | 1,151,902,000 | $ 28,680,000. | 33,190,000. |
| 1915 | 991,780,000 | 29,150,000. | 58,075,000. |
| 1916 | 1,161,750,000 | 35,588,000. | 48,976,000. |
| 1917 | 1,545,482,000 | 48,300,000. | 43,923,000. |
| 1918 | 1,761,184,000 | 54,152,000. | 88,069,000. |
| 1919 | 1,758,389,000 | 70,285,000. | 106,872,000. |
| 1920 | 2,046,409,000 | 92,628,000. | 146,624,000. |
| 1921 | 1,700,000,000 | | 188,671,000. |

| Pulp and Paper | Boxes |
|---|---|
| $ 2,730,000. | |
| 3,200,000. | $ 750,000. |
| 3,590,000. | 1,832,000. |
| 6,915,000. | 1,612,000. |
| 10,517,000. | 1,845,000. |
| 13,554,000. | 2,142,000. |
| 21,012,000. | 3,650,000. |

Taking the export business for the past six years we find the percentage of the total to be;

| | |
|---|---|
| 1916 | 3.7% |
| 1917 | 2.5% |
| 1918 | 5.0% |
| 1919 | 6.2% |
| 1920 | 7.0% |
| 1921 | 11.0% |

As the cut for 1918 and 1919 were practically the same it will be noticed that lumber began to seek an outlet by export immediately following the close of the war. Each year the relative importance of the export trade has increased attaining the figure of 11% the past year, these percentages being based on the total amount of timber scaled in the province, and the export of water borne lumber only.

### Development of Trade with United States

The development of the trade with the United States is of great importance as shown by the following figures.

| | |
|---|---|
| 1916 | 2,565,000 |
| 1917 | No figures given |
| 1918 | 3,013,000 to California |
| 1919 | 5,259,000 Principally to Cal. |
| 1920 | 4,162,000 Principally to Cal. |
| 1921 | 30,712,000 of this 5,431,000 to Atlantic Seaboard and 20,000,000 to California |

The demand from California in 1921 was probably an abnormal one. In fact, the slackening of that trade would indicate that such was the case. However, there will undoubtedly be a good volume of business from that section. What is likely to offer the most interesting opportunities for the development of the export trade is the Atlantic seaboard business. In 1921 5,431,000 was shipped by water from British Columbia to the east coast of the States. During the same period Washington and Oregon shipped 206,000,000 feet to the same section, Washington shipping 161,450,000 and Oregon 44,550,000 feet.

British Columbia should find it easy to secure more than one fortieth of the Atlantic business and the development of facilities for handling will without doubt have a great effect in getting a stronger representation of it.

### Pulp, Paper and Box Business

The pulp and paper and the box business have undergone a rapid development and play an important part in the total timber business of British Columbia. The following table will show the relative importance of these industries :—

| Percentage of total cut | Pulp & Paper | Boxes |
|---|---|---|
| 1916 | 10% | 5.3% |
| 1917 | 14% | 3.3% |
| 1918 | 19.4% | 3.4% |
| 1919 | 17.8% | 3. % |
| 1920 | 23% | 2.8% |

The 1921 figures on these lines are not yet available. It is also noticed that the percentage of boxes in 1916 was unusually large. This was due to war demands. The pulp and paper business shows one of the most consistent developments of any branch of the timber industry. There which doubtless develop a coordination between the lumber loggers and the pulp makers that will utilize to the utmost the waste that now occurs in many of the logging operations.

A comparison of the exports of lumber from Washington and Oregon as to that of British Columbia in reference to the principal markets may also be of interest.

The following figures are from the water borne shipments as given by the Pacific Lumber Inspection Bureau and are substantially complete and accurate :—They are the figures of 1921:—

| Ports | Wash & Ore. | B. C. |
|---|---|---|
| Australia | 38,880,000 | 27,276,000 |
| China | 90,125,000 | 41,790,000 |
| Egypt | | 8,566,000 |
| India & Str. Set | 1,599,000 | 8,429,000 |
| Japan | 325,982,000 | 32,601,000 |
| New Zealand | 3,268,000 | 4,554,000 |
| South America East | 1,053,000 | 23,000 |
| South America West | 51,945,000 | 1,285,000 |
| United K'G &Cst. | 13,558,000 | 13,593,000 |
| Domestic Totals | 1,234,731,000 | 26,712,000 |

Perhaps the last figures are the most illuminating. they cover the shipments to Atlantic Coast, Hawaiian Islands, Philippine Islands, San Francisco Bay, San Pedro Bay (Los Angeles Harbor), California Unclassified. The British Columbia shipments are only 2.2% of those from Oregon and Washington. It is true that these markets are the domestic markets of the States but the above figures indicate the tremendous possibilities as the timber resources of British Columbia and methods of handling are developed to their fullest capacity.

### Australian Exports Fell Down

The British Columbia exports to Australia for 1921 showed a loss of 4,942,000 feet as against 1920: To China, 1921 gave a gain of 26,879,000 over, 1920; Japan a gain of 46,000,000; India and Straits Settlement a gain of 2,809,000 while the United Kingdom and Continent shipments showed a loss in 1921 of 47,624,000 feet as against 1920.

It would be impossible to attempt the analysis of the foregoing figures as to the causes of the fluctuations of the different markets in the space available for this article. However, a study of the figures given will disclose many interesting possibilities. We have given our entire attention in the above to the export conditions attending the British Columbia operations because of the dormant condition of the domestic markets, and the fact that the greater number of the large producing mills are looking to the export trade more and more.

One conclusion that might be drawn is the need to stabilize conditions in the timber arena. This would tend to do away with the unusual and, to a degree at least, unwarranted, fluctuations of volume.

# Northern Ontario and Georgian Bay Output

## Big Decrease in Amount of Lumber Sawn Last Year—Lath Production also Shows Decided Decline—Some Operators Still Have Considerable 1921 Logs on Hand

The annual review of statistics from northern Ontario and Georgian Bay districts tells the story of 1921 production in cold figures, "a period which everyone wishes to forget." The early months of the past year found many operators with high-priced stocks on hand and prices dwindling. Months of deflated quotations ensued in the hope of securing business and holding trade connections until the market righted itself, but it was late in the fall before the decline ceased. As a result, buyers seeing values on the downward path, augmented by large stocks and keen competition, waited for the lowest figure. Even to-day many operators have considerable of last year's cut still on hand. Some mills did not operate at all when they found there were very few requisitions for their 1920 output, and others, who anticipated a better demand last year and made an average cut, were naturally disappointed. The outlook, however, is brightening.

Profits were in the vast majority of cases out of the question and values were about 30 per cent to 50 per cent below those of the "peak period", according to the various estimates given. At the time of the slump, which hit the lumber enterprises early, labor was still demanding top wages, and good bushmen, in fact any kind of labor, were scarce. Operators certainly had their troubles for a while, but wages began to sag, there was a surplus of men and efficiency of the workers became evident on all sides.

The 1921 cut, as everyone knows, was much below that of 1920, which year was characterized by just an average production. Returns from forty operating centres in the Georgian Bay and northern Ontario districts afford a good idea of how the different sections produced last season in comparison with 1920.

In lumber, including soft and hardwoods, the decrease in 1921 was over 104,000,000 feet compared with 1920; doubtless smaller than anticipated viewing the depression that the industry faced at the outset of 1921.

In view of the discouraging nature of the market, the fact that representative producers in Ontario reduced their cut only so far, coupled with the majority predicting 1922 prospects as "fair" goes to show that the manufacturers are hopeful and reasonably sure that the market is moving in the right direction and that the bend in the road has been passed.

The lath market also suffered. The cut in Northern Ontario and the Georgian Bay districts last year was 119,000,000 pieces in comparison with 164,000,000 pieces in 1920, a decrease of 45,000,000 pieces.

The shingle and picket market, in spite of the year's unfavorable showing in the other lines registers an increase of 5,000,000. The principle shingle producting points are Peterboro, Fenelon Falls, Parry Sound, Penetang and Midland.

The following statistics were obtained through the courtesy of the operators in the districts named and the "Canada Lumberman" desires to tender its appreciation for the information.

### Lumber Production

| | 1921 Feet | 1920 Feet |
|---|---|---|
| Bala | 3,000,000 | 3,000,000 |
| Biscotasing | 3,913,000 | 1,370,000 |
| Bracebridge | 5,450,000 | 7,300,000 |
| Byng Inlet | 29,000,000 | 24,000,000 |
| Cache Bay | 18,899,000 | 18,644,000 |
| Cutler | 27,800,000 | 40,084,971 |
| Callander | 27,299,000 | 27,298,000 |
| Fenelon Falls | 3,000,000 | 3,500,000 |
| Field | 6,443,000 | 23,580,000 |
| Foleyet | 4,500,000 | 4,500,000 |
| Fort Frances | 48,000,000 | 75,000,000 |
| Gravenhurst | 7,000,000 | 7,600,000 |
| Haileybury | 3,580,000 | 6,000,000 |
| Huntsville | 11,280,400 | 16,106,610 |
| Jacksonboro | 5,800,000 | 6,700,000 |
| Jarlsberg | 1,500,000 | 3,000,000 |
| Keewatin | 18,694,241 | 23,000,000 |
| Kearney | 1,700,000 | 2,250,000 |
| Latchford | 1,000,000 | 2,500,000 |
| Little Current | 12,521,443 | 11,353,000 |
| Marksville | 1,915,000 | 3,250,000 |
| Marmora | 1,900,000 | 2,100,000 |
| Midland | 23,708,403 | 50,000,000 |
| Milnet | 18,000,000 | 18,000,000 |
| Nesterville | 20,000,000 | 12,000,000 |
| North Bay | 9,874,000 | 8,850,000 |
| Owen Sound | 19,500,000 | 11,500,000 |
| Pakesley | 17,250,000 | 21,750,000 |
| Parry Sound | 7,636,334 | 6,404,481 |
| Penetanguishene | 14,886,676 | 34,500,000 |
| Peterboro | 4,300,000 | 5,300,000 |
| Pine | 3,145,000 | 4,200,000 |
| Port Arthur | 1,943,133 | 5,821,900 |
| Powassan | 5,000,000 | 5,000,000 |
| Sarnia | 10,395,000 | 10,060,000 |
| Sprague | 23,758,000 | 36,000,000 |
| Thessalon | 16,000,000 | 16,000,000 |
| Victoria Harbor | 15,892,133 | 30,371,654 |
| West River | 7,000,000 | 5,000,000 |
| Other Places | 35,060,000 | 35,900,000 |

Total ... 488,253,661 ft. ... 589,657,516 ft.
Decrease == 104,403,855 feet.

### The Lath Output

| | 1921 Pieces | 1920 Pieces |
|---|---|---|
| Biscotasing | 2,945,000 | 550,000 |
| Bracebridge | 1,400,000 | 1,800,000 |
| Byng Inlet | | 7,000,000 |
| Cache Bay | 4,810,000 | 4,510,000 |
| Callander | 10,790,000 | 14,287,000 |
| Fenelon Falls | 1,000,000 | 900,000 |
| Field | 3,935,000 | 1,643,800 |
| Foleyet | 3,000,000 | 3,000,000 |
| Fort Frances | 11,721,300 | 21,543,700 |
| Gravenhurst | 2,163,000 | 3,136,000 |
| Huntsville | 300,000 | 700,000 |
| Jacksonboro | 3,600,000 | 1,900,000 |
| Keewatin | 3,077,120 | 4,516,010 |
| Little Current | 6,163,850 | 5,476,150 |
| Marmora | 100,000 | |
| Midland | 12,024,250 | 12,000,000 |
| Milnet | 9,000,000 | 9,000,000 |
| Nesterville | 4,072,000 | 2,000,000 |
| North Bay | 3,000,000 | 3,600,000 |
| Pakesley | 5,500,000 | 7,000,000 |
| Parry Sound | 4,789,960 | 3,896,660 |
| Penetang | 13,929,100 | 13,789,800 |
| Peterboro | 3,500,000 | 400,000 |
| Pine | 3,878,850 | 2,300,000 |
| Port Arthur | 893,000 | 40,000 |
| Sarnia | 7,773,000 | 6,944,000 |
| Sprague | 13,990,250 | 12,000,000 |
| Thessalon | 7,500,000 | 8,000,000 |
| Victoria Harbor | 7,655,000 | 8,621,000 |
| West River | 5,000,000 | 3,000,000 |
| Other Places | 9,000,000 | 3,000,000 |

Total ... 119,143,610 ... 164,833,320
Decrease == 45,689,710 pieces.

### Next Convention of Retailers in Windsor

It has been decided by the executive of the Ontario Retail Lumber Dealers' Association that the 6th Annual Convention of that body will be held at the New Prince Edward Hotel in Windsor, Ont., on January 24th, 25th and 26th, 1923. Among the speakers who will address the gathering will be Douglas Malloch of Chicago, the widely known lumberman poet. The convention next year will embody many new features including the presence of the ladies and a day for sight-seeing and pleasure in Detroit, for the retail lumbermen of the City of the Straits have announced that they intend to extend a cordial welcome to the Canadian visitors.

It is probable that there will also be an exhibit of building materials, equipment and other accessories of the retail lumber yard and arrangements will be made for a number of firms to have booths for display purposes. J. C. Scofield, the energetic president of the O.R.L.D.A. is a live wire of the industry and resides in Windsor. He and secretary Boultbee are already at work making preparations for the great event of next year.

James C. Miller, Owen Sound, recently passed away at his home in that city. Mr. Miller, who in his 70th year, was well-known in the commercial life of Western Ontario, having for 53 years been connected with the woodworking firm of John Harrison & Sons Co., Limited. For the greater part of this time he acted as treasurer. He is survived by his wife and two sons, Victor, of Peace River, district, and W. Harrison Miller, of the Phillips Mfg. Co., of Toronto.

# Looking for Steady Business at Fair Prices

*Montreal Lumber Market Went Through Rather Anxious Period—While Fair Amount of Material*
*Was Sold It Carried With It No Profit and Frequently Loss—Export of Forest Products from the*
*Commercial Metropolis Was Small—Pulpwood Demand Fell Off as All Mills Were Well Supplied*
*—Cost of Production Now Low and Conditions Point More to Stabilization in Output and Values.*

The Montreal lumber market in 1921 was disappointing, and thus by the nature of events any review of the year must be written in a more or less sombre vein. However optimistically inclined one may be, the facts have to be recognized; these do not warrant a rose coloured view of the situation in 1921, neither do they call for gloomy prophecies as to the immediate future. On the contrary, the fact that business failures were practically nil is indicative of the strong financial position of the lumber trade as a whole. There were certain redeeming features, but unfortunately they were not sufficiently numerous to counterbalance the unfavorable circumstances. It was a difficult and anxious period which required all the ability and patience of manufacturers, wholesalers and retailers to keep things running. They were not found wanting.

### Some Features of the Year

The year was characterized by an almost continuous decline in prices, which at the end of the period showed substantial reductions as compared with values when the year opened. The losses were due, mainly, to liquidation of stocks purchased at high prices—liquidation forced in many instances in order to secure money to meet bank and other obligations.

In the aggregate a fair amount of lumber was sold, but in a buyers' market of this description demand has little effect on prices, especially at a time when wholesalers were underselling one another in order to secure ready money. The position as compared with the boom days was reversed. Then buyers were willing to pay exceptionally high prices to obtain lumber; last year, for at least a portion of the period, sellers were disposing of stocks for almost any price they could get. The result was, of course, serious losses. The lumber trade was in no worse condition than others, in some respects it was better off. The period of readjustment naturally involved writing down values to meet the new conditions. These manufacturers and wholesalers who heeded the warning of the previous fall and who adopted the policy of liquidating during the early months were more fortunate than those who believed that the market would recover and held on to their stocks. It did not recover—on the contrary the movement was the other way, with the result that quotations showed a gradual but certain decline as the months went on.

### Disposing of Surplus Spruce

Manufacturers, particularly of spruce, found it difficult to sell during the days when wholesalers were liquidating, but later were able to dispose of fair amounts at prices which left little or no margin. Wholesalers who held only small stocks were thus able to secure lumber at comparatively low rates and were in a position, especially in the fall, to make some profit. Pine held up more strongly than spruce, due to the policy of the Ottawa Valley manufacturers of maintaining quotations as high as possible.

In considering the factors which influenced the market, the slackness in general trade must not be overlooked. Large consumers of lumber, such as the industrial and railway companies, bought very sparingly, depending as far as possible, upon the reserve stocks.

Hardwoods, which soared to such tremendous heights, reacted more sharply than soft woods. Buying was very slow, owing to the dullness in the trades which are the chief customers for these grades, and which are more or less in the luxury class.

The American demand was not any too good; although in the fall it improved a little. On the whole the call for B. C. products was fair. The lull in shipbuilding adversely affected the timber business. Two cargoes arrived in the St. Lawrence via the Panama Canal, these being consigned to a Montreal firm of wholesalers. The competition for orders for Western stocks was keen and some low prices were taken.

### The Local Position in Brief

Local retailers were not extensive buyers. Their policy was as a rule, to purchase only such lumber as they needed for immediate wants. The position was so uncertain that they preferred to have low stocks and to buy as required rather than run the risk of stocking up and later finding values on a lower basis. The market-

ing of a large block of what was formerly British Government spruce proved an unfavorable factor for a time, as it intensified competition at a period when there were large offerings. Building was moderately brisk, but wholesalers and retailers had to meet the competition of certain manufacturers who offered stocks direct to the contractors at low prices. The Montreal Building permits totalled $21,381,273, an increase of $7,313,664 over 1920, while those in the outlying municipalities also showed substantial gains. The bulk of the work was in the form of residences, apartment houses, and flats, the need for which is as acute as ever. The indications are for a still more active season this year. Costs are down to a point where construction is now more profitable than it was, and the loan companies are not holding the purse strings as tight as they did a year ago. Local sash and door factories were fairly well employed, partly owing to contracts for work outside the city.

### Labor Costs Lower

The cut in 1920-21 was comparatively small. Prices of camp supplies and of labor remained high, the downward movement in commodities and in help not having made themselves felt to any extent. Woods operations in 1921-22 in the Province of Quebec are also on a small scale, with labor plentiful at about thirty dollars per month, a considerable reduction over the preceding year.

Manufacturers with old logs will have to take a loss on them, but will probably be able to make a reasonable profit on this year's cut. The outlook in Montreal may be described as satisfactory—nothing in the way of a runaway market, but rather that of a steady business with prices a little higher.

### Pulpwood Dull and Depressed

The past year was a lean period for the farmers who cut pulpwood and for the dealers in that commodity. Although Canadian pulp and paper mills supplement their supplies from outside sources, the chief customers are the U. S. mills, and the great decline in exports to that country illustrate the comparative paucity of their purchases. The position is this: Canadian and U. S. mills have tremendous stocks on hand, which were purchased at very stiff prices, and in the belief that the boom in pulp and paper would continue. As everybody knows, the market fell away and the companies thus have very large wood piles, which cost very large sums. Under these circumstances, they did not require to purchase their usual supplies and the price materially declined. The large pulp and paper companies have written off substantial sums to bring down the value of their pulpwood to something like replacement values, and two or three have cut considerable quantities this year, at a low rate, in order to average the cost of their piles. Until the size of these have been reduced, prices are not likely to improve.

### A Fall in Exports

The exports for the past season—39,272,000 feet—were the lowest, with one exception, in the history of the port of Montreal. The exception was in 1917, when 30,303,737 feet were exported, the small total that year being due to the restricted amount of shipping space allowed by the Government. As compared with 1920, the past year showed a decline of 70,083,497 feet. The loss in trade was owing to heavy stocks in the U. K., a sluggish demand, low prices, and competition by the Scandinavian countries and the Baltic States. The competition was very sharp, and in face of cheaper shipping rates and a favorable exchange Canada was unable to meet the offers of her trade rivals. During the early months of the season, our exporters sent very little, and it was only when business in the U. K. picked up that they were able to ship any quantity of lumber. As it was, some firms who ordinarily send large quantities shipped only a few standards, preferring to remain idle rather than lose money on consignments. The shipping rate was one hundred shillings per standard compared with three hundred shillings in the early part of 1921 and two hundred shillings in fall of that year. According to British advices there is likely to be considerable diminution in low priced stocks sent to the U. K. by European countries during the current year, thus improving the outlook for Canadian products. The following are the exports since 1903:

1903 .................................................... 223,468,093

| | |
|---|---:|
| 1904 | 140,972,953 |
| 1905 | 148,649,976 |
| 1906 | 141,672,081 |
| 1907 | 111,819,995 |
| 1908 | 108,186,777 |
| 1909 | 110,006,619 |
| 1910 | 109,076,506 |
| 1911 | 93,871,940 |
| 1912 | 101,400,869 |
| 1913 | 97,890,047 |
| 1914 | 66,423,321 |
| 1915 | 98,121,864 |
| 1916 | 95,978,013 |
| 1917 | 90,808,727 |
| 1918 | 58,441,373 |
| 1919 | 144,375,182 |
| 1920 | 109,355,497 |
| 1921 | 99,879,000 |

The pulp industry is not strictly within the lumbering fields, but it has some interest to our readers in that many of the large pulp and paper companies are manufacturers of lumber for the do-

mestic, British and American markets. Those companies, which experienced a period of boom, shared in the general reaction. They depend to a large extent upon foreign business for pulp and paper, and naturally this showed a substantial decline, both in volume and in prices. European countries were competitors and were able to offer pulp and paper at quotations which were below those of Canadian mills, a favourable exchange and cheap water transportation being important factors in this connection. There were additions to the equipment of several mills, increasing the capacity; it is doubtful, however, if any of the mills worked up to the maximum production during the year. Some other projects were held up. The cost of production was considerably reduced, but not in relation to the lower prices of the products. There is every indication that the present year will be a more active and prosperous period than 1921, as although prices show a very substantial decline as compared with the peak period, they have recovered somewhat from the lowest ruling last year.

## Retail Lumbermen Will Charter Big Steamer for Five Days

President J. C. Scofield of the Ontario Retail Lumber Dealers' Association was in Toronto recently in conference with Secretary Boultbee and many matters of importance were considered. Mr. Scofield had an interview with L. H. Richards of Sarnia, Chairman of the Excursion Committee, who has made some happy suggestions regarding the change of route for the annual outing which will take place in June. Instead of taking the boat for Duluth as originally proposed, an offer has been made by the Northern Navigation Company to place the "Huronic" at the disposal of the party. The retailers will charter the boat and will leave Windsor and Sarnia on Friday, June 23rd and the steamer will arrive on Friday night at St. Mary's River and on Saturday morning, June 24th, will proceed up the River to the Canadian Soo where a warm welcome will be extended to the party. Several lumber yards will be visited and also the big plant of the Spanish River Pulp and Paper Mills.

On Saturday night the excursionists will again board the craft and sail down the North Channel passing Little Current, Blind River, Spragge, Cutler and other points and it is probable that part of Sunday will be spent at either Thessalon or Killarney. The sail down the inside channel will be a delightful one and the staff of the

Northern Navigation steamer have promised to give the members of the party a meal on the rocks. Other interesting events will come off, after which the "Huronic" will resume her trip, sailing down Georgian Bay to Midland, where Monday, June 26th will be spent. After spending several hours in that enterprising saw-mill town, the party will depart and enjoy another long sail to Sarnia, reaching there on Tuesday afternoon, June 27th.

The entire cost of the trip including meals on board the boat, will be fifty dollars and the O.R.D.L.A. has to guarantee 150 members. It is probable that the Michigan Retail Lumber Dealers' Association will join with their brethren from Ontario in this enjoyable excursion. The Michigan men intended to make the journey last year but delayed it until too late and they are planning, with President Scofield, to have a union outing from June 23rd until June 27th, on board the Huronic that will in every way be memorable, and profitable. It is expected that practically all the retail lumbermen will be accompanied by their wives or daughters. L. H. Richards, chairman of the Excursion Committee has associated with him the presidents and secretaries of the various district bodies and says that this year's trip will be the greatest ever.

## Mr. Barnjum Shows Practical Interest in Forestry Methods

There has been so much fruitless discussion regarding the conservation of our remaining wood supply, and reforestation, and so little actually accomplished, and the situation is so alarming, owing to the tremendous devastation by the spruce bud worm and forest fires, that I am moved by the urgency of the situation to make the following offers, applying in the provinces of Nova Scotia, New Brunswick and Quebec, says Frank J. D. Barnjum, of Annapolis Royal N. S.

### Open to Any Citizen of Canada

A prize of $1,000.00 divided as follows:—$500.00 first prize: $250.00 second prize—150.00 third prize and $100.00 fourth prize for the best essay on the regulation of the Forest Fire menace, with suggestions for the enactment of laws for the prevention of the same or for any other methods for the protection and retention of our home grown forests for our home industries, Judges to be the two Provincial Foresters of Quebec and New Brunswick, the Dean of the Faculty of Forestry of the University of Toronto, and the Director of the Dominion Forestry Branch; essays to be mailed to my address on or before June 1st, 1922, prizes to be awarded and paid July15th, 1922. For the help and information of those who are not familiar with this particular subject, I will mail my bulletins on conservation free on application.

### Nova Scotia

$250.00 for the best municipal or town forest plantation, plantations to be made this spring and prizes to be awarded September 15th, 1922, the judges to be the Commissioner of Crown Lands of Nova Scotia and Professor M. Cumming of Truro.

$250.00 to the Chief Fire Ranger whose district shows the most efficient organization and best results, and showing proportionately the least fire loss as determined by his activity in fire fighting, and application of the best preventative methods, the prize to be awarded and paid on the 30th day of November, 1922, and the judge to be the Commissioner of Crown Lands of Nova Scotia.

A cash bonus of $2.00 per acre to the farmers of Nova Scotia for every acre of spruce of pine seedlings planted by them on their farms, the coming spring of 1922, no one farmer to be paid a bonus on more than 100 acres, so as to distribute the plantings as widely as possible over the province. Location and method of planting must be approved by Government Forester of Nova Scotia if one is appointed, otherwise, by Mr. Barnjum's Forester, to insure satisfactory results.

### New Brunswick

$250.00 for the best municipal or town forest plantation, planting to be done this spring and prize to be awarded September 15th, 1922, the Judges to be the Minister of Lands and Forests of New Brunswick, the Professor of Forestry, University of New Brunswick, and the Provincial Forester, of New Brunswick.

$250.00 to the Chief Fire Ranger whose district shows the most efficient organization and best results, and showing proportionately the least fire loss as determined by his activity in fire fighting, and by the application of the best preventative methods, the Judge to be the Provincial Forester for the Province of New Brunswick, prize to be awarded and paid on November 30th, 1922.

### Quebec

$250.00 for the best municipal plantation, planting to be done this spring, and prize to be awarded September 15th, 1922, the Judges to be the Minister of Lands and Forests of Quebec, the Director of the School of Forestry, Laval University, Quebec, the Chief Forester of Quebec.

$250.00 to the Chief or District Fire Ranger whose district shows the most efficient organization and best results and showing proportionately the least fire loss as determined by his activity in fire fighting, and by the application of the best preventative methods, the Judge to be the Chief Forester of Quebec, and prize to be awarded, and paid on November 30th, 1922.

# Manufactures Cheese Boxes from Big Elm Logs

"Since I started business in 1884, I have seen the cost of elm timber increased tenfold," declares Mark Armstrong, manufacturer of rotary cut veneer, Markdale, Ont.

Mr. Armstrong is not only a lumberman but a magistrate whose juridiction covers nearly as wide a territory as his lumber operations, for he administers justice in six townships and three incorporated villages in the county of Grey.

His connection with the lumber industry dates back as far as

An old Ontario winter scene. Sleighloads of logs being hauled to the veneer factory of M. Armstrong, Markdale, Ont.

Mark Armstrong, Markdale, Ont.

1884 when the present business was started under the name of Armstrong Bros. Mark Armstrong was the senior member of the firm and during the last thirteen years has been the sole proprietor. He

says that he does not run what one would call an extensive business, but makes a specialty of cheese box stock of No. 1 quality, getting in his elm logs during the winter and operating his rotary cut veneer factory in the summer. During a good season he has taken out as much as 500,000 feet of logs. These are brought in by teams and also by rail while the finished product is shipped principally in car lots, to different jobbers and box manufacturers throughout Ontario, Quebec and the Maritime Provinces.

Mr. Armstrong has a complete factory fitted with Coe veneer-making equipment, large cement tanks for steaming purposes, travelling crane for handling the logs, drying racks and other requisites. The capacity of his plant is about 4,000 feet of logs per day. The logs seen in the accompanying illustration, which are being drawn by team from a considerable distance out in the country, to Markdale, are soft elm and an average of about 5 feet in diameter.

Mr. Armstrong has always been a public spirited resident of Markdale and is a former reeve of that village. He also served in the council a number of years and was chairman of the public and high school boards. His only son, Flight Lieut. H. M. Armstrong, went overseas and was killed during the great war.

Mr. Armstrong reports that the business outlook is steadily improving and he expects that conditions will show considerable betterment during the coming year.

## New Secretary for Ottawa Bureau

George W. Ewan has been appointed secretary-treasurer of the Ottawa Lumbermen's Credit Bureau. He succeeds H. A. L. Swan, who filled the position for a number of years but last October removed to Nashville, Tenn., where he is now residing. Since Mr. Swan's departure, A. G. Rose, chairman of the Bureau has been acting secretary-treasurer.

Mr. Ewan, the new secretary, was for several years with the Continental Paper Bag Co. and later was a member of the firm of Cameron & Ewan, stock brokers. He has entered upon his new duties with the best wishes of many friends.

## Improved Method of Handling Logs

### By J. S. Innes, Montreal

It occurs to the writer as a result of close observation over a widespread forest area in Eastern Canada, and in the North-Eastern section of the United States, that the Woods Managers in Ontario, Quebec and the Maritime Provinces will soon be making some definite and beneficial changes in their methods of handling their drives.

Up to date, it appears to have been the popular method to dam small creeks and streams and create a landing or dump above the dam, and when the spring freshet came, drive the logs to the main river or lake.

In some cases, this plan may have been satisfactory, but as it seems a generally acknowledged fact that the ice in lakes and large rivers passed down before the ice of creeks and streams, the main force of the freshet on the main river, or the maximum rise of the lake, is lost, or passed down rather, before the operator can get his wood down the stream to the main water. Therefore, the delayed drive, the sweeping of the creek or stream, and the cleaning up of the main water.

Last summer, (in August) I took a trip a short distance up the

St. Maurice River, only as far as Grand Mere, but in that comparatively short distance, I saw a very large quantity of wood stranded. It is true that the St. Maurice and its tributaries had not a heavy freshet last spring, and, never having visited the upper St. Maurice Valley, I do not know about the tributary waters, but I feel safe in the assumption that, had these logs been all dumped on the St. Maurice, or the lakes in its course, no such amount of wood would have been anchored, high and dry, in late August.

And yet, heretofore, the woods operators could not have been considered at fault in their methods. Some of their creeks and streams were probably eight to fourteen miles in length, and as it would have been the height of false economy to haul their logs to the main river or lake by teams, they must, perforce, dump in the most convenient water, flowing in the right direction.

However, a corrective element has arisen; where the horse could not be used to haul a paying quantity to the main water, the logging tractor can be relied upon to do so.

## Shantymen's Christian Association Work

Wm. Henderson, general superintendent of the Shantymen's Christian Association, 15 Toronto St., Toronto, says the work is progressing favorably in all the camps of the various provinces, and the results have been most encouraging. The annual conference of the Association will be held next month, and it is expected that workers will be present from every branch to tell of what has been accomplished in spreading the Gospel tidings in the shanties.

One missionary writing from Quebec says,—"In all the camps I had real good attention. The men were quite interested and asked me to come again. They sent a team and cutter with me for the whole trip."

"No less than seven missionaries have for a season been kept off their fields through sickness either of themselves or those in their homes. It is also desirable that a second boat and two more missionaries should be available for British Columbia."

# The Lumbering Industry of Canada in Statistical Summary

The Dominion Bureau of Statistics, Ottawa, presents an advance report on the Lumbering Industry in Canada for the calendar year 1920 in two sections (a) operations in the woods and (b) mill operations. The number of operating plants in each section is shown by provinces in the following summary for the years, 1919 and 1920.

| | Logging operations | | Sawmill operations | |
|---|---|---|---|---|
| | 1920 | 1919 | 1920 | 1919 |
| Alberta | 16 | | 47 | 34 |
| British Columbia and Yukon | 268 | included | 313 | 259 |
| Manitoba | 16 | in | 40 | 38 |
| New Brunswick | 69 | | 324 | 349 |
| Nova Scotia | 117 | sawmill | 476 | 486 |
| Ontario | 208 | operations | 745 | 852 |
| Prince Edward Island | 1 | in | 53 | 63 |
| Quebec | 225 | 1919 | 1,853 | 1,419 |
| Saskatchewan | 5 | | 27 | 10 |
| Canada | 925 | | 3,481 | 3,610 |

## Production

The total value of production in 1919 under both heads amounted to $222,322,975, of which sawn lumber represented $122,030,653, lath, $2,157,758, shingles, $13,525,625, and other mill products $6,086,715, while forest products during the same year totalled $77,922,224. In 1920 the total value amounted to $311,815,293, comprising sawn lumber valued at $168,368,437, lath at $5,248,879, shingles at $14,695,159, other mill products at $7,496,706 and forest products at $116,006,112, the increased value over 1919 being $89,492,318, or approximately 40 per cent. The values are computed from the selling prices at the mill or point of production.

| Items of Production | Unit of measure | Sawmill Plants Quantity Selling Value | |
|---|---|---|---|
| Sawn lumber, merchant | m.ft.b.m. | 3,795,754 | 148,132,044 |
| Sawn lumber, custom | m.ft.b.m. | 545,901 | 20,225,393 |
| Lath | M | 760,031 | 5,248,879 |
| Shingles | M | 2,855,706 | 14,695,159 |
| Other miscellaneous mill products | | | 7,496,706 |
| TOTAL MILL PRODUCTION | | | 195,909,181 |

| Items of Production | Unit of measure | Forest Production Quantity Selling Value | |
|---|---|---|---|
| Logs cut in year | m.ft. | 2,282,826 | 87,857,209 |
| Timber squared | m.ft. | 46,897 | 1,180,492 |
| Pulpwood | cords. | 1,616,495 | 21,751,961 |
| Shingle and stave bolts | cords. | 225,344 | 995,534 |
| Poles, all kinds | no. | 451,406 | 411,867 |
| Ties, hewn | no. | 3,906,815 | 2,707,281 |
| Posts | no. | 1,468,749 | 148,434 |
| Piling | | | 95,555 |
| Firewood cut for sale | cords | 29,949 | 148,526 |
| Other miscellaneous forest products | | | 646,532 |
| TOTAL FOREST PRODUCTION | | | 116,006,112 |

"Other miscellaneous mill products" includes—

| | |
|---|---|
| Veneer | $1,022,540 |
| Cooperage stock | 818,758 |
| Dressed lumber | 896,580 |
| Ties sawn | 3,978,489 |
| Piling | 54,256 |

| | |
|---|---|
| Mine timbers | 16,316 |
| Poles | 40,974 |
| Posts | 80,947 |
| Slabs and edgings, sold | 835,919 |
| Other miscellaneous mill products | 1,456,947 |

a "Other miscellaneous forest products" includes—

| | |
|---|---|
| Bark for tanning | $ 79,524 |
| Masts and spars | 954 |
| Mine timbers | 119,139 |
| Unspecified forest products | 446,615 |

## Classification of the Products

In the subjoined table will be found a classification of the cut of sawn lumber, lath and shingles by kinds of wood, quantity of the cut and value at the mill.

### Kinds of Wood

| Sawn lumber— | M.H. B.M. Quantity | Selling Value at mill |
|---|---|---|
| Soft wood— | | |
| Spruce | 1,490,098 | 56,089,633 |
| Douglas fir | 901,915 | 34,413,916 |
| White pine | 541,687 | 29,607,605 |
| Hemlock | 319,393 | 11,306,062 |
| Balsam fir | 133,290 | 4,733,598 |
| Cedar | 197,004 | 7,159,963 |
| Red pine | 96,853 | 3,925,008 |
| Jack pine | 81,885 | 3,203,812 |
| Western yellow or Bull pine | 80,575 | 3,899,820 |
| Tamarack or Larch | 73,891 | 2,815,932 |
| Other kinds | 32,449 | 1,263,368 |
| Totals for soft wood | 4,047,742 | 157,417,607 |
| Hardwoods— | | |
| Birch | 93,930 M | 4,367,680 |
| Maple | 57,714 M | 2,513,079 |
| Basswood | 29,428 M | 1,359,478 |
| Elm | 30,458 M | 1,265,721 |
| Birch | 8,494 M | 330,040 |
| Ash | 10,145 M | 422,549 |
| Poplar, all kinds | 13,530 M | 563,659 |
| Oak | 4,797 M | 222,761 |
| Hickory | 165 M | 6,005 |
| Chestnut | 693 M | 33,690 |
| Walnut | 107 M | 6,130 |
| Butternut | 478 M | 19,259 |
| Cherry | 983 M | 40,129 |
| Red alder | 35 M | 1,380 |
| Totals for hardwoods | 254,883 | 10,930,830 |

| Kinds of Wood | Unit | Shingle production Quantity Sell. Val. | | Lath production Quantity Sell. Val. | |
|---|---|---|---|---|---|
| White Pine | M | 8,341 | 48,455 | 143,816 | 1,169,918 |
| Hemlock | M | 5,339 | 33,177 | 97,063 | 658,449 |
| Spruce | M | 55,379 | 969,113 | 359,994 | 3,313,384 |
| Cedar | M | 2,773,392 | 14,284,132 | 49,375 | 341,371 |
| Balsam Fir | M | 7,830 | 34,425 | 3,496 | 27,283 |
| Jack Pine | M | 1,304 | 6,504 | 34,586 | 305,063 |
| Poplar, aspen | M | 432 | 1,611 | .. | .. |
| Poplar, balsam | M | 189 | 526 | .. | .. |
| Poplar, cottonwood | M | 15 | 150 | 13 | 144 |
| Douglas fir | M | 964 | 5,769 | 97,311 | 435,532 |
| Other kinds | M | 2,371 | 12,297 | 16,329 | 99,370 |
| Totals | | 2,855,706 | 14,695,159 | 760,031 | 5,248,879 |

## Lumber Cut, 1920, by Provinces, Kinds of Wood, Quantity and Value

### SOFTWOODS

| Kinds of Wood | CANADA | Alberta | British Columbia | Manitoba | New Brunswick | Nova Scotia | Ontario | P. E. Island | Quebec | Saskatchewan |
|---|---|---|---|---|---|---|---|---|---|---|
| White Pine M. ft. | 541,687 | | 20,100 | | 33,524 | 16,063 | 320,306 | 12 | 61,792 | |
| $ | $29,607,605 | .... | 760,912 | 56,110 | 956,436 | 563,572 | 24,450,177 | 720 | 2,801,786 | 53,268 |
| M. ft. | 1,490,098 | 35,529 | 132,096 | 1,981,396 | 368,103 | 176,715 | 109,766 | 2,493 | 557,018 | 3,034,534 |
| Spruce M. ft. | 56,089,633 | 1,373,869 | 5,185,309 | | 13,329,672 | 6,137,144 | 4,378,501 | 97,635 | 21,757,658 | |
| Douglas Fir M. ft. | 901,915 | | 901,915 | | | | | | | |
| $ | $34,413,916 | .... | 34,413,916 | | | | | | | |
| M. ft. | 319,952 | | 37,227 | | 25,865 | 44,261 | 89,539 | 283 | 72,413 | |
| Hemlock $ | $11,306,062 | .... | 146,173 | | 977,747 | 1,455,461 | 2,836,410 | 10,545 | 2,714,857 | |
| M. ft. | 197,004 | | 144,173 | | 90,145 | 1,601 | 7,891 | 195 | 23,199 | |
| Cedar $ | $7,159,963 | | 5,341,327 | | 715,846 | 51,035 | 359,197 | 7,809 | 894,756 | |
| M. ft. | 133,290 | 875 | 11,384 | 10 | 52,150 | 10,982 | 7,108 | 1,771 | 47,116 | |
| Balsam Fir $ | $4,733,598 | 27,000 | 434,918 | 350 | 1,759,233 | 346,877 | 257,475 | 67,005 | 1,859,740 | |
| M. ft. | 96,853 | | | | 3,243 | 2,803 | 80,511 | 145 | 9,549 | |
| Red Pine $ | $3,925,008 | | | | 101,937 | 93,756 | 3,349,339 | 5,900 | 376,076 | |
| M. ft. | 73,891 | | 49,232 | 350 | 8,593 | 660 | 11,803 | 2 | 2,719 | 628 |
| Tamarack $ | $2,815,932 | 130 | 1,891,524 | 10,140 | 968,965 | 33,760 | 489,995 | 80 | 106,398 | 23,130 |
| M. ft. | 81,885 | 4,092 | 13,537 | 577 | 1,727 | 1,453 | 44,236 | 88 | 15,679 | 396 |
| Jack Pine $ | $3,203,812 | 153,623 | 557,540 | 17,530 | 54,863 | 50,090 | 1,639,715 | 3,430 | 730,025 | 13,907 |
| M. ft. | 80,575 | | 80,575 | | | | | | | |
| Bull Pine $ | $3,899,820 | | 3,899,820 | | | | | | | |
| M. ft. | 32,449 | | 750 | | 4,578 | 163 | 5,046 | 276 | 20,536 | |
| All other kinds | 1,263,368 | | 90,000 | | 101,580 | 4,435 | 295,607 | 11,060 | 880,286 | |
| TOTALS FOR M. ft. | 4,047,742 | 40,500 | 1,441,082 | 56,957 | 509,028 | 254,693 | 875,900 | 5,364 | 810,026 | 54,292 |
| CANADA | $157,417,607 | 1,454,611 | 54,305,298 | 3,009,416 | 19,139,608 | 8,755,130 | 38,265,246 | 204,165 | 22,314,482 | 2,071,551 |

## HARDWOODS

| Kinds of Wood | | CANADA | Alberta | British Columbia | Manitoba | New Brunswick | Nova Scotia | Ontario | P. E. Island | Quebec | Saskatchewan |
|---|---|---|---|---|---|---|---|---|---|---|---|
| Birch | M. ft. | 95,920 | | 34 | 386 | 4,635 | 10,344 | 24,776 | 457 | 55,398 | |
| | $ | 4,297,480 | | 855 | 12,900 | 157,741 | 350,514 | 1,108,389 | 17,860 | 2,619,341 | |
| Maple | M. ft. | 87,714 | | 801 | | 1,642 | 2,978 | 37,012 | 116 | 15,165 | |
| | $ | 2,512,079 | | 31,025 | | 61,780 | 97,880 | 1,560,913 | 4,748 | 755,734 | |
| Basswood | M. ft. | 29,428 | | | | 296 | 35 | 13,835 | 55 | 15,277 | |
| | $ | 1,259,478 | | | | 6,944 | 1,065 | 569,780 | 2,100 | 670,589 | |
| Beech | M. ft. | 8,494 | | | | 27 | 1,872 | 4,531 | 207 | 2,157 | |
| | $ | 330,040 | | | | 1,063 | 54,145 | 175,680 | 9,230 | 89,852 | |
| Elm | M. ft. | 30,458 | | | | 6 | 2,821 | 30,954 | 10 | 5,667 | |
| | $ | 1,265,751 | | | | 183 | 191,050 | 838,940 | 409 | 235,178 | |
| Poplar | M. ft. | 15,530 | 729 | 1,396 | 1,176 | 218 | 354 | 7,352 | 80 | 4,319 | 73 |
| | $ | 563,650 | 25,575 | 55,071 | 36,374 | 6,539 | 10,460 | 261,081 | 3,300 | 161,780 | 3,070 |
| Ash | M. ft. | 10,145 | | | | 3 | 27 | 3,845 | 12 | 6,258 | |
| | $ | 422,549 | | | | 112 | 830 | 151,463 | 480 | 209,664 | |
| Cherry | M. ft. | 983 | | | | | | 155 | | 828 | |
| | $ | 40,139 | | | | | | 6,564 | | 23,575 | |
| Oak | M. ft. | 4,727 | | | | | 163 | 3,564 | 40 | 960 | |
| | $ | 222,701 | | | | | 5,910 | 164,767 | 1,000 | 50,484 | |
| Chestnut | M. ft. | 699 | | | | | | 699 | | | |
| | $ | 33,690 | | | | | | 33,690 | | | |
| Butternut | M. ft. | 478 | | | | | 5 | 51 | | 428 | |
| | $ | 19,259 | | | | | 156 | 2,460 | | 16,643 | |
| Hickory | M. ft. | 165 | | | | | | 155 | | 10 | |
| | $ | 6,605 | | | | | | 6,115 | | 490 | |
| Walnut | M. ft. | 107 | | | | | | 72 | | 25 | |
| | $ | 6,120 | | | | | | 4,640 | | 1,480 | |
| Red Alder | M. ft. | 35 | | 35 | | | | | | | |
| | $ | 1,220 | | 1,220 | | | | | | | |
| TOTALS FOR CANADA | M. ft. | 354,882 | 729 | 2,186 | 1,462 | 6,757 | 19,394 | 117,001 | 977 | 106,396 | 79 |
| | $ | 10,980,830 | 25,575 | 88,771 | 49,174 | 234,518 | 711,854 | 4,884,431 | 39,718 | 4,913,719 | 3,070 |

### Capital Investment

The amount of capital invested in the lumbering industry is given under two heads, (a) forest operations, (b) mill operations for the various items of capital by provinces. The total capital in 1920 amounted to $234,793,646, while in 1919 it stood at $231,203,247, or an increase during the year of $3,590,399.

### Popular Lumberman Becomes Benedict

A scion of an old-established house with a long and honorable record is Mr. Frank Power, Treasurer of Messrs. W. & J. Sharples, Limited, Quebec City, who was united in marriage on March 6th. to Miss Germaine Garneau, daughter of the late Hon. E. B. Garneau. Frank is of the younger generation of lumbermen in the Old Capital

Frank Power, Quebec, P.Q.

on the St. Lawrence and has a host of good friends. He enters upon the matrimonial venture under the most promising circumstances, for the reason that both his own and his bride's family are an integral, if not an indispensable, part of the activities of a particularly charming and hospitable community. Mr. and Mrs. Power sailed from New York on the "Arabic" on March 8th. for the Mediterranean trip.

### Exports at Campbellton Show Decrease

G. C. Woodward, American Consul, Campbellton, N. B., has sent the "Canada Lumberman" an interesting report showing the invoiced exports of forest products to the United States from the Campbellton consular district during the calendar years 1920 and 1921. The consular district at Campbellton includes the agencies at Gaspe, Que., and Bathurst, N. B., and covers the counties of Restigouche and Gloucester in the province of New Brunswick, and Gaspe, Matane and Bonaventure in the province of Quebec.

The statement is as follows:—

| Articles | Unit Qty. | Quantity 1920 | Value 1920 | Quantity 1921 | Value 1921 |
|---|---|---|---|---|---|
| Wood & Products: | | | | | |
| Lath: | M | 36,187 | $ 330,435 | 96,205 | $ 530,871 |
| Lumber: | | | | | |
| 1 Miscellaneous | M | 175 | 8,900 | 37 | 1,579 |
| Pine | M | 1,924 | 78,684 | 1,790 | 64,110 |
| Spruce | M | 46,235 | 1,853,022 | 44,599 | 1,331,054 |
| 2 Miscellaneous | | | | | 723 |
| Poles | pc. | | | 13,711 | 62,967 |
| Pulpwood | cd. | 30,972 | 777,831 | 14,323 | 224,813 |
| Shingles | M | 49,572 | 314,647 | 65,225 | 293,723 |
| Ties | pc. | 141,183 | 137,655 | 35,903 | 36,140 |
| Trees, fir | bdl. | | | 5,695 | 1,655 |
| Woodpulp | lb. | 71,778,000 | 4,270,537 | 22,227,616 | 682,612 |
| Total | | | $7,761,821 | | $3,230,247 |

1-Includes Cedar, hardwood, poplar, etc.
2-Includes Ship's knees, spars, logs, posts, etc.

### Will Test the Strength of Timbers

Announcement is made at the testing laboratories of the Department of Civil Engineering at Columbia University, New York that it would be two months before experiments were completed to determine the strength of Southern yellow pine and Douglas fir timbers available in commercial lumberyards in New York.

The tests are being made under the auspices of the superintendents of building in New York's five boroughs to establish equitable grading rules and working stresses for submission to the Board of Alderman to be considered in connection with recommended revisions of the sections of the Building Code governing timber construction.

The New York Lumber Trade Association, Southern Pine Association, West Coast Lumbermen's Association and National Lumber Manufacturers' Association assisted in selections of specimens.

### Lumber Company Suffers Fire Loss

The offices and finished lumber shed of the Citizens' Lumber Co., at Shaunavon, Sask., were recently destroyed by fire, causing a loss of over $12,000. The blaze originated in the living rooms of Manager Orvik above the office. The fire had made good headway before being discovered.

# Ups and Downs of the Lumber Industry in the Ottawa Valley

## By EVERETT ANDREW

The lumber trade of the Ottawa Valley after emerging from one of, if not the worst year of its history, looks out on 1922 with hope and a large degree of confidence. The trade expects the coming season to be productive of better business, and indications in early March pointed toward a more active market.

Trade in 1921, both from a production and sales end reached the lowest ebb of many years, and while the going out of the business tide caused considerable concern, and incidentally several losses, the belief prevails that the tide is returning and better days are ahead for the lumbering industry.

Lumbermen the world over are gamblers in the nature of their enterprise. They stake their money and assets in one form or another against the forces of nature and take a chance on growth, fires, water conditions, camp and mill costs, labor costs and a variety of unforseen contingencies. Lose, win, or draw the industry persists with a large degree of optimism.

During the last two years public opinion tried to make a football of lumber. Anytime, anybody wanted to kick at something he or she usually singled out the lumberman or the price of lumber. Many are the alleged sins of commission and omission that the lumberman has been supposed to have committed, and chief among them was that the high price of wood goods was directly responsible for the shortage of building, subsequently high rents, and profits to landlords, and the oppression of the ordinary wage earner.

Still not a single municipal or co-operative lumber firm has been established in the Ottawa Valley, not a stick of lumber has been produced by the public; which seems very remarkable, if the immense profits imagined by the public, and voiced by its utterances, actually exist?

Still thousands upon thousands of dollars have been lost in the two years by established lumbering companies, and the heads are not going around whining and pleading with the public to give their losses back to them. The assumption that immense "clean-ups" have been made by lumbermen during the last two years, through the high cost of lumber, is just about as reasonable as an expert poker player expecting to fill a straight flush on a three card draw.

The depression in the lumber trade in 1921 was caused by a lack of demand on the part of the buying public, in Canada, the United States and European Countries. Members of the trade attribute the falling away to a variety of causes, one of which was the ordinary course of depression which history shows has followed periods of undue prosperity occasioned by wars. Another was the entertaining of the belief that lumber sooner or later would have to return to 1912 or 1913 prices.

### Business Spotty During the Year

Let it be said here and now, and the writer has the opinions of many representative lumbermen, that the, days of low cost boards and 2 by 4, 2 by 8 etc. in the Ottawa Valley are just about gone. Lumber may come down a little in price this year, but it is not going to get back to 1912 or 1913 standards. Several manufacturers in the Valley cannot see, even with reduced labor costs and food costs in the camps, where they can produce lumber and make an ordinary profit on a pre-war price basis.

The market in 1921 was characterized by very spotty business, with no one stock or grade being in special demand throughout the year. Trade was poor from the manufacturers end to the retail yards, and thanks to the lessened production which has gone on since 1914, top heavy stocks, or even pre-war stocks were not carried by many firms.

The lack of building and the incentive toward building was really the cause of the depression. This could be traced back to the shortage of money and the high interest rates which had been charged. During the closing period of the year the adverse balance between the United States and Canada got closer together, with the result that the trade entered 1922 with a much more favorable money market.

Labor of all kinds, both in the bush and out of it, was plentiful and wages showed a considerable decrease. Camp supplies also came down in price. Exorbitant freight rates hit the trade harder than perhaps anything else. The general opinion of lumber shippers in the Ottawa Valley was that freight rates were altogether out or reason, and that while the public was complaining about the tall figure for forest products, it took very scant notice of the freight charges and earnings of the railway companies.

The outlook for 1922 is much more favorable than a year ago as to bush operations and building. Carpenters, bricklayers, and stone masons unions have already agreed to accept a cut of five or more cents per hour, and it is altogether probable that other crafts embraced in the building trades council will follow in their footsteps. This year the members of the Ottawa branch of the Canadian Building and Construction Building Industries Association has got away from the former principle of collective bargaining, and are dealing separately with the members of the unions involved. This should help building a great deal, and besides restoring public confidence in building should ultimately work to the advantage of the lumberman, and be a stimulus to the movement of stock.

### All Firms Report No Profits

Stocks in the Ottawa market are fairly heavy with some concerns and decidedly light with others. Reports from companies show that profits during the past year have been considerably less. In fact one company reported that there were no profits in 1921.

The outlook for the woods programme is hopeful of an increased cut as several of the companies in their returns to the "Canada Lumberman" reported that their production would be greater. With labor costs and conditions beginning to right themselves on a sane basis there seems reason why public confidence in building should not be restored.

There was practically little or no business as far as European export was concerned. Bottoms were plentiful, shipping rates were pretty stiff but, notwithstanding this there were very few requisitions from the Old Country for Canadian stocks.

Exports to the United States fell away off and dropped over four million dollars in value.

### Exports From the Ottawa District

The report of the American Consul for the Ottawa district, covering exports to the U. S. during 1921, is as follows;

**Lumber**

|  | 1921 Feet | Value | 1920 Feet | Value |
|---|---|---|---|---|
| Dressed lumber | 6,867,781 | $ 874,099 | 18,456,596 | $ 997,977 |
| Rough lumber | 20,666,306 | $ 1,428,397 | 106,667,976 | 5,319,522 |
| Tongue and grove | | Practically none | 406,855 | 23,228 |
| Total | 27,534,087 | $ 1,802,496 | 127,531,430 | $ 6,340,727 |
| Decrease in feet over 1920 | 99,997,343 | | | |
| Decrease in Value over 1920 | $ 4,538,301 | | | |

**Lath, Pickets and Shingles**

|  | 1921 Pieces | Value | 1920 Pieces | Value |
|---|---|---|---|---|
| Lath | 42,262,000 | $ 358,905 | 3,647,000 | $ 72,041 |
| Pickets | 14,224,000 | 179,091 | 21,270,000 | 228,556 |
| Shingles | 5,519,000 | 27,037 | 2,274,000 | 15,366 |
| Total | 62,005,000 | $ 556,033 | 28,191,000 | $ 315,963 |
| Total increase in pieces over 1920 | 34,614,000 | | | |
| Total decrease in value over 1920 | $ 243,070 | | | |

**Pulpwood, peeled**

|  | 1921 Cords | Value | 1920 Cords | Value |
|---|---|---|---|---|
| Peeled pulpwood | 52,075 | $ 640,490 | 34,144,00 | $ 374,566 |
| Total | 52,075 | $ 640,490 | 34,144,000 | $ 374,566 |
| Total increase in cords over 1920 | 17,893 | | | |
| Total increase in value over 1920 | $ 265,924 | | | |

**Exports for Last Five Seasons**

|  | | Lumber | Lath etc. | Pulpwood |
|---|---|---|---|---|
| Value | 1921 | $ 1,802,496 | $ 558,033 | $ 630,490 |
| Feet, pieces or cords | 1921 | 27,534,087 | 62,005,000 | 52,075 |
| Value | 1920 | $ 6,340,727 | $ 315,963 | $ 374,566 |
| Feet, pieces or cords | 1920 | 127,531,430 | 23,191,000 | 34,144 |
| Value | 1919 | $ 4,631,996 | $ 431,560 | $ 491,863 |
| Feet, pieces or cords | 1919 | 104,750,981 | 104,016,000 | 49,202 |
| Value | 1918 | $ 4,965,463 | $ 157,752 | $ 174,392 |
| Feet, pieces or cords | 1918 | 165,454,448 | 59,308,000 | 17,146 |
| Value | 1917 | $ 3,995,388 | $ 292,528 | $ 33,416 |
| Feet, pieces or cords | 1917 | 148,970,659 | 68,300,000 | 4,847 |

# An Expert Analysis of Your Truck Problems

### By the "MOTORMAN"

Editor, Canada Lumberman,—

An article on "How Live Yardman May Speed Up His Deliveries," which appeared in the January 15th edition of the "Canada Lumberman" appealed to us and we are writing to ask you to assist us in deciding a problem which we have been considering for some time. We are endeavoring to reach a conclusion whether or not to buy a truck, and hope that you may be able to give us some advice or data.

We are located in a town of 3,400 people and there is no sawmill nearer us than 16 miles. We run a general lumber yard and planing mill but have no railway siding on the property. We have to haul all our lumber by horses from the G. T. R. station which is about half a mile from our premises. Perhaps you can tell us whether we should buy a truck and of what size and give us some information on the cost of its operation and maintenance.

Thanking you for any trouble you may take to oblige us along the line indicated, we are

Sincerely yours,

The planing mill man and retail lumber merchant must look around today and conserve his time and energy as never before. The man in the medium-sized town has before him the economic problem of delivery, and it is more acute than that of the city retailer. He must go out more and more into the country, and bring home the business, and not only bring it home but deliver the completed order.

Looking over his hauling problem, we find that in the course of a year he will receive about twenty cars of lumber, lath, shingles and fence posts, also a number of smaller shipments of wall board, nails, prepared roofing, doors, etc. This is, possibly, spread over the months when he is able to handle outside work in comfort and also at a time when contractors and other customers are clamouring insistently for their orders to be delivered. To be able to accommodate them, he has been keeping an extra horse and wagon busy during these months, yet has not found it possible to go out into the surrounding district for new business because he could not give delivery. The farmers could not come for the material, so he really was losing business which he should have had coming to him.

The firm have no competition nearer than sixteen miles, also their yard is half a mile from the railroad siding. Evidently they have no previous experience upon which to figure present requirements, and so must be guided by what others tell them about truck operation in connection with a yard and mill.

They may safely invest in a motor truck but must get one which will be both economical and satisfactory to their business, and for which purpose I would recommend that they obtain a two-ton truck with long wheel base and equip it with a stake body, having racks about three feet high, also a roller at the back, and a closed cab. This equipment will give them a truck which has long enough body space and also would be prepared to handle a load of trim or manufactured material which requires racks to keep it in place, and yet could be used to unload the cars of lumber arriving. They would simply remove the racks for this purpose and utilize the roller to unload at the yard; also, if necessary, they could have a trailer to attach to the truck and thus handle considerably more lumber in the one operation.

Roughly we have outlined what to buy and now it follows that there are only one or two other questions to settle; first of which is, possibly, which shall we buy, and second, what will it cost us to run the truck after purchasing it?

To the first question, we would state that only one answer can be given, namely, buy equipment manufactured by an organization of known stability so that when the truck is in need of adjustment and replacement parts, these will be obtainable, or, in other words, purchase from a manufacturer sufficiently sound financially who will

be in business during the lifetime of the truck; for then a firm can always obtain assistance and service.

Secondly, your costs may be approximated for you, and we append herewith a cost analysis to which we would draw your attention, and will endeavor to explain a few of the items therein.

We have figured an investment of a truck of known quantity and feel that it is much better to do that than on a price basis. Our interest on the investment is figured over a period of six years and is based on a formula as

$$\frac{x \quad 1 \quad I \times C}{x \qquad 2} \text{ when } x \text{ is the number of}$$

years of life estimated for the truck. "I" is the rate of interest and "C" is the capital invested.

You might, in computing your own personal costs, eliminate garage rent as it would possibly be taken care of in your general overhead expenditure.

The items composing running expenses per mile are easily understood and require no other explanation except that, in some instances, the prices of gasoline oil and tires will vary and must be taken care of as they fluctuate.

The daily mileage might be decreased in certain cases and yet will in some occasions be higher than given.

The wage scale will, no doubt, be somewhat lower in the towns than in the cities; yet quite often an extra man is employed which will be an adequate reason for allowing the yearly wage rate to remain as is shown.

From the total operating costs you made, deduct your mileage costs and costs per unit for your deliveries, as, for instance, you might do nothing but unload cars with the truck, in which case your unit mile cost would be per foot or per thousand feet.

The unit mile cost as shown allows for a load of two tons carried

### Analysis Form of Truck Delivery

| | |
|---|---|
| 1. Total Investment (2-ton truck) | $4300 |
| 1. Tire Cost | 300 |
| 8. Investment Less Tire Cost (Amount to be Depreciated) | 4000 |

#### Overhead Expense

| | |
|---|---|
| 4. Interest on Total Investment 7% on Item No. 1 per year | $163 |
| 5. License, per year | 35 |
| 6. Insurance per year | 250 |
| 7. Garage, per year | 100 |
| Total, per year | $548 |
| 8. Total Overhead Cost for Period | $548 |

#### Running Expense

| | | |
|---|---|---|
| 9. Depreciation, 900,000 mile truck life basis | per mile | $.02 |
| 10. Tires, $300.00 for 10,000 mile life | per mile | .03 |
| 11. Fuel, 10 miles per gallon at 8.35 per gallon | per mile | .035 |
| 12. Repairs and Maintenance | per mile | .02 |
| 13. Cylinder Oil 300 mile per gallon and $1.00 per gallon | per mile | .005 |
| 14. Total Running Expense | per mile | $.11 |
| 15. Miles operated per day | | 100 |
| 16. Days operated for year | | 300 |
| 17. Total Miles operated for year | | 30,000 |
| 18. Total Running Expense for year (Item 14 times Item 17) | | $3300.00 |

#### Payroll Expense

| | |
|---|---|
| 19. Driver's Wage per day | $4.00 |
| 20. Driver's Wage for year (Item 19 times, Item 16) | $1200.00 |
| 21. Total Payroll Expense for year | $1200.00 |
| 22. Total Operating Cost for Year, (Sum of Items 8, 18, 21) | $5048.00 |
| 23. Total Operating Cost per Day (Item 22 divided by Item 16) | $16.83 |
| 24. Total Operating Cost Per Mile (Item 22 divided by Item 17) | .1683 |
| 25. Average Round Trips per Day | .10 |
| 26. Average Miles per Round Trip | 10 |
| 27. Average Tonnage per Trip | .4 |
| 28. Average Unit Miles per Trip | 30 |
| 29. Average Unit Miles per Day (Item 28 times Item 25) | 200 |
| 30. Unit Miles for Period (Item 29 times Item 16) | 60000 |
| 31. Cost Per Unit Miles (Item 22 divided by Item 30) | $ 3/5c. |
| | (carrying one ton one mile.) |

The "Canada Lumberman" will be pleased to be of help to any of its subscribers who may daire suggestions or information on any of the following points:

(1) Cost of operation for any size of truck.
(2) Analysis of your truck requirements, or any other points relating to the advantages or advisability of using motor delivery.

# Nearly All Plants Show Lessened Cut

## Comparisons for Seven Years Shows Annually Decreasing Output in Ottawa District —Many Omens that Conditions May Change in Near Future

"The seven good kine are seven years; the seven good ears are seven years; the dream is one."

"And the seven thin and ill favored kine that came up after them are seven years; and the seven empty ears blasted with the east wind shall be seven years of famine."

The forthcoming is the prophecy contained in the book of Genesis and is applicable to the lumbering operations of the mills in the Ottawa Valley, from a production standpoint, the prophecy has been fulfilled and there has resulted, seven years of famine.

Figures, covering operations for 1921, the seventh of the famine years, show a still further decrease in lumber production, as compared with 1920, of over thirty seven million feet.

Lath went down, one million, seven hundred and ten thousand, six hundred and eighty nine pieces, and shingles dropped a little over four million pieces.

The production of the Ottawa Valley plants, with all companies reporting to the "Canada Lumberman" was, lumber 236,660,764 feet; lath 55,041,470 pieces; shingles 25,615,850 pieces.

The seven famine years cover a production period of from 1921 to 1915 inclusive. Available figures show the lumber yield of the Ottawa Valley mills, over the period covered by figures, to have been 2,431,643,388 feet. The total production of lumber in 1915 is shown as 485,096,969 feet, which had it been carried through as a normal production, would have revealed a total of 3,395,678,783 feet. Thus it is evident that an abnormal decrease of 964,035,395 feet, or around two pre-war years', total production, has taken place.

In other words the lumber trade of the Valley, from a productive angle is about two full years behind normal production, due to the conditions brought about by the world war and the depression of business. Truly the scriptural blast of the "east wind" has swept for seven years through the lumber producing and manufacturing industry in the Ottawa Valley, until it has cut the production in half.

The seven year "east wind", however, is apparently about due

to change its direction and begin to shift to or veer from the west. The year 1922 should mark the change of the wind and reports of some companies in regard to 1922 operations show that the famine period is due for a change of location.

Meanwhile the lumber trade of the Ottawa Valley is waiting for the re-appearance of the seven fat and favored kine to come along and pick the full ears. Omens, in 1922, in the financial, real estate, and building circles, tinkle like the good cows are coming home.

The Gatineau Company Limited, with only two of its mills, (Rockland and Hull,) operating was by far the biggest lumber producing organization in the Ottawa Valley during 1921. John R. Booth Ltd., ranked second, but its cut of 23,000,000 ft. of lumber was only a shadow of its 80,000,000-foot production in 1915, when J. R. Booth was the greatest lumber producer in the entire Ottawa district. In the intervening years W. C. Edwards and Co., and in 1920 the Gatineau Co., Ltd. held first place in regard to output.

About the only real surprise furnished in the 1921 returns occurred in the lath arena, where the Gatineau Co., Ltd., at its Rockland plant, produced eighteen million pieces, the greatest lath cut of any Ottawa Valley mill within the last seven years. The former Gilmour and Hughson mill in Hull Que., (now a part of the Gatineau Co., Ltd.,) added another two million lath, making a total of 20,000,000 for this concern without the Ottawa plant operating. The Hawkesbury Lumber Company ranked second with a yield of six million pieces, which equalled its 1920 lath production.

James MacLaren, Buckingham, was the largest producer of shingles in 1921. His mill went well over ten million pieces being an increase of over three million pieces, as compared with 1920. The Gatineau Co., Ltd. was second with a production of six million pieces, which was four million less than its production of 1920.

Production figures covering the last seven years, which are based on returns from the mills and published figures, are as follows:—

### Some Productive Figures Covering Last Seven Years

| | 1921 | 1920 | 1919 | 1918 | 1917 | 1916 | 1915 |
|---|---|---|---|---|---|---|---|
| W. C. Edwards & Co., Ottawa .. Gatineau Co. | | Limited | 60,000,000 | 65,000,000 | 72,000,000 | 40,000,000 | 76,000,000 |
| Gatineau Co. Ltd., Ottawa .......... | none | | W. C. Edwards | | | | |
| Gatineau Co. Ltd., Rockland ........ | 35,000,000 | 80,000,000 | W. C. Edwards | | | | |
| Gatineau Co. Ltd., Hull ........... | 20,000,000 | 17,000,000 | W. C. Edwards | | | | |
| John R. Booth, Co. Ltd., Ottawa ... | 23,000,000 | 48,000,000 | 40,000,000 | 45,000,000 | 50,000,000 | 40,000,000 | 80,000,000 |
| Colonial Lumber Co., Pembroke, Ont., | 20,500,000 | 17,500,000 | 27,000,000 | 28,000,000 | 13,000,000 | 15,500,000 | 25,000,000 |
| Gillies Bros., Braeside, Ontario, .... | 19,000,000 | 8,500,000 | 12,000,000 | 27,300,000 | 28,250,000 | 20,500,000 | 25,500,000 |
| McLachlin Bros., Arnprior, Ontario, | 18,000,000 | 18,000,000 | 27,000,000 | 49,000,000 | 34,000,000 | 26,000,000 | 45,000,000 |
| Hawkesbury Lumber Co., Ottawa, .. | 18,000,000 | 13,000,000 | 15,000,000 | 25,000,000 | 40,000,000 | 33,000,000 | 58,000,000 |
| Pembroke Lumber Co., Pembroke Ont., | 17,000,000 | 22,000,000 | 22,000,000 | 13,000,000 | 25,000,000 | 28,500,000 | 19,000,000 |
| Gilmour & Hughson, Hull, Que., ... Gatineau Co. | | Limited | 20,000,000 | 82,000,000 | 25,000,000 | 19,000,000 | 25,000,000 |
| James Maclaren, Buckingham, Que... | 15,994,000 | 13,682,000 | 20,000,000 | 20,000,000 | 25,700,000 | 26,500,000 | 26,000,000 |
| Riordon Co., Ltd., Calumet and . | | | | | | | |
| Northern mills ................. | 10,466,764 | 6,123,631 | 6,000,350 | 3,500,000 | 6,300,000 | 13,188,687 | 14,982,969 |
| Fassett Lumber Co., Fassett, Que.,.. | 10,000,000 | 14,000,000 | 18,000,000 | 17,600,000 | 17,785,000 | 18,480,000 | 17,904,000 |
| James Davidson's Sons, Ottawa, .... | 6,500,000 | 7,000,000 | 6,000,000 | 7,500,000 | 9,000,000 | 6,000,000 | |
| J. Lumaden, Lumadens Mills, .... | | | | | | 12,000,000 | 15,000,000 |
| Shepard and Morse, Ottawa, ........ | 5,000,000 | 7,000,000 | 8,000,000 | 10,500,000 | 16,355,000 | 12,330,000 | 13,754,000 |
| Petawawa Lumber Co., Petawawa, Ont., | | | | | 3,000,000 | 5,000,000 | 10,000,000 |
| Dennis Canadian Co., Whitney, Ont., | 4,500,000 | 7,200,000 | 4,250,000 | 5,000,000 | 4,600,000 | 7,050,000 | 6,500,000 |
| R. & T. Ritchie, Aylmer, Que., ..... | 3,000,000 | 4,000,000 | 3,000,000 | 5,000,000 | 5,000,000 | | 5,000,000 |
| Smith Bros., Campbell's Bay ...... | 1,500,000 | 2,280,000 | 2,300,000 | 1,600,000 | 1,155,987 | 180,000 | 156,000 |
| Papineauville Lumber Co., | | | | | | | |
| Papineauville, Que., ........ | 1,200,000 | 1,500,000 | 2,000,000 | 1,500,000 | 1,040,000 | 3,600,000 | 5,000,000 |
| Rideau Lumber Co., Ottawa, ........ | D. N. O. | D. N. O. | D. N. O. | D. N. O. | 1,075,000 | | 3,000,000 |
| Fraser Lumber Co., Ottawa, ........ | D. N. O. | D. N. O. | D. N. O. | D. N. O. | D. N. O. | 5,000,000 | |
| St. Lawrence Lmb. & Box Factory, | | | | | | 1,500,000 | |
| Other Places ....... ........ . | 8,000,000 | 18,000,000 | 15,000,000 | 20,000,000 | 30,000,000 | 15,000,000 | 20,000,000 |
| Total. | 235,660,764 | 273,325,631 | 297,950,350 | 359,000,000 | 485,300,987 | 350,906,687 | 485,096,696 |

## Ottawa Valley Lath Production

Returns show that almost as many laths were produced in the Ottawa Valley in 1921 as in 1920. The returns furnish an interesting comparison.

| | 1921 | 1920 |
|---|---|---|
| Gatineau Co., (W. C. Edwards & Co.) | | |
| (Rockland & Hull plants) | 20,000,000 | 17,150,000 |
| J. R. Booth Limited ..................... | 3,000,000 | 4,500,000 |
| Colonial Lumber Co. ..................... | 2,500,000 | 2,300,000 |
| Gillies Bros. ............................ | 600,000 | 2,500,000 |
| McLachlin Bros. ......................... | 3,000,000 | 3,000,000 |

| | 1921 | 1920 |
|---|---|---|
| Hawkesbury Lumber Co. ................... | 6,000,000 | 6,000,000 |
| Pembroke Lumber Co. .................... | 4,000,000 | 6,000,000 |
| James MacLaren ......................... | 3,755,000 | 2,099,000 |
| Riordon Co. ............................. | 3,689,350 | 2,080,259 |
| Fassett Lumber Co. ...................... | 1,087,120 | 1,480,000 |
| James Davidson's Sons ................... | 3,500,000 | 3,000,000 |
| Shepard & Morse Lumber Co. ............. | 1,500,000 | 2,250,000 |
| Dennis-Canadian Co. ..................... | | 1,093,000 |
| R. & T. Ritchie Limited ................. | 3,000,000 | 2,000,000 |
| Smith Bros. ............................. | 300,000 | 100,000 |
| Other places ............................ | 1,000,000 | 1,000,000 |
| Total ............................. | 55,041,470 | 56,752,258 |

The total production in laths in the Ottawa Valley for the last seven years has been as follows:—

| 1921 | 1920 | 1919 | 1918 | 1917 | 1916 | 1915 |
|---|---|---|---|---|---|---|
| 55,041,470 | 56,752,259 | 45,900,000 | 45,184,000 | 74,466,250 | 50,560 | 81,721 |

### Shingle Output on the Decline

The production of shingles showed a falling off of over 4,000,000 during the past year as compared with 1920. The returns are:—

| | 1921 | 1920 |
|---|---|---|
| Gatineau Co. | 6,000,000 | 10,000,000 |
| (Rockland plant) | 1,250,000 | 2,500,000 |
| J. R. Booth Limited | 10,309,000 | 7,048,000 |
| James MacLaren | 2,518,850 | 3,962,750 |

| | 1921 | 1920 |
|---|---|---|
| Riordon Co. | 1,500,000 | 1,250,000 |
| James Davidson's Sons | 2,888,000 | 2,652,000 |
| Dennis-Canadian Co. | | 500,000 |
| R. & T. Ritchie | 150,000 | 200,000 |
| Smith Bros. | 1,000,000 | 1,500,000 |
| Other places | | |
| Total | 25,615,850 | 29,783,750 |

There has been a reduction in the manufacture of shingles to the extent of over 10,000,000 during the last seven years. The records during recent years for the district are as follows:—

| 1921 | 1920 | 1919 | 1918 | 1917 | 1916 | 1915 |
|---|---|---|---|---|---|---|
| 25,615,850 | 29,783,750 | 33,012,000 | 19,268,000 | 21,802,000 | 27,224,750 | 35,993,250 |

# Statement of Exports of Timber Stocks at Quebec

## By "Statistician"

There is published on this page a comparative statistical return of the exports of square timber and lumber from the port and district of Quebec during each of the fiscal years ending March 31st, for the period extending from 1912 to 1921. The statement does not include the shipments from the port during the season of 1921.

### Some of the Details

The table sets forth separately the exports to the United Kingdom and those to other countries and also shows in the square tim-ber line goods of Canadian origin in contrast with those of foreign origin exported at Quebec.

Under the heading of "lumber" all the exports are of domestic origin. It will be noted that, in the last two years, the exports of certain square timbers have been grouped together under the head-ing of "Hardwood," instead of being shown separately, this being due to a change made in the classification at the beginning of the fiscal year 1920.

### SQUARE TIMBER

| Fiscal Year | ASH United Kingdom Domestic Produce | Foreign Produce | BIRCH United Kingdom Domestic Produce | Foreign Produce | Other Countries Domestic Produce | ELM United Kingdom Domestic Produce | Foreign Produce | Other Countries Domestic Produce | OAK United Kingdom Domestic Produce | Foreign Produce |
|---|---|---|---|---|---|---|---|---|---|---|
| 1912 | $ 386 | $ | $ 53,496 | $ | $4,461 | $113,231 | $107,484 | $ | $134,489 | $ 52,327 |
| 1913 | 498 | 170 | 62,949 | 3,060 | 5,870 | 73,333 | 171,189 | 4,194 | 24,541 | 329,147 |
| 1914 | 1,961 | | 50,135 | | 2,726 | 67,707 | 333,396 | 4,205 | 71,835 | 186,784 |
| 1915 | 290 | | 46,758 | | | 60,929 | 153,039 | 5,490 | 71,578 | 143,380 |
| 1916 | 1,881 | | 103,088 | | | 50,786 | 111,414 | | 26,357 | 107,944 |
| 1917 | 33 | | 40,748 | 898 | | 137,979 | 109,927 | 18,774 | 13,662 | 223,943 |
| 1918 | | | 10,277 | | | 331,732 | | | | |
| 1919 | | | | 12,715 | | | 1,784 | | | |
| 1920 | | | | | | | | | | |
| 1921 | | | | | | | | | | |

| Fiscal Year | WHITE PINE United Kingdom Domestic Produce | Foreign Produce | Other Countries Domestic Produce | RED PINE United Kingdom Domestic Produce | Foreign Produce | MAPLE United Products | HARDWOOD United Kingdom Domestic Produce | Foreign Produce | OTHER SQ. TIMBER United Kingdom Domestic Produce | Foreign Produce |
|---|---|---|---|---|---|---|---|---|---|---|
| 1912 | $776,580 | $ 26,212 | $ | $39,578 | $ | $ | $ | $ | $ 351 | $ |
| 1913 | 917,780 | 2,840 | 2,693 | 64,144 | | | | | 599 | |
| 1914 | 302,273 | 107,408 | 2,995 | 13,150 | 19,192 | | | | 2,506 | |
| 1915 | 335,546 | 151,004 | | 2,652 | | | | | | |
| 1916 | 129,539 | 191,645 | | | | 690 | | | 15,923 | 1,260 |
| 1917 | 56,043 | 53,897 | | | | | | | | 1,965 |
| 1918 | 101,306 | | | | | | | | | |
| 1919 | 6,415 | | | | | | | | | |
| 1920 | 865,566 | 71,773 | | | | | 171,345 | 103,686 | 19,641 | |
| 1921 | 311,431 | 9,084 | | | | | 165,964 | 100,914 | | |

### PLANKS & BOARDS / SPRUCE DEALS / PINE DEALS DEAL ENDS

| Fiscal Year | United Kingdom M. Ft. | Value | Other Countries M. Ft. | Value | United M. Ft. | Kingdom Value | Other Countries M. Ft. | Value | United Kingdom M. Ft. | Value | United Kingdom M. Ft. | Value |
|---|---|---|---|---|---|---|---|---|---|---|---|---|
| 1912 | 8,006 | $ 122,195 | 3,399 | $ 67,861 | 41,393 | $ 613,941 | 978 | $ 8,438 | 347 | $ 8,850 | 176 | $3,289 |
| 1913 | 4,160 | 89,842 | | | 28,137 | 533,326 | 360 | 12,964 | | | 39 | 492 |
| 1914 | 3,672 | 84,378 | 6,133 | 116,778 | 28,639 | 598,884 | 7 | 316 | 360 | 9,735 | | |
| 1915 | 4,985 | 102,025 | 1 | 6 | 19,947 | 390,155 | | | 1 | 39 | | |
| 1916 | 1,965 | 45,094 | 1,350 | 20,278 | 46,310 | 963,716 | 1,291 | 36,144 | 189 | 6,298 | | |
| 1917 | 3,463 | 65,437 | | | 50,284 | 1,214,459 | | | 306 | 15,126 | | |
| 1918 | 557 | 24,348 | | | 5,969 | 156,803 | | | | | | |
| 1919 | 386 | 9,970 | | | 975 | 156,803 | 140 | 2,780 | 1,110 | 77,187 | | |
| 1920 | 71,527 | 2,750,119 | 381 | 20,346 | 975 | 27,407 | | | | | | |
| 1921 | 27,377 | 3,151,310 | 190 | 9,535 | | | | | | | | |

### SCANTLING / BASSWOOD LUMBER:N.O.P. / SHOOKS / STAVES

| Fiscal Year | Other Countries M. Ft. | Value | United Kingdom M. Ft. | Value | United Kingdom Value | United Kingdom Value | United Kingdom Value |
|---|---|---|---|---|---|---|---|
| 1912 | 3,914 | $67,439 | 80 | $1,100 | $ 84,660 | $ | $1,130 |
| 1913 | | | 185 | 2,950 | 28,795 | | 3,114 |
| 1914 | 991 | 16,115 | 42 | 2,385 | 118,298 | 9,939 | 640 |
| 1915 | | | | | 38,177 | | 1,745 |
| 1916 | | | | | | | |
| 1917 | | | | | 16,772 | | |
| 1918 | | | | | | | |
| 1919 | | | | | 517,287 | | |
| 1920 | | | | | | 8,300 | |
| 1921 | | | | | | 38,775 | 1,200 |

# Opportunity Offered by Fire Resistive Frame Construction

By EDGAR P. ALLEN
Publicity Director, National Lumber Manufacturers' Association.

In spite of the singularly adroit and in many instances ingenuous arguments in favor of substitutes for lumber in home building, the home of wood has always been the most economical and the most beautiful, giving widest scope to architectural expression, lending itself most readily to alterations, additions and redecoration, and harmonizing in every variation of setting. Wood substitutes in house construction are "frozen" in place. Once erected the building can seldom be changed except at great expense, and who has ever built a home that instantly met every expectation and requirement; that did not become the theme of constant domestic speculation and expanded desire? The man or woman who builds a residence never

( 1) Fire stopping at all intersections of walls and partitions with floors, ceilings and roof.
( 2) Herring bon fire stopping in partitions midway between floor levels.
( 3) Partition and wall corners framed solid.
( 4) Wall between porch attic, and house sheathed solid.
( 5) Header beams 20 inches from the fireplace breast. Incombustible hearth.
( 6) Wood members 2 inches from chimney, space between filled with loose incombustible material.
( 7) Plaster applied directly to chimney breast.
( 8) Flue lining in chimneys.
( 9) Top of chimney 2 feet above peak of roof
(10) Protection over heating plant.
(11) Roof framing 2 inches from chimney, flashed, permitting free movement of chimney.
(12) Top of heating plant 15 inches from ceiling.
(13) Furnace 2 feet from warm air riser.
(14) Smoke pipe 1½ times its diameter below the ceiling.
(15) Heat pipes 6 inches below ceiling.
(16) Doubled tin pipes, ¾-inch air space between in partitions, kept 1 inch from all woodwork. Steam and hot water pipes 1 inch from woodwork.
(17) Heat pipes running through floors, fire stopped with loose incombustible material.

**SCIENCE CONTRIBUTES IMPROVED FRAME CONSTRUCTION** *for* Fire Prevention Week

The above illustration points out many of the ways to make a wooden house fire resistive. Other means that suggest themselves are the use of zinc coated nails to hold the shingles on the roof, painting the house with a fire resistant paint, especially at points of greatest fire hazard, use of a fire resistant stain on the shingles, and the use of metal lath in places subject to especial fire risk.—

really finishes it, for the residence, if it be truly a home, grows constantly with the richer lives of the occupants. Other means that suggest themselves are the weaving of fancies about the new room, that additional porch, the proposed back stairway and the thousand and one minor changes that, in homes of wood, are easily made, but in homes built of heavier and more unyielding materials can not come without appalling expense.

The lasting quality of frame construction is attested by the survival of thousands of beautiful old homes through generations of use. The material in them is exactly the same as may now be purchased

from any progressive lumber dealer, and their workmanship can be duplicated by any conscientious builder. The true Colonial home of a century ago, if kept in reasonable repair, is as good to-day as it ever was. Every home must be kept from deterioration and the frame house is most easily, conveniently and economically repaired, where the heavy, stiff and immobile wood substitutes present serious architectural problems. Homes of wood grow more beautiful in their mellow coloring with the passing years. They radiate hospitality and typify the tranquil domestic life within their walls. Homes of wood alone have true character, for which there is no substitute.

But, say the advocates of wood substitutes in final appeal, our structures are fireproof. Here is the Big Bertha of the substitute broadside. It is supposed to silence every argument, to drown every possible objection, to relegate to the limbo of forgotten things every stick of construction lumber and to disturb and alarm every owner of a wooden house. Yet the owner of a wooden home need not worry unduly on this score. About the only type of construction that will not burn under easily conceivable circumstances is the steel and concrete jail. But who wants to live in a jail? If our wood substitute friends should press their arguments to their logical conclusion—if in fact the perfect fireproof house were evolved—it would more nearly resemble a jail than a home. The evidences of our senses convince use that there are many more American homes built of wood than of any other material. To be more exact, engineers have figured it out that 83 per cent. of the homes built in 1920 were of wood. Previous to that year the percentage in favor of frame construction would run much higher, for 1920 was not a year of real home building. And how often does one see the charred remains of a dwelling that is not duplicated in the same neighborhood by the ruins of a home built in its major construction parts, of other materials? Of course wood will burn if conditions of conflagration are favorable. But the less favorable these conditions, the less hazard there is of a home either catching fire or being consumed before the fire is extinguished.

This is the thought behind the most modern type of frame construction known as "fire resistive." During the last year the most improved designs in frame construction with a view chiefly to the competent engineers in the lumber industry have been working out reduction of the fire hazard to a minimum. So successful has been this work that the authoritative announcement has just been made that through better building methods, and at very little increased cost, the danger from fire in frame houses has been reduced 50 per cent. In all respects these houses are similar in appearance to those of usual construction, but they possess many, and for the most part hidden, protective features that make them essentially fire resistive.

The accompanying diagram graphically illustrates many of these modifications in construction. It will be observed, by noting the number indicated and the reference below, that fire stopping is of primary importance. This means the interposing of panels and short pieces within spaces that ordinarily serve as flues for the rapid spread of combustion. Most of the other improvements are protective in their nature and prevent wooden parts catching fire from chimneys, fireplaces, heating plants, steam and hot water pipes, etc. While, of course, wood will burn, it is also true that there is really no such thing as a "fireproof" house within the reach of the ordinary pocketbook. What is now offered is a type of construction that is fire resistive and as nearly fireproof as frame construction as now developed can be made. It conforms strictly to the scientific building codes of the most progressive cities and carries a minimum of fire risk to the occupants, because of the necessarily slow spread of combustion in such a building as is here described.

There is a strong demand for lath at the present time and many inquiries are received. A large number of wholesalers have no stock on hand and others, who have, are holding out for pretty firm prices in the belief that the coming year will be a very good one in the building line.

George Mason, of Manchester, England, head of the firm of G. Mason & Co., accompanied by his sales manager, Mr. Nelson, spent a few days in Toronto recently upon the trade and also visited the mills of the company at Midland, Ont.

# Statement Showing Quantity and Value of Canadian Forest Products (Unmanufactured and Manufactured) Exported from Canada Years Ended March 31, 1911 and 1921

| UNMANUFACTURED | | Year ended March 31, 1911 | | | Year ended March 31, 1921 | | |
|---|---|---|---|---|---|---|---|
| | | Total Exports | Exports to United Kingdom | United States | Total Exports | Exports to United Kingdom | United States |
| **Logs and Timber—** | | | | | | | |
| Fence posts | $ | ..... | ..... | ..... | 158,915 | ..... | 158,915 |
| Logs, cedar | M. Ft. | ..... | ..... | ..... | 19,561 | ..... | 19,326 |
| | $ | 202 | ..... | 202 | 484,097 | ..... | 476,543 |
| Logs, elm | $ | 23,983 | 10,877 | 13,106 | ..... | ..... | ..... |
| Logs, hardwood | M ft. | ..... | ..... | ..... | 11,196 | 1,567 | 9,611 |
| | $ | ..... | ..... | ..... | 330,775 | 95,504 | 219,791 |
| Logs, hemlock | $ | 7,581 | ..... | 6,946 | ..... | ..... | ..... |
| Logs, pine | M ft. | 4,726 | ..... | 4,726 | 1,780 | 1,409 | 371 |
| | $ | 26,510 | ..... | 26,510 | 160,325 | 149,878 | 10,447 |
| Logs, spruce | M ft. | 13,760 | ..... | 13,760 | 6,045 | 5 | 5,897 |
| | $ | 153,327 | ..... | 153,327 | 198,545 | 284 | 197,324 |
| Logs, all other, n.o.p. | M ft. | 103,441 | 704 | 102,397 | 22,350 | 3,693 | 18,561 |
| | $ | 982,750 | 15,812 | 962,834 | 493,189 | 155,136 | 336,338 |
| Masts and spars | $ | 3,960 | ..... | 456 | 23,426 | ..... | 140 |
| Piling | Lin. Ft. | ..... | ..... | ..... | 3,022,764 | ..... | 1,964,795 |
| | $ | 171,748 | ..... | 170,734 | 273,434 | ..... | 251,950 |
| Poles, hop, hoop, telegraph and other | $ | 78,085 | ..... | 78,055 | ..... | ..... | ..... |
| Poles, telegraph and telephone | No. | ..... | ..... | ..... | 116,982 | ..... | 116,555 |
| | $ | ..... | ..... | ..... | 485,512 | ..... | 485,542 |
| Poles, other | $ | ..... | ..... | ..... | 1,847 | ..... | 1,582 |
| Posts, sleepers and railroad ties | No. | 391,489 | ..... | 390,929 | ..... | ..... | ..... |
| Railroad ties | No. | ..... | ..... | ..... | 2,545,351 | 912,136 | 1,401,269 |
| | $ | ..... | ..... | ..... | 3,272,714 | 1,303,196 | 1,396,580 |
| **Sawmill and Planing Mill Products—** | | | | | | | |
| **Bolts and Blocks—** | | | | | | | |
| Match blocks | $ | 63,801 | 56,706 | 6,095 | ..... | ..... | ..... |
| Shingle bolts of pine and cedar | Cord | 10,894 | ..... | 10,894 | 4,905 | ..... | 4,905 |
| | $ | 37,002 | ..... | 37,002 | 30,720 | ..... | 30,720 |
| Stave and other bolts | $ | ..... | ..... | ..... | 30,045 | ..... | ..... |
| **Lumber and Timber—** | | | | | | | |
| Basswood | M Ft. | 4,010 | 331 | 3,514 | ..... | ..... | ..... |
| | $ | 93,444 | 11,755 | 75,844 | ..... | ..... | ..... |
| Battens | M Ft. | 39,297 | 34,398 | ..... | ..... | ..... | ..... |
| Deals, pine | $ | 66,628 | 59,686 | 5,313 | ..... | ..... | ..... |
| | $ | 1,564,518 | 1,406,444 | 115,589 | ..... | ..... | ..... |
| Deals, spruce and other | M Ft. | 435,971 | 408,790 | 14,550 | ..... | ..... | ..... |
| | $ | 6,929,010 | 6,471,153 | 247,708 | ..... | ..... | ..... |
| Deal ends | M Ft. | 22,800 | 19,931 | 674 | ..... | ..... | ..... |
| | $ | 344,811 | 310,395 | 6,888 | ..... | ..... | ..... |
| Hickory | M Ft. | ..... | ..... | ..... | ..... | ..... | ..... |
| Planks and boards | M Ft. | 1,127,783 | 79,778 | 847,948 | ..... | ..... | ..... |
| | $ | 21,509,769 | 1,659,701 | 15,948,790 | ..... | ..... | ..... |
| Planks and boards, fir | M Ft. | ..... | ..... | ..... | 129,390 | 12,644 | 76,936 |
| | $ | ..... | ..... | ..... | 4,738,525 | 606,019 | 2,569,572 |
| Planks and boards, pine | M Ft. | ..... | ..... | ..... | 453,306 | 75,253 | 356,789 |
| | $ | ..... | ..... | ..... | 23,454,856 | 5,579,967 | 16,439,746 |
| Planks and boards, spruce | M Ft. | ..... | ..... | ..... | 894,528 | 325,274 | 517,979 |
| | $ | ..... | ..... | ..... | 35,826,462 | 13,279,552 | 20,144,979 |
| Planks and boards, other | M Ft. | ..... | ..... | ..... | 137,230 | 14,888 | 110,273 |
| | $ | ..... | ..... | ..... | 7,059,952 | 982,235 | 5,953,124 |
| Scantling | M Ft. | 88,092 | 35,584 | 41,532 | ..... | ..... | ..... |
| | $ | 1,202,832 | 434,534 | 571,733 | ..... | ..... | ..... |
| Timber, square, Douglas fir | M Ft. | ..... | ..... | ..... | 34,893 | 3,391 | 3,723 |
| | $ | ..... | ..... | ..... | 1,393,524 | 169,459 | 108,824 |
| Timber, square, ash | $ | 4,189 | 3,779 | ..... | ..... | ..... | ..... |
| Timber, square, birch | $ | 117,006 | 113,551 | 2,141 | ..... | ..... | ..... |
| Timber, square, elm | $ | 157,996 | 155,554 | ..... | ..... | ..... | ..... |
| Timber, square, oak | $ | 151,299 | 143,021 | 6,463 | ..... | ..... | ..... |
| Timber, square, hardwood | M Ft. | ..... | ..... | ..... | 3,866 | 3,533 | 399 |
| | $ | ..... | ..... | ..... | 265,240 | 245,557 | 16,993 |
| Timber, square, red pine | $ | 33 | ..... | ..... | ..... | ..... | ..... |
| Timber, square, white pine | M Ft. | 9,145 | 9,118 | 16 | 2,042 | 1,961 | 77 |
| | $ | 598,774 | 597,131 | 580 | 219,653 | 215,631 | 3,585 |
| Timber, square, other, n.o.p. | M Ft. | 575 | 440 | 108 | 1,443 | 17 | 1,083 |
| | $ | 14,259 | 11,304 | 2,772 | 53,519 | 740 | 35,764 |
| Oter lumber, n.o.p. | $ | 391,864 | 174,368 | 195,303 | 230,916 | 114,035 | 105,521 |
| **Other Sawmill and Planing Mill Products—** | | | | | | | |
| Doors, sashes and blinds | $ | 20,326 | 9,696 | 2,594 | 212,087 | 79,550 | 8,103 |
| Knees and futtocks | No. | 4,772 | ..... | 4,772 | ..... | ..... | ..... |
| | $ | 3,068 | ..... | 3,068 | 8,705 | ..... | 8,180 |
| Laths | M | 700,041 | 15,637 | 667,503 | 428,644 | 7 | 414,097 |
| | $ | 1,706,035 | 37,588 | 1,627,518 | 3,767,820 | 65 | 3,636,924 |
| Mouldings, trimmings and other house furnishings | $ | 1,786 | ..... | 7 | 75,328 | 43,741 | 16,174 |
| Paling | M | 4,508 | 528 | ..... | ..... | ..... | ..... |
| | $ | 72,322 | 10,390 | ..... | ..... | ..... | ..... |
| Pickets | M | 35,052 | 4,186 | 27,176 | 50,005 | 488 | 48,546 |
| | $ | 191,993 | 21,196 | 148,390 | 576,483 | 11,315 | 539,512 |
| Shingles | M | 735,557 | ..... | 711,634 | 1,851,559 | 33 | 1,796,865 |
| | $ | 1,585,751 | ..... | 1,648,448 | 9,230,581 | ..... | 9,058,127 |
| Shooks | $ | 289,074 | 231,703 | 8,323 | 1,062,390 | 209,072 | 90,263 |

## Canadian Forest Products Exported—Continued

| | | Year ended March 31, 1911 | | | Year ended March 31, 1921 | | |
|---|---|---|---|---|---|---|---|
| | | Total Exports | Exports to United Kingdom | Exports to United States | Total Exports | Exports to United Kingdom | Exports to United States |
| **Other Unmanufactured Wood—** | | | | | | | |
| Bark for tanning | Cord | 12,949 | ..... | 12,949 | 3,504 | ..... | 3,504 |
| | $ | 78,138 | ..... | 78,138 | 37,010 | ..... | 37,010 |
| Firewood | Cord | 19,446 | ..... | 19,804 | 29,358 | ..... | 29,035 |
| | $ | 46,366 | ..... | 45,965 | 115,973 | ..... | 115,471 |
| Lathwood | Cord | 400 | ..... | 400 | ..... | ..... | ..... |
| | $ | 1,600 | ..... | 1,600 | ..... | ..... | ..... |
| Pulpwood | Cord | 936,791 | ..... | 936,791 | 1,615,467 | ..... | 1,615,467 |
| | $ | 6,092,713 | ..... | 6,092,713 | 21,513,594 | ..... | 21,513,594 |
| Other articles of forest produce | $ | 4,071 | ..... | 4,071 | ..... | ..... | ..... |
| **TOTAL UNMANUFACTURED** | $ | 45,261,114 | 11,919,694 | 28,680,154 | 115,554,475 | 23,336,125 | 83,957,338 |
| **MANUFACTURED** | | | | | | | |
| **Cooperage—** | | | | | | | |
| Barrels, empty | No. | 16,091 | 219 | 9,846 | 20,448 | 80 | 18,539 |
| | $ | 15,703 | 140 | 7,284 | 55,934 | 200 | 45,961 |
| Pails, tubs, churns and other hollow woodenware | $ | 15,050 | 2,438 | 905 | 49,701 | 9,990 | 15,531 |
| Staves and headings | $ | 104,982 | 24,904 | 46,250 | 198,356 | 29,945 | 105,699 |
| **Wood Pulp—** | | | | | | | |
| Chemically prepared pulp | Cwt. | 731,428 | 4,112 | 716,347 | ..... | ..... | ..... |
| | $ | 1,305,101 | 8,219 | 1,296,153 | ..... | ..... | ..... |
| Chemical pulp, sulphate (Kraft) | Cwt. | ..... | ..... | ..... | 2,254,002 | ..... | 2,226,839 |
| | $ | ..... | ..... | ..... | 18,160,725 | ..... | 18,046,063 |
| Chemical pulp, sulphite, bleached | Cwt. | ..... | ..... | ..... | 1,941,922 | 27,906 | 1,606,834 |
| | $ | ..... | ..... | ..... | 15,195,065 | 264,581 | 13,820,526 |
| Chemical pulp, sulphite, unbleached | Cwt. | ..... | ..... | ..... | 4,785,040 | 835,891 | 3,531,184 |
| | $ | ..... | ..... | ..... | 37,704,419 | 4,190,567 | 31,583,349 |
| Mechanically ground pulp | Cwt. | 3,567,227 | 958,765 | 4,673,522 | 5,833,043 | 1,397,783 | 3,358,653 |
| | $ | 4,407,431 | 488,709 | 3,796,422 | 16,491,818 | 3,472,454 | 11,552,473 |
| **Other Manufactured Wood—** | | | | | | | |
| Ashes | $ | 95,122 | 30,229 | 61,734 | 40,414 | ..... | 40,414 |
| Charcoal | $ | 6,092 | ..... | 3,045 | 75,749 | ..... | 75,749 |
| Coffins, caskets and parts of | $ | ..... | ..... | ..... | 14,156 | ..... | 1,534 |
| Furniture | $ | 253,336 | 24,300 | 23,953 | 804,964 | 271,729 | 57,939 |
| Handles of all kinds | $ | ..... | ..... | ..... | 137,988 | 22,095 | 86,076 |
| Matches and Match Splints | $ | 85,663 | 83,611 | 297 | ..... | ..... | ..... |
| Matches | $ | ..... | ..... | ..... | 131,157 | 1,856 | 9 |
| Match splints | $ | ..... | ..... | ..... | 215,454 | 59,100 | 4,450 |
| Spool wood | $ | 95,053 | 94,063 | 450 | 863,521 | 764,302 | 99,328 |
| All other manufactures of wood | $ | 459,558 | 237,050 | 78,953 | 1,705,066 | 405,578 | 790,841 |
| **TOTAL MANUFACTURED** | $ | 6,845,344 | 994,102 | 5,316,469 | 75,833,467 | 9,492,328 | 59,336,772 |

---

# Statement Showing Quantity and Value of Forest Products Unmanufactured and Manufactured Imported into Canada for Consumption, Years Ended March 31, 1911 and 1921

| | | Year ended March 31, 1911 | | | Year ended March 31, 1921 | | |
|---|---|---|---|---|---|---|---|
| **UNMANUFACTURED** | | Total Imports | Imports to United Kingdom | Imports to United States | Total Imports | Imports to United Kingdom | Imports to United States |
| **Canes, Reeds, Willows, Etc.—** | | | | | | | |
| Bamboo-reed, not further manufactured than cut and bamboos, unmanufactured | $ | 11,097 | 5 | 7,785 | 46,045 | 3,977 | 33,225 |
| Cane and rattans, not manufactured, and not further manufactured than split, when for use in Canadian manufactures | $ | 14,823 | 3,043 | 11,771 | 280,986 | 2,328 | 209,109 |
| Cane, reed or rattan, not further manufactured than split, n.o.p. | $ | 42,932 | 174 | 42,414 | 12,750 | ..... | 10,371 |
| Osiers or willows, unmanufactured | $ | 5,481 | 4,634 | 495 | 13,293 | 12,309 | 894 |
| **Corkwood or Cork Bark—** | | | | | | | |
| Corkwood or cork bark, unmanufactured, imported by manufacturers for use in their own factories in the manufacture of corks and washers of cork | $ | ..... | ..... | ..... | 68,196 | ..... | 68,196 |
| Corkwood, unmanufactured, n.o.p. | $ | 64,182 | 1,562 | 47,246 | 4,064 | ..... | 3,957 |
| **Logs and Timber—** | | | | | | | |
| Fence Posts— | | | | | | | |
| Fence posts and railroad ties | $ | 1,197,805 | ..... | 1,197,805 | 28,813 | ..... | 28,813 |
| Hickory billets | $ | 62,532 | ..... | 62,532 | 184,374 | ..... | 184,374 |
| Hop poles | $ | ..... | ..... | ..... | ..... | ..... | ..... |
| Logs and round unmanufactured timber, n.o.p. | $ | 699,107 | ..... | 698,386 | 480,407 | 3,860 | 479,751 |
| Poles, telegraph and telephone | $ | ..... | ..... | ..... | 282,614 | ..... | 282,614 |
| Railroad ties | $ | ..... | ..... | ..... | 1,720,379 | ..... | 1,720,379 |
| **Sawmill and Planing Mill Products—** | | | | | | | |
| Bolts, Blocks, Felloes, etc. | | | | | | | |
| Felloes of hickory or oak, not further manufactured than rough sawn or bent to shape | $ | 57,775 | ..... | 37,776 | 199,440 | ..... | 199,440 |
| Handle, heading, stave and shingle bolts, n.o.p. | $ | 139,328 | ..... | 139,228 | 466,246 | ..... | 466,246 |

## Canadian Forest Products Imported—Continued

| | | Year ended March 31, 1911 | | | Year ended March 31, 1921 | | |
|---|---|---|---|---|---|---|---|
| | | Total Imports | Imports to United Kingdom | Imports to United States | Total Imports | Imports to United Kingdom | Imports to United States |
| Heading and stave bolts in the rough of poplar ...... $ | | 100,297 | 25 | 100,272 | 226,597 | 83 | 226,128 |
| Hub, last, wagon, oar, for cheese boxes ............ $ | | ..... | ..... | ..... | ..... | ..... | ..... |
| Ten-pin blocks, rough, for the manufacture of ten-pins $ | | 75 | ..... | 75 | ..... | ..... | ..... |
| Lumber and timber, planks and boards, when not otherwise manufactured than rough sawn or split or creosoted, vulcanized, or treated by any other preserving process or not,— | | | | | | | |
| African teak, amaranth, black heart, ebony, boxwood, cocobarol, dogwood, lignum vitæ, persimmon, red cedar and satin wood ............................ $ | | 33,875 | 1,296 | 28,193 | 67,965 | 17,744 | 44,340 |
| Cherry, chestnut and hickory .................... M Ft. | | ..... | ..... | ..... | 10,024 | ..... | 10,024 |
| $ | | ..... | ..... | ..... | 1,136,901 | ..... | 1,136,901 |
| Cherry, chestnut, gumwood, hickory and whitewood ........................................ M Ft. | | 16,739 | 1 | 16,485 | ..... | ..... | ..... |
| $ | | 670,775 | 61 | 656,510 | ..... | ..... | ..... |
| Gumwood ...................................... M Ft. | | ..... | ..... | ..... | 11,630 | ..... | 11,627 |
| $ | | ..... | ..... | ..... | 1,008,015 | ..... | 1,007,697 |
| Mahogany ...................................... Feet | | 3,023,008 | 218,291 | 2,524,921 | 2,258,003 | 1,230 | 2,146,590 |
| $ | | 347,730 | 23,833 | 309,253 | 561,371 | 638 | 548,325 |
| Oak ........................................... M Ft. | | 57,593 | 15 | 57,519 | 37,413 | ..... | 37,327 |
| $ | | 2,321,935 | 3,378 | 2,315,518 | 4,517,795 | ..... | 4,506,307 |
| Pitch Pine .................................... M Ft. | | 94,048 | ..... | 94,048 | 37,468 | ..... | 37,468 |
| $ | | 2,111,818 | ..... | 2,111,818 | 1,773,164 | ..... | 1,773,164 |
| Redwood ...................................... Feet | | 81,308 | ..... | 77,398 | 242,375 | ..... | 235,375 |
| $ | | 5,117 | ..... | 4,593 | 15,990 | ..... | 15,750 |
| Rosewood ...................................... Feet | | 45,752 | ..... | 14,304 | 9,121 | ..... | 9,121 |
| $ | | 4,492 | ..... | 1,615 | 3,818 | ..... | 3,818 |
| Sandalwood .................................... Feet | | ..... | ..... | ..... | 4,610 | ..... | 4,610 |
| Spanish cedar ................................. Feet | | 967,259 | ..... | 967,259 | 68,783 | ..... | 68,783 |
| $ | | 57,109 | ..... | 57,109 | 14,680 | ..... | 14,680 |
| Sycamore ...................................... Feet | | 7,040 | 632 | 6,608 | 75,962 | ..... | 75,962 |
| $ | | 301 | 49 | 252 | 7,404 | ..... | 7,404 |
| Walnut ........................................ Feet | | 594,395 | 4,368 | 589,927 | 1,489,523 | ..... | 1,489,523 |
| $ | | 22,685 | 653 | 22,022 | 287,060 | ..... | 287,060 |
| White ash ..................................... Feet | | 2,425,974 | ..... | 2,425,974 | 674,342 | ..... | 674,342 |
| $ | | 127,674 | ..... | 127,674 | 115,748 | ..... | 115,748 |
| Whitewood or yellow poplar .................... M Ft. | | ..... | ..... | ..... | 4,610 | ..... | 4,610 |
| $ | | ..... | ..... | ..... | 558,632 | ..... | 558,632 |
| **Lumber and Timber, n.o.p.—** | | | | | | | |
| Lumber, rough sawn or dressed on one side only, n.o.p. ...................................... M Ft. | | 193,583 | 1 | 193,177 | 49,510 | 1 | 49,320 |
| $ | | 3,500,066 | 22 | 3,495,496 | 3,119,994 | 114 | 3,107,519 |
| Sawed boards, planks, deals, planed or dressed on one or both sides, or tongued and grooved ............ M Ft. | | 22,850 | 1 | 22,849 | 3,060 | 17 | 3,001 |
| $ | | 315,621 | 45 | 315,576 | 223,697 | 25,794 | 196,018 |
| Timber, hewn or sawn, squared or sided or creosoted .. $ | | 333,927 | ..... | 333,927 | 142,968 | 33 | 142,935 |
| **Other Sawmill and Planing Mill Products—** | | | | | | | |
| Doors of wood .................................. $ | | ..... | ..... | ..... | 230,357 | ..... | 230,357 |
| Laths ......................................... M | | 17,349 | ..... | 17,338 | 12,898 | ..... | 12,898 |
| $ | | 49,056 | ..... | 49,027 | 115,319 | ..... | 115,319 |
| Mouldings, plain, gilded or otherwise further manufactured ..................................... $ | | 65,364 | 96 | 64,415 | 67,311 | 106 | 67,025 |
| Pickets ....................................... $ | | ..... | ..... | ..... | 3,755 | ..... | 3,755 |
| Pine and spruce clapboards .................... M Ft. | | ..... | ..... | ..... | ..... | ..... | ..... |
| Shingles ...................................... M | | 5,754 | ..... | 5,750 | 8,645 | ..... | 8,642 |
| Veneers of oak, rosewood not over 3/32 of an inch in thickness ..................................... $ | | 11,379 | ..... | 11,368 | 29,752 | ..... | 29,744 |
| Veneers of wood, n.o.p., not over 3/32 of an inch in thickness ..................................... $ | | 245,933 | 344 | 245,589 | 649,862 | 17 | 649,845 |
| Window sash ................................... $ | | 53,133 | ..... | 53,133 | 261,837 | ..... | 261,837 |
| $ | | ..... | ..... | ..... | 19,423 | ..... | 19,413 |
| **Other Unmanufactured Wood—** | | | | | | | |
| Bark, hemlock ................................. Cord | | 79 | ..... | 79 | ..... | ..... | ..... |
| $ | | 515 | ..... | 515 | ..... | ..... | ..... |
| Sawdust of wood of all kinds .................... $ | | 21,976 | 8,793 | 17,460 | 17,660 | ..... | 17,660 |
| Wood for fuel ................................. Cord | | 28,109 | ..... | 28,109 | 10,334 | ..... | 10,336 |
| $ | | 77,922 | ..... | 77,922 | 38,007 | ..... | 37,964 |
| **TOTAL, UNMANUFACTURED** .............. $ | | 12,772,009 | 41,811 | 12,660,202 | 19,024,778 | 69,235 | 18,877,713 |
| **MANUFACTURED** | | | | | | | |
| **Cooperage—** | | | | | | | |
| Barrels, empty ................................. No. | | 83,525 | 2,076 | 81,300 | 205,077 | 1,425 | 202,496 |
| $ | | 91,389 | 1,240 | 90,035 | 330,970 | 1,871 | 333,370 |
| Barrels containing petroleum or its products, or any mixture of which petroleum forms a part, when such contents are chargeable with specific duty .......... No. | | 44,937 | 3,448 | 41,430 | 7,107 | 952 | 6,017 |
| $ | | 44,508 | 3,486 | 41,003 | 14,300 | 2,104 | 11,935 |
| Staves of oak, sawn, split or cut, not further manufactured than listed or jointed ...................... M | | 6,967 | ..... | 6,967 | 6,359 | ..... | 6,359 |
| $ | | 195,354 | ..... | 195,354 | 450,106 | ..... | 450,106 |
| Staves and stave materials of wood, other than oak or poplar, listed or jointed and improved in condition but not bevelled at the ends ........................ $ | | ..... | ..... | ..... | 233,444 | ..... | 233,444 |
| Woodenware pails and tubs ...................... $ | | 13,945 | 53 | 13,797 | 53,104 | 213 | 52,591 |

## Canadian Forest Products Imported—Continued

| | | Year ended March 31, 1911 | | | Year ended March 31, 1921 | | |
|---|---|---|---|---|---|---|---|
| | | Total Imports | Imports to United Kingdom | United States | Total Imports | Imports to United Kingdom | United States |
| **Corkwood Manufactures—** | | | | | | | |
| Corks, manufactured from corkwood, over three fourths of an inch in diameter measured at the larger end .. | Lb. | 480,409 | 60,773 | 8,774 | 369,530 | 48,482 | 74,838 |
| | | 129,514 | 27,686 | 3,798 | 212,377 | 45,058 | 51,587 |
| | $ | 48,724 | 1,949 | 4,589 | 156,468 | 579 | 22,879 |
| Corks, manufactured from corkwood, three fourths of an inch and less in diameter, measured at the larger end .. | Lb. | 10,413 | 743 | 2,866 | 117,343 | 819 | 27,601 |
| Cork slabs, boards, planks and tiles produced from cork waste or granulated or ground cork........... | $ | ..... | ..... | ..... | 178,224 | 155 | 31,941 |
| Manufactures of corkwood or cork bark, n.o.p., including strips, shives, shells and washers of cork ........... | $ | 185,021 | 8,369 | 116,143 | 283,622 | 6,505 | 198,253 |
| **Turned and Carved Wood Products—** | | | | | | | |
| Handles "D" shovel, wholly of wood and wood handles for manufacture of "D" shovel handles ........... | $ | 49,906 | ..... | 49,906 | 118,904 | ..... | 118,904 |
| Handles of all kinds, ash ........................... | $ | 25,190 | 387 | 24,909 | 107,231 | ..... | 107,231 |
| Handles of all kinds, hickory ...................... | $ | 65,532 | 639 | 64,883 | 78,739 | ..... | 78,739 |
| Handles of all kinds, n.o.p. ........................ | $ | ..... | ..... | ..... | 109,948 | 492 | 108,450 |
| Lasts of wood ..................................... | d | 22,953 | ..... | 22,953 | 31,328 | ..... | 31,328 |
| Mexican saddle trees and stirrups of wood ......... | $ | 13,384 | 29 | 13,355 | 21,950 | 10 | 21,940 |
| Rakes, hay ........................................ | No | 5,340 | ..... | 5,340 | ..... | ..... | ..... |
| | $ | 792 | ..... | 792 | ..... | ..... | ..... |
| Spokes, hickory and oak, not further manufactured than rough turned, and not tenoned, mitred or sized ...... | $ | 230,309 | ..... | 229,309 | 278,831 | ..... | 278,831 |
| Snaths ........................................... | Doz. | 15 | ..... | 15 | 6 | 4 | 2 |
| | $ | 30 | ..... | 30 | 102 | 84 | 18 |
| Treenails ......................................... | M | ..... | ..... | ..... | 89 | ..... | 89 |
| | $ | ..... | ..... | ..... | 4,113 | ..... | 4,113 |
| Walking sticks and walking canes of all kinds ...... | $ | 18,414 | 8,156 | 9,295 | 28,812 | 10,567 | 17,873 |
| **Wood Pulp and Fibre—** | | | | | | | |
| Fibre, kartavert, indurated fibre, vulcanized fibre and like materials, and manufactures of, n.o.p. ............... | $ | 83,171 | 695 | 81,673 | 480,386 | 2,299 | 478,073 |
| Bleached sulphite pulp ............................ | Lb. | ..... | ..... | ..... | ..... | ..... | ..... |
| | $ | ..... | ..... | ..... | ..... | ..... | ..... |
| Soda pulp ........................................ | Lb. | ..... | ..... | ..... | 1,415,561 | ..... | 1,415,561 |
| | $ | ..... | ..... | ..... | 94,898 | ..... | 94,898 |
| Unbleached sulphite pulp ......................... | Lb. | ..... | ..... | ..... | 28,985,667 | ..... | 28,985,667 |
| | $ | ..... | ..... | ..... | 1,301,266 | ..... | 1,301,266 |
| Wood pulp, mechanically or chemically prepared, n.o.p. ............................................ | Lb. | ..... | ..... | ..... | 19,766,282 | 3,145 | 19,764,137 |
| | $ | ..... | ..... | ..... | 1,271,493 | 652 | 1,270,841 |
| Wood pulp ........................................ | $ | 52,526 | 4,088 | 38,291 | ..... | ..... | ..... |
| Lumber and Timber manufactured, n.o.p. ........... | $ | 182 | 132 | 50 | ..... | ..... | ..... |
| **Other Manufactures of Wood—** | | | | | | | |
| Caskets and coffins and metal parts thereof ......... | $ | 24,822 | ..... | 24,822 | 87,406 | 15 | 87,357 |
| Charcoal .......................................... | $ | 24,905 | 9 | 23,234 | 88,628 | 132 | 88,887 |
| Certain stretchers ................................. | $ | 7,632 | 191 | 7,441 | 1,353 | ..... | 1,353 |
| Furniture, house, office, cabinet or store furniture of wood or other material n.o.p. in parts or finished ..... | $ | 1,339,898 | 136,795 | 1,119,379 | 1,686,159 | 112,054 | 1,433,518 |
| Matches of wood .................................. | $ | ..... | ..... | ..... | 129,949 | 181,700 | 7,818 |
| Woodenware, churns, n.o.p. washboards, pounders and rolling pins ..................................... | $ | 17,056 | 206 | 16,699 | 21,267 | 87 | 20,980 |
| Manufactures of wood, n.o.p. ...................... | $ | 1,613,661 | 87,614 | 1,489,118 | 3,451,701 | 154,586 | 3,187,363 |
| **TOTAL MANUFACTURED** ...................... | $ | 4,301,202 | 380,297 | 3,699,265 | 11,213,750 | 629,613 | 10,128,543 |

---

## Basic Trade Factors are all Very Favorable
### By George H. Holt

Our opinion of trade outlook for 1922 is decidedly favorable. All of the basic factors of demand, finance, reduced stocks on hand, low input of logs, improved prices for the farmers, diversion of interest and financial waste from war preparations to civil development, reduction of wages, greater efficiency in industry, a general improvement in the mental attitude, and the moral attitude of the world toward peace and progress, the settlement or improvement of a large percentage of the Political questions, including Japan and Ireland, a general recognition of the fact that War prices and boom prices are a thing of the past, are highly favorable.

The public sentiment that is forcing all governments to equalize their budgets, the disposition to take measures to stimulate as well as stabilize industry, the closer working relations existing between governments which assures an extended period of freedom from aggression, the disposition to develop great power resources which will permanently reduce costs of operation and transportation and of any trend towards Bolshevism, decrement but in foreign commerce, important development of new or enlarged waterways, intelligent stimulation and control of immigration, the reduction of danger from strikes in industry and transportation and of and trent towards Bolshevism, decreasing interest rates on high grade securities, tending to force capital into enterprise rather than fixed investment, revolutionary developments in the departments of power transmission and radio activities, (stimulating enormous activities in new fields of enterprise), and many other positive factors which are beginning the urge of a new ear, are all of enormous importance in estimating not only the distant but also the near future.

The competition of debased currencies in Europe has probably reached its maximum and with a readjustment of political factors there is good reason to expect within the year a tremendous improvement in that respect and increased purchasing power on the part of the European populations which will permit them to buy raw materials and food products which this continent desires to sell and transport.

Increase of commerce (home and foreign), calls for increased interest in mining and production of precious and semi-precious metals greatly in excess of the present quantity. Commerce requires exchange in finance as well as materials, and international exchange requires a sound metallic basis not (with alldue respect to your profession) an increase of printing presses.

# Lower Stumpage Rate Sought by Lumbermen

## Operators of New Brunswick Hold Annual Gathering and Make Several Representations to Government—Mr. Brankley is New President

The annual meeting of the New Brunswick Lumbermen's Association was held in Fredericton on March 2. One of the chief topics of conversation was the proposed change in the method of protecting the forests against fire.

The election of directors for the ensuing year resulted as follows:—Donald Fraser, Plaster Rock; William Richards, Campbellton; Angus McLean, Bathurst; W. B. Snowball, Chatham; J. W. Brankley, Chatham; T. Henry McEvoy, Dalhousie; J. Herbert Irving, Buctouche; George H. King, M. P. P., Chipman.

Officers were selected by the executive for the year as follows:—
President, J. W. Brankley, Chatham.
Vice-president, Angus McLean, Bathurst.
Secretary-treasurer, R. W. McLellan, Fredericton.

The retiring president F. C. Beattey, of St. John, N. B. presented a report upon the activities of the association during the year. The matter of fire protection in the forests was fully considered. The proposal that the lumbermen undertake the protection against fire themselves by forming a forest protective association instead of

J. W. Brankley, Chatham, N.B.
Newly elected President

F. C. Beattey, St. John, N.B.
The retiring President

the province, was talked over. The province of Quebec has such a system, and by some it is said that it would be more efficient and economical in New Brunswick.

The following resolutions were carried at the annual meeting:—
Resolved that a committee be named to meet the Minister of Lands and Mines to again take up with him the Petition presented to the Government in August last, and also the matter of Forest Fire Protection and report back to a special meeting of the Association. The Chairman appointed such committee, as follows:—Angus McLean, Hon. J. P. Burchill, Donald Fraser, George Schryer, R. W. McLellan.

Resolved that a Committee of J. Fraser Gregory, Donald Fraser, J. W. Brankley (with power to add to their numbers) be appointed to represent this Association and appear before the Railway Commission on the 7th March 1922 to press for a reduction in freight rates.

On motion resolved the following be and constitute the Executive for the ensuing year.
Messrs. Donald Fraser, William Richards, W. B. Snowball, J. H. Irving, George King, F. C. Beattey, Angus McLean, J. W. Brankley, T. H. McEvoy.

## They Want Reduction in Stumpage

Writing to the "Canada Lumberman," a member of the New Brunswick Lumber Dealers' Association says—You are no doubt

aware that we are paying $5 per M on spruce and fir in this province, and there has been an agitation to reduce this to $2.50. The main argument is on the ground of the depressed condition of the trade and the fact that Quebec has reduced its stumpage from $2.70 to $1.60. Quebec is our heaviest competitor.

The present N. B. scale was adopted as far back as 1870, and the lumber operator cannot commence to saw out the scale charged by our Government and he always runs from ten to fifteen per cent short. This is the reason that we are asking for the adoption of the Quebec scale.

It cost this province $140,000 last year for forest fire protection. As yet we have no association for this purpose the same as in the Province of Quebec, and we have been pressing upon the Government to turn over the protection of the forests to the lumbermen, thereby removing this important work from the operation of politics, and the lumbermen also feel they could do the work much more efficiently and economically.

Under the Workmen's Compensation Act, manufacturers, and particularly lumbermen, are being over assessed, and we claim that the Act as administered by the New Brunswick Board is a heavy tax, particularly under present conditions in the depressed state of the lumber market. The Bathurst Lumber Company have at present a case before the courts testing out the validity of the Board's assessments, and our main contention is that any over-assessment in one year should be credited against the following year's assessment. Notwithstanding that this is especially provided for in the Workmen's Compensation Act, the Board continues from year to year to over-assess with the result that they have on hand at the present time an enormous surplus which we claim should be either refunded or credited as above. The financial stringency makes it hard to do otherwise.

## New Brunswick Lumbermen Get Cold Comfort

The New Brunswick Lumbermen's Association have asked a reduction of the stumpage rate upon lumber cut upon the Crown Lands of the Province to $2.50 per thousand feet.

They want this rate with the Quebec scale in effect and have told the Provincial Government that unless such conditions obtain there will inevitably follow a complete shut-down of operations next session as banks cannot be shown that it is safe to advance funds for carrying on the work with so much less profitable operating conditions in New Brunswick than in Quebec. The Quebec stumpage rate has been quoted as reduced to $1.60 per thousand.

The lumbermen's requests have been under consideration for some time and inaction by the Government has caused them to be placed in the form of demands now. A system of fire protection for the forests controlled by the lumbermen so as to replace what they characterize as Government control by private efficiency is also asked by the lumbermen, who have given the government to understand that there must be an immediate decision or the time will be too late to get supplies into the woods over the snow for carrying on any operations next winter.

There are said to be millions of feet of budworm-infected timber standing in the province which will be useless unless it is cut and taken out by next season, one authority stating that fully 98 per cent of the fir upon the Crown Lands of the province has been affected. This, it is urged, adds to the seriousness of the situation. It is said that the attitude of the Government on all points raised has been anything but sympathetic or helpful to the lumber interests.

Premier Foster replied that he could not agree with the statement that the forest protection service was not efficient. The present service was a good one. He was in favor of any plan that would bring about a reduction in the cost. Mr. Foster also said that the present system of collecting stumpage was a great improvement over what was in effect previous to the present government coming into power in 1917. The Premier added that the government did not object to trying out the Quebec system of stumpage for a few years, particularly as the cut would be smaller.

# Some Facts About Quebec Log Crop

### Big Decline in Pulpwood Output but Cut of Timber is up to Average in Some Districts

Lumber operations in the woods this winter are being carried on in the province of Quebec as extensively as in the year previous. This applies to the manufacture of timber and deals. In the case of pulpwood there is less activity on account of continued slump in demand and the low prices prevailing, as well as the terms of purchase offered by the American pulp and paper mill owners.

The Quebec limit holders in their general operations this winter, who cut but a small percentage of logs in the woods last winter, are now cutting 50 per cent. of normal, not, however, in anticipation of a favorable reaction in the United Kingdom market or any appreciable rise in prices, but on account of the small cut in the winter of 1920-21, diminishment of stock and suspense by the provincial government of the Order-in-Council until May next of the rise in operation rates, likewise the lower cost of labor and supplies.

The total quantity of wood cut in the winter of 1920—21 in the province of Quebec under government contract was 1,173,849,000 feet, board measure. This includes the exploitation of pine and production in the Ottawa Valley for the manufacture of pulp and paper, and gave a revenue to the Department of Lands and Forests for the fiscal year ending June 1st, $4,000,000 in comparison to $900,000 received in revenue by the department in 1910, which was then considered a banner year. This increase in revenue received by the government of Quebec is due to successive advances in dues from time to time during the past decade and the organization and surveillance of the forestry service in control of operations.

The chief of the forestry service, G. C. Piche, in his annual report to the government, not yet published, attributes the results so satisfactory to his department, to the forestry service in its control that has given a satisfactory and sensible amelioration in the exploitation of the forest operations for the year of 1920-21, especially as regards the amendments made to the rules and regulations in connection with cutting and the mobilization of inspectors to take care that these regulations are observed, and if violated, fines imposed for infractions.

### Some Interesting Provincial Statistics

The number of woodsmen employed during the following years, with horses employed in camps were:—

1918-19, men 22,265; horses, 7,468; camps 2,850;
1919-20, men 28,633; horses 10,234; camps 3,304;
1920-21, men, 29,270; horses, 9,752; camps 3,387.

No definite figures as to the cut in progress this winter are available, neither as to the men, horses employed or camps, but it is estimated that fully as many are engaged in the woods as last winter owing of the increase in the cut for timber and deals to make up for the decrease in the making of pulpwood in comparison to the active operations last year in this particular respect.

The personnel in the employ of the Department of Lands and Forests in controll of the work of exploitation in the woods, has been increased by 28 men, and now comprises 30 forest engineers, and 99 guards or cullers, a total of 129 men in comparison to 101 the year previous.

There are in the province of Quebec over 2,600 establishments in which wood is the main raw material distributed as follows:— 2,200 sawmills; 369 sash and door factories; 281 planing mills; 34 furniture and chair factories; 30 pulp and paper mills;30 box and crate factories; 23 farm implement factories; 22 carriage and other vehicle factories; 14 butter tub and box factories; 12 broom factories; 16 shipbuilding plants; 8 casket and coffin factories and 8 flooring factories. Through raw lumber has been reduced in price, the manufactured products of nearly all the above factories still maintain high prices.

---

### Eastern Exporters Want Cut in Ocean Rates

The question of ocean freights is receiving much attention and it is felt by the lumber manufacturers in eastern Canada that a much larger business could be done with the Old Country if carrying charges were reduced in order to meet competition from the Baltic and other competing points in Europe.

It is understood that representative lumbermen from various parts of Nova Scotia and New Brunswick had interviews recently with Hon. W. C. Kennedy, Minister of Trade and Commerce, and Mr. R. B. Teakle, of Montreal, manager of the Canadian Merchant Marine, pointing out that rates are altogether too high on shipments across the Atlantic, and many vessels have been lying idle, which might, at least, have made an experimental trip regarding the possibilities of developing overseas trade at a lessened price per standard.

It is charged by several lumbermen that shipping federation is responsible for the stiff levies which now prevail. It seems almost impossible to break the rigid regulations although the lumbermen are

doing everything in their power to show that, with reduced costs, a much larger export trade could be done in spruce and pine deals and even hardwoods.

The matter was thoroughly discussed at a recent gathering in Ottawa and R. L. Sargant, traffic manager of the C. L. A., is acting in conjunction with the Maritime Province men to bring about the desired change.

As showing how high the rates are at the present time compared with those of eight or nine years ago, the following table is of interest:

**Schedule of Ocean Freight from Montreal, Quebec and St. John to London, Liverpool, Glasgow and Manchester**

|  | 1912 | 1913 | 1914 | 1922 |
|---|---|---|---|---|
| Timber and Logs— |  |  |  |  |
| Hardwood and Pine | 65 to 70 S | 65 to 70 S | 65 to 70 S | 165 S |
| Deals— |  |  |  |  |
| Spruce and Pine | 40 S | 40 to 42 S | 35 to 40 S | 100 S |
| Hardwood | 42 S | 48 S | 35 to 42 S | 100 S |
| Boards— |  |  |  |  |
| Spruce and Pine | 43 S | 49 S | 35 to 42 S | 110 S |
| Hardwood— | 60 S | 60 to 65 S | 65 to 70 S | 120 S |

### New Hardwood Flooring Plant in Trenton

The Trenton Hardwood Flooring Co., Limited, of Trenton, Ont. was granted a provincial charter, and will engage in the manufacture of standard grades of hardwood flooring in that town. The company have secured lands and buildings with suitable trackage, and are installing dry kilns and other hardwood flooring equipment. The capacity of the plant will be in the neighborhood of 15,000 feet of finished flooring a day. The firm will also put in equipment for dressing lumber in transit.

W. A. Fraser, managing-director of the Trenton Cooperage Co., is the president of the newly-organized Trenton Hardwood Flooring Co., Limited. R. A. R. Allen of Mill Bridge, is secretary-treasurer and J. B. Morgan one of the directors.

### Well Deserved Promotion for Mr. McNutt

James K. McNutt, for years Secretary-Treasurer of Geo. W. Reed & Co., Limited, Montreal, was, at a recent meeting of the Board of Directors, elected President and Managing Director of the Company.

Mr. McNutt spent the earlier years of his career in the lumber business. His experience in this line goes back to the source, for

he was born in York County, New Brunswick, when lumbering operations were the chief industry in that section. His father owned and operated "McNutt's Mill," a familiar landmark, on Tay Creek.

Geo. W. Reed & Company had been in business over half a century when Mr. McNutt joined it in 1905, as collection clerk. Mr. McNutt's abilities received high recognition, when two years later—1907 the Company was incorporated and he was appointed Secretary-Treasurer. He was so successful in handling the Company's rapidly expanding business that his recent election to the Presidency was the logical result of his seventeen years constructive work with this well known firm. The "Canada Lumberman" congratulates Mr. McNutt and wishes him every success.

# Past Year was Fraught with Many Difficult Problems in the Lumber Arena

### BY R. F. LOGAN, HALIFAX, N. S.

R. F. Logan, Halifax, N. S.

The year 1922 will long be remembered by the lumbermen of Nova Scotia as one presenting great difficulties and problems to those engaged in every branch of the industry. The quantity of lumber produced during the year was probably not over 30% of an average cut, but the large quantity of old lumber carried over from the previous year, more than counterbalanced any salutary effect this curtailment might otherwise have had.

These old stocks were forced on the market early in the season, and under ever increasing pressure, the market, which at no period of the year displayed any strength to speak of, sagged off continually until it reached a very low level, netting the shipper for narrow randoms, anything from $15.00 to $20.00 per M according to local conditions.

While it is too early to predict with any degree of certainty whether the present year has anything better in store than the past, it seems to be the general impression that as the season advances, there will be a gradual resumption of business along lines approaching normal. Certainly prices today show very little if any improvement over those ruling for the past several months, and there does not appear to be any inclination on the part of buyers to enter the market. There seems every indication, both at home, and in the United States that building will be resumed during the coming summer on a large scale and this would certainly produce a very healthy condition in the lumber business.

The great bulk of the old stock in Nova Scotia last year if we except the stock held in storage by the British Government was liquidated during the year, and the stocks of good quality and specification on hand now, are comparatively light for the time of year.

The output of new lumber for the year 1922 will not be much over 50% of an average cut. Operations have been seriously hampered during the winter by the unfavorable weather conditions, the deep snow in some localities forcing the camps to close down.

While the supply of labor has been abundant, there is no reason for good woodsmen to be out of work. Supplies, with the exception of hay, are considerably lower than last winter, and on the whole costs have been reduced to a point which should have the effect of stimulating business in all lines related to the lumber industry.

With the exception of a short period at the beginning and end of last year, shipments to the British market were practically suspended. During this time our market in Britain was largely supplied by the product of European countries, principally Czecho-Slovakia, who were able to compete with our lumber under conditions particularly favorable to them. Their greatest advantage was probably in the matter of freight rates, the Steamship Companies showing no disposition to reduce their rates from this country to allow Canadian shippers to compete with the shorter haul from the Continent. Shippers are looking forward to substantial reductions on liner rates in the near future.

Rates by sailing vessels are already down, and it is altogether likely, that if the market should improve on the other side to any extent, a decided increase in the quantity of lumber shipped to the British market may be experienced. Probably the most encouraging feature of the whole situation so far as the British market is concerned is the continued advance in the rate of Sterling Exchange. All authorities were agreed that with the Sterling at the very low rate prevalent during the past year, and subject to violent fluctuations as it was, that business could be done at only a greatly restricted basis, and as it returns more nearly to par, it may be inferred that export business will be stimulated correspondingly.

Late reports from the United States are optimistic regarding the outlook for building there during the coming season.

According to one very reliable trade report, the building permits for twenty of the largest cities in the New England States for the month of January just past is more than double the value of any previous January since 1914, and if this record is kept up for the balance of the building season, this improvement must necessarily be reflected in an increased demand for building sizes.

The West India market, which usually absorbs a fair amount of Nova Scotia stock, principally pine and spruce boards, has not yet shown very much indication of revival. This is no doubt due to the fact that the present stocks on hand are sufficient for the limited demand in those Islands, coupled with the fact that Southern and Western lumber, which has fallen greatly in price is being used to a great extent. However as Canadian woods have been found to be more suitable for the needs of the West Indies, shippers in Halifax will be prepared to supply this market, when the demand arises.

There is every indication that the local demand will show a decided improvement over last year. The same conditions that are bringing about a resumption of building activity in the United States and other countries, are at work in Nova Scotia, and the cities and towns throughout the province are expected to consume a great deal more stock than last year.

There is one point upon which opinion seems to be unanimous not only among lumbermen, but among all branches of industry in the province, and that is, that the greatest factor in retarding business at the present time is the excessive freight rates. It is to be hoped that the pressure being brought to bear on the Railway Commission by trade organizations and other delegations throughout the country may have the desired effect in bringing about a more equitable freight tariff. There is no question that the present tariff bears more heavily on the shippers and manufacturers in this Eastern portion of the Dominion than any other, and that shippers have suffered very seriously ever since the present tariff went into effect. It is felt that a proper readjustment of freight rates, in conjunction with other improved conditions, would contribute greatly toward restoring the industry to a satisfactory basis.

### Some Exports From Eastern Ports

Figures compiled showing the exports of lumber and lumber products from the port of St. John should be of interest to the trade as they give a comparison for the years 1920 and 1921 and back as far as 1913 and 1914.

A statement issued by the firm of George McKean & Company, Ltd., shows that they handled the enormous amount of 639,892,573 superficial feet from 1913 until 1921. The figures as compiled show their shipments from the port of St. John, from Halifax, N. S., and from Out Ports as follows:—

| | Saint John N.B. | Halifax N.S. | Out Ports |
|---|---|---|---|
| 1913 | 17,948,692 S ft. | 10,409,315 S ft. | 52,073,507 S ft. |
| 1914 | 23,398,599 " | 70,291,336 " | 59,068,634 " |
| 1915 | 36,977,730 " | 20,886,783 " | 55,303,943 " |
| 1916 | 39,730,289 " | 61,132,904 " | 33,100,540 " |
| 1917 | 50,878,602 " | 33,357,757 " | 8,590,472 " |
| 1918 | 9,034,781 " | 3,822,919 " | 1,430,225 " |
| 1919 | 41,084,531 " | 3,844,208 " | 12,518,870 " |
| 1920 | 20,953,387 " | 3,271,154 " | 8,748,371 " |
| 1921 | 33,991,353 " | 3,354,181 " | 13,301,314 " |
| | 305,084,966 | 149,670,039 | 233,137,384 |

### Shipments From St. John to United States

One of the most interesting statments is that compiled by the Consular District for New Brunswick, showing the amount of all lumber and lumber products shipped to the United States through St. John in 1914-15-20-21. The figures follow:—

| | 1914 | 1915 | 1920 | 1921 |
|---|---|---|---|---|
| Lumber | $647,940.89 | $445,035.37 | $2,222,660.74 | $1,134,437.00 |
| Laths | 236,351.76 | 335,319.93 | 374,925.45 | 371,815.00 |
| Pine Boards | 18,725.52 | 28,067.05 | 100,703.86 | |
| Pulp Wood | 75,457.36 | 60,538.10 | 296,001.33 | 148,518.00 |
| Shingles | 414,749.91 | 29,030.98 | 15,362.25 | 12,510.00 |
| Ships' Knees | 594.55 | 152.50 | | |
| Wood Pulp | 432,687.58 | 471,736.52 | 1,827,680.61 | 888,930.00 |
| Ship Timber | | | 1,803.50 | |
| Snow Fences | | | 520.80 | |
| Spruce Filling | | | 20,264.10 | 3,396.00 |
| Wood Cross Arms | | | 1,296.00 | 110.00 |
| Cedar Poles | | | | 6,010.00 |
| | 1,895,507.67 | 1,370,570.35 | 4,861,220.33 | 2,565,726.00 |

# LUMBER CUT IN NEW BRUNSWICK WILL BE SMALL

### By Hon. C. W. Robinson,
#### Minister of Lands and Mines for New Brunswick

Hon. C. W. Robinson Moncton, N.B.

That the estimate made recently in the press regarding the cut of timber on Crown Lands of New Brunswick for the present season is approximately correct, I am now in a position to confirm. The total cut will not exceed 100,000,000 feet. Our forestry department has fairly complete returns by this time and this figure is reliable.

The cut of the previous year was about 200,000,000 feet and the cut of 1919 was about 365,-000,000 feet. These figures will give you an idea of the operations on Crown Lands in the Province of New Brunswick during the past three years. Our normal cut is from 200,000,000 feet to 300,000,000 feet

The winter cut has been light on private lands as a rule. Very few portable mills are in operation, through some few have started in much later in the season than I have ever known, largely encouraged by the attractive prices for lath, and are making a cut of entirely, or almost entirely, lath, for the American market.

The pulp wood situation is very quiet. The operations for pulp wood are few and the quantity is in about the same proportion as the cut of lumber.

The Government has been very much interested of late in discussing with the Committee of the Lumbermen, the question of Quebec scale vs New Brunswick scale, and Quebec system of fire protection vs New Brunswick system of fire protection. No definite conclusion has been reached at the time of writing.

It is generally admitted that the New Brunswick scale on small logs is unfair but it has been in vogue for a long time, and as a matter of fact, it is only a scale by custom as there is no lawful scale in New Brunswick which extends lower than eleven inches. I have thought it advisable to have a legal scale, but before adopting one, am trying to get the best possible advice as to just what scale to adopt.

The system of fire protection in Quebec is in the hands almost entirely of the licensees, who form associations in which the membership is voluntary and they receive some assistance from the Government.

In New Brunswick on the other hand, the system is all controlled by the Forestry Department, with head office at Fredericton, the capital of New Brunswick, and a tax of one cent an acre is placed upon the licensees to assist in carrying out the law. The New Brunswick service has made considerable success in curtailing fires caused by settlers. The restrictions placed upon the burning of slash have been very beneficial and last season fires which occurred in this way, were reduced to a minimum. The most of our fires were caused by sportsmen.

The cost of fire fighting was somewhere about $120,000 which seems excessive for the small province of New Brunswick, but when we consider the meteorological conditions of 1921, and the experience of the State of Maine and the Province of Quebec, I think it will be found that we were just as well off as any of them. The actual damage to Crown lands was light.

Whether any better results could have been obtained under associations such as they have in Quebec is a question, and even with such associations the problem of taking care of that portion of the province which is not under license is a big factor to consider.

So you can see we are not yet settled upon a change in policy, though we have an open mind on the question and would be only too glad to adopt anything that would seem to be an improvement and help to preserve this wonderful natural resource which we have in our forest lands.

## New Lumber Firm Starts in Hamilton

The NorWood Lumber Co., of Hamilton, Ont., have started in the wholesale and retail lumber business on Sherman Ave. North, at the G. T. R. station. The members of the organization M. B. Zimmerman, B. L. Harper and D. G. Webster are widely known to the trade.

Mr. Zimmerman is in charge of the retail yard and will devote his whole time to that end. Mr. Harper and Mr. Webster will work principally in the wholesale branch. Mr. Zimmerman has been in the lumber business for over twenty years, having operated in a retail yard at Grimsby prior to entering the service of the Consumers' Lumber Co., Hamilton, being manager of the yard and factory. He is well versed in all angles of the retail business.

Mr. Harper was for eight years city traveller for the Long Lumber Co., of Hamilton, and Mr. Webster was with the same firm for twelve years, latterly as accountant. The NorWood Lumber Co. starts off under favorable auspices.

## What It Costs to Operate Tractor

David Conklin, of Kingsville, Ont., who is well known as a manufacturer and dealer in hardwood and softwood lumber, is one of those who has used a tractor for a number of years. Mr. Conklin says that he had a tract of timber on the shores of Lake Erie which had to be drawn through the lake sand for some distance. The tractor travelled over the sand like a turtle, drawing her load of 2,000 feet of oak and hickory which is very heavy timber. The fuel for the tractor along with the driver, cost Mr. Conklin $7.50 to make

the trip of about 28 miles loaded one way, whereas four teams and their drivers drawing the same load or number of feet cost $18.00.

Mr. Conklin says he is disposing of his tractor, not on the ground that it did not give him satisfaction, but because he has no particular use for it now as the timber in Essex County is about done. He is an ardent believer of tractor haul and says that in economy, convenience, service and quantity it has team haul beaten in every way.

One of the great advantages the tractor has over the horses, is when the days and roads are not suitable for hauling, the engine is costing nothing for fuel, just the driver to pay, whereas the horses must be fed whether they work or not, and there are the wages of four or five teamsters to meet as well.

## Port Arthur Firm Is Very Busy

John Stirrett & Sons, Limited, of Port Arthur, Ont., have recently become incorporated as a limited liability company. W. C. Willson is the vice-president and managing director. The firm have been running five camps to full capacity during the past winter, and the season's cut will run into large proportions. From every indication the company believe that business in the lumber line is coming back gradually and they will have an active season during the summer and fall of 1922.

John Stirrett & Sons say they have booked some very nice pulpwood orders and are also working on tie orders for the Canadian National and the C. P. Railways. Their output of railway ties will be more than double that of last year,

# NEW LUMBER COMPANY OPENS RETAIL YARD

The Myers Lumbering and Manufacturing Company, of Toronto has been formed and will embark in the lumber business on Eglinton Avenue, at the top of Spadina Road on the old Belt Line The company has a splendidly located site consisting of six acres and will organize a planing mill and factory capable of turning out all kinds of wood work. The President of the company is W. J. Myers, who was for several years in the cooperage business in Toronto and, after retirement for quite a period, has decided to enter the lumber industry.

The managing-director of the new company is W. Warren, who for the past seven years has been in charge of the lumber yard and plant of the R. Laidlaw Lumber Company at the corner of Dundas and Bloor Streets. Previous to coming to Toronto, Mr. Warren was associated with Cushing Bros. of Saskatoon, where he held a responsible position. He is widely known in the trade and on his retirement from the service of the R. Laidlaw Lumber Company, was presented by the staff of the West end yard with a handsome silver tea service and an appreciative address.

# Importance of Proper Dry Kiln Facilities

## Drying of Green Lumber by Right Method Means Saving Money on Freight Bills, Quicker Turnover of Stock and Less Expense in the Yard

By KENNETH REDMAN*

The subject of properly kiln drying lumber is one which may be considered in two lights, either from a strictly technical standpoint, or from a practical trade-point of view. It is along the latter line that I intend to consider the subject and if the only result is to start your readers thinking about modern practice in kiln drying, it will be well worth while. One has only to pick up any of the trade papers today to observe several short articles from different kiln engineers stating the importance of this or that factor in properly seasoning lumber. The fact that these papers are publishing kiln drying articles is, itself, evidence that there is a keen appreciation of the importance of this phase of the lumber industry. These mediums are not only publishing the short articles contributed by various men but are establishing Dry Kiln Departments with technical and practical men in charge and are prepared to give expert service to the lumber men along this line. The more progressive kiln companies in addition to selling the equipment for dry kilns, keep a staff of experienced operators, always subject to the service of their clients to maintain the kilns at maximum efficiency and to instruct the lumber companies' operators in case they are falling down in production. All of this activity denotes that there is a widespread interest and this generally denotes that there is money to be made in bringing your dry kilns up to modern standards.

Now, let us look to the benefits which may be derived by carefully watching this one phase of your business. First of all, you are going to reduce the weight of your lumber and save good money on your freight bill, either for yourself or for your purchaser, and in either case this is going to mean more business for you whether you sell f. o. b. plant or destination. The customer who can buy f. .o. b. plant and only has a small freight bill to pay is going to come back for more lumber and is going to come to the man who gives him dried lumber of proper grade

If you dry your lumber directly from the saw, taking it from the sorting table and loading into your kiln trucks with a proper trackage layout directly to your dry kilns, you will not only effect a great saving in handling charges, but in from two to fourteen days depending upon the species of lumber which you handle, your log is available for the market and ready to be turned into dollars and cents. Contrast this with the expense of stacking in the yard and waiting from four to eight months or more before you have any market for your lumber. Think of the ease with which you can deliver an order which at the time of taking you have not in stock. Think of your investment of capital which is tied up in your yard, on which you are paying interest and insurance, possibly endangering your entire mill operation by fire risk.

Those who depend upon yard seasoning, expect as inevitable, a good heavy loss and degrade in their lumber due to end checks and warping etc. These can be entirely eliminated by a modern kiln, and your total degrade will not amount over 2% or 3%. This drying of green lumber, however, is one which must be undertaken with a good deal of common sense, because not every mill is in a position to undertake it profitably.

I should say, that the large established mill, which has a more or less constant market, is the one which can most profitably at this time undertake to dry, green from the saw. The expense to the small portable type of mill cutting only a few M feet per day would not justify an installation of a battery of kilns at this time, but, the big established mills will not only can save money on proper dry kiln installation, but they can increase their business through judicious advertising of their dry kiln equipment, featuring this to the trade and showing that they are in a position to make immediate shipment on standard and special dimensions if needed, and that the shipment will come through with minimum freight rates and

* Manager Dry Kiln Department B. F. Sturtevant Co.

high quality. This sort of advertising is in effect with several companies today and they are meeting with marked success. It used to be that a firm advertised the excellence of their standing timber, but, I believe within five years they will be advertising the excellence of their dry kilns and the skill of their dry kiln engineer.

### What Constitutes Good Dry Kiln?

Now let us examine what constitutes a good dry kiln. First of all the building should be of substantial fire proof construction of a good insulating material, perfectly hollow tile, or brick. Cement blocks and wood are used, but they are subject to more rapid deterioration, cement to cracking and wood to warping, due to the high humidity used today in most all dry kilns. The kiln must be so designed as to be capable of drying both air seasoned lumber, or green from the saw. Now that we come to the question of design of the dry kiln we come to the point that I wish to drive home.

The drying of lumber does not vary a particle from the modern commercial methods of drying lots of other materials with the one exception that wood is much more complex substance than is usually encountered in the industrial drying of chemicals, fabrics etc. The principle underlying the drying of all these substances is identical, and briefly stated, is that the moisture must not be taken from the surface at a rate faster than the moisture from the centre can work to the surface. This is the golden rule of lumber drying.

Now, what design of kiln will most certainly meet these conditions? If one should write to the Forest Products Laboratory one would undoubtedly receive a reply to the effect that any kiln in which the temperature, humidity and circulation is uniform, ample and under control of the operator, is a good kiln and should give any desired results and this is true but in the late war, we learned very clearly that ample circulation means a great deal more than what had been customary up to that time.

It is a comparatively simple matter to supply a sufficient amount of heat and moisture to the air within a kiln. It is also easy to control the degree of heat and the amount of moisture, but the most important feature of all, namely, the circulation, has only recently come to the front when the stress of war demanded that spruce and mahogany be dried perfectly without loss of strength or tendency to warp after manufacture. Under war conditions, a drying machine was demanded which did not permit a variation of 6% or 8% in the moisture content of the lumber at the end of the run. There could be no pockets in the kiln which remain wet while the majority of the lumber was dried. For this wet lumber when worked into propellers of 6 or 7 laminations would cause the propeller to be thrown out of line. It was then found that, in order to be absolutely certain of uniform drying, that a much larger volume of air was necessary which would carry to the lumber constantly the proper amount of heat and moisture. In other words, look at the circulation in your dry kiln as the railroad system of the country delivering to all parts of the pile the proper amount of heat and moisture, depositing some of the heat and picking up in exchange additional water vapor, the loss of which vapor is the drying of the lumber. If this system falls down, or is inadequate, your drying is retarded and uniform. The mere fact that you have certain conditions in a part of your kiln is of no use whatsoever, unless the kiln is so designed that you are sure that the same conditions exist in all parts of the kiln.

Now the circulation in the pipe coil kiln is caused by convexion currents of air due to an unequal distribution of heat. In other words,hot air rises, cools and then drops and the operation is repeated with a continual intake of fresh air and exhaust of heated air through a system of vents. On the face of it, the fact, that there must be warmer and cooler places within the kiln in order to get circulation, indicates that the rate of drying must vary according to whether the lumber happens to be situated in one of the warmer spots or in a cooler spot. Naturally, the lumber subjected to the warmer air will dry more rapidly than the lumber subjected to the cooler air, with the result that the entire charge of lumber must remain in the kiln until the more slowly drying portions have finished drying.

Further more, the circulation in the centre of the pile is much more sluggish than around the edges and this has its effects in re-

tarding the drying. The result of these uneven conditions is that the drying time is prolonged longer than is necessary and the operation is more difficult due to the varying conditions within the different parts of the dry kiln. During the war I personally examined some 200 to 250 kilns of this type and have yet to find a pipe coil kiln where there are not differences as much as 20. deg. to be found in the pile of lumber. As a result of this deficiency I believe it is safe to say that the majority of the inspectors engaged on this work were convinced of the necessity of a forced circulation of air which would carry the desired conditions of temperature and humidity to all the lumber every minute and hour of the night and day without being effected by the setting of the sun and other climate changes.

### Drying Both Sides of Lumber Uniformly

Thus the modern moist air fan kiln was developed which substituted a rapid movement of air in place of high temperature and which also operated at high humidities. In other words, the climatic conditions of the month of March, are closely imitated when we get the warm moist air breeze which you all know is the safest and quickest condition for drying lumber. Instead of using 170 deg. to 190 deg. of heat, 120 deg. to 140 deg. was used and the air was kept very moist throughout the greater part of the run. As a result of these conditions the lumber comes out soft and workable, caseardening stresses are reduced to a minimum and as a result, the glue work stays in place.

Another feature of a forced air circulation is the fact that the air passes through the lumber in a horizontal plane drying both sides of the lumber uniformly. Compare this with the ordinary pipe coil kiln where the air circulates upwards striking the downfaced surface of the lumber only and practically ignoring the top face surface. This cannot help but produce uneven drying and is one of the causes of most of the cupping of lumber.

I will not attempt to give a word description of the fan kiln except to say that this kiln embodies all of the features of automatic temperatures and humidity control with a uniform and positive circulation at all times. It is a fact, that by merely changing the weight on the lever arm that, within two minutes, the changed conditions are uniformly distributed throughout the entire kiln and are recorded on the recording psychometer for that purpose. When such a kiln is delivered to you it becames strictly a point of intelligent operation from then on to secure quick, high grade drying. Our company does not stop with the selling of the equipment and the installation of it, but maintains a corps of experienced operators who are sent out on every job to make certain that your dry kiln engineer is acquainted with the most approved methods of kiln drying lumber.

The heat efficiency of this kiln, due to the return of nearly all of the air, must be apparent at first glance. The power cost is an additional one to that encountered in a pipe coil kiln, which is partly offset in the saving of steam and more than made up for the speed and quality of drying. Where a plant generates its own electricity the additional power charge is not a noticeable factor and in any event, the saving experienced in the time and quality while drying your lumber more that offsets this power cost.

The equipment for these kilns going into Canadian plants is entirely manufactured at our plant in Galt so that you have first and last a Canadian product. The engineering for this kiln originated in the United States to be sure, but just as soon as conditions warrant we will put on Canadian operators and you will then be getting a dry kiln manufactured in Canada and installed by Canadian engineers.

I want to say that this dry kiln is a mechanical drying machine for drying lumber, and that, if our engineers could advise any further means of making it more efficient or more simple in operation that we would submit any expense in doing so. We have gone into this game with the idea of making this kiln the best one on the market and its performance today justifies our belief that we have succeeded. The drying of lumber is bound, as the years go by, to play an ever increasing and more important part in the economic operation of a saw mill and its product.

### Southern Pine and Douglas Fir Test

Announcement was made recently at the testing laboratories of the Department of Civil Engineering at Columbia University, New York, that it would be two months befors experiments were completed to determine the strength of southern yellow pine and Douglas fir timbers available in commercial lumber yards in New York.

The tests are being made under the auspices of the superintendents of buildings in the city's five boroughs to establish equitable grading rules and working stresses for submission to the Board of Alderman to be considered in connection with recommended revisions of the sections of the building code governing timber construction.

---

## Mr. Clark Reviews Hardwood Outlook

A. E. Clark of Toronto, president of the Canadian Lumbermen's Association, was in South Bend, Ind., recently as the guest of Charles O. Maus, of the Charles O. Maus Lumber Co., and while there had the pleasure of addressing the members of the South Bend Hardwood Club. There was a large attendance and the Canadian lumberman was given a warm welcome. He referred to the deflation that had taken place in all lines of industry and each one was inclined to think that the business with which he was connected had been the hardest hit. Nearly every activity had felt the depression keenly and the agriculture branch was about the last to feel the defects. This, in his opinion, was one of the causes why recovery was not more rapid. Other industries had been struck about the same time, but agriculture being the basic one and the last to suffer, it took longer for the process of readjustment to re-assert itself.

There were those who still thought that hardwood lumber might be reduced to the prices of pre-war years, but this was manifestly impossible owing to various economic and manufacturing conditions. In 1920 the entire cut of lumber in the United States was 28,000,000,000 feet and this was smaller than usual. However, taking this figure as an average for the past seven years and using the average number of feet obtained from the acre in hardwoods, viz., 2,000 feet per acre, the cut of the United States would cover 14,000,000 acres, or in seven years a total of 98,000,000 acres, which represented in all a territory of 154,000 square miles. Thus the timber resources were receding, and while it might be possible for a mill whose limits were located right at the source of supply, to produce lumber at practically the same prices as pre-war years, it could not be carried out in the majority of plants who had to bring their timber from not only rapidly-diminishing but farther-removed areas.

Mr. Clark went on to deal with the freight rates, the high cost of distribution and the likelihood of shortage in supply of thick hardwood stock, particularly if there was any active demand. All these factors meant a readjustment in the basis of prices, and the speaker doubted if values would go any lower. Owing to decreased production, with anything like a normal demand and an improvement in the export situation, there might be another cause for anxiety regarding the future.

Mr. Clark strongly emphasized the necessity for stabilization of quotations, and pointed out that it was only by co-operation and getting fair values that the best interest of the industry were maintained. When the slump set in a year and a half ago, there was a development of that disease sometimes known as "cancelitis." Should a real demand start in the near future, there might be a similar danger if firms began bidding against one another just to get the order: those, who cut prices simply to land the business, might, on turning around to ascertain where they can locate the stock, find themselves sadly disappointed and unable to "make good." The latter remarks were addressed to a number of purchasing agents who were guests at the Hardwood Club.

Mr. Clark touched upon several other phases of the industry and was accorded a hearty vote of Thanks.

### Prominent Peterboro Lumberman Missing

It is believed that John Duignan, a well-known lumberman of Peterboro, Ont., recently met death in the Otonabee river as his coat was found on the C. P. R. bridge. Mr. Duignan disappeared from his home only a few hours before, his family believing that he had retired for the night. The body has not yet been recovered.

Mr. Duignan was for many years manager of the Estate of the Alfred McDonald Lumber Co., of Peterboro, and during the past two years was at the head of the Lakefield Lumber Co., which built and operated a modern mill of medium capacity in that town.

Mr. Duignan leaves a wife and two sons. He had not been in good health for some months and is said to have been despondent over the set-back in the lumber business that followed the boom at the time the new company was organized.

Eastern Distributors, Ltd., St. John, N. B. have been incorporated to conduct a general lumber business, with O. Ring and A. W. Carter, of St. John among the incorporators. Capital $50,000.

# PULPWOOD and PULP

## Many New Drum Barkers Installed

The Canadian Barking Drum Company, Limited, Toronto, have recently installed in the new ground wood plant of the Temiskaming Pulp &Paper Company; at Haileybury, Ontario, a new drum barker, 10 feet in diameter by 30 feet in length. The drum shell is constructed of U-Bars which, it is stated, increase the efficiency of the drums considerably as they practically eliminate all brooming of the wood. The company are now rolling all these U-Bars from their own rolls at the steel mill by which method they have been able to improve further on this important feature of the drum.

The drum is suspended by heavy chains running over heavy traction wheels with chilled rim. There are no bearings or trunions underneath the drum to interfere with the bark and the company say they are in a position to submerge the drum in water held in a cylindrical concrete tank. It is contended that this method of barking is the correct one for getting high capacity and clean wood, as water in connection with the rubbing of the wood plays an important part in the barking action.

The Canadian Barking Drum Company have also recently installed two, 10 by 30 feet drums in the enlarged wood room of the Mattagami Pulp and Paper Company, of Toronto, at their plant which is located at Smooth Rock Falls. The drums are installed side by side, the wood being distributed to both of them.

The Hawk Lake Lumber Company, of Monteith, Ontario, are also putting in one of these barking drums, 8 by 20 feet for rossing wood. The Hawk Lake Company are taking out a considerable quantity of pulpwood, which they will ship barked. The Canadian Barking Drum Company have in Canada and the United States either in operation or construction some 186 barkers and, in Northern Ontario, there are several in use by the Abitibi Power and Paper Company, the Northern Ontario Colonization and other organizations. Pulp and paper plants are calling more and more for wood that is barked and contractors report that it is becoming increasingly difficult to sell rough wood. A large amount is saved in freight, handling charges, etc. by having the product barked.

## Says Pulpwood Situation Is Quiet

Such a slump in demand and in wages in the lumber and pulpwood industry in Quebec as has been prevalent has not been known for a long period. This is the opinion expressed by J. G. Coulombe of the St. Lawrence Lumber Company, Quebec.

In an interview Mr. Coulombe stated that one of the anomalies of human nature was the fact that great pulp concerns piled up huge supplies of wood at top-hole prices during the war although realizing that prices and demand would come down before long.

Continuing, he said that the bottom in wages had not yet been reached. The decline in woods operations in 1920-21 was such that wages went down from $3.50 and $3.00 a day to $1.25, and there were many more men than jobs.

"And yet, you know," he said, "my father can recall the days when the best of native woodsmen were glad to get their $16.00 a month "all found," during the rigors of the winter months. They would walk as much as 60 to 100 miles, dunnage on their backs to the jobs they desired to undertake during the winter months. Their diet then was just pork and beans and molasses. And let me tell you, they were the finest woodsmen in the world. Nowdays the companies house the men in warm log cabins and feed them, as though they were guests at the Ritz or some other big hostelry."

## Using Clean Water for Preserving Pulp

R. J. Blair, Pathologist of the Forest Products Laboratories, McGill University, who has been experimenting over a period of many months in the use of clean water as a preservative for stored mechanical pulp, states that the various forms of pulp deterioration are due to the action of wood destroying fungi and moulds. To keep pulp free from attacks of any of these it is necessary to store the material in such a way that one or more of the requirements of the mould or fungus plants will be lacking. Starting from the accepted fact that wood which is immersed in water, or is covered with water-

saturated soil, is not destroyed by agencies which bring about ordinary decay, he has experimented in the use of clean water for preserving pulp. He makes public the following summary and conclusions of the experiments:

Of the pulp received only part was stored in water. The remaining laps and sheets were left in the building with the storage tanks and were freely exposed to the air. After seventeen months this latter material was found to be in very bad condition.

A comparison between fresh lapped pulp and that stored in water shows that after seventeen months there was slight deterioration in all cases. For pressed pulp the same condition held but was more noticeable.

....In stored slush stock the freeness was higher that in the case with either laps or pressed pulp stored for the same length of time under the same conditions, and the strength tests were also somewhat lower.

In making a comparison between different methods of water storage running water apparently gave a better result than either a weekly or daily change.

In cold storage little deterioration seems to occur.

The results indicate that water storage is superior to air storage for groundwood pulp.

## Paper Mills Win Safety Awards

At a meeting of the directors of the Ontario Pulp & Paper Makers' Safety Association, held in Toronto recently, the trophies for competition for the best accident record among the pulp and paper mills in Ontario for the past year were awarded.

In Class A—mills employing 200 people or over, the Dryden Pulp & Paper Co., of Dryden, Ont., was given the award with 24 non-fatal accidents, involving a loss of time of 374½ days, which is equal to 2.31 lost time per full time worker.

In Class B—mills employing 200 hands or over, the award went to the Don Valley Paper Co., of Toronto. This plant had 1 non-fatal accident during the year, involving a loss of time of one day, or .028 days per full time worker.

One shield and one flag will be presented to the Dryden Co. and the Don Valley Co., respectively. The shield will stay in their possession during the current year but the flag will remain their property for all time.

## Mr. Barnjum Pays Visit to Ontario

Mr. Frank J. D. Barnjum, of Annapolis Royal, N. S. who is an extensive timber limit holder in the Bluenose province, and also a manufacturer of groundwood pulp, was in Toronto recently, calling upon a number of friends in the forest products line. Mr. Barnjum is widely known as an able authority and convincing writer on the conservation of Canada's forest resources and the urgent necessity of more protective steps being taken to guard these holdings for the future. He is an ardent advocate of reforestation, the burning of slash, an export duty on pulpwood, elimination of waste, more careful cutting and an intensive fight against the destructive spruce bud-worm, and other measures of an effective nature.

## General Summary of Western Outlook

Writing the "Canada Lumberman" a leading British Columbia firm say that stocks have been reduced sixty per cent during the past year and that prices fell 30 to 40 per cent. They look for an increased demand and better quotations in 1922.

Regarding the general situation, they say labor costs are somewhat lower and efficiency higher, making for a considerable lower cost of production. There is a gradually increasing demand for specialties and uppers with a tendency to slightly higher prices. There is but little call for lower grades at prices below cost of production. An increasing activity in export is noted as transportation rates are lowered. Jap squares are active at prices little more than cost of production.

# CURRENT LUMBER PRICES—WHOLESALE

## TORONTO

(In Car Load Lots, F.O.B. cars Toronto)

**White Pine**

| | | |
|---|---|---|
| 1 x 4/7 Good Strips | $100.00 | $110.00 |
| 1¼ & 1½ x 4/7 Good Strips | 120.00 | 125.00 |
| 1 x 8 and up Good Sides | 150.00 | 160.00 |
| 2 x 4/7 Good Strips | 130.00 | 140.00 |
| 1¼ & 1½ x 8 and wider Good Sides | 185.00 | 190.00 |
| 2 x 8 and wider Good Sides | 190.00 | 200.00 |
| 1 in. No. 1, 2 and 3 Cuts | 75.00 | 80.00 |
| 5/4 and 6/4 No. 1, 2 and 3 Cuts | 95.00 | 100.00 |
| 2 in. No. 1, 2 and 3 Cuts | 105.00 | 110.00 |
| 1 x 4 and 5 Mill Run | 52.00 | 55.00 |
| 1 x 6 Mill Run | 53.00 | 56.00 |
| 1 x 7, 9 and 11 Mill Run | 53.00 | 56.00 |
| 1 x 8 Mill Run | 55.00 | 58.00 |
| 1 x 10 Mill Run | 60.00 | 62.00 |
| 1 x 12 Mill Run | 65.00 | 70.00 |
| 5/4 and 6/4 x 5 and up Mill Run | 58.00 | 60.00 |
| 2 x 4 Mill Run | 52.00 | 53.00 |
| 2 x 6 Mill Run | 53.00 | 56.00 |
| 2 x 8 Mill Run | 55.00 | 58.00 |
| 2 x 10 Mill Run | 58.00 | 62.00 |
| 2 x 12 Mill Run | 60.00 | 64.00 |
| 1 in. Mill Run Shorts | 35.00 | 40.00 |
| 1 x 4 and up 6/16 No. 1 Mill Culls | 32.00 | 34.00 |
| 1 x 10 and up 6/16 No. 1 Mill Culls | 36.00 | 38.00 |
| 1 x 12 and up 6/16 No. 1 Mill Culls | 37.00 | 39.00 |
| 1 x 4 and up 6/16 No. 2 Mill Culls | 25.00 | 27.00 |
| 1 x 10 x 12 6/16 No. 2 Mill Culls | 28.00 | 30.00 |
| 1 x 4 and up 6/16 No. 3 Mill Culls | 17.00 | 22.00 |

**Red Pine**

(In Car Load Lots, F.O.B. Toronto)

| | | |
|---|---|---|
| 1 x 4 and 5 Mill Run | $35.00 | $36.00 |
| 1 x 6 Mill Run | 38.00 | 40.00 |
| 1 x 8 Mill Run | 40.00 | 42.00 |
| 1 x 10 Mill Run | 42.00 | 44.00 |
| 2 x 4 Mill Run | 38.00 | 40.00 |
| 2 x 6 Mill Run | 40.00 | 42.00 |
| 2 x 8 Mill Run | 41.00 | 43.00 |
| 2 x 10 Mill Run | 44.00 | 47.00 |
| 2 x 12 Mill Run | 49.00 | 50.00 |
| 1 in. Clear and Clear Face | 70.00 | 72.00 |
| 2 in. Clear and Clear Face | 70.00 | 72.00 |

**Spruce**

| | | |
|---|---|---|
| 1 x 4 Mill Run | 35.00 | 36.00 |
| 1 x 6 Mill Run | 36.00 | 37.00 |
| 1 x 8 Mill Run | 38.00 | 40.00 |
| 1 x 10 Mill Run | 45.00 | 47.00 |
| 1 x 12 Mill Run Spruce | 48.00 | 50.00 |
| Mill Culls | 25.00 | 27.00 |

**Hemlock (M R)**

(In Car Load Lots, F.O.B. Toronto)

| | | |
|---|---|---|
| 1 x 4 and 5 in. x 9 to 16 ft | $26.00 | $27.00 |
| 1 x 6 in. x 9 to 16 ft | 33.00 | 35.00 |
| 1 x 8 in. x 9 to 16 ft | 34.00 | 36.00 |
| 1 x 10 and 12 in. x 9 to 16 ft | 35.00 | 37.00 |
| 1 x 7, 9 and 11 in. x 9 to 16 ft | 33.00 | 35.00 |
| 2 x 4 to 12 in., 18 ft | 37.00 | 39.00 |
| 2 x 4 to 12 in., 20 ft | 40.00 | 42.00 |
| 1 in. No. 2, 6 ft. to 16 ft | 23.00 | 25.00 |

**Fir Flooring**

(In Car Load Lots, F.O.B. Toronto)

| | | |
|---|---|---|
| Fir flooring, 1 x 3 and 4", No. 1 and 2 Edge Grain | | $73.00 |
| Fir flooring, 1 x 3 and 4", No. 1 and 2 Flat Grain | | 48.00 |
| (Depending upon Widths) | | |
| 1 x 4 to 12 No. 1 and 2 Clear Fir, Rough | | 77.00 |
| 1¼ x 4 to 12 No. 1 and 2 Clear Fir, Rough | | 81.00 |
| 2 x 4 to 12 No. 1 and 2 Clear Fir, Rough | | 77.00 |
| 3 & 4 x 4 to 12 No. 1 & 2 Clear Fir, Rough | | 84.00 |
| 1 x 4, 5 and 6 in. Fir Casing | $73.00 | 80.00 |
| 1 x 8 and 10 Fir Base | 78.00 | 86.00 |
| 1¼ and 1½ 8, 10 and 12 in. E.G. Stepping | 90.00 | 95.00 |
| 1¼ and 1½ 8, 10 and 12 in. F.G. Stepping | 80.00 | 85.00 |
| 1 x 4 to 12 Clear Fir, D4S | 72.50 | 79.50 |
| 1¼ and 1½ x 4 to 12 Clear Fir, D4S | 75.25 | 82.25 |
| XX Shingles, 6 butts to 2", per M | | 3.20 |
| XXX Shingles, 6 butts to 2", per M | | 5.25 |
| XXXXX Shingles, 5 butts to 2", per M | | 6.10 |

**Lath**

(F.O.B. Mill)

| | |
|---|---|
| No. 1 White Pine | $11.00 |
| No. 2 White Pine | 10.00 |
| No. 3 White Pine | 8.00 |
| Mill Run White Pine, 32 in | 5.00 |
| Merchantable Spruce Lath, 4 ft | 6.50 |

## TORONTO HARDWOOD PRICES

The prices given below are for car loads f.o.b. Toronto, from wholesalers to retailers, and are based on a good percentage of long lengths and good widths, without any wide stock having been sorted out.

The prices quoted on imported woods are payable in U. S. funds.

**Ash, White**

(Dry weight 3800 lbs. per M. ft.)

| | 1s & 2s | No. 1 Com. | No. 2 Com. |
|---|---|---|---|
| 1" | $100.00 | $ 60.00 | $ 35.00 |
| 1¼ and 1½" | 105.00 | 65.00 | 35.00 |
| 2" | 110.00 | 70.00 | 45.00 |
| 2½ and 3" | 125.00 | 80.00 | 55.00 |
| 4" | 140.00 | 95.00 | 60.00 |

**Ash, Brown**

| | 1s & 2s | No. 1 Com. | No. 2 Com. |
|---|---|---|---|
| 1" | $ 95.00 | $ 55.00 | $ 30.00 |
| 1¼ and 1½" | 100.00 | 60.00 | 30.00 |
| 2" | 105.00 | 65.00 | 33.00 |
| 2½ and 3" | 125.00 | 80.00 | 55.00 |
| 4" | 140.00 | 95.00 | 60.00 |

**Birch**

(Dry weight 4000 lbs. per M. ft.)

| | 1s & 2s | Sels. | No. 1 Com. | No. 2 Com. |
|---|---|---|---|---|
| 4/4 | $105.00 | $ 80.00 | $ 50.00 | $ 32.00 |
| 5/4 | 110.00 | 85.00 | 55.00 | 35.00 |
| 6/4 | 115.00 | 90.00 | 60.00 | 38.00 |
| 8/4 | 120.00 | 100.00 | 65.00 | 42.00 |
| 12/4 | 125.00 | 105.00 | 70.00 | 50.00 |
| 16/4 | 130.00 | 110.00 | 80.00 | 55.00 |

**Basswood**

(Dry weight 2500 lbs. per M. ft.)

| | 1s & 2s | No. 1 Com. | No. 2 Com. |
|---|---|---|---|
| 4/4 | $ 80.00 | $ 50.00 | $ 25.00 |
| 5/4 and 6/4 | 85.00 | 60.00 | 30.00 |
| 8/4 | 90.00 | 65.00 | 35.00 |

**Chestnut**

(Dry weight 2800 lbs. per M. ft.)

| | 1s & 2s | No. 1 Com. | Sound Wormy |
|---|---|---|---|
| 1" | $130.00 | $ 80.00 | $ 40.00 |
| 1¼" to 1½" | 135.00 | 85.00 | 43.00 |
| 2" | 145.00 | 90.00 | 48.00 |

**Maple, Hard**

(Dry weight 4200 lbs. per M. ft.)

| | F.A.S. | Sels. | No. 1 Com. | No. 2 Com. |
|---|---|---|---|---|
| 4/4 | $ 80.00 | $ 65.00 | $ 45.00 | $ 33.00 |
| 5/4 | 80.00 | 65.00 | 45.00 | 38.00 |
| 6/4 | 85.00 | 70.00 | 50.00 | 45.00 |
| 8/4 | 95.00 | 75.00 | 60.00 | 50.00 |
| 12/4 | 100.00 | 75.00 | 65.00 | 60.00 |
| 16/4 | 120.00 | 100.00 | 70.00 | 65.00 |

**Elm, Soft**

(Dry weight 3100 lbs. per M. ft.)

| | 1s & 2s | No. 1 Com. | No. 2 Com. |
|---|---|---|---|
| 4/4 | $ 75.00 | $ 50.00 | $ 25.00 |
| 6/4 and 8/4 | 80.00 | 60.00 | 30.00 |
| 12/4 | 96.00 | 70.00 | 35.00 |

**Gum, Red**

(Dry weight 3300 lbs. per M. ft.)

| | Plain 1s & 2s | Plain No. 1 Com. | Quartered 1s & 2s | Quartered No. 1 Com. |
|---|---|---|---|---|
| 1" | $120.00 | $ 70.00 | $133.00 | $ 83.00 |
| 1¼" | 120.00 | 70.00 | 148.00 | 88.00 |
| 1½" | 130.00 | 75.00 | 148.00 | 88.00 |
| 2" | 135.00 | 95.00 | 158.00 | 103.00 |

Figured Gum, $10 per M. extra, in both plain and quartered.

**Gum, Sap**

| | 1s&2s | No. 1 Com. |
|---|---|---|
| 1" | $ 55.00 | $ 40.00 |
| 1¼" and 1½" | 60.00 | 44.00 |
| 2" | 65.00 | 50.00 |

**Hickory**

(Dry weight 4500 lbs. per M. ft.

| | 1s&2s | No. 1 Com. |
|---|---|---|
| 1" | $120.00 | $ 60.00 |
| 1¼" | 145.00 | 65.00 |
| 1½" | 145.00 | 65.00 |
| 2" | 150.00 | 70.00 |

**Plain White and Red Oak**

(Plain sawed. Dry weight 4000 lbs. per M. ft.)

| | 1s&2s | No. 1 Com. |
|---|---|---|
| 4/4 | $120.00 | $ 75.00 |
| 5/4 and 6/4 | 130.00 | 80.00 |
| 8/4 | 135.00 | 85.00 |
| 10/4 | 145.00 | 90.00 |
| 12/4 | 145.00 | 90.00 |
| 16/4 | 150.00 | 95.00 |

**White Oak, Quarter Cut**

(Dry weight 4000 lbs. per M. ft.)

| | 1s&2s | No. 1 Com. |
|---|---|---|
| 4/4 | $160.00 | $ 90.00 |
| 5/4 and 6/4 | 170.00 | 95.00 |
| 8/4 | 190.00 | 105.00 |

**Quarter Cut Red Oak**

| | 1s&2s | No. 1 Com. |
|---|---|---|
| 4/4 | $145.00 | $ 80.00 |
| 5/4 and 6/4 | 160.00 | 90.00 |
| 8/4 | 165.00 | 95.00 |

**Beech**

The quantity of beech produced in Ontario is not large and is generally sold on a log run basis, the locality governing the prices. At present the prevailing quotation on log run, mill culls out, delivered in Toronto, is $35.00 to $40.00.

## OTTAWA

Manufacturers' Prices

**Pine**

| | | |
|---|---|---|
| Good sidings: | | |
| 1 in. x 7 in. and up | | $140.00 |
| 1¼ in. and 1½ in., 8 in. and up. | | 165.00 |
| 2 in. x 7 in. and up | | 165.00 |
| No. 2 cuts 2 x 8 in. and up | | 80.00 |
| Good strips: | | |
| 1 in. | $100.00 | $105.00 |
| 1¼ in. and 1½ in. | | 120.00 |
| 2 in. | | 125.00 |
| Good shorts: | | |
| 1 in. x 7 in. and up | | 110.00 |
| 1 in. 4 in. to 6 in. | 85.00 | 90.00 |
| 1¼ in. and 1½ in. | | 110.00 |
| 2 in. | | 125.00 |
| 7 in. to 9 in. A sidings | 54.00 | 56.00 |
| No. 1 dressing sidings | 70.00 | 74.00 |
| No. 1 dressing strips | | 62.00 |
| No. 1 dressing shorts | 50.00 | 53.00 |
| 1 in. x 4 in. s.c. strips | | 48.00 |
| 1 in. x 5 in. s.c. strips | | 48.00 |
| 1 in. x 6 in. s.c. strips | | 50.00 |
| 1 in. x 7 in. s.c. strips | 63.00 | 64.00 |
| 1 in. x 8 in. s.c. strips, 12 to 16 ft. | | 54.00 |
| 1 in. x 10 in. M.R. | | 58.00 |
| S.C. sidings, 1½ and 2 in. | 58.00 | 60.00 |
| S.C. strips, 1 in. | | 45.00 |
| 1¼, 1½ and 2 in. | 50.00 | 55.00 |
| S.C. shorts, 1 x 4 to 6 in. | 34.00 | 36.00 |
| S.C. and bet., shorts, 1 x 5 | | 36.00 |
| S.C. and bet., shorts, 1 x 6 | | 42.00 |
| S.C. shorts, 6-11 ft., 1 x 10 in. | | 48.00 |
| Box boards: | | |
| 1 in. x 4 in. and up, 6 ft.-11 ft. | | 34.00 |
| 1 in. x 3 in. and up, 12 ft.-16 ft. | 35.00 | 37.00 |
| Mill cull shorts, 1 in. x 4 in. and x 4 in. and up, 12 ft. and up | 24.00 | 26.00 |
| Mill culls, strips and sidings, 1 in. up, 6 ft. to 11 ft. | | 22.00 |
| O. culls r and w p | 18.00 | 20.00 |

**Red Pine, Log Run**

| | | |
|---|---|---|
| Mill culls out, 1 in. | 32.00 | 34.00 |
| Mill culls out, 1¼ in. | 32.00 | 34.00 |
| Mill culls out, 1½ in. | 32.00 | 34.00 |
| Mill culls out, 2 in. | 32.00 | 34.00 |
| Mill Culls, white pine, 1 in. x 7 in. and up | | 20.00 |

**Mill Run Spruce**

| | | |
|---|---|---|
| 1 in. x 4 in. and up, 6 ft.-11 ft. | | 23.00 |
| 1 in. x 4 in. and up, 12 ft.-16 ft. | 30.00 | 32.00 |
| 1" x 9"-10" and up, 12 ft.-16 ft. | | 35.00 |
| 1¼" x 7, 8 and 9" up, 12 ft.-16 ft. | | 53.00 |
| 1¼ x 10 and up, 12 ft.-16 ft. | 38.00 | 42.00 |
| 1½" x 12" x 12" and up, 12'-16' | | 42.00 |
| Spruce, 1 in. clear fine dressing and B | | 55.00 |
| Hemlock, 1 in. cull | | 20.00 |
| Hemlock, 1 in. log run | 24.00 | 26.00 |
| Hemlock, 2 x 4, 6, 8, 10 12/16 ft. | | 28.00 |
| Tamarac | 25.00 | 28.00 |
| Basswood, log run, dead culls out | 45.00 | 50.00 |
| Basswood, log run, mill culls out. | 50.00 | 54.00 |
| Birch, log run | 45.00 | 50.00 |
| Soft Elm, common and better, 1, 1½, 2 in. | 58.00 | 68.00 |
| Ash, black, log run | 62.00 | 65.00 |
| 1 x 10 No. 1 barn | 57.00 | 62.00 |
| 1 x 10 No. 2 barn | 51.00 | 56.00 |
| 1 x 8 and 9 No. 2 barn | 47.00 | 52.00 |

# CURRENT LUMBER PRICES—WHOLESALE

**Lath per M.:**

| | | |
|---|---|---|
| No. 1 White Pine, 1¼ in. x 4 ft. | | 8.00 |
| No. 2 White Pine | | 6.00 |
| Mill run White Pine | | 7.00 |
| Spruce, mill run, 1½ in. | | 6.00 |
| Red Pine, mill run | | 6.00 |
| Hemlock, mill run | | 5.50 |

**White Cedar Shingles**

| | | |
|---|---|---|
| XXXX, 18 in. | 9.00 | 10.00 |
| Clear butt, 18 in. | 6.00 | 7.00 |
| 18 in. XX | | 5.00 |

## QUEBEC

**White Pine**
(At Quebec)

| | Cts. Per Cubic Ft. | |
|---|---|---|
| First class Ottawa wancy, 18 in. average according to lineal | 100 | 110 |
| 19 in. and up average | 110 | 120 |

**Spruce Deals**
(At Mill)

| | | |
|---|---|---|
| 3 in. unsorted, Quebec, 4 in. to 6 in. wide | $ 20.00 | $ 25.00 |
| 3 in. unsorted, Quebec, 7 in. to 8 in. wide | 26.00 | 28.00 |
| 3 in. unsorted, Quebec, 9 in. wide | 30.00 | 35.00 |

**Oak**
(At Quebec)

| | Cts. Per Cubic Ft. | |
|---|---|---|
| According to average and quality, 55 ft. cube | 125 | 130 |

**Elm**
(At Quebec)

| | | |
|---|---|---|
| According to average and quality, 40 to 45 ft. cube | 100 | 120 |
| According to average and quality, 30 to 35 ft. | 90 | 100 |

**Export Birch Planks**
(At Mill)

| | | |
|---|---|---|
| 1 to 4 in. thick, per M. ft. | $ 30.00 | $ 35.00 |

## ST. JOHN, N.B.

(From Yards and Mills)

**Rough Lumber**

| | | |
|---|---|---|
| 2x3, 2x4, 3x3, 3x4. Rgh Merch Spr | $30.00 | |
| 2x3, 2x4, 3x3, 3x4, Dressed 1 edge | 31.00 | |
| 2x3, 2x4, 3x3, 3x4, Dressed 4 sides | 31.00 | |
| 2x6, 2x7, 3x5, 4x4, 4x6, all rough. | 30.00 | |
| 2x6, 2x7, 3x5, 4x4, 4x6, all rough. | 34.00 | |
| 2x8, 3x7, 5x5, 6x6 | 37.00 | $ 40.00 |
| 2x9, 3x8, 6x8, 7x7 | 37.00 | 40.00 |
| 2x10, 3x9 | 45.00 | |
| 2x12, 3x10, 3x12, 8x8 and up | 45.00 | |
| Merch. Spr. Bds., Rough, 1x3-4 & 5 | 30.00 | |
| Merch. Spr. Bds., Rough, 1x6 | 34.00 | |
| Merch. Spr. Bds., Rough, 1x7 & up | 40.00 | |
| Refuse Bds., Deals and Setgs | 18.00 | 20.00 |

Above random lengths up to 18-0 long.
Lengths 19-0 and up $5.00 extra per M.
For planing Merch. and Refuse Bds. add $2.00 per M. to above prices.
Laths, $7.00.

**Shingles**

| | Per M. |
|---|---|
| Cedar, Extras | $6.00 |
| Cedar, Clears | 5.25 |
| Cedar, 2nd Clears | 4.25 |
| Cedar, Extra No. 1 | 2.90 |
| Spruce | 4.50 |

## SARNIA, ONT.

**Pine, Common and Better**

| | |
|---|---|
| 1 x 6 and 8 in. | $110.00 |
| 1 in., 8 in. and up wide | 130.00 |
| 1¼ and 1½ in. and up wide | 180.00 |
| 2 in. and up wide | 180.00 |

**Cuts and Better**

| | |
|---|---|
| 4/4 x 8 and up No. 1 and better | 125.00 |
| 5/4 and 6/4 and up No. 1 and better | 150.00 |
| 8/4 and 8 and up No. 1 and better | 150.00 |

**No. 1 Cuts**

| | |
|---|---|
| 1 in.. 8 in. and up wide | 110.00 |
| 1¼ in., 8 in. and up wide | 125.00 |
| 1½ in., 8 in. and up wide | 125.00 |
| 2 in., 8 in. and up wide | 130.00 |
| 2½ in. and 3 in., 8 in. and up wide | 175.00 |
| 4 in., 8 in. and up wide | 185.00 |

**No. 1 Barn**

| | | |
|---|---|---|
| 1 in., 10 to 16 ft. long | $ 75.00 | $ 85.00 |
| 1¼, 1½ and 2 in., 10/16 ft. | 80.00 | 85.00 |
| 2½ to 3 in., 10/16 ft. | 85.00 | 100.00 |

**No. 2 Barn**

| | | |
|---|---|---|
| 1 in., 10 to 16 ft. long | 65.00 | 75.00 |
| 1¼, 1½ and 2 in., 10/16 ft. | | 66.00 |
| 2½, 1½ and 3 in. | | 85.00 |

**No. 3 Barn**

| | | |
|---|---|---|
| 1 in., 10 to 16 ft. long | 48.00 | 55.00 |
| 1¼, 1½ and 2 in., 10/16 ft. | 50.00 | 56.00 |

**Box**

| | | |
|---|---|---|
| 1 in., 1¼ and 1½ in., 10/16 ft. | 33.00 | 35.00 |

**Mill Culls**

Mill Run Culls—

| | |
|---|---|
| 1 in., 4 in. and up wide, 6/16 ft. | 27.00 |
| 1¼, 1½ and 2 in. | 28.00 |

## WINNIPEG

**No. 1 Spruce**

| Dimension | S.1.S. and 1.E. | | | |
|---|---|---|---|---|
| | 10 ft. | 12 ft. | 14 ft. | 16 ft. |
| 2 x 4 | $30 | $29 | $29 | $30 |
| 2 x 6 | 31 | 29 | 29 | 30 |
| 2 x 8 | 32 | 30 | 30 | 31 |
| 2 x 10 | 33 | 31 | 31 | 32 |
| 2 x 12 | 34 | 32 | 32 | 33 |

For 2 inches, rough, add 50 cents.
For S1E only, add 50 cents.
For S1S and 2E, S4S or D&M, add $3.00.
For timbers larger than 8 x 8, add 50c. for each additional 2 inches each way.
For lengths longer than 20 ft., add $1.00 for each additional two feet.
For selected common, add $5.00.
For No. 2 Dimension, $3.00 less than No. 1.
For 1 x 2 and 2 x 2, $2 more than 2 x 4 No. 1.
For Tamarac, open.

## BUFFALO and TONAWANDA

**White Pine**
Wholesale Selling Price

| | |
|---|---|
| Uppers, 4/4 | $225.00 |
| Uppers, 5/4 to 8/4 | 225.00 |
| Uppers, 10/4 to 12/4 | 250.00 |
| Selects, 4/4 | 200.00 |
| Selects, 5/4 to 8/4 | 200.00 |
| Selects, 10/4 to 12/4 | 225.00 |
| Fine Common, 4/4 | 155.00 |
| Fine Common, 5/4 | 160.00 |
| Fine Common, 6/4 | 160.00 |
| Fine Common, 8/4 | 160.00 |
| No. 1 Cuts, 4/4 | 115.00 |
| No. 1 Cuts, 5/4 | 130.00 |
| No. 1 Cuts, 6/4 | 135.00 |
| No. 1 Cuts, 8/4 | 140.00 |
| No. 2 Cuts, 4/4 | 70.00 |
| No. 2 Cuts, 5/4 | 100.00 |
| No. 2 Cuts, 6/4 | 105.00 |
| No. 2 Cuts, 8/4 | 110.00 |
| No. 3 Cuts, 5/4 | 60.00 |
| No. 3 Cuts, 6/4 | 65.00 |
| No. 3 Cuts, 8/4 | 67.00 |
| Dressing, 4/4 | 95.00 |
| Dressing 4/4 x 10 | 98.00 |
| Dressing, 4/4 x 12 | 110.00 |
| No. 1 Moulding, 5/4 | 150.00 |
| No. 1 Moulding, 6/4 | 150.00 |
| No. 1 Moulding, 8/4 | 155.00 |
| No. 2 Moulding, 5/4 | 125.00 |
| No. 2 Moulding, 6/4 | 125.00 |
| No. 2 Moulding, 8/4 | 130.00 |
| No. 1 Barn, 1 x 12 | 90.00 |
| No. 1 Barn, 1 x 6 and 8 | 76.00 |
| No. 1 Barn, 1 x 10 | 80.00 |
| No. 2 Barn, 1 x 6 and 8 | 62.00 |
| No. 2 Barn, 1 x 10 | 63.00 |
| No. 2 Barn, 1 x 12 | 75.00 |
| No. 3 Barn, 1 x 6 and 8 | 42.00 |
| No. 3 Barn, 1 x 10 | 44.00 |
| No. 3 Barn, 1 x 12 | 47.00 |
| Box, 1 x 6 and 8 | 36.00 |
| Box, 1 x 10 | 38.00 |
| Box, 1 x 12 | 39.00 |
| Box, 1 x 13 and up | 40.00 |

## BUFFALO

The following quotations on hardwoods represent the jobber buying price at Buffalo and Tonawanda.

**Maple**

| | 1s & 2s | No. 1 Com. | No. 2 Com. |
|---|---|---|---|
| 1 in. | $ 80.00 | $ 45.00 | $ 30.00 |
| 5/4 to 8/4 | 85.00 | 50.00 | 30.00 |
| 10/4 to 4 in. | 90.00 | 55.00 | 30.00 |
| **Sap Birch** | | | |
| 1 in. | 90.00 | 48.00 | 30.00 |
| 5/4 and up | 100.00 | 53.00 | 30.00 |
| **Soft Elm** | | | |
| 1 in. | 70.00 | 45.00 | 30.00 |
| 5/4 to 2 in. | 75.00 | 50.00 | 30.00 |
| **Red Birch** | | | |
| 1 in. | 120.00 | 75.00 | |
| 5/4 and up | 125.00 | 80.00 | |
| **Basswood** | | | |
| 1 in. | 70.00 | 45.00 | 30.00 |
| 5/4 to 2 in. | 80.00 | 55.00 | 35.00 |
| **Plain Oak** | | | |
| 1 in. | 95.00 | 55.00 | 35.00 |
| 5/4 to 2 in. | 105.00 | 65.00 | 40.00 |
| **Ash** | | | |
| 1 in. | 85.00 | 50.00 | 30.00 |
| 5/4 to 2 in. | 95.00 | 55.00 | 30.00 |
| 10/4 and up | 110.00 | 70.00 | 30.00 |

## BOSTON

Quotations given below are for highest grades of Michigan and Canadian White Pine and Eastern Canadian Spruce as required in the New England market in car loads.

| | | |
|---|---|---|
| White Pine Uppers, 1 in. | | |
| White Pine Uppers, 1¼, 1½, 2 in. | | |
| White Pine Uppers, 2½, 3 in. | | |
| White Pine Uppers, 4 in. | | |
| Selects, 1 in. | | $190.00 |
| Selects, 1¼, 2 in. | | 200.00 |
| Selects, 2½, 3 in. | | |
| Selects, 4 in. | | |
| Prices nominal | | |
| Fine Common, 1 in., 30%, 12 in. and up. | | 165.00 |
| Fine Common, 1 x 8 and up | | 165.00 |
| Fine Common, 1¼ to 2 in. | $165.00 | 170.00 |
| Fine Common, 2½ and 3 in. | | 180.00 |
| Fine Common, 4 in. | | 195.00 |
| 1 in. Shaky Clear | | 100.00 |
| 1¼ in. to 2 in. Shaky Clear | | 110.00 |
| 1 in. No. 2 Dressing | | 95.00 |
| 1¼ in. to 2 in. No. 2 Dressing | | 95.00 |
| No. 1 Cuts, 1 in. | | 110.00 |
| No. 1 Cuts, 1¼ to 2 in. | | 140.00 |
| No. 1 Cuts, 2½ to 3 in. | | 180.00 |
| No. 2 Cuts, 1 in. | | 80.00 |
| No. 2 Cuts, 1¼ to 2 in. | | 110.00 |
| Barn Boards, No. 1, 1 x 12 | | 88.00 |
| Barn Boards, No. 1, 1 x 10 | | 84.00 |
| Barn Boards, No. 1, 1 x 8 | | 82.00 |
| Barn Boards, No. 2, 1 x 12 | | 75.00 |
| Barn Boards, No. 2, 1 x 8 | | 71.00 |
| Barn Boards, No. 2, 1 x 10 | | 68.00 |
| Barn Boards, No. 3, 1 x 12 | | 48.00 |
| Barn Boards, No. 3, 1 x 10 | | 47.00 |
| Barn Boards, No. 3, 1 x 8 | | 47.00 |

**No. 1 Clear**

| | | |
|---|---|---|
| Can. Spruce, No. 1 and clear, 1 x 4 to 9" | | $ 78.00 |
| Can. Spruce, 1 x 10 in. | | 78.00 |
| Can. Spruce, No. 1, 1 x 4 to 7 in. | | 75.00 |
| Can. Spruce, No. 1, 1 x 8 and 9 in. | | 75.00 |
| Can. Spruce, No. 1, 1 x 10 in. | | 76.00 |
| Can. Spruce, No. 2, 1 x 4 and 5 in. | | 34.00 |
| Can. Spruce, No. 2, 1 x 6 and 7 in. | | 36.00 |
| Can. Spruce, No. 2, 1 x 8 and 9 in. | | 38.00 |
| Can. Spruce, No. 2, 1 x 10 in. | | 41.00 |
| Can. Spruce, No. 2, 1 x 12 in. | | 45.00 |
| Spruce, 12 in. dimension | | 46.00 |
| Spruce, 10 in. dimension | | 45.00 |
| Spruce, 9 in. dimension | | 43.00 |
| Spruce, 8 in. dimension | | 42.00 |
| 2 x 10 in. random lengths, 8 ft. and up | | 40.00 |
| 2 x 12 in., random lengths | | 43.00 |
| 2 x 3, 2 x 4, 2 x 5, 2 x 6, 2 x 7 | | 30.00 |
| 3 x 4 and 4 x 4 in. | | 31.00 |
| 2 x 9 | | 38.00 |
| All other random lengths, 7 in. and under, 8 ft. and up | 30.00 | 34.00 |
| 5 in. and up merchantable boards, 8 ft. and up, D 1s | 30.00 | 32.00 |
| 1 x 2 | 30.00 | 32.00 |
| 1 x 3 | | 30.00 |
| 1⅝ in. Spruce Lath | | 8.75 |
| 1½ in. Spruce Lath | | 8.00 |

**New Brunswick Cedar Shingles**

| | |
|---|---|
| Extras | 5.25 |
| Clears | 4.25 |
| Second Clear | 3.75 |
| Clear Whites | 3.00 |

Second Hand Machinery & Equipment Wanted & For Sale

# Quick Action Section

Special Lots Of Lumber— —Positions Wanted & Vacant

## Lumber Wanted

### Wanted

One half million feet of each Pine, Spruce and Hemlock. Dry stock or stock now being sawn. Box 835, Canada Lumberman, Toronto. 6

### Wanted

To contract a large quantity of 5/8" x 4" and 5" log run spruce with mill culls out. Address H. V. Berry, Fort Plain, N.Y. 3-6

### Hard Maple Wanted

Several cars 8/4 and 12/4 dry stock, No. 1 and 2 Common. For further particulars apply. Box No. 826 Canada Lumberman, Toronto. 5-8

### Wanted

Sawdust and Baled or Loose. Shavings. Pine or Hardwood. Quote f.o.b. mill and describe. Apply Box 789 Canada Lumberman, Toronto. 4-8

### Hard Maple Wanted

A number of cars each of 1"; 1-1/8" and 1¼" dry; quote lowest price, stating grade and shipping point. Box 805 Canada Lumberman, Toronto. 4-7

### We Will Buy

A block of Hemlock, Spruce, Red or White Pine that is sawn or will be sawn before the 15th of March. Box 770 Canada Lumberman, Toronto. 2 T.f.

### Hard Maple and Birch Wanted

A limited quantity of 4/4 and 8/4 dry stock No. 2 Common and Better. For further particulars apply Box 761 Canada Lumberman, Toronto, Can. 2-7

### Hemlock Wanted

We are in the market for a few blocks of Mill Run or No. 1 and No. 2 Hemlock lumber and lath.

The Elgie & Jarvis Lumber Co. Limited,
18 Toronto St., Toronto 6

### Wanted, Dry Birch and Hemlock

We are open to purchase dry Birch lumber, all thicknesses, and also 2" good Merchantable Hemlock. Will also contract for one or two good mill cuts. Box 827 Canada Lumberman, Toronto. 5-6

### Wanted

To contract for supply of ROCK ELM for bending purposes Cut 3¼" thick for delivery June, July and August. No substitute for Rock Elm will be accepted. Quote price to St. Mary's Wood Specialty Co. Ltd., St. Mary's Ont. 5-8

### Hard Maple Wanted

Carload lots 1¼" x 6 x 10'—1sts and 2nds, dry.
Carload lots (1¼" x 2½" x 49", 1" x 3½" x 49" clear, dry, equal number of pieces each size in each car.
Box 782 Canada Lumberman, Toronto. 3-7

## Lumber For Sale

### For Sale

250,000 feet Soft Elm Lumber.
1,000 Cords Slabs, mostly Pine and Hemlock.
John Harrison & Sons Co. Limited,
Saw and Planing Mills,
Owen Sound, Ont. 6

### PUBLISHER'S NOTICE

Advertisements other than "Employment Wanted" or "Employees Wanted" will be inserted in this department at the rate of 25 cents per agate line (14 agate lines make one inch). $3.50 per inch, each insertion, payable in advance. Space measured from rule to rule. When four or more consecutive insertions of the same advertisement are ordered a discount of 25 per cent. will be allowed.

Advertisements of "Wanted Employment" will be inserted at the rate of one cent a word, net. Cash must accompany order. If Canada Lumberman box number is used, enclose ten cents extra for postage in forwarding replies. Minimum charge 25 cents.

Advertisements of "Wanted Employees" will be inserted at the rate of two cents a word, net. Cash must accompany the order. Minimum charge 50 cents.

Advertisements must be received not later than the 10th and 20th of each month to insure insertion in the subsequent issue.

### Cherry in Logs

I have on hand 200,000 ft. of cherry in logs to be cut in the spring. If you are in the market to buy, please advise me what price you are able to pay on the cars. Box 836, Canada Lumberman, Toronto. 6

### For Sale

Two million feet dry merchantable spruce from 1" to 4" thick, dry on sticks. Can be shipped rough or dressed. Also approximately two million feet Birch, Beech and Maple, 1", 2" and 3", Mill Run, Culls out. Prices right All dry. Sawn during season 1920-21. Rhodes, Curry Ltd., Amherst, N.S. 5-8

### For Sale

10 Cars of Mill Run Beech Sawed approximately 65%—6/4 Balance 4/4.
9 Cars 1" & 2" Hard Maple Chiefly second Growth straight grain White Lumber suitable for Bending.
1 Car 6/4 Soft Elm No. 2 & Better.
1 Car 8/4 Soft Elm No. 2 & Better.

The above is all Bone Dry and we can make Prompt Shipment.

Apply Box 887 Canada Lumberman, Toronto. 6-7

### WHITE PINE LUMBER
### For Immediate Shipment—1920 Cut—Should Be Bone Dry

About 30,000 ft. 2 in.
" 18,000 ft. 1 in.
" 2,000 ft. 3 in.

Apply to J. A. Farnsworth, Cookshire, Quebec. 6-T.f.

### "Canadian Lath"

All grades White Pine, Red Pine, Jack Pine, Spruce, and Hemlock. Carefully manufactured ⅜ x 1½"-4' and 32".

Brewster Loud Lumber Co.,
508 Lincoln Building,
5-6 Detroit, Michigan.

### For Sale

At Blind River, Ontario, Pine and Spruce Lath, also some Cedar and Hemlock Lath. Grades, four foot mill run, 32" mill run, and four foot No. 3.

F. P. Potvin,
Blind River, Ont.
2-T.f.

### Lumber for Sale

| | | | |
|---|---|---|---|
| 100 | M. 1" Basswood | 15 | M. 1" Soft Maple |
| 15 | M. 2" Rock Elm. | 15 | M. 1¼" " |
| 25 | M. 2" Soft Elm. | 50 | M. 2 x 4/6/8" x 12 |
| 25 | M. 1" Soft Elm. | | Spruce |
| 8 | M. 1" Ash. | 3 | M. 1½" Hickory |

All last winter's cut.
Also 10,000 Cedar fence posts.

Glenn A. Shaver,
5-8 Lunenburg, Ont

## Machinery For Sale

### For Sale

30-18 Monarch Tractor with five sets of heavy log trucks and chains, if needed for good roads building, log bunks can be removed and boxes put on. Apply Box 834, Canada Lumberman, Toronto. 6

### Saw Mill Machinery for Sale

Including Engine, Boilers, Edger, Shafting, Solid Iron Pulleys, Gears etc. Attractive prices for immediate sale. Box 790 Canada Lumberman, Toronto. 4-7

### For Sale

Neverslip Monarch Tractor 20-12 H.P. in first-case condition, only used short time. Will sacrifice for quick sale. Apply Rhodes, Curry Limited, Amherst, N.S. 5-8

### For Sale

One Buffalo-Pitts Road tractor, 65 H.P. good for 180 lbs. steam. Would make good Saw-mill outfit or roadmaking, also two heavy freight wagons. For particulars apply to Bancroft Lumber and Mfg. Co. Ltd., Bancroft, Ont. 6

### For Sale
#### Second Hand Machinery

1—35 H.P. John Inglis & Son Boiler.
1—45 H.P. Perkins Engine.
1—Lloyd Manfg. Co., Double Edger
1—16 foot Robbs Carriage.
1—Trimmer, 1-14" Belt 40 feet, 1-12" Belt 85 feet.

Shafting and pulleys, to put a small portable mill together. Address D. N. Therlault, Burnsville, Glou., Co., N.B. 6

### Wickes Gang

GANG: No. 12 Wickes Gang, 40" sash, 15" stroke, steam binder rolls, front and back in two sections, feed and oscillation combined, 1908 model, and has been in use for five years. We furnish with this gang 11 rolls for cants and stock, one filing machine, and 4 sets of saws.

THE PEMBROKE LUMBER CO.,
1t.f. Pembroke, Ont.

### For Sale

Band Resaw, 54" Berlin with 3—5½" saws, $1000.00
Box-Board Printer, one-color, Con. & Deng. 10" x 44" $400.00
Box-Board Printer, two-color, 19" x 44" Hooper Late type, Chain feed $800.00
Box-Board Squeezer, 40" x 48", Mereen-Johnson automatic $700.00
Corrugated Fastener Driver, Doig 2-head $475.00
Equalizer, Berlin No. 229 automatic, Cap. up to 8' 6" long $675.00
Lock-Corner Cutter, Morgan No. 8 double end, $600.00
Lock-Corner Setting-Up machine, Morgan No. 2, $400.00
Nailing machines, all styles, Morgan & Doig. State your wants.
Sander, double-disc, 48" Fischer, all iron $285.00
Screw Driving Machines, Reynolds No. 2 $250.00 Each. (2).
Surfacer, single, 24" x 8" J. A. Fay & Co. Sectional Roll, $850.00
Surfacer, double, 30" x 7" Whitney, Sectional roll, $1150.00.

Chas. N. Braun Machinery
4-7 Fort Wayne, Indiana.

### For Sale En-Bloc

Complete Saw Mill equipment, including one Four Block Hamilton Carriage. One pair heavy twin engines, feed complete and steam nigger. One three block E. Long Carriage with eight inch gun shot feed and steam nigger. One heavy three saw edger, W. Hamilton, make. Three 75 H.P. Boilers complete with dutch ovens and stacks. One 90 H.P. engine and fly-wheel complete. One lath and shingle mill. Complete filing equipment. One refuse burner. Shafting pulleys, transmission, etc., complete. Apply Box 788 Canada Lumberman, Toronto. 3-8

### Engines, Boilers, etc., for Sale

One "Williams" Upright Engine 6" x 6"
One Upright Engine 5" x 6"
Six Return tubular boilers of following dimensions:-
One "Butterfield" 72" x 14' - 3¼" tube - ⅝" shell.
One "Polson" 64" x 14' - 3¼" tube - ½" shell
One "Doty" 60" x 15' - 4" tube - ½" shell
One "Doty" 60" x 14½" - 4" tube - ½" shell
One "Doty" 60" x 15' -4" tube - ½" shell
One "Inglis" 60" x 16' - 3" tube - ½" shell
One double acting "Northey" Fire pump, 6" suction, 5" discharge, 14" steam cylinder, 8" water cylinder, 13" stroke, Capacity 450 gallons per minute.
One "Northey" feed pump 6 x 4 x 7" stroke, Capacity 60 gallons per minute.
One brass Mill steam whistle.

For further particulars apply The Conger Lumber Co Limited., Parry Sound. Ontario. 24 T.f.

## Machinery Wanted

### Wanted

Right Hand carriage for Mill 30 M. capacity. Must be in good condition. Box 806 Canada Lumberman, Toronto. 4-7

### Wanted
#### Following Used Machines

Matcher six inch drop rip saw, swing cut-off saw, band saw, Jointer, Planer. State particulars and price. Reply Box 838 Canada Lumberman, Toronto. 6

## Situations Wanted

Band Sawyer with thirteen years experience and A1 references and fast Niggerman. Apply Box No. 813 Canada Lumberman, Toronto. 5-6

Filer, band or circular, open for position best of references. 20 years experience in saw works and mills. Box 808 Canada Lumberman, Toronto. 5-6

POSITION WANTED: As manager for a good responsible Lumber Co., 36 years experience in Lumbering. Box 729 Canada Lumberman, Toronto. 1-6

Want positon, as bandsaw filer, double cut preferred. Worked for the same company last four seasons. A1 references. Box 759 Canada Lumberman, Toronto. 4-7

Young man 28, wishes permanent position in lumber camp, preferably outdoor work, have had several years experience in office work. Box 840 Canada Lumberman, Toronto. 6-7

WANTED POSITION: for 1922 as head filer in good large Band Mill. Expert in every detail. Satisfaction guaranteed. Apply Box 780 Canada Lumberman, Toronto. 1-6

Lumber salesman, good connection, Toronto to Montreal, fifteen years experience, moderate salary. Open for engagement after the 25th inst. Box 807 Canada Lumberman, Toronto. 6

Wanted position as Mill Superintendent. Eight years experience as Mill Superintendent fifteen years as sawyer. Can furnish best references. Box 747 Canada Lumberman, Toronto. 1-6

Position of responsibility wanted by man thoroughly familiar with the retail lumber, sash and door and millwork business. Twelve years experience, several of which as estimator and in charge of order department in one of the largest plants in the West. Take off own bills of quantities. First class testimonials. Age 38. Good salary expected. At present employed in the East but desire change. Go anywhere. What can you offer? Reply to Box 842 Canada Lumberman, Toronto 7

# Review of Current Trade Conditions

### Montreal Reports Business as Improving

It is difficult to write in definite terms of the Montreal lumber market. At the present time conditions are of such a mixed character that, as one wholesaler put it, "we hardly know where we are." Business is by no means bad so far as volume is concerned, but it has not reached the proportions that were expected, neither have prices settled down to a firm basis. According to some wholesalers, prices are not as satisfactory as could be desired, and offerings are being made at a very low rate. The large spruce mills are still asking higher values, but some of the smaller manufacturers are quoting comparatively low figures. Some good orders for the American market have been received.

Hardwoods, especially birch, are a little firmer, although it is difficult to dispose of the lower grades.

B. C. woods are somewhat slow of sale, the recent advance on fir not having been maintained. The rise checked the demand, consequently it was found advisable to go back to the old terms.

Spruce lath continues strong, while white pine lath is scarce and high in price.

A letter received from England refers in pessimistic terms to the hardwood market there. Heavy stocks of birch are still held and with the furniture trade in a depressed condition, sales, even at reduced prices, are difficult to negotiate, only the highest grade having any chance of disposal.

Although the building permits for February—$561,100—show a decrease of $62,505 as compared with the corresponding month last year, there is evidence that construction will be of a satisfactory amount during the season. Several large projects are contemplated, and tenders are out for some of these. The total permits for the two months amount to $777,560, a decrease of $199,270 compared with 1921.

Many lumber firms in the Province will be hit by the Provincial Government's proposals to double the tax on motor trucks, making it $50 per ton, and also to prohibit heavy trucks operating in certain parts of the Province. The Government feel that the trucks destroy the roads and that the owners of the vehicles should be made to pay more for the maintenance of the highways. The result will be, no doubt, to check the use of trucks, in fact, it was stated by a member of the Government that the legislation is proposed in order to restrict the use of heavy vehicles.

Reports have been circulated regarding the condition of the British Government lumber piled at various points in the Maritime Provinces. It has been asserted that the stock, or, at least the greater portion of it, is in very bad shape. Official information, however, is to the effect that although a comparatively small portion is of little value, by far the greater part is in good condition and that much of it is 1920 sawing. It is understood that it is intended to offer some of the stock through wholesalers only.

Exports of pulpwood continue to diminish. For the month of January the total was 66,094 cords, of a value of $696,943, compared with 155,752 cords and $2,271,464 last year. During the ten months of the fiscal year, the exports were 630,540 cords, valued at $7,926,536 as against 1,243,112 cords, valued at $16,396,940 for the corresponding period in 1921.

### Ottawa Lumber Prices Drop on Several Lines

Substantial decreases, in many grades of pine and spruce lumber, were announced by some lumber manufacturers in the Ottawa lumber market during the early period of March. The decreases are in contrast with prices which have prevailed more or less generally since the early part of the year and will likely be the basis of the spring and summer prices.

The best grades of pine good sidings, good strips, and good shorts, were not affected and held firm as to their price. There were some of the trade, however, who intimated that the prices on the better grades of stock might show a reduction in the future.

No. 1, dressing shorts, showed the greatest decrease, falling down from a previous quotation of from $68 to $73, down to a quotation of from $50 to $53. Other grades of dressing shorts, also came down very considerably, as did box boards, mill culls, and old culls.

Red pine, log run, in all grades, dropped heavily on the top price quotations and from two to three dollars per M on the previously lowest figure which had been quoted.

Mill run spruce, in grades 1 and 4 in. and up to 9 and 10 in.,

also dropped slightly. The lowest lumber quotation on the market under the new schedule is from $18 to $20 per M, which is the figure for old pine culls, r. and w.p.

The exact reason for the considerable reduction had not yet been made clear, but it was unofficially believed that the lack of demand during 1921, was the chief factor. Some of the trade, on the other hand, thought it was a move on the part of the manufacturers to add an early stimulus toward increased building, restore public confidence in building, and bring about a more normal movement of stock.

Another view taken of the situation is that logs in the woods have been much more cheaply produced this year, than in past years, and that some manufacturers knowing their woods conditions, are ready to make sacrifices to create sales and get old high cost stock off their hands, to meet competition in the new stock market.

However, as said before, the real factors for the decreased prices, whether the ones given above are correct or not, are not definitely stated, and it will probably be from one to two weeks or perhaps longer, before the real reasons for the substantial drop, will be explained.

The market for the last month so far as demand was concerned remained very poor. Very few orders filtered through which were mostly from the United States for middle grades of stock.

In early March the outlook of the trade was for better business which was largely based with the settlement of conditions and wage questions between contractors and members of labor unions. The settlement of, carpenters, bricklayers, and stone masons, all of whom accepted lowered wages was taken as a most favorable sign.

Export to European countries continued negligible.

Bush operation progressed in a most satisfactory manner. The snow was not too deep, and the temperature was very favorable. Wages paid amounted to from $26 to $32 with board.

### Eastern Conditions Will Depend on Demand

Just what the condition of the lumber industry in New Brunswick will be this year depends entirely on the demand. From present indications the trade is slowly but surely picking up and in time will be back to normal.

With a feeling of optimism operators throughout the province went ahead and cut during the winter considerably more than had been planned last fall hoping that market conditions would improve and the demand for New Brunswick's leading product throughout the United Kingdom increase.

At the present time leading operators and shippers are not prone to join the ranks of the prophets and are merely marking time and waiting for a revival of trade. Just what the outcome will be time alone can tell and lumber dealers are non-commital when approached regarding prospects during 1922.

The present state of the lumber market was indicated recently at a meeting of the St. John city council when tenders were received from firms in Halifax and Amherst, N. S., among local bids for a supply of lumber for harbor and ferry departmental uses. A list of the tenderers and prices submitted follows:— J. S. Gregory—588 pieces spruce logs, $1,911.

Union Lumber Co.—$52.25 a thousand for Douglas fir; 38c. a foot for spruce logs.

J. A. Likely, Ltd.—Douglas fir, $47.50 a thousand.

Thos. Bell,—$53.75 a thousand for Douglas fir.

W. Malcolm Mackay—Spruce deals, $25.75 and $34 a thousand, according to size.

J. A. Gregory—Spruce deals, $24 to $45 a thousand, according to size; spruce logs, $38 a thousand feet.

J. Roderick & Sons— Spruce deals, $26.90 to $35; Douglas fir, $52.50; hemlock, $33.

Musgrave & Co., Halifax, hemlock, $32.50; Douglas fir, $54.75 to $55.25.

Rhodes, Curry, Ltd., Amherst—Spruce deals, $28.90 to $33; Douglas fir, $55.

### Contemplated New Work Shows Big Volume

The volume of contemplated new work reported in Canada during February according to MacLean Building Reports, Limited amounted to $27,011,200 compared with $22,391,600 in January. Construction contracts awarded in February amounted to $10,718,300 compared with $8,392,600 in January. Residential buildings

accounted for 37.8% of the February total and amounted to $4,049,200. Business buildings amounted to $2,539,600 or 23.7% of the total; industrial buildings $610,000 or 5.7%; public works and utilities $3,519,500 or 32.8%. Industrial building, although small, showed a gratifying increase over the previous month.

During January, the Wholesale price Index of 48 Building Materials receded to a point 6.1% below December 1921 and is now 88.3% above 1913 compared with a peak of 183.8% reached in May, 1920. Prices have now declined 51.9% from the high.

There seems no good reason why we should not witness in 1922, a revival in building construction upon the largest scale since the boom days of 1912 and 1913. Wages have come down in a considerable degree, and labor in the building trades is easy to secure, and, in general more efficient than it has been for several years. Building costs, while still above the level of pre-war times, have gone through a considerable deflation, and it is probable that they will not recede any lower until the edge is taken off demand by a year or two active building. Money for building purposes will be available in a plentiful supply and interest will probably be lower in the near future. All these factors unite with the great need for housing facilities to bring about a situation which should result in a general resumption of construction all along the line in the year 1922.

## Gives an Estimate of Decreased Cut

A representative lumberman, whose business takes him through all portions of Northern Ontario, in conversation with the "Canada Lumberman" recently regarding the cut during the present winter, stated that it would be larger in some sections than was anticipated, although not as large as during the season of 1920 and 1921. The decrease in the amount of hemlock taken out he estimates will be from 25% to 30%, hardwoods 60% to 65%, white pine about 10%. While spruce will be about the same as a year ago and jack pine may show a gain of from 5% to 10%. The month of March has been particularly favorable in getting out timber and everything in connection with logging operations was conducted on a satisfactory basis. The men in the bush are much more content and efficient than a year ago and it is stated that the logs delivered at the mills in various points in Northern Ontario, will not cost as much as those of last winter, the decrease being variously estimated all the way from 25% to 40%.

It is generally thought that the lumber business will pick up materially by the end of March. More enquiries are being received all the while and some of them have been translated into orders. As the spring approaches, the feeling of confidence increases and this is noticeable especially in the larger cities and growing towns. In the villages and other centres which depend mostly upon the agricultural population for their support, things are not so bright. The farmers are waiting for another crop before launching out in any heavy expenditure for new buildings. In the meantime, the alert retailer is doing all in his power to push the repair trade and is losing no opportunity to drive home the fact that it is false economy for the agriculturist to allow his fences, barns and outbuildings and sheds to become delapidated through not buying the necessary boards and nails to keep his property in presentable shape.

## New Aerial System of Lumber Drying

The Canadian Vatu Drying and Woodworking Co., Limited, whose plant and limits are located at Island Lake, Ont., sixteen miles from Sault Ste Marie on the Algoma Central Railway, recently spent a considerable sum in overhauling their sawmill and water power. The President and General Manager of the company is J. A. Craig, formerly of Peekskill, N. Y., who is the inventor of a natural air lumber dryer. The other directors of the company are business men of Sault Ste. Marie, who joined with the inventor in organizing the Canadian Vatu Drying & Woodworking Co. Mr. Craig says his invention has been patented in Canada, the United States and several foreign countries. The company are also manufacturing in their factory baseball bats made out of yellow birch.

Mr. Craig says that this new natural air drier, which he has perfected, will dry all kinds of lumber from the saw including any variety of southern pine, gum, poplar and oak taking out as high as from eight to forty per cent. moisture in a two hour run according to the percentage of moisture the lumber contains. Mr. Craig adds that the first drier, a small one, was installed at Island Lake, Ont., a year and half ago and the initial test was on round green birch dowels, 38 inches long, two and three quarter inches in diameter and weighing 5,500 pounds to the thousand feet. A run of two hours was made and twenty per cent. of moisture was taken out. The dowels were then piled up for six days and reweighed, which according to Mr. Craig, they showed that all of the moisture in the saturated fibre had been removed, the wood weighing 3,000 pounds to the

thousand feet. The drier has been in the use ever since drying out baseball stocks.

Writing to the "Canada Lumberman", Mr. Craig says—"We have just finished several successful tests in frozen green pine and hardwood at Island Lake in zero weather and even up to twenty below. The drier is in a building where the temperature ranges from 60 to 70 Fah. The lumber is run for two hours and then is taken out and kept seven days in the same temperature and, in every case the moisture came out to the required weight, the stock being free from checks or warping. The dry of green frozen white pine and all Canadian hardwoods is done equally satisfactory, according to the moisture content of the wood. Dryers can be built to take care of drying any amount of lumber or timber and the largest task undertaken so far was for 4,000 feet per drier in two hours, taking eight horse power to run the dryer. The lumber is run into the drier in cars from the sorting table and locked in, to run at 3,500 feet per minute for a period of one to two hours. The cars are next unlocked and run into drysheds and, in seven days in winter and five days in summer, the stock is ready to ship or work up into whatever is required. The dryer was invented for the small lumber manufacturer so that he could cut his green logs into lumber one week, and dry and ship the product the next week, thus getting the highest market price and saving insurance, freight, interest etc."

## Cost of Operating Logging Railway

In connection with the operation of logging railways, it may be stated that the cost of the installation and operation can only be approximated as conditions differ so widely.

The Dennis-Canadian Co., of Whitney, Ont., who have ten miles of track and built their own railroad nine years ago, say that they have been operating in a very rough country, using standard guage track with 56 lb. rail. If a fairly level section, the cost of making grade is about double that of good roads for sleigh haul. The ties, if they can be made along the track, cost about $500.00 per mile, and will last about ten years. Rails can be considered as an investment with the exception of freight, as re-laying rail can usually be sold at what it cost, subject to market fluctuation. Where there is no rocky cutting to be done, the grade for standard guage and laying of rails will cost about $3,000. per mile, exclusive of material used. For lighter operations a 36-guage is a much more economical outfit all the way through, the cost of rail equipment and the cost of installation and in making changes on branches in the woods.

Mr. L. Van Meter, manager of the company, states they use a 40-ton locomotive of the geared type, which is more flexible and permits of shorter curves and will work on grades where a road locomotive would be useless. Grades up to 10% can be used where the train can be handled in sections and 30% curves are not a serious proposition.

The company use 10-foot bunks with 3-foot drop stakes on their logging cars, and, on a 10-mile haul, are bringing in two trains of 12 cars each per day, and this could be done on a much longer haul. Where logs are assembled to the track by sleigh during the winter or where they are taken from the water it permits of continuous operation.

....As a general proposition where there is, say, five years supply of timber to be handled, Mr. Van Meter is of the opinion that $1.00 per M should be sufficient to take care of railroad depreciation and construction.

## Fire Losses in Canada are Amazing

The sum of $5.52 per capita is the amount of the fire loss chargeable to every man, woman and child in Canada for 1921, or a total of over $45,000,000. In spite of fire prevention propaganda carried out by various organizations, the losses from fire seem to be increasing from year to year. In 1919 the figure was, roughly, $25,000,000; 1920, $28,000,000; and in 1921 $45,000,000; an increase of approximately 60%.

A deplorable feature is that the greater part of this loss need not have occurred, for simple precautionary and preventative measures would have reduced the loss in many cases if they would not have prevented it altogether. When it is considered that the per capita loss in Canada is the highest in the world and is nearly six times as great as the per capita loss of Great Britain, thinking persons are forced to the conclusion that Canadians are not as careful or as progressive in regard to fire and prevention as the citizens of other countries.

Total expenditure for building throughout the United States for the year 1921 was $1,595,165,192, a gain of 14.9 per cent over the record year of 1920, according to Bradstreet's. Reports from 150 cities showed that $120,594,839 had been expended for building in December, a gain of 112.8 per cent over December, 1920.

# *The Ten Commandments of Present Day Business*

The science of proper merchandising, plainly teaches us the following Ten Commandments:

1. That all commodities offered for sale to the public, should be offered in quantity or measurement terms, easily and fully understandable to the public.

2. No one should be asked, or expected to buy any commodity under quotation or price denominations that are in the least mysterious to the buyers, or by which they themselves cannot easily compute and determine the relation of price to quantity.

3. That the use of "Trade Terms" for quantities and prices is entirely ethical and proper as between the different branches of the trade, who fully understand their quantitive proportions and relative values, but they are not ethical or proper in retailing to the public which does not understand them and cannot calculate or estimate them.

4. That the public must and will mistrust the merchants who force it to buy their line of goods under terms of measurement and price, that it does not understand and cannot calculate.

5. If you wish to gain and hold the confidence, trust and good will of the trade, then you must abandon the high sounding prices of "Trade Terms" quantities and treat and trade with them in terms entirely understandable to them.

6. That the customers who buy from you under measurement and prices bases that are mysterious to them, are justifiably apt to be apprehensive and suspicious as to having gotten an honest and square deal. You wouldn't like to buy that way yourself. Why ask them to?

7. It is good business practice to reduce all of your quantity and price units to the smallest and simplest forms possible to the commodity handled, so as to bring it within the ready intelligence and understanding of those to whom it is offered.

8. Prices per piece in any commodity of piece units is the simplest and most easily understood form for selling that commodity.

9. Selling lumber under prices per piece or per lineal foot makes it so easily comprehensible that a child can figure it, or calculate the cost of any amounts needed, and it will reduce the dealers time spent in figuring and estimating under the per thousand feet board measure system by two-thirds and eliminate most of his errors.

10. The retail merchants of every important commodity sold, EXCEPT LUMBER, have reduced their measurement and price standards and terms to the simplest possible units, placing them fully within the understanding of any customer. NOW WHY NOT LUMBER? It is easy to do: It cuts your work in half: It eliminates you your errors: It will make and satisfy your customers: It is good merchandising.

There is a right way and a wrong way of doing things and the fore going Bulletin, (No. 306) recently sent out by the Ontario Safety League, shows how accidents may be avoided when carrying boards from one part of the lumber yard to another.

# EDGINGS

The Big Bear Lumber Co., was recently registered in Toronto.

Frank D. Barnjum, of Annapolis Royal, N. S., was a recent visitor to Montreal.

George Hughes is rebuilding the shingle mill at Trout Mills, near North Bay which was burned down.

The Howard Smith Paper Co., of Montreal, contemplate the erection of a portable pulp mill at Gaspe, Quebec.

James W. E. Elliott, a New Toronto lumber merchant, who died intestate on December 23, 1921, left an estate of $68,560.

At the present time there are approximately 35,000,000 feet of logs in J. Holly & Sons booms in South Bay, N. B. At this time last year, there were 23,000,000.

Robert Imrie of the R. Imrie Lumber Co., Toronto, is receiving the congratulations of his many friends in the industry on the advent of a son and heir in his home.

Gordon G. Scott, a lumberman of Fredericton, N. B., has assigned. His liabilities are placed at $125,000, while it is said that the assets amounted to approximately $70,000.

George Wagner was seriously injured while working in the lumber woods at Jemseg, N. B., a few days ago. He was struck in the face with a peavy and for a time his condition was critical.

The Ottawa City Council has awarded the contract for rough lumber required during the present year in the Board of Works Department to the Independent Coal & Wood Co., Ottawa.

Herbert Comba, foreman of a sawmill near Perth, Ont., was instantly killed on Tuesday morning when he was struck on the face by a huge splitter which had been hurled from a log by a circular saw.

It is expected that the new machines of the Abitibi Power & Paper Co., at Iroquois Falls, Ont., which are now turning out about 450 tons daily, will soon be producing over 500 tons. They are being speeded up all the time.

John W. Gerney recently visited relatives in Fredericton, N. B. He is president of the Garvey Lumber Corporation of New York, which operates a number of mills. He predicts an early improvement in the lumber market in the United States.

The sawmill of the A. L. M. & D. Co., Limited, at Abbotsford, B. C., recently resumed after being shut down for two months, the longest period in several years, owing to the cold weather. During the time of the frost the plant was completely overhauled.

Rev. Dixon Smith who has returned recently from India, has purchased the equipment of a sawmill belonging to Joseph Wrightson at Cargill, Ont. Mr. Smith has had it crated and shipped to India to be used in connection with his work in the industrial school at Cocanada.

The Sheppard & Gill Lumber Co., Limited, Toronto, was recently incorporated with provincial charter to acquire the firm known as Sheppard & Gill Lumber Co., and to operate sawmills, pulp mills and conduct a general lumber business in all branches. Capital $150,000.

John Howes & Sons, Ltd., Harriston, Ont., were recently granted a provincial charter to operate sawmills and conduct a general lumber business manufacturing and dealing in forest products. Capital $40,000. Two of the incorporators are John Howes and N. J. Howes, both of Harriston, Ont.

Provincial Homebuilders, Ltd., Toronto, have been incorporated to erect all kinds of buildings and deal in building materials and to acquire the business and good will of the Mutual Home Builders Syndicate. Capital $40,000. Among the incorporators are C. E. Ring and J. W. Siddall, both of Toronto.

A. M. B. Stevens, Director of the Timber Disposal Department, Board of Trade, London, England, is on an official visit to Canada, in connection with the stocks of British Government lumber in this country. Mr. Stevens will interview the various shippers, and make arrangements for the future. He will also inspect the stocks, and make himself generally acquainted with the position and conditions on this side.

W. J. Hughes, who is the Ontario Government homestead inspector in the Thunder Bay district, says that pulpwood has been taken out in certain sections. Mr. Hughes' territory extends from Shabaqu on the west to Nipigon on the east, and he declares that more pulpwood is being cut this season than ever by the settlers, many having harvested as much as 200 cords, while in a few instances the amount runs as high as 600 cords.

Sir Frederick Becker, chairman of Becker & Co., London, England, and chairman of Becker & Co. of America, Ltd., Montreal, is in

Canada in connection with his pulp interests. He is very optimistic as to the outlook in Great Britain for pulp and paper and predicts a rise in the price of the latter during the year. British manufacturers had suffered severely from dumping by European countries, but there were signs of a cessation of this practice.

Rumors from Three Rivers are to the effect that preliminary steps for the construction of the plant of the "Three Rivers ?ulp and Paper Company with a capital of $3,000,000 or more, will be ta'en up shortly according to some contractors who state that they have been approached to undertake the construction. The Three Rivers Pulp and Paper plant has located near the Three Rivers Ship Yard now occupied by the Fraser Brace Company.

Wm. J. Markle, who was for several years with the Boake Mfg. Co., Toronto, has been appointed manager of the lumber yard and planing mill of the Consumers' Lumber Co., Hamilton, and entered upon his new duties last month. He succeeds M. B. Zimmerman, one of the members of the newly-formed Norwood Lumber Co., Hamilton, which recently started in both the wholesale and retail line on Sherman Ave. North, in that city.

Dan McLachlin of Arnprior, Ont., Brig.-General J. B. White of Montreal and J. A. Gillies of Braeside, Ont., who are directors of the Ottawa Valley section of the Forest Protective Association were in Quebec lately in conference with Paul G. Owens and other directors of the Quebec section of the same association relative to the matter of better forest protection from fire. They stated that because of the vigilance of the association forest fires were less frequent than many years ago when co-operation in this matter was lacking.

Following a recommendation of the Logging Committee, the Woodlands section of the Canadian Pulp and Paper Association has decided to appoint a forester, who will act as secretary, for the purpose of advising the members on forestry and logging operations. The executive council of the association has given the necessary authority and promised financial support. The section will hold a summer meeting in July and will visit the Saranac nurseries of the New York State Forestry Commission, with trips to limits in the vicinity.

George Chahoon, president of the Laurentide Paper Co., and E. A. Dunlop, the well-known lumberman of Pembroke, are two of the directors of the newly-formed Canadian Match Co., which recently began operations in Canada. Among the notable features of the Canadian-made article is the chemical treatment of the matches, which is of such a kind that rats and mice will not gnaw them. The sticks are also unusually long and strong and one of the outstanding features it is said is that the matches are absolutely non-poisonous.

Chas. Huard, aged 48 years, while working in the pulp plant of the Bathurst Lumber Co., Bathurst, N. B., fell in one of the digesters, which was being charged with chips and caustic liquor. Huard was engaged in keeping a chute, which leads into the digester, clear of chips, but he and an associate failed to notice the signal given by the pulp cooks that they were about ready to drop the chips into the digester. He dropped with the chips when the digester was opened and was immersed in the deadly caustic of the digester. He leaves a wife and large family.

Doaktown, N. B., has been a busy place during the past winter, although the lumber cut is small in comparison with previous years. Several mills have been in operation, James Holmes & Son, cutting white birch, F. D. Swim and Alex. Storey cutting lath, Everett Weaver and L. Bamos following the same occupation. The woodworking factory of Henry Swim is also running to capacity, supplying materials for various contracts in Fredericton. Mr. Swim has also lately fitted up a lath mill, which is kept very busy. Doaktown is at the base of the lumbering operations of the Miramichi Lumber Co.

When the 40-ton groundwood pulp plant of the Kaministiquia Pulp & Paper Co., Port Arthur, was sold by auction recently to the Consolidated Water Power & Paper Co., Wisconsin Rapids, Wis., for $175,000., this did not include about 4982 cords of pulpwood on the property. The wood was offered for sale a few days later by Sheriff Thompson in order to satisfy a lien held by a cartage company. There were several bidders and the successful one was Thomas Falls, who is a well-known timber and pulpwood contractor of Port Arthur. It is understood that the price paid for the wood was around $40,000.

H. R. Christie, of the Faculty of Forestry, Toronto University, gave an interesting address in Vancouver recently in which he said that as regards climate in general, forests do not exert any influence. Contrary to the popular belief, forests have a beneficial effect on climate locally, but the evidence does not support the theory that over large areas, deforestation leads to arid conditions. Forests are really the effect, not the cause, of precipitation. It was shown that areas of dense forests were due to the greater rainfall. "Rainfall," Mr. Christie said, "was brought about by great causes,—as ocean currents, mountain ranges, relation of the earth to the sun, etc." Climatic conditions go in cycles. An interesting evidence of this was brought out by Mr. Christie, who said that rainfall was not influenced by any form of plant life on the planet.

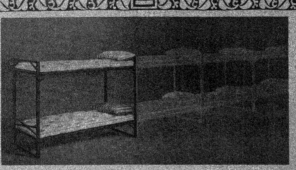

START WITH ANY NUMBER OF UNITS — EXPAND AS ADDITIONAL SLEEPING ACCOMMODATIONS ARE REQUIRED

## Standardized Bunks of Steel

### Comfortable—Sanitary—Enduring

**Used by Industrial, Lumber and
Construction Camps Everywhere**

FROM the standpoint of comfort and lasting service, no other type of bunk so fully meets the labor-housing requirements of large industrial or lumber camps as satisfactorily as *steel bunk units*, as illustrated above.

Bunks of this type are strong, sanitary and comfortable. They may be had in either single or double deck units and in any quantity, upon short notice.

They are easily assembled — may be quickly taken down, moved or stored, and are adaptable to the varying needs of any camp.

Where sleeping accommodations must be provided for vast armies of industrial workers, Simmons sanitary steel bunk *units* become a very necessary part of the camp equipment.

Write today. Complete specifications and descriptions of all styles of Bunks for any purpose, will be furnished promptly upon request.

SIMMONS LIMITED
Executive Office, Montreal
MONTREAL    TORONTO    WINNIPEG    CALGARY    VANCOUVER

# SIMMONS BEDS
## Built for Sleep

Tractor and Train at foot of 35% down grade from Fish's Camp.

# THE LINN LOGGING TRACTOR

### Designed and developed for winter log hauling, in the North Woods

To fulfill all requirements of the Northern Logger a tractor must:—
Haul heavy trains of sleighs down steep sandhills and around sharp curves.
Haul with absolute safety over lakes and rivers, where the ice is sometimes not thicker than fourteen inches.
Haul heavy trains over main hauls over all encountered grades—to landings.
Have carrying capacity on itself, so that it can be used for supply haulage over Portage roads.
Must have a fast high speed so that return trips to rollways may be rapid.
Must be foolproof and easily operated and controlled.
All these requirements are fulfilled only, by The Linn Logging Tractor.
Ask the operator who uses Linn.

*—Logging Department—*

## MUSSENS LIMITED

Dubrule Building                    MONTREAL

The machine shown above is our No. 177 Double Surfacer, a sturdy heavy and powerful machine, that will handle your big timbers, as well as thin stock ¼ of an inch in thickness. Wide floor flanges which form a strong sturdy foundation for the working parts that is practically vibrationless, thus insuring a fine finish.

Chipbreaker has heavy coil tension springs, which allows for uneven or crooked stock. Bed of machine may be raised or lowered by either hand or power hoist. All adjustments handy to operator, easily controlled and accurate.

Rates of feed 35 to 90 feet per minute. Built 30 inches wide 12 inch opening.

## P. B. Yates Machine Co. Ltd.
### Hamilton    Canada

# YATES

Eastern Sales Office
263 St. James St.              Montreal, Que.

PUTS AIR TO WORK

# HIGH HUMIDITY DRY KILN——

### EXPERTS PREDICT
a heavy demand and small stocks of K. D. lumber this Spring

### BE PREPARED
by installing a modern moist air fan kiln now

### AS COMPARED
to steel our prices are relatively lower than in 1913

### REQUEST OUR LITERATURE
and learn where your dollars will dry the most lumber

"THE KILN WITH THE CIRCULATION YOU CAN UNDERSTAND"

## B. F. STURTEVANT COMPANY of CANADA, LTD.

HEAD OFFICE AND WORKS:     GALT, ONTARIO

Sales Offices:     TORONTO and MONTREAL

—Territorial Representatives—

Empire Engineering & Supply Co., Edmonton, Alberta — Pryer-Barker Co., Vancouver, B. C. — Kipp-Kelly Ltd., Winnipeg, Man.

## ALPHABETICAL INDEX TO ADVERTISERS

## Subscribers' Information Form

Many letters reach us from subscribers enquiring where a certain machine, a certain kind of lumber or veneer, or some other class of goods, can be obtained. We can usually supply the information. We want to be of service to our subscribers in this way, and we desire to encourage requests for such information. Make use of this form for the purpose.

"CANADA LUMBERMAN"
340 Adelaide Street West, Toronto

Date ............................................ 19...

Please tell us where we can procure ................................................................................

..............................................................................................................................

..............................................................................................................................

..............................................................................................................................

Name ............................................

Address ............................................

# CITY OF SHERBROOKE, P.Q.

Rock Forest Plant, Sherbrooke Municipal System
One of Six Water Powers Belonging to City

## MANUFACTURERS!

### Locate in Sherbrooke!

Excellent Factory Sites
Good Shipping Facilities
Five Railroads
Plentiful Supply of Skilled Labor
Ideal Living Conditions
Low Taxation
Plentiful Housing

## CHEAP POWER

For further information, apply
**THE MANAGER**
Gas and Electricity Department
SHERBROOKE, P.Q.

# ATKINS

### STERLING QUALITY

# SAWS

## Mill Owners, Managers, Superintendents & Filers

Ever try to saw a log or board with a poor saw? Or—let us put the question differently—have you ever tried to do a job without the proper tools?

The mill man who thinks he is saving money by putting off the purchase of an

### Atkins Sterling Quality Saw

or Machine Knives, Saw Tools or Atkins-Coleman Feed Rollers—that fellow is figuring backwards; he's not a money maker; he's his own worst enemy.

We are ready to furnish you with the proper Saws (Sterling Quality) also Machine Knives and Feed Rollers. They aren't luxuries for the mill that needs them, but real necessities. Write nearest point for catalog and prices.

## E. C. ATKINS & CO.

**Established 1857    The Sterling Quality Saw People**
Home Office and Factory, Indianapolis, Indiana

**Canadian Factory, HAMILTON, Ontario**
Branch carrying complete stock, VANCOUVER, B. C.

# CANADA LUMBERMAN BUYERS' DIRECTORY

The following regulations apply to all advertisers:—Eighth page, every issue, three headings;
quarter page, six headings; half page, twelve headings; full page, twenty-four headings

**ALLIGATORS**
Payette Company, P.
West, Peachy & Sons

**BABBITT METAL**
Canada Metal Company
General Supply Co. of Canada, Ltd.

**BALE TIES**
Canada Metal Co.
Laidlaw Bale Tie Company

**BAND MILLS**
Hamilton Company, William
Waterous Engine Works Company
Yates Machine Company, P. B.

**BAND SAW BLADES**
Simonds Mfg. Co.

**BAND RESAWS**
Mershon & Company, W. B.

**BARKERS**
Bertrand, F. X., La Compagnie Manufactiere.
Smith Foundry & Machine Co.

**BEARING METAL**
Canada Metal Co.
Beveridge Supply Co., Ltd.

**BEDSTEADS (STEEL)**
Simmons Limited

**BELT DRESSING**
Dominion Belting Co.
General Supply of Canada, Ltd.

**BELTING**
Canadian Consolidated Rubber Co.
Dominion Belting Co.
General Supply Company
Goodhue & Co., J. L.
Gutta Percha & Rubber Company
D. K. McLaren, Limited
McLaren Belting Company, J. C.
York Belting Co.

**BLOWERS**
Reed & Co., Geo. W.
B. F. Sturtevant Co. of Canada, Ltd.
Toronto Blower Company

**BOILERS**
Engineering & Machine Works of
Canada
Hamilton Company, William
Waterous Engine Works Company

**BOILER PRESERVATIVE**
Beveridge Supply Company
Shell-Bar, Boice Supply Co. Ltd.

**BOX MACHINERY**
Yates Machine Company, P. B.

**CABLE CONVEYORS**
Engineering & Machine Works of
Canada.
Hamilton Company, Wm.
Waterous Engine Works Company

**CAMP SUPPLIES**
Davies Company, William
Dr. Bell Veterinary Wonder Co.
Johnson, A. H.
Turner & Sons, J. J.
Woods Manufacturing Company. Ltd.

**CANT HOOKS**
General Supply Co. of Canada, Ltd.
Pink Company, Thomas

**CEDAR**
Bury & Co., Robt.
Cameron Lumber Co.
Canadian Western Lumber Company
Chesbro, R. G.

Dry Wood Lumber Co.
Fesserton Timber Company
McElroy Lumber Co., Ltd.
Muir & Kirkpatrick
Rose, McLaurin, Limited
Terry & Gordon
Thurston-Flavelle Lumber Company
Vancouver Lumber Company
Victoria Lumber & Mfg. Co.

**CHAINS**
Canadian Link-Belt Company, Ltd.
General Supply Co. of Canada, Ltd.
Engineering & Machine Works of
Canada
Hamilton Company, William
Pink & Co., Thomas
Waterous Engine Works Company

**CLOTHING**
Woods Mfg. Company

**CONVEYOR MACHINERY**
Canadian Link-Belt Company, Ltd.
General Supply Co. of Canada, Ltd.
Hamilton Company, Wm.
Hopkins & Co., Ltd., F. H.
Waterous Engine Works Company

**CORDWOOD**
McClung, McLellan & Berry

**COUPLING (Shaft)**
Engineering & Machine Works of
Canada

**CRANES**
Hopkins & Co., Ltd., F. H.
Canadian Link-Belt Company

**CUTTER HEADS**
Shimer Cutter Head Company

**CYPRESS**
Wistar, Underhill & Nixon

**DERRICKS AND DERRICK
FITTINGS**
Hopkins & Co., Ltd., F. H.

**DOORS**
Canadian Western Lumber Co.
Gardiner, P. W. & Son
Mason, Gordon & Co.
Midland Wood Products, Ltd.
Terry & Gordon

**DRAG SAWS**
Gerlach Company, Peter
Hamilton Company, William

**DRYERS**
Coe Manufacturing Company
B. F. Sturtevant Co. of Canada, Ltd.

**DUST COLLECTORS**
Reed & Co., Geo. W.
B. F. Sturtevant Co. of Canada, Ltd.
Toronto Blower Company

**EDGERS**
Hamilton Company, Ltd., William
Green Company, G. Walter
Long Mfg. Company, E.
Payette Company, P.
Waterous Engine Works Company

**ELEVATING AND CONVEYING
MACHINERY**
Canadian Belt-Link Company, Ltd.
Engineering & Machine Works of
Canada
Hamilton Company, William
Waterous Engine Works Company

**ENGINES**
Engineering & Machine Works of
Canada
Hamilton Company, William

Payette Company, P.
Waterous Engine Works Company

**EXCELSIOR MACHINERY**
Elmira Machinery & Transmission
Company

**EXHAUST FANS**
B. F. Sturtevant Co. of Canada, Ltd.
Toronto Blower Company

**EXHAUST SYSTEMS**
Reed & Co., Geo. W.
B. F. Sturtevant Co. of Canada, Ltd.
Toronto Blower Company

**FIBRE BOARD**
Manley Chew

**FILES**
Disston & Sons, Henry
Simonds Canada Saw Company

**FIR**
Apex Lumber Co.
Associated Mills, Limited
Bainbridge Lumber Company
Cameron Lumber Co.
Canadian Western Lumber Co.
Canfield, P. L.
Chesbro, R. G.
Dry Wood Lumber Co.
Fesserton Timber Co.
Grier & Sons, Ltd., G. A.
Heeney, Percy E.
Knox Brothers
Mason, Gordon & Co.
McElroy Lumber Co., Ltd.
Robertson & Hacket Sawmills
Rose, McLaurin, Limited
Terry & Gordon
Timberland Lumber Company
Timms, Phillips & Co.
Underhill Lumber Co.
Vancouver Lumber Company
Vanderhoof Lumber Co.
Victoria Lumber & Mfg. Co.

**FIRE BRICK**
Beveridge Supply Co., Ltd.
Elk Fire Brick Company of Canada
Shell-Bar, Boice Supply Co. Ltd.

**FIRE FIGHTING APPARATUS**
Waterous Engine Works Company

**FITTINGS**
Crane Limited

**FLOORING**
Cameron Lumber Co.
Chesbro, R. G.
Long-Bell Lumber Company

**GEARS (Cut)**
Smart-Turner Machine Co.

**GUARDS (Machinery and Window)**
Canada Wire & Iron Goods Co.

**HARDWOODS**
Anderson Lumber Company, C. G.
Anderson Shreiner & Mawson
Barrett, Wm.
Bury & Co., Robt.
Cameron & Co.
Edwards & Co., W. C.
Fassett Lumber Co., Ltd.
Fesserton Timber Co.
Gillespie, James
Gloucester Lumber & Trading Co.
Grier & Son, G. A.
Hart, Hamilton & Jackson
Heeney, Percy E.

Knox Brothers
Mason & Co., Geo.
McDonagh Lumber Co.
McLennan Lumber Company
McLung, McLellan & Berry
Pedwell Hardwood Lumber Co.
W. & J. Sharples.
Spencer, Limited, C. A.
Strong, G. M.
Summers, James R.
Webster & Brother, James

**HARDWOOD FLOORING**
Grier & Son, G. A.

**HARNESS**
Beal Leather Co., R. M.

**HEMLOCK**
Anderson Lumber Company, C. G.
Anderson, Shreiner & Mawson
Bartram & Ball
Beck Lumber Co.
Bourgouin, H.
Canadian General Lumber Company
Edwards & Company, W. C.
Fesserton Timber Co.
Grier & Sons, Ltd., G. A.
Hart, Hamilton & Jackson
Hocken Lumber Company
Mason, Gordon & Co.
McCormack Lumber Co.
McDonagh Lumber Co.
McElroy Lumber Co., Ltd.
Robertson & Hacket Sawmills
Spanish River Lumber Co.
Spencer, Limited, C. A.
Stalker, Douglas A.
Terry & Gordon
Vancouver Lumber Co.
Vanderhoof Lumber Co.

**HOISTING AND HAULING
ENGINES**
General Supply Co. of Canada, Ltd.
Hopkins & Co., Ltd., F. H.

**HOSE**
General Supply Co. of Canada, Ltd.
Gutta Percha & Rubber Company

**INSURANCE**
Barton & Ellis Co.
Burns Underwriting Co.
Hardy & Co., E. D.
Lumbermen's Underwriting Alliance
Rankin Benedict Underwriting Co.

**INTERIOR FINISH**
Cameron Lumber Co.
Canadian Western Lumber Co.
Canfield, P. L.
Eagle Lumber Company
Mason, Gordon & Co.
Rose, McLaurin, Limited

**KILN DRIED LUMBER**
Bury & Co., Robt.

**KNIVES**
Disston & Sons, Henry
Simonds Canada Saw Company
Waterous Engine Works Company

**LARCH**
Otis Staples Lumber Co.

**LATH**
Anderson, Shreiner & Mawson
Apex Lumber Co.
Austin & Nicholson
Beck Lumber Co.
Brennen & Sons, F. W.
Cameron Lumber Co.
Canadian General Lumber Company
Carew Lumber Co., John
Chaleurs Bay Mills
Dadson, A. T.
Dupuis, Limited, J. P.

Eagle Lumber Company
Fassett Lumber Co., Ltd.
Foley Lumber Company
Fraser Bryson Lumber Co., Ltd.
Gloucester Lumber & Grading Co.
Grier & Sons, Ltd., G. A.
Harris Tie & Timber Company, Ltd.
Larkin Co., C. A.
Mason & Co., Geo.
McLennan Lumber Company
Miller, W. H. Co.
New Ontario Colonization Company
Otis Staples Lumber Company
Power Lumber Co.
Price Bros. & Company
Shevlin-Clarke Co.
Spencer, Limited, C. A.
Terry & Gordon
U. G. G. Sawmills. Limited
Union Lumber Company
Victoria Harbor Lumber Company

**LATH BOLTERS**

General Supply Co. of Canada, Ltd.
Hamilton Company, Wm.
Payette & Company, P.

**LOCOMOTIVES**

Engineering & Machine Works of
   Canada
General Supply Co. of Canada, Ltd.
Hopkins & Co., Ltd., F. H.
Climax Manufacturing Company
Montreal Locomotive Works

**LINK-BELT**

Canadian Link-Belt Company
Hamilton Company, Wm.

**LOCOMOTIVE CRANES**

Canadian Link-Belt Company, Ltd.
Hopkins & Co. ,Ltd., F. H.

**LOGGING ENGINES**

Engineering & Machine Works of
   Canada
Hopkins & Co., Ltd., F. H.
Mussens Ltd.

**LOG HAULER**

Engineering & Machine Works of
   Canada
Green Company. G. Walter
Holt Manufacturing Co.
Hopkins & Co., Ltd., F. H.
Payette Company, P.

**LOGGING MACHINERY AND
EQUIPMENT**

General Supply Co. of Canada, Ltd.
Hamilton Company, William
Holt Manufacturing Co.
Hopkins & Co., Ltd., F. H.
Payette Company, P.
Waterous Engine Works Company
West, Peachey & Sons
Mussens Ltd.

**LUMBER EXPORTS**

Fletcher Corporation

**LUMBER TRUCKS**

Hamilton Company, Wm.
Waterous Engine Works Company

**LUMBERMEN'S BOATS**

Adams Engine Company
Gidley Boat Co.
West, Peachey & Sons

**LUMBERMEN'S CLOTHING**

Kitchen Overall & Shirt Co.

**MATTRESSES**

Simmons Limited

**METAL REFINERS**

Canada Metal Company

**OAK**

Long-Bell Lumber Company

**PACKING**

Beveridge Supply Company
Gutta Percha & Rubber Company

**PANELS**

Bury & Co., Robt.

**PAPER**

Beveridge Supply Co., Ltd.
Price Bros. & Co.

**PINE**

Anderson Lumber Company, C. G.
Anderson, Shreiner & Mawson
Atlantic Lumber Co.
Austin & Nicholson
Barratt, William
Beck Lumber Co.
Cameron & Co.
Cameron Lumber Co.
Canadian General Lumber Company
Canadian Western Lumber Co.
Canfield, P. L.
Cheabro, R. G.
Cleveland-Sarnia Sawmills Company
Cox, Long & Company .
Dadson, A. T.
Dudley, Arthur N.
Eagle Lumber Company
Edwards & Co.. W. C.
Excelsior Lumber Company
Fesserton Timber Company
Fraser Bryson Lumber Co., Ltd.
Gillies Bros. Limited
Gloucester Lumber & Trading Co.
Gordon & Co. George
Goodday & Company, H. R.
Grier & Sons, Ltd., G. A.
Harris Tie & Timber Company, Ltd.
Hart, Hamilton & Jackson
Hettler Lumber Company, Herman H.
Hocken Lumber Company
Julien, Roch
Lay & Haight
Lloyd, W. Y.
Loggie Co., W. S.

Long-Bell Lumber Company
Mason, Gordon & Co.
Mason & Co., Geo.
McCormack Lumber Co.
McFadden & Malloy
McLennan Lumber Company
Montreal Lumber Company
Muir & Kirkpatrick
Northern Lumber Mills.
Otis Staples Lumber Co.
Parry Sound Lumber Company
Pigeon River Lumber Co., Ltd.
Rolland Lumber Co.
W. & J. Sharples.
Shevlin-Clarke Co.
Spanish River Lumber Co.
Spencer, Limited, C. A.
Stalker, Douglas A.
Strong, G. M.
Summers, James R.
Terry & Gordon
Union Lumber Company
Victoria Harbor Lumber Co.
Watson & Todd, Limited

**PLANING MILL EXHAUSTERS**

Toronto Blower Co.

**PLANING MILL MACHINERY**

Mershon & Co., W. B.
B. F. Sturtevant Co. of Canada, Ltd.
Toronto Blower Co.
Yates Machine Company, P. B.

**PORK PACKERS**

Davies Company, William

**POSTS AND POLES**

Anderson, Shreiner & Mawson
Canadian Tie & Lumber Co.
Dupuis, Limited, J. P.
Eagle Lumber Company

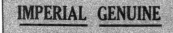

Harris Tie & Timber Co., Ltd.
Long-Bell Lumber Company
Mason, Gordon & Co.
McLennan Lumber Company
Terry & Gordon

**POST GRINDERS**

Smith Foundry Co.

**PULLEYS AND SHAFTING**

Canadian Link-Belt Company
General Supply Co. of Canada, Ltd.
Green Company, G. Walter
Engineering & Machine Works of
    Canada
Hamilton Company, William

**PULP MILL MACHINERY**

Canadian Link-Belt Company, Ltd.
Engineering & Machine Works of
    Canada
Hamilton Company, William
Payette Company, P.
Waterous Engine Works Company

**PULPWOOD**

British & Foreign Agencies
D'Auteuil Lumber Co.
Price Bros. & Co.
Scott, Draper & Co.

**PUMPS**

General Supply Co. of Canada, Ltd.
Engineering & Machine Works of
    Canada
Hamilton Co., William
Hopkins & Co., Ltd., F. H.
Smart-Turner Machine Company
Waterous Engine Works Company

**RAILS**

Gartshore, John J.
Hopkins & Co., Ltd., F. H.

**ROOFINGS**

. (Rubber, Plastic and Liquid)
Beveridge Supply Company
Reed & Co., Geo. W.

**RUBBER GOODS**

Dunlop Tire & Rubber Goods Co.
Gutta Percha & Rubber Company

**SASH**

Midland Woodworkers
Midland Wood Products, Ltd.

**SAWS**

Atkins & Company, E. C.
Disston & Sons, Henry
General Supply Co. of Canada, Ltd.
Gerlach Company, Peter
Green Company, G. Walter
Hoe & Company, R.
Radcliff Saw Mfg. Co.,
Shurly Co., Ltd., T. F.
Shurly-Dietrich Company
Simonds Canada Saw Company

**SAW GRINDERS**

Smith Foundry Co.

**SAW MILL LINK-BELT**

Canadian Link-Belt Company.

**SAW MILL MACHINERY**

Canadian Link-Belt Company, Ltd.
General Supply Co. of Canada, Ltd.
G. Walter Green Co., Ltd.
Hamilton Company, William
La Compagnie Manufacture, F. X.
    Bertrand
Long Manufacturing Company, E.
Mershon & Company, W. B.
Parry Sound Lumber Company
Payette Company, P.
Waterous Engine Works Company
Yates Machine Company, P. B.

**SAW SHARPENERS**

Hamilton Company, William
Waterous Engine Works Company

**SAW SLASHERS**

Hamilton Company, Wm.
Payette Company, P.
Waterous Engine Works Company

**SHINGLES**

Apex Lumber Co.
Associated Mills, Limited
Brennen & Sons, F. W.
Cameron Lumber Co.
Campbell-MacLaurin Lumber Co.
Canadian Western Lumber Co.
Carew Lumber Co., John
Chaleurs Bay Mills
D'Auteuil Lumber Co.
Dry Wood Lumber Co.
Eagle Lumber Company
Fraser, Companies Limited
Gillespie, James
Gloucester Lumber & Trading Co.
Grier & Sons, Limited, G. A.
Harris Tie & Timber Company, Ltd.
Heaps & Sons
Heeney, Percy E.
Mason, Gordon & Co.
McLennan Lumber Company
Miller Company, Ltd., W. H.
Rose, McLaurin, Limited
Stalker, Douglas A. .
Terry & Gordon
Timms, Phillips & Co.
Vancouver Lumber Company
Vanderhoof Lumber Co.

**SHINGLE & LATH MACHINERY**

Green Company, G. Walter
Hamilton Company, William
Long Manufacturing Company, E.
Payette Company, P.
Smith Foundry Co.

**SILENT CHAIN DRIVES**

Canadian Link-Belt Company, Ltd.

**SLEEPING EQUIPMENT**

Simmons Limited

**SLEEPING ROBES**

Woods Mfg. Company, Ltd.

**SMOKESTACKS**

Hamilton Company, Wm.
Reed & Co., Geo. W.
Waterous Engine Works Company

**SNOW PLOWS**

Pink Company, Thomas

**SOLDERS**

Canada Metal Co.

**SPARK ARRESTORS**

Reed & Co., Geo. W.
Waterous Engine Works Company

**SPRUCE**

Anderson, Shreiner & Mawson
Barrett, Wm.
Cameron Lumber Co.
Campbell, McLaurin Lumber Co.
Canadian Western Lumber Co.
Chesbro, R. G.
Cox, Long & Co,.
Dadson, A. T.
Oudley, Arthur N.
Fassett Lumber Co., Ltd.
Fraser, Companies Limited
Fraser-Bryson Lumber Company
Gillies Brothers
Gloucester Lumber & Trading Co.
Goodday & Company, H. R.

Grier & Sons, Ltd., G. A.
Harris Lumber Co., Frank H.
Hart, Hamilton & Jackson
Hocken Lumber Company
Julien, Roch
Larkin Co., C. A.
Lay & Haight
Lloyd, W. Y.
Loggie Co., W. S.
Mason, Gordon & Co.
McCormack Lumber Co.
McDonagh Lumber Co.
McElroy Lumber Co., Ltd.
McLennan Lumber Company
Muir & Kirkpatrick
New Ontario Colonization Company
Northern Lumber Mills
Pigeon River Lumber Co.
Power Lumber Co.
Price Bros. & Co.
Rolland Lumber Co.
Rose, McLaurin, Limited
W. & J. Sharples.
Spencer, Limited, C. A.
Strong, G. M.
Terry & Gordon
U. G. G. Sawmills. Limited .
Vanderhoof Lumber Co.

**STEAM SHOVELS**

Hopkins & Co., Ltd., F. H.

**STEEL CHAIN**

Canadian Link-Belt Company, Ltd.
Hopkins & Co., Ltd., F. H.
Waterous Engine Works Company

**STEAM PLANT ACCESSORIES**

Waterous Engine Works Company

**STEEL BARRELS**

Smart-Turner Machine Co.

**STEEL DRUMS**

Smart-Turner Machine Co

**TARPAULINS**

Turner & Sons, J. J.
Woods Manufacturing Company, Ltd.

**TANKS**

Hopkins & Co., Ltd. F. H.

**TENTS**

Turner & Sons, J. J.
Woods Mfg. Company

**TIES**

Austin & Nicholson
Carew Lumber Co., John
Canadian Tie & Lumber Co.
Chaleurs Bay. Mills
D'Auteuil Lumber Co.
Gloucester Lumber & Trading Co.
Harris Tie & Timber Company. Ltd.
McLennan Lumber Company
Miller, W. H. Co.
Price Bros. & Co.
Scott, Draper & Co.
Terry & Gordon

**TIMBER BROKERS**

Bradley, R. R.
Cant & Kemp
Farnworth & Jardine
Wright, Graham & Co.

**TIMBER CRUISERS AND
ESTIMATORS**

Savage & Bartlett.
Sewall, James W.

**TIMBER LANDS**

Department of Lands & Forests, Ont.

**TOWING MACHINES**

Corbet Foundry & Machine Co.
Payette Company, P. .
West, Peachy & Sons

**TRACTORS**

Holt Manufacturing Co.
Hopkins & Company, Ltd., F. H. .
Mussens Ltd.

**TRANSMISSION MACHINERY**

Canadian Link-Belt Company, Ltd.
Engineering & Machine Works of
    Canada
General Supply Co. of Canada. Ltd.
Grand Rapids Vapor Kiln
Hamilton Company, Wm.
Waterous Engine Works Company

**TURBINES**

Engineering & Machine Works of
    Canada
Hamilton Company, William
B. F. Sturtevant Co. of Canada, Ltd.

**VALVES**

Crane Limited

**VAPOR KILNS**

Grand Rapids Vapor Kiln
B. F. Sturtevant Co. of Canada, Ltd.

**VENEERS**

Bury & Co., Robt.

**VENEER DRYERS**

Coe Manufacturing Company
B. F. Sturtevant Co. of Canada, Ltd.

**VENEER MACHINERY**

Coe Machinery Company

**VETERINARY REMEDIES**

Dr. Bell Veterinary Wonder Co.
Johnson, A. H.

**WARPING TUGS**

West, Peachey & Sons

**WATER WHEELS**

Engineering & Machine Works of
    Canada
Hamilton Company, William

**WIRE**

Canada Metal Co.
Laidlaw Bale Tie Company
Canada Wire & Iron Goods Co.

**WIRE CLOTH**

Canada Wire & Iron Goods Co.

**WIRE ROPE**

. Canada Wire & Iron Goods Co.
Hopkins & Co. .Ltd., F. H.
Dominion Wire Rope Co.
Greening Wire Co., B.

**WOODWORKING MACHINERY**

General Supply Co. of Canada, Ltd.
Long Manufacturing Company, E.
Mershon & Company, W. B.
Waterous Engine Works Company
Yates Machine Company, P. B.

**WOOD PRESERVATIVES**

Beveridge Supply Company .

**WOOD PULP**

Austin & Nicholson
New Ontario Colonization Co.
Power Lumber Co.

Waterous Bandmills hold their leadership in the sawmill industry simply because they do the *most* work for the *least* money. Business *needs* that kind of machinery now more than ever.

Molson's Bank Bldg., Vancouver, B. C.                                                    Winnipeg, Manitoba.

# Waterous
### BRANTFORD, ONTARIO, CANADA

Vol. 42        Toronto, April 1, 1922        No. 7

# Canada Lumberman

Founded 1880

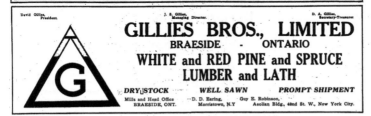

# *The Same Old Story*

**W**E base our claim for
a share of your busi-
ness on the service we
give you plus the quality
of our lumber.

If our traveller does not
call on you this week
send your inquiries
direct to the office.

## UNION LUMBER COMPANY LIMITED
### 701 DOMINION BANK BUILDING
### TORONTO          CANADA

# FRASER COMPANIES, Limited

### Bleached Sulphite Pulp Mill.    Saw Mills (all Band Saw Mills).   Shingle Mill
### HERE THEY ARE ON THE MAP

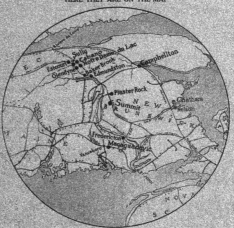

## Mills and Railway Connections

| Saw and Shingle Mills | Railway Connections |
|---|---|
| Cabano, Que. | Temiscouata Ry. |
| Notre Dame du Lac, Que. | Temiscouata Ry. |
| Glendyne, Que. | C. N. Ry. |
| Estcourt, Que. | C. N. Ry. |
| Sully, N. B. | C. N. Ry. |
| Edmundston, N. B. C.P.R., C.N.R. and Temiscouata Ry. | |
| Magaguadavic, N.B. | C. P. R. |

| Saw and Shingle Mills | Railway Connections |
|---|---|
| Baker Brook, N. B. | C.N.Ry., Temiscouata Ry. |
| Plaster Rock, N.B. | C. N. R. |
| Summit, N. B. | C. N. R. |
| Fredericton, N. B. | C.P.Ry. and C.N.Ry. |
| Nelson, N. B. | C. N. Ry. |
| Campbellton, N. B. | C. N. R. |

Bleached Sulphite Mill, Edmundston, N. B. .... Railway Connection, C.P.R., C.N.R. and Temiscouata Ry.
Sulphite, Mill, Chatham, N. B. .... Railway Connection, C. N. R.

Bleached Sulphite.    Rough and Dressed Spruce.    White Cedar Shingles.    Railway Ties
Piano Sounding Board Stock a Specialty.

## Selling and Purchasing Offices :--    EDMUNDSTON, N. B.

**DOUGLAS FIR LUMBER**
**RED CEDAR SHINGLES**

### The Question of Supply

During the past two months our mill
connections have been handicapped
by unusual weather conditions, but
we are glad to state that we are now
in a position to give our usual prompt
service in your requirements.

**Timms Phillips & Co., Ltd.**
Vancouver, B. C.

TORONTO OFFICE: Canada Permanent Bldg.
Phone Adel. 6490
MONTREAL OFFICE: 23 Marconi Bldg.
Phone M 2999

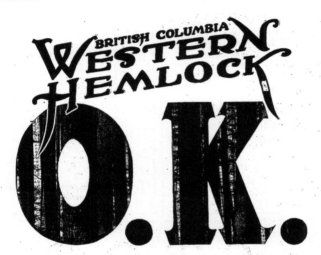

## Ask the Man Who Has Used it

The proof of the value of wood is in the service obtained therefrom.

Lumber dealers and their customers are getting to like BRITISH COLUMBIA WESTERN HEMLOCK better the more they deal in it or use it.

It is not a hardwood but is possessed of a grain that is externally beautiful. It takes a high polish, is free from pitch and "shakes" and possesses great strength.

Don't wait until all your competitors have established a reputation for handling BRITISH COLUMBIA WESTERN HEMLOCK.

We'll be glad to send you BRITISH COLUMBIA WESTERN HEMLOCK in mixed carloads along with our other BIG CHIEF Brand Specialties, British Columbia Red Cedar Shingles, and Cedar and Fir lumber in all sizes known to high-class manufacture.

# VANCOUVER LUMBER CO., LIMITED, Vancouver, B.C.

Branch Sales Offices at Toronto, Ont., Winnipeg, Man., Chicago, Ill

# BUY
## BRITISH COLUMBIA
# Red Cedar Shingles

The life of a British Columbia Red Cedar Shingle Roof can almost be gauged by the life of the nail with which the shingle is nailed in place. Judging from available data, the average life of the ordinary steel wire nail, which has been in such common use, is only from seven to twelve years. Some wire nails will last longer, depending upon the condition of exposure, climate and similar features, but considering our climate as a whole, at the end of from seven to twelve years a large percentage of wire nails will have rusted either completely through or so extensively that the first strong wind will complete the work. The shingles that have been held in position by such nails are then free to work down, permitting rains or melting snows to leak through and damage the interior of the structure. Examination will disclose that the fibre of the shingle itself is still in perfect condition, and a leaky roof, in the majority of occasions is due entirely to the use of faulty nails, but the average home owner, placed at such inconvenience, will not stop to reason this out and the poor wooden shingle comes in for more unjust abuse.

There are several kinds of nails which experience has proven will give lasting satisfaction, and the wise dealer will advise his customers of these satisfactory nails. A pure zinc shingle nail meets all the demands of durability required. Its principal drawback is its high cost and a slight tendency to bend under careless driving. Galvanized wire nails theoretically are rust proof, and if the galvanized coating is properly applied, and of sufficient thickness, such a nail will last as long as the shingle it holds in place. The life of this shingle roof, properly applied with these nails then is from 40 to 50 years. Pure iron nails, or the old cut or wrought nails are ideal but difficult to secure. Copper nails also constitute a perfect shingle nail.

| | |
|---|---|
| **Timms Phillips & Co., Ltd.**<br>Yorkshire Bldg., Vancouver<br>Manufacturers and Wholesalers<br>**Red Cedar Shingles**<br>3x-5x- Perfections, Royals, Imperials<br>**Red Cedar Bevel Siding** | **Vancouver Lumber Co., Ltd.**<br>Manufacturers<br>**XXX—XXXXX CEDAR<br>SHINGLES**<br>(Rite Grade Inspected)<br>Head Office,    Eastern Sales Office<br>Vancouver, B.C.    Toronto, Ont. |
| **Westminster Mill Co.**<br>LIMITED<br>New Westminster, B.C.<br>**Red Cedar Shingles**<br>**Cedar Bevel Siding** | **Dominion Timber Products Ltd.**<br>Vancouver Block<br>Vancouver<br>Largest Manufacturers of<br>**Perfection Shingles**<br>in Canada |
| **Underhill Lumber Co., Ltd.**<br>Dominion Bldg., Vancouver<br>**RED CEDAR SHINGLES**<br>3x-5x- Perfection and Eurekas<br>**CEDAR BEVEL SIDING**<br>**CEDAR BUNGALOW SIDING** | **Shull Lumber & Shingle Co**<br>Limited<br>New Westminster B. C.<br>Trade Mark<br>**RED BAND SHINGLES**<br>XXX  XXXXX  Stars Clears<br>From Mill to You |
| If you want a market<br>for B. C. Red Cedar<br>Shingles put an advert-<br>isement on this page. | **Kootenay Shingle Co. Ltd.**<br>Salmo, B. C.<br>**Red Cedar Shingles**<br>xxx and xx.<br>Packed by the thousand |

# Let us know your requirements in

Pine

Spruce

Hemlock

Hardwoods

Lath and
Hardwood
Flooring

B.C. Lumber
and Timber

WE CAN GIVE YOU IMMEDIATE DELIVERIES.

*Established 1871*

# G. A. GRIER & SONS
## LIMITED

MONTREAL                                    TORONTO
1112 Notre Dame St. W.                  22 Royal Bank Chambers, 484 King St. W.

*We have no connection with or interest in any other firm bearing a name similar to ours.*

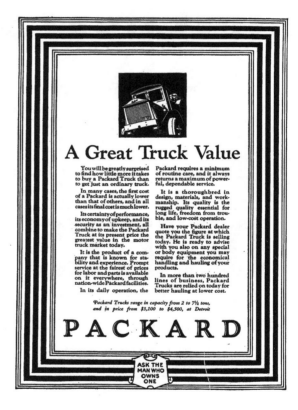

# A Great Truck Value

You will be greatly surprised to find how little more it takes to buy a Packard Truck than to get just an ordinary truck.

In many cases, the first cost of a Packard is actually lower than that of others, and in all cases its final cost is much lower.

Its certainty of performance, its economy of upkeep, and its security as an investment, all combine to make the Packard Truck at its present price the greatest value in the motor truck market today.

It is the product of a company that is known for stability and experience. Prompt service at the fairest of prices for labor and parts is available on it everywhere, through nation-wide Packard facilities.

In its daily operation, the Packard requires a minimum of routine care, and it always returns a maximum of powerful, dependable service.

It is a thoroughbred in design, materials, and workmanship. Its quality is the rugged quality essential for long life, freedom from trouble, and low-cost operation.

Have your Packard dealer quote you the figure at which the Packard Truck is selling today. He is ready to advise with you also on any special or body equipment you may require for the economical handling and hauling of your products.

In more than two hundred lines of business, Packard Trucks are relied on today for better hauling at lower cost.

*Packard Trucks range in capacity from 2 to 7½ tons, and in price from $3,100 to $4,500, at Detroit*

# PACKARD

ASK THE MAN WHO OWNS ONE

# THE GREAT NATIONAL LUMBER JOURNAL

Pioneer and Leader
in the Industry

## Canada Lumberman
founded 1880

Recognized Authority
for Forty Years

Vol. 42     Toronto, April 1, 1922     No. 7

# How to Cut Costs in Your Logging Operations

### By W. F. V. Atkinson

W. F. V. Atkinson Dryden, Ont.

Among other practical benefits obtained from recent conventions of lumbermen, foresters and paper makers are suggestions regarding ways and means of reducing logging costs.

A well-known official of a large paper company recently stated that while progress was continually being made in methods of manufacture of paper and in saw-milling, nothing had been done to improve logging methods during the last fifty years. Is this true? If not, it is, at least, a reason to throw some light on the subject and was probably suggested by noting the increased cost of logging without personal experience of any great length in this country.

What are the facts? A close inspection and experience of job-bers and of company camps in many parts of Canada and in the border states, under very varied conditions and climate, shows that very great changes have been made in camps, equipment and methods. Were it not so, the present cost of logging would be much higher than it now is. This is obvious when it is known that wages are higher, skilled woodsmen are scarce and the logs or wood are brought great distances and from rougher districts, being cut sometimes two or more years before they reach the mills. The old style ox-team, the single horse, the single ten foot wooden sleigh with runners unshod and six inches wide,—the "chienne" or hand log sleigh, the snow roads, the drag chain, axe felling, and topping," etc., may be contrasted with the modern snow-ploughs and rutters, sprinklers, cable brakes, hoists, jammers, log sleighs with twelve-foot bunks and trip stakes, as well as the Western high lead cable and steam logging railroad; the old maple pry which the "peavie" replaced on the drive; the uses of dynamite that the old black powder could not fill. Yes, changes and improvements too numerous to mention here.

Think of the old "Cambuse" camps which were bunkhouses and cook camps at the same time. The beans and the bread, both baked under hot sand and ashes. Then there were, the pork, pea soup, molasses and tea which were after all the whole bill of fare. Compare these with the present bright and dry camps, steel bunks, mattresses and pillows, the wash-room, the van or camp store with all a man needs in the woods; the clean, airy cook-camp with its kitchen and tables piled high with the best of all kinds, jams, cakes and pies. This, indeed, has been overdone so that men are heard to say "less frills and more wages," but it has come to this to avoid grumbling.

### In the Days of Old "Cambuse"

The old ways have changed, indeed. One change, however, is much to be deplored. The well-skilled lumberjacks are few. One of the old-time men could do two or three times the work and was worth twice the wages of the class of men recently going to camps. Pride in skill and strength is dying out. Surely there is a defect here in our methods when our young men do not seek to qualify in this vocation. Are not the operators as much to blame as the men? With the right leaders and a well-defined and fixed policy this de-

fect can be revived in the camps of any company which has the foresight to take it up. Just think what it means.

Operators generally are wide awake and ready to grasp any improvements that will reduce costs per thousand feet or per cord. That the cost has risen depends on changed conditions which have to be faced. Some of these can be remedied. It is not the purpose of this article to deal with a subject so large, and be it said so local, as each operation had its own problems.

### Motor Tractors for Log Hauling

Two general points were discussed at the recent meetings, comparative costs and motor tractors for log hauling. Some interesting figures were cited on logging costs, but it is manifest that such figures cannot be used for comparison unless there is a similarity of conditions and methods of bookkeeping.

Great differences in the following, for instance, would preclude comparison:—

1st. Timber, average size and quantity per acre, log-scale or method measurement used.

2nd. Topography, with all that entails in skidding, road-making, bridging, etc. Grading, lifts-muskegs, open spaces, lakes and ponds.

3rd. Hauling distances, loading and unloading advantages, grades, road maintenance, etc.

4th. Bookkeeping, i.e., method of charging labor, overhead and depreciation to each subdivision of the work.

5th. The drive which is a matter apart but a large factor in cost. This will pay investigating more than ever since some of the provinces have begun to regulate the use of the water.

It is presumed the cost of these works is now kept and divided to suit the operator, but if costs are to be compared, a standard method and standard forms are needed. These might be drafted by a committee of the Woodlands Section of the Canadian Pulp and Paper Association, and if approved after amendment, adopted by those interested in comparing costs, with the object of reducing them.

With regard to tractors, some one said that new machinery was more readily sought after across the border. This may be so, as Canadians who have been logging, sawing and building ships

Tractor pulling two big loads uphill in soft snow

Tractor pulling two heavily loaded sleighs over soft snow roads

Three teams of horses needed to pull load out to main road

for over 250 years, have been taught to be cautious. Some of our recent operators came here with ready-made plans and rigging. They changed them where they found what it cost their neighbors to do the same work. Some kinds of tractors have not been found suitable, that is, convenient and profitable, for the work expected of them.

Steam tractors are dangerous in our woods, as are the "donkeys" in the west. It is only, after a careful summing up of all the individual requirements and conditions, that a decision can be made. For instance, a certain tractor may be able to pull the biggest load on a straight, level and hard road and might seldom or never be needed for that condition, much like the "Sunday loads," so well known, and like them, of no practical value.

### Some Items to be Considered

It would appear to be wise to sit down, first what you can do with teams on your job and the cost of same, purchase price of horses, care and drivers, feed, risk of loss and depreciation.

Second,—If you cannot do all of these things with a tractor, what can you do and what more can be done with a tractor than with your teams, and again set down the cost of a tractor or tractors, repairs, fuel and oil (only when working) driver, depreciation and a small loss risk.

Let us, therefore, list the work at which horses are used and we will find on enquiry that there are tractors that will do enough of different kinds of work to keep busy more days in the year than their equivalent in teams. There is the camp-building, road-making, and grading, "toting," skidding, snowploughing and rutting, breaking roads after heavy snow, sprinkler drawing, side road pulling out and main road haul; also sundry, such as "making" heavy boom timber, etc.; then, camp being over, spring road-making, grading, etc., of which there is always some to be done in your district, work on company's farm or possibly odd heavy jobs about the depot camps or down at the mills.

We cannot do without horses, but apart from very short hauling, skidding, light toting and livery work, tractors can be had to do the work required better than horses because, faster and strong-

er and never-tired in an emergency, tractors can be run with an extra crew day and night, and thus effect a clean-up on a log haul that would otherwise be impossible.

Again where a cable team and match block or a hoist can be used for a short time only, a tractor can be used until the small "corner" had been cleaned up. A light-weight tractor is essential when lakes, small ponds, or wet muskegs have to be crossed, or where the teams are usually carried in scows to reach the job. Weight on the tractor is needed where the road is hard and the load heavy. This should and can be adjustable at the foreman's discretion.

### The Mechanism Should be Simple

Again the parts and mechanism should be simple. The work is generally far from the machine shop. Some tractors are hard to steer and accidents have happened. A tractor will travel more than twice as fast as a team of horses, loaded or otherwise, and thus fully double the number of trips that can be made. 50 cords of pulp logs may be considered a reasonable sleigh train-load. Unless the road is properly iced, this load is best carried on six sleighs rather than on five, and saves side cutting. Three trains of sleighs, to save time, should be used with each tractor. A little planning is needed in arranging the loaded sleighs to prevent delay. Turnouts are as usual though fewer are needed and "go back" hills are not required. Sanding is needed a little less than with teams. Sleigh poles and draw-bars which are quickly interchangeable, can be used so that single loads can be brought out of side roads by teams, if desired.

A great saving in cost is made by using standard sleighs which can be used again elsewhere when needed. The only material changes are in the rutter which can be replaced by flanges the width of the tractor treads, say 18 inches each, and the sprinkler openings changed so as to flood this channel or wider rut.

This applies especially to a type of tractor with which some recent tests were made. Under no possible circumstances could the same loads have been moved by teams. Uphill and on soft snow roads when done with this small tractor, showed that it was specially adapted to logging purposes generally under rough and varying conditions. Some of the tests referred to are shown in the accompanying pictures.

With the right kind of tractor in the hands of a good foreman much money can be saved if you can use it to advantage. If it is to be used only for log hauling seventy-five or eighty days in the year, one might hesitate with reason before making a change over from horses to power.

Most lumbermen are glad to learn of the experiences of their fellow-workers, as, matters of a practical nature of mutual interest and profit. The discussions and expressions of views at the recent conventions may lead to wide benefit and, best of all, to co-operation, greater economy and expedition in the all important work of improved methods of logging in Eastern Canada.

Type of load drawn showing soft state of roads

The Agent-General for Ontario in the British Isles, Mr. Wm. C. Noxon, has just arranged for an Ontario Government film illustrating lumbering in Ontario to be shown at more than 1,000 cinemas in Great Britain and Ireland during the next twelve months. This is in addition to a large number of Ontario films which are in constant circulation in the Old Country.

# Toronto Wholesalers Are Hospitable Hosts

## Entertain Retail Lumbermen at Enjoyable Dinner—Interesting Addresses Delivered by Lieut.-Governor of Ontario and Douglas Malloch Lumberman Poet

Representative in its character, enthusiastic in its welcome and happy in its associations was the regular monthly meeting of the Wholesale Lumber Dealers' Association held at the King Edward Hotel, Toronto, on March 20 when that body welcomed the retailers of the Queen City as their guests. The gathering was held in the Pompeian Room and there were over 100 lumbermen in attendance.

There were two outstanding events of the evening. One was the presence of his Honor, Harry Cockshutt, Lieutenant-Governor of Ontario, and the other was the witty and racy address of Douglas Malloch, Chicago, the widely-known lumberman poet. Mr. Malloch spoke for an hour and was accorded a rousing reception.

H. J. Terry, chairman of the Association, proved to be an admirable presiding officer and kept things running in a masterly manner.

All regular business was dispensed with until the next meeting. One of the first duties of the chairman, after the toast to "the King" had been loyally honored, was the introduction of the Lieutenant-Governor of the province. Mr. Terry said that the firm of which Mr. Cockshutt had for many years been connected in the city of Brantford, had bought a large amount of lumber, and he thought it was in order for the Wholesale Lumber Dealers' Association to elect his Honor an honorary member. The suggestion was received with appreciative applause.

In responding, the recipient thanked the Association for the distinction conferred upon him. He was glad to learn that the Association existed for service and the betterment of conditions in the lumber industry generally and that prices were never discussed. As a customer for many years he knew something about the prices of lumber and realized that the situation was gradually growing more difficult. The sources of supply wer receding all the time and operators were gradually encroaching upon our reserves of timber. The hardwood limits of Ontario were becoming almost a thing of the past.

### Emphasizes Great Need of Reforestation

Mr. Cockshutt dwelt strongly upon the needs of reforestation, which had been neglected in our hardwood and softwood timbers, and said that it was the duty of lumbermen to "root for reforestation." "We may have," he added, "enough timber for our own times but we have not enough for the future. Our sons will come after us and surely we want to leave them some heritage." The lumbermen's interests have been largely spoiled by the axemen, who have gone in and cut down timber promiscuously. "In furthering this object," declared his Honor, "we are performing a service for our country and timber supply. We are all interested in the province of Ontario and its natural wealth, and can make it a great thing for those coming after us. Let us all feel that we have some interest in our own country after we are dead and gone, for I believe, we owe something to posterity."

His Honor said he had already met a number of the lumbermen and would be pleased to meet as many as possible at Government House, which existed for service. "We are all members of one community and the cause for service to humanity calls for our best efforts and thought in the welfare and advancement of our own people and our province," he concluded.

W. E. Bigwood, who was to have delivered the address of welcome to the retailers on behalf of the wholesalers, was absent by reason of illness. His task was performed by A. C. Manbert in his usual happy style. Mr. Manbert's remarks were brief, but hearty, and he assured the retailer guests that it was a great pleasure to have them around the festive board.

T. A. Patterson responded for the retailers in the absence of W. C. Irvin, who was not able to be present owing to illness. In the course of his reply, Mr. Paterson said in part:

"This lavish banquet, which we have just partaken of, shows that the wholesalers wish us well. When we hear their side of the tales of grievances that they have to contend with in selling to the retailers, they should just hear some of the difficulties of the retail trade in selling the consumer—specifications running like this:—'This hemlock, must be exact sizes, free from wane, shake, large or loose knots, etc.'

The retail lumber business looks to be on a return to fairly busy proportions, especially in house-building, which is opening up very early this year. I think there will be plenty of business in To-ronto this season to keep all the yards going at capacity output and avoid the hazardous and reckless slashing of prices, often below the cost of replacement, which has been our misfortune to have during the past winter in an effort to keep business up to normal when the supply was greater than the demand.

"In respect to our reception here, this bringing together of the two branches of the marketing of lumber and other products renews friendships which may have been upset through misunderstanding of grades and other things entering into the buying and selling of lumber. If there are any of us who feel that way, after hearty greetings and shaking of hands, let us forget old sores and renew business dealings which should be pleasant and mutually profitable to buyer and seller." The retailer guests then rose in a body and sang "For they are jolly good fellows."

It was intended that greetings should be borne from the Rotary Club, Kiwanis Club, Lions Club and Gyro Club. F. H. Bigwood, who was to have represented the Kiwanis Club, could not attend but John J. Gibson, president of the Rotary Club, and R. E. Whitehead, president of the Gyro Club, extended felicitations and spoke of the benefits and advantages of service and co-operation. Both gentlemen were well received.

### Some Sinners I Have Met

Douglas Malloch was then introduced and at once plunged into his subject, "Some Sinners I Have Met". He told many humorous stories and took a few pleasant "cracks" at the chairman and several members of both the wholesale and retail lumber trade. Mr. Malloch declared that the lumber salesman was the most independent man in the world to-day as he was taking orders from nobody.

The speaker dwelt upon the relations between man and man, the value of friendship and co-operation, association and fellowship. He stressed these points with many stirring incidents and said that some fellows never set foot on the ship of good-fellowship.

Proceeding, Mr. Malloch recited from time to time several of his own stimulating poems and referred to sinners that he had met, which he dealt with seriatim. These were the gossip, the grouch, the pessimist, the quitter, the loafer, the liar, the man who talks too much, the fiend for work, etc. Each of these "species" encountered in business life were described in a forceful way by Mr. Malloch. With subtle flashes of wit and apt story, he drove home point after point, which was heartily applauded. He sent his hearers away all feeling better and brighter for they realized that, amid much mirth, wisdom and philosophy, they had listened to something which stirred the best and purest in them and aroused them to a larger sense and appreciation of self, their duty to their fellowmen, their outlook on business and their contribution to the cause of humanity.

Mr. Terry announced that the next meeting of the Ontario Wholesale Lumber Dealers' Association would be held on Friday, April 21, when A. J. Brady, of Brady Bros., North Tonawanda, N. Y., who is a speaker of force and earnestness, would deliver an address on "Salesmanship."

### "Passing the Buck" in Lumber Prices

Passing the buck is a favorite pastime, and in times of business depression or uncertainty is the greatest indoor or outdoor sport extant.

During the past few months in the lumber arena, whenever the question of prices and production was discussed, the manufacturers frequently blamed the wholesaler and the wholesaler the retailer for the somewhat unsatisfactory state of affairs and for holding up values. Then a cross current would set in from another direction and the retail dealer would blame the wholesalers and the wholesaler the manufacturer. Nearly everyone seemed to be shifting the onus and responsibility on to someone else. It was always the other fellow who was at fault.

The offices of the Burns Underwriting Co. have been removed from Room 556, Insurance Exchange Building, Chicago, Ill., to Room 1106, O. C. L. Building, 166 West Jackson Boulevard, Chicago.

The Fletcher Lumber Co., Windsor, Ont., have commenced work on a planing mill and general office. The planing mill is to be one-storey 30 x 50 while the office building is to be 24 x 24.

# Retailers Are Getting Ready For Fine Lake Trip

Further details have been completed by L. H. Richards, chairman of the Excursion Committee of the Ontario Retail Lumber Dealers' Association for the annual outing which takes place on June 23rd. The "Huronic," of the Northern Navigation Co., has been chartered and everything promises to be carried out successfully and enjoyably.

In writing to the "Canada Lumberman" regarding the outing, Mr. Richards says the steamer will leave Windsor at 5 p.m. on Friday, June 23rd, and reach Sarnia at 11 p.m. She will arrive at Owen Sound at 7 o'clock the next evening, June 24th, and leave there at 11 p.m., arriving at Killarney at 7 a.m. Sunday the 25th. Killarney will be left at 9 a.m. and the boat will travel via the North Channel route, passing Little Current and all the North Shore mills during the day on Sunday; then up through the St. Mary's River and the Canadian locks into Lake Superior far enough to turn the boat, and down through the American locks, arriving at Sault Ste. Marie at 7 p.m. Sunday June 25th. The vessel will then leave the Soo about midnight and arrive at Mackinaw Island at 10 a.m. on Monday, June 26th, leaving there at 12 o'clock, and will arrive at Sarnia at 10 a.m., Tuesday. Leaving there at noon, the "Huronic" will reach Windsor about 5 p.m. the same evening. The boat will take on passengers at Windsor, Sarnia or Owen Sound.

The fares will be,—for twenty five of the preferred staterooms $60.00 per person, and for all the other rooms on the boat $50.00 per person, including meals. Children between the ages of 5 and 12 years will travel half fare. Those under 5 years of age, who occupy chairs in the dining room, will be charged $6.00 each. Children who do not occupy chairs in the dining room and are under the age of 5, will be taken along free.

The "Huronic" will have on board a social hostess and an orchestra. The committee in charge of the outing will arrange other forms of entertainment and it is expected that the touring retail lumbermen will have automobile drives in Owen Sound and Sault Ste. Marie.

For the northern section, including North Bay, Sudbury and Sault Ste. Marie, the Northern Navigation Co. have agreed to carry members of the Ontario Retail Lumber Dealers' Association and their friends from Sault Ste. Marie to Sarnia on the "Huronic," leaving the Soo June 22nd and returning with the party on June 23rd from Sarnia or Windsor. The excursionists will leave the boat at the Soo on Sunday, June 24th. This will make a complete round trip for the retail dealers and members of the O.R.D.L.A. who reside in the north and should prove to be a drawing card from that section.

# More Effective Protection of Quebec Forests

The Quebec Department of Lands and Forests is seeking legislation for drastic measures of protection of the provincial forests from fire. Careless operation in the past has been productive of so much waste and destruction. G. C. Piche, superintendent of forestry in connection with the Lands and Forests Department, in an interview said the provincial government had viewed with alarm reports submitted by the Forestry Branch of the Department of Lands and Forests, and had given the minister in charge of the department, Hon. Mr. Mercier, a free hand to use whatever measures he judged best to cope with the situation. "This freedom of action," said Mr. Piche, "has given the forestry branch of the service wide latitude in judgment and effective action. It has caused a reorganization of the forest protective service especially against the danger of fire, that has wrought incalculable loss to the province in recent years.

One of the very first essential things in connection with the reorganization is the naming of 500 additional rangers to search out fires in the woods and subdue the flames before they can develop into destructive proportions, to spread and cause serious loss to the province and limit holders. The latter, who in the past contributed ½ cent per acre of their holdings towards the government expense for fire ranger protection, have agreed to raise the amount of 1 cent per acre. This is in addition to the various fire protective associations equipped and manned at the expense of the limit holders in the various sections of the province.

"With the addition of 500 fire rangers," said Mr. Piche, "the pro-

J. B. Burke Ottawa Ont.
Who has opened an office in Toronto and represents the Allen-Stoltze Lumber Co., of Vancouver, in Eastern Canada

vince will have over 1500 such protectors against forest fires. In the meantime the Lands and Forests Department intends to organize a staff of lecturers and send them out to educate the farmers and settlers in every district on how to guard gainst and fight fire in its begining, and by co-operation and co-ordination, control spreading fires should they get beyond the control of the district rangers.

"What I want to see accomplished," added Mr. Piche, "is to awaken the French Canadian farmers and settlers in remote districts, to the old idea and system of protection, as we in past generations practised in the province of Quebec, and now carried on with such splendid results in Sweden, Norway and Finland, commonly known as a "Ber" or congregation of neighbors to assist in each other in building projects or any matters of farm or household improvement.

Mr. Piche wishes to see organized in every section of the province in the vicinity of forest lands, settlers' associations who will always be on the lookout for the prevention of and subjection of forest fires. The department also is sending out 250,000 post cards to be distributed to all the children attending rural schools, on which is printed a message calling upon the rising generations to study the value of the forest resources of the province, and with the request that the children, as well as the adult population, co-operate to guard the forest against the dangers of fire.

Mr. Piche, discussing the bill before the legislature recently approved, said it was specially legislated in the interest of forest protection Article 1581 to be inserted in the revised statistics of 1909, deals with locators or squatters and every person who without authorization either through himself or any other person, takes possession of and occupies any part of public domain, shall be liable to a penalty of not less than $1.00 or more than $1,000, per day during which time he is or has been wrongfully in possession of such public land.

In all forest belonging to the Crown no clear cutting and no operations constituting an exception to the regulations in force, may be carried on without the authority from the Lieutenant Governor in Council. License holders wishing to obtain authority must make application to the minister, and at the same time produce a working plan based on a proper inventory made in accordance with the instructions of the department; and license holders wishing to obtain authorizations to do extraordinary cutting in his forest on account of windfalls, fire, epidemics of insects etc. must apply to the minister.

Article 1610 inserted in the revised statistics of 1909, sets forth that no person shall establish a sawmill in Crown Lands and have them a mile from any timber limit without the authority of the Department, and when so authorized, shall comply with the regulations of the department respecting the manner of disposing of the waste from the sawmill, the piling of the products and all other matters relating to the protection of forests against fire.

These two articles are supplemented by others for protection against fire and infractions of the law carry heavy penalties. An amendment much needed to prevent settlers from carelessness in making clearances of their land, that have frequently been responsible for forest fires, is included in the bill and makes the owner or occupant responsible for any fire that occurs on such owned land, and will incur penalties unless he can satisfy the court that such fire was not lighted by himself or anyone in his employ or under his direction.

# Progressive Firm Operates Four Busy Mills

Hon. J. K. Flemming Juniper, N.B.

*Former Premier of New Brunswick, Who Has Regained His Health, Is Now an Aggressive Factor in the Lumber Arena — Believes That Birch of Eastern Province, when Properly Manufactured, Will Hold High Place Among Hardwoods — Expansion of Flemming and Gibson, Limited, Has Been Steady.*

Hugh J. Flemming Juniper, N.B.

Operating four busy mills with an annual production of over 10,000,000 feet, one of the most progressive firms in the lumber line is Flemming & Gibson, Limited, of Juniper, N. B. Its history has been progressive and its development steady. The firm manufactures and deals in many specialties, including railway shims.

It was in 1910 that Hon. James K. Flemming, John Gibson and C. F. Rogers formed the organization. Mr. Gibson retired a few months later and the others then carried on until 1917 when Mr. Rogers withdrew, leaving Mr. Flemming in complete control. It was at this period that Mr. Flemming's sons and S. A. Billings, who is superintendent and in complete charge of the milling plants, came into the organization and continued the lumber business on the Miramichi River at Juniper, which is also located on the Canadian National Railways and is a live community.

In 1920 Flemming & Gibson, Limited, and the Welch Company, established a mill at Welch Siding on the C. N. R., a short distance above Juniper. This organization was incorporated as The Juniper Lumber Company, and began work immediately. A year or so later the Welch Company's property, which had been operated for a long period by that firm and also their interests in the Juniper Lumber Company, were purchased by Flemming & Gibson, Limited. This deal included the steam sawmill at Foreston, nearly 5,000 acres of freehold lands, 21 square miles of Crown lease and 16 miles of railway lands.

Flemming & Gibson, Limited, now have mills at Foreston, Juniper, Clearwater and Welch Siding, with a total daily capacity of about 100,000 feet of long lumber and a large quantity of by-products such as lath, shingles, railway shims, etc. Special machinery has been installed for the manufacture of hardwood in small pieces,

and the company are now in a position to work up hardwood economically and profitably.

In connection with each mill a shingle machine has been set up and a quantity of shingles is turned out annually. The company also handles a good many cedar telegraph poles, railway ties, etc. Each sawmill is steam-driven, having a large enough engine and boiler to supply ample motive power. The kinds of timber cut are principally spruce, balsam fir, birch and maple.

The yards and shipping facilities of the mills are excellent and from Juniper Station are dispatched the product to Foreston, Clearwater and Juniper plants, while the Welch Siding mill ships its own production. In each yard the company has a quantity of lumber always on hand although its stock was pretty low at the end of the last fiscal year of the firm, for which, in view of the existing state of the market, no sorrow was expressed.

The company employs directly and indirectly in its operations about 500 men and some 50 teams of horses. All log hauling is done by horse-power although the company is considering the advisability of using a tractor in the near future.

A wholesale business is also carried on, a reliable connection having been established in northern New York, New Jersey, and New York City, to which shipments are made. New England points, with Boston as the centre, get the most of the product. Some attention has also been devoted to the handling of lumber manufactured by other mills, and the firm has been successful in disposing of various cuts to good advantage.

The members of the firm of Flemming & Gibson, Limited, are keenly interested in the development of the hardwoods of New Brunswick which they have cut for some years, and believe that

Glimpse of the store, office, and residences at Juniper

Over 5,000 ft. of lumber on one load, 6 ft. high, 6 ft. wide and 12 ft. long

Some big loads of lath, each load weighing about seven and a half ton.

General view of Juniper mill and yard of the company, a scene in mid-winter

the birch of that province, properly manufactured, will hold a high place among hardwoods that are in public favor. They declare that its beauty is fully the equal of oak for interior finish. As members of the National Hardwood Lumber Association, they are deeply concerned in the expansion of the hardwood activities of the East.

Hon. J. K. Flemming, the president and manager of the company, is widely known throughout the province, being a man of extensive business experience and insight. He was formerly Premier and Minister of Lands and Mines in the Government of New Brunswick, retiring in 1914. For a number of years after he was in impaired health, but during the past few months he has regained his former vigor and now gives careful attention to the company's affairs. Mr. Flemming has three sons, all filling important positions in the organization, one of whom, Hugh J. Flemming, secretary-treasurer of the firm has spent the last six years in the company's offices and is conversant with the various phases of the business. Although in the early twenties, he was elected last fall to represent his parish at the Municipal Council Board for Carleton, and has the distinction of being the youngest member who ever sat as a member of that body.

S. A. Billings, is superintendent and has complete charge of the manufacturing units of the company. His insight and ability in the production end have contributed materially to the success of the operations.

# How Lumberman Borrows Money from Banks

### By W. P. Rapley.

It is always interesting to publish articles dealing with the manufacture, sale and distribution of lumber. From time to time there have appeared in the "Canada Lumberman" contributions dealing with practically every phase of the industry from bush operations to the disposition of the finished product.

Recently a timely and instructive article on "Lumber and the Banks", was published in "Caduceus", the staff magazine of the Canadian Bank of Commerce. The author is W. P. Rapley of Sherbrooke, Que., who shows an intimate acquaintance with the various processes of lumber production and an appreciation of the difficulties which sawmill men encounter at all periods of the year and more particularly in the winter and spring. He has a grasp of the speculative nature of the lumber business, its open, pioneer character, the hazard that the exponents of this great national activity assume at all times, and the cheerful, confident spirit which animates him in this undertaking.

On the other hand many retailers and wholesale lumbermen who, perhaps, are not thoroughly conversant with the perplexities which many a sawmill man has in financing his enterprise, particularly during a year of depression or falling values, may after perusing the observations of the writer see that the manufacturer has no primrose path, but is, at all times, confronted with obstacles and dangers. If his rewards now and then seem to be a little larger than ordinary, it must be remembered that he assumes greater risks and waits a long time for results. The lumber business is a long-range one, peering far into the future and taking chances with wind, weather, building operations, labor conditions, supply and demand, railway facilities, fire, flood, famine, etc.

Then again, while certain members of the trade have in the past been referred to as "lumber kings" or "lumber barons", these examples are few and far between. No mention is made of the scores and scores who have gone down in the conflict and lost vast fortunes; neither does the average person realize that, outside of the speculative character of the industry itself, the investment in limits, driving equipment, mills, yards, etc., is very heavy and the returns received are comparatively small when all these outstanding facts are taken into consideration.

The embryo banker has a wonderful source of information at his disposal, which may or may not be appreciated; he has the opportunity to obtain a fundamental knowledge of the various industries conducted by customers of the branch at which he is stationed. If the desire exists, and it should be cultivated if it does not, he has only to take advantage of his environment to acquire an education which will never be regretted and which will be an important factor in preparing him for the responsibility of a managerial appointment. There is one industry producing a commodity second in importance only to wheat, the details of which are known to comparatively few of the branches—and that is lumbering. With the lure of the woods and rivers strong with us, there cannot be many who are not familiar with the romance of lumber from log to mill, but this article is written in the belief that there are unusual and interesting features in connection with its financing of which many of the staff are not aware.

Credit is granted for lumbering on a more generous scale than is the case with any other industry; the proportion between liquid assets and floating liabilities seems at certain seasons to violate every rule of safe banking, but the vital importance of the product guarantees a market, and the security from the standpoint of reasonable liquidation may be regarded as imperishable except from fire. In every lumbering centre the inhabitants will point out to the newly-arrived banker the residence of local millionaires who, having begun with nothing, have become wealthy through lumber or pulpwood. This at first gives him the impression that the forest offers the surest and easiest road to fortune. He soon learns, however, that many have ventured without success, and when he considers the attributes of energy, ability and courage that a lumberman must possess to begin with the proverbial "shoestring" and year after year place his entire capital at the mercy of the elements, he is forced to the conclusion that the reward is well deserved.

In order to consider comprehensively some of the salient features peculiar to the industry, let us assume that, as bank manager, it is our duty and privilege to watch the account of a lumberman, who after operating successfully for a certain number of years has acquired a handsome surplus of say $150,000, but has cut over his limits and is compelled to seek a fresh field. He disposes of his cut-over lands, mill, stock, etc., and purchases a substantial limit, intending to operate on a more extensive scale. To secure a property of any magnit-

ude, probably means moving to the outskirts of civilization, as each year results in the exhaustion of forests in the more settled districts The account may previously have been carried with a bank not represented at the town where we are stationed, and upon learning of the sale of the limits in question and after instituting enquiries and assuring ourselves of the purchaser's standing, we formulate our plans to secure the connection.

. If our efforts meet with success the account is opened in the spring. We are informed that a mill will be erected and roads built with a view to commencing operations in the fall. No advances will be required until cutting commences, but we arrange for a statement to be submitted on 31st August in order that a line of credit may be established in plenty of time.

On the date mentioned our new customer calls at the office and presents us with the following figures:

Statement as at 31st August

| | |
|---|---|
| Cash in Bank .......... ......... ......... ....... | $17,000 |
| Accounts Receivable ...... ......... ......, ....... | 18,000 |
| | $35,000 |
| Limits ...... ......... ......... ......... ......... | 80,000 |
| Roads, camps, etc. ......... ......... ......... ....... | 3,000 |
| Interest in Booming Co. ...... ......... ......... | 3,000 |
| Horse, sleighs, etc. ......... ......... ......... ....... | 7,000 |
| Camp and mill supplies ......... ......... ......... | 3,500 |
| Mill and machinery ......... ......... ......... | 40,000 |
| Railway sidings ...... ......... ......... ......... | 1,500 |
| Residence ......... ......... ......... ....... | 5,000 |
| | 178,000 |
| Accounts payable ......... ......... ......... | 3,000 |
| | 3,000 |
| Due on limits, payable $5,000 per annum, first payment due July of following year ....... | 25,000 |
| Surplus ......, ...... ......... ......... | 150,000 |
| | $178,000 |

He states that he wishes to get out about 5,000,000 feet of logs and requests a credit of $100,000 to be secured in the usual manner by assignments under Section 88 of the Bank Act.

## Observations of the Banker

We have now had sufficient time to become well acquainted with our customer, have seen the mill erected; and after studying the assets, arrived at the conclusion that we are prepared to recommend the account. However, our superintendent remains to be convinced, and we must consider the information to be embodied in our communication in order that the application may be viewed in a comprehensive manner. Let us ask ourselves the following questions.

What do we know of our customer's ability, reputation, etc.?

We have found by means of mercantile and bankers' reports that he was well and favorably known at his former place of residence, and has had many years of experience as a lumberman. He had cut over his lands and was able to sell his mill and real estate and was therefore possessed of sufficient ready money to develop his new property. His eldest son has assisted him for five years and has been trained in every branch of the business. This is an important feature as providing against mismanagement in case of the father's demise or long illness.

What do we know of the limits?

While we have not had them cruised, we know from reports that they are looked upon by lumbermen as equal to any in the district and were carefully inspected by our customer before the purchase was consummated. They are reported to contain an abundance of spruce, which can be lumbered at a minimum of expense. The property lies along the banks of an easily driven river, and is intersected by small streams and brooks, which ensures a short haul. While the limits are not freehold, the land is not suited to agriculture and no difficulty will be experienced in obtaining renewals of the licenses in due course. When the large timber is cut, the property should have value as a pulpwood investment.

What is the nature of the drive?

The limits are about twenty-five miles up stream from the mill, and there are only two other concerns driving the river. These three have joined in forming a booming company for the purpose of making what is known as a "corporation drive." That is, the company has constructed the necessary piers and booms and will handle the three drives which will come down simultaneously in the spring, and the logs will be sorted and boomed and the expense divided pro rata. The river empties into a small lake on which the mills are located,

and there is absolutely no danger of loss if the booms should be carried away by a freshet.

## Inside Knowledge

What is the equipment of the mill?

The mill is complete and well constructed, considering the cost, and at a conservative estimate the limits provide for a life of fifteen years. Its capacity can be increased by a small outlay should additional limits be purchased or more extensive operations be carried on. The mill is not of steel construction, but is what is known as an "open burner." For this reason the insurance rate will be considerably higher, but the additional cost of a steel burner would have been prohibitive at this juncture. A high-pressure pump has been installed to provide protection against fire. Adequate insurance is carried on the mill and every care will be taken to avoid fire, as the loss of the mill in the sawing season would result in a "lock up" until a new mill could be erected. There will be no expense for fuel as the sawdust is available for this purpose.

What are the railway facilities?

The town is situated on a transcontinental railway, and our customer will not be at a disadvantage with competitors as regards freight rates. The yards are served by a siding, and loading can be carried on expeditiously.

What labor is available?

Plenty of local labor is available, and our customer has brought a number of his foremen with him. They have been in his employ for years, and their loyalty is an indication that there is little likelihood of his having troubles in that direction.

## The Financial Statement

The items composing the balance sheet are for the most part self-explanatory. We might mention that the accounts receivable appear to be first-class, and should all be paid during the next three or four months. We shall not show them in our declarations, as they represent the former business, and do not in reality pertain to our security by way of Section 88. We should, however, be justified in doing so, as we have obtained a general assignment of accounts. The timber licenses have been registered in our customer's name, and he has assigned them to the vendors to secure the unpaid portion of the purchase price. The agreement permits him to complete the transaction at any time, but he cannot be called upon to pay more than $5,000 per annum, provided the cut does not exceed 6,000,000 feet.

While there is apparently a lack of liquid assets for a credit of $100,000, we must remember that with that amount he should eventually convert 5,000,000 feet of logs into at least 5,750,000 feet of lumber, allowing for a modest overrun of 150 feet per thousand. Estimating that this lumber should realize say $34 per thousand, or $195,500, we feel satisfied that after allowing for all reasonable shrinkages, the bank will be provided with ample security. However, it is likely to be over a year from the time the cutting commences until the sawing is completed and in the meantime operations will have commenced for the next season. As a result we shall never be able to show a liquid surplus to confirm the figures we have used, and as the reason may not be clear to any one not familiar with the industry, we shall endeavor to explain as we go on why a lumber account generally appears to be receiving unusually generous treatment from its banker.

## Advancing the Credit

After complying with the usual formalities, the credit is granted, embodying the stipulation "relative insurance in favor of the bank." This clause is of great importance, and we must be alert to see that it is observed. There can be no loss by fire until the logs are hauled from the water and sawn into lumber, but we must see that sufficient insurance is placed and lodged with us at frequent intervals as the manufactured stock accumulates. Many lumbermen cancel the insurance on their manufactured stock as soon as snow falls and do not replace it until spring, as there is not considered to be any risk during the winter. This is a matter which must be carefully considered according to the circumstances and conditions surrounding the account.

Our customer will be anxious to commence cutting as early as possible, as with deep snow he will not be able to cut as close to the ground, and valuable timber will be left on the stump, but the date will depend upon the labor situation. If he employs farmers from the surrounding country, they will not be able to leave their farms until the harvest is gathered. Under present conditions large operators in the Province of Quebec prefer to have the cutting done by contractors or jobbers as they are called, who undertake the work at so much per thousand feet to be paid at intervals as the work progresses. These jobbers will fell the trees and yard the logs but the hauling to the banks of the rivers in most cases will be undertaken by the operator. There are several reasons for employing jobbers who are generally farmers well known as to their ability and

integrity, but the chief advantage is the fact that there is less likelihood of labor trouble. A jobber may have a small contract necessitating the assistance of three or four men, or it may be larger. He will naturally engage his own relatives or friends, and it has been found that he obtains much better results when gangs of men are supervised by foremen. Which course is pursued depends to a great extent upon the location of the limits and their distance from civilization. If there are no settlements close by it will be difficult to secure a sufficient number of capable jobbers.

### Customer's Declaration

To return to the hypothetical account in question, we must obtain declarations in connection with our security, and our customer should be asked to compile these figures once a month. We will say that on 31st December we receive a declaration as follows:—

Advance to jobbers, $20,000.
Bank loan, $5,000.

Not much information, and one not familiar with conditions would naturally ask for more particulars. However, it would be impossible to record exactly how many feet of logs the jobbers have cut and the security shown represent the amount paid out to them together with other expenses incidental to the work. So far the bulk of the money required has been furnished by the customer.

On 31st January the estimate stands at:—

Advances to jobbers, $35,000.
Bank loan, $20,000.

Cutting is now in full swing and the logs are being hauled up the rivers.

Declaration 28th February:—
Advance to jobbers, $55,000.

Our customer is still using moneys received from accounts receivable, but this is not apparent, as there are certain overhead expenses which are not yet reflected in our security.

### Second Declaration

By 31st March, when the next declaration is received, the hauling has been completed and the logs are on the banks or in the streams ready for the drive. The jobbers have been paid in full, and the scale shows the total cut, and the declaration received for the first time shows something tangible:—

5,075,000 feet logs at $15, $76,125.
Bank loan, $60,000.

The winter has been favourable, and no logs have been left in the woods; the scale is gratifying inasmuch as it shows that our customer has to all intents and purposes kept within his estimate which confirms our confidence and furthermore indicates that his credit should prove ample.

With a normal spring providing plenty of water, no difficulty should be experienced in the drive, and we will say that on 30th April the logs are boomed and the mill put in operation. The declaration reads:—

Logs in streams, 275,000 feet at $15 ...................... $ 4,125
Logs in booms, 4,800,000 feet at $18 ...................... 86,400

Bank loan ...................... $90,525
Bank loan ...................... $75,000

It is evident that 275,000 feet of logs were "hung up" in the drive. These logs should come down next spring, and as they bear our customer's special mark they constitute good security. There will, of course, be some shrinkage, but we shall not take it into consideration, as we know the figures and valuations to be sufficiently conservative to allow for this contingency.

### Third Declaration

We will assume that on 31st May, after the mill has been running a month, the following declaration is received:—

Logs in stream, 275,000 feet at $15 ...................... $ 4,125
Logs in booms, 4,175,000 at $18 ...................... 75,150
Lumber, 800,000 feet at $30‡ ...................... 24,000
Overrun of 15 p.c. allowed for

                               $103,275
Bank loan ...................... $ 80,000
Fire Insurance ...................... 16,000

Our margin of security should continue to improve steadily from now on. In the early stages we may have experienced some misgiving that there might be a hitch, but our security is now in a condition where we can verify it from a personal inspection.

The mill functions properly and sawing is carried on, and during the summer we visit the mill frequently. Our observations show that the book-keeping provides for a complete record of each day's sawing, loss of time through accidents, etc. The lumber is carefully sorted and piled and the stipulation of the insurance companies strictly carried out.

On 31st August our customer advises that his entire output has been contracted for by responsible firms at an average of $34

per thousand run of the mill. His statement is now a year old, but he advises that he would prefer not to tender an audited statement until 31st December, when the yards should be clear of lumber and the results of the year can be comprehensively reviewed.

He submits a declaration and estimate of profit, and requests that a fresh credit should be granted to finance a similar cut for the coming season. The proceeds of sales will meanwhile take care of operations and permit him to keep within the present and anticipated credit. The profit is estimated at $25,000, and we might reasonably ask why the application could not be reduced to this extent, but it is important to remember that we have assumed for convenience that no logs or lumber were held over and that the circumstances were propitious throughout. If our customer had not been starting a new venture, it is doubtful if he could have got out 5,000,000 feet with loans of $100,000, as he would likely carry over a portion of his stock to meet with some slight reverse, and he will do well to keep within this figure next year, allowing for the $25,000 additional capital provided from profits.

Declaration 31st August:—

Logs in streams, 275,000 feet at $15 ...................... $ 4,125
Logs in booms, 1,500,000 feet at $18 ...................... 27,000
Lumber, 22,800,000 feet at $30 ...................... 84,000
Accounts receivable for lumber sold at $34 ...................... 33,400

                              $148,525
Bank loan ...................... $100,000
Insurance ...................... 80,000

It would appear that on 31st December with the entire stock sold at $34, the account should show a much larger margin of liquid assets, but we must remember that there will be advances to jobbers, with the result that the ratio may not reach more than 1·50 to 1. This we regard as highly satisfactory for an account of this nature, and to confirm our views we would mention that the Federal Reserve Banks in the United States, while demanding assets of 2 to 1 when offered paper for re-discount, make an exception in favor of the lumberman and are satisfied with a margin of 1.50 to 1.

Space will not permit us to go into details regarding the estimated net profit of $25,000. Suffice it to say that we believe it to be conservative. According to the original estimate which has proved approximately correct, there should be a profit of say $45,000 which would leave $20,000 to take care of depreciations, interest, taxes, etc.

Now while our experience has been most satisfactory, our observations of the past year have given us a pretty good idea as to what pitfalls exist and what contingencies may arise, and we will record them herewith.

1. Owing to the distance to the limits, it is impossible actually to check the operations and the normal security must be first-class.

2. The success or failure depends on the customer's ability, and once the bank has made advances it must carry the operation through as the security cannot be realized until manufactured into lumber. For instance, if a credit were granted to cut 5,000,000 feet and the customer, either through poor judgment or by taking advantage of his position cut 7,000,000 feet, the bank would in self protection be obliged to increase the loans in order to make the security marketable.

3. It is impossible to avoid seasons overlapping. That is, the loan will not be liquidated before it will be necessary to make advances for the next season. For this reason it would be advisable to review the account at the end of the summer with a view to ascertaining the customer's plans. If contracts have not been made for the manufactured lumber and the demand should fall off, the bank might unwillingly find itself committed to finance another cut, which would necessitate much higher advances than it would have cared to entertain.

4. No matter how able the operator may be, he is at the mercy of the elements. There may be too much or too little snow. The spring may be open before his hauling is completed, or there may not be sufficient water to float his logs to the main river, and the mill may be so located that there is danger of a sudden freshet carrying away the booms with a total or partial loss.

5. The life of the mill depends upon the life of the limit. Its valuation should be written down, or a reserve set aside each year, if fresh limits are purchased.

There is a great deal to learn in connection with lumbering. Those who are fond of outdoor life can combine business with pleasure, shoot over the limits in the fall and fish the streams in the spring, and thereby familiarize themselves with the property and the various stages of operation.

Note:—The figures used in the foregoing are, of course, not based on actual facts, and could not be used for the purpose of comparison. It would be difficult to arrive at an estimate that could be regarded as correctly proportioned, as costs and selling prices vary according to the physical aspects of the property and its distance from the market, either for domestic use or export.

# Hauling Logs From Roll-way to River Landing

### Interesting Operations Carried on by the St. Maurice Paper Company—Eleven Logging Tractors in Action—Delivering the Goods in Record Time and Under Difficult Conditions

#### By J. S. INNES

Tank Tractor taking on water. The tank is 14' x 6' x 8' and is filled, in from three to five minutes

In the woodlands end of the lumber business probably the most worrying problem has been that of log haulage. The continual demand for cost reduction has, as far as the woods operations are concerned, pointed the accusing finger to the problem of log haulage.

It has long been recognized by the Canadian woods manager, that a mechanical means for log haulage must be adopted in order to reduce haulage costs.

The inevitable answer to the woodsman's query was the tractor; and when a survey was made, many tractors were heard of, for which were claimed marvellous haulage performance. Some operators accepted the vendors' statement of capacity, and soon found themselves the possessors of equipment which would not do their work. They realized, too late that a log hauling tractor must do the work of many teams, under all encountered conditions, in order to create the desired economy. It certainly must "deliver the goods."

Safety in handling long trains of logs down steep sand hills; up such grades as are encountered in our woods, over lake and river ice; through deep snow.

The St. Maurice Paper Company had a tractor in operation, but, when it was decided to visit their operations, it was found

Tractor and train at foot of 35% down grade from Fish's Camp

that this logging tractor had moved all their logs in three weeks, and was in its garage.

The writer, therefore, in company with some Ontario and Quebec operators, visited the operations of the Gould Paper Company, at Forestport, N. Y., where twelve logging tractors were in operation.

We arrived at Forestport, and were hospitably received by the superintendent of logging operations, Mr. J. B. Todd, and the following day were driven the 26 miles into their limits on North Lake, where they were engaged in hauling 17,000 cords of 12 ft. pulp wood, over the height of land, from the watershed of North Lake to the Moose River waterway.

Their hauling distance from rollway to landing was 12 miles. Rollways were located at three points, about five miles separated from each other.

Eleven logging tractors are in operation on this limit, and the

twelfth at a small operation known as Tugg Hill. Five of the eleven logging tractors carry tanks for water, each tank being 14 ft. by 8 ft. by 6 ft. Four of these tank tractors operate from camp No. 9 rollways to the summit yard. The summit yard is at the top of a 2½ mile, 7½% up grade. Each of these tank tractors haul a train of six sleds, each sled being loaded with five cords of spruce and hemlock logs. The tank is filled at the foot of the up-grade, and when returning from the summit yard to the rollways at camp No. 9, it waters the roads. The distance from the summit yard to camp No. 9 is a little over 12 miles. Six filling stations are located on the main hauls for tank filling.

Each of the remaining six logging tractors carries a load of two cords on their own bolsters. Three of these logging tractors operate between camp No. 8 and the landing or dump. They take a train of six sleds from camp No. 8, and couple on to an additional train of six sleds (hauled to the summit by tank tractors from camp No. 9) and proceed to the landing with the long train.

Three river tractors operate between Fish's camp and the river. They haul four or five sleds from the rollways at Fish's camp to the river landing. Immediately upon leaving Fish's camp, a very steep grade of 15% is encountered. One tank tractor located at Fish's camp doubleheads with the river tractor to the top of the grade, and the river tractor proceeds to the summit yard alone.

Between Fish's camp and the summit a steep curving sand hill of nearly 35% down grade and 350 yards in length, is encountered, and yet the logging tractor handles its train of logs down this mountain side without any difficulty whatever.

After leaving the summit yard, the drop to the river landing is commenced. This drop is estimated to be about 25% down grade, of half a mile in length. The river tractors handle all these long trains down this grade. All tractors returning haul back their empty sled train to the rollways.

At the landing solid log bridges are formed at the commencement of the hauling, nine of these being formed as rapidly as logs are brought to the landing. When the bridge is completed, the tractor pulls its train of sleds on to the bridge, and the landing crews empty the train load on to the ice. The tractor, of course, leaves its loaded train at once, couples up with an empty train, and returns to the rollways. Each tractor must make two complete round trips each day.

Hauling had been commenced on January 15, and at the time of our visit (Feb. 2) 9,600 cords or 192,000 logs were at the landing. Tanks are filled in from three to five minutes. Road plowing and icing are done during the day, the tractors accomplishing these operations on their regular trips.

At headquarters camp, known as camp No. 7, is located the general foreman, the logging tractor garage, machine shop, gasoline filling station, stove, cookhouse and sleep camp. Both the main haul and the go back pass directly in front of this camp.

Last year, with nine logging tractors in operation on this territory, the company moved 24,000 cords of wood to the landing in 38 days, at an approximate haulage cost of 72 cents per cord.

I have this winter visited some operations in the Adirondacks. and I found no dumps in small streams. The dumps were located on main rivers and lakes. True, the haul was sometimes as great as fourteen miles, but the method cut the cost in half. The cost of improvements on the stream or creek was saved; the cost of the drive on the stream or creek was eliminated. and the expense of sweeping the main river was eliminated. and—pleasant to relate—the actual haulage cost with the logging tractor for the necessary extra distance, from six to fourteen miles, was practically no greater than the previous cost with teams, for the usual two or three mile haul to the landing at creek or stream.

I show a picture taken of a dump at the main river of one

Linn logging tractor and train on bridge at landing.   Train is left here to be unloaded by landing crews

operation I visited. These people hauled twelve miles to their main river. At the time the photo was taken (Feb. 2nd.) there were 9,600 cords in the river, and hauling had only been going on since Jan. 15th., and the haulage cost of that wood was only 72 cents per cord. These people have absolutely no dams or improvements whatsoever on their main river.

Last year, when they finished hauling they had in their dump on the river, 28,000 cords of spruce and hemlock. The freshet came in the night, and, in the morning, not a log was left at the landing.

At the top of up-grade from Fish's Camp. Tractors double head to this point and from here one tractor takes the train down 55% grade

They drive 54 miles, and, in 18 days, the entire 28,000 cords was at their mill storage, 54 miles distant. Had they driven creeks and streams, they would, no doubt, have been driving on into August, at any rate.

This method of main river driving is, to my mind, one of the principal factors in woods cost reduction; that, coupled with reliable mechanical log hauling, appears to be the only factors at present presenting themselves for cost reduction.

### Death of Esteemed Lumber Retailer

Many friends in the retail lumber ranks will regret to learn of the death of John Howes of Harriston, Ont., who passed away recently after a long illness. Mr. Howes was born and raised on a farm near Harriston. There was considerable hardwood bush on the property and he started in to dispose of this, eventually going into the lumber line himself, his sons now being associated with him. Recently a charter was granted, incorporating the firm of John Howes & Sons, Limited. One of his sons, N. J. Howes, is head of the new organization. The late Mr. Howes was a man of kindly disposition, and sympathetic nature and always took a deep interest

in the work of the Ontario Retail Lumber Dealers' Association and particularly the activities of the Orangeville district. He always attended the annual gatherings where he was a welcome visitor. His passing removes a man who was well thought of and well spoken of by all with whom he came in contact.

### Stocks Low at Manchester and Liverpool

It is interesting to note both Canadian and Baltic stocks that were held in Manchester and Liverpool, England, at the end of February and to compare them with what was on hand in the same period of 1921 and 1920.

Canadian Stocks, imports, at Manchester and Liverpool,—1920, 2,260 standards; 1921, 1,440; 1922, 970. Consumption—1920, 2,990 standards; 1921, 4,080; 1922 1, 670. Stocks on hand— 1920 23,380 standards; 1921, 29,560; 1922, 7,080.

Baltic stocks held at Manchester and Liverpool:— 1922, 3,710 standards; 1921, 1,560; 1922, 3,500. Consumption,—1920 4,860 standards, 1921, 3,580; 1922, 5,880. Stocks on hand—1920, 24,770 standards; 1921, 30,610; 1922, 12, 600.

### General and Personal Notes of Interest

Frank L. Adolph, sales manager of the Adolph Lumber Company, Baynes Lake, B. C, who has been in Toronto for some time in the interests of the firm, has opened an office at 41 Victoria Street, Mr. Adolph is specializing in the Western soft white pine, mountain fir and larch and has called upon a large number of the retailers and wholesalers in Ontario. He is a former Ontario boy being born in Bruce County, where his father ran a sawmill for a number of years.

Chas J. Brooks, of the sales staff of the Toronto office of the Canadian Western Lumber Company, returned recently from a business trip throughout the Maritime provinces. He reports that while trade is quiet at present, the prospects down East are getting brighter and there is a growing feeling of confidence in the betterment of business conditions generally.

J. L. Nevison has removed his office from 43 Adelaide Street East to 302 Brass Building corner of Adelaide and Yonge Streets, Toronto. Mr. Nevison represents the McElroy Lumber Company of Winnipeg, the North West Lumber Co., of Edmonton and the Theo. A. Burrows Lumber Co., of Winnipeg. He reports a considerable improvement in business during the past few weeks.

### Say Cut Will be Down by One Half

The Bancroft Lumber & Mfg. Co., of Bancroft, Ont. say they did not take out any logs this winter and only intend making shingles and running their planing mill at Paudash Lake, Ont. In this stock there is a part of their 1920 cut. It is said that the production of lumber in the vicinity of Bancroft, which is in the northern part of Hastings County, will only be about 50% of what it was last year.

The officers of the Bancroft Lumber & Mfg. Co. are D. W. Avey, president, D. S. Hubbel, vice-president, M. E. Davis, secretary, and D. A. Davis, treasurer and manager. The latter recently returned from an extensive business trip of several weeks through Michigan, Ohio and Indiana.

The will of the late Joseph Oliver, lumber merchant, of Toronto, who died on January 8th, 1922, has been filed for probate. He left an estate of $58,380.

# The "Grain" of Wood with Reference to Direction of Fibre

### By ARTHUR KOEHLER
#### Specialist in Wood Identification, Forest Products Laboratory, Madison, Wisconsin.

Upon the direction of the grain in woods used in airplane construction may depend the strength of the machine and the safety of the pilot. It is, therefore, of great importance that the inspector be familiar with the different kinds of "grain" and be able to determine the direction and slope of the fibers, so that he may eliminate pieces which, on account of their cross-grain, would be likely to reduce seriously the margin of safety.

There are various kinds of "grain" in wood, and various uses of the word. The annual rings are often considered as constituting the grain. Woods with wide and conspicuous rings are said to be "coarse grained," and those with narrow rings, "fine grained." If each annual ring is composed of a hard and a soft layer, as, for example, in the yellow pines, Douglas fir, oak, and ash, the wood is said to have an "uneven grain," as contrasted with the "even grain" of white pine, basswood, maple, and mahogany. Occasionally "uneven grain" is used with reference to woods in which the annual rings are very irregular in width. Cypress is often of this nature.

When lumber is sawed along the radius of the annual rings, it is said to show "edge grain," that is, the "edge" of the annual ring shows on the face. This is also known as "comb grain" and "vertical grain." When lumber is cut parallel or tangent to the annual rings, it is said to show "flat grain." In grading rules a slope of 45 degrees for the annual rings is considered the line of demarcation between edge grain and vertical grain. The cross-section of timber is usually called the "end grain."

For woods in which the annual rings are inconspicuous as in maple, red gum, and mahogany, the word "grain" is rarely used with reference to the annual rings. Thus the expression "coarse-grained maple," "uneven grained red gum," or "edge-grained mahogany" is seldom used.

The word "grain" is also used with reference to the size of the pores; woods with comparatively large pores, such as oak, chestnut, ash, and African mahogany, are said to have a "coarse grain," while those with small pores, such as maple, cherry, basswood, and red gum are called "fine-grained." Painters designate them as "open" and "close grained" respectively, the former requiring a filler. Occasionally the word "texture" is used in place of "grain" in describing the width or uniformity of the rings or the size of the pores.

Since the term "grain" is used in describing a number of different characteristics of wood, it would help considerably to avoid confusion if the width of the rings were expressed by the terms "wide-ringed," "narrow-ringed," or "with rings of medium width;" the uniformity or irregularity in the structure or width of the rings, by "even texture" or "uneven texture"; and the size of the pores, by "coarse texture," or "fine texture." The terms "edge grain" and "flat grain" are more definitely fixed in their meaning and should be retained.

A common use of the term "grain" is to describe the direction in which the fibres extend in a tree or piece of lumber.

"Straight grain" means that the fibres run practically parallel with the main axis of a tree, or are parallel with the main axis of any given piece.

"Spiral grain" means that the fibres extend in an oblique direction circumferentially in the tree, so that if extended they would wind around the tree trunk, forming a spiral, (see Fig. 1). Wood which has a spiral grain, when split radially, produces a twisted surface.

"Interlocked grain," also called "cross grain," is caused by alternating layers of wood being spirally grained in reverse directions; that is, the fibres put on for a number of years may slope in a right-handed direction, and then for a number of years the slope reverses to a left-handed direction, and later changes back to a right-handed pitch, and so on, (see Figure 2). Such wood is exceedingly difficult to split radially, although tangentially it splits fairly easily. Interlocked grain is common in black gum, red gum, some cottonwood, eucalyptus, and many tropical trees.

Diagonal grain is the slanting of the wood fibres brought about by causes other than spiral grain in the tree. Usually it is due to sawing straight grained timber in a direction not parallel with the fibres, a procedure to be avoided, if possible, in cutting stock in which

strength is an essential feature. Curvature in the tree trunk and other irregularities in the grain outside of local wavy and curly grain may, however, make it impossible to avoid the production of diagonal grain in cutting up certain logs. The common method of cutting lumber is to saw parallel with the central axis, which produces more or less serious diagonal grain in the lumber, depending on the taper of the log, (see Figure 3). Obviously, diagonal grain weakens the lumber, and several mills cutting airplane stock are not cutting parallel to the outer surface of the log. Diagonal grain may also be produced by

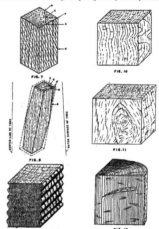

FIG. 7        FIG. 10
FIG. 8        FIG. 11
FIG. 9        FIG. 12

cutting up quarter-sawed lumber and not getting the faces parallel to the annual layers of growth, (see Figure 4). or by cutting up plain sawed lumber and not getting the faces parallel to the direction of the fibres (see Figure 5). Diagonal grain produced in the latter way is difficult to distinguish from natural spiral grain in the tree. However, since so far as is known, they are equally weakening, there usually is no need to distinguish between the two.

Both spiral grain and diagonal grain are also called "cross grain." Natural spiral grain can be detected by the twisted surface produced in splitting long pieces, and, according to Oakleaf*, usually by the fact that the parabolas and elipses produced by the intersection of the annual rings with the flat surface, do not extend in the same direction as the fibres.

### How to Determine the Presence and Slope of Spiral Grain on the Tangential Faces

Spiral grain can be detected most easily by splitting wood in a radial direction. This, of course, mutilates the piece and is not always

permissible. The direction of seasoning checks on the tangential surface also indicates the direction of the fibres. If no checks are present the direction of the resin ducts (brownish hair-like lines), which are found only in pines, spruces, Douglas fir, and larch or tamarck, serves as a guide for determining the slope of the grain. In the hardwoods, especially in species in which the pores are distinct, such as ash, oak, hickory, walnut, mahogany, and birch, the direction of the pores indicates the direction of the grain. Coniferous woods seem to be more subject to spiral grain than hardwoods. If the resin ducts are absent or obscure, or if the pores in hardwoods are obscure, the direction in which the ink spreads will indicate the direction of the grain. This test can best be applied by using a fine pointed pen and an alcohol solution (about ¾ alcohol and ¼ water) of some dye-like safranin. If the pen, dipped in the dye, is pressed slightly into the wood, the dye will spread from about ⅛ to ¼ of an inch along the fibres. The direction of the grain can be followed up by again placing the pen point at the extreme to which the ink has spread along the fibres, and so on until a line sufficiently long to determine the slope of the grain has been made.

Some determine the direction of the fibres by picking up the fibres with a knife and observing in which direction they tear out. The presence, but hardly the slope, of spiral grain may also be determined by the dip of the fibres where chips are torn out of the radial surface by the planer. With a hand lens magnifying about 15 diameters the direction of the fibres can plainly be seen. In no case should the direction of the annual rings on the tangential face be taken as the direction of the grain.

The slope of the grain on the tangential face is usually expressed as the number of units (inches or other units) along the length of the stick in which the grain deviates one unit from a radial plane parallel to the main axis of the stick. This is expressed as 1 in 12, 1 in 30, etc.

Diagonal grain on the radial surface can usually be easily detected by the direction of the annual rings. The slope of the grain on the radial face is expressed as the number of units along the length of the stick in which the grain (annual rings) deviates one unit from a tangential plane parallel to the main axis of the stick.

Diagonal grain on the tangential surface and its slope can be determined in the same manner as spiral grain, from which it need not be differentiated.

It must be remembered that if the stick has any taper, the slope of the fibres with respect to its main axis, and not to the surface of the stick, gives the true slope of the grain. This is equally true for spiral grain.

The slope of either spiral or diagonal grain may be more in one portion of the stick than in another; therefore, the entire length of the stick should be examined.

### How to Determine the Presence and the Slope of Spiral or Diagonal Grain When the Surfaces Are Not Truly Radial or Tangential

On shaped sticks which are round or oval in cross-section, surfaces sufficiently tangential or radial to determine the direction and slope of the grain may be found. The direction of the grain in rectangular pieces may be determined as in other pieces in which the faces are truly tangential or radial, that is, by splitting, checks, direction of resin ducts, pores, medullary rays, and annual rings, or by the ink test, depending on whether spiral or diagonal grain is being looked for.

The slops of the grain in rectangular pieces may be determined as follows:

Diagonal grain—Starting some distance from the end and on the edge farthest from the centre of the tree, or on the edge nearest to the centre, trace back an annual ring to the end of the stick, as O B in Figure 6. Follow the ring across the stick, as B C D. Measure the distance from the corner A to the ring B C D. Then (the distance) A C in (the distance) A O is the true slope of the grain.

Spiral grain—Starting some distance from the end of one of the two edges which are neither farthest from nor nearest to the centre of the tree, trace back the grain to the end of the stick, as O B in Figure 7. Draw the radial line B C D and connect A with the nearest point on the line B C D, then (the distance) A C in (the distance) A O is the true slope of the grain at that part of the stick. In some woods, and even in conifers containing resin ducts, it is often exceedingly difficult to find the proper direction for the line O B, so that splitting of a corner may be the only accurate way of finding the slope the grain.

If both spiral and diagonal grain are present in a stick the direction and slope of each may be determined separately by the methods above.

If the stick has any taper, as is often the case in fuselage struts (the distance A C in (the distance) A O (Figure 8) is the true slope of the grain where A O is parallel to the main axis of the stick.

True wavy grain is due to a wavy arrangement of the fibres, producing undulation on a split radial surface. (See Figure 9.) Wavy

grained wood will split straight tangentially, but the wavy direction of the fibres can be seen on the tangential surface. Irregular protuberances on the tree trunk may produce one or several "waves" in the annual rings. This is seen best on the radial face, (See Figure 10.) In this case the waves are not as regular as when the undulations occur on the radial face. A bulge in the annual rings may indicate the presence of a pitch pocket toward the inner side of the tree.

Curly grain is an irregular distortion of the fibres as seen on the tangential surface. (See Figure 11.) It is produced in the healing over of knots or injuries received by the growing tree. It can be detected by noting carefully the direction of the fibres or the irregular way in which the fibres are chipped out by the planer knives. The ink test is also good for determining the direction of the fibres in curly grain.

Knots are weakening because of the distortion of grain which they produce, although they are denser as a rule than the surrounding

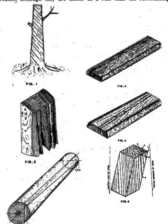

wood. Knots start nearly always at the pith and grow in diameter from year to year, so that they are cone-shaped, with the apex at the pith (Figure 12). Knots from sprouts which come out of the side of the tree trunk do not, of course, originate at the centre.

"Live" or "sound" knots are intimately connected with the fibre of the surrounding wood, especially from the lower side, because here the sap brought up from the roots must flow from the sapwood of the trunk to the sapwood of the branch and thence to the leaves. From the upper side the connection is less intimate, and for this reason the cleft in a knotty piece of wood split from the lower side usually runs into the knot, but the cleft in a piece split from above may run around the knot, and the wood is more easily split.

After the limbs have served the tree for some time, the lower ones may become overshadowed by the growing crown to such an extent that they die. After a branch is dead it forms no further connection with the surrounding wood, and often if cut across, as in plain sawed lumber, it can be removed. Such a knot is called a "loose knot." If the knot is firmly held in position but is surrounded by bark or pitch, it is termed an "encased knot." A knot cut lengthwise is called a "spike knot," and a knot less than one-half inch in diameter is called a "pin knot."

*Oakleaf, H. B.—"Inspectors' Manual, Equipment Division Signal Corps."

# Nova Scotia Lumbermen Form an Association

## Rousing Meeting Held at Halifax Elects Officers and Gets off to Good Start— Much Business Comes up for Consideration—Enjoyable Social Function

Rufus E. Dickie, President of Nova Scotia Lumbermen

An enthusiastic gathering of the lumber operators and wholesalers of the province of Nova Scotia was held at Halifax on March 23rd. for the purpose of organizing a lumbermen's association along the lines of those already in existence in other parts of Canada. There was a large representative attendance from all sections of the province. Every branch of the industry manifested its interest in the meeting and it was generally conceded that the need for such an organization was keenly felt.

The sessions were held in the Board of Trade Rooms on Hollis St., which were kindly placed at the disposal of the lumbermen. R. E. Dickie, of Stewiacke, N. S., is the new president of the Association,, and I. J. Soy, of the Maple Leaf Lumber Co., Ltd., Londonderry, vice-president. A strong executive has also been elected. A. E. Saunders, Secretary of the Halifax Board of Trade, is acting secretary until the services of a permanent official can be secured. Mr. Saunders greatly assisted the lumbermen in the matter of organization as also did Mr. Thompson, secretary of the Canadian Manufacturers' Association. Their efforts in this respect are much appreciated.

The morning session was devoted chiefly to a discussion as to what form the organization should take. It was suggested that the lumbermen might form a trade section of the Canadian Manufacturers' Association, and many strong arguments were advanced favoring such a course. It seemed to be the sentiments of the meeting however, that the best interests of the industry would be served by having a separate organization, thus establishing a distinct identity. At this session a committee was appointed to draw up a constitution to be submitted to the afternoon session for ratification and adoption.

At the afternoon session the following officers were nominated to serve for the ensuing year:—
President R. E. Dickie; Vice-President I. J. Soy; Executive M. R. Chappell, Chas. Hill, C. A. Founes, A. S. MacMillan C. H. Read, Fred Campbell, Colin C. Tyrer, Eric Curry, Mr. Whitman, F .G. Boutilier, Mr. Godding, R. E. Dickie, Fred Chambers, I. J. Soy, J. R. Gordon, Louis W. Logan, Percy Spicer, G. T. MacNutt.
Mr. A. E. Saunders, Secretary of the Halifax Board of Trade is acting Secretary.

Practically all the time of both afternoon and evening session was devoted to organizing work, which was only natural in view of the fact that this was the first meeting. There were enough matters touched upon of particular interest to the lumbermen of the province by some of those present to indicate that the newly elected Executive will have a number of problems to absorb their attention during their term of office.

### Enjoyable Banquet was Held

In the evening a banquet was held at the Green Lantern, followed by a moving picture which was put on in the banqueting hall, and was greatly enjoyed by all present.

After refreshments had been disposed of the meeting was addressed by the newly elected President, who was followed by V. J. Paton, the Chairman of the Workmen's Compensation Board. Mr. Paton explained the working of the Workmen's Compensation Act, and gave some interesting statistics in connection with the operations of the Board since its inception five years ago. His statement that the rate struck for 1922 would be 2% was greeted by unanimous applause, and should be highly gratifying to all the lumbermen of the province.

Mr. Thompson of the Canadian Manufacturers' Association spoke briefly on Compensation, and Mr. Fraser of the Accident Prevention Association made an eloquent plea for the adoption of sane methods for the prevention of unnecessary accidents in industry.

A vote of thanks was heartily tendered to Mr. Dickie, the newly elected President, to whose initiative and energy the gathering was largely due, and after enjoying "the Saw Mill" by Larry Semon which was very appropriate to the occasion, the meeting dispersed.

The success of the new Association now rests with the individual members and those who will join later.. As stated, the need for an organization of this kind embracing the whole province had for a long time been keenly felt and repeatedly urged by all those who have given thought to the matter. The machinery for concerted action is now available.

The members of the lumbering industry are the ones who will benefit. It is now up to each individual member to support the work so well begun.

The Nova Scotia Lumbermen's Association is off to a good start and the "Canada Lumberman" wishes the newly formed body every success, usefulness and prosperity.

### Laboratories are For Use of Lumbermen

The worth and work of the Forest Products Laboratories of Canada, which are in affiliation with McGill University, Montreal, are not sufficiently appreciated by the lumberman of the Dominion. While the splendid facilities of the institution are becoming more widely known, much more extended use could and should be made of them.

A cynic once remarked of "a friend—oh, he's a fellow of whom I can make good use to further my own personal interests." While this conception or definition may be selfish and circumscribed, even if given a literal interpretation so far as the research and technical service departments of the Forest Products Laboratories are concerned, no member of the staff will offer the slighest protest.

The scope of the work undertaken, its character, practical benefits, educational development, economic suggestions, research advantages and co-operation with the lumber and pulp and paper industries have been referred to many times in the past. Its facilities should, however, be more widely recognized and appreciated by the lumber interests of Canada, as the Laboratories' courteous co-operation in the solution of any problem encountered in the uses of wood is available at all times.

It is a common occurrence for some doubt to arise in the mind of the manufacturer or wood user as to the exact identity of a particular consignment or piece of wood. Such doubt arises, for example, when the grain, color, strength or other properties appear unusual or when a hitherto unfamiliar wood is being tried for a certain purpose for which it may have been recommended.

As a result of the numerous requests for the identification of woods received by the Forest Products Laboratories of Canada a wood identification service was recently announced.

Identification of a sample of timber is frequently possible only by means of microscopic examination, a process for which most woodworking organizations are not equipped. The Laboratories possess every facility for this work and have pleasure in placing them at the disposal of the woodusing industries.

The Laboratories are equipped to examine any samples submitted and will do so without charge. Such samples should be accompanied by a statement as to the country of origin. In the case of North American woods the district of origin should be stated if possible. .

In a recent leaflet, the Forest Products Laboratories of Canada point out that they have adequate modern machinery and equipment for research in the mechanical, physical, chemical and other properties of forest products to their use, etc. The Laboratories have made thousands of tests of the strength of Canadian woods by modernized standard methods, have investigated conditions in several hundred mills, factories and other buildings in Canada and the United States with respect to decay of timber in such buildings, and published numerous technical articles and bulletins which are of timely instruction and interest.

It is also emphasized that the Laboratories have dealt with great numbers of technical inquiries, frequently involving experimental investigations or tests,

### Mr. Brooks Joins Black Rock Lumber Co.

H. Brooks, for the past sixteen years associated with the Fesserton Timber Co., of Toronto, is now a member of the Black Rock Lumber Co., of Buffalo, N. Y., wholesale dealers in pine and hardwood. The officers are W. E. Bernhard, president and treasurer; H. Brooks, vice-president, and G. H. Klaes, secretary. All are well-known in the lumber arena and they have opened offices at 421 and 422 Fidelity Building, Buffalo, and are specializing in Canadian hard and softwoods and southern hardwoods. The firm are looking after the ter-

H. Brooks Buffalo, N.Y.

ritory between Buffalo and Detroit and Detroit and Toronto. Mr. Brooks will continue to call upon his Canadian friends in the trade, as usual, and will be a frequent visitor to Ontario.

The reason of the location of the Black Rock Lumber Company's offices in Buffalo is that it is the most central point for their activities.

Mr. Bernhard, the president, has long been associated with the lumber industry and is thoroughly familiar with its requirements, while Mr. Brooks is a practical man, serving several years in the camps and mill of the Fesserton Timber Co. before going on the sales staff.

Mr. Klaes is the executive and financial man of the Black Rock Lumber Co., which was recently incorporated with a capital stock of $100,000, to engage in the wholesale trade.

### Mr. Hazen Starts in Wholesale Line

Harry Hazen, who was for several years in the retail lumber business in Tillsonburg, Ont., sold out some months ago to M. L. Burwell, has decided to go into the wholesale line and opened up an office in Tillsonburg, as eastern representative for the Robinson Lumber Co. He is also in touch with eastern stocks as well.

Mr. Hazen recently returned from a trip to British Columbia and says that he found things rather quiet there owing to the export trade. Some of the larger firms are able to operate with some advantage, but, taking all things into consideration, conditions are rather unsettled. Mr. Hazen says "We are not looking for much change in prices as no one is realizing any profits, simply moving along until the depression in business and financial standing of the country improves.

### Quebec City Needs Twelve Hundred Houses

Scarcely a week passes but what your Quebec correspondent comes into contact with a variety of European financiers or business men who, while optimistic of the future, speak in depreciating terms of the present. They all admit that the aftermath of the war was expected to make men and people generally better, but instead has caused a spirit of materialism more pronounced than before, which will take years to eradicate. They wonder at the happy condition in Canada in comparison to the European world and even in the United States where the politicians in Congress and the Senate are juggling with momentous questions for political ends to the detriment of their country. Its people as well as those of the world have been casting longing eyes in that direction, accompanied by the wish that the United States with its horde of gold would take a sane, human view of the situation and help to rescue the universe from its slough of despondency. Captains of wealth and industry, discussing the economic situation generally, are not pessimists by any means. They are men of supreme commercial and industrial minds who have their capital invested in various parts of the world which they are endeavoring to save. They, however, take a gloomy view of conditions and speak with regret, that the wholesale and retail commodity interests as well as labor, will not understand the situation as governed by basic laws of economy, by leaving to the profiteers, the immense amount of construction needed, especially in the building channels of Europe which are being held up by the high prices of every material except lumber and by the price of labor. Until the leaders of labor unions drawing fat salaries at the expense of the worker and the consumer, come to realize that they are so stopping the wheels of human machinery and financial activities to the destruction of the sources of supply and demand for labor, the situation cannot be improved.

Here is the city of Quebec with a population of approximately 116,000 and perhaps one of the most richest and most contented cities in Canada, can be found glaring evidence of the economic situation which is demoralizing the world. The city is growing larger in population every year, due to the farmers' sons and daughters leaving the lands for the excitement of civic life and the fact that they made more money during the time of the war than they had ever previously dreamed of. The result is that though some 300 new dwellings were erected in Quebec City during the past year, there is still a shortage of over 1200 houses to accommodate the needs of the people seeking domiciles. These conditions are well known to citizen of means, who say they are looking for places and opportunities of investment, but will not place their money in property holdings. The result is that they are buying stocks or investing in bonds issued from all countries of Europe and the United States. In the meantime, the landlords have raised the rents sky high.

### Making Profitable Use of Sawmill Waste

The problem of sawmill waste was almost unknown fifty years ago to the wood working industries of Canada. Today, however, the closer utilization of our forest resources is one of the greatest problems of all wood users. Until very recent years, the aim of all sawmill superintendents was to obtain the greatest possible production (his ability being rated accordingly) and in this, quality was, necessarily sacrificed for quantity. Quantity production, as we all know, is very essential, but quantity without quality creates a very serious waste and is one of the conditions which must be remedied if a mill is to stand up under to-day's severe competition.

In this country, estimates and figures go to show that, so far as the ultimate consumer is concerned, about 50% of the tree is lost in the process of manufacture, while in most European countries, where the scarcity of timber is felt on all sides, this waste has been reduced to about 14%. Many will no doubt question this figure but when one stops to consider the amount of timber left in the woods in the form of high stumps and tops, that which is usually lost in saw dust, slabs and edgings, and compare the lost product with that which is actually used, one will find it stands very near a fifty fifty basis. While much is being accomplished in this work, there are also a great many obstacles to overcome. A great many plants have not enough waste to warrant the purchase of the special machinery necessary to work this into a merchantable product. In other cases the waste varies so greatly in size, shape and species that the cost of assorting is almost prohibitive, and freight rates to consuming centers more than absorb any visible profit.

In a great many mills the hardwood waste is very profitably converted into squares and other small dimensions and turning stock which finds a ready market with manufacturers of furniture, toys, novelties, etc.

The greatest difficulty in the utilization of stock of this character is in the disposal of assorted lengths and sizes, the assorting and assembling of sufficient quantities of each to justify carload lots and the avoidance of loss in seasoning.

One New York firm, which has a number of mills in the East, has during the past year of business depression, not only utilized every piece of slab, edging, etc., coming from the various mills, but has reduced thousands of feet of manufactured lumber to small squares, etc., as this class of material found a ready market, lumber itself being stagnant.

Shavings and sawdust are sold as bedding and packing for refrigerator cars, etc., instead of being burned as fuel or in large refuse burners built to reduce this character of waste material. In many mills, the soft wood slabs are burned as fast as produced while in others they are worked up into lath or sold to pulp mills which reduce them to a good grade of pulp while other mill men who are more favorably located find a ready and profitable market in slab wood cut and sold for fuel.

## The New President is Aggressive

J. W. Brankley Chatham, N.B.
Newly Elected Presiding Officer of the New Brunswick Lumbermen's Association

The new president of the New Brunswick Lumbermen's Association is J. W. Brankley, of Chatham, general manager of the Miramichi Lumber Co., Mr. Brankley was vice-president last year and has always taken a warm interest in Association work. He is an enthusiastic member of the Canadian Lumbermen's Association and at the annual gathering is always a well-known figure. Mr. Brankley who was born in Lincolnshire, England, in 1865 came to Canada in 1882. His first job was with E. F. Keene & Co., at Megantic, Que., when he went to work in the woods. His insight into the vocation which he has followed with such success, has been practical in all its branches. In 1898 the Keene Company sold out to Frank C. Dudley of Portland, Me., and when the change took place Mr. Brankley was made manager. Nine years later he severed his connection with that company and went as manager to the Shawmut Mfg. Co., of Shawmut, Me., where a large sawmill and pulp mill were operated. About twelve years ago the subject of this reference started with the International Paper Co., and cruised the limits of the Van Dyke Estate in New Hampshire. In the following year he cruised the Gilmour & Hughson limits in the Gatineau Valley, comprising some 3,500 square miles.

About ten years ago Mr. Brankley went to Chatham, N. B., as general-manager of the Miramichi Lumber Co., and the following year built a large rossing mill at Gaspe, Que., for the St. Maurice Lumber Co., of which he is now general-manager. He also occupies a similar position in regard to the Dalhousie Lumber Co. In 1915 Mr. Brankley was made manager of the American Realty Co. In Sheet Harbor, N. S., where a large tract of timberland is owned by that organization.

Mr. Brankley is the representative of the lumbermen on the Forest Advisory Board of the province. He is also president of the South West River Driving Co., and of the South West River Boom Co., and, naturally in the course of his many duties has not much spare time on his hands, but industry and he have always been on most cordial terms.

## Mr. Lambert Given Silver Loving Cup.

S. L. Lambert, of Welland, Ont., who is a widely-known sawmill man and lumber dealer, is one of the live-wire residents of Welland, Ont. He is a member of the City Council and has great faith in the future of Welland. Ald. Lambert has given practical expression to this belief by erecting the Reeta Hotel and theatre which are a credit to the city.

The annual banquet of the Welland Board of Trade was recently held in the new Reeta Hotel and that body presented Mr. Lambert with a magnificent silver loving cup. The recipient suitably acknowledged the kindness of the Board.

An important address was delivered by Premier Drury on "The Conservation of Ontario's Timber Resources." He said that in the north country there is an immense problem to solve,—that of reforestation. At the present time Ontario was cutting 400,000,000 feet of timber a year, and at the present rate the supply would be exhausted in about thirty-five years. This problem demanded instant and intelligent action. The provincial government is taking measures along the lines of more efficient fire control and reforestation of Crown Lands. Between the Georgian Bay and the Ottawa River there are 10,000 square miles of barren lands. If these lands are treated in a proper manner, in sixty years the Premier declared the people would cut 50,000,000 more feet than they are cutting to-day. If no preservation was undertaken, the virgin timber would be exhausted in thirty years.

## Lumber News and Personal Notes

L. L. Brown, B. C. Lumber Commissioner, who was called to Vancouver owing to the illness of his wife, is expected to return

East in a few days. Mrs. Brown is now greatly improved and has regained her former health.

Edward Sweeney, of the Western Cooperage Co., Victoria, B. C., is spending some time in Ontario, calling upon the trade.

E. J. L. Esperance, Montreal, has been elected a director of the Bridge River Timber & Manufacturing Company, Limited.

W. B. Snowball, of J. B. Snowball & Co., Chatham, N. B., spent a few days in Toronto recently, calling upon members of the trade.

C. F. Wilson, of Callander, Ont., has joined the buying staff of the Fesserton Timber Co., Toronto, and entered upon his new duties.

C. W. Wilkinson, of the Union Lumber Co., Toronto, and Mrs. Wilkinson, who have been spending the past month in Cuba, have returned home.

Representatives of B. C. mills report that while the demand is quiet at the present time, there are quite a few inquiries for long joisting and timbers.

The Myers Lumber & Manufacturing Co., Limited, of which W. Warren is managing-director, have opened an office on the third floor at 15 Toronto St., Toronto.

Wm. Laking, of the Wm. Laking Lumber Co., Toronto, has been spending the past few weeks in St. Petersburg, Florida, where he has been having an enjoyable time.

J. T. Todd, sales manager of the Adams River Lumber Co., Chase, B. C., who arrived in Toronto some time ago, has opened an office at 1305, Bank of Hamilton Building.

A. E. Gordon, of Terry & Gordon, Limited, Toronto, who has been on an extended holiday trip to British Columbia and the South, has returned. He had a very enjoyable outing.

Hugh A. Rose of Rose-McLaurin, Limited, wholesale lumber dealers, Toronto, returned recently from a successful three weeks' business trip throughout the Maritime Provinces.

Mr. Marks, of St. Catharines, Ont., formerly with the Midland Woodworkers, Limited, and also the Lincoln Construction Co., has joined the sales staff of the Fesserton Timber Co. Toronto.

International Tank & Silo Co., Ltd., Toronto have been incorporated to manufacture and deal in lumber and other building supplies. Capital $40,000. L. V. Sutton and A. B. Mortimer are two of the incorporators.

A Boisvert & Sons have lately built a sawmill at Sorel, Que., making a specialty of rock elm. The plant is now in operation. The firm are doing a wholesale business and expect soon to embark in the manufacture of clothespins, axe handles and other lines.

Anderson, Shreiner and Mawson, wholesale lumber dealers, Toronto, who have offices on the corner of Victoria and Adelaide Sts., East, will shortly remove to more commodious quarters in the new Childs' Building near the corner of King and Yonge Streets.

It is understood that the Bathurst Company, Bathurst, N. B., may erect a mill for manufacturing newsprint paper. It is said the plans for the new plant are well under way and that construction will start about June 1st. Angus McLean is the president and general manager of the Bathurst Co.

Sir William Price and George McKee have been appointed by the executive of the Canadian Pulp & Paper Association to act as an advisory committee when requested to do so by the Minister of Lands & Forests of the Province of Quebec. The subject has also been before the Quebec Limit Holders' Association.

Among the new lumber companies recently incorporated in British Columbia are: Cobble Hill Logging Company, Limited, $25,000, Victoria; Pacific Shingle Company, Limited, $50,000, New Westminster; Rotary Shingle Company, Limited, $20,000, Vancouver; Euclataws Lumber Company, Limited, $20,000, Vancouver.

# CURRENT LUMBER PRICES—WHOLESALE

## TORONTO

(In Car Load Lots, F.O.B. cars Toronto)

### White Pine

| | | |
|---|---|---|
| 1 x 4/7 Good Strips | $100.00 | $110.00 |
| 1¼ & 1½ x 4/7 Good Strips | 120.00 | 125.00 |
| 1 x 8 and up Good Sides | 150.00 | 160.00 |
| 2 x 4/7 Good Strips | 130.00 | 140.00 |
| 1¼ & 1½ x 8 and wider Good Sides | 185.00 | 190.00 |
| 2 x 8 and wider Good Sides | 190.00 | 200.00 |
| 1 in. No. 1, 2 and 3 Cuts | 75.00 | 80.00 |
| 5/4 and 6/4 No. 1, 2 and 3 Cuts | 95.00 | 100.00 |
| 2 in. No. 1, 2 and 3 Cuts | 105.00 | 110.00 |
| 1 x 4 and 5 Mill Run | 52.00 | 55.00 |
| 1 x 6 Mill Run | 53.00 | 56.00 |
| 1 x 7, 9 and 11 Mill Run | 53.00 | 56.00 |
| 1 x 8 Mill Run | 55.00 | 58.00 |
| 1 x 10 Mill Run | 60.00 | 62.00 |
| 1 x 12 Mill Run | 65.00 | 70.00 |
| 5/4 and 6/4 x 5 and up Mill Run | 58.00 | 60.00 |
| 2 x 4 Mill Run | 52.00 | 53.00 |
| 2 x 6 Mill Run | 53.00 | 56.00 |
| 2 x 8 Mill Run | 55.00 | 58.00 |
| 2 x 10 Mill Run | 58.00 | 60.00 |
| 2 x 12 Mill Run | 63.00 | 65.00 |
| 1 in. Mill Run Shorts | 35.00 | 40.00 |
| 1 x 4 and up 6/16 No. 1 Mill Culls | 30.00 | 32.00 |
| 1 x 10 and up 6/16 No. 1 Mill Culls | 34.00 | 36.00 |
| 1 x 12 and up 6/16 No. 1 Mill Culls | 34.00 | 36.00 |
| 1 x 4 and up 6/16 No. 2 Mill Culls | 23.00 | 25.00 |
| 1 x 10 x 12 6/16 No. 2 Mill Culls | 26.00 | 28.00 |
| 1 x 4 and up 6/16 No. 3 Mill Culls | 17.00 | 18.00 |

### Red Pine

(In Car Load Lots, F.O.B. Toronto)

| | | |
|---|---|---|
| 1 x 4 and 5 Mill Run | $34.00 | $35.00 |
| 1 x 6 Mill Run | 35.00 | 36.00 |
| 1 x 8 Mill Run | 37.00 | 38.00 |
| 1 x 10 Mill Run | 42.00 | 44.00 |
| 2 x 4 Mill Run | 38.00 | 40.00 |
| 2 x 6 Mill Run | 40.00 | 42.00 |
| 2 x 8 Mill Run | 41.00 | 43.00 |
| 2 x 10 Mill Run | 44.00 | 47.00 |
| 2 x 12 Mill Run | 49.00 | 50.00 |
| 1 in. Clear and Clear Face | 70.00 | 72.00 |
| 2 in. Clear and Clear Face | 70.00 | 72.00 |

### Spruce

| | | |
|---|---|---|
| 1 x 4 Mill Run | 34.00 | 35.00 |
| 1 x 6 Mill Run | 35.00 | 36.00 |
| 1 x 8 Mill Run | 37.00 | 38.00 |
| 1 x 10 Mill Run | 45.00 | 47.00 |
| 1 x 12 Mill Run Spruce | 48.00 | 50.00 |
| Mill Culls | 25.00 | 27.00 |

### Hemlock (M R)

(In Car Load Lots, F.O.B. Toronto)

| | | |
|---|---|---|
| 1 x 4 and 5 in. x 9 to 16 ft | $26.00 | $27.00 |
| 1 x 6 in. x 9 to 16 ft | 33.00 | 35.00 |
| 1 x 8 in. x 9 to 16 ft | 34.00 | 36.00 |
| 1 x 10 and 12 in. x 9 to 16 ft | 35.00 | 37.00 |
| 1 x 7, 9 and 11 in. x 9 to 16 ft | 33.00 | 35.00 |
| 2 x 4 to 12 in. 10/16 ft | 33.00 | 34.00 |
| 2 x 4 to 12 in., 18 ft | 37.00 | 39.00 |
| 2 x 4 to 12 in., 20 ft | 40.00 | 42.00 |
| 1 in. No. 2, 6 ft. to 16 ft | 23.00 | 25.00 |

### Fir Flooring

(In Car Load Lots, F.O.B. Toronto)

| | | |
|---|---|---|
| Fir flooring, 1 x 3 and 4", No. 1 and 2 Edge Grain | | $72.00 |
| Fir flooring, 1 x 3 and 4", No. 1 and 2 Flat Grain | | 46.00 |
| (Depending upon Widths) | | |
| 1 x 4 to 12 No. 1 and 2 Clear Fir, Rough | | 77.00 |
| 1¼ x 4 to 12 No. 1 and 2 Clear Fir, Rough | | 81.00 |
| 2 x 4 to 12 No. 1 and 2 Clear Fir, Rough | | 77.00 |
| 3 & 4 x 4 to 12 No. 1 & 2 Clear Fir, Rough | | 84.00 |
| 1 x 4, 5 and 6 in. Fir Casing | $73.00 | 80.00 |
| 1 x 8 and 10 Fir Base | 78.00 | 86.00 |
| 1¼ and 1½ 8, 10 and 12 in. E.G. Stepping | 90.00 | 95.00 |
| 1¼ and 1½ 8, 10 and 12 in. F.G. Stepping | 80.00 | 85.00 |
| 1 x 4 to 12 Clear Fir, D4S | 72.50 | 79.50 |
| 1¼ and 1½ x 4 to 12 Clear Fir, D4S | 75.25 | 82.25 |
| XX Shingles, 6 butts to 2", per M | | 3.35 |
| XXX Shingles, 6 butts to 2", per M | | 5.35 |
| XXXXX hingles, 5 butts to 2", per M | | 6.15 |

### Lath

(F.O.B. Mill)

| | |
|---|---|
| No. 1 White Pine | $11.00 |
| No. 2 White Pine | 10.00 |
| No. 3 White Pine | 8.00 |
| Mill Run White Pine, 32 in | 3.50 |
| Merchantable Spruce Lath, 4 ft | 6.50 |

## TORONTO HARDWOOD PRICES

The prices given below are for car loads f.o.b. Toronto, from wholesalers to retailers, and are based on a good percentage of long lengths and good widths, without any wide stock having been sorted out.

The prices quoted on imported woods are payable in U. S. funds.

### Ash, White

(Dry weight 3800 lbs. per M. ft.)

| | 1s & 2s | No. 1 Com. | No. 2 Com. |
|---|---|---|---|
| 1" | $100.00 | $ 65.00 | $ 40.00 |
| 1¼ and 1½" | 110.00 | 70.00 | 45.00 |
| 2" | 115.00 | 75.00 | 50.00 |
| 2½ and 3" | 125.00 | 85.00 | 60.00 |
| 4" | 140.00 | 95.00 | 70.00 |

### Ash, Brown

| | | | |
|---|---|---|---|
| 1" | $ 95.00 | $ 55.00 | $ 30.00 |
| 1¼ and 1½" | 100.00 | 60.00 | 30.00 |
| 2" | 105.00 | 65.00 | 33.00 |
| 2½ and 3" | 125.00 | 80.00 | 55.00 |
| 4" | 140.00 | 95.00 | 60.00 |

### Birch

(Dry weight 4000 lbs. per M. ft.)

| | 1s & 2s | Sels. | No. 1 Com. | No. 2 Com. |
|---|---|---|---|---|
| 4/4 | $105.00 | $ 80.00 | $ 50.00 | $ 32.00 |
| 5/4 | 110.00 | 85.00 | 55.00 | 35.00 |
| 6/4 | 115.00 | 90.00 | 60.00 | 38.00 |
| 8/4 | 120.00 | 100.00 | 65.00 | 42.00 |
| 12/4 | 125.00 | 105.00 | 70.00 | 50.00 |
| 16/4 | 130.00 | 110.00 | 80.00 | 55.00 |

### Basswood

(Dry weight 2500 lbs. per M. ft.)

| | 1s & 2s | No. 1 Com. | No. 2 Com. |
|---|---|---|---|
| 4/4 | $ 80.00 | $ 50.00 | $ 25.00 |
| 5/4 and 6/4 | 85.00 | 60.00 | 30.00 |
| 8/4 | 90.00 | 65.00 | 35.00 |

### Chestnut

(Dry weight 2800 lbs. per M. ft.)

| | 1s & 2s | No. 1 Com. | Sound Wormy |
|---|---|---|---|
| 1" | $130.00 | $ 80.00 | $ 40.00 |
| 1¼ to 1½" | 140.00 | 85.00 | 43.00 |
| 2" | 150.00 | 90.00 | 48.00 |

### Maple, Hard

(Dry weight 4200 lbs. per M. ft.)

| | F.A.S. | Sels. | No. 1 Com. | No. 2 Com. |
|---|---|---|---|---|
| 4/4 | $ 85.00 | $ 65.00 | $ 45.00 | $ 33.00 |
| 5/4 | 85.00 | 65.00 | 45.00 | 38.00 |
| 6/4 | 90.00 | 70.00 | 50.00 | 45.00 |
| 8/4 | 100.00 | 75.00 | 60.00 | 50.00 |
| 12/4 | 105.00 | 75.00 | 65.00 | 60.00 |
| 16/4 | 125.00 | 100.00 | 70.00 | 65.00 |

### Elm, Soft

(Dry weight 3100 lbs. per M. ft.)

| | 1s & 2s | No. 1 Com. | No. 2 Com. |
|---|---|---|---|
| 4/4 | $ 75.00 | $ 50.00 | $ 30.00 |
| 6/4 and 8/4 | 80.00 | 60.00 | 35.00 |
| 12/4 | 95.00 | 70.00 | 40.00 |

### Gum, Red

(Dry weight 3300 lbs. per M. ft.)

| | Plain 1s & 2s | Plain No. 1 Com. | Quartered 1s & 2s | Quartered No. 1 Com. |
|---|---|---|---|---|
| 1" | $115.00 | $ 70.00 | $130.00 | $ 75.00 |
| 1¼" | 120.00 | 75.00 | 130.00 | 80.00 |
| 1½" | 120.00 | 75.00 | 130.00 | 80.00 |
| 2" | 125.00 | 90.00 | 135.00 | 90.00 |

Figured Gum, $10 per M. extra, in both plain and quartered.

### Gum, Sap

| | 1s&2s | No. 1 Com. |
|---|---|---|
| 1" | $ 55.00 | $ 40.00 |
| 1¼" and 1½" | 60.00 | 44.00 |
| 2" | 65.00 | 50.00 |

### Hickory

(Dry weight 4500 lbs. per M. ft.

| | 1s&2s | No. 1 Com. |
|---|---|---|
| 1" | $120.00 | $ 60.00 |
| 1¼" | 145.00 | 65.00 |
| 1½" | 145.00 | 65.00 |
| 2" | 150.00 | 70.00 |

### Plain White and Red Oak

(Plain sawed. Dry weight 4000 lbs. per M. ft.)

| | 1s&2s | No. 1 Com. |
|---|---|---|
| 4/4 | $120.00 | $ 75.00 |
| 5/4 and 6/4 | 130.00 | 80.00 |
| 8/4 | 135.00 | 85.00 |
| 10/4 | 145.00 | 90.00 |
| 12/4 | 145.00 | 90.00 |
| 16/4 | 150.00 | 95.00 |

### White Oak, Quarter Cut

(Dry weight 4000 lbs. per M. ft.)

| | 1s&2s | No. 1 Com. |
|---|---|---|
| 4/4 | $160.00 | $ 90.00 |
| 5/4 and 6/4 | 170.00 | 95.00 |
| 8/4 | 190.00 | 105.00 |

### Quarter Cut Red Oak

| | 1s&2s | No. 1 Com. |
|---|---|---|
| 4/4 | $145.00 | $ 80.00 |
| 5/4 and 6/4 | 160.00 | 90.00 |
| 8/4 | 165.00 | 95.00 |

### Beech

The quantity of beech produced in Ontario is not large and is generally sold on a log run basis, the locality governing the prices. At present the prevailing quotation on log run, mill culls out, delivered in Toronto, is $35.00 to $40.00.

## OTTAWA

Manufacturers' Prices

### Pine

| | | |
|---|---|---|
| Good sidings: | | |
| 1 in. x 7 in. and up | | $140.00 |
| 1¼ in. and 1½ in., 8 in. and up | | 165.00 |
| 2 in. x 7 in. and up | | 165.00 |
| No. 2 cuts 2 x 8 in. and up | | 80.00 |
| Good strips: | | |
| 1 in. | $100.00 | $105.00 |
| 1¼ in. and 1½ in. | | 120.00 |
| 2 in. | | 125.00 |
| Good shorts: | | |
| 1 in. x 7 in. and up | | 110.00 |
| 1 in. 4 in. to 6 in. | 85.00 | 90.00 |
| 1¼ in. and 1½ in. | | 110.00 |
| 2 in. | | 125.00 |
| 7 in. to 9 in. A sidings | 54.00 | 56.00 |
| No. 1 dressing sidings | 70.00 | 74.00 |
| No. 1 dressing strips | | 62.00 |
| No. 1 dressing shorts | 50.00 | 53.00 |
| 1 in. x 4 in. s.c. strips | | 48.00 |
| 1 in. x 5 in. s.c. strips | | 48.00 |
| 1 in. x 6 in. s.c. strips | | 50.00 |
| 1 in. x 7 in. s.c. strips | 63.00 | 64.00 |
| 1 in. x 8 in. s.c. strips, 12 to 16 ft. | | 54.00 |
| 1 in. x 10 in. M.R. | | 58.00 |
| S.C. sidings, 1½ and 2 in. | 58.00 | 60.00 |
| S.C. strips, 1 in. | | 45.00 |
| 1¼, 1½ and 2 in. | 50.00 | 55.00 |
| S.C. shorts, 1 x 4 to 6 in. | 34.00 | 36.00 |
| S.C. and bet., shorts, 1 x 5 | | 36.00 |
| S.C. and bet., shorts, 1 x 6 | | 42.00 |
| S.C. shorts, 6-11 ft., 1 x 10 in. | | 48.00 |
| Box boards: | | |
| 1 in. x 4 in. and up, 6 ft.-11 ft. | | 34.00 |
| 1 in. x 3 in. and up, 12 ft.-16 ft. | 35.00 | 37.00 |
| Mill cull shorts, 1 in. x 4 in. and x 4 in. and up, 12 ft. and up | 24.00 | 26.00 |
| Mill culls, strips and sidings, 1 in. up, 6 ft. to 11 ft. | | 22.00 |
| O. culls r and w p | 18.00 | 20.00 |

### Red Pine, Log Run

| | | |
|---|---|---|
| Mill culls out, 1 in. | 32.00 | 34.00 |
| Mill culls out, 1¼ in. | 32.00 | 34.00 |
| Mill culls out, 1½ in. | 32.00 | 34.00 |
| Mill culls out, 2 in. | 32.00 | 34.00 |
| Mill Culls, white pine, 1 in. x 7 in. and up | | 20.00 |

### Mill Run Spruce

| | | |
|---|---|---|
| 1 in. x 4 in. and up, 6 ft.-11 ft. | | 23.00 |
| 1 in. x 4 in. and up, 12 ft.-16 ft. | 30.00 | 32.00 |
| 1" x 9"-10" and up, 12 ft.-16 ft. | | 35.00 |
| 1¼" x 7, 8 and 9" up, 12 ft.-16 ft. | | 35.00 |
| 1¼ x 10 and up, 12 ft.-16 ft. | 38.00 | 42.00 |
| 1½" x 12" x 12" and up, 12'-16' | | 42.00 |
| Spruce, 1 in. clear fine dressing and B | | 55.00 |
| Hemlock, 1 in. cull | | 20.00 |
| Hemlock, 1 in. log run | 24.00 | 26.00 |
| Hemlock, 2 x 4, 6, 8, 10 12/16 ft. | | 28.00 |
| Tamarac | 25.00 | 28.00 |
| Basswood, log run, dead culls out | 45.00 | 50.00 |
| Basswood, log run, mill culls out. | 50.00 | 54.00 |
| Birch, log run | 45.00 | 50.00 |
| Soft Elm, common and better, 1, 1½, 2 in. | 58.00 | 68.00 |
| Ash, black, log run | 62.00 | 65.00 |
| 1 x 10 No. 1 barn | 57.00 | 62.00 |
| 1 x 10 No. 2 barn | 51.00 | 56.00 |
| 1 x 8 and 9 No. 2 barn | 47.00 | 52.00 |

# CURRENT LUMBER PRICES—WHOLESALE

**Lath per M.:**

| | | |
|---|---|---|
| No. 1 White Pine, 1¼ in. x 4 ft. | | 8.00 |
| No. 2 White Pine | | 6.00 |
| Mill run White Pine | | 7.00 |
| Spruce, mill run, 1½ in. | | 6.00 |
| Red Pine, mill run | | 6.00 |
| Hemlock, mill run | | 5.50 |

**White Cedar Shingles**

| | | |
|---|---|---|
| XXXX, 18 in. | 9.00 | 10.00 |
| Clear butt, 18 in. | 6.00 | 7.00 |
| 18 in. XX | | 5.00 |

## QUEBEC

**White Pine**

(At Quebec)

| | Cts. Per Cubic Ft. | |
|---|---|---|
| First class Ottawa waney, 18 in. average according to lineal | 100 | 110 |
| 19 in. and up average | 110 | 120 |

**Spruce Deals**

(At Mill)

| | | |
|---|---|---|
| 3 in. unsorted, Quebec, 4 in. to 6 in. wide | $ 20.00 | $ 25.00 |
| 3 in. unsorted, Quebec, 7 in. to 8 in. wide | 26.00 | 28.00 |
| 3 in. unsorted, Quebec, 9 in. wide | 30.00 | 35.00 |

**Oak**

(At Quebec)

| | Cts. Per Cubic Ft. | |
|---|---|---|
| According to average and quality, 55 ft. cube | 125 | 130 |

**Elm**

(At Quebec)

| | | |
|---|---|---|
| According to average and quality, 40 to 45 ft. cube | 100 | 120 |
| According to average and quality, 30 to 35 ft. | 90 | 100 |

**Export Birch Planks**

(At Mill)

| | | |
|---|---|---|
| 1 to 4 in. thick, per M. ft. | $ 30.00 | $ 35.00 |

## ST. JOHN, N.B.

(From Yards and Mills—Retail)

**Rough Lumber**

| | | |
|---|---|---|
| 2x3, 2x4, 3x3, 3x4. Rgh Merch Spr | $30.00 | |
| 2x3, 2x4, 3x3, 3x4, Dressed 1 edge | 31.00 | |
| 2x3, 2x4, 3x3, 3x4, Dressed 4 sides | 31.00 | |
| 2x6, 2x7, 3x5, 4x4, 4x6, all rough. | 30.00 | |
| 2x6, 2x7, 3x5, 4x4, 4x6, all rough. | 34.00 | |
| 2x8, 3x7, 5x5, 6x6 | 37.00 | $ 40.00 |
| 2x9, 3x8, 6x8, 7x7 | 37.00 | 40.00 |
| 2x10, 3x9 | 45.00 | |
| 2x12, 3x10, 3x12, 8x8 and up | 45.00 | |
| Merch. Spr. Bds., Rough, 1x3-4 & 5 | 30.00 | |
| Merch. Spr. Bds., Rough, 1x6 | 34.00 | |
| Merch. Spr. Bds., Rough, 1x7 & up | 40.00 | |
| Refuse Bds., Deals and Setgs. | 18.00 | 20.00 |

Above random lengths up to 18-0 long.

Lengths 19-0 and up $5.00 extra per M.

For planing Merch. and Refuse Bds. add $2.00 per M. to above prices.

Laths, $7.00.

**Shingles**

| | Per M. |
|---|---|
| Cedar, Extras | $6.00 |
| Cedar, Clears | 5.25 |
| Cedar, 2nd Clears | 4.25 |
| Cedar, Extra No. 1 | 2.50 |
| Spruce | 4.00 |

## SARNIA, ONT.

**White Pine—Fine, Com. and Better**

| | |
|---|---|
| 1 x 6 and 8 in. | $110.00 |
| 1 in., 8 in. and up wide | 130.00 |
| 1¼ and 1½ in. and up wide | 180.00 |
| 2 in. and up wide | 180.00 |

**Cuts and Better**

| | |
|---|---|
| 4/4 x 8 and up No. 1 and better | 125.00 |
| 5/4 and 6/4 and up No. 1 and better | 150.00 |
| 8/4 and 8 and up No. 1 and better | 150.00 |

**No. 1 Cuts**

| | |
|---|---|
| 1 in., 8 in. and up wide | 105.00 |
| 1¼ in., 8 in. and up wide | 125.00 |
| 1½ in., 8 in. and up wide | 125.00 |
| 2 in., 8 in. and up wide | 130.00 |
| 2½ in. and 3 in., 8 in. and up wide | 175.00 |
| 4 in., 8 in. and up wide | 185.00 |

**No. 1 Barn**

| | | |
|---|---|---|
| 1 in., 10 to 16 ft. long | $ 75.00 | $ 85.00 |
| 1¼, 1½ and 2 in., 10/16 ft. | 80.00 | 85.00 |
| 2½ to 3 in., 10/16 ft. | 85.00 | 100.00 |

**No. 2 Barn**

| | | |
|---|---|---|
| 1 in., 10 to 16 ft. long | 65.00 | 75.00 |
| 1¼, 1½ and 2 in., 10/16 ft. | | 66.00 |
| 2½, 1½ and 3 in. | | 85.00 |

**No. 3 Barn**

| | | |
|---|---|---|
| 1 in., 10 to 16 ft. long | 48.00 | 55.00 |
| 1¼, 1½ and 2 in., 10/16 ft. | 50.00 | 56.00 |

**Box**

| | | |
|---|---|---|
| 1 in., 1¼ and 1½ in., 10/16 ft. | 33.00 | 35.00 |

**Mill Culls**

Mill Run Culls—

| | |
|---|---|
| 1 in., 4 in. and up wide, 6/16 ft. | 26.00 |
| 1¼, 1½ and 2 in. | 27.00 |

## WINNIPEG

**No. 1 Spruce**

| Dimension | S.1.S. and 1.E. 10 ft. | 12 ft. | 14 ft. | 16 ft. |
|---|---|---|---|---|
| 2 x 4 | $30 | $29 | $29 | $30 |
| 2 x 6 | 31 | 29 | 29 | 30 |
| 2 x 8 | 32 | 30 | 30 | 31 |
| 2 x 10 | 33 | 31 | 31 | 32 |
| 2 x 12 | 34 | 32 | 32 | 33 |

For 2 inches, rough, add 50 cents.

For S1E only, add 50 cents.

For S1S and 2E, S4S or D&M, add $3.00.

For timbers larger than 8 x 8, add 50c. for each additional 2 inches each way.

For lengths longer than 20 ft., add $1.00 for each additional two feet.

For selected common, add $5.00.

For No. 2 Dimension, $3.00 less than No. 1.

For 1 x 2 and 2 x 2, $2 more than 2 x 4 No. 1.

For Tamarac, open.

## BUFFALO and TONAWANDA

**White Pine**

**Wholesale Selling Price**

| | |
|---|---|
| Uppers, 4/4 | $225.00 |
| Uppers, 5/4 to 8/4 | 225.00 |
| Uppers, 10/4 to 12/4 | 250.00 |
| Selects, 4/4 | 200.00 |
| Selects, 5/4 to 8/4 | 200.00 |
| Selects, 10/4 to 12/4 | 225.00 |
| Fine Common, 4/4 | 155.00 |
| Fine Common, 5/4 | 160.00 |
| Fine Common, 6/4 | 160.00 |
| Fine Common, 8/4 | 160.00 |
| No. 1 Cuts, 4/4 | 115.00 |
| No. 1 Cuts, 5/4 | 130.00 |
| No. 1 Cuts, 6/4 | 135.00 |
| No. 1 Cuts, 8/4 | 140.00 |
| No. 2 Cuts, 4/4 | 70.00 |
| No. 2 Cuts, 5/4 | 100.00 |
| No. 2 Cuts, 6/4 | 105.00 |
| No. 2 Cuts, 8/4 | 110.00 |
| No. 3 Cuts, 5/4 | 60.00 |
| No. 3 Cuts, 6/4 | 65.00 |
| No. 3 Cuts, 8/4 | 67.00 |
| Dressing, 4/4 | 95.00 |
| Dressing 4/4 x 10 | 98.00 |
| Dressing, 4/4 x 12 | 110.00 |
| No. 1 Moulding, 5/4 | 150.00 |
| No. 1 Moulding, 6/4 | 150.00 |
| No. 1 Moulding, 8/4 | 155.00 |
| No. 2 Moulding, 5/4 | 125.00 |
| No. 2 Moulding, 6/4 | 125.00 |
| No. 2 Moulding, 8/4 | 130.00 |
| No. 1 Barn, 1 x 12 | 90.00 |
| No. 1 Barn, 1 x 6 and 8 | 76.00 |
| No. 1 Barn, 1 x 10 | 80.00 |
| No. 2 Barn, 1 x 6 and 8 | 62.00 |
| No. 2 Barn, 1 x 10 | 63.00 |
| No. 2 Barn, 1 x 12 | 75.00 |
| No. 3 Barn, 1 x 6 and 8 | 42.00 |
| No. 3 Barn, 1 x 10 | 44.00 |
| No. 3 Barn, 1 x 12 | 47.00 |
| Box, 1 x 6 and 8 | 36.00 |
| Box, 1 x 10 | 38.00 |
| Box, 1 x 12 | 39.00 |
| Box, 1 x 13 and up | 40.00 |

## BUFFALO

The following quotations on hardwoods represent the jobber buying price at Buffalo and Tonawanda.

**Maple**

| | 1s & 2s | No. 1 Com. | No. 2 Com. |
|---|---|---|---|
| 1 in. | $ 75.00 | $ 45.00 | $ 28.00 |
| 5/4 to 8/4 | 80.00 | 50.00 | 28.00 |
| 10/4 to 4 in. | 85.00 | 55.00 | 28.00 |

**Sap Birch**

| | | | |
|---|---|---|---|
| 1 in. | 90.00 | 45.00 | 30.00 |
| 5/4 and up | 100.00 | 50.00 | 30.00 |

**Soft Elm**

| | | | |
|---|---|---|---|
| 1 in. | 70.00 | 45.00 | 30.00 |
| 5/4 to 2 in. | 75.00 | 50.00 | 30.00 |

**Red Birch**

| | | | |
|---|---|---|---|
| 1 in. | 120.00 | 75.00 | |
| 5/4 and up | 125.00 | 80.00 | |

**Basswood**

| | | | |
|---|---|---|---|
| 1 in. | 70.00 | 45.00 | 30.00 |
| 5/4 to 2 in. | 80.00 | 56.00 | 36.00 |

**Plain Oak**

| | | | |
|---|---|---|---|
| 1 in. | 95.00 | 55.00 | 35.00 |
| 5/4 to 2 in. | 105.00 | 65.00 | 40.00 |

**Ash**

| | | | |
|---|---|---|---|
| 1 in. | 80.00 | 48.00 | 30.00 |
| 5/4 to 2 in. | 85.00 | 52.00 | 30.00 |
| 10/4 and up | 100.00 | 65.00 | 30.00 |

## BOSTON

Quotations given below are for highest grades of Michigan and Canadian White Pine and Eastern Canadian Spruce as required in the New England market in car loads.

| | | |
|---|---|---|
| White Pine Uppers, 1 in. | | |
| White Pine Uppers, 1¼, 1½, 2 in. | | |
| White Pine Uppers, 2½, 3 in. | | |
| White Pine Uppers, 4 in. | | |
| Selects, 1 in. | | $190.00 |
| Selects, 1¼, 2 in. | | 200.00 |
| Selects, 2½, 3 in. | | |
| Selects, 4 in. | | |

Prices nominal

| | | |
|---|---|---|
| Fine Common, 1 in., 30%, 12 in. and up. | | 165.00 |
| Fine Common, 1 x 8 and up | | 165.00 |
| Fine Common, 1¼ to 2 in. | $165.00 | 170.00 |
| Fine Common, 2½ and 3 in. | | 180.00 |
| Fine Common, 4 in. | | 195.00 |
| 1 in. Shaky Clear | | 100.00 |
| 1¼ in. to 2 in. Shaky Clear | | 110.00 |
| 1 in. No. 2 Dressing | | 95.00 |
| 1¼ in. to 2 in. No. 2 Dressing | | 95.00 |
| No. 1 Cuts, 1 in. | | 110.00 |
| No. 1 Cuts, 1¼ to 2 in. | | 140.00 |
| No. 1 Cuts, 2½ to 3 in. | | 180.00 |
| No. 2 Cuts, 1 in. | | 80.00 |
| No. 2 Cuts, 1¼ to 2 in. | | 110.00 |
| Barn Boards, No. 1, 1 x 12 | | 95.00 |
| Barn Boards, No. 1, 1 x 10 | | 87.00 |
| Barn Boards, No. 1, 1 x 8 | | 83.00 |
| Barn Boards, No. 2, 1 x 12 | | 82.00 |
| Barn Boards, No. 2, 1 x 8 | | 69.00 |
| Barn Boards, No. 2, 1 x 10 | | 70.00 |
| Barn Boards, No. 3, 1 x 12 | | 48.00 |
| Barn Boards, No. 3, 1 x 10 | | 47.00 |
| Barn Boards, No. 3, 1 x 8 | | 47.00 |

**No. 1 Clear**

| | | |
|---|---|---|
| Can. Spruce, No. 1 and clear, 1 x 4 to 9" | | $ 78.00 |
| Can. Spruce, 1 x 10 in. | | 78.00 |
| Can. Spruce, No. 1, 1 x 4 to 7 in. | | 75.00 |
| Can. Spruce, No. 1, 1 x 8 and 9 in. | | 75.00 |
| Can. Spruce, No. 1, 1 x 10 in. | | 76.00 |
| Can. Spruce, No. 2, 1 x 4 and 5 in. | | 34.00 |
| Can. Spruce, No. 2, 1 x 6 and 7 in. | | 36.00 |
| Can. Spruce, No. 2, 1 x 8 and 9 in. | | 38.00 |
| Can. Spruce, No. 2, 1 x 10 in. | | 41.00 |
| Can. Spruce, No. 2, 1 x 12 in. | | 45.00 |
| Spruce, 12 in. dimension | | 44.00 |
| Spruce, 10 in. dimension | | 42.00 |
| Spruce, 9 in. dimension | | 41.00 |
| Spruce, 8 in. dimension | | 40.00 |
| 2 x 10 in. random lengths, 8 ft. and up | | 40.00 |
| 2 x 12 in., random lengths | | 43.00 |
| 2 x 3, 2 x 4, 2 x 5, 2 x 6, 2 x 7 | | 30.00 |
| 3 x 4 and 4 x 4 in. | | 31.00 |
| 2 x 9 | | 38.00 |
| All other random lengths, 7 in. and under, 8 ft. and up | 30.00 | 34.00 |
| 5 ls. and up merchantable boards, 8 ft. and up, D 1s | 30.00 | 32.00 |
| 1 x 2 | 30.00 | 32.00 |
| 1 x 3 | | 30.00 |
| 1⅝ in. Spruce Lath | | 8.50 |
| 1½ in. Spruce Lath | 7.25 | 7.50 |

**New Brunswick Cedar Shingles**

| | | |
|---|---|---|
| Extras | 5.25 | 5.50 |
| Clears | 4.25 | 4.50 |
| Second Clear | 3.73 | 4.15 |
| Clear Whites | | 3.00 |

Second Hand Machinery & Equipment Wanted & For Sale

# Quick Action Section

Special Lots Of Lumber— —Positions Wanted & Vacant

## Lumber Wanted

### Hard Maple Wanted

Several cars 8/4 and 12/4 dry stock, No. 1 and 2 Common. For further particulars apply Box No. 826 Canada Lumberman, Toronto. 5-8

### Hard Maple Wanted

A number of cars each of 1", 1-1/8" and 1¼" dry; quote lowest price, stating grade and shipping point. Box 806 Canada Lumberman, Toronto. 4-7

### We Will Buy

A block of Hemlock, Spruce, Red or White Pine, that is sawn or will be sawn before the 15th of March. Box 770 Canada Lumberman, Toronto. 2-T.f.

### Hard Maple and Birch Wanted

A limited quantity of 4/4 and 8/4 dry stock No. 2 Common and Better. For further particulars apply Box 761 Canada Lumberman, Toronto, Can. 2-7

### Wanted

To contract for supply of ROCK ELM for bending purposes Cut 8¼" thick for delivery June, July and August. No substitute for Rock Elm will be accepted. Quote price to St. Mary's Wood Specialty Co. Ltd., St. Mary's Ont. 5-8

### We Will Buy

Clear Eastern cedar, suitable for boat building in large or small quantities. This is of interest to small saw mills cutting cedar. For particulars write the Peterborough Canoe Co. Limited, Peterborough, Ont. 7

### Hard Maple Wanted

Carload lots 1¼" x 6 x 10'—1sts and 2nds dry.
Carload lots (1¼" x 2½" x 49", 1" x 3½" x 49" clear, dry, equal number of pieces each size in each car.
Box 782 Canada Lumberman, Toronto. 3-7

## Lumber For Sale

### For Sale in Carload Lots

Telegraph Poles, Cedar Ties, Poplar, Spruce and Balsam Pulpwood.

Jas. Thos. Clair,
Clair, N.B.
7

### For Sale

Two million feet dry merchantable spruce from 1" to 4" thick, dry on sticks. Can be shipped rough or dressed. Also approximately two million feet Birch, Beech and Maple, 1", 2" and 3", Mill Run, Culls out. Prices right All dry. Sawn during season 1920-21. Rhodes, Curry Ltd., Amherst, N.S. 5-8

### For Sale

10 Cars of Mill Run Beech Sawed approximately 65%—6/4 Balance 4/4.
9 Cars 1" & 2" Hard Maple Chiefly second Growth sraight grain White Lumber suitable for Bending.
1 Car 6/4 Soft Elm No. 2 & Better.
1 Car 8/4 Soft Elm No. 2 & Better.
The above is all Bone Dry and we can make Prompt Shipment.
Apply Box 887 Canada Lumberman, Toronto. 6-7

### For Sale

At Blind River, Ontario, Pine and Spruce Lath, also some Cedar and Hemlock Lath, Grades, four foot mill-run, 32" mill-run, and four foot No. 3.

F. P. Potvin,
Blind River, Ont.
2-T.f.

#### PUBLISHER'S NOTICE

Advertisements other than "Employment Wanted" or "Employees Wanted" will be inserted in this department at the rate of 25 cents per agate line (14 agate lines make one inch). $3.50 per inch, each insertion, payable in advance. Space measured from rule to rule. When four or more consecutive insertions of the same advertisement are ordered a discount of 25 per cent. will be allowed.

Advertisements of "Wanted Employment" will be inserted at the rate of one cent a word, net. Cash must accompany order. If Canada Lumberman box number is used, enclose ten cents extra for postage in forwarding replies. Minimum charge 25 cents.

Advertisements of "Wanted Employees" will be inserted at the rate of two cents a word, net. Cash must accompany the order. Minimum charge 50 cents.

Advertisements must be received not later than the 10th and 20th of each month to insure insertion in the subsequent issue.

### Lumber for Sale

| | | | |
|---|---|---|---|
| 100 | M. 1" Basswood | 15 | M. 1" Soft Maple |
| 15 | M. 2" Rock Elm. | 15 | M. 1¼" " " |
| 25 | M. 2" Soft Elm. | 50 | M. 2 x 4/6/8" x 12 |
| 25 | M. 1" Soft Elm. | | Spruce |
| 8 | M. 1" Ash. | 8 | M. 1½" Hickory |

All last winter's cut.
Also 10,000 Cedar fence posts.

Glenn A. Shaver,
Lunenburg, Ont.
5-8

### WHITE PINE LUMBER
### For Immediate Shipment—1920 Cut—Should Be Bone Dry

About 30,000 ft. 2 in.
" 18,000 ft. 1 in.
" 2,000 ft. 3 in.

Apply to J. A. Farnsworth, Cookshire, Quebec. 6-T.f.

### Sale of Timber
### to
### Close an Estate

South East Quarter of Township of PROUDFOOT containing twenty-three and a quarter square miles, and known as Berth No. 2. Containing the following timber as cruised by one of the most reliable timber cruisers in Ontario.

Favorable terms can be arranged:—

| | |
|---|---|
| BIRCH | 10,950,000 ft. |
| MAPLE | 4,000,000 ft. |
| HEMLOCK | 2,000,000 ft. |
| ELM | 100,000 ft. |
| PINE | 100,000 ft. |
| CEDAR poles 25' up 50' | 5,000 |
| SPRUCE & BALSAM Cordwood | 5,000 cords |
| HARDWOOD CORDWOOD first-class | 80,000 cords |
| PRICE | $26,184.00 |

F. C. Clarkson, Assignee,
E. R. C. Clarkson & Son,
TORONTO
E.o.I. 5-11

## Machinery For Sale

### For Sale

8 inch Steam Feed. First class condition L. Robertson, Ardbeg, Ontario. 7-9

### Saw Mill Machinery for Sale

Including Engine, Boilers, Edger, Shafting, Solid Iron Pulleys, Gears etc. Attractive prices for immediate sale. Box 790 Canada Lumberman, Toronto. 4-7

### For Sale

Neverslip Monarch Tractor 20-12 H.P. in first-cass condition, only used short time. Will sacrifice for quick sale. Apply Rhodes, Curry Limited, Amherst, N.S. 5-8

### For Sale

30-18 Monarch Tractor with five sets of heavy log trucks and chains, if needed for good roads building, log bunks can be removed and boxes put on. Apply Box 884, Canada Lumberman, Toronto. 6-9

### Wickes Gang

GANG: No. 12 Wickes Gang, 40" sash, 18" stroke, steam binder rolls, front and back in two sections, feed and oscillation combined, 1908 model, and has been in use for five years. We furnish with this gang 11 rolls for cants and stock, one filing machine, and 4 sets of saws.

THE PEMBROKE LUMBER CO.,
Pembroke, Ont.
1t.f.

### Engines, Boilers, etc., for Sale

One "Williams" Upright Engine 6" x 6"
One Upright Engine 5" x 6"
Six Return tubular boilers of following dimensions:-
One "Butterfield" 72" x 14' - 3¼" tube - ¼" shell.
One "Polson" 64" x 14' - 3¼" tube - ¼" shell
One "Doty" 50" x 15' - 4" tube - ¼" shell
One "Doty" 60" x 14½' - 4" tube - ½" shell
One "Doty" 60" x 15' - 4" tube - ½" shell
One "Inglis" 60" x 16' - 3" tube - ½" shell
One double acting "Northey" Fire pump, 6" suction, 5" discharge, 14" steam cylinder, 8" water cylinder, 13" stroke, Capacity 450 gallons per minute.
One "Northey" feed pump 6 x 4 x 7" stroke, Capacity 60 gallons per minute.
One brass Mill steam whistle.
For further particulars apply The Conger Lumber Co Limited., Parry Sound, Ontario. 24 T.f.

### For Sale

Band Resaw, 54" Berlin with 3—5½" saws, $1000.00
Box-Board Printer, one-color, Con. & Deng. 19" x 44" $400.00
Box-Board Printer, two-color, 19" x 44" Hooper Late type, Chain feed $800.00
Box-Board Squeezer, 40" x 48", Mereen-Johnson automatic $700.00
Corrugated Fastener Driver, Doig 2-head $475.00
Equalizer, Berlin No. 229 automatic, Cap. up to 6' 6" long $675.00
Lock-Corner Cutter, Morgan No. 8 double end, $600.00
Lock-Corner Setting-Up machine, Morgan No. 2, $400.00
Nailing machines, all styles, Morgan & Doig, State your wants.
Sander, double-disc, 48" Fischer, all iron $235.00
Screw Driving Machines, Reynolds No. 2 $250.00 Each. (2).
Surfacer, single, 24" x 6" J. A. Fay & Co. Sectional Roll, $250.00
Surfacer, double, 30" x 7" Whitney, Sectional roll, $1150.00.

Chas. N. Braun Machinery
Fort Wayne, Indiana.
4-7

### Good Values
### Subject to Prior Sale

Band Resaw, Connell & Dengler, 54 and 60"
Band Rip Saw, Yates No. 281.
Circular Resaw, 44"
E. B. Hayes Dowell Gluer and Driver.
E. B. Hayes Standard Power Door Clamp.
Jointers, 16" and 24".
Matcher and Sizer, 30" x 12" American.
Matcher, 14" Woods.
Matcher, Hardwood American, No. 229.
Matcher, 30" x 8" Connell & Dengler.
Moulder, Hermance 10" wide open side.
Moulder Woods No. 2 light inside.
Moulder, C. B. Rogers, 6" outside.
Moulder, Berlin 10" No. 118, inside.
Moulder, Woods 5 head, inside.
Planers, all sizes single and double.
Sanders, 3-drum, 30, 42, 48, and 60".
Saws, circular, power feed, several makes.
Woodworking Machinery Company of Buffalo,
54 Mechanic St.,
Buffalo, N.Y.
5-E.o.I. - T.f.

### For Sale En-Bloc

Complete Saw Mill equipment, including one Four Block Hamilton Carriage. One pair heavy twin engines, feed complete and steam nigger. One three block E. Long Carriage with eight inch gun shot feed and steam nigger. One heavy three saw edger, W. Hamilton, make. Three 75 H.P. Boilers complete with dutch ovens and stacks. One 90 H.P. engine and fly-wheel complete. One lath and shingle mill. Complete filing equipment. One refuse burner. Shafting pulleys, transmission, etc., complete. Apply Box 783 Canada Lumberman, Toronto. 8-8

## Machinery Wanted

### Wanted

A 54" or 60" Used Band Resaw. Apply—The St. Catharines Box & Lumber Co. Ltd., 78 Niagara St., St. Catharines, Ont. 7

## Situations Wanted

Filer, band or circular, open for position best of references. 20 years experience in saw works and mills. Box 808 Canada Lumberman, Toronto. 5-7

Position wanted for the coming season to make lath or Pickets by thousand. Can give good references if required. Box 849 Canada Lumberman, Toronto. 7-9

Wanted—Position by bookkeeper with a high knowledge of double entry also pay roll etc. Lumber business preferred. Box 864 Canada Lumberman, Toronto. 7-8

Want positon as bandsaw filer, double cut preferred. Worked for the same company last four seasons. A1 references. Box 759 Canada Lumberman, Toronto. 4-7

Young man 28, wishes permanent position in lumber camp, preferably outdoor work, have had several years experience in office work. Box 840 Canada Lumberman, Toronto. 6-7

Wanted position as Mill Superintendent. Eight years experience as Mill Superintendent fifteen years as sawyer. Can furnish best references. Box 747 Canada Lumberman, Toronto. 1-7

Experienced Shipper—wants position in Sash, Door and Planing Mill plant. 20 years experience, steady, reliable, and capable of handling orders from office to completion. Familiar with Planing Mill Machinery, also good Glazier.. A 1 references, Box 847, Canada Lumberman, Toronto. 7-8

Aggressive Young Man with ability, integrity and five years experience Lumber and Woodworking offices, desires permanent position with progressive concern in a town. Am adaptable to any phase of work. Replies treated confidential. Excellent references. Box 845 Canada Lumberman, Toronto. 7

Young Scotchman married, abstainer, wishes permanent progressive position as bookkeeper, stenographer and general office man. Have had following experience: Six years banking, two years assistant bookkeeper and stenographer, London, England; eight years lumber office experience. Willing to go anywhere. Salary $100/$125. Apply Box 799 Canada Lumberman, Toronto, 4-8

Employment wanted by man in the prime of life, married and a Canadian, well experienced in all branches of Lumbering, from road-cutting to manager, Saw-mill and Yard, Driving and Rafting and Timber Estimating, am a Licensed Culler and have office experience. Would like executive position with Company who are lumbering for profits, not pastime. Am at present employed in executive position but scope is limited, and wish to change. Box 851 Canada Lumberman, Toronto. 7-8

# The Spanish River Lumber Co. Limited
## LUMBER MANUFACTURERS     CUTLER, ONTARIO

WHITE PINE,
   NORWAY PINE,
      HEMLOCK

Shipments
   by Rail
      or Water

# Review of Current Trade Conditions

## Ontario and the East

There is no particular change in the general lumber situation. The market in some respects is in a chaotic condition and various reports are heard from wholesalers. Some declare that business is picking up materially while others say that there is a disposition on the part of many concerns to hang back in their purchases. They are still waiting to find out how business conditions will shape up during the present month and what the prospects are for building in their respective communities. In Toronto, a great deal of construction work has started early and many business blocks and private dwellings are already well on the way to completion. The result is that yards are kept fairly busy and things are looking particularly bright in the newer sections of the city.

In Ontario some retailers appear to be pretty well stocked up and are buying only in mixed carload lots. The revival of trade, which it was predicted, would be brought about this year, is not likely to materialize suddenly, but that there will be a gradual improvement is acknowledged on all sides although no boom is likely to result. Never was the general situation in lumber so hard to analyze as at present. Each one seems to have a different view regarding the spring activities. While there are no pessimists, still some concerns are not exactly optimists and are adopting a conservative policy. Collections are still reported to be rather slow.

The situation regarding hardwoods is fairly active; the demand from the United States being stronger than the domestic requisitions. Automobile concerns have been buying to some extent but not in any huge quantities. Furniture factories are fairly busy; agricultural implement concerns are not calling for any great supplies of lumber. The farmer is backward about undertaking any heavy expenditure until he is sure of a good crop and better prices for his products. Retailers in the smaller towns feel this worse than those in the larger centres. Alterations and repair work, however, are reported to be very good.

There is a fair call for hemlock, which is reported to be none too plentiful. Spruce is one of the dullest features of the market and prices are inclined to soften. It is expected that most of the saw-mills will get off to a fairly early start, but just how large a quantity they will cut or how long they will operate, remains to be seen. Some manufacturers are prepared to turn out as much lumber as last season while others will produce only about half the amount.

The lath market is active at the present time and there is a scarcity in all lines except 32" lath, which are plentiful and easy in price. Quotations on No. 1's and No. 2's are very firm at present but whether they will hold remains to be seen.

Early this year, there was some talk of a shortage of dry lumber stocks and a runaway market if a normal demand set in. As the days go by, less is heard concerning a runaway episode and the great desideratum is stabilization in prices. It is contended that costs are now down to the lowest basis so far as the woods end is concerned. When the mills start up there is likely to be a further reduction in wages of mill hands, other than skilled help, the scale being 25 to 30 cents an hour. The whole lumber situation is one so closely linked up with industrial and building activities that whatever affects the latter will have its reflex on the former. If the showing is good in the building line, lumber dealers believe that they should enjoy a fair turnover this season.

No decision as yet has been given in the matter of reduction in freight rates, which was applied for by the lumberman some time ago. It is still contended by all those engaged in the industry, that were carrying charges to revert to what they were previous to September 1920, considerable impetus would be given to the moving of stock. In the present uncertainty a number of purchasers, particularly of lumber which comes from distant points, are holding back in the hope that the drop in transportation may take place in the near future.

In the Speech from the Throne at Ottawa it was stated that conferences had been arranged between the railway authorities of Canada with respect to a reduction in the freight rates on basic commodities. This reference is of particular interest to lumbermen, many of whom have written the Prime Minister of Canada, congratulating him upon this step and urging upon him the great necessity for a substantial reduction in the carrying tolls on lumber.

It is stated that a number of Nova Scotia lumbermen are feeling the effects of the competition of B. C. forest products in the Boston market by reason of the low water carrying charges on material from the West. It is said that 2 x 4, 2 x 6 and 2 x 8 fir are being brought around via the Panama Canal and delivered in cargo lots at a lower figure than B. C. spruce can be shipped from Halifax to the New England market, that is, unless the eastern water rates are substantially reduced.

A recent dispatch from St. John, N. B., says—It is reported by local shipping men that the lumber shipping market for this spring shows little improvement over last spring. The freights are fairly firm with orders mostly for small vessels. The American market does not appear to be especially bright and $6 is the prevalent rate, although there was a flurry in laths in New York recently which advanced the rate for the time being to $8. The English outlook is not promising as large supplies are held on the other side by the British government and little inducement is offered to local shippers. Deals are offered at 85s. for medium sized steamers and 80s. for large ones. It is reported that eighty million feet of lumber is yarded at West St. John, mostly by the government and associated interests.

## How Timber Exporters View Outlook

Judging by the advices during March from Quebec exporters, salesmen and agents, in the United Kingdom, the forecasts, which have been made during the past few months in the "Canada Lumberman" have been verified by J. G. Leyie, Vice President of W. & J. Sharples, Limited, who proceeded to Great Britian two months ago to look over conditions, consult with the firm's agents and at the same sime solicit business. In letters received from Mr. Leyie he is not optimistic regarding trade. He holds out little hope for the betterment of conditions abroad during the spring and early summer and bases his judgment on many things, among them being the unsettled financial situation, the continued non-amelioration of the European political horizon, fear in all lines of commercial and trade circles and the ultra caution of the nation's banking system.

From other sources of information the statements contained in Mr. Levie's letters contain the same story. It should be considered that no solution for economic difficulties will ever succeed permanently that is not in agreement with basic economic laws. In the present emergency, as has been previously stated, the great trouble is that the people are looking for a miracle to occur and for prosperity to come back in a jump. Prosperity will return to the United Kingdom only with a settlement of the European political questions, adjustment of the rates of exchange, with the operation of basic economic laws and the people ceasing to call for political assistance for industry. They will have to learn that what they are seeking, is an interference with the operation of those basic laws that, work a country out of a situation which is the aftermath of the great war. This also applies to the lumberman, the farmer and every other worker in the avenue of the world's industrial and commercial life. Trust is centred in the speedy alignment of wages and prices, which are now out of line with the general level; by a quick reduction of taxation, transportation rates, and in a restoration of sound conditions of finance. In particular, the schemes of co-operative marketing, and the facilitating of the investment of capital, together with better and cheaper carrying rates will contribute immensely to correct present conditions. But withal, the thought needs to be constantly kept in mind that underlying every disturbance at home, is the disturbed state of the world at large. On the amending of the disturbance of the world depends the correction of most of the troubles at home. It is only as the plight of the Canadian farmer in the prairie provinces, manufacturer, merchant and workman is viewed in the larger aspect as a part of the world condition and as Canadians keep their true sense of relationship with the inevitable, can we look for a starting-point toward working for the proper remedies? These conditions are reviewed are generally admitted by the financial interests of the world which makes them reluctant to take chances in investment that would oil and keep the wheels of industry moving and help along the basic laws of economy.

The Elliott Woodworking Co., of Belleville, have started manufacturing electric washing machines at their plant in that city.

The next monthly meeting of the Wholesale Lumber Dealers' Association will be held in Toronto on Friday April 21. A. J. Brady, of North Tonawanda, N. Y., will give an address on "Salesmanship."

## Montreal Lumbermen Think Spruce Prices Too High

In the view of some Montreal lumbermen, the prices of spruce at the mills will have to be reduced if business is to be stimulated. It is stated that lumber is being offered at very low quotations, presumably the product of some of the smaller mills, the evidence being that the larger mills are holding out for what they believe to be fair prices. It is difficult to see how the mill prices can be reduced to any appreciable extent having regard to the cuts already made and to the cost of operation. A fair amount of business is passing but it is nothing like the volume which was expected about this time.

The hardwood market is a little better although it is almost impossible to dispose of the lower ends. This particularly applies to birch.

The mills have advanced the price of spruce lath fifty cents; this is not likely to hold in view of the weakness which has developed in the American market. Stocks, however, are not in large supply.

A fair number of orders for spruce have been received for American account, but here again there are complaints of the difficulty in securing satisfactory prices.

Pulpwood is almost dead. The price at Watertown for sap peeled wood is $17.50. Reports from the province are to the effect that very little wood has been cut this season.

Mr. A. M. B. Stevens, Director of the Timber Disposal Department, Board of Trade, London, and Mr. S. G. Denman, Representative of the Department in Canada, have been on visits to Ottawa, Toronto, New York and Boston. The report that British government stocks in the Maritime Provinces have been sold as low as $16, is, we understand, without foundation. There is no idea of dumping the entire stocks on to the Canadian market; these will be sold gradually and in such quantities as to obviate the danger of a menace to the Canadian market.

The protest against the Bill of the Quebec Government amending the Motor Vehicle Act has resulted in a modification of the measure as it effects trucks, a form of transportation which is being more freely used by the lumber industry. The schedule of taxes in the original draft has been reduced; the rate for one ton vehicles is left at $25 per annum, while that for every additional ton is $12.50, until two and a half tons are reached. For three ton vehicles $40 per ton is charged, the object being to entirely eliminate heavy trucks. From the owners' point of view the proposals are still very unfair, not only as to the taxes which are higher than any other province, but as to the restriction that no truck over two and a half tons shall be allowed outside the limits of towns and cities. There is an exception to this when trucks are engaged on the construction and maintenance of roads. Many truck owners state that the bill will mean the entire scrapping of some of their vehicles and the partial unemployment of others.

## Western Veneer Plant May Be Enlarged

The busy veneer manufacturing plant of the Canadian Western Lumber Co. Limited at Fraser Mills, B. C., may be enlarged in the near future. The company states that the veneer business has certainly made vast strides during the past few years and that they are at present marketing considerable of their product in Ontario. They are now making three grades and say they are able to compete with composition board of various kinds. A large quantity is being shipped to Australia and the prairie provinces are using increasing supplies.

In visiting the plant the first objects that attract attention are the large steam vats in which the selected logs are subjected to live steam for a period of thirty six hours. Only certain portions of the Douglas fir tree can be used for the manufacture of veneer. It must be free from knots, shake pitch and such other defects. After being subjected to the steam treatment the log is moved to the peeling room where the thick bark is stripped. It is then mounted on the lathe, a powerful machine equipped with a peeling knife ninety six inches long and eight inches wide. Instead of the knife turning against the log, the log is turned against the knife. The thin sheet of veneers runs out on a long table to the cutting knife, where it is sliced into various lengths required to fill orders on hand.

From here it goes to another room and goes through a drying process. The Canadian Western Lumber Company have installed an up-to-date dryer costing in the neighborhood of thirty thousand dollars. It doesn't look very complicated from the outside but it's insides are filled with steam pipes, fans for the circulation of hot air and other various contrivances calculated to dry out even, the oldest mummy in Egypt. After thoroughly drying the sheets they are sent to the glue machine. Fir veneer is built up by glueing three sheets together, the grain of one sheet running crossways of the other two sheets. As an absolutely waterproof glue is used Fir veneer is one of the few veneers that can be used successfully in the open.

Three grades are manufactured. The first grade is used for paneling and other inside work where a stain or varnish finish is desired. The second grade is intended for enamel or paint finish jobs while the third grade is manufactured where just a rough finish is wanted. No special varnish or stain is necessary to finish these panels. But results are obtained by using the standard varnishes and stains now on the market. The finished work shows a very smooth, satin like panel requiring no repairs for years. The panels fit in exceptionally well where fir lumber is used as interior trim.

## Calls for Prompt Readjustment of Rates

Robert E. Stocking, of the New York lumber firm of Messrs. Power, Moir & Stocking, arrived in Quebec during the latter part of March to consult with the president of the company, Mr. W. Gerard Power on business in connection with the company, and railway shipments of lumber to New York and other United States Atlantic States.

In the course of an interview Mr. Stocking said, "I have come to discuss with Mr. Power and the lumber interests here the question of obtaining lower transportation rates from the railroads if we wish to conserve the eastern Canada lumber trade with the eastern and central states of the United States. Railroads were deaf to the appeals of West Coast lumbermen for a reduction in freight rates until after it was demonstrated to them by the lumbermen that they were not wholly dependent upon them, by moving the bulk of their stock by water. When the railroads woke up to this fact they made a belated reduction which, however, came too late, and, perhaps, having learned a lesson in this case, may take it as a warning and listen to the advice of the eastern lumber interests or else suffer the chances of killing our trade and, of course, these channels of supply and revenue.

"Business was remarkable with our and other Quebec firms in the eastern States markets up to the end of last December, or until cheaper wood was being brought to New York, Pennsylvania, Massachusetts, Connecticut and other states in the Atlantic Board of the United States, at cheaper prices on account of lower transportation rates, of waterway which had the effect of underselling us in our offer of Canadian lumber products, and products from the eastern mills along railroads. For example, steamships arriving from South American ports in the Pacific ports, and even U. S. Atlantic ports, having no return cargo, instead of taking on water ballast, now go to Pacific ports at Oregon, Seattle, Washington, etc., and purchase a cargo of lumber which they convey back and through the Panama Canal and sell for a profit sufficient to compensate them in the freight values they would otherwise receive if carrying the same cargoes across the seas in ordinary export trade, with the profits which would accrue to the legitimate export selling trade. In the meantime these steamers charge themselves only $5. freight rate, including the charges of the Panama Canal, a carrying distance of 6,000 miles, while the Canadian and eastern lumber exporters are called upon to pay double freight rates. The cost for shipment of lumber from the port of Quebec to English ports, a voyage of, approximately, 3,000 miles, costs the exporter $11.36 per 1,000 feet, board measure.

"Even if the freight rates on transcontinental railways were cut down and made low, we in the eastern lumber trade could not compete in the foreign markets under such conditions. We are, therefore, seeking as much as possible from the competition now offering from the West Coast lumber export trade, where the mills are not located inland and depend upon railroad transportation, but on the coast and close to the waterways to give them the advantage of cheap water transportation. We are, for these reasons, endeavoring to conserve our eastern United States trade and production of the mills that lie along and depend upon railroad transportation to the New York zone, and the existence of Canadian mills.

"It is well known in the lumber trade that while there is considerable clear wood in the Pacific Coast fir, due to the nature of its growth, the Canadian spruce is more knotty; consequently the clear wood of the fir commands higher prices than the Canadian spruce, which allows the fir lumber interests to sell the knotty production cheaper than the eastern spruce, and thus given an advantage over the eastern lumber export trade.

"In the interest of Canadian manufacturers of lumber, the Canadian export trade, and our relations with the Canadian lumber trade, has caused me to take the matter up with the Canadian railroads, particularly the Grand Trunk Railway System, which operates over 600 miles of railway in the eastern United States. We have asked for serious consideration of lower freight rates on the transportation of lumber from Canada to the eastern United States. I have written to Mr. R. L. Sargant, manager of the Transportation Department of the Canadian Lumbermen's Association, Ottawa, respecting the matter with a view to warning Canadian railroad interests of what is taking place, and regret to say that as the situation at present stands,

all the representatives of all-rail mills in the eastern territory, are practically taking little notice and standing aside and looking on, while the Pacific Coast shippers are getting the business.

"In the letter to Mr. Sargant, I called his attention to the circulars letters of the 16th and 27th of February, issued from his office, relative to the hearing of C. L. A. applications arranged March 7th. I pointed out to him that we refrained from expressing ourselves because we understood the hearing was in connection with railway rates within Canada, and the firm I was a member of, in its business connections was engaged in entirely shipping Canadian lumber to the American market, and that any observations we might advance would lack point; also that whether or not at this time any references to the effect of the predominating very high freight rates on lumber from Canada to the United States, would be considered out of place. I pointed out the recent alarming developments in connection with the transportation of lumber to the American eastern States markets from mills located in Eastern Canada, who largely depend upon the states of New York, New Jersey, Pennsylvania, Connecticut, Massachusetts and the Atlantic seaboard in general, and did not see how the subject to be discussed at the C. L. A. meeting would concern any gathering of lumbermen or carriers of lumber, having in mind the state of affairs brought on by the large amount of tonnage in lumber now being handled from the Pacific Coast and shipped through the Panama Canal to the Atlantic seaboard for distribution in New York and distribution by reshipment inland.

"I called the attention of Mr. Sargant to the original conference rates on lumber through the Panama Canal, put into effect last year which was set at $20, per 1,000 feet, board measure. This rate was later reduced to $18, and quite recently the conference rate was dropped and open competition substituted, with the result that freights commenced to drop, and in the first part of the month of March we were advised of quotations of $14; and even $12, to New York. It is also of common in New York that some of the steamships have been buying lumber cargoes in lieu of water ballast, which they are willing to sell at cost, making their profit out of what they get, which was placed to the credit of freight charges. The outcome is that Pacific Coast fir, spruce and hemlock are daily arriving at the American ports of Norfolk, via Philadelphia, Baltimore, New York and Boston, at the present time in large quantities and at such low prices that the eastern inland mills, entirely dependent on railroad means of transportation, are finding their old-time markets closed to them."

## Permanent Display of Canadian Products

Consolidated Exports Displays of Canada, Limited, has been organized with a capital stock of $100,000. The head office of the company is in Toronto. Col. Chas. R. Hill is president and managing-director and Lieut. Col. A. B. Kenny, president of Big Bear Lumber Co., is vice-president.

The company has been formed to supply a medium for Canadian manufacturers to display and sell their products in the overseas buying centres. London will be made the starting point, and it is intended that the exhibits shall be permanent in character. By co-operative effort it is believed that the expense of exhibition and salesmanship under the company's permanent plan, will cost little more than a two weeks' display under short-term arrangements.

The exhibits will likely consist of building material, machinery, household furnishings, etc., each in charge of a special salesman.

It is said that not 1% of Canadian manufacturers show a full range of samples with sales representation and that the time has come when Canada must let her resources be known by proofs and not just commercial intelligence.

## How Budworm Has Ravaged Eastern Timber

At the annual meeting of the Acadian Entomological Society held in St. John N. B. a few days ago Dr. J. H. Tothill said that the loss in lumber in the province of New Brunswick due to the ravages of the spruce budworm have been estimated at 700,000,000 board feet of spruce and 7,267,000,000 board feet of fir. The progress of the outbreak was studied by the speaker and assistants and a reconnaissance survey of budworm conditions was made in co-operation with the Crown lands department. Figuring the value of this timber at the present stumpage rate on crown lands for green timber $4.50 per thousand for fir and $5.00 per thousand for spruce the loss in stumpage value alone to the province is $3,500,000 for spruce and $32,701,500 for fir a grand total of about $36,000,000. This, he pointed out, represents the stumpage value of the standing dead timber in the province had the bud worm not destroyed it. In addition to the loss of raw material, Dr. Tothill said, there is also an industrial loss that is reflected back on the province as a whole. The dead material cannot be worked up into the finished product, so that the

operators and the wage earners will necessarily forgo the financial benefits ordinarily derived from the use of such raw materials. He said that it is conceivable that there may be an industrial loss for nearly half a century due to a lessened activity in the lumber industry due to the lessening of the forest resources for the period.

Another result of the budworm attack is, he said, that, with so much dead material in the woods, favorable conditions have been produced for an increase of other injurious insects such as bark beetles. These have increased noticeably during the last five years. Another somewhat similar result is that with the thinning out of the forests the losses from blow-downs are becoming more severe. Even if unprotected trees are not actually blown down the increased swaying increases the snapping off of rootlets which in turn lowers the resistance to insects and fungus attacks.

A further result, he pointed out, of the outbreak is that the fire hazard has been considerably increased and will remain so for about the next five years.

## Lumber Company Becomes Incorporated

The Michener Lumber Co. has been formed with a capital stock of $40,000, and head office in Smithville, Ont. As previously announced, Wm. Michener, who has carried on a lumber business, planing mill and retail yard for the last twenty- five years in Smithville, is president of the company. Wallace Glintz is secretary-treasurer and Harold Gowland is vice-president. The new company deals in all kinds of lumber, lath, shingles, posts, interior and exterior trim, etc., and has taken over the business formerly conducted by Mr. Wm. Michener.

## Two Good Men on Advisory Board

The appointment by the Canadian Pulp and Paper Association of Sir William Price and G. M. McKee to act with two members of the Quebec Limit Holders' Association as an advisory board is calculated to make for greater harmony in the discussion of questions affecting the Quebec lumber and pulp and paper industries. Sir William Price represents lumber as well as paper, while Mr. McKee is more particularly interested in pulp and paper, although his company, the Donnacona Paper Company, are large limit holders.

Hon. E. Mercier, Minister of Lands & Forests for Quebec has publicly stated that he welcomes the appointment of such a Board, believing that conferences between representatives of the lumbermen and pulp and paper industries and the department will be of mutual benefit. The idea is to see that proper legislation is passed, and the only way that this can be accomplished is by taking an active interest in the matter and by co-operating with the Government in everything that has reference to forestry legislation."

The Pulp and Paper Association is no doubt looking at the subject from the point of view of the production of pulpwood, but as has been previously pointed out, some of the companies have also large lumber interests and are, therefore, affected by legislation which touches both sides of their business. Questions are bound to arise which will concern both lumber and pulp and paper.

Mr. Mercier intimated that it would be advisable to appoint men on the advisory board who are representative and can speak with authority. No one can question the qualifications of Sir William Price and Mr. McKee in these respects.

## Builders Want Lumber Grades Standardized

The subject of the standardization of lumber was briefly discussed at a meeting of the Montreal Builders' Exchange on March 15. The topic was brought up by Mr. Church, the president who stated that there were no standards for lumber. Some of the contractors bought merchantable spruce and got good lumber, while other purchases of the same grade resulted in the receipt of very poor stuff. He desired standards in order to secure something like uniformity.

Mr. A. Plamondon pointed out that the same grades form different mills varied widely in quality. In ordering, a contractor had no guide as to what he would receive. Standardization would give him this guide, while it would also be of benefit to the lumbermen as it would place them on an equality in quoting to customers. Other trades had standards of quality, but in lumber there was no such thing. In hardwoods he had found great variation in what were supposed to be identical grades.

The Chairman remarked that in cement and other builders' supplies there were standards, which if not lived up to would justify the return of the goods, but in lumber there was no remedy. He added "When you buy fifths and better in spruce you generally get fifths and no better."

## Pulpwood May be Scarce This Fall

A. L. Perkins & Co., Powassan, Ont., who are extensive dealers in pulpwood in the Parry Sound district, say that production of spruce, balsam and poplar in that section this season is the lightest on record. What new wood has been delivered has been practically all absorbed as hauled to the railways. The surplus from last season's bumper cut is also moving freely and this stock will very soon be exhausted. The demand is improving and a number of mills which could not be interested a few months ago, are now looking around for pulpwood.

Mr. Perkins says that supplies are low, and, as deliveries are now over for this winter, no large quantities will be available until the winter of 1923. It, therefore, looks like a real shortage of pulpwood of all kinds for the summer and fall months of 1922. In his opinion, any mill well stocked with wood at the present time even at a little higher price than at present replacement values, is in a fortunate position.

During the last six months the market offered nothing but discouragement to producers, jobbers and shippers, and there was, therefore, very little wood produced, and what was delivered to the railways this winter was produced at a loss.

Mr. Perkins adds that shippers must go farther afield every year, which means higher haulage or teaming costs, and at the price offered by the mills, purchasers simply could not deliver for the money. The unreasonable freight rates prevailing also add considerably to the curtailing of production, as purchasers cannot see the point of giving their timber away, after paying cutting, hauling and loading costs, which they kept down to about $7.00 per cord, and handing it over to the railways to charge $14.00 per cord freight on their product. Such an arrangement is badly out of balance.

"I am," declares Mr. Perkins, "of the opinion that the worst is over and as pulpwood was one of the first commodities to suffer drastic declines, it should likewise be one of the first to recover, and any change must necessarily be for the better. If our exports of paper, pulp and wood continue on the increase, there will, certainly, not be sufficient pulpwood to go around before another cut can be brought out to the railways."

## Biggest Pulp Contract Ever Signed in Canada

What is considered the largest pulp contract ever negotiated in Canada reached its final stages recently. The contract is between Sir Frederick Becker, of London, Eng., and the Saguenay Pulp and Power Company, Limited. Sir Frederick, in signing the contract, represents what is known as the Ludgate syndicate, composed of between twenty and twenty-five consumers of mechanical and sulphite pulp in England, France and Belgium.

A rough calculation makes the contract worth between $70,000,000 and $75,000,000. It will extend for 10 years, and calls for production by the Saguenay Pulp and Power Company of 500 tons of mechanical pulp and 250 tons of sulphite pulp per day. This production automatically sold, by the terms of the contract, on a basis of cost plus .$10 per ton for mechanical pulp, and cost plus $15 per ton for sulphite pulp. The value of the mechanical pulp over the term of the contract will be roughly $52,000,000, and of the sulphite pulp, $22,000,000.

It will assure practically capacity operations over the period of 10 years to the producing company.

## Too Much Pulpwood Exported From Quebec

A topic of interest to lumbering companies and pulp organizations was brought up in the Quebec legislature recently with regard to the embargo on pulpwood. The legislature heard from the member for Bonaventure of a leak in the embargo and the assertion was made that millions of feet of pulpwood was being cut in the province and being shipped to New Brunswick, and thence exported to the United States. This is a contravention, in spirit at any rate, of the law passed by the Quebec legislature, the object of which is to ensure that all pulpwood cut in the province on Crown lands shall be manufactured within the limits of the province. Since this law has been in force quite a number of large pulp mills have been established

in the province by American organizations, and a great proportion of the paper used by the leading papers of the United States is manufactured in Quebec Province, thus giving employment to hundreds of people.

Quoting statistics, Fabien Bugeaud, member for Bonaventure, informed the House that during the years 1918-19 there had been exported from the Province of Quebec 296,068,343 feet of wood cut from Crown lands and 27,998,445 feet cut from private lots, making a total of 324,066,754 feet. In 1919-20 there had been 380,964,232 feet cut from private lots, making a total of 394,411,630 feet. In 1920-21 there had been cut 379,407,720 feet from Crown lands and 42,853,225 feet from private lots, making a total of 422,260,945 feet. These figures, he said, showed an increase of 26,000,000 feet for 1920-21, indicating that the evil of exporting instead of decreasing was being aggravated and that very rapidly. This would strike the House even more forcibly when it was realized that this amount represented 30 per cent of the total export of forest products, that is to say, one-third of the wood of the Province of Quebec was being manufactured outside of the province. Lumber merchants and mill owners whom he had consulted told him that once the wood reached the mill the cost of making it a manufactured product was $15 per thousand feet, but in view of the decrease in wages this year he would reckon it at $10 per 1,000 and this meant that the enormous sum of $4,220,000 had been earned by the workmen of other provinces in the manufacture of Quebec wood. During these times of unemployment such a sum would have gone far to relieve the hardships that had existed in many parts.

Mr. Bugeaud, continuing, said that 49,180,751 feet of wood had been cut in Bonaventure county last year. This was a decrease of 6,000,000 feet, however, over the preceding year, and out of that enormous quantity only 15,000,000 had been manufactured in the county. This meant that 34,000,000 feet were manufactured in New Brunswick or elsewhere, representing a loss for Bonaventure and a gain for New Brunswick, or elsewhere of $340,000. These figures, he said, would prove how right he was in stating that the Province of Quebec was suffering.

Hon. H. Mercier, Minister of Lands and Forests, in reply, pointed out that the matter was not one that could be considered solely from a provincial point of view, but because of the inter-provincial relations law it had to be considered from a Canadian viewpoint. In consequence it was a matter that had to be very carefully studied before any action was taken. He admitted that the question was a grave one and the situation demanded attention. He pointed out that certain lumber companies in the Baie de Chaleur district had amalgamated and formed the Bathurst Lumber Company; it being found to be cheaper to send the wood across the bay and out by the Intercolonial than to ship it by rail along the bay and trans-ship at Matapedia over the Intercolonial. The question, however, was a complex one and it was being carefully studied, and an easy solution was not to be expected because there was a question of inter-provincial trade to be considered.

The embargo in regard to the United States had undoubtedly brought a great industry into the province.

## Abitibi Earnings Are Very Encouraging

Net earnings of $4,678,172, the second largest in the history of the company are shown in the eighth annual report of the Abitibi Power & Paper Company, Montreal, whose plant is located at Iroquois Falls, Ont. The most noteworthy feature of the exhibit lies in the drawing upon surplus to the extent of over $2,000,000 to provide for depreciation of inventories and for the wiping out of an item of nearly half a million for Government taxes for the years 1919 and 1920. This naturally leaves a surplus comparing unfavorably with that of the previous year, but the company, through this drastic action, would seem to be starting the year 1922 with a clean slate and in a favorable position to take advantage of the gradually improving business opportunities.

Gross earnings for the year were $8,861,810, as compared with $10,580,142 the previous year. After operating expenses of $4,183,637, net operating revenue stands at $4,678,172, as compared with $5,043,133 in 1920, the latter having been the highest in the history of the company.

# New Brunswick Spruce Will Soon Take Its Proper Place

### Hon Mr. Robinson Declares Heavy Cost of Forest Fire Protection is Justified—Proposed Change of Scale

That the cost of forest fire protection is heavy, but the saving justified it, was a statement made by Hon. C. W. Robinson, Minister of Lands and Mines for New Brunswick in a strong address made in the New Brunswick legislature a few days ago. He explained with regard to the estimates of his department that fire protection alone cost $144,000 an amount greatly in excess of what was anticipated. He also gave a minute and enlightening review of the lumber situation, showing the causes of the present situation and what could be expected in the future. During the course of his speech he added that there were 10,000,000,000 feet of standing lumber on the crown lands and 20,000,000,000 feet in the province, including Crown and private lands.

The chief item of expenditure in his department had been for forest fire protection, and he maintained that he did not believe that the greatest asset that the province possessed should be neglected. The minister contended that there might be better ways of fighting forest fires, but he believed that the system in vogue in New Brunswick was the best that they could devise. Under the forest fire law the department took control of all fires. The fires in the province last year were the worst in its history. No less than 485 fires were fought by the department and in addition there were numerous small fires put out by people in the neighborhood. He thought they could afford to expend considerable money for the protection of the forests, but if any member could show how a reduction might be made without impairing the efficiency of the service, he would be glad to adopt such a proposal. Many suggestions, he said, had been put forth by the lumbermen and had been given careful consideration, but the department wanted to be sure of a better system before deciding on a change. He pointed out that in 1920 there had been 227 forest fires against 348 for the year 1921. In addition there were eighty-five railway fires in 1920 and 147 in the following year. The losses in 1920 totaled $663,000 against $427,000 last year. The total area burned in 1920 was 94,787 acres against 84,783 last year. The number of fires that burned over 1,000 acres in 1920 was twenty-three, while last year there were only ten. The figures give some idea of the work performed by the forest service during the year. Had there been no forest service in 1921, Hon. Mr. Robinson said, the damage might have been beyond all comprehension. In fact, he said, it was little short of a miracle that they did not have a tremendous conflagration in the province. He paid a glowing tribute to the work of the chief forest ranger Mr. Prince. He recalled the disastrous fire at Westfield, the cost of fighting amounted to $18,000.

Hon. Mr. Robinson said that the lumbermen's associations of the province had been urging the government to adopt the system now in vogue in Quebec. He had been looking into the matter and had found that the cost of fighting fires in that province were fully as great as in New Brunswick. In the State of Maine where there were fifty lookout towers and an area as large as New Brunswick the cost of protection, he said, exceeded $200,000 a year.

#### Caution Needed Before Changing Scale

Referring to other section of the Crown land department there were a number of scalers employed to scale the logs. The minister said it was the ambition of the department to scale every log and collect 100 per cent of stumpage and he had reason to believe that this was being accomplished. He now had under consideration proposals of the lumbermen to have the province adopt the Quebec system, and while it had some attractive features, he felt that New Brunswick could not afford to make a sudden change as caution was needed before adopting any new system. He spoke of a report that lumbermen in session advocated a reduction from $5 to $2.50 as far as spruce was concerned and proportionately with regard to other lumber. It was urged that the lumbermen were operating under undue costs and against severe competition from other provinces; also that an early reply should be given to enable the operators to enter the woods at an early date and prepare for the next logging season. The matter, he said, was a serious one to decide. The head of the Lands & Mines Department spoke of the original object of the stumpage rates. He said many factors entered into the lumber situation and he believed that the stumpage was one of the most important. Manufactured lumber was piled in the millyards, the product of several years. Many logs were in the booms and some operators had enough logs on hand to run their mills without cutting a single log. The lumbermen, he said, were in a serious condition, many with logs which cost from twenty to thirty per cent more than their present value and the price of lumber half what it was. One factor in the situation, he said, was mismanagement of railways of the province. When the lumber mar-

ket was at its peak there were excellent chances to sell in the United States, but the railroads could not furnish cars. One operator had told him that he lost an order for several hundred carloads through the manner in which the C. N. R. board, sitting in Toronto, had handled the situation. The difficulty was wider than the province; it was Dominion wide.

Another serious matter was the bud worm-killed timber standing in the province. Every encouragement for its removal had been given, but unfortunately the ravages of this pest came at a most inopportune time, when there was no demand even for the best. Statistics from the chief forester showed that four million acres had been cruised up to the present time. He said that eight billion feet were estimated to be standing on three and a half million acres. Two billion could be easily added for the small trees overlooked making a total of ten billion. A report of 460 square miles surveyed in 1921 showed that merchantable green timber was 294,272,000 feet; under-sized green timber 536,896,000 feet; and dead standing timber 278,537,000 feet, making a grand total of 1,109,705,000 feet. Of that quantity 258,190,000 was dead standing fir. Dead spruce was 3.6 per cent; dead fir 56 per cent; dead spruce was sixty feet to the acre and dead fir 877 feet to the acre. The chief feature of the statement was that the damage by the bud worm was chiefly confined to fir.

Mr. Robinson predicted that it would be only a few years before New Brunswick spruce would take its proper place in the world's market.

When asked regarding re-seeding he said he believed that the province was particularly fortunate in the fact that nature did more towards reforestation than man could do.

## Norway Maples for the Fallen Heroes

Norway maples are the trees selected for planting Montreal's Road of Remembrance for her fallen soldiers. They have been selected because they are declared to be less liable to destruction by caterpillars and cement dust from sidewalks, than other varieties of maples, and because in five years they produce a nice shade and are full grown in about 20 years. They are, moreover, the hardiest variety of soft maples and are considered by the civic authorities, with whom the final choice lies, the best trees for street planting in Montreal. Norway maples are planted extensively throughout New York state, where they are also considered the most suitable variety for streets.

Careful consideration was given before the choice was made, it is stated. Sugar maples were dropped from consideration because they take twice as long to grow and also because they are so attractive to insects.

## Canadian Trees for Great Britain

In carrying out reforestation of the British Isles, the Forestry Commission is depending chiefly on Canada for tree seeds. The collecting, threshing and shipping of these seeds is done by the Forestry branch of the Department of the Interior. The threshing and cleaning is done at a very efficient plant in New Westminster, B. C. Before Christmas a shipment of 3,000 pounds was made evenly divided between Douglas fir and Sitka spruce seed. Just lately the second shipment was made consisting of 1,800 pounds of Douglas fir, 1,500 pounds of Sitka spruce and 100 pounds of western hemlock seed. A third shipment which will be made as soon as possible will conclude the despatch of the seed collected during the season of 1921. It is reported from Great Britain that the trees above mentioned grow exceptionally well in the British Isles.

Mr. Peters of J. E. Moore & Company, St. John, N. B., has been on a visit to Montreal.

The plant of the Kastner Lumber Co. at Wiarton, Ont., was recently destroyed. The loss is $10,000. It is believed that the fire was the work of an incendiary.

The capital stock of the Hope Mfg. Co., Limited, 456 Gilbert St., Toronto, Ont., has been increased from $40,000 to $100,000. The company are large manufacturers of doors and other lines.

During the period 1917 to 1920, 2,300 forest fires in Quebec were attributed to carelessness of sportsmen and workmen. These 2,300 fires swept over approximately 377,000 acres, of which at least 273,000 acres were estimated to be green timber and young growth.

The Algoma Lumber Co., Limited, has been incorporated with a capital stock of $50,000 and headquarters in Wiarton, to carry on the business of timber merchants, sawmill owners, logging operations, etc. Among the incorporators of the company are E. W. Geddes of Blyth; James J. Tyson of Wiarton; Robert T. Wright of Thorndale and James R. Bogue, of Strathroy. The company is empowered to acquire the undertakings and assets in the district of Algoma of the partnership or syndicate subsisting between Messrs. Geddes, Tyson, Wright and Bogue.

# EDGINGS

The Great Lakes Pulp and Paper Co. will erect a large paper mill in Fort William, Ont.  The capacity will be 100 tons a day and the plant must give employment to 600 men by February 1st, 1925.  A satisfactory agreement has been reached with the Ontario Government.

The W. Williamson Lumber Co., with headquarters in Toronto and a capital stock of $100,000, has been incorporated to take over the business of Wm. Williamson, 601 Woodbine Ave., Toronto.  The company is composed of W. T. Williamson, Frederick F. Williamson and others.

It is said that the Donnacona Paper Co. is considering the erection of a new wood pulp mill and electric power house during the coming summer at Port Rouge, Que.  It is reported the company will move part of the wallboard plant to that place.

Joseph and Henry Gibson, who have been associated with their father, James Gibson, of Hadlow, Levis, Que., in the lumber and square timber business for the past twenty years, have just opened a retail lumber business at the corner of St. Valier & Incarnation streets, Quebec City, and if knowing the business spells success, they should succeed.

The St. Croix Pulp & Paper Company is reported to have been organized and will in future be known as the Premier Power & Pulp Company, with a capitalization of $2,000,000.  About $1,000,000 will be invested in renovating the old plant, and, with proposed improvements, it is expected that the output will be about 8,000 tons of newsprint and 5,000 tons of wrapping paper a year.  Any surplus pulp will be sold in the markets of United States and Great Britain.

John B. Reid, of Toronto, honorary president of the Ontario Retail Lumber Dealers' Association, who is spending the winter at St. Petersburg, Florida, has been creating quite a name for himself in that southern city.  Some time ago he was elected vice-president of the newly-formed Canadian Club, and now his rink of lawn bowlers has carried off the international cup on the bowling green.  Mr. Reid's quartette is composed of all Toronto men with the exception of one who came from Kingston.

There are many important changes in the laws relative to woods and forests in the bill presented to the Quebec Legislature by Hon. H. Mercier, Minister of Lands and Forests for Quebec, all aiming at the better protection of the timber limits of the province and the prevention of their destruction by fire.  Any person who without authorization takes possession of any part of the public domain shall be liable to a penalty of not less than a dollar or more than $1,000 a day during the period he is in wrongful possession of such public lands.

No cutting of timber will be allowed on ungranted lands without an authorization from the Lieutenant-Governor-in-Council.  Failure to report, at the expiration of a permit, the quality and character of trees cut on a location will in future be punishable by a fine of ten dollars a day.  No sawmill may be established on Crown lands and less than a mile from any timber limits without special authorization from the Department on penalty of a similar fine.

The plant of the Wayagamack Pulp & Paper Co., of Three Rivers, Que., is now operating to capacity, turning out about 240 tons of kraft pulp daily and 150 tons of kraft paper.  The fact that the export demand for kraft paper has revived to such a marked extent is accepted, as auguring well for the future, and an active year for the district is now conceded.  It is understood that the enquiry for Wayagamack's products comes to a considerable extent from the company's customers in the United States, while enquiries are being received in gratifying measure from foreign countries.  One of these has been Japan, which has been a good buyer in the past.

On the North Shore of the province of New Brunswick where the economic conditions have been anything but cheerful for many months the signs of renewed activity are apparent on every side.  Arrangements are being made for the opening and running of mills that have remained idle for many months and in some instances for over a year.  Bathurst is looking forward to the re-opening of the Gloucester Lumber and Trading Company's mill, the Northern Workmen's mill and also to the resumption of the larger milling activities of the Bathurst Company, Ltd.  In the Miramichi district a similar state of affairs exists.  Further north Campbellton, which did not suffer as heavily as other sections during the prolonged depression owing to its railroad activities, is also lining up and the anticipations are that the lumbering conditions are slowly but surely working back to normal.

Donald Urquhart, well-known manufacturer and exporter, passed away recently at Hensall, Ont., after a month's illness.  He first embarked in business in Thamesville, and after a few years moved to

Hensall where he established and carried on until recently an extensive lumber, grain and milling business. He is survived by his wife and two daughters. Mr. Urquhart was in the 77th year of his age.

The Nashwaak Pulp & Paper Co., St. John, N. B., have closed down recently for an indefinite period. It is announced that the conditions of the pulp market was the reason for the cessation of operation. About 200 men are thrown out of employment.

Fire recently visited the town of Picton, Ont., and destroyed the planing mill, stables, flour and grist mill of Hyatt & Hart. The origin of the fire is unknown. It is thought to have been started from electric wiring. The damage is estimated to be $20,000 and is partially covered by insurance, the greatest loss being on the machinery. All the horses of the firm were saved.

At a meeting of the board of directors of the Bridge River Timber & Manufacturing Co., Ltd., held recently in Montreal, E. J. L'Esperance was elected a member of the board, which, with the addition named, is now composed as follows.—C. B. Graddon, president; Herbert Grier, Hon. W. H. Sharpe, M. J. McNeill and Patrick Donnelly.

E. D. Warner, who for some time has been with the Kingston Road Lumber Co., is once more on the road selling for the Adams River Lumber Co. and the Associated Mills. He is associated with J. T. Todd, who has opened an office at 1305 Bank of Hamilton Building, Toronto.

R. S. Gilchrist, for the past three years with the Boake Mfg. Co., Limited, has been appointed sales manager of the firm, succeeding W. J. Markle, now manager of the Consumers' Lumber Co., Hamilton. Mr. Gilchrist spent several years with the Evans Co., of Sudbury, and during the war was with the R. A. F. in the engineering headquarters, after which he joined the Boake Mfg. Co.

The McNeil Lumber Co., Limited, of Montreal, Que., recently applied for membership in the National Hardwood Lumber Association, Chicago, Ill. The annual meeting of the latter body will be held in Chicago on June 22nd and 23rd. It will mark the silver anniversary of the organziation which is now one of the most important and influential in the whole field of trade bodies.

Armstrong & Savage, Limited, wholesale and retail lumber dealers, have taken over the yard and business formerly conducted by the Eastern Wrecking Co. at 2647 Danforth Ave., Toronto. E. E. Armstrong is the president of the company; H. C. Strange, secretary-treasurer and Wm. Barratt, who was formerly with the Canada Lumber Co., at Weston, is the manager of the company.

Among the most encouraging developments in the newsprint industry of late, is the annoucement of an order for 14,000 tons, received by Price Bros. & Co., Limited, for export to England. This is said to be the first English order for Canadian newsprint received in Quebec since the war. The order is from the London Daily Express and calls for delivery over a period of nine months. The first shipment of 1,000 tons will be made on March 11th.

J. L. McNicol of Hamilton, formerly assistant paper controller for Canada under the War-Measures Act, left recently for Siam to assume the duties of pulp and paper expert for the Siamese Government with whom he has enterd into a two-year contract. He will establish and put into operation a complete pulp and paper mill for the government of Siam and will afterwards train the youth of that country in the art of pulp and paper-making.

In the 61st annual report of the Crown Land Department of New Brunswick, extensive information is given respecting the progress that had been made up to the close of the last fiscal year with the survey of the Crown lands of the province which has been going on for several years. The area covered up to October 31, 1921, was 3,951,-610 acres, or approximately 6,174 square miles. Of this area the drafting of the timber plans and compiling of the timber estimates has been completed for 3,645,899 acres, or approximately 5,697 square miles.

The sulphate pulp mill of the Canada Paper Company is no longer in operation in accordance with the judgment of the Supreme Court. Some time ago, the Supreme Court confirmed the judgment of a lower court, in the action taken by A. J. Brown, K. C., of Montreal, to prevent the company from using sulphate and soda for the manufacture of paper at the plant at Windsor Mills, P. Q. Mr. Brown claimed the odor from the use of sulphate and soda prevented him from enjoying his country residence. The closing of the plant throws about 75 men out of work.

A provincial charter has been granted to the Toronto Hardwood Lumber Co., with headquarters in Toronto and a capital stock of $40,000. The new organization is an associate one of the Toronto Veneer Co., 1104 Queen St., West, and among the incorporators are,—Joseph A. Houde, Wm. A. Dugit, Herbert T. Brewitt, W. R. Jones and Ernest Houde, all of whom are associated with the Toronto Veneer Co. The Toronto Hardwood Lumber Co. will handle all kinds of hardwoods, both foreign and domestic, and is engaging in the business both in a wholesale and retail way. The yards are at the corner of Atlantic Ave. and the G. T. R.

## This Mark of Dependability

There are many substitutes for the Genuine Oak-tanned product. To avoid being misled, always look for the Oak Leaf trade mark. The genuine product always bears this mark.

# Mr. Mill Owner

### —are you tired of accepting substitutes?

There was a time when out of necessity or for patriotic reasons you were asked to accept substitutes for the genuine in the articles you wore, ate or used. Often these were unsatisfactory and in the end more expensive.

Particularly is this true of belting.

You may be quoted prices which at first seam cheaper than the price of a D. K. McLAREN GENUINE BRITISH OAK-TANNED LEATHER BELT but it is well to remember that belting costs are based on ultimate service, not the purchase price.

For you, Mr. Millman who are tired of accepting substitutes, demand the genuine—made by

## D·K·M̄cLAREN LIMITED

| Head Office and Factory: | 351 St. James Street, MONTREAL |
|---|---|

| TORONTO, ONT. | VANCOUVER, B.C. | St. JOHN, N.B. |
|---|---|---|
| 194 King St. W. | 334 Cordova St. W. | 90 Germain St. |

## ALPHABETICAL INDEX TO ADVERTISERS

Tractor and Train at foot of 35% down grade from Fish's Camp.

# THE LINN LOGGING TRACTOR

## Designed and developed for winter log hauling, in the North Woods

To fulfill all requirements of the Northern Logger a tractor must:—
Haul heavy trains of sleighs down steep sandhills and around sharp curves.
Haul with absolute safety over lakes and rivers, where the ice is sometimes not thicker than fourteen inches.
Haul heavy trains over main hauls over all encountered grades—to landings.
Have carrying capacity on itself, so that it can be used for supply haulage over Portage roads.
Must have a fast high speed so that return trips to rollways may be rapid.
Must be foolproof and easily operated and controlled.
All these requirements are fulfilled only, by The Linn Logging Tractor.
Ask the operator who uses Linn.

*—Logging Department—*

## MUSSENS LIMITED

Dubrule Building                    MONTREAL

*Installation at the Housing Corporation, Waltham, Mass.*

## A Vacuum Cleaner at Every Cutting Head

That is exactly what a correctly designed collecting and conveying system means in your plant.

But the system must be installed so that the mill may be kept entirely free from refuse and waste, even when you are running at maximum speed and capacity. There are many other problems connected with your output which must also be taken into consideration.

And that is where the long, varied experience of our collecting and conveying specialists can be of inestimable value to you.

Our engineers will be glad to look over your plant—without the slightest obligation.

*Send for Catalog No. 261*

Sturtevant
PUTS AIR TO WORK

## B. F. STURTEVANT COMPANY OF CANADA, LIMITED
TORONTO  -  GALT  -  MONTREAL

—Territorial Representatives—

Empire Engineering & Supply Co., Edmonton, Alta.—Fryer-Barker Co., Vancouver, B.C.—Kipp-Kelly Ltd., Winnipeg, Man.

# CANADA LUMBERMAN BUYERS' DIRECTORY

The following regulations apply to all advertisers:—Eighth page, every issue, three headings;
quarter page, six headings; half page, twelve headings; full page, twenty-four headings

**ALLIGATORS**
Payette Company, P.
West, Peachy & Sons

**BABBITT METAL**
Canada Metal Company
General Supply Co. of Canada, Ltd.

**BALE TIES**
Canada Metal Co.
Laidlaw Bale Tie Company

**BAND MILLS**
Hamilton Company, William
Waterous Engine Works Company
Yates Machine Company, P. B.

**BAND SAW BLADES**
Simonds Mfg. Co.

**BAND RESAWS**
Mershon & Company, W. B.

**BARKERS**
Bertrand, F. X., La Compagnie Manu-
factiere.
Smith Foundry & Machine Co.

**BEARING METAL**
Canada Metal Co.
Beveridge Supply Co., Ltd.

**BEDSTEADS (STEEL)**
Simmons Limited

**BELT DRESSING**
Dominion Belting Co.
General Supply of Canada, Ltd.

**BELTING**
Canadian Consolidated Rubber Co.
Dominion Belting Co.
General Supply Company
Goodhue & Co., J. L.
Gutta Percha & Rubber Company
D. K. McLaren, Limited
McLaren Belting Company, J. C.
York Belting Co.

**BLOWERS**
Reed & Co., Geo. W.
B. F. Sturtevant Co. of Canada, Ltd.
Toronto Blower Company

**BOILERS**
Engineering & Machine Works of
Canada
Hamilton Company, William
Waterous Engine Works Company

**BOILER PRESERVATIVE**
Beveridge Supply Company
Shell-Bar, Boice Supply Co. Ltd.

**BOX MACHINERY**
Yates Machine Company, P. B.

**CABLE CONVEYORS**
Engineering & Machine Works of
Canada.
Hamilton Company, Wm.
Waterous Engine Works Company

**CAMP SUPPLIES**
Davies Company, William
Dr. Bell Veterinary Wonder Co.
Johnson, A. H.
Turner & Sons, J. J.
Woods Manufacturing Company, Ltd.

**CANT HOOKS**
General Supply Co. of Canada, Ltd.
Pink Company, Thomas

**CEDAR**
Bury & Co., Robt.
Cameron Lumber Co.
Canadian Western Lumber Company
Chesbro, R. G.

Dry Wood Lumber Co.
Fesserton Timber Company
McElroy Lumber Co., Ltd.
Muir & Kirkpatrick
Rose, McLaurin, Limited
Terry & Gordon
Thurston-Flavelle Lumber Company
Vancouver Lumber Company
Victoria Lumber & Mfg. Co.

**CHAINS**
Canadian Link-Belt Company, Ltd.
General Supply Co. of Canada, Ltd.
Engineering & Machine Works of
Canada
Hamilton Company, William
Pink & Co., Thomas
Waterous Engine Works Company

**CLOTHING**
Woods Mfg. Company

**CONVEYOR MACHINERY**
Canadian Link-Belt Company. Ltd.
General Supply Co. of Canada, Ltd.
Hamilton Company, Wm.
Hopkins & Co., Ltd., F. H.
Waterous Engine Works Company

**CORDWOOD**
McClung, McLellan & Berry

**COUPLING (Shaft)**
Engineering & Machine Works of
Canada

**CRANES**
Hopkins & Co., Ltd., F. H.
Canadian Link-Belt Company

**CUTTER-HEADS**
Shimer Cutter Head Company

**CYPRESS**
Wistar, Underhill & Nixon

**DERRICKS AND DERRICK
FITTINGS**
Hopkins & Co., Ltd., F. H.

**DOORS**
Canadian Western Lumber Co.
Gardiner, P. W. & Son
Mason, Gordon & Co.
Midland Wood Products, Ltd.
Terry & Gordon

**DRAG SAWS**
Gerlach Company, Peter
Hamilton Company. William

**DRYERS**
Coe Manufacturing Company
B. F. Sturtevant Co. of Canada, Ltd.

**DUST COLLECTORS**
Reed & Co., Geo. W.
B. F. Sturtevant Co. of Canada, Ltd.
Toronto Blower Company

**EDGERS**
Hamilton Company, Ltd., William
Green Company, G. Walter
Long Mfg. Company, E.
Payette Company, P.
Waterous Engine Works Company

**ELEVATING AND CONVEYING
MACHINERY**
Canadian Belt-Link Company, Ltd.
Engineering & Machine Works of
Canada
Hamilton Company, William
Waterous Engine Works Company

**ENGINES**
Engineering & Machine Works of
Canada
Hamilton Company. William

Payette Company, P.
Waterous Engine Works Company

**EXCELSIOR MACHINERY**
Elmira Machinery & Transmission
Company

**EXHAUST FANS**
B. F. Sturtevant Co. of Canada, Ltd.
Toronto Blower Company

**EXHAUST SYSTEMS**
Reed & Co., Geo. W.
B. F. Sturtevant Co. of Canada, Ltd.
Toronto Blower Company

**FIBRE BOARD**
Manley Chew

**FILES**
Disston & Sons, Henry
Simonds Canada Saw Company

**FIR**
Apex Lumber Co.
Associated Mills, Limited
Bainbridge Lumber Company
Cameron Lumber Co.
Canadian Western Lumber Co.
Canfield, P. L.
Chesbro, R. G.
Dry Wood Lumber Co.
Fesserton Timber Co.
Grier & Sons, Ltd., G. A.
Heeney, Percy E.
Knox Brothers
Mason, Gordon & Co.
McElroy Lumber Co. Ltd.
Robertson & Hacket Sawmills
Rose, McLaurin, Limited
Terry & Gordon
Timberland Lumber Company
Timms, Phillips & Co.
Underhill Lumber Co.
Vancouver Lumber Company
Vanderhoof Lumber Co.
Victoria Lumber & Mfg. Co.

**FIRE BRICK**
Beveridge Supply Co., Ltd.
Elk Fire Brick Company of Canada
Shell-Bar, Boice Supply Co. Ltd.

**FIRE FIGHTING APPARATUS**
Waterous Engine Works Company

**FITTINGS**
Crane Limited

**FLOORING**
Cameron Lumber Co.
Chesbro, R. G.
Long-Bell Lumber Company

**GEARS (Cut)**
Smart-Turner Machine Co.

**GUARDS (Machinery and Window)**
Canada Wire & Iron Goods Co.

**HARDWOODS**
Anderson Lumber Company, C. G.
Anderson, Shreiner & Mawson
Atlantic Lumber Company
Barrett, Wm.
Bury & Co., Robt.
Cameron & Co.
Edwards & Co., W. C.
Fassett Lumber Co., Ltd.
Fesserton Timber Co.
Gillespie, James
Gloucester Lumber & Trading Co.
Grier & Son, G. A.
Hart, Hamilton & Jackson
Heeney, Percy E.

Knox Brothers
Mason & Co., Geo.
McDonagh Lumber Co.
McLennan Lumber Company
McClung, McLellan & Berry
Pedwell Hardwood Lumber Co.
W. & J. Sharples.
Spencer, Limited, C. A.
Strong, G. M.
Summers, James R.
Webster & Brother, James

**HARDWOOD FLOORING**
Grier & Son, G. A.

**HARNESS**
Beal Leather Co., R. M.

**HEMLOCK**
Anderson Lumber Company. C. G
Anderson, Shreiner & Mawson
Bartram & Ball
Beck Lumber Co.
Bourgouin, H.
Canadian General Lumber Company
Edwards & Company, W. C.
Fesserton Timber Co.
Grier & Sons, Ltd., G. A.
Hart, Hamilton & Jackson
Hocken Lumber Company
Mason, Gordon & Co.
McCormack Lumber Co.
McDonagh Lumber Co.
McElroy Lumber Co., Ltd.
Robertson & Hacket Sawmills
Spanish River Lumber Co.
Spencer, Limited, C. A.
Stalker, Douglas A.
Terry & Gordon
Vancouver Lumber Co.
Vanderhoof Lumber Co.

**HOISTING AND HAULING
ENGINES**
General Supply Co. of Canada, Ltd.
Hopkins & Co., Ltd., F. H.

**HOSE**
General Supply Co. of Canada, Ltd.
Gutta Percha & Rubber Company

**INSURANCE**
Barton & Ellis Co.
Burns Underwriting Co.
Hardy & Co., E. D.
Lumbermen's Underwriting Alliance
Rankin Benedict Underwriting Co.

**INTERIOR FINISH**
Cameron Lumber Co.
Canadian Western Lumber Co.
Canfield, P. L.
Eagle Lumber Company
Mason, Gordon & Co.
Rose, McLaurin, Limited
Terry & Gordon

**KILN DRIED LUMBER**
Bury & Co., Robt.

**KNIVES**
Disston & Sons, Henry
Simonds Canada Saw Company
Waterous Engine Works Company

**LARCH**
Otis Staples Lumber Co.

**LATH**
Anderson, Shreiner & Mawson
Apex Lumber Co.
Austin & Nicholson
Beck Lumber Co.
Brennen & Sons, F. W.
Cameron Lumber Co.
Canadian General Lumber Company
Carew Lumber Co., John
Chaleurs Bay Mills
Dadson, A. T.
Dupuis, Limited, J. P.

81

Eagle Lumber Company
Fassett Lumber Co., Ltd.
Foley Lumber Company
Fraser Bryson Lumber Co., Ltd.
Gloucester Lumber & Grading Co.
Grier & Sons, Ltd., G. A.
Harris Tie & Timber Company, Ltd.
Larkin Co., C. A.
Mason & Co., Geo.
McLennan Lumber Company
Miller, W. H. Co.
New Ontario Colonization Company
Otis Staples Lumber Company
Power Lumber Co.
Price Bros. & Company
Shevlin-Clarke Co.
Spencer, Limited, C. A.
Terry & Gordon
U. G. G. Sawmills, Limited
Union Lumber Company
Victoria Harbor Lumber Company

**LATH BOLTERS**

General Supply Co. of Canada, Ltd.
Hamilton Company, Wm.
Payette & Company, P.

**LOCOMOTIVES**

Engineering & Machine Works of Canada
General Supply Co. of Canada, Ltd.
Hopkins & Co., Ltd., F. H.
Climax Manufacturing Company
Montreal Locomotive Works

**LINK-BELT**

Canadian Link-Belt Company
Hamilton Company, Wm.

**LOCOMOTIVE CRANES**

Canadian Link-Belt Company, Ltd.
Hopkins & Co. ,Ltd., F. H.

**LOGGING ENGINES**

Engineering & Machine Works of Canada
Hopkins & Co., Ltd., F. H.
Mussens Ltd.

**LOG HAULER**

Engineering & Machine Works of Canada
Green Company, G. Walter
Holt Manufacturing Co.
Hopkins & Co., Ltd., F. H.
Payette Company, P.

**LOGGING MACHINERY AND EQUIPMENT**

General Supply Co. of Canada, Ltd.
Hamilton Company, William
Holt Manufacturing Co.
Hopkins & Co., Ltd., F. H.
Payette Company, P.
Waterous Engine Works Company
West, Peachey & Sons
Mussens Ltd.

**LUMBER EXPORTS**

Fletcher Corporation

**LUMBER TRUCKS**

Hamilton Company, Wm.
Waterous Engine Works Company

**LUMBERMEN'S BOATS**

Adams Engine Company
Gidley Boat Co.
West, Peachey & Sons

**LUMBERMEN'S CLOTHING**

Kitchen Overall & Shirt Co.

**MATTRESSES**

Simmons Limited

**METAL REFINERS**

Canada Metal Company

**OAK**

Long-Bell Lumber Company

**PACKING**

Beveridge Supply Company
Gutta Percha & Rubber Company

**PANELS**

Bury & Co., Robt.

**PAPER**

Beveridge Supply Co., Ltd.
Price Bros. & Co.

**PINE**

Anderson Lumber Company, C. G.
Anderson, Shreiner & Mawson
Atlantic Lumber Co.
Austin & Nicholson
Barratt, William
Beck Lumber Co.
Cameron & Co.
Cameron Lumber Co.
Canadian General Lumber Company
Canadian Western Lumber Co.
Canfield, P. L.
Cheshro, R. G.
Cleveland-Sarnia Sawmills Company
Cox, Long & Company
Dadson, A. T.
Dudley, Arthur N.
Eagle Lumber Company
Edwards & Co., W. C.
Excelsior Lumber Company
Fesserton Timber Company
Fraser-Bryson Lumber Co., Ltd.
Gillies Bros., Limited
Gloucester Lumber & Trading Co.
Gordon & Co., George
Goodday & Company, H. R.
Grier & Sons, Ltd., G. A.
Harris Tie & Timber Company, Ltd.
Hart, Hamilton & Jackson
Hettler Lumber Company, Herman H.
Hocken Lumber Company
Julien, Roch
Lay & Haight
Lloyd, W. Y.
Loggie Co., W. S.

Long-Bell Lumber Company
Mason, Gordon & Co.
Mason & Co., Geo.
McCormack Lumber Co.
McFadden & Malloy
McLennan Lumber Company
Montreal Lumber Company
Muir & Kirkpatrick
Northern Lumber Mills
Otis Staples Lumber Co.
Parry Sound Lumber Company
Pigeon River Lumber Co., Ltd.
Rolland Lumber Co.
W. & J. Sharples.
Shevlin-Clarke Co.
Spanish River Lumber Co.
Spencer, Limited, C. A.
Stalker, Douglas A.
Strong, G. M.
Summers, James R.
Terry & Gordon
Union Lumber Company
Victoria Harbor Lumber Co.
Watson & Todd, Limited

**PLANING MILL EXHAUSTERS**

Toronto Blower Co.

**PLANING MILL MACHINERY**

Mershon & Co., W. B.
B. F. Sturtevant Co. of Canada, Ltd.
Toronto Blower Co.
Yates Machine Company, P. B.

**PORK PACKERS**

Davies Company, William

**POSTS AND POLES**

Anderson, Shreiner & Mawson
Canadian Tie & Lumber Co.
Dupuis, Limited, J. P.
Eagle Lumber Company

# DUNLOP

## Means Transmission
## Belt Supremacy

### Note the Long Grain Rubber Friction

Dunlop "GIBRALTAR REDSPECIAL" has a Friction of Special Dunlop Rubber that retains its life indefinitely.

"Note the Long Grain Rubber Friction" as illustrated.

Elasticity has not been sacrificed for Abnormal Friction Pull.

*Also makers of High-Grade Conveyor and Elevator Belts; Packing, Hose, etc.*

## Dunlop Tire & Rubber Goods Co., Limited
Head Office and Factories: TORONTO          Branches in the Leading Cities

Harris Tie & Timber Co., Ltd.
Long-Bell Lumber Co.
Mason, Gordon & Co.
McLennan Lumber Company
Terry & Gordon

**POST GRINDERS**

Smith Foundry Co.

**PULLEYS AND SHAFTING**

Canadian Link-Belt Company
General Supply Co. of Canada, Ltd.
Green Company, G. Walter
Engineering & Machine Works of Canada
Hamilton Company, William

**PULP MILL MACHINERY**

Canadian Link-Belt Company, Ltd.
Engineering & Machine Works of Canada
Hamilton Company, William
Payette Company, P.
Waterous Engine Works Company

**PULPWOOD**

British & Foreign Agencies
D'Auteuil Lumber Co.
Price Bros. & Co.
Scott, Draper & Co.

**PUMPS**

General Supply Co. of Canada, Ltd.
Engineering & Machine Works of Canada
Hamilton Co., William
Hopkins & Co. ,Ltd., F. H.
Smart-Turner Machine Company
Waterous Engine Works Company

**RAILS**

Gartshore, John J.
Hopkins & Co. ,Ltd., F. H.

**ROOFINGS**

(Rubber, Plastic and Liquid)
Beveridge Supply Company
Reed & Co., Geo. W.

**RUBBER GOODS**

Dunlop Tire & Rubber Goods Co.
Gutta Percha & Rubber Company

**SASH**

Midland Woodworkers
Midland Wood Products, Ltd.

**SAWS**

Atkins & Company, E. C.
Disston & Sons, Henry
General Supply Co. of Canada, Ltd.
Gerlach Company, Peter
Green Company, G. Walter
Hoe & Company, R.
Radcliff Saw Mfg. Co.,
Shurly Co. Ltd., T. F.
Shurly-Dietrich Company
Simonds Canada Saw Company

**SAW GRINDERS**

Smith Foundry Co.

**SAW MILL LINK-BELT**

Canadian Link-Belt Company

**SAW MILL MACHINERY**

Canadian Link-Belt Company, Ltd.
General Supply Co. of Canada, Ltd.
G. Walter Green Co., Ltd.
Hamilton Company, William
La Compagnie Manufacture, F. X. Bertrand
Long Manufacturing Company, E.
Mershon & Company, W. B.
Parry Sound Lumber Company
Payette Company, P.
Waterous Engine Works Company
Yates Machine Co., P. B.

**SAW SHARPENERS**

Hamilton Company, William
Waterous Engine Works Company

**SAW SLASHERS**

Hamilton Company, Wm.
Payette Company, P.
Waterous Engine Works Company

**SHINGLES**

Apex Lumber Co.
Associated Mills, Limited
Brennen & Sons, F. W.
Cameron Lumber Co.
Campbell-MacLaurin Lumber Co.
Canadian Western Lumber Co.
Carew Lumber Co., John
Chaleurs Bay Mills
Cheshro, R. G.
D'Auteuil Lumber Co.
Dry Wood Lumber Co.
Eagle Lumber Company
Fraser, Companies Limited
Gillespie, James
Gloucester Lumber & Trading Co.
Grier & Sons, Limited, G. A.
Harris Tie & Timber Company, Ltd.
Heaps & Sons
Heeney, Percy E.
Mason, Gordon & Co.
McLennan Lumber Company
Miller Company, Ltd., W. H.
Rose, McLaurin, Limited
Stalker, Douglas A.
Terry & Gordon
Timms, Phillips & Co.
Vancouver Lumber Company
Vanderhoof Lumber Co.

**SHINGLE & LATH MACHINERY**

Green Company, C. Walter
Hamilton Company, William
Long Manufacturing Company, E.
Payette Company, P.
Smith Foundry Co.

**SILENT CHAIN DRIVES**

Canadian Link-Belt Company, Ltd.

**SLEEPING EQUIPMENT**

Simmons Limited

**SLEEPING ROBES**

Woods Mfg. Company, Ltd.

**SMOKESTACKS**

Hamilton Company, Wm.
Reed & Co., Geo. W.
Waterous Engine Works Company

**SNOW PLOWS**

Pink Company, Thomas

**SOLDERS**

Canada Metal Co.

**SPARK ARRESTORS**

Reed & Co., Geo. W.
Waterous Engine Works Company

**SPRUCE**

Anderson, Shreiner & Mawson
Barrett, Wm.
Cameron Lumber Co.
Campbell, McLaurin Lumber Co.
Canadian Western Lumber Co.
Cheshro, R. G.
Cox, Long & Co.
Dadson, A. T.
Dudley, Arthur N.
Fassett Lumber Co., Ltd.
Fraser, Companies Limited
Fraser-Bryson Lumber Company
Gillies Brothers
Gloucester Lumber & Trading Co.
Goodday & Company, H. R.

Grier & Sons, Ltd., G. A.
Harris Lumber Co., Frank H.
Hart, Hamilton & Jackson
Hocken Lumber Company
Julien, Roch
Larkin Co., C. A.
Lay & Haight
Lloyd, W. Y.
Loggie Co., W. S.
Mason, Gordon & Co.
McCormack Lumber Co.
McDonagh Lumber Co.
McElroy Lumber Co., Ltd.
McLennan Lumber Company
Muir & Kirkpatrick
New Ontario Colonization Company
Northern Lumber Mills
Pigeon River Lumber Co.
Power Lumber Co.
Price Bros. & Co.
Rolland Lumber Co.
Rose, McLaurin, Limited
W. & J. Sharples
Spencer, Limited, C. A.
Strong, G. M.
Terry & Gordon
U. G. G. Sawmills, Limited
Vanderhoof Lumber Co.

**STEAM SHOVELS**

Hopkins & Co., Ltd., F. H.

**STEEL CHAIN**

Canadian Link-Belt Company, Ltd.
Hopkins & Co.,Ltd., F. H.
Waterous Engine Works Company

**STEAM PLANT ACCESSORIES**

Waterous Engine Works Company

**STEEL BARRELS**

Smart-Turner Machine Co.

**STEEL DRUMS**

Smart-Turner Machine Co

**TARPAULINS**

Turner & Sons, J. J.
Woods Manufacturing Company, Ltd

**TANKS**

Hopkins & Co., Ltd., F. H.

**TENTS**

Turner & Sons, J. J.
Woods Mfg. Company

**TIES**

Austin & Nicholson
Carew Lumber Co., John
Canadian Tie & Lumber Co.
Chaleurs Bay Mills
D'Auteuil Lumber Co.
Gloucester Lumber & Trading Co.
Harris Tie & Timber Company. Ltd.
McLennan Lumber Company
Miller, W. H. Co.
Price Bros. & Co.
Scott, Draper & Co.
Terry & Gordon

**TIMBER BROKERS**

Bradley, R. R.
Cant & Kemp
Farnworth & Jardine
Wright, Graham & Co.

**TIMBER CRUISERS AND ESTIMATORS**

Savage & Bartlett.
Sewall, James W.

**TIMBER LANDS**

Department of Lands & Forests, Ont.

**TOWING MACHINES**

Corbet Foundry & Machine Co.
Payette Company, P.
West, Peachy & Sons

**TRACTORS**

Holt Manufacturing Co.
Hopkins & Company, Ltd., F. H.
Mussens Ltd.

**TRANSMISSION MACHINERY**

Canadian Link-Belt Company, Ltd.
Engineering & Machine Works of Canada
General Supply Co. of Canada, Ltd.
Grand Rapids Vapor Kiln
Hamilton Company, Wm.
Waterous Engine Works Company

**TURBINES**

Engineering & Machine Works of Canada
Hamilton Company, William
B. F. Sturtevant Co. of Canada, Ltd.

**VALVES**

Crane Limited

**VAPOR KILNS**

Grand Rapids Vapor Kiln
B. F. Sturtevant Co. of Canada, Ltd.

**VENEERS**

Bury & Co., Robt.

**VENEER DRYERS**

Coe Manufacturing Company
B. F. Sturtevant Co. of Canada, Ltd.

**VENEER MACHINERY**

Coe Machinery Company

**VETERINARY REMEDIES**

Dr. Bell Veterinary Wonder Co.
Johnson, A. H.

**WARPING TUGS**

West, Peachey & Sons

**WATER WHEELS**

Engineering & Machine Works of Canada
Hamilton Company, William

**WIRE**

Canada Metal Co.
Laidlaw Bale Tie Company
Canada Wire & Iron Goods Co.

**WIRE CLOTH**

Canada Wire & Iron Goods Co.

**WIRE ROPE**

Canada Wire & Iron Goods Co.
Hopkins & Co. ,Ltd. F. H.
Dominion Wire Rope Co.
Greening Wire Co., B.

**WOODWORKING MACHINERY**

General Supply Co. of Canada, Ltd.
Long Manufacturing Company, E.
Mershon & Company, W. B.
Waterous Engine Works Company
Yates Machine Company, P. B.

**WOOD PRESERVATIVES**

Beveridge Supply Company

**WOOD PULP**

Austin & Nicholson
New Ontario Colonization Co
Power Lumber Co.

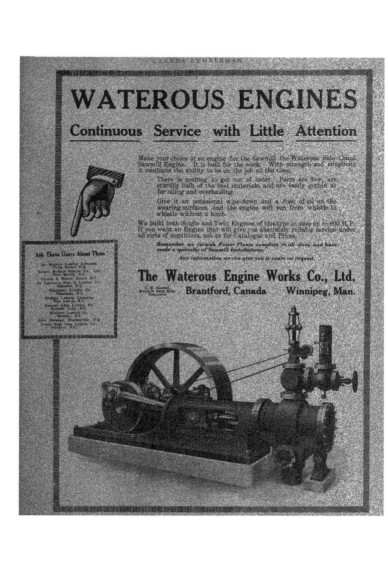

# TWO MINUTES

IT takes just two minutes to write us a letter asking how International Time Recorders will save money for you.

It will be the most profitable two minutes you have spent so far this year.

Why not do it now?

## International Business Machines Co., Ltd.

F. E. MUTTON, Vice-President and General Manager

Head Office and Factory:   300-350 Campbell Avenue, Toronto

HALIFAX, 44 Granville St. ST. JOHN, 39 Dock St.   QUEBEC, 306 Merger Bldg
MONTREAL, 1 and 8 Notre Dame St. OTTAWA, 190 Queen St.  TORONTO, 36
Grain St.  HAMILTON, Bank of Hamilton Bldg. LONDON, 480 Richmond St.
WALKERVILLE, 44 Lincoln Rd.  WINNIPEG, 207 McDermott Ave.  VANCOUVER,
300 Cambie St.  SASKATOON, 354 Third Ave. S.

*Also manufacturers of International Dayton Scales and International Electric Tabulators*

Vol. 42     Toronto, April 15, 1922     No. 8

# Canada Lumberman

*Founded 1880*

# "HAMILTON" LATH MACHINES

## "Hamilton" Lath Mill

All iron frame, exceptionally heavy, rigid and strongly braced, top and bottom rolls power driven. Extra wide table.

Carries six 14" saws.

Guaranteed capacity 50,000 lath in ten hours.

**Get Our Special Catalogue**

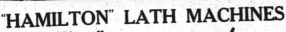

## "Hamilton" Lath Bolter

Extra heavy all iron frame, Feed Rolls driven, top and bottom, fitted with adjustable steel guide.

Carries four 20" saws. Saws readily changed for filing.

Both of above Machines Carried in Stock

We also manufacture single end Bolters, double end Picket Machines, and also Combined Lath Mill & Bolter for use where space in your mill is limited.

Write us for prices.

### WILLIAM HAMILTON CO., LIMITED, Peterboro, Ontario

Agents:—J. L. Neilson & Co., Winnipeg, Man.

# NATURE PRODUCES the TREES

The Lumber produced is poor or good in proportion to the care and attention given to manufacture.

Handling well manufactured Lumber is a serious business with us.

Properly manufactured
Properly graded
And shipped as and when you
want it.

*Try us with that order you have in mind*

## UNION LUMBER COMPANY LIMITED
701 DOMINION BANK BUILDING
TORONTO            CANADA

# LUMBER
## —Wanted—
## Mill-cuts in

# W. Pine
# Hemlock
# Birch
# Elm
# Maple

## C. G. Anderson Lumber Company, Limited

Manufacturers and Strictly Wholesale
Dealers in Lumber

SALES OFFICE

### 705 Excelsior Life Building
## Toronto

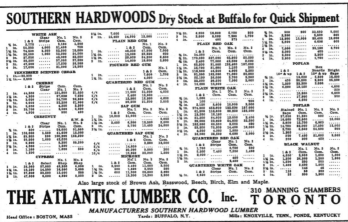

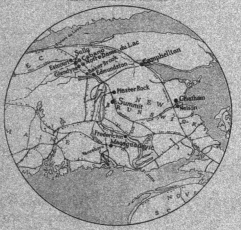

## ARKANSAS SOFT PINE SATIN-LIKE INTERIOR TRIM

ITS FINE GRAIN, close texture and tough fiber are particularly suited to the type of work illustrated. A wood of perfect physical and chemical make-up for white enamel, eliminating, as it definitely does, every hazard of raised grain or ultimate discoloration.

Technical literature, samples, both finished and natural, sent by the Bureau on request. Write mills direct for price

*All stock bearing the Arkansas Soft Pine trade mark is manufactured and sold exclusively by the following companies:*

| | |
|---|---|
| Arkansas Lumber Company · · · Warren, Arkansas | Gates Lumber Company · · · · · Wilmar, Arkansas |
| Cotton Belt Lumber Company · Bearden, Arkansas | Ozan-Graysonia Lumber Company · · Prescott, Ark. |
| Crossett Lumber Company · · · · Crossett, Arkansas | Southern Lumber Company · · · Warren, Arkansas |
| Eagle Lumber Company · · · · Eagle Mills, Arkansas | Stout Lumber Company · · · · Thornton, Arkansas |
| Edgar Lumber Company · · · · · Wesson, Arkansas | Union Saw Mill Company · · · · · Huttig, Arkansas |
| Fordyce Lumber Company · · · · Fordyce, Arkansas | *Sales Office, Boatmen's Bank Bldg., St. Louis, Mo.* |
| Freeman-Smith Lumber Company · · Millville, Ark. | Wisconsin & Arkansas Lumber Co. · Malvern, Ark. |

COMPOSING THE

# Arkansas Soft Pine Bureau
LITTLE ROCK · ARKANSAS

CANADA LUMBERMAN

**DOUGLAS FIR LUMBER**
**RED CEDAR SHINGLES**

## The Question of Supply

During the past two months our mill connections have been handicapped by unusual weather conditions, but we are glad to state that we are now in a position to give our usual prompt service in your requirements.

**Timms Phillips & Co., Ltd.**
Vancouver, B. C.

TORONTO OFFICE: Canada Permanent Bldg.
Phone Adel. 6490
MONTREAL OFFICE: 23 Marconi Bldg.
Phone M. 2999

# BUY
## BRITISH COLUMBIA
# Red Cedar Shingles

The life of a British Columbia Red Cedar Shingle Roof can almost be gauged by the life of the nail with which the shingle is nailed in place. Judging from available data, the average life of the ordinary steel wire nail, which has been in such common use, is only from seven to twelve years. Some wire nails will last longer, depending upon the condition of exposure, climate and similar features, but considering our climate as a whole, at the end of from seven to twelve years a large percentage of wire nails will have rusted either completely through or so extensively that the first strong wind will complete the work. The shingles that have been held in position by such nails are then free to work down, permitting rains or melting snows to leak through and damage the interior of the structure. Examination will disclose that the fibre of the shingle itself is still in perfect condition, and a leaky roof, in the majority of occasions is due entirely to the use of faulty nails, but the average home owner, placed at such inconvenience, will not stop to reason this out and the poor wooden shingle comes in for more unjust abuse.

There are several kinds of nails which experience has proven will give lasting satisfaction, and the wise dealer will advise his customers of these satisfactory nails. A pure zinc shingle nail meets all the demands of durability required. Its principal drawback is its high cost and a slight tendency to bend under careless driving. Galvanized wire nails theoretically are rust proof, and if the galvanized coating is properly applied, and of sufficient thickness, such a nail will last as long as the shingle it holds in place. The life of this shingle roof, properly applied with these nails then is from 40 to 50 years. Pure iron nails, or the old cut or wrought nails are ideal but difficult to secure. Copper nails also constitute a perfect shingle nail.

# Is Your Fire Protection Equipment Adequate ?

Fire Hose is a necessary feature of the equipment of every Factory, Mill or Public Building.

The outlay is small in comparison to the loss and inconvenience that even a small fire entails, let alone a fire that destroys an entire plant.

*Quick action is essential to prevent a bad "blaze."*

That quick action can only be secured where your plant is adequately prepared for such an emergency.

## Dunlop Mill Fire Hose

offers you efficient Fire protection through being of a quality that stands up under the kind of service that a hose of this type has to give.

The Dunlop Hose Service Department will be glad to estimate on your requirements.

## Dunlop Tire & Rubber Goods Co., Limited

Head Office and Factories: TORONTO
Branches in the Leading Cities

*Also makers of High-Grade Water Hose, Belting, Packing, etc.*

# THE GREAT NATIONAL LUMBER JOURNAL

Pioneer and Leader
in the Industry

Canada Lumberman
Founded 1880

Recognized Authority
for Forty Years

Vol. 42        Toronto, April 15, 1922        No. 8

# Logging By Railroad Has Decided Advantages

The "Canada Lumberman" has recently been presenting some interesting information in regard to the operating cost and maintenance of logging railroads as a means of transporting hardwoods from the bush to the scene of their conversion into lumber.

Among organizations that have operated a logging railroad for the last seventeen years, is the Fassett Lumber Co., Limited, of Fassett, Labelle county, Quebec. Their line, which was started in 1905, is known as the "Salmon River & Northern Railroad". The company have constructed since that time 42 miles in all, of which at present they have in use 28 miles, including branch lines and switches. The steel used is 56 lbs. and the company find it heavy enough except that they would recommend a heavier rail for an operation covering a period of years. The road is a standard gauge one and all the main line is ballasted.

When building through a rough, mountainous country, such as this line traverses, the company naturally ran up against what, at first, seemed insurmountable obstacles in the way of rock and boggy places, but so far they have always managed to overcome them without too great an expense. They have at all times figured the percentage of grade against the load. They have no grade at the present time greater than 3 per cent against the load on the mainline, and the highest grade with load is 5.4 per cent.

One instance, which the company cites, is worthy of mention. They pulled up a grade of 9 per cent over 30,000,000 feet of logs and 20,000 cords of 4 foot hardwood, not saying anything about bark and pulp. This was done without any serious mishap, "but operating on grades as steep as this is dangerous work and we aim to keep away from them as far as possible," said E. J. Staniforth, manager of the company.

Regarding costs of construction, it is not possible to give this in detail, but, taking grading since 1912—some ten years back,—the company built 21 miles of standard gauge railway. The average cost covering this period for grading—ready for ties and steel—was $2,410. per mile. This average is high as when labor was at its peak, the cost ran as much as 250 per cent higher than under normal conditions. Ties are usually made along the line and run from 18 to 35 cents each, according to the distance they have to be hauled to the track. The cost of laying the steel runs from $300 to $500 per mile, according to the conditions.

Speaking of ballasting, Mr. Staniforth says the outlay for this depends on the distance the ballast has to be hauled. The loading in itself is not a large factor as the company uses a grab bucket in connection with one of their steam loaders, which will load in one day twenty cars.

### The Equipment and Its Operation

The equipment of the road consists of the following rolling stock which is now in service,—3 Shay-geared locomotives, of 70, 65 and 50 tons respectively; two Barnhardt steam loaders, 55 logging cars and 25 flat cars. The locomotives are of a type particularly adapted to logging railroads and will handle 20 to 22 cars of logs each trip to the plant, representing about 65,000 feet at a haul. Mr. Staniforth says the company have not had any other type of geared locomotive and he believed the ones in use are equal to anything on the market for this class of work.

The Barnhardt loaders which were built by the Marion Steam Shovel Co., of Marion, O., are similar in operation to a steam shovel, and will handle from 600 to 1,000 logs per day, according to the size of the log. Three men, (one engineer and two tong hookers) will load 22 cars a day under favorable conditions. The loaders pull themselves from car to car by cable, each car being equipped with

Hardwood activities, of the Fassett Lumber Co., of Fassett, Que., showing stacks of bark which are being loaded as well as a log train in operation

Another view of a log train on its way to the plant of the Fassett Lumber Co. at Fassett, Que.

steel rails for this purpose, and are economical and adaptable to this class of timber.

Each of the fifty-five logging cars is of a skeleton type. The bunks are 12 feet and are equipped with binding chain and two steel rails running the full length of the car for the steam loader to operate on. The twenty-five flat cars of the firm are of the ordinary type, 32 feet long and are racked for hauling 4-foot cordwood of which the company freight each year from 10,000 to 12,000 cords.

So far as the cost of maintenance is concerned, Mr. Staniforth says the Fassett Lumber Co. cannot give the cost of upkeep of the track on a mileage basis. They have taken a period of ten years, 1912-22, and averaged the price per thousand feet, which includes freighting of logs, upkeep of rolling stock and maintenance of track, viz., $2.95 per thousand. This figure was based on a production of 162,500,000 feet. It is rather interesting comparing costs over this period. The highest peak over normal was 289 per cent. To-day the company's cost for this part of the operation are high owing to the heavy cost of coal, which is 107 per cent greater than normal on account of the excessive freight rates now in effect.

Mr. Staniforth says that much can be said pro and con in regard to logging by rail, but that he is not in a position to give any comparison of rail haul cost with river driving, as the Fassett Lumber Co. have never done anything extensively in the latter line. It seems to him, however, that the following facts speak out, and this is how Mr. Staniforth sums up the advantages of logging by rail :—

Logging by railroad enables you to manufacture hardwoods, which cannot be floated successfully or hauled any distance in quantities to a plant by any other method, without high cost.

The plant can be kept in operation the year round re-

Log train in operation on the limits of Fassett Lumber Co.

gardless of weather conditions, and the supply of logs is not subject to "conditions beyond your control," as in the case of floating the logs.

Investment in logging operations is smaller, owing to the fact that a large supply of logs has not to be carried over from year to year. In some operations logs are delivered to the mill as they are cut in the woods, without practically any surplus supply on hand. But in our operation, owing to the nature of the timberlands, a year's supply is usually delivered to the railroad during sleigh hauling. Of course, when the road is extended into the timberland from time to time, there is always a limited supply that can be skidded to the track without being hauled on sleighs.

There is no loss to be charged off for sinkage or loss of logs, as in the case of river driving.

Special timber bills can be cut and put on the market very quickly. Often orders can be accepted, timber cut, sawn and delivered on the job, inside of one week. Other products

One of the landings of the company.

such as hemlock bark, ties, pulpwood, posts, poles and cordwood, can be loaded direct on standard cars, and shipped to destination without further handling. This gives a revenue for that class of material which is usually left untouched in the woods, owing to the high cost of putting it on the market.

"In my opinion," Mr. Staniforth concludes, "logging by rail with a mixed timber proposition is the only practical method, providing, of course, you are in possession of sufficient stumpage to warrant the outlay. I think that a number of lumbermen are sceptical about an operation of this description on account of the initial cost and upkeep. I believe that a great many manufacturers are not getting any benefit from their hardwood stumpage, cutting softwoods and leaving the hardwoods to become over-matured, blown over, or destroyed by fire, which they must realize sooner or later means a serious loss.

# Standardization of Lumber Grades Needed

## Montreal Contractors Say That Variations in Quality, Though Nominally of the Same Character, are Wide—Interesting Views on Important Topic

At the last general meeting of the Montreal Builders' Exchange, a brief discussion of the standardization of lumber grades was followed by the appointment of a small committee to study the subject.

The complaint was that, owing to absence of definite grades, contractors received from different firms lumber varying widely in quality, although nominally of the same character and ordered under the same classification. For instance, merchantable spruce will differ very materially according to the mill, wholesaler or yard supplying lumber. It is suggested that the compilation and enforcement of positive grades will enable the contractor to order exactly what he requires and what he will expect to revevie, and will help the lumberman to the extent that he will be able to quote more accurately on definite specifications.

It is further suggested that it would put all lumbermen on an equality in competing for business and do away with any incentive to cut prices in the hope of securing orders and then making up for the low quotations by furnishing say, a large proportion of culls, when merchantable was called for. Even allowing for some inevitable differences, owing to the manufacture of lumber by various mills, it is contended that the differences are so wide as to call for a system of grading which will establish something approaching uniformity.

The following interviews with representative contracting firms in Montreal explain their opinions in greater detail.

### Says Montreal Gets all the Culls

A. Plamondon, of Arsenault & Plamondon, Limited, said.—Any one in the building trade in Montreal is impressed by the absence of any recognized standard in lumber used in construction. He is entirely at a loss in comparing the different prices quoted for this kind of material, either from retailers or wholesalers. What seems to be the height of unfavorable conditions is when lumber is ordered and unloaded at the works and then is refused by the inspector, architect or engineer. Unless the lumber merchant is willing to take it back, although no law can force him to do so, the contractor is obliged to dispose of this scrap lumber at a loss.

In these times of efficiency, when standards are adhered to in any other class of building material, such as cement, sand, stone, steel, etc., we fail, at the first glance, to understand the causes which are keeping lumber, one of the most important materials used in construction work, from obtaining a recognized standard upon which all those concerned can reply.

Inquiries from reliable sources in connection with this matter reveal the following facts: one of the main reasons for this state of affairs is a question of supply and demand, due to the poor quality of lumber employed in building construction. One other reason is the keen competition of buyers in their attempt to obtain the lowest prices without specifying any special quality of lumber. The market has developed to such an extent, that Montreal is recognized by the lumbermen of Canada and the States as the dumping ground of the continent for all kinds of cull lumber.

For instance, all lumber sold in Toronto is merchantable lumber, where no local dealer will handle culls, whereas Montreal will absorb any amount of this trash in building construction. Were it otherwise culls could be employed only for crating and the like.

To emphasize this point, I wish to mention the significant fact that on price lists furnished by Mills from time to time, to dealers, all over the Country, special attention is drawn at the bottom of the list that all culls will find a favorable market in Montreal, and will sell only $3.00 cheaper than the merchantable grades.

### Must be Superman to get out Even

The Montreal dealer today in order to meet competition must be an expert in buying cheap grade lumber and a superman in grading what he buys. For instance, let us call retail dealer "A" and the prospective buyer "B".

"A" buys from the mill 100,000 ft. B. M. of lumber of the following specified width:—5% of 4", 10% of 5", 15% of 6", 15% of 7", 12% of 8", 10% of 9", 10% of 10" and 20% of 11" and over. It cost him say $32.00 M. Ft. B.M. f.o.b. his yard. "B" the client, asks for a quotation on this lumber and informs "A" that dealers quoted him $30 00 M. ft. B. M. delivered on job. "A", to meet competition, will

have to juggle with his 100-M of lumber recently bought, and if he is an expert in the game will arrange his lumber in the following manner to return him a good profit:—He will separate prices in the following way:— His 11" and over at $40.00, 10" at $37.50, 9" at $36.00, 8" at $33.00, 7" at 32.00, 6" at $30.00, 5" at $29.00, 4" at $25.00. Then "A" will quote "B" a price of $29.00 M and will deliver a large proportion of 4" and 5" and mix a small percentage of 6" and 7".

Continuing Mr. Plamondon said, the Montreal dealers are not to blame for this state of affairs as they have to meet unfair competitions. They know that it would be to their advantage if lumber could be graded to a recognized standard, which would be accepted by the interested parties such as the Building Contractors, Architects and Engineers. The lumber merchants would then be on a fair level when they quoted prices for lumber with definite recognized standards, and furthermore by selling only merchantable lumber they could reduce their turnover by half, and make as much profit in proportion to what they make at present.

There is no doubt that it would be to the advantage of everyone concerned, especially to the wholesalers, who could base their quotations on something definite, if this question of grading lumber was standardized, and one way to arrive at this would be to specify the width of lumber when asking quotations.

To obtain the standardization of lumber we suggest that the Builders' Exchange of Montreal form a special committee for a study of this question of standardization of lumber, and officially ask the Lumbermen's Association, the Architects' Association of Quebec, and the Professional Engineers' Corporation, to submit their opinions upon this subject. Furthermore we think that the Builders' Exchange should ask those in charge of the Forest Products Laboratories, to make a special study of the question; we believe this bureau, which is composed of specialists, and which has obtained interesting developments in certain lines, would be of great help.

The construction industry is deeply interested in this matter and is anxious to receive any suggestions regarding the proposed plan, and will welcome any comment that will ensure enlightment on the matter, concluded Mr. Plamondon.

### Should Get Grade He Pays For

K. D. Church, president of the Montreal Builders' Exchange:— We want some means by which the contractor can make certain of getting what he orders. Under present conditions he is not sure that he will get the grade he pays for. The difficulty is not with the larger mills, but with the smaller ones, where apparently little or no grading is done. You will order say merchantable stock from one mill, and the same thing from another and find that there is a wide difference in the quality. The reputable firms will supply reliable lumber—they grade it, and if one firm can do this there is no reason why others cannot do the same. As regards orders given to the yards, I find that as a rule the goods come up to what has been ordered. In one instance I ordered some 2 in. lumber from a small mill and then found that it varied from 1½ to 2½ inches on the same specifications. We want to get together in order to avoid this matter on a basis which will help the contractor and lumberman, and do away with disputes regarding the quality of the lumber ordered and supplied.

T. A. Somerville, manager of E. G. M. Cape & Co., Ltd. This is a matter for the lumber firms, in so far as drawing up standardization rules is concerned. Our experience is that the only way to obtain what is ordered is to return the lumber if it does not come up to expectations. Naturally there will be some variation but good firms as a rule, supply according to orders.

H. C. Johnson, of the H. C. Johnson Co., Limited: We have found great varation in the lumber received from different lumbermen, al-

though the orders have been for identical grades. The only way to get satisfaction is to return the lumber if it is not up to expectations. Probably the establishment of grades would be of considerable value, but it would still be up to the contractor to see that he receives what he pays for. Grades are no protection against the dishonest lumberman or against any other class of trader. Comparatively few contractors know much about lumber and it might be a good thing if they would obtain more knowledge as to the various classes.

Douglas Bremner, of Norris, Bremner & Co., Limited: I think that the suggested grading rules would be of value to the contractor. Our experience has been similar to that of other contractors in ordering lumber—a considerable difference in the same class of stock according to the source of purchasing. Our complaint is not so much as to quality but as to sizes. In calculating the strength of certain work we order certain sizes of lumber, sometimes we find, however, that either the stock is too narrow or too thin, with the result that if used, the estimated strength of the work would be lessened. Moreover, we should be paying for more lumber than we received. Our experience is that it pays to buy good lumber, even of the cost be higher, as good lumber is the cheapest in the long run, of course, we regret any lumber which does not come up to what we order, but at the same time we would welcome any method which would lessen the chances of dispute.

## John Barry Joins the Silent Majority

Many friends in the lumber trade will regret to learn of the death of John Barry, who since 1885 had been associated with the historic firm of John B. Smith & Sons, Limited, Toronto. Mr. Barry had been suffering from an attack of influenza, but had rallied and was at the office a couple of days before his death. The end came rather suddenly-at his home on Indian Road, and caused a great shock to his host of acquaintances in all ranks of the industry.

The late Mr. Barry, who was 54 years of age leaves a widow, one son, Frank, (of John B. Smith & Sons,) and a daughter Mrs. Kennedy. He was a devout member of St. Cecilia's Church and his benefactions among the needy will long be remembered.

Mr. Barry was a practical lumberman and knew every operation from the felling of the tree to the marketing of the finished product. He spent several years in the woods for John B. Smith & Sons, and on the occasion of the annual excursion of the Ontario Retail Lumber Dealers' Association to North Bay and Lake Nipissing in August 1920 he conducted several lumbermen through the camps of the Indians on the French River Reserve, calling upon Chief Dokies and other leading members of the contingent who are descendants from the Chippawas. Mr. Barry was the life of the party on that outing, having captured a large porcupine which was exhibited among some of the late sleepers as a fine specimen of the "New Ontario bed-bug".

Mr. Barry was genial, kind-hearted and well thought of; a friend to everybody with whom he came in contact. For several years past he was manager of the lumber yards of John B. Smith & Sons, at the Dundas bridges, Toronto. He represented the firm on the road for a long period and was a welcome caller on every customer.

## Southwestern Retailers Will Meet in Windsor

At the annual meeting of the South Western Ontario Retail Lumber Dealers' Association, which will be held in the Scottish Rite rooms Windsor, on April 27th., it is expected that there will be a large attendance, and every preparation is being made by the local representative to give the visitors a cordial welcome. There will be morning and afternoon sittings. A number of important matters are to be discussed, officers will be elected for the ensuing year, and in the evening there will be a banquet tendered the delegates at which W. P. Flint, secretary of the Millwork Cost Bureau, of Chicago, will give an address.

The annual gathering of the South Western Ontario Retail Lumber Dealers' Association is always an important occasion and one of the outstanding features in retailers' meetings. It is believed that this year's session will be equally representative in character, fruitful in results and instructive in proceedings as any of the previous ones and there will be several features about it which will be worth while.

Every member should make it a point to be present in Windsor on Thursday April 27th.

## Rise in Values—Increase in Volume

In the Eastern States the lumber business has been showing considerable improvement during the past few weeks.

While buying is not brisk for this period of the year, there is a steadily growing volume of business and wholesale prices for the most part are being well maintained. North Carolina pine has been

holding up exceptionally well, and some items are very active; notably dimension and roofers. Southern hardwoods are also firm and the demand for the upper grades is growing. There has been a softening of the market on Pacific Coast due to the heavy movement of Douglas fir by awter to the Atlantic Seaboard territory, and the keen competition between Pacific Coast operators. Northern hardwoods are holding an even keel, except in a few of the lower grades, which are rather weak in demand and price.

The most important factors to-day are the expansion of building activities throughout the country, and especially in the Eastern States; the small lumber stocks in the hands of the retailers and the gradual revival of operators by the lumber consuming industrial plants, whose products consist largely of wood, are not overly stocked with lumber, and the lumber manufacturer who caters to the industrial trade may expect a fairly good volume of business during the coming year. Thretail yards are coming back into the market slowly, but during the past ten days inquiries from this source have been numerous, this being especially true of the retailers in the rural and suburban districts of the North Atlantic States. In a number of instances the market has taken an upward trend since the middle of March, but price advances, on the whole, are not expected to be rapid.

## Nova Scotia Lumbermen Object to Tax

A deputation from the newly-formed Nova Scotia Lumbermen's Association recently conferred with the provincial government in Halifax with respect to the proposed cent an acre extra tax on land which automatically came into force this year. Hitherto the land tax has been one cent an acre but on January 1, 1922 it became two cents an acre. This levy is strongly objected to by the industry and the conference disclosed the fact that as regards the tax, both the government and the men engaged in the lumber line in Nova Scotia, the only province in which the tax is being increased, have troubles of their own.

Among the speakers, on behalf of the lumbermen, were Rufus E. Dickie, president; I. J. Soy, vice-president; Frank J. D. Barnjum, of Annapolis Royal, and Mr. Anderson, M.P.P. for Guysboro.

The conference brought out the fact that the men engaged in the lumber industry in Nova Scotia have to pay a school and county tax. Mr. Soy stated that his company were paying $1500 annually for the upkeep of three schoolhouses, more than all the rest of the district put together.

Hon. G. H. Murray, premier, in the course of a candid reply, stated that he had not personally thought the lumbermen of Nova Scotia would feel themselves excessively taxed by the additional imposition of the 1c an acre. He had looked over the Dominion and seen the amount which other governments were receiving from their lumber industries, and had come to the conclusion that Nova Scotia should be obtaining more in this direction.

The Premier further said he wished it to be understood that there was no scientific principle about this taxation. It was simply a question of getting needed money from every possible source in a crucial, abnormal period—an altogether unprecedented time. Hands were, so to speak, being laid on any and everybody who could contribute a dollar to the provincial treasury.

## Mr. Lambert's Enterprise Appreciated

S. L. Lambert, retail lumber dealer, Welland, Ont., has just completed the erection of a handsome and attractive new hotel and theatre in that progressive city, and his enterprise is much appreciated by the public. The structure is of solid brick with spacious dining room which has a seating accommodation for 175 persons. The interior of the hotel has tile walls and is beautifully decorated throughout. There is a telephone and bath in connection with each bedroom. The kitchen is fitted with the latest cooking appliances and ice machine installed by the Canadian Ice Machine Co., which will make a half a ton of congealed moisture daily. The building is well ventilated by a fresh air fan system.

The hotel, which was opened recently and has already met with a large measure of patronage, is under the management of B. Morgan Smith, late of the Mossop Hotel, Toronto.

## B. C. Timber Exports were Heavy

An increase in the lumber export trade of Canada for the past year, is indicated in the records of the Canadian Government Merchant Marine, the headquarters of which are in Montreal. To practically all parts of the world vessels of the Merchant Marine carried cargoes of lumber, and for the Province of British Columbia alone all previous records for shipping were surpassed.

During the year, from British Columbia, 188,000,000 feet of lumber were exported to various foreign countries, as compared with an average of 40,000,000 feet for several preceding years.

# Lumber Concern Has Most Progressive Policy

### Kaministiquia Company of Fort William Possesses Well Equipped Plant and Conducts Aggressive Advertising Campaign in the Press—Yards Cover City Block and are Admirably Laid Out

E. Sutcliffe Fort William, Ont. Manager Kaministiquia Lumber Co

The Kaministiquia Lumber Co., Limited, of Fort William, Ont., is one of the live organizations in that part of the province. It has been forcing its way steadily to the front during the last two or three years and now is in the vanguard of the retail establishments.

In a recent issue of the "Canada Lumberman" reference was made to the effective advertising campaign conducted by the company which believes in a liberal use of printers' ink. Its slogan is "One foot or a million." The company has a well-equipped planing mill and shop with driveways through both sides.

The office of the company is commodious and comfortable, occupying half of the building seen in the accompanying cut, and at the rear are sheds where large quantities of sash, door, interior trim and other products are carried. The company prides itself on having one of the best lumber yards in the Dominion, always aiming to keep its alleyways as clean as possible and the lumber piles straight at all times.

The well laid-out yards of the company cover about one city block. The planing mill is situated in the lumber yard and the equipment consists of a timber surfacer, band resaw, large planer and matcher, rip saw, pony planer, jointer and small sticker.

The construction of the planing mill and shop is such that the firm can unload from a driveway on one side and feed direct from the wagon to the machine and take direct from machine and load in a driveway on the opposite side of the mill. The company can operate any machine from the rough to the finished product with two men.

The company is now buying logs as well as lumber and expect to have a small sawmill operating in the near future as it intends going into the manufacture of birch flooring and is buying birch logs extensively. The materials used by the firm are grown in the vicinity of Fort William, and are white spruce, balsam, jack pine and white pine. The lumber is sawn full size so as to finish one quarter inch less when dressed. The company also handles large quantities of B. C. products and timber, long joints, finish, etc. and contemplates branching out considerably in the near future.

In the matter of deliveries, the Kaministiquia Lumber Co. uses both horses and trucks. Horses are the most serviceable in the winter as snow usually falls in heavy quantities in Fort William. The truck is found to be the most useful in good weather, and on

small orders the firm say that it is almost impossible to get along without such a conveyance. "For real service under favorable conditions we would use trucks only," declared the manager.

In regard to advertising, an enterprising policy is followed by the firm and well-written, effective and admirable display ads. inserted in the local press. The company spends about ⅓ of 1% of its turnover in printing and publicity. This department is ably handled by Wm. J. Waters. He is an ex-service man and quite an artist in his line. Mr. Waters devotes special attention to drawing up convincing and attractive announcements regarding quality and service and his work has been favorably commented upon by a large number of customers.

E. Sutcliffe, manager of the company, began his career with the Pigeon River Lumber Co. in 1906. For a few months he acted as collector and then worked in the yard learning the business. Mr. Sutcliffe started at the bottom unloading cars of 3 x 12/16 right from the saw. He found this was "some job" but he determinedly stuck to it. The next few months he spent in scaling and loading cars and learning the grades. Then he was taken into the office where he acted as counter clerk and also looked after the invoicing. Mr. Sutcliffe next became city salesman and assistant manager, which position he held for several years.

In July, 1920 the Kaministiquia Lumber Co., Limited, bought out the interests of the Pigeon River Lumber Company in Fort William, and Mr. Sutcliffe was appointed manager in November of the same year. He has made several improvements, including the build-

An alley in the lumber yards, showing loads on sleighs being delivered to a customer. The company has a well-kept yard

ing of a planing mill which, he says, should have been erected a year ago in order to take care of the growing trade. Mr. Sutcliffe reports that the volume of business each month since November 1920 has shown a steadily gratifying gain.

The Kaministiquia Lumber Co. has at the present time approximately 1,000,000 feet of lumber bought, all in the rough, and intend buying quite heavily all winter to take care of the coming season's trade which it anticipates will be somewhat larger than it has been for the last few years.

#### Some Advts. That Say Something

Speaking of the aggressive publicity program of the firm, here is a sample of its advertisement which appeared in the press the first working day after the Christmas holiday:—

Some are full of puddin' and pessimism, others with bank books full of debit ink. Our yards are chock full of selected Lumber and we are full of optimism and selling zeal.

Why not wake from that high cost of building sleep and call around early in the game and see us and be convinced that building is once more back to its old place?

Cedar Shiplap!

Just the kind of material you want to re-line that garage

The offices of the Kaministiquia Lumber Co., Fort William, Ont., occupy the right half of the building which has sheds at the rear where the company stocks large quantities of sash and doors, interior trim, etc.

or chicken pen to make it warm for the winter. Get yours now while the getting's good.

### Storm Sash!

Now is the time to get the measurements for those storm sash you'll be needing this coming Fall and Winter. Do not leave it till the cold weather gets you. See us for prices.

### Storm Sash and Doors

Order your Storm Sash early. We are now prepared to take care of the fall rush on Storm Sash and Doors.

What about those odd repair jobs you have to do before the cold weather sets in this fall?

Why not get started and have the job done while the weather is warm? We handle all kinds of building material and lumber.

### Special Notice To Builders

We have a number of odd sized doors at a remarkably low price. It will pay you to drop in and look them over before building that house of yours.

### Economize

Economy is a good habit. See us before you build that store, house, garage, shed or barn. You can save dollars by buying your material from us.

### He is a Wooden Head!

How often have you heard that expression? We fight shy of the man with a mahogany dome. But to the man with wood on the brain—who is building?—going to build?—or would like to build?—that is the man we want to talk to. We can make it worth his while to listen and show him that now is the time to profit by our liberal quotations on all classes of lumber. Follow the timber talks in our ads. for reasons.

### Storm Sash

Give us your order for your Storm Sash. We are equipped to give you the best of service.

We have the Largest Retail Stock of Lumber at the head of the Lakes. Our prices and quality cannot be beat. See us before buying.

### Quality—Not Value—Makes the Home

Have you ever stopped to think that it is quality and not value that makes the home?

Let us prove this to you. Our stock of lumber is up-to-date in every respect. Drop in and see it before you build. We handle a complete line of interior and exterior finishes. Our retail stock of lumber is the best in the Twin Cities.

### Lumber, Building Material and Finishes

Let us straighten out your building propositions for you. We are experts at the job and our information is free. Consult us before you build.

### Attention Mr. House Owner

Is that roof of yours in bad condition? We handle a large assortment of roofing materials. Just the ideal thing to make your roof weatherproof. See us for prices.

You'll be convinced that you can afford to build if you get our prices on lumber.

### Hardwood Flooring at Pre-War Prices

We Lead, Others Follow—Call around and give us the once over, and be convinced that our prices on lumber and all building materials are at rock bottom.

Shavings Free—Come and take all you want.

## Reaction Sets in on Pulpwood Shipments

The pulpwood situation in so far as it concerns the district of Quebec, gives little evidence of appreciable improvement, and about the middle of March a slump set in which has affected the activities of all Quebec dealers.

A reaction, that promised good business, came into effect in the latter part of last December, which brought about a change for the better to hearten the markets, and during the months of January and February, up to the middle of March, a demand for wood reached the Quebec shippers from Ontario and American pulp and paper mills to lend encouragement. The orders received were in a large measure for the filling of old contracts which have been held up. There being a plentiful supply of railway freight cars at the command of the Quebec shippers, they took advantage of the situation to forward as rapidly as possible to their customers all the wood they could handle from the well-stored bases of supply. This resulted in a revival of shipping activities in which all the Quebec shippers participated, and

during the two and a half months mentioned, over 40,000 cords had been shipped to the Ontario and American Mills. In the beginning of March the mills notified the shippers that the movement would have to be eased, as the quantities they were receiving were congesting their storage capacity, and on March 15 an embargo was placed by order on all shipments, with the result that a slump set in which is now in effect, and likely to continue until the opening of navigation and shipment by water to escape the high freight rates.

The Quebec shippers, who purchased the pulpwood supplies from the farmers along the lines of the Intercolonial Railway, as part of the system of the Canadian National Railways, paid $11.00 per cord; likewise along the line of the Lake St. John and Quebec Central Railways paid $10.00 per cord. The farmers, who have immense supplies of the wood piled all along the lines of these railroads, are seemingly very independent in their sale transactions under the impression that there will be a big demand in the near future, which will give them high prices for their wood. The shippers, however, who are in close touch with conditions which prevail at the American mills, are not quite so sanguine, and are endeavoring to educate the farmers to observe things in their proper light, but the latter seem too optimistic in their sense of visualization to be influenced. The slump, which set in last month, however, has given them an unexpected jar, and it is probable that before long the prices of pulpwood may take a further drop.

The vital question to be considered is the present tariff in railway freight rates, which is greatly disturbing the minds of the Quebec lumber manufacturers, as well as the pulpwood interests shipping to the New York, Massachusetts and Pennsylvania markets, on account of the competition from the Pacific woods, the latter arriving in these American centres by water at much lower rates than demanded by the railroads.

In the meantime the Quebec shippers are filled with a spirit of hope. They say that they are not worrying as they look for a change in conditions which will even up prospects for better results.

### Continued by Simpson

Quebec pulpwood shippers, interviewed, say, they did not make much of a turn-over in their shipment of pulpwood during January and up to the middle of March, because they had contracted for the purchase of their wood when the prices were higher than at present; nevertheless they were satisfied. They were asked if they expected the price at the base of production and supply to go lower than $10. per cord and replied in the negative, saying present quotations were exceptional, as many producers could afford to wait and refuse to part with their wood, convinced that there was bound to come a big demand from the mills whose stock was running low, especially in the United States, which would bring about higher prices.

## St. Maurice Company Earnings Fall Off

The annual financial statement of the St. Maurice Paper Co., Montreal, whose mills are at Cap de la Madeleine, near Three Rivers, Que., shows the result of the uncertainty in the paper industry. The company, of which Alex. MacLaurin, Montreal, is vice-president and general-manager, is a subsidiary of the Union Bag & Paper Co., of New York, and turns out 110 tons of news a day, 200 tons of groundwood pulp, 60 tons of sulphite and 60 tons of sulphate. Operating profits, after all expenses, amounted to $1,046,679, as compared with $2,976,636 for the previous year. After deduction of $339,951 depreciation of plant and equipment, and provision for exhaustion of timber areas, net profits amounted to $706,728, down from $1,769,989 the previous year, after an additional charge of $800,000 to contingent reserve and $43,352 interest had been deducted. With addition of previous surplus, a balance remained of $1,953,179, out of which dividends of $631,992 were paid.

---

### Determination to Win Decides Issue

They had just finished the last rubber of bridge—a young man and the president of a large corporation. The stakes were small and the young man paid the toll. To show his indifference to the loss, the young man said: "I don't care whether I win or lose; I enjoy the game."

The president looked at him and said: " If I didn't want to win I wouldn't care to play. If I lost the desire to win I should not care to live. The desire to win is the one thing that makes life worth living. No man can be happy—no man can be successful—who does not desire to win.

"A determination to win—not once in a while but all the time—is responsible for the success of every big man. A man cannot always win, but he can always try to win, and the more he tries to win the oftener he will win.

# Lumbermen's Safety Association Assembles

### Fatal Accidents During Past Year are Greatly Reduced—Adoption of Current Cost Plan and Other Changes in Compensation Act Strongly Recommended

Of relative importance and outstanding interest to the lumber industry in Ontario were many matters taken up at the annual meeting of the Lumbermen's Safety Association, held at the King Edward Hotel, Toronto, on April 5th. All the sawmill men of the province automatically belong to the Lumbermen's Safety Association, and in becoming members there is no fee whatever. The Association is a body to look after its own interests individually and collectively reduce hazards to labor as much as possible, adopt all safety precautions and enlist the interest and co-operation of workmen in the great task of prevention of accidents.

A number of lumbermen were in Toronto attending the Joint Safety Convention, and advantage was taken of the occasion to hold hte annual session at the same time and place. H. I. Thomas, of Ottawa, who has been chairman for several years, presided, and the discussions were lively and interesting. The report of the secretary-treasurer was presented and officers elected for the coming year.

On motion of G. E. Spragge, and seconded by A. E. Beck, it was decided that the Board of Directors for 1922 be the same as for 1921. These consist of the following:—H. I. Thomas, Ottawa, W. E. Bigwood, Byng Inlet, Sir H. K. Egan, Ottawa, D. McLachlin, Arnprior, Hon. George Gordon, North Bay, J. S. Gillies, Braeside, and D. R. Thomas, Ottawa.

At a subsequent meeting of the directors, W. E. Bigwood was elected chairman for the coming year, and D. McLachlin, vice-chairman.

In opening the proceedings, Mr. Thomas said that the Lumbermen's Safety Association had urged upon the Workmen's Compensation Board the advisability of adopting the current cost plan as being both wise and expedient, particularly so as the benefit reserve fund had now reached $10,000,000.00, and he believed that this should not now be added to. Then there was the question of interprovincial relationships between Ontario and Quebec, whereby he thought the industry should not be assessed in the province of Ontario for labor living in Quebec, or in the event of an accident, resulting in death, the awards in another province should be passed in accordance with the Ontario practice.

The question of merit rating had also been taken up and given favorable endorsation by the lumbermen. If such a method was adopted it would act as a stimulus on the part of manufacturers to use every means in their power to reduce accidents to a minimum and see that annually a better showing was made than that of the previous one. Mr. Thomas believed that the assessments should be based upon the frequency or absence of accidents in each individual industry, and considered this of the most importance. He said that he had applied to the chairman of the Board for a statement, showing the amount of compensation paid in by each firm in the lumbermen's group, and the sum that had been paid back in the way of compensation, but he had not yet been able to obtain such a compilation. The number of fatal accidents in the lumber industry in Ontario had decreased from 53 in 1920 to about 20 during the past year.

In discussing the composition of the Board, Mr. Thomas was of the opinion that this body should be constituted and continued as a judicial one and not as a class representation. It was regrettable that there should be any suggestion of class distinction at all in the personnel of the Board, such as one might be led to suppose from the recent appointment made of a labor man.

Mr. Bigwood, in discussing matters, thought that the impartial and judicious character of the Board should be preserved, and that while there had been some talk of employers nominating a man to occupy a position on the Commission, he did not think the lumbermen should make any recommendation in this direction at present.

#### Should be Two Divisions of Mills

The working of the Act and other features came up for discussion. It was suggested by Mr. McLachlin and others that Class 1 should be divided into two groups, the big mills and the smaller mills. According to the present assessment, the larger concerns were carrying the little ones. Mr. McLachlin said that he felt the burdens should be more properly applied. When asked his opinion regarding the advisability of the workmen paying part of the assessment, which had been suggested during the Safety Convention by J. R. Shaw, of Woodstock, Ont., vice-president of the Canadian Manufacturers' Association, Mr. McLachlin replied that it might work out in other

industries but he was not in favor of any assessment being made upon the men in lumbering, which comprised distinctly two branches, that of logging and manufacturing. The occupation was of a seasonable character and the number of employees changed frequently.

Mr. Thomas also thought that it would be advisable to urge that sawmills be divided into two classes. He spoke strongly in favor of merit rating, particularly in regard to accidents which could in no way be traced as a fault or oversight of the manufacturer. If the accidents are not due to any contributory cause, he did not see why firms should be penalized. Among other things he mentioned was where men suffered an abrasion of the skin but would not consult a doctor, the result being that blood poisoning frequently set in, necessitating the loss of a limb or eventuating in the death of the careless one.

C. J. Mickle stated that there seemed to be a tendency on the part of a number of employees since the compensation pending sickness had been increased to 66 2/3 per cent., to do some malingering.

H. I. Thomas Ottawa, Ont., who presided at annual meeting of Lumbermen's Safety Association

This was particularly the case where a man was injured, was examined by the doctor and then left for his home many miles away, where the doctor could not see him to know whether he was in a fit state to return to work. Such a fellow frequently laid off as long as possible because he was drawing two-thirds of his pay. Mr. Mickle referred to the carelessness of many employees who were deliberate parties to fatal accidents, and in his own operations he mentioned special hazard assessments that had been unjustifiably made.

Mr. McLachlin said he favored the lumber mills being divided up and a special assessment made on the larger and smaller mills. Those owning and operating timber limits should come under the first class, while men who had an engine and a saw frame, but were really not lumbermen and only did custom cutting, should come under a special group of their own.

Mr. Thomas drew attention to the fact that a number of deck lines (chains) which had been used in the woods, had been found too weak and had snapped with the result that in their own operations (Booth) two fatal deaths had occurred last season. The attention of the manufacturers of these chains was drawn to the fact, and they had decided to turn out a stronger and better article and to replace all the old chains with those of a new type.

After some other discussion along various lines of the operation of the Act, which was taken part in by Messrs. Spragge, Atkinson, Gillies and others, the meeting adjourned.

Among those present were:—H. I. Thomas (J. R. Booth, Lim-

ited) Ottawa, chairman; J. S. Gillies, (Gillies Bros.) Braeside; Wm. McLachlan, Magnetawan; W. J. Fry, Kirkfield; J. G. Morrison, Brechin; W. E. Bigwood, (Graves, Bigwood & Co.) Byng Inlet; G. E. Spragge, (Victoria Harbor Lumber Co.) Toronto; Dan. McLachlin, (McLachlin Bros.) Arnprior; C. J. Mickle, (Mickle, Dyment & Son) Gravenhurst; A. E. Beck, (C. Beck Mfg. Co.) Penetang; W. F. V. Atkinson (Dryden Pulp & Paper Co.) Dryden; Frank Hawkins (Secretary Lumbermen's Safety Association) Ottawa; G. B. Van Blaricom (Editor, "Canada Lumberman") Toronto, and R. F. Milne, (Inspecting Staff, Lumbermen's Safety Association) Ottawa, and others

### Secretary Reviews Operations for Year

Frank Hawkins of Ottawa, secy-treas. of the Lumbermen's Safety Association presented the following interesting report on the activities for 1921.

At the last annual meeting, adjourned from May 27th, 1921, to June 6th, it was decided to lay before the Workmen's Compensation Board the views of members regarding Schedule 1, of Class1 operations, and a letter was written to Mr. Samuel Price, Chairman of the Board, on June 21st, as follows:—

Your letter of June 11th came duly to hand, but owing to the absence of the writer a reply has been unavoidably delayed.

With reference to the reserve of over $8,000,000.00 in the hands of the Board and the remarks in our letter to you of June 8th in this particular, we are very firmly of the opinion, and urge upon your Board not merely the desirability but the urgent necessity of arriving at some system whereby the current Cost Plan may be put into operation. We desire to assure you and your Board that this is not merely a question of asking for our own way in this matter; it is because we feel that there has now been built up a very large reserve fund which would be more than ample to meet any possible contingencies that could arise and employers feel that they would rather face the payment of actual awards in each year than continue contributing the very high rated assessments now charged, out of which still further considerable increases of reserve would be made. You say that the question of the adoption of the Current Cost Plan has often been considered by the Board but that your Board has felt wholly unable to entertain the idea, and you refer us to the report for 1916, page 39, and we assume that your present decision is the same as it was then. According to your report for 1916, page 15, the Pensions Reserve Fund at that time was $1,046,810.07 and now this fund is over $8,000,000.00. In other words your Board has taken out of the productive working capital of the Province the sum of over $8,000,000.00 which more than fully provides for the payment of all claims. Our strong feeling is that this Fund should not be added to. We are willing to concede that a reserve fund should be retained at this figure, and we think the industries in Schedule 1 would be prepared to pay assessments large enough to provide for current accidents and maintain this amount in the hands of the Board, but so far as Class 1 industry is concerned we are emphatically opposed to further increases of the Pension Reserve Fund, as distinguished from the adoption of the Current Cost Plan. You will pardon us for saying that we consider that your argument, as contained in the report for 1916 when the reserve fund was only a little over a million dollars, loses entirely its effectiveness as applied to conditions which exist to-day when the Board has a reserve fund of over $8,000,000.00 and under the law has the power to assess as often and for amounts which the Board may consider to be necessary.

### Matter of Interprovincial Payments

Another question which we have taken up with your Board on previous occasions is one referring to interprovincial relationships. As an example: a man employed in Ontario, carried on the pay roll of an Ontario employer but whose residence is in the Province of Quebec, is accidentally killed. The employer has been paying to the Board assessments based on the award which would be given in the event of injury or death. But because the man resided with his family in the Province of Quebec an award is given only on the basis of what the Quebec laws would give, and as this is on a very much lower basis than award which would be given to an Ontario resident extreme hardships, if not absolute, positive distress and want, are placed upon the widow and children. There are two points in connection with this matter (a) assessments are paid by the industry for the higher rate of protection, (b) the widow and children suffer because of the fact that under the Quebec Act or some other Provincial Act, the death claim would be very much less than if assessed and paid in Ontario.

We are of the opinion that arrangements should be made between Provinces where such a condition as this exists, whereby either the industry should not be assessed in the Province of Ontario or that in the event of accident resulting in death the awards should be based in accordance with the Ontario practice.

We can only repeat what we have always urged upon your

Board, that assessments should be based upon the frequency or absence of accidents in each individual industry concerned.

With reference to the detailed statement of contributions and accident cost, we again regret to say that we cannot agree with the attitude which you take when you say that the issue of such a statement would not be justified so soon after the one previously made and distributed. We are very firmly of the opinion that this information should be given to all industries annually.

On June 25th, 1921, Mr. Price replied as follows:—

We have your favor of the 21st inst.

Though I think it is only right to say frankly I feel there is no possibility of the Board changing its attitude upon a number of the questions which you mention, we shall be glad to meet a deputation of the lumbermen at any time that they may find it convenient to come if you will let us know a reasonable length of time beforehand.

### Reserve Fund Over Ten Millions

"Several matters covered in your letter to the Chairman of the Board of June 21st, were pretty fully discussed.

With reference to the Reserve Fund of over $8,000,000, Mr. Price advised that it was only fair to say that this Fund had now reached over $10,000,000. Your Secretary represented to him that it was the very strong feeling of the employers in Class 1, Schedule 1, that this fund was now adequate to take care of any possible contingencies that might arise, and that we believe that the time had come, in view of the six and a half years' exprtience, when assessments should be based on the current cost of damages awarded during the year. Mr. Price asked if your Secretary considered it a fair proposition to place the responsibility upon future operators who might begin business for the accidents which are occurring today. Your Secretary replied that the whole scheme of the Workmen's Compensation Board was not based on the operation of one individual firm but on all firms in that industry and inferred that the Board's basis went even further than this and included all industries in Schedule 1 and further that he considered it as fair to do this as it was to make the larger operators carry the losses of the smaller operators, as undoubtedly was the case now and had been from the start.

### Glaring Instance of Injustice

Another question which was fully discussed was that of Interprovincial relationships. Your Secretary objected strongly to the Board making assessments on the basis of the Ontario pay-roll, thereby providing adequately in case of accident on the basis of an Ontario award, whereas, if the injured workman happened to reside in another province the award was based on what was considered could be collected either under suit or by mutual arrangement and paid out, not in a lump sum but a monthly sum on the basis of this lower award.

The case of Mrs. Deschamp, whose husband had been employed for a number of years by J. R. Booth, Limited, and who was unfortunately electrocuted, leaving her with three or four small children, was a glaring instance of what could only be regarded as an injustice. Mr. Deschamp during his life had been in receipt of a wage of $150. a month, and owing to the fact that the family lived in Hull, an award had been given to the widow of some $22.00 a month, whereas if the case had been dealt with on the basis of an "Ontario resident she would have received $70.00 a month now and $80.00 a month later. The result is that the widow has taken suit in the Province of Quebec against J. R. Booth, Limited for $25,000. Mr. Price seemed to think that there wasn't any possibility whattver of the Quebec Court awarding damages in this case, but your Secretary indicated that had the Ontario Workmen's Compensation Board awarded the $70.00 or $80.00 a month as the case might be and as would have been due to the widow had her family resided in the Province of Ontario, there would have been no proceedings against the firm. Mr. Price pointed out that the same conditions existed in all parts of Canada as between the provinces of Canada and adjoining states of the Union. Your Secretary's reply was that that seemed to emphasize the absolute necessity that existed for satisfactory arrangements being made whereby the interests of the workmen and his family; the interests of the employers individually and industries as a whole be fully protected.

Your Secretary referred again to the detailed statement showing the contributions by the industries and the accident awards in each case, and Mr. Price promised that he would give consideration to this matter.

We received a letter from the Chairman of the Workmen's Compensation Board dated June 27th, stating that the Board had decided for the future to make the payments for the weekly expense bills of the inspectors made direct by this office, and commencing July 1st,

1921, we have been doing this. We think it simplifies matters considerably and that it is a more satisfactory arrangement all round.

We append herewith Inspector Milne's report covering 1921 operations:—

"As requested, I give you herewith a resume of the work on which I have been engaged during the year 1921.

In January 1921, I started at Austin & Nicholson's on the C. P. R., and inspected all the camps en route East to North Bay. I then took the C. N. R., and inspected all camps between North Bay and Foleyet; then came Back to North Bay and taking the T. N. & O.Ry., covered all the camps as far as mileage 136.

All told I inspected 62 camps and found quite an improvement as regards sanitary conditions and any of the firms that had built new camps had complied very well with the Provincial regulations, and a vast improvement was shown between conditions as they existed to day and when everyone built to suit themselves.

A large percentage have adopted wooden cuspidors and find they are a decided improvement. When they were first suggested many foremen were strongly opposed to their use, but they all seem to be falling in line now and sanitary conditions are very much improved.

As regards sleeping conditions, I find that about seventy-five per cent. (75%) of the firms have installed steel beds and mattresses, which are very much appreciated by the men.

In all the camps the general health of the men was good and everyone eagerly listened to the talk on First Aid and seemed to be eager for all the information they could obtain. In March I started to inspect the mills East of Ottawa and up until some time in December I had visited 476 saw mills and found in almost every case the lumbermen have decided that "Safety First" is their motto and comply very willingly and readily with any suggestions I have to make.

### Record of Accidents During Year

With regard to the number of accidents in Class 1, Schedule1, the total number reported to the Board during the year 1921, is

Owing to the absence of the Secretary's stenographer through illness, the total tabulation of these accidents has not been completed, but the following is a partial analysis and may be regarded as typical of the general result,—

Bruises, contusions, abrasions, 487; cuts, lacerations, punctures, 430; fractures, 179; crushes, 56; sprains, strains, twistings, wrenchings, 112; burns, scalds, 20; eye injuries, 25; hernias, 11; internal injuries, 35; contusions (brain & spine) 7; dislocations, 14; frost bite, 16; slivers, infected, 32; poison ivy, 1; broken blister, 1; Total 1426.

Deaths :—Falling logs and trees,10; drowned,6; falling on head, 1; caught in machinery, 1; dynamite and explosions, 1; caught between cars, 1.                                         Total .... 20

                                                         1446

Additional accidents memos not analyzer      1299

Total Accident Memos during 1921          2745

### The Rates For The Coming Year

The following letter was read from S. Price, Chairman, of the Workmen's Compensation Board:—

"We are enclosing herewith provincial statement concerning Class 1, for the year 1921. The accident expenditure, as you will see, is exceedingly bad, with the result that the rates assessed are necessarily very materially increased.

"The Board's report for the year is not yet ready, but is now being compiled, and before it is presented to the legislature, will be printed. The report for the previous year was very greatly delayed in the hands of the printer. Perhaps this is the report to which you refer, and a copy is being sent you herewith.

"The adjusted rates of assessment in Class 1, and the provisional rates for 1922 are as follows:—

| Provisional Adjusted Group | Class | 1921 Adjusted | 1922 Provisional |
|---|---|---|---|
| Logging, woods operations, river driving, rafting, booming or loading as a business or as an industry in this class except as otherwise specified. | | $3.00 | $2.50 |
| Creosting of timbers | | 1.50 | 1.50 |
| Sawmills, shingle mills, lath mills or rossing plants as a business or in an industry in this class except as otherwise specified. | | 4.00 | 3.50 |
| Cooperage stock, spokes, veneer or excelsior manufacturing. | | 4.00 | 3.50 |
| (1) Kiln drying | | 1.50 | 1.50 |
| (2) Operations which would otherwise be in more than one group in this class and in which the usual annual payroll does not exceed $10,000. | | 4.00 | 3.50 |
| Lumber yards, including the delivery of lumber carried on in connection with sawmills are to be included with the sawmills. | | | |

"Regarding the matter of permanent investments full details are always given in the Board's annual report. The accident fund, however, under the provisions of the Act, is to be deemed one and indivisible, and the investments are not to be apportioned to the different classes of industry."

### Provisional Statement of Income and Expenditure
#### Class 1, for Year 1921

| | |
|---|---|
| Assessment collected on estimated payrolls | $511,639.78 |
| Interest on current funds, Section 9-93 a and 99 (3) | |
| Payments | 5,683.19 |
| Estimated adjustment 1921 payrolls | 158,094.36 |
| Carried forward from 1920 | 19,158.73 |
| Total | $656,278.60 |

#### Expenditures

| | |
|---|---|
| Compensation paid other than pensions | $196,063.47 |
| Transferred from pensions award | 136,276.00 |
| Paid to Safety Associations | 5,271.00 |
| Administration Expenses | 11,870.65 |
| Compensation deferred | 3,125.00 |
| Paid for medical aid | 74,270.90 |
| Set aside for disaster reserve | 5,135,43 |
| Compensation estimated for continued disabilities | 135,252.40 |
| Compensation estimated for outstanding accidents | 94,763.38 |
| Estimate for medical attendance | 35,694.54 |
| Total | $700,822.79 |

Provisional balance    44,544.19

Note. The above figures are on the adjusted (increase) rates of assessment.

# How Quebec Will Conserve Its Timber Wealth

The Quebec Lands and Forest Department have decided to lose no more time in the work of reforestation which will entail a big organization and expenditure of considerably more to carry out and bring to a successful issue.

G. C. Piche, chief of the Forestry Branch of the department, discussing the important question in an interview with the Quebec correspondent of the "Canada Lumberman" respecting the future forests of Quebec, said :—

The reforms made during the last decade and the rigid control of the operations of settlers and limit holders have modified completely the aspect of the problem. Where in the past the lumberman and the settler were antagonistic, harmony now exists. The members of the Forest Service who were then accused of being only the agents of the lumbermen are now respected and well considered by everyone, thanks to the introduction of the professional men, of the forest engineers. The lumbering operations are controlled more closely, not only upon the settlers lots, but also upon the timber limits. Our system of fire protection leads us to hope that within a few more years we will have the situation well in hand, as our people are becoming more careful and all the interested take more pains to prevent these accidents. We also admit that with a larger technical personnel, as we now have, we can turn our attention to other problems, which we had been obliged to neglect.

We must frankly admit that the present methods of lumbering are not fully conducted according to the principles of sylviculture, but it was yet the best system that could be devised under the prevailing conditions and, in many cases, could not have been done better. It must not be forgotten, that if we were to apply faithfully the European methods of exploiting forests, lumbering would cost so much that it would discourage any well disposed man. Notwithstanding the danger of fire and the lack of railway facilities, the absence of a market for every type of product, and the low cost of stumpage, compels us to adopt more elastic methods, as the expenditures must be made in direct proportion to the benefit of the enterprise. In other words, the additional value of the timber limit after its lumbering should limit the extra cost of lumbering involved by the introduction of the forestry methods.

The actual consumption of timber upon the forests under license

is practically one billion feet, board measure, which gives an average cut for these 45 million acres of about 20 superficial feet. This is very small, and certainly below the annual growth. In fact, it is admitted that the annual growth of trees in volume will vary from 50 to 600 feet per acre and sometimes more, according to the conditions of the locality; therefore we feel pretty sure in stating that we can largely increase our operations if we will take the necessary means of handling our forests according to scientific principles. In fact, if the forests under license were handled properly, they could produce five times as much wood as they do now and this without the least danger of exhausting them, each operation leaving them in a better producing state. Let us not forget, that there are some 75,000,000 acres of virgin forest lands, containing on an average at least, 3 cords per acre, or 225,000,000 cords of pulpwood, which we consider as a reserve.

### Operations Over Too Small Areas

One of the drawbacks of the present time is that the lumbering operations are concentrated over too small areas: in order to reduce the cost of logging, the limit holders have a tendency to cut too much material per acre, leaving behind only a small forest capital to reproduce the future stand. As the average rate of annual growth in volume is about 2 per cent. we could afford to come back every 40 years at the same place by removing only half of the actual stand, but if more than that is taken out, it means that the tract cannot be lumbered before a longer period. The larger you leave the trees or the more timber you leave behind, the sooner you are in position to log again at the same place. We fully agree with Mr. Geo. Chahoon, of the Laurentide Company when he says that we will have to regulate the volume of the cut hereafter, reducing it where it is needed; this will mean an increase in the logging expenses, but our lumbermen and papermen are certainly ready to stand this expenditure, they will certainly make this little sacrifice, knowing that their woodlands, instead of loosing value, are enriching themselves, with the prospect that they will be able in the future to cut much more per acre than now. Of course, the limit holders will have to seek elsewhere the quantities of timber they cannot find on their limits, but this will not be difficult as there are still immense areas under license that are not operated and which should be lumbered now before the timber dies of over maturity or disease, as it is the case with balsam fir. They could also buy part of the 900,000 cords pulpwood offered for sale every year by the private forest owners. It is a pity to see each year so much timber leaving this Province to feed the foreign mills whereas it could be used here with so much profit and whereas it would lessen by so much the drain upon our forests. I cannot understand the indifference of some of our paper companies in this regard as it would prolong the life of their woodlands if they entered into competition for this wood, which they are in a position to buy at a higher price than their competitors. A few years ago, I tried in vain to interest some papermen to the pulpwood of the Abitibi district; but they would not consider my proposal saying they could not afford it on account of the freight, yet the same pulpwood from Abitibi is shipped every year to numerous points of the United States at distances twice as great as that to their mills. The measures to be adopted for the welfare of our forests are the following:—

An inventory of all the forest lands; we ignore all of the Northern forests, the Ungava is still an unknown factor. There are in these Northern lands immense tracts of forests. We should know of them as soon as possible. These explorations will require many years, but with the modern conveniences, with the use of airplanes, the work can be shortened to a great degree.

### The Classification of Lands

The next point is to devote much attention to the classification of lands. The agricultural soils should be mapped and organized for the establishment of settlers under the best conditions. The experiment of the Abitibi is a direct proof that it is yet possible to colonize with success in our province, and the same methods should be repeated wherever there is a group of suitable lands that may form several parishes. The separation of the forest lands from the cultivable tracts is progressing rapidly but the work could be yet accelerated for the greater good of the settler and the lumberman.

Technical studies of the growth of our forest trees, of their reproduction, of the best methods to handle our woodlands should be continued so as to organize solidly the management of our forests in order to insure their perpetuity and to increase their possible annual yield.

Much economy has already been brought in the lumbering methods but there is still a great amount of waste in the woods operations and a large loss in the driving of logs owing to the long distance between the mills and the forest. New methods of transportation may have to be devised to avoid this loss and especially to allow the removal of the hardwood, which, in many cutover sections, are crowding out the resinous trees that have been left. I do not doubt that the birch and the maple will be utilized before long for making pulp; their value for lumber is now very high, therefore it will not take long before it may pay to operate railways to lumber tracts.

Of course, the protective systems and organizations elaborated recently should be rapidly extended all over the province, so as to safeguard the remaining forests against fires. If we can protect the actual reproduction against fires, we need not be afraid of the future, because our forest trees will seed over the cutover lands and over the brules, and a new forest will soon spring up. We have, and this is often forgotten by many extensive areas of young forests, forming the reserves of the future, which must be protected as well as the old forests so as to insure the perpetuity of our forests wealth.

### Planting More Waste Lands

Now that our forests are becoming effectively protected against fire, we can devote our attention to reforestation, but it will be necessary to do this work in a business way. First all the waste lands belonging to private people should be planted so as to furnish the necessary supply to our villages. The reforestation of the timber limits is also included in our program. The government owning the land, not the limit holder, is the first interest in this work. We shall do this work where we are confident there will be no immediate danger of fire and where we can protect the plantation against this enemy. The government has no intention of saddling the cost of this work upon the lumberman, but, in cases where the lumberman is directly responsible for the deterioration of the forest either through his neglect or through wasteful lumbering, he should be compelled to repair the damages he has caused by planting. Plans are under progress to set soon millions of trees yearly, and we ought before long to be planting each year twice as many trees as there will be cut in the province.

"I have the greatest faith in the future of our forests as we have the material to work with, as we have a progressive class of lumbermen, perhaps better than anywhere else on the continent, as we have the population desirous of seeing this province advancing, progressing, showing the lead to others."

## Mr. Booth Passes His Ninety Fifth Milestone

The many friends of J. R. Booth, of Ottawa, Canada's veteran lumber king, railway builder and pulp and paper manufacturer, will congratulate him on his celebration of another birthday. Mr Booth was 95 years of age on April 5th and observed his natal anniversary by doing a good day's work. He was around his mills and yards as usual and is enjoying good health. The great Canadian captain of industry received congratulatory messages from scores of persons all over Canada and the United States, and the members of his staff sent up to his home a basket of beautiful roses, 95 in all. The wonderful vitality of Mr. Booth and the amount of work that he is able to accomplish in a day, needs no extended reference. It is familiar to all who have any occasion to visit the yards or watch him as he makes his daily rounds of inspection from one activity to another.

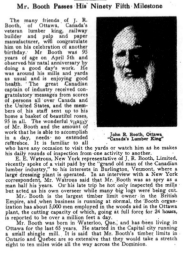

John R. Booth, Ottawa
"Canada's Lumber King"

E. E. Watrous, New York representative of J. R. Booth, Limited, recently spoke of a visit paid by the "grand old man of the Canadian lumber industry," to his interests in Burlington, Vermont, where a large dressing plant is operated. In an interview with a New York correspondent, Mr. Watrous said that Mr. Booth was as spry as a man half his years. On his late trip he not only inspected the mills but acted as his own overseer while many big logs were being cut.

Mr. Booth is the largest timber limit owner in the British Empire, and when business is running at normal, the Booth organization has about 5,000 men employed in the woods and in the Ottawa plant, the cutting capacity of which, going at full force for 24 hours, is reported to be over a million feet a day.

Mr. Booth was born in Waterloo, Que., and has been living in Ottawa for the last 65 years. He started in the Capital city running a small shingle mill. It is said that Mr. Booth's timber limits in Ontario and Quebec are so extensive that they would take a stretch eight to ten miles wide all the way across the Dominion.

# The Tale of A Log

## BY HARRY A. AUBREY
### Quitman, Mo.

As many of my friends and relatives have gone before me, so shall I now go, for with a crash, the tree of which I am a part has been felled to the earth.

We stand in the forests as monuments of the handiwork of God in the form of trees. When the time comes for us to be cut down and made into lumber the same care should be taken of us and follow us as was given throughout our growth. Then our maturing will not have been in vain, and the loss to the forest will be greatly over-balanced in the gain by mankind.

I had often observed, from my lofty height, the operations of men in the forests, as tree after tree dropped from view, so, therefore, I was not surprised, when on falling, to see men pounce upon me with an instrument called a saw and glide it quickly back and forth until the tree fell apart in divers lengths, and it dawned upon me that I was a log.

To me it was a very important moment, for the time had come for me to show my colors; in other words, what I was made of. I had no doubt as to my being able to show quality on being made into lumber, if handled with skill and judgment, coupled with sound practical sense, on the part of all who would guide me on my way, until, eventually, in many forms, I would be part piece by piece into a building, and live again, as a monument to modern machinery and the hands of men.

After being cut into a log, I was, as it is called, skidded along the ground to the right of way of a railroad, there to be picked up by a great hook attached to both ends of me, called a loader, and deposited on a car with other logs, which, like myself, were going on their last excursion. Soon our trip was over. We had gone what appeared to be only a short distance.

That, I afterwards found out, was caused by my riding on a well balanced roadbed behind a high powered locomotive, with the throttle in the hands of an expert engineer, a man who never wished to lose any of us in transit.

A few moments later, we were being backed upon a slight incline or dike, for a brief respite while men were unhooking the chains that had girded us on the cars. I looked about me. To my amazement, I beheld a large building with half a dozen stacks reaching upward as I used to stand in the forest, With smoke or black heat pouring out of the tops.

On inquiry I was told we were at the mill and it was Quitman, a Long-Bell plant. I certainly was pleased to hear this, as I had often heard men in the woods speak of this place, but I was hardly prepared for what I saw. But it was enough for me to say: "Any log coming to this plant is sure of getting justice as far as quality is concerned," for I found out the watch-word of this plant was "Efficiency."

All the chains having by this time become loose with a roar and a splash, I, with a dozen others, was hurled into the pond, or miniature lake, such as all high-class lumber manufacturers have connected with their plants, to move us logs about easily.

After my immersion into the pond, which was a sort of a hazing introduction to the mill, in which I was soon to play an active part, in many parts, I arose to the surface blowing for breath, and then floatel idly about, wondering, "Where do I go from here?"

### Stinging Sensations in My Sides

I did not have long to wait and wonder, for very soon I felt some stinging sensations in my sides, such as I had often heard produced by Jersey mosquitoes. But this, being far from their haunts, I again sought information and was enlightened by a friendly little log that it was a pond-man. He had a long pole with a sharp spike in the end, and jabbed this into me to roll me over, in order to get a line on my general make-up, size, species and so forth.

He towed me toward a trough with a chain of what appeared to me to be full of spikes. This, was called the log-conveyor, which was soon to carry me up into the mill, where I would be operated on in a short time. I felt myself being moved upward with no exertion whatever on my part, and

into the mill. I had at last arrived on what could be called the last lap in my crude raw condition.

I noted there were other logs already there, lying on what was called decks, but I soon staisfied myself that none could compare with me. I had taken the best care of myself all my life, growing from a small sapling into my present magnificent girth, I was filled with pride as I looked on my dimensions, knowing soon I was to pass from an ornament in the forest, to be worked into other forms of usefulness, and thus to fulfill my mission on eath. So, in all fairness to myself and without conceit, I may say I was a good log.

At this stage a flat stick was laid across one end of me by a young man, for the purpose of finding out what was in me in measurements—called scaling—which apparently pleased him, for without a warning, I was kicked out on the conveyor on to the deck. In a few minutes it would be my turn to be thrown on the carriage, and appliances used to run us logs back and forth, while a man called the sawyer takes a slice off of us as we go to and fro.

### One Fleeting Glance at the Sawyer

As I felt myself being thrown on the carriage a fear overcame me as to whether I would be cut up by a real live sawyer, or, as "Jim" White would say, by a carriage runner. Well, after several turns and twists, and being hit with a nigger made of steam, and several other niggers on the carriage pinching me with doghooks, we were off. I gave one fleeting glance at the face of the man who had hold of the levers in the box as I flew by, and saw the look of intelligence stamped on him, his every action showing he admired me. I knew I was in the hands of a sawyer, one who would use all his skill and knowledge on such a fine log as I was to get the utmost out of me, both for quality and scale, and not simply cut me up alive, rebardless of the nice sap-clears which might be in me.

After a few sidings were taken off, I saw the sawyer turn me and look closely at my ends, as soon as my heart began to appear, he cut some beautiful edge grain flitches off of me.

After utilizing all he could of me in this form he again turned, twisted and looked me over, without any stopping of the carriage, and I soon realized he was going to box my heart and turn the balance of me out as a timber in a bridge stringer form, which was very gratifying to me, for as a bridge stringer would I not be in a position of trust, helping to hold up the great railroad trains as they passed over a structure of which I was a part?

One may ask, if I were such a good log, as I have stated, why the sawyer did not get two stringers out of me instead of one. Dear reader, as I have herein stated, the man at the throttle was a sawyer. He noticed my ends as they passed to and fro on the carriage, and perceived that I was afflicted with a heart-shake, which was better left boxed up in one place where it was not injurious, rather than to square me up and burst me open, possible through the shake, thereby ruining my whole career.

I wish to say right here that there is nothing so pleasing to a good log as to see a sawyer note carefully its general appearance, as to dimensions, amount of sap or heart it may contain, and for natural defects, hidden within, which appear in sidings, many of which, by constant turning, are avoided, thus making the product of a higher degree.

The reader may ask, what became of my sidings, or uppers, as lumbermen generally call the material cut off of us before we are squared to timbers. It would be a treat for me to carry you with me and follow each piece which came from me through the stages of manufacture, but space and your patience forbid it, so I will just take you with me in a dream which came to me of late, in which I saw plainly a large building in a city. On looking about I was greeted here and there by many pieces of lumber which had their source from me.

There was flooring, ceiling, wainscoting, the interior with

beautiful finish, picture mouldings; in fact, in any part of the large beautiful home I could see pieces of myself. I had a word with some of them, and I was informed that from the time of leaving me at the mill, through all the stages and process of manufacture, until they were put into their present places each to do its share of usefulness, they received the same care and skill in making that I had received on first going into the mill.

Many pieces told me they never would have occupied the place they now were in but for the knowledge of the workman putting them there by ripping or cutting out a defect. I heard a voice overhead, saying, "I expected nothing else but the burner, but here I am in the form of a plastering lath," so you will note there was little waste out of me, even the sawdust going for fuel, and I heard it remarked in the woods that the time was coming when only the moisture would be lost.

Wood is an indispensable part of the material structure upon which civilization rests, and the demand for wood in all forms will be greater in the future than ever before. Therefore, wanton waste from destructive and careless lumbering should cease. Waste should be eliminated at every angle of the game, so that every foot of material possible in a log may be brought out with the best results and we, as logs, will be a credit to the trees from which we come. Here ends my tale.— The Log of Long-Bell.

## The Question is Often Asked

# Is Unemployment Essential to Industry?

### By Harry P. Mix

Whether or not unemployment is essential is a problem on which there is scope for a wide difference of opinion. Much might be advanced both for and against the question, whether considered in the abstract or concrete. It is the affirmative phase of the subject which I intend to present to the readers of the "Canada Lumberman".

Practically all authorities agree that as long as time lasts, there will be periods of rapid development, followed by those of stagnation or depression, in which unemployment becomes acute and pronounced. This has been the history of the world in all ages. No more striking example of this state of affairs has been furnished than by the abnormal activity, which ensues a few months after the recent war and characterized all lines of enterprise; and its gradual subsidence during the process of deflation and readjustment, until the bottom seemed to have dropped out of almost every undertaking except those of the indispensable requirements of daily life.

It is doubtful if in any decade during the last fifty years, have there been more evidences of wide-spread unemployment than within the past twelve or eighteen months. We are now happily emerging from this quietude and unrest, but the era through which we have gone, has emphasized many points that cannot be successfully assailed.

If there had been no surplus labor, expansion and advancement could not have taken place during the boom period, when there was unexampled prosperity in all trades. If that be true, there must of necessity be at intervals a superabundance of labor to meet varying conditions.

### No Even Keel Industrially

From my own observations and deductions, there is no even keel on which industrial and financial matters can rest. Stabilization and equilibrium are desirable, but it is an ideal towards which both capital and labor have looked in vain. It is a well-known, economic fact that market prices are regulated by the law of supply and demand. At times there is overproduction and at others, the output is not sufficient in many lines to meet ordinary needs. The industrial pendulum has always swung both ways in the supplying of the marketable commodities of the day, and it is not possible to gauge things industrial, economic, financial or commercial like one might the production of a purely mechanical contrivance.

That unemployment is essential to industry is demonstrated by the increase or decrease in residents in all centres. In mining, lumbering, fishing, building and other avenues of activity, there is bound to be great differences in production, demand and distribution. This fact is self-evident. Were all things balanced, there would be no openings for the increasing population of the world.

It is well known that nothing stands still in the manufacturing arena. Undertakings of all kinds employing labor either go forward or backward. What enables the process of growth and development but the reserves of humanity which can be called up to meet existing needs and conditions. One might as well contend that concerns could get along on a fixed capital, without ever increasing their issues of stock or adding to "rest" funds as to contend that only a fixed, definite amount of labor is required at all times and under all circumstances.

### Raising Efficiency to Higher Plane

There must be a give and take situation; a taut and loose state of affairs prevailing. Without it there would be no safety valve or outlet. Unemployment serves to regulate conditions in many walks such as the prevention to a large extent of strikes, avoiding dissension, eliminating disputes and raising efficiency to a higher plane. If it were not so,—there would be a natural tendency toward monopoly, stagnation and incompetency on the part of labor. There would be little incentive for men to exert themselves, grow more proficient in their calling or increase production and thus reduce the cost of the ordinary requirements of life. Labor would also be inclined to become shiftless, careless and inefficient if there was no supply that could be called upon to keep things up to the mark in both equality and quantity. Without this protection in the employment world, there would be no opportunity on the part of employers to fill the places of laggards in the service; output would be limited or tied up, public demands go unsatisfied, and no expansion be possible.

Wealth increases as labor increases and, without a surplus of the latter, there would be lacking capital with which to broaden out industrially and in every other avenue of human achievement and discovery.

Again, unemployment is essential to industry in curbing and controlling high prices. A scarcity of labor would result in rising values higher than justified and so create an abnormal and fictitious state which would be neither sound, healthy nor satisfactory. In almost every business special call arises at times to take on more workers for a few days or months, and if there was no idle labor, how could these demands be met? Therefore, I contend that reserves are as essential in labor as any other sphere to meet seasonable, fluctuating and economic requirements and conditions, for we have not yet reached the millenium of a job for every man.

# Should Leather Belt be Run With Grain or Flesh Side Next to Pulley?

The question of whether a leather belt should be run with the grain or flesh side next to the pulley has been, until quite recently in the same category as the old saw: "How old is Ann?" From the time when leather belts were first used for power transmission until the present, men have argued the matter pro and con without having any definite facts upon which to base their opinions or any more really concrete evidence than that of individual observation. The very natural result has been as many opinions on the matter as there were men to voice them.

It appeared to some men that a closer contact with the pulley could be had by putting the grain side of the belt next to it. Others have contended with equal conviction that the flesh side, being tough-

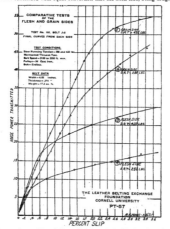

er, was better able to withstand friction. And still others have gone into the realm of metaphysics for their argument, maintaining stoutly that a wise Providence had placed the flesh side of leather next to the animal deliberately and it was not for man to reverse that order on a pulley. But speculation on the matter is at an end; scientific experimental evidence has been obtained to settle the controversy once for all.

During the latter part of last summer, tests of the capacity of the grain and flesh sides of leather belts were begun by the Leather Belting Exchange in its Research Laboratory at Cornell University. They were under the direction of Mr. R. F. Jones, Director of the Laboratory. Covering a period of more than two months continuous tests were run on the testing apparatus belonging to the Leather Belting Exchange, which is being operated under the supervision of Cornell University, using five 4 inch single belts, 30 feet long, of different manufacture. They weighed from 16 to 18 ounces. Every effort was made throughout the tests to standardize conditions and to reduce the probable error to a minimum, and this unquestion-

ably was accomplished. All five belts were run long enough previous to the experiments to have been thoroughly "run-in," and had reached a condition of constant capacity when the records were taken.

The method of procedure was to take horse-power readings from the belts first when running on the grain sides, and then when running on the flesh, the power being gradually increased until about 4 per cent slip had been reached.

In considering the results, it must be remembered that a leather belt is at its lowest point of capacity when new, largely because of the elasticity of the leather and the newness of its surface. Leather belts are well stretched in the process of manufacture, so that when the belt is put on the pulley there may be as little stretch as possible consistent with thorough lubrication and retaining the natural life or elasticity, which is such a valuable property of the leather belt. When a new leather belt is placed on the pulleys, however tightly, it will elongate under load. But after the tension of the load has been removed it returns very nearly to its original length. This stretch is an annoyance when installing a new belt, but it is of the nature of a safety valve, protecting both belt and machinery.

The newness of the surface, however, makes it necessary to "run in" the belt when testing it. That is, to run it for a sufficient time to permit the belt to attain its maximum capacity in transmission. As an illustration, one belt under test at the Cornell Laboratory transmitted 12 h.p. when first put on the pulley at a slip of 1.2 per cent. After five hours running it reached 19 h.p. with the same percentage of slip and the same tension. At the end of 13 hours it transmitted 24 h.p., and reached 31 h.p. after 20 hours with a slip of 1.6 per cent. According to horsepower tables, its scheduled transmission should have been 26 h.p.

Inasmuch as the belts used in the Leather Belting Exchange tests seemed to be typical, and the apparatus at hand was such as to

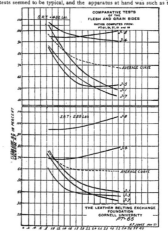

give the most accurate readings of performance, it is safe to conclude that the results are scientifically acceptable.

To review the details of each individual test would require more space than is here available. Suffice it to say that a summary of all of the results is clearly in favor of the grain side from the standpoint of power transmission. In fact, it may be concluded from it that under reasonable shop tension, the flesh side will average only 50 to 60 per cent as much horsepower as the grain side. At higher tensions the flesh side will do better, averaging from 50 to 100 per cent as much power as the grain, depending upon the belt, the tension and conditions of service.

A curve plotted from the readings taken when the belts were running on the flesh side is similar both in shape and capacity to that given by many of the leather belt substitutes. All that can be said of the test belts run on the flesh side is that the data obtained from them were more uniform than that taken when they were running on the grain.

Using the horsepower transmitted and the percentage of slippage as the coordinates, on Chart PT 57, which is representative, the

grain tests showed an almost curveless gain in horsepower up to 53, when the slip reached about 3 per cent for belts running at a slow running tension of 432 pounds. In the case of the test belts operated at a slow running tension of 288 pounds, the 3 per cent slippage was reached at about 44 h.p. With the belts running on the flesh side, however, the 3 per cent slippage marks was reached at 28 h.p. when operated at a slow running tension of 432 pounds, and at 16 h.p. when the tension was 288 pounds.

In short, the evidence produced from the mass of data obtained leaves no reasonable doubt but that there are distinct advantages to be had from running leather belts on the grain side. It is simply another case where scientifically obtained evidence must outweigh arbitrary opinions held usually by reason of personal and, oftentimes inaccurate observation. It would seem to indicate that all those who have held the flesh side in favor in years past would do well to readjust their opinions, and if there be any alive to-day who are still determined to bring Providence into the discussion, they must find some providential reason for putting the flesh side of leather next to the animal and the grain side next to the pulley.

## What Should the Lumber Dealer Spend on Advertising?

The question is often asked—What percentage of sales should a live, retail lumberman spend on advertising? This has always been a moot proposition on which no apparent unanimity of opinion exists in the trade.

A great many different kinds of people go to make up a world. There are some dealers who declare that they can get along very well without advertising as they are handling basic products; their business has been established so many years that everybody knows they sell lumber, posts and shingles, and comes to them, etc. This kind of soothing sentimentalism or egotism might have got by in the past before advertising was brought up to the status that it enjoys at present and the strong position it now commands. To-day the retail lumberman who does not believe in advertising of some kind, either in the press or through booklets, leaflets, circulars, novelties, fence signs or other means of publicity, is a rarity.

There are others who go much farther and contend that advertising is the whole life of business, and is the channel through which all activity flows. Some men even wander beyond this and trust everything to advertising and let their stock and service run down, which, of course, is a fatal mistake. Some retail lumbermen so far as an advertising appropriation is concerned declare that much depends upon circumstances, location and business methods, the kind of times trade is passing through and the general feeling in the community.

Inquiries made by the "Canada Lumberman" from a number of retailers who advertise—and there are quite a number who still are apprehensive of making any investment in this line—show their outlay for publicity ranges all the way from ¼% to 2½% of the total sales. The average, however, is about 1%.

Some misunderstanding frequently arises regarding the term "advertising." How broad and comprehensive should it be? Generally speaking, advertising does not mean the use of printers' ink alone or a space taken in the daily or weekly paper, but all other means used to call attention to the fact that one deals in lumber and has certain milling facilities, yard service and supplies for the interior and exterior trim of houses, shingles, lath, fence posts, roofing, etc. Some lumber merchants get out booklets of their own; others send out blotters; a few get up a seasonable letter to customers, and others distribute mementos at fall fairs, farmers institutes and other gatherings. Some use billboards and zinc signs. All this should, of course, be included in advertising because anything that serves to make you or your business more widely and favorably known and to establish a closer connection with your customers so that the facilities of your yard, stocks and service are appreciated, is good advertising; in fact one Western Ontario man remarked the other day to the "Canada Lumberman," "Anything that makes me or my business spoken of advantageously, is advertising. Of course a police court conviction or something of that character is unfavorable advertising. I want my name so associated and linked up with the public mind that when any man is considering the building of a sleeping porch, an implement house, a silo, a hennery, a pig sty or even a dog house, he at once begins to think of lumber, and my name consciously or unconsciously comes to his mind and he will drive right to my yard here to get his supplies."

Of course, advertising, in order to get results, must be seasonable, forceful and attractive. It has to receive attention and be looked after as carefully as any other department of business. It cannot

be neglected and picked up only at such times as convenient or when there is nothing else to do. Just how much advertising the average lumber dealer should do, depends on the amount of his sales, the results he gets, the efficacy of the mediums used, the value of his mailing list and the size of the business that he desires to develop. There are instances of where alert and aggressive dealers have trebled their business in a few years by effective publicity backed up, of course by service that is in every way sufficient and satisfactory.

One Northern Ontario dealer says—" I would as soon think of getting along without a sign or a motor truck as to attempt to do business without advertising. It has brought me good results."

A Huron County man says,—"I set aside $1.00 for advertising from every $100.00 sale I make. I think is about a fair balance, and under the heading of "Advertising" I include my dues as a member of the Ontario Retail Lumber Dealers' Association, the local association, convention expenses, etc., all of which I believe are gladdening and stimulating agencies."

Another Eastern Ontario dealer says,—"I spend about 1½% and advertise the year round. I use a page, two colums wide and 4 inches deep, in the local paper and change my ad. every two weeks. Occasionally I increase the size of the space when I have something special to offer in the line of hardwood flooring or interior trim. At other times I use readers or liners. Advertising is a judicious and efficient means of extending business."

More expressions of opinion were received along this line and some who do advertising, admit they have not got it down so fine as to figure out the percentage of what they spend. One dealer declared that he does not use newspapers to any great extent, but he has made himself solid in the towns and surrounding country with every farmer and carpenter by giving them an apron. He presents all callers at his office with a calendar and, sends out a greeting card every Christmas to an up-to-date mailing list of about 1800 names. All within a radius of fifteen miles. He believes that to create an impression with his customers, a lumber merchant must constantly drive home the fact that he is right there to do business and he values all trade that comes his way, great or small. Most people like to receive some personally addressed mail matter, and when they are remembered in this way, it leaves a very good impression with them.

Another dealer says "My appropriation for advertising does not trouble me very much. I expend what I consider sufficient and vary it according to the season and the stock I carry."

Thus views differ, but the main thing with the average retailer to-day is to convince him that he should advertise and to do it as effectively, aggressively and convincingly as possible.

H. J. Terry, Chairman of the Wholesale Lumber Dealers' Association, Toronto, has been elected a director of the Toronto Rotary Club for the coming year.

A. McKelvey, secretary and treasurer of the McLeod Sash and Door Company, Vancouver, states that conditions in the trade have improved greatly in the past few weeks, featured by a growing demand from the prairie provinces and Eastern Canada. Shipments are being made from the factory to points as far east as Halifax.

A view of the sawmill of the Indian Lake Lumber o., Osaquan, Ont. The plant has a capacity of 3,000 railway ties a day and 20,-000 feet of lumber.

A record haul of ties at Dalton, in Northern Ontario. Each team is hauling about 225 ties taken out by Austin & Nicholson, of Chapleau, Ont.

A bird's eye view from the sulphate boiler house chimney, showing the lumber yard of the Brompton Pulp & Paper Co. at East Angus, Que., and also a section of the town.

## Retailers Lake Outing Will be Winner

**L. H. Richards Sarnia, Ont.**
**Chairman of Excursion Committee**

L. H. Richards, of Sarnia, chairman of the Ontario Retail Lumber Dealers' Association midsummer outing committee, J. C. Scofield, Windsor, president of the O. R. L. D. A. and F. D. Geoghegan, General Passenger Agent for the Northern Navigation Company, Limited, are working diligently to make the event in June next an outstanding success. The steamer "Huronic" of the Northern Navigation Co., has been chartered for a four days' trip from Windsor and Sarnia to Owen Sound, Killarney, Sault Ste. Marie, Mackinac and return by Sarnia and Windsor. In order to make the trip a success the Ontario Association must guarantee 173 full fare tickets by June 10th.

President Scofield is making arrangements with the Michigan Retail Lumber Dealers' Association to join with the Ontario Retail Lumber Dealers' Association in this outing. The members from Michigan are to be assigned 75 berths on the vessel. The total capacity of the "Huronic" is about 225 berths. This will leave about 150 berths available for the Ontario lumbermen. Ladies are particularly requested to join in the outing and all dealers are asked to bring along their wives and families.

L. H. Richards of the Laidlaw-Belton Lumber Co., Sarnia, will issue the tickets to members of the O. R. L. D. A. Reservations will be made by him and held upon payment of half of the purchase price of the ticket. Tickets for staterooms and berths reserved and marked will be mailed to members upon receipt of the full purchase price.

The trip will commence on Friday June 23rd at 5 P. M., from Windsor and will end on Tuesday June 27th at 5 P. M. at Windsor. The route and time table will be as follows:—

Leave Windsor. 5 P. M. Friday, June 23rd.
Leave Sarnia, 11 P. M. Friday, June 23rd.
Arrive Owen Sound, 7 P. M. Saturday, June 24th.
Leave Owen Sound, 11 P. M. Saturday, June 24th.
Arrive Killarney, 7 A. M. Sunday, June 25th.
Leave Killarney, 9 A. M. Sunday, June 25th.
Arrive Sault Ste. Marie, 7 P. M. Sunday, June 25th.
Leave Sault Ste. Marie, midnight Sunday, June 25th.
Arrive Mackinac, 10 A. M. Monday, June 26th.
Leave Mackinac noon Monday, June 26th.
Arrive Sarnia, 10 A. M. Tuesday, June 27th.
Leave Sarnia, noon, Tuesday, June 27th.
Arrive Windsor, 5 P. M. Tuesday, June 27th.

As already explained, the cost per person for the boat trip from Windsor and return will be $50.00. In further explanation of this, it may be said this figure will cover all the expenses from the moment the excursionist goes on board until he steps ashore again at Windsor four days later.

There will, however, be an addition of 1% sales tax making the $50.00 ticket will cost $50.50, while the $60.00 ticket will cost $60.60. Children between five and twelve years of age will be carried at half fare two children as one full fare in connection with the guarantee. Children under five will be charged for at the rate of $6.00 each for the trip to cover meals when occupying a seat at the table.

Twenty-five preferred state-rooms have been set aside at a cost of $60.00 per person, for those who desire to pay the extra charge in order to have one of the more favorably located state-rooms. The preferred state-rooms all accommodate three persons. About half of them have an upper berth for one person and a double lower berth. The other half have an upper berth for one person, a lower berth for one person and a couch on the opposite side of the room. All other rooms are similarly equipped. The special price for the preferred rooms is charged in consideration of the fact that they are in the centre of the ship and on the promenade deck. All state-rooms on the vessel are outside rooms.

## How Reforesting is Done by Nature

In nearly all the talks about reforestation — which deserves a great deal more attention than the public yet has given to the subject — there is too much said about the part man is to play, and not enough about nature's part. It is all right for man to plant trees where there are no trees. It is often necessary. But speaking in general, nature understands such work far better than man, and does it more effectually and is always working on the job.

Observe the edge of any forest or wood lot—how the trees are always crowding out and encroaching on the cleared land. The woods grow of their own accord, laterally as well as vertically wherever they have a chance. The wind and the birds and the squirrels scatter seeds, and the saplings spring up, and the first thing one knows there are new trees, added to the old and replacing the dead ones.

Observe any fence or cleared space between fields, when left to itself. In a few years, if there are any trees in the neighbourhood there is an inevitable line of trees and scrubs, often of many kinds some of them not traceable to any visible source. Nature is taking advantage of the only ground left her, and using it for reseeding.

Nature only asks to be let alone and given a little time, and she will take care of the work of reforestating the country. She only asks man to give her a little space to work in, and not thwart her efforts by cutting or grubbing up or burning down every little tree as soon as she has it started, and to let a mature tree stand here and there in the fields to provide newseed. But if man wants to do a little positive and constructively helpful work, he might take the trouble to thin out, prune and otherwise encourage the trees that nature sends him, thereby showing his appreciation. All a tree needs is about as much work as a farmer gives to a hill of corn, though it's worth far more than the corn.—Concord Monitor.

## Sudden Death of John R. Davidson

Many friends will regret to learn of the death of John R. Davidson, of Winnipeg, who passed away in that city on March 27 at the early age of 36 years, following an operation. Born in South Shields, England, he came to Canada ten years ago and located at Prince Albert, Sask., where he was secretary of the Builders' Exchange. In 1914 he removed to Winnipeg where he was editor of several publications of Hugh C. MacLean, Western, Limited.

Mr. Davidson was a member of the Fort Rouge Bowling Club, and in 1920 was the winner in the Winnipeg and Provincial Double Championships, in addition to numerous other trophies captured during his connection with the Fort Rouge Club. Surviving him are his wife, who resides in Winnipeg, and his mother who is living in England. Mr. Davidson was a big, broadminded, highly esteemed gentleman who made warm friends of all with whom he came in contact.

## National Executive Committee Appointments

W. H. Schuette, President of the National Wholesale Lumber Dealers' Association, announces the Executive Committee of the Association to serve for the ensuing year as follows:—W. H. Schuette, Pittsburgh, Pa., President; C. A. Goodman, Marinette, Wis., 1st Vice-President; Dan McLachlin, Arnprior, Ont., 2nd Vice-President; J. W. McClure, Memphis, Tenn.; F. R. Babcock, Pittsburgh, Pa.

At the closing session of the Annual Meeting at Washington March 23rd, a very strong invitation was received from the Pittsburgh delegation inviting the Association to hold its 31st Annual Meeting in 1923 in the City of Pittsburgh.

The by-laws provide that the Trustees shall decide the time and place of the Annual Meeting. The Convention unanimously and enthusiastically recommended that the Trustees accept this invitation and an early definite announcement may be expected.

# Nova Scotia's Lumber Interests are Growing

### Industry Suffered During Past Year Owing to Depression but Reduction of Stocks and Lowered Production Costs Should Result in Revival in Near Future

By Hon. O. T. Daniels

Hon. O. T. Daniels Halifax, N.S.

In common with other lines of business the lumber industry of Nova Scotia suffered in 1921 a season of depression and readjustment. After the war a great demand for lumber for reconstruction purposes was anticipated. This led to a considerable increase in production in the season of 1919-20. The expected great demand, however, did not materialize. The depression in business which began to be felt in the spring of 1920 soon developed, in the case of lumber, a condition of comparative stagnation. Operators found themselves with large stocks, produced at the highest cost and unsaleable at profitable rates. As prices fell stocks gradually became reduced, but in the fall of 1920, because of the considerable stocks on hand and the high costs of production then prevailing, there was nothing to encourage large operations in the season then beginning. The cut for the season of 1920-21 was estimated to have been about half of that for the previous season. The estimated production of long lumber for export and sale to local yards in the season of 1919-20 was 350,000,000 feet, board measure, valued at $10,500,00.00, and for last season 175,000,000, feet valued at $3,500,00.00. The average value in the former year is put at $30.00 per thousand and in the latter at $20.00, these figures indicating approximately the difference in prices in the two seasons.

The foregoing figures represent only a part of the forest products of Nova Scotia, there are besides pulp, cordwood, railroad ties, barrel staves, pit props, ship timber, laths, shingles and other miscellaneous items of considerable importance. The total value of the forest products of the Province for the year 1921 is estimated at $10,325,000.00.

#### Cut This Year Will Be Half

It is too early to estimate closely the cut for the present season. Owing to market conditions prevailing and the stocks still in the hands of producers and dealers the cut is likely this year to be considerably smaller than in 1921. It has been estimated at one half. The outlook as regards the market conditions is more favorable. There is prospect of more active demand. Improved trade and consequent reduction of stocks, together with lower production costs, should open the way to increased activity in lumber operations in the season of 1922-23.

Among the difficulties which beset the lumber operator in 1921 were the high freight rates. In the case of vessel freights the rate dropped to less than one half of the highest figure reached in 1920, but the rate by rail scarcely dropped at all. These high freight rates were an element in keeping up the price of lumber for home consumption as well as for export, and helped to retard building operations. Reduced rail freight rates are, it is hoped, on the way. These with lower wages cannot but hasten the recovery of business in the line of construction work and improve the demand for lumber.

The summer of 1921 is likely to be long remembered in Nova Scotia because of the unusually severe and prolonged drought. Forest fires were numerous in all parts of the province. Usually May is the worst month for fires, the danger not being so great in the season when the woods are green with the leafing out of the trees. Under the exceptional conditions of last year, however, fires were most numerous in the months of June, August and September.

The number of acres burned over in Nova Scotia last year is estimated at 77,000. The cost of fighting the fires was about $40,000, and the estimated damage $120,000. The fire damage was less than might have been expected in view of the unusual conditions. The

matter of the protection of the forests from fire has received attention from the government during the past year and measures have been adopted to improve facilities for lighting fires and provide additional funds for this purpose.

In value of product lumbering cannot be said to be the chief industry of Nova Scotia, but its importance can hardly be overstated. A considerable area of the province suitable for forest growth could not be profitably used for any other purpose. Climate conditions favor an unusually rapid growth. Damage from the ravages of insects has not been as great in Nova Scotia as in some other provinces. Overcutting and the menace of fire are the things chiefly to be guarded against. The lumber industry provides profitable employment for an important section of the population, and at a season when other work could not easily be obtained. This applies not only to lumbering, as that term is usually employed, but to the gathering, manufacture, and utilization of all forest products.

#### New Company Operating at Longford Mills

The Canada Wood Specialty Co., Limited, of Orillia, Ont., have purchased the entire stock of unsold lumber and logs from the Standard Chemical Co., at Longford Mills, Ont., and have also taken a lease of the mills for the present season. The stock consists of about 2,000,000 feet of dry birch, maple, elm, ash and basswood lumber, and upwards of 2,000,000 feet of hard and softwood logs.

A. F. Cooper, who has superintended the lumber operations of the Standard Chemical Co. since 1910, will continue to act in the same capacity for the Canada Wood Specialty Co., with headquarters at Longford Mills.

#### Ocean Freight Rate War is Now On

Prospect of an "aggressive steamship rate war" at Vancouver, B. C. affecting all commodities carried between Canada and the Orient was reported to the Department of Commerce, Washington by American Council-General Ryder at Vancouver.

The rate on lumber, he said, recently was reduced from $15 to $12 per thousand feet, and this caused a general reduction in other lines. Lumber exporters, he said, are rushing to take full advantage of the reduced rates. The rate of $6 a ton for wheat flour was reduced to $5, and that on general merchandise reduced to an average of $2 a ton.

The Blue Funnel and Japanese Lines are the principal companies involved, Mr. Ryder said, the managers admitting that "a rate war is on in earnest." The Canadian Pacific Ocean Service, while not apparently directly concerned, he added, has declared its intention of meeting all competition.

#### New Association is Already at Work

The newly-formed Nova Scotia Lumbermen's Association is off to a good start. A constitution has been drawn up and meetings of the Executive have already been held.

E. A. Saunders, who is secretary pro tem., states that he is obliged to decline the secretaryship of the Nova Scotia Lumbermen's Association owing to the many organizations in which he holds a similar position.

A complete list of the members of the Executive is as follows:— T. G. Boutilier, Musquodoboit, N. S.; Fred Campbell, Clarkesville, N. S.; Fred Chambers, New Glasgow, N. S.; M. R. Chappell, Sydney, N. S.; Eric Curry, Brooklyn, Hants Co., N. S.; C. A. Fownes, North Sydney, N. S.; G. M. Godding, Liverpool, N. S.; J. R. Gordon, Liverpool, N. S.; Chas. Hill, Truro, N. S.; L. W. Logan, Musquodoboit, N. S.; A. S. McMillan, Halifax, N. S.; G. T. McNutt, Halifax, N. S.; C. H. Ried, Amherst, N. S.; Percy L. Spicer, Parrsboro, N. S.; and F. C. Whitman, Annapolis, N. S.

It is believed that the Nova Scotia Lumbermen's Association will prove a very successful and aggressive body. A deputation had an interview with the government recently, protesting against the increased land tax which automatically came into force this year.

## The Lumber Outlook in Ontario

There is no marked change in the general situation and the market, while improving in certain lines, has shown advancement only on a few items during the past two or three weeks. In the larger cities there is a fair amount of hemlock moving, some of the grades are reported rather scarce. The business with the United States, particularly in white pine has opened up a little more auspiciously and some shipments are taking place. Building operations continue brisk in the larger centres and each week encouraging reports are received. It is now believed costs are down about as low as they will be and that prices will hold firm on the majority of woods, except that a few re-adjustments may take place on slow moving lines

Winter logging operations are now over and all the camps have been broken up. As soon as the ice gets out of the rivers and lakes, the drives to the mills will begin. Manufacturers are preparing to open their plants as soon as their log ponds are free of ice and a number of mills have large stocks of last year's logs on hand with which to begin sawing.

Very few sales of stocks have taken place as yet, for wholesalers contend that manufacturers are asking altogether too much for their product. There is a difference in the figure which many producers are naming and that which wholesalers are willing to pay. Probably negotiations which are now pending in several instances may be closed up a little later on. Retail yards are not buying extensively at the present time, being pretty well sorted up. The yardsmen are waiting for developments.

In hardwoods, while there are numerous enquiries, the market continues quiet. It is reported that in certain cities across the border, motor firms have pooled their stock, which shuts off any immediate buying. The outlook, however, is growing brighter and is reflected more in the confidence expressed on all sides that 1922 will likely be a fair year, rather than in any immediate and augmented turn-over.

Eastern representatives of Western mills say that trade has been rather quiet for some time. There has been quite a call for long joists and fir timbers especially when offered at bargain prices. The shingle market has shown some strengthening of late and it is expected that buying will develop to a larger extent as building operations develop. The Toronto Transportation Commission has been calling for three-quarter million feet in oak, hemlock, fir and yellow pine cross ties. Some of these tenders have already been awarded. It is hoped that the latter part of April and the beginning of May will witness larger purchases in general lumber requirements.

Interviews with leading wholesalers and manufacturers elicit the information that no pronounced tendencies in the trade have developed during the past few months. The cut during the past winter was small, but it is anticipated that unless an abnormal demand sets in there will be sufficient stock to meet all ordinary requirements. The industry is looking forward with expectation to the lowering of freight rates in the near future and it is announced that encouraging reports have been received that the carrying charges on basic commodities may be reduced. If the rates revert to what they were previous to September 1920 there is no doubt there would be a freer movement of forest products particularly on long hauls. B.C. woods have had to come in competition with Ontario and Michigan hemlock, Southern pine and spruce and it has been difficult to move Coast products in any large volume. It is believed that next month will witness considerable impetus in the lumber business. A revival is on the way but from one cause and another its arrival has been slower than was predicted some weeks ago.

If certain reductions, now being made by the railways, are straws indicating which way the wind is blowing, it would appear as if there would be an extension of these concessions on carrying charges in the near future.

A recent Supplement No. 104 has been issued, setting forth a reduction in the arbitrary rates on lumber and forest products from stations along the Temiskaming & Northern Ontario Railway to points in Ontario. The rate from Uno Park is reduced 3½c per 100 lbs.; Cobalt 3c; Cochrane 7c, etc. The rate from New Liskeard to Toronto on lumber, etc., is decreased from 25c to 22c per 100lbs.; from Cochrane to Toronto from 33c to 26c per 100 lbs., and other northern points like proportion.

There has also been a lessening in rates on wood commodities on the Canadian National Railway from New Brunswick and Nova Scotia to Montreal and terminals. The former rate, for instance, from Caledonia, N.S., to Montreal, was 39c per 100 lbs.; it is now 36½c; from Bridgewater, N.S. it was 36½c.; now 34c, etc.

### General Jottings of Trade Interest

The Wilson Lumber Co., Limited, who have offices in the Confederation Life Building, Toronto, will remove in a few days to their new office on Fleet St. at the foot of Spadina Ave., where their yards are located. The new building is a convenient and well arranged one and being in connection with the yards will enable the company to extend their activities and specialize more in hardwoods in mixed cars and less than car lots. The Wilson Lumber Co. also handle softwoods as well.

Edwards & Ames have begun the erection of a new shingle mill at the foot of Trinity Street in Vancouver.

Louis Pelletier, St. Donat, Rimouski County, Que., intends erecting a sawmill at Luceville, Que.

C. Gagnon of St. Cecile de Whitton, Compton County, Que., recently had his sawmill destroyed by fire.

The Kastner Lumber Co., whose plant at Wiarton was destroyed by fire recently, will rebuild. The firm has purchased the equipment of the Niebergal mill.

Rose McLaurin, Limited, wholesale lumber dealers, Toronto, have removed their office from 1 Toronto St. to Rooms 1226 and 1227, Bank of Hamilton Building, Toronto.

F. H. Bigwood of the Canadian General Lumber Co., Toronto, is chairman of the Committee on Arrangements for the great international Kiwanian Convention which will be held in Toronto in June.

The C. A. Larkin Co. are removing their office from 630 Confederation Life Building to 229 in the same building with entrance at 12 Richmond St. East, Toronto, where they will have much larger quarters.

J. L. MacFarlane, of the Canadian General Lumber Co., Toronto, who was ill for many weeks, is once more able to appear at the office. He is greatly improved in health and his many friends in the industry are pleased to see him around again.

Frank W. Gordon has opened offices in the Northwest Building, Vancouver, B. C., where he will carry on the wholesale lumber business. Mr. Gordon was formerly with the firm of Terry & Gordon, Limited, Toronto.

Harry Hardy, 204 Woodbine Ave., Toronto, who for several years past has been a member of the sales staff of the Union Lumber Co., Toronto, has retired in order to go into the lumber business on his own behalf.

Many friends in the lumber trade will regret to learn of the death of Daniel Marsh of Grimsby, Ont., a veteran retail lumberman and contractor of that town. One of his sons Henry Marsh died a few weeks ago and the passing of the father makes the second and occurrance since the beginning of the present year. The late Mr. Marsh was highly esteemed for his enterprise, kindliness and integrity. The business, with which he was so long associated, is being carried on by his son, J. Albert Marsh.

A. M. B. Stevens, Director of the Timber Disposal Dept., Board of Trade, London, England, left Montreal on April 2nd. On his return to London, sailing from New York on the 4th. As a result of Mr. Stevens' visit to Canada, it is understood that active steps are being taken to dispose promptly of the British Government stock in the Dominion. Lieut. Col. R. M. Beckett, of Quebec, is acting as advisor on behalf of the Board of Trade, in conjunction with Mr. Blakeley of Cox, Long & Company, Ltd., 433 Coristine Building, Montreal, the selling agents, and Mr. Denman, of the Timber Disposal Department, 604 Shaughnessy Building, Montreal. All inquiries as to the lumber should be made to the above addresses.

The Citizens' Lumber Co., of Regina, Sask., have purchased N. J. Uglum's lumber yard in that city and at Shaunavon. A deal was completed a month ago in which the Barr Lumber Co., and the N. J. Uglum Lumber Co., took over the East End yard site of the Citizens' Lumber Co., as the Citizens' were closing out at East End. Just following this move, a fire consumed the Citizens' office and warehouses in Shaunavon. The new deal gives possession of the Uglum office and warehouses at both places to the Citizens' Lumber Co., who will transfer the lumber to the Uglum yard. The Citizens' Co., will operate the Uglum yard at Shaunavon and expect to dispose of the East End yard through a series of consolidations which are taking place among the retail companies of Manitoba, Saskatchewan and Alberta.

Hon. T. D. Pattullo, of Victoria, B. C., Minister of Lands and Forests, is spending some time in the East, being called to Ontario owing to the illness of his father, George R. Pattullo, Woodstock, Ont., the veteran Registrar of Oxford County. Mr. Pattullo also has conferred with various representatives of the lumber industry in Ottawa, Montreal, Toronto, and other places. One of his missions is to interview Angus McLean, of the Bathurst Co., Bathurst, N. B., and his associates in regard to the proposed pulp and paper mill which these gentlemen have planned to establish at Prince George, B. C. The mill will be of 200 tons capacity if the original plans are not modified. Its organizers have made a careful and exhaustive survey of the country east of Prince George, and have developed their project to the utmost, so far as gathering information is concerned.

## Mr. Rolland Finds British Market Dull

Louis S. Rolland, exporter, of Montreal, recently returned from a two months' business visit to Great Britian. He was accompanied by his wife, Mr. Rolland having been married just prior to the voyage. He visited London, Manchester, Bristol, Cardiff, Newcastle, Edinburgh, and Glasgow, and made a large number of inquiries as to present conditions and prospects.

His opinion, based on those inquiries made from representative firms, is that there is no hope of any immediate improvement in the Canadian export trade. Speaking to a representative of the "Canada Lumberman," Mr. Rolland said: "General business conditions in the basic industries, with the exception of coal, are not satisfactory. Lumber stocks are ample for present and prospective demands. Canadian stocks in most lines are plentiful, with the exception of a few choice sizes in pine. So far as hardwoods are concerned, there is no demand except at figures far below those at which Canadian mills can afford to sell."

Louis S. Rolland, Montreal

"There is no chance for Quebec spruce at the prices which our mills are quoting. The competition from Europe is very keen. One of the largest Scandinavian importers stated that Sweden has about ten times as much lumber as under ordinary conditions, while Norway and Finland have about normal stocks. Finnish goods are being imported into Great Britain as a substitute for white pine, owing to the reason that they can be purchased for considerably less money. One factor that is making for low prices for spruce is that previous to the war, Germany was an importer of spruce from Scandinavia, whereas now Germany is exporting that lumber at attractive prices. The Baltic States are also shipping at quotations which appeal to British buyers.

"The consumptive demand is limited, and with this condition some of the importers of Canadian goods, who previously had done at least a small amount of business, are apparently holding off together, fearing that Sweden may export to Great Britain on a very large scale. Swedish banks have loaned very freely against lumber stocks in Sweden and it is believed that liquidation of the stocks will be made during the current year. One of the largest Swedish banks has one third of its money tied up in lumber, and it looks as if action will be taken to obtain, at least, some of that money by forcing the goods on to the market.

"As the result of my visit, I have come to the conclusion that Canadian exporters will find it impossible to ship much lumber during the coming season. Not only are commercial conditions in the Old Country adverse, but the prices now obtained do not represent any profit—in fact, a loss is far more likely.

"From the shipping point, the situation favors Scandinavian exporters, owing to the fact that the shipping companies have been quicker to realize the necessity of reducing rates on lumber, almost disregarding the profit or loss sustained, thus affording great help to Scandinavian exporters. Against this Canadian shippers have been up against a strong combine holding firm on the rates agreed upon at the periodical meetings of the North American Conference, which has unfortunately not taken into consideration the fact that, generally speaking, the Canadian exporters have been taking considerable losses on merchandise held, thus impairing any prospects or efforts made to meet outside competition. Undoubtedly the modification of the existing rates would advance the possibilities of placing Canadian stocks on the English market; the shipping companies would in this way help to stimulate our exports, a class of trade which Canada very much needs. With cheaper shipping rates, we should be in a better position to take advantage of a revived demand for lumber in the United Kingdom."

## Lumber Salesman Who Gets the Orders

"A lumberman salesman is different than most salesman," said a well known business man the other day. "All he needs is a good personality. If he has this he will sell lumber."

"I think you are wrong," said a dealer who has bought a great deal of lumber during his time. "I like the good fellows and the fellows with pleasing personality, and I do buy lumber from them. but the most of my business has gone to salesmen who are substantial, hardworking, earnest, practical men and who know their business from A to Z.

"I think that selling lumber is no different than anything else. The man who knows the most about the thing that he is selling will get the bulk of the business."

Selling is a business just the same as the running of a retail yard is a business.

Very often we hear salesmen say: "I am going to get into business." Too many salesmen feel that way about it.

We were talking to a salesman the other day who earns on an average of $5,800.00 every year.

His friend who lives across the street from him is running a retail business. Last year he lost several thousand dollars.

Last year was not a fair year, however, to make a comparison. On the average both men will probably make nearly the same amount of money with the salesman having an advantage of $1,000.00 or $1,500.00 in most years.

Yet the dealer is looked upon as being much better off than the salesman. This is not the case.

The salesman's selling ability, which is his capital, is worth just as much as the retailer's entire business in that it earns its owner the same amount of money, or more, each year.

The retailer has had to invest nearly $60,000.00 in order to earn as much as his salesman friend, and then very often does not succeed in doing so.

## Bounty on Porcupines to Save Trees

On account of the large amount of damage being done in the woods by porcupines, I will personally pay a bounty of ten cents each for every porcupine killed during the month of April, 1922, anywhere within the Province of Nova Scotia. By actual count it has been found that a porcupine will destroy about 100 fully grown trees in a winter, so that the total loss from this animal runs into very large figures. Every fully grown tree that is saved is worth more for present needs than 100 seedlings planted, though both are urgently needed.

No bounty will be paid after May 1st, on account of the added fire risk caused by having hunters in the woods after that date.

An extra cash bonus of one hundred dollars will be paid at the end of April to the one who actually kills the largest number during the month. In the event that two contestants should kill exactly the same number the bonus will be paid to the one who sends in the largest returns early in the month before the female reproduces.

All that will be necessary will be to cut off the snouts and forward same by parcel post or express to me at Annapolis Royal, Nova Scotia, stating location where porcupines were killed and giving name and address of the sender, and a check for the bounty will be forwarded by return mail. As porcupines are quite plentiful in many parts of Nova Scotia, hunters and a large number of the unemployed should make good wages out of this bounty and be at the same time saving their own or their neighbors' trees from destruction.

Porcupines cannot throw their quills, this is simply an old superstition, you have to come in actual contact with the animal before it can shed its quills. They are comparatively tame and can often be killed with a stick.

I intend renewing this offer in the fall after snow comes again.
Frank J. D. Barnjum. Annapolis Royal, N. S.

| DATE | HEMLOCK | W.PINE | SPRUCE | B.C.FIR | CEDAR | SHINGLES | LATH | POSTS | PLASTER | DOORS | CEMENT |
|------|---------|--------|--------|---------|-------|----------|------|-------|---------|-------|--------|
| Feb. 1 | | | | | | | | | | | |
| " 2 | | | | | | | | | | | |
| " 3 | | | | | | | | | | | |
| " 4 | | | | | | | | | | | |
| " 5 | | | | | | | | | | | |
| " 6 | | | | | | | | | | | |
| " 24 | | | | | | | | | | | |
| " 25 | | | | | | | | | | | |
| " 26 | | | | | | | | | | | |
| " 27 | | | | | | | | | | | |
| " 28 | | | | | | | | | | | |
| TOTAL | | | | | | | | | | | |

## How Busy Retailer May Keep Monthly Record of Sales

In the last issue of the "Canada Lumberman" reference was made to a system by which a southwestern Ontario retail lumber dealer kept tab on the quantity of the different kinds of lumber, etc., sold each day. By reference to his book, he is enabled to tell exactly in what months white pine, hemlock, spruce, hardwood flooring, shingles, fence posts,etc., moved most freely and to gauge his stock and purchases accordingly. The reference aroused considerable interest and a number of inquiries have been received in regard to the system.

The lumber merchant, who has carried this into effect during the past four years is K. J. Shirton, of Dunnville, vice-president of the Ontario Retail Lumber Dealers' Association and Mayor of the progressive southwestern Ontario town.

The accompanying cut is a sample of the plan which he uses in keeping a record of the different items such as lumber, shingles,

lath, posts, plaster, doors, cement, etc. · The system can be extended, if desired, to show all the kinds of lumber sold, by merely adding more columns. The quantities disposed of are entered daily while posting the cash sales and accounts. At the end of each month the respective totals are learned by adding up the daily quantities. Mr. Shirton says an ordinary small book of about 50 pages is used, each month requiring a page, or two and in this way he has the data for several years which is handy for comparative purposes.

In speaking to the "Canada Lumberman," Mr. Shirton said,—"It never occurred to me to bring this idea up before our Association as the system appeared rather crude and homemade, but, after reading your article in a recent edition, I began to see how this method can be of real benefit to all dealers. As it exists now, the plan has been of great assistance to us, and with a few more columns added, we can give more definite information. It is a system that is easily expanded and can be worked out on a comprehensive basis."

### The Cordwood Market Around Fort William

Approximately 6,000 cords of firewood were brought into Fort William from the surrounding district during the past season. The average price was about 25% lower than last year.

The wood is shipped chiefly in cordwood length, but according to dealers, most of the customers prefer it in stove-lengths, ready for use, and this, of course, adds to the price. The day has long since past when the man of the house takes out his bucksaw and gets to work at this back-breaking job.

Jackpine and birch are the two most popular woods on the market. Tamarac is becoming very scarce and will soon be unobtainable. Those who understand the wood situation claim that between seven and eight years ago practically all the large tamarac was killed off by a blight. This was general throughout the country. The young growth was uninjured, but will not be available for the purpose for which tamarac is used, that of piling for a great number of years.

Poplar makes a good summer wood, and is one of the cheapest on the market, but is not well known, and, therefore, hard to sell, so it is stated.

### The Forest Area of Quebec Province

The total area of forest land in the Province of Quebec is 450,-337,761 acres, or 703,653 square miles, according to the Provincial Lands and Forests Department. This does not include the Ungava territory annexed in 1912, which practically doubles the surface. According to the last census, taken in 1911, the properties belonging to private individuals, companies and communities covered at that time 15,613,267 acres.

### News Happenings in Brief Form

The Canadian Pulp and Paper Association has appointed Mr. P. B. Wilson, Spanish River Paper Mills, Limited, Sault Ste. Marie and Mr. I. H. Weldon, Provincial Paper Mills, Toronto, to act as an advisory board with the Minister of Lands, Forests and Mines of the Province of Ontario. These gentlemen will act when requested.

The Horticultural Society, of Hastings, Ont., will make it possible

for the village to have a memorial avenue by planting a tree for every soldier from Hastings who served in the war. The tree to be planted is the Norway maple, which is considered one of the best shade trees, and which thrives well.

Recent advices received from Arnprior, Ont., state that the prospects for an active lumbering season are very bright. Both Gillies Bros., at Braeside, and McLachlin Bros., at Arnprior, have a large supply of logs in the river and streams adjacent to the Ottawa. It is expected that the mills will start up during the latter part of April. The general opinion of lumbermen in the Arnprior district is that while the lumber markets must, of course, have an effect on operations the prospects for the season are considered very good. Building activities which have been delayed, are increasing. Arnprior and the surrounding district depend to a great extent on the lumber mills in Arnprior and in Braeside, and from present indications there is every reason for optimism.

The Myers Lumber and Manufacturing Co., Limited, Toronto, was recently incorporated to manufacture and deal in all kinds of forest products. Capital $200,000. Among the incorporators are W. J. Myers, W. Warren and E. Crowe, all of Toronto.

The Company, who have opened an office at 15 Toronto St., are establishing a lumber yard and woodworking plant on Spadina Road and Eglinton Ave.

John Waugh, retail lumber dealer, of Niagara Falls, Ont., was in Toronto recently and as usual came over on the first boat from Port Dalhousie. He holds a record for being the first lumberman to arrive in Toronto by boat each spring and he generally manages to take in the last trip on the steamer "Dalhousie City" each season.

The April meeting of the Wholesale Lumber Dealers' Association, Inc., will be held at the Albany Club, Toronto, on Friday 21st inst. A. J. Brady, Jr., of North Tonawanda, N. Y., who will deliver an address upon "Salesmanship," is a fluent and forceful speaker.

M. B. King, of the King-Farris Lumber Co., Vancouver, was in Toronto, Montreal and Ottawa on business during the past few days. He is a brother of Hon. J. H. King, Minister of Public Works, Ottawa.

H. R. Van, of the Louise Lumber Co., Quebec, P. Q., recently returned from a business trip to the Old Country.

Bruce Woodworkers, Limited, Chesley, Ont., have commenced manufacturing a line of beech and maple flooring.

## Pulpwood Cut Small Around Jacksonboro

The New Ontario Colonization Co. Limited, whose land office and mills are at Jacksonboro, Ont., say they do not expect to have an extended sawing season this year as they did not operate heavily in the bush during the past winter. They confined their efforts to taking out what logs their regular jobbers and settlers could get out, and, in addition, a limited amount of pulpwood. The company add that they have a fair stock of lumber on hand, slightly more than the amount at this time in 1921. The pulpwood situation has been quiet and the immediate outlook for improvement in the Jacksonboro district is not encouraging. The company believe that the market will strengthen as the season progresses as it is their ppinion wood will be in fair demand this fall. The production of pulpwood in the vicinity of Jacksonboro, was considerably reduced during the past winter. Concluding the New Ontario Colonization Co., say—We feel that the lumber situation should progress to a more stabilized basis during the year and believe that prices will show a firmer tendency as the year advances. There seems to be an inclination on the part of some manufacturers to weaken slightly here and there, but when full costs of logging and manufacturing are reckoned up for the season, undoubtedly values will strengthen rather than go lower.

## Reduced Rates Granted on Pulpwood

Through the influence of the Quebec Board of Trade, says the Quebec correspondent of the "Canada Lumberman," and at the unanimous request of the 15,000 French Canadians who have settled in the Abitibi district, along the line of the Transcontinental Railway, the one-third reduction in railway rates has, it is said, been granted to relieve the situation of the settlers who have been unable to transport their pulpwood and lumber under the old rates without an appreciable loss in the manufacture.

Recently the Abitibi Pulp and Paper Co., have purchased several thousand cords of pulpwood from the Abitibi settlers, for which they paid $4.25 per cord, loaded on cars, and at a cost of $8.25 delivered to the company's mills. This pulpwood in the rough cost the Abitibi settlers $5.25 to cut and place on the cars, which entailed a direct loss of $1.25 per cord to the settlers.

In the meantime purchasers for American pulp and paper mills acquired 30,000 cords of pulpwood from the same district, taking advantage of the low price of the wood and reduction in Transcontinental Railway transportation. This goes to show the change that has come over the pulpwood situation in the province of Quebec on account of the slump in demand for wood and the tremendous quantity cut and lying along the various railways awaiting sale.

## Pulpwood May Advance Slightly in Price

Pulpwood, both rough and peeled, has been moving very freely in the Haileybury district and Northern Ontario during the past month. The demand seems good for any quantity but the prices remain unchanged. There is an indication that, at least, $2.00 more will be paid for wood that can be taken out during the coming summer as, at the present rate of loading, all the pulpwood along the line of the Temiskaming and Northern Ontario Railway will be shipped out before May 1st.

Very few ties have been taken out this season in and around Haileybury, and practically no shipments have been made. During the month the Grand Trunk shipped out a few small lots of ties left over from the last year, but they are not buying any just now.

Speaking to the "Canada Lumberman," a leading representative of the North said, "Lumber is moving freely in the larger sizes, viz., 2 by 8, 2 by 10 and 8 by 8, being used chiefly by the mines for shaft timber. A large number of inquiries would denote that there will be a bigger amount of spring building on this line than in any year since 1914. The roads in the North have been in great shape for drawing out logs. Small mills are all through for the winter with a lesser cut than was generally expected. Wholesalers are not buying much up around Haileybury at present owing to the high freight rate. Unless the price is an exceptionally favorable one."

## Men Did Not Legally Seize Proper Logs

A judgment of considerable interest was recently rendered by the Superior Court at Perce, Gaspe Co., Quebec.

The Great Eastern Paper Co., which owns a tract of timberland on the Magdalen River last fall, gave out several contracts to jobbers. These jobbers carried on operations during the winter and this spring it was discovered that one of the number had become insolvent. As a natural result the men employed by this party demanded that the paper company come good for the amount of their wages. This was refused by the company. The men then took a seizure against the logs, claiming a privilege thereon for their labor.

In virtue of the writ of seizure the bailiff seized a quantity of logs in the company's boom at Magdalen River, and in which was contained the timber these labourers had worked. However, the logs on which these men had worked were mixed in the boom with the company's total winter cut and the company maintained that the amount due the men was owing by the jobber and cut by themselves, and that the men had no authority to seize wood other than that of the jobber for whom they had worked. This meant that the wood on which the laborers had worked for the jobber had to be identified in order for them to realize the amount due them as wages. Under existing circumstances, this was impossible.

The Superior Court at Perce upheld the contention of the paper company, declaring that the laborers had a just claim against the jobber for whom they had worked, but none against the company itself, and that they could not legally seize the logs generally in the boom.

## Enough Pulpwood to Last Sixty Years

The annual meeting of the Abitibi Power & Paper Co., whose plants are located at Iroquois Falls, Ont., was held in Montreal recently. A. J. Brown, K.C. was elected to the Board to fill the vacancy created by the retirement of Shirly Ogilvie. This was the only change and the following officers were elected:—President, F. H. Anson; vice-president, Alex. Smith; Directors, Sir Thos. Tait; George H. Kilmer, K. C.; George E. Challes; W. K. George; Victor E. Mitchell, K. C.; and W. A. Black.

Mr. Anson said that the mills are at present operating to capacity, turning out daily 500 to 550 tons of newsprint. In February 12,200 tons of newsprint was manufactured and 13, 000 tons were sold. He further stated that the company had contracted far enough ahead to assure a favorable average for the year.

Mr. Anson pointed out that the organization had during the past few years carried on quite an extensive programme in the matter of expansion, with the result that it is now in a position to cope with the readjusting conditions, having enough wood enough on its limits to last for about sixty years, and a present surplus of developed waterpower. In this connection he pointed out that shareholders would be looking for dividends and when disbursements are resumed, he wished to see it done on a permanent basis.

Mr. Anson was also asked as to what he figured to be the working capital of the company, and stated that it was shown in the annual report as $1,300,000. In reply to the suggestion that there had been a certain difference of opinion in the matter, the president stated that such differences possibly arose from varied systems of bookkeeping. He intimated that the pulpwood of the company was carried at a very conservative figure.

## Western Company Bondholders Will Meet

A special meeting of the debenture holders of the Western Canada Pulp & Paper Co. has been called for April 24th to consider ways and means of protecting their interests in this concern. The Western Canada Pulp Co. has encountered adversity and is forced to pass interest on the bonds which fell due in February last. It is understood the bondholders have given notice of foreclosure although no definite proceedings are announced. The company's plant is located at Port Mellon, on Howe Sound, B. C., about twenty-five miles from Vancouver. The company owns its own townsite which is located on navigably deep water and is located with a dock 600 feet long.

# CURRENT LUMBER PRICES—WHOLESALE

## TORONTO

(In Car Load Lots, F.O.B. cars Toronto)

### White Pine

| | | |
|---|---|---|
| 1 x 4/7 Good Strips | $100.00 | $110.00 |
| 1¼ & 1½ x 4/7 Good Strips | 120.00 | 125.00 |
| 1 x 8 and up Good Sides | 150.00 | 160.00 |
| 2 x 4/7 Good Strips | 130.00 | 140.00 |
| 1¼ & 1½ x 8 and wider Good Sides | 185.00 | 190.00 |
| 2 x 8 and wider Good Sides | 190.00 | 200.00 |
| 1 in. No. 1, 2 and 3 Cuts | 75.00 | 80.00 |
| 5/4 and 6/4 No. 1, 2 and 3 Cuts | 95.00 | 100.00 |
| 2 in. No. 1, 2 and 3 Cuts | 105.00 | 110.00 |
| 1 x 4 and 5 Mill Run | 52.00 | 55.00 |
| 1 x 6 Mill Run | 53.00 | 56.00 |
| 1 x 7, 9 and 11 Mill Run | 53.00 | 56.00 |
| 1 x 8 Mill Run | 55.00 | 58.00 |
| 1 x 10 Mill Run | 60.00 | 62.00 |
| 1 x 12 Mill Run | 65.00 | 70.00 |
| 5/4 and 6/4 x 5 and up Mill Run | 58.00 | 60.00 |
| 2 x 4 Mill Run | 52.00 | 53.00 |
| 2 x 6 Mill Run | 53.00 | 56.00 |
| 2 x 8 Mill Run | 55.00 | 58.00 |
| 2 x 10 Mill Run | 58.00 | 60.00 |
| 2 x 12 Mill Run | 63.00 | 65.00 |
| 1 in. Mill Run Shorts | 35.00 | 40.00 |
| 1 x 4 and up 6/16 No. 1 Mill Culls | 30.00 | 32.00 |
| 1 x 10 and up 6/16 No. 1 Mill Culls | 34.00 | 36.00 |
| 1 x 12 and up 6/16 No. 1 Mill Culls | 34.00 | 36.00 |
| 1 x 4 and up 6/16 No. 2 Mill Culls | 23.00 | 25.00 |
| 1 x 10 x 12 6/16 No. 2 Mill Culls | 26.00 | 28.00 |
| 1 x 4 and up 6/16 No. 3 Mill Culls | 17.00 | 18.00 |

### Red Pine

(In Car Load Lots, F.O.B. Toronto)

| | | |
|---|---|---|
| 1 x 4 and 5 Mill Run | $34.00 | $35.00 |
| 1 x 6 Mill Run | 35.00 | 36.00 |
| 1 x 8 Mill Run | 37.00 | 38.00 |
| 1 x 10 Mill Run | 42.00 | 44.00 |
| 2 x 4 Mill Run | 38.00 | 40.00 |
| 2 x 6 Mill Run | 40.00 | 42.00 |
| 2 x 8 Mill Run | 41.00 | 43.00 |
| 2 x 10 Mill Run | 44.00 | 47.00 |
| 2 x 12 Mill Run | 49.00 | 50.00 |
| 1 in. Clear and Clear Face | 70.00 | 72.00 |
| 2 in. Clear and Clear Face | 70.00 | 72.00 |

### Spruce

| | | |
|---|---|---|
| 1 x 4 Mill Run | 34.00 | 35.00 |
| 1 x 6 Mill Run | 35.00 | 36.00 |
| 1 x 8 Mill Run | 37.00 | 38.00 |
| 1 x 10 Mill Run | 45.00 | 47.00 |
| 1 x 12 Mill Run Spruce | 48.00 | 50.00 |
| Mill Culls | 25.00 | 27.00 |

### Hemlock (M R)

(In Car Load Lots, F.O.B. Toronto)

| | | |
|---|---|---|
| 1 x 4 and 5 in. x 9 to 16 ft | $26.00 | $27.00 |
| 1 x 6 in. x 9 to 16 ft | 33.00 | 35.00 |
| 1 x 8 in. x 9 to 16 ft | 34.00 | 36.00 |
| 1 x 10 and 12 in. x 9 to 16 ft | 35.00 | 37.00 |
| 1 x 7, 9 and 11 in. x 9 to 16 ft | 33.00 | 35.00 |
| 2 x 4 to 12 in. 10/16 ft | 33.00 | 34.00 |
| 2 x 4 to 12 in., 18 ft | 37.00 | 39.00 |
| 2 x 4 to 12 in., 20 ft | 40.00 | 42.00 |
| 1 in. No. 2, 6 ft. to 16 ft | 23.00 | 25.00 |

### Fir Flooring

(In Car Load Lots, F.O.B. Toronto)

| | |
|---|---|
| Fir flooring, 1 x 3 and 4", No. 1 and 2 Edge Grain | $72.00 |
| Fir flooring, 1 x 3 and 4", No. 1 and 2 Flat Grain | 46.00 |

(Depending upon Widths)

| | |
|---|---|
| 1 x 4 to 12 No. 1 and 2 Clear Fir. Rough | 77.00 |
| 1¼ x 4 to 12 No. 1 and 2 Clear Fir, Rough | 81.00 |
| 2 x 4 to 12 No. 1 and 2 Clear Fir, Rough | 77.00 |
| 3 & 4 x 4 to 12 No. 1 & 2 Clear Fir, Rough | 84.00 |
| 1 x 4, 5 and 6 in Fir Casing | 73.00 |
| 1 x 8 and 10 Fir Base | 78.00 |
| 1¼ and 1½ 8, 10 and 12 in. E.G. Stepping | [illegible] |
| 1¼ and 1½ 8, 10 and 12 in. F.G. Stepping | 80.00 |
| 1 x 4 to 12 Clear Fir, D4S | 72.00 |
| 1¼ and 1½ x 4 to 12 Clear Fir, D4S | 75.25 |
| XX Shingles, 6 butts to 2", per M | 3.35 |
| XXX Shingles, 6 butts to 2", per M | 5.35 |
| XXXXX Shingles, 5 butts to 2", per M | 6.15 |

### Lath

(F.O.B. Mill)

| | |
|---|---|
| No. 1 White Pine | $11.00 |
| No. 2 White Pine | 10.00 |
| No. 3 White Pine | 8.00 |
| Mill Run White Pine, 32 in | 3.50 |
| Merchantable Spruce Lath, 4 ft | 6.50 |

## TORONTO HARDWOOD PRICES

The prices given below are for car loads f.o.b. Toronto, from wholesalers to retailers, and are based on a good percentage of long lengths and good widths, without any wide stock having been sorted out.

The prices quoted on imported woods are payable in U. S. funds.

### Ash, White

(Dry weight 3800 lbs. per M. ft.)

| | 1s & 2s | No. 1 Com. | No. 2 Com. |
|---|---|---|---|
| 1" | $100.00 | $ 65.00 | $ 40.00 |
| 1¼ and 1½" | 110.00 | 70.00 | 45.00 |
| 2" | 115.00 | 75.00 | 50.00 |
| 2½ and 3" | 125.00 | 85.00 | 60.00 |
| 4" | 140.00 | 95.00 | 70.00 |

### Ash, Brown

| | 1s & 2s | No. 1 Com. | No. 2 Com. |
|---|---|---|---|
| 1" | $ 95.00 | $ 55.00 | $ 30.00 |
| 1¼ and 1½" | 100.00 | 60.00 | 30.00 |
| 2" | 105.00 | 65.00 | 33.00 |
| 2½ and 3" | 125.00 | 80.00 | 55.00 |
| 4" | 140.00 | 95.00 | 60.00 |

### Birch

(Dry weight 4000 lbs. per M. ft.)

| | 1s & 2s | Sels. | No. 1 Com. | No. 2 Com. |
|---|---|---|---|---|
| 4/4 | $105.00 | $ 80.00 | $ 50.00 | $ 32.00 |
| 5/4 | 110.00 | 85.00 | 55.00 | 35.00 |
| 6/4 | 115.00 | 90.00 | 60.00 | 38.00 |
| 8/4 | 120.00 | 100.00 | 65.00 | 42.00 |
| 12/4 | 125.00 | 105.00 | 70.00 | 50.00 |
| 16/4 | 130.00 | 110.00 | 80.00 | 55.00 |

### Basswood

(Dry weight 2500 lbs. per M. ft.)

| | 1s & 2s | No. 1 Com. | No. 2 Com. |
|---|---|---|---|
| 4/4 | $ 80.00 | $ 50.00 | $ 25.00 |
| 5/4 and 6/4 | 85.00 | 60.00 | 30.00 |
| 8/4 | 90.00 | 65.00 | 35.00 |

### Chestnut

(Dry weight 2800 lbs. per M. ft.)

| | 1s & 2s | No. 1 Com. | Sound Wormy |
|---|---|---|---|
| 1" | $130.00 | $ 80.00 | $ 40.00 |
| 1¼ to 1½" | 140.00 | 85.00 | 43.00 |
| 2" | 150.00 | 90.00 | 43.00 |

### Maple, Hard

(Dry weight 4200 lbs. per M. ft.)

| | F.A.S. | Sels. | No. 1 Com. | No. 2 Com. |
|---|---|---|---|---|
| 4/4 | $ 85.00 | $ 65.00 | $ 45.00 | $ 33.00 |
| 5/4 | 85.00 | 65.00 | 45.00 | 38.00 |
| 6/4 | 90.00 | 70.00 | 50.00 | 45.00 |
| 8/4 | 100.00 | 75.00 | 60.00 | 50.00 |
| 12/4 | 105.00 | 75.00 | 65.00 | 60.00 |
| 16/4 | 125.00 | 100.00 | 70.00 | 65.00 |

### Elm, Soft

(Dry weight 3100 lbs. per M. ft.)

| | 1s & 2s | No. 1 Com. | No. 2 Com. |
|---|---|---|---|
| 4/4 | $ 75.00 | $ 50.00 | $ 30.00 |
| 6/4 and 8/4 | 80.00 | 60.00 | 35.00 |
| 12/4 | 96.00 | 70.00 | 40.00 |

### Gum, Red

(Dry weight 3300 lbs. per M. ft.)

| | Plain 1s & 2s | Plain No. 1 Com. | Quartered 1s & 2s | Quartered No. 1 Com. |
|---|---|---|---|---|
| 1" | $115.00 | $ 70.00 | $125.00 | $ 76.00 |
| 1¼" | 120.00 | 75.00 | 130.00 | 80.00 |
| 1½" | 120.00 | 75.00 | 130.00 | 80.00 |
| 2" | 125.00 | 90.00 | 135.00 | 90.00 |

Figured Gum, $10 per M. extra, in both plain and quartered.

### Gum, Sap

| | 1s&2s | No. 1 Com. |
|---|---|---|
| 1" | $ 55.00 | $ 40.00 |
| 1¼" and 1½" | 60.00 | 44.00 |
| 2" | 65.00 | 50.00 |

### Hickory

(Dry weight 4500 lbs. per M. ft.

| | 1s&2s | No. 1 Com. |
|---|---|---|
| 1" | $120.00 | $ 60.00 |
| 1¼" | 145.00 | 65.00 |
| 1½" | 145.00 | 65.00 |
| 2" | 150.00 | 70.00 |

### Plain White and Red Oak

(Plain sawed. Dry weight 4000 lbs. per M. ft.)

| | 1s&2s | No. 1 Com. |
|---|---|---|
| 4/4 | $120.00 | $ 75.00 |
| 5/4 and 6/4 | 130.00 | 80.00 |
| 8/4 | 135.00 | 85.00 |
| 10/4 | 145.00 | 90.00 |
| 12/4 | 145.00 | 90.00 |
| 16/4 | 150.00 | 95.00 |

### White Oak, Quarter Cut

(Dry weight 4000 lbs. per M. ft.)

| | 1s&2s | No. 1 Com. |
|---|---|---|
| 4/4 | $160.00 | $ 90.00 |
| 5/4 and 6/4 | 170.00 | 95.00 |
| 8/4 | 190.00 | 105.00 |

### Quarter Cut Red Oak

| | 1s&2s | No. 1 Com. |
|---|---|---|
| 4/4 | $145.00 | $ 80.00 |
| 5/4 and 6/4 | 160.00 | 90.00 |
| 8/4 | 165.00 | 95.00 |

### Beech

The quantity of beech produced in Ontario is not large and is generally sold on a log run basis, the locality governing the prices. At present the prevailing quotation on log run, mill culls out, delivered in Toronto, is $35.00 to $40.00.

---

## OTTAWA

Manufacturers' Prices

### Pine

| | | |
|---|---|---|
| Good sidings: | | |
| 1 in. x 7 in. and up | | $140.00 |
| 1¼ in. and 1½ in., 8 in. and up. | | 165.00 |
| 2 in. x 7 in. and up | | 165.00 |
| No. 2 cuts 2 x 8 in. and up | | 80.00 |
| Good strips: | | |
| 1 in. | $100.00 | $105.00 |
| 1¼ in. and 1½ in. | | 120.00 |
| 2 in. | | 125.00 |
| Good shorts: | | |
| 1 in. x 7 in. and up | | 110.00 |
| 1 in. 4 in. to 6 in. | 85.00 | 90.00 |
| 1¼ in. and 1½ in. | | 110.00 |
| 2 in. | | 125.00 |
| 7 in. to 9 in. A sidings | 54.00 | 56.00 |
| No. 1 dressing sidings | 70.00 | 74.00 |
| No. 1 dressing strips | | 62.00 |
| No. 1 dressing shorts | 50.60 | 53.00 |
| 1 in. x 4 in. s.c. strips | | 48.00 |
| 1 in. x 5 in. s.c. strips | | 48.00 |
| 1 in. x 6 in. s.c. strips | | 50.00 |
| 1 in. x 7 in. s.c. strips | 63.00 | 64.00 |
| 1 in. x 8 in. s.c. strips, 12 to 16 ft. | | 54.00 |
| 1 in. x 10 in. M.R. | | 58.00 |
| S.C. sidings, 1½ and 2 in. | 58.00 | 60.00 |
| S.C. strips, 1 in. | | 45.00 |
| 1¼, 1½ and 2 in. | 50.00 | 55.00 |
| S. . shorts, 1 x 4 to 6 in. | 34.00 | 36.00 |
| S. . and bet., shorts, 1 x 5 | | 36.00 |
| S.C. and bet., shorts, 1 x 6 | | 42.00 |
| S.C. shorts, 6-11 ft., 1 x 10 in. | | 48.00 |
| Box boards: | | |
| 1 in. x 4 in. and up, 6 ft.-11 ft. | | 34.00 |
| 1 in. x 3 in. and up, 12 ft.-16 ft. | 35.00 | 37.00 |
| Mill cull shorts, 1 in. x 4 in. and x 4 in. and up, 12 ft. and up | 24.00 | 26.00 |
| Mill culls, strips and sidings, 1 in. up, 6 ft. to 11 ft. | | 22.00 |
| O. culls r and w p | 18.00 | 20.00 |

### Red Pine, Log Run

| | | |
|---|---|---|
| Mill culls out, 1 in. | 32.00 | 34.00 |
| Mill culls out, 1¼ in. | 32.00 | 34.00 |
| Mill culls out, 1½ in. | 32.00 | 34.00 |
| Mill culls out, 2 in. | 32.00 | 34.00 |
| Mill Culls, white pine, 1 in. x 7 in. and up | | 20.00 |

### Mill Run Spruce

| | | |
|---|---|---|
| 1 in. x 4 in. and up, 6 ft.-11 ft. | | 23.00 |
| 1 in. x 4 in. and up, 12 ft.-16 ft. | 30.00 | 32.00 |
| 1" x 9"-10" and up, 12 ft.-16 ft. | | 35.00 |
| 1¼" x 7, 8 and 9" up, 12 ft.-16 ft. | | 33.00 |
| 1¼ x 10 and up, 12 ft.-16 ft. | 38.00 | 42.00 |
| 1½" x 12" x 12" and up, 12'-16' | | 42.00 |
| Spruce, 1 in. clear fine dressing and B | | 55.00 |
| Hemlock, 1 in. cull | | 20.00 |
| Hemlock, 1 in. log run | 24.00 | 26.00 |
| Hemlock, 2 x 4, 6, 8, 10 12/16 ft. | | 28.00 |
| Tamarac | 25.00 | 28.00 |
| Basswood, log run, dead culls out | 45.00 | 50.00 |
| Basswood, log run, mill culls out. | 50.00 | 54.00 |
| Birch, log run | 45.00 | 50.00 |
| Soft Elm, common and better, 1, 1½, 2 in. | 58.00 | 68.00 |
| Ash, black, log run | 62.00 | 65.00 |
| 1 x 10 No. 1 barn | 57.00 | 62.00 |
| 1 x 10 No. 2 barn | 51.00 | 56.00 |
| 1 x 8 and 9 No. 2 barn | 47.00 | 52.00 |

# CURRENT LUMBER PRICES—WHOLESALE

**Lath per M.:**

| | | |
|---|---|---|
| No. 1 White Pine, 1¼ in. x 4 ft. | | 8.00 |
| No. 2 White Pine | | 6.00 |
| Mill run White Pine | | 7.00 |
| Spruce, mill run, 1½ in. | | 6.00 |
| Red Pine, mill run | | 6.00 |
| Hemlock, mill run | | 5.50 |

**White Cedar Shingles**

| | | |
|---|---|---|
| XXXX, 18 in. | 9.00 | 10.00 |
| Clear butt, 18 in. | 6.00 | 7.00 |
| 18 in. XX | | 5.00 |

## QUEBEC

**White Pine**
(At Quebec)

| | Cts. Per Cubic Ft. | |
|---|---|---|
| First class Ottawa wancy, 18 in. average according to lineal | 100 | 110 |
| 19 in. and up average | 110 | 120 |

**Spruce Deals**
(At Mill)

| | | |
|---|---|---|
| 3 in. unsorted, Quebec, 4 in. to 6 in. wide | $ 20.00 | $ 25.00 |
| 3 in. unsorted, Quebec, 7 in. to 8 in. wide | 26.00 | 28.00 |
| 3 in. unsorted, Quebec, 9 in. wide | 30.00 | 35.00 |

**Oak**
(At Quebec)

| | Cts. Per Cubic Ft. | |
|---|---|---|
| According to average and quality, 55 ft. cube | 125 | 130 |

**Elm**
(At Quebec)

| | | |
|---|---|---|
| According to average and quality, 40 to 45 ft. cube | 100 | 120 |
| According to average and quality, 30 to 35 ft. | 90 | 100 |

**Export Birch Planks**
(At Mill)

| | | |
|---|---|---|
| 1 to 4 in. thick, per M. ft. | $ 30.00 | $ 35.00 |

## ST. JOHN, N.B.

(From Yards and Mills—Retail)

**Rough Lumber**

| | | |
|---|---|---|
| 2x3, 2x4, 3x3, 3x4. Rgh Merch Spr | $30.00 | |
| 2x3, 2x4, 3x3, 3x4, Dressed 1 edge | 31.00 | |
| 2x3, 2x4, 3x3, 3x4, Dressed 4 sides | 31.00 | |
| 2x6, 2x7, 3x5, 4x4, 4x6, all rough. | 30.00 | |
| 2x6, 2x7, 3x5, 4x4, 4x6, all rough. | 34.00 | |
| 2x8, 3x7, 5x5, 6x6 | 37.00 | $ 40.00 |
| 2x9, 3x8, 6x8, 7x7 | 37.00 | 40.00 |
| 2x10, 3x9 | 45.00 | |
| 2x12, 3x10, 3x12, 8x8 and up | 45.00 | |
| Merch. Spr. Bds., Rough, 1x3-4 & 5 | 30.00 | |
| Merch. Spr. Bds., Rough, 1x6 | 34.00 | |
| Merch. Spr. Bds., Rough, 1x7 & up | 40.00 | |
| Refuse Bds., Deals and Setgs. | 18.00 | 20.00 |

Above random lengths up to 18-0 long.
Lengths 19-0 and up $5.00 extra per M.
For planing Merch. and Refuse Bds. add $2.00 per M. to above prices.
Laths, $7.00.

**Shingles**

| | Per M. |
|---|---|
| Cedar, Extras | $6.00 |
| Cedar, Clears | 5.25 |
| Cedar, 2nd Clears | 4.25 |
| Cedar, Extra No. 1 | 2.50 |
| Spruce | 4.00 |

## SARNIA, ONT.

**White Pine—Fine, Com. and Better**

| | |
|---|---|
| 1 x 6 and 8 in. | $110.00 |
| 1 in., 8 in. and up wide | 130.00 |
| 1¼ and 1½ in. and up wide | 180.00 |
| 2 in. and up wide | 180.00 |

**Cuts and Better**

| | |
|---|---|
| 4/4 x 8 and up No. 1 and better | 125.00 |
| 5/4 and 6/4 and up No. 1 and better | 150.00 |
| 8/4 and 8 and up No. 1 and better | 150.00 |

**No. 1 Cuts**

| | |
|---|---|
| 1 in., 8 in. and up wide | 105.00 |
| 1¼ in., 8 in. and up wide | 125.00 |
| 1½ in., 8 in. and up wide | 125.00 |
| 2 in., 8 in. and up wide | 130.00 |
| 2½ in. and 3 in., 8 in. and up wide | 175.00 |
| 4 in., 8 in. and up wide | 185.00 |

**No. 1 Barn**

| | | |
|---|---|---|
| 1 in., 10 to 16 ft. long | $ 75.00 | $ 85.00 |
| 1¼, 1½ and 2 in., 10/16 ft. | 80.00 | 85.00 |
| 2½ to 3 in., 10/16 ft. | 85.00 | 100.00 |

**No. 2 Barn**

| | | |
|---|---|---|
| 1 in., 10 to 16 ft. long | 65.00 | 75.00 |
| 1¼, 1½ and 2 in., 10/16 ft. | | 66.00 |
| 2½, 1½ and 3 in. | | 85.00 |

**No. 3 Barn**

| | | |
|---|---|---|
| 1 in., 10 to 16 ft. long | 48.00 | 55.00 |
| 1¼, 1½ and 2 in., 10/16 ft. | 50.00 | 56.00 |

**Box**

| | | |
|---|---|---|
| 1 in., 1¼ and 1½ in., 10/16 ft. | 33.00 | 35.00 |

**Mill Culls**

| | |
|---|---|
| Mill Run Culls— | |
| 1 in., 4 in. and up wide, 6/16 ft. | 26.00 |
| 1¼, 1½ and 2 in. | 27.00 |

## WINNIPEG

**No. 1 Spruce**

| Dimension | S.1.S. and 1.E. 10 ft. | 12 ft. | 14 ft. | 16 ft. |
|---|---|---|---|---|
| 2 x 4 | $30 | $29 | $29 | $30 |
| 2 x 6 | 31 | 29 | 29 | 30 |
| 2 x 8 | 32 | 30 | 30 | 31 |
| 2 x 10 | 33 | 31 | 31 | 32 |
| 2 x 12 | 34 | 32 | 32 | 33 |

For 2 inches, rough, add 50 cents.
For S1E only, add 50 cents.
For S1S and 2E, S4S or D&M, add $3.00.
For timbers larger than 8 x 8, add 50c. for each additional 2 inches each way.
For lengths longer than 20 ft., add $1.00 for each additional two feet.
For selected common, add $5.00.
For No. 2 Dimension, $3.00 less than No. 1.
For 1 x 2 and 2 x 2, $2 more than 2 x 4 No. 1.
For Tamarac, open.

## BUFFALO and TONAWANDA

**White Pine**
Wholesale Selling Price

| | |
|---|---|
| Uppers, 4/4 | $225.00 |
| Uppers, 5/4 to 8/4 | 225.00 |
| Uppers, 10/4 to 12/4 | 250.00 |
| Selects, 4/4 | 200.00 |
| Selects, 5/4 to 8/4 | 200.00 |
| Selects, 10/4 to 12/4 | 225.00 |
| Fine Common, 4/4 | 155.00 |
| Fine Common, 5/4 | 160.00 |
| Fine Common, 6/4 | 160.00 |
| Fine Common, 8/4 | 160.00 |
| No. 1 Cuts, 4/4 | 115.00 |
| No. 1 Cuts, 5/4 | 130.00 |
| No. 1 Cuts, 6/4 | 135.00 |
| No. 1 Cuts, 8/4 | 140.00 |
| No. 2 Cuts, 4/4 | 70.00 |
| No. 2 Cuts, 5/4 | 100.00 |
| No. 2 Cuts, 6/4 | 105.00 |
| No. 2 Cuts, 8/4 | 110.00 |
| No. 3 Cuts, 5/4 | 60.00 |
| No. 3 Cuts, 6/4 | 65.00 |
| No. 3 Cuts, 8/4 | 67.00 |
| Dressing, 4/4 | 95.00 |
| Dressing 4/4 x 10 | 98.00 |
| Dressing, 4/4 x 12 | 110.00 |
| No. 1 Moulding, 5/4 | 150.00 |
| No. 1 Moulding, 6/4 | 150.00 |
| No. 1 Moulding, 8/4 | 155.00 |
| No. 2 Moulding, 5/4 | 125.00 |
| No. 2 Moulding, 6/4 | 125.00 |
| No. 2 Moulding, 8/4 | 130.00 |
| No. 1 Barn, 1 x 12 | 90.00 |
| No. 1 Barn, 1 x 6 and 8 | 76.00 |
| No. 1 Barn, 1 x 10 | 80.00 |
| No. 2 Barn, 1 x 6 and 8 | 62.00 |
| No. 2 Barn, 1 x 10 | 68.00 |
| No. 2 Barn, 1 x 12 | 75.00 |
| No. 3 Barn, 1 x 6 and 8 | 39.00 |
| No. 3 Barn, 1 x 10 | 39.00 |
| No. 3 Barn, 1 x 12 | 45.00 |
| Box, 1 x 6 and 8 | 33.00 |
| Box, 1 x 10 | 33.00 |
| Box, 1 x 12 | 36.00 |
| Box, 1 x 13 and up | 37.00 |

## BUFFALO

The following quotations on hardwoods represent the jobber buying price at Buffalo and Tonawanda.

**Maple**

| | 1s & 2s | No. 1 Com. | No. 2 Com. |
|---|---|---|---|
| 1 in. | $ 75.00 | $ 45.00 | $ 28.00 |
| 5/4 to 8/4 | 80.00 | 50.00 | 28.00 |
| 10/4 to 4 in. | 85.00 | 56.00 | 28.00 |

**Sap Birch**

| | | | |
|---|---|---|---|
| 1 in. | 90.00 | 45.00 | 30.00 |
| 5/4 and up | 100.00 | 50.00 | 30.00 |

**Soft Elm**

| | | | |
|---|---|---|---|
| 1 in. | 70.00 | 45.00 | 30.00 |
| 5/4 to 2 in. | 75.00 | 50.00 | 30.00 |

**Red Birch**

| | | | |
|---|---|---|---|
| 1 in. | 120.00 | 75.00 | |
| 5/4 and up | 125.00 | 80.00 | |

**Basswood**

| | | | |
|---|---|---|---|
| 1 in. | 70.00 | 45.00 | 30.00 |
| 5/4 to 2 in. | 80.00 | 55.00 | 35.00 |

**Plain Oak**

| | | | |
|---|---|---|---|
| 1 in. | 95.00 | 55.00 | 35.00 |
| 5/4 to 2 in. | 105.00 | 65.00 | 40.00 |

**Ash**

| | | | |
|---|---|---|---|
| 1 in. | 80.00 | 48.00 | 30.00 |
| 5/4 to 2 in. | 85.00 | 52.00 | 30.00 |
| 10/4 and up | 100.00 | 65.00 | 30.00 |

## BOSTON

Quotations given below are for highest grades of Michigan and Canadian White Pine and Eastern Canadian Spruce as required in the New England market in car loads.

| | | |
|---|---|---|
| White Pine Uppers, 1 in. | | |
| White Pine Uppers, 1¼, 1½, 2 in. | | |
| White Pine Uppers, 2½, 3 in. | | |
| White Pine Uppers, 4 in. | | |
| Selects, 1 in. | | $190.00 |
| Selects, 1¼, 2 in. | | 200.00 |
| Selects, 2½, 3 in. | | |
| Selects, 4 in. | | |
| Prices nominal | | |
| Fine Common, 1 in., 30%, 12 in. and up. | | 165.00 |
| Fine Common, 1 x 8 and up | | 165.00 |
| Fine Common, 1¼ to 2 in. | $165.00 | 170.00 |
| Fine Common, 2½ and 3 in. | | 180.00 |
| Fine Common, 4 in. | | 195.00 |
| 1 in. Shaky Clear | | 100.00 |
| 1¼ in. to 2 in. Shaky Clear | | 110.00 |
| 1 in. No. 2 Dressing | | 95.00 |
| 1¼ in. to 2 in. No. 2 Dressing | | 95.00 |
| No. 1 Cuts, 1 in. | | 110.00 |
| No. 1 Cuts, 1¼ to 2 in. | | 140.00 |
| No. 1 Cuts, 2½ to 3 in. | | 180.00 |
| No. 2 Cuts, 1 in. | | 80.00 |
| No. 2 Cuts, 1¼ to 2 in. | | 110.00 |
| Barn Boards, No. 1, 1 x 12 | | 95.00 |
| Barn Boards, No. 1, 1 x 10 | | 87.00 |
| Barn Boards, No. 1, 1 x 8 | | 83.00 |
| Barn Boards, No. 2, 1 x 12 | | 82.00 |
| Barn Boards, No. 2, 1 x 8 | | 69.00 |
| Barn Boards, No. 2, 1 x 10 | | 70.00 |
| Barn Boards, No. 3, 1 x 12 | | 48.00 |
| Barn Boards, No. 3, 1 x 10 | | 47.00 |
| Barn Boards, No. 3, 1 x 8 | | 47.00 |

**No. 1 Clear**

| | | |
|---|---|---|
| Can. Spruce, No. 1 and clear, 1 x 4 to 9" | | $ 78.00 |
| Can. Spruce, 1 x 10 in. | | 78.00 |
| Can. Spruce, No. 1, 1 x 4 to 7 in. | | 75.00 |
| Can. Spruce, No. 1, 1 x 8 and 9 in. | | 75.00 |
| Can. Spruce, No. 1, 1 x 10 in. | | 76.00 |
| Can. Spruce, No. 2, 1 x 4 and 5 in. | | 34.00 |
| Can. Spruce, No. 2, 1 x 6 and 7 in. | | 36.00 |
| Can. Spruce, No. 2, 1 x 8 and 9 in. | | 38.00 |
| Can. Spruce, No. 2, 1 x 10 in. | | 41.00 |
| Can. Spruce, No. 2, 1 x 12 in. | | 45.00 |
| Spruce, 12 in. dimension | | 44.00 |
| Spruce, 10 in. dimension | | 42.00 |
| Spruce, 9 in. dimension | | 41.00 |
| Spruce, 8 in. dimension | | 40.00 |
| 2 x 10 in. random lengths, 8 ft. and up | | 40.00 |
| 2 x 12 in., random lengths | | 43.00 |
| 2 x 3, 2 x 4, 2 x 5, 2 x 6, 2 x 7 | | 30.00 |
| 3 x 4 and 4 x 4 in. | | 31.00 |
| 2 x 9 | | 38.00 |
| All other random lengths, 7 in. and under, 8 ft. and up | 30.00 | 34.00 |
| 5 in. and up merchantable boards, 8 ft. and up, D 1s | 30.00 | 32.00 |
| 1 x 2 | 30.00 | 32.00 |
| 1 x 3 | | 30.00 |
| 1⅝ in. Spruce Lath | | 8.50 |
| 1½ in. Spruce Lath | 7.25 | 7.50 |

**New Brunswick Cedar Shingles**

| | | |
|---|---|---|
| Extras | 5.25 | 5.50 |
| Clears | 4.25 | 4.50 |
| Second Clear | 3.75 | 4.15 |
| Clear Whites | | 3.00 |

Second Hand Machinery & Equipment Wanted & For Sale

# Quick Action Section

Special Lots Of Lumber——Positions Wanted & Vacant

## Lumber Wanted

### Want

Mill output of Lath. Give prices on grades. Apply Box 863, Canada Lumberman, Toronto. 8-9

### Oak Wanted

Canadian Plain Red Oak wanted. A few cars of 4/4 and 8/4 No. 2 Common and Better. Apply Box 866 Canada Lumberman, Toronto. 8-9

### Wanted

Will buy Hemlock, Spruce and Pine, in blocks of 50 M. ft. to one million feet, send list of sizes. Box 873 Canada Lumberman, Toronto. 8

### Hard Maple Wanted

Several cars 8/4 and 12/4 dry stock, No. 1 and 2 Common. For further particulars apply Box No. 826 Canada Lumberman, Toronto. 5-8

### We Will Buy

A block of Hemlock, Spruce, Red or White Pine that is sawn or will be sawn before the 15th of March. Box 770 Canada Lumberman, Toronto. 2 T.f.

### Wanted

By wholesaler in New York State 4/4, 5/4, 6/4, and 8/4 Log Run Birch. Quote prices F.O.B. mills, giving description of stock. Box 868 Canada Lumberman, Toronto. 8-T.f.

### Wanted

Sawdust—Dry Hardwood and Pine, Ungraded. Quote F.O.B. Cars Mill in bulk for Pine, and in bulk and bags for Hardwood. Describe fully. Box 860, Canada Lumberman, Toronto. 8

### Wanted

By
GIDLEY BOAT CO. LTD.,
Penetang, Ontario.

4/4 Clear Cedar, Ontario or Quebec stock; 8/4 Clear Spruce. 8-9

### Lath for Sale

White Pine and Jack Pine. Write or wire for prices.

Brewster Loud Lumber Co.,
508 Lincoln Bldg.,
Detroit, Mich.
8-11

### Wanted

10 Cars No. 3 Jack Pine Lath also White Pine and Hemlock Lath in all grades.

Brewster Loud Lumber Co.,
508 Lincoln Bldg.,
Detroit, Mich.
8-11

### Wanted

To contract for supply of GREY ELM for bending purposes Cut 3¼" thick for delivery June, July and August. Quote price to St. Mary's Wood Specialty Co. Ltd., St. Mary's Ont. 5-8

## Lumber For Sale

### Lumber for Sale

75 M 1½" Maple No 2 Common & Better 60 M 1" Soft Elm Log Run Dry Stock. A. J. McEwen, Box No. 294 Maxville, Ont. 8-11

**PUBLISHER'S NOTICE**

Advertisements other than "Employment Wanted" or "Employees Wanted" will be inserted in this department at the rate of 25 cents per agate line (14 agate lines make one inch). $3.50 per inch, each insertion, payable in advance. Space measured from rule to rule. When four or more consecutive insertions of the same advertisement are ordered a discount of 25 per cent. will be allowed.

Advertisements of "Wanted Employment" will be inserted at the rate of one cent a word, net. Cash must accompany order. If Canada Lumberman box number is used, enclose ten cents extra for postage in forwarding replies. Minimum charge 25 cents.

Advertisements of "Wanted Employees" will be inserted at the rate of two cents a word, net. Cash must accompany the order. Minimum charge 50 cents.

Advertisements must be received not later than the 10th and 20th of each month to insure insertion in the subsequent issue.

### For Sale

At Blind River, Ontario, Pine and Spruce Lath, also some Cedar and Hemlock Lath. Grades, four foot mill run, 32" mill run, and four foot No. 3.

F. P. Potvin,
Blind River, Ont.
2-T.f.

### For Sale

Two million feet dry merchantable spruce from 1" to 4" thick, dry on sticks. Can be shipped rough or dressed. Also approximately two million feet Birch, Beech and Maple, 1", 2" and 3", Mill Run, Culls out. Prices right All dry. Sawn during season 1920-21. Rhodes, Curry Ltd., Amherst, N.S. 5-8

### Lumber for Sale

| | | | |
|---|---|---|---|
| 100 | M. 1" Basswood | 15 | M. 1" Soft Maple |
| 15 | M. 2" Rock Elm. | 15 | M. 1¼" " |
| 25 | M. 2" Soft Elm. | 50 | M. 2 x 4/6/8" x 12 |
| 25 | M. 1" Soft Elm. | | Spruce |
| 8 | M. 1" Ash. | 8 | M. 1½" Hickory |

All last winter's cut.
Also 10,000 Cedar fence posts.

Glenn A. Shaver,
5-8 Lunenburg, Ont

### WHITE PINE LUMBER

**For Immediate Shipment—1920 Cut—Should Be Bone Dry**

About 30,000 ft. 2 in.
" 18,000 ft. 1 in.
" 2,000 ft. 3 in.

Apply to J. A. Farnsworth, Cookshire, Quebec. 6-T.f.

## Machinery For Sale

### For Sale

8 inch Steam Feed. First class condition. L. Robertson, Ardbeg, Ontario. 7-9

### Machine for Sale

1 new type C-3 Yates Moulder. For price and particulars regarding equipment apply Box 864 Canada Lumberman, Toronto. 8-11

### For Sale

Neverslip Monarch Tractor 20-12 H.P. in first-case condition, only used short time. Will sacrifice for quick sale. Apply Rhodes, Curry Limited, Amherst, N.S. 5-8

### For Sale

1—250 H.P. Steam Plant complete; will sell whole plant or part. In excellent condition. Bargain price for quick sale. Box 875 Canada Lumberman, Toronto. 8

### Wickes Gang

GANG: No. 12 Wickes Gang, 40" sash, 15" stroke, steam binder rolls, front and back in two sections, feed and oscillation combined, 1908 model, and has been in use for five years. We furnish with this gang 11 rolls for cants and stock, one filing machine, and 4 sets of saws.

THE PEMBROKE LUMBER CO.,
1t.f. Pembroke, Ont.

### For Sale

30-18 Monarch Tractor with five sets of heavy log trucks and chains, if needed for good roads building, log bunks can be removed and boxes put on. Apply Box 834, Canada Lumberman, Toronto. 6-9

### For Sale En-Bloc

Complete Saw Mill equipment, including one Four Block Hamilton Carriage. One pair heavy twin engines, feed complete and steam nigger. One three block E. Long Carriage with eight inch gun shot feed and steam nigger. One heavy three saw edger, W. Hamilton, make. Three 75 H.P. Boilers complete with dutch ovens and stacks. One 90 H.P. engine and fly-wheel complete. One lath and shingle mill. Complete filing equipment. One refuse burner. Shafting pulleys, transmission, etc., complete. Apply Box 783 Canada Lumberman. Toronto. 3-8

### Engines, Boilers, etc., for Sale

One "Williams" Upright Engine 6" x 6"
One Upright Engine 5" x 6"
Six Return tubular boilers of following dimensions:-
One "Butterfield" 72" x 14' - 3¼" tube - ½" shell.
One "Polson" 64" x 14' - 3¼" tube - ½" shell
One "Doty" 60" x 15' - 4" tube - ½" shell
One "Doty" 60" x 14½" - 4" tube - ½" shell
One "Doty" 60" x 15' - 4" tube - ½" shell
One "Inglis" 60" x 16' - 3" tube - ½" shell
One double acting "Northey" Fire pump, 6" suction, 5" discharge, 14" steam cylinder, 8" water cylinder, 13" stroke, Capacity 450 gallons per minute.
One "Northey" feed pump 6 x 4 x 7" stroke, Capacity 60 gallons per minute.
One brass Mill steam whistle.

For further particulars apply The Conger Lumber Co Limited., Parry Sound. Ontario. 24 T.f.

## Situations Wanted

Wanted—a good Lath Mill to run by the M. by an A1 man. Box 874 Canada Lumberman, Toronto. 8

Band Sawyer, either right or left, 10 years experience on fast niggerman, first class references. Will go anywhere. Box 858 Canada Lumberman, Toronto. 8

Position wanted for the coming season to make lath or Pickets by thousand. Can give good references if required. Box 849 Canada Lumberman, Toronto. 7-9

Wanted—Position by bookkeeper with a high knowledge of double entry also pay roll etc. Lumber business preferred. Box 854 Canada Lumberman, Toronto. 7-8

Wanted position as Mill Superintendent. Eight years experience as Mill Superintendent fifteen years as sawyer. Can furnish best references. Box 747 Canada Lumberman, Toronto. 1-9

Experienced Shipper—wants position in Sash, Door and Planing Mill plant. 20 years experience, steady, reliable, and capable of handling orders from office to completion. Familiar with Planing Mill Machinery, also good Glazier.. A 1 references, Box 847, Canada Lumberman, Toronto. 7-8

Position wanted: As retail manager or travelling salesman, 17 years business experience, thoroughly acquainted with all phases of the retail trade, total abstainer. Apply Box 889 Canada Lumberman, Toronto. 6-8

Position Wanted as Lumber Inspector and Scaler, by young Russian, four years experience on Rough and Dressed lumber, can handle yard work and Shipping, has good connection with the Saw Mill. Single, can go anywhere. First Class Canadian references. Apply Box 812, Canada Lumberman, Toronto, Ont. 5-8

Aggressive Young Man with ability integrity and five years' experience Lumber and Millwork offices, desires permanent position with progressive concern in a town. Can handle Orders, Sales and Correspondence etc. Replies treated confidential. Excellent credentials. Box 869 Canada Lumberman, Toronto. 8

Estimator. Lumber, Sash and Doors, Factory work. Gilt edge testimonials. Twelve years experience, Sales Manager, Estimator and general office man. Age 37. Energetic, reliable and accurate. Open for engagement with wide awake and up-to-date concern where above qualities and abilities would be appreciated. Reply to Box 872 Canada Lumberman, Toronto. 8

Young Scotchman married, abstainer, wishes permanent progressive position as bookkeeper, stenographer and general office man. Have had following experience: Six years banking, two years assistant bookkeeper and stenographer, London, England; eight years lumber office experience. Willing to go anywhere. Salary $100/$125. Apply Box 799 Canada Lumberman, Toronto. 4-8

Employment wanted by man in the prime of life, married and a Canadian, well experienced in all branches of Lumbering, from roadcutting to manager, Saw-mill and Yard, Driving and Rafting and Timber Estimating, am a Licensed Culler and have office experience. Would like executive position with Company who are lumbering for profits, not pastime. Am at present employed in executive position but scope is limited, and wish to change. Box 851 Canada Lumberman, Toronto. 7-8

## Situations Vacant

Wanted—Head shipper for retail lumber yard in Toronto. Apply giving experience and salary expected. Box 857, Canada Lumberman, Toronto. -8

Wanted active young man having good sales connection amongst the Canadian and American trade. Must be of good appearance and a proven salesman. Salary or commission basis. Apply to Box. 99 Canada Lumberman, Montreal. 8
8

## Business Chances

### Wanted

To contract for entire cut White Pine, Spruce, Jack and Norway Pine up to twenty million feet, also lath. Give full particulars and address. Box 853 Canada Lumberman, Toronto. 7-8

### Wanted

To make arrangements with good lumber firm in Canada handling Spruce and Lath on commission basis in New York and New Jersey States, good connections, resident New York. Apply Box 828 Canada Lumberman, Toronto. 7-8

### Wanted

By wholesaler in New York State, Spruce connection with mill in position to ship 2". Merchantable, sizes surfaced to ¼" scant on a competitive basis into New York State. We discount all our bills. Box 867 Canada Lumberman, Toronto. 8 T.f.

### New Forests for Great Britain

A shipment of seven hundred pounds of Douglas fir seed was recently forwarded from the Dominion Forestry Branch seed-extracting plant at New Westminster, B.C. to Great Britain. This is the final shipment of seed collected in 1921. The total quantity of each kind of seed shipped for the season was: Douglas fir, 4,000 pounds; Sitka spruce, 3,000 pounds; and western hemlock, 100 pounds. As tree seed is very small and light, ranging from an average of forty-three thousand seeds to the pound of Douglas fir to four hundred thousand seeds to the pound of Sitka spruce, it will be seen that many millions of seedlings will be germinated from these shipments for planting in the extensive reforestation scheme which the British Forestry Commission has in hand.

Canada's forests belong to the whole people. They have an important bearing on climate and water supply. They enter into the daily life of the Canadian, both in a business and a domestic sense to a degree of which few are conscious. The public unfortunately is a strong contributing factor in the origin of most forest fires, and education in this matter will do much to reduce the present enormous fire waste.

A few rows of trees on the side of the prevailing winter winds will make a world of difference in the comfort of the farmstead.

# Review of Current Trade Conditions

### St. John Reports Some Improvement in Demand

The lumber trade at St. John, N. B. at the present moment seems to be in a somewhat improved condition in so far as demand is concerned. Prices have certainly not increased. As a matter of fact they are less, perhaps, by a dollar a thousand than a month ago. Demand for lumber seems quite fair, but the trouble is to buy at prices offered. The sellers, cannot make a new dollar for an old one and stand to lose at the quotations proferred in the American market.

Many steamers are at present in port. All the Irish boats are taking small parcels of good deals at prices which lead for scantling about $22.00 to $23.00 at the mills and broader deals $28.00 to $35.00 per M. Quite a quantity of old government stocks are being shipped to Manchester and Liverpool as both of the English houses here have bought back several millions of the stock at bargain prices and are dumping it over to England taking what they can get for it. They are culling out some sizes and shipping to the United States where it is being sold at a profit, simply because it has been bought back from the government at ridiculously low prices. This, has its serious effect upon the manufacturers who are forced either to sell at these prices and take enormous losses or hold on if they can and await better times. In the meantime, they must pay interest on borrowings which increase the value of the old lumber, and as a matter of fact any new logs as yet will not show a profit in the manufactured lumber at prices pertaining.

Certainly lumber is moving and every day the old stocks are being absorbed all over this country. New cut stock is not yet ready for shipment and the cut is anything but heavy in New Brunswick, while in Nova Scotia it is the lightest it has ever been. The next month or two is bargain time for those with money, but later on the lumber manufacturer must assuredly get a reward for his labors and this noble business will be back on its feet. One mill at St. John started operations the 25th of March, viz., Murray & Gregory, Ltd. They are sawing largely English deals, well graded, and well manufactured. They will have only about a three-quarter cut for the season.

Wages are about 15 per cent. lower than last year and men quite plentiful and willing to work.

Laths are not as steady in price as a month ago, and may weaken during the next two weeks or they may go higher.

The winter mills are practically done sawing but the larger mills will start before long and will be producing at a heavy rate but no old stocks are on hand and it is believed the lath market will remain steady around $5.00 at mills.

The driving season has not started as yet in full swing. Only the smaller streams are open. Men for this work can be hired around $1.50 per day and board but there is only a limited quantity of logs to drive.

### Quebec Exporters Say Outlook is Not Bright

Capt. John Burstall, senior member of the Quebec timber firm of John Burstall & Co., and H. R. Van, manager of the Louise Lumber Co., Limited, Quebec, who returned from the United Kingdom at the end of March, have not much to say in regard to condition in the timber and lumber markets in the United Kingdom.

Capt. John Burstall, who is one of the best-known representatives in the overseas trade markets, when requested to give his impressions on the timber and lumber situation in England, said that he did not care to discuss the situation. He made a few sales, but on the while, the situation in the United Kingdom was not encouraging. He referred to the strike of the engineers as a disturbing factor, and when asked if the Genoa conference was looked forward to ameliorate the political and trade situation, said opinions were divided in England on this question.

H. R. Van said he did not wish to make any statement in regard to his impressions overseas. There was nothing very good to tell, he added.

J. G. Levie, vice-president of the Quebec shipping firm of W. & J. Sharples, after two months' observance during which time he toured England, Ireland and Scotland, to confer with the firm's representatives, and the United Kingdom lumber trade in general, will return about the middle of the month. It is expected that he will not have encouraging news to communicate on his return, judging from weekly letters received by his firm. According to the information gained from the senior member, W. Gerard Power, reports of Mr. Levie are but confirmation of the trade letters which have appeared in the "Canada Lumberman" for several months past.

It is fully recognized, however, that these unsettled conditions cannot endure for a much longer period of time. Quebec shippers, who have their ear constantly to the ground, are encouraged by the belief that the coming summer will bring a change, but say it is better to look clearly into the present condition of things with a philosophical mind than otherwise, and await with patience the opportunities to be presented in the near future, which are bound to lift the clouds and clear the business horizon.

Labor is beginning to realize that it cannot proceed towards the goal of progress without capital, and, therefore, inclined to view the situation with a saner vision. The high salaried leaders or paid agitators are beginning to understand that they have shot their bolt and should capital crawl much deeper into its shell of self-preservation, there will be little construction activities for the wage earner, which will revolve against the tyranny of trade unionism, and landlord and retail trade profiteering as well.

The inclination for investment in bond and gilt-edged stocks, which has been brought about by the fear of the money interests to invest in business, especially construction for the circulation of money in trade activities, is beginning to take a more optimistic observation of the situation. Judging by appearance, more wealth will be loosened this summer in business activities than at any period since the signing of the armistice, which will affect the lumber trade and bring it back to its own.

### Ottawa Lumber Interests are More Hopeful

Indications that a revival of building on something approaching a pre-war scale loomed up at Ottawa, during the early part of April and though the lumber market in general did not show any great increase in activity, the underlying factors seemed much better than they did a year ago. The trade though it has not yet experienced good business, which apparently is ahead, holds a large degree of optimism regarding the future.

The chief hope is that building will increase this spring, and judging from the number of permits issued during March, there is going to be a considerable increase of activity in this direction. In March 1922, there were 80 permits issued as compared with 45 in March the previous year. Many permits call for the erection of new homes, and while the amounts in most instances are not exceptionally large, they indicate a healthy growth of structural operations.

A year ago permits for several large works were taken out early, but as the season progressed or strikes occurred the projects were abandoned. One of such works was the new Bank of Commerce building on Sparks Street, which was to cost $300,000. Tenders for this work are now being called for after a revision of the plans. Another was the $750,000.00 theatre on Queen Street by the Famous Players corporation. This work after being gotten under way was stopped nearly nine months ago, and has not been proceeded with.

Another satisfactory factor is the general labor situation in regard to the crafts embraced in the building trades. The majority of the trades have either settled or have negotiations under way which bear promise of a satisfactory agreement at lower wages, without strikes taking place. The members of the Laborers' Union who have been negotiating with the contractors for the last three weeks finally went to arbitration, the proceedings commencing on April 5th. The contractors offered 45 cents per hour and it was rejected. Last year the men received 50 cents per hour.

A still further hopeful sign is the reported easing of the American money market, it being stated by the Ottawa lumber trade that plenty of money was available in the U. S. at four and one half per cent. interest, which is in decided contrast with the rate of a year ago and the adverse exchange.

Several predicted that if the easy money in the U. S. went into building this spring, that there was bound to be a good market for eastern lumber stocks.

"The American market for the last couple of weeks, has been if anything, worse than it was a month or six weeks ago so far as orders are concerned," was the comment of one lumberman. The demand was spotty and was practically for any one of a mixture of grades. He believed, however, that if American building opened up well that there would be a fair demand for practically all grades.

Though business was slow the market did not show any further

View of Mills in Sarnia.

# BUY THE BEST

Retailers and woodworking establishments who like to get A1 NORWAY and WHITE PINE LUMBER always buy their stocks from us because we can ship them on quick notice. It pays to have the goods, but it pays better to "deliver" them.

We also make a specialty of heavy timbers cut to order any length up to 60 feet from Pine or B. C. Fir.

*"Rush Orders Rushed"*

## Cleveland-Sarnia Sawmills Co., Limited
### SARNIA, ONTARIO

B. P. Bole, Pres.    F. H. Goff, Vice-Pres.    E. C. Barre, Gen. Mgr.    W. A. Saurwein, Ass't. Mgr.

sign of weakening as regards price. The best stocks were reported to be fairly low and it was not anticipated that any great reduction in price would be experienced. The middle grades some weeks ago underwent a considerable drop and dealers say that the cull stock is practically down to as low level as it can go.

The final March blizzard which raged March 31st and April 1st, set back building in Ottawa about a week or ten days, according to contractors.

Reports from the woods indicate that the operations are in most cases in good shape for the spring drive, and some companies especially, John R. Booth Ltd., have a considerable log supply on hand, or near the mills. One report was current that the Booth Company intended to open its sawmill on April 15th, and work on day and night shifts as before the war. Definite announcement as to this was with-held by the Company. The Booth and the Hawkesbury mills, it was expected, would be among the first of the valley mills to commence operations.

Trade with the wholesale yards and the retailers was only fair, the majority of the stock bought being for repairs and alterations. Factory conditions showed little or no change with respect to volume of output or labor conditions.

## No Distinct Tendencies in Montreal Markets

The Montreal market is characterized by absence of distinct tendencies, and a divergence of opinion as to the immediate future. A fair amount of business is moving, but while some wholesalers state that the prices, particularly for spruce, are low, others state that they are obtaining fair rates. The latter applies especially to orders for American account. There are reports as to mills selling at cheap prices; these, however, appear to be of a more or less nebulous character. On this point, one wholesaler stated "I have made many inquiries as to this alleged cheap lumber and have found in every case that there is no foundation for the report. In every instance where the price is apparently low, the quality is on a par with the quotation, and the lumber is by no means cheap."

There is some doubt as to the course of prices, combined with uncertainty as to the general business situation, which is having its effect on the market. Certain wholesalers insist that mill prices must come down if the buying is to be encouraged, and that this must be backed up by lower freight rates.

Hardwoods are dull, with the lower ends practically unsaleable.

B. C. stocks are moving slowly, at prices which represent a reduction from the recent advance for upper grades.

The Riordon Company has sold large blocks of stock to United States customers at what are regarded as satisfactory prices.

The building season has not opened very well. A large amount of work is in prospect, particularly in the way of schools and similar buildings, but so far few contracts have been placed.

With regard to the allegation in the Quebec Parliament that pulpwood from Crown lands is reaching the States via the Maritime Provinces, the buyer of wood for a large American mill expressed doubt as to whether any large amount is being sent across the border. He based his opinion on the ground that the transportation charges would add to the cost to such an extent as to make the price prohibitive.

## March Building Operations Show Gain

The volume of contemplated new work reported in Canada during March, according to MacLean Building Reports, Ltd., amounted to $23,773,100. Construction contracts awarded throughout the Dominion amounted to $13,465,000, compared with $10,718,300 in February, and $10,256,700 in March, 1921. Residential buildings accounted for 44.6 per cent. of the March total, and amounted to $5,930,800. Business buildings amounted to $5,267,200, or 39 per cent. of the total; industrial buildings $260,000, or 1.9 per cent.; public works and utilities, $2,007,000, or 14.5 per cent. A significant feature of the March construction record is the increase in business buildings over February.

## Nova Scotia Lumbermen are Alert

The lumbermen of Nova Scotia are to be congratulated on organizing a provincial body. Their brethren from the other provinces fell into the line some years ago and while the forest products men down by the sounding sea have, perhaps, been a little backward in getting together, nevertheless, they have taken a step in the right direction. There are several live-wire representatives who will see that no stone is left unturned to make the new Association a success.

There are many problems of a local character, to which it is necessary to direct attention from time to time. These apply to freight and water rates, car supply, general shipping facilities and other matters with which a provincial body can deal effectively.

R. E. Dickie, who is at the head of the new organization is a live-wire lumberman, and will, if he is accorded proper support, see that the Nova Scotia Lumbermen's Association continues to grow in strength and influence.

Everything betokens a useful career for this new body of forest products producers and distributors.

## High Honor for Dan McLachlin

It is pleasing to announce that a Canadian in the person of Dan McLachlin of Arnprior, Ont., was elected second vice-president of the National Wholesale Lumber Dealers' Association, at the annual convention held in Washington recently. Mr. McLachlin is the present presiding officer of the Canadian Forestry Association.

The other officers elected were,—President, W. H. Schuette, Pittsburgh, Pa.; First vice-president, Chas. A. Goodman, Marinette, Wis. Horace F. Taylor, of Buffalo who is well-known in Canada, was re-elected one of the trustees for the next three years. Henry Cape, of New York, was re-elected treasurer, and W. W. Schupner, of New York, was re-elected secretary.

The retiring president, Mr. McClure, declared that he believed the Association to be on the verge of great expansion, and predicted that, at least, 100 new members would join up during the coming year. The banquet was one of the enjoyable features of the gathering. Mr. McClure was toast master and the speakers were,—Senator George W. Pepper, of Pennsylvania, and Col. H. S. Osborne, who is a Canadian. The latter told of Canadian ineals and purposes, and was given a splendid reception.

At the gathering in Washington there were several Canadians in attendance and gratifying reports were presented from the various departments of the organization. There was throughout the gathering a feeling of optimism, the general opinion being that the worst of the depression is over and that the future can be looked forward to with confidence.

J. W. McClure, of Memphis, Tenn., the retiring president, gave a stirring address in which he predicted better business for 1922. He said in part:—The year 1921 did not leave many pleasant memories for the most of us. At times it seemed that all precedent was shattered, all experience worthless, and business seemen to be without a compass to guide its course through uncharted seas. It should be said, however, that the lumber industry showed remarkable stability and less wreckage than most other important industries. We now have the satisfaction of knowing that the worst is behind us and that the future course is turning upward toward better things. There are many reasons for believing that 1922 will show a substantial improvement in business over 1921, even though that improvement may come so closely as to be scarcely perceptible. The volume of building now under way and in prospect for this year is probably the greatest in the history of our country. The enormous amounts appropriated and being expended for road building, while perhaps not directly affecting the lumber business, will give employment to large numbers and will add to the general purchasing power of the country. Recent improvements in the value of stocks and in the iron and steel trade, in the prices of grains and other agricultural products all forecast better conditions for the future. However, there are many brakes retarding this progress, the principal one being the unstable conditions in Europe, so that the best we can expect perhaps for this year and probably next is a slow and halting improvement. If we recognize the change in the rules of the game under new conditions, we need not be content to break even or to make small profits. If we cannot make money through advancing values we can still profit by decreasing costs and cutting down overhead.

## Planting Trees on Waste Lands

A large number of interests throughout Ontario are heartily endorsing the reforestation of the pine ridges and waste lands of Ontario and also the encouragement of wood lots. The Canadian Forestry Association is doing a good work. Its propaganda is having an excellent effect.

Recently a delegation from the Canadian Forestry Association waited upon the Ontario Government, asking for a grant of $10,000. for the coming year. It was suggested that such a grant would be fruitful economy rather than postponable expenditure.

With lecturers and demonstrators skilled in the work as is now planned for Ontario and with such unique facilities as two railroad cars, one a forest exhibits-car dealing with forest protection, the other a tree planting-car equipped as a motion picture auditorium, the Association is prepared to give more extensive educational service than has been the case in any previous year.

### How Simcoe County Starts Reforestation

The County of Simcoe has closed a deal for the purchase of an
additional 100 acres to its 800-acre reserve for reforestation at
Anten Mills.

The purchase comprises the west half of lot one on the sixth
concession, Vespra, adjoining the reserve, and the price was $20.00
an acre.   There is a house, barn and stable on the property.   It is
understood there is another 100 acres, the east half of lot one,
available, but whether the price talked of will be met is, as yet,
uncertain.

In making the additional purchase, the Reforestation committee
is acting on the suggestion of Chief Forester Zavitz, with whom a
county delegation held a conference two weeks ago.

The committee again visited Toronto, recently meeting Premier
Drury as well as department heads.   The result was that the Government
promised to start planting young trees from the St. Williams
nursery about April 15.   Ten acres of the newly-acquired 100 acres
will be immediately developed into a nursery for the country.   Skilled
men will be assigned to the task of planting both seed and transplanting
tree sprouts, the Government to pay the cost of planting
and labor.   Young trees from the Anten Mills, or Hendrie Station
nursery will be distributed free to all persons in Simcoe county who
will undertake to replant them.   Development of the larger area will
also be started this summer.   From the activities of the reforesting
committee a real benefit to the country in future years has been put
in course of development and its progress doubtless will be watched
with keen interest.

### Last Cent of Firm's Debts Paid

Fulfilling an obligation to which he had committed himself in
March 1915, W. H. C. Mussen, of Mussens, Limited, Montreal is freed
of the liabilities which existed when the firm was placed in voluntary
liquidation seven years ago.   Cheques and drafts have been forwarded
to creditors providing for the final dividend of ten per cent., thus
completing payment of one hundred cents on the dollar.

Mussens, Limited, as now, engaged in the sale of railway,
mining and contractors and municipal supplies and in common with
such enterprises, sharply experienced the business depression which
affected Canadian contractors during that period of the war.   Faced
by the difficulties of collections and the further difficulty of profitably
disposing of the heavy stock on hand, Mr. Mussen, president of the
firm, decided that it was then advisable to apply for the appointment
of a liquidator.   It was announced at the time the liabilities of Mussens,
Limited totalled $300,000, while the assets comprising merchandise
on hand, realty holdings, open accounts, and bills receivable amounted
to $550,000, or approximately $250,000 in excess of the liabilities.
As the stock carried by the firm was not of a character to be
readily placed on the market, particularly during a period of depression
with no construction work in sight, the action taken was regarded
as offering the greatest possible protection to the creditors.

During the seven year period since 1915 Mussens, Limited have
received the support of the manufacturing firms represented by them
at the time of the liquidation, with one or two exceptions.   With these
exceptions, the organization continues to represent the firms who
were their creditors.   During the period several other concerns requested
Mussens, Limited, to represent them, showing the confidence
which the firm was regarded.   It had been necessary to reduce the
staff to a minimum, but all the heads of departments had been retained
so that the efficiency of the organization is unimpaired.

The company which has branches at Toronto, Winnipeg and
Vancouver, was established by Mr. Mussen in 1901.   In 1906 it was
organized as a joint stock company.

### New Sluiceway to Handle Pulpwood

The Fort William Pulp & Paper Co. are making many improvements
to their pulp mill at Fort William.   There is being constructed
at present a sluiceway nearly ¼ mile long, running from the wood
room to the reservoir in which the pulpwood is boomed.   This sluice
is being installed to handle the wood into the mill in a more convenient
manner, and will do away with the costly method heretofore in
use in handling from the cars.   The sluiceway will have a heavy steel
bottom, and with its conveyor and other parts, will represent expenditure
of $100,000.00.   Other improvements are also contemplated
at the plant.

Sir Frederick Becker left Montreal on April 2 on his return to
England.   During this month's visit to Canada he inspected the pulp
mills in Quebec and the Maritime Provinces in which he if financially
interested.

# EDGINGS

W. B. Blair, of Blair Bros., Ltd., Montreal, is suffering from an attack of grippe. He has been confined to the house some time.

Fire caused by friction broke out recently at the convergence of the mill waste conveyors to the boiler room of the Fraser Companies pulp mill at Edmundston, N. B. Prompt action saved the mill from much damage being done.

The Black River Pulpwood Co., Limited, Montreal, have been granted a provincial charter with a capital of $1,000,000 to conduct a general lumber business, manufacturing and dealing in all kinds of forest products.

Immeubles Landry, Limited, Mont Joli, Que., have been incorporated with a capital of $48,000 to conduct logging operations and to manufacture and sell forest products of all kinds. L. P. Landry and A. Landry, both of Mont Joli, are tow of the incorporators

Phippen Bros., lumber dealers, 746 Pape Ave., Toronto, recently opened a yard on Danforth Ave., East of the city limits. A new dressed lumber shed has been erected on the premises and considerable stock is being carried.

The Donnacona Paper Company of Donnacona, Que., is considering the erection of a new wood pulp mill and electric power house during the coming summer and it is reported they will move part of their wallboard plant to Pont Rouge.

It is understood that the Bathurst Co., Bathurst, N. B., may erect a mill for manufacturing newsprint paper. It is said the plans for the new plant are well under way and that construction will start about June 1st. Angus McLean is the president and general-manager of the Bathurst Co.

B. C. Howard & Company, Limited, Sherbrooke, Que., have been incorporated and will take over the firm of B. C. Howard & Co., manufacturing and marketing wood products of all kinds. Capital $599,000. B. C. Howard and C.B. Howard, both of Sherbrooke, are two of the incorporators.

The Laberge Lumber Co., of Sudbury, Ont., will erect a handsome new office building on their premises at the corner of Notre Dame and Louis Sts. The structure will be two storeys high 40 x 60 feet, brick with hot water heating and hardwood trim and floors. The cost will be about $25,000.

The Eastern Wrecking & Construction Co., of which W. Posnik is manager, have sold their premises at 2741 Danforth Ave., and purchased a lumber yard on the corner of Trent & Danforth Aves. They will occupy their new premises about June 1st. The company deal in all kinds of new and second-hand building material.

The Kastner Lumber Co., whose sawmill was recently destroyed by fire, expect to rebuild as soon as possible as the company has all its winter's stock to cut. Mr. Kastner reports that all the stock was saved except some that was stored in the mill. The loss of the firm in the recent fire is estimated at $15,000, with insurance of $4,800.

John T. James, of Bridgeburg, Ont., has sold his planing mill and lumber yard at Crystal Beach, to J. Russel Carrick, late of Buffalo, N. Y., who has taken possession. Mr. Carrick is a son-in-law of C. H. Hann, who for the last fifteen years has been foreman of the plant.

N. M. Bearinger, of the Elmira Planing Mills, Elmira, Ont., has erected an attractive new office which is one of the best fitted and most commodious in Western Ontario. It is finished in hardwood and the exterior is strucco. Every feature of the building embodies all the latest ideas in construction and display.

The Canadian Splint Co., Pembroke, Ont., which has been in operation for some months and the Diamond Match Co., which supplies the ignition for matches made, are being united under the name of the Canadian Match Co. (There are more than 250 men and girls on the payroll and changes are contemplated whereby the output of the plant will be increased.

W. A. Nichols of Carleton Place, Ont., who is a well-known sawmill operator and lumber dealer in that town, recently bought some fine limits near Hopetown in Lanark County. From a huge white pine tree on these limits Mr. Nichols recently cut 10 logs each 12 feet long. The tree measured 36 inches at the butt, and according to the Doyle rule contains 3,610 feet of lumber.

The Forest Exhibits Car of the Canadian Forestry Association, which has been touring the East for some months, has just been

It is understood that Mickle, Dyment & Son, whose headquarters are at Barrie, will operate their sawmill at Severn River, Ont., during the coming season. It has been idle for some time.

British Columbia. During the past month the car was completely made over by a staff of workmen and artists so as to adopt its visual instructions to B. C. conditions. Daily lectures will be given in the car by members of the B. C. Forest Service.

J. D. Forsythe was instantly killed in his sawmill at West Huntington, in Hastings County. He was reaching in front of the carriage to put a wedge behind a log when in some manner the carriage started up, carrying him against the circular saw. His body was literally severed in twain. Mr. Forsythe leaves a widow and one daughter to mourn his loss.

The Double Diamond Lumber Co., Limited, has been granted a charter with a capital stock of $100,000 and head offices at Mattagami Heights, in the district of Temiskaming, Ont. Among the incorporators are Eugene Bradeau and Annette Wallingford, both of the Township of Mountjoy. The company is empowered to carry on the business of timber merchanes, sawmill operators, loggers, etc.

A. H. Richardson, of the Provincial Forestry Department, in an illustrated address recently given in Toronto, showed how deforestation in some districts had released loose sandy soil which by wind action principally, drifted over nearby productive lands sometimes burying it 30 feet deep in sand. In regard to the work of the Forestry Department Mr. Richardson showed how this was carried on from the covering of the seed to the plantations of 4, 7, 12, 25, and 50 years.

The St. Croix Pulp and Paper Company of Hartville, N. S., is reported to have been reorganized and will in future be known as the Premier Power and Pulp Company, with a capitalization of $2,000,000. About $1,000,000 will be invested in renovating the old plant, and with proposed improvements, it is expected that the output will be about 8,000 tons of news print and 5,000 tons of wrapping paper a year. Any surplus pulp will be sold in the markets of United States and Great Britain.

The Hope Mfg. Co., Limited, 456 Gilbert St., Toronto, who recently increased its capital stock from $40,000 to $100,000, is devoting more attention to the retail lumber line and has gradually increased its facilities in this line. The company also continues to manufacture sash, doors and interior and exterior trim of all kinds, and report that business has been remarkably good during the past few weeks. There is considerable activity in both the yard and factory of the organization.

More than five million seedings and cuttings of trees will be distributed from the Dominion nurseries throughout the Prairie Provinces in Western Canada during the coming season. Most of them will go into the farm shelter belts. Forestry experts say that it would have been only a question of time before the prairies would have been forest if settlement and cultivation had not interfered. As it is, the establishment of shelter belts of trees around farmsteads is helping to break not only the winds but the winds but the monotony of the surrounding country.

A recent report from the West says that the spring-like weather on the prairies has improved business conditions greatly and considerable lumber has been moving as a result. Building permits taken out in Winnipeg and other centres are on such a scale as to suggest much construction. The one discouraging feature is that rents for office and residential property are still maintained at high pressure. This is declared to be one of the most discouraging features of all large western cities, which boards of trade assert can only be relieved by increasing building operations.

Writing to the "Canada Lumberman" a subscriber in the province of Quebec says that it would be of great interest to know the quantity of 1921 burned timber that is being salvaged at the present time. He says that salvaging the budworm-affected trees will not effect the output very materially as this timber is so spread out that is not possible in the majority of operations to go after it. It is stated that approximately 95 square miles of timber were burned over in 1921 in the Gaspe Peninsula, Que., but owing to the conditions of business, one of which was unusually heavy supply of logs and pulpwood at the mills, no companies affected in this district attempted any salvaging last year, but will do so more or less heavily during the coming year.

In an investigation conducted by several persons in Toronto it is stated that the cost of house building has come down slightly this year and that an ordinary six roomed, solid brick detached house can now be built on a twenty-five foot lot—the land remaining at the same figure as last year—for between two and three hundred dollars less than in 1921. The present figure represents about five thousand dollars. It is said that the same kind of a dwelling could be built in 1917 for about three thousand five hundred dollars but the land at that time cost some four or five hundred dollars less than it does today. The estimated outlay for the course lumber is given as follows—1917—$420; 1921—$232; 1922—$200. Inside trim and finish—1917—$420; 1921—$600; 1922—$500. The price of hardwood flooring is estimated to be about the some as last year or slightly more.

## Subscribers' Information Form

Many letters reach us from subscribers enquiring where a certain machine, a certain kind of lumber or veneer, or some other class of goods, can be obtained. We can usually supply the information. We want to be of service to our subscribers in this way, and we desire to encourage requests for such information. Make use of this form for the purpose.

"CANADA LUMBERMAN"
345 Adelaide Street West, Toronto

Date........................19....

Please tell us where we can procure ...........................................................

.................................................................................................................

.................................................................................................................

.................................................................................................................

Name ....................................................................

Address ....................................................................

## ALPHABETICAL INDEX TO ADVERTISERS

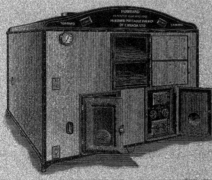

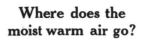

# CANADA LUMBERMAN BUYERS' DIRECTORY

The following regulations apply to all advertisers:—Eighth page, every issue, three headings;
quarter page, six headings; half page, twelve headings; full page, twenty-four headings

**ALLIGATORS**
Payette Company, P.
West, Peachy & Sons

**BABBITT METAL**
Canada Metal Co.
General Supply Co., of Canada, Ltd.

**BALE TIES**
Canada Metal Co.
Laidlaw Bale Tie Company

**BAND MILLS**
Hamilton Company, William
Waterous Engine Works Company
Yates Machine Company, P. B.

**BAND SAW BLADES**
Simonds Mfg. Co.

**BAND RESAWS**
Mershon & Company, W. B.

**BARKERS**
Bertrand, F. X., La Compagnie
Manufacturiere.
Smith Foundry & Machine Co.

**BEARING METAL**
Canada Metal Co.
Beveridge Supply Co., Ltd.

**BEDSTEADS (STEEL)**
Simmons Limited

**BELT DRESSING**
Dominion Belting Co.
General Supply of Canada, Ltd.

**BELTING**
Canadian Consolidated Rubber Co.
Dominion Belting Co. .......
General Supply Company
Goodhue & Co., J. L.
Gutta Percha & Rubber Company
D. K. McLaren, Limited
York Belting Co.

**BLOWERS**
Reed & Co., Geo. W.
B. F. Sturtevant Co., of Canada, Ltd.
Toronto Blower Company

**BOILERS**
Engineering & Machine Works of
Canada
Hamilton Company, William
Waterous Engine Works Company

**BOILER PRESERVATIVE**
Beveridge Supply Company
Shell-Bar, Boico Supply. Co., Ltd.

**BOX MACHINERY**
Yates Machine Company, P. B.

**CABLE CONVEYORS**
Engineering & Machine Works of
Canada.
Hamilton Company, William
Waterous Engine Works Company

**CAMP SUPPLIES**
Davies Company, William
Dr. Bell Veterinary Wonder Co.
Johnson, A. H.
Turner & Sons, J. J.
Woods Manufacturing Co., Ltd.

**CANT HOOKS**
General Supply Co., of Canada, Ltd.
Pink & Company, Thomas

**CEDAR**
Bury & Co., Robt.
Cameron Lumber Co.
Canadian Western Lumber Co.
Chesbro, R. G.
Dry Wood Lumber Co.
Fesserton Timber Company
Fesserton Timber Company
McElroy Lumber Co., Ltd.
Muir & Kirkpatrick
Rose, McLaurin, Limited
Terry & Gordon
Thurston- Flavelle Lumber Co.
Vancouver Lumber Company.
Victoria Lumber & Mfg. Co.

**CHAINS**
Canadian Link-Belt Company, Ltd.
General Supply Co., of Canada. Ltd.
Engineering & Machine Works of
Canada
Hamilton Company, William
Pink & Company, Thomas
Waterous Engine Works Company

**CLOTHING**
Woods Mfg. Company

**CONVEYOR MACHINERY**
Canadian Link-Belt Company, Ltd.
General Supply Co., of Canada, Ltd.
Hamilton Company, William
Hopkins & Co., Ltd., F. H.
Waterous Engine Works Company

**CORDWOOD**
McClung, McLellan & Berry

**COUPLING (Shaft)**
Engineering & Machine Works of
Canada

**CRANES**
Hopkins & Co., Ltd., F. H.
Canadian Link-Belt Company, Ltd.

**CUTTER HEADS**
Shimer Cutter Head Company

**CYPRESS**
Wistar, Underhill & Nixon

**DERRICKS AND DERRICK
FITTINGS**
Hopkins & Co., Ltd., F. H.

**DOORS**
Canadian Western Lumber Co.
Gardiner, P. W. & Son
Mason, Gordon & Co.
Terry & Gordon

**DRAG SAWS**
Gerlach Company, Peter
Hamilton Company, William

**DRYERS**
Coe Manufacturing Company
B. F. Sturtevant Co. of Canada, Ltd.

**DUST COLLECTORS**
Reed & Co., Geo. W.
B. F. Sturtevant Co. of Canada, Ltd.
Toronto Blower Company

**EDGERS**
Hamilton Company, Ltd., William
Green Company, G. Walter
Long Mfg. Compay, E.
Payette Company, P.
Waterous Engine Works Company

**ELEVATING AND CONVEYING
MACHINERY**
Canadian Link-Belt Company, Ltd.
Engineering & Machine Works of
Canada
Hamilton Company, William
Waterous Engine Works Company

**ENGINES**
Engineering & Machine Works of
Canada
Hamilton Company, William
Payette Company, P.
Waterous Engine Works Company

**EXCELSIOR MACHINERY**
Elmira Machinery & Transmission
Company

**EXHAUST FANS**
B. F. Sturtevant Co. of Canada, Ltd.
Toronto Blower Company

**EXHAUST SYSTEMS**
Reed & Co., Geo. W.
B. F. Sturtevant Co. of Canada, Ltd.
Toronto Blower Company

**FIBRE BOARD**
Manley Chew

**FILES**
Disston & Sons, Henry
Simonds Canada Saw Company

**FIR**
Apex Lumber Co.
Associated Mills, Limited
Bainbridge Lumber Company
Cameron Lumber Company
Canadian Western Lumber CO.
Canfield, P. L.
Chesbro, R. G.
Dry Wood Lumber Co.
Fesserton Timber Co.
Grier & Sons, Ltd., G. A.
Heeney, Percy E.
Knox Brothers
Mason, Gordon & Co.
McElroy Lumber Co., Ltd.
Robertson & Hackett Sawmills
Rose, McLaurin, Limited
Terry & Gordon
Timberland Lumber Company
Timms, Phillips & Co.
Underhill Lumber Co.
Vancouver Lumber Company
Vanderhoof Lumber Company
Victoria Lumber & Mfg. Company

**FIRE BRICK**
Beveridge Supply Co., Limited
Elk Fire Brick Company of Canada
Shell-Bar, Boico Supply Co., Ltd.

**FIRE FIGHTING APPARATUS**
Waterous Engine Works Company

**FITTINGS**
Crane Limited

**FLOORING**
Cameron Lumber Co.
Chesbro, R. G.
Long-Bell Lumber Company

**GEARS (Cut)**
Smart-Turner Machine Company

**GUARDS (Machinery and Window)**
Canada Wire & Iron Goods Co.

**HARDWOODS**
Anderson Lumber Company, C. G.
Anderson, Shreiner & Mawson
Atlantic Lumber Company
Barrett, Wm.
Black Rock Lumber Co.
Bury & Co., Robt.
Cameron & Company
Edwards & Co., W. C.
Fassett Lumber Company, Limited
Fesserton Timber Co.
Gillespie, James
Gloucester- Lumber & Trading Co.
Grier & Sons, Ltd., G. A.
Hart, Hamilton & Jackson
Heeney, Percy E.
Knox Brothers
Mason & Company, Geo.
McDonagh Lymber Company
McLennan Lumber Company
McLung, McLellan & Berry
Pedwell Hardwood Lumber Co.
W. & J. Sharpies
Spencer, Limited, C. A.
Strong, G. M.
Summers, James R.

**HARDWOOD FLOORING**
Grier & Sons, Ltd., G. A.

**HARNESS**
Beal Leather Company, R. M.

**HEMLOCK**
Anderson Lumber Company, C. G.
Anderson, Shreiner & Mawson
Bartram & Ball
Beck-Lumber Company.
Bourgouin, H.
Canadian General Lumber Company
Edwards & Co., W. C.
Fesserton Timber Co.
Grier & Sons, Ltd., G. A.
Hart, Hamilton & Jackson
Hocken Lumber Company
Mason, Gordon & Company
McCormack Lumber Company
McDonagh Lumber Company
McElroy Lumber Co., Ltd.
Robertson & Hacket Sawmills
Spencer, Limited, C. A.
Stalker, Douglas A.
Terry & Gordon
Vancouver Lumber Company
Vanderhoof Lumber Company

**HOISTING AND HAULING
ENGINES**
General Supply Co., of Canada, Ltd.

Tractor and Train at foot of 35% down grade from Fish's Camp.

# THE LINN LOGGING TRACTOR

## Designed and developed for winter log hauling, in the North Woods

To fulfill all requirements of the Northern Logger a tractor must:—

Haul heavy trains of sleighs down steep sandhills and around sharp curves.

Haul with absolute safety over lakes and rivers, where the ice is sometimes not thicker than fourteen inches.

Haul heavy trains over main hauls over all encountered grades—to landings.

Have carrying capacity on itself, so that it can be used for supply haulage over Portage roads.

Must have a fast high speed so that return trips to rollways may be rapid.

Must be foolproof and easily operated and controlled.

All these requirements are fulfilled only, by The Linn Logging Tractor.

Ask the operator who uses Linn.

*—Logging Department—*

# MUSSENS LIMITED

**Dubrule Building**                    MONTREAL

Hopkins & Co., Ltd., F. H.

**HOSE**
General Supply Co. of Canada, Ltd.
Gutta Percha & Rubber Company

**INSURANCE**
Barton & Ellis Company
Burns Underwriting Company
Hardy & Company, E. D.
Rankin Benedict Underwriting Co.

**INTERIOR FINISH**
Cameron Lumber Company
Canadian Western Lumber Co.
Canfield, P. L.
Eagle Lumber Company
Mason, Gordon & Co.,
Rose, McLaurin, Limited
Terry & Gordon

**KILN DRIED LUMBER**
Bury & Co., Robt.

**KNIVES**
Disston & Sons, Henry
Simonds Canada Saw Company
Waterous Engine Works Company

**LARCH**
Otis Staples Lumber Company

**LATH**
Anderson, Shreiner & Mawson
Apex Lumber Company
Austin & Nicholson
Beck Lumber Company
Brennen & Sons, F. W.
Cameron Lumber Company
Canadian General Lumber Company
Carew Lumber Company, John
Chaleurs Bay Mills

Dadson, A. T.
Eagle Lumber Company
Fassett Lumber Company, Limited
Foley Lumber Company
Fraser Bryson Lumber Co., Ltd.
Gloucester Lumber & Trading Co.
Grier & Sons, Ltd., G. A.
Harris Tie & Timber Company, Ltd.
Larkin Company, C. A.
Mason & Company, Geo.
McLennan Lumber Company
Miller, W. H. Company
New Ontario Colonization Company
Otis Staples Lumber Company
Power Lumber Company
Price Bros. & Company
Shevlin-Clarke Company
Spencer, Limited, C. A.
Terry & Gordon
U. G. G. Sawmills, Limited
Union Lumber Company
Victoria Harbor, Lumber Company

**LATH BOLTERS**
General Supply Co. of Canada, Ltd.
Hamilton Company, William
Payette & Company, P.

**LOCOMOTIVES**
Engineering & Machine Works of Canada
General Supply Co. of Canada, Ltd.
Hopkins & Co., Ltd., F. H.
Climax Manufacturing Company
Montreal Locomotive Works

**LINK-BELT**
Canadian Link-Belt Company
Hamilton Company, William

**LOCOMOTIVE CRANES**
Canadian Link-Belt Company
Hopkins & Co., Ltd., F. H.

**LOGGING ENGINES**
Engineering & Machine Works of Canada

Hopkins & Co., Ltd., F. H.
Mussens Limited

**LOG HAULER**
Engineering & Machine Works of Canada
Green Company, G. Walter
Holt Manufacturing Company
Hopkins & Co., Ltd., F. H.
Payette & Company, P.

**LOGGING MACHINERY AND EQUIPMENT**
General Supply Co. of Canada, Ltd.
Hamilton Company, William
Holt Manufacturing Company
Hopkins & Co., Ltd., F. H.
Payette & Company, P.
Waterous Engine Works Company
West, Peachey & Sons
Mussens Limited

**LUMBER EXPORTS**
Fletcher Corporation

**LUMBER TRUCKS**
Hamilton Company, William
Waterous Engine Works Company

**LUMBERMEN'S BOATS**
Adams Engine Company
Gidley Boat Company
West, Peachey & Sons

**LUMBERMEN'S CLOTHING**
Kitchen Overall & Shirt Company

**MATTRESSES**
Simmons Limited

**METAL REFINERS**
Canada Metal Company

**OAK**
Long-Bell Lumber Company

**PACKING**
Beveridge Supply Company
Gutta Percha & Rubber Company

**PANELS**
Bury & Company, Robt.

**PAPER**
Beveridge Supply Company
Price Bros. & Company

**PINE**
Anderson Lumber Company, C. G.
Anderson, Shreiner & Mawson
Atlantic Lumber Company
Austin & Nicholson
Barratt, William
Beck Lumber Company
Black Rock Lumber Co.
Cameron & Company
Cameron Lumber Company
Canadian General Lumber Company
Canadian Western Lumber Co.
Canfield, P. L.
Cheabro, R. G.
Cleveland-Sarnia Sawmills Company
Cox, Long & Company
Dadson, A. T.
Dudley, Arthur N.
Eagle Lumber Company
Edwards & Co., W. C.
Excelsior Lumber Company
Fesserton Timber Co.
Fraser Bryson Lumber Co., Ltd.
Gillies Bros, Limited
Gloucester Lumber & Trading Co.
Gordon & Company, George
Goodday & Company, H. R.
Grier & Sons, Ltd., G. A.
Harris Tie & Timber Company, Ltd.
Hart, Hamilton & Jackson
Hettler Lumber Co., Herman H.
Hocken Lumber Company
Julien, Roch
Lay & Haight
Lloyd, W. Y.
Loggie Company, W. S.

**POST GRINDERS**
Smith Foundry Company

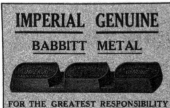

# IMPERIAL GENUINE
## BABBITT METAL

### FOR THE GREATEST RESPONSIBILITY THE BEST THAT MONEY CAN BUY
(Contains No Lead)

**Harris Heavy Pressure**
BEARING METAL
For All General Machinery Bearings

### The CANADA METAL CO., Limited
Hamilton   Montreal   TORONTO   Winnipeg   Vancouver

# Put your problem up to us

We are specialists in building locomotives. We build all types and sizes, also all kinds of repair parts for locomotives and tenders.

Our experience puts us in a position to give you expert advice as to what particular type and size of locomotive is best suited to your needs.

*Put Your Locomotive Problem up to us.*

## Montreal Locomotive Works
Limited
Dominion Express Building,   :   Montreal, Canada

**POSTS AND POLES**
Anderson, Shreiner & Mawson
Canadian Tie & Lumber Co.
Dupuis, Limited, J. P.
Eagle Lumber Company
Harris Tie & Timber Company, Ltd.
Long-Bell Lumber Company
Mason, Gordon & Co.
McLennan Lumber Company
Terry & Gordon

**PLANING MILL EXHAUSTERS**
Toronto Blower Company

**PLANING MILL MACHINERY**
Mershon & Company, W. B.
B. F. Sturtevant Co. of Canada, Ltd.
Toronto Blower Company
Yates Machine Company, P. B.

**PORK PACKERS**
Davies Company, William
Long-Bell Lumber Company
Mason, Gordon & Co.
McCormack Lumber Company
McFadden & Malloy
McLennan Lumber Company
Montreal Lumber Company
Muir & Kirkpatrick
Northern Lumber Mills
Otis Staples Lumber Company
Parry Sound Lumber Company
Rolland Lumber Company
W. & J. Sharples
Shevlin-Clarke Company
Spencer, Limited, C. A.
Stalker, Douglas A.
Sommers, James R.
Union Lumber Company
Victoria Harbor Lumber Company
Watson & Todd, Limited

**PULLEYS AND SHAFTING**
Canadian Link-Belt Company
General Supply Co. of Canada, Ltd.
Green Company, G. Walter
Engineering & Machine Works of
Canada
Hamilton Company, William

**PULP MILL MACHINERY**
Canadian Link-Belt Company
Engineering & Machine Works of
Canada
Hamilton Company, William
Payette & Company, P.
Waterous Engine Works Company

**PULPWOOD**
British & Foreign Agencies
D'Auteuil Lumber Company
Price Bros. & Company
Scott, Draper & Company

**PUMPS**
General Supply Co. of Canada, Ltd.
Engineering & Machine Works of
Canada
Hamilton Company, William
Hopkins & Co., Ltd., F. H.
Smart-Turner Machine Company
Waterous Engine Works Company

**RAILS**
Gartshore, John J.
Hopkins & Co., Ltd., F. H.

**ROOFINGS**
(Rubber, Plastic and Liquid)
Beveridge Supply Company
Reed & Co., Geo. W.

**RUBBER GOODS**
Dunlop Tire & Rubber Goods Co.
Gutta Percha & Rubber Company

**SASH**
Midland Woodworkers

**SAWS**
Atkins & Company, E. C.
Disston & Sons, Henry
General Supply Co. of Canada, Ltd.
Gerlach Company, Peter

Green Company, G. Walter
Hoe & Company, R.
Radcliff Saw Mfg. Company
Shurly Company, Ltd., T. F.
Shurly-Dietrich Company
Simonds Canada Saw Company

**SAW GRINDERS**
Smith Foundry Company

**SAW MILL LINK-BELT**
Canadian Link-Belt Company

**SAW MILL MACHINERY**
Canadian Link-Belt Company
General Supply Co. of Canada, Ltd.
G. Walter Green Company, Ltd.
Hamilton Company, William
La Compagnie Manufacture, F. X.
Bertrand
Long Mfg. Company, E.
Mershon & Company, W. B.
Parry Sound Lumber Company
Payette & Company, P.
Waterous Engine Works Company
Yates Machine Company, P. B.

**SAW SHARPENERS**
Hamilton Company, William
Waterous Engine Works Company

**SAW SLASHERS**
Hamilton Company, William
Payette & Company, P.
Waterous Engine Works Company

**SHINGLES**
Apex Lumber Company
Associated Mills, Limited
Brennen & Sons, F. W.
Cameron Lumber Company
Campbell-MacLaurin Lumber Co.
Canadian Western Lumber CO.
Carew Lumber Company, John
Chaleurs Bay Mills
Chesbro, R. G.
D'Auteuil Lumber Company
Dry Wood Lumber Co.
Eagle Lumber Company
Fraser, Companies Limited
Gillespie, James
Gloucester Lumber & Trading Co.
Grier & Sons, Ltd., G. A.
Harris Tie & Timber Co., Ltd.
Heaps & Sons
Heeney, Percy E.
Mason, Gordon & Co.
McLennan Lumber Company
Miller Company, Ltd., W. H.
Rose, McLaurin, Limited
Stalker, Douglas A.
Terry & Gordon
Timms, Phillips & Company
Vancouver Lumber Company
Vanderhoof Lumber Company

**SHINGLE & LATH MACHINERY**
Green Company, C. Walter
Hamilton Company, William
Long Manufacturing Company, E,
Payette & Company, P.
Smith Foundry Company

**SILENT CHAIN DRIVES**
Canadian Link-Belt Company

**SLEEPING EQUIPMENT**
Simmons Limited

**SLEEPING ROBES**
Woods Mfg. Company, Ltd.

**SMOKESTACKS**
Hamilton Company, William
Reed & Co., Geo. W.
Waterous Engine Works Company

**SNOW PLOWS**
Pink & Company, Thomas

**SOLDERS**
Canada Metal Company

**SPARK ARRESTORS**
Reed & Company, Geo. W.
Waterous Engine Works Company

**SPRUCE**
Anderson, Shreiner & Mawson
Barrett, Wm.
Cameron Lumber Company
Campbell, McLaurin Lumber Co.
Canadian Western Lumber Co.
Chesbro, R. G.
Cox, Long & Company
Dadson, A. T.
Dudley Arthur N.
Fassett Lumber Company, Ltd.
Fraser, Companies Limited
Fraser Bryson Lumber Co., Ltd.
Gillies Brothers
Gloucester Lumber & Trading Co.
Goodday & Company, H. R.
Grier & Sons, Ltd G. A.
Harris Lumber Co., Frank H.
Hart, Hamilton & Jackson
Hocken Lumber Company
Julien, Roch
Larkin Co., C. A.
Lay & Haight.
Lloyd, W. Y.
Loggie Co., W. S.
Mason, Gordon & Co.
McCormack Lumber Co.
McDonagh Lumber Co.
McElroy Lumber Co., Ltd.
McLennan Lumber Company
New Ontario Colonization Co.
Northern Lumber Mills
Power Lumber Co.
Price Bros. & Company
Rolland Lumber Co.
Rose, McLaurin, Limited
W. & J. Sharples
Spencer, Limited, C. A.
Strong, G. M.
Terry & Gordon
U. G. G. Sawmills, Limited
Vanderhoof Lumber Company

**STEAM SHOVELS**
Hopkins & Co., Ltd., F. H.

**STEEL CHAIN**
Canadian Link-Belt Company
Hopkins & Co., Ltd., F. H.
Waterous Engine Works Company

**STEAM PLANT ACCESSORIES**
Waterous Engine Works Company

**STEEL BARRELS**
Smart-Turner Machine Company

**STEEL DRUMS**
Smart-Turner Machine Company

**TARPAULINS**
Turner & Sons, J. J.
Woods Manufacturing Company Ltd.

**TANKS**
Hopkins & Co., Ltd., F. H.

**TENTS**
Turner & Sons, J. J.
Woods Mfg. Company

**TIES**
Austin & Nicholson
Carew Lumber Co., John
Canadian Tie & Lumber Co.
Chaleurs Bay Mills
D'Auteuil Lumber Co.
Gloucester Lumber & Trading Co.
Harris Tie & Timber Company Ltd.
McLennan Lumber Company
Miller, W. H. Co.
Price Bros. & Company
Scott, Draper & Co.
Terry & Gordon

**TIMBER BROKERS**
Bradley, R. R.
Cant & Kemp
Farnworth & Jardine
Wright, Graham & Co.

**TIMBER CRUISERS AND
ESTIMATORS**
Savage & Bartlett.
Sewell, James W.

**TIMBER LANDS**
Department of Lands & Forests, Ont.

**TOWING MACHINES**
Payette & Company, P.
West, Peachey & Sons

**TRACTORS**
Holt Manufacturing Company
Hopkins & Co., Ltd., F. H.
Mussens Limited

**TRANSMISSION MACHINERY**
Canadian Link-Belt Company
Engineering & Machine Works of
Canada
General Supply Co. of Canada, Ltd.
Grand Rapids Vapor Kiln
Hamilton Company, William
Waterous Engine Works Co.

**TURBINES**
Engineering & Machine Works of
Canada
Hamilton Company, William
B. F. Sturtevant Co. of Canada, Ltd.

**VALVES**
Crane, Limited

**VAPOR KILNS**
Grand Rapids Vapor Kiln
B. F. Sturtevant Co. of Canada, Ltd.

**VENEERS**
Bury & Co. Robt.

**VENEER DRYERS**
Coe Manufacturing Company
Sturtevant Co., B. F. of Canada Ltd.

**VENEER MACHINERY**
Coe Manufacturing Company

**VETERINARY REMEDIES**
Dr. Bell Vetinerary Wonder Co.
Johnson, A. H.

**WARPING TUGS**
West, Petchey & Sons

**WATER WHEELS**
Engineering & Machine Works of
Canada
Hamilton Company, William

**WIRE**
Canada Metal Co.
Laidlaw Bale Tie Company
Canada Wire & Iron Goods Co.

**WIRE CLOTH**
Canada Wire & Iron Goods Co.

**WIRE ROPE**
Canada Wire & Iron Goods Co.
Hopkins & Co., Ltd., F. H.
Dominion Wire Rope Co.
Greening Wire Co., B.

**WOODWORKING MACHINERY**
General Supply Co. of Canada, Ltd.
Long Manufacturing Company, E.
Mershon & Company, W. B.
Waterous Engine Works Co.
Yates Machine Company, P. B.

**WOOD PRESERVATIVES**
Beveridge Supply Company
Austin & Nicholson
New Ontario Colonization Company
Power Lumber Co.

**WOOD PULP**
Austin & Nicholson
New Ontario Colonization Co.
Power Lumber Co.

# Heaviest and Most Rigid Band Mills on the Market

A DISTINCT step forward in the march of sawmill equipment progress—that is the verdict of those who have seen the bandmill here illustrated. Embodying all the modern and approved features of up-to-date band mill design and many refinements in their minor details, they are an improvement over anything heretofore produced in this type of machine.

Their installation provides the most rapid and economical means of manufacturing lumber.

Space does not permit a detailed description here but we have prepared a small bulletin giving the complete facts and will be pleased to forward a copy to you upon request.

*Drop us a line now, while it is in your mind*

# The E. Long Manufacturing Co., Limited

### Orillia                                    Canada

Robt. Hamilton & Co., Vancouver
Gormans, Limited,
    Calgary & Edmonton

A. R. Williams Machinery Co.,
    of Canada, Ltd.
Williams & Wilson Ltd., Montreal

Vol. 42      Toronto, May 1, 1922      No. 9

# Canada Lumberman

*Founded 1880*

# "Kendall" Gang Circular

## The Machine that will convert your small logs into more and better lumber quicker than ever before

This illustration shows the latest design of 12″ "Kendall" gang circular which takes 21-36″ saws No. 10 gauge and cuts cants up to 12″ in thickness. Like the other models it has a hollow mandrel 5-3/16″ diameter, and water cooled saws. Each saw has a separate guide easily accessible and readily adjustable and the end bridge-tree is so designed that it swings back out of place for changing saws. As can be seen from the cut the feed, which is variable, is driven independent of the mandrel and the press rolls are steam operated. Feed rolls are 36″ long—drive pulley 30 x 22″, floor space 9′-0″ x 11′-0″.

We have no hesitation in saying that this gang circular cuts lumber absolutely the smoothest and truest to size of any machine on the market today.

These machines are made in the following sizes:
26″ Saws for 8″ Cants using weight press rolls.
32″ Saws for 10″ Cants using steam press rolls.
36″ Saws for 12″ Cants using steam press rolls.
We also make a complete line of twin circulars with either chain, rope or steam feed for slabbing logs for these machines.

### CONSULT US FOR ANY OF YOUR SAWMILL NEEDS

# William Hamilton Co., Limited

Agents: J. L. Neilson & Company, Winnipeg, Man.        PETERBORO, ONT.

# White Pine
# Red Pine
# Jack Pine
# Spruce
# Lumber
# and Lath

## UNION LUMBER COMPANY LIMITED
701 DOMINION BANK BUILDING
TORONTO          CANADA

# CO-OPERATION---

## *The Life-Blood of*
## Successful Enterprise

CENTURIES and centuries ago the early Britons first discovered the value of co-operation. Instead of each man continuing to build his own hut, hunt his own food and make his own apparel, it was conceived that greater speed and better workmanship could be accomplished when one group of men built all the huts, another group did all the hunting and so on. Thus the first principals of successful co-operation took root and flourished.

To-day co-operation is the life-blood of successful enterprise. On every hand we see striking examples of it's wondrous power. It has bridged rivers, spanned continents, harnessed torrents. It has given us homes, pleasures, prosperity—all the necessities and luxuries of life. It is striving, and will eventually succeed, in bringing permanent peace to a war-scarred world,

The principles of co-operation are not hard to master. We found long ago that co-operation meant giving the best quality and service we could—filling every order with satisfaction—thinking from the buyer's standpoint. Our business has grown through rigid adherence to this policy.

May we co-operate with you when you are ready to place orders for lumber?

## TERRY AND GORDON
### LIMITED
### CANADIAN FOREST PRODUCTS

BRANCH
MONTREAL

HEAD OFFICE
TORONTO
EUROPEAN AGENTS

BRANCH
VANCOUVER

SPENCER LOCK & Co., LONDON, ENG.

Ontario Representatives for
THE BRITISH COLUMBIA MILLS TIMBER AND TRADING CO., VANCOUVER, B. C.

# LUMBER

## ─Wanted─

### Mill-cuts in

# W. Pine
# Hemlock
# Birch
# Elm
# Maple

## C. G. Anderson Lumber Company, Limited

Manufacturers and Strictly Wholesale
Dealers in Lumber

SALES OFFICE

## 705 Excelsior Life Building
## Toronto

**DOUGLAS FIR
LUMBER
RED CEDAR
SHINGLES**

We mauufactnre all grades of

# RedCedarShingles

Which are inspected by
**the British Columbia Inspestor**

We can give Mixed or Straight cars of

# Rough K.D. Clear Fir

Manufactured from
old growth logs

## Timms Phillips & Co., Ltd.
Vancouver, B. C.

MONTREAL OFFICE: 23 Marconi Bldg.
Phóne M 2999

TORONTO OFFICE: Canada Permanent Bldg.
Phone Adel. 6490

# BUY
# BRITISH COLUMBIA
# Red Cedar Shingles

The life of a British Columbia Red Cedar Shingle Roof can almost be gauged by the life of the nail with which the shingle is nailed in place. Judging from available data, the average life of the ordinary steel wire nail, which has been in such common use, is only from seven to twelve years. Some wire nails will last longer, depending upon the condition of exposure, climate and similar features, but considering our climate as a whole, at the end of from seven to twelve years a large percentage of wire nails will have rusted either completely through or so extensively that the first strong wind will complete the work. The shingles that have been held in position by such nails are then free to work down, permitting rains or melting snows to leak through and damage the interior of the structure. Examination will disclose that the fibre of the shingle itself is still in perfect condition, and a leaky roof, in the majority of occasions is due entirely to the use of faulty nails, but the average home owner, placed at such inconvenience, will not stop to reason this out and the poor wooden shingle comes in for more unjust abuse.

There are several kinds of nails which experience has proven will give lasting satisfaction, and the wise dealer will advise his customers of these satisfactory nails. A pure zinc shingle nail meets all the demands of durability required. Its principal drawback is its high cost and a slight tendency to bend under careless driving. Galvanized wire nails theoretically are rust proof, and if the galvanized coating is properly applied, and of sufficient thickness, such a nail will last as long as the shingle it holds in place. The life of this shingle roof, properly applied with these nails then is from 40 to 50 years. Pure iron nails, or the old cut or wrought nails are ideal but difficult to secure. Copper nails also constitute a perfect shingle nail.

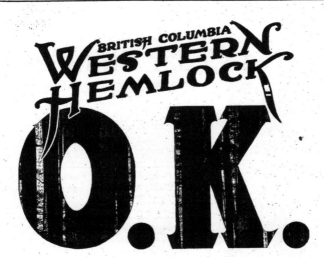

# THE GREAT NATIONAL LUMBER JOURNAL

| Pioneer and Leader in the Industry |  Canada Lumberman /founded 1880 | Recognized Authority for Forty Years |

Vol. 42        Toronto, May 1, 1922        No. 9

# How Ontario Is Insuring Future Wood Supply

### By E. J. Zavitz.
#### Head of Provincial Forestry Department.

E. J Zavitz, Toronto
Provincial Forester

In this article I desire to give a description of the reforestation work in the Provincial Forest Station in Norfolk County, as related to the general problem of reforestation in Ontario. Following an agitation in agricultural circles a Forestry Department was established at the Ontario Agricultural College at Guelph in 1905. In connection with this Department a forest nursery was established which was to supply forest planting material to those land owners desiring to reforest.

This movement was chiefly concerned with the problem of reforestation in Southern Ontario, a region which had been largely settled and cleared for agriculture. In this region there are two distinct problems, namely:

1. Encouragement of reforestation on private lands.
2. Reforestation of the large areas of waste land which occur in numerous localities throughout old agricultural Ontario.

The private woodlot which is usually of small acreage and only an adjunct to the farm represents in the aggregate a considerable and important factor in our problems. It is estimated that there is about 8,500 square miles of this class of land in the old, settled part of Ontario. It is important that the private land owners be urged to protect and replant the woodlot and to reforest waste portions of his land. These small areas are, in the aggregate, of vital importance from the standpoint of fuel and local wood supplies.

It is, with the second problem, that of reforesting the larger waste areas in older Ontario, that I wish to deal more in detail.

We have in older Ontario numerous large areas, chiefly of sand formation which were denuded of trees, and are today barren wastes, threatening the safety of the surrounding farm land. These waste land areas are to be found in nearly every portion of the older part of the Province.

### Twofold Use of Waste Lands

By establishing forest stations in these waste land areas where forest planting can be carried out and demonstrated, the influence will be felt throughout the surrounding districts. In addition to reclaiming waste land and making it productive these forest station centres can provide planting material to supply prospective private owners who wish to re-stock depleted woodlots or reforest waste portions of their farms.

The policy of establishing forest stations of this nature was adopted in 1908 when land was secured in Norfolk County, and the Provincial Forest Nursery was moved from the Ontario Agricultural College to this area. The forest station in Norfolk comprises 1,680 acres and is situated in the southern portion of the County at the border of a district which has large sand formations. This part of Norfolk was settled over one hundred years ago, and the particular land comprising the forest station was granted to settlers about 1804. At this time this area was covered with a magnificent forest with

pure stands of white pine on the lighter soils and valuable hardwoods, as oak, chestnut and ash, in the swales.

After the area was logged for the merchantable timber futile attempts at farming commenced. At first crops were obtained but as soon as the vegetable mould was depleted from these light soils, it became very difficult to produce crops, in many cases fields cleared began to break up and blow. Upon securing this area as a forest station the following phases of work were undertaken: Development of nurseries for growing forest planting material; forest planting on the drifting sands; forest planting in the cut over areas on which a poor second growth existed; thinnings and improvement of the small areas on which satisfactory second growth existed.

### Collecting Coniferous Seed

The first step in growing forest nursery stock is the securing of seed. This is complicated by the fact that we cannot depend upon a good crop of seed every year. Little difficulty is met in collecting hardwood seed and for the purposes of this article I will refer more particularly to the collecting of coniferous seed.

Coniferous seed such as pine is secured by collecting the cones and extracting the seed. All of our coniferous trees mature their cones in the autumn and it is important to note that the cone remains on the trees until it opens and allows the seed to escape. It will therefore be seen that it would be useless to collect the cones which have fallen to the ground in order to secure seed.

White pine produces a heavy crop of cones about every five years. The cones mature by the end of August and the seed has usually fallen from the cone by the fifteenth of September. The cones are collected by picking them from the tree or obtaining them from squirrel caches. The bulk of the seed is extracted by spreading the cones out on sheets in the sun and depending on solar heat to open them. One cone has from 20 to 40 fertile seeds and a bushel of cones

Ontario Forestry Branch collects hundreds of bushels of red pine cones which are spread out for drying to assist in extracting the seed

Red pine seedlings two years old. Lath shades have been removed at the end of the first season

Showing seed beds with lath screens for shade and overhead pipes for watering

Three year old transplants of white pine (on left) and scotch pine ready for final planting

Block of 3 year old scotch pine nursery lines ready for final planting

produces about one pound of seed. One pound of white pine seed contains from 25 to 28 thousand seeds. The cost of collecting white pine seed runs from 75 cents to $3.00 per pound, depending on the abundance of cones.

Red or norway pine cones, which mature a few days later than white pine, can be collected at the same time or even a few days later. A small proportion of the red pine seed can be extracted by solar heat but the usual method employed by the Ontario Forestry Branch is to extract the seed with artificial heat in a specially arranged building. This season several hundred bushels of red pine cones were collected in Simcoe County and the seed extracted for use in the Provincial Forest Nurseries. One pound of seed contains about 50,000 seeds. The cost of collecting red pine seed varies from $3.00 to $5.00 per pound.

White spruce cones are collected and handled in a similar manner to those of white pine. The seed is much similar and contains about 130,000 seeds to the pound.

Jack pine cones mature in the autumn but remain on the trees for several years. The cheapest method of collecting is to pick cones from trees which are being felled in a tie or logging operation. One pound of seed contains about 100,000 seeds and cost from $3.00 to $5.00 per pound.

## Growing Coniferous Seedlings

The seed is sown in autumn or early spring in seed beds which are usually four feet wide. The unit of size used at the Ontario forest station is 4 x 30 feet. The young seedlings are protected from the sun by a protective screen which is made of lath woven with wire so that it will roll out over the bed as illustrated. Additional covering with burlap or straw is kept on the seed beds just after sowing until germination is well advanced. At the end of the first season the 4 x 30 seed bed will contain 20,000 to 35,000 one year old plants.

While the above process is a simple one, considerable difficulty is encountered during the first few weeks of the life of the seedling. This difficulty arises from sun scorch and from attacks by organisms in the soil which cause what is commonly known as "damping off".

Water is supplied by a system of overhead pipes giving a fine shower whenever required and making our nurseryman in dependent of the weatherman.

Various methods are employed in handling forest nursery stock. Frequently the seedlings of scotch pine and jack pine can be transplanted at the end of the first season. Where plants are used in final planting on areas which are protected the seedlings remain in the seed beds for two years and are transplanted at once to their final location. Where stocky plants are required for exposed forest planting the seedlings are lifted and transplanted to nursery lines where they remain for one to two years. These one or two year old transplants have a large amount of fibrous roots and will stand extreme planting conditions.

This season (1921) we have five acres in seed beds with about seven million seedlings. These are chiefly white pine, white spruce, scotch pine and jack pine. Of these about one million scotch pine have been lifted and transplanted into nursery lines.

Reforesting with conifers, such as pine and spruce, is usually

Showing blow sand area with jack pine planted to stop movement of sand.
Note the old white pine stumps

done early in the spring, from April 15th to May 15th. The plants
are lifted in the nursery and taken to the planting area where they
are "heeled in," that is, the roots are placed in a trench and covered
with soil for temporary protection. In forest planting two men usually form a working unit. One man prepares the planting spot and
makes the hole with a mattock or spade, the other sets the plant.
The plants are usually carried in pails filled with water to protect
the roots and prevent them from drying out, which is a very necessary precaution. Plants are spaced from five to six feet apart each
way, this close planting being followed in order to force the trees
in height growth and to produce clear timber. Spacing at six feet
requires 1,210 plants to the acre.

About 500 acres of forest plantations have been made at the
Norfolk Forest Station since 1909. Following is a brief description
of some of the older plantations.

At the entrance to the property, along the main highway there
existed a ridge of blow sand which had covered the original fence.
In 1909 this ridge was planted with imported scotch pine and jack
pine transplants from 12 to 15 inches in height. The plants were
spaced about four feet apart each way and on the worst blow sand,
pine brush was thrown down to give protection to the plants. In
this plantation there was only about two per cent. loss. Measurements made of these trees in 1920 showed dominant trees 22 to 24
feet high with an average height growth of 21 feet and diameter at
4½ feet from the ground of 3.5 inches. An interesting feature of this
first plantation was that the local people thought it a waste of time
and money to plant little evergreen trees in this sterile sand and
looked upon the experiment with scorn. The success of this planting has since been an incentive to a large number of private owners
in the district to carry out similar work.

One of the interesting plantations at this station is that of 12
acres of red pine made in 1913. Plants used in this work were grown
at the local station from seed collected in Simcoe County. This
planting was made on an old pasture where there was a light turf.
Shallow plow furrows were run every five feet and the plants placed
every five feet in the furrow. There was a loss of less than one per
cent. In 1920 or after eight years of growth this plantation averaged
9.4 feet in height.

### The Nursery Work At Norfolk

Space will not permit of detailed reference to other plantations
at this station. White pine has been planted on the various types of
land. On the blowing sands in the open fields white pine does not
thrive as well as scotch or red pine. Wherever protection exists it
does well and promises to eventually surpass the others.

A considerable portion of the area at this station is covered with
a growth of scrub oak and poplar, through which ground fires have
run in the past, killing any young pine seedlings which may have existed. Areas of this kind are being underplanted with white pine and
in these conditions white pine gives splendid results.

Plantations of red oak and mixed hardwoods have been started
on the better classes of soil at the station. Only a small percentage
of the land is suited for hardwoods but these plantations will be of
future interest as experiments.

The cost of forest planting varies a great deal depending upon
the nature of the planting area, the class of labor and upon the kind
of plants used. Planting in sand formations is usually low in cost
and for the Norfolk plantations costs have run from six to twelve

White pine plantation made in 1907 on light sandy soil. Dominant trees
6 inches in diameter

1 and 2. Showing mature White Pine cones. 3.
Showing one-year-old seeding. 4 and 5. Seedling
just after germination. 6. Individual scale from
cone. 7. Scale showing winged seeds.

dollars an acre.

A portion of the land secured for this work has second growth
white pine and hardwoods. These areas are being protected and
thinned and are a valuable asset to an experimental forest station.

In addition to the material required for the above planting we
ship from these nurseries stock for experimental and demonstration
planting on private lands in many parts of Ontario. From material
thus supplied plantations have been started in nearly every county of
older Ontario.

# Majority Favor Standardization of Grades

### Question Arises How Could Rules be Impartially Enforced—Eastern Lumbermen Have Various Views on Definite Grades— Price Governs Quality

In the last issue of the "Canada Lumberman" there was published interviews with several Montreal contractors on the Standardization of lumber. All those interviewed were favorable to more definite grades being drawn up, naturally viewing the subject from the standpoint of their interests as users of lumber. Below, are given the opinions of a number of Montreal wholesalers, who, in the main, are favorable to standardization. There are, however, divergences when it comes to the enforcement of any rules. It is clear, from the opinions expressed, that grading, especially of spruce, is a more or less uncertain quantity, taking the mills as a whole, and that there is a very wide interpretation of the term "merchantable." The complaint is mainly as to the lumber supplied by the small mills, it being generally agreed that the larger mills can be relied upon to supply the quality ordered.

The following views will be read with interest.

H. C. Campbell of the C. H. Russell Company, Limited:—I certainly favor the Standardization of lumber. In pine and spruce we have too many grades, which can be reduced with advantage to all concerns. In the West and in the States they are standardized and reduced to book form, and I can see no reason why this cannot be done in Eastern Canada, thus replacing the present uncertain condition of grading with something approximating definite rules. I would suggest that spruce should be divided into the following grades: Third quality and better or merchantable, which should be square edged, absolutely sound, tight red knotted; fourth quality, square edged but to admit splits, gum seams, and a small amount of shake, really outs from the merchantable; fifth quality, sound boards, containing red heart, occasional worm holes, and a limited amount of w4ne—in fact lumber suitable for ordinary construction and for resawing purposes; mill culls, in which a limited amount of rot would be allowed; dead culls, boards only fit for dunnage and the like. In the case of a mill-run grade the manufacturer should guarantee the percentage of the different grades. I would make the following grades in pine: good sidings, 8 inches and up, and good strips, 4 to 7 inches, both 10 to16 feet long; good siding shorts, 8 inches and up, and good strip shorts, 4 to 7 inches, both 6 to 9 feet long; No. 1 factory or shop, suitable for window and door stock, admitting coarse knots, but to have definite percentages of clear cuttings; Nos. 1 and 2 fine dressing, for siding , flooring and ceiling, which would include a limited amout of tight, pin knots, stock suitable for interior trim; Nos. 1 and 2 shelving, which would permit sap stain, a limited number of knots, slight shakes and check, but edges free from knots; No. 1 common, with medium sized knotted stock, some shake, stain, etc,; No. 2 common, box board and cheap construction grade; No. 1 mill culls practically sound on one face; No. 2 mill culls, allowing rot on both faces to some extent, and worm holes; No. 3 mill culls, comprising the low ends.

In order to enforce such grade rules, I suggest appointment of cullers by the Provincial Government, who would certify that the lumber sold by the mills was according to the printed rules. This would safeguard the wholesaler and the retailer, while the consumer would be able not only to order on straight specifications but would be in a position to effectively check the lumber on its receipt. The rules could be arranged between the Lumbermen's Association and the Builder's Associations.

### Proposed Grading Would Be of Value

H. Bourgouin—In considering the subject, one must not overlook the fact that in spruce, the grades of Quebec are different from those of Ontario and the Maritime Provinces. The large mills in the St. Maurice district have practically the same grades; they are very good, but I cannot say the same of the small mills of Quebec. Naturally the cuts of the larger mills command more money. It is true that consumers receive lumber described as merchantable, which varies greatly in quality, according to the source from which it is purchased, that is largely a question of price. A contractor who pays a low price for fourths and better will no doubt receive fifths and better—in other words, he gets what he pays for. Some contractors know this, but others do not. This practice of substituting lumber inferior to that called for works to the disadvantage of the wholesaler or retailer who quotes a fair price on the specifications and intends to supply the right goods. Other lumbermen will quote

a lower price for the same grade and take the chance of getting through with inferior stock. Occasionally they are held to a strict interpretation of the specifications as for instance, in the case of a large building now in course of construction where the rejections have run into a large percentage. Montreal is the dumping ground for all the rubbish of the country, and it is a shame to see the rotten lumber which is being used . Apparently, many contractors will not see it pays to buy and insist on getting good lumber. At present, roofing is selling in Montreal for $27.00, all widths and lengths. If contractors would pay $33.00, they would get a better grade, save the waste entailed by the lumber coming in odd lengths, and also save on the lumber of handling.

There are certain yards which will sell at your own price, but do you expect to get the qualities and quantities bargained for? My experience as a wholesaler is that you have to be very careful in seeing that you get what you pay for, as the description given by some sellers is exaggerated, to use a mild term. The proposed gradings will be of great value, provided that they are enforcable by law. Then every man will know exactly what he is ordering, and will be in a legal position to secure it. At present, the term "merchantable" spruce covers many varieties of lumber. This should be made more definite. Of course, those who have been in the busintss for a long time know what to expect from the different mills, but the consumer, as a rule, lacks this knowledge, although he probably makes a shrewd guess that if there is a difference of several dollars in the prices quoted, there will be a corresponding difference in the lumber supplied—but it all comes under the head of "merchantable." I am strongly of opinion that the grading rules suggested will prove of advantage to manufacturer, honest wholesaler or retailer, and the contractor. What applies to spruce also applies to pine—make the rules compulsory.

### Can Rules Be Reduced To Writing

J. S. Bock, of the Eagle Lumber Co., Limited:—I am very doubtful of the general value of the proposed grading rules, so far as reducing them to writing is concerned. As a matter of fact, definite grades are in operation in practice. Culling is essentially a business which can only be efficiently learnt by practical training, although I recognize that printed rules might be of some assistance to those who desire to become cullers. However, I do not think that contractors would derive much benefit from them. The weak point relates to the means to enforce the rules. No doubt contractors receive lumber of varying qualities, although sold under the general term of merchantable. I suggest that greater uniformity could be secured if every yard appointed a culler licensed by the Provincial Government, such culler being made responsible for grades and measurements. I attach more importance to measurements than to grades. Such a man could not only check lumber received from the mill, but also that sold by the retailer to the consumer. The culler would be empowered to check the orders with the lumber loaded in the yard, and to give a ticket, certifying that the lumber was according to the order. Cullers would be paid by the lumber dealers, and could, I think, be depended upon to deal fairly with the buyers and sellers. In woods operations they are paid by the companies, but their figures are accepted by the Provincial Government. The fact that the yards employed cullers would be a check on the mills, all of whom would be forced, in turn, to engage licensed cullers—in the case of a dispute between a buyer and a seller, a culler would always be available for a re-inspection. Under the arrangement suggested, which would be a voluntary one, retailers and contractors would be in a better position as regards lumber grades which were ordered.

### Should Be Welcome to Yards

Louis S. Rolland, of Rolland Lumber Co., Ltd.—The subject of overcoming the present difficulties of being able to purchase a uniformity of grading of soft woods from retail merchants, and manufacturers, should be very welcome to the yards in general. The present great difficulties is very well known—the fact is, there are several gradings in spruce and white pine. The trouble in the past has been that Montreal has been buying a lot of inferior classified wood, that has been manufactured by small indifferent mills, whose grading and manufacture is of great variety. The market has also been

troubled from white pine coming from similar sources, causing some difficulties when determining specified grades.

In my opinion, if a grading was established based on the Quebec Rules, all possible trouble would be materially eliminated. As lumber of this particular classification is now being manufactured by mills worth while considering, it would not only simplify the difficulties experienced by the yards, but it would be of great assistance to the customer of these yards, as well as greatly determining the true value of the lumber manufactured by mills of reputation, which after all is the only sure manner of buying to supply the requirements of the ultimate consumer without causing him any inconvenience.

If this, therefore, was adopted, it would greatly eliminate a lot of possible controversy, starting from the manufacturer all the way down to the ultimate consumer, for the reason, it might be pointed out, that even taking into consideration some of the best mills manufacturing spruce and pine, there is bound to be some difference in the classification of the lumber manufactured. This would bring out the true value of the lumber inasmuch, as this is hardly recognized at the present time, and is due to the nature of the logs, some mills, being in position to offer better value for the same money, or a little more money, than the mills manufacturing from a poorer class of logs.

By having a definite and stipulated grading, the results of all this would be that the market would gradually, with a lot of patience and time, arrive at a uniformity of grading, and would result in a clear and definite understanding of what a buyer might expect to receive when he orders a particular grade.

Spruce, which is a species that is consumed to a great extent on this market, has been sold in a variety of grades, and in particular mill run stock, in which, when comparing the grading of responsible mills with indifferent ones, there is a vast difference. This should be recognized when prices are being considered, and which so far has not been considered, for the reason that the ultimate consumer has not been able to determine just what grade is right. By establishing a uniformity of grading true value would be brought forth, and present difficulties eliminated.

Considering whitepine, I will illustrate a particular case—"Mill Run" grade. This particular "term" "covers a multitude of Sins." On account of the quality of the logs coming down to one mill, being superior to what a neighboring mill might get from its limits, the mill run grade of one plant would contain a much higher percentage of the better grade, than the other mill, who having inferior logs, would have a very small percentage of the good end, and a comparatively higher percentage of the lower grade, so that by the adoption of the rules of grading, true value would be brought forth and recognized, and any particular grade that the ultimate consumer required could be very easily acquired.

In the past the great difficulty that the better class of producers of pine and spruce have experienced is the indifference of many manufacturers to the true value for their money, which at the present time is more or less nonexistant, and I firmly believe that not only will the mills be pleased to learn that a definite grading has been established, but the wholesalers will welcome this as it would help fair competition. At the present time a well graded and manufactured article is very seldom considered when offered to the retailer; in some cases he is content to pay less money for inferior graded and manufactured stock, as it seems to be more a question of price, than the value you offer for the money. In the end, however, the article sometimes considered a very good purchase, turns out a rather expensive one.

### How Could Uniformity be Enforced

C. M. Bartram:—There is no question of the desirability of obtaining uniform grades, but the important point is how to enforce them. It would be necessary to recast the present grading, so as to make the rules of Quebec and the Maritime Provinces uniform. I suggest that the Lumbermen's Association should undertake a campaign of education in order to bring home to everybody the present chaotic condition and to gradually bring the mills to their grading. Later it would no doubt be possible to enforce these rules. The conditions which obtain today have been so long in existance that, in my opinion, it would be unfair to ask the small mills to, at once, put into operation any new grading rules—in fact, I think it would be impossible. It would have to be a gradual process and one which would be the outcome of education. In the end the small mills would benefit by the results of education.

G. W. Grier:—It comes down to this—contractors get the grade they pay for: you cannot get something for nothing, and no rules will alter this fact. If contractors want good lumber, they must pay a fair price. They cannot expect to get merchantable spruce for the price of culls.

# Motor Movement Has it Over Horse Haul

### By Warren B. Bullock

Detailed statistics providing the superiority and greater economy of the power machine to horses in getting out timber from forest operations have been prepared by the Woodlands Seition of the American Paper and Pulp Association, in a summary of reports by various operators made at the convention of the section, says Warren B. Bullock in the "Commercial Vehicle."

The summary of the comparative efficiency of power and horse as prepared by Secretary O. M. Porter of the Woodlands, Section, is not only of value to the paper industry, whose particular operations were described, but to the lumber industry and to those interested in power vehicles as well, for the conditions described by the paper company woods superintendents are exactly those faced by the woods departments of the lumber companies.

Detailed comparisons on various operations as given by the men who have made tests show that the power equipment costs only one-third to one-fourthof animal equipment, in consideration of work accomplished.

The figures are of particular value for they were given by the woods operations superintendents and not by the representatives of tractor manufacturers, though the equipment manufacturers were represented at the conference.

Operations in New York, Minnesota, Wisconsin, as well as in Canada, were included in the discussions, and the figures ,while given by men skilled in getting out pulpwood, are for the same type of woods operations as would be found in lumber operations.

### Some Interesting Comparative Figures

Stanley H. Sisson of the Racquette River Co. told of hauling 23,000 cords of 16 foot peeled-wood 10 to 12 miles, making an average of 65½ cords per day per tractor, handling 15,000 cords in thirty-eight days. His comparison was as follows: One team hauling nine cords to the trip, double headers at landings, cost $15.50 per

day, or $1.72 per cord. The tractor cost, on a basis of 60 cords, with two trips to the landing, was $43.06 per day, or $.717 per cord. The tractor dispatch systems to provide empty sleds, and to keep the tractors moving, and particularly proper garage and repair attention.

O. L. E. Weber of the Watab Paper Co., Sartell, Minn, told of extensive use of tractors under conditions where horses could not be used at times, and figured the 10-ton tractor would do the work of 36 horses, and a 5-ton tractor of 16 horses. He figured the cost of hauling 5,000 cords of pulp wood, 35,000 tamarack and cedar ties, 30,000 cedar posts, and 750,000 feet of Norway pine, over the haul which was required in this operation, as being $10,100 with horses.

Ellwood Wilson, of the Laurentide Company, Grand Mere, Que., gave the actual cost of handling his pulp wood on the Ste. Maurice as being 65 cents per cord-mile, and 21 cents per ton-mile, the timber hauled being 4 foot green hard wood.

C. L. Tolles of the Phoenix Manufacturing Company of Eau Claire, said that one of his operations showed the total cost per 1000feet of timber on a 3-mile haul including repairs to sleighs, and upkepp of the main road, together with the cost of operating a pumping station, was $.783 per 1000 feet, board measure. One of his log haulers, he said, making three trips a day on a 10-mile haul or a 60-mile per day of 24 hours, hauled two train loads of logs, seven sleighs per train, of 35,000 feet each, and one train load of eight sleighs of 12 cords each, or 96 cords.

### What Steam Haulers Can Do

"If worked to capacity," he said, "the steam log haulers will travel 50 miles in 12 hours, or 80 in 24 hours, working four men, and burning 5 tons of coal, hauling 35,000 to 80,000 feet. Horses will work only 10 to 12 hours, will not-average over 20 miles a day, and six four-horse teams will aevrage only 24,000 to 48,000 feet,

and will cost as much as the engine. It will require six men to handle them and 36 bushels of oats a day for feed. The total day's work, therefore, is about one-fourth that of the log-hauler."

E. A. Drott of Drott and Newall, giving figures on a Wisconsin operation, said the hauling cost $1.50 per thousand feet, on a 10½ mile road. Natives using horses were compelled to pay $10 per

thousand, and then had some logs hung up in the woods. On a 7½ mile haul, the Drott & Newall cost was $1 per thousand, where jobbers were paying $7 for horse hauls. He and Mr. Wilson both pointed out, however, that to get proper results, it was necessary to take great care of the tractors, to keep them in good operating conditions.

# Different Lumber Grades and Their Value

## To be Successful Salesman You Must First Sell Yourself and Have Confidence in the Firm and the Goods You are Selling—Hard Work Helps Out

"How to be a Lumber Salesman" was the subject of an interesting and convincing address delivered recently before the Association of Lumber Salesmen at Pittsburg, Pa., by C. V. McCreight. He dealt with the matter from the standpoints of work, knowledge, service, personality, appearance and responsibility. In the analysis of the personal tributes and preparations requisite to efficient lumber salesmanship, the speaker brought out many points, together with some principles which might well be embodied in a salesmen's code of ethics. Mr. McCreight, in the course of his illuminating talk, said:

To be a "real" lumber salesman, you must have certain qualifications and requirements which places you in position to handle your problem intelligently.

To be a salesman, you must first sell yourself, and have confidence in the firm and the goods you are selling.

Lumber is usually bought, and not sold. This is true from the fact that the salesman in most cases accepts the customer's requisition rather than consulting his stock list, or determining in his own mind as to whether the item the customer requires can be furnished special.

The difficulty with most salesmen is to know when to refuse an order, consequently, that is why I say lumber is usually bought, and not sold.

In order to be a successful salesman, you should know the different grades, and the comparative values of different kinds of lumber and lumber products.

You should make yourself acquainted with the various uses of lumber, and with this knowledge, you should help the buyer to obtain stock suitable to his needs.

To sell lumber successfully you must use different tactics than those applicable many years ago. In the early days the qualifications of a salesman were based on his ability to "tell stories" which is of course entirely out of date at the present time. Selling is a science, and because of that fact, you must use constructive methods.

### Necessity for Hard Work

Hard work is essential to success. With proper application, and by using your resources, and making use of the opportunities that present themselves, one can be a "success." A salesman must be industrious. He must dig up work, rather than depend upon the Sales Manager, or the head of the firm to develop the outline of possibilities. Lack of initative or work is the chief difficulty of the average salesman.

Today, we have the automobile, the moving picture, and many other kinds of amusement which takes up quite a portion of the salesman's time. In fact the salesman is inclined to go to bed late, and get up late, consequently he pursues a life of ease. This practice develops "laziness" which is a disease, and of course the result is detrimental.

The only remedy for this difficulty is "hard work." Hard work promotes happiness. It drives away frets and cares. It ushers in ability and contentment. It makes time pass quickly. It opens up new avenues of pleasure, and leads to full enjoyment of the better things of human life. It is said that "Those who do not work should not eat. No man has a right to be a consumer, unless he is also a producer. I don't say that a man should not "play." Labor without "play" kills. Every man should get away from his business long enough to breathe deeply and eat heartily.

The principal function of a salesman today is service. When we speak of service, we do not necessarily refer to price. Service means the help that you can render your customer by advising him the kinds of lumber he should use, the manner in which you can expedite his order, and the kind of grade, class of lumber produced from various sections of the country that are most useful to him.

There are many suggestions made as to how to develop a salesman. Most of us have been asked at one time or another how we sell.

I find it rather difficult to answer this question. The only way to develop salesmanship is by personal contact. The most important factor is having that essential element "personality."

There are two qualities which are opposite one another. Strength or personality, and the knack or power of putting one's self in touch with another man's mind which is tact. The power of arresting attention, and making an impression, which is "personality" is essential to salesmanship. Personality is the bed rock of character without which the salesman can not get along.

### How Personality Comes to Front

Personality is not one's "looks," nor is it an exaggerated opinion of one's self, nor does it mean that one has a complete knowledge of his product. Personality gives one the confidence to bring out the good that is within, and to hide the evil. The good things comprise: Honesty, intelligence, kindness, forebearance, appreceation, humidity, pleasing manner and appearance. Evil in ones self is: Deceit, stupidity, impatience, obstinacy, ingratitude, egotism, and trickery.

The thing that concerns us most is not to try to be something that we are not. We should not try to deceive our fellow men. When we try to be unnatural, we only deceive ourselves, as the effort is to apparent.

Appearance has a lot to do with the meeting of your customer. The eye is quick to observe, consequently appearance aids in approach. Through this, you must have confidence in yourself: confidence in your firm; confidence in the goods which you are selling. If you have these qualifications of confidence you at once reflect on your customer, and of course he must have confidence in you. If you can not develop confidence in yourself and customer you of course can not make the sale.

Friendship should be cultivated, but you must remember, that your mission is to sell lumber, and that friendship is incidental. You must also realize that your customer has "friends," and that it is impossible for you to sell all on whom you call.

The main difficulty with many salesmen is to close the deal. The last stroke as it were is the essential thing. Salesmanship depends on the power of clinching the bargain. It is to this climax that the whole conversation must lead. The sales man must have this decisiveness of mind, which enables him to grasp at the right moment and close in an instant. It is the lack of sheer resolution which invalidates the great majority of those negotiations which fail.

### Mission is to Close Business

The salesman is too often like the second class tennis player. He has a pretty stroke, but he can not land the order.

Your mission on the road is to talk business. Of course if your customer develops some other subject, it is the logical thing to discuss it with him. The average buyer does not have much time to give to other things than business during office hours.

Brevity is a jewel, and should be practiced at all times. We can be brief, and yet not dis courteous. A salesman must expect disappointments, and if he is a bool salesman will meet these disappointments in a cheerful manner.

If he knows his business, he will not sell his customer against his own judgment. Of course, you may say the buyer should know his business, but yet you must admit that the buyer is easily open to conviction, or willing to listen to new ideas which may be presented by a salesman.

As stated above, personality it a factor which in many cases makes the sale. Human effort and honest toil contributes all wealth, and all prosperity.

A salesman should know when to take an order, and when not to take an order. He should know the desirable orders, and those that are not difficult and hard to fill. I of course admit that it is very hard thing for a salesman to refuse or turn down orders, yet if he

qualifies as a salesman; these essentials or requirements govern.

A salesman should not be a "beggar," or a "complainer."—He should present his case to his customer in an intelligent manner. He should be able to answer all questions intelligently and concisely, and rely on his ability, rather than on the mercy of the buyer.

**Give the Customer all the Facts**

Facts are the essential things that the salesman should give the customer, he should not misrepresent, nor make promises that can not be fulfilled in order to obtain an order. Nine kicks out of every ten are made when the order is taken, or when the sale is made.

A good salesman, or one that has the qualifications will never ask a customer to cancel an order on a fellow salesman. In fact this

is one of the most contemptible, and unfair practices known in the business.

A salesman should never sell lumber by comparison. Lumber should be sold on grade only. A salesman never should pass judgment on another man's lumber, misrepresents grades, or sell lumber other than on standard grades as established by the various associations.

Your employer entrusts to you his most precious asset. i.e., good will. Goodwill is the foundation on which every successful business house is built, consequently it behooves us to build on this foundation. Your success does not only depend on the success of the firm, but on your carrying out the principles established by the firm.

# "Lumber Business is the Finest and Cleanest"

### Everyone Engaged in the Great Industry Should Feel Tingle in His Blood and Realize That it is Real Man's Job, says A. J. Brady to Toronto Wholesalers

**Alex. C. Gordon**
Who presided at the meeting

"Salesmanship" was the subject of a stirring and practical address delivered by A. J. Brady, Jr., of Brady Bros., wholesale lumbermen, North Tonawanda, N. Y., at the regular monthly meeting of the Wholesale Lumber Dealers' Association, Inc., which was held at the Albany Club, Toronto, on April 21st. The attendance was large and representative, and the remarks by Mr. Brady were both witty and helpful. He drove home many timely lessons and his observations afforded much food for thought. Alex. C. Gordon, vice-chairman, presided in the absence of H. J. Terry, chairman, who was in New York on business. Under the direction of Mr. Gordon everything moved along satisfactorily and pleasantly and the meeting was voted one of the best that has been held in some time, quite a number of new faces being around the board.

J. L. MacFarlane, of the Canadian General Lumber Co., who has been ill for the past four months, was in attendance and was given a cordial welcome. He sang with good effect "The Standard on the Braes of Mars." It was announced that the next meeting, which will be held on May 18th, will partake of the nature of a round-table conference on "Conditions in the lumber trade and the outlook."

Mr. Brady said there had been so much said on "Salesmanship" that it was difficult to present anything original. It had been said that there was nothing new under the sun and that anything which had appeared as new, was simply the application of something old in a slightly different fashion. Good times and bad times had been experienced and conditions of selling became more difficult in periods of depression. It was necessary to be more watchful, alert, industrious and energetic.

Mr. Brady said his object was to bring to mind certain cardinal features, and he believed that every man should be in love with the business in which he was engaged. Each must have love, respect and veneration for his calling if desirous of making it a success, backed up by application, judgment, self-reliance and dependability. Selling is absolutely a personal affair. It was the go-getter who captured the business to-day, and it was in the old problem of work that a whole lot of our difficulties could be solved. The impression that the other fellow has the softest job is a delusion.

There was no finer, cleaner, more honorable business on God's footstool to-day than that of the lumber industry, which from the felling of the tree to the marketing of the finished product was one of romance, a real man's business and work. All these associations should send a tingle through the blood and arouse a just pride. "It is well to remember in salesmanship," he added, "that we are not disposing of so many 2 x 4s or dimension timber but a product wrought by the brain and power of man."

Mr. Brady dwelt upon the personal side; how it stood highest between men and business in all relations and was a trade-controlling

factor when upheld by honesty, service and dependability. The speaker quoted from J. Ogden Armour on "The Dependable Man," in which it was pointed out that such a man was a safe man; duties may be entrusted to him and he will handle them with diligence, good sense and earnestness. Mr. Armour had declared "If you are looking for the quickest route to opportunity, learn to be this type of man. There is no better time for sowing the seed of dependableness than right now. Make yourself dependable and you world come as near being indispensable as any of us can hope to be, but do not be deceived. Dependableness is a rare accomplishment, so rare that every Executive is on the look-out for it wherever it may be found. It cannot be acquired by wishing for it. It is the prize that comes from self-mastery."

Mr. Brady dwelt upon the abuse of the telephone, whereby men were inclined to remain in their office and call up the other party rather than go out and see him, thus losing the personal touch. There was too much of a disposition also on the part of certain salesmen to pass up the "hike towns" and call on only those in the larger places. The speaker said by personal calls the first order was secured and by means of repeated visits there was the gaining of confidence, the getting of repeat orders, the establishment of goodwill and many other things not secured by the absent treatment.

Goodwill is the foundation of all business success. It meant the establishment of reputation, repeat business, the settlement of kicks, and the absence of "peanut salesmanship" which, he said, was, in other words, price-cutting. Mr. Brady quoted from an article which stated in part,—"The price-cutter is worse than a criminal. He is a fool who not only pulls down the standard of his goods; he not only pulls down his competitors; he pulls down himself and his whole trade. He scuttles the ship in which he himself is afloat. Nothing is so easy as to cut prices and nothing is so hard as to get them back when once they have been pulled down. Any child can throw a glass of water on the floor but all the wisest scientists in the world cannot pick that water up. Who gets the benefit of price-cutting? Nobody. The man who sells makes no profit and the man who buys finds himself getting an inferior article. Price-cutting is not business any more than smallpox is health."

In closing, Mr. Brady asked if they had ever noticed those climbing to the top and wondered who they were and why they were there. They were there because they had faced all difficulties, were sane optimists and had courage, judgment, application and self-reliance. The man on the job was the man who brought home the bacon. This year was a salesman's year, not that of an order-taker, and a salesman had to be a go-getter. The greatest factor of all in successful salesmanship was work. Elbow grease and labor were to-day the strongest combination in the world to win in any conflict.

A hearty vote of thanks was tendered Mr. Brady for his able and logical address, by D. C. Johnston and J. B. Jarvis. It was carried amid much applause. Several speakers followed with short remarks on various phases of salesmanship, among them being A. G. Wilmot, of the Otis, Staples Lumber Co., Wycliffe, B. C.; J. T. Todd, of the Adams River Lumber Co., Chase, B. C.; Frank Sweeney, of the Canadian Western Cooperage Co., Victoria; W. J. Lovering; F. M. Hendricks, of the Hendricks Caskey Co., Buffalo, N. Y.; W. M. Gilbert, of Terry & Gordon, Limited; K. M. Brown, of the Vancouver Lumber Co.; Alf. Read, of Read Bros.; L. D. Barclay, of the Canadian Western Lumber Co.; G. B. Van Blaricom, Editor, "Canada Lumberman," and others. The discussion was very interesting and many strong points were brought out.

## Recalls Early Logging Days in Ontario

**Capt. Robert Dollar**
Veteran Lumberman and Shipping Magnate

"Thinking back 57 years ago, or to be more exact, it was in the fall of 1865 that I was working as a common hand at the munificent salary of $16.00 a month in a lumber shanty, (now called camp) at the head of the Peache Creek, a tributary of the Gatineau River, when a letter came to Brooks, the foreman, telling him to send me to Ottawa. I could. thing of no other reason for this action than that I was fired, but I could not bring myself to believe it, as I never had worked harder in my life than the few months I had been in this camp. However, I had to obey orders and reluctantly started on my journey to the office in Ottawa," said Captain Robert Dollar, of the Robert Dollar Co., San Francisco, Cal., who is known all over the lumber and shipping world, and has many friends throughout the industry in Canada.

"Little did I think or could have imagined that in leaving that camp with all my belongings in a bag on my back, that I was starting out on a new road that even in the most fantastic dream could I ever have imagined what the end was going to be. With fear and trembling I reported at the office in Ottawa to hear my fate. I was at once reassured that it was not something unfortunate but the reverse. The kind face and words of Hiram Robinson soon set me at rest. What a fie policy it is to talk kindly to everyone you meet. How much it helps a poor fellow.

"I soon learned the purpose for which they had sent me. It was that Hamilton Brothers, the company for whom I was working, had bought the D. Moine timber limits from Egan estate and I was to go to their depot on the Du Moine and receive and look after all the outfit, stores, and supplies that went with the purchase of the limits. I well remember stating that having no experience and being only twenty years old that this was a job far too big for me. However, I was told that for sometime back I had been closely watched and had been seen trying to learn writing and arithmetic, and that in sending me the risk, if any, was theirs not mine.

"How a young man should and watch and consider his action as he comes to the forks of the road when starting out in the world, as I had to do at this time. One road would take me back to working without advancement, the other road lead to advancement and success.

"In the pesent days of fast railways and automobiles, it might not be amiss to describe my trip from Ottawa to show the wonderful change and advancement that has been made in the mode of travel as well as all other conditions. From Ottawa I took a stage to Aylmer going from there by steamer to Chats Falls. A light railroad had been laid over the portage and light cars hauled by horses carried the passengers to the head of the rapids and from there a steamer took us to portage du Fort. This occupied a full day. The next day I went by stage to Hevelock (now called Bryson) where we got another small steamer up past calument Island across Coulonge Lake and on to Chapeau. This completed another day. The following day I drove by stage across Allumette Island then crossed in a boat to Pembroke, completing the third day. Next day I walked over the portage and secured passage on a new boat which landed at the mouth of the Du Moine river. Here I hired an Indian with a small bark canoe to take me to my destination, portaging over the numerous falls and rapids. This occupied three days more. I expect all this could be accomplished in about a day with the present rapid means of communication.

"After receiving all the material I hired a few Indians, and trappers, a pair of oxen, and build a storehouse to store the goods that would come when the winter would set in, and a small camp to accommodate the teamsters. In this store house sufficient provisions were safely housed for next years lumbering operations.

"The next thing I did was to clear fifty of sixty acres of land, which were planted in potatoes and oats. A summer road had to be made next, as the only communication in winter was over the ice. so I cut out a wagon road about thirty miles long to connect with the outside world at all seasons of the year.

"The next winter we were busy getting out the logs and in the spring running them down the creeks and rivers to the Joachin boom where they were boomed out and with a capstan crib taken taken on their way, run over the rapids, assembled again at the foot, and so on until we finally reached the Chaudiere Falls at Ottawa, where we made an inefficient attempt to run them through. We then ran them through the north slide at Hull. Those were the first logs that ever passed Ottawa City, and those were only the forerunners of many millions of logs that were to follow. This was certainly pioneering.

"Out of a small acorn the great oak grows, and from that small beginning great growth has been made, for the great lumbering operations still continue under the same name and management of the Hawkesbury Lumber Company. They are there but I have certainly moved around a long way throughout the world from that good start I got on the Ottawa river."

## Should Adopt Definite Names for Grades

James Charron, of Kirkland Lake, Ont., writing to the "Canada Lumberman" says:—

I am pleased to see that the Montreal Builders' Exchange have taken up this matter of standardizing grades of lumber. I am sure that if they would send some of their delegates to the next meeting of the Wholesale Lumber Association with a proper list of names for grades and their definition, that they would have their support in adopting a standard for the different grades and the names of those grades.

The exact grade that Mr. Church, President of the Montreal Builders' Exchange, named in his address is an illustration of what I would like to make clear. For instance, why should Mr. Church want to make a purchase of lumber from any mill under the name of 5ths and better. According to that, the wholesaler could send him all 5ths, putting in as small a percentage of better grades as he liked and Mr. Church would have to accept the shipment.

Now if there was a definite understanding between the wholesalers and everyone concerned that when Mr. Church ordered a car of 5ths and better anywhere in Quebec or Ontario, that he would get, say, 5% 1 and 2 spruce and 75% commen and 20% cull, then the wholesaler would knew that unless he got, at least that percentage, that Mr. Church would be justified in refusing the shipment. My object in this is not to protect the retailer or consumer, but I think it would be of mutual interest to all concerned if one name for each grade were adopted all over the country, or, in other words, call a spade a spade.

## Roads of Remembrance are Fitting Memorials

The annual convention of the Intercollegiate Association of Forestry Clubs and Foresters' and Lumbermen's Association was held recently in the New York State College of Forestry, Syracuse University. Among those who took part in the proceedings was Ellwood Wilson, chief forester of the Laurentide Paper Co., Grand Mere, Que., who spoke on "the professional spirit in forestry." He also delivered a similar address before the Northern Retail Lumbermen's Association, at their gathering in Syracuse, N. Y.

One outstanding feature of the conclave of foresters and lumbermen was that it was a reflection of the growing interest in forestry and its continued problems. It proved to be a great get-together occasion and a manifestation of the desire on the part of professional foresters and the big lumber interests to co-operate in the production, preservation and management of the forests which are essentially a national resort.

One pleasing feature of the proceedings was the dedication of the Roads of Remembrance on the main automobile route from Buffalo to New York. This marked the beginning of a project for roadside tree-planting which will extend across the State and will, it is expected, lead to the development of widespread highway beautification by planting of trees. Other sections have taken up this inspiring idea and are preparing to make the roads attractive with arboreal adornment. The planting of the highway is in memory of those who fell in the world-war and the event synchronized with Arbor Day and Forest Production Week, which was set aside by President Harding for the purpose of stimulating interest in trees and their conservation.

The example presented by New York state in the Roads of Remembrance might well be emulated by Ontario, Quebec and other provinces. Such a project would constitute a constant reminder of the heroism of The Canadian boys who lived and fought and died in order that the British Empire might endure. Such an undertaking would be a touching tribute, not to any particular community, but to all Canada if the scheme became a comprehensive one. No more fitting commemoration of the sentiment and patriotic sacrifices of Canadian veterans who contributed their all that posterity might still enjoy freedom, liberty and life, could be conceived and executed.

# Niagara District Retailers Meet at Welland

## Annual Gathering Held in Handsome Hotel Built by Progressive Lumberman Who is Elected Chairman for Coming Year—Business Outlook Brightening Considerably

S. L. Lambert, of Welland, Ont., who recently erected the handsome and attractive Reeta Hotel and Lambert Theatre in that progressive city, was elected chairman of the Niagara Peninsula Lumber Dealers' Association at the annual meeting, which was held at the hotel on April 22nd. There was a good attendance and much interest was taken in the proceedings. Mr. Lambert has been a resident of Welland for the last 15 years and has built up a large business in the lumber and woodworking line. He has of late years put up about 450 houses in Welland which he has disposed of to contented home owners. Last session Mr. Lambert recognized the need of the city for a commodious, up-to-date hotel and attractive theatre. This work he undertook and carried it out successfully, the actual opening taking place on March 22nd last, on which occasion he was presented by the citizens of Welland with a handsome loving cup. In the rotunda of the imposing interior stands this silver trophy with the following inscription,—"Presented to S. L. Lambert as a token of esteem and appreciation for his enterprise and public spirit in the erection of the Reeta Hotel and Lambert Theatre in the city of Welland March 22nd 1923."

The new hotel is a four-storey structure and contains 40 rooms, 27 of them with bath. The building is a solid brick one with spacious dining room, which will seat 175 persons. The interior of the hotel has tiled walls and is beautifully decorated while a fresh air fan system supplies ventilation throughout the whole edifice. E. M. Smith, late of the Mossop Hotel, Toronto, is the manager of the Reeta Hotel, the name "Reeta" being selected by Mr. Lambert in honor of his elder daughter who is a bright girl in her teens. The Lambert Theatre represents the last word in comfort and convenience and has a handsome entrance. It will seat 1700 persons.

The foregoing is a short reference to the enterprise of Mr. Lambert and no doubt he will show in connection with the Niagara Peninsula district of the Ontario Retail Lumber Dealers' Association the same progressive spirit as has characterized his record in Welland, where he has been a member of the municipal council for the last four or five years and has always supported every move for the welfare and advancement of the city.

The other officers elected at the gathering were,—Vice-chairman, A. Bailey, Hagersville; Secy-treas, O. W. Rice, Welland, (re-elected); Directors,—M. A. Wills, St. Catharines; Jas. Harriman Niagara Falls; A. M. Wise, St. Catharines; R. E. Reid, Niagara Falls; P. Barraclough, Cayuga, and K. J. Shirton, Dunnville. The latter is the retiring chairman of the Niagara District and is vice-president of the Ontario Retail Lumber Dealers' Association. A hearty vote of thanks was tendered Mr. Rice for his able and faithful work as secretary-treasurer.

### Getting Out After New Members

Various important matters were discussed at the session, including the necessity of increasing the membership of the district. Chairman Shirton announced that he would devote several days to getting more to join. The present membership was fourteen but he felt that this could be nearly doubled by aggressive action. Several others also intimated that they would do their part.

It was explained that there seemed to be in some towns a dealer or two who was content merely to do business, and two or three instances were referred to of retailers who had been established for years, being no further ahead of the game financially than when they began. They conducted their affairs on a hit-and-miss plan without any co-operation with their fellows and no definite idea of what constituted costs or overhead. In many cases they were price-cutters, and at the end of each year when the inventories were taken, some were worse off than when they began. It was thought that if these fellows—happily not many—were approached in a proper spirit and were shown the benefits of co-operation, education and association which a district body presents, they would be only too happy to come in and link forces with the others.

H. Boultbee, of Toronto, secretary of the Ontario Retail Lumber Dealers' Association was present and addressed the gathering on the progress made by the Mechanics' Lien Law and the amendments that had been proposed. This measure is still before the House, and, while the original draught has been changed in some particulars, there is yet hope that greater protection may be afforded the retail lumbermen and the building material men. The present law is regarded as obsolete and affording little or no safeguarding of the interests of those who supply lumber, etc. for various jobs in the home-building line. As the bill introduced by the Government is liable to come

S. L. Lambert, Welland Ont.
New Chairman of Niagara District

O. W. Rice, Welland
Re-elected Secy-Treas

James Harriman, Niagara Falls
Re-elected on Executive

K. J. Shirton, Dunnville
The Retiring Chairman

R. E. Reid, Niagara Falls
Member of the Executive

up any day, it is expected that more definite data will be forthcoming in the near future. It is proposed by the retail lumbermen, under the new measure, to place upon the owner and upon the mortgagee responsibility for the payment of material accounts up to the extent of 35 per cent. of the total cost of the building instead of 15 and 20 per cent., as is now the case.

### Getting Ready For Summer Outing

A letter was read from J. C. Scofield, of Windsor, president of the Ontario Retail Lumber Dealers' Association, regretting his inability to attend the annual meeting of the Niagara District, but inviting the members to take part in the annual outing up the lakes which will be held from June 23rd to June 27th. Various details of

The new Reeta Hotel and Lambert Theatre in Welland, Ont.

the trip were explained and those present announced that they would be only too glad to join in the excursion which will leave Sarnia and Windsor on June 23rd and return on the 27th. It is expected to be the best trip that the lumber merchants of the province have ever enjoyed.

A general discussion took place on "Trade Conditions and the Outlook for the Coming Season." One member announced that the farmers had started to loosen up and do a little more buying.. In the larger towns it was also explained that more inquiries were being received and the prospects for activity were growing more promising each day.

Among those present were.—K. J. Shirton, Dunnville; James Harriman, Niagara Falls; A. Bailey, Hagersville; O. W. Rice, Welland; S. L. Lambert, Welland; M. A. Wills, St. Catharines; H. Boultbee, secretary O.R.L.D.A., Toronto; G. B. Van Blaricom. Editor "Canada Lumberman," Toronto, and others.

In the report of the secretary-treasurer it was shown that a good balance was on hand and the membership fee for 1922 was fixed at $3.00. Several meetings were held last season, which were fairly well attended and an effort will be made to have gatherings at different points during the coming twelve months. The next meeting will likely take place in St. Catharines.

### No Fresh Outbreaks of Spruce Bud Worm

The reconnaissance survey of the forests of New Brunswick, made under the direction of John Tothill, of the Dominion Entomological Branch, for the purpose of determining the extent of the ravages of the spruce bud-worm shows that this pest has about run its course. No new outbreaks have been discovered for some time though some slight infestations were reported last summer in Gloucester County, near Quebec border. A gratifying feature of the situation is that the spruce which was attacked is making a rapid recovery, and will show little effects of the attacks in a few years' time beyond the slight suppression in growth. The percentage of attacked balsam fir which is recovering is however, very small. The bud-worm plague has proved the greatest calamity to befall the forests of the Province since the larch saw-fly plague which broke out in the early eighties of the last century and killed practically all the tamarac. It is estimated that the bud-worm pest destroyed four

million feet of balsam fir and practically destroyed 360 million feet of spruce on the Crown Lands of the Province. The damage done to private timber lands also serious. The amount of timber destroyed is equal to the amount cut on the Crown Lands for the period of sixteen years, and according to the estimates of Hon. C. W. Robinson, Minister of Lands and Mines, represents a stumpage value of about $19,000,000 which should have flowed into the Provincial treasury during the next fifty years.

Many of the forest areas in which balsam predominated are now a vast wilderness of dead trees, mostly fallen and partly decayed. Much of the dead timber was salvaged, but the larger percentage could not be removed for various reasons and so became a dead loss. The accumulation of so much dead material has left the forests in a rather serious state, providing a stamping ground for the development of bark beetles and wood-boring insects, as well as forming a dangerous fire hazard, and a menace to the forest in general.

Considered collectively, however, the loss due to the bud-worm, while serious, is by no means disastrous. The stands of spruce are, the backbone of the lumber industry, aggregate nearly twice the quantity of fir, and valuable stands of cedar, hemlock, pine, maple, birch, beech, and poplar have been untouched by the plague.

### Mr. Mathieu Resigns Important Position

James A. Mathieu, M. L. A. vice-president and general manager of the Shevlin-Clarke Company, Fort Frances has resigned as a protest against the adjustment of the company's difference with the Ontario Government. In a statement made public, Mr. Mathieu says:—

"It is with keen regret that I have found it necessary to sever my connection with the Shevlin-Clarke Company. The events of the past two years have, however, led up to an adjustment of the Company's differences with the Ontario Government of which I cannot approve."

"It is necessary for the executive head of the company, he adds "to accept, and to some extent, at all events, personally ratify a settlement with the Government which is unjust and unfair and brought about by strangulation methods.

"The truth is that the Government has extorted a large sum of money for timber, which was not due it, for political purposes.

"Every practical lumberman, every politican and every lawyer knows this, and every financier knows how the screws were applied."

### Would Extend Accident Prevention Effect

An attempt to extend the accident prevention effect of the Workmen's Compensation Act is being made by a bill which J. C. Tolmie, of Windsor, submitted to the Ontario Legislature recently. The member explained that it was his object to encourage manufacturers who were trying to protect their workmen, and to penalize those who were careless, and this could best be done by rating that would give a lower rate to the employer with the most modern protective equipment and the lowest accident ratio, and imposing a penalty rate on others.

At the present time, he pointed out, the workmen's board has power to adopt a rating system but it was permissive only and it was his purpose to make it obligatory upon the board to take such matters into consideration in establishing rates.

### Pioneer Lumberman Passes Away in Winnipeg

Another of the fast vanishing little band of 'Old Timers of Western Canada has passed in the person of Alex. Brown, Sen., who died at his Winnipeg residence on April 13th. He had been in very poor health for a number of years and lately had been confined to his home.

Alex. Brown or "Sandy" as he has always been best known to his many friends, was born in Ayrshire, Scotland but came to Canada when a young man. In these days Winnipeg was in swaddling clothes, and he watched the city grow to what he had always predicted for it; the bustling importance of a metropolis. He came west in 1872, and formed the partnership which still exists today the firm of Brown and Rutherford, lumber merchants. The partnership was formed with Thomas Rutherford who had come from Galt, Ont. The business started in a small factory and grew gradually into the present large plant and lumber yards.

"Sandy" used to take a great delight in telling of the "social" life of the earlier days when there were only very few "first families." A retiring man of quiet dignity who never cared to follow the band wagon or figure in any public capacity, he could however, not entirely escape the honors and trust, the people of the early settlement forced upon him. He was one of the first fire chiefs of Winnipeg and at one time occupied a seat in the city council.

# Mackenzie's Building Service Wakes 'Em Up

### Georgetown, Ont., Lumber Merchant Makes Many Friends Among the Farmers With His Building Helps—Draws Plans of Homes and Farm Buildings

J. B. Mackenzie, Georgetown, Ont.

It is often a matter of service and facilities. To the one who can provide these in the largest measure, the rewards go. The retail lumberman who can supply or draw plans, furnish specifications and bills of material, and, if necessary, carry out a contract, has an advantage over the yardman who merely carries a stock and is not in a position to give definite information in connection with any construction or building problem.

As a builder of barns and other structures, no one in his line is more widely known in Western Ontario than J. B. Mackenzie of Georgetown and Acton, Ont. Being an all-round man, he knows everything about business in the structural line, and he has gained a stronghold upon the community.

In Georgetown, Ont., you can't miss seeing J. B. Mackenzie's retail lumber establishment and planing mill if you happen to breeze into that busy little town some fine spring morning on the Guelph radial which passes his front door.

J. B. Mackenzie, who is well known in the Ontario Retail Lumber Dealers Association circles, enjoys a wide business acquaintance and may well be termed a live wire lumber merchant as he not only supplies the materials for a building or home but can draw blue prints, furnish a statement of quantities, quote a finished price and erect the building. The rural trade around Georgetown is none too bright at the present, the farmers feeling the low prices and poor soil returns as in many other parts of Ontario and naturally decline to make heavy expenditures on new buildings. Many who are striving to get on their feet have to invest their cash in feed and other requirements and have no surplus money to build or make extensive repairs. Others, who are more fortunate, claim that last year they only realized 3% on the year's investment which is a fair example of the position of the farmer in many districts of Ontario today.

#### Believes in Aggressive Publicity

Of course there are some who can afford to build and to those Mr. Mackenzie has been strongly appealing with a fair degree of success. Advertisements are carried in the Farmers' Sun and other papers announcing the plan service and a price on the finished structure, requesting the farmers to inquire about the prices on the different buildings. Circulars and advertising are used consistently to help build up a strong public confidence in the firm whose policy is "once a customer always a customer."

The Mackenzie plant is well laid out to handle all kinds of mill work and is operated by hydro and equipped with a 20 h.p. Westinghouse motor, 25 cycle, 3 phase, 550 volts which has given every satisfaction. The mill proper is a two storey building 60 feet by 66 feet. On the main floor is the heavier machinery, band saw, variety saw, sticker, self feed rip saw, surface planer, buzz planer and swing saw. Adjoining the mill in the rear is a drying room 14 feet by 60 feet heated by a pipeless furnace with a 26 inch fire pot where a temperature of 110 degrees can be obtained. The lumber is piled on the floor of the drying room with stickers in between to give a free air passage. The register is in the floor at the middle of the room and is about three feet square. A large sash and door business is done by him in Toronto, and this lumber drying contrivance is giving satisfactory results.

On the upper floor of the mill are the lighter woodworking machines such as the shaper, cut off saw, hollow chisel mortiser, sander tenoner, chain mortiser, sash sticker, pony planer and light variety saw. At present the firm employs seven men in the mill and yards but this number will be increased as business gets on a better footing. Mr. Mackenzie makes a strong appeal to home lovers in his advertising literature requesting them to inquire without obligation at his office about the building of their new home. To quote from a Mac-

kenzie circular: "Bring me your own individual ideas in house building and I have the building knowledge and experience to incorporate your ideas into a practical plan."

The farmer is not neglected. Although the farm trade affords a stumbling block today, this does not dampen the spirit of the Georgetown merchant who believes in the future of his farmer friends and offers them every help and building service to save them money by drawing the plans for their new barns or implement houses. Along with the plan a complete list of materials is given and the cost complete,if he is erecting the structure for the prospect. Last year Mr. Mackenzie drew the plans for and built several barns and supplied the lumber for others. The implement house is another farm building that is of first importance on the modern farm and an advertisement special for the implement house in a Mackenzie circular runs something like this.

#### Build A Snug Implement House

Implement houses are cheap and necessary. Farm machinery are necessary but not cheap. One thousand dollars worth of farm machinery with best of care will depreciate about 10% each year. The loss on some farms is more than that amount because valuable

## Plank Frame Barn

The above picture shows a barn of plank frame construction covered with British Columbia Cedar dressed 1 side, edged and shiplapped which we built for Prof. Hutt, near Georgetown. This makes a close job of sides without it being necessary to batten cracks. Roof is covered with 3 X B. C. shingles and will wear and give satisfaction for 30 years or more.

Wooden clad barns look cosier and are easily painted and trimmed up to give a good appearance and the cost is 25% less.

We handle only a strictly good grade of shingle and always carry large stocks of 3 X and 5 X quality.

Cedar shiplap in 8, 10, 12 widths makes a good outside siding as it stands the weather and sun without twisting or checking.

It can be put on either vertical or horizontal. We have it in lengths from 10 ft. to 18 ft.

For repairs to old buildings it makes splendid doors, feed boxes, etc.

### J. B. MACKENZIE
### Acton and Georgetown

Phone Office 36W  
Residence 35J Georgetown

farm implements are left out under the weather, when they should be under cover. Each farmer needs a building separate from his other farm buildings designed for storage of implements away from poultry roost nuisance and danger of fire. Poultry are interesting and profitable on a farm, but not among implements and wagons. You can turn a wagon wheel into a hen roost by rolling it in. Frequently the hens turn the whole wagon into a roost without turning a wheel.

Better adopt the safety first plan and build a tasty good appearing house with close fitting doors. It's a good way to fool the implement dealer. He expects you to buy new in place of taking care of the old.

"We have plans for several implement houses prepared and will tell you what the materials will cost or the cost of the building erected."

When the "Canada Lumberman" interviewed Mr. Mackenzie recently he was busily at work on the design of a colonnade. He takes great pleasure in working into practical plans the different ideas of the public in the rejuvenation of their homes, by tasty installations of interior woodwork such as a colonnade and other features afford. The busy Georgetown retailer has both the machinery

and knowledge to turn out in first class shape all the interior woodwork that goes to complete the modern home.

Mr. Mackenzie himself has many original and workable ideas of his own, especially in the layout of a home, which he makes use of in his plandrawing work. The farm dwelling as everyone knows is usually approached from the kitchen side or the door nearest the barn which is different to the home in the city or town which is entered generally only from the street giving the front door the most use. The so called front door on many farms is generally an ornament and although is supposed to be the main entrance, is usually isolated.

Mr. Mackenzie has a plan in mind that will no doubt prove popular with the farmer who intends building a new residence. This plan is not an extravagant one but renders the different parts of the farm house easy of access. The main door of the house is adjacent to the barn and other buildings and could face, say, a lane that runs at right angles to the main road. A bright hall reaches every room on the ground floor, and many other features such as closets and the all important position of the kitchen have been considered and thought out by Mr. Mackenzie who believes it is something that is needed on many farms— a convenient farm house.

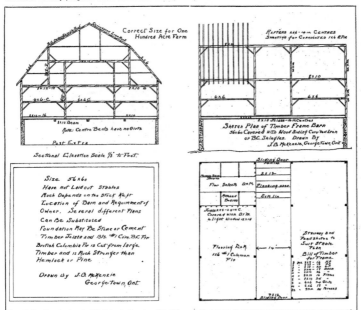

Copy of a barn blue print drawn by J. B. Mackenzie, Georgetown, Ont., for a prospective customer. In the right hand corner is a complete list of materials for the frame. If Mr. Mackenzie is building the barn a price is quoted on the barn complete.

# "Nearer the Bottom the Better the Outlook"

## B. C. Forest Products Are in Fair Demand with Export Trade Slackening Some-what—Millmen Cannot Pay Loggers' Prices and Meet Competition

### By H. C. Copeland, Vancouver

The nearer the approach to the absolute bottom of things the better the outlook for improvement. That seems to be tht real underlaying principle of the optimistic opinion of the lumber market today. Of course there is some lumber business. The local markets are quite active but at prices which are based entirely on "keep it moving at any price" rather than a fair figure based on the price of logs and the manufacturing costs.

As the writer sees the matter it is simply this, there are still certain points in industrial lines where the prices are too high as based upon relative production costs of other lines. This brings about a degree of fear among the prospective investors that prices have not reached the bottom, the result is what we have been calling a "buyer's strike." Among the producers themselves a man getting a relative low wage resents, in fact refuses, to pay producers in other lines relative high prices for their products.

It may be that there are individual attempts at securing profits that are too high. However, that may be, the profits are always the small end, and futhermore the commercial stream always insists upon a proper equalization of levels. As a matter of fact the entire commercial body responds to the same law as does water—a matter of seeking its level. Any more that tends to hold one part of the body above the rest produces the same relative effect that it does to raise an amount of water above the main body. It requires a great effort to raise it and a yet greater one to hold it there and in the end it must all come back to the same level. The above analogy can be followed in the lumber markets very closely.

As we have stated the local markets for lumber are rather active, but at low and competitive prices. The principle advantage to the manufacturers is that it helps clear the yards of the commons which accumulate from the export trade.

### Prairie Trade Has Been Slow

The prairie trade is extremely slow. A few stocking up orders are coming through but it is evident that the retail yards are not going to tie up their money until they can see in actual demand a reason for their so doing. When the crop conditions have advanced to a point where a fair crop is a practical certainty the orders from this market will likely come in with a rush. Many possibilities may result. If the mills have out and stocked large amounts of lumber everything will be lovely, otherwise the prairie yards will find themselves up against a strong demand for lumber and no lumber. It takes several months from the purchase in B. C. to the prairie consumer.

It would seem as if the wisest course on the part of the retailer would be to finance a reasonable stock and be ready which ever way the market breaks, with the advantage of having all the odds his way.

It is not our intention to be pessimistic but on the other hand do not believe in optimism that is based only on a fond hope. British Columbia timber interests have yet a long way to go as regards team work, and when we enter the markets of the world it is only team work that can win. The loggers claim at present that they cannot sell at lower figures and make a profit. Mill men say that they cannot pay the logger's prices and meet their competition in the exports markets. The fact is lumber is being sold at certain prices in certain markets. If we want our share of that business we must make the prices on the goods wanted. It should be a case of "get together." That means get "two-gether." No one man can get "together," it must be a case of give and take. The other fellow is likely no more of a ——— than you are if, —IF—, you are honest with yourself and him, that goes both ways.

The stabilizing of exchange in reference to the Canadian dollar and sterling will doubtless have a favorable effect on loosening conditions. The stronger prices of grain is another favorable condition as it will help bring the farmers out in the clear or with less loss at least, making them more active possibilities.

### Should Not Kill Potential Buying Power

The credit retrenchment campaign, while it may have been called for and thoroughly needed, can be carried too far. It may easily be carried to a point where it will kill the potential buying powers of many an otherwise sound prospect. It might be that the better way would be to help finance the good moral hazard where he needed the material for the development of his plant, even though he was unable to pay up at present on his old account. Another possible consideration is that a farmer forced to pay up now may be so handicapped that he can not make the grade the next year.

An extremely gratifying condition is the building permits from the States. One authority reports from 194 cities that the permits for January 1922 exceed by 125% those of 1921. Last year British Columbia shipped 5½ million feet to Atlantic seaboard points and this was only 2½% of the amount shipped from B. C., Washington and Oregon. It would seem as if these figures should mean a great deal as regards B. C. possibilities.

The above in connection with the fact that one Vancouver mill shipped one order of 500,000 feet of shiplap—No. 1 with up to 15% No. 2, to the Atlantic coast last month and has already shipped 250,000 feet to the same market so far this month, and that, at least, one other mill has received large orders for the same kind of business would indicate one of he brightest points in the business.

The Japanese export trade has slowed down, several reasons are alleged, one is the effort for still lower charter rates, another is saturation of the market, yet another is the desire to buy the standing timber and handle it with Japanese labor and make all the profits. At any rate while there is yet a considerable volume moving the general condition is uncertain.

Australian trade is off to a marked degree, the Chinese market is slow. In general there is a great deal of pessimism heard on the street. This is unfortunate in that it may hold back the real onward movement that is not far away. In this article we may be accused of pessimism, but that is not our opinion. We do feel that there has been a large degree of boosting for boom times that was not justified by the facts and that in effect could only hold back the true toward movement. There are certain fundamental indications that there will be a demand for lumber that should make extremely healthly markets. The rest just remains in getting together and pulling together and the advantage will be felt by everyone.

### Last Season of Dennis Canadian at Whitney

L. Van Meter, of the Dennis Canadian Co. Whitney, Ont., was in Toronto recently, calling upon many friends in the lumber trade. He reports that the mill at Whitney has started operations for the season and will cut about 6,000,000 feet, principally of hardwoods.

The Dennis Canadian Co., have been operating in Canada for the last ten years, having in 1912 taken over the plant and limits at Whitney from the Munn Lumber Co. who succeeded the St. Anthony Lumber Co. The mill has a sawing capacity of about 100,000 feet a day, the equipment consisting of two single-cut band saws and a vertical resaw. This is the last season which the Dennis-Canadian Co., will run the mill ,which at the close of 1922 will likely be dismantled. All the timber on the holdings of the company has been used up, and the balance, of about 10,000 acres, composed of hardwoods, hemlock and spruce, was disposed of a few weeks ago to Murray & Omanique, who run a sawmill at Barry's Bay, Ont.

Mr. Van Meter expects that, while the sawing of the Dennis-Canadian Co., will be completed this fall, it will take another year to clean up what stock they have in the yard, so that it is not likely that the company, whose headquarters are at Grand Rapids, Mich., will close out their entire interests in Canada until the fall of 1923.

### British Government Stocks Being Sold

The British Government stocks of lumber are gradually being sold. The entire stocks in the yards of the J. B. Snowball Co., Ltd., Chatham, N. B., have been disposed of. These amount to about ten million feet, the greater part of which is held for early loading for the U. K. A large block of Campbellton stock has been sold for export by the steamer "Skrymer." This lumber, totalling 1000 standards, fetched $22.50 per 1000 feet F.O.B.

The following were recent visitors to Montreal:—Messrs. A. C. Manbert, Canadian General Lumber Co., Ltd., Toronto; R. L. Montgomery, Montgomery & Sons, Co., New Richmond, P. Q.; H. F. Foy, Goodday & Co., Quebec; H. R. Van, Louise Lumber Co., Quebec; J. C. Bartram, Ottawa; W. B. Snowball Co., Ltd., Chatham, N. B.; R. Loggie, Loggieville, N. B.

**Canada Lumberman**

*founded 1880*

*The National Lumber Journal for Forty Years*

Issued on the 1st and 15th of every month by

**HUGH C. MACLEAN PUBLICATIONS, Limited**

THOS. S. YOUNG, Managing Director

HEAD OFFICE  - - - -  347 Adelaide Street, West, TORONTO

Proprietors and Publishers also of Electrical News, Contract Record,
Canadian Woodworker and Footwear in Canada.

VANCOUVER  - - - - - - -   Winch Building
MONTREAL  - - - -  119 Board of Trade Bldg.
WINNIPEG  —  —  302 Travellers' Bldg.
NEW YORK  - - - -  296 Broadway
CHICAGO  - - - -  14 West Washington Street
LONDON, ENG.  - - - -  16 Regent Street, S.W.

TERMS OF SUBSCRIPTION
Canada, United States and Great Britain, $3.00 per year, in advance; other
foreign countries embraced in the General Postal Union, $4.00.
Single copies, 30 cents.

Authorized by the Postmaster-General for Canada, for transmission as
second-class matter.

Vol. 42          Toronto, May 1, 1922          No. 9

## What Is Wrong with Lumber Industry?

Considerable discussion has been heard of late regarding what is wrong with the lumber business. One man advances a certain theory and another strongly advocates something of a diametrically opposite character. Each believes that he has put his finger on the vital spot and diagnosed the case correctly, and if his suggestions were carried out, all would be smooth sailing in the near future.

There is no universal panacea for industrial ills any more than there is for every variety of human ailments. There are certain basic principles, however, which it is well to recognize and study.

In directing attention to the lumber business to-day it is interesting to observe the way in which certain exponents view matters. Some take a selfish and superficial view of things in general, others seek to delve deeply into economic sources and fundamental principles, and still others declare that present-day grievances are largely of a mental nature and, if a more buoyant and optimistic frame of mind and attitude prevailed, conditions would soon be satisfactorily adjusted.

In conversation with one of the leading figures of the lumber trade in Canada, who has for years been connected with the industry in both a wholesale and manufacturing capacity, he said that the chief difficulties at this juncture are lack of confidence and weakness of purpose, coupled with too much concern regarding the future and what the other fellow is doing or going to do.

We are too prone to indulge in speculation and too much inclined to concern ourselves about the price the other chap is asking or what stock he has to offer. Instead of a manufacturer fixing his figure for his product on what it has cost him on his own operation, and deciding that his hemlock, white pine or spruce must be sold for such and such a sum—and sticking to that quotation—he is anxiously enquiring about what his neighbor or competitor is naming, and whether his stock is moving, if he has made any sales, how he feels regarding the future etc.

What is required to-day is that when salesman should say.— "This is our price for such and such a grade, width and thickness," and adhere to it. As it is now, a salesman goes in to a retail lumber man who asks him what his 1 x 4 spruce flooring is worth and the representative replies, ' oh, $35.00. Now that figure is not the traveller's price at all. He immediately begins, by specious processes and arts, circumlocution or some other subtle means, to try and find out if the dealer has been offered spruce flooring at a lower figure. If so, he promptly proceeds to cut under the quotation, and seeks to land the business. The ordinary salesman is much more concerned in getting ahead of the other fellow and beating him out in a rivalry of price slashing than he is of sticking steadfastly to his own list of values.

Then salesmen adopt other expedients to demoralize and unsettle the market. A retailer will make an offer for a certain lot, naming $2.00 or $3.00 less than the salesman has the power to quote. The latter sends in the order subject to "approval of head office," which

is sometimes conceded and sometimes not. Other representatives, of course, are granted leeway and have the power to reduce their quotation on certain lines to certain figures or to practically make their own price if they can land the business.

The result is that orders to-day are accepted at a loss. There is a lack of stability in many lines of lumber and a decided want of confidence on the part of the customer. Until a more rigid stand prevails regarding prices, there is not likely to be that improvement which we hope will soon be witnessed in the general situation so far as forest products are concerned.

You may think from these remarks that I am casting some reflections upon the salesman. Not at all. Manufacturers and wholesalers are equally to blame. They are constantly poking their head through the veil of the future and seeking to spy out what is beyond. They utter predictions about a growing demand, increase in prices and a runaway market; now is the time to buy, now is the time to sell, etc., making the lumber industry much more hazardous and speculative in character than it was ever intended to be.

Now I have been in the lumber business quite a number of years and I have never seen any firm make itself wealthy by essaying all the while to read the future and to cash in at certain particular periods. So many imagine that they are prophets, natural born speculators or shrewd guessers when they are nothing of the sort. Because they have happened to make a lucky hit once or twice, does not endow them with any special predictive talents or bestow upon them the gifts of talismans.

We are more immediately concerned ourselves with the present, the costs of production or operating conditions, the stock on hand, getting our price for it, how we can move it, etc. I cannot better illustrate my conception of this than to refer to my early days on the farm. That was away back in the eighties when barley was the chief grain of interest in the locality where I was brought up. In one or two autumns it rose to a $1.00 per bushel, and some farmers who had held on and got $1.05, thought they were the cleverest and most prescient individuals in the entire community. They gave others who held on too long or who sold their season's crop too early the merry Ha Ha, intimating that "We are intellectually superior to you. Why have not you our discernment?" Well, one swallow does not make a summer and one fortunate bargain does not create a Croesus.

One prudent and well-balanced resident in the community, who had been chaffed by some neighbors for selling his barley too soon, was in a reflective mood one night when I happened to be at his house, he said, "Young man, don't try to read the future too much. Don't imagine that you are a born speculator or a soothsayer of Old Testament times. We hear of such men to-day but they are gone to-morrow. The lucky strokes that they make are well advertised but the reverses, which are many, are hushed up.

It is the same in connection with betting on horse races. You hear of the fellow, who makes a killing one day, tells it far and wide, but on the other day when he suffers a loss, he is discreetly silent. It is the same, too in connection with the marketing of grains. " For the last five years I have kept tab" he continued," on my neighbors, and I found that the man who sold when he was ready, that is, after his harvest was over, and the grain cleared up and he had the time and opportunity to market the product, got on the average, more for his barley than the fellow who was disposing of his early one year and late the next or holding over a year for in the hope of realizing a huge price and subsequently having to take a sacrifice.

"Success," he went on, " consists largely in doing the proper thing at the proper time, and the proper period is generally when one is ready to sell."

You will pardon this digression from the lumber field, but it illustrates very pointedly what I have in mind regarding lumber stocks that are on hand to-day. We should not seek so eagerly to descry the future, worry about the other fellow or endeavor to undersell him; but should face conditions as they are. We should make the price for our product based on the decreased cost of logging, driving, sawing etc., and adhere to that figure, showing that we have confidence in our selling values, faith in ourselves and assurance that the present state of affairs is not half as depressing as many who, by their course and conduct, are leading others in the trade to believe. Stabilization, conservation, a cool head, firm decision and a grasp of the present, are elements that will contribute to bring about prosperity than all the theorizing and speculating in the wide world.

The Hammermill Paper Co., of Erie, Pa who have an office at Port Arthur, bought through jobbers 45,000 cords of pulpwood during the past season. It is said that this company, along with others who have taken out considerable wood through contractors, will be shipping out all told 125,000 cords of pulpwood during the coming season, from the Port Arthur district.

# Mr. Levie Returns from Trip Overseas

### Says Ocean Freight Rates Are Still too High and Seriously Handicap Canadians in Business

John G. Levie, Quebec, P.Q.

Mr. John G. Levie, vice-president of the well-known Quebec export lumber firm of W. & J. Sharples, Quebec, who went abroad in the early part of February last in the interest of the firm on April 22nd, is satisfied with the result of his visit to the British Isles. In an interview with the Quebec correspondent of the 'Canada ' Lumberman," Mr. Levie said,—"I visited England, Ireland and Scotland, spending ample time in these countries to confer with the firm's agencies, and talk business with customers, knowing the existing conditions before I went to the United Kingdom. I am satisfied with the result of my business visit. I sold some wood in England and Scotland, but did better in Ireland, and feel confident that I would have done much better if the steamship companies would only take a sane view of conditions and reduce freight rates.

"Last fall we received quotations from steamship companies of 100 shillings, and as a natural consequence had to write business at these high rates, which handicapped our selling. Since my return to Quebec on April 21st. we have received advices by cable that the rate had dropped to 85 shillings. This is not enough. We insist upon 60 shillings which is a fair rate. At the higher rates, even 85 shillings the Canadian export trade is unable to compete with Poland, Germany, Finland and Norway and Sweden, countries whose work is coming into the United Kingdom markets to the discrimination of Canadian wood. Nevertheless if the steamships had given us the 85 shilling rate last fall, instead of at this date. we would have been better guided in our last winter's business, and I would have been in a position to have done a great deal more business than I did in the British Isles during my visit just completed.

Therefore is is up to the shipping companies to reduce the freights on lumber if they have any wish to see the export lumber trade from Canada rejuvenated, and made active. They must realize that the war was over by the signing of the Armistice, and over three years have elapsed since that period. If they desire to see shipping more actively employed, especially in the Canadian lumber trade. they will have to reduce their freight rates to bring about, or at the least,' assist in bringing about normal conditions. The lumber trade of Canada has made sacrifices during the past two years to meet exigencies, and we do not see why the steamship companies should not meet the situation at least half way. Until they do, they must not expect the Canadian trade to sell when there is no profit and with the risk of loss, as we cannot compete with the wood trade from European continental countries, now shoving the Canadian trade out of the United Kingdom markets by excessive steam freight rates in the Atlantic carrying trade together with the differences in exchange which discriminates against Canada, and in order to demonstrate this evil, I quote you the eve of my departure from Liverpool, April 11th, as to the value of the pound sterling in various countries, as follows:—

New York, 18, 18/1, Paris £1 18/1, £1 18/3, Brussels, £2 1/, £2 1/3, Geneva, 17/11, 17/11, Madrid, £1 2/8, £1 2/5½, Rome, £3 5/6, £3 5/6, Berlin. £70, £57, Vienna, £1332, £1332, Warsaw, £832 10/, £832 10/, Amsterdam, 19/2, 19/1½, Christiania, £1 6/8½, £1 6/11, Copenhagen, £1 2/11, £1 2/10, Stockholm, 18/6, 18/6, Helsingfors. £8 17/6, £8 15/6.

Speaking of conditions in general as viewed by Mr. Levie during his sojourn in the United Kingdom, Mr. Levie said:— "They are really better than I expected. There is a good deal of construction in progress, but the purchasers are nervous owing to unsettled political conditions, consequently are buying with caution. Stocks are low but still the producers are reluctant to buy big lots, content with small lots to tide them over in the present. Construction and consumption of lumber is going on well, and would be better only for the engineering strike, which has affected and tied up all work in British ship yards. Then again, there is the Genoa Conference which

is being watched with a tremor of anxiety, which caused building interests to act with caution.

"But, taking everything into consideration, as I visualized the situation, I am of the opinion that the bottom of the Canadian trade with the United Kingdom has been reached, and should the steamship companies lower their freight rates in compatibility with conditions to put new life in shipping, a new life will be put in the Canadian labor trade with Great Britian before very long to encourage all concerned.

---

## Getting Ready for Big Summer Trip

Arrangements are being further perfected for the annual midsummer outing of the Ontario Retail Lumber Dealers' Association. which will take place from June 23rd to June 27th on board the S. S. "Huronic" of the Northern Navigation Co. L. H. Richards, of Sarnia, is the energetic chairman of the excursion, and along with J. C. Scofield, of Windsor, president of the Ontario Retail Lumber Dealers' Association, and secretary Boultbee, of Toronto, no stone is being left unturned to insure the success and enjoyment of the trip.

The Ontario Association must guarantee 175 full-fare tickets by June 10th. While this is a rather big proposition, still the organization has never fallen down on anything it has undertaken, and there is every reason to believe that success will crown its efforts in connection with the forthcoming jaunt which will be a delightful one from Windsor and Sarnia to Owen Sound, Killarney, Sault Ste Marie, Mackinac and return.

In this issue the "Canada Lumberman" presents a view of the S. S. "Huronic." which has been chartered for the occasion. It will be observed that it is a staunch, well-built and comfortable craft. The cost per person for the boat trip from Windsor and return will be $50.00. This will cover all expenses from the moment the tra-

Northern Navigation Company Steamer "Huronic" Chartered by Retail Lumbermen of Ontario for their outing up the Lakes in June

veller crosses the gang-plank until he disembarks on his return to the point from which he started. Members of the Ontario Retail Lumber Dealers' Association are invited to bring along their wives and the members of their families. President Scofield is making arrangements with the Michigan Retail Lumber Dealers' Association to join the Ontario Association on this outing. The Michigan men will be assigned 75 berths.

The total carrying capacity of the vessel is about 250. Twenty-five preferred staterooms have been set aside at a cost of $60.00 per person. These staterooms will all accommodate three persons. About half of them have upper berths for one person and a double lower. The other half have an upper berth for one person and a lower berth for one person and a couch on the opposite side of the room. All other rooms are similarly equipped. Outside of the 25 preferred staterooms the entire fare for the round trip is $50.00 as already stated.

The itinerary of the trip is as follows:— Leave Windsor 5 P. M. June 23rd; leave Sarnia 11 P. M. same day; arrive Owen Sound 7 P. M. June 24th. leave Owen Sound 11 P. M. same day; arrive Killarney 7 A. M. June 25th, leave Killarney 9 A. M. same day; arrive at Sault Ste Marie midnight same day; arrive at Mackinac 10 A. M. June 26th; leave Mackinac noon same day; arrive Sarnia 10 A. M. June 27th; leave Sarnia noon same day; arrive Windsor 5 P.M. same day.

L. H. Richards, of Sarnia, will issue tickets to the members. Reservations will be made by him and held upon payment of one half the purchase price of the tickets.

## Personal Paragraphs of Interest

Ray B. Maxson, a member of the Chas. O. Maus Lumber Co., South Bend, Ind., was in Toronto recently ,calling upon the trade.

H. D. Joyce, a well-known figure in Montreal lumbering circles, has opened an office in the new Canada Cement Building Montreal.

C. H. Belton, of the Laidlaw-Belton Lumber Co., Sarnia, Ont., recently returned from an extended business trip to British Columbia.

E. D. Harper has joined the sales staff of Terry & Gordon, Ltd., Toronto, and will cover part of Western and Northern Ontario. He has entered upon his new duties.

Knox Bros., Limited, of Montreal, have opened a purchase and sales office at 511 McLeod Building, Edmonton, Alta., under the management of Hugh R. Patriarche.

Andrew Stark, of the selling staff of the Elgie & Jarvis Lumber Co., Toronto, recently joined the ranks of the benedicts and is receiving the congratulations of his friends.

Wm. F. Baker, president of the Crow's Nest Pass Lumber Co., Wardner, B. C., and a director of the B. C. Spruce Mills, Lumberton, B. C., was in Toronto recently on business.

W. C. Laidlaw, of the R. Laidlaw Lumber Co., Toronto sailed recently from New York on the "Homeric" on a business trip to Great Britain. He will be absent about three months.

Wiley N. Scholes, late of Stewart & Wood, Limited, Toronto, has been appointed secretary-treasurer of the C. G. Anderson Lumber, Co., Limited, Toronto and has entered upon his new duties.

V. A. Barnett, who has been connected with the wholesale and retail lumber business all his life, has started in the retail lumber line at Stop 24, New Toronto. The firm name is Barnett-Hewlett Lumber Co.

Wm. B. Cole, of Sparta, Ont., passed away recently in his 83rd year. For many years he was engaged in lumbering and milling operations. He was a Justice of the Pease and at one time a member of Elgin County council.

George H. Holt, of the Holt Timber Co., Chicago, was in Toronto recently after an absence of several weeks. Mr. Holt spent some time in Florida and lately recovered from an attack of pneumonia. He is gradually regaining his strength.

J. J. Miller, of the Anderson-Miller Lumber Co., Toronto, who is the Canadian member of the National Hardwood Lumber Association Committee on Rules for Measurement and Inspection, was in Chicago recently attending a meeting of that body.

E. H. Port, who was for some years in the office of the Eastern Wrecking & Construction Co., Toronto, has started in the retail lumber business under the name of the Long Branch Lumber Co. He has established a yard at Stop 28¾ Long Branch.

Alvin E. Smith, who for several years past has been a member of the sales staff of Read Bros., Limited, wholesale lumber dealers. Toronto, has joined the travelling force of the C. G. Anderson Lumber Co., Limited, Toronto, and entered upon his new duties.

J. P. Johnson, of J. P. Johnson & Son, Toronto, was in Peterboro recently, attending the funeral of the late John Duignan, of the Lakefield Lumber Co. Mr. Duignan was for many years manager of the mills and lumber business of the late Alfred McDonald, Peterboro.

The many friends of Hon. T. D. Pattullo, of Victoria, Minister of Lands in British Columbia, will sympathize with him in the death of his father, George R. Pattullo, registrar of Oxford County, who passed away at his home in Woodstock, Ont., recently. Mr. Pattullo had long been one of the best-known men in Western Ontario.

L. L. Brown, B. C., Lumber Commissioner, has returned from a visit to Victoria where he was called owing to the illness of his wife who is now completely restored to health. Mr. Brown states that the permanent exhibit of B. C. forest products which the province will make in the new display rooms at 51 Yonge St., Toronto is now on the way and should be in place within the next few weeks. He reports that the lumber business in British Columbia is generally picking up in volume and more mills are resuming operations.

J. Gordon Walklate, the secretary-treasurer of the recently formed Trans-Canada Lumber Co., Limited Drummond Building, Montreal, was for several years in the mill department of W. C. Edwards & Co., Ottawa, and later with the Pine Lake Lumber Company, Pickerel, Ontario. He left to go overseas and on returning to Canada, started in business in Montreal under his own name. In the early part of this year, the Trans-Canada Lumber Company was formed with O. L. Pope, Bury, Que., as president, and N. L. Wilson, Ottawa, as vice-president. M. Pope is the owner of two hardwood mills at Bury, Que.

John B. Reid, of Toronto, honorary-president of the Ontario Retail Lumber Dealers' Association, who with his wife and daughter has been spending the last six months at St. Petersburg, Florida, has

George W. Ewan Ottawa, Ont. Newly appointed Secretary-Treasurer of the Lumbermen's Credit Bureau of Capital City.

Harold D. Joyce, Montreal Who has opened wholesale lumber office in new Canada Cement Building in that city

returned home. Mr. Reid greatly enjoyed his extended holiday and is looking remarkably well. He speaks in the highest terms of Southern hospitality and says a great many Canadians spent the winter in the "Sunshine City" as St. Petersburg is frequently styled. Mr. Reid won several honors at bowling and was elected vice-president of the Canadian Club. He also took part in other activities during his residence in St. Petersburg.

## Good Price for Second Growth Timber

Fifteen acres of second-growth hardwood, on the shores of Lake Simcoe, east of Barrie, were sold last winter for $600. That was the price paid for the standing timber, the land remaining in the hands of the original owner. From half an acre 35 cords of hardwood were cut.

It is only 80 years since settlement began in the section in which this sale took place, and probably not over 60 since the original timber was cut on the land that has since grown a second crop.

## London Citizen Is Building His Own Coffin

The absolute limit in spare-time occupations have been discovered. A man living in the east end of London, Ont., is spending his evenings making coffins for himself and his wife. He has been engaged at the task for about two years.

He came into possession of some beautiful walnut lumber a number of years ago and stored it in his attic. A cabinet maker by trade, he thought it a shame not to be making use of the boards. He intended to build a mausoleum of his own but has given up this idea and has purchased crypts in a public mausoleum. He is busy at his trade every day and is cheerful and a good citizen.

## Snowball Company Has Added Planing Mill

W. B. Snowball, of the J. B. Snowball Co., Limited, Chatham, N. B., states that while business still continues quiet in the lumber line, some English buying has commenced. His firm recently sold about 10,000,000 feet of stock to go to the British market.

The J. B. Snowball Co., have a new planing mill in operation and are now turning out stock. The mill is fitted with a No. 341 Berlin resaw and a Yates No. 91 planer and profiler, with all attachments for doing the class of work that can be turned out by such a machine. The mill building itself is 80 feet long by 28 feet wide and there is a separate structure for the boiler and engine. The J. B. Snowball Co., have stop-off privileges and are now doing milling in-transit as well as looking after the dressing of all their own lumber as required. Mr. Snowball says that the planing mill will afford the company splendid facilities for extending their service and meeting the wants of their customers in different parts of Canada.

The J. B. Snowball Co., are among the oldest lumber operators in the Maritime Provinces and produce spruce, pine and hemlock lumber, as well as shingles and lath. They have always done a large export trade and also considerable business across the line.

## Lieut-Col. Milne Honored at North Bay

On the occasion of the recent visit of his Excellency, Lord Byng, to North Bay, Ont., one of the features was the decoration of Lieut-Col. W. H. Milne, formerly of the 159th Battalion, with the Order of the British Empire. The ceremony was performed by Canada's Governor-General in the presence of a large gathering. Lieut-Col. Milne is a son of Wm. Milne, the veteran lumber manufacturer of North Bay and Trout Mills, and is a member of the firm of Wm. Milne & Sons. He has for a number of years looked after the logging end of the business. The Colonel served with distinction with the Canadian Forestry Corps in France and has long taken an active interest in military matters. Lieut-Col.

**Lieut-Col. W. H. Milne
North Bay, Ont.**

Milne enlisted with the 159th (Northern Battalion) for overseas service in February 1916 and reverted to a captaincy in order to get over to France. In March 1917 he was transferred to the Canadian Forestry unit and two months later was promoted to rank of major. A year afterwards he became Lieut-Colonel, and after the European conflict was over, he returned to Scotland where certain forestry operations were carried out until May 1919 when he returned to North Bay and resumed his associations with the firm.

Lieut-Col. Milne was connected with No. 6 District in the Vosges Mountains, France, and had charge of three sawmills. Of the progressive character and practical nature of his work with the Forestry Corps little need be said as it is widely known among all Canadian foresters and lumbermen who went overseas. Many friends will congratulate him on the recent honor which he has received.

---

### General Jottings of Trade Interest

Lumber Mfrs Yards, Ltd., Lebret, Sask., recently opened a branch yard in that town.

C. Lloyd & Sons, Limited, Wingham, Ont., have been incorporated with a capital of $40,000 to manufacture and deal in wood products. A. E. Lloyd and R. H. Lloyd, both of Wingham, are two of the incorporators.

Hall Bros., wholesale lumber dealers, of Toronto, who operate a mill at Marlbank, in Hastings County, completed their cut of about 750,000 feet, their mill having been in operation since January last. The cut consists of maple, basswood and elm, and is about the same as last year.

Greater activity was indicated in the lumber business in the district of New Westminster, B. C., during 1921 than the previous one. The receipts at the Crown Timber Office for the last fiscal year ending March 31st 1922 were $149,546. During the year previous twelve months they were $138,086.

Col. C. H. L. Jones, of Sault Ste Marie, Ont., general manager of the Spanish River Pulp & Paper Mills, who took the 227th Battalion overseas and later was head of the forestry operations in France, was tendered a hearty welcome recently by the war veterans of Sault Ste Marie, Col. Jones being the president of the organization.

The Tionaga Lumber Co., has begun sawing at Tionaga on the C. N. R. west of Sudbury. R. B. Herron, who is managing-director of the company, says that the firm will take out between 5,000,000 and 6,000,000 feet of jack pine and spruce this year, or about the same quantity as last, although the number of railway ties will not be as large.

International Burr Corporation of Canada, Limited, Belleville, Ont., were recently granted a federal charter with a capital of $40,000, to manufacture and market a product used in dressing pulp mill stones in the manufacture of paper and pulp. W. P. Aiken, of Watertown, N. Y., and C. B. Aiken, of Belleville, Ont., are among the incorporators of the company.

Pacific coast and north-western lumber and shingle interests in their fight to get the 50 cent duty on shingles restored to the tariff bill, are working to effect a combination among the senators who want the finance committee rates increased. These include a part of agricultural senators and a number who are trying to boost other schedules, says a recent despatch from Washington.

The planing mill compensation rate has been reduced in Ontario by the Workmen's Compensation Board. The mills had a good record during the past year, so far as accident showing was concerned, and the Board has been enabled to decrease the rate from $2.40 to $2.00. This announcement was made in a report recently issued by the W.C.A. under the heading "Useful Information for the Employer."

An order was issued recently at Washington by the Interstate Commerce Commission requiring transcontinental railroads to establish on or before June 12, new standards and regulations to remove unjust disadvantages to which the commission found lumber producers of the north-western Pacific Coast States to be subjected by present railroad regulations fixing minimum weights for carloads shipments.

Canadian spruce is wanted in India according to recent advices received from London, England. The Indian Government is calling for tenders for a year's supply of lumber for packing cases and has specified Canadian spruce as the material. The Government requires 140 standards 3x11 inches, 400 standards 3x9 inches, and 300 standards 3x7 inches, all of a length from 10 to 16 feet and of the quality known as "good commercial."

According to the best estimates 50,000,000 feet is the total quantity of logs that will come out of the Miramichi River in New Brunswick this year. Out of this quantity 35,000,000 feet will come from the southwest Miramichi and the remaining 15,000,000 feet through the northwest branch. Practically all the logs on both branches are old ones which were cut a year ago last winter and have since been on the banks or in the streams. It is said that the average wages being paid the drivers on the Nashwaak River and other streams is $2.20 per day, or about 50% less than last year.

The sawmill of Stanley Douglass, Limited, at South Devon. N. B., has started the season's operations as well as the resawing and planing mill departments. Between 5,000,000 and 6,000,000 ft. will be cut this year. All the drives of the Fraser Companies, Limited, comprising the supply of lumber for their Victoria Mills in Fredericton, N. B., have reached safe waters. The drives which are now out, consist of about 5,600,000 feet. The balance of the supply of logs for the season's cut at the Victoria mills, which will total upwards of 9,000,000 feet, will be bank logs, all of which have been contracted for.

Advices received from Sydney, N. S., state that John E. Moore, a well-known lumberman of St. John, N. B., has been appointed by the Minister of Labor to represent the British Empire Steel Corporation on the new Conciliation Board which will rehear the wage dispute between the company and its mining employees, according to a telegram received by Isaac D. MacDougal, the U. M. W. member of the board. Mr. Moore and Mr. MacDougal meet soon at Truro to select a chairman. If they fail to agree the chairman will be chosen by Hon. James Murdock. Although the time for the British Empire Steel Corporation was extended by the Labor Department the company declined to nominate a representative.

The wood room of the Abitibi Co., made a unique record for output and efficiency during February and March. Owing to the fact that there was not so much pulpwood cut in the North last year, as usual, and a lot of the companies were not cutting at all, many settlers were up against it with wood on their hands for which there was no demand. The Abitibi Co., although it had big crews in the bush, decided to purchase a good deal of the wood from the settlers, which relieved the strain on the latter to a large extent. This meant a lot of 4-foot wood to handle. The first move was to build a special slasher to handle this length of wood, cutting off the 42-inch block required by the grinders and carrying the short block to the chippers. When the slasher started running, the amount of cords handled and barked was 200 a day. This was later increased to 300 cords and eventually to 550. The average cords per barker per hour showed a similar increase, running as high as 2.5 cords.

## Will Dispose of British Stocks Speedily

A. M. B. Stevens, director of the Timber Disposal Department, Board of Trade, London, England, who came to Canada with the object of disposing of as promptly as possible the British Government's stock of wood in Canada, amounting to 100,000,000 feet, b.m., recently paid a visit to Quebec to confer with Lieut.-Col. R. M. Beckett, of the firm of Dobell, Beckett & Co., who is acting as adviser on behalf of the British Board of Trade in connection with Mr. Blakely of Cox, Long & Co., Limited, Montreal. Lieut.-Col. Beckett and Mr. Stevens held a conference with the Quebec timber export firms of Price Bros. & Co., W. Gerard Power, president of W. & J. Sharples, Regd., and other Quebec export concerns, and after going into the matter thoroughly, came to the conclusion that it was in the best interests of the Canadian lumber trade to have this large stock of lumber owned by the British Government, disposed of to the best advantage as quickly as possible.

Lieut.-Col. Beckett, in a talk with the Quebec correspondent of the "Canada Lumberman," said the Quebec conference was most satisfactory, the Quebec export firms agreeing that the disposal of the stock of lumber would result in clarifying the situation, and no matter the sacrifice, it had to come sooner or later, and the sooner the better.

Lieut.-Col. Beckett, who is taking an active part as advisor to the British Board of Trade, also said that he had succeeded in a disposal of 25,000,000 feet of the stock.

## Ocean Freight Rates on Deals too High

R. L. Sargant the manager of the Transportation Department of the Canadian Lumbermen's Association, in a recent interview with "Canada Lumberman," said the rate on deals from Canadian ports to those of the United Kingdom has been reduced from 100s to 85s per standard. "This rate of 85s is" he added not of much benefit to the Canadian exporter by reason of the fact that the rate from Scandinavian ports to those of Great Britain has been as low as 55s. The Canadian exporter should, at least, have a rate not exceeding 60 to 65s per standard if he is to be in a position to compete with these Scandinavian interests."

## Hocken Lumber Company Opens Retail Yard

The Hocken Lumber Co., Limited, manufacturers and wholesalers, whose head office is in Toronto and mills at West. River and Deer Lake, Ont., are opening up a retail lumber yard at the north-east corner of Dovercourt Road and Van Horne St., Toronto, where white pine, hemlock, spruce and other building materials will be handled. The manager of the retail business will be Harry N. Hocken, who is a brother of Norman C. Hocken, president if the company. Osborne Smith, who was for several years in the retail lumber line in Toronto, will have charge of the yard.

The Hocken Lumber Co., sawed about 1,000,000 feet of hemlock at their mill at Deer Lake last winter, and have now started up their plant at West River where over 6,000,000 feet of white and red pine will be cut during the coming season.

## Japan in the Market for Western Woods

Y. Sito, of Kobe, Japan, and a party of Japanese lumber and wood pulp buyers, who are said to represent a capital of $35,000,000, arrived recently in Victoria, B. C. It is stated that the unprecedented demand of Japan for British Columbia lumber last year was not merely a temporary development but an indication that Japan will be in the market for B. C. forest products in large volume for many years to come.

"We are looking for cedar principally," said Mr. Sito. "in Japan we do not paint our building material, so that only lumber that retains its natural color is acceptable. Cedar is also light and easy to handle. The use of hemlock in Japan is rapidly growing, and Douglas fir is also finding an important place in the market."

## Early Lumbering Activities at Braeside

A copy of Neilson's Weekly the pioneer newspaper published in Arnprior, Ont., fifty three years ago gives an interesting account of the lumber enterprise in Braeside, (near Arnprior) which was just commencing in 1869.

Concerning the origin of the big lumber industry (Gillies Bros., Limited.) now at Braeside, Neilson's Weekly said that Mr. Purvis, Manager of the Osborne mills at Portage du Fort, had purchased a number of acres of land on the river, about half way between Arnprior and Sand Point, which he was fitting up for a lumber yard "for receiving and piling the boards sawn at the Portage," which were to be floated to the spot. As the railway track was just at

hand the lumber could be re-shipped without cartage. It was reported that Mr. Purvis would immediately put up a steam sawmill on the property to run in connection with the upper mill. The prediction as made by the Weekly that all the sites along the Ottawa above Arnprior, and particularly McNab's grove, would be taken up ere long. "The convenience to the railway, and the ability to get any quantity of logs by water for fifty or a hundred years to come, renders this vicinity a most desirable one for such purposes." A directory of Renfrew County was published. The South Riding was represented in the Commons by Daniel McLachlin of Arnprior, and in the Legislature by J. L. McDougall of Renfrew.

## Toronto Lumberman Heads Young Men's Club

C. A. Westley, who was recently elected president of the Young Men's Club of the Toronto Board of Trade, which was organized three years ago, is one of the best-known of the younger members of the industry.

Mr. Westley has long been an active worker in the Board of Trade and other organizations. He began his career with the lum-

C. A. Westley, Toronto

ber industry with Church & Fee, (now Church & Church )at Labelle, Que., where he was clerk in the bush, culler, etc., for four years. Then he joined G. A. Grier & Sons, Limited, Montreal, and was in their yard and office for some time, after which he took a position on the road. In 1914 Mr. Westley came to Toronto and has since been associated with the Toronto branch of this widely-known lumber firm. He has covered various parts of Ontario and is a capable and aggressive salesman.

## Continental Wood Products Elect Officers

The annual meeting of the Continental Wood Products Co., Limited, 107 St. James St., Montreal, was held recently and the following directors were elected:—Philip T. Dodge (President of the International Paper Co., New York); Herman Elsas (President of the Continental Paper & Bag Mills, New York); Thomas Fynes; Louis Gosselin, K. C.; C. A. L. Hibbard; Isidore Kuhe; Chester W. Layman.

The directors subsequently met when the following Executive was elected:— President, Louis Gosselin, K.C.; Vice-President and Treasurer, Thomas Fynes; Secretary, E. B, Segendorf.

The woods headquarters of the company are at Devon, (Pine P. O.) Ont., and their plants are located at Elsas, Ont., on the C. N. Ry., and Lachevrotiere, Que., on the C. P. R., and C. N. Ry. The company produce lumber, pulpwood, ties, lath, shingles, and cedar poles.

E. L. Bliss, who is well known in Ontario and has had considerable experience in the exportation of the forests and mill operations has been appointed manager of the company's operations in Ontario and, in particular, manager of the company's Ontario plant situated at Elsas. Under his direction much is expected from this plant supplied from the company's extensive timber limits in the district of Sudbury.

## New Pulp and Paper Making Process
### By "A Canadian"

Not a few Canadian lumbermen have for some years been studying and investigating the process of manufacturing jack pine and princess pine into a commercial article that would have a large demand, and meet the requirements of the public. In this they have been assisted by many bureaus of research and scientific authorities.

The investigations carried on in all countries where paper is a requirement in nearly every walk of life, have stimulated investigators and others to considerable activity and have aroused an interest in the study of various kinds of grasses and timber for the production of paper in order to take the place of the spruce, balsam and other woods which are now used so extensively. Experiments and tests to employ various kinds of timber carrying a high percentage of pitch but containing excellent fibre, have been carefully carried out by existing methods, but the latter have proven to be too expensive to meet the economical cost of converting timber used at present when these same methods were applied to woods carrying a large percentage of pitch. It was found when the problems were considered, that the present methods could be employed with such modifications that each process should be incorporated in the new method; and the results have been successful. Instead of the pitch being an injurious product, it becomes a source of revenue. The process combines those used in both chemical and groundwood pulp manufacture.

The new method is now in successful operation, and with large amounts of princess and jack pine in Canada, should merit the consideration of those financially interested in forest products. It is believed that a new industry started along this line, would insure satisfactory returns from the beginning. The cost of manufacture is the prime factor in the production of any article and when a new industry looms up, not only is the cost of buildings and machinery taken into consideration, but that of the manufactured article as well. The building and equipment for using princess and jack pine in the production of pulp and paper are of standard design and the cost can be readily determined. The manufacturing cost of the finished pulp will be from 50 to 75% less than the manufacture of any chemical pulp now made, and from 10 to 20% more than the expense in turning out groundwood.

The process is semi-chemical and the yield is about 65% greater per cord than any known chemical process and about 20% less per cord than the mechanical groundwood process. The fact is that it combines the two. The strong features are the extracting of the gums, leaving the fibre strong in character, easily bleached and readily converted into paper, making papers of its own natural color, of excellent character, tough and durable, or when bleached into the higher grades of book and writing papers, without the assistance of stronger fibres, as is now necessary in paper-making.

Canadian forests of princess and jack pine, when this process is employed in the Dominion, will become as valuable as spruce and white pine. Canadians will then add another industry to their country which will not only contribute wealth to the population, but employ labor and increase other resources of the Dominion to meet the requirements of this new development.

## Fairly Good Cut in Pulpwood

Chas. W. Cox, Port Arthur, Ont., who is a well-known contractor for pulpwood, says that although the output was not as large last season as the one previous, on the whole the business was fairly successful.

Mr. Cox declares that while the prices he has received do not come up to those of a year ago, the cost of production has been considerably reduced. Roughly speaking, supplies for the camps, such as hay, oats, potatoes, etc., have been purchased locally at, approximately, 50% reduction below last year's quotation. Labor has been most plentiful and bushmen have been satisfied with a decrease in wages of comparatively the same per cent over last year. The cutting price, paid generally during the winter was $2.00 a cord, while a year ago it was $4.00, $5.00 and in some cases as high as $6.00 a cord.

Mr. Cox reports that the general wage for bush labor this winter was $30.00 to $40.00 a month and in 1920-21 the figure was from $75.00 up. He has model, well laid out and sanitary camps, which have won much favorable comment.

Regarding the pulpwood outlook for 1922, Mr. Cox adds that it is perhaps too early yet to make any prediction but he feels that the market will be getting a little stronger. On account of the unusual depth of snow, production was somewhat hampered in the northern woods last winter. Possibly a few concerns did not secure the amount of stock they had at first anticipated taking out.

With these facts in view, Mr. Cox feels that next year operators may look, for a somewhat increased demand for their product. He supplies a lot of pulpwood for the Detroit Sulphite Pulp & Paper Co. of Detroit, and when the season for navigation starts, sends forward several loads regularly by water.

## British Columbia has Much Pulpwood

C. J. Kay, president of the Canadian Paper Trade Association, and head of the Columbia Paper Co., Limited, Vancouver, recently delivered an interesting and timely address before the Wholesale Bureau of the Board of trade in that city on the importance of the industry to Canada. He said that the total output of pulp and paper for export in 1890 was $120.00 and the output in 1921 was valued at $174,000,000. Canada's pulp and paper industry had grown to become the second largest in the world. Mr. Kay said that while the total newsprint manufactured in the United States last year was 1,116,000 tons. Canada was not far behind in producing 800,000 tons. In emphasizing the importance of the industry in regard to the exchange situation, he mentioned that no less than 85% of Canada's newsprint production was exported to the United States and other countries, leaving 15% to be consumed in the Dominion.

Mr Kay estimated the available pulpwood of British Columbia at 225,000,000 cords and said there could be no denying that with the industry still in its infancy on the Coast, British Columbia would be regarded as the great source of supply for the West in the future and the province upon which other rapidly depleting sections would have to rely.

## Fraser Companies in Good Position

The annual statement of, the Fraser Companies, Limited, of New Brunswick, for the year ending December 31, 1921, was recently issued. The net profits for the year amounted to $1,001,459, from which was deducted $199,227 for bond interest and $333,073 for other interests, leaving a balance of $468,359. Then came special deductions in an effort to discount absolutely depreciation of inventories and to bring the balance sheet down to a rock bottom basis as dictated by a conservative management. Depreciation was taken off amounting to $445,572; depletion of $235,463, annual proportion of discount in securities sold, $31,500 and for payment of Dominion Government taxes for previous years, $249,462. Then as a further measure of safety the directors decided to provide $1,000,000 for depreciation of inventories in view of the decline in replacement value of logs and manufactured lumber, pulpwood and supplies. These deductions made from the balance at profit and loss of $2,745,141 at the end of the year left a balance to carry froward or surplus account of $783,142. In spite of the heavy write-offs it is gratifying to note that the net working capital of the company amounted to $2,504,406 at the end of the year, an actual increase over the total of 2,431,681 at the end of 1920. In addition during the year the company redeemed and cancelled $25,000 par value of its first mortgage 6 per cent. bonds, leaving the general mortgage issue of $2,000,000, which was distributed during the year, that much nearer a first mortgage position This amount it is proposed to cancel every year

The president, Archibald Fraser, in his report states that the company's operations were steadily carried on throughout the year, thus carrying out the process of liquidation of high priced inventories. "Since the first of this year," he states, "there has been some improvement in business conditions. Your company's pulp mills have operated full since January first."

# CURRENT LUMBER PRICES—WHOLESALE

## TORONTO

(In Car Load Lots, F.O.B. cars Toronto)

### White Pine

| | | |
|---|---|---|
| 1 x 4/7 Good Strips | $100.00 | $110.00 |
| 1¼ & 1½ x 4/7 Good Strips | 120.00 | 125.00 |
| 1 x 8 and up Good Sides | 150.00 | 160.00 |
| 2 x 4/7 Good Strips | 130.00 | 140.00 |
| 1¼ & 1½ x 8 and wider Good Sides | 185.00 | 190.00 |
| 2 x 8 and wider Good Sides | 190.00 | 200.00 |
| 1 in. No. 1, 2 and 3 Cuts | 75.00 | 80.00 |
| 5/4 and 6/4 No. 1, 2 and 3 Cuts | 95.00 | 100.00 |
| 2 in. No. 1, 2 and 3 Cuts | 105.00 | 110.00 |
| 1 x 4 and 5 Mill Run | 52.00 | 55.00 |
| 1 x 6 Mill Run | 53.00 | 56.00 |
| 1 x 7, 9 and 11 Mill Run | 53.00 | 56.00 |
| 1 x 8 Mill Run | 55.00 | 58.00 |
| 1 x 10 Mill Run | 60.00 | 62.00 |
| 1 x 12 Mill Run | 65.00 | 70.00 |
| 5/4 and 6/4 x 5 and up Mill Run | 58.00 | 60.00 |
| 2 x 4 Mill Run | 52.00 | 53.00 |
| 2 x 6 Mill Run | 53.00 | 56.00 |
| 2 x 8 Mill Run | 55.00 | 58.00 |
| 2 x 10 Mill Run | 58.00 | 60.00 |
| 2 x 12 Mill Run | 63.00 | 65.00 |
| 1 in. Mill Run Shorts | 35.00 | 40.00 |
| 1 x 4 and up 6/16 No. 1 Mill Culls | 30.00 | 32.00 |
| 1 x 10 and up 6/16 No. 1 Mill Culls | 34.00 | 36.00 |
| 1 x 12 and up 6/16 No. 1 Mill Culls | 34.00 | 36.00 |
| 1 x 4 and up 6/16 No. 2 Mill Culls | 23.00 | 25.00 |
| 1 x 10 x 12 6/16 No. 2 Mill Culls | 26.00 | 28.00 |
| 1 x 4 and up 6/16 No. 3 Mill Culls | 17.00 | 18.00 |

### Red Pine

(In Car Load Lots, F.O.B. Toronto)

| | | |
|---|---|---|
| 1 x 4 and 5 Mill Run | $34.00 | $35.00 |
| 1 x 6 Mill Run | 35.00 | 36.00 |
| 1 x 8 Mill Run | 37.00 | 38.00 |
| 1 x 10 Mill Run | 42.00 | 44.00 |
| 2 x 4 Mill Run | 37.00 | 38.00 |
| 2 x 6 Mill Run | 37.00 | 38.00 |
| 2 x 8 Mill Run | 38.00 | 39.00 |
| 2 x 10 Mill Run | 41.00 | 42.00 |
| 2 x 12 Mill Run | 46.00 | 47.00 |
| 1 in. Clear and Clear Face | 70.00 | 72.00 |
| 2 in. Clear and Clear Face | 70.00 | 72.00 |

### Spruce

| | | |
|---|---|---|
| 1 x 4 Mill Run | 34.00 | 35.00 |
| 1 x 6 Mill Run | 35.00 | 36.00 |
| 1 x 8 Mill Run | 37.00 | 38.00 |
| 1 x 10 Mill Run | 45.00 | 47.00 |
| 1 x 12 Mill Run Spruce | 48.00 | 50.00 |
| Mill Culls | 25.00 | 27.00 |

### Hemlock (M R)

(In Car Load Lots, F.O.B. Toronto)

| | | |
|---|---|---|
| 1 x 4 and 5 in. x 9 to 16 ft. | $26.00 | $27.00 |
| 1 x 6 in. x 9 to 16 ft. | 32.00 | 33.00 |
| 1 x 8 in. x 9 to 16 ft. | 33.00 | 34.00 |
| 1 x 10 and 12 in. x 9 to 16 ft. | 35.00 | 37.00 |
| 1 x 7, 9 and 11 in. x 9 to 16 ft. | 32.00 | 33.00 |
| 2 x 4 to 12 in. 10/16 ft. | 32.00 | 33.00 |
| 2 x 4 to 12 in., 18 ft. | 37.00 | 39.00 |
| 2 x 4 to 12 in., 20 ft. | 40.00 | 42.00 |
| 1 in. No. 2, 6 ft. to 16 ft. | 23.00 | 25.00 |

### Fir Flooring

(In Car Load Lots, F.O.B. Toronto)

| | |
|---|---|
| Fir flooring, 1 x 3 and 4", No. 1 and 2 Edge Grain | $72.00 |
| Fir flooring, 1 x 3 and 4", No. 1 and 2 Flat Grain | 46.00 |

(Depending upon Widths)

| | |
|---|---|
| 1 x 4 to 12 No. 1 and 2 Clear Fir, Rough | 77.00 |
| 1¼ x 4 to 12 No. 1 and 2 Clear Fir, Rough | 81.00 |
| 2 x 4 to 12 No. 1 and 2 Clear Fir, Rough | 77.00 |
| 3 & 4 x 4 to 12 No. 1 & 2 Clear Fir, Rough | 84.00 |
| 1 x 4, 5 and 6 in Fir Casing | 73.00 |
| 1 x 8 and 10 Fir Base | 78.00 |
| 1¼ and 1½ 8, 10 and 12 in. E.G. Stepping | 90.00 |
| 1¼ and 1½ 8, 10 and 12 in. F.G. Stepping | 80.00 |
| 1 x 4 to 12 Clear Fir, D4S | 72.00 |
| 1¼ and 1½ x 4 to 12 Clear Fir, D4S | 75.25 |
| XX Shingles, 6 butts to 2", per M | 3.35 |
| XXX Shingles, 6 butts to 2", per M | 5.45 |
| XXXXX Shingles, 5 butts to 2", per M | 6.25 |

### Lath

(F.O.B. Mill)

| | |
|---|---|
| No. 1 White Pine | $11.00 |
| No. 2 White Pine | 10.00 |
| No. 3 White Pine | 8.00 |
| Mill Run White Pine, 32 in. | 3.50 |
| Merchantable Spruce Lath, 4 ft. | 6.50 |

## TORONTO HARDWOOD PRICES

The prices given below are for car loads f.o.b. Toronto, from wholesalers to retailers, and are based on a good percentage of long lengths and good widths, without any wide stock having been sorted out.

The prices quoted on imported woods are payable in U. S. funds.

### Ash, White

(Dry weight 3800 lbs. per M. ft.)

| | 1s & 2s | No. 1 Com. | No. 2 Com. |
|---|---|---|---|
| 1" | $100.00 | $ 65.00 | $ 40.00 |
| 1¼ and 1½" | 110.00 | 70.00 | 45.00 |
| 2" | 115.00 | 75.00 | 50.00 |
| 2½ and 3" | 125.00 | 85.00 | 60.00 |
| 4" | 140.00 | 95.00 | 70.00 |

### Ash, Brown

| | | | |
|---|---|---|---|
| 1" | $ 95.00 | $ 55.00 | $ 30.00 |
| 1¼ and 1½" | 100.00 | 60.00 | 30.00 |
| 2" | 105.00 | 65.00 | 33.00 |
| 2½ and 3" | 125.00 | 80.00 | 55.00 |
| 4" | 140.00 | 95.00 | 60.00 |

### Birch

(Dry weight 4000 lbs. per M. ft.)

| | 1s & 2s | Sels. | No. 1 Com. | No. 2 Com. |
|---|---|---|---|---|
| 4/4 | $105.00 | $ 80.00 | $ 50.00 | $ 32.00 |
| 5/4 | 110.00 | 85.00 | 55.00 | 35.00 |
| 6/4 | 115.00 | 90.00 | 60.00 | 38.00 |
| 8/4 | 120.00 | 100.00 | 65.00 | 42.00 |
| 12/4 | 125.00 | 105.00 | 70.00 | 50.00 |
| 16/4 | 130.00 | 110.00 | 80.00 | 55.00 |

### Basswood

(Dry weight 2500 lbs. per M. ft.)

| | 1s & 2s | No. 1 Com. | No. 2 Com. |
|---|---|---|---|
| 4/4 | $ 80.00 | $ 50.00 | $ 25.00 |
| 5/4 and 6/4 | 85.00 | 60.00 | 30.00 |
| 8/4 | 90.00 | 65.00 | 35.00 |

### Chestnut

(Dry weight 2800 lbs. per M. ft.)

| | 1s & 2s | No. 1 Com. | Sound Wormy |
|---|---|---|---|
| 1" | $130.00 | $ 80.00 | $ 40.00 |
| 1¼ to 1½" | 140.00 | 85.00 | 43.00 |
| 2" | 150.00 | 90.00 | 43.00 |

### Maple, Hard

(Dry weight 4200 lbs. per M. ft.)

| | F.A.S. | Sels. | No. 1 Com. | No. 2 Com. |
|---|---|---|---|---|
| 4/4 | $ 85.00 | $ 65.00 | $ 45.00 | $ 33.00 |
| 5/4 | 85.00 | 65.00 | 45.00 | 38.00 |
| 6/4 | 90.00 | 70.00 | 50.00 | 45.00 |
| 8/4 | 100.00 | 75.00 | 60.00 | 50.00 |
| 12/4 | 105.00 | 75.00 | 65.00 | 60.00 |
| 16/4 | 125.00 | 100.00 | 70.00 | 65.00 |

### Elm, Soft

(Dry weight 3100 lbs. per M. ft.)

| | 1s & 2s | No. 1 Com. | No. 2 Com. |
|---|---|---|---|
| 4/4 | $ 75.00 | $ 50.00 | $ 30.00 |
| 6/4 and 8/4 | 80.00 | 60.00 | 35.00 |
| 12/4 | 96.00 | 70.00 | 40.00 |

### Gum, Red

(Dry weight 3300 lbs. per M. ft.)

| | —Plain— | | —Quartered— | |
|---|---|---|---|---|
| | 1s & 2s | No. 1 Com. | 1s & 2s | No. 1 Com. |
| 1" | $115.00 | $ 70.00 | $125.00 | $ 75.00 |
| 1¼" | 120.00 | 75.00 | 130.00 | 80.00 |
| 1½" | 120.00 | 75.00 | 130.00 | 80.00 |
| 2" | 125.00 | 90.00 | 135.00 | 90.00 |

Figured Gum, $10 per M. extra, in both plain and quartered.

### Gum, Sap

| | 1s&2s | No. 1 Com. |
|---|---|---|
| 1" | $ 53.00 | $ 38.00 |
| 1¼" and 1½" | 58.00 | 42.00 |
| 2" | 63.00 | 48.00 |

### Hickory

(Dry weight 4500 lbs. per M. ft.

| | 1s&2s | No. 1 Com. |
|---|---|---|
| 1" | $120.00 | $ 60.00 |
| 1¼" | 145.00 | 65.00 |
| 1½" | 145.00 | 65.00 |
| 2" | 150.00 | 70.00 |

### Plain White and Red Oak

(Plain sawed. Dry weight 4000 lbs. per M. ft.).

| | 1s&2s | No. 1 Com. |
|---|---|---|
| 4/4 | $130.00 | $ 70.00 |
| 5/4 and 6/4 | 135.00 | 75.00 |
| 8/4 | 140.00 | 80.00 |
| 10/4 | 145.00 | 90.00 |
| 12/4 | 145.00 | 90.00 |
| 16/4 | 150.00 | 95.00 |

### White Oak, Quarter Cut

(Dry weight 4000 lbs. per M. ft.)

| | 1s&2s | No. 1 Com. |
|---|---|---|
| 4/4 | $160.00 | $ 90.00 |
| 5/4 and 6/4 | 170.00 | 95.00 |
| 8/4 | 190.00 | 105.00 |

### Quarter Cut Red Oak

| | 1s&2s | No. 1 Com. |
|---|---|---|
| 4/4 | $145.00 | $ 80.00 |
| 5/4 and 6/4 | 160.00 | 90.00 |
| 8/4 | 165.00 | 95.00 |

### Beech

The quantity of beech produced in Ontario is not large and is generally sold on a log run basis, the locality governing the prices. At present the prevailing quotation on log run, mill culls out, delivered in Toronto, is $35.00 to $40.00.

## OTTAWA

Manufacturers' Prices

### Pine

| | | |
|---|---|---|
| Good sidings: | | |
| 1 in. x 7 in. and up | | $140.00 |
| 1¼ in. and 1½ in., 8 in. and up. | | 165.00 |
| 2 in. x 7 in. and up | | 165.00 |
| No. 2 cuts 2 x 8 in. and up | | 80.00 |
| Good strips: | | |
| 1 in. | $100.00 | $105.00 |
| 1¼ in. and 1½ in. | | 120.00 |
| 2 in. | | 125.00 |
| Good shorts: | | |
| 1 in. x 7 in. and up | | 110.00 |
| 1 in. 4 in. to 6 in. | 85.00 | 90.00 |
| 1¼ in. and 1½ in. | | 110.00 |
| 2 in. | | 125.00 |
| 7 in. to 9 in. A sidings | 54.00 | 56.00 |
| No. 1 dressing sidings | 70.00 | 74.00 |
| No. 1 dressing strips | | 62.00 |
| No. 1 dressing shorts | 50.00 | 53.00 |
| 1 in. x 4 in. s.c. strips | | 48.00 |
| 1 in. x 5 in. s.c. strips | | 48.00 |
| 1 in. x 6 in. s.c. strips | | 50.00 |
| 1 in. x 7 in. s.c. strips | 63.00 | 64.00 |
| 1 in. x 8 in. s.c. strips, 12 to 16 ft. | | 54.00 |
| 1 in. x 10 in. M.R. | | 58.00 |
| S.C. sidings, 1½ and 2 in. | 58.00 | 60.00 |
| S.C. strips, 1 in. | | 45.00 |
| 1¼, 1½ and 2 in. | 50.00 | 55.00 |
| S. . shorts, 1 x 4 to 6 in. | 34.00 | 36.00 |
| S. . and bet., shorts, 1 x 5 | | 36.00 |
| S.C. and bet., shorts, 1 x 6 | | 42.00 |
| S.C. shorts, 6-11 ft., 1 x 10 in. | | 48.00 |
| Box boards: | | |
| 1 in. x 4 in. and up, 6 ft.-11 ft. | | 34.00 |
| 1 in. x 3 in. and up, 12 ft.-16 ft. | 35.00 | 37.00 |
| Mill cull shorts, 1 in. x 4 in. and x 4 in. and up, 12 ft. and up | 24.00 | 26.00 |
| Mill culls, strips and sidings, 1 in. up, 6 ft. to 11 ft. | | 22.00 |
| O. culls r and w p | 18.00 | 20.00 |

### Red Pine, Log Run

| | | |
|---|---|---|
| Mill culls out, 1 in. | 32.00 | 34.00 |
| Mill culls out, 1¼ in. | 32.00 | 34.00 |
| Mill culls out, 1½ in. | 32.00 | 34.00 |
| Mill culls out, 2 in. | 32.00 | 34.00 |
| Mill Culls, white pine, 1 in. x 7 in. and up | | 20.00 |

### Mill Run Spruce

| | | |
|---|---|---|
| 1 in. x 4 in. and up, 6 ft.-11 ft. | | 28.00 |
| 1 in. x 4 in. and up, 12 ft.-16 ft. | 30.00 | 32.00 |
| 1" x 9"-10" and up, 12 ft.-16 ft. | | 35.00 |
| 1¼" x 7, 8 and 9" up, 12 ft.-16 ft. | | 35.00 |
| 1¼ x 10 and up, 12 ft.-16 ft. | 38.00 | 42.00 |
| 1½" x 12" x 12" and up, 12'-16' | | 42.00 |
| Spruce, 1 in. clear fine dressing and B | | 55.00 |
| Hemlock, 1 in. cull | | 20.00 |
| Hemlock, 1 in. log run | 24.00 | 26.00 |
| Hemlock, 2 x 4, 6, 8, 10 12/16 ft. | | 28.00 |
| Tamarac | 25.00 | 28.00 |
| Basswood, log run, dead culls out | 45.00 | 50.00 |
| Basswood, log run, mill culls out | 50.00 | 54.00 |
| Birch, log run | 45.00 | 50.00 |
| Soft Elm, common and better, 1, 1½, 2 in. | 58.00 | 68.00 |
| Ash, black, log run | 62.00 | 65.00 |
| 1 x 10 No. 1 barn | 57.00 | 62.00 |
| 1 x 10 No. 2 barn | 51.00 | 56.00 |
| 1 x 8 and 9 No. 2 barn | 47.00 | 52.00 |

# CURRENT LUMBER PRICES—WHOLESALE

**Lath per M.:**

| | | |
|---|---|---|
| No. 1 White Pine, 1¼ in. x 4 ft. | | 8.00 |
| No. 2 White Pine | | 6.00 |
| Mill run White Pine | | 7.00 |
| Spruce, mill run, 1½ in. | | 6.00 |
| Red Pine, mill run | | 6.00 |
| Hemlock, mill run | | 5.50 |
| **White Cedar Shingles** | | |
| XXXX, 18 in. | 9.00 | 10.00 |
| Clear butt, 18 in. | 6.00 | 7.00 |
| 18 in. XX | | 5.00 |

## QUEBEC

**White Pine**
(At Quebec)

| | Cts. Per Cubic Ft. | |
|---|---|---|
| First class Ottawa waney, 18 in. average according to lineal | 100 | 110 |
| 19 in. and up average | 110 | 120 |

**Spruce Deals**
(At Mill)

| | | |
|---|---|---|
| 3 in. unsorted, Quebec, 4 in. to 6 in. wide | $ 20.00 | $ 25.00 |
| 3 in. unsorted, Quebec, 7 in. to 8 in. wide | 26.00 | 28.00 |
| 3 in. unsorted, Quebec, 9 in. wide | 30.00 | 35.00 |

**Oak**
(At Quebec)

| | Cts. Per Cubic Ft. | |
|---|---|---|
| According to average and quality, 55 ft. cube | 125 | 130 |

**Elm**
(At Quebec)

| | | |
|---|---|---|
| According to average and quality, 40 to 45 ft. cube | 100 | 120 |
| According to average and quality, 30 to 35 ft. | 90 | 100 |

**Export Birch Planks**
(At Mill)

| | | |
|---|---|---|
| 1 to 4 in. thick, per M. ft. | $ 30.00 | $ 35.00 |

## ST. JOHN, N.B.

(From Yards and Mills—Retail)

**Rough Lumber**

| | | |
|---|---|---|
| 2x3, 2x4, 3x3, 3x4. Rgh Merch Spr. | $28.00 | |
| 2x3, 2x4, 3x3, 3x4, Dressed 1 edge | 30.00 | |
| 2x3, 2x4, 3x3, 3x4, Dressed 4 sides | 31.00 | |
| 2x6, 2x7, 3x5, 4x4, 4x6, all rough. | 28.00 | |
| 2x6, 2x7, 3x5, 4x4, 4x6, all rough. | 30.00 | |
| 2x8, 3x7, 5x5, 6x6 | 35.00 | $40.00 |
| 2x9, 3x8, 6x8, 7x7 | 37.00 | $40.00 |
| 2x10, 3x9 | 40.00 | |
| 2x12, 3x10, 3x12, 8x8 and up | 42.00 | |
| Merch. Spr. Bds. Rough, 1x3-4 & 5 | 28.00 | |
| Merch. Spr. Bds., Rough, 1x7 & up | 35.00 | |
| Refuse Bds., Deals and Setgs. | 18.00 | 20.00 |

Above random lengths up to 18-0 long.
Lengths 19-0 and up $5.00 extra per M.
For planing Merch. and Refuse Bds. add $2.00 per M. to above prices.
Laths, $7.00.

**Shingles**

| | Per M. |
|---|---|
| Cedar, Extras | $6.00 |
| Cedar, Clears | 5.00 |
| Cedar, 2nd Clears | 4.00 |
| Cedar, Extra No. 1 | 2.50 |
| Spruce | 3.50 |

## SARNIA, ONT.

**White Pine—Fine, Com. and Better**

| | |
|---|---|
| 1 x 6 and 8 in. | $110.00 |
| 1 in., 8 in. and up wide | 130.00 |
| 1¼ and 1½ in. and up wide | 180.00 |
| 2 in. and up wide | 180.00 |
| **Cuts and Better** | |
| 4/4 x 8 and up No. 1 and better | 125.00 |
| 5/4 and 6/4 and up No. 1 and better | 150.00 |
| 8/4 and 8 and up No. 1 and better | 150.00 |
| **No. 1 Cuts** | |
| 1 in., 8 in. and up wide | 105.00 |
| 1¼ in., 8 in. and up wide | 125.00 |
| 1½ in., 8 in. and up wide | 125.00 |
| 2 in., 8 in. and up wide | 130.00 |
| 2½ in. and 3 in., 8 in. and up wide | 175.00 |
| 4 in., 8 in. and up wide | 185.00 |

**No. 1 Barn**

| | | |
|---|---|---|
| 1 in., 10 to 16 ft. long | $ 75.00 | $ 85.00 |
| 1¼, 1½ and 2 in., 10/16 ft. | 80.00 | 85.00 |
| 2½ to 3 in., 10/16 ft. | 85.00 | 100.00 |
| **No. 2 Barn** | | |
| 1 in., 10 to 16 ft. long | 65.00 | 75.00 |
| 1¼, 1½ and 2 in., 10/16 ft. | | 66.00 |
| 2½, 1½ and 3 in. | | 85.00 |
| **No. 3 Barn** | | |
| 1 in., 10 to 16 ft. long | 48.00 | 55.00 |
| 1¼, 1½ and 2 in., 10/16 ft. | 50.00 | 56.00 |
| **Box** | | |
| 1 in., 1¼ and 1½ in., 10/16 ft. | 33.00 | 35.00 |
| **Mill Culls** | | |
| Mill Run Culls— | | |
| 1 in., 4 in. and up wide, 6/16 ft. | | 26.00 |
| 1¼, 1½ and 2 in. | | 27.00 |

## WINNIPEG

**No. 1 Spruce**

| Dimension | S.1.S. and 1.E. 10 ft. | 12 ft. | 14 ft. | 16 ft. |
|---|---|---|---|---|
| 2 x 4 | $29 | $28 | $28 | $29 |
| 2 x 6 | 30 | 28 | 28 | 29 |
| 2 x 8 | 31 | 29 | 29 | 30 |
| 2 x 10 | 32 | 30 | 30 | 31 |
| 2 x 12 | 33 | 31 | 31 | 32 |

For 2 inches, rough, add 50 cents.
For S1E only, add 50 cents.
For S1S and 2E, S4S or D&M, add $3.00.
For timbers larger than 8 x 8, add 50c. for each additional 2 inches each way.
For lengths longer than 20 ft., add $1.00 for each additional two feet.
For selected common, add $5.00.
For No. 2 Dimension, $3.00 less than No. 1.
For 1 x 2 and 2 x 2, $2 more than 2 x 4 No. 1.
For Tamarac, open.

## BUFFALO and TONAWANDA

**White Pine**
Wholesale Selling Price

| | |
|---|---|
| Uppers, 4/4 | $225.00 |
| Uppers, 5/4 to 8/4 | 225.00 |
| Uppers, 10/4 to 12/4 | 250.00 |
| Selects, 4/4 | 200.00 |
| Selects, 5/4 to 8/4 | 200.00 |
| Selects, 10/4 to 12/4 | 225.00 |
| Fine Common, 4/4 | 155.00 |
| Fine Common, 5/4 | 160.00 |
| Fine Common, 6/4 | 160.00 |
| Fine Common, 8/4 | 160.00 |
| No. 1 Cuts, 4/4 | 115.00 |
| No. 1 Cuts, 5/4 | 130.00 |
| No. 1 Cuts, 6/4 | 135.00 |
| No. 1 Cuts, 8/4 | 140.00 |
| No. 2 Cuts, 4/4 | 70.00 |
| No. 2 Cuts, 5/4 | 100.00 |
| No. 2 Cuts, 6/4 | 105.00 |
| No. 2 Cuts, 8/4 | 110.00 |
| No. 3 Cuts, 5/4 | 60.00 |
| No. 3 Cuts, 6/4 | 65.00 |
| No. 3 Cuts, 8/4 | 67.00 |
| Dressing, 4/4 | 95.00 |
| Dressing 4/4 x 10 | 98.00 |
| Dressing, 4/4 x 12 | 110.00 |
| No. 1 Moulding, 5/4 | 150.00 |
| No. 1 Moulding, 6/4 | 150.00 |
| No. 1 Moulding, 8/4 | 155.00 |
| No. 2 Moulding, 5/4 | 125.00 |
| No. 2 Moulding, 6/4 | 125.00 |
| No. 2 Moulding, 8/4 | 130.00 |
| No. 1 Barn, 1 x 12 | 90.00 |
| No. 1 Barn, 1 x 6 and 8 | 76.00 |
| No. 1 Barn, 1 x 10 | 80.00 |
| No. 2 Barn, 1 x 6 and 8 | 62.00 |
| No. 2 Barn, 1 x 10 | 63.00 |
| No. 2 Barn, 1 x 12 | 75.00 |
| No. 3 Barn, 1 x 6 and 8 | 39.00 |
| No. 3 Barn, 1 x 10 | 39.00 |
| No. 3 Barn, 1 x 12 | 45.00 |
| No. 1 Box, 1 x 6 and 8 | 36.00 |
| No. 1 Box 1 x 10 | 37.00 |
| No. 1 Box, 1 x 12 | 38.00 |
| No. 1 Box, 1 x 13 and up | 39.00 |

## BUFFALO

The following quotations on hardwoods represent the jobber buying price at Buffalo and Tonawanda.

**Maple**

| | 1s & 2s | No. 1 Com. | No. 2 Com. |
|---|---|---|---|
| 1 in. | $ 75.00 | $ 46.00 | $ 28.00 |
| 5/4 to 8/4 | 80.00 | 50.00 | 28.00 |
| 10/4 to 4 in. | 85.00 | 56.00 | 28.00 |
| **Sap Birch** | | | |
| 1 in. | 90.00 | 45.00 | 30.00 |
| 5/4 and up | 100.00 | 50.00 | 30.00 |
| **Soft Elm** | | | |
| 1 in. | 70.00 | 45.00 | 30.00 |
| 5/4 to 2 in. | 75.00 | 50.00 | 30.00 |
| **Red Birch** | | | |
| 1 in. | 120.00 | 75.00 | |
| 5/4 and up | 125.00 | 80.00 | |
| **Basswood** | | | |
| 1 in. | 70.00 | 45.00 | 30.00 |
| 5/4 to 2 in. | 80.00 | 55.00 | 35.00 |
| **Plain Oak** | | | |
| 1 in. | 95.00 | 55.00 | 35.00 |
| 5/4 to 2 in. | 105.00 | 65.00 | 40.00 |
| **Ash** | | | |
| 1 in. | 80.00 | 48.00 | 30.00 |
| 5/4 to 2 in. | 85.00 | 52.00 | 30.00 |
| 10/4 and up | 100.00 | 65.00 | 30.00 |

## BOSTON

Quotations given below are for highest grades of Michigan and Canadian White Pine and Eastern Canadian Spruce as required in the New England market in car loads.

| | | |
|---|---|---|
| White Pine Uppers, 1 in. | | |
| White Pine Uppers, 1¼, 1½, 2 in. | | |
| White Pine Uppers, 2½, 3 in. | | |
| White Pine Uppers, 4 in. | | |
| Selects, 1 in. | | $190.00 |
| Selects, 1¼, 2 in. | | 200.00 |
| Selects, 2½, 3 in. | | |
| Selects, 4 in. | | |
| Prices nominal | | |
| Fine Common, 1 in., 30%, 12 in. and up. | | 165.00 |
| Fine Common, 1 x 8 and up | | 165.00 |
| Fine Common, 1¼ to 2 in. | $165.00 | 170.00 |
| Fine Common, 2½ and 3 in. | | 180.00 |
| Fine Common, 4 in. | | 195.00 |
| 1 in. Shaky Clear | | 100.00 |
| 1¼ in. to 2 in. Shaky Clear | | 110.00 |
| 1 in. No. 2 Dressing | | 95.00 |
| 1¼ in. to 2 in. No. 2 Dressing | | 95.00 |
| No. 1 Cuts, 1 in. | | 110.00 |
| No. 1 Cuts, 1¼ to 2 in. | | 140.00 |
| No. 1 Cuts, 2½ to 3 in. | | 180.00 |
| No. 2 Cuts, 1 in. | | 80.00 |
| No. 2 Cuts, 1¼ to 2 in. | | 110.00 |
| Barn Boards, No. 1, 1 x 12 | | 95.00 |
| Barn Boards, No. 1, 1 x 10 | | 87.00 |
| Barn Boards, No. 1, 1 x 8 | | 83.00 |
| Barn Boards, No. 2, 1 x 12 | | 82.00 |
| Barn Boards, No. 2, 1 x 8 | | 69.00 |
| Barn Boards, No. 2, 1 x 10 | | 70.00 |
| Barn Boards, No. 3, 1 x 12 | | 48.00 |
| Barn Boards, No. 3, 1 x 10 | | 47.00 |
| Barn Boards, No. 3, 1 x 8 | | 47.00 |
| **No. 1 Clear** | | |
| Can. Spruce, No. 1 and clear, 1 x 4 to 9" | | $ 78.00 |
| Can. Spruce, 1 x 10 in. | | 78.00 |
| Can. Spruce, No. 1, 1 x 4 to 7 in. | | 75.00 |
| Can. Spruce, No. 1, 1 x 8 and 9 in. | | 75.00 |
| Can. Spruce, No. 1, 1 x 10 in. | | 76.00 |
| Can. Spruce, No. 2, 1 x 4 and 5 in. | | 34.00 |
| Can. Spruce, No. 2, 1 x 6 and 7 in. | | 36.00 |
| Can. Spruce, No. 2, 1 x 8 and 9 in. | | 38.00 |
| Can. Spruce, No. 2, 1 x 10 in. | | 41.00 |
| Can. Spruce, No. 2, 1 x 12 in. | | 45.00 |
| Spruce, 12 in. dimension | | 44.00 |
| Spruce, 10 in. dimension | | 42.00 |
| Spruce, 9 in. dimension | | 41.00 |
| Spruce, 8 in. dimension | | 40.00 |
| 2 x 10 in. random lengths, 8 ft. and up | | 40.00 |
| 2 x 12 in., random lengths | | 43.00 |
| 2 x 3, 2 x 4, 2 x 5, 2 x 6, 2 x 7 | | 30.00 |
| 3 x 4 and 4 x 4 in. | | 31.00 |
| 2 x 9 | | 38.00 |
| All other random lengths, 7 in. and under, 8 ft. and up | 30.00 | 34.00 |
| 5 in. and up merchantable boards, 8 ft. and up, D 1s | 30.00 | 32.00 |
| 1 x 2 | 30.00 | 32.00 |
| 1 x 3 | | 30.00 |
| 1⅝ in. Spruce Lath | | 8.50 |
| 1½ in. Spruce Lath | 7.25 | 7.50 |
| **New Brunswick Cedar Shingles** | | |
| Extras | 5.25 | 5.50 |
| Clears | 4.25 | 4.50 |
| Second Clear | 3.75 | 4.15 |
| Clear Whites | | 3.00 |

# Quick Action Section

Second Hand Machinery & Equipment Wanted & For Sale

Special Lots Of Lumber—Positions Wanted & Vacant

**PUBLISHER'S NOTICE**

Advertisements other than "Employment Wanted" or "Employees Wanted" will be inserted in this department at the rate of 36 cents per agate line (14 agate lines make one inch). $2.50 per inch, each insertion, payable in advance. Space measured from rule to rule. When four or more consecutive insertions of the same advertisement are ordered a discount of 25 per cent. will be allowed.

Advertisements of "Wanted Employment" will be inserted at the rate of one cent a word, net. Cash must accompany order. If Canada Lumberman box number is used, enclose ten cents extra for postage in forwarding replies. Minimum charge 25 cents.

Advertisements of "Wanted Employee" will be inserted at the rate of two cents a word, net. Cash must accompany the order. Minimum charge 50 cents.

Advertisements must be received not later than the 10th and 20th of each month to insure insertion in the subsequent issues.

## Lumber Wanted

### Want

Mill output of Lath. Give prices on grades. Apply Box 868, Canada Lumberman, Toronto.

### Wanted to Buy

Peeled spruce and balsam pulpwood. 50% cash, balance on arrival. Write P. O. Box 983, Montreal.

### Oak Wanted

Canadian Plain Red Oak wanted. A few cars of 4/4 and 8/4 No 2 Common and Better. Apply Box 866 Canada Lumberman, Toronto.

### We Will Buy

A block of Hemlock, Spruce, Red or White Pine that is sawn or will be sawn before the 15th of March. Box 770 Canada Lumberman, Toronto.

### Wanted

By wholesaler in New York State 4/4, 5/4, 6/4 and 8/4 Log Run Birch. Quote prices F.O.B. mills, giving description of stock. Box 866 Canada Lumberman, Toronto.

### Wanted

By
GIDLEY BOAT CO. LTD.,
Penetang, Ontario.
4/4 Clear Cedar, Ontario or Quebec stock; 8/4 Clear Spruce.

### Lath for Sale

White Pine and Jack Pine. Write or wire for prices.
Brewster Loud Lumber Co.,
566 Lincoln Bldg.,
Detroit, Mich.

### Wanted

10 Cars No. 3 Jack Pine Lath also White Pine and Hemlock Lath in all grades.
Brewster Loud Lumber Co.,
566 Lincoln Bldg.,
Detroit, Mich.

## Lumber For Sale

### Sawdust

For sale, in car lots.
The London Box Mfg. & Lumber Co., Limited.

### For Sale in Carload Lots

Telegraph Poles, Cedar and Hardwood Ties, Spruce Balsam and Poplar Pulpwood. Jas. Thos. Clair, Clair, N. B.

### Lumber for Sale

75 M 1½" Maple No 2 Common & Better 90 M 1" Soft Elm Log Run Dry Stock. A. J. McEwen, Box No. 294 Maxville, Ont.

### For Sale

Several Car Loads of 4 x 4; 4 x 6; 6 x 6; 8 x 8; 10 x 10; 12 x 12 Fir and large Timber Lengths 12, 14, 16. Price $26.00 f.o.b. Car Bridesville, B. C. Michael Dumont, Bridesville, B. C.

### For Sale

At Blind River, Ontario, Pine and Spruce Lath, also some Cedar and Hemlock Lath, Grades, four foot mill run, 32" mill run, and four foot No. 3.
F. P. Potvin,
Blind River, Ont.

### WHITE PINE LUMBER

For Immediate Shipment—1920
Cut—Should Be Bone Dry

About 30,000 ft. 2 in.
    12,000 ft. 1 in.
    2,000 ft. 3 in.
Apply to J. A. Farnsworth, Cookshire, Quebec.

### For Sale

50,000 Ft. dry oak plank, eight, nine, and ten quarter, No. 2 Common and Better.

5,000 Ft. dry hickory, four, six and eight quarter, No. 3 Common and Better.

5,000 Ft. white ash, eight quarter, No. 2 Common and Better.

15,000 Ft. dimension stock.
1 car of 2 x 2 19" and 2 x 2 30" furniture squares, oak.

Apply to The Crown Lumber Co. Ltd., Woodstock, Ontario.

## Sale of Timber
### to
### Close an Estate

South East Quarter of Township of PROUDFOOT containing twenty-three and a quarter square miles, and known as berth No. 2. Containing the following timber as cruised by one of the most reliable timber cruisers in Ontario.

Favorable terms can be arranged:—

| | |
|---|---|
| BIRCH | 10,000,000 ft. |
| MAPLE | 4,000,000 ft. |
| HEMLOCK | 100,000 ft. |
| HEMLOCK | 100,000 ft. |
| PINE | 100,000 ft. |
| CEDAR poles 25' up 50' | 5,000 |
| SPRUCE & BALSAM | 5,000 wood 5,000 cords |
| HARDWOOD CORDWOOD | first-class |
| | 80,000 cords |
| PRICE | $36,136.00 |

F. C. Clarkson, Assignee,
15 & R. C. Clarkson & Son,
TORONTO

## Machinery Wanted

### Wanted

One Circular Saw Hand Gummer for use on Saws from 33" to 60". Submit cut and prices. Box No. 891, Canada Lumberman, Toronto.

## Machinery For Sale

### For Sale

8 inch Steam Feed. First class condition. L. Robertson, Ardbeg, Ontario.

## Machinery for Sale

One pony, double cutting, six foot, band mill in good condition—S. L. Lambert, Welland, Ontario.

### Machine for Sale

1 new type C-8 Yates Moulder. For price and particulars regarding equipment apply Box 864 Canada Lumberman, Toronto.

### Used Machinery

Boilers, Generator Sets, belted and direct drive, pumps, concrete mixers, pipe and saw-mill machinery. Specialty Equipment Co., 66 Ottawa Street, Montreal.

### For Sale

1 E. Long Mfg. Co. Lath Mill with 11 saws.
1 Standard Machinery Co. 7 Saw Lath Bolter with 44 saws.
1 Diamond Iron Works 5 Ft. Horizontal Band Resaw, slat bed, with 3 saws.
1 26 Ton Lima Geared Locomotive, standard gauge.
Schroeder Mills & Timber Co., Pakesley, Ontario.—Milwaukee, Wis.

## Wickes Gang

GANG: No. 13 Wickes Gang, 40" cash, 38" stroke, steam binder rolls, front and back in two sections, feed and oscillation combined, 1908 model, and has been in use for only a few months. We furnish with this gang 13 rolls for cants and stock, one filing machine and 4 sets of saws.
THE PEMBROKE LUMBER CO., Pembroke, Ont.

## For Sale

One ten-ton Holt Caterpillar tractor, can be used for log hauling and road building, complete with $700.00 worth of spare parts. Box 901, Canada Lumberman, Toronto.

## Engines, Boilers, etc., for Sale

One "Williams" Upright Engine 6" x 6"
One Upright Engine 8" x 8"
Six Return tubular boilers of following dimensions:
One "Butterfield" 72" x 16' - 3¼" tube - 16" shell.
One "Polson" 64" x 14' - 3¼" tube - 16" shell
One "Duty" 60" x 15' - 4" tube - 14" shell
One "Duty" 60" x 14½" - 4" tube - 14" shell
One "Duty" 60" x 16' - 4" tube - 16" shell
One "Inglis" 60" x 12' - 4" tube - 12" shell
One double acting "Northey" Fire Engine, 9" suction, 5" discharge, air steam cylinder, 5" water cylinder, 12" stroke, capacity 450 gallons per minute.
One Ship Pump 6 x 4 x 7" stroke.
Capacity 90 gallons per minute.
One brass Mill steam whistle.
For further particulars apply The Conger Lumber Co. Limited, Parry Sound, Ontario.

### For Sale

850—H.P. Goldie Corliss heavy duty compound condensing Engine, cylinders 20-40, stroke 42", in use less than two years, also 1—750 Gallon fire underwriters pump and other smaller engines. Apply T. Hobbs, 202 Howland Ave., Toronto.

### For Sale

20-25 Monarch Tractor with five sets of heavy log trucks and chains, if needed for good roads building, log bunks can be removed and boxes put on. Apply Box 684, Canada Lumberman, Toronto.

## Good Values
### Subject to Prior Sale

Band Resaw, Connell & Dengler, 54 and 60".
Band Rip Saw, Yates No. 281.
Circular Resaw, 54".
E. B. Hayes Dowell Gluer and Driver.
Matcher, Hardwood American No. 229.
Matcher, 30" x 8" Connell & Dengler.
Moulder, Harmon 10" wide open side.
Moulder, Woods No. 2 light inside.
Moulder, Berlin 10" No. 115, inside.
Moulder, Woods 5 head, inside.
Planers, all sizes, single and double.
Sanders, 3-drum, 30, 42, 48 and 60".
Saws, circular, several makes.
Timber Sizers, Yates and American.
Woodworking Machinery Co. of Buffalo
84 Mechanic St.,
Buffalo, N. Y.

## Situations Wanted

Position wanted for the coming season to make lath or Pickets by thousand. Can give good references if required. Box 849 Canada Lumberman, Toronto.

Lath Maker wants position to run Lath or Picket Mill by the Day. 14 years' experience. References if required. Box No. 862 Canada Lumberman, Toronto.

Wanted position as Mill Superintendent. Eight years experience as Mill Superintendent fifteen years as sawyer. Can furnish best references. Box 747 Canada Lumberman, Toronto.

Wanted position as Superintendent or yard foreman in a large wholesale lumber yard or with a large manufacturing company. Can furnish best of references. Box 590 Canada Lumberman, Toronto.

Position wanted as lumber buyer and inspector on the road. Also good log seller. Have had 14 years' experience buying and shipping lumber. Box No. 584 Canada Lumberman, Toronto.

Wanted position—As lumber buyer and inspector on the road, have had twelve years experience, buying and shipping hardwood lumber, can furnish good references. Box 900 Canada Lumberman, Toronto.

Scotchman, married, 20, desires position as Accountant-Bookkeeper or general office work. Twelve years experience payrolls, cashier, bookkeeper and general office routine. Total abstainer. Excellent references. Box 860 Canada Lumberman, Toronto.

Position wanted in a wholesale lumber yard doing a thriving business or would accept position as yard foreman in sawmill yard or with large furniture company. Understand grading and inspection rules. Box 883 Canada Lumberman, Toronto.

Ambitious young man with good education and five years experience in sales and factory department of large wholesale and retail woodworking and lumber concern in the east, desires position with progressive concern. Will go anywhere. First class ability to handle correspondence, orders, sales, etc. Good knowledge of factory cost recording. Also have taken a six months' course in bookkeeping. Very best reference. Box 881 Canada Lumberman, Toronto. 9

## Situations Vacant

Experienced Woods Superintendent for Pulp Company operating extensive limits, also Junior Forestry Engineer as assistant. Applicants must give full business and personal history. Box 880 Canada Lumberman, Toronto. 9-10

## Business Chances

### Timber Limit Wanted

We want a freehold timber limit near Sault Ste. Marie, Sudbury and North Bay, accessible to a River, about one million cords of pulpwood. Destination of that wood will be Niagara Falls, Michigan and Illinois. Full particulars will be appreciated. Apply to Quebec Lumber Co. 140 St. Peter St., Quebec 8-11

### For Sale

One heavy portable sawmill, three bunk steel carriage, two inserted tooth saws, double edger, trimmers, slab saw, 20 H.P. centre crank engine, 80 H.P. locomotive boiler on wheels, 8 sets sleighs, 8 sets wagons, three teams of horses, camp equipment and bunk tools for 30 men. Capacity of mill 32,000 to 38,000 ft. of hardwood per day winter sawn. Could be seen in operation during the next three weeks. The above equipment is good as new. Attractive price. Also 3½ ton Motor Truck nearly new. Apply Box 850 Canada Lumberman, Toronto. 7-10

## Newfoundland Limits and Sawmill for Sale

Timber licenses for 110 square miles of good limits in the vicinity of Gambo, Newfoundland. Mill on Tide water and near Gambo Railway Station. Large portion virgin about 90 years to run. Large portion virgin timber,—pine, spruce and fir. Timber estimated 30 million feet pine, 60 million spruce and fir, 100,000 cords Pulpwood.

J. R. Walker & Co. Ltd., 85 Common St., Montreal. 7-38

## FOR SALE
### RETAIL LUMBER YARD

Good going concern, situated in the heart of the building district.

This yard is being offered for sale to close an Estate.

Address enquiries to The Trusts and Guarantee Company, Limited, 120 Bay Street, Toronto.

### Wanted

By wholesaler in New York State, Spruce connection with mill in position to ship 8'. Merchantable, sizes surfaced to ¼" scant on a competitive basis into New York State. We discount all our bills. Box 887, Canada Lumberman, Toronto § T-f.

### Wanted

Small tract of timber from 500 to 1,000 acres. To be good Merchantable saw timber. Prefer soft woods, but will consider hardwoods. Easy to operate. Give full description and price in first letter. Address, Samuel Whitenmyer, Harrisburg, Pa. 9-10

### Mills and Limits for Sale

145 sq. miles of standing spruce, close to railway.
Mill well equipped, capacity 75,000 to 100,000 ft.
Mill, well equipped, capacity 30,000 ft.
Phoenix Logging Engine.
Sheds and numerous other equipment.
Write for particulars.

The Saskatchewan Lumber Co. Limited, Crooked River, Sask. 6-T-f

## Miscellaneous

### Lumber Waggons for Sale

20 Rain Wagons almost new, 6" tires, 4" and 4¾" steel axe.
6-8 Barrett Bros. 890 Catharine St., Ottawa, Ont.

### Airplanes and the Forests

Airplanes were used with great advantage in forest protection work in five provinces of the Dominion last year, and the work is likely to be extended in the coming season. The advantage of an airplane patrol over that by canoe is illustrated by the following extract from a report of one of the airmen engaged in protecting the forests in northern Manitoba last year: "We could always see from 30 to 50 miles on either side of the plane, and it would be no difficulty to locate smoke at this distance. When you compare this with a canoe travelling up a river with high banks, where it is impossible to see more than a hundred yards in either direction, and where the patrol would be unable to notice smoke unless it was driven down over him, the advantage is entirely on the side of the plane."

### Tree Planting in the West

The civic authorities of Calgary are aiming to have 10,000 trees planted in the parks and on the streets of that city in 1922. Other cities and towns on the prairies have also planned tree-planting campaigns. This planting of trees in urban communities, along with the millions of trees now being planted annually on prairie farms, will in a few years make a great change in the aspect of the Prairie Provinces.

## MacLean Building Reports
Limited

MacLean Building Reports will give you accurate, advance information on every building and engineering contract of consequence in the Dominion.

These Reports are issued daily and reach subscribers in ample time to bid on the work or submit prices for the machinery, equipment, materials or supplies required.

Hundreds of firms are deriving much financial benefit from the use of MacLean Building Reports. Tell us what territory you cover and put it up to us to show how we can help you get more business. Be sure to write to-day for rates and free sample reports.

**MacLean Building Reports, Ltd.**
345 Adelaide St. W. - TORONTO
119 Board of Trade Bldg. - MONTREAL
348 Main St. - WINNIPEG
212 Winch Bldg. - VANCOUVER

## TIMBERLANDS FOR SALE

The Bradley Sales Agency has taken over the Timberland Business carried on for some years by Mr. R. R. Bradley, Consulting Forester.

The Agency is open to receive listings of Timberlands in all parts of Canada and Newfoundland but more particularly in Easter Canada. There is an active demand at present for hardwood tracts and freehold pulpwood lands.

Clients may rest assured that their confidence will be protected and that the identity of the property and ownership will be disclosed only to p e r s o n s and corporations who we have every reason to believe are serious in their inquiries and are strong enough financially to buy.

### Bradley Sales Agency

512 Bank of Montreal Bldg., 205 St. James St., MONTREAL, P. Q.

## EXECUTOR'S SALE
### of old established
## PLANING MILL and LUMBER BUSINESS
Situate in the
### TOWN OF TILBURY, ONTARIO
### THE CANADA TRUST COMPANY

Executors of Estate of the late E. B. Richardson, offer for sale the following assets of the Estate.

**BUILDINGS—**
Factory building, cement block construction with dry kiln and offices.
Frame store-house, two storeys.
Frame dry shed.

**MACHINERY, Etc.—**
Steam engine and boiler.
15 H.P. Motor.
10" three sided moulder.
Hand Feed Sawmill.
Wood frame cut off saw
Planer 24" x 10".
Power Feed Rip saw
Planer and Matcher with heads.
Circular Re-saw.
Sash Moulder.
Shaper.
Tenoner with swing arm.
Power stroke Mortiser.
12" Jointer.
Roller table Rip and Cross cut off saw.
Tilting table Rip saw.
20" Band Saw M. 202.
Door clamp.
Double Emery grinder.
18" Wood Lathe.
Belt driven post borer.
50" Fan.
All machines are on concrete bases and fully equipped with bearings, hangers, line shafts, counter shafts, belting etc.

**LAND—**
Lots No. 2, 3, & 4, Queen Street and
Lots No. 5, 6, & 7, Smith Street, Tilbury.
TILBURY is situate in a splendid farming section on the C.P.R., M.C.R. and Toronto to Windsor Highway. There is positively no other Planing Mill or lumber business within many miles of Tilbury. There is a good manufacturing trade in Mill work, builders' supplies, tanks, etc.—all waste can be used in manufacturing fish boxes at a good profit.
Good trade in Cement, Lime, Roofing materials wire, etc.
The stock of lumber on hand is very well assorted—no dead stock.

—For further particulars write—
## THE CANADA TRUST COMPANY
London • Ontario

# Review of Current Trade Conditions

## Ontario and the East

There have been no marked changes in conditions since the middle of April, although business generally appears to be improving and buying is a little freer. The month of May is expected to show considerable impetus in the way of meeting building requirements and catering to the need of extensive repairs which are being carried on or contemplated in various parts of the country. Reports on the whole differ as to the volume and extent of car and yard sales. Some firms declare that April was the best month they have had this year, while other concerns assert that it was nothing to boast about.

Many sawmills in different parts of the country started up last week and others will be in full operation early in May. Labor is reported plentiful and there has been a considerable reduction in wages. Skilled help around the mills have had their pay cut from 10 to 15%, while ordinary labor on a ten-hour basis, has been put on a 25 to 30 cents an hour schedule. Manufacturers realize that they have to get their costs of production down to the lowest notch. They have been taking a loss on high-priced lumber produced last season and the season before, and unless they can break even on their product, they cannot stand the financial strain of operating.

The hardwood market has shown some improvements and there is some scarcity of birch and maple in firsts and seconds and selects, particularly in 1, 1½ and 2 inch. There is plenty of the low ends offering for which the demand is limited, while some of the bigger holders are endeavoring to make the higher quality carry the low ends in all sales transactions. Any substantial increase in demand would, doubtless, bring advances in prices, but buyers are not yet showing insistence and there is a wide range in quotations. The building boom, which is going on in various cities, has added considerable strength to the hardwood situation. Wholesalers report some mill men want more for their stocks at the mills then the wholesaler can realize for what material he has on hand or is seeking to replace.

Hemlock continues to show considerable activity, and generally the market is retaining well. The white pine situation is fairly good and prices in the upper grades are, certainly, holding their own. Mill culls are yet weak and there is an abundance on the market. Other lines of wood are showing a moderate activity although spruce and jack pine are not robust. Unless prices advance on jack pine some manufacturers in Northern Ontario declare they will not cut any this season. They are not able to cover themselves on what they are being offered and they decidedly object to taking further losses or lower prices.

Some discussion is heard as to whether values in the lumber business have touched bottom, or not. In most woods it is believed they have, but a few adjustments may take place on certain slow moving grades. There has been considerable material bought recently in Eastern Canada for the building of refrigerator cars, while the T. & N. O. recently purchased several hundred thousand feet of B. C. fir timbers for bridge work.

Shingles are a little stronger, and owing to many mills being shut down in the west, there is no surplus of this product.

The lumber trade is still looking forward to the long-anticipated announcement of a radical reduction in freight rates, and particularly on the basic commodities of which lumber is one of the chief.

"The lumber business in Toronto is in a peculiar shape at the present time in that competition is probably keener here and hereabouts than any other place in the Dominion," remarked a leading wholesale lumberman the other day. "There is a good volume of business going but there is so much rivalry that it has to be taken at a price, and when an acceptance is received there are many firms who wish they had not entered into the deals for the simple reason that there is no profit in them.

"We're here have to face more competition from other woods than any similar city. The word has gone out that there is a building boom in Toronto where the permits are running around $2,000,000 a month, and scores of houses and stores are in course of erection. This has brought in salesmen for Southern pine, Michigan and Wisconsin hemlock, extra representatives for B. C. fir, many eastern Quebec and New Brunswick spruce, with the result that the field is vastly over-crowded. Everyone is saying big business is being done in Toronto and that is the place to go, with the corollary that there has been an influx of various woods and salesmen such as I have never seen before at this period. However, matters may right themselves in the near future and it will likely be a case of a survival of the fittest."

## Montreal Market Remains Practically the Same

When the year commenced it was generally expected that the Montreal market would gradually improve as far as business was concerned, and that prices would, at least, keep at the same level. These hopes have not been realised. Trade has been dull, while prices have declined. Wholesalers whose business is chiefly of a local character state that excessive competition has resulted in spruce prices being seriously cut, and that it is difficult to secure orders which show a fair margin of profit. The competition among retailers is also keen, with the result that trade will take no risks of stocking up, and are buying only for immediate requirements.

The interviews on the Standardization of Lumber quoted in another column explain to some extent the reason for this cutting of values at periods when there is anxiety to secure trade. With many consumers price is the essential factor, quality being a secondary matter. Contractors who complain that they get a quality lower than they expected leave out of consideration the fact that they too often accept very low offers—and they naturally obtain lumber on a par with the price paid. Wholesalers with connections outside the Montreal district state that they are getting fair prices.

Spruce orders from the States are coming in on a market scale, but practically nothing is doing in pine. The demand for lath has slackened off, although mill prices still keep firm.

The trade in B. C. forest products is dull, with reports of a weakening in quotations. The low prices at which other woods can be purchased has made it difficult to sell B. C. products in large quantities.

There is a decidedly more optimistic feeling as to building prospects. According to information supplied to the Builders' Exchange, an extensive program is in sight, but much depends upon costs. The Exchange is considering the question of the men's wages, the idea being that a further reduction of about ten per cent. is necessary if the greater part of the proposed work is to materialise. The men are naturally opposed to any reduction, arguing that the shortness of the building season and the comparative high cost of living does not warrant any lower scales than those in operation last year. At the same time it is admitted that these schedules were not then adhered to owing to the lack of work and the desire of the men to secure jobs at almost any price.

## St. John Believes Things are on the Mend

A general feeling is prevalent in St. John, N. B., that we have reached the end of the low prices for lumber and that the corner has been well turned; that before long new and higher prices will be in effect. Certainly if ever any industry has gone through severe liquidation the lumber business has, and deserves a permanent change for the better.

Demand is, certainly, improving from the American side, and prices have stiffened and steadied. While as yet they are unprofitable, with an increase in demand sure and steady, advances will follow.

The New York market is using large quantities of lumber, and while a good deal of western fir is finding its way there, as well as in New England, this condition will not continue, for as soon as other business offers to the transportation by water companies, they will go elsewhere or more profitable return cargoes will be taken. When this happens spruce will certainly come into its own and ere long with broken stocks and a general shortage of good material, we will get back to prices which will leave a profit. No more stocks will be sacrificed in the East as the banks are holding up the inventories rather than have the manufacturers throw away everything.

The Government stocks are fast disappearing and old stocks of poor material are speedily passing away. A great many cargoes have gone into vessels both for American and English ports, and even though it is bought at very low prices, it is being used up. It surely had to be cleaned up and, when well out of the road, new and better stocks will bring the prices asked for.

There are very few large deals to be had either now in stock or to be cut from this year's logs, and if Irish ports call for any cargoes, it will only take a reasonable demand to inflate prices to a profitable point.

Two mills, viz., Murray & Gregory, and Randolph & Baker are now running at St. John.

Driving has begun but only a few logs have been put in this

winter and, no doubt, by fall this shortage of good stocks will be felt all over the country. Buyers of lumber will certainly have to be wise or they will be caught without an opportunity to fill their schedules.

## Quebec Exporters Say Conditions are Unsettled

The river St. Lawrence is clear of ice from the sea to the head of navigation, but notwithstanding there is no sign of any vessel arriving until towards the end of April. This in itself graphically elucidates the dearth of shipping, the absence of freight in demand by the United Kingdom, as well as unsettled conditions of business owing to the political uncertainty and economic situation in European and continental countries.

Quebec timber and manufactured lumber exporters interviewed have little to say except that the outlook for the spring and early trade with the United Kingdom is, to say the least, at the present very discouraging. The export firms of John Burstall & Co., Dobell, Beckett & Co., and W. & J. Sharples, Reg., have small parcels ordered for shipment to the United Kingdom, but as yet have chartered no space in ocean steamers on account of the high freight rates. At the time of writing the rate of freight on timber and deals to British and Glasgow ports, is 100 shillings per standard, and to the Irish ports of Dublin and Belfast, 90 shillings. Infinitely too high is the verdict of the Quebec shippers, especially taking into consideration the competition from the Sweden and Finland source of supply.

Mill owners and shippers of lumber to the United States market complain of a big drop in their export trade across the border, which they attribute to the prevailing excessive railway freight rates. They are fully cognizant of the tremendous amounts of construction in progress in the Atlantic centres of the United States, but say on account of the railway freight rates, they are cut out of the market by the Pacific fir coming by water at very low rates in freightage to American Atlantic ports, which they are not able to compete with.

## Ottawa Reports But Little Change in Trade

The Ottawa lumber market during the latter part of April underwent some what of an improvement, but trading generally was not as brisk as it had been expected it would be. The improvement was chiefly noted in increased inquiries and orders from the United States. They were mostly for mill run and the lower grades of lumber.

Stocks with the manufacturers remained pretty much the same as they had been, though the retail yards were doing an increased business. Manufacturers pointed out that while trade with the retailers was improving they were using stocks which they purchased some time ago, and that the majority had not had to come into the market to purchase new supplies.

Building prospects remained bright, and the trade in general, feels that if the present rate of new building continues that stocks will soon begin to move quickly. Locally there were very few sales by manufacturers for Ottawa consumption. Prices, though trading was not heavy remained firm.

The price of certain grades of lumber on the Ottawa market, some dealers pointed out, was higher than at Montreal and Toronto, for the reason that Ottawa to a certain extent was in a "pocket." Down east, it was stated there were very large stocks of spruce, and buyers were turning to these on account of the lower quotations. In Toronto and Western Ontario, it was asserted, that the British Columbia stocks were getting the preference for the same reason.

Conditions as regard freight and labor remained the same. The woodworking factories reported business beginning to pick up a little.

With several manufacturers, the abnormally high water in the Ottawa river, which was the highest for 20 years, caused most concern and prevented the re-opening of sawmills. During the flood tide of the waters a boom containing 60,000 logs belonging to John R. Booth, Ltd., broke loose from above Woodroffe, and swent down the river. In the course of the logs was the sorting gap of Shepard and Morse Lumber Company which was carried away, and several thousand logs of this concern were cast loose and floated to Rochester Bay. The Booth logs were later caught in a large boom near the head of Chaudiere Falls.

Though the high waters caused lumbermen considerable concern as to the safety of booms, it also brought with it a blessing in the form of washing out logs that had been stranded for years, and bringing them down to the mill ponds.

The sawmilling season was expected to get under way around May 1st. There appears to be plenty of labor available, and the prospect of any strike or holdout for higher wages on the part of the workers, appears very remote. Most companies reported an abundance of labor, and several of them state that they will select only the best workers, and give preference to their former employees.

## Wages are Cut in Eastern Sawmills

The question of the cost of the manufacturing of lumber is always an interesting one, particularly at the present time when the aim of every producer is to get basic costs down to the lowest possible amount. In the readjustment of things it is generally conceded that labor has played its part, and if railway rates and other levies came down in proportion, there would be a freer movement of forest products and a livelier demand from every quarter.

Mills which have resumed operations in Ontario and the East have cut the wages of their employees down to the lowest possible scale, and such cuts have been accepted without question. The price of board has also been reduced. The whole situation regarding labor is summed up by a representative manufacturer of Northern Ontario, who recently declared, "I believe that wages are about as low now as they will get. I do not think they will ever get back to the basis of 1914. Events move along in cycles to higher levels, especially the reward for services, and while there have been several cuts from the peak of 1919-20, wages are, on the whole, 25% more than they were prior to the war. We are paying our rough labor in the yards 25 cents an hour and in a few cases 30 cents, on a ten-hour basis. This is at the rate of $2.50 a day. Prior to the war men were receiving only $1.50 to $2.00.

Skilled help is also getting fully 25 to 40% more than it received in 1914. This includes band sawyers, doggers, edgermen, trimmers, millwrights, saw-filers and others. The wages of these have been reduced this season from 10 to 15%, and in all cases the decreases have been accepted. Many of the mills have lowered the board of their men from $7.00 to $6.00 per week. The pay for the "boys on the drive" is now $1.50 to $2.00 a day, with board. Last spring the figure was $2.00 to $3.00.

In the bush during the past winter the schedule for ordinary labor was $26.00 to $32.00 per month and board, which is about one-half of what it was early in the previous year.

While there may be a few drops during the season on certain classes of labor, it is felt by a number of operators that the bottom has about been reached and it is generally conceded that the efficiency of men is much greater than it was two or three years ago. Now any fellow who has a job, is hanging on to it for dear life and is seeking to render all that is in him. He knows that if he does not measure up to the mark, there are half a dozen others ready to take his place. This is keeping him up to the scratch and doing a full day's work for his pay.

Many lumber manufacturers contend that since labor has played its part and played it courageously in the readjustment of affairs, that other agencies might well contribute to lowering costs, and thus assist in the stabilization of prices and the getting of the industry generally down to a bed-rock basis.

The lumber business is slowly but surely moving ahead. Although there are flurries here and there and trade is spotty, still things are in the right direction and the month of May is likely to witness an improvement.

## The Proposed McCumber Tariff

The proposed McCumber tariff bill, which is now being brought up at Washington is arousing much interest, particularly that portion dealing with lumber. The "Canada Lumberman" has been fortunate in obtaining an advance copy of this bill on "Wood and Manufactures of Wood, Schedule 4." The following clauses are worth perusing. It is not thought the measure will pass in its proposed form.

Par. 402.—Logs of fir, spruce, cedar, or Western hemlock, $1 per thousand feet board measure: Provided, that any such logs cut from any particular class of lands shall be exempt from such duty if imported from any country, dependency, province, or other subdivision of government which has at no time during the twelve months immediately preceding their importation into the United States maintained any embargo, prohibition, or other restriction (whether by law, order, regulation, contractual relation or otherwise, directly or indirectly) upon the exportation of such logs from such country, dependency, province, or other subdivision of government, if cut from such class of lands.

Par. 403.—Brier root or brier wood, ivy or laurel root, and similar wood unmanufactured, or not further advanced than cut into blocks suitable for the articles into which they are intended to be converted, 10 per centum ad valorem.

Par. 404.— Sawed boards, planks, deals, and all forms of sawed cedar, commercially known as Spanish cedar, lignum-vitae, lancewood, ebony, box, granadilla, mahogany, rosewood, satinwood, Japanese white oak, Japanese maple, and all other woods not further manufactured than sawed 15 per centum ad valorem; veneers of

wood, and wood unmanufactured, not specially provided for, 20 per centum ad valorem.

Par. 405.—Paving posts, railroad ties, and telephone trolley, electric-light, and telegraph poles of cedar or other woods, 10 per centum ad valorem.

Par. 406.—Hubs for wheels, posts, heading bolts, stave bolts, lastblocks, wagon blocks, oar blocks, heading blocks, and all like blocks or sticks, rough hewn, sawed, or bored, 10 per centum ad valorem.

Par. 407.—Pickets, palings, hoops, and staves of wood of all kinds, 10 per centum ad valorem.

Par. 409.—Casks, barrels, and hogsheads (empty), sugar-box shooks, and packing boxes, (empty), and packing box shooks, of wood, not specially provided for, 15 per centum ad valorem.

Par. 410.—Boxes, barrels, and other articles containing oranges, lemons, limes, grapefruit, shaddocks or pomelos, 25 per centum ad valorem: Provided, that the thin wood, so called, comprising the sides, tops, and bottoms of fruit boxes of the growth or manufacture of the United States, exported as fruit box shooks, may be reimported in complete form, filled with fruit, by the payment of duty at one-half the rate imposed on similar boxes of entirely foreign growth and manufacture: but proof of the identity of such shooks shall be made under regulations to be perscribed by the Secretary of the Treasury.

Par. 411.—Reeds wrought or manufactured from rattan or reeds, whether round, flat, split, oval, or in whatever form, cane wrought or manufactured from rattan, not specially provided for in this section 15 per centum ad valorem. Furniture made with frames wholly or in part of wood, rattan, reed, bamboo, osier or willow, or malacca, and covered wholly, or fiver of any kind 60 per centum ad valorem: split bamboo, 1 cent per pound; osier or willow, including chip of and split willow, prepared for basket makers' use, 35 per centum ad valorem; all articles not specially provided for, wholly or partly manufactured of rattan, bamboo, osier or willow, 45 per centum ad valorem.

Par. 412.— Toothpicks of wood or other vegetable substance, 25 per centum ad valorem; butchers' and packers' skewers of wood, 25 cents per thousand.

## Quebec Ready to Fight Forest Fires

The Department of Lands and Forests is getting ready to fight forest fires in spring and summer in the province of Quebec. Mr. G. C. Piche, chief superintendent of the Forestry Service, informs the "Canada Lumberman," through its Quebec correspondent, that the Department has fears of great devastation by fires during the coming summer. He explains that the unusually early spring has caused the snow in the woods to disappear very rapidly, and he is of the opinion that the entire land will be clear of snow before the trees begin to bud, and dry trees without leaves will be great fuel for fires, which would spread with rapidity, devastating forest areas of incalculable value.

For this reason the Dep't. is taking no chances. 1,500 fire rangers, inspectors and their assistants have been engaged, and no money will be spared by the Department to protect the provincial forests. The four protective associations organized and controlled by the limit holders and subsidized by the provincial government, are also close to the prospective fire menace and doing their part to protect forest property. Mr. Piche on account of the early spring, is preparing for all emergencies to combat fire. He points to a forest fire at Boulogne, France, in the middle of March which destroyed 40 sq. miles of valuable pine forest, and said this was a warning to the Quebec Department of Lands and Forests to take every possible precaution to guard against fire. He said there were 6,000 clearances at the Abitibi, which the Department was carefully watching, and had there 112 fire rangers on the look-out day and night.

## Act to Extend Lumber Cutting Privileges

An important bill has been introduced in the Ontario legislature which is likely to become law. It covers a number of salient matters in regard to the granting of timber limits and the privileges of cutting the product thereon. The bill, which received its first reading early in April, was introduced by Hon. Beniah Bowman, Minister of Lands and Forests. It reads as follows:—

"Whereas from time to time certain privileges in respect to the cutting of Crown timbers upon Crown and patented lands, has been granted without competition as required by Section 3 of the Crown Timber Regulations; and whereas in the granting thereof the provisions with respect to ground rent and fire protection were not uniform; and whereas for the purposes of maintaining intact lumbering organizations and timber operations, the time in which to exercise such privileges has in certain cases been extended; and whereas

serious doubts have arisen as to the validity of all such cutting privileges, it is deemed expedient to remove the doubts by granting to the Minister of Lands and Forests, the power so to do."

There has, therefore been introduced, as stated, the present Act, which is known as the "Timber Cutting Privilege Act", which comes into force on the day it receives royal assent, which will likely be within the next few weeks. This Timber Cutting Privilege Act says the Minister of Lands and Forests is authorized when he deems it in the public interests so to do, to confirm, vary or cancel any timber-cutting privileges heretofore granted on timber areas without public competition, as required by the Crown Timber Regulation.

Another clause reads as follows:—"Whenever a timber limit or area is offered for sale by public competition, the Minister of Lands and Forests may stipulate a time in which the timber is to be cut and left subject to the acquiring by the operator of an annual license to cut as required by Crown Timber Act and may also when he deems it in the public interest, extend the time for cutting beyond the time prescribed in the terms and conditions of any sale.

## $5,000 Prize for Suppression of Bud Worm

A prize of five thousand dollars is offered by Mr. Frank J. D. Barnjum, of Annapolis Royal, N. S., for a practical method of combatting and suppressing the spruce bud worm, bark beetle and borer which have caused such tremendous damage in the forests of Eastern Canada and the United States. The Province of Quebec alone has suffered a loss during the past ten years of 150,000,000 cords of standing pulpwood by these pests, which represents a market value in pulpwood of three billion dollars, or if manufactured into paper, of seven billion dollars. This represents a loss of wood sufficient for forty-five years requirements for newsprint for the North American continent. This staggering loss has prompted Mr. Barnjum to offer this substantial prize.

Competition will close August 1st and the $5,000 will be paid in cash for the successful suggestion that is accepted by the judges, who will be Sir William Price of Messrs. Price Bros., Quebec; Dr. C. D. Howe, Dean of the Faculty, Toronto University; Mr. Fred A. Gilbert, Great Northern Paper Company, Bangor, Maine; Mr. G. C. Piche, Chief of Forest Service, Quebec, and Mr. Ellwood Wilson, Laurentide Company, Grand Mere, P. Q.

Competitive suggestions are to be mailed to Mr. Frank J. D. Barnjum, New Birks Building, Montreal, Canada, previous to August 1st.

Mr. Barnjum recently received the following appreciative letter from R. W. Hibberson, of Hibberson Bros., timber factors, Victoria, B. C.,—I have read with great interest your excellent article on the "Depletion of the Eastern Timber Supply". The facts which you very ably brought out should do a great deal of good and we sincerely hope that the Government will take immediate steps to conserve the supply of pulp timber for our Canadian mills.

We are faced with very much the same situation in the West,— our large pulp mills, which according to their prospectuses, had sufficient timber to last them periods varying from twenty-five to forty years, are now buying heavily for future supplies; they are realizing that instead of twenty-five years supply, they have had barely ten years and the immense areas which they understood were heavily timbered, on investigation proved to be barren, unmerchantable timber and large areas were inaccessible.

On the 31st day of December, some four thousand Special Timber Licenses reverted to the Provincial Government,—these Licenses on examination have proved to be of little commercial value; only a few of them contained good timber.

Many of our prominent loggers are today engaged in a fruitless search for good logging chances on the mainland and on the Coast of Vancouver Island. Several of them told me that they have been engaged for the past year looking for a good logging chance, but up to date have been unable to find it.

Stumpage prices have risen for Special Licensed timber to $2.50 and $3.00 per thousand feet, which a year ago could be bought for $1.00 Crown lands in certain sections of Vancouver Island are bringing as high as $6.00 per thousand feet stumpage, and several large sales have been made during the past three months at prices varying from $3.00 to $6.00.

Already, the loggers are invading various points on the West Coast of Vancouver Island, establishing camps and putting in new mills, with a view to using the mills for export business.

We have had a very considerable export business during the past year and are now not only shipping timber, but are shipping whole logs, just as they come out of the woods, to Japan and certain Chinese points. The logs are cut in 13 and 14 foot lengths and are taken in diameters up to 36 inches. We have now new orders for many million of feet of logs.

### Mr. Marsh was Veteran Lumberman

Daniel Marsh, pioneer and lumber dealer and contractor Grimsby, Ont., who passed away recently in that town at the age of 81 years and whose death was referred to in a recent issue of the "Canada Lumberman," was one of the veteran figures in the district where he carried on business successfully for some 60 years. During his career he constructed in the Grimsby fruit district a number of the finest residences which stand as a monument to his skill as a contractor and builder.

Mr. Marsh was born in Somerset, England, and came to Grimsby at the age of 18 years. His wife predeceased him by some 26 years. He is survived by four sons and four daughters, Albert and Fred associated with him in the business, Wm. J. of Iowa Falls, Iowa, and Wesley of Fort Myers, Florida. All the daughters reside in Grimsby.

The contracting and building business, as well as that of the Grimsby planing mill, which was carried on by the late Mr. Marsh, will be continued by his two sons, J. A. and F. M. Marsh. It will be remembered that another son, Henry Marsh, passed away a few months ago.

### Manitoba Forest Patrols will Use Radio System

If present plans mature, two radio stations will be installed this season for the use of the forest aeroplane patrols at Norway House and Victoria Beach, was announced by Major B. D. Hobbs, of Winnipeg Station of the Canadian Air Board.

The outfits will be able to transmit by key only and to receive key or phone calls.

The advantages of the methods, said Major Hobbs, will be that speedy communication may be made between bases in the matter of reporting fires to the district inspector of forestry at Winnipeg, so that help may be sent to the scene of fires with the least possible delay, and for the broadcasting of reliable weather reports from the northern country.

The flying boats will not be equipped with wireless outfits since already they carry reliable homing pigeons. The planes were used last year with very satisfactory results, making the trip from Norway House to Winnipeg in a very few hours.

Four or five machines will be sent from Winnipeg to the bases in the last week in May, while six machines will be operating before the middle of June.

### Fire Damages Manitoba Airplane Station

The five airplanes belonging to the Winnipeg branch of the Canadian Air Board are rapidly being rigged for their season's work in the Northern part of the province. Some slight delay in getting the machines into service will be occasioned by an explosion which, with the resulting fire destroyed equipment and spare parts to the value of $10,000.

The building in which the fire started was practically destroyed and two of the mechanics injured by the explosion of a gasoline tank which was being repaired.

Four of the five machines, including one hydroplane, will be ready for fire service by the end of May according to Major Hobbs, who has charge of the Winnipeg station.

Equipment to replace that destroyed at the station is being shipped from the east, so practically no delay will be occasioned in the erection of machines.

### No Particular Tariff Needed on Lumber

The new duties on lumber, as provided for in the tariff bill reported by the Senate Finance Committee, were branded as ridiculous by J. H. Bloedel, of Seattle, Wash., head of the Bloedel-Donovan Lumber Mills, with offices in New York, on his arrival from Washington.

Mr. Bloedel assailed the Senate bill for removing the 50c. rate on red cedar shingles as fixed in the House bill and placing a duty of $1 on fir, cedar and hemlock logs, which, he said created the anomaly of taxing raw material and letting the manufactured product in free.

"There should be a tariff on shingles," Mr. Bloedel asserted; "whether 50 cents or some other figure I am not prepared to state. No particular tariff is needed on lumber unless Canada should place a discriminatory rate on U. S. products. In that case United States should follow with a reciprocal tariff."

The Thomson-Kneeland Lumber Co., have opened an office and yard at 3441 William St., Montreal, and are carrying a full line of building material, doors, trim, flooring, etc.

# Our Log Carriages

are now equipped with

## Payette's
## New 1921 Improved Patent
## Sawmill Dog

This dog handles with equal ease
Pine or Hardwood Logs from 3" to
48" diam. or 1" x 3" boards.

We can equip YOUR PRESENT
CARRIAGE with our 1921 Patent
Dog

### P. Payette Co., Penetang, Ont.

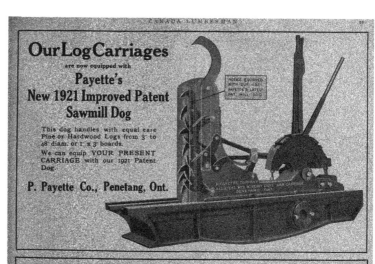

# The Machine That Made a Record in a Recent
# Lath Cutting, 10 Hour Test

Four Hundred Sawmills in
the Dominion are to-day using this machine.

It has all the latest im-
provements and for quick,
clean work has no equal.

The Payette No. 1 Bolter
and No. 2 Lath Mill will cut,
count, tie and pile 128,350
laths in a period of ten hours.
The above consisted of 4 foot
laths 1½ by ⅜ inches, and
constitutes a record in rapid
lath cutting.

If you are not using a
Payette No. 1 Bolter you
should be.

Also manufacture lath trimmers tiers and splitters.

Shall we send you full particulars
and prices?

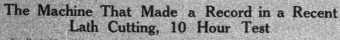

# P. PAYETTE & CO.,

J. T. Payette, Prop.        PENETANG, ONT.

# EDGINGS

The Reliance Lumber Co., Langenburg, Sask., recently opened a branch in that town.

The lumber cut in Nova Scotia for the winter will be 50 per cent. of last year's, according to a recent report of the government employment bureaus in the province.

S. Hayward, Port Elgin, N. B., sawmill operator, recently passed away. He was well-known and had been identified with the industry for many years.

A. E. Belanger, Valleyfield, P. Q., is remodelling a factory for the purpose of manufacturing sash, doors and general woodwork. Some equipment will be required.

The Donaconna Papar Co., Donaconna, Ont., has obtained a permit from the provincial government of Quebec to build a large dam on the Jacques Cartier River at the foot of Jacques Cartier Lake.

T. D. Robinson & Sons; Brown & Rutherford and McDonald-Dure Lumber Co., Winnipeg, were recently awarded the contract for supplying lumber for the city of Winnipeg for the coming season.

James B. Hall, Vancouver, B. C., president of the Hall Machine Works, manufacturers of logging and box making machinery died recently in his 69th year. He moved from Toronto to Vancouver twelve years ago.

The J. R. Morgan Co., Limited, of Prince Rupert, B. C., have secured a contract to get out 6,000,000 feet of logs for the Pacific Mills, Limited, at Ocean Falls, B. C. The logs will be cut on Surf Inlet, Princess Royal Island.

The Fesserton Timber Co., of Toronto, have begun the operation of their sawmill at Krugersdorf on the T. & N. O. Railway, above Englehart, Ont. The mill will turn out about 35,000 feet a day, the product being principally spruce and jack pine.

La Compagnie Blanchette, Limited, Chicoutimi, Que., were recently granted a provincial charter to operate sawmills and carry on a general lumbering business. Capital $20,000. T. Blanchette, and W. Blanchette, both of Chicoutimi, are two of the incorporators.

Cox, Long, & Co., Ltd., Montreal, the agents in Canada for the Timber Disposal Department, Board of Trade, London, have sold 1,000 standards of the British Government stock to the Associated Importers, Limited, London, England. The stocks will be shipped to the U. K.

Thompson-Kneeland Lumber Co., Limited, Montreal, were recently granted a provincial charter to conduct a wholesale and retail lumber business. Capital $49,000. W. H. Thompson, and A. T. Kneeland, lumber merchants, both of Outremont, Que., are two of the incorporators.

A. N. Dudley, wholesale lumberman of Toronto, who last month spent a few days at Summerville, S. C., took part in a golf tournament there, and was the winner in the second flight in which there were sixteen competitors. He brought home a handsome silver trophy as the result of his success on the links.

The Haight & Dickson Lumber Co., Sudbury, Ont., has commenced the operation of its sawmill at Bethnal, Ont., Mileage 93½, on the C. N. R. The company will cut about 4,000,000 feet of jack pine and spruce along with a quantity of white pine. The firm is having about 2,000,000 feet of logs sawn at Pine, Ont.

Dwyer Couts, aged 22 years who was employed in the sawmill at Kinburn, Ont., suffered instant death recently. He had gone to the mill to get a drink of water, and when turning, his trouser became caught in the main drive shaft, throwing him back with terrific violence. Both his legs were severed and his spine fractured.

Word was received in Toronto that the steamship companies had reduced the ocean freight rates from Montreal, Halifax, Quebec and St. John from 100 S. per standard to 50 S. While the reduction is not nearly as large as was anticipated by some of the exporters, still it is felt that it is a move in the right direction and may stimulate overseas business.

It is stated that the Ontario Government recently granted leases of two more waterpowers in Northern Ontario to E. W. Backus, of the Fort Frances Pulp & Paper Co., Fort Frances, who secured the English River pulpwood limits about a year ago, and is erecting a new pulp plant at Kenora. Both of the waterpowers are on the Ontario-Minnesota border.

International Burr Corporation of Canada, Limited, Belleville, Ont., were recently granted a federal charter with a capital of $40,000 to manufacture and market a product used in dressing pulp mill stones in the manufacture of paper and pulp. W. P. Aiken of Water-

town, N. Y., and C. B. Aiken of Belleville, Ont., are among the incorporators of the company.

The Abitibi Power and Paper Co. of Iroquois Falls, Ont., in order to facilitate transportation of raw material, is building a railway of its own from Iroquois Falls branch of the Temiskaming & Northern Ontario Railway up with the village of Hughes on the mainline of the Transcontinental Railway. The private line will pass through the townships of Edward, Mortimer and part of Stimson.

The Abitibi Power & Paper Co., of Iroquois Falls, Ont., have thoroughly overhauled and repaired their drum barkers, making them ready for spring operation. The drums are each giving as high as 400 cords per day or 1,600 cords in all when going at full spead. The conveyors running to and from the barking drums have been repaired, and when the first logs come down the river, everything will be in readiness.

C. Russell Carrick, Crystal Beach, Ont., has purchased the Crystal Beach Planing Mill and Lumber Yard from J. T. James. This business will be carried on under the management of C. H. Haun. In all probability a few changes and improvements will be made, including the installation of a 60 h.p. electric motor. Mr. Haun reports that business is extremely good in the Crystal Beach district.

: An urgent plea is being made by all public bodies interested in the forests of Ontario. It is being sent to campers, hunters, fishermen and others having occasion to use the woods for recreation . All such parties are asked to join hands with the forest rangers of Ontario this season in eliminating at least half of the enormous forest fire losses which were chargeable last summer to human agencies.

Brunette Sawmills, Sapperton, near New Westminster, B. C., whose plant was totally destroyed by fire some time ago contemplate rebuilding on a larger scale with a capacity for 1,000,000 feet of lumber per day and at an approximate cost of $250,000. This is in accordance with the by-law giving the company a special tax rate of $5,000 a year or 20 years, which has just been ratified by ratepayers. The agreement calls for the mills to be rebuilt and operating within six months.

W. H. Johnston, of Pefferlaw, Ont., who is a widely-known sawmill man of York County, the Johnston mill having been in the family for over 100 years, was in Toronto recently. Mr. Johnston states that his mill has been in operation a month and that he expects to saw about 600,000 feet during the spring season. He is also making arrangements to erect summer cottages at Port Bolster, on Lake Simcoe. Last year he put up several and this year will add materially to the number.

Hon. L. A. Taschereau, Prime Minister of Quebec, who recently returned from a visit to the United States, says that the Fordney Traiff Bill did not seem very popular with the Government of the United States. Instead of raising the duty on Canadian woods, he is of the opinion that the federal authorities at Ottawa should levy an export duty on pulpwood, which would greatly handicap a number of large U. S. manufacturing firms who are dependent upon Canada for their supply of pulpwood.

Parrsboro, N. S., have recently entered into an agreement with a large firm in Maine, who intends storing 100,000 cords of pulpwood on the shores of Lake Glooscap, covering a period of ten years. The average amount stored annually will be 10,000 cords at 25 cents a cord. The starting of this industry means an outlay of a considerable amount in acquiring wharfs properties, providing for the conveyance across a roadway lying between the storage yards and shipping piers, together with a considerable expenditure of cutting, hauling and transferring to the upper waters of the lake the timber required for the cord waning.

J. A. Hawtin, of Kinmount, Ont., who formerly ran a sawmill at Kettleby, in York County, until his limits were cut out, was in Toronto recently calling upon the trade. He now operates a sawmill at Lochlin, which is located on Lake Kushog, in Victoria County. Last year Mr. Hawtin sawed about a million and a half feet of mixed timber and his cut this season will be nearly as large. He buys considerable material from the farmers and does a large custom business as well. Mr. Hawtin furnished the lumber for several cottages on the shore of Lake Kushog, and expects to do considerable in that line this summer.

Recently a deputation from the Abitibi district, headed by Hector Authier and supported by the Quebec Board of Trade, waited upon Hon. W. C. Kennedy, Minister of Railways at Ottawa, and urged that the freight rates on pulpwood and lumber be reduced 50% to bring them to an equal basis with the rates charged in Nova Scota coal mines. It was pointed out by the deputation that about $2,000,000. worth of wood was piled along the lines of the railway and could not be moved on account of excessive freight rates and that this would not only bring on a financial crisis but might result in setting the whole country on fire during the warm weather in summer. Hon. Mr. Kennedy said he had given instructions that the rates on pulpwood be reduced by one-third.

**CAMP HEATER**

| No. | Length of wood | Diameter of Steel Body | Weight |
|-----|------|------|------|
| 30 | 30 | 18 | 100 |
| 36 | 36 | 28 | 150 |
| 44 | 44 | 23 | 160 |
| 50 | 50 | 25 | 175 |

## Comfort, Service, and Good Cheer

ADAM HALL heaters and ranges are the result of many years study of the camp's requirements. The range shown below is one that helps the cook to get the meals on time, and cooked to the whole camp's satisfaction. It burns both coal and wood, fires up quickly and is very convenient to work with. It is built to give years of service.

*May we send you full information?*

**COAL OR WOOD—In Two Sizes**

| Ovens, widths | Depth | Height | Fire Boxes, Wood |
|-----|-----|-----|-----|
| 24-in. | 26-in. | 16-in. | 28-in. |
| 30-in. | 26-in. | 16-in. | 28-in. |

# ADAM HALL, LTD.
## PETERBOROUGH - ONT.

# What Keeps The Bunch Smilin'—

WHEN you roll out in the morning—one of those real, "up-an'-at'em" mornings—and go over and stow away the best the cook has to offer, doesn't it help a lot to know that you've got the best saw in the world—all shining and fixed up just right—waiting to help you through the day's work? Oh Boy! how tired you get when you've got a poor saw. It takes the life right out of a fellow when he tries to use a saw that goes dull about as often as he looks at it.

You know a lot of fellows have found the kind of saw that keeps away a grouch. They're the ones who use Disston Cross-cuts.

They've found that a Disston holds a sharp cutting-edge—that it doesn't crumble off at the points after you tune it up. That's because Disston Cross-cuts are made of the famous Disston-made Steel. Disston Saws run easy and fast, too—the way they are ground and tensioned takes care of that.

So the next time you see a fellow coming in from a day's work ahead of the rest of the crowd, singing and smiling and happy—look at him and then look at his saw—we're layin' long odds you'll see a real fellow and a Disston Saw.

Is there anything you would like to know about Disston Cross-cut Saws? More than likely you've got about three questions right now. We'll be glad to answer them. Just send your letter to Department H or the right fellow will get it and attend to it at once.

**HENRY DISSTON & SONS, LIMITED**
TORONTO, CANADA
Branch: Vancouver, B.C.

# DISSTON
## CROSS-CUT SAWS

# ALPHABETICAL INDEX TO ADVERTISERS

...of the Sturtevant fan circulation principle.

"Yellowwood, being the most abundant indigenous wood, has been placed foremost in the seasoning program. A quantity of 312 cubic feet of faluate yellowwood was received from the Transkei forests. The green logs were sawed into 1¼-inch boards immediately afterwards placed in the fan kilns. The load was subjected to a drying temperature of 120° F. to 175° F. with humidity varying from 30 to 100 per cent and was steamed at intervals to relieve case-hardening stresses. In 16 days the wood dried from 70 to 7 per cent moisture content. Since then a further quantity of yellowwood has been seasoned and no matter how the boards are cut, flat or deep, there is no warping and cracking. This is most satisfactory."

## A South African Report

Note that the green lumber was immediately placed in the fan Kilns.

Note also that in sixteen days it was ready to ship; no tied up capital here.

And, further, "no matter how the boards are cut, flat or deep, there is no warping and cracking."

Catalog 268 is full of interesting information and data on lumber drying; a copy will be mailed you free on request.

# Sturtevant

PUTS AIR TO WORK

## High Humidity Dry Kiln

*The kiln with a circulation you can understand*

## B. F. Sturtevant Co. of Canada, Ltd.

Montreal        Galt        Toronto

Territorial Representatives:

Empire Engineering & Supply Co.        Kipp-Kelly Ltd.
Edmonton, Alberta.        Winnipeg, Man.

# CANADA LUMBERMAN BUYERS' DIRECTORY

The following regulations apply to all advertisers:—Eighth page, every issue, three headings;
quarter page, six headings; half page, twelve headings; full page, twenty-four headings

**ALLIGATORS**
Payette Company, P.
West, Peachy & Sons

**BABBITT METAL**
Canada Metal Co.
General Supply Co., of Canada, Ltd.

**BALE TIES**
Canada Metal Co.
Laidlaw Bale Tie Company

**BAND MILLS**
Hamilton Company, William
Waterous Engine Works Company
Yates Machine Company, P. B.

**BAND SAW BLADES**
Simonds Mfg., Co.

**BAND RESAWS**
Mershon & Company, W. B.
Yates Machine Co., P.B.

**BARKERS**
Bertrand, F. X., La Compagnie
Manufacturiere.
Smith Foundry & Machine Co.

**BEARING METAL**
Canada Metal Co.
Beveridge Supply Co., Ltd.

**BEDSTEADS (STEEL)**
Simmons Limited

**BELT DRESSING**
Dominion Belting Co.
General Supply of Canada, Ltd.

**BELTING**
Canadian Consolidated Rubber Co.
Dominion Belting Co. . . . . . . . . . . .
General Supply Company
Goodhue & Co., J. L.
Gutta Percha & Rubber Company
D. K. McLaren, Limited
York Belting Co.

**BLOWERS**
Reed & Co., Geo. W.
B. F. Sturtevant Co., of Canada, Ltd.
Toronto Blower Company

**BOILERS**
Engineering & Machine Works of
Canada
Hamilton Company, William
Waterous Engine Works Company

**BOILER PRESERVATIVE**
Beveridge Supply Company
Shell-Bar, Boico Supply Co., Ltd.

**BOX MACHINERY**
Yates Machine Company, P. B.

**CABLE CONVEYORS**
Engineering & Machine Works of
Canada.
Hamilton Company, William
Waterous Engine Works Company

**CAMP SUPPLIES**
Davies Company, William
Dr. Bell Veterinary Wonder Co.
Johnson, A. H.
Turner & Sons, J. J.
Woods Manufacturing Co., Ltd.

**CANT HOOKS**
General Supply Co., of Canada, Ltd.
Pink & Company, Thomas

**CEDAR**
Bury & Co., Robt.
Cameron Lumber Co.
Canadian Western Lumber Co.
Chesbro, R. G.
Dry Wood Lumber Co.
Fesserton Timber Company
Fesserton Timber Company
McElroy Lumber Co., Ltd.
Muir & Kirkpatrick
Rose, McLaurin, Limited
Terry & Gordon
Thurston- Flavelle Lumber Co.
Vancouver Lumber Company.
Victoria Lumber & Mfg. Co.

**CHAINS**
Canadian Link-Belt Company, Ltd.
General Supply Co., of Canada, Ltd.
Engineering & Machine Works of
Canada
Hamilton Company, William
Pink & Company, Thomas.
Waterous Engine Works Company

**CLOTHING**
Woods Mfg. Company

**CONVEYOR MACHINERY**
Canadian Link-Belt Company, Ltd.
General Supply Co., of Canada, Ltd.
Hamilton Company, William
Hopkins & Co., Ltd., F. H.
Waterous Engine Works Company

**CORDWOOD**
McClung, McLellan & Berry

**COUPLING (Shaft)**
Engineering & Machine Works of
Canada

**CRANES**
Hopkins & Co., Ltd., F. H.
Canadian Link-Belt Company, Ltd.

**CUTTER HEADS**
Shimer Cutter Head Company
Yates Machine Co., P.B.

**CYPRESS**
Maus Lumber Co., Chas. Q.
Wistar, Underhill & Nixon

**DERRICKS AND DERRICK
FITTINGS**
Hopkins & Co., Ltd., F. H.

**DOORS**
Canadian Western Lumber Co.
Gardiner, P. W. & Son
Mason, Gordon & Co.
Terry & Gordon

**DRAG SAWS**
Gerlach Company, Peter
Hamilton Company, William

**DRYERS**
Coe Manufacturing Company
B. F. Sturtevant Co. of Canada, Ltd.

**DUST COLLECTORS**
Reed & Co., Geo. W.
B. F. Sturtevant Co. of Canada. Ltd.
Toronto Blower Company

**EDGERS**
Hamilton Company, Ltd., William
Green Company, G. Walter
Long Mfg. Company, E.
Payette Company, P.
Waterous Engine Works Company
Yates Machine Co., P.B.

**ELEVATING AND CONVEYING
MACHINERY**
Canadian Link-Belt Company, Ltd.
Engineering & Machine Works of
Canada
Hamilton Company, William
Waterous Engine Works Company

**ENGINES**
Engineering & Machine Works of
Canada
Hamilton Company, William
Payette Company, P.
Waterous Engine Works Company

**EXCELSIOR MACHINERY**
Elmira Machinery & Transmission.
Company

**EXHAUST FANS**
B. F. Sturtevant Co. of Canada, Ltd.
Toronto Blower Company

**EXHAUST SYSTEMS**
Reed & Co., Geo. W.
B. F. Sturtevant Co. of Canada, Ltd.
Toronto Blower Company

**FIBRE BOARD**
Manley Chew

**FILES**
Diston & Sons, Henry
Simonds Canada Saw Company.

**FIR**
Apex Lumber Co.
Associated Mills, Limited
Bainbridge Lumber Company.
Cameron Lumber Co.
Canadian Western Lumber CO.
Canfield, P. L.
Chesbro, R. G.
Dry Wood Lumber- Co.
Fesserton Timber Co.
Gejer & Sons, Ltd., G. A.
Heeney, Percy E.
Knox Brothers.
Mason, Gordon & Go.
McElroy Lumber Co., Ltd.
Robertson & Hackett Sawmills
Rose, McLaurin, Limited
Terry & Gordon
Timberland Lumber Company
Timms, Phillips & Co.
Underhill Lumber Co.
Vancouver Lumber Company
Vanderhoof Lumber Company
Victoria Lumber & Mfg. Company

**FIRE BRICK**
Beveridge Supply Co., Limited
Elk Fire Brick Company of Canada
Shell-Bar, Boico Supply Co., Ltd.

**FIRE FIGHTING APPARATUS**
Waterous Engine Works Company

**FITTINGS**
Crane Limited

**FLOORING**
Cameron Lumber Co.
Chesbro, R. G.
Long-Bell Lumber Company

**GEARS (Cut)**
Smart-Turner Machine Company

**GUARDS (Machinery and Window)**
Canada Wire & Iron Goods Co.

**HARDWOODS**
Anderson Lumber Company, C. G.,
Anderson, Shreiner & Mawson
Barrett, Wm.
Black Rock Lumber Co.
Bury & Co., Robt.
Cameron & Company
Edwards & Co., W. C.
Fassett Lumber Company, Limited
Fesserton Timber Co.
Gillespie, James
Gloucester Lumber & Trading Co.
Grier & Sons, Ltd., G. A.
Hart, Hamilton & Jackson
Heeney, Percy E.
Knox Brothers
Kinnon Lumber Co.
Mason & Company, Geo.
Maus Lumber Co., Chas. O.
McDonagh Lumber Company
McLennan Lumber Company
McLung, McLellan & Berry
Pedwell Hardwood Lumber Co.
W. & J. Sharples
Spencer, Limited, C. A.
Strong, G. M.
Summers, James R.

**HARDWOOD FLOORING**
Grier & Sons, Ltd., G. A.

**HARNESS**
Beal Leather Company, R. M.

**HEMLOCK**
Anderson Lumber Company, C. G.
Anderson, Shreiner & Mawson
Bartram & Ball
Beck Lumber Company
Bourgouin, H.
Canadian General Lumber Company
Edwards & Co., W. C.
Fesserton Timber Co.
Grier & Sons, Ltd., G. A.
Hart, Hamilton & Jackson
Hocken Lumber Company
Mason, Gordon & Company
McCormack Lumber Company
McDonagh Lumber Company
McElroy Lumber Co. Ltd.
Robertson & Hacket Sawmills
Spencer, Limited, C. A.
Stalker, Douglas A.
Terry & Gordon
Vancouver Lumber Company
Vanderhoof Lumber Company

**HOISTING AND HAULING
ENGINES**
General Supply Co., of Canada, Ltd.

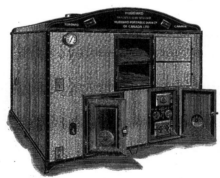

Hopkins & Co., Ltd., F. H.

**HOSE**
General Supply Co., of Canada, Ltd.
Gutta Percha & Rubber Company

**INSURANCE**
Barton & Ellis Company
Burns Underwriting Company
Hardy & Company, E. D.
Rankin Benedict Underwriting Co.

**INTERIOR FINISH**
Cameron Lumber Company
Canadian Western Lumber Co.
Canfield, P. L.
Eagle Lumber Company
Mason, Gordon & Co.
Rose, McLaurin, Limited
Terry & Gordon

**KILN DRIED LUMBER**
Bury & Co., Robt.

**KNIVES**
Disston & Sons, Henry
Simonds Canada Saw Company
Waterous Engine Works Company

**LARCH**
Otis Staples Lumber Company

**LATH**
Anderson, Shreiner & Mawson
Apex Lumber Company
Austin & Nicholson
Beck Lumber Company
Brennen & Sons, F. W.
Cameron Lumber Company
Canadian General Lumber Company
Carew Lumber Company, John
Chaleurs Bay Mills

Dadson, A. T.
Eagle Lumber Company
Fassett Lumber Company, Limited
Foley Lumber Company
Fraser Bryson Lumber Co., Ltd.
Gloucester Lumber & Trading Co.
Grier & Sons, Ltd., G. A.
Harris Tie & Timber Company, Ltd.
Larkin Company, C. A.
Mason, & Company, Geo.
McLennan Lumber Company
Miller, W. H. Company
New Ontario Colonization Company
Otis Staples Lumber Company
Power Lumber Company
Price Bros. & Company
Shevlin-Clarke Company
Spencer, Limited, C. A.
Terry & Gordon
U. G. G. Sawmills, Limited
Union Lumber Company
Victoria Harbor Lumber Company

**LATH BOLTERS**
General Supply Co. of Canada, Ltd.
Hamilton Company, William
Payette & Company, P.

**LOCOMOTIVES**
Engineering & Machine Works of Canada
General Supply Co. of Canada, Ltd.
Hopkins & Co., Ltd., F. H.
Climax Manufacturing Company
Montreal Locomotive Works

**LINK-BELT**
Canadian Link-Belt Company
Hamilton Company, William

**LOCOMOTIVE CRANES**
Canadian Link-Belt Company
Hopkins & Co., Ltd., F. H.

**LOGGING ENGINES**
Engineering & Machine Works of Canada

Hopkins & Co., Ltd., F. H.
Mussens Limited

**LOG HAULER**
Engineering & Machine Works of Canada
Green Company, G. Walter
Holt Manufacturing Company
Hopkins & Co., Ltd., F. H.
Payette & Company, P.

**LOGGING MACHINERY AND EQUIPMENT**
General Supply Co. of Canada, Ltd.
Hamilton Company, William
Holt Manufacturing Company
Hopkins & Co., Ltd., F. H.
Payette & Company, P.
Waterous Engine Works Company
West, Peachey & Sons
Mussens Limited

**LUMBER EXPORTS**
Fletcher Corporation

**LUMBER TRUCKS**
Hamilton Company, William
Waterous Engine Works Company

**LUMBERMEN'S BOATS**
Adams Engine Company
Gidley Boat Company
West, Peachey & Sons

**LUMBERMEN'S CLOTHING**
Kitchen Overall & Shirt Company

**MATTRESSES**
Simmons Limited

**METAL REFINERS**
Canada Metal Company

**NAILING MACHINES**
Yates Machine Co., P.B.

**OAK**
Long-Bell Lumber Company
Maus Lumber Co., Chas. O.

**PACKING**
Beveridge Supply Company
Gutta Percha & Rubber Company

**PANELS**
Bury & Company, Robt.

**PAPER**
Beveridge Supply Company
Price Bros. & Company

**PINE**
Anderson Lumber Company, C. G.
Anderson, Shreiner & Mawson
Atlantic Lumber Company
Austin & Nicholson
Barratt, William
Beck Lumber Company
Black Rock Lumber Co.
Cameron & Company
Cameron Lumber Company
Canadian General Lumber, Company
Canadian Western Lumber Co.
Canfield, P. L.
Chesbro, R. G.
Cleveland-Sarnia Sawmills Company
Cox, Long & Company
Dadson, A. T.
Dudley, Arthur N.
Eagle Lumber Company
Edwards & Co., W. C.
Excelsior Lumber Company
Fesserton Timber Co.
Fraser Bryson Lumber Co., Ltd.
Gillies Bros, Limited
Gloucester Lumber & Trading Co.
Gordon & Company, George
Goodday & Company, H. R.
Grier & Sons, Ltd., G. A.
Harris Tie & Timber Company, Ltd.
Hart, Hamilton & Jackson
Hettler Lumber Co., Herman H.
Hocken Lumber Company
Julien, Roch
Keewatin Lumber Co.
Lay & Haight
Lloyd, W. Y.
Loggie Company, W. S.
Long-Bell Lumber Company
Mason, Gordon & Co.
Mason & Company, Geo.

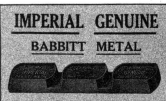

# Dunlop Belts Respond With Economy and Long Life to all Uses.

They are built with an eye to long Service.

They save machinery by their ability to run smoothly, and easily yet they transmit the required power.

The special frictioned-surface of "Gibraltar RedSpecial," and the great flexibility of this Belt, ensure close pulley contact. It Masters straining drives and off-and-on loads.

Heat and cold, wet and dryness do not affect it.

The Dunlop process eliminates stretch, This saves constant adjustments and undue waste of time.

For Belt Economy and Belt Satisfaction use "Gibraltar RedSpecial" frictioned-surface. This belt will adapt itself to any drive.

## Dunlop Tire & Rubber Goods Co., Limited

Head Office and Factories: TORONTO
Branches in the Leading Cities

McCormack Lumber Company
McFadden & Malloy
McLennan Lumber Company
Montreal Lumber Company
Muir & Kirkpatrick
Northern Lumber Mills
Otis Staples Lumber Company
Parry Sound Lumber Company
Rolland Lumber Company
W. & J. Sharples
Shevlin-Clarke Company
Spencer, Limited, C. A.
Stalker, Douglas A.
Strong, G. M.
Summers, James R.
Terry & Gordon
Union Lumber Company
Victoria Harbor Lumber Company
Watson & Todd, Limited

**PLANING MILL EXHAUSTERS**
Toronto Blower Company

**PLANING MILL MACHINERY**
Mershon & Company, W. B.
B. F. Sturtevant Co. of Canada, Ltd.
Toronto Blower Company
Yates Machine Company, P. B.

**POPLAR**
Keewatin Lumber Co.

**POST GRINDERS**
Smith Foundry Company

**POSTS AND POLES**
Anderson, Shreiner & Mawson
Canadian Tie & Lumber Co.
Dupuis, Limited, J. P.
Eagle Lumber Company
Harris Tie & Timber Company, Ltd.
Long-Bell Lumber Company
Mason, Gordon & Co.
McLennan Lumber Company
Terry & Gordon

**PULLEYS AND SHAFTING**
Canadian Link-Belt Company
General Supply Co. of Canada, Ltd.
Green Company, G. Walter
Engineering & Machine Works of
  Canada
Hamilton Company, William

**PULP MILL MACHINERY**
Canadian Link-Belt Company
Engineering & Machine Works of
  Canada
Hamilton Company, William
Payette & Company, P.
Waterous Engine Works Company

**PULPWOOD**
British & Foreign Agencies
D'Auteuil Lumber Company
Price Bros. & Company
Scott, Draper & Company

**PUMPS**
General Supply Co. of Canada, Ltd.
Engineering & Machine Works of
  Canada
Hamilton Company, William
Hopkins & Co., Ltd., F. H.
Smart-Turner Machine Company
Waterous Engine Works Company

**RAILS**
Gartshore, John J.
Hopkins & Co., Ltd., F. H.

**ROOFINGS**
(Rubber, Plastic and Liquid)
Beveridge Supply Company
Reed & Co., Geo. W.

**RUBBER GOODS**
Dunlop Tire & Rubber Goods Co.
Gutta Percha & Rubber Company

**SASH**
Midland Woodworkers

**SAWS**
Atkins & Company, E. C.
Disston & Sons, Henry
General Supply Co. of Canada, Ltd.
Gerlach Company, Peter

Green Company, G. Walter
Hoe & Company, R.
Radcliff Saw Mfg. Company
Shurly Company, Ltd., T. F.
Shurly-Dietrich Company
Simonds Canada Saw Company

**SAW GRINDERS**
Smith Foundry Company

**SAW MILL LINK-BELT**
Canadian Link-Belt Company

**SAW MILL MACHINERY**
Canadian Link-Belt Company
General Supply Co. of Canada, Ltd.
G. Walter Green Company, Ltd.
Hamilton Company, William
La Compagnie Manufacture, F. X.
  Bertrand
Long Mfg. Company, E.
Mershon & Company, W. B.
Parry Sound Lumber Company
Payette & Company, P.
Waterous Engine Works Company
Yates Machine Company, P. B.

**SAW SHARPENERS**
Hamilton Company, William
Waterous Engine Works Company

**SAW SLASHERS**
Hamilton Company, William
Payette & Company, P.
Waterous Engine Works Company

**SHINGLES**
Apex Lumber Company
Associated Mills, Limited
Brennen & Sons, F. W.
Cameron Lumber Company
Campbell-MacLaurin Lumber Co.
Canadian Western Lumber Co.
Carew Lumber Company, John
Chaleurs Bay Mills
Chebro, R. G.
D'Auteuil Lumber Company
Dry Wood Lumber Co.
Eagle Lumber Company
Fraser, Companies Limited
Gillespie, James
Gloucester Lumber & Trading Co.
Grier & Sons, Ltd., G. A.
Harris Tie & Timber Co., Ltd.
Heaps & Sons
Heeney, Percy E.
Mason, Gordon & Co.
McLennan Lumber Company
Miller Company, Ltd., W. H.
Rose, McLaurin, Limited
Stalker, Douglas A.
Terry & Gordon
Timms, Phillips & Company
Vancouver Lumber Company
Vanderhoof Lumber Company

**SHINGLE & LATH MACHINERY**
Green Company, C. Walter
Hamilton Company, William
Long Manufacturing Company, E.
Payette & Company, P.
Smith Foundry Company

**SILENT CHAIN DRIVES**
Canadian Link-Belt Company

**SLEEPING EQUIPMENT**
Simmons Limited

**SLEEPING ROBES**
Woods Mfg. Company, Ltd.

**SMOKESTACKS**
Hamilton Company, William
Reed & Co., Geo. W.
Waterous Engine Works Company

**SNOW PLOWS**
Pink & Company, Thomas

**SOLDERS**
Canada Metal Company

**SPARK ARRESTORS**
Reed & Company, Geo. W.
Waterous Engine Works Company

**SPRUCE**
Anderson, Shreiner & Mawson
Barrett, Wm.
Cameron Lumber Company
Campbell, McLaurin Lumber Co.
Canadian Western Lumber Co.
Chesbro, R. G.
Cox, Long & Company
Dadson, A. T.
Dudley Arthur N.
Fassett Lumber Company, Ltd.
Fraser, Companies Limited
Fraser Bryson Lumber Co., Ltd.
Gillies Brothers
Gloucester Lumber & Trading Co.
Gooday & Company, H. R.
Grier & Sons, Ltd G. A.
Harris Lumber Co., Frank H.
Hart, Hamilton & Jackson
Hocken Lumber Company
Julien, Roch
Keewatin Lumber Co.
Larkin Co., C. A.
Lay & Haight.
Lloyd, W. Y.
Loggie Co., W. S.
Mason, Gordon & Co.
McCormack Lumber Co.
McDonagh Lumber Co.
McElroy Lumber Co., Ltd.
McLennan Lumber Company
Muir & Kirkpatrick
New Ontario Colonization Co.
Northern Lumber Mills
Power Lumber Co.
Price Bros. & Company
Rolland Lumber Co.
Rose, McLaurin, Limited
W. & J. Sharples.
Spencer, Limited, C. A.
Strong, G. M.
Terry & Gordon
U. G. G. Sawmills, Limited
Vanderhoof Lumber Company

**STEAM SHOVELS**
Hopkins & Co., Ltd., F. H.

**STEEL CHAIN**
Canadian Link-Belt Company
Hopkins & Co., Ltd., F. H.
Waterous Engine Works Company

**STEAM PLANT ACCESSORIES**
Waterous Engine Works Company

**STEEL BARRELS**
Smart-Turner Machine Company

**STEEL DRUMS**
Smart-Turner Machine Company

**TARPAULINS**
Turner & Sons, J. J.
Woods Manufacturing Company Ltd.

**TANKS**
Hopkins & Co., Ltd., F. H.

**TENTS**
Turner & Sons, J. J.
Woods Mfg. Company

**TIES**
Austin & Nicholson
Carew Lumber Co., John
Canadian Tie & Lumber Co.
Chaleurs Bay Mills
D'Auteuil Lumber Co.
Gloucester Lumber & Trading Co.
Harris Tie & Timber Company Ltd.
McLennan Lumber Company
Miller, W. H. Co.
Price Bros. & Company
Scott, Draper & Co.
Terry & Gordon

**TIMBER BROKERS**
Bradley, R. R.
Cant & Kemp
Farnworth & Jardine
Wright, Graham & Co.

**TIMBER CRUISERS AND
ESTIMATORS**
Savage & Bartlett
Sewell, James W.

**TIMBER LANDS**
Department of Lands & Forests, Ont.

**TOWING MACHINES**
Payette & Company, P.
West, Peachey & Sons

**TRACTORS**
Holt Manufacturing Company
Hopkins & Co., Ltd., F. H.
Mussens Limited

**TRANSMISSION MACHINERY**
Canadian Link-Belt Company
Engineering & Machine Works of
  Canada
General Supply Co. of Canada, Ltd.
Grand Rapids Vapor Kiln
Hamilton Company, William
Waterous Engine Works Co.

**TURBINES**
Engineering & Machine Works of
  Canada
Hamilton Company, William
B. F. Sturtevant Co. of Canada, Ltd.

**VALVES**
Crane, Limited

**VAPOR KILNS**
Grand Rapids Vapor Kiln
B. F. Sturtevant Co. of Canada, Ltd.

**VENEERS**
Bury & Co. Robt.

**VENEER DRYERS**
Coe Manufacturing Company
Sturtevant Co., B. F. of Canada Ltd.

**VENEER MACHINERY**
Coe Manufacturing Company

**VETERINARY REMEDIES**
Dr. Bell Vetinerary Wonder Co.
Johnson, A. H.

**WARPING TUGS**
West, Peachey & Sons

**WATER WHEELS**
Engineering & Machine Works of
  Canada
Hamilton Company, William

**WIRE**
Canada Metal Co.
Laidlaw Bale Tie Company
Canada Wire & Iron Goods Co.

**WIRE CLOTH**
Canada Wire & Iron Goods Co.

**WIRE ROPE**
Canada Wire & Iron Goods Co.
Hopkins & Co., Ltd., F. H.
Dominion Wire Rope Co.
Greening Wire Co., B.

**WOODWORKING MACHINERY**
General Supply Co. of Canada, Ltd.
Long Manufacturing Company, E.
Mershon & Company, W. B.
Waterous Engine Works Co.
Yates Machine Company, P. B.

**WOOD PRESERVATIVES**
Beveridge Supply Company
Austin & Nicholson
New Ontario Colonization Company
Power Lumber Co.

**WOOD PULP**
Austin & Nicholson
New Ontario Colonization Co.
Power Lumber Co.

# The Waterous Combination Setworks

## A setting mechanism and friction receder in one machine

Quick, powerful, safe and absolutely accurate. Can be attached to any rack carriage having set shaft not larger than 2-15/16". Easy on the operator and easy on itself.

## This Setworks
### Cannot Develop Lost Motion

In the ordinary set works the setting lever movement that determines the amount of set is controlled by stop pins placed in a stationary quadrant. As soon as the connections between the lever and the pawl cages become worn, lost motion is bound to develop, and the accuracy of the set is lost.

#### We overcome this in our set works

The quadrant carrying the stop pins is fastened to one of the pawl cages—on the movement of the setting lever the cages start from the home stop, advance until they strike and then return to the home stop. For the same position on the stop pins the travel of the cages will be the same, no matter how much the connecting links are worn. All wear comes behind the pins and the absolute accuracy of the set is a permanent feature.

### Other Features:

1. The Friction Receder Lever lifts the pawl automatically from the ratchet wheel before receding can commence. This does away with a pawl-lifting lever.

2. Only Two Levers are Required for both operations of setting and receding, both are placed most conveniently for the setter, no stooping is necessary. The operator can thus work quickly, accurately, and without fear of stripping his ratchet wheel.

3. Tool Steel Pawls extend full across the 4" face of the wheel, three pawls are carried in each cage, the latter made very wide and open for quick adjustment and to prevent clogging by saw dust.

4. Quadrant is Double Slotted, carries our patented knockback pins, arranged to give four standard cuts without shifting.

5. Pawls are arranged to set 1/32" up to 3" at one full throw of lever.

6. Every Part is Made to Template, repairs can be quickly furnished. The set works can be supplied without receder attachment if desired.

## The Waterous Engine Works Co., Ltd.
### BRANTFORD    -    CANADA

Agency—C. E. Kendall Molson's Bank Bldg., Vancouver                Branch—WINNIPEG, MAN.

ol. 42        Toronto, May 15, 1922        No. 10

# Canada Lumberman
*Founded 1880*

# "HAMILTON"
# Twin Circular Machine

Above cut illustrates one design of Twin or Span Circular used for slabbing logs for the gang or for making ties. With this machine chain feed is used. We also manufacture other designs with steam or rope feed.

The chain feed circular shown above will slab logs 16 ft. long into cants from 16" down to 4" in thickness, and this style of feed meets with most favor from millmen.

The saw frames are adjustable by rack and pinion controlled by handwheel with locking device, and a flat scale marked off at the mill shows distance between saws at all times. Saws used vary from 42" to 50" in diameter.

A special centering device operated by 6" steam cylinder is used to place logs to best advantage on track before going through the saws and the slabs coming off behind the machine are taken care of by means of chains or rollers.

The drive for feed chains which is variable is controlled by Sawyer and can be stopped or started at will.

Standard length of track supplied when cutting 16 ft. logs is 56 feet.

## *Consult us for any of your Sawmill Needs*

# William Hamilton Co., Limited

Agents: J. L. Neilson & Company, Winnipeg, Man.     PETERBORO, ONT.

# FESSERTON

**S E R V I C E**

The size of your order should have little bearing on the service you have a right to expect from the wholesaler.

It has no bearing whatever on the service *Fesserton* give their customers.

We try to make every order the forerunner of a repeat later on.

So don't think your order too small for us to handle—we'll appreciate it and show our appreciation by giving you the best service that is possible.

## The Fesserton Timber Company, Limited
15 Toronto Street    MAIN 795-6    **TORONTO**
Western Office Winch Building   -   Vancouver, B. C.

# Knox Brothers, Limited

### LIST OF SPECIALS AT VANCOUVER
Delivered Toronto or Monteal rate

3 cars 1 x 3 No. 1 Common Fir V. Joint V2S Bone Dry $30.50
4 cars 1 x 4 No. 1 Common Fir V. Joint V2S Bone Dry 30.50
2 cars 1 x 3 No. 1 Common Fir Flooring Bone Dry .. 31.00
5 cars 1 x 4 No. 1 Common Fir Flooring Bone Dry 30.50
2 cars 1 x 3 No. 1&2 Edgegrain Fir Flooring Kiln Dried 69.00
3 cars 1 x 4 No. 1&2 Edgegrain Fir Flooring Kiln Dried 69.00
1 car 1 x 5 Bull Nose Casing No. 1 ............... 71.00
2 cars No. 2 Common Fir Flooring 1 x 4 ........... 27.50

### LIST OF SPECIALS AT QUEBEC
Prices F.O.B. our Mill, Levis, Que.

3 cars Clear Birch Flooring 13/16 x 2" face ......... $85.00
5 cars Clear Birch Flooring 13/16 x 2¼" face ........ 85.00
5 cars Clear Birch Flooring 13/16 x 2½" face ........ 85.00
2 cars Clear Birch Flooring 13/16 x 1¾" face ........ 85.00
1 car ½ x 4 No. 1 Clear Cedar Bevel Siding Kiln Dried Shorts 3/7".................................. 37.00
2 cars 1 x 3 No. 1&2 Clear Fir Flooring Kiln Dried ... 46.00
1 car 1 x 4 No. 1&2 Clear Fir Flooring Kiln Dried ... 46.00
1 car 1 x 3 No. 1&2 Clear Fir V. Joint Kiln Dried .... 46.00
2 cars 1 x 4 No. 1&2 Clear Fir V. Joint Kiln Dried .... 46.00
2 cars ½ x 3&4 No. 1&2 Clear Fir V. Joint Kiln Dried 38.00
1 car 1 x4 No. 3½ Fir Flooring Kiln Dried ......... 40.00
1 car 1 x 4 No. 3½ Fir V. Joint Kiln Dried ......... 40.00

#### WIRE YOUR ORDERS COLLECT

Eastern Canadian Mill Address
P. O. Box 27
Lauzon Quebec
(opposite Quebec City)

**Head Office**
**512-513 Drummond Bldg.**
**Montreal**

At Quebec we specialize in dressing in transit for wholesalers and manufacturers.

# White Pine
# Red Pine
# Jack Pine
# Spruce
# Lumber
# and Lath

**UNION LUMBER COMPANY LIMITED**
701 DOMINION BANK BUILDING
TORONTO            CANADA

# RIGHT NOW

## Opportunity is Knocking

## at

## Your Door

YOU don't need to wait for to-morrow to meet opportunity face to face. It is here to-day in the form of a **bigger building movement**—a movement that means bigger business for you.

All over Canada a remarkable change has taken place. People have come back to one-family houses. They have tired of living in apartments, duplexes and the like. They want their own homes and they are building them. Building reports show a surprising increase.

The important factor in this new construction is seeing that houses are more substantially built—that they are good investments which will interest new capital.

Home builders know that houses built of high grade lumber satisfy all demands for permanence and beauty. In your locality there are many builders who will require high quality lumber. Are you prepared to do the business you should.

We are ready to fill your orders at once. Shipments are made from Ontario, Quebec or British Columbia. Every order will receive the careful attention that it is our custom to give.

### Send in your enquiries to-day

# TERRY AND GORDON
### LIMITED
## CANADIAN FOREST PRODUCTS

BRANCH      HEAD OFFICE      BRANCH
MONTREAL    TORONTO    VANCOUVER
     EUROPEAN AGENTS
SPENCER LOCK & Co., LONDON, ENG.

Ontario Representatives for
THE BRITISH COLUMBIA MILLS TIMBER AND TRADING CO., VANCOUVER, B. C.

## "Well Bought is Half Sold!"

Building
Boom
Boosting
Business

means

Badly
Broken
Bins

causing

Rushing
Retailers
Replace
Ravages!

Byng Inlet

Superior
Service
Supplies
Shortages
Swiftly

from

Gilt-edge
Guaranteed
Goods
"Graded

for use."

---

# Canadian General Lumber Co.
Limited

# FOREST PRODUCTS

TORONTO OFFICE :— 712-20 Bank of Hamilton Building
Montreal Office :—514 Canada Cement Company Bldg.
Mills : Byng Inlet, Ont.

# FRASER COMPANIES, Limited

Bleached Sulphite Pulp Mill.    Saw Mills (all Band Saw Mills).    Shingle Mill '
## HERE THEY ARE ON THE MAP

## Mills and Railway Connections

| Saw and Shingle Mills | Railway Connections |
|---|---|
| Cabano, Que ... ... ... .. Temiscouata Ry. |
| Notre Dame du Lac, Que. ... ... .. Temiscouata Ry. |
| Glendyne, Que ... ... ... ... ... C. N. Ry. |
| Estcourt, Que. ... ... ... ... ... C. N. Ry. |
| Sully, N. B. ... ... ... ... ... C. N. Ry. |
| Edmundston, N. B. C.P.R., C.N.R. and Temiscouata Ry. |
| Magaguadavic, N.B. ... ... ... ... C. P. R. |

| Saw and Shingle Mills | Railway Connections |
|---|---|
| Baker Brook, N. B. ... ... C.N.Ry., Temiscouata Ry. |
| Plaster Rock, N.B. ... ... ... ... ... C. P. R. |
| Summit, N. B. ... ... ... ... ... C. N. R. |
| Fredericton, N. B. ... ... ... C.P.Ry and C.N.Ry. |
| Nelson, N. B. ... ... ... ... ... C. N. Ry. |
| Campbellton, N. B. ... ... ... ... C. N. Ry. |

Bleached Sulphite Mill, Edmundston, N. B. ....Ra ilway Connection, C.P.R., C.N.R. and Temiscouata Ry.
Sulphite Mill, Chatham, N. B. .................Ra ilway Connection, C. N. R.

Bleached Sulphite.      Rough and Dressed Spruce.      White Cedar Shingles.      Railway Ties
· Piano Sounding Board Stock a Specialty.

## Selling and Purchasing Offices :--    EDMUNDSTON, N. B.

# BUY
## BRITISH COLUMBIA
# Red Cedar Shingles

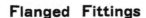

# THE GREAT NATIONAL LUMBER JOURNAL

Pioneer and Leader
in the Industry

# Canada Lumberman
/ounded 1880

Recognized Authority
for Forty Years

Vol. 42        Toronto, May 15, 1922        No. 10

# Increasing Wood Supply of Old Quebec

By H. R. Wickendon, Wayagamack Pulp and Paper Company, Limited,
Three Rivers, Que.

When one compares the evolution of forest exploitation in other countries with that which has taken place in our province, it becomes evident that we have been and are now passing through the same stages of development as others did under similar conditions What appear as errors in our past and even in the present seem to have been made in such countries at some time or other. These apparent errors were to a great extent unavoidable, due to the necessarily slow improvements in forest exploitation in conjunction with the development of wood using industries.

It is evident that all the changes which took place elsewhere were gradual, and carried out with a view to the economic working of the forests.

In considering the progress in forest management which has been made abroad during periods of one hundred years or more, we should not get discouraged at the progress which we are making in our Province as, benefiting by the experience of these other countries, we will undoubtedly attain to their standard in a much shorter time.

In the early days the forest was cut for lumbering purposes only; forest exploitation was hampered by distance and difficult means of communication. Market requirements compelled the lumberman to take out the largest and best trees, paying little heed to the balance, and generally without any view to perpetuating the forest which to them seemed inexhaustible. To-day, with the large demand for wood for pulp and paper, it is necessary to exploit the entire forest, thus calling for a careful system of reforestation, to ensure a continuous supply of wood. Improved means of communication and the presence of communities where woods labor is available makes this more intensive forest exploitation possible. These communities have been built and developed by the lumberman.

As appears above, one finds first a period when the lumberman pure and simple have gone into the forest taking out the choicest trees, with a consequent heavy loss; secondly comes the time when the pulp and paper manufacturer, combined with the lumbermen, are able to take out practically every thing found in the full grown forest,

Successful Regeneration of Balsam and spruce under cover of old hardwoods. This area was cut seven years ago removing all soft woods with the exception of a few healthy spruce seed trees near by. There are now 1000 to 3000 young spruce and balsam growing per acre.

and consequently study carefully the means of reproducing the forest.

To meet present day requirements, the following points should be considered :—

### Wood Economy

This can be effected principally through confining the yearly cut to the smallest area possible, by taking out all the merchantable timber, excepting the necessary health seed trees, in the places where the cutting is carried on. If this is done it will be found that the debris left in cut over areas will lie closer to the ground and decay faster. Thus the loss due to pests and insects and the fire risk will be diminished; moreover, conditions will be favorable to the developments of natural regrowth.

If on the other hand the forest is not cut clean, larger areas must be dealt with each season in order to get the required amount of timber. The trees that are left at present, as all lumbermen know, are mostly those which are stunted and diseased and have failed to attain a required size due to the crowding and consequent lack of light. These form the majority of the seed sowers intended to perpetuate the forest. In other words, the forest perpetuation is effected mostly by the seeds of the unhealthiest specimens that are to be found.

Partial cutting of the forest whereby weak trees are left exposed to storm ravage occasions a great deal of wind fall. These fallen trees together with the debris left from the cutting make a well prepared hot bed for insects and a fire trap. Fire once started in such places is favored by the wind fall and a fair amount of timber still standing. It is more rapidly carried forward from tree to tree by the wind and assumes greater proportions than in a relatively clean cut over area. Fire loss on the whole is therefore likely to be larger where the cutting is irregular and incomplete than where it is thorough and well confined.

Wood loss from sinkage in driving will be diminished if operations are well planned so that logs are not kept in the water too long.

### Economy in the Exploitation of the Forest

It is possible to do a great deal in this direction by careful and proper survey and investigation of the forest before making roads, building dams, or carrying out other work necessary for the getting out of the timber. It also goes without saying that with these careful surveys the cutting of the forest can be carried out with the greatest economy.

In order to operate the forest to the best advantage both as regards the safeguarding of the forest itself and the cost and efficiency of logging operations, it is very essential that operators should have full assurance that they will be able to operate in a certain manner in any one region during as great a term of years as is reasonably possible. The past system of diameter cutting is being acknowledged

Forty year old mixed softwood and hardwood forest. The spruce and balsam are starting to come through the hardwoods. A good crop of wood will be available here in 20 to 30 years

in many cases and under certain conditions, to be out of date, and is to be replaced by a system which will avoid frequent changes in cutting regulations.

### Greatest Perpetual Wood Yield

This item is one that has not been considered seriously heretofore. If the total quantity of wood which has been got out of a particular well defined area, during a long period of years were ascertained, and from this total the average wood production per acre were determined, it would be found that this yearly wood production in our province was small when compared to the yearly wood production obtained for similarly situated forests in foreign countries. In our case the wood yield can be increased; the forest lands of the north can be made to produce more wood. Rational forestry does not aim at preventing full grown forests from being cut but rather at doing everything to keep all areas occupied by growing forests rather than over mature or decrepit forest. This increases or at least maintains the perpetual wood yield. A great deal can be done in this respect without much expenditure by judicious location of cutting operations on the following general principles.

By cutting first in matured areas where wood loss is taking place, or where the growth is practically nil. By preserving areas where young or thrifty timber is standing which will be available after the matured timber above mentioned is exhausted. By care of areas where seedlings and regrowth are to be found. By giving the great-

Seed trees left after clear cutting. Healthy trees will produce good seed in large quantities and are less liable to blow down

est possible production from fire to the entire forest, thus conserving the full grown timber, the young and thrifty timber and the seedling areas.

To successfully carry out the above cutting idea, it is necessary first, to prepare general reconnaissances and preliminary estimates and, secondly, in conjunction with logging operations, to prepare local and more detailed maps and wood inventories.

In the past the fear of additional expense has deterred many from carrying out the survey work. If the surveys are well planned, the saving in operating expenses will more than compensate for the cost of carrying out this work, and will also prevent misplacing of logging improvements, overloading of driving lakes and streams with the ensuing heavy sinkage in logs, and tying up of capital, the waste of time and money in haphazard yearly repeated so-called explorations which are not carried out with the knowledge of trained or experienced men and, lastly, the the leaving of patches of timber which becomes either an expense to salvage later on or must be left to waste. With these details, the practical knowledge and experience of woods managers can be used to the best advantage.

### Ascertaining the Best Method

The thorough knowledge of forest conditions which is obtained by a survey will help to determine what method of reforestation is best suited to the region and will prevent the undertaking of unduly expensive or impractical programs of reforestation in an attempt to provide for the future.

The types of cruising and mapping which should be followed are, first of all, one which is not intensive but comprises making recon-

Fifty year old forest of jack pine and spruce. There is an average of 25 cords of pulp wood per acre on this area

naissance of large areas (general reconnaissance and preliminary estimates and maps), secondly, a system which secures details (local detailed maps and inventories), which are necessary for the immediate cutting requirements and which would include topography maps for use in locating roads, dams and extent of watersheds.

The general reconnaissances or preliminary estimates without going into details, furnish the information of the amount of merchantable timber available and its location, likewise the location and area of young forest and of regrowth such as found on cut over ground or new burns. It will also give sufficient data to establish the growth conditions and what the total yearly continuous wood production ought to be in the limits which are to be operated as a working unit.

From the information obtained by a general reconnaissance the progress of logging operations will be determined. The expenditure for logging improvements can also be kept in proportion to the amount of wood available in each region.

A plan of operating the forest in a working unit can be formulated so that, as far as economically possible, the cutting will progress as follows: (1) immediate cutting to be carried out where the maturity of the wood calls for cutting; (2) cutting of the near future: will take place in what is now younger timber requiring a few years more to fully develope and (3) cutting of the distant future: areas now covered with regrowth will eventually develop into full growth forest and be then available for cutting. Thus, in a cycle of say 60 years or more, the whole forest area will have been gone over once. Such methodical progression of cutting operations will greatly increase the yearly wood production per acre principally because growing forests eventually replace those which are at present either not growing or even deteriorating.

Present forest conditions warrant full confidence for the obtaining of future wood supplies from the forest areas of the Laurentians if operations are carried on in such a manner.

A type of forest which is of importance in providing a future wood yield is the young forest and regrowth which occurs in old burns. Large areas of old burn covered with what is now 20—50 year old forest exists from which a timber and pulp wood supply of the near future will be obtained. An average softwood production of

Heavy windfall of small trees left after cutting to a diameter limit

Partly cut over land after a forest fire. This area was covered with dead trees and debris. As appears in the picture, the fire has been very intense.

A cut over area where only trees over a certain size were taken, the poorest trees being left. These left-over trees have died rotted or blown down. They are a total loss and form a fire trap. This method of cutting is wasting forest resources.

1/5 to ½ cord per acre per year is a usual production on such areas. More recent burns where the fire has neither occurred more than once nor destroyed the surface soil, are to a great extent covered with a fair quantity of healthy softwood seedlings sprung up from seed which survived the fire and are benefiting by the improved soil conditions due to the action of a light fire.

### Hardwood vs. Softwood

Fears are often expressed that hardwoods will encroach upon and greatly diminish the softwood crops of the future. This is, to some extent, true in certain parts of this Province. Fortunately, the shade enduring qualities of certain conniferous trees help them to resist the crowding of hardwoods which do not tolerate shading so well; thus in the Laurentian regions of this Province where poplar and birch, and occasionally yellow birch, occur, mixed in with the softwoods, one finds spruce and balsam seedlings thriving under the cover of tall old birches or poplars, while the birch or poplar seedlings themselves do not seem to develop. For this reason I feel certain that the softwoods will not be harmed by hardwoods competition in such areas.

In many cases the sofwoods rather seem to benefit by the presence of birch and poplar. It should also be kept in mind that a mixed forest of hardwoods and softwoods is the one claimed by the entomologists in Canada, and specially abroad, to be best suited to resist insects or other ravages. It was noticed that in the last epedemic of the balsam budworm, areas which were covered by pure softwood stands were in most instances the worst affected.

It is misleading to judge what our Province can do in wood production if one judges by most of the stands of virgin forest which at present exist. In the natural course of events, a forest is always subjected to attacks by disease and storms, and the older it gets the more it becomes affected. Once having reached a certain age, a steady deterioration takes place, due to decay, pests, wind falls, etc., which offset any growth which may be taking place on the sound trees still existing in the forest. Investigation in any region will reveal an age at which the average production of wood per acre per year will be at a maximum. This is the possible wood growth to be expected in that region and that age will be the most suitable cycle of cutting, since the greatest quantity of wood will be produced continuously. It is obviously not correct to use figures merely obtained in overmatured and uncared for stands in making economical calculations of the future wood supply.

With the Forestry Department of the Province working along these lines, as they are now doing, it only needs a hearty co-operation of the lumbermen in order to attain a perpetual ond increased production.

In summing up, everything goes to show that all efforts must be devoted to forest protection and to the gathering knowledge of forest resources and conditions, to enable one to carry on cutting operations with a view to prevent wood waste and helping natural reforestation.

It is clear that the present natural reproduction is the only one which can renew the forest in the timber limits on a sufficiently large scale to supply future needs and do it in these large regions at a cost that is less than any artificial method.

This, and the fact that natural reproduction does not involve large and immediate cash outlays, more than warrants the adoption and carrying out of well planned forest policies.

## Live Lumber Dealers Talk Quality, not Price

How many lumber dealers really talk about lumber? Prices of lumber—oh, yes! Per M feet—to be sure! But to what extent does a lumber dealer talk about the kind of board, and what the user can get out of it? asks the Long Bell Service Bulletin.

Look down your Main Street a moment, into the stores that are building up trade, stores that are prospering. Outside of special sales, what are they talking to their customers The grocer is telling how good his best grade of flour is, and what kind of bread and cake the housewife can make with it. The dry goods store is laying out its best quality of goods, talking value to the woman patron and, when price is mentioned, pointing out how the customer economizes by buying the best. All down the street, the aggressive lumber dealer included, sales are being made of reputable goods, known goods, because the buyer has been convinced that he usually gets no more than he pays for, and that price is of not so much importance as quality and economical buying.

The talk about lumber often has been how cheap it is and not

how good it is or how useful and dependable it is. Lumber has been sold some times with more worry over what a competitor will ask for the same bill than how well pleased the customer will be with the material. It takes a salesman to get enthused over a pile of good boards and then make the customer see the added values of such boards. But it takes salesmen to sell things these days, no matter whether the article is pins or lumber.

Aggressive dealers are not satisfied just to quote a price on material and let it go at that. Especially when a man is building a house or a barn or any good sized structure that must last, price is not the only thing to be considered. The average man wants to build as economically as he can, but if he knew it he wouldn't cut the quality just to save fifty or a hundred dollars.

K. M. Brown, of the Vancouver Lumber Co., Toronto, returned recently from a business trip to St. John, N. B. and other points east.

# South Western Dealers Assemble in Windsor

## Many Subjects Discussed and Officers Elected for Coming Year—Able Address on "How Building Associations Can Help the Lumberman" —Trade is Improving

John T. Wallace, London
Retiring President S.W.O.R.L.D.A.

Satisfactory in results and enthusiastic in character. was the eigth annual meeting of the South Western Ontario Retail Lumber Dealers' Association, held on April 27th in the Scottish Rite Club Rooms in Windsor. The attendance was representative, and the discussions interesting and profitable. One of the features of the gathering was the visit of W. P. Flint, of Chicago, secretary of the Millwork Cost Bureau, who gave a practical and pointed address at the evening session on "Millwork Costs." Mr. Flint's timely remarks on factory operation certainly opened the eyes of a number of the members to the necessity and advisability of making proper and reliable estimates on all woodworking jobs and eliminating guesswork and cut-throat competition. In the past there has been too much taking certain charges for granted and proceeding on the principle of "Well, if we loose on this, we will make on the next job," or "If Smith can do it for so and so, we can do it for a little less." Mr. Flint showed the basis on which estimates were made, the amount that should be charged for material, work, wastage, overhead, etc. His address is dealt with more fully in another column of the "Canada Lumberman."

Other subjects discussed during the convention were,—"A Universal Catalogue;" "Forming Building and Loan Associations in Ontario;" "The Proposed Mechanics' Lien Act;" "Advertising." "Cost of Motor Truck Operation;" "Summer Outing" and "Trade Prospects."

The Border City dealers were accorded a hearty vote of thanks for their hospitality, an motion of J. L. Naylor, of Essex, and John McGibbon, of Sarnia.

John T. Wallace, of the Dyment-Baker Lumber Co., London, President of the Southwestern Ontario Retail Lumber Dealers Association, presided at the morning session and announced that they were assembling in their annual gathering under somewhat brighter prospects than they did a year ago at Sarnia. The outlook was more promising and a more optimistic feeling prevailed. The membership of the S.W.O.R.L.D.A. was increasing and the organization was stronger than it was a year ago.

On calling for nominations, W. A. Hadley, of Chatham, and J. C. Scofield, of Windsor, promptly proposed that E. C. Russell be made the presiding officer for the coming year. This was carried unanimously. A nominating committee was appointed, consisting of Messrs. Scofield, Hadley and Wallace, to name the Executive for the coming year.

The officers for 1922 are as follows:—
President, E. C. Russell (Walker Sons, Limited) Walkerville;
Vice-President, George N. Kernohan, London;
Secretary-treasurer, B. F. Clarke, Glencoe, (re-elected);
Executive committee,—E. C. Poisson, Ford; Allan McPherson, Glencoe; H. S. Ludlam, Leamington; L. H. Richards, Sarnia; George H. Belton, London; A. J. Clatworthy, Granton; E. O. Penwarden, St. Thomas, and A. W. Osborne, Sandwich.

Among those present during the convention were:—P. G. Piggott, Chatham; M. Hardy, (George H. Belton Lumber Co., Limited) London; J. T. Wallace, London; E. C. Russell, Walkerville; George N. Kernohan, London; Chas. Hubbell, Thamesville; L. H. Laird, Dresden; W. A. Hadley, Chatham; M. R. Bogart, Chatham; J. L. Naylor, Essex; E. C. Poisson, Ford; F. Villineuve,

Walkerville; S. C. Hadley, Chatham; A. D. Park (Dyment-Baker Lumber Co.) London; L. H. Richards, Sarnia; J. C. Scofield (president of the O.R.L.D.A.) Windsor; A. McPherson. Glencoe; B. F. Clarke, Glencoe; T. C. Warwick, Blenheim; Archie Warwick, Blenheim; A. W. Osborne, Sandwich; W. J. Taylor, Ridgetown; H. S. Ludlam. Leamington; C. E. Naylor, Essex; S. Herath, Ojibway; Chester H. Belton, Sarnia; G. D. McPherson, Merlin; Robert Binnie, Leamington; C. P. Wellman, Amherstburg; C. R. Blair, Chatham, Ont.; C. S. Hadley, Chatham; Walter T. Piggott, Windsor; H. Boulbes,(secretary O.R.L.D.A.) Toronto; G. B. Van Blaricom (editor "Canada Lumberman,") Toronto, and others.

These gentlemen were all all in attendance during the day session and at the banquet in the evening when "Millwork Costs" were discussed. Many others were present, including several representatives from Detroit, giving the assembly an international character.

Among the visitors from the City of the Straits were,—R. C. Restrick, of the Restrick Lumber Co.; John Stewart, president of the Detroit Lumber Dealers' Association; John Commelord, former president of the National Retail Lumber Dealers' Association, and George Howenstein, secretary of the Detroit Lumber Dealers' Association and Credit Bureau. These gentlemen were given a warm welcome and all conveyed fraternal greetings.

### Universal Catalogue and Standardization

S. Herath, of Ojibway, dealt with the subject of a Universal Catalogue. He said all dealers had surplus materials, odds and ends that they did not know what to do with unless they disposed of them at a bargain price. They were oddments of flooring, ceiling, mouldings, etc. He thought the adoption of certain standard types and designs in woodwork would eliminate much of this waste from time to time. If a Universal Catalogue was printed, it could be employed by the dealers who could order from it. Different lines of flooring were used by retail lumbermen, and there was no standard type of matching. If an order was placed with another concern, the matching would not come together. It was thus difficult to keep down the tail ends of stock. The same thing applied to mouldings, base, trim, doors, etc.

A Universal Catalogue, which is published in Chicago, was exhibited by the speaker, who said he thought such a step was a good idea. From this catalogue standard sizes in mouldings, panels, trim, etc., could be ordered. The catalogue was attractively illustrated and he was of the opinion that the S. W. O. R. L. D. Association should consider the matter of a Universal Catalogue and urge upon the manufacturers to adopt a standard system of various sizes and dimensions. If such a plan were carried out, all could work on a more economic and satisfactory basis. Manufacturers and dealers would have to co-operate in the project which would take considerable time to perfect, but eventually orders could be made by naming a certain number and design in the book.

A short discussion followed, in which Mr. Herath was asked a number of questions and in reply he stated that he thought that such a move would have to come first from the manufacturers.

### Work of Building and Loan Bodies

"Forming Building and Loan Associations in Canada," is a subject of much interest at the present time and, on the invitation of W. A. Hadley, of Chatham, the gathering was addressed by K. V. Haymaker, Secy-Treas of the Home Building Savings and Loan Co. of Detroit. Mr. Haymaker described the function and purpose of building and loan associations, saying they were mutual, co-operative concerns, operating on the basis of the members uniting together for financial well being. They had both investing and borrowing members. Any movement that assisted in the erection of homes was of interest to the lumbermen, and the speaker pictured the many buildings that could be put up with the aid of such an association. Building and loan societies restricted their investments to home building or the purchases of homes. House building added the speaker, is a vital part of the business in which you gentlemen are interested and, with out that feature you know what the lumber

business to day would be. The bulk of the business of the world was done on some line of credit. Banks were limited in their investments or loans to comparatively short terms and were circumscribed by so many federal regulations that they would never be a factor in supplying funds for mortgage loans.

The building and loan societies relied on the small savings of the people and the average person building a dwelling desired a long time loan, which could be paid off in weekly or monthly installments by the owner. Such men are the best types of citizens and made payments on their places like rent. In the state of Ohio in order to stimulate building operations, there are 800 building and loan associations formed and they have 530 millions in assets There are more such associations in America to day than there are national banks and the amount paid in was more than double the capital stock of the national banks. Building and loan bodies restricted their operations to houses principally and the people used such organizations to deposit their savings. Every time such an association makes a loan on a building, it meant the sale of a bill of lumber. The rich man was so taxed on income etc., that he did not care to advance money and the banks and life insurance companies were cut down to short time loans. There was little relief to be afforded from these sources and in consequence great stimulus had been given to such associations as he had referred to. The latter had made it convenient, easy and cheap to borrow money and had been of much benefit to the public at large. The speaker suggested that the Southwestern Lumber Dealers Association should look in the matter and see what they could do along this line. He thought a number of building and loan associations could be formed in Ontario to supply mortgage money, which would mean more building, employment for workmen, the sale of lumber and the ushering in of good times, thus helping to solve many problems which different committees faced today.

On motion of J. C. Scofield and W. A. Hadley, a hearty vote of thanks was tendered Mr. Haymaker for his instructive remarks, Mr. Scofield said the banks were of little help as a loaning proposition and loan associations would, he thought, prove advantageous to the people and the retail lumberman. A committee of Messrs. Herath, J. L. Naylor and J. C. Scofield was appointed to look into the matter and report at a future meeting on the advisability of forming a building and loan association.

### When Should the Retailer Buy

"Is this a good time for lumbermen to stock up" was discussed by W. A. Hadley, of Chatham. He said that it would be presumptuous on his part to suggest a proper period to purchase lumber. He thought the average dealer should buy only for his needs as he saw them but should not go beyond the point where the interest on the money invested, taxes, insurance etc. added to the cost of lumber in the yard faster than the advance in price. Replacing stock under such circumstances was not profitable. Each dealer must be governed largely by local conditions. He thought no retailer should stock up simply to fill up his yard space or increase his piles. Local surroundings, Mr. Hadley asserted, had much to do with the situation and materials that were called for in Chatham might not be sought at all in Windsor or some other city. Each lumber merchant had to use his own judgment. Many a traveller would say buy now as the price is going up and probably on the following week there would be a decline in the figure. It was therefore, up to every man to learn by present experience, and what he had undergone in the past. This should be the best guide and lesson for the future.

### Mechanics' Lien Act for the Dominion

"What are we going to do about a new Lien Act?" was the subject dealt with by H. Boultbee, of Toronto, secretary of the Ontario Retail Lumber Dealers' Association. Mr. Boultbee explained that steps had been taken to have the new bill passed and the various features in the proposed measure. The latest word received was that nothing would be done this session in the provincial legislature in the way of passing a new Mechanics' and Wage Earners' Lien Act, The Attorney-General of Ontario had received word from Ottawa in which it was pointed out that the Dominion Government was considering the passing of a uniform law, applicable to the various provinces of the Dominion. The federal authorities were desirous of securing the views of the different sections in order to draft the proposed legislation.

It was thought by Messrs. C. H. Belton, W. A. Hadley, John T. Wallace and others that the co-operation of other organizations interested in the house-building line should be secured, particularly in regard to the amount which the owner should be compelled to hold back in order to satisfy claims for material and wages. In the bill, (which it was until lately thought would be brought down,) it has been suggested by the lumberman that the hold-back should be 35%.

If other organizations joined with the retail lumbermen, greater strength and influence would be brought to bear upon the representatives of the lumber dealers.

A motion was passed expressing approval of the work that had been done and is being done by the O. R. L. D. A. in connection with the securing of a new Mechanics' Lien Act, and that an endeavor be made to have a round table session at which representatives of contractors' associations, builders' exchanges and other bodies might be called in to discuss the measure. This was moved by C. H. Belton and seconded by J. T. Wallace.

### Tells of the Great Summer Outing

L. H. Richards, of Sarnia, chairman of the Excursion Committee, explained in detail the summer outing, which will take place up the lakes on the S S "Huronic," of the Northern Navibation Co., starting at Windsor and Sarnia on June 23 and returning on June 27. He stated that a large number of reservations had already been made and the success of the trip seemed assured. It was necessary that the complement of 175, which must be secured by the lumbermen before June 10th, should be guaranteed at the earliest possible date. A number of the Michigan retailers would also participate in the jaunt.

Mr. Richards explained many other details, all of which have been outlined in previous editions of the "Canada Lumberman," and will be found in another page of the present issue. He urged upon all the necessity of sending in cheques, covering the amount of the fare, by return mail. The committee wished to get the reservations and tickets cleaned up as quickly as possible so that there would not be a rush at the last moment.

### Some Terse Talks on Advertising

A logical and edifying address was given by Chester H. Belton, of Sarnia, on "What Form of Advertising is Most Productive?" He said all should believe in the business in which they were engaged. They had to make a living out of the lumber line and were naturally anxious to see sales increase and home-building proceed on a larger scale. Too many lumbermen took it for granted that people when requiring anything in their line would come to their door and that there was no necessity for them advertising since they were dealing in a more or less staple product. There was grave danger of getting in a rut and thinking that people will bring in their house plans whenever they were prepared to build and the dealers would thus sell lots of lumber.

The retail lumberman was a real force and factor in the progress and upbuild of his community. He should believe in his business and go out and talk about it. Dealers did not boost their own business enough in the district in which they lived, and advise people as to the best methods to employ in matters of construction. Sometimes an outsider stepped in where business was stagnant, bringing in new ideas and wakening up all the other men in the town. By initiative and foresight, such a merchant forced his way to the front.

There were several means of advertising. One was in the columns of the press or the indirect method of appeal. Another was the direct method of sending to a selected list illustrated literature, booklets, circulars, etc., with the idea of creating in the mind of the people a desire to build. He said there were numerous booklets sent out indiscriminately, but he thought that there should be some attention and thought given to the appropriateness of the advertising matter before it was posted in order that it might reach the most likely prospects. Cuts in catalogues would often pull more quickly than to simply advertise John Smith, lumber dealer etc. The main idea was not for a dealer to advertise himself so much as to make known his service, to create the idea and desire for building, and show the people something tangible in the way of completed homes, barns, garages, etc.

Mr. Belton went on to say that when one wished for anything he usually got it in the end if he kept after it, and dealers should put the same feeling into the advertising, so far as stimulating the home-owning instinct was concerned.

The speaker strongly advised each dealer to circularize his own territory with literature, howing cuts of homes, barns, sheds, etc., pointing out that he, (the dealer,) could supply bills of material for such structures and that further detailed information and prices would be gladly given at the office. He did not believe in advertising lumber prices too strongly, as such a proceeding often aroused in a competitor a feeling of resentment. Frequently prices were presented merely as a bait and used to get men into the office in an effort to sell them something else.

Mr. Belton again emphasized in his remarks the necessity of advertising in order to create the desire to build and to show the people something tangible in that line. No narrow minded policy should be pursued. While the advertising of one firm might send a customer

George N. Kernohan, London,
Elected Vice-President.

B. F. Clarke, Glencoe,
Re-elected Secy.-Treas.

George H. Belton, London,
Re-elected Director.

E. C. Poisson, Ford,
Newly-elected Director.

A. W. Osborne, Sandwich,
Newly-elected Director.

T. C. Warwick, Blenheim,
Retiring Director.

W. J. Greer, St. Thomas,
Retiring Director.

M. R. Bogart, Chatham,
Retiring Director.

John McGibbon, Sarnia,
Retiring Director.

S. Herath, Oilbway,
Retiring Director.

J. A. McPherson, Merlin,
Retiring Director.

Chas. Hubbell, Thamesville,
Retiring Director.

Some Newly-elected Officers and Retiring Directors of the South Western
Ontario Retail Lumber Dealers' Association

to another man in the same line to get material for a home, still the procedure might work both ways and, perhaps, a competitor's customer would come to you.

Mr. Belton rather favored the idea in the lumber trade of direct advertising on a number of lines rather than indirect through the newspapers. All kinds of publicity had their advantages and a retailer should use the means which brought him the best results. The main thing was for the retailer to advertise and show that he was a real, progressive, constructive factor in the community.

S. Herath, of Ojibway, thought that in many cases advertising through the press was just as essential and effective as direct advertising by means of the mail. To make known a special article to a special class, often cost as much, when sending out printed matter through the post, as it would to use advertising space in the papers, when the public at large would be made acquainted with the line and much wider publicity received. Persons liked to look over what appeared in the newspapers, and he had great faith in this kind of publicity, particularly in connection with real estate in which activity he was engaged, as well as the lumber business. "We are all doing too little advertising to market our products," concluded Mr. Herath.

G. B. Van Blaricom, editor, "Canada Lumberman," Toronto, was also asked to give his views on publicity for retail lumbermen, and pointed out that, as a class, retailers of forest products are not doing the amount of advertising that they should, particularly in the press. Any form of publicity was better than none at all, and the lumber dealer should be to the forefront, especially at this season of the year, in fostering the home-building idea, showing what service he can render and the material he can supply in connection with house construction and other work being carried out. Too many yardmen took it for granted that because they had been established so many years or were known personally, that this in itself was sufficient. Some instances were given of the effective and timely publicity of certain lumber firms who have built up large businesses through the use of printers' ink.

# How Millwork Cost Bureau Applies Burden

## Splendid Address Delivered at South Western Ontario Retail Lumber Dealers' Association by Mr. Flint, of Chicago, on Proper Way to Figure Costs—What Estimating Embraces

W. P. Flint, of Chicago, who is Secretary of the Millwork Cost Bureau, gave an able and comprehensive address on "Millwork Costs" at the banquet held in connection with the annual convention of the Southwestern Ontario Retail Lumberman at Windsor on April 27th. His remarks were followed with great interest. Mr. Flint answered many questions that were put to him by different retail dealers, clearly and promptly. In order that there might be no misunderstanding regarding the functions of the Millwork Cost Bureau, he stated at the outset that the Bureau was not a commercial organization. It was a co-operative association of sash, door, and millwork manufacturers of the United States and Canada, not organized for profit but for the sole purpose of supplying the industry with accurate information covering the cost of manufacturing millwork and the education of the estimators in properly surveying quantities from architects' plans and the use of Cost Schedules as a basis for accurately predetermining cost of production.

The Bureau's activities cover the following service, known as "General Service," with the cost absorbed by dues, and "Special Service" entailing an extra charge.

### General Service—Cost Absorbed by Dues

Cost Book "A" was designed to assist manufacturers of special or odd millwork in predetermining the probable cost of the varied product on which they are required to furnish estimates. It is particularly adapted to the figuring of architects' plans and special lists. The book is made up of over seventy-five printed schedules in loose-leaf form. Its entire contents represent the composite data of the Bureau's membership—which now numbers approximately 500 firms—and its schedules present to the estimator cost guides that because of their arrangement and scope, are applicable to practically every class of work ranging from the most simple to the extremely intricate constructions. This flexibility is accomplished through the employment of what are termed "Basis List Prices" and "Extras." Each schedule includes also "Specifications" indicative of the construction contemplated by the Basis List Prices. Any variance from the specifications is then adjusted by applying to the Basis Prices the additions or deductions—as the case may require—shown under Extras. All prices in the Cost Book "A" are list, subject to discount.

It is evident, therefore, that the whole Cost Book "A" procedure is entirely devoid of arbitrary costs and that it will assist the estimator to attain an accurate conception of values by impelling him to dissect the work he estimates.

### Cost Exhibit File

A set of Cost Exhibits in binder form. These exhibits are copies of cost records of especial significance, received from those of the membership who operate our Standard Cost Finding System. Each week new exhibits are mailed to be inserted in the binder. All exhibits are a scientific analysis of actual cost experience of member factories, and indicate on the adverse side the quantities of material and the hours of labor consumed, together with the proper burden or overhead applicable to the material and labor elements. Waste of course is accounted for in the material costs. In order that each record may be thoroughly comprehensive, a sketch is supplied also of the work under consideration. On the reverse side of the cost exhibits a blank form is provided, by means of which members are enabled to insert their own rates and thus build up cost on a basis of the labor hours supplied by the contributor of the original record.

### Estimator's Correspondence Course

A Course in Modern Estimating Procedure, which expounds not only estimating proper, but also the subjects of PLAN INTERPRETATION and QUANTITY SURVEY. Five sets of plans and specifications,—composed of three residences, one store and Boat building and one school-house—together with a binder of proper explanatory text constitute the working material of the study. Enrollments are not confined to experienced estimators—both the novice and the seasoned man will find it equally instructive and interesting. This course does not require the students to occupy themselves with anything except such matters as pertain to millwork estimating. Neither is it of a theoretical nature, but because the student figures precisely such jobs as occur in the every-day operation of a millwork establishment, he is trained in an altogether practical manner.

In addition to Plan Interpretation and Quantity Survey, the course teaches the Practical Application of Cost Book "A"; in fact, the student is not called upon to formulate any price from an outside source. Through this supervisory service, members are therefore assured that the whole subject of estimating is thoroughly understood and disposed of in a manner that makes of the estimator's every-day work a pleasant and interesting science, rather than a nerve-wracking, "hit or miss" problem.

Enrollments are accepted from member-firms only—not from individuals—and while no extra charge is made, a deposit to the amount of $10.00 is required for each person entered in the study. This deposit is returned at such time as the entrant completes the study or for a legitimate reason is excused from doing so.

### Special Service—Entailing an Extra Charge

For those who are conducting cost systems, or desire to install one, the service of our travelling Cost Accountants is available. These accountants are capable of compiling from your past operating period a scientific schedule of equitable burden rates and to arrange your accounts in such manner as will automatically develop future burden rates.

We maintain also a Supervisor of Cost Recording, whose function it is to train your employees to proficiently compile cost records.

These two branches of service entail an extra charge that represents only cost to the Bureau. About one third of our membership, in addition to being subscribers for our General Service, have also availed themselves of our accounting service.

In any community where a substantial number of members desire to do so, they may procure the services of one of our represen-

tatives for a series of lectures in their city. Inasmuch as all subjects pertaining to cost and estimating procedure are thoroughly expounded during the course of these lectures, they have been found particularly appealing to Estimators' Clubs. The number of lectures before any given group varies, it being dependent upon local conditions and the wishes of the individual members.

No charge is made for the lecturer's time, but the participating members are rendered an invoice which absorbs railroad fare, hotel and living expenses.

The above sets forth our service to the industry and the cost therefor is as follows :

The membership is divided into 3 classes; viz., "Active members—Class 1," "Active Members—Class 2" and "Associate Members—Class 3."

These classifications are dependent upon the amount of annual sales. Firms whose annual sales exceed $300,000.00 are required to subscribe as Class 1 members. Firms whose annual sales exceed $100,000.00, but are not more than $300,000.00, are required to subscribe as Class 2 members. Firms whose annual sales do not exceed $100,000.00 are required to subscribe as Class 3 members.

An Initiation Fee of $50.00 is charged each member. The dues

W. P. Flint, Chicago
Secretary Millwork Cost Bureau

are, for Class 1, $240.00 per year; for Class 2, $120.00 per year; for Class 3, $50.00 per year. All dues are payable quarterly in advance.

Now that you are familiar with the object and service rendered by the Bureau, I wish to say a few words on Cost Finding and Burden Compilation, without any attempt at technical elaboration, and this subject may be briefly depicted by means of the following "Statement of Cost." These figures are taken from an actual cost audit and have been revised only so far as to eliminate odd numbers, thus making the process of burden compilation readily discernible. Each of the burden unite; that is, items 5, 6, 7, 8 and 9, includes its proper share of interest on investment for land, buildings, equipment and average stock; taxes on the same items; depreciation on buildings and equipment and insurance on buildings, equipment and average stock, and of course also the supplies, repair and labor expenses peculiar to each unit.

### Cost Statement—12 Months

Direct Material
1. Lumber (1,000,000 board ft.)........................$50,000.00
2. Glass, Veneers, Screen Wire, Pulleys, Weights, ....
   Cord, Stock Millwork, etc. .......... ......... ...  14,000.00
Direct Labor
3. Machine Labor (26,000 hours) .........  18,000.00
4. Bench Labor (40,000 hours) .............  26,000.00

                 Direct Cost ...................... $108,000.00

Yard and Factory Burden
5. Yard Expense (1,000,000 bd ft)    $6,000.00
6. Kiln Expense (500,000 bd ft)        4,000.00
7. Machine Expense (26,000 hours)     13,000.00
8. Bench Expense (40,000 hours)       12,000.00   35,000.00

                 Factory Cost ........             $143,000.00
Commercial Burden
9. Warehouse, Delivery, Selling and Administrative
   Expense ................. ......... ....... .......   28,000.00

                 Total Cost .... .. ..... ... .. ... .. $171,000.00

The respective burden rates would be calculated in this fashion :
Lumber—Yardage and Handling Burden
   Item No. 5, Yard Expense $6,000 divided by 1,000,000 board ft.
   handled equals $6 per M. B. M. burden rate.
Lumber—Kiln Burden
   Item No. 6, Kiln Expense $4,000 divided by 500,000 board ft.
   dried, equals $8 per M. B. M. burden rate. This rate is in addition to the $6 per M. B. M. rate for Yardage and Handling.
Machine Burden
   Item No. 7, Machine Expense $13,000 divided by 26,000 hours
   equals 50c. per hour burden rate.
Bench Burden
   Item No. 8, Bench Expense $12,000 divided by 40,000 hours,
   equals 30c. per hour burden rate.
Commercial Burden ............ ............ .......... .....
   Item No. 9, Commercial Expense $28,600 divided by Factory
   Cost $143,000 equals 20 per cent burden rate.

#### Application of the M. C. B. Burdens

Under the M. C. B. cost plan the burden application to a cost record of six yellow pine stair newels, using the foregoing rates, would be :

### Example "I"

| Material | | |
|---|---:|---:|
| Delivered Purchase Price 1" B & B Yel. Pine | $90.00 | |
| Yardage and Handling Burden .............. | 6.00 | |
| 70 Board ft BM (including waste) @........ | $96.00 | $ 6.72 |
| Machine | | |
| Labor (3 hours) ........ | $ 2.00 | |
| Burden (3 hours) ........ @ $.50 | 1.50 | 3.50 |
| Bench | | |
| Labor (28 hours) ........ | $20.10 | |
| Burden (28 hours) ........ @ $.30 | 8.40 | 28.50 |
| | Factory Cost......... | $38.72 |
| Commercial Burden 20 per cent .............. | | 7.74 |
| | Total Cost............ | $46.46 |

While this method is primarily for a Millwork Manufacturer, the principles are applicable to a retail lumber yard, as the lumber handling expense of both branches of the industry is identical and can be applied in the same manner, which loads the lumber on the wagon ready for delivery in the retail business and takes it up to the saws in a manufacturing plant. The commercial expense can be applied in the same manner and should prove equally usable in either branch.

The question now arises as to how the schedules in Cost Book "A" are compiled. This is best demonstrated by the following figures, which are a part of our Moulding Reference Schedule :

| Wood 1" Thick | | Uns Birch | Fir | P1RO | YP |
|---|---|---|---|---|---|
| Grade | | FAS | No. 2C1&Btr | FAS | B&Btr |
| Waste—Percent of net footage | | 30% | 20% | 30% | 10% |
| Rip. & Cut. Hours per M gross bd. ft. | | 11.33 | 8.67 | 11.33 | 6.00 |
| Delivered Purchase Price | | 105.00 | 63.00 | 105.00 | 68.50 |
| Yard Burden | | 5.30 | 5.30 | 5.30 | 5.30 |
| Kiln Burden | | 6.00 | .00 | 6.00 | .00 |
| Ripping & Cutting : | | | | | |
| | .60 Wages | | | | |
| | .57 Burden | | | | |
| Hours as above @ | 1.17 | 13.26 | 10.14 | 13.26 | 7.02 |
| Without Waste | | 139.56 | 78.44 | 139.56 | 74.82 |
| Waste | | 38.87 | 15.69 | 38.87 | 7.48 |
| Sticking & Sanding : | | | | | |
| | .60 Wages | | | | |
| | .57 Burden | | | | |
| 11.67 hours @ | 1.17 | 13.65 | 13.65 | 13.65 | 13.65 |
| Factory Cost | | 192.08 | 107.78 | 192.08 | 95.96 |
| Commercial Burden 20% | | 36.42 | 21.56 | 36.42 | 19.19 |
| Total Cost per M net bd. ft. | | $219.50 | $129.34 | $219.50 | $115.14 |

Total Cost divided by $125.00 equals
"Percentage Of" Standard Mould-
ing Basis                        174.80%   103.47%   174.80%   92.11%
2½ times above equals Cost Book "A"
"Percentage Of" Standard Moulding
Basis                        *437.00%  *258.65%  *437.00%  *230.28%

NOTE—The "Standard Moulding Basis" on Page 5 B of Cost Book "A" is equivalent to $125.00 per M; hence the division by $125.00 to produce a "Percentage Of" the Standard Moulding Basis.

These are so arranged that the individual firm is enabled to supply the actual cost of lumber, labor, and burdens applying in any plant, thereby developing the cost for that plant. To demonstrate how easily this can be accomplished I will call on Mr. M. R. Bogart, of Chatham, to give me this information as pertaining to his own plant, and will work it out on the blackboard, using as a basis oak,

at $125.00 per M with wages of 75c. per hour and burdens of 75cts. per hour. The cost of producing oak moulding is shown to be $2.05 per inch per 100 lineal feet, or 203.60 per cent of the Universal List.

**Lumber Waste.—the Percentages**

Mr. Flint gave the waste percentages occasioned in the production of first clear lumber, including grade, all defects eliminated (clear one face and two edges) from first and second or B and B stock. "These figures," he said, include all waste incidental to kiln-drying, planing, ripping, cutting and sticking and are to be added to the net lumber realized—not the amount cut up.

| | Stock 4/4 in. and under | Stock 5/4 in. and up |
|---|---|---|
| Basswood | 15% | 20% |
| Red Birch | 35 | 45 |
| Unselected Birch | 30 | 40 |
| Cypress | 15 | 20 |
| Fir | 30 | 35 |
| Fir Squares | | 12% |
| Red Gum | 20 | 25 |
| Unselected Gum | 20 | 25 |
| Mahogany | 20 | 25 |
| Plain Red Oak | 30 | 40 |
| Plain White Oak | 40 | 50 |
| Quartered Red Oak | 30 | 40 |
| Quartered White Oak | 35 | 45 |
| White Pine | 15 | 20 |
| Yellow Pine | 10 | 15 |
| Poplar | 25 | 30 |
| Spruce | 20 | 25 |
| Quartered Sycamore | 30 | 40 |
| Walnut | 35 | 45 |

Of utmost importance to the industry is the New Correspondence Course for Estimators, which is conducted by the Bureau, the cost thereof being absorbed by the dues.

The new Course, in addition to teaching the correct application of Cost Book "A," also clearly and completely covers the subjects of Plan Interpretation and Quantity Survey, and embraces six assignments.

Five sets of plans and specifications covering various types of buildings, and one set of "Test Questions" are employed to illustrate the work of the Course. A perspective drawing of the building involved in each assignment is furnished to assist the student in visualizing how the structure will appear when completed. All data except the blue prints, are contained in a loose-leaf binder, so that the text and student's solutions of problems will in the future form a neat and valuable reference volume. Special printed work sheets properly punched so as to fit binder, are furnished to the student free of charge.

**Course is Comprehensive and Thorough**

Preceding Assignment I are eighteen pages of text, covering general information pertaining to Plan Interpretation and Quantity Survey. The first plan and accompanying data constitute Assignment I, which is the "Example" or model procedure to be followed in the remaining four plan assignments. Assignments I, III, and IV cover residences, while Assignment V embraces a store and flat building, and Assignment VI a school. Assignment II comprises a set of "Test Questions," to ascertain if the estimator is thoroughly familiar with all the preceding work. All assignments, except II, are subdivided into a convenient number of parts, each involving a department, such as exterior frames, stairs, etc., which subdivisions are known as "Lessons."

In Assignment I the items of millwork are surveyed by us from the "Example" plan and the TOTAL Cost Book "A" list, with page references for each item is shown. This list of items is known as a "General Estimate," owing to the fact that it is to illustrate the manner in which a commercial estimate should appear. Each "Lesson" of Assignment I illustrates the ITEMIZED application of Cost Book "A" and also contains a discussion of the Quantity Survey principles involved, and a discussion of the Cost Book "A" schedule applying to the department under consideration. In solving Assignments III to VI inclusive, the omitting, of course, the Quantity Survey and Cost Book "A" discussions. The list of millwork surveyed from the plan in each case by the student, also the application of Cost Book "A," will be checked at our office and the duplicate copy returned to the student with corrections and suggestions as required.

Experience in figuring architects' plans nor a knowledge of Cost Book "A" is not required of those who wish to be enrolled in the new Course, as these subjects will be thoroughly covered, so that even the novice should experience no difficulty in satisfactorily proceeding with the study.

**Enrollment for New Course**

Applications for enrollment must be made on our regular printed form and signed by an officer of the firm. You will note from Enrollment Form, that each member is to furnish a deposit of $10.00 per student, which deposit is to be returned upon completion of the course, or where a legitimate excuse for failure to do so exists. The new Course, will constitute a branch of the Bureau's regular service, entailing no additional expense, and the deposit or temporary charge referred to above is required merely as an assurance that only such parties will be enrolled as are sincerely interested in an early and successful conclusion of their study.

Much time and money have been expended in the compilation of this Course, and those who have examined the work have pronounced it to be the most complete and comprehensive technical Course ever placed at the disposal of an industry or the public. In addition to the expert knowledge in the possession of our Estimating Department, this Course also reflects the opinions of over one hundred experienced estimators, who were interviewed and consulted during the progress of the work.

This new branch of our service embodies almost limitless possibilities, as it is a well-known fact that the industry in the past has suffered immeasurably from the effects of inaccurate plan interpretation and quantity survey. It is obvious that the good effects accruing from a knowledge of one's cost can be largely nullified where the list of material surveyed from the plan is inaccurate to the extent of from ten to twenty per cent. The Course is an exposition of the most practical and meritorious methods in vogue in our industry today and should appeal to the student, as the mass of irreverent matter which most students of commercial courses are obliged to contend with has been eliminated. The magnitude of the above work is being fully appreciated and, while it has been in the hands of the industry for only the last thirty days, the response has been greater than was even expected both from our Canadian members as well as those in the States.

### Thirty-Three Years with Walker Sons

Eben Campbell Russell, who was named after a good Scotch uncle, is the new president of the South Western Ontario Retail Lumber Dealers' Association, in which body he has always taken an active interest since its inception in 1914. Mr. Russell was vice-president last year, and his elevation to chief executive of this live and energetic body, was well received. He has been in the lumber business for practically 50 years, starting as a boy in Williamsport, Pa., where he did tallying for Dodge & Co., with whom his father was engaged for many years. The Dodge Company later acquired extensive timber limits in Ontario and operated mills on the Severn, at Byng Inlet, Collingwood, Waubaushene and other points. It was in the early 70's that the new president of the South Western Ontario Retail Lumber Dealers' Association came to Canada at the request of his firm, and began measuring lumber in their Severn mill. The following year he moved to Collingwood where he remained seven years, working in the mill yard. He left Dodge & Co., in 1887 to go with Secord, Cousins & Co., at their plant in Goderich, where he was an inspector for some months.

E. C. Russell, Walkerville
New President S.W.O.R.L.D.A.

The next position held by Mr. Russell was with the Muskoka Mill & Lumber Co., (whose headquarters were at Albany), when he scaled logs in a Muskoka camp for one winter. On completing the operation he returned to Goderich where he was engaged by Williams & Murray as manager of their mill-yard for several years. His next job was with the Georgian Bay Lumber Co., of Waubaushene, where he took charge of their yard and remained with them for nearly three years, and in November 1889 he entered the services of Walker Sons, (then Hiram Walker & Sons, Limited,) at Walkerville, which town in those days was not the up-to-date, progressive community that it is to-day, with its paved streets and all modern improvements.

Mr. Russell has been with Walker Sons, as manager of their yard and woodworking plant for 33 years, and is still going strong. He has evinced deep interest in Walkerville, being a member of the council for nine years and mayor for two terms. He has served on the Public Library Board and other public bodies and has always taken a prominent part in Masonic activities, having gone through the chairs in the Blue Lodge, Chapter and Preceptory.

# *How Motor Truck Solves the Delivery Problem*

### *Representative Dealer Tells South Western Ontario Lumber Merchants That its Use Pays Every Time and is More Economical than Horse Haul*

P. G. Piggott, Chatham, Ont.

"The Cost of Operation and Maintenance of Motor Trucks" was dealt with by Percy G. Piggott, of the P. G. Piggott Lumber Co., Chatham Ont., who said that they had just completed one year, operating a ton and a half truck in connection with their business and that it was their first experience in this line of merchandising. Continuing he gave his personal views on the truck delivery problem and the expense of the same as follows:—

I am thoroughly convinced, figuring a motor truck against horses, that according to money invested, the investment is about the same. Say $2,000.00 worth of truck will do equally as much as $2,000.00 put into horses and waggons, or vice versa; therefore, it develops into a problem of service and maintenance. In the first place I estimate it takes the time of one and three quarters men against one man's time on a truck. As there are times with teams, the two drivers work together, I figure that I save three quarters of one man's pay in getting the same work done by truck.

Then the item of insurance, I can have my outfit protected for about half the cost as to horses.

In cases of deliveries, when one man is used, the quickness of the truck will make the difference of one fraction a man's time, or I have the use of a man at actual work in my yard one quarter longer; therefore, I estimate I actually save the maintenance of one man.

We now come to the time of the season where a truck is at a disadvantage, or I might say, more so than horses, for when a truck is at a disadvantage, horses are also handicapped. There are about ten weeks of the year when our truck is at a three quarters disadvantage, and horses one half, due to spring and fall conditions of road, but you will agree this is one of our quietest times in business, therefore, the actual loss is not large, but is hard to estimate, as our roads are getting better which makes, and will make in the future, big differences. The advantage that the truck imparts to merchandising and service, I can only leave to your own good judgment.

Now, to get down to actual figures as I find them, considering we have the same amount invested in equipment, our interest on investment and our depreciation will be about the same.

We will now take the truck end of maintenance, as my figures show:

|  | DR. |  |  |
|---|---|---|---|
| Oil, Gas, repairs | $ 529.81 |  |  |
| Estimate, to put it low, | 3/4 | man's pay | $700.00 |
| Credit balance | $170.19 |  |  |

I estimate that a truck does the work of three single horses or one team a nd one single horse, and figure up-keep of horses at:

.75 cents per day ......................................$ 814.25
Pay to cartage for goods during 10 weeks
    truck was at disadvantage        121.75

                 Dr. banance   $ 682.50

So my figures show me that I am making a saving of $852.69 per year without any charge for up-keep or horse equipment.

It is recognized by the "Engineering Society of America" "Dominion Government" & U. S. Government, that the actual investment as to horses and trucks relating to work is about even, with a lean-to the truck of 1/8. It is also recognized under the same investment that the truck saves one man's pay. Big merchandising concerns argue that the motor truck opens up 20 miles of radius more business, and is worth 1-1/2 against one in service.

Some will question you about accidents which run into big money, but you must remember that both equipments will be subjected to accidents. In the matter of mishaps much depends on the driver, whether he is careful or careless.

## South Western Ontario Retailers Banqueted at Windsor

At the banquet in the evening a number of Detroit lumbermen were present. The spread in the ball room of the Scottish Rite Club was an inviting one and the menu was most tempting. Over fifty lumbermen were in attendance.

E. C Russell, the newly-elected president of the Association, presided and welcomed the visitors from the City of the Straits. J. C. Scofield, president of the O.R.L.D.A., and Mr. Russell both joined in greeting the men from across the border, which gave the assembly an international character. Messrs. R. C. Restrick, who had the pleasure of addressing the South Western Association members at Sarnia last year, and John Stewart, president of the Detroit Lumber Dealers' Association, extended best wishes from the Detroit dealers.

John Commeford, former President of the National Retail Lumber Dealers' Association, expressed his pleasure at being present, and thought that much good could come by an association of the National body with that of Ontario. Both organizations had many things in common. There were several matters of mutual interest in which he believed the two bodies could join forces. Mr. Commeford spoke of the great importance and responsibility of the retail lumber interests in the United States, and said the latter had more money invested in the lumber line than had the manufacturers.

Touching again, on the National and Ontario Associations, the speaker said their aims were identical, and he could only emphasize the advisibility of affiliation. One feature, that might be of interest to the Ontario body was insurance, which was furnished to the members of the National Association at actual cost, and this figure was much less than that of the old line insurance companies.

J. C. Scofield, of Windsor, the president of the Ontario Retail Lumber Dealers' Association, reciprocated the kind expressions of the American visitors, and invited them to attend the next annual convention of the O.R.L.D.A., which would be held at the new Prince Edward Hotel, Windsor, on January 24th, 25th and 26th. There was no reason why the Ontario and National Associations of the United States should not be affiliated in some way. They had many interests in common, and questions often arose on which unity of action might be taken. There were also problems in the solution of which the wisdom and co-operation of the two Associations would be of advantage, and the subject would be taken up at the next convention.

George Howenstein, secretary of the Detroit Lumber Dealers' Association, also spoke briefly.

Mr. Flint was next introduced and gave an able address on "Millwork Costs." At the close a hearty vote of thanks was tendered him by Messrs. W. A. Hadley and J. T. Wallace, on behalf of the Association.

J. C. Scofield was appointed chairman of a committee, with power to add to the number in regard to starting a class on millwork cost and estimating in the Windsor distrilt.

Some wholesale lumber salesmen calling upon the retailers are said to be getting themselves and the companies they represent, "in dutch" by the indiscriminate manner in which they employ the word "service." To quote the words of an Ontario retailer:—"Several lumber salesmen who call upon me are no sooner inside my office than they begin to tell me I must give more and better service than ever before. These chaps are, no doubt, saturated with the talks on "Service" from listening to their bosses and manufacturers."

As a matter of fact, this same retailer is one of the most wideawake in the Ontario lumber business and anybody who would dictate to him about service would have to include some real ideas and not hot air. It might be a good thing for lumber salesmen who really believe in "Service" to find out first what kind of service the retailer whom he is calling upon, is giving his community before speaking

# Survey of the Log and Lumber Market of British Columbia

### By Henry C. Copeland, Vancouver.

The nearest approach to finding a single word that will in any degree reflect the condition of the B. C. timber markets at the present is "nebulous." There are many indications of renewed activity in the lumber section of the market and on the other hand logging men are talking about the possibility of a shut down within the next ninety days.

A large order was offered at a firm price for water shipment a couple of weeks ago. There were no takers at the figure with the result that a few days later the order was placed at $2.00 a thousand more than the first offer.

One of the large operators stated lately that they were going to hold off until the prices strengthened. It is natural that the buyer should work to secure as low a price as possible and the seller to get as much as he can. At the present time we seem to be on the break of conditions and there is considerable jockeying as to the final basis on which the larger business is to be done.

Without doubt one of the most important factors is the price of logs. The ancient argument between the logger and mill man is yet going on. It is also claimed that some loggers sell their products across the line at prices that are less than the same buyers are paying for U. S. timber. Then the Fordney bill in the U. S. Congress would put a tariff on B. C. logs of $1.00 a thousand. And so it goes on. The great need of a stabilized market is growing from day to day:

Perhaps one of the best statements of the logger's side of the question can be given in the answer to our question as to the condition of the lumber market as given by one of the informed men in the business :

"I hardly know what to say as to the situation; all reports indicate that increased orders are being placed for lumber throughout the East, South and the Pacific Coast mills, with a slight stiffening in price in all the districts except the Pacific Coast. I also understand considerable business is being offered to Pacific Coast mills at what they claim is too low a figure for them to participate, considering the cost of logs and the cost of production.

#### Logs are High in Price

"There has been much talk of late re the high price of logs and I will grant that the price of logs is high compared to pre-war days but by careful analyzation you will find that the operating costs in logging camps are a long way from being down to a pre-war basis. In pre-war days the camps were working anywhere from 10 to 12 hours per day and the scale of wages not a great deal more than half of what they are at present. I also venture to say that labour of today does not show the same kick it did some years ago; in any event the production per man in a camp today is much less than we used to obtain.

"As to supplies and other expenses entering into the cost of operating a logging camp; machinery is much higher, many classes being still more than twice the price they were some years ago, also tools of various descriptions are still very high. Looking at the matter from a stumpage point of view, for stumpage, of course, must enter into the cost of operating, the ordinary holder of stumpage considers the value of his stumpage as doubled in 8 years, otherwise he is not obtaining a revenue from the money invested in stumpage; therefore stumpage which prior to 1914 figured at $1.00 per M. ft., should now be considered at $2 and stumpage more accessible, which in those days had an operating value of $2.00 per M. ft., should now be considered at $4 per M. ft. If you will carefully consider the increase necessary in order for one to retain his stumpage, you will find that it works out pretty close to this proportion.

#### The Future Value of Stumpage

"In considering these various phases, I feel that logs today should be worth at least twice the price they were prior to 1914, in order for the operator to make the same proportion of profit on his operation as he did in those days. It is possible, with constant agitation and propaganda, to reduce the price of logs so they will be brought down to a point less than the figure I mentioned, in which case it would be necessary for many of the logging operations to be

closed down, otherwise they would be sacrificing their best asset and the best asset of the country, which is stumpage.

"It is economically wrong, I think you will agree, were this country to sell lumber or logs to markets outside of the country, without obtaining a figure which will give a good return on the raw material, meaning by the raw material the stumpage value. Stumpage value some day will be worth what it costs to grow a tree. It is possible that the community and industry will wake up too late to the fact that its good stumpage has been depleted, and in many instances the industry and the province generally have not received for this stumpage a new dollar for an old one."

Granting our informant's contention, and there can be no doubt as to the facts as to what he states, it appears that there are still some elements that enter into the logging business that have to readjust themselves before we can reach a stabilized condition. It is evident that when we go out of our own country for business that we must meet competition. If one branch of the industry, or if any of the elements entering into that branch, demand a higher price than all the others in the industry are relatively getting, then only one of two things can happen, either they lose out on the business or the other branches of the industry have to carry the burden.

Fir logs are now firm at $10, $16 and $24. Hemlock, $11 to $14.75, Spruce same as fir or better. Cedar, shingle $20.

#### Good Season from the East

The lumber markets are showing a considerable degree of activity. There is nothing to cause us to become unduly enthusiastic as yet, as a matter of fact our domestic markets are yet very slack so far as the prairies are concerned. The mountain mills all have large yard stocks that the prairies usually absorb, they will also begin cutting again very soon, if they have not already begun. However, prices of grains and live stock are improving, the retailers are down to the last sticks in the yards, we heard of one who had to go out and borrow kindling wood, and on general condition there must be some business begin to come from that section, in fact there is already a slow movement discernable.

Eastern Canada is potentially good. A considerable number of enquiries and some orders are coming in. The building program already in sight is considerable and there is every reason to believe that we will have a satisfactory season from this section.

An important market for B. C. lumber lies in the States, both for water and rail shipments. Prices there seem to have stiffened, that has sent their attention to this side for mixed cars and at satisfactory prices. It may be generally stated that when Seattle wholesalers begin to buy mixed cars at good prices over here that markets are going to be good. Stocks appear to be badly broken and the calls are for dimension, boards, siding, shiplap, in fact pretty general stock.

#### Japanese Buying is Only Fair

Water shipments to the Atlantic seaboard are moving a considerable quantity. Two ships loaded for that market at the Fraser Mills during the last month. These two cargoes were nearly one-half the entire amount shipped from B. C. to that section by water during 1921. We are informed from several quarters that there are many enquiries from the Atlantic but the prices offered are not attractive, in fact are being largely turned down. But one of our sources of information tells us that they feel that with the large amount of building permits being taken out and the improved money situation that there can be no doubt as to the betterment of this field to a large extent.

Almost every item on the list is being asked for from this market, cedar poles, fir poles, cedar posts, bevel siding, dimension, matched stock, 1-inch stock, hemlock, etc. 7,600 fir piles were sent out in one order.

The Japanese buying is only fair, the demand is for cedar logs, baby squares of cedar, round logs and "waney" squares. The Australian business shows some improvement, but the prices are too low to be attractive. China is picking up, there is a considerable improvement, the enquiries are for the usual Shanghai specifications covering almost the entire list, although many large and long timbers are called for. These are mostly for resawing.

## Canada Lumberman
### Founded 1880

*The National Lumber Journal for Forty Years*

Issued on the 1st and 15th of every month by

HUGH C. MACLEAN PUBLICATIONS, Limited

THOS. S. YOUNG, Managing Director

HEAD OFFICE - - - - 347 Adelaide Street, West, TORONTO

Proprietors and Publishers also of Electrical News, Contract Record, Canadian Woodworker and Footwear in Canada.

| | |
|---|---|
| VANCOUVER - - - - - | Winch Building |
| MONTREAL - - - - | 119 Board of Trade Bldg. |
| WINNIPEG - - - - | 302 Travellers' Bldg. |
| NEW YORK - - - - - | 296 Broadway |
| CHICAGO - - | 14 West Washington Street |
| LONDON, ENG. - - - - | 16 Regent Street, S.W. |

TERMS OF SUBSCRIPTION

Canada, United States and Great Britain, $3.00 per year, in advance; other foreign countries embraced in the General Postal Union, $4.00.

Single copies, 20 cents.

Authorized by the Postmaster-General for Canada, for transmission as second-class matter.

Vol. 42                Toronto, May 15, 1922                No. 10

### Evolution in Retail Lumber Business

It is interesting to watch the evolution in business. It matters not in which department you enter, there have been many innovations and successful reforms carried out. In the restaurant, grocery, meat, merchant tailoring, men's furnishing, millinery, house-furnishing or other lines, radical alterations in methods of service, display, design and delivery have been effected. Thus we have today the cafeteria, grocetria, the cash-and-carry store, the ready-towear shop, the quick service "purveyor." There is no delivery expenses and the elimination of various other "frills" have not detracted from the value of the goods, but rather have helped to cut down overhead and reduce their cost to the public. Considerable saving has been effected this way in nearly all lines of produce and household articles.

The changes that have taken place in other avenues of business will soon be witnessed in the retail lumber arena. The day of the ramshackle office, the illkept and tumbledown piles, the muddy roadways, the dilapidated fence, the out-at-the-elbows dressed lumber shed, have passed away.

To-day the retailer who wants to succeed must create a good impression upon the public. A merchant tailor would soon lose his reputation as a maker of superior suits if he went around attired in a dowdy, vile-fitting one: a shoe merchant would lose prestige if he wore a down-in-the-heel, shabby shoe, and the lumber merchant must give some thought to the appearance and attractiveness of his surroundings. He is supposed to be the embodiment of a clean-up and uplift sentiment, and must show by his surroundings that he is a patron of his own product. His office, yards, fences, sheds, delivery outfits, signs,—in fact everything pertaining to his property, —should reflect the spirit of progress and present an outward evidence of prosperity, and orderliness.

This article is not intended to emphasize service, which has been referred to times without number in these columns, but is aimed to arouse some of the careless or hesitant to a realization of what should be done by them to keep pace with the march of events, and demonstrate that they are catching some conception of advancement. The lumber merchant has but to look around him and find in all cities and towns muddy streets giving way to paved thoroughfares and hundreds of thousands of dollars being spent in Ontario and other provinces in order to have hard, smooth and well-kept highways. In the urban and suburban districts verandahs are now painted, lawns are kept clean and well-trimmed, gardens are a thing of beauty, business fronts have fine, plate glass windows with artistic, airy awnings. Everywhere there is beauty and arrangement except in the case of certain outlying lumber yards, a few of which yet partake of the nature of an ordinary junk shop. The majority of dealers have brushed up considerably, but there is still a long way for some to travel.

However, it is pleasing to state that more new offices have been erected by retail lumbermen during the past year than in any previous one since the days of the war. This is an encouraging sign and affords probable purchasers of forest products ideas of how certain kinds of flooring look when laid, as well as interior and exterior trim, panels, ceiling, base, stairways, etc. The ordinary retailer should, however, go a step farther and have a service or display room. It is one of the best assets which he can possess. It arouses the interest of the women who after all, are the determining factors when it comes to the matter of deciding the style, type and location of a home.

In coming issues, the "Canada Lumberman" intends to devote more attention to service rooms of retailers which, it may be pointed out, are large dividend payers. This feature has been the development of the retail lumber yard during the last decade and has now to be added to meet changing conditions. It fills a long-felt want, gives practical demonstration to the appearance and finish of windows, panelling, built-in features and other "conceits" with regard to well-planned houses. A built-in writing desk, folding breakfast table, bookcase, cupboard, linen closet, buffet, china cabinet, etc., can all be shown to good advantage. Several live retailers of Eastern Canada are now installing such service departments, and it will be a pleasure for the "Canada Lumberman" from time to time to show what can and is being done in the way of retailing building material on a higher, broader and more serviceable plan in accordance with the progress and policy of present-day home-builders.

### The Girl in the Lumber Office

Are women as efficient as men; are they capable of taking hold of a position and showing as much adaptability, resource and energy as an earnest-minded and industrious young man? No doubt many women are competent, alert and progressive as they have risen to executive, management, sales and other posts where they have become factors of influence and prestige in the business world. There is, however, one class of females that is often amazing to the average caller on either wholesale or retail firms—the lackadaisical lady in the lumber line.

Perhaps the institution is a one-man affair and the only assistance the proprietor has is a girl in the office. Now, the latter cannot be in and out at the same time, and by the law of fate if he steps out, several people call on business and get contrary if he remains in no one comes around. Thus it devolves upon the assistant to answer the phone and any other queries that may arise from visitors when the boss is absent.

Some female assistants might well be called co-workers. They are so adaptable, interested and business-like in manner and speech. On the other hand, there is the disinterested and languishing stenographer or bookkeeper, who, in response to a personal call or to the query if Mr. S. is in, will reply "No, he is not." Of course, the caller might see this for himself, but Miss Assistant never ventures another word. She does not intimate whether Mr. S. has stepped out for three or four minutes, whether he is across the hall, has gone out for an hour, is out of the city, is at home indisposed, or will be back in the afternoon, to-morrow, next week or next year. She does not endeavor to get the name of the visitor, the nature of his business or even accost him with the stereotyped inquiry "Will you call again?" The result is that the information sought as well have in his office a cigar store Indian or one of the statues from Queen's Park, so far as any usefulness, information or practical aid from Miss Assistant is concerned, particularly when Mr. S. himself is not on the job. Now this is the view expressed by numerous lumbermen and others who have to do all the enquiring and almost furnish the answers to their own queries regarding Mr. S.

The outstanding shortcoming of the present day on the part of clerical help is either "don't know" or "don't care." Both delinquincies come under the same category. When these sweeping assertions are made regarding lady assistants in lumber offices, one wonders if the latter are really to blame for the censure or criticism heaped upon them. Is not the boss himself often culpable? He never volunteers any information when he puts on his coat to leave, and when he goes out of town, may not intimate where he can be found or when he will be back. He issues no explicit instructions, neither does he teach the girl anything outside of the most ordinary clerical work. No doubt he is accessory to her incompetence and indifference.

There are many lumber offices in the larger cities where only a girl is in charge for several hours a day as the principals of the firm are out making calls or selling. Very few of these ladies can tell what stock their employer has on hand, of what thicknesses, widths and grades, when shipments have been made, what the prevailing price is, etc., although they are left a list covering such data. There are, probably, two or three real salesladies out of scores employed in wholesale or retail offices in Toronto. When such a girl is secured, she, naturally, commands a generous return for her services. Her value to the firm is much more than a mere dollar and cents basis.

# All Aboard for Retailers' Big Trip up the Lakes

Many reservations have already been made for the annual outing of the Ontario Lumber Dealers' Association up through the Lakes on June 23 to 27.

L. H. Richards, of the Laidlaw-Belton Lumber Co., Sarnia, the hustling chairman of the committee, is leaving nothing undone to insure the success of the gathering, and has been kept busy answering a multitude of inquiries and letters from far and near points.

Reservations are being made rapidly and it is necessary that before June 10, 175 full-fare tickets should be taken up by members of the O. R. L. D. A. and their wives and families. Some dealers have taken as many as five tickets as they are convinced that the outing will be thoroughly enjoyable and refreshing from start to finish. After May 15 if a sufficient number of retailers have not "signed up" the reservations will be thrown open to wholesale lumbermen.

Chairman Richards has been in communication with the Chambers of Commerce at Owen Sound, Sault Ste Marie and Sarnia, and at each of these points automobiles will be provided for driving the excursionists around and showing them the sights and all points of interest. Certainly the Chambers of Commerce will give the touring lumbermen and their wives a splendid time.

On Monday evening on the "Huronic" June 26 there will be a concert, and a humorous lecture by Douglas Malloch, of Chicago. This talk has made a killing wherever it has been heard and those who have listened to Mr. Malloch in the past know what a treat is in store for them. He will join the party at Mackinac.

The total cost of the trip is $50.00, plus a war tax of 50c. This includes everything from the time one steps on the boat at Windsor on the afternoon of Friday June 23, until he disembarks in the same city at 5 P. M. on June 27. There are 25 preferred staterooms set aside for those who desire to pay an extra charge of $10.00. These will accommodate three persons, and the fee is $60.00, plus the war tax of 60c, which sum also includes everything. It may be said that

all staterooms on the vessel are outside rooms, airy and comfortable.

On the "Huronic" there will be music, dancing, concerts, afternoon tea, publication of a daily paper and many other livening features. It is expected that a number of Michigan dealers will also take in the outing. This will be entirely a lumbermen's party and the boat is capable of carrying 250 persons.

The following is the time table and route of the forthcoming midsummer jaunt.

Leave Windsor, 5 P. M. Friday, June 23rd.
Leave Sarnia, 11 P. M. Friday, June 23rd.
Arrive Owen Sound, 7 P. M. Saturday, June 24th.
Leave Owen Sound, 11 P. M. Saturday, June 24th.
Arrive Killarney, 7 A. M. Sunday, June 25th.
Leave Killarney, 9 A. M. Sunday, June 25th.
Arrive Sault Ste Marie, 7 P. M. Sunday, June 25th.
Leave Sault Ste. Marie, midnight Sunday, June 25th.
Arrive Mackinac, 10 A. M. Monday, June 26th.
Leave Mackinac, noon Monday, June 26th.
Arrive Sarnia, 10 A. M. Tuesday, June 27th.
Leave Sarnia, noon, Tuesday, June 27th.
Arrive Windsor, 5 P. M. Tuesday, June 27th.

Once again it is urged that all reservations be made early with L. H. Richards, of Sarnia, chairman of the Excursion Committee, or H. Boultbee, of Toronto, secretary of the O. R. L. D. A.

J. C. Scofield, of Windsor, president of the Ontario Retail Lumber Dealers' Association, in speaking to the "Canada Lumberman." stated that he would be very glad, indeed, if the retail lumber dealers of Montreal, Quebec or any other city in the East, would join in this outing. He extends to them a special invitation to come and mingle with their brethren from Ontario in one of the most delightful and picturesque sails that it is possible to take in fresh waters.

---

## The Dependable Man

There is a type of man who is built for success. He may have genius or just ordinary talent—no matter. The point is that he always "arrives." While others plod a weary way, he gets ahead, says J. Ogden Armour.

Those who take note of his progress often cannot account for it. So they say he is "lucky." Or they whisper it about that he has a "pull with the boss."

But the secret is deeper than that. He is a man who is absolutely dependable.

Make yourself dependable, and you will come as near being indispensable as any of us can hope to be. You will be the last one your employer will wish to part with, and the first one that he will want to promote to greater responsibilities.

But do not be deceived. Dependableness is a rare accomplishment—so rare that every executive is on the lookout of it wherever it may be found. It cannot be acquired by wishing for it. It is the price that comes from self-mastery.

What is a dependable man? You can tell by these earmarks:

First, he is one that you can rely upon to do his own thinking. Business requires thinking, and someone must do it. The dependable man never sidesteps his share nor tries to pass it along to someone else. You always find him on the alert. His brains do not flit away on vacations, leaving his job without a guardian.

Next, he is one whose judgment you can trust. He doesn't do foolish things. He knows his own abilities; and not being conceited, he is equally aware of his own weaknesses. He has the happy faculty of understanding other people's viewpoints and of seeking their advice when he ought. Also he knows when to act on his own initiative.

Finally, he is a man you can listen to, taking stock in whatever he says. You are sure that he speaks only after due reflection. He does not talk to the galleries or for the purpose of "grinding his own ax." He makes his suggestions and pleads his causes solely in the interest of the business.

Such a man is safe. Important duties may be entrusted to him and he will handle them with diligence, good sense and earnestness. If you are looking for the quickest route to opportunity, learn to be this type of man. There is no better time for sowing the seeds of dependableness than the dawn of the New Year. This is when one should take inventory of himself and set out to attain those qualifications which are essential to success.

## Have Mercy on the Forests

There should be no need to make an appeal to campers, fishermen, hunters, picknickers, to seek to preserve the forests which are at once the pride and profit of British Columbia, says the "Vancouver World." More damage has been done by dropped matches and lack of care in extinguishing camp fires than in any other way. And—with the exception of picknickers, who are proverbially a careless people out for pleasure—all the classes mentioned should appreciate the heinousness of such offence. Most of them do, for it is not the man of the woods, the hunter, who does not carefully extinguish his fire. But the picknicker—there's the rub! And especially the picnicker who has not been "raised" in a country such as this, or who has spent most of his life in a town!

The destruction of forest life through carelessness should rank as one of the most serious offences which a man in this province can commit. That seems to be the only way in which its heinousness can be brought home to the careless person who takes the attitude' "what has posterity done for me," or who simply does not think at all.

It is a comparatively simple matter for any camper or fisherman to take such sensible precautions as to extinguish a camp fire before leaving camp, to put out a cigarette before throwing it away or to avoid throwing matches into inflammable leaves, twigs or moss. A great many campers show very little caution in selecting a spot to build their camp fires. In no case should a camp fire be built against a tree or in an old log or in a dry bog; but wherever possible on a rocky shore or on a gravel or sand base. A small fire always cooks better than a large one and is much easier to extinguish. When through with the cooking fire a few quarts of water or a shovel or two of earth will easily extinguish it. No glowing coals or smoking embers should be left under any circumstances.

## Mr. Todd Opens Office in Toronto

J. T. Todd, who represents the Adams River Lumber Co., of Chase, B. C., The Associated Mills, Limited, of Vancouver, and the Edgecombe-Newham Co., Limited, has opened a joint sales and service office at 1305 Bank of Hamilton Building, Toronto. The Adams River Lumber Co., with which Mr. Todd has been associated for many years, is one of the largest mountain manufacturers and produces about 150,000 feet per nine-hour day of fir, cedar, spruce and

**J. T. Todd, Toronto**

pine, all of which is air dried. The Associated Mills, which is the centralized selling department of seven Coast mills, represent a joint daily capacity of 500,000 feet, and are specializing in all kinds of Coast uppers, yard stocks, timber, etc. Edgecombe-Newham Co. are widely known, being large producers of B. C. shingles, with a daily capacity of 500,000.

E. D. Warner, who is favorably known to the lumber industry, in Ontario is a member of the selling staff of Mr. Todd, who reports that business is improving and the outlook getting better.

## Stratford District Annual Gathering

The annual meeting of No. 7 District, Ontario Retail Lumber Dealers' Association, will be held at the Mansion House, Stratford, on Monday May 15th, at 1:30 p.m. Election of officers for the coming year and other important business will come up. Secretary Kalbfleisch of Stratford, says that the gathering has been delayed to make it more convenient for members coming in motor cars. It is hoped that there will be a large and representative attendance as the roads are now in splendid shape for driving.

## Ottawa Lumber Firms Suffer Fire Losses

Two Ottawa lumber firms, James Hill, Pretoria Ave., and the extensive wood yards of Barrett Bros., Catharine Street were threatened by fire, on the night of May 4th. Both fires occured almost simultaneously and the origin is unknown. At the Barrett yard a loss of about $50,000 was incurred, while at the Hill factory the damage was less than $10,000 owing to the presence of mind of a neighbor who saw the blaze and sent in an alarm. Insurance protects the greater part of both losses.

## Booms Break Owing to High Water

James Davidson's Sons, Ottawa, whose log booms broke loose late last month in the Calumet river, estimate between fifty and seventy thousand logs have gone out of their usual course and entered the Ottawa river. They will likely be rounded up around Quyon, Que. Arrangements will be made with either the Shepard and Morse Lumber Company or Ritchie Bros., to take care of the sawing. The break in the Davidson booms was due to abnormally high water. The logs on their way down, carried away portions of the timber slides of the Upper Ottawa Improvement Company, causing a loss of several thousand dollars.

## Erecting New Sawmill at Deer Lake

Tudhope & Ludgate are erecting a circular sawmill at Deer Lake on the C. N. R. to cut the timber that they have in the township of Ferry, consisting of pine, spruce and hemlock. The firm have also a quantity of cedar poles there.

James Ludgate says that driving commenced in the section around Pakesley during the last two weeks in April and the lakes opened up with a snap.

The Schroeder Mills & Timber Co., of which Mr. Ludgate is manager, started their mill at Pakesley early in May and they have logs enough for a full season's cut of about 15,000,000 feet of lumber. The Schroeder Company took out about 25,000,000 feet of logs last season, half of which they have at the French River and Key Harbour on Georgian Bay. Mr. Ludgate reports that lumber is moving fairly well now and they have several men shipping.

## Twenty One Years in Lumber Line

J. H. Jones, of Thamesford, Ont., who has been for 21 years in the lumber and timber business, is widely known in Western Ontario. Previous to the war he did considerable export trade. Mr. Jones specializes in beech, which is used for flooring as well as for chairs, ladders and various other lines. He operates a circular sawmill of medium capacity and conducted three small camps during the past winter. Mr. Jones took out a little over half million feet of hardwoods, chiefly of elm and basswood, which he is sawing to order at a good price. He also cut about 2,000 cords of wood for fuel purposes.

## Lumbermen May Build Emergency Dams

Hon. G. H. Ferguson, former Minister of Lands and Forests, and Z. Mageau, M. L. A. of Sturgeon Falls, who is a well-known lumberman, made representations recently to Hon. Harry Mills, Minister of Lines, whereby the latter consented in the legislature to an amendment of his Rivers and Streams Act, which will allow lumbermen, without permit, to construct emergency dams on Ontario rivers. The bill introduced by Mr. Mills required the consent of the Minister before any work could be gone on with in the Ontario rivers and streams and the point was pressed that this might prove a hardship on lumbermen, who, finding their dams giving way, under the act, could not build an emergency dam further up the river. The bill received a second reading.

## Eastern Lumber Yards Need Cleaning Up

Chief Forester C. G. Piche, of Quebec, has received a report from Lake Frontier that the fire which destroyed three million feet of lumber as well as a sawmill and two houses had been completely extinguished. The fire was attributed to some careless person discarding a lighted match or a cigarette butt. Mr. Piche said that in the yards of railway stations in lumbering districts there was a great deal of waste bark and wood lying about, which was a decided menace. He urged that all this waste be cleared away as soon as possible, for with dry spells which occur every spring there was need of every precaution being taken.

## Litigation Starts Over Power Dam

Litigation which owes its origin to the construction of the power dam above the Chaudiere Falls in 1909, was started recently before Judge Surveyer in the Hull Superior Court. The Scott estate, through Captain W. F. Hadley, has instituted action for $84,000 damages against the E. B. Eddy Company, Limited, J. R. Booth, Limited, and the Hull and Ottawa Power Company. Damages are claimed on account of alleged flooding of lands. It is claimed that the flooding is caused by the waters being held back for power purposes by the big concrete dam which spans the river immediately above the Falls.

## Western Pulp Plant Will be Sold

The properties of the Western Canada Pulp & Paper Co., which are located at Howe Sound, B. C., will be sold. This discussion arrived at recently by a meeting of the debenture-holders, which was held in the offices of the Chartered Trust & Executor Co., Toronto. In February last the company defaulted in the payment of interest on its bonds and the bondholders started foreclosure proceedings with the intention of disposing of the plant of the company. The debenture-holders, who have second claim upon the assets of the Western Canada Pulp & Paper Co., unanimously agreed to allow the sale to proceed. If any proceeds are left after the claim of the bondholders are satisfied, the debenture-holders will share in them.

The aggressive dealer who really sells lumber knows that he is building future business when he satisfies a customer. He quotes as fair a price as is consistent with the quality of the material that ought to go into a certain job; then he sells that quality of material to the buyer. The dealer makes sure in that way of the buyer's satisfaction; he is building future business, too, because he holds these customers on the basis of quality, and the customer comes back because he can get this quality, not price.

# Definite Grading Rules Desirable

## Representative Lumbermen Think There Is a Need for More Uniform Standards in Classification

Further interviews with lumbermen on the Standardization of Lumber are given in this issue. Practically all those spoken to state that conditions are very unsatisfactory and that more precise gradings are desirable. The difficulty is how to obtain an amelioration of conditions, having regard to the number of small manufacturers whose output is poorly graded. It would seem to be a matter of education rather than an attempt to take drastic measures. Contractors, who complain of the quality of lumber received, are probably mainly those who buy in the cheapest market, and it is pointed out, they cannot expect to receive good lumber when paying the price of inferior descriptions. There is strong evidence to support the contention that, as a rule, Montreal builders are using the poorest grades and that a large amount of what one lumberman describes as "refuse" lumber goes into many buildings.

W. K. Grafftey, managing director of the Montreal Lumber Company, Limited:—While I agree that the Standardization of Lumber is desirable, I see no way of enforcing the rules. In fact, I think it impracticable in view of the number of small mills. Existing conditions are chaotic. We can, of course, depend on the large manufacturers as to grade but in too many other instances the position is unsatisfactory. With regard to O and dead culls, there should be some recognized basis, as to what should be allowed under these classifications—a qualification as to what can be sent in when ordering these grades. Some of the lumber being used in Montreal is of the poorest type, and to prevent this, a civic inspector should insist that the lumber going into buildings should be of fair and reasonable quality.

### Difficult to get Small Mills in Line

C. B. Graddon, of the Graddon Lumber Company:—There has been in existance for many years a Quebec Cullers' Act, but it is disregarded as far as the domestic trade is concerned. In my opinion, it will be very difficult to get the small mills to conform to any grading rules. The question of grades is after all a matter of price, and the production of the large mills all command a higher price than that of the small mills. Contractors apparently want lumber o fa very cheap description, and they are supplied with a quality in accordance with the price paid. The lumber which goes into many buildings in Montreal is so poor that its use should be prohibited. How it passes inspection is beyond me. How can contractors expect to obtain merchantable lumber as specified when many are paying even low prices for culls? Contractors can get all the good lumber they want if they are willing to pay reasonable prices for it.

J. A. Laferte:—I am of opinion that the suggested grading rules for softwoods would be of benefit to the industry. The National Hardwoods Association is a similar system as applies to softwoods would prove the solution of putting into operation the proposed Standardization rules. The arrangement would have to be voluntary, and would involve education of the smaller mills to the point of manufacturing better grades. The effect would be that higher prices would be obtained which would be a greater factor in inducing many mills to comply with the rules. Naturally this would take considerable time. It would be a good thing for all concerned if we could secure the use of lumber of the better grade than that which comes to Montreal in such large quantities.

### How Could System Be Enforced

F. H. Stearns, of F. H. Stearns & Co.,:—This is a question which mainly concerns the retailer and his customers. I doubt if the ordinary builder has sufficient knowledge of lumber to judge as to the quality and a book of grading rules would not help to any extent. It would, of course, be very desirable to have a system by which the wholesaler could be certain that when he orders, say, merchantable spruce from a small mill, he will get that quality, thus avoiding a considerable amount of trouble with the retail customers of the wholesalers, the former being pretty competent judges of what lumber should be. But how could such a system be enforced?

### Depends on Co-operation of Smaller Mills

A. W. Barnhill:—The question of securing more strict definitions of grades, particularly in spruce, depends upon the amount of co-operation which could be obtained from the smaller manufacturers. Present uncertain conditions are not conducive to smoothness in business, and more strict interpretation would be of benefit to manufacturers, wholesalers, retailers and consumer. There would undoubtedly be some difficulty in getting the co-operation to which I referred, especially from those owning portable mills, but if these owners could be shown that it would pay them to grade their lumber

better, it would, I think, gradually force them to realize that it would compensate them for the extra trouble and also for any additional equipment required. It is largely a matter of education. In the West grading rules are in operation with success. Up to 1908 there was trouble concerning grading, and as a result of a meeting in Winnipeg, it was decided to standardize grades and sizes for spruce, such rules applying to Manitoba, Saskatchewan and the Prairie section of Alberta, an arrangement which I believe worked out very well.

## Newsy Jottings from Far and Near

The office of the Abitibi Power & Paper Co., Limited, has been removed to the Canada Cement Building, Montreal.

The Marshay Lumber Co., have begun sawing at Laforest, Ont., and will start up their mill at Milnet, on the C.N.R., about the 1st of June.

Graves, Bigwood & Co., began operations in their mills at Byng Inlet early in May and will cut about the same quantity of logs as last season.

The National Lumber Co., have started operations in their sawmill at L'Orignal, Ont., and will cut a large stock of white pine. The mill was not in operation last year.

A. B. Gordon, of Toronto, president of the Canadian Timber Co., recently spent a couple of weeks on the drive at Sturgeon River. The company's mill at Callander, Ont., began operations for the season last week.

At the annual banquet of the Canadian Daily Newspapers' Association, held in Montreal, on May 3rd, the film of the operation of Price Bros., was shown. This illustrates the process of producing newsprint—from the forest to the press.

The planing mill of A. Henderson, of Cheltenham, Ont., was recently destroyed by fire. It is understood that Mr. Henderson, who is a well-known member of the Ontario Retail Lumber Dealers' Association and has always taken an active interest in the Orangeville District, is moving to Orangeville, where he is establishing a new yard and factory.

With both legs broken, one arm dislocated at the elbow, a jaw fractured and his body badly covered with bruises as a result of being caught in a flywheel of the sawmill of Hubey & MacDonald at Seabright, N. S., Byron MacDonald has been in a critical condition. He was working in the mill, of which his father, Neil MacDonald, has been a partner for ten years.

The annual report of the Saguenay Pulp & Paper Company, Limited, for the year 1921 shows a surplus of $64,982. after providing for bond interest and depreciation. Net profits were $2,433,429, and after deducting bond interest of $1,214,529, a balance remained of $1,-218,900. Depreciation on buildings took up $325,865; on limits,$298,-195; and on inventories, $529,838, a total of $1,153,918.

The pulp mill of the Kaministiquia Pulp & Paper Co., at Port Arthur, which was sold recently by auction to the Consolidated Waterpower & Paper Co., of Wisconsin, has commenced operations. It has been closed since early last summer. A number of improvements have been made to the plant, including the installation of a new intake pipe. Earl Smith, of Port Arthur, is the superintendent.

Russell Harris Lumber Co., 34 Victoria St., Toronto have been appointed exclusive handlers in the province of "Velvet Brand" Short Leaf yellow pine, (the softest pine that grows,) and are selling large quantities of it, both steam dried and smoke dried. This pine is practically free from pitch and is used for many purposes, particularly for high-class interior trim, ceiling etc. The Russell Harris Co., report that the demand for "Velvet Brand" which is manufactured by the George Surmeyer Lumber Co., of St. Louis, Mo., is increasing steadily.

There has been a lot said of reforestation in Grey County, Ont., but practically nothing has been done by public bodies. It remained for Dr. Jamieson, Ex-M.P.P., of Durham, to take a practical interest in the matter. He has purchased about 250 acres in North Egremont in and near where the McLean saw mill used to operate. Mr. Jamieson intends to have it fenced to allow nature to have her way with the growth at present existing, but purposes to plant out under expert advice some thousands of butternut and other trees of commercial value.

The Canadian Forestry Exhibit car, which has been on Vancouver Island for the past ten days has been brought to the main land. The car is making a tour of Canada under the direction of the Canadian Forestry Association, an organization including over 13,000 members engaged in various branches of the lumbering industry. It receives a grant from the Dominion government and from several of the provinces. It aims to give the people an adequate idea of forest resources of Canada and to educate them as to the importance of preventing forest fires.

## Personal Paragraphs of Interest

D. Ritchie, of D. & J. Ritchie, Newcastle, N. B., was in Montreal recently on business.

N. J. Tierney, St. Omer, Bonaventure County, Que., was in Toronto recently calling upon the lumber trade.

Roch Julien, wholesale lumber dealer, Quebec, was in Toronto recently calling upon a number of friends in the trade.

W. Blair, of Blair Bros., Limited, Montreal, has returned to business after an absence of over two months, due to illness.

W. R. Sayre, manager of the W. R. Sayre Lumber Co., San Francisco, Cal., was in Toronto lately calling upon the trade.

E. S. Hoag, late of Laforest, Ont., has joined the selling staff of the Union Lumber Co., Toronto and is covering part of Ontario.

J. B. Snowball, of the W. B. Snowball Co., Chatham, N. B., was in Toronto recently calling upon a number of friends in the lumber trade.

John Rowland, of the Sprague-Rowland Lumber Co., Winnipeg, Man.,was in Toronto recently, calling upon a number of friends in the trade.

The offices of the Canadian General Lumber Co., Ltd., in Montreal, have removed from the McGill Building to Room 514, Canada Cement Building.

Edward Clark, of Edward Clark & Sons, Limited, Toronto, has gone to the Guelph Sanitarium for special treatment. He has not been in good health for some weeks past.

The Montreal offices of Timms, Phillips and Co., Ltd., have been removed to 33 C. P. R. Telegraph Chambers, Hospital Street. A. W. Barnhill has also removed to the same address.

W. H. Kelly, of W. H. Kelly Lumber Co.,Buckingham, Que., passed away on April 25th in his 65th year. He leaves a wife and family and during his business career he made many warm friends throughout the community.

J. H. Lavallee, president and manager of the Anglo-Canadian Lumber Co., Iberville, Que., left Montreal recently on the "Montcalm" on a business trip to England and France. He expects to return about the end of June.

J. B. Burke, of Ottawa, who represents the Allen-Stoltze Lumber Co., of Vancouver, in Ontario and the Eastern provinces, and some time ago opened an office in the Manning Chambers, Toronto, has returned to Ottawa in which city he will make his headquarters, his office being at 117 Bell St.

Mason, Gordon & Co., who have been in the wholesale lumber business in Montreal for several years, have been granted a federal charter, and the new style of the firm is Mason, Gordon & Co., Limited. The capital stock is $100,000. and the firm is empowered to carry on a general lumber business in all its branches. Among the members are W. T. Mason, P. D. Gordon and others.

Mrs. Shuster, of Belleville, wife of the late Rev. A. Shuster, passed away recently in Pittsburg, Pa., where she had been living with her son, Chas. Shuster. She was one of the most enthusiastic workers in social reform, and was the mother of W. E. Shuster, of the Shuster Co., Belleville, where the remains were interred. The death of Mrs. Shuster was caused by her clothes igniting when standing in front of a grate. She was 88 years old.

## Menace of Cigarette in Forest Fires

Notwithstanding the repeated warnings issued from the Quebec Department of Lands and Forests against the danger of fire in the woods, and the menace of the cigarette, the amateur hunters and fishermen will insist upon throwing away carelessly, lighted matches and butts of cigarettes to cause forest fires.

Chief Forester G. C. Piche, is extremely nervous over the possibilities of forest fires this spring due to the dry season, and, as already pointed out in the "Canada Lumberman," has augmented the fire protective service in the woods to 1500 rangers, inspectors and their assistants. The department does not feel satisfied, even with protective service of the four provincial Limit Holders' Protective Associations.

The fire which occurred at Lake Frontier on May 2nd, which resulted in the destruction of 3,000,000 feet of lumber, as well as a sawmill and two dwellings, has caused the forestry branch of the Lands and Forests Department to redouble their vigilance, and the Government has decided to spare no expense for protection against fire this season. Mr. Piche has ordered an investigation into the origin of the Lake Frontier fire, and has received a report, in which it is stated that the blaze was caused by some careless person, discarding a lighted cigarette butt among a heap of waste bark and wood allowed to accumulate and spread over the railway station property and yards of the lumbering districts.

It is beyond comprehension why men will smoke and throw away lighted cigarette butts, and it is suggested that a law should be passed against cigarette smoking in the woods and in lumber yards. "This menace, "says Mr. Piche, "not only applies to the province of Quebec, but as well the forest resources of Ontario and all other Canadian provinces where lumber operations are being carried on."

## Conger Co. Gets Sawing Done at Penetang

The Conger Lumber Co., of Parry Sound, Ont., whose mill and yards were destroyed by fire last fall will not rebuild. This decision was arrived at some time ago. W. B. Maclean, of Toronto president of the company, says that arrangements have been made with the C. Beck Mfg. Co., of Penetanguishene, for sawing their stock of hemlock logs during the coming season. The logs were cut in Gibson township and floated down the Moon River. They are now being towed to Penetanguishene, a distance of about 45 miles. The Conger Lumber Company's cut of hemlock will be over 3,000,000 feet, or about the same quantity as last year.

## Million Dollars to Protect Western Lumber

A vote of $1,000,000 was recently made in the House of Commons at Ottawa, for the protection of timber in Manitoba, Saskatchewan, Alberta and the railway belt of British Columbia. The same will be used for the preservation and replenishing of the forests. H. H. Stevens, M.P., of Vancouver, said the condition of Canadian forests was becoming alarming owing to the wasteful methods of lumbering, forest fires and destructive insects. He asked whether the Government was re-considering reforestation and what steps were being taken to take care of existing forests. Hon. Chas. Stewart, Minister of the Interior, replied that reforestation was not being undertaken on a large scale as reproduction was fairly satisfactory. Good work was being performed by the Air Fire Patrol Service.

## Roses Bloom Near the Lumber Piles

J. C. Scofield, president of the Ontario Retail Lumber Dealers' Association, and head of the Windsor Lumber Co., Windsor, has one of the finest and best laid-out yards in Western Ontario. It comprises a little over six acres, has two private sidings running the full length of the property and everything about the premises is neat and orderly. The ground is well drained, the foundations for the piles are kept in good repair and permit of free ventilation, and the work of tile draining in all parts is now under way. The yard is so laid out as to enable the company by the use of gravity rollers to unload the bulk of lumber and flooring direct from the car to the pile or shed, thus keeping the expense of handling down to a minimum.

It is not often that one sees growing in a lumber yard roses and flowers of various hues. In front of the office set out in long rows are many beautiful plants, which are given the personal attention of Mr. Scofield. This adds a touch of the artistic to the well-kept premises and makes the surroundings most inviting.

## Surplus of Fir on Atlantic Seaboard

Last month inquiries were generally not so active as in the previous month, although certain lines showed enough improvement so that production in two of the greatest lumber districts reached normal, viz: the South and North West.

Eastern Spruce dimension is hardly entering the New York market, because of the railroad differential and the high base in Boston. To a certain extent this is true of West Virginia.

The most active factor in the lumber business in the past month, has been the market for Douglas fir. Unfortunately concerns which should have known better, brought tremendous quantities of the New York lumber to the Atlantic Seaboard and all on consignment, with the consequence that this stock was dumped at ruinous prices.

Coinciding with this deluge of unsold lumber was a further drop in freight rates, so that the market had no general level and depended entirely upon circumstances. This is unfortunate from every point of view, as it is especially hard on the retail yards to have the value of their stocks on hand thus depreciated by transit levels. However, this movement has eased off, and prevailing levels are around $28.00 for average dimension schedule.

Some Eastern random has arrived by schooner and due to the price of fir as outlined has been sold at low levels. Inquiry for lath has fallen off and the market is slipping. Several big cargoes arrived in April and offerings have lately been in excess of yard requirements.

# Exporters Score High Ocean Rates

## Impossible to Enter into Overseas Competition, Declare Quebec Lumber Merchants.

The first shipment of timber from the port of Quebec to the United Kingdom will consist of part cargo of oak shipped on the Canadian Government Merchant Marine steamer "Canadian Navigator," scheduled to sail for Greenock during the end of the second week in May. This oak is being shipped by two Quebec export firms, Messrs. John Burstall & Co., and W. J. Sharples. The next lots of timber and deals sold by the Quebec export firms to British, Scotch and Irish ports, will be forwarded later in the season.

Though the situation of the timber and lumber markets in the United Kingdom are practically the same as they were last month, there seems to be a rift in the dark clouds, which may bring about a better condition in the fall. The ocean liner freight rates from ports in the St. Lawrence route are without question the responsible embargo on Canadian sales and shipments of lumber. In the first week of May, Quebec firms received cablegrams with offers of prices to be paid for Canadian lumber to be shipped to the United Kingdom, which the exporters had to refuse on account of the high freight rates. The rates in the present are 85 shillings per standard from Quebec to the United Kingdom, altogether too high to permit the Canadian exporters to compete with the selling powers of Sweden, Finland, Poland and Germany. But if the steamship companies had agreed to give this rate in the beginning of last winter instead of the end of April, when the representatives of Canadian export firms had returned to Canada they would undoubtedly, have brought back more orders.

But the whole crux of the Canadian lumber situation as it applies to the United Kingdom rests with the combination of steamship interests, especially referring to the liners, who cannot be brought to visualize the situation as it exists. The Quebec exporters, realize the high cost of operating big ocean liners, with their increased over head charges these days, agree that for the present or until the cost of operation is lowered, 60 shillings would not be sufficient in rate to pay the companies. They contend, however, by mathematical calculation, that 75 shillings would give the liners sufficient return, and would help out the export lumber situation from Canada in its trade relations with the United Kingdom.

Lt. Col. R. M. Beckett, of the firm of Dobell, Beckett & Co., discussing the situation with the Quebec correspondent of the "Canada Lumberman," said he felt confident that the year 1922 would bring an improvement over the lumber trade conditions in the United Kingdom in comparison with 1921. Of course, he realized that there still existed a feeling of unrest in England and a nervousness on the part of the money powers to invest in Government securities. This feeling, however, was gradually giving way to a better spirit of confidence, as the United Kingdom was gradually receiving its equilibrium, and if it were not for the labor difficulties and the strikes, including the engineers' strike, the trade conditions in England would be in a much better position than it is to-day.

Referring to the Canadian lumber trade and the export of timber and deals from the port of Quebec to the United Kingdom, Col. Beckett said: "It is impossible for the Canadian exporter of lumber to ship overseas and compete with the lumber interests of Sweden, Finland, Poland, etc., at the prevailing high rates of the steamships in the present day, and unless they come down to 65 shillings, Canada cannot export, and the movement of lumber across the sea embargoed. There is no competition in the steamship companies carrying trade these days. It is a combination of interests which dictates and maintains the present high freight rates, and this combination does not seem to understand that Canadian exporters cannot afford to sell their lumber at a loss, which they would be compelled to do if they were to submit to the present high ocean rates, which prevent them from competing with the lumber interests of European continental countries.

"We have a Canadian Merchant Marine Service," said Col. Beckett, "and a number of these steamers laid up for want of service demand, and it sounds reasonable that these Government ocean freight steamers should step in to ease off the situation. But I understand that the Canadian Government Merchant Marine forms part of the steamship combine and must abide by the ruling of the steamship federation. It does seem strange that a Government Marine Service, built and paid for by the people, should engage to form part of a combine or oligarchy rather than come to the assistance of Canadian trade interests and detriment of the lumber trade of Canada. This Government Marine fleet should be immune from all features of combine. It is owned by the Canadian people at large and should be operated in the interest of Canadian trade instead of being managed and operated to suit the big interests of steamship monopoly in freight rates.

"I am given to understand that there are several of the Canadian Government Merchant Marine boats lying idle. It is a question for the Canadian government, as the constitutional representatives of the Canadian people, to decide.

"In the meantime, if 60 or 65 shillings is not sufficient to provide a profit for the operation of these Government ships, why should not the management accept a rate of 75 shillings, which would give a fair profit."

The firm of Dobell & Co. have received an offer from the owner of a tramp steamer to carry wood freight to the United Kingdom for 80 shillings, and from others, 72 shillings. It is rumored that one important Quebec firm endeavored to charter one of the Canadian Government steamers to carry lumber to the United Kingdom at the rate of 60 shillings, and received the reply that a ship would be supplied at current rates, which means the same rate as the liners, 85 shillings.

## Woodworking Team Won Championship in Ottawa

To go through the season with only a loss of two games out of thirty played is the enviable record of the John Davidson's Sons hockey team, champions of the Manufacturers' League, Ottawa, the premier industrial hockey circuit of the Capital City. Winners of the first section, consisting of Woodroffe, Grant-Holden-Graham, and the Royal Mint teams, along with the champions, the race was an interesting one all the way through. James Davidson's Sons team went through the last six games without a goal being scored against them.

The champions had the hearty co-operation and assistance of Messrs. Grant and Keith Davidson, sons of the founder of the well-known establishment that bears their name. Always eager to render assistance to the team whenever the occasion demanded, the heads of the company were most enthusiastic in their support.

The second section of the Manufacturers' League was made up of the Dominion Express, Just Motors, Capital Wire Cloth and C. P. R. teams. The C. P. R. squad were victors after a hard struggle and met Davidson's team for the final. The latter won out by a score of 1 to 0 after one of the most gruelling contests ever witnessed in the industrial league.

As a token of appreciation of the honor that they have brought to their employers as well as themselves, the hockey champions were guests at a banquet which was given in the British Hotel, Aylmer, their chiefs acting as hosts.

## News Happenings in Paragraphic Form

Dutton Wall Lumber Co., Ltd., Blucher, Sask., have closed their yard in that town.

Northern Woodlands, Limited, with a capital stock of $100,000, and headquarters in Montreal, have been granted a federal charter to make, sell and deal in pulpwood, wood pulp, paper, roofing material, beaver board, straw board, fibre board, wrapping paper, etc. Among the incorporators of the new company are Harley W. Gross and Harry C. Chesley, of Montreal.

Information has been received in Vancouver that shipments of B. C. Douglas Fir which have been sent into the Boston market have made much more favorable impression than some of the red fir from the other side which has gone into the same market. This preference was so strong that it was considered that it would create a stronger demand for material from British Columbia mills.

A federal charter has been granted to Hollingsworth & Whitney, Limited, with headquarters in Halifax, N. S., and a capital stock of $4,000,000, to purchase, hold and lease timber lands in the province of Nova Scotia, and to buy, sell and deal in lumber, paper, veneer, pulpwood and wooden goods of all kinds. Among the incorporators are S. D. Jenks W. C. Macdonald, Frank B. A. Chipman, Norman A. MacKay and Russell Y. Findley.

James Murray, one of the pioneer millwrights of the Central country, recently left Prince George for his farm on the prairies. He has been for a number of years millwright for the Alexa Lake Mills Ltd. Mr. Murray was for many years with John B Smith & Sons, of Toronto. He is unlikely to remain long on the prairies, and stated when he left the tall timber that he expected to return to the mountains before many months had passed.

The work of fire rangers in Northern Manitoba this summer will be facilitated by the introduction of a water plane, which will make regular patrols through the district. Supplies of gasoline will be established throughout the North, but the long canoe patrols which have been a part of the rangers' duties in the past will be unnecessary owing to the presence of the plane. Last summer 28 rangers were employed in Northern Manitoba patrolling the mineral belt, and the southern skirts of the fur area, but this number will be reduced during the coming summer.

# Budget of Newsy Briefs From Eastern Canada

Bank logs were arriving in fairly large quantities at Springhill, N.B., for some time past and were offered at $11 to $15 per thousand. They are mainly fir and spruce.

J. A. Gregory's mill at Ketepec has been operating for some time and the Bonny River mill started a few days ago. Mr. Gregory has a large number of logs on hand and the outlook is for a busy season.

On May 4 a new sash and door mill in Charlottetown, P.E.I., was destroyed by fire. The mill, which was owned by Messrs. Barnard, had been running only one day and the fire is thought to have started in the furnace room.

The mill and lumber yard of the Portage Lumber Company were burned at Portage, Aroostook County, on May 3. The fire originated from a hot box in the mill. The disastrous fire throws over 100 men out of employment. The loss is estimated at $150,000.

A report from Sussex, N.B., says that a large quantity of lumber has been shipped away from there during the last couple of months. About eighty cars were sent forward to points in the United States and large quantities sent to St. John for shipment overseas.

The Bonny River Company in St. George, N.B., started sawing operations recently. They expect to have a cut of 4,000,000 or 5,000,000 feet. The major portion of their drive arrived down river and the remaining amount is said to be all out of their brooks.

J. J. Herb, who was formerly superintendent of the Interlake Tissue Mills, Merritton, Ont., was recently in the West in consultation with the municipal authorities regarding the securing of a site on the Indian reserve on Lulu Island for the erection of a paper mill.

Among the losses this spring by fire was that of a lumbering manufacturing plant at Bantalor Station, which is situated on the National Transcontinental Ry. The mill was owned by Alderman Harold M. Young and had been running for a year and a half. The loss was estimated at $25,000 and only $8,000 insurance was carried. It is understood that plans are being made to erect a new plant.

According to late reports from the Miramichi, fully fifty million feet of logs will be brought down the river. The majority of these logs were cut last season and had been lying on the banks of the various streams. Some of the mills along the Miramichi have resumed operations.

Hon. F. P. Thompson, of Fredericton, N.B., who died recently in St. Luke's hospital, Ottawa, after a short illness, was a well-known member of the Senate. He was interested for years in the lumbering and milling business and had a most successful career. For many years he was in New Brunswick politics.

Dion's sawmill was destroyed by fire lately at Thetford Mines, Que. For a time it was feared that the flames woud spread to other nearby buildings, owing to the strong wind blowing, but after a hard fight the firemen managed to get control of the situation. The mill is a total loss. Mr. Dion having withdrawn his insurance only about one month ago.

A resident of Hartland, N.B., who was in St. John recently, said that the loss of the Hatfield Lumber Company's mill by fire in March, last, will mean a set back to men seeking employment. The mill, which was situated at Deerville, Carleton County, was destroyed by fire, which started from an unknown origin during the night. He said the owners placed the loss at about $6,000.

The St. John Log Driving Company are now actively engaged with their respective duties along the river. Prior to the opening of navigation on the river a meeting of the company was held and the following board of directors appointed: J. Fraser Gregory, chairman; W. E. Gunter, F. C. Beatteay, C. A. Beatteay, A. F. Randolph, St. John, and Mr. Walker of Fredericton, secretary and manager.

Men who have been employed for many years in Stetson, Cutler & Company's large mill at Indiantown, St. John, are anxiously awaiting word of the big plant's resumption of sawing operations. There is no word at the time of writing regarding the company's plans. In the meanwhile they are disposing of stock piled on their wharves. recently the three masted schooner Charles C. Lister, loaded a cargo for an American port.

Losses estimated at about $100,000 were caused by a fire which broke out in the lumber mills owned by Fraser Companies, Limited, at Bakerbrook, 13 miles from Woodstock, N.B. The spruce and shingle mills and all the lumber piled in one of the yards were completely destroyed. The fire spread rapidly and as it went it consumed ten dwellings, a store, a dozen out-buildings, the C.N.R. section house, the Temiscouata railway bridge over Baker Brook, and a box car loaded with lumber.

J. H. Johnson, mayor of Prince George, B.C., who is one of the promoters of the new pulp mill in the vicinity of that city, recently stated that it was hoped construction would commence in June, and if everything went well, operation of the plant would start in 1928. The mill will have a 150-ton daily capacity. A title on 200 square miles of timber limits has been secured East of Prince George on the Fraser River, all of which is considered the best quality for making a high grade of pulp.

Rain is badly needed along the St. John river and tributaries in order to swell the streams and give lumbermen a chance to get their drives out. The River Valley Lumber Company have two drives, one on the Otnabog and the other on Back Creek, aggregating 1,000,000 feet hung up. This represents about a third of their total cut and will mean a big loss if they cannot get the logs out this season. The company have been shipping lumber cut last season and hope to have their yard cleaned out in the near future.

The forest fire menace which promised to become serious in the central and south portions of New Brunswick, has been stamped out for the time being by the heaviest rain which has occurred in New Brunswick since last autumn. The rain has been general all over the province, according to reports reaching here this morning. While a considerable territory was burned over in the several fires in Sunbury County and in the southeastern corner of the parish of St. Mary's, York County, the total loss from fires was not large.

Chief Forester Prince, of New Brunswick, announced in Fredericton on May 5 that it was his intention to have the lookout stations manned the following week. The C.P.R. had been ordered to establish their thirty motor patrols on their lines of railways and some are now on duty. Motor patrols are also being established in the C.N.R. lines in New Brunswick.

W. H. Kelly died recently in Buckingham, Que., of which town he had been a resident for upwards of 25 years. He was a contractor for the building of tugs and bridge apparatus for the Dominion Government, and furnished the Montreal Harbor Commission with a large proportion of the timber used in their many schemes of improvement. Mr. Kelly came to Buckingham at the time when Grondin & Racicot, sawmillers, were being forced out of business through stress of falling markets. Mr. Kelly secured the mill and brought it to Buckingham, where after it had been in operation for some time, it was destroyed by fire. He had previously formed the W. H. Kelly Lumber Co. and rebuilt the plant immediately, carrying on sawing operations until the taking over of the mill and interests by Shear, Brown & Wills, some years ago. Mr. Kelly was also interested in farming and stock-raising and was in his 63rd year. He was a former Mayor of Buckingham.

In a recent report published by the American consul in St. John, N.B., it was shown that lumber exports to the United States during the first quarter of the year had been slightly smaller than during the corresponding period in 1921. This year's statement for the first quarter follows:

| | |
|---|---:|
| Laths | $ 91,614.92 |
| Lumber | 176,290.21 |
| Pine boards | 3,437.98 |
| Pulp wood | 677.60 |
| Shingles | nil |
| Hemlock boards | 456.60 |
| Wood pulp | 309,742.79 |
| | $582,220.10 |

Exports for the corresponding quarter in 1921 were valued at $616,966.11.

# PULPWOOD and PULP

## Pulpwood Business in Quebec is Dull

The purchasing power of pulp wood in the district of Quebec is still inactive, and the dealers are in a state of gloom, especially those with large stocks stored along the railway lines who are unable to sell their wood except at a loss. The Quebec dealers, spoken to on the subject, are crestfallen over the situation. One of those interviewed said his last sale to the American mills took place in January last, when he disposed of 1,000 cords and not one cord since, and furthermore, he had not as yet made the delivery.

The price of pulpwood has, in consequence, fallen, and the American concerns who give out the statement that their storage capacity at their mills is congested with wood are offering $14 per cord delivered, a price that cannot be entertained.

There is a tremendous quantity of rough pulpwood piled along the railroads going to decay. It is suggested that the Canadian mills instead of cutting wood on their limits should purchase the pulpwood cut and piled along the various railroads throughout the province of Quebec. One dealer informed the "Canada Lumberman's" correspondent that the last sale he made to American mill purchasers only gave him the price of $17 per cord, delivered at the mill, and besides he had to accept the purchaser's note for payment in three months.

The slump in demand and the unusually large quantity of pulpwood cut and falling into decay along the railway lines, has caused the government forestry service to watch the scientific end of independent interests in their laboratories for the prevention of decay in groundwood pulp used in the manufacture of paper. The interesting investigation recently completed at the Forest Products Laboratories of the Department of Interior is likely to have practical results for the prevention of decay in groundwood pulp, which frequently deteriorates through the action of mould and wood-destroying fungi. This creating considerably monetary loss to the owners is being watched with interest. The discovery which will, probably, mean the saving of millions of dollars to the pulp and paper industry and the industry, has come out of the investigations as to the practicability of pulping fire-killed trees. The forest fires which every year destroy millions of dollars' worth of Canadian timber, leave behind them immense numbers of trees which are killed, but not destroyed, by the fire. Such trees are never logged, and the wood becomes a total loss. These fire-killed trees are attacked by insects and fungi and are a menace to sound trees, one very common result being the sap-stain, a dark discolouration of the wood next to the bark, due to microscopic fungi. It has been discovered that these trees can be saved and utilized for commercial purposes by ordinary bleaching methods, and that the sap-stain need not prevent the material.

These experiments being conducted in the laboratories of the Canadian Department of Interior, are being watched with interest in an investigation into the pulping qualities of fire-killed woods in general, and if results are satisfactory, a vast quantity of wood, hitherto wasted, will be converted into a valuable resource.

## Fire-Killed Trees May be Used for Pulp

The forest fires which every year destroy millions of dollars worth of Canadian timber leave behind them immense numbers of trees which are killed but not destroyed by the fire. Such trees are seldom logged and the wood usually becomes a total loss.

Fire-killed trees are readily attacked by insects and fungi, one very common result being the so-called sap-stain, and coloration of the wood next the bark, due to invasion by microscopic fungi. As the value of sap-stained wood for making paper pulp has been questioned by manufacturers an investigation on the subject was recently undertaken at the Forest Products Laboratories of the Department of the Interior, Canada. It was found that pulping by the sulphite process failed to remove the coloration but that it could be completely eliminated by the ordinary bleaching methods. The sap-stain therefore need not prevent the material from being used for bleached sulphite pulp.

This is the first step in an investigation into the pulping qualities of fire-killed woods in general. If other results are equally satisfactory a large amount of wood, hitherto wasted, will be converted into a valuable resource.

## How Leading Industry is Expanding

Seven new machines with a total rated capacity of 558 tons daily of newsprint, were brought into operation in Canada during the last year, bringing the maximum daily production of newsprint up to 3,342 tons, or 1,002,600 tons a year. Two additional mills are in course of construction and will be in operation in the near future. This will bring Canada's maximum newsprint capacity up to 1,082,600 tons annually and amount to approximately 30% of the total newsprint consumption on the American continent.

## Storing Pulp in Water Saves Losses

An interesting investigation recently completed at the Forest Products Laboratories of the Department of the Interior, Canada, which is likely to have important practical results, relates to the prevention of decay in stored ground-wood pulp used in the manufacture of newspaper. Wood-pulp is sometimes stored in large quantities for several months and frequently deteriorates through the action of moulds and wood-destroying fungi, thus creating considerable monetary loss to the owners. The Laboratories, basing their experiments on the fact that wood submerged in water is immune to fungal decay, have investigated the preservative effect on pulp of storage in water and have found this method to give results so favorable as to warrant a trial on a commercial scale. The experiments were performed with several kinds of commercial pulp and were continued for seventeen months, after which time it was found that the pulp was unaffected by decay and could be made into a paper of good quality.

## Men Leave to Work on the Drives

Several gangs of men left Toronto recently to work on the log drives in various parts of Northern Ontario.

Employment Service Superintendent Wm. Mead, of Toronto, says, and there is a better prospect of work in the bush next winter for men seeking that class of employment. Last year very few men were sent out from Toronto as the different logging companies could obtain all the labor they required in their own towns and villages.

It is reported that in the winter of 1920-21, about 6,000 men left Toronto to work in the bush. Then business was lately active. During the past winter there were only a few hundred men able to secure jobs in the shanties.

The Victoria mill of the Fraser Companies Ltd., at Fredericton, N.B., is now in full operation having started sawing on May 1. They expect the cut this year to be in the vicinity of 9,000,000 feet. During the winter months the mill confined its operations to sawing laths.

Pulpwood handled by C. W. Cox, of Port Arthur, Ont., being hauled to the landing at Nipigon on Lake Superior for shipment by water.

# CURRENT LUMBER PRICES—WHOLESALE

## TORONTO

(In Car Load Lots, F.O.B. cars Toronto)

### White Pine

| | | |
|---|---|---|
| 1 x 4/7 Good Strips | $100.00 | $110.00 |
| 1¼ & 1½ x 4/7 Good Strips | 120.00 | 125.00 |
| 1 x 8 and up Good Sides | 150.00 | 160.00 |
| 2 x 4/7 Good Strips | 130.00 | 140.00 |
| 1¼ & 1½ x 8 and wider Good Sides | 185.00 | 190.00 |
| 2 x 8 and wider Good Sides | 190.00 | 200.00 |
| 1 in. No. 1, 2 and 3 Cuts | 75.00 | 80.00 |
| 5/4 and 6/4 No. 1, 2 and 3 Cuts | 95.00 | 100.00 |
| 2 in. No. 1, 2 and 3 Cuts | 105.00 | 110.00 |
| 1 x 4 and 5 Mill Run | 52.00 | 55.00 |
| 1 x 6 Mill Run | 53.00 | 56.00 |
| 1 x 7, 9 and 11 Mill Run | 53.00 | 56.00 |
| 1 x 8 Mill Run | 55.00 | 58.00 |
| 1 x 10 Mill Run | 60.00 | 62.00 |
| 1 x 12 Mill Run | 65.00 | 70.00 |
| 5/4 and 6/4 x 5 and up Mill Run | 58.00 | 60.00 |
| 2 x 4 Mill Run | 52.00 | 53.00 |
| 2 x 6 Mill Run | 53.00 | 56.00 |
| 2 x 8 Mill Run | 55.00 | 58.00 |
| 2 x 10 Mill Run | 58.00 | 60.00 |
| 2 x 12 Mill Run | 63.00 | 65.00 |
| 1 in. Mill Run Shorts | 35.00 | 40.00 |
| 1 x 4 and up 6/16 No. 1 Mill Culls | 30.00 | 32.00 |
| 1 x 10 and up 6/16 No. 1 Mill Culls | 34.00 | 36.00 |
| 1 x 12 and up 6/16 No. 1 Mill Culls | 34.00 | 36.90 |
| 1 x 4 and up 6/16 No. 2 Mill Culls | 23.00 | 25.00 |
| 1 x 10 x 12 6/16 No. 2 Mill Culls | 26.00 | 28.00 |
| 1 x 4 and up 6/16 No. 3 Mill Culls | 17.00 | 18.00 |

### Red Pine

(In Car Load Lots, F.O.B. Toronto)

| | | |
|---|---|---|
| 1 x 4 and 5 Mill Run | $34.00 | $35.00 |
| 1 x 6 Mill Run | 35.00 | 36.00 |
| 1 x 8 Mill Run | 37.00 | 38.00 |
| 1 x 10 Mill Run | 42.00 | 44.00 |
| 2 x 4 Mill Run | 37.00 | 38.00 |
| 2 x 6 Mill Run | 37.00 | 38.00 |
| 2 x 8 Mill Run | 38.00 | 39.00 |
| 2 x 10 Mill Run | 41.00 | 42.00 |
| 2 x 12 Mill Run | 46.00 | 47.00 |
| 1 in. Clear and Clear Face | 70.00 | 72.00 |
| 2 in. Clear and Clear Face | 70.00 | 72.00 |

### Spruce

| | | |
|---|---|---|
| 1 x 4 Mill Run | 34.00 | 35.00 |
| 1 x 6 Mill Run | 35.00 | 36.00 |
| 1 x 8 Mill Run | 37.00 | 38.00 |
| 1 x 10 Mill Run | 45.00 | 47.00 |
| 1 x 12 Mill Run Spruce | 48.00 | 50.00 |
| Mill Culls | 25.00 | 27.00 |

### Hemlock (M R)

(In Car Load Lots, F.O.B. Toronto)

| | | |
|---|---|---|
| 1 x 4 and 5 in. x 9 to 16 ft | $26.00 | $27.00 |
| 1 x 6 in. x 9 to 16 ft | 32.00 | 33.00 |
| 1 x 8 in. x 9 to 16 ft | 33.00 | 34.00 |
| 1 x 10 and 12 in. x 9 to 16 ft | 35.00 | 37.00 |
| 1 x 7, 9 and 11 in. x 9 to 16 ft | 32.00 | 33.00 |
| 2 x 4 to 12 in. 10/16 ft | 32.00 | 33.00 |
| 2 x 4 to 12 in., 18 ft | 37.00 | 39.00 |
| 2 x 4 to 12 in., 20 ft | 40.00 | 42.00 |
| 1 in. No. 2, 6 ft. to 16 ft | 23.00 | 25.00 |

### Fir Flooring

(In Car Load Lots, F.O.B. Toronto)

| | |
|---|---|
| Fir flooring, 1 x 3 and 4", No. 1 and 2 Edge Grain | $75.00 |
| Fir flooring, 1 x 3 and 4", No. 1 and 2 Flat Grain | 48.00 |

(Depending upon Widths)

| | |
|---|---|
| 1 x 4 to 12 No. 1 and 2 Clear Fir, Rough | 77.00 |
| 1¼ x 4 to 12 No. 1 and 2 Clear Fir, Rough | 81.00 |
| 2 x 4 to 12 No. 1 and 2 Clear Fir, Rough | 77.00 |
| 3 & 4 x 4 to 12 No. 1 & 2 Clear Fir, Rough | 84.00 |
| 1 x 4, 5 and 6 in Fir Casing | 76.00 |
| 1 x 8 and 10 Fir Base | 83.00 |
| 1¼ and 1½ 8, 10 and 12 in. E.G. Stepping | 95.00 |
| 1¼ and 1½ 8, 10 and 12 in. F.G. Stepping | 85.00 |
| 1 x 4 to 12 Clear Fir, D4S | 75.00 |
| 1¼ and 1½ x 4 to 12 Clear Fir, D4S | 78.00 |
| XX Shingles, 6 butts to 2", per M | 3.35 |
| XXX Shingles, 6 butts to 2", per M | 5.75 |
| XXXXX Shingles, 5 butts to 2", per M | 6.40 |

### Lath

(F.O.B. Mill)

| | |
|---|---|
| No. 1 White Pine | $11.00 |
| No. 2 White Pine | 10.00 |
| No. 3 White Pine | 8.00 |
| Mill Run White Pine, 32 in | 3.50 |
| Merchantable Spruce Lath, 4 ft | 6.50 |

## TORONTO HARDWOOD PRICES

The prices given below are for car loads f.o.b. Toronto, from wholesalers to retailers, and are based on a good percentage of long lengths and good widths, without any wide stock having been sorted out.

The prices quoted on imported woods are payable in U. S. funds.

### Ash, White

(Dry weight 3800 lbs. per M. ft.)

| | 1s & 2s | No. 1 Com. | No. 2 Com. |
|---|---|---|---|
| 1" | $105.00 | $ 65.00 | $ 30.00 |
| 1¼ and 1½" | 110.00 | 70.00 | 45.00 |
| 2" | 120.00 | 75.00 | 50.00 |
| 2½ and 3" | 140.00 | 85.00 | 60.00 |
| 4" | 155.00 | 95.00 | 70.00 |

### Ash, Brown

| | 1s & 2s | No. 1 Com. | No. 2 Com. |
|---|---|---|---|
| 1" | $120.00 | 60.00 | $40.00 |
| 1¼ and 1½" | 130.00 | 65.00 | 45.00 |
| 2" | 150.00 | 70.00 | 55.00 |
| 2½ and 3" | 160.00 | 85.00 | 55.00 |
| 4" | 175.00 | 95.00 | 60.00 |

### Birch

(Dry weight 4000 lbs. per M. ft.)

| | 1s & 2s | Sels. | No. 1 Com. | No. 2 Com. |
|---|---|---|---|---|
| 4/4 | $105.00 | $ 80.00 | $ 50.00 | $ 32.00 |
| 5/4 | 110.00 | 85.00 | 55.00 | 35.00 |
| 6/4 | 115.00 | 90.00 | 60.00 | 38.00 |
| 8/4 | 120.00 | 100.00 | 65.00 | 42.00 |
| 12/4 | 125.00 | 105.00 | 70.00 | 50.00 |
| 16/4 | 130.00 | 110.00 | 80.00 | 55.00 |

### Basswood

(Dry weight 2500 lbs. per M. ft.)

| | 1s & 2s | No. 1 Com. | No. 2 Com. |
|---|---|---|---|
| 4/4 | $ 80.00 | $ 50.00 | $ 25.00 |
| 5/4 and 6/4 | 85.00 | 60.00 | 30.00 |
| 8/4 | 90.00 | 65.00 | 35.00 |

### Chestnut

(Dry weight 2800 lbs. per M. ft.)

| | 1s & 2s | No. 1 Com. | Sound Wormy |
|---|---|---|---|
| 1" | 135.00 | 80.00 | 40.00 |
| 1¼ to 1½" | 145.00 | 85.00 | 43.00 |
| 2" | 155.00 | 90.00 | 43.00 |

### Maple, Hard

(Dry weight 4200 lbs. per M. ft.)

| | F.A.S. | Sels. | No. 1 Com. | No. 2 Com. |
|---|---|---|---|---|
| 4/4 | $ 85.00 | $ 65.00 | $ 45.00 | $ 33.00 |
| 5/4 | 85.00 | 65.00 | 45.00 | 38.00 |
| 6/4 | 90.00 | 70.00 | 50.00 | 45.00 |
| 8/4 | 100.00 | 75.00 | 60.00 | 50.00 |
| 12/4 | 105.00 | 75.00 | 65.00 | 60.00 |
| 16/4 | 125.00 | 100.00 | 70.00 | 65.00 |

### Elm, Soft

(Dry weight 3100 lbs. per M. ft.)

| | 1s & 2s | No. 1 Com. | No. 2 Com. |
|---|---|---|---|
| 4/4 | $ 75.00 | $ 50.00 | $ 30.00 |
| 6/4 and 8/4 | 80.00 | 60.00 | 35.00 |
| 12/4 | 96.00 | 70.00 | 40.00 |

### Gum, Red

(Dry weight 3300 lbs. per M. ft.)

| | Plain | | Quartered | |
|---|---|---|---|---|
| | 1s & 2s | No. 1 Com. | 1s & 2s | No. 1 Com. |
| 1" | $120.00 | $ 72.00 | $ 125.00 | $ 76.00 |
| 1¼" | 122.00 | 75.00 | 130.00 | 80.00 |
| 1½" | 125.00 | 78.00 | 130.00 | 80.00 |
| 2" | 130.00 | 90.00 | 135.00 | 90.00 |

Figured Gum, $10 per M. extra, in both plain and quartered.

### Gum, Sap

| | 1s&2s | No. 1 Com. |
|---|---|---|
| 1" | $ 55.00 | $ 38.00 |
| 1¼" and 1½" | 58.00 | 42.00 |
| 2" | 63.00 | 48.00 |

### Hickory

(Dry weight 4500 lbs. per M. ft.

| | 1s&2s | No. 1 Com. |
|---|---|---|
| 1" | $120.00 | $ 60.00 |
| 1¼" | 145.00 | 65.00 |
| 1½" | 145.00 | 65.00 |
| 2" | 150.00 | 70.00 |

### Quarter Cut Red Oak

| | 1s&2s | No. 1 Com. |
|---|---|---|
| 4/4 | $145.00 | $ 80.00 |
| 5/4 and 6/4 | 160.00 | 90.00 |
| 8/4 | 165.00 | 95.00 |

### Plain White and Red Oak

(Plain sawed. Dry weight 4000 lbs. per M. ft.)

| | 1s&2s | No. 1 Com. |
|---|---|---|
| 4/4 | $130.00 | $ 70.00 |
| 5/4 and 6/4 | 135.00 | 75.00 |
| 8/4 | 140.00 | 80.00 |
| 10/4 | 145.00 | 90.00 |
| 12/4 | 145.00 | 90.00 |
| 16/4 | 150.00 | 95.00 |

### White Oak, Quarter Cut

(Dry weight 4000 lbs. per M. ft.)

| | 1s&2s | No. 1 Com. |
|---|---|---|
| 4/4 | $160.00 | $ 90.00 |
| 5/4 and 6/4 | 170.00 | 95.00 |
| 8/4 | 190.00 | 105.00 |

## OTTAWA

Manufacturers' Prices

### Pine

| | | |
|---|---|---|
| **Good sidings:** | | |
| 1 in. x 7 in. and up | | $140.00 |
| 1¼ in. and 1½ in., 8 in. and up. | | 165.00 |
| 2 in. x 7 in. and up | | 165.00 |
| No. 2 cuts 2 x 8 in. and up | | 80.00 |
| **Good strips:** | | |
| 1 in. | $100.00 | $105.00 |
| 1¼ in. and 1½ in. | | 120.00 |
| 2 in. | | 125.00 |
| **Good shorts:** | | |
| 1 in. x 7 in. and up | | 110.00 |
| 1 in. 4 in. to 6 in. | 85.00 | 90.00 |
| 1¼ in. and 1½ in. | | 110.00 |
| 2 in. | | 125.00 |
| 7 in. to 9 in. A sidings | 54.00 | 56.00 |
| No. 1 dressing sidings | 70.00 | 74.00 |
| No. 1 dressing strips | | 62.00 |
| No. 1 dressing shorts | 50.00 | 53.00 |
| 1 in. x 4 in. s.c. strips | | 48.00 |
| 1 in. x 5 in. s.c. strips | | 48.00 |
| 1 in. x 6 in. s.c. strips | | 50.00 |
| 1 in. x 7 in. s.c. strips | 51.00 | 54.00 |
| 1 in. x 8 in. s.c. strips, 12 to 16 ft. | | 54.00 |
| 1 in. x 10 in. M.R. | | 58.00 |
| S.C. sidings, 1½ and 2 in. | 58.00 | 60.00 |
| S.C. strips, 1 in. | | 45.00 |
| 1¼, 1½ and 2 in. | 50.00 | 55.00 |
| S. shorts, 1 x 4 to 6 in. | 34.00 | 36.00 |
| S. and bet., shorts, 1 x 5 | | 36.00 |
| S.C. and bet., shorts, 1 x 6 | | 42.00 |
| S.C. shorts, 6-11 ft., 1 x 10 in. | | 48.00 |
| **Box boards:** | | |
| 1 in. x 4 in. and up, 6 ft.-11 ft. | | 34.00 |
| 1 in. x 3 in. and up, 12 ft.-16 ft. | 35.00 | 37.00 |
| Mill cull shorts, 1 in. x 4 in. and x 4 in. and up, 12 ft. and up | 24.00 | 26.00 |
| Mill culls, strips and sidings, 1 in. up, 6 ft. to 11 ft. | | 22.00 |
| O. culls r and w p | 18.00 | 20.00 |

### Red Pine, Log Run

| | | |
|---|---|---|
| Mill culls out, 1 in. | 32.00 | 34.00 |
| Mill culls out, 1¼ in. | 32.00 | 34.00 |
| Mill culls out, 1½ in. | 32.00 | 34.00 |
| Mill culls out, 2 in. | 32.00 | 34.00 |
| Mill Culls, white pine, 1 in. x 7 in. and up | | 20.00 |

### Mill Run Spruce

| | | |
|---|---|---|
| 1 in. x 4 in. and up, 6 ft.-11 ft. | | 23.00 |
| 1 in. x 4 in. and up, 12 ft.-16 ft. | 30.00 | 32.00 |
| 1" x 9"-10" and up, 12 ft.-16 ft. | | 35.00 |
| 1¼" x 7, 8 and 9" up, 12 ft.-16 ft. | | 35.00 |
| 1¼ x 10 and up, 12 ft.-16 ft. | 38.00 | 42.00 |
| 1½" x 12" x 12" and up, 12'-16' | | 42.00 |
| Spruce, 1 in. clear fine dressing and B | | 55.00 |
| Hemlock, 1 in. cull | | 20.00 |
| Hemlock, 1 in. log run | 24.00 | 26.00 |
| Hemlock, 2 x 4, 6, 8, 10 12/16 ft. | | 28.00 |
| Tamarac | 25.00 | 28.00 |
| Basswood, log run, dead culls out | 45.00 | 50.00 |
| Basswood, log run, mill culls out. | 50.00 | 54.00 |
| Birch, log run | 45.00 | 50.00 |
| Soft Elm, common and better, 1, 1½, 2 in. | 58.00 | 68.00 |
| Ash, black, log run | 62.00 | 65.00 |
| 1 x 10 No. 1 barn | 57.00 | 62.00 |
| 1 x 10 No. 2 barn | 51.00 | 56.00 |
| 1 x 8 and 9 No. 2 barn | 47.00 | 52.00 |

# CURRENT LUMBER PRICES—WHOLESALE

**Lath per M.:**

| | | |
|---|---|---|
| No. 1 White Pine, 1¼ in. x 4 ft. | | 8.00 |
| No. 2 White Pine | | 6.00 |
| Mill run White Pine | | 7.00 |
| Spruce, mill run, 1½ in. | | 6.00 |
| Red Pine, mill run | | 6.00 |
| Hemlock, mill run | | 5.50 |
| **White Cedar Shingles** | | |
| XXXX, 18 in. | 9.00 | 10.00 |
| Clear butt, 18 in. | 6.00 | 7.00 |
| 18 in. XX | | 5.00 |

## QUEBEC

**White Pine**
(At Quebec)

| | Cts. Per Cubic Ft. | |
|---|---|---|
| First class Ottawa waney, 18 in. average according to lineal | 100 | 110 |
| 19 in. and up average | 110 | 120 |

**Spruce Deals**
(At Mill)

| | | |
|---|---|---|
| 3 in. unsorted, Quebec, 4 in. to 6 in. wide | $ 20.00 | $ 25.00 |
| 3 in. unsorted, Quebec, 7 in. to 8 in. wide | 26.00 | 28.00 |
| 3 in. unsorted, Quebec, 9 in. wide | 30.00 | 35.00 |

**Oak**
(At Quebec)

| | Cts. Per Cubic Ft. | |
|---|---|---|
| According to average and quality, 55 ft. cube | 125 | 130 |

**Elm**
(At Quebec)

| | | |
|---|---|---|
| According to average and quality, 40 to 45 ft. cube | 100 | 120 |
| According to average and quality, 30 to 35 ft. | 90 | 100 |

**Export Birch Planks**
(At Mill)

| | | |
|---|---|---|
| 1 to 4 in. thick, per M. ft. | $ 30.00 | $ 35.00 |

## ST. JOHN, N.B.

(From Yards and Mills—Retail)

**Rough Lumber**

| | | |
|---|---|---|
| 2x3, 2x4, 3x3, 3x4. Rgh Merch Spr. | $28.00 | |
| 2x3, 2x4, 3x3, 3x4, Dressed 1 edge | 30.00 | |
| 2x3, 2x4, 3x3, 3x4, Dressed 4 sides | 31.00 | |
| 2x6, 2x7, 3x5, 4x4, 4x6, all rough. | 28.00 | |
| 2x6, 2x7, 3x5, 4x4, 4x6, all rough. | 30.00 | |
| 2x8, 3x7, 5x5, 6x6 | 35.00 | $40.00 |
| 2x9, 3x8, 6x8, 7x7 | 37.00 | $40.00 |
| 2x10, 3x9 | 40.00 | |
| 2x12, 3x10, 3x12, 8x8 and up | 42.00 | |
| Merch. Spr. Bds. Rough, 1x3-4 & 5 | 28.00 | |
| Merch. Spr. Bds., Rough, 1x7 & up | 35.00 | |
| Refuse Bds., Deals and Setgs. | 18.00 | 20.00 |

Above random lengths up to 18-0 long.
Lengths 19-0 and up $5.00 extra per M.
For planing Merch. and Refuse Bds. add $2.00 per M. to above prices.
Laths, $7.00.

**Shingles**

| | Per M. |
|---|---|
| Cedar, Extras | $6.00 |
| Cedar, Clears | 5.00 |
| Cedar, 2nd Clears | 4.00 |
| Cedar, Extra No. 1 | 2.50 |
| Spruce | 3.50 |

## SARNIA, ONT.

**White Pine—Fine, Com. and Better**

| | |
|---|---|
| 1 x 6 and 8 in. | $110.00 |
| 1 in., 8 in. and up wide | 130.00 |
| 1¼ and 1½ in. and up wide | 180.00 |
| 2 in. and up wide | 180.00 |
| **Cuts and Better** | |
| 4/4 x 8 and up No. 1 and better | 125.00 |
| 5/4 and 6/4 and up No. 1 and better | 150.00 |
| 8/4 and 8 and up No. 1 and better | 150.00 |
| **No. 1 Cuts** | |
| 1 in., 8 in. and up wide | 105.00 |
| 1¼ in., 8 in. and up wide | 125.00 |
| 1½ in., 8 in. and up wide | 125.00 |
| 2 in., 8 in. and up wide | 130.00 |
| 2½ in. and 3 in., 8 in. and up wide | 175.00 |
| 4 in., 8 in. and up wide | 185.00 |

| | | |
|---|---|---|
| **No. 1 Barn** | | |
| 1 in., 10 to 16 ft. long | $ 75.00 | $ 85.00 |
| 1¼, 1½ and 2 in., 10/16 ft. | 80.00 | 85.00 |
| 2½ to 3 in., 10/16 ft. | 85.00 | 100.00 |
| **No. 2 Barn** | | |
| 1 in., 10 to 16 ft. long | 65.00 | 75.00 |
| 1¼, 1½ and 2 in., 10/16 ft. | | 66.00 |
| 2½, 1½ and 3 in. | | 85.00 |
| **No. 3 Barn** | | |
| 1 in., 10 to 16 ft. long | 48.00 | 55.00 |
| 1¼, 1½ and 2 in., 10/16 ft. | 50.00 | 56.00 |
| **Box** | | |
| 1 in., 1¼ and 1½ in., 10/16 ft. | 33.00 | 35.00 |
| **Mill Culls** | | |
| Mill Run Culls— | | |
| 1 in., 4 in. and up wide, 6/16 ft. | | 26.00 |
| 1¼, 1½ and 2 in. | | 27.00 |

## WINNIPEG

**No. 1 Spruce**

| Dimension | S.1.S. and 1.E. 10 ft. | 12 ft. | 14 ft. | 16 ft. |
|---|---|---|---|---|
| 2 x 4 | $29 | $28 | $28 | $29 |
| 2 x 6 | 30 | 28 | 28 | 29 |
| 2 x 8 | 31 | 29 | 29 | 30 |
| 2 x 10 | 32 | 30 | 30 | 31 |
| 2 x 12 | 33 | 31 | 31 | 32 |

For 2 inches, rough, add 50 cents.
For S1E only, add 50 cents.
For S1S and 2E, S4S or D&M, add $3.00.
For timbers larger than 8 x 8, add 50c. for each additional 2 inches each way.
For lengths longer than 20 ft., add $1.00 for each additional two feet.
For selected common, add $5.00.
For No. 2 Dimension, $3.00 less than No. 1.
For 1 x 2 and 2 x 2, $2 more than 2 x 4 No. 1.
For Tamarac, open.

## BUFFALO and TONAWANDA

**White Pine**
Wholesale Selling Price

| | |
|---|---|
| Uppers, 4/4 | $225.00 |
| Uppers, 5/4 to 8/4 | 225.00 |
| Uppers, 10/4 to 12/4 | 250.00 |
| Selects, 4/4 | 200.00 |
| Selects, 5/4 to 8/4 | 200.00 |
| Selects, 10/4 to 12/4 | 225.00 |
| Fine Common, 4/4 | 155.00 |
| Fine Common, 5/4 | 160.00 |
| Fine Common, 6/4 | 160.00 |
| Fine Common, 8/4 | 160.00 |
| No. 1 Cuts, 4/4 | 115.00 |
| No. 1 Cuts, 5/4 | 130.00 |
| No. 1 Cuts, 6/4 | 135.00 |
| No. 1 Cuts, 8/4 | 140.00 |
| No. 2 Cuts, 4/4 | 70.00 |
| No. 2 Cuts, 5/4 | 100.00 |
| No. 2 Cuts, 6/4 | 105.00 |
| No. 2 Cuts, 8/4 | 110.00 |
| No. 3 Cuts, 5/4 | 60.00 |
| No. 3 Cuts, 6/4 | 65.00 |
| No. 3 Cuts, 8/4 | 67.00 |
| Dressing, 4/4 | 95.00 |
| Dressing 4/4 x 10 | 98.00 |
| Dressing, 4/4 x 12 | 110.00 |
| No. 1 Moulding, 5/4 | 150.00 |
| No. 1 Moulding, 6/4 | 150.00 |
| No. 1 Moulding, 8/4 | 155.00 |
| No. 2 Moulding, 5/4 | 125.00 |
| No. 2 Moulding, 6/4 | 125.00 |
| No. 2 Moulding, 8/4 | 130.00 |
| No. 1 Barn, 1 x 12 | 90.00 |
| No. 1 Barn, 1 x 6 and 8 | 76.00 |
| No. 1 Barn, 1 x 10 | 80.00 |
| No. 2 Barn, 1 x 6 and 8 | 62.00 |
| No. 2 Barn, 1 x 10 | 63.00 |
| No. 2 Barn, 1 x 12 | 75.00 |
| No. 3 Barn, 1 x 6 and 8 | 39.00 |
| No. 3 Barn, 1 x 10 | 39.00 |
| No. 3 Barn, 1 x 12 | 45.00 |
| No. 1 Box, 1 x 6 and 8 | 36.00 |
| No. 1 Box 1 x 10 | 37.00 |
| No. 1 Box, 1 x 12 | 38.00 |
| No. 1 Box, 1 x 13 and up | 39.00 |

## BUFFALO

The following quotations on hardwoods represent the jobber buying price at Buffalo and Tonawanda.

| | 1s & 2s | No. 1 Com. | No. 2 Com. |
|---|---|---|---|
| **Maple** | | | |
| 1 in. | $ 75.00 | $ 46.00 | $ 28.00 |
| 5/4 to 8/4 | 80.00 | 50.00 | 28.00 |
| 10/4 to 4 in. | 86.00 | 56.00 | 28.00 |
| **Sap Birch** | | | |
| 1 in. | 90.00 | 45.00 | 30.00 |
| 5/4 and up | 100.00 | 50.00 | 30.00 |
| **Soft Elm** | | | |
| 1 in. | 70.00 | 45.00 | 30.00 |
| 5/4 to 2 in. | 75.00 | 50.00 | 30.00 |
| **Red Birch** | | | |
| 1 in. | 120.00 | 75.00 | |
| 5/4 and up | 125.00 | 80.00 | |
| **Basswood** | | | |
| 1 in. | 70.00 | 45.00 | 30.00 |
| 5/4 to 2 in. | 80.00 | 55.00 | 35.00 |
| **Plain Oak** | | | |
| 1 in. | 95.00 | 55.00 | 35.00 |
| 5/4 to 2 in. | 105.00 | 65.00 | 40.00 |
| **Ash** | | | |
| 1 in. | 80.00 | 48.00 | 30.00 |
| 5/4 to 2 in. | 85.00 | 52.00 | 30.00 |
| 10/4 and up | 100.00 | 65.00 | 30.00 |

## BOSTON

Quotations given below are for highest grades of Michigan and Canadian White Pine and Eastern Canadian Spruce as required in the New England market in car loads.

| | | |
|---|---|---|
| White Pine Uppers, 1 in. | | |
| White Pine Uppers, 1¼, 1½, 2 in. | | |
| White Pine Uppers, 2½, 3 in. | | |
| White Pine Uppers, 4 in. | | |
| Selects, 1 in. | | $190.00 |
| Selects, 1¼, 2 in. | | 200.00 |
| Selects, 2½, 3 in. | | |
| Selects, 4 in. | | |
| Prices nominal | | |
| Fine Common, 1 in., 30%, 12 in. and up. | | 165.00 |
| Fine Common, 1 x 8 and up | | 165.00 |
| Fine Common, 1¼ to 2 in. | $165.00 | 170.00 |
| Fine Common, 2½ and 3 in. | | 180.00 |
| Fine Common, 4 in. | | 195.00 |
| 1 in. Shaky Clear | | 100.00 |
| 1¼ in. to 2 in. Shaky Clear | | 110.00 |
| 1 in. No. 2 Dressing | | 95.00 |
| 1¼ in. to 2 in. No. 2 Dressing | | 95.00 |
| No. 1 Cuts, 1 in. | | 110.00 |
| No. 1 Cuts, 1¼ to 2 in. | | 140.00 |
| No. 1 Cuts, 2½ to 3 in. | | 180.00 |
| No. 2 Cuts, 1 in. | | 80.00 |
| No. 2 Cuts, 1¼ to 2 in. | | 110.00 |
| Barn Boards, No. 1, 1 x 12 | | 95.00 |
| Barn Boards, No. 1, 1 x 10 | | 87.00 |
| Barn Boards, No. 1, 1 x 8 | | 83.00 |
| Barn Boards, No. 2, 1 x 12 | | 82.00 |
| Barn Boards, No. 2, 1 x 8 | | 69.00 |
| Barn Boards, No. 2, 1 x 10 | | 70.00 |
| Barn Boards, No. 3, 1 x 12 | | 48.00 |
| Barn Boards, No. 3, 1 x 10 | | 47.00 |
| Barn Boards, No. 3, 1 x 8 | | 47.00 |
| **No. 1 Clear** | | |
| Can. Spruce, No. 1 and clear, 1 x 4 to 9" | | $ 78.00 |
| Can. Spruce, 1 x 10 in. | | 78.00 |
| Can. Spruce, No. 1, 1 x 4 to 7 in. | | 75.00 |
| Can. Spruce, No. 1, 1 x 8 and 9 in. | | 75.00 |
| Can. Spruce, No. 1, 1 x 10 in. | | 76.00 |
| Can. Spruce, No. 2, 1 x 4 and 5 in. | | 34.00 |
| Can. Spruce, No. 2, 1 x 6 and 7 in. | | 36.00 |
| Can. Spruce, No. 2, 1 x 8 and 9 in. | | 38.00 |
| Can. Spruce, No. 2, 1 x 10 in. | | 41.00 |
| Can. Spruce, No. 2, 1 x 12 in. | | 45.00 |
| Spruce, 12 in. dimension | | 44.00 |
| Spruce, 10 in. dimension | | 42.00 |
| Spruce, 9 in. dimension | | 41.00 |
| Spruce, 8 in. dimension | | 40.00 |
| 2 x 10 in. random lengths, 8 ft. and up | | 40.00 |
| 2 x 12 in., random lengths | | 43.00 |
| 2 x 3, 2 x 4, 2 x 5, 2 x 6, 2 x 7 | | 30.00 |
| 3 x 4 and 4 x 4 in. | | 31.00 |
| 2 x 9 | | 38.00 |
| All other random lengths, 7 in. and under, 8 ft. and up | 30.00 | 34.00 |
| 5 in. and up merchantable boards, 8 ft. and up, D 1s | 30.00 | 32.00 |
| 1 x 2 | 30.00 | 32.00 |
| 1 x 3 | | 30.00 |
| 1⅝ in. Spruce Lath | | 8.50 |
| 1½ in. Spruce Lath | 7.25 | 7.50 |
| **New Brunswick Cedar Shingles** | | |
| Extras | 5.25 | 5.50 |
| Clears | 4.25 | 4.50 |
| Second Clear | 3.75 | 4.15 |
| Clear Whites | | 3.00 |

# Quick Action Section

## Construction Industry Is Decidedly Active

The volume in building is developing—says MacLean Building Reports, Limited. It is, in fact, the chief influence in improved business conditions in Canada. To-day, with but one exception, the construction industry is busier than it has been at any time since 1914. It is busy on private construction and that is the important thing. The public is setting out to satisfy long deferred requirements in housing, in business building and in plant facilities.

During April, construction contracts awarded in Canada, amounted to $29,428,400, compared with $13,465,000 in March, and $21,622,000 in April 1921. Residential building accounted for 42.8% of the April total, and amounted to $12,472,200. Business building amounted to $8,203,300, or 27.9% of the total; industrial buildings, $3,176,400, or 10.8%; public works and utilities, $5,576,500, or 18.5%. The amount of contemplated new work reported during April was $29,427,600.

The trend of building costs is still slightly downward. During March, the wholesale price index of 48 building materials declined 5%, and is now 79.7% above 1913, compared with a peak of 183.8% reached in May, 1920. Prices have now declined 56.6% from the high. The confidence of building investors is mounting rapidly because they are learning that we have really entered the period of stabilization in building costs and that there is no danger of too great a depreciation in the replacement values of buildings constructed now.

Its time to build. The convincing proof is that thousands and thousands of projects are going ahead; that builders are finding conditions favorable, that labor is settling down to a sound basis of production, and the flow of money into building channels is increasing. Many of the big projects under-way have been undertaken only after careful study of the situation and only after the investor has come to realize that the major conditions in the building field now are favorable.

---

## Price Bros. Issue Annual Statement

The annual statement of Price Bros. & Co., Quebec, shows the effect of the labor troubles which were experienced at one of their plants last year. The statement issued covers the fiscal year ended February 28th last. The adverse market for newsprint earlier in the year, reduced the earning power of the company to some extent. The report shows the results of the economies effected, and Sir Wm. Price, president of the company, expressed the belief that everything is now on a sound working basis and the future is brighter.

The company's profit for the fiscal year amounted to $1,327,332, as compared with $1,135,450 in the four months of the company's existance in the previous fiscal period. Comparisons must be made between the full year just ended and the preceding broken period. After bond and note interest, net profits were $906,356, against $993,458 in the previous period, payment of dividends of $651,992 necessitating a withdrawal from surplus of $161,992 and reducing profit and loss balance to $490,372.

It is notable that during the year dividends were at the higher rate for the first half of the period, so that 2½ per cent. was actually paid. The 2 per cent. dividend was earned in the year, net earnings being equal to 2.07 per cent. on the outstanding capital stock.

The company's working capital position is satisfactory in view of the fact that inventories in the year were written down to replacement values, or less. Current assets amounted to $5,703,390. as against $7,592,144 a year ago, and current liabilities to $3,014,042, against $3,780,183. This indicates net working capital of $2,689,347, compared with $3,814,961. a year ago, a reduction of little over $1,000,000

Property account is carried at $46,119,892., compared with $45,497,018, bond debit has been reduced about $200,000. to $4,770,696, while reserves are $1,107,239, against $1,192,937. Total assets stand at $52,134,698., against $53,386,710.

---

## Captured Tarpon After Strenuous Fight

W. J. Pulling, of Sandwich, Ont., who is well-known in lumber circles, and Mrs Pulling, recently returned after spending the winter in Naples, Florida.

Mr. Pulling scored the 1922 Naples record by landing three members of the tarpon tribe, one fish being 6 feet, 8 inches in length and weighing 125 lbs. It took an hour and a quarter for Mr. Pulling to get the finny monster into the boat, but the task was worth while. Mrs. Pulling hooked a tarpon 6 feet long and weighing 95 lbs., which is a splendid showing for a lady angler.

Hunting tarpon is one of the most exciting of water sports

---

## Hemp Hurds for Paper Making

An interesting investigation recently carried out at the Forest Products Laboratories of the Department of the Interior, Canada, relates to the value of hemp hurds as a paper-making material. Hemp hurds are the waste stalks of hemp from which the fibre has been removed. Considerable quantities of the hurds, at present a mere waste product, are available in Canada. Some attention has been given to this subject in the United States where experiments have been made in which the soda process was used. The work at the Laboratories however has been directed towards the application of the sulphite process, widely used in Canadian pulp mills for the manufacture of chemical wood-pulp. The results obtained indicate that while the material lends itself to sulphite cooking the resulting pulp has an extremely short fibre and is somewhat hard to bleach. The yield however is large and the pulp might advantageously be used as a filler with pulps of longer fibre.

---

## County Forests

It is announced that already twelve counties have taken advantage of the Ontario Government's plan for assisting municipal forestry. These counties have acquired blocks of non-agricultural land which, in co-operation with the Provincial Forest Service, will be planted with pine, spruce, and other trees. The blocks of land vary in size from 100 acres up to 1,000 acres. It is expected that several other counties will take up reforestation within the coming year.

The man who goes fishing or camping and who carelessly throws cigarette stubs about or neglects to put out the last vestiges of any fire he starts to boil a pot of water may do more damage to his native province than he can repay by a lifetime of hard work.

---

# Review of Current Trade Conditions

## Conditions in Ontario and the East

May is expected to be a very good month in the lumber arena and the first few days showed considerable improvement over what has prevailed for some time. In the country, trade is not opening out rapidly but the signs are hopeful. The farmers are, of course, busy seeding and planting and until spring operations are over, will not direct a great deal of their attention to building or repairs. In the cities, however, conditions are different and all places from 10,-000 up are reporting a building boom, practically in the line of modern-priced dwellings.

It begins to look as if this year's activities will contribute very largely toward satisfying the need of houses in most communities. From nearly every populous centre come reports of record-breaking building permits, and in some centres more houses are going up during present month than were erected during a whole year in the war-time period. All this has created a sturdy movement in hemlock, white pine, chestnut and other trim, while flooring manufacturers are reported to be exceptionally busy. The demand is keen for birch and maple flooring, while oak also is in strong requisition.

There is reported in many places a scarcity of 2 x 4 x 10 and 2 x 8 x 10 in hemlock. No. 1 white pine, mill culls are moving quite freely and there is a pretty fair call for good sides, good strips and No. 1, 2 and 3 cuts. There is a fair movement of white pine across the border so Easter wholesalers report.

Most of the Toronto firms specializing in softwoods, are quite optimistic over the local building boom. All the woodworking plants in the Queen City are working to capacity, and retail yards are buying freely and delivering the material on more jobs than they have at any time during the past few years. One representative yardman, who conducts a large establishment (but by no means the largest in Toronto,) stated recently that during April his firm had made 2800 deliveries, sold over 2,000,000 feet of hemlock and over 10 cars of shingles. The latter are in urgent demand and exceptionally scarce.

Prices are ascending all the while and will ntaurally continue to do so until some B. C. mills, which were closed down owing to the snow and cold weather last winter, get in operation once more and satisfy the call for shingles which have to be favored more this season than ever as a roof covering.

There are no cars in transit and it may be quite a while yet before those who desire shingles, are able to get them in the quantities which their trade demands. There are no "lame ducks" at Cartier at the present time, as cars loaded with shingles under demurrage are frequently called. There is a fair movement of white pine across the border, so eastern wholesalers report.

In the hardwood market conditions are more difficult to analyze. Manufacturers and wholesalers generally agree that in Ontario and the East the market is not nearly as active as it is across the border where prices on the scarcer lines show a distinct upward tendency. Producers declare that advances are bound to become effective unless the old economic law of supply and demand miscarries. On the other hand, stocks in Ontario are getting badly shot, and what orders are being taken locally, they are described by one dealer as being "accepted at ruinous prices." No large blocks of stock have changed hands, and buying and selling occur largely as the market situation develops from week to week.

In birch, 6/4 and up, the demand is easing off, but there is a steady call for 1 inch birch in firsts and seconds and No. 1 common, which are reported to be scarce and getting higher in price. In maple, the largest demand is for 6/4 No. 1 common and better. Other lines are comparitively quiet. Requisitions for basswood are few and far between at the present time, but elm is picking up somewhat. More inquiries are being received from week to week for hardwoods, but most of them are what are termed an "impossible character," or the price set is too low for wholesale dealers to obtain in the stock and turn it over profitably. Those who have hardwood stocks for sale are holding them at firm prices and one exponent declares that producers ask more for their stuff than the wholesaler is getting and he wants to know where the latter comes in. Owing to the floods in the south, white and red oak, both plain and quartered, are stiffening in price.

Automobile factories are extending their operations and are buying in, increased quantities of hardwood, especially ash. The furniture factories are not rushed at the present juncture and few of them are factors in the market. Railway demand and agricultural implement and vehicle interests evince very little desire to buy, as most of these organizations have plenty of stock on hand. One large agricultural concern has at one of its factories 25,000,000 feet of hardwood, some of which has been in the yard for years.

On the whole, however, the lumber situation is improving slowly, but steadily. There is a better tone prevailing, and while 1922 may not be a record year, it is significant that there is some demand for various materials which twelve months ago could not be peddled at any price.

All the sawmills in Ontario have practically started up for the season and will likely cut as much, or more, than last year, when a number of them shut down early owing to the dull state of the market. This left several with a large quantity of logs on hand which will be used up this season along with what was cut in the bush.

It is interesting to note that so far as Toronto is concerned, the permits for April reached $3,555,000, as against $2,617,000, for the corresponding month in 1921. In April the permits were for 532 dwellings, the average cost of which would be from $4,000, to $5,000, During the last year of the war, 1918, there was only 743 dwellings put up in Toronto, so that this year practically three-quarers as many domiciles are being built in a single month as came into existence during the whole year of 1918.

There is still a great deal of talk heard in regard to railway rate situation, and eastern representatives of B.C. mills are hoping that the predicted decrease will soon eventuate. Now that Parliament is devoting attention to the transportation problem, and has appointed a House Committee to enquire into the whole situation, it is felt that something definite may result so far as basic commodities are concerned, on July 6th next, which is the date of the expiration of the suspension of the Crow's Nest Pass agreement.

Much interest is being taken in the whole traffic situation. One eastern representative of a leading B.C. mill stated that there was still a disposition on the part of a number of Ontario dealers to hold back waiting for diminished carrying costs. He asserted this might come in the near future, any reduction in delivered price would be more than offset by the increase in the f.o.b. figure at the mill. This condition would be brought about by the augmented demand following the reduction in transportation tolls.

White pine lath are very scarce and stiff in price owing to the active house-building campaign in the different cities. No. 1 white pine culls and mill cull siding are moving steadily.

The bridge and building of the Grant Trunk Railway, Montreal, have been calling for over 3,000,000 ft. of material for switch and cross ties, general bridge timbers and planking. The order runs heavy for cross ties, 10 x 10 x 14, while a number of switch ties are also being purchased, these being 7 x 9 and from 8 to 15-ft. in length. All the material being awarded by the railway is for B. C. fir.

## St. John Market has Several Ups and Downs

The lumber trade at St. John, N. B., does not show any change during the last two weeks. During some weeks a firmer tone seems to take place, then comes a waiting period in which sales seem to die out, demand is limited and prices, which appear to be ready to advance, stop and forward march and halt entirely.

Manufacturers do not know which way to turn, each hoping for better things. The better prices and demand do not seem to come. Certain lumber propositions over the country, have cheap and handy stumpage and are able to sell at very low prices and still have a profit. When they sell at these figures, all buyers believe that others must also dispose of their material at the same low price, and any proposition which have not these conditions as the base of their foundation, must also sell and take heavy losses. Largely all lumber organizations in the east have about the same cost of logging and stumpage, with manufacturing costs much the same, so taken as a whole what price effects one, effects all.

Quotations remain to-day unchanged. Some inquiries coming from England leave only prices even at 75 shillings, freight of $22.00 to $23.00 at the mill all around for 3 x 4 and up. The specifications contain large quantities of 9 inch, which are hard to get as logs are small, being chiefly second growth timber running to 8 inch and under with only limited quantities of 9 inch and up.

The American market remains unchanged and demand is fair. It should show some advance in the near future, but for narrow stock after all charges are paid, there is not left over $17.00 per M.

View of Mills in Sarnia.

# BUY THE BEST

Retailers and woodworking establishments who like to get A1 NORWAY and WHITE PINE LUMBER always buy their stocks from us because we can ship them on quick notice. It pays to have the goods, but it pays better to "deliver" them.

We also make a specialty of heavy timbers cut to order any length up to 60 feet from Pine or B. C. Fir.

*"Rush Orders Rushed"*

# Cleveland-Sarnia Sawmills Co., Limited

### SARNIA, ONTARIO

B. P. BOLE, Pres.    F. H. GOFF, Vice-Pres.    E. C. BARER, Gen. Mgr.    W. A. SAURWEIN, Ass't. Mgr.

on cars at mills or shipping centres, these are certainly unprofitable prices, even on low logging and sawing costs. No one seems to see any change ahead for considerable time to come.

Local building is limited and as a good deal of British Government stock is being sold locally at reduced prices, that no manufacturer of ordinary priced logs can compete and show profits. All this stock of material is slowly being absorbed. Buyers are reaping the benefit which will not be in existence long as it is impossible to keep it up. The forests of the east are fast passing and enormous waste has taken place during the past two years which, in the next fire, will be sorely felt by the public. Houses to-day are being erected at prices which will never again be duplicated.

Laths still remain at around $5.00 per M at mills. Logs are coming in slowly and many drives are in need of rain to bring them forward. A good many buyers from the United States are in this section of the country looking for bargains and finding them, and yards across the border are certainly reaping the reward of low prices.

Only two mills are running in St. John, mostly sawing English deals, unsold as yet.

## Business in Montreal Shows Improvement

The volume of business in Montreal has improved, with the prospect of a still greater increase, due to the general anticipation of a busy building season. Contractors are figuring on a large amount of construction of an important character, while there is a very extensive programme of apartment houses and other residences. A possible source of trouble is the attitude of labor to the proposed reduction in wages, but judging by previous experience this will not amount to a great deal. The April building permits totalled $2,038,-834, the largest this year and an increase of $593,194 over the corresponding period last year.

While this is incouraging, there is another side to the shield. The disquieting feature is that prices, especially of spruce, are being cut, the competition between retailers being especially keen. This is also reflected to a certain extent in the business of the wholesalers, some of whom say that it is becoming harder to obtain orders on a profitable basis. The condition referred to applies especially to the local trade.

There are reports of an increasing number of small mills selling not only to the retailers but to the consumers at prices which are low, even taking into account the character of the lumber. Inquiries from across the border have increased and the orders too are on the upgrade.

Business in B. C. Forest products is on the quiet side, with fir prices inclined to harden, especially for upper stock.

A large block of British Government stock has been sold to New York buyers, and some further sales have also been made for domestic account. The Government stocks are being disposed of at a good rate, the sales have been very large this year. An offer of 75 shillings per standard has been received from the owners of a tramp boat for shipping some British stock to the U. K.

So far very little lumber has been sent to the U. K. by export firms. What shipments have gone consisted of parcels of hardwood. It is of course too early to say anything definite as to probable exports from the past but the outlook is that the season will not be a busy one.

There is very little doing in pulpwood. The March shipments to the United States totalled 96,998 cords values at $955,983, as against 589,287 cords, valued at $2,521,863 in March, 1921. For the year, wood exports totalled 825,967 cords, valued at $9,879,150. In 1921 1,615,467 cords, valued at $21,513,594, were exported, and in 1920, 838,732 cords, valued at $8,454,803.

## Ottawa Reports Demand is Looking Up

The long awaited movement of stock, on the Ottawa lumber market actually began during the first part of May, when increased orders from the United States started and sent a better feeling through the trade.

The optimistic view did not have sufficient length or radius to reach all of the trade, for here and there a manufacturer complained of things in general, but the manufacturing wholesalers were sitting up and taking notice of the increase in business.

The demand came principally from the United States and was for spruce and the better grades of pine. The tendency toward the better grades, point toward a stronger market in pine and prices continued to keep up.

The increase in the demand while not as heavy as had been expected earlier in the year, was such that hope was revived. Reports from exporters to the United States are that a building boom is

about to set in across the border and the feeling in this direction is strongest in New York State.

By the same sources the information is conveyed that a good deal of lumber from the southern states and British Columbia lumber, is arriving and entering into competition with the shipments from the Ottawa Valley; on the New York market.

The existing freight rate, Ottawa Valley dealers proclaimed, seriously mitigated against the chances of the local trade entering into full fledged competition with the competitive market. "If freight rates come down to a reasonable basis we may look forward to a good volume of business, occurring before the middle of June" was the conservative comment of one of the largest shippers in the Valley.

The person who voiced this opinion also added, "give us a decreased freight rate and domestic business will also pick up." Beyond any question the present freight rates have considerable bearing on the movement of stock, and also have had a further moral effect of preventing people from purchasing lumber and undertaking new jobs.

Dealers claim, regarding what promises to be re-opened business, that the question of freight charges fundamentally works down to the consumer, and the consumer and the public have seen this, and delayed construction.

Reports from down east indicate there is no price on spruce and that quotations for a certain grade fluctuates from five to eight dollars per M. Besides freight levies, it is pointed out, a good deal depends on the location, yard, room, stocks, etc. of the seller.

As indicated by building permits for April, the Ottawa market is a most hopeful one. New structures in Ottawa have this season swept well past the million dollar mark. The total of estimated new buildings for the first four months was $1,149,945 as compared with $757,235 a year ago. The number of individual permits for April alone, which amounted to 162, were more than for the whole of the first four months of 1921.

Taking the first four months of 1922 as a criterion it compares favorably with the record breaking building year of 1919, the greatest in Ottawa since the century began.

The demand for stocks in retail yards remained good. Wholesalers were considerably more hopeful, but some manufacturers were not inclined to take a quick guess at the pickup of business. High water in the Ottawa river prevented some sawmills from getting under way on May 1st, as they had intended to do. Sawmill labor remained plentiful, and while the sawmills had not got actually underway it was reported that the wages to be paid this year would be from ten per cent lower than those paid in 1921.

Conditions with the woodworking factories brightened, and inquiries indicated that business would soon likely be on the up trend.

With transportation opened May 1st, and several shipments which had been loaded last fall, went down with the high water.

## New System of Checking Lumber

At a meeting of the Montreal Lumber Association, held on May 1st, a letter from the Monreal Harbor Commissioners on the subject of checking lumber was considered. Hitherto the custom has been to check up the lumber at the end of the season. The letter from the commissioners stated that for the present season the driver of every vehicle bringing lumber, etc., for ship lining or other purposes from the city to the wharves, will have to deposit with the official at the gate a certificate giving the number of feet, b.m., on the vehicle. The certificate must be signed by those sending the lumber and specifically stating that the signer will be responsible for the wharfage thereon. A monthly account will be subsequently ordered. Any deviation from this practice will result in the vehicle being turned back until the request is complied with.

The meeting agreed that the request was reasonable and approved the new system.

## Pembroke Sawmills are now Operating

The Pembroke Lumber Co., of Pembroke, Ont., opened its mill recently with a staff of 200 men, and the Colonial Lumber Co. is also starting up with about the same number of employees. With the big raft of logs which came down the Indian and Muskrat rivers to Pembroke a few days ago, there is ample material for the industries to make a nice beginning. The water in the Ottawa river is still very high and a big raft of 200,000 logs broke loose recently in a heavy storm at Rapides des Joachims, 50 miles up the Ottawa. The tugs have gathered up most of the logs but some of them went down the stream beyond Westmeath before they could be corralled. The general report of millmen is that too much water and high winds have been playing havoc with log booms generally on the Ottawa.

# EDGINGS

Lac La Biche Lumber Co., Limited, Lac La Biche, Sask., was recently incorporated.

Citizens Lumber Co., Admiral, Sask., has been taken over by Galvin & Security Lumber Co.

R. Border, Ebenezer, Sask., lumber and implement dealer recently sold his implement business to Clark Bros.

The Kastner Lumber Co., of Wiarton, Ont have in the foundations for a new sawmill, which will be 75 x 125 feet, and will replace the mill which was burned some time ago.

E. J. Mahon, Lumber Co., who recently opened a retail lumber yard on Howard Ave., Windsor, Ont., report that they are doing a good trade and that the prospects are bright for the coming season.

The sawmill of Mickle, Dyment & Son, at Severn River, Ont., which it was reported that the firm intend to operate this year, will not be put in commission according to advices received from head office.

A reduction of twenty per cent. in wages of employees went into effect at the Victoria Mills with the commencement of lumber sawing operations at the Fredericton, N. B. plant of the Fraser Companies, Limited.

There is an immence traffic in the yards of the Abitibi Power & Paper Co., at Iroquois Falls, there being a mile of cars entering the yards every day and a mile of cars going out. The average number daily is about 275 cars.

The manufacturers of Ottawa are forming a baseball league and several woodworking teams have entered, among the firms represented on the diamond being James Davidson's Sons; J. R. Booth, Ltd., and McAuliffe-Davis Lumber Co.

Pierre Letourneau & Fils, Ltd., La Sarre, Que., have been granted a provincial charter to operate sawmills and deal in forest products. Capital $19,000. P. Letourneau and A. Letourneau, both of La Sarre, Que., are two of the incorporators.

The Home Lumber Co., of which J. H. Lapointe is manager, have opened a retail yard at 245 Garnier St., near Mount Royal Ave., East, Montreal. The company are carrying a complete stock of lumber, lath, shingles and general building material, and report business as improving.

The sawmill of Harold M. Young, of Fredericton, and John A. Young, M.P.P. of Tavmouth, N. B., located at Bantalour Station sixteen miles south of McGivney on the Transcontinental Division of the C.N. R., was recently destroyed by fire with a loss of approximately $25,000.

Permits for more than 100 residences have been issued in Kitchener, Ont., this spring. In April there were 39, for $169,600. The total value of the permits for the month was $280,220, bringing the total for the first four months to $686,025, nearly three times the total for the same period of last year.

In 1918, the last year of the war, the population of Toronto increased 15,852, yet only 743 new dwellings were added to the assessment roll. During April of this year permits were issued for 532 dwellings. The scarcity of housing accommodation will be less marked this fall than at any time since 1915.

It is said that the Belgian Industrial Co., of Shawinigan Falls, Que., is preparing to extend its paper mill, the cost of which will be between $1,500,000. and $2,000,000. This does not include the outlay for machinery. Preparations are now being made for excavation work, and it is expected that the plant will be completed some time in 1923.

The Fletcher Lumber Co., Limited, are moving from Marenette St., to Howard Ave., Windsor, Ont., where a suitable site has been secured with good railway facilities on the Essex Terminal. A new planing mill has just been erected by the company and the equipment installed. An attractive office has also been put up. Mr. Fletcher now has a well laid out and admirably located yard.

Water power now developed in Canada represents an investment of $530,000,000, according to a report issued by the Water Power branch of the Department of the Interior, Ottawa. The present development represents an annual equivalent of 20,500,000 tons of coal. By 1940, should the rate of growth of installation during the past fifteen years be continued, the amount of investment will have grown to $1,000,000,000.

Clarke Bros., Limited who are widely known lumbermen and also operate a sulphate pulp plant at Bear River N. S., which was erected and put in commission during the past year, intend providing for the additional water facilities required for the mill. The

bondholders at a recent meeting in Toronto, approved and ratified a proposal to sell $600,000 first lien, sinking fund bonds. The bonds bear interest at 7% and are for a period of 15 years. Provision is made for the establishment of a sinking fund after the first 5 years with the addition of $50,000 yearly.

Restoration of the House tariff bill duty of 50 cents a thousand on shingles was asked of the Senate finance committee at Washington recently by the 25 senators of the Republication agricultural tariff bloc. Shingles are now on the free list. At the same time, the bloc presented requests for increases in the rates on a number of agricultural products over the figures fixed in the administration bill.

E. C. Poisson, who has been in the retail lumber business for the last eight years at Ford, Ont., and is a former mayor of that progressive town, recently suffered a loss by fire when part of his dressed lumber shed and office was destroyed, although very little stock was lost. Mr. Poisson has now rebuilt the structure, and his office and the front of the building is finished in stucco, presenting a handsome appearance.

The Argenteuil Lumber Co., of Morin Heights, P. Q., are operating their sawmill this season, but their run will not be as long as it was last year. The log output of the firm during the past winter was only about one-third of the total of the year previous. The Company report that the demand for lumber as regards the wholesale trade, has not improved very much in the past few months, but that local trade shows a considerable gain over last year, more especially on dressed stock and shingles.

The shipments of tree seedlings and cuttings going out this spring from the Dominion forest nursery station at Indian Head, Saskatchewan, will be among the largest in the past five years. The kinds sent out are chiefly Russian poplar, willow, and caragana. They are used solely for planting shelter belts on prairie farms. Since the nursery was established about sixty million seedlings and cuttings have been distributed to prairie farmers.

There is quite a boom in building lines in Toronto, and during the month of April permits were issued to the extent of $3,555,000, as against $261,269 for the corresponding month in 1920. During the same period construction contracts to the value of $29,428,400, were issued for the whole of Canada. Since the first of the year the permits issued in Toronto have run over $9,000,000. During April 1,841 building prospects were undertaken throughout Ontario, valued at $17,110,700.

An important conference of the Abitibi Power & Paper Co., the T. & N. O. Railway Commission, the Ontario Government and other interests was held recently in Toronto to come to some disposition of a large part of the electrical power stored in the Abitibi River. It is understood that it has been decided to reserve the Long Sault Rapids, for future disposition. The T. & N. O. Railway has also waived its rights to any powers for electrification or other purposes on the river between Iroquois Falls and Tin Can Portage, a distance of 40 miles.

It is not very long ago since sawdust at the mills was considered a nuisance and for the greater part was thrown into the water. If a small quantity of it could be sold now and again, it brought a price of from 1 to 1½ cents per bushel. The largest mills in Norway thought they did well when they could earn from sawdust $2,000 to $3,000 a year. Now this refuse has become valuable, the price having risen from 10 to 15 cents, and from the large quantities sold forms a considerable item in the incomes of the mills, some of them now earning from this source $30,000 to $40,000 a year. The reasons for this heavy rise in the value of sawdust are several. The high prices of fuel during the last few years have caused sawdust to be employed as fuel. However, sawdust attained its principal value after the cellulose mills commenced to use this material; and thereby it has secured a steady demand, and what is very important for the future, a comparatively high price, when the prices of fuel again become normal.

Secretary Ritter, of the Western Retail Lumbermen's Association, Winnipeg, says that the building department is still kept busy, which is rather unusual for this time of the year. Association members, he stated, report numerous inquiries but not a great many actual sales being made. The results from the silo campaign have really been wonderful, continued Mr. Ritter. "The farmers are certainly sold on the idea, and I expect by this time next year you will see the silo being built before anything else. We have had such a demand for sunflower seed that we have just about cleaned out all the seed houses. There is hardly a farmer in western Canada who will not have a small patch of sunflowers planted, and every patch of sunflowers means a silo prospect. This silo campaign has been one of the greatest things our association has ever undertaken, and I believe the co-operative idea of promoting sales has firmly established itself as one of our biggest association activities."

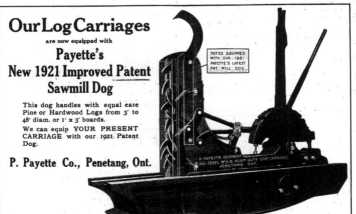

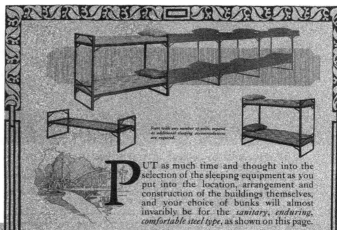

*Start with any number of units, expand as additional sleeping accommodations are required.*

**P**UT as much time and thought into the selection of the sleeping equipment as you put into the location, arrangement and construction of the buildings themselves, and your choice of bunks will almost invariably be for the *sanitary, enduring, comfortable steel type*, as shown on this page.

*Simmons Bed and Bedding Equipment*

Large employers of labour will find the services of this organization of Sleep Equipment specialists adequate to their every need.

Simmons Standardized Steel Bunk Units and Simmons Bunk Mattresses and Pillows cost but little if any more than haphazard equipment, so difficult and costly to move or renovate.

From the plain, commonsense standpoint of comfort, portability and lasting service, no other type of bunk meets the labour-housing needs of large industrial or lumber camps, so completely as STEEL Bunk UNITS. They are strong, sanitary and comfortable. They may be had in either single or double-deck units. You can start with a few or many units and be sure of getting the identical units, when expansion of operations, or as the needs of an increased working force require.

SIMMONS STANDARDIZED STEEL BUNK UNITS are built by the makers of Simmons Beds, Built for Sleep. They are specially designed to satisfy the need for comfortable beds in the sleeping quarters of industrial, lumber and construction camps.

Where clean, attractive and comfortable beds must be provided for vast armies of workers, bunks of this character become a very necessary part of the camp's equipment. Complete descriptions, specifications and prices will be promptly furnished upon request.

SIMMONS LIMITED
Executive Offices, Montreal
MONTREAL   TORONTO   WINNIPEG   CALGARY   VANCOUVER

# SIMMONS BEDS
### *Built for Sleep*

## LINK-BELT CHAINS FOR SAW MILLS
### CARRIED IN STOCK FOR PROMPT SHIPMENT

In our endeavor to match the high quality of Link-Belt chains, with an equally high standard of service, we carry large stocks of the principal sizes of chains for saw mill service. Prompt shipment can be made from all of the offices listed below.

This trade >——< mark identifies genuine Link-Belt chains.

### CANADIAN LINK-BELT COMPANY, LTD.

TORONTO—Wellington and Peter Streets.                    MONTREAL—10 St. Michael's Lane

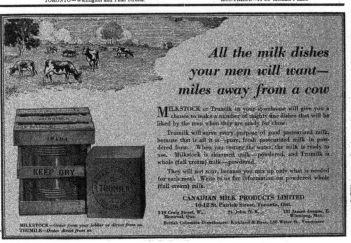

# ATKINS SAWS

STERLING
QUALITY

## HAVE YOU PLACED
## YOUR ORDER?

The sound of the saw and the hammer is in the air.
Everywhere new buildings are being built. Saw
mills are getting busier. Those who have good Saws
and Machine Knives—

### ATKINS Sterling Quality SAWS

and Machine Knives—are in shape to turn out lumber quickly, economically and in large volume. How
about your order? If you have not used Atkins
Saws and Machine Knives, give them a trial. They
will make good.

*We manufacture Atkins-Coleman
Feed Rollers, Saw Tools and Saw
Specialties. Address nearest
point.*

## E. C. ATKINS & CO.

Established 1857     The Sterling Quality Saw People
Home Office and Factory, Indianapolis, Indiana

Canadian Factory, HAMILTON, Ontario
Branch carrying complete stock, VANCOUVER, B. C.

# ALPHABETICAL INDEX TO ADVERTISERS

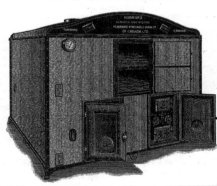

# CANADA LUMBERMAN BUYERS' DIRECTORY

The following regulations apply to all advertisers:—Eighth page, every issue, three headings;
quarter page, six headings; half page, twelve headings; full page, twenty-four headings

**ALLIGATORS**
Payette Company, P.
West, Peachy & Sons

**BABBITT METAL**
Canada Metal Co.
General Supply Co., of Canada, Ltd.

**BALE TIES**
Canada Metal Co.
Laidlaw Bale Tie Company

**BAND MILLS**
Hamilton Company, William
Waterous Engine Works Company
Yates Machine Company, P. B.

**BAND SAW BLADES**
Simonds Mfg., Co.

**BAND RESAWS**
Mershon & Company, W. B.
Yates Machine Co., P.B.

**BARKERS**
Bertrand, F. X., La Compagnie
Manufacturiere.
Smith Foundry & Machine Co.

**BEARING METAL**
Canada Metal Co.
Beveridge Supply Co., Ltd.

**BEDSTEADS (STEEL)**
Simmons Limited

**BELT DRESSING**
Dominion Belting Co.
General Supply of Canada, Ltd.

**BELTING**
Canadian Consolidated Rubber Co.
Dominion Belting Co. .......... ......
General Supply Company
Goodhue & Co., J. L.
Gutta Percha & Rubber Company
D. K. McLaren, Limited
York Belting Co.

**BLOWERS**
Reed & Co., Geo. W.
B. F. Sturtevant Co., of Canada, Ltd.
Toronto Blower Company

**BOILERS**
Engineering & Machine Works of
Canada
Hamilton Company, William
Waterous Engine Works Company

**BOILER PRESERVATIVE**
Beveridge Supply Company
Shell-Bar, Boico Supply Co., Ltd.

**BOX MACHINERY**
Yates Machine Company, P. B.

**CABLE CONVEYORS**
Engineering & Machine Works of
Canada.
Hamilton Company, William
Waterous Engine Works Company

**CAMP SUPPLIES**
Davies Company, William
Dr. Bell Veterinary Wonder Co.
Johnson, A. H.
Turner & Sons, J. J.
Woods Manufacturing Co., Ltd.

**CANT HOOKS**
General Supply Co., of Canada, Ltd.
Pink & Company, Thomas

**CEDAR**
Bury & Co., Robt.
Cameron Lumber Co.
Canadian Western Lumber Co.
Chesbro, R. G.
Dry Wood Lumber Co.
Fesserton Timber Company
Fesserton Timber Company
McElroy Lumber Co., Ltd.
Muir & Kirkpatrick
Rose, McLaurin, Limited
Terry & Gordon
Thurston- Flavelle Lumber Co.
Vancouver Lumber Company
Victoria Lumber & Mfg. Co.

**CHAINS**
Canadian Link-Belt Company, Ltd.
General Supply Co., of Canada, Ltd.
Engineering & Machine Works of
Canada
Hamilton Company, William
Pink & Company, Thomas
Waterous Engine Works Company

**CLOTHING**
Woods Mfg. Company.

**CONVEYOR MACHINERY**
Canadian Link-Belt Company, Ltd.
General Supply Co., of Canada, Ltd.
Hamilton Company, William
Hopkins & Co., Ltd., F. H.
Waterous Engine Works Company

**CORDWOOD**
McClung, McLellan & Berry

**COUPLING (Shaft)**
Engineering & Machine Works of
Canada

**CRANES**
Hopkins & Co., Ltd., F. H.
Canadian Link-Belt Company, Ltd.

**CUTTER HEADS**
Shimer Cutter Head Company
Yates Machine Co., P.B.

**CYPRESS**
Maus Lumber Co., Chas. O.
Wistar, Underhill & Nixon

**DERRICKS AND DERRICK FITTINGS**
Hopkins & Co., Ltd., F. H.

**DOORS**
Canadian Western Lumber Co.
Gardiner, P. W., & Son
Mason, Gordon & Co.
Terry & Gordon

**DRAG SAWS**
Gerlach Company, Peter
Hamilton Company, William

**DRYERS**
Coe Manufacturing Company
B. F. Sturtevant Co. of Canada, Ltd.

**DUST COLLECTORS**
Reed & Co., Geo. W.
B. F. Sturtevant Co. of Canada, Ltd.
Toronto Blower Company

**EDGERS**
Hamilton Company, Ltd., William
Green Company, G. Walter
Long Mfg. Company, E.
Payette Company, P.
Waterous Engine Works Company.
Yates Machine Co., P.B.

**ELEVATING AND CONVEYING MACHINERY**
Canadian Link-Belt Company, Ltd.
Engineering & Machine Works of
Canada
Hamilton Company, William
Waterous Engine Works Company

**ENGINES**
Engineering & Machine Works of
Canada
Hamilton Company, William
Payette Company, P.
Waterous Engine Works Company

**EXCELSIOR MACHINERY**
Elmira Machinery & Transmission
Company

**EXHAUST FANS**
B. F. Sturtevant Co. of Canada, Ltd.
Toronto Blower Company

**EXHAUST SYSTEMS**
Reed & Co., Geo. W.
B. F. Sturtevant Co. of Canada, Ltd.
Toronto Blower Company

**FIBRE BOARD**
Manley Chew

**FILES**
Disston & Sons, Henry
Simonds Canada Saw Company

**FIR**
Apex Lumber Co.
Associated Mills, Limited
Bainbridge Lumber Company
Cameron Lumber Co.
Canadian Western Lumber CO.
Canfield, P. L.
Chesbro, R. G.
Dry Wood Lumber Co.
Fesserton Timber Co.
Grier & Sons, Ltd., G. A.
Heeney, Percy E.
Knox Brothers
Mason, Gordon & Co.
McElroy Lumber Co., Ltd.
Robertson & Hackett Sawmills
Rose, McLaurin, Limited
Terry & Gordon
Timberland Lumber Company
Timms, Phillips & Co.
Underhill Lumber Co.
Vancouver Lumber Company
Victoria Lumber & Mfg. Company

**FIRE BRICK**
Beveridge Supply Co., Limited
Elk Fire Brick Company of Canada.
Shell-Bar, Boico Supply Co., Ltd.

**FIRE FIGHTING APPARATUS**
Waterous Engine Works Company

**FITTINGS**
Crane Limited

**FLOORING**
Cameron Lumber Co.
Chesbro, R. G.
Long-Bell Lumber Company

**GEARS (Cut)**
Smart-Turner Machine Company

**GUARDS (Machinery and Window)**
Canada Wire & Iron Goods Co.

**HARDWOODS**
Anderson Lumber Company, C. G.
Anderson, Shreiner & Mawson
Atlantic Lumber Company
Barrett, Wm.
Black Rock Lumber Co.
Bury & Co., Robt.
Cameron & Company
Edwards & Co., W. C,
Fassett Lumber Company, Limited
Fesserton Timber Co.
Gillespie, James
Gloncester Lumber & Trading Co.
Grier & Sons, Ltd., G. A.
Hart, Hamilton & Jackson
Heeney, Percy E.
Knox Brothers
Kinnon Lumber Co.
Mason & Company, Geo.
Maus Lumber Co., Chas. O.
McDonagh Lumber Company
McLennan Lumber Company
McLung, McLellan & Berry
Pedwell Hardwood Lumber Co.
W. & J. Sharples
Spencer, Limited, C. A.
Strong, G. M.
Summers, James R.

**HARDWOOD FLOORING**
Grier & Sons, Ltd., G. A.

**HARNESS**
Beal Leather Company, R. M.

**HEMLOCK**
Anderson Lumber Company, C. G.
Anderson, Shreiner & Mawson
Bartram & Ball
Beck Lumber Company
Bourgouin, H.
Canadian General Lumber Company.
Edwards & Co., W. C.
Fesserton Timber Co.
Grier & Sons, Ltd., G. A.
Hart, Hamilton & Jackson
Hocken Lumber Company
Mason, Gordon & Company
McCormack Lumber Company
McDonagh Lumber Company
McElroy Lumber Co., Ltd.
Robertson & Hacket Sawmills
Spencer, Limited, C. A.
Stalker, Douglas A.
Terry & Gordon
Vancouver Lumber Company
Vanderhoof Lumber Company

**HOISTING AND HAULING ENGINES**
General Supply Co. of Canada, Ltd.

Climbing a 7½ per cent grade of 6½ Miles in length

# THE LINN LOGGING TRACTOR

The Canadian Lumberman of today is finding increasingly difficult woods problems confronting him.

His Hauls are each season becoming longer, and the efficiency of the horse, as a haulage factor, is, in the same ratio, decreasing.

The stream drive is expensive and troublesome.

Therefore—Reliable, Economical Mechanical haulage must be resorted to—and the only medium that will fulfill all the requirements of the Canadian Logger is the Linn Logging Tractor—designed and developed during the past eight years—exclusively for log hauling in the North Country.

During the past season, we had a very comprehensive motion picture taken—showing Linn Logging Tractors in operation over various limits—If you have not already seen this film, we will gladly arrange to show it to you, in your own office—it is a revelation of logging methods—and not a set and arranged picture—it was taken over different operations, under ordinary working conditions.

And we also have a very comprehensive catalogue about to come from the printers. Your request for a copy will be immediately honored.

*—Logging Department—*

## MUSSENS LIMITED

Dubrule Building      Philips Place      MONTREAL

Hopkins & Co., Ltd., F. H.

**HOSE**
General Supply Co. of Canada, Ltd.
Gutta Percha & Rubber Company

**INSURANCE**
Barton & Ellis Company
Burns Underwriting Company
Hardy & Company, E. D.
Rankin Benedict Underwriting Co.

**INTERIOR FINISH**
Cameron Lumber Company
Canadian Western Lumber Co.
Canfield, P. L.
Eagle Lumber Company
Mason, Gordon & Co.
Rose, McLaurin, Limited
Terry & Gordon

**KILN DRIED LUMBER**
Bury & Co., Robt.

**KNIVES**
Disston & Sons, Henry
Simonds Canada Saw Company
Waterous Engine Works Company

**LARCH**
Otis Staples Lumber Company

**LATH**
Anderson, Shreiner & Mawson
Apex Lumber Company
Austin & Nicholson
Beck Lumber Company
Brennen & Sons, F. W.
Cameron Lumber Company
Canadian General Lumber Company
Carew Lumber Company, John
Chaleurs Bay Mills

Dadson, A. T.
Eagle Lumber Company
Fassett Lumber Company, Limited
Foley Lumber Company
Fraser Bryson Lumber Co., Ltd.
Gloucester Lumber & Trading Co.
Grier & Sons, Ltd., G. A.
Harris Tie & Timber Company, Ltd.
Larkin Company, C. A.
Mason & Company, Geo.
McLennan Lumber Company
Miller, W. H. Company
New Ontario Colonization Company
Otis Staples Lumber Company
Power Lumber Company
Price Bros. & Company
Shevlin-Clarke Company
Spencer, Limited, C. A.
Terry & Gordon
U. G. G. Sawmills, Limited
Union Lumber Company
Victoria Harbor Lumber Company

**LATH BOLTERS**
General Supply Co. of Canada, Ltd.
Hamilton Company, William
Payette & Company, P.

**LOCOMOTIVES**
Engineering & Machine Works of Canada
General Supply Co. of Canada, Ltd.
Hopkins & Co., Ltd., F. H.
Climax Manufacturing Company
Montreal Locomotive Works

**LINK-BELT**
Canadian Link-Belt Company
Hamilton Company, William

**LOCOMOTIVE CRANES**
Canadian Link-Belt Company
Hopkins & Co., Ltd., F. H.

**LOGGING ENGINES**
Engineering & Machine Works of Canada

Hopkins & Co., Ltd., F. H.
Mussens Limited

**LOG HAULER**
Engineering & Machine Works of Canada
Green Company, G. Walter
Holt Manufacturing Company
Hopkins & Co., Ltd., F. H.
Payette & Company, P.

**LOGGING MACHINERY AND EQUIPMENT**
General Supply Co. of Canada, Ltd.
Hamilton Company, William
Holt Manufacturing Company
Hopkins & Co., Ltd., F. H.
Payette & Company, P.
Waterous Engine Works Company
West, Peachey & Sons
Mussens Limited

**LUMBER EXPORTS**
Fletcher Corporation

**LUMBER TRUCKS**
Hamilton Company, William
Waterous Engine Works Company

**LUMBERMEN'S BOATS**
Adams Engine Company
Gidley Boat Company
West, Peachey & Sons

**LUMBERMEN'S CLOTHING**
Kitchen Overall & Shirt Company

**MATTRESSES**
Simmons Limited

**METAL REFINERS**
Canada Metal Company

**NAILING MACHINES**
Yates Machine Co., P.B.

**OAK**
Long-Bell Lumber Company
Maus Lumber Co., Chas. O.

**PACKING**
Beveridge Supply Company
Gutta Percha & Rubber Company

**PANELS**
Bury & Company, Robt.

**PAPER**
Beveridge Supply Company
Price Bros. & Company

**PINE**
Anderson Lumber Company, C. G.
Anderson, Shreiner & Mawson
Atlantic Lumber Company
Austin & Nicholson
Barratt, William
Beck Lumber Company
Black Rock Lumber Co.
Cameron & Company
Cameron Lumber Company
Canadian General Lumber Company
Canadian Western Lumber Co.
Canfield, P. L.
Cheabre, R. G.
Cleveland-Sarnia Sawmills Company
Cox, Long & Company
Dadson, A. T.
Dudley, Arthur N.
Eagle Lumber Company
Edwards & Co., W. C.
Excelsior Lumber Company
Fesserton Timber Co.
Fraser Bryson Lumber Co., Ltd.
Gillies Bros, Limited
Gloucester Lumber & Trading Co.
Gordon & Company, George
Goodday & Company, H. R.
Grier & Sons, Ltd., G. A.
Harris Tie & Timber Company, Ltd.
Hart, Hamilton & Jackson
Hettler Lumber Co., Herman H.
Hocken Lumber Company
Julien, Roch
Keewatin Lumber Co.
Lay & Haight
Lloyd, W. Y.
Loggie Company, W. S.
Long-Bell Lumber Company
Mason, Gordon & Co.
Mason & Company, Geo.

# A SUPERIOR RESAW

# 341

Among millmen the 341 has become very popular as a medium capacity resaw. It has extraordinary capacity for its size, takes stock up to 30 inches wide 12 inches thick. A very compact machine, sturdy, all adjustments handy, easily controlled and accurate. Rolls may be tilted for bevel siding. Eight rates of feed up to 185 feet per minute.

We have a Circular which explains this machine fully—we'll gladly send you copy upon request, and this, without the slightest obligation on your part. Will we send you copy?

### P. B. Yates Machine Co. Ltd.

**Hamilton        Canada**

Eastern Sales Office
263 St. James St.                Montreal, Que.

McCormack Lumber Company
McFadden & Malloy
McLennan Lumber Company
Montreal Lumber Company
Muir & Kirkpatrick
Northern Lumber Mills
Otis Staples Lumber Company
Parry Sound Lumber Company
Rolland Lumber Company
W. & J. Sharples
Shevlin-Clarke Company
Spencer, Limited, C. A.
Stalker, Douglas A.
Strong, G. M.
Summers, James R.
Terry & Gordon
Union Lumber Company
Victoria Harbor Lumber Company
Watson & Todd, Limited

**PLANING MILL EXHAUSTERS**
Toronto Blower Company

**PLANING MILL MACHINERY**
Mershon & Company, W. B.
B. F. Sturtevant Co. of Canada, Ltd.
Toronto Blower Company
Yates Machine Company, P. B.

**POPLAR**
Keewatin Lumber Co.

**POST GRINDERS**
Smith Foundry Company

**POSTS AND POLES**
Anderson, Shreiner & Mawson
Canadian Tie & Lumber Co.
Dupuis, Limited, J. P.
Eagle Lumber Company
Harris Tie & Timber Company, Ltd.
Long-Bell Lumber Company
Mason, Gordon & Co.
McLennan Lumber Company
Terry & Gordon

**PULLEYS AND SHAFTING**
Canadian Link-Belt Company
General Supply Co. of Canada, Ltd.
Green Company, G. Walter
Engineering & Machine Works of
Canada
Hamilton Company, William

**PULP MILL MACHINERY**
Canadian Link-Belt Company
Engineering & Machine Works of
Canada
Hamilton Company, William
Payette & Company, P.
Waterous Engine Works Company

**PULPWOOD**
British & Foreign Agencies
D'Auteuil Lumber Company
Price Bros. & Company
Scott, Draper & Company

**PUMPS**
General Supply Co. of Canada, Ltd.
Engineering & Machine Works of
Canada
Hamilton Company, William
Hopkins & Co., Ltd., F. H.
Smart-Turner Machine Company
Waterous Engine Works Company

**RAILS**
Gartshore, John J.
Hopkins & Co., Ltd., F. H.

**ROOFINGS**
(Rubber, Plastic and Liquid)
Beveridge Supply Company
Reed & Co., Geo. W.

**RUBBER GOODS**
Dunlop Tire & Rubber Goods Co.
Gutta Percha & Rubber Company

**SASH**
Midland Woodworkers

**SAWS**
Atkins & Company, E. C.
Disston & Sons, Henry
General Supply Co. of Canada, Ltd.
Gerlach Company, Peter

Green Company, G. Walter
Hoe & Company, R.
Radcliff Saw Mfg. Company
Shurly Company, Ltd., T. F.
Shurly-Dietrich Company
Simonds Canada Saw Company

**SAW GRINDERS**
Smith Foundry Company

**SAW MILL LINK-BELT**
Canadian Link-Belt Company

**SAW MILL MACHINERY**
Canadian Link-Belt Company
General Supply Co. of Canada, Ltd.
G. Walter Green Company, Ltd.
Hamilton Company, William
La Compagnie Manufacture, F. X.
Bertrand
Long Mfg. Company, E.
Mershon & Company, W. B.
Parry Sound Lumber Company
Payette & Company, P.
Waterous Engine Works Company
Yates Machine Company, P. B.

**SAW SHARPENERS**
Hamilton Company, William
Waterous Engine Works Company

**SAW SLASHERS**
Hamilton Company, William
Payette & Company, P.
Waterous Engine Works Company

**SHINGLES**
Apex Lumber Company
Associated Mills, Limited
Brennen & Sons, F. W.
Cameron Lumber Company
Campbell-MacLaurin Lumber Co.
Canadian Western Lumber Co.
Carew Lumber Company, John
Chaleurs Bay Mills
Chesbro, R. G.
D'Auteuil Lumber Company
Dry Wood Lumber Co.
Eagle Lumber Company
Fraser, Companies Limited
Gillespie, James
Gloucester Lumber & Trading Co.
Grier & Sons, Ltd., G. A.
Harris Tie & Timber Co., Ltd.
Heaps & Sons
Heeney, Percy E.
Mason, Gordon & Co.
McLennan Lumber Company
Miller Company, Ltd., W. H.
Rose, McLaurin, Limited
Stalker, Douglas A.
Terry & Gordon
Timms, Phillips & Company
Vancouver Lumber Company
Vanderhoof Lumber Company

**SHINGLE & LATH MACHINERY**
Green Company, C. Walter
Hamilton Company, William
Long Manufacturing Company, E.
Payette & Company, P.
Smith Foundry Company

**SILENT CHAIN DRIVES**
Canadian Link-Belt Company

**SLEEPING EQUIPMENT**
Simmons Limited

**SLEEPING ROBES**
Woods Mfg. Company, Ltd.

**SMOKESTACKS**
Hamilton Company, William
Reed & Co., Geo. W.
Waterous Engine Works Company

**SNOW PLOWS**
Pink & Company, Thomas

**SOLDERS**
Canada Metal Company

**SPARK ARRESTORS**
Reed & Company, Geo. W.
Waterous Engine Works Company

**SPRUCE**
Anderson, Shreiner & Mawson
Barrett, Wm.
Cameron Lumber Company
Campbell, McLaurin Lumber Co.
Canadian Western Lumber Co.
Chesbro, R. G.
Cox, Long & Company
Dadson, A. T.
Dudley Arthur N.
Fassett Lumber Company, Ltd.
Fraser, Companies Limited
Fraser Bryson Lumber Co., Ltd.
Gillies Brothers
Gloucester Lumber & Trading Co.
Goodday & Company, H. R.
Grier & Sons, Ltd G. A.
Harris Lumber Co., Frank H.
Hart, Hamilton & Jackson
Hocken Lumber Company
Julien, Koch
Keewatin Lumber Co.
Larkin Co., C. A.
Lay & Haight
Lloyd, W. Y.
Loggie Co., W. S.
Mason, Gordon & Co.
McCormack Lumber Co.
McDonagh Lumber Co.
McElroy Lumber Co. Ltd.
McLennan Lumber Company
Muir & Kirkpatrick
New Ontario Colonization Co.
Northern Lumber Mills
Power Lumber Co.
Price Bros. & Company
Rolland Lumber Co.
Rose, McLaurin, Limited
W. & J. Sharples.
Spencer, Limited, C. A.
Strong, G. M.
Terry & Gordon
U. G. G. Sawmills, Limited
Vanderhoof Lumber Company

**STEAM SHOVELS**
Hopkins & Co., Ltd., F. H.

**STEEL CHAIN**
Canadian Link-Belt Company
Hopkins & Co., Ltd., F. H.
Waterous Engine Works Company

**STEAM PLANT ACCESSORIES**
Waterous Engine Works Company

**STEEL BARRELS**
Smart-Turner Machine Company

**STEEL DRUMS**
Smart-Turner Machine Company

**TARPAULINS**
Turner & Sons, J. J.
Woods Manufacturing Company Ltd.

**TANKS**
Hopkins & Co., Ltd., F. H.

**TENTS**
Turner & Sons, J. J.
Woods Mfg. Company

**TIES**
Austin & Nicholson
Carew Lumber Co., John
Canadian Tie & Lumber Co.
Chaleurs Bay Mills
D'Auteuil Lumber Co.
Gloucester Lumber & Trading Co.
Harris Tie & Timber Company Ltd.
McLennan Lumber Company
Miller, W. H. Co.
Price Bros. & Company
Scott, Draper & Co.
Terry & Gordon

**TIMBER BROKERS**
Bradley, R. R.
Cant & Kemp
Farnworth & Jardine
Wright, Graham & Co.

**TIMBER CRUISERS AND
ESTIMATORS**
Savage & Bartlett.
Sewell, James W.

**TIMBER LANDS**
Department of Lands & Forests, Ont.

**TOWING MACHINES**
Payette & Company, P.
West, Peachey & Sons

**TRACTORS**
Holt Manufacturing Company
Hopkins & Co., Ltd., F. H.
Mussens Limited

**TRANSMISSION MACHINERY**
Canadian Link-Belt Company
Engineering & Machine Works of
Canada
General Supply Co. of Canada, Ltd.
Grand Rapids Vapor Kiln
Hamilton Company, William
Waterous Engine Works Co.

**TURBINES**
Engineering & Machine Works of
Canada
Hamilton Company, William
B. F. Sturtevant Co, of Canada, Ltd.

**VALVES**
Crane, Limited

**VAPOR KILNS**
Grand Rapids Vapor Kiln
B. F. Sturtevant Co. of Canada, Ltd.

**VENEERS**
Bury & Co. Robt.

**VENEER DRYERS**
Coe Manufacturing Company
Sturtevant Co., B. F. of Canada Ltd.

**VENEER MACHINERY**
Coe Manufacturing Company

**VETERINARY REMEDIES**
Dr. Bell Vetinerary Wonder Co.
Johnson, A. H.

**WARPING TUGS**
West, Peachey & Sons

**WATER WHEELS**
Engineering & Machine Works of
Canada
Hamilton Company, William

**WIRE**
Canada Metal Co.
Laidlaw Bale Tie Company
Canada Wire & Iron Goods Co.

**WIRE CLOTH**
Canada Wire & Iron Goods Co.

**WIRE ROPE**
Canada Wire & Iron Goods Co.
Hopkins & Co., Ltd., F. H.
Dominion Wire Rope Co.
Greening Wire Co., B.

**WOODWORKING MACHINERY**
General Supply Co., of Canada, Ltd.
Long Manufacturing Company, E.
Mershon & Company, W. B.
Waterous Engine Works Co.
Yates Machine Company, P. B.

**WOOD PRESERVATIVES**
Beveridge Supply Company
Austin & Nicholson
New Ontario Colonization Company
Power Lumber Co.

**WOOD PULP**
Austin & Nicholson
New Ontario Colonization Co.
Power Lumber Co.

# Horizontal Band Resaw

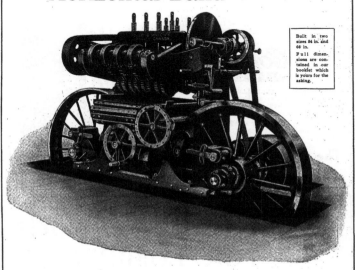

Built in two
sizes 84 in. and
66 in.

Full dimen-
sions are con-
tained in our
booklet which
is yours for the
asking.

The splendid qualities of this machine are known throughout the industry. It is a machine that gets every dollar's worth of merchantable lumber from each log. More and more it is commending itself to the wide-awake lumberman, who is on the alert for greater efficiency and increased profits in his mill.

The fact has been kept in mind that the resaw is in most instances to be installed in mills already operating. For this reason conditions that are liable to exist have been kept in mind and it has been made to take up as little space, both in length, width and head room is as consistent with good design.

# The E. Long Manufacturing Co., Limited
## Orillia                                      Canada

Robt. Hamilton & Co., Vancouver
Gormans, Limited,
    Calgary & Edmonton

A. R. Williams Machinery Co.,
of Canada, Ltd.
Williams & Wilson Ltd., Montreal

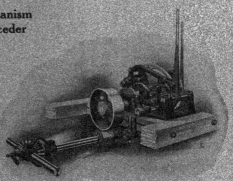

# "HAMILTON" LOG CARRIAGES

Above cut shows one of our **No. 2 HEAD BLOCK CARRIAGES** with knee opening 40″ from saw line. Note the sturdy compact lines of this carriage, built for heavy but accurate service weight properly distributed, and the dogs set low on the knees to insure gripping of the smallest logs.

We make these Carriages with pine or oak frames any length—having cast iron, or steel cast head blocks—with knee opening of 33″, 40″, and 54″, and equipped with any number of head blocks of any spacing required. Hand or Steam Set may be used, and carriages are designed for either steam or rope feed. They are built of the best materials obtainable for fast and accurate cutting, are equipped with **NEW DESIGN AXLE RECEDING WORKS** and have carriage wheels 14″, 16″ or 18″ diameter. We have installed hundreds of these carriages in Mills from Coast to Coast, and we guarantee them in material, workmanship, and design to equal any on the market to-day, and to give thorough satisfaction wherever used.

**OUR CARRIAGE CATALOGUE IS YOURS UPON REQUEST**

Consult us for any of your saw mill needs, and you will have a Plant looking after your ests that has been in the Sawmill Machinery game for over sixty-five years.

## William Hamilton Co., Limite

Agents: J. L. Neilson & Co., Winnipeg, Man.   Peterborough, Ont.

# White Pine
# Red Pine
# Jack Pine
# Spruce
# Lumber
# and Lath

**UNION LUMBER COMPANY LIMITED**
701 DOMINION BANK BUILDING
TORONTO          CANADA

# Take a Tip From the Business Barometer

### *It Says*
## "NOW IS THE TIME TO STOCK UP"

"Is this a good time for lumbermen to stock up" is a question commanding universal attention. The answer is found in a survey of existing conditions in the building trade.

### Now is the Time to Buy Lumber Because

All sections of the country appear to be sharing to a greater or lesser degree in the general revival of business. Building reports show a surprising increase. There is a big demand all along the line for building materials. You can only meet this demand by having a thoroughly complete stock on hand.

### And Because

According to every indication there will be no further decline in lumber prices. To take full advantage of favorable prices means placing your orders now.

### And Finally Because

Procrastination is the thief of time—and profits. Carefulness is a virtue but confidence is better. You know your own local conditions—your good judgment tells you there is no time like the present to act.

> In placing your orders remember our reputation for quality and service. We can make immediate shipments from Ontario, Quebec or British Columbia. Write us to-day for quotations.

## TERRY AND GORDON
### LIMITED
## CANADIAN FOREST PRODUCTS

HEAD OFFICE
**TORONTO**

BRANCH
MONTREAL

EUROPEAN AGENTS
SPENCER LOCK & Co., LONDON, ENG.

BRANCH
VANCOUVER

Ontario Representatives for
THE BRITISH COLUMBIA MILLS TIMBER AND TRADING CO., VANCOUVER, B. C.

*"Well Bought is Half Sold!"*

Building
Boom
Boosting
Business

means

Badly
Broken
Bins

causing

Rushing
Retailers
Replace
Ravages !

**Byng Inlet**

Superior
Service
Supplies
Shortages
Swiftly

from

Gilt-edge
Guaranteed
Goods
" Graded

for use."

**Canadian General Lumber Co.**

Limited

# FOREST PRODUCTS

TORONTO OFFICE :— 712-20 Bank of Hamilton Building

Montreal Office :—514 Canada Cement Company Bldg.

**Mills : Byng Inlet, Ont.**

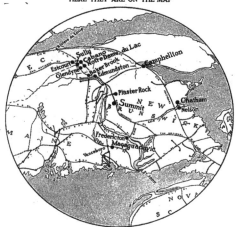

**DOUGLAS FIR
LUMBER**
**RED CEDAR
SHINGLES**

We mauufactnre all grades of

## Red Cedar Shingles

Which are inspected by
the British Columbia Inspestor

We can give Mixed or Straight cars of

## Rough K.D. Clear Fir

Manufactured from
old growth logs

### Timms Phillips & Co., Ltd.
Vancouver, B. C.

MONTREAL OFFICE: 23 Marconi Bldg.
Phone M 2999

TORONTO OFFICE: Canada Permanent Bldg
Phone Adel. 6490

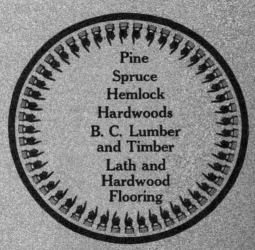

# BUY
## BRITISH COLUMBIA
# Red Cedar Shingles

The life of a British Columbia Red Cedar Shingle Roof can almost be gauged by the life of the nail with which the shingle is nailed in place. Judging from available data, the average life of the ordinary steel wire nail, which has been in such common use, is only from seven to twelve years. Some wire nails will last longer, depending upon the condition of exposure, climate and similar features, but considering our climate as a whole, at the end of from seven to twelve years a large percentage of wire nails will have rusted either completely through or so extensively that the first strong wind will complete the work. The shingles that have been held in position by such nails are then free to work down, permitting rains or melting snows to leak through and damage the interior of the structure. Examination will disclose that the fibre of the shingle itself is still in perfect condition, and a leaky roof, in the majority of occasions is due entirely to the use of faulty nails, but the average home owner, placed at such inconvenience, will not stop to reason this out and the poor wooden shingle comes in for more unjust abuse.

There are several kinds of nails which experience has proven will give lasting satisfaction, and the wise dealer will advise his customers of these satisfactory nails. A pure zinc shingle nail meets all the demands of durability required. Its principal drawback is its high cost and a slight tendency to bend under careless driving. Galvanized wire nails theoretically are rust proof, and if the galvanized coating is properly applied, and of sufficient thickness, such a nail will last as long as the shingle it holds in place. The life of this shingle roof, properly applied with these nails then is from 40 to 50 years. Pure iron nails, or the old cut or wrought nails are ideal but difficult to secure. Copper nails also constitute a perfect shingle nail.

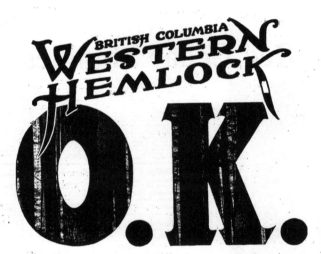

## Ask the Man Who Has Used it

The proof of the value of wood js in the service obtained therefrom.

Lumber dealers and their customers are getting to like BRITISH COLUMBIA WESTERN HEMLOCK better the more they deal in it or use it.

It is not a hardwood but is possessed of a grain that is externally beautiful. It takes a high polish, is free from pitch and "shakes" and possesses great strength.

Don't wait until all your competitors have established a reputation for handling BRITISH COLUMBIA WESTERN HEMLOCK.

We'll be glad to send you BRITISH COLUMBIA WESTERN HEMLOCK in mixed carloads along with our other BIG CHIEF Brand Specialties, British Columbia Red Cedar Shingles, and Cedar and Fir lumber in all sizes known to high-class manufacture.

## VANCOUVER LUMBER CO., LIMITED, Vancouver, B.C.

Branch Sales Offices at Toronto, Ont., Winnipeg, Man., Chicago, Ill

## ARKANSAS SOFT PINE SATIN-LIKE INTERIOR TRIM

ITS FINE GRAIN, close texture and tough fiber are particularly suited to the type of work illustrated. A wood of perfect physical and chemical make-up for white enamel, eliminating, as it definitely does, every hazard of raised grain or ultimate discoloration.

Technical literature, samples, both finished and natural, sent by the Bureau on request. Write mills direct for price

*All stock bearing the Arkansas Soft Pine trade mark is manufactured and sold exclusively by the following companies:*

| | |
|---|---|
| Arkansas Lumber Company · · · Warren, Arkansas | Garst Lumber Company · · · · Wilmar, Arkansas |
| Gurdon Belt Lumber Company · Bearden, Arkansas | Ozan-Graysonia Lumber Company · Prescott, Ark. |
| Crossett Lumber Company · · · Crossett, Arkansas | Southern Lumber Company · · · Warren, Arkansas |
| Eagle Lumber Company · · · · Eagle Mills, Arkansas | Stout Lumber Company · · · · Thornton, Arkansas |
| Edgar Lumber Company · · · · Wesson, Arkansas | Union Saw Mill Company · · · Huttig, Arkansas |
| Fordyce Lumber Company · · · Fordyce, Arkansas | Saco Office, Boettner's Bend Bldg., St. Louis, Mo. |
| Freeman-Smith Lumber Company · Millville, Ark. | Wisconsin & Arkansas Lumber Co. · Malvern, Ark. |

COMPOSING THE

# Arkansas Soft Pine Bureau
LITTLE ROCK · ARKANSAS

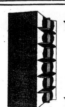

# THE GREAT NATIONAL LUMBER JOURNAL

Pioneer and Leader
in the Industry

**Canada Lumberman**
*founded 1880*

Recognized Authority
for Forty Years

Vol. 42          Toronto, June 1, 1922          No. 11

# Clarion Call for Reproduction on Cut-over Lands

### By Roland D. Craig

Roland D. Craig, Ottawa, Ont.

That the exhaustion of the accessible supplies of virgin timber in Ontario is now within the industrial horizon is conceded by practically everyone connected with utilization of these resources. The subject has been discussed in the public press so frequently that the average citizen is beginning to realize that it is only a matter of a comparatively short time until the forests once considered unlimited, will cease to supply our needs. In the local markets lumber shipped from the Southern States and the Pacific Coast is already replacing to an increasing extent our native pines and hemlock. The seriousness of the situation does not seem, however, to be fully realized, if one may judge from the lack of effort being made to produce new forests to take the place of those which are being cut or destroyed by fire.

Of the 260 million acres in Ontario, only about 15 million acres has been cleared for agricultural purposes and there is not more than 20 million acres still uncleared, which is likely to be suitable for cultivation. Of the remaining 225 million acres, one half may be considered as potential, if not at present forest land. How much of this carries timber of commercial value is not known yet, but since only about 25 million acres is held under cutting licenses and a large proportion of this has been cut-over or burned, it is doubtful if on more than one third, or 35 million acres, of the forest land there is timber of a size that would be considered suitable for present utilization and a considerable proportion of this timber is so situated that it is inaccessible to the existing industries.

It is not of this remnant of the mature forests that I wish to call attention, but to the 75 million acres of cut-over and burned-over land which should be producing wood at a rate very much faster than we are using it, but which through carelessness and indifference is being allowed to degenerate into barren wastes. There is an evident lack of appreciation of the fact that trees grow, and that the tiny seedlings or young saplings which come up on the denuded lands will in a not-too-distant future produce a crop of pulpwood or sawlogs. The destruction of a thousand acres of reproduction by fire is considered of little or no consequence, and the periodic burning of this "brush" is even advocated as a means of preventing forest fires. The result is that on vast areas, in spite of nature's efforts to produce forests, the more valuable timber species are being exterminated.

During the past summer, I had occasion to study the effects of fire on the reproduction of white and red pine in the vicinity of Quetico Park, Rainy River District, and a brief outline of my observations, illustrated with a few photos, may be of interest to the readers of the "Canada Lumberman."

This region was generally well forested with pine and still has some of the finest stands in the province, but it has suffered severely from fire, both before and since logging operations were commenced. There were fires of considerable extent in the virgin timber about forty years ago and again eleven years ago. On these areas there is almost everywhere a good young growth of pine which started under the preliminary growth of white birch and poplar but, in the older stands, is beginning to out-grow the deciduous trees. Jack pine, as one would expect, is more prevalent in the new growth than in the original forest but there is a good proportion of white and red pine. The satisfactory reproduction is due to the fact that there was a scattering of seed trees which though injured were not killed and also that the fire was not severe enough on the ground to kill all the seeds in the soil.

A second fire in this reproduction destroyed both seedlings and seed trees and, even after 10 years there was practically no new

Area on which a second fire about eleven years ago destroyed the first reproduction leaving it practically barren

Broad cast burned and all advanced growth and hardwood killed, these falling down making serious fire hazard

Area logged and slash burned as cut without destroying the young growth.

Area on which the logging slash was burned broad-cast

reproduction of red and white pine and, only scattered patches of jack pine, aspen, and white birch.

The broad-cast burning of logging slash appears to have been an established practice in this district, as elsewhere. Sooner or later (usually sooner), the slash catches fire and it makes such a hot fire that every tree, large or small, is killed, and later the dead trees fall down and create a fire menace as bad as the logging slash. Fire frequently recurs in this debris shortly after a new crop has started and there being no seed trees left and the supply of seed in the ground being exhausted, the hope of natural reforestation is remote. This almost prairie condition exists over many thousands of acres which a few years ago supported heavy stands of pine. If the first fire occurs late in the season when the ground is dry all the humus and tree seeds in the soil are destroyed and reproduction is practically precluded until the land is reseeded from surrounding forests.

The question naturally arises as to how this devastation can be avoided. Intensive fire patrol and efficient fire fighting equipment are essential and will help, but the most effective preventative is to remove the chief cause of the fires by disposing of the slash before it becomes a menace. This was done on one area with the result that after the logging a thrifty young stand, in which there was a fair proportion of pine, was left unharmed, the ground-cover was undisturbed and the danger of fire was very little, if any greater than in a virgin forest. The seed bed was left in good condition for the

germination of pine seed and millions of seedlings are coming up, whereas it was difficult to find one on a broad-cast burned area.

The polewood stand left on the ground has a start equivalent to thirty or forty years of growth, and another crop will be available that much sooner than it would have been if the slash had been burned broad-cast. The limbs and tops in this case were piled and burned as the trees were cut, on the ground or on the snow. No kerosene or torch was required to start the fires; a few pieces of birch-bark sufficed for that purpose. One extra swamper per cutting gang was required to handle the slash and as it was all out of the way of the skidders, the saving in the cost of skidding would offset, at least to some extent, the cost of the slash disposal.

Nature endowed the province of Ontario with a wonderful and varied forest, capable of supplying practically every requirement for wood. She will continue to do so if, when we upset the equilibrium established after centuries, we leave her the material and conditions to work with. If our forests are to continue to be a great industrial factor, as they should, provisions for their regeneration must be made in their exploitation. On much of our forest land it is now too late to do anything but to plant artificially but there are vast areas of young forests whose potential value should be fully realized and which should receive as great a measure of protection as the mature timber.

Old burn on Quetico Lake where scattered seed-trees of pine escaped and where a good reproduction of pine is just beginning to outgrow the concomitant aspen and white birch

Area broad-cast burned two or more times after logging. No coniferous and very little deciduous reproduction left

# Operators Discuss the Shrinkage of Lumber

### Representative Manufacturers Give Their Ideas on What Allowance Has to be Made in Sawing Certain Thicknesses of Wood—Opinions Differ

A representative Eastern lumber firm recently sent the following querry to the "Canada Lumberman":—

"If we were to saw logs (spruce and fir) which have been in the water for two years, into stock of 1 and 2 inches, how much would a piece,—say 2 x 6 x 16—shrink both in thickness and width in three years?"

The opinion of manufacturers of lumber in various provinces was sought and the replies received contain much interesting information.

An Ottawa Valley firm says that a piece 2 x 6 x 16 ft. air-dried spruce after three years' exposure would shrink about 3/32 in. in width or thickness.

A New Brunswick operator furnishes the following view—"We figure that a 2 x 6 x 16 ft, piece of spruce will shrink about 1/8 in. in thickness and about 1/4 in. in width in three years drying. There must be a little variation in this as it depends somewhat on the density of the wood; that is, there is some spruce that will shrink a little more than others. Taking it on the average, however, this is a fair statement, and we believe you will find it borne home by many practical lumbermen who express an opinion."

#### Not Shrunk as Much as Expected

Another New Brunswick firm declares:—"We find that lumber that we have that is three and four years old has not shrunk as much as we really anticipated. Our 2 in. stock, which we are resawing and selling as boards, is in almost every case resawing and dressing two sides to 13/16 in. We have looked over a large bunch of our stock recently, and as closely as we could judge, we would say that 2 x 6 shrink about 1/32 in. in thickness and about 1/16 in. in width. Of course, we have some cases of miss sawing, but we cannot blame this on shrinkage. We try to saw plump in thickness and the same too in width. Fir and white spruce would shrink much more than black spruce."

Here is the opinion of a Quebec lumberman,—"We have no actual data in this regard as we have never made any experiments, but we always saw our lumber between 1/8 and 1/4 in. over in width, and about 1/8 in. in thickness. We have never had any difficulty with our customers or received any complaints of stock being under-size though we have had large quantities of lumber in our yards for two or three years at different times. In our opinion 2 in. lumber should not shrink any more than the figures we have mentioned, when thoroughly air-dried."

A Northern Ontario concern says,—"We have sawn considerable spruce but never have had it in pile for a year. The shrinkage from being in pile three years would be more than for one year. We would judge that spruce sawn under the conditions you speak of, would shrink about 1/8 in. in thickness and 3/16 in. in width."

#### Very Much Depends on Conditions

An Eastern Ontario manufacture says,—"It is difficult to estimate the shrinkage of lumber after sawing as the kind of wood, time of year sawn which effects road drawing, etc., all influence shrinkage. Our practice is to allow 1/4 inch in width 1/8 inch in thickness and 1/2 inch in length over the nominal size of the board. This we have found to be ample."

Another Northwestern Ontario producer observes,—"On account of never having given the subject any consideration, we hesitate to make any statements as to how much 2-inch spruce stock would shrink in thickness and width in three years. We believe the shrinkage after the first six months would be almost negligible."

The president of a leading lumber company in the Sudbury district offers the following views:—"We allow enough so that lumber will dry out full thickness in width, but to give the actual shrinkage in thickness and width in three years, is something that is beyond us. This is a technical question and so many others enter into the matter, that it is only the research departments of some technical school that could give you a reply that would be correct, and possibly then their decision would be only partly true. In our own op-

eration we have watched shrinkage sufficiently to make safe the manufacture of white pine, hemlock and spruce."

#### The Ordinary Shrinkage in Hardwoods

The head of a well-known lumber company in Western Ontario states that as their business is confined largely to hardwoods, they do not care to express an opinion as to what shrinkage would take place in spruce. The shrinkage in hardwoods varies a great deal, depending upon the texture of the particular kind of wood. Basswood, for instance, shows much more shrinkage than oak or hard maple. It is customary for hardwood men to cut basswood 1 1/8 inches to dry 1 inch, while in hard maple the practice is to cut 1 1/16 inch to dry 1 inch, and 3-inch hard maple is reasonably safe if cut 3/18 inches. The same regulation applies to shrinkage as to width. Basswood and soft elm will shrink from 1/4 inch to 3/8 inch on a 6 inch board. Hard maple will not shrink much over half of this. We would think that spruce would show a shrinkage intermittent between basswood and hard maple.

Another firm in the North say that the shrinkage will be about 1/32 in. on 1 in. and about 1/16 in. on 2 in. spruce.

Another widely-known New Brunswick lumberman writes,—

"We are not in a position to give you an intelligent answer on the question of the shrinkage of lumber. We know a good deal about shrinkage, but in lumber it varies so much that it is difficult to get any idea which would be of any practical value. Take black spruce, for instance—you cannot compare it with white spruce nor could you compare rapid-growing spruce with slow-growing white spruce; neither could you compare slow-growing fir with rapid-growing fir, and the air-dried proposition varies so much. If we had any ideas that would be of any value, we would gladly give them to you. We have a rule to go by in sawing lumber which requires to be a certain size after dried, but at different mills we have to make a slightly different allowance. In regard to the shrinkage of lumber which has been in the water, we cannot tell you whether there would be any difference between the shrinkage of a green spruce tree and one which has laid in the water for over two years."

#### Mr. Little Recalls Early Timber Days

Mr. William Little, one of the directors of the Canadian Forestry Association, who attended the board meeting of the Association in Quebec lately, is the son of the late James Little, who came from Ireland over one hundred years ago and was one of the early pioneers in the Canadian lumber trade who died at the age of 82 years. His son, William Little, was born at Caledonia, Ont., and is now 86 years of age, and himself a pioneer in the lumber operating business. He is still in good physical health, tall and well built in stature, with a constitution that is likely to cause him to live to be a nonogenarian. He still takes an active interest in the lumber business and is endowed with a memory which makes him an interesting raconteur of the past.

"It is nearly forty years," said Mr. Little in an interview with the Quebec correspondent of the "Canada Lumberman," "since I last visited Quebec City, and I am certainly impressed with the many changes which have taken place since that time. The upper and lower town landmarks still remain to remind one of the past, but, on the other hand, the city has extended and the population doubled, but, alas, the old friends and business men of the city in the lumber export trade, have all passed away and with them the once picturesque shipping of the port.

"I remember when I came to Quebec to attend to the export shipping of my father's timber and later my own, I could stand on Dufferin Terrace and in looking over the expanse of the large and beautiful harbor,my vision would permit me to count hundreds of ships lying at anchor in the centre of the stream, while the quays lining both sides of the river would have many more ships moored, to take into their hold timber, which would come down the St. Lawsence in rafts to be shipped across the Atlantic. "What a contrast to-day. A beautiful deep-water harbor the finest in the world, empty of shipping in comparison with the past.

## Wholesalers at Table Conference

### Many Matters Discussed at the Regular Session of Toronto Dealers—Big Picnic Will Be Held

A round-table conference was held by the Wholesale Lumber Dealers' Association, Inc., at the Albany Club, Toronto, on May 19th. It was the occasion of the monthly session of the members and there was a fair attendance. H. J. Terry presided and everyone took part in the discussion which ranged over a variety of topics but centered principally on how a larger representation of "the boys" could be brought out at the regular gatherings. Some helpful hints were offered by G. E. Spragge, Alfred Read, K. M. Brown, A. E. Clark, A. C. Gordon and others. The talk was a heart-to-heart one as nothing was held back, and much constructive criticism was heard. It was felt that a greater number of concrete subjects should be discussed, that there should be a more outspoken attitude on the part of any members who had a grievance, criticism or complaint of any kind, that there should be a give-and-take spirit and more vital topics discussed, such as the shortage of supply in certain lines, the trend of the market, eastern and western conditions, trade ethics, etc.

The outcome of the discussion was a decision to hold the June meeting on a Monday instead of a Friday. It will be a noon-day gathering from 12.30 to 2 o'clock, and the fee for the dinner will be $1.00. Many successful clubs and trade organizations are holding their sessions at noon-day instead of in the evening, and the lumbermen decided to try out the plan in the hope that it will meet with encouragement and recognition.

Another matter brought up was a suggestion by K. M. Brown that the Association should issue a trade-mark which could be used by all the members in their advertising. Nearly all other bodies have a trade-mark, and Mr. Brown was of the opinion that the lumbermen could well follow in this course.

Another suggestion was the holding of a picnic. Two years ago a very successful outing took place at Grimsby Beach and added considerably to the prestige of the wholesale lumbermen. A. E. Clark, who has a summer residence at Grimsby, invited the members to come there again. The entertainment committee was instructed to make full arrangements for an outing at an early date. The proposed picnic was heartily endorsed by everyone.

A. E. Clark brought up the matter of the wholesalers being represented before the special parliamentary committee on freight rates. He thought the wholesale lumbermen should favor such a move and the matter was left with the board of directors to take such action as they deem necessary on the date when the forest products men were afforded a hearing before the committee. Mr. Clark said that the case presented some months ago by the Canadian Lumbermen's Association before the Railway Commission when there was a large attendance of members of the C.L.A. from all parts of Canada, was ably handled. Chairman Carvell said that no interests had made stronger representation to the board for the lessening of carrying charges than had the lumbermen. On the forthcoming occasion before the members of the house committee on freight rates Mr. Clark thought the wholesale lumber dealers should make as effective a showing as possible in numbers and influence.

The delinquency of several firms in making their monthly trade reports to the secretary was talked over. It was felt that something should be done to secure a larger number of firms reporting at the end of each month. Various suggestions were made which will be considered by the board of directors. The worth of the reports was commented upon and it was realized that in order to attain their full value more firms should be more prompt in sending them in.

Various other matters of a minor character were referred to the board of directors.

### Western Loggers Ask too Much, Say Millmen

The difficulties which some manufacturing firms in British Columbia have to encounter at the present time and a review of conditions as they exist, is furnished in a recent communication received by H. A. Rose, of Rose, McLaurin, Limited, Toronto, from a progressive concern in Victoria. The following paragraphs will be read with much interest:—

"The conditions under which we are operating are probably more difficult than they have been for a long time. We have been trying to keep our plants running and obtain sawing business that will enable us to deliver logs to the mills at the market prices for same. This, of course, necessitates our obtaining only sawing orders where there are some unusual conditions which will enable us to obtain a better price.

"Towing conditions have been very difficult and we have had

booms tied up for extended periods causing us to close down for several days at a time pending arrival of logs. At Victoria we have been out of logs for three or four weeks and have not turned a wheel. We do not intend going out on the market to buy logs and pay the prices which the loggers are asking as we can secure no business that will justify the payment of these prices. Conditions to-day are such that when a mill pays a logger the prices asked, the logger is making a profit on his operations, of fully as much as the mills will lose in sawing such logs, and until conditions right themselves, we will not be factors in the B. C. lumber industry.

"So far as our stocks are concerned we have not been making any real effort to sell the same, and now find that the increased building activities all over the U. S. have created a demand for such sizes as are usually used in house construction, with the result that prices have advanced several dollars per thousand. We are able to quote, for instance on dimensions sold direct to the trade, prices that are the equivalent of net price list "E-1." There are no 6 in. clear strips on the coast and drop siding is now being sold on the American side at about $35.00 mill. There are also enormous amounts of car building material being bought and the prices realized are in many cases as much as $10.00 per M. more than our Canadian railroads will pay.

"We do not look for a material improvement in the Canadian market this year. Export conditions are chaotic and will probably not right themselves for some months to come. There is a considerable quantity of common grades of lumber now being purchased from tide-water mills for shipment to the Atlantic seaboard and the Californian market is improving so that it is possible to make substantial shipments to this market which will realize for the mills a much better price than can be obtained for the same lumber from the northwest trade."

### Progressive Eastern Lumber Company

The Argenteuil Lumber Co., Limited, Morin Heights, Que., are one of the widely-known lumber organizations in the county of Argenteuil. They have been operating since 1907 and their present mill was built in 1914, the old one having been burned the previous year.

The mill is run by waterpower, operating under a 40-foot average head, but steam is also used. The plant is equipped with a Waterous steam nigger and loader and heavy steam feed carriage, a Waterous 12-inch double cast band mill, a circular resaw, edger, trimmer, slab slashers, etc. The capacity is about 40,000 feet per day. The company also have one Berlin 108 planer, a shingle machine, a clapboard

Sawmill of the Argenteuil Lumber Co., at Morin Heights, Que

sawing machine and a clapboard planer. There is a small electric plant that generates sufficient power for their own use and for which the company supply light to the village.

The limits of the company are situated in Howard and Wentworth townships, Argenteuil County, and for the past few years the company have hauled all their logs to the mill on sleighs. The products are spruce and birch lumber, cedar shingles, sheathing, soft and hardwood flooring and clapboards.

Sir George H. Perley, of Ottawa, is president of the company; J. E. Seale, of Morin Heights, vice-president; H. Jekill, of Montreal, secretary-treasurer, and J. P. Middleton, of Morin Heights, managing-director.

The company are operating their mill this season on a limited scale only as their log output last winter was only about one-third of their total in 1920-21. They report that the local trade shows a considerable improvement over last year, especially on dressed lumber and shingles.

# How Product of Small Sawmills May be Much Improved

## By "Observer"

The complaints, voiced against certain sawmill men at a recent meeting of the Montreal Builders' Exchange when that body discussed at length the subject of grade standardization of soft-wood, were timely and interesting. However, granting that the output of several of the smaller mills in both Ontario and Quebec may be indifferently manufactured in some cases, the fact that Montreal has become "the dumping ground for this material," as one contractor put it, would appear to demonstrate that wholesalers are not functioning uniformly as a lumber Association should, or they are not making sufficient effort to secure from the mills what they agree is the correct grading for the different pieces that are later to be used in building construction. In other words, they are apparently not protecting their own markets as they should.

Here is a good chance for the wholesalers to prove their worth and co-operation in the industry by educating the small mills to improve their output. Standardization is a desirable thing, but it cannot be accomplished over night; it is up to purchasers to get together and educate the small millmen to better and more uniform grading, for apparently the larger and permanently established mills, produce dependable accurately graded lumber.

It is, of course, out of the question to expect the small sawmill to turn out as many grades as the large mill, but a larger proportion of clear cuttings could be obtained by remanufacture in many cases, while the quality should be every bit as good as the larger mill.

The small millman's chief aim should be to cut as much high-grade stock as possible and also to see that both high and low grades can be readily sold. Upon the grader lies the result. If his judgment is good, the mill will make proportionate profits, but if he does not know when to trim or rip a board, or, on the other hand, if it be advisable to leave it as it is, to bring the highest return, then the mill will lose profits that otherwise would be made.

I think the following observations from the "American Lumberman" are well worth reproducing in our columns—To every grader comes the question in the course of his daily work, whether to trim or rip a board, and for the man who is new at the job of grading, it is a live question to answer. Here is a good way to figure it. Rip or trim only when: 1. The remanufactured board is worth as much as the original board, plus the cost of reworking, plus a profit. 2. When the remanufactured board is not of a size of which there is a surplus in stock. The good grader knows the market values of the different grades but that is where many fall down. For most experienced graders, a glance at a board tells them whether to rip or trim to raise the grade, but how many know whether the operation is worth it. For instance, if a 10-foot board is trimmed one foot or one-tenth, the remanufactured board must yield one-ninth more per thousand in order to break even. By the same method, if one-eighth is trimmed, the remainder must be worth one-seventh more per thousand than the original board. A knowledge of values is, of course, important, and if the grader can be taught to trim with the above rule in mind, the trimming question is readily solved.

In trimming lumber a 2 or 4-foot piece is of practically no value and the price received for 2 or 4-foot trims simply covers the cost of handling these small pieces.

For example, a 1 x 6 inch, 16-foot piece of No. 4 white pine is worth 22.4 cents. After trimming it 2 feet to rise the grade, the piece of 1 x 6 inch, 14-foot No. 3 white pine secured is worth 23.8 cents. The gain is 1.4 cent, which is offset by the labor in trimming, and by the possibility of the 1 x 6 inch 14 foot No. 3 again dropping to a No. 4, as a result of additional handling in stocking the 1 x 6 inch, 14 foot, No. 3 in the dry shed. But a 1 x 6 inch 18-foot No.2 white pine is worth 49.5 cents, and a 1 x 6 inch, 16-foot No. 1 white pine is worth 69.6 cents, so that the difference makes possible a gain of 20.1 cents, which is obvious when the labor of trimming.

In ripping lumber to raise the grade, you have a larger item of labor to consider. It is necessary to return the stock to the planing mill or rip saw, and again regrade, and to sort the ripped products. Estimating the cost of this work at $3 a thousand board feet, it would cost about 5 cents a piece to rip and regrade a thousand feet of 1 x 2 inch 16-foot.

Ripping a 1 x 12 inch, 16-foot No. 3 white pine worth 64 cents for a 1 x 4 inch, 16-foot No. 2 white pine worth 58.6 cents and a 1 x 4 inch, 16-foot No. 4 white pine worth 14.9 cents, we have a total value of 73.5 cents, but considering the cost of ripping, regrading and sorting, there is nothing to be gained.

Ripping a 1 x 12 inch, 16-foot No. 3 white pine to a 1 x 6 inch, 16-foot "C" white pine worth 88 cents and a 1 x 6 inch, 16-foot No. 3 worth 31.2 cents, gives a total of 119.2 cents, which, compared with the value of a 1 x 12-inch, 16-foot No. 3 at 64 cents, shows a gain that amply repays for the labor of ripping and regrading. In marking a piece of lumber for ripping or trimming, put the marks on the part to be trimmed off, or on the lower grade as far as possible, in order to keep the higher grade piece free from unnecessary crayon marks.

The production of better grades is sometimes a difficult doctrine to preach to the small sawmill man who must invest in additional equipment if he decides to better his grades. However, if the millman is shown that in freight alone he will save the cost of the additional equipment every month and, at the same time, get more for his lumber, he will see the reason of the argument and act accordingly. Here is a chance also for live-wire manufacturers of mill machinery to help push better grading by showing the small mills the saving and profits to be made by installing equipment, such as trimmers, edgers and other machines, for the remanufacture into better and more profitable lumber.

---

## Competent Supervision of Timber Needed

"Nature has no economic sense, but she accepts direction." This is how Dr. C. D. Howe, dean af the faculty of forestry of the University of Toronto, summarizes Canada's forest difficulties, in an able article in the University of Toronto Monthly, in which he stresses the need for the exercise over Canadian timber lands of competent supervision.

Dr. Howe points out that without strenuous efforts on the part of government forestry officials Western timber lands will shortly succumb to the combined attacks of fire, disease and indiscriminate cutting operations and will cease to be a source of revenue.

"It does not follow that an area covered with forests is commercially valuable because of their presence," Dr. Howe states in dispelling the prevalent idea that trees are equally valuable for market purposes. "Seventy kinds of trees have been used in this country in the wood and timber trade, but only a few species contribute to the annual Canadian output of four billion feet of lumber. In terms of manufactured lumber products, forests contribute to our national wealth a quarter of a billion dollars a year, but of this sum two-thirds is paid for by only six kinds of trees."

Using pulpwood as an example of the value of some timbers and the worthlessness of others, "four million cords of pulpwood are cut each year to be worked into paper products worth $200,000,000," Prof. Howe states. "But the wood of only four kinds of trees is used in most of this output of pulp.

"No wood fits purposes as well as the Canadian white pine, but our commercial supply of this species is fast disappearing," Dr. Howe warns. "We are already using poorer wood as substitutes."

Detailing the relatively small fraction of forest lands which are of commercial interest, "of Canada's 3.5 million square miles 1.6 million are too cold, too high, or too dry to grow trees attractive to lumbermen," the article reads. "Deducting cultivated and grass lands, we have left a billion acres of forest, but more than a quarter of this area won't grow trees of saw log size."

Areas bearing trees of saw log size are a still smaller proportion, it appears, because trunks twelve inches in diameter are needed for this purpose.

Telling of the fire loss experienced each year, "Destruction of our forests by fire has been incomprehensibly great," Dr. Howe writes, "Saw timber thus destroyed amounts to more than has been removed by logging and farming operations together, since the settlement to the country began. Half to two-thirds of Canada's forested area do not to-day contain forests of sawlog size, because they have been burned within the past seventy-five years.

"Much of the burned over area has been visited by fire two, three or even half a dozen times. These repeated fires on the same area make abortive nature's attempt to reclothe the old burns with commercially valuable trees. Worthless brush and trees of no market value are replacing magnificent forests of pine, devastated by repeated burning."

Records show that the fire danger is still a serious menace.

"Devastation by fire is not a thing of the past, but it still continues unabated," Dr. Howe reports. "A million and a half acres of forest fell prey to flames in Eastern Canada last summer."

# Wholesalers Invited on Trip

### Annual Outing up the Lakes During Latter Part of June Promises to be Largely Attended.

Arrangements are now practically complete for the annual mid-summer outing of the Ontario Retail Dealers' Association, which will be held up the lakes June 23rd to June 27th.

L. H. Richards, of Sarnia, chairman of the outing committee, reports that reservations have been coming in very satisfactorily from retail lumbermen and the O.R.L.D.A. has extended an invitation to all wholesale dealers to join them in this enjoyable midsummer trip on board the "Huronic" of the Northern Navigation Co. A large number of wholesalers have accepted the invitation and it is expected that there will be four days of delightful association.

The visitors will be entertained by the Chamber of Commerce at Owen Sound, Sault Ste Marie and Sarnia, and automobiles will be provided for sight-seeing. There will not be a dull moment from the beginning to the end of the jaunt.

All details are now arranged and it is expected that a number of retail lumbermen from Michigan will be members of the party. On board the boat there will be music, dancing, concerts, afternoon tea, the publication of a daily paper and other diverting features.

On Monday evening June 26 on the "Huronic" there will be a concert, and a humorous lecture by Douglas Malloch, of Chicago, the lumberman poet. This talk has made "a killing" wherever it has been heard and those who have listened to Mr. Malloch in the past know what a treat is in store for them. He will join the lumbermen at Mackinac.

The steamer is capable of accommodating 250 persons, and the fact that members of the party will be away from business only two or three days, is appealing strongly to many forest product merchants who will be accompanied by their wives and families.

So much has been said in previous editions regarding the details of the trip that little more can be added. Any who have not yet made their reservations should do so immediately with L. H. Richards, of the Laidlaw-Belton Lumber Co., of Sarnia.

The time table and route of the party is as follows:—
Leave Windsor, 5 P.M. Friday, June 23rd.
Leave Sarnia, 11 P.M. Friday, June 23rd.
Arrive Owen Sound, 7 P.M. Saturday, June 24th.
Leave Owen Sound, 11 P.M. Saturday, June 24th.
Arrive Killarney, 7 A.M. Sunday, June 25th.
Leave Killarney, 9 A.M. Sunday, June 25th.
Arrive Sault Ste Marie, 7 P.M. Sunday, June 25th.
Leave Sault Ste Marie, midnight Sunday, June 25th.
Arrive Mackinac, 10 A.M. Monday, June 26th.
Leave Mackinac, noon Monday, June 26th.
Arrive Sarnia. 10 A.M. Tuesday, June 27th.
Leave Sarnia, noon Tuesday, June 27th.
Arrive Windsor, 5 P.M. Tuesday, June 27th.

The retail lumbermen have undertaken a big task and are assuming heavy obligations in connection with the forthcoming excursion. The project is an ambitious one and it is hoped that wholesalers and retailers will join whole-heartedly in taking advantage of the splendid opportunity for a sail up the lakes and the many enjoyable events that will be associated with it. The Ontario Retail Lumber Dealers' Association has always made a success of anything it has undertaken, and does not want to see this splendid record of achievement shattered. It is, therefore, up to every man to take hold and push unitedly and aggressively for the big outing on June 23rd to 27th.

### How Delivery Cost is Overcome

An Ontario retailer asks if it is customary to make an extra charge for delivering small quantities, such as 100 or 300 feet, or less than 500.

Where what is termed free delivery is practiced there is no specific charge for delivery on any amount. A pound of nails or a single piece of lumber is delivered just the same as a whole house pattern, without any specific item of charge for this service.

To offset this, however, it is a practice to make the specific price for the smaller quantities higher than for larger quantities. Some dealers set a fifty dollar value as a minimum, although there is no uniformity in this respect. The idea is that measuring out and delivering small quanties of any merchandise costs more in proportion than delivery in larger quantities; therefore the price schedule on smaller quantities is made higher so as to absorb this extra cost.

This is simpler than making specific charges for all deliveries. Some have had plans of making a specific or percentage charge for delivery, but it is a hard thing to keep balanced up fairly. The charge to be equitable for small items might easily exceed the original cost of the material itself. Therefore, the better practice seems to be that of making what is termed free delivery within certain limits, and including the cost of this delivery service in the original price of the products, using a slightly higher list for the small quantities.

### Coralling Lumber Business of the Farmer

Loud and emphatic is the "dull times" cry from the farm trade these days and lumber retailers who handle what little business offering for repair work are finding no sinecure in the job of making collections. Dealers who depend largely on the farmers for a big portion of their trade are finding it difficult to console themselves with the idea of attracting and getting the farmer to do his repair work and building now. In districts, where the farmers depend solely on one certain kind of crop, and in these days of deflating prices and poor soil returns, business is by no means brisk even in the mixed farming communities. However unsatisfactory as the situation is, there is always a solution. We have had many solutions offered, however, to our present problems by all sorts of people in all lines of business, but no one can tell you what to do in your particular position. You have to solve your own peculiar problem. Retailing lumber to farmers is not the easiest thing in the world to-day; in fact, selling anything, apparently, is no cinch.

But the farmers are not bankrupt and in this new day of economical readjustment the agriculturist will be taught industrial economy in the same manner as the others are learning it. The manufacturer is looking for machines that will reduce his production costs and the farmer will be approached by people who will show him, in dollars and cents, how a certain machine will enable him to produce more cheaply; and mark you, the farmer, as "near" as the class is reputed to be, will loosen up and buy, if he is convinced the equipment is a money maker.

Where does the retailer of lumber stand in this new economic game? What can he do to show the farmer how to save actual money on his repairs or buildings?—only real honest economies will convince the yeoman.

Are you studying the farmer's problems or just looking after the area within your yard. Have you thought about the different farms in your district and what in the way of lumber each requires, if the market for each is improving and larger production is contemplated.

Some dealers are going a step farther to get this first hand knowledge by establishing an information bureau for the benefit of the farm trade, such as displaying a list of farmer's names who want seed for spring sowing and those who have seed on hand to sell.

Another dealer has a black board in his window where he is listing names of farmers who have farm implements to sell and another section for equipment wanted. This scheme of studying the farm trade at close range is even closer to the lumber dealer's own business as he can learn what buildings the farmers have for their machinery. This service is, of course free to anyone who wishes to buy or sell rural requisites.

These are only a couple of ways the lumber merchant may get inside knowledge of the news of the surrounding district and perhaps put a farmer friend on the track of a good purchase or, on the other hand a market for a piece of equipment for another.

These little services—which perhaps some will say are not practical, and too troublesome for the retail lumber dealer to perform,—are after all the foundation of a wider acquaintance and stronger friendship that will go a long way when the farmer is buying lumber instead of machinery.

Of course, these services to the farmer are not immediate money makers, but if such plans can enable you to learn the needs or the actual standing of a farmer, and more than that, if a visit to the farm itself is the outcome, then certainly they are good business leaders.

If you can learn what size of a hog or cattle business a man does, or if he specializes in one or more lines, you are undoubtedly in a better position to advise him convincingly when he needs new or additional accommodation to look properly after his stock. It goes without saying, of course, that retail lumber merchants doing business among the farmers are keen observers of the produce market, but today these matters should be given more attention than ever in order to talk intelligently with farmer friends when you meet them or when they call to make enquiries regarding the price of lumber.

If the retail lumber merchant is wise he can make his place of business a valuable bureau of local information for the farmers and a rendezvous for them when they come to town. They will come to know that they can call around for a chat and get a market tip perhaps, without being under any obligation for the information handed out. From these little, seemingly unimportant interviews there may be gleaned what the lumber merchant is always looking for —new business.

# District Dealers Hold Rally at Stratford

## Retail Lumbermen Discuss Many Subjects of Vital Interest—Officers Elected for the Coming Year—Trade Picking Up and Building Fairly Active

George S. Zimmerman, Tavistock. Retiring Chairman District No. 7

The sales tax, mechanics' lien, credit bureau, collections, building prospects, advertising, cost of doing business, profit figuring, retail advertising, and Midsummer outing up the lakes, were all informally discussed at the annual meeting of the Stratford District (No. 7,) of the Ontario Retail Lumber Dealers' Association, which was held in the "Mansion House" in the Classic City on May 15th. There was a good attendance and much interest was evinced in the proceedings.

George S. Zimmerman, of Tavistock, chairman of the district, presided, and stated that the outlook throughout the district was much better than a year ago. Considerable building was going on in some of the smaller towns and many people were seriously considering the project of erecting homes. He found in some quarters, however, there was a disposition to hang back in the expectation that prices would still be further reduced and that wages, now regarded as too high, would decline.

Mr. Zimmerman spoke of the value of association and the good effect of mingling together and rubbing shoulders with the other fellow. It broadened men out and they learned to understand one another better. He believed that an association was more needed in times like these—during a period of recovery and readjustment—than when things were at their peak and all was plain sailing. A local body could do much in the way of eliminating prejudice, misunderstanding and straightening out affairs between dealers, while the Ontario Association, which was the parent body, dealt with larger matters, such as the sales tax, mechanics' lien act, legislation, insurance, house plans, trade ethics, etc. Mr. Zimmerman strongly advised everyone to become identified with both organizations and they would reap great good from membership. In closing he referred briefly to the instructive character of the work and business done at conventions throughout the year.

One of the first items at the Stratford session was the collection of the annual fee for the coming year which was fixed at $2.00, and retiring secretary E. K. Kalbfleisch gave a brief report of his work during the past twelve months.

### The New Officers for 1922

The election of officers was then proceeded with and resulted as follows:—

Chairman,—J. J. Cluff, Seaforth;
Vice-Chairman,—E. K. Kalbfleisch, Stratford.
Secretary-Treasurer,—E. Fleischauer, (Peffer & Co.) Stratford;
Executive Committee,—D. C. Baird, St. Mary's; Robert Oliver, Listowel; G. M. McKenzie, Clinton; T. A. Pounder, Stratford; George S. Zimmerman, Tavistock.

Among those present at the gathering were:—George S. Zimmerman, Tavistock; E. K. Kalbfleisch, Stratford; N. M. Bearinger, Elmira; A. F. Cluff, Seaforth; D. C. Baird, St. Mary's; G. M. McKenzie, Clinton; E. Fleischauer, Stratford; T. A. Pounder, Stratford; Horace Boultbee, (secretary O.R.L.D.A.,) Toronto, G. B. Van Blaricom, (editor "Canada Lumberman,") Toronto and others.

A general discussion took place in reference to the sales tax. It is explained by Secretary Boultbee that a late ruling of the department at Ottawa was to the effect that the retailer was not obliged to collect a tax on lumber which was converted into flooring or planed and matched. It was only when lumber was converted into boxes, window frames, sash or something of that character that the term "manufacturing" applied, and the 1½% had to be returned to the government. Lumber that did not change its original form when handled by the retailer, was not subject to a tax. This, included flooring, matching, dressing, etc., but where cut up and sent out in a different shape from that originally received, the sales tax applied. Secretary Boultbee of the O.R.L.D.A. read the following letter form the Collector of Customs and Exise Ottawa, in regard to the sales tax.

"Charges for customs sawing took effect October 1st, 1921, but the Department of Customs and Excise later, to be precise, November 8th, 1921, ruled that Sales Tax does not apply upon charges for custom sawing and planing of lumber, which has previously borne the payment of Sales Tax of 2%.

"A manufacturer or dealer owning lumber for resale is not required to pay Sales Tax on custom sawing or planing thereof if the lumber has been previously subjected to Sales Tax at the rate of 2%; in the event that the tax has not been so paid, the lumber is subject to 2% when sold by the manufacturer."

The matter of the mechanics' lien act was also discussed and it was the unanimous opinion that the present measure was weak, unworkable and inadequate and afforded little or no protection to the retail lumber merchant or the builders' supply men. Secretary Boultbee explained that efforts to have the provisions changed had not been effective although considerable money had been spent in legal services, etc. In view of the request received from Ottawa that no legislation along this line be introduced by the provinces, it is the hope meanwhile that a Dominion measure might be formulated, which would be applicable to the various districts of Canada, and would possess some measure of uniformity, the present legislation might have to be endured for some time. Many members gave instances of how they had suffered losses under the present act which was full of loop-holes and practically worthless.

It was intimated that some members of the district who had been doing price-cutting, evidently did not know how to figure costs or take into consideration all that overhead meant. One dealer explained that there was little use trying to educate certain yardmen or factory men, as they knew it all and nobody could teach them anything. The only way was to let such fellows run their course and, in the end when they ran up against a stone wall or tumbled over a precipice, they would discover that something had gone wrong with their business machine. Now and then there sprang up in every community and in every line of business the price-cutter who seemed to glory in taking the job from the other fellow, no matter even if it was at a loss.

### Keeping a Tab on Delinquents

Then the matter of collections was discussed, and it appears that in every district there are certain builders, contractors or others who are always going out of their own town to a neighboring dealer to get prices on lumber or other supplies. They pretend to have good credit, but inquiry often reveals that they are dead-beats or slow-pay. In order that dealers in other towns and villages may not get stung, it was decided to further strengthen the credit bureau of the district. Those customers who owe certain lumbermen in different towns and seek to obtain supplies in a new quarter, may find that they are up against it. A Credit Bureau will be operated by the Stratford district and E. Fleischauer, secretary-treasurer, who will have the names of both slow and bad patrons. It was felt that a district bureau would be of much benefit to the dealers, and they could do much to protect one another from losses.

Another type of individual who appears to be flourishing at the present time is the fellow who can always" buy it for less." He comes into town, and, after getting a price from a local lumberman, will casually remark that Mr. J. of the neighboring burgh is $10.00 cheaper on his hemlock, or $15.00 on his white pine strips or so much less on lath, shingles, etc. Most dealers know that callers of this type are deliberately falsifying, but have not the moral courage to tell them so in a pointed manner. Others have the lists of what lumber is commanding in adjacent towns, and, as soon as these bargain-hunting individuals talk about how much better they can do some place else, the yardmen produce the lists. In many cases the visitor

J. J. Cluff, Seaforth,
Newly-elected Chairman

E. K. Kalbfleisch, Stratford,
Newly-elected Vice Chairman

Robert Oliver, Listowel,
Re-elected Member of the Executive

who has sprung this bluff, begins to hedge or finds it convenient to retire rather speedily.

One dealer stated that as soon as a man talked about how cheap he could get it in a neighboring town, he would say,—"My car is right at the door here. Jump in with me and we will go over to K's place right away. I would like to get some of that stuff myself at the figure you mention." The visitor generally says that he has not time just then or temporizes in some other way to escape a "show down."

The subject of advertising was also taken up, and it was agreed that more dealers should use the local papers in order to make known the service they can render, the goods they carry and what they can do in the way of furnishing interior and exterior trim and other material for home building.

### Say Something in Lumber Advertising

N. M. Bearinger, of Elmira, gave one of the most effective talks on "Publicity" that has been delivered before a district Association in a long period. He said that he used double-column space in a local paper, changed the reading matter of his ad. every week, and endeavored to make it original, effective and striking. The announcement always appeared in the same place and the people in the district now looked for his ad. as one of the regular features of the paper. Ministers, school teachers and others had come up to Mr. Bearinger and had a good laugh at some witty sally contained in his announcements or complimented him upon the novel presentation in print of his wares. Mr. Bearinger said that he used some rather catchy captions, such as "Not Guilty," "The Dutchman," "Efficiency," etc., rather than the mere word "Lumber." After the heading he sought to draw a parallel between some incident, with which they were all familiar and the service which he was able to give in his mill and yard.

Mr. Bearinger added that he could trace many orders direct to the space used in the press and he had also cultivated friendly relations with the editor of the paper. In conversation with him, Mr. Bearinger had remarked that by the middle of the summer, if enough houses were not put up by private enterprise in Elmira to satisfy the demand, he, (Bearinger) would erect a number, which would be disposed of on favorable terms. This was what he intended to do, and the announcement appeared in several papers. The result was that many farmers, who had been hesitating about buying material for construction, reading that a building boom was about to start in Elmira, had come in and bought their joists, studding, siding, flooring and other supplies in great haste: "in fact," said Mr. Bearinger, "they almost cleaned me out."

Other dealers present at the meeting also gave some instances in connection with publicity and agreed that it was advisable to advertise, particularly at this season of the year.

Another matter taken up was how more interest in the district meetings could be developed and the attendance augmented. It was thought that certain local dealers should speak on vital questions and give their views and the programme should be announced in advance. It was suggested that W. P. Flint, of Chicago, secretary of the Millwork Cost Bureau, might be asked to come over a little later on in the season and give the members an address on "Millwork Costs.". It is probable that the next district gathering may be held in the evening following a dinner.

Secretary Boultbee drew attention to the annual midsummer outing which will take place up the lakes starting at Windsor on Friday June 23rd and ending on June 27th. The steamer "Huronic" had been chartered and a large number of reservations had already been made. The trip would be full of delightful associations and would be entirely a lumbermen's party. Many members would bring their wives and daughters; in fact some dealers were purchasing as many as five tickets. A number of those present intimated that they would be only too happy to take in the trip.

### Quit Quoting by the Thousand Feet

One thing that every retailer should discard is the habit of quoting price to consumers at so much per thousand feet. The retailer still buys by the thousand, and perhaps thinks in the thousand feet units, but it is time to get away from this and to think in hundred feet units. Not only are wise salesmen representing the mills now talking and selling in hundred feet units, but the retailer should invariably use this basis in preference to the thousand feet units in figuring with the individual customer or contractor, says the "Southern Lumberman."

With the individual customer it is best to leave out the feetage unit entirely in talking prices. Find out exactly what the man wants, then give him a price on it. Most live retailers have reduced their prices to a piece basis so that they can take any item of framing, or boards and name the customer a price on one or more pieces by the piece.

That is good where the customer asks for lumber by the piece. Where the customer wants material to do a certain bit of work, figure what it is he needs and name a price on the whole amount.

The flooring matter has been illustrated several times. The right thing to do is to find out the size of the room, the kind of floor wanted, then figure up and make the price on the amount necessary to lay that floor. The same idea holds if it was a pig trough, chicken house or anything else. Figure out the material for whatever it is someone wants to construct, and then make a price on the whole lot.

The one thing to keep persistently in mind is to break yourself from the habit of thinking and quoting in the thousand feet units. It does not convey a definite idea to the average mind and does carry the idea of a big price,—big compared with single foot or the hundred feet amount, thus creating an impression that lumber costs too much, a thing that plainly we want to avoid.

### Location for London Lumber Yard

The city council of London, Ont., has granted a permit to the Mathews Lumber Co. to locate a lumber yard on Horton St. in that city. Since early last summer the Matthews Company has been battling with the city council for a lumber yard location. They were ordered to move from the site, which the council has now granted them a permit to occupy. They did not get a new site quickly enough, and, after sundry threats, were made, a limited time was set by which the Mathews Company had to move. The threat was taken seriously and a new site was then secured. Though this was outside the fire limits, being on Simcoe St., the council would not let the firm locate there. Finally the civic authorities concluded that the matter had been played with long enough and granted the permit for the location on Horton St.

## New Insect Danger Threatens Timber

Two species of destructive insects are making their reappearance in the forests of New Brunswick.

These insects are known as the larch sawfly and the larch case borer, and steps are already being taken by the Department of Lands and Mines to minimize or prevent the danger of destruction similar to that which occurred in the province some forty or fifty years ago, when these insects wiped out completely the valuable tamerack stands of the province.

Col. T. G. Loggie, of Fredericton, Deputy Minister of Lands and Mines, has forwarded a communication to Dr. J. H. Grisdale, of the Federal Department of Agriculture at Ottawa, who has charge of the Dominion Entomological Branch operations, asking for information regarding the ways and means by which to combat this new danger. It is suggested by Col. Loggie that some parasite destructive to these insects could be introduced in the province as a means of fighting the threatened destruction of the new stands of tamarack.

Tamarack is especially valuable in shipbuilding operations the lumber being used in the construction of ships knees, and New Brunswick has only recently recovered from the devastation wrought by these insects during their first ravages almost half a century ago.

## Japan Wants High Grade B.C. Lumber

"Vancouver Quality" is the high-grade lumber that is popular in Japan, according to information received by the Vancouver Board of Trade from Mr. A. E. Bryan, Canadian Trade Commissioner at Yokohama.

Mr. Bryan draws the attention of all exporters from Canada to the fact that there is a decided preference on the Japanese market for Canadian quality, and that firms should always point out clearly whether they are offering Canadian or United States lumber.

"When buyers on this side of the Pacific place orders with Canadian mills" he says, "it is because they want Canadian lumber or as it is known on this market—Vancouver quality."

Considerable trouble, he states, has been caused lately by Canadian exporters shipping lumber of United States origin to firms in Japan, who took it for granted that as they were buying from Canada they would receive Canadian quality, but who found on examining inspection certificates that the lumber was shipped from the United States.

Where this procedure is followed without the Japanese buyer being notified it is liable to cause much trouble, and is not conducive to building up a good name for Canadian lumber exporters Mr. Bryan adds.

## Stirring Up Interest in Forestry

A board meeting of the Canadian Forestry Association was held at Quebec recently to develop further plans for the extension of propaganda in forest fire protection. The meeting was presided over by the president, Dan. McLachlin, of Arnprior, Ont. The directors present were Messrs. Robson Black, (manager) Ottawa; W. Little; General J. B. White and C. E. E. Ussher, Montreal; J. A. Gillies, of Braeside; R. H. Campbell, Ottawa; G. H. Prince, Fredericton; G. C. Piche, Quebec, and others.

This Association, which is not identified with any government or commercial board, has a score of educational methods in operation by which public interest in forest protection is stimulated. It was decided that the Forest Exhibition Car newly equipped and improved upon, will tour the province of Quebec for a period to last several months with three lecturers attached and with motion pictures to show the causes which lead to forest fires, illustrated literature to educate and appeal to children, adults, boy scouts and every class of citizens in regard to forest protection.

It was also decided at the meeting to institute a National Essay Competition with twenty-seven cash prizes, for children to promote juvenile interest in forest protection, tree planting, care of the farm, woodlot and allied topics. The tree planting on the prairies was also discussed, by which thousands of settlers on the bare prairie lands have been assisted to start shelter belts of trees to beautify their homes and thus lead to ambitious ones for general tree-planting on bare lands.

## Should Keep His Feet off Ground

A college graduate applied for work in a Northern Ontario lumber camp and was assigned to one end of a cross-saw, the other end being in charge of an old and experienced lumberman. At the end of an hour the veteran stopped sawing and regarded his weary partner with pitying eyes.

"Sonny," he said, "I don't mind you riding on this saw, but it it's just the same to you, I wish you'd quit scraping your feet on the ground."

## General Jottings in Short Shape

The British Columbia Timber Export Association held its annual meeting recently in Vancouver, and the members reported a promising outlook, with a very good list of orders for the immediate future. J. D. McCormick was elected president; J. O. Cameron, vice-president; H. J. Mackin, F. R. Pendleton, W. W. Harvey, A. E. Wood, E. S. Sanders and E. J. Palmer, directors. J. G. McConville was re-elected manager and R. H. H. Alexander, secretary. Mr. McConville reported 133,000,000 feet of lumber was exported by the Association during 1921.

The Canadian Forestry Association announces a prize essay competition for the school children of Canada whereby rewards of $25.00, $15.00 and $10.00 will be given in each of the nine provinces to those writing the most intelligent essays dealing with some phase of forestry or tree-planting based upon local conditions. The object of the competition is to stimulate study and inquiry as to the forest resources of Canada and their protection against the devastation of fire; the planting of trees on urban streets; the establishing and improving of farm woodlets, and the developing of tree-planting on the bare prairies.

Allan McPherson, Glencoe, Ont. Newly-elected Director     E. O. Penwarden, St. Thomas, Newly-elected Director     A. J. Clatworthy, Granton, Newly-elected Director     H. S. Ludlam, Leamington, Newly-elected Director

Some New Members of the Executive of the South Western Ontario Retail Lumber Dealers' Association, who were elected at the Annual Meeting held recently in Windsor, Ont.

## Fred Bigwood Takes Hold of Big Job

Fred. H. Bigwood, who is the chairman of the committee of arrangements for the international Kiwanian convention, which will be held in Toronto during the latter part of June, is a busy man these days. It is expected that thousands of visitors from all over America will be flocking to the Queen City, and the man who has to direct the forces for the reception and entertainment of the invading host, is Mr. Bigwood, who is vice-president of the Kiwanis Club, Toronto, of which he is an enthusiastic exponent. He is also a widely-known lumberman and a brother of W. E. Bigwood, Toronto, former president of the Canadian Lumbermen's Association. Fred H. Bigwood was born at Winooski, near Burlington, Vermont, and

**F. H. Bigwood, Toronto**

has been identified with the forest products line practically all his life. While in Vermont he was largely engaged in the screen door business, and in 1908 came to Canada entering the sales department of Graves, Bigwood & Co., whose mills are at Byng Inlet. About that time the company started extensively into the manufacture of box shooks, and the subject of this reference has devoted particular attention to the management of that department. On the formation of the Canadian General Lumber Co., Mr. Bigwood became identified with the organization both as a stockholder and a director. He has looked after the sales of the box shook branch of Graves, Bigwood & Co. and the office sales of the Canadian General Lumber Co. Of a modest, retiring citizen, Mr. Bigwood is a silent and aggressive worker in anything that he undertakes. The Kiwanians could not have picked a better man for the work he is called upon to do in connection with the great gathering. It may be of interest to note that two years ago Mr. Bigwood was awarded the prize at the Wholesale Lumbermen's picnic at Grimsby Beach, Ont., for being "the handsomest man on the grounds."

## Integrity of the Wholesale Lumberman

W. W. Schupner of New York, Secretary of the National Wholesale Lumber Dealers' Association, writes as follows:—

The trade press reports an address made by Mr. Edward Hines at the annual meeting of the Southern Pine Association in New Orleans, March 28th, in which reference was made to alleged practices on the part of certain unnamed so-called wholesale lumber dealers. During the American Lumber Congress at Chicago the substance of his remarks was frequently referred to, not in the Congress itself, but in private conversations, especially among some members of the wholesale delegation who felt that the integrity of the wholesale industry as a whole might be unnecessarily questioned because of statements intended to cover rare isolated instances, and, further, that wholesalers as a class should not permit such statements to pass unheeded, particularly where they might prejudice the opinion of the general public.

To the members of our Association, or to any lumberman conducting business on ethical lines, the effect of such statements on the lumber industry may seem remote, and it should be stated that in the address before the Southern Pine Association Mr. Hines is reported as saying, "Now I do not wish to make any broad charge nor have I any quarrel with the many reputable, substantial, high moral firms doing business as wholesalers." Nevertheless, such remarks can and do have their effect as will be noted from the following extract of Secretary of Commerce Hoover's address before the National Lumber Manufacturers' Association and the National Federation of Construction Industries, Chicago:

"Let us take a single material—lumber. Several leading manufacturers inform me that the time has come when we must have a guaranty against short deliveries and fraudulent alterations of qualities. The product of the honest millman must reach the consumer as the manufacturer wishes his product to reach the consumer. Also, he must have protection from the crooked competitor. Is it not possible for the National Lumber Manufacturers' Association to take upon itself the duty of giving a brand to lumber that will show its content and grade? Many commodities are assured as to quantity and grade under the inspection and rules of our voluntary trade associations. If you think it wiser to do so we

could probably secure the enactment of a "pure food law" in all building materials. I would much rather see the trades themselves establish their own standards."

The function of the wholesaler is well recognized as an economic factor in the distribution of lumber whether or not the wholesaler distributes stock of his own manufacture. This service to the industry was decidedly emphasized in the very harmonious sessions of the American Lumber Congress just held at Chicago, consisting of delegates representing manufacturers, wholesalers and retailers.

It is unnecessary to say that the wholesale lumber industry is conducted on a high plane of business integrity, and while an occasional offender may have to be eliminated, such rare instances must not confuse the public in its high estimation of the industry in its entirety. The National Wholesale Lumber Dealers Association, in adhering to its high standard of membership, is rendering an effective service in its efforts to assure the trade and public that membership in the Association carries a stamp of business integrity and reliability.

It is expected to hold an early conference at Washington between Secretary of Commerce Hoover and a committee of lumbermen, at which this Association will be ably represented. In issuing this statement the officers of the Association wish to again assure the members that no opportunity will be lost to protect the interests and foster the welfare of the wholesaler, while at the same time we endeavor to protect the interests of the entire lumber industry, recognizing the essential unity of all its branches.

## The Standardization of Lumber Grades

In recent issues the "Canada Lumberman" has published a large number of interviews with eastern contractors and wholesale and retail lumber on the Standardization of Lumber. Montreal is mainly a spruce market, and naturally the discussion chiefly dealt with the grading of that lumber. The case for the contractors is that they are handicapped in ordering and receiving lumber owing to the indefinite character of grading, and that standardization will enable them to more clearly specify what they desire to order. Further, that there is a wide variation in quality, although the lumber is specified to be of the same grade. While it is admitted that there is justification for the latter statement, it is asserted that the contractors are largely to blame for the conditions prevailing. In their anxiety to obtain the lowest prices, contractors will only pay the figure for culls while specifying a higher quality, which the buyers, of course, do not obtain.

The interviews have brought out the fact that some Montreal builders, in purchasing lumber, give little or no consideration to quality—price being the only factor, with the result that a large quantity of the very poorest material is used in construction. Some of this is described as rotten, refuse, and quite unfit for building, but it has the redeeming virtue, from the purchaser's point, of being cheap. How it passes civic inspection is a mystery to some of those who condemn the use of this class of material.

In the opinion of the great majority of those interviewed, there is an imperative need for a change in existing grading conditions. The position is asserted to be so unsatisfactory as to be almost chaotic. The well-known manufacturers supply well-graded lumber, but too many of the smaller mills, it is stated, are not to be depended upon, and will send good, bad and indifferent stuff under the general classifications of "merchantable" and "culls."

Several opinions are expressed on the subject of how to secure better and more definite grading. Proposals to enforce rules by law would undoubtedly meet with strong opposition, not only from the small mills but also from those manufacturers who have established their own grades and have built up extensive businesses in those grades. Any regulation on this subject would be necessarily Provincial in its scope, which would make it difficult to enforce legal grades on lumbermen outside, say, the Province of Quebec, many of whom do a large trade with Quebec wholesalers and retailers. Some wholesalers believe that better grading can only be secured by a process of education regarding the benefits which would accrue from producing a well-manufactured article; that, in the course of time, it would be brought home to the small mills that it was to their financial interest to put on the market lumber of a better grade, and that the contractors would also be educated to the point of purchasing the higher grades of forest products. The obstacles in the way of a general application of such rules are many but it is held that they can be overcome. As evidence of this the examples of the National Hardwood Lumber Association and the enforcement of grading rules in the West and, in many parts of the United States are cited. The discussion arose out of a meeting of the Montreal Builders' Exchange, a small committee of which is considering the subject. The next move will probably be in the direction of consulting the Lumbermen's Associations interested.

## Service In the Yard and Out of It

Some wise man once breathed a truth when he said, "Genius is merely an infinite capacity for taking pains."

How many men who know they have the ability to go after some big undertaking which may be hard to handle, let time slip away and never get started.

The man they call the genius is after all only human. You find him wherever you go, whether it be at the head of manufacturing departments or higher up in financial departments. But the difference between him and other men is in one point. He stops and balances things, and says to himself: My company needs an improved method of accounting: I may either make the system better or I may not—which shall it be? And so he starts that minute on the new system —and they call him a genius.

It is the same in everything, whether undertaken by an individual or a company. If the heads of a firm go into conference and find out their service is falling down—talk won't make the service better. How much misuse and abuse this word "service" has come in for. Men who have smeared their building with signs painted in big red letters announcing their superior service to the public have been known to lose all interest, and in many cases courtesy, towards a prospect who calls seeking advice about materials, but who is not in the market at the moment.

Making a determined effort to give better service will never be accomplished until pains are taken in every department of the business. Co-operation must be employed. The spirit of accomplishment and pride in their work must first be born in the minds of the employees. Harmony must exist in every department and those who do not harmonize and who plainly care nothing for their own advancement, let alone the company's, should be dismissed. For what good is the efficiency of manufacturing, the speed and accuracy in which the material is turned out, if the shipping department is slow and the men take no pains in the handling and the placing of the product before the consumer.

Many companies to-day where wood materials are retailed and partly manufactured on the premises, have reduced wages and made announcement to their employees that the company service has deteriorated and that only a personal interest taken by each man in every department of the plant to produce more efficient work and to increase production, could ever place the company in a position to meet the close competition of present day business.

Co-operation amongst employees is another phrase which has been thrown around mercilessly by insincere business men. Many firms talking co-operation do not give their employees a square deal; they want service to be given to the public, but forget about the men upon whom depends that quality of service. In their wild clamour for reformation they start at the wrong rung in the ladder. First harmony and company interest must prevail among the employees before a company can really render perfect service.

Another common point of discord in manufacturing firms is the element of misunderstanding. Firms who are really on the square with their men, often find, especially nowadays, a reduction of wages imperative, if the business be kept on its feet during some trying period. It is then that employers must bring into force all their tact and foresight if they would keep that contented state of mind amongst the men, for a man, who is discontented and suspicious, is a hard person to talk company service to.

After settling all civil questions, then is the time to turn your undivided attention to the public—not before. Many lumber merchants selling materials to customers, who know little or nothing about the construction of the building they are financing, never try to learn the circumstances and details of the job, but are content to merely sell the materials. If the customer is put to a lot of additional expense through unwise planning and consequent wasting of material, these men see no reason why they should bother their heads. But these same retailers will in many cases be the biggest advertisers of service.

An interesting story was told once of a man who bought a new car and drew a rough plan of the style of garage he wished to build in the rear of his premises. The plan, as the owner drew it, called for a modest structure to be covered with corrugated iron and ready roofing. The retailer was to supply the wood for the frame, floor, roof and the mill-work for three doors and frames. The owner had a flat roof for his plans.

The retailer suggested a change in the roof, making a difference of two feet, front to back, and giving a nice slant for drainage. He explained as best he could to the customer the way the 2 by 4's should be cut, all of different lengths to make posts that would give the required slant to the roof. Although the retailer knew the customer did not understand the construction sufficient enough to explain it to a carpenter, he neglected stepping over to the home of the customer, which was only two blocks away, and talking to the carpenter.

Two days later the customer called again and said he did not receive enough lumber for the job. The dealer assured him he had enough if the carpenter hadn't wasted the material. However, the merchant promised to drop in the same evening on his way home and see the garage. When he arrived at the customer's home the carpenter had gone home for the day. One glance at the half finished garage told him the carpenter was not following the plans; he had cut the posts all one length, leaving a whole bunch of small pieces over; and the roof slant would have to be made separately from the rest of the frame by cutting more material different lengths. This method required many additional feet of material for extra beams and bracing which would not have been necessary under the dealer's plans. The garage cost the owner ten dollars more than was estimated, because the dealer did not inject action into his service.

# Canada Lumberman
### founded 1880

### The National Lumber Journal for Forty Years

Issued on the 1st and 15th of every month by

**HUGH C. MACLEAN PUBLICATIONS, Limited**
THOS. S. YOUNG, Managing Director

HEAD OFFICE - - - - 347 Adelaide Street, West, TORONTO
Proprietors and Publishers also of Electrical News, Contract Record,
Canadian Woodworker and Footwear in Canada.

VANCOUVER - - - - - - - - Winch Building
MONTREAL - - - - - 119 Board of Trade Bldg.
WINNIPEG - - - - - 302 Travellers' Bldg.
NEW YORK - - - - - - 296 Broadway
CHICAGO - - - - 14 West Washington Street
LONDON, ENG. - - - - 16 Regent Street, S.W.

### TERMS OF SUBSCRIPTION

Canada, United States and Great Britain, $3.00 per year, in advance; other
foreign countries embraced in the General Postal Union, $4.00.
Single copies, 20 cents.

Authorized by the Postmaster-General for Canada, for transmission as
second-class matter.

| Vol. 42 | Toronto, June 1, 1922 | No. 11 |

## Why Lumber Prices will not Recede

"Oh!" "Lumber is so high in price." "It is a caution what I have to pay for a few boards." "Everything else has come down but lumber." "I will not build this year until there is a further reduction." "The only trade that is making a profit now is in the lumber line."

These and like expressions are frequently heard from prospective home builders, landlords and others, who are delaying construction in certain towns and cities. The "Canada Lumberman" has always contended that, with many prejudiced and narrow-minded individuals who have little or no practical acquaintance with forest products, lumber has been made "the goat."

There are many things that enter into the ordinary house, which involve a much larger expenditure than the comparatively small outlay for lumber, yet the latter is the target at which many recklessly fire.

Too long have retail lumbermen and others allowed their product to be the mark of sarcasm, derision and ignorance. If the most superficial observer will stop to give consideration to the lumber question, he must realize that prices will never recede to where they were before the war. The deduction is perfectly logical and needs no elaborate explanation or defence. Among the contributing causes of augmented cost, are higher wages, longer hauls from the sources of supply, increased freight rates, added overhead for mill operation and equipment and many others.

Once in a long while a daily newspaper or widely-read weekly publication points out these patent facts to readers, but ordinarily publishers do not travel much out of their way to enlighten the public on the facts that govern lumber prices, which have been referred to time and time again in these columns. It is refreshing to learn that a Southern paper (Louisville Courier-Journal) recently came out with a forceful and convincing editorial, and the data set forth practically applies the same to every locality in Canada as in the United States.

Some of the points raised might be presented by the average retail lumberman to customers who come in with the monotonous or stereotyped complaint about "Your lumber being too high in price," or, "Can get it cheaper elsewhere."

The editorial follows:—Lumber has not come down in the degree that many prospective builders believed it would in the general recession of prices which followed the large increase of prices between 1917 and 1920.

There are perfectly good reasons why lumber will not be sold again at what the average home builder of this generation believes the prices should be.

"Glass," observes an economist, "is merely white sand plus labor." Assuming that there is white sand in inexhaustible supply, glass would be a commodity governed in price by labor cost largely, provided the supply of sand were distributed that freight would not be a large element in making of the price.

Lumber is labor plus freight plus timber. The timber grows scarcer each year. The supply of raw material was distributed by nature over a very large part of the continent of North America and existed in sufficient quantity at points within easy reach of every piece of every State.

It now is existent in areas which grow remoter every year, from scenes of consumption.

The cost of lumber is the cost of labor plus an increasing cost of freight and the value of material which grows costlier as the supply diminishes.

Two generations ago in Kentucky it was customary to saw ash and poplar logs into firewood lengths to be split and burned. It was customary to fell black walnut and split it for rails. It was not necessary to buy shingles to roof a farm building unless the builder preferred the shingles upon account of their appearance. Boards which made a very good roof could be riven with a frow from cuts of oak. Joists and sills were made from tree trunks hewn square. There remained plenty of timber at hand which a local, or movable, sawmill could transform into the various kinds of lumber used in building.

Labor was cheaper than now, but the great difference between lumber cost then and now is a difference in the quantity of timber available and the remoteness of remaining sources of supply; the average haul, by rail and otherwise, between the stump left where the tree is cut and the point at which ground is broken for the foundation of the building.

Neither propaganda against high prices nor legislation to reduce the home builder's burdens can bring lumber down to former levels until there is reproduced a well distributed supply of the raw material.

The Forest Service of the Department of Agriculture tells the Senate, in response to a request for information, that the United States is using 26,000,000,000 cubic feet of wood every twelve months and growing 6,000,000,000 cubic feet. And 4,000,000 acres of cutover land is added annually to an area of cut-over or burned-over forest land now amounting to about 300,000,000 acres.

As this destructiveness proceeds the cost of the commodity and the cost of freight on the commodity must be reflected in increasing prices of every forest product. There are Kentucky residences floored with flint-like ash or oak, weather-boarded with yellow poplar good for a century's service under paint applied at right intervals, which could not be rebuilt with the same materials for less than what it cost to build them. But outcries will not affect the conditions under which the advance of cost has been inevitable, and under which, despite occasional fluctuations, the general tendency of prices will be upward.

Quarreling with lumber prices and not producing timber is like kicking about the cost of potatoes and not raising potatoes.

## Forest Fire is Early on the Job

Nearly every community has its speed maniacs, its radio fans and baseball enthusiasts, not to speak of its flappers, bootleggers and other products of modern civilization. It would appear, too, that the poor are always with us and that we will always have forest fires, which seem almost as impossible to eradicate as petty thieving or disorderly conduct.

It was announced that, although the spring has been wet, the first forest blaze of the season occurred on May 3 on the Ellis timber limits two miles north of Burnt River, Ont. It is stated that considerable damage was done to young timber. Quebec was not to be outdone in any sense, and its first fire in 1922 occurred three or four days before at Deschaillons, County Lotbiniere, where large tracts of the forest were wiped out, and men direct from the forest service in Quebec City had to be sent to supervise the suppression of the flames.

If forest fires make their appearance so early in the season and cause so much damage before they are extinguished, what may be expected later on when everything becomes parched and dry? Eternal vigilance is the price of safety, and there should be no cessation of activity in the line of stamping out this arch enemy.

In a recent address a leading authority pointed out that forest fires in Canada were destroying from five to ten times the amount of timber that is annually turned to commercial use, and that most of such fires are humanly set. Last year the chief causes of the fire losses were camping parties, fishermen and men direct from travellers of the woods.

Commenting upon the rapid reduction of our timber wealth, its wastage by operators and its devastation by flame, C. Price Green, Chief Commissioner of Natural Resources for the Canadian National Railway, in a recent address said:—

"Let us briefly review the situation in Canada which has about half the forest resources of the United States or about 260 million acres of commercial forest. About half her forest areas have been burnt over in the past 100 years, some several times. British Columbia alone has lost over 600 million feet from fire.

"At the present rate of consumption, about 14 billion feet a year, we have lost by fire the equivalent of 450 years' supply. On the basis of tax of 50 cents per 1,00 feet B.M., the lowest in effect, it means that the people from this cause have lost 1,000 million dollars.

The United States cannot look to Canada for any alleviation of her situation with respect to sawn lumber; in fact it has been estimated that if Canada were called upon to supply the total demand of the United States, the supply would not last much more than 15 years.

"It may be thought that the picture I have drawn is one of blue ruin, but it is simply a presentation of facts that must be faced."

## Getting on in the Lumber Business

Recently a Canadian retail lumber dealer who spent some time across the border, got a few ideas in literature which he had posted in the office. There are two cards containing certain printed matter. The verse on one is headed "To Success" and the other "To Failure."

Under the caption "Success appears the following verse.—
"Early to bed, early to rise,
Work like H—— and advertise."

Under the heading "To Failure," there is the following:—
"Late to bed, late to rise,
Loaf like H—— and criticize."

. The printed signs have naturally made quite a hit and stimulate the members of the dealer's staff to action.

In another retail lumber office recently the appended sign appeared in a prominent place.—"Do not fail to ask for credit," and below this, in smaller letters, were the significant words,—"You'll not get it."

Other retail lumber dealers have mottos or printed cards on their office walls or desks. In a Northern town was noted the following:—"To H—— with worry, that's the place for it." Asked as to the meaning of this rather cryptic epigram, the retailer of wood goods said,—"Why, worry has no place in a man's business, consuming his time, talent and energy, destroying his power of initiative and his capacity for creative work. Worry works endless harm and never wrought good to anyone; therefore the proper place for such an enemy to our peace of mind, progress and outlook is the 'lower regions. That is what is meant exactly by that motto,—'To H—— with worry, that's the place for it."

Much depends upon service. We hear a great deal about its use and abuse, and many people who talk on this subject, furnish the least in the matter of satisfying their patrons. The individual, who is eternally prating of his honesty, the woman always proclaiming her virtue, and the speculator ever vaunting his "clean-up," may all be viewed with a certain amount of suspicion. It does not need reiterated statments to establish certain self-evident facts. They stand out clearly and are visible from many standpoints. 

It is the same, too, with service. Speaking of this much maligned word, a leading retailer of wood products the other day said, "It is most amusing, not to say annoying, to hear certain fellows in other towns talk about service. They know not what the first syllable of the word means. Now, I am not going to give you a talk on service in my own line, but all lumber purchasers know when they are getting it, just the same as I do in connection with the grocery, butcher or barber business. I am not acquainted with the details of management of these establishments, yet when I go to my barber for a haircut, no matter whether he executes the job or one of his assistants, he knows exactly the way I want my locks trimmed. I don't have to give him any instructions. He learned this the first time, and it is a pleasure to go there and sit in a chair and not be plied with a plethora of questions about 'do you want this' and 'do you want that.' Then he does not urge upon me to take a lot of extras, and keep me saying "no" until one feels as if he were a tightwad or a cynic.

"It is the same, too, in connection with my grocer. If he says the goods will be delivered to my house by a certain time, they are there. In taking down my orders, he does not have to ask every time as many grocers do'. By the way, "Mr. J. what is the number of your house on B.—St. A young grocer that I had dealt with, asked me this question, at least, twenty times a month. If I could not remember the street number and addresses of my patrons, I would have a handy list ready, so that I could refer to it and not be plying my patrons or callers with the same query day after day, and putting up the plausible plea about being so rushed or doing so much business that is was impossible to remember where each patron lives.

"After all, it is the individual that counts. He is a unit of the mass, and each mortal likes to be well thought of and well spoken of. It gratifies our pride—whether we are willing to admit it or not—that Mr. So and So knows our name, how to spell it correctly, where we live, our street number, the kind of goods we buy, etc.

"The same remarks that I have made apply largely to a meat merchant, who will not have to inquire every time what my wife or fami-

ly desire. He should know that each family has a preference, and what that preference is.

"I have digressed somewhat from the lumber business just to show others what service means. We should occasionally detach ourselves from our own environs and interests and take a wider view of our vocation. We should approach it from different angles and remember that as long as business exists there will be different ideals and vantage points. We have to take a sweep of the whole in order to be broadminded, progressive and efficient. Too often we see things from our own standpoint alone and not from our customer's. We can learn something useful, practical and helpful from nearly every mortal if we are receptive to new conceptions and willing to give suggestions serious consideration, before declaring that they possess neither value, point nor pith.

## Making Forest Protection Wider Yet

The Canadian Forestry Association is doing valuable work in sending out periodically to the press, schools and members of the Association, and others interested a series of questions and answers on "Forestry." These queries or forest protection propaganda are of a timely and practical character and present ideas on the reforestation, conservation and protection of our wooded wealth, that the average Canadian should have at his finger ends. The matter is entertainingly written and is being published in a number of papers and periodicals as a special weekly feature which has become poplar.

As an illustration of the questions answered in this literature, two are taken at random from a recent issue and are herewith appended. They show the effective and valuable work which is being done.

Q. How much of Canada's forests is denuded each year for the manufacture of pulp and paper?

A. About four million cords are cut each year in this country, valued in the rough at forty-five million dollars and from which pulp and paper products are produced to the value of over two hundred million dollars. More than ninty per cent. of these values is furnished by the wood of four kinds of trees of which spruce is chief.

Q. Is there any reliable information as to how much of our Dominion forests has been sacrificed to forest fires in the past century?

A. Dr. C. D. Howe, head of the Forest School of the University of Toronto, estimates that from one half to two-thirds of the forested area of Canada, or, in other words, around one million square miles has been burned within the past 55 years. Dr. Howe further estimates that the forest areas have been so denuded of the larger-sized timbers that to-day less than twelve per-cent. of the land area of the country contains timber of the size demanded by a modern lumber mill.

Dr. Howe's comment as to the effect of forest fires is highly interesting. He says that "of the million square miles of our forest inheritance that has been devastated by fire, much has been burned not only once but two, three and even half a dozen times. These repeated fires on the same area render abortive nature's attempt to reclothe the old burns with commercial valuable trees. Whole townships that once supported magnificent forests of pine or spruce are now, because of repeated burning, covered with worthless brush of no market value.

## The One Quality That Wins

"It was the determination to win which eventually won the war.

"It is the desire of the doctor to win that enables him to pull the patient through. The doctor is not fighting for his fee—he is fighting to win.

"I have employed a good many men in the last forty years" said the president, "and I never employed one until I was satisfied that he had above all other qualifications a firm determination to win.

"But you can't win at bridge if you don't have the cards!", said the young man.

"Some men do", replied the president. "If you doubt it, try duplicate bridge. One man plays the hand and loses one trick; the hands are reversed and his opponent gains one. You will say the opponent was a better player. So he was. But he was a better player because he possessed the desire to win. The desire to win made him study the game—know it—and play it well.

"Whether you are playing or working, it is the determination to win that decides the issue."

## Budget of Brief From the Busy East

Within the last two weeks there have been a number of bad fires in the Maritime Provinces, which have caused heavy losses to lumbermen. A few days ago over one million feet of pine lumber on Bay du Vin Island was destroyed by fire. It was owned by T. B. Williston and is said to have been insured for $33,000. It is reported that he was offered a much larger price for it before the slump but held out for a rising market.

Word was received in Yarmouth N. S., a few days ago telling of a disasterous fire at Richfield, a village on the Carleton branch of the Tusket river, where a big lumber plant known as the French Mills was totally destroyed by fire. It is said that the blaze originated from a pile of burning edgings and other waste a short distance from the mill.

A fire, which broke out in the cook house of Hick's mill at Dalhousie Junction a few days a go did considerable damage before it was extinguished. The cook house was destroyed in a remarkably short time and the flames spread to five shingle sheds where about sixty carloads of shingles were stacked and these were completely destroyed. Fortunately the mill was saved and is continuing operations.

Fire recently destroyed a planing mill and contents consisting of some valuable machinery belonging to John H. Crandall in Moncton. The loss was estimated at $5,000 and was covered by insurance.

The Fraser Companies Limited have announced that their loss in the destruction by fire of their plant at Baker Brook, Madawaska County, was covered by insurance. It is understood that the plant had a value of not less than $150,000, while the manufactured lumber and other losses at the place brought the total damage up to over $200,000. The mill was equipped for manufacturing from 120,000 to 130,000 cedar shingles daily, in addition to 50,000 feet of long lumber and 30,000 laths.

The larch sawfly and the larch case borer have made a reappearance in the forests of New Brunswick. Dr. Grisdale, federal department of agriculture at Ottawa, who has charge of Dominion entomogical operations, has been notified that these destructive pests have reappeared in this province by Colonel T. G. Loggie, deputy minister of Lands and Mines. Colonel Loggie has asked for information regarding the ways and means to combat the evil. About forty or fifty years ago these insects wiped out the valuable tamarack stands in the province.

Late reports from Salisbury say that the big log drive on the Little River, owned by the Salisbury Lumber Company, has reached safe water and the head of the drive is now at the mill pond. This lot of logs comprises about 4,000,000 feet is the output of two winters' operations.

Anderson Bros., saw mill at Brockway, N. B., was destroyed by fire recently. There was practically no insurance. The winter cut had just been finished but fortunately lumber piled near the mills was not destroyed.

A report from the Nashwaak on May 17 said that the river is clear of lumber. At the mouth of the Nashwaak, the report stated, rafting operations of the Nashwaak Pulp & Paper Company are proceeding rapidly. At that date 4,234,000 feet, or a total of 124,543 pieces, had been put through the rafting grounds.

At Kennebecasis Island a few miles above Indiantown, St. John, the St. John Log Driving Company is rafting the product of the drift drive and it is expected to be completed in the near future. The corporation drive of the company was at Little Bear Island a couple of days ago and work was being carried on among the islands at that point. The water was reported to be falling and as the rafting this year is being done at the Mitchell boom, Lincoln, the drive still had a long distance to go.

A few days ago the Shives Lumber Company's shingle mill at Campbellton shut down because the sawyers refused to work for the scale of wages offered. When the whistle blew to start operations in the morning the men were all at their posts but some of the sawyers left and approaching the superintendent asked what the company intended to pay. They were informed that eighteen cents a thousand, at which rate they had been paid for the previous weeks would be the rate for the immediate future, but in event of the shingle market improving, rate would be improved. They were also shown figures quoting the market prices of shingle and that on every thousand manufactured there was a loss of fifty-three cents. Notwithstanding this the sawyers walked out and the mill had to be closed down. About one hundred men were thus thrown out of employment. The men say that if the company will give them twenty-three cents per thousand for the season they will return to work. The Shives mill is the largest shingle mill in the Maritime Province and has eighteen shingle machines.

## National Hardwood Gathering in Chicago

It is expected that a large number of Canadian members of the National Hardwood Lumber Association will attend the twenty-fifth annual convention of that body which will be held in Chicago on June 22nd to 23rd at the Congress Hotel. An interesting and varied programme has been prepared.

On the morning of Thursday June 22nd Horace F. Taylor, Buffalo, N. Y., president of the N.H.L.A., will deliver his annual address, and Frank F. Fish, of Chicago, secretary-treasurer, will present his report. In the afternoon among the speakers will be Hon. Henry J. Allen, Governor, of Kansas; Herbert C. Hoover, secretary of Commerce, Washington, and Alex. H. Oxholm, chief of the lumber division, Department of Commerce, Washington. A complimentary banquet will be tendered the visitors and invited guests in the evening in the Gold Room of the Congress Hotel by the National Hardwood Lumber Association.

Friday June 23rd will be "Lumbermen and Lumber Buyers Day." At the morning session there will be a report of the committee and from the officers. Chas. N. Perrin, chairman, will present the report of the Inspection Rules Committee. In the afternoon Earl Palmer, chairman, will bring down the statement of the committee for the purpose of formulating a sales code. Other items on the agenda are a discussion of sales codes, report of Committee on Resolutions, new business, election of president and three vice-presidents to serve one year, and the choice of eight directors to serve three years. In the evening there will be a dinner and smoker in the Gold Room of the Congress Hotel.

The Association announces that owing to the amount of important business the forthcoming convention has to deal with, and the attendance expected of those directly interested, no provision has been made for the entertainment of ladies.

George C. Goodfellow, of Montreal, is the Canadian member of the Board of Directors of the N.H.L.A. It is likely that John W. McClure, of Memphis, Tenn., first vice-president of the Association, will be made president for the coming year.

It is expected that the attendance at the convention in Chicago on June 22nd and 23rd will break all previous records, and the official bulletin of the Association announces that " there is every reason to believe that when it has come and gone the gathering will stand as the apogee of all lumber trade conventions which have preceded it. As an exceptionally strong programme has been arranged."

## Lumber Conditions in the South Improve

W. H. Harris, of the Frank H. Harris Lumber Co., Toronto, returned lately after spending about three months across the border, principally at Meridian, Miss., and Summerville, N. C. Mr. Harris was accompanied by his wife, and reports that conditions are up, so far as hardwoods are concerned. Owing to the high water in the Mississippi Bottoms, mills have been hard hit and have not been able to produce anything like capacity. The wet weather has interfered to some extent with several Southern pine mills. During a long period in 1921 when business was so dull that manufacturers could not get cost out of their product, a number of plants were shut down and these are only beginning to get under way again. Orders and shipments are both higher than production, which was down over 13,000,000 feet one week recently, due to a shortage of logs. Shipment was about normal by about 6% and orders were 21% in excess of normal production.

All lumber prices are stiffening and Mr. Harris is of the opinion that, owing to the scarcity of dry stocks, there is not any prospect of a recession in values. Business on the whole is much improved in the South and a more optimistic feeling prevails. Mr. Harris reports that his own firm are handling considerable quantities of Southern pine and hardwoods, and are finding business favorable at the present time.

## Timberland Business Becoming More Active

James W. Sewall, forest engineer and timber expert, with offices at Washington, D. C. and Old Town, Maine, reports that while business in his line is still quiet he is satisfied that conditions are very steadily improving. Activity in timberland purchases cannot as yet be said to exist, but some lands and timber are now being optioned with view to purchase and operation. This is decidedly different from last year at this time when the market was quiescent.

Mr. Sewall has recently been on quite an extended trip through the eastern states and looks forward to a reasonably busy season. His organization has over fifty men engaged in timber cruising and valuation now, and has kept its entire force intact throughout the period of general business depression.

# How Old Established Firm Advertises

## Chatham Concern has Been in Business for Over Seventy-Five Years and Believes in Publicity

One of the firms in Western Ontario which is making effective use of newspaper publicity and taking large space in the daily papers, is the S. Hadley Lumber Co., Limited, of Chatham, Ont. This concern is the oldest in the lumber business west of Toronto, being launched in 1846 and still going strong. W. A. Hadley is president and general manager of the concern, and M. R. Bogart, secretary-treasurer. Associated with Mr. Hadley are his sons, S. C. and C. S. Hadley, who take deep interest in the welfare of the industry. The company have an attractive office and large factory on Wellington St. and their yards are at Thomas, Adelaide & Wellington Sts. Chatham. The firm manufactures interior and exterior finish, store office and bank fixtures, and has built up an enviable reputation in the latter line, having furnished the wood fittings for many financial, commercial and other concerns, not only in Western Ontario, but in various other parts of the Dominion.

However, this is another story, and it is in reference to the advertising of the Hadley organization to which the "Canada Lumberman" desires to direct attention at present. The publicity is being looked after by Mr. Bogart, who in the choice of illustrations and reading matter, shows good thought and judgment. There is plenty of white space around each announcement and there is not too much reading matter. One or two salient points are driven home, and just now a particularly active appeal is being made to home-builders. At this season of the year the mind of nearly everyone turns to outdoor life or to a dwelling of his own. and to stimulate and strengthen this desire to build, is appropriate, opportune and advisable.

In a recent announcement this old-established Chatham firm said:—"Put your money into your own home." On one side was shown a beautiful bungalow and on the other side a waste basket with a lot of rent receipts filling the receptacle to the top. The announcement went on "Make your home distinctive by buying quality. If you don't buy quality at the time of purchase, you pay for it in what you use during the period of material service—and penalize your satisfaction on top of it. It costs no more." The S. Hadley

THE RAY OF SUNSHINE

## "Build with the Birds"

### You'll never build cheaper

LET US HELP YOU REALIZE YOUR DREAM THIS SEASON
BUILD IT THIS SPRING

Not in several years have conditions been so favorable as they are right NOW. The period of building inactivity is passing. Prices of materials, cost of labor etc. are stable. Authorities who have studied the situation declare that in a few months, the tide of building activity will have risen to a point that will create shortages.

There is every reason for building now. Plans to choose from.

### Everything For the Builder

## THE S. HADLEY LUMBER CO.
(Established 1846) LIMITED
(Oldest established lumber business in Western Ontario.)

## THE CHATHAM SAND & GRAVEL CO.
### Building Supplies
FULL STOCKS — ECONOMY PRICES.

An attractive advertisement by live Chatham, Ont. firm

Lumber Co., add,—"We have a building service you like. Let us assist you in your plans." The slogan of the firm is "Full stock and economy prices."

Another announcement read,—"Emerson was right. 'The world does find its way to the doors of men who do things better.' Quality has an almost magic way of making every customer a booster. Why?—Satisfaction which costs no more. If building or repairing, may we assist you in your preparations?"

Various other means of advertising are also followed by the Chatham firm who might have adopted the policy of some dealers, —lean back and say,—"Oh, well! There is no use of us spending any money in publicity. We have been doing business here for three-quarters of a century and everybody for miles around knows we sell lumber, shingles, lath, cedar posts, etc. When they want any of this material, they will come to us as we have been the longest in business."

This is the narrow-minded, short-sighted, selfish attitude taken by a number of retail lumber firms who have not been in business one-third of the time that the Hadley Co., have. The latter, however, are giving a practical demonstration of their faith in the value and efficiency of advertising by using as much as a quarter-page in an issue of the Chatham dailies on Saturdays and smaller space on other days of the week. They believe that carefully-prepared, attractively-displayed and clearly worded publicity is both convincing and instructive and a powerful lever in inducing many people who might otherwise hesitate, to build homes, erect barns, put up garages, add sun rooms, verandahs or porches etc., to their property.

## Starting New Course in Cost Figuring

The Millwork Cost Bureau, of Chicago, has just issued a new Estimators' Correspondence Course as a service to members. This is one of the most valuable and comprehensive courses of its kind which has ever been offered to woodworkers It consists of work on five sets of plans and includes the taking off of quantities and the application of Cost Book "A," which is the basic cost list issued by the Bureau, to the special millwork required for these structures. The student is thus given a thorough grounding in the reading of plans, the taking off of quantities, in making out lists of material and in the figuring of costs through the application of Cost Book "A". The course is open to members, who may enroll as many of their staffs as they like without extra charge. When the work has been covered in a satisfactory manner and the Bureau is satisfied that the student has a thorough grounding in the various phases of estimating and costing covered, a certificate or diploma is issued which indicates that the student has mastered the Millwork Cost Bureau's system.

## Opens Lumber Yard in Orangeville

A retail lumber yard has been opened in Orangeville, Ont., by A. Henderson, late of Cheltenham, Ont., where he conducted a planing mill and lumber business for several years and had the misfortune to be burned out some time ago. In Orangeville, Mr. Henderson has secured a factory 36 x 100 feet, two storeys, and fair-sized yard for a piling ground. He has installed machinery for a planing mill. The citizens of Cheltenham and vicinity presented Mr. Henderson with an address and a purse of gold on May 8th, along with expressions of sincere regret at his departure from among them.

## Airplane Service Reveals New Lakes

Several hitherto unknown lakes and river valleys have been discovered in Jasper Park, Canadian Rockies, through the use of government airplanes. This work was undertaken by the High River air station, Alberta, and three experimental flights were carried out over the region for the purpose of exploration and reconnaissances. The Canadian Air Board report states: "A flight was made on each of three successive days with gratifying success and the possibilities of the use of air craft for exploration in mountain regions and in the administration and general maintenance of the park system were proved without a doubt."

At the conclusion of the operation, Colonel Maynard Rogers, Park superintendent, who was taken as observer on each of the three flights, expressed himself as highly pleased with the results obtained and with the rapidity with which it was possible to reach any part of the park as compared with making a similar trip by trail. In the seven hours flying over the park he claimed he travelled more distance and inspected more country than he could possibly have done by trail in six weeks' or two months' hard travelling. Col. Rogers also expressed the opinion that sufficient flying had been done to demonstrate the absolute necessity of having machines stationed at Jasper Park to continue this exploration and general reconnaissance work, as well as for the purpose of forest fire protection.

## Personal and General Paragraphs

S. G. Denman, of the British Government Timber Department, Montreal, has returned from a trip to the Maritime Provinces.

G. E. Wightman, of the Wightman Lumber Company, Montreal, has been on a visit to the Maritime Provinces.

W. T. Mason, of Mason, Gordon and Company, Limited, Montreal has returned from a business visit to the Pacific Coast.

Allison Peck, of Hillsboro, Albert County, N. B., is contemplating erecting a woodworking factory in Moncton, N. B.

F. C. Baker, of the Devon Lumber Co., Sherbrooke, Que., was in Toronto lately calling upon a number of friends in the trade.

Chas. O. Maus, of Chas O. Maus Lumber Co., South Bend, Ind., was a recent visitor to Toronto and reports business in the hardwood line as constantly improving.

F. W. Adolph, general-manager of the Adolph Lumber Co., Baynes Lake, B. C., spent a few days in Toronto recently with his brother, F. L. Adolph, eastern representative of the firm.

The plant of the Dominion Match Co., Deseronto, Ont., is being sold under the Bankruptcy Act. F. C. Clarkson, of Toronto, is trustee for the creditors.

D. L. O'Gorman, of the Brewster Loud Lumber Co., Detroit, Mich., was in Toronto lately calling upon a number of members of the trade.

Jacob Hazelton, a former well known lumberman of New Brunswick passed away recently at Lower Southampton, York County, N. B., at the ripe age of 87 years.

A. T. Wilmot of Toronto, representing the Otis-Staples Lumber Co., of Wycliffe, B. C., and the East Kootenay Lumber Co., of Jaffray, B. C., has returned from a business trip to the Pacific Coast.

A. C. Manbert, of the Canadian General Lumber Co., Toronto, who was confined to his home at Oakville for several days owing to an attack of bronchitis, is able to be around again.

E. Lord, who for several years was with the Georgian Bay Lumber Co., Waubaushene, Ont., has joined the sales staff of the Fesserton Timber Co., Toronto, Ont., and is covering the London-Windsor district.

Mrs. F. N. Pardy, who has been a member of the staff of the C. G. Anderson Lumber Co., Toronto, has gone to Bobcaygeon, where she will conduct the White House, a popular summer resort for the coming season.

The new 40-ton groundwood pulp plant which has been erected at Dickson Creek, near Haileybury, by the Temiskaming Pulp & Paper Co., will be put in operation about the middle of June. All the equipment is now being installed.

The pulp and paper companies in the district of Three Rivers, Que., are working to capacity. The St. Maurice Paper Co. has sufficient orders to keep it going to full capacity until late in the fall, while the Wayagamack Pulp & Paper Co. is running full in turning out kraft, both glazed and unglazed.

Hon. E. C. Drury, premier of Ontario, is an ardent advocate of reforestation, and on May 24th took part in an interesting ceremony at Sharon, York County, held under the auspices of the York Pioneer and Historical Association. The new grounds were formally opened and there was a series of tree planting along the front.

The Gravel Lumber Company, Limited, Etchemin Bridge, Que., of which Sir William Price is president, has opened an office at 501 Drummond Building Montreal, under the management of Mr. L. G. Gravel, the assistant general manager of the company. The company, which has been established 42 years, specializes in Quebec spruce, birch flooring, and boxes.

H. G. McDermid, of the Union Lumber Co., Toronto, met with a rather painful accident the other day while motoring. A little child suddenly came out from behind another car, and, in order not to run down the youngster, Mr. McDermid, in leaning forward to grasp the gear shift lever, struck his head against the front of the car and sustained a nasty cut on the chin from which he is now recovering.

R. Lockhart, of R. Lockhart & Co., Limited, of Fort Frances, Ont., and R. P. Westcott, formerly connected with the McDonald Lumber Co., Limited, and the McDonald Lumber Yards, Limited, have opened a wholesale lumber office in the McIntyre Building, Winnipeg, Man., and will be known as the Lockhart-Westcott Lumber Co., Limited.

H. J. Terry, of Terry & Gordon, Limited, Toronto, who is chairman of the Wholesale Lumber Dealers' Association Inc., and a director of the Rotary Club of Toronto, left on May 30th for Los Angeles, Cal., to attend the International Convention of Rotary Clubs. There were about 140 Rotarians and their wives who travelled by special train, taking in all the principal points en route. Mr. Terry

is chairman of the Fourth District, Canadian Rotary Division, and was accompanied by Mrs. Terry. After the convention they will spend several weeks in the South.

The annual meeting of Price Bros. & Co., Quebec, was held recently but only routine business was transacted owing to the absence of the president, Sir Wm. Price in Europe. All the old officers of the company were re-elected as follows:—President, Sir Wm. Price; vice-presidents, George S. Thomson and James M. McCarthy; managing-director, J. Leonard Apedaile; secretary-treasurer, H. E. Price.

The annual midsummer outing and meeting of the Technical Section of the Canadian Pulp & Paper Association will be held on June 20th and 21st at Iroquois Falls, Ont., where the mill and power plants of the Abitibi Power & Paper Co. will be visited. R. A. McInnis, general-manager of the Abitibi Company, is making full arrangements for the success of the summer outing.

J. Walter & Sons, Kitchener, Ont., manufacturers of fibre products, including furniture trimmings, ship and home decorations, will erect a new factory. A suitable site has been secured and the capacity of the plant will be three times that of the present one. The demand for the company's products has been exceptionally active during the last few months.

An important meeting of the Paper Club was recently held in Montreal, to see the showing of Price Bros. & Company's pictures which depicted in detail the manufacture of newsprint from the woods operation to the finished product. A. L. Dawe, former secretary of the Canadian Pulp & Paper Association, and now with the Canadian Export Paper Co., Limited, gave a short address on the aims and objects of the club which has planned a picnic to one of the paper mills near Montreal some time during the summer.

Paul E. Joubert, of Lamontagne, Limited, has been elected vice-chairman of the Montreal branch of the Canadian Manufacturers Association. Messrs. S. F. Rutherford, Dominion Box and Package Company, Limited, and A. D. Huff, Riordon Company, Limited, are on the Executive Council of the branch. The following are members of the committee of the Quebec Division of the Association: Messrs. H. C. Price, Price Brothers and Company, and A. O. Gignac, Quebec City; H. Biermans, Belgian-Industrial Company, Shawinigan Falls, and J. Alain, Victoriaville Furniture, Limited, Victoriaville.

Mrs. Adolph, wife of the late Frederick Adolph, Sr., died recently at Baynes Lake, B. C. in her 86th year. She had resided in the West for the past sixteen years and was a former resident of Chesley, Ont., to which town the remains were brought for interment. The late Mrs. Adolph was a woman who enjoyed the respect and confidence of a wide circle of friends, and leaves to mourn her death F. W. Adolph, of the Adolph Lumber Co., Baynes Lake, B. C., F. L. Adolph, of Toronto, eastern representative of the same company, and H. L. Adolph, barrister, of Brandon, Man. Two daughters are also left, Miss Jennie Adolph, of Baynes Lake, and Mrs. W. H. Griffith, of Jaffray, B. C.

G. W. Boake, of the Boake Mfg. Co., Toronto, who is receiving the congratulations of many friends on his recent marriage to Miss Elliott, of Chicago. Mr. Boake was presented with a handsome cabinet of silver by the members of his staff and a number of lumbermen friends.

## New Manager for Shevlin Clarke Co.

B. W. Lakin, who for past fifteen years has been the logging superintendent for the Cookston Lumber Co., of Bemidji, Minn., has been appointed general-manager of the Shevlin-Clarke Lumber Co., at Fort Frances, Ont., and entered upon his new duties last month. He succeeds J. A. Mathieu, M. L. A. who resigned a few weeks ago. Mr. Lakin has been with the Shevlin-Clarke Co. for 24 years, having charge of lumber and logging operations for them in Oregon as well as in Minnesota. He is a member of the Kiwanis Club, Bemidji Country Club and the Masonic Order. The esteem in which he is held as a citizen and a business man, is attested by a reference in the "Bemidji Daily Pioneer," which says in part:—"The Fort Frances plant has two large sawmills and is doing a big logging

B. W. Lakin, Fort Frances, Ont.

business. Mr. Lakin has been identified with the Bemidji business affairs in many ways, being one of the owners of the Bemidji Lumber & Fuel Co., a director of the Northern National Bank and a director of the Bemidji Civic Commerce Association. He will retain his interests in the Bemidji Lumber & Fuel business and carries with him the best wishes of many friends."

Mr. Lakin has already created a favorable impression in Fort Frances and won the appreciation of those associated with him. M. A. Malone is the new assistant manager of the Shevlin-Clarke Co. He has been with the company for several years and his promotion is well deserved.

The Shevlin-Clarke Co. report that orders are coming in satisfactorily at the present time and business has been steadily improving for some weeks.

## Quebec Coping With Insect Plague in Forests

Forest destruction by insects is at present commanding the serious consideration of the Department of Lands and Forests in the province of Quebec. The tremendous loss annually of valuable forest resources of the province, which surpasses in destruction forest fires, has caused the forestry heads of the department to make a determined effort to combat the costly evil before the entire forest resources of Quebec are destroyed.

Up to the present the Quebec Government has an Entomological Branch Service connected with the forestry service, and has depended upon the Federal Government Entomological organization to assist in this work. The situation having opened a serious aspect to threaten the whole fabric of the lumber trade and pulp and paper manufacturing business of the country, the Quebec Government has decided to organize an Entomological Branch of the forestry service to cope with the insect plague. The seriousness of the question is recognized by the fact that every season in the eastern forests the tops and dying branches and dying tree give evidence of the incalculable injury caused by destructive insects.

Mr. J. M. Swaine, chief of the Entomological Branch of the Department of Agriculture at Ottawa, and his assistant, Mr. F. C. Craighead, who have devoted much study, scientific research and practical work on the insect problem, have from time to time in their reports warned the Dominion provincial governments and lumber interests

in general on the seriousness of the insect destruction of Canadian forest resources, and the many millions of dollars lost each year by the insects in their periodical invasions.

Mr. Avila Bedard, assistant chief of the Quebec Forest Service, is at present engaged in writing a treatise on the insect menace, which will be published in the near future, and acting under instructions from the Minister, Hon. Mr. Mercier, with the co-operation of Mr. G. C. Piche, chief of the forestry service, the Quebec students in scientific forestry are following a course of studies in scientific entomology to prepare for the work of the extermination of the forest insects. It would also be advisable for the Canadian Limit Holders'Association to have their engineers take a course in Entomology and thus combine their efforts with the Government to arrest and, if possible, discover a means to exterminate the insect pest before the entire forest resources of Canada are destroyed by this most insidious insect enemy of the trees, which in its ramificating work of destruction, attack the very vitals of future Canadian lumber operations.

Over-matured and weakened trees or injured branches are usually attacked and killed by various species of bark and sapwood, boring beetles and their quibs, is the statement made by Mr. J. M. Swaine, the scientific entomologist in the employ of the Agricultural Branch of the Federal Department of Agriculture. Many of these species feed normally in dying trees, and they are the first of the forest scavengers, whose function it is to reduce the useless wood again to plant food for the succeeding timber stand. They are accompanied or immediately followed by wood boring species in eastern conifers, destroying the commercial value of the trunk within two years from its death. In large quantities of wind-blown timber and in extensive bodies of recent slash, these beetles find abundant food supply and feed in enormous numbers, so that when the windfalls or slash are gone, the normal amount of over-mature and dying bark is not sufficient for them and then for a few years, at least, a much larger proportion of the standing timber is killed.

## Mr. Cooke Opens an Office in Toronto

S. P. W. Cooke, who for many years has been connected with the lumber business and for some time past was Ontario representative of Mason, Gordon & Co., Montreal, has opened an office at 209 Confederation Life Bldg., Toronto.

"Doc" Cooke, as he is familiarly styled, is an old Ottawa boy, who first became identified with forest products when he joined the

S. P. W. Cooke, Toronto, Ont.

staff of the East Kootenay Lumber Co., Jaffray, B. C. with whom he was for a considerable period. Afterwards he sold for several Western mills, making his headquarters in Moose Jaw, Sask. Three years ago he located in Montreal and became associated with the lumber industry in the East. He is now representing in Ontario the Allen-Stoltze Lumber Co., of Vancouver, B. C.; J. Hanbury & Co., of Vancouver; the Forest Mills, Limited, of Revelstoke, B. C.; and G. M. Strong, Cambria, Que.

Mr. Cooke is specializing in all lines of B. C. forest products as well as Quebec spruce and hemlock, and reports that business is opening up nicely.

## Change in Well Known Toronto Lumber Firm

The wholesale lumber firm of Campbell, Welsh & Paynes, Toronto, has been dissolved by mutual consent, the partnership agreement having expired, and Mr. Campbell, the senior member of the organization being desirous of retiring. The business will in future be carried on by W. G. Paynes.

Maurice Welsh, who has been identified with the firm for the last five years, has purchased Mr. Paynes' interest in the Algonquin Lumber Co., Limited, and is now at the head of that organization, which conducted an operation last year and handled considerable quantities of jack pine, lath, etc.

Mr. Paynes is retaining the same office in the Bank of Hamilton Building as was occupied by the old firm, and the Algonquin Lumber Co. is also in the same quarters for the present.

W. G. Paynes, who as already stated, will continue the business, is well-known to the lumber trade of Ontario. Born in England in 1876 in the county of Surrey, he came to Canada when thirteen years of age. He spent his school days in Simcoe, after which he taught for some time. Teaching, however, did not appeal to him and at the first opportunity he took a position in the office of the Turner Lumber Co. at Midland. He spent four years with them in that town and then came to Toronto to look after their interests in the Queen City. He remained with the firm four years more and secured a good knowledge and experience in both shipping and office end of

J. L. Campbell, Toronto, Ont.
Retiring from lumber business

W. G. Paynes, Toronto, Ont.
Who continues the business

the industry. Mr. Paynes then joined the firm of Campbell & Johnson as a salesman and has been associated with Mr. Campbell up to the recent dissolution.

In January 1916 the firm of Campbell & Johnson was dissolved after ten years association, J. P. Johnson retiring and going in partnership with his son, A. K. Johnson.

Campbell & Paynes was formed and continued until May 1917 when Maurice Welsh joined the firm which became Campbell, Welsh & Paynes. Mr. Welsh had been with the Campbell, McLaurin Lumber Co., of Montreal, as Ontario manager for ten years previous to becoming identified with Campbell & Paynes.

Mr. Campbell who is now retiring from the lumber business and will enjoy a well-earned rest, has been in the wholesale lumber line in Toronto about fifteen years and has always been highly regarded for his integrity and sound business principles. Previous to coming to Toronto, he spent some twenty-one years in the West in the district of Melita, Man., where he was engaged successfully in the farming, the retail lumber and hardware business. He was also the first registrar of deeds in Melita, was reeve for four years and later mayor of the town. He was the pioneer returning officer in the first election that ever took place in that district, and occupied other important positions, among them being president of the Board of Trade.

Mr. Campbell has always been interested in lumbermen's organizations, and was for four years a director and later president for the same length of time of the Western Retail Lumber Dealers' Association. In Toronto he has been a warm supporter of the Wholesale Lumber Dealers' Association, Inc., and other bodies.

## Mr. Wilmot Speaks Hopefully of the West

A. G. Wilmot, of Toronto, eastern manager of the Otis Staples Lumber Co, Limited, Wycliffe, B. C., and the East Kootenay Lumber Co., Limited, of Jaffray, returned recently from a flying business trip to the West.

He reports that the lumber business in British Columbia is rapidly improving. The demand from across the border and also from the Prairie yards where stocks had almost run down to the vanishing point, set in ratherly suddenly. The result is that many mills have been cleaned out of certain lines of stock and just at present cannot handle some of the business offering. With the excellent drying weather now prevailing the lumber being cut at present will shortly be available for shipment.

Mr. Wilmot reports that no lumberman on the Coast desires to see a runaway market and all are endeavoring to control the situation as much as possible in order that conditions may be stabilized and production and consumption balanced as nearly as possible.

The East Kootenay Lumber Co., is not operating at Jaffray this season, having cut out its limits at that point. A new location is now being sought. The Otis Staples Lumber Co., are very busy at Wycliffe, and turning out about 120,000 feet a day, 75% of which is Western soft pine and the remainder larch and mountain fir.

Mr. Wilmot says that a feeling of optimism is now growing throughout the manufacturers on both the Coast and mountain districts and while no boom is on, things are steadily on the mend and demand increasing to an extent that is encouraging after a rather prolonged period of depression in domestic trade. Mr. Wilmot reports that the crop prospects in the West are most promising.

## Thinks Camp Regulations are Too Rigid

During consideration of Board of Health estimates in the Ontario Legislature lately, Hon. G. H. Ferguson protested that regulations issued by the Provincial Department to govern sanitary conditions in lumber camps were more adapted to "summer resort" requirements than to the practical lumbering field. Z. Mageau, Sturgeon Falls, who is a well-known lumber manufacturer also objected to the expense devolving upon lumbermen in adhering to the regulations.

Hon. Walter Rollo, arose to explain that the regulations had been the subject of a conference between the lumbermen, employees and the department. He, however, could not name the individuals present at such conference, nor was he prepared to give the necessary detailed information which Opposition members required concerning the various items.

Hon. G. H. Ferguson regarded seriously the inability of the Minister to furnish all the required information, and Hon. Manning Doherty, who was leading the Government forces at the time, finally acquiesced in the demand of Hon. Mr. Ferguson that all the Minister's estimates stand over until the latter was able to acquaint himself with the complete details.

## New Kind of Oak Logs Offered

It would seem as if all conditions of men would like to enter the lumber business. A story is going the rounds that the purchasing agent of a large organization in Montreal was approached the other day by a would-be timber salesman who enquired if he did not want to buy some oak logs.

"Well I don't know" answered the purchasing agent, "What kind of oak is it?"

"Well" replied the amateur dispenser of wood products "I don't know exactly but I think it is either fumed or quartered oak, but I tell you sir, I will find out and let you know."

Needless to say the foreflushing salesman has not yet turned up with the necessary data about the logs.

## "We Use Creosote Sir not—"

The story is going the rounds that an English timber purchaser accompanied by a gentleman from Victoria recently paid a visit to one of the large saw-mills in Vancouver. The general manager of the concern showed the visitors around the extensive yards and they came upon some timbers, the ends of which were painted red.

"Why do you color the ends like that?" inquired the British visitor.

"Oh" replied the general manager "We believe that giving the sticks a coat of paint it prevents them from checking. At least that is our opinion" he added.

The English gentleman spoke up and said that they did things differently "at 'ome." They treated their timber so that there was no doubt about it being well preserved.

"Oh, that is all bull," interrupted the resident of Victoria.

"Not at all sir, not at all" was the rejoinder of the Old Country timber merchant. "It is not bull at all that we use sir, Allow me to inform you that it is creosote."

## Now Cutting Pulpwood for Next Season

The Thompson & Heyland Lumber Co., of Toronto, who are extensive dealers in pulpwood, report that there is practically no change in the demand at the present time and that settlers are now beginning to cut wood for delivery during next season. Spruce and balsam can be peeled from now any time up to August 15th.

Mr. Heyland states that his company have shipped since the first of the year about 25,000 cords to Thorold, Niagara and Pennsylvania mills. Nearly all the wood along the T. & N. O. Ry. has been moved, but there is a certain amount of old wood on the Transcontinental, east and west of Cochrane, which has become worm-eaten and fire-killed and is pretty well culled, so that what remains is not of any great value.

There seems to be an impression that the price for pulpwood will strengthen this fall as a number of mills who had large stocks on hand, may be requiring supplies. This view is not shared by Mr. Heyland who sees nothing to warrant any increased activity in the pulpwood output or prices for months to come; in fact, a number of mills declare they have supplies enough on hand to satisfy their requirements for another year or two.

South of North Bay peeled spruce and balsam is selling from $11.00 to $12.00 per cord, f.o.b. cars, and north of North Bay and east and west of Cochrane the figures run from $7.50 to $9.50 a cord. Peeled poplar south of North Bay is bringing about $7.50 and peeled hemlock around $8.00 f.o.b. cars. Rossed spruce on the Transcontinental Railway is being sold at $9.00 to $10.00 a cord. There is a fair demand for poplar at the present time and some mills across the border have ordered a considerable supply.

## Big Change in Eastern Timber Lands

Hollingsworth & Whitney, Limited, were recently granted a federal charter with a capital stock of $4,000,000, and headquarters in Halifax. This new organization is a subsidiary of the Hollingsworth & Whitney Co., of Boston, who are well-known paper manufacturers.

Hollingsworth & Whitney, Limited, have acquired the timberlands of the Davison Lumber & Mfg. Co., of Bridgewater, N. S., now in liquidation, which are located in Lunenburg, King's, Annapolis and Queen's Counties. The timber lands of C. T. White, Limited, of Sussex, N. B., in St. John, King's and Albert Counties, New Brunswick, and in Cumberland, N. S., have also been acquired. The purchase price for both these large properties is not announced but it is said to represent $2,000,000.

It is reported that Hollingsworth & Whitney, Limited, will erect pulp mills in New Brunswick and Nova Scotia.

The timberlands in New Brunswick of C. T. White, Limited, have an approximate acreage over all of 125,000 acres with an estimated cordage of over 1,000,000 cords of softwood and approximately 60,000,000 feet of hardwood. The property just bought by Hollingsworth & Whitney, Limited, was sold by the Timberlands Department of the Quebec Savings & Trust Co., of Montreal.

## Pulp Plant Ordered to be Sold

An order for the sale of the Western Canada Pulp and Paper Company, formerly the Rainy River Pulp Company—was recently made by Mr. Justice Macdonald, Vancouver, and is said to presage a reorganization whereby the bondholders will take charge, expend $250,000 on water power and other development and make the property a paying concern. The shareholders and creditors will have a chance to bid on the property at the sale on June 15. Neither of these bodies are opposing the sale.

The application was made by Mr. J. G. Gibson on behalf of the holders of first mortgage debenture bonds, amounting to $1,000,000, and claims for $105,000 interest. The property, consisting of a forty-ton mill and timber limits, is valued at about $1,000,000.

There is little or no equity left for the shareholders who hold

the second issue of $1,200,000 of debentures or for the unsecured creditors with claims of $552,000.

In 1919 the property was sold under similar circumstances by order of Mr. Justice Murphy not only operated for four months when it is said to have lost $100,000. It has been idle since April, 1921.

To make the property pay, it is said to require water power development at a cost of $125,000 and certain new equipment. It is the intention of the bondholders if they buy the property in to raise $250,000 to refinance the concern.

## Belgian Industrial Company is Expanding

The Belgian Industrial Co., Shawinigan Falls, Que., are erecting a machine building to house two newsprint machines, each of which will have a width of 228 inches. Only one machine will be installed at the present time and it is estimated to have a daily capacity of 80 tons.

The contract for the Fourdrinier has been awarded to Chas. Walmsley & Sons of Bury, England, but the auxiliary equipment has not yet been ordered. The drawings for steel work have been completed and about 400 tons of steel will be required in the building. The entire construction and engineering work will be taken care of by the Belgian Industrial Company's own organization. The expenditure involved in the extension will be somewhat less than $1,000,000.

## Good Season for Driving Pulpwood

The past spring has been an exceptionally good one for driving logs and pulpwood down the St. Francis river. Most of the companies have been able to get their drives cleared successfully.

The Brompton Pulp & Paper Co., of East Angus, Que., reported that they had had a satisfactory drive, while it is understood those of B. C. Howard & Co., the Lacroix Lumber Co., and others have been very successful. The Chaudiere river was low for some days, but recent rains raised the level of the water enough to permit Price Bros. & Co., to complete their pulpwood drive.

## Ontario Will Have Four Free Nurseries

The Ontario Government expects to have four nurseries in operation raising young trees for reforestation before the end of this year. The Government has quadrupled the capacity of the nursery at Norfolk and has taken options on land for another near Durham. Two more are planned, one in the eastern portion of the province. The Department of Lands and Forests has been advised by botanical experts against importing seeds from Europe owing to the danger of disease. It is to stick to the practice of collecting seeds from northern Ontario, and the outlook is that the development along this line will be limited only by the capacity to collect seeds.

## Simcoe County Leads Way in Reforestation

The county of Simcoe, Ont., the first of the counties to adopt the county good roads system, is to the fore again with a plan to replant its waste places with trees, being the first of the counties to thus engage in the movement for reforestation. The area bought consists of one thousand acres of sandy land which was once covered with the finest of white pine. Quite unfit for agricultural purposes it is claimed to be admirably suited for reforestation. For this land the county paid from two to twenty dollars per acre. Six hundred thousand, year-old seedlings of Scotch pine are being planted in the nursery park. Some that are three years old will be set out this year and in succeeding years one hundred acres annually will be planted until the whole thousand acres is filled. Scientific direction is given the planting by a representative of the Forestry department of the Ontario government.

# CURRENT LUMBER PRICES—WHOLESALE

## TORONTO

(In Car Load Lots, F.O.B. cars Toronto)

### White Pine

| | | |
|---|---|---|
| 1 x 4/7 Good Strips | $100.00 | $110.00 |
| 1¼ & 1½ x 4/7 Good Strips | 120.00 | 125.00 |
| 1 x 8 and up Good Sides | 150.00 | 160.00 |
| 2 x 4/7 Good Strips | 130.00 | 140.00 |
| 1¼ & 1½ x 8 and wider Good Sides | 185.00 | 190.00 |
| 2 x 8 and wider Good Sides | 190.00 | 200.00 |
| 1 in. No. 1, 2 and 3 Cuts | 75.00 | 80.00 |
| 5/4 and 6/4 No. 1, 2 and 3 Cuts | 95.00 | 100.00 |
| 2 in. No. 1, 2 and 3 Cuts | 105.00 | 110.00 |
| 1 x 4 and 5 Mill Run | 52.00 | 55.00 |
| 1 x 6 Mill Run | 53.00 | 56.00 |
| 1 x 7, 9 and 11 Mill Run | 53.00 | 56.00 |
| 1 x 8 Mill Run | 55.00 | 58.00 |
| 1 x 10 Mill Run | 60.00 | 62.00 |
| 1 x 12 Mill Run | 65.00 | 70.00 |
| 5/4 and 6/4 x 5 and up Mill Run | 58.00 | 60.00 |
| 2 x 4 Mill Run | 52.00 | 53.00 |
| 2 x 6 Mill Run | 53.00 | 56.00 |
| 2 x 8 Mill Run | 55.00 | 58.00 |
| 2 x 10 Mill Run | 58.00 | 60.00 |
| 2 x 12 Mill Run | 63.00 | 65.00 |
| 1 in. Mill Run Shorts | 35.00 | 40.00 |
| 1 x 4 and up 6/16 No. 1 Mill Culls | 30.00 | 32.00 |
| 1 x 10 and up 6/16 No. 1 Mill Culls | 34.00 | 36.00 |
| 1 x 12 and up 6/16 No. 1 Mill Culls | 34.00 | 36.00 |
| 1 x 4 and up 6/16 No. 2 Mill Culls | 23.00 | 25.00 |
| 1 x 10 x 12 6/16 No. 2 Mill Culls | 26.00 | 28.00 |
| 1 x 4 and up 6/16 No. 3 Mill Culls | 17.00 | 18.00 |

### Red Pine

(In Car Load Lots, F.O.B. Toronto)

| | | |
|---|---|---|
| 1 x 4 and 5 Mill Run | $34.00 | $35.00 |
| 1 x 6 Mill Run | 35.00 | 36.00 |
| 1 x 8 Mill Run | 37.00 | 38.00 |
| 1 x 10 Mill Run | 42.00 | 44.00 |
| 2 x 4 Mill Run | 37.00 | 38.00 |
| 2 x 6 Mill Run | 37.00 | 38.00 |
| 2 x 8 Mill Run | 38.00 | 39.00 |
| 2 x 10 Mill Run | 41.00 | 42.00 |
| 2 x 12 Mill Run | 46.00 | 47.00 |
| 1 in. Clear and Clear Face | 70.00 | 72.00 |
| 2 in. Clear and Clear Face | 70.00 | 72.00 |

### Spruce

| | | |
|---|---|---|
| 1 x 4 Mill Run | 34.00 | 35.00 |
| 1 x 6 Mill Run | 35.00 | 36.00 |
| 1 x 8 Mill Run | 37.00 | 38.00 |
| 1 x 10 Mill Run | 45.00 | 47.00 |
| 1 x 12 Mill Run Spruce | 48.00 | 50.00 |
| Mill Culls | 25.00 | 27.00 |

### Hemlock (M R)

(In Car Load Lots, F.O.B. Toronto)

| | | |
|---|---|---|
| 1 x 4 and 5 in. x 9 to 16 ft. | $26.00 | $27.00 |
| 1 x 6 in. x 9 to 16 ft. | 32.00 | 33.00 |
| 1 x 8 in. x 9 to 16 ft. | 33.00 | 34.00 |
| 1 x 10 and 12 in. x 9 to 16 ft. | 35.00 | 37.00 |
| 1 x 7, 9 and 11 in. x 9 to 16 ft. | 32.00 | 33.00 |
| 2 x 4 to 12 in. 10/16 ft. | 32.00 | 33.00 |
| 2 x 4 to 12 in., 18 ft. | 37.00 | 39.00 |
| 2 x 4 to 12 in., 20 ft. | 40.00 | 42.00 |
| 1 in. No. 2, 6 ft. to 16 ft. | 23.00 | 25.00 |

### Fir Flooring

(In Car Load Lots, F.O.B. Toronto)

| | |
|---|---|
| Fir flooring, 1 x 3 and 4", No. 1 and 2 Edge Grain | $75.00 |
| Fir flooring, 1 x 3 and 4", No. 1 and 2 Flat Grain | 52.00 |
| 1 x 4 to 12 No. 1 and 2 Clear Fir Rough | 81.50 |
| 1¼ x 4 to 12 No. 1 and 2 Clear Fir, Rough | 85.50 |
| 2 x 4 to 12 No. 1 and 2 Clear Fir, Rough | 81.50 |
| 3 & 4 x 4 to 12 No. 1 & 2 Clear Fir Rough | 89.50 |
| 1 x 4, 5 and 6 in Fir Casing | 80.00 |
| 1 x 8 and 10 Fir Base | 85.00 |
| 1¼ and 1½ 8, 10 and 12 in. E.G. Stepping | 95.00 |
| 1¼ and 1½ 8, 10 and 12 in. F.G. Stepping | 85.00 |
| 1 x 4 to 12 Clear Fir, D4S | 78.00 |
| 1¼ and 1½ x 4 to 12 Clear Fir, D4S | 100.00 |
| XX Shingles, 6 butts to 2", per M. | 3.35 |
| XXX Shingles, 6 butts to 2", per M. | 5.75 |
| XXXXX Shingles, 5 butts to 2", per M. | 6.40 |

### Lath

(F.O.B. Mill)

| | |
|---|---|
| No. 1 White Pine | $11.00 |
| No. 2 White Pine | 10.00 |
| No. 3 White Pine | 8.00 |
| Mill Run White Pine, 32 in. | 3.50 |
| Merchantable Spruce Lath, 4 ft. | 6.50 |

## TORONTO HARDWOOD PRICES

The prices given below are for car loads f.o.b. Toronto, from wholesalers to retailers, and are based on a good percentage of long lengths and good widths, without any wide stock having been sorted out.

The prices quoted on imported woods are payable in U. S. funds.

### Ash, White

(Dry weight 3800 lbs. per M. ft.)

| | 1s & 2s | No. 1 Com. | No. 2 Com. |
|---|---|---|---|
| 1" | $115.00 | $ 65.00 | $ 45.00 |
| 1¼ and 1½" | 120.00 | 75.00 | 50.00 |
| 2" | 130.00 | 80.00 | 50.00 |
| 2½" and 3" | 150.00 | 100.00 | 60.00 |
| 4" | 165.00 | 120.00 | 70.00 |

### Ash, Brown

| | 1s & 2s | No. 1 Com. | No. 2 Com. |
|---|---|---|---|
| 1" | $120.00 | 60.00 | $40.00 |
| 1¼ and 1½" | 130.00 | 65.00 | 45.00 |
| 2" | 150.00 | 70.00 | 55.00 |
| 2½ and 3" | 160.00 | 85.00 | 55.00 |
| 4" | 175.00 | 95.00 | 60.00 |

### Birch

(Dry weight 4000 lbs. per M. ft.)

| | 1s & 2s | Sels. | No. 1 Com. | No. 2 Com. |
|---|---|---|---|---|
| 4/4 | $110.00 | $ 80.00 | $ 50.00 | $ 32.00 |
| 5/4 | $115.00 | $ 85.00 | $ 55.00 | $ 35.0 |
| 6/4 | 115.00 | 90.00 | 60.00 | 38.00 |
| 8/4 | 120.00 | 100.00 | 65.00 | 42.00 |
| 12/4 | 125.00 | 105.00 | 70.00 | 50.00 |
| 16/4 | 130.00 | 110.00 | 80.00 | 55.00 |

### Basswood

(Dry weight 2500 lbs. per M. ft.)

| | 1s & 2s | No. 1 Com. | No. 2 Com. |
|---|---|---|---|
| 4/4 | $ 80.00 | $ 50.00 | $ 30.00 |
| 5/4 and 6/4 | 85.00 | 60.00 | 30.00 |
| 8/4 | 90.00 | 65.00 | 35.00 |

### Chestnut

(Dry weight 2800 lbs. per M. ft.)

| | 1s & 2s | No. 1 Com. | Sound Wormy |
|---|---|---|---|
| 1" | $140.00 | $ 85.00 | $ 40.00 |
| 1¼ to 1½" | 145.00 | 93.00 | 40.00 |
| 2" | 158.00 | 103.00 | 42.00 |

### Maple, Hard

(Dry weight 4200 lbs. per M. ft.)

| | F.A.S. | Sels. | No. 1 Com. | No. 2 Com. |
|---|---|---|---|---|
| 4/4 | $ 90.00 | $ 65.00 | $ 50.00 | $ 33.00 |
| 5/4 | $ 90.00 | 65.00 | 50.00 | 38.00 |
| 6/4 | $ 90.00 | 70.00 | 55.00 | 45.00 |
| 8/4 | 100.00 | 75.00 | 60.00 | 50.00 |
| 12/4 | 105.00 | 75.00 | 65.00 | 60.00 |
| 16/4 | 125.00 | 100.00 | 70.00 | 65.00 |

### Elm, Soft

(Dry weight 3100 lbs. per M. ft.)

| | 1s & 2s | No. 1 Com. | No. 2 Com. |
|---|---|---|---|
| 4/4 | $ 75.00 | $ 50.00 | $ 30.00 |
| 4/4 | $ 85.00 | 60.00 | 35.00 |
| 12/4 | 100.00 | 70.00 | 40.00 |

### Gum, Red

(Dry weight 3800 lbs. per M. ft.)

| | Plain 1s & 2s | Plain No. 1 Com. | Quartered 1s & 2s | Quartered No. 1 Com. |
|---|---|---|---|---|
| 1" | $125.00 | $ 80.00 | $135.00 | $ 95.00 |
| 1¼" | 130.00 | 80.00 | 140.00 | 95.00 |
| 1½" | 130.00 | 85.00 | 140.00 | 100.00 |
| 2" | 130.00 | 90.00 | 150.00 | 105.00 |

Figured Gum, $30 per M. extra in both plain and quartered.

### Gum, Sap

| | 1s&2s | No. 1 Com. |
|---|---|---|
| 1" | 60.00 | $ 40.00 |
| 1¼ and 1½" | 60.00 | 45.00 |
| 2" | 65.00 | 50.00 |

### Hickory

(Dry weight 4500 lbs. per M. ft.

| | 1s&2s | No. 1 Com. |
|---|---|---|
| 1" | $125.00 | $ 70.00 |
| 1¼" | 145.00 | 70.00 |
| 1½" | 145.00 | 75.00 |
| 2" | 150.00 | 80.00 |

### Quarter Cut Red Oak

| | 1s&2s | No. 1 Com. |
|---|---|---|
| 4/4 | $145.00 | $ 80.00 |
| 5/4 and 6/4 | 160.00 | 90.00 |
| 8/4 | 165.00 | 95.00 |

### Plain White and Red Oak

(Plain sawed. Dry weight 4000 lbs. per M. ft.)

| | 1s&2s | No. 1 Com. |
|---|---|---|
| 4/4 | $130.00 | $ 75.00 |
| 5/4 and 6/4 | 135.00 | 80.00 |
| 8/4 | 140.00 | 85.00 |
| 10/4 | 145.00 | 95.00 |
| 12/4 | 145.00 | 100.00 |
| 16/4 | 150.00 | 105.00 |

### White Oak, Quarter Cut

(Dry weight 4000 lbs. per M. ft.)

| | 1s&2s | No. 1 Com. |
|---|---|---|
| 4/4 | $165.00 | $ 95.00 |
| 5/4 and 6/4 | 175.00 | 100.00 |
| 8/4 | 190.00 | 105.00 |

## OTTAWA

Manufacturers' Prices

### Pine

| | | |
|---|---|---|
| **Good sidings:** | | |
| 1 in. x 7 in. and up | | $140.00 |
| 1¼ in. and 1½ in., 8 in. and up. | | 165.00 |
| 2 in. x 7 in. and up | | 165.00 |
| No. 2 cuts 2 x 8 in. and up | | 80.00 |
| **Good strips:** | | |
| 1 in. | $100.00 | $105.00 |
| 1¼ in. and 1½ in. | | 120.00 |
| 2 in. | | 125.00 |
| **Good shorts:** | | |
| 1 in. x 7 in. and up | | 110.00 |
| 1 in. 4 in. to 6 in. | 85.00 | 90.00 |
| 1¼ in. and 1½ in. | | 110.00 |
| 2 in. | | 125.00 |
| 7 in. to 9 in. A sidings | 54.00 | 56.00 |
| No. 1 dressing sidings | 70.00 | 74.00 |
| No. 1 dressing strips | | 62.00 |
| No. 1 dressing shorts | 50.00 | 53.00 |
| 1 in. x 4 in. s.c. strips | | 48.00 |
| 1 in. x 5 in. s.c. strips | | 48.00 |
| 1 in. x 6 in. s.c. strips | | 50.00 |
| 1 in. x 7 in. s.c. strips | 51.00 | 64.00 |
| 1 in. x 8 in. s.c. strips, 12 to 16 ft. | | 54.00 |
| 1 in. x 10 in. M.R. | | 58.00 |
| S.C. sidings, 1½ and 2 in. | 58.00 | 60.00 |
| S.C. strips, 1 in. | | 45.00 |
| 1¼, 1½ and 2 in. | 50.00 | 55.00 |
| S.C. shorts, 1 x 4 to 6 in. | 34.00 | 36.00 |
| S.C. and bet., shorts, 1 x 5 | | 36.00 |
| S.C. and bet., shorts, 1 x 6 | | 42.00 |
| S.C. shorts, 6-11 ft., 1 x 10 in. | | 48.00 |
| **Box boards:** | | |
| 1 in. x 4 in. and up, 6 ft.-11 ft. | | 34.00 |
| 1 in. x 3 in. and up, 12 ft.-16 ft. | 35.00 | 37.00 |
| Mill cull shorts, 1 in. x 4 in. and x 4 in. and up, 12 ft. and up | 24.00 | 26.00 |
| Mill culls, strips and sidings, 1 in. up, 6 ft. to 11 ft. | | 22.00 |
| O. culls r and w p | 18.00 | 20.00 |

### Red Pine, Log Run

| | | |
|---|---|---|
| Mill culls out, 1 in. | 32.00 | 34.00 |
| Mill culls out, 1¼ in. | 32.00 | 34.00 |
| Mill culls out, 1½ in. | 32.00 | 34.00 |
| Mill culls out, 2 in. | 32.00 | 34.00 |
| Mill Culls, white pine, 1 in. x 7 in. and up | | 20.00 |

### Mill Run Spruce

| | | |
|---|---|---|
| 1 in. x 4 in. and up, 6 ft.-11 ft. | | 23.00 |
| 1 in. x 4 in. and up, 12 ft.-16 ft. | 30.00 | 32.00 |
| 1" x 9"-10" and up, 12 ft.-16 ft. | | 35.00 |
| 1¼" x 7, 8 and 9" up, 12 ft.-16 ft. | | 35.00 |
| 1¼ x 10 and up, 12 ft.-16 ft. | 38.00 | 42.00 |
| 1½" x 12" x 12" and up, 12'-16'. | | 42.00 |
| Spruce, 1 in. clear fine dressing and B | | 55.00 |
| Hemlock, 1 in. cull | | 20.00 |
| Hemlock, 1 in. log run | 24.00 | 26.00 |
| Hemlock, 2 x 4, 6, 8, 10 12/16 ft. | | 28.00 |
| Tamarac | 25.00 | 28.00 |
| Basswood, log run, dead culls out | 45.00 | 50.00 |
| Basswood, log run, mill culls out. | 50.00 | 54.00 |
| Birch, log run | 45.00 | 50.00 |
| Soft Elm, common and better, 1, 1½, 2 in. | 58.00 | 68.00 |
| Ash, black, log run | 62.00 | 65.00 |
| 1 x 10 No. 1 barn | 57.00 | 62.00 |
| 1 x 10 No. 2 barn | 51.00 | 56.00 |
| 1 x 8 and 9 No. 2 barn | 47.00 | 52.00 |

# CURRENT LUMBER PRICES—WHOLESALE

**Lath per M.:**

| | | |
|---|---|---|
| No. 1 White Pine, 1¼ in. x 4 ft. | | 8.01 |
| No. 2 White Pine | | 6.00 |
| Mill run White Pine | | 7.00 |
| Spruce, mill run, 1½ in. | | 6.00 |
| Red Pine, mill run | | 6.00 |
| Hemlock, mill run | | 5.50 |

**White Cedar Shingles**

| | | |
|---|---|---|
| XXXX, 18 in. | 9.00 | 10.00 |
| Clear butt, 18 in. | 6.00 | 7.00 |
| 18 in. XX | | 5.00 |

## QUEBEC

**White Pine**
(At Quebec)

| | Cts. Per Cubic Ft. | |
|---|---|---|
| First class Ottawa wancy, 18 in. average according to lineal | 100 | 110 |
| 19 in. and up average | 110 | 120 |

**Spruce Deals**
(At Mill)

| | | |
|---|---|---|
| 3 in. unsorted, Quebec, 4 in. to 6 in. wide | $ 20.00 | $ 25.00 |
| 3 in. unsorted, Quebec, 7 in. to 8 in. wide | 26.00 | 28.00 |
| 3 in. unsorted, Quebec, 9 in. wide | 30.00 | 35.00 |

**Oak**
(At Quebec)

| | Cts. Per Cubic Ft. | |
|---|---|---|
| According to average and quality, 55 ft. cube | 125 | 130 |

**Elm**
(At Quebec)

| | | |
|---|---|---|
| According to average and quality, 40 to 45 ft. cube | 100 | 120 |
| According to average and quality, 30 to 35 ft. | 90 | 100 |

**Export Birch Planks**
(At Mill)

| | | |
|---|---|---|
| 1 to 4 in. thick, per M. ft. | $ 30.00 | $ 35.00 |

## ST. JOHN, N.B.

(From Yards and Mills—Retail)

**Rough Lumber**

| | | |
|---|---|---|
| 2x3, 2x4, 3x3, 3x4. Rgh Merch Spr. | $28.00 | |
| 2x3, 2x4, 3x3, 3x4, Dressed 1 edge | 30.00 | |
| 2x3, 2x4, 3x3, 3x4, Dressed 4 sides | 31.00 | |
| 2x6, 2x7, 3x5, 4x4, 4x6, all rough. | 28.00 | |
| 2x6, 2x7, 3x5, 4x4, 4x6, all rough. | 30.00 | |
| 2x8, 3x7, 5x5, 6x6 | 35.00 | $40.00 |
| 2x9, 3x8, 6x8, 7x7 | 37.00 | $40.00 |
| 2x10, 3x9 | 40.00 | |
| 2x12, 3x10, 3x12, 8x8 and up | 42.00 | |
| Merch. Spr. Bds. Rough, 1x3-4 & 5 | 28.00 | |
| Merch. Spr. Bds., Rough, 1x7 & up | 35.00 | |
| Refuse Bds., Deals and Setgs. | 18.00 | 20.00 |

Above random lengths up to 18-0 long.
Lengths 19-0 and up $5.00 extra per M.
For planing Merch. and Refuse Bds. add $2.00 per M. to above prices.
Laths, $7.00.

**Shingles**

| | Per M. |
|---|---|
| Cedar, Extras | $6.00 |
| Cedar, Clears | 5.00 |
| Cedar, 2nd Clears | 4.00 |
| Cedar, Extra No. 1 | 2.50 |
| Spruce | 3.50 |

## SARNIA, ONT.

**White Pine—Fine, Com. and Better**

| | |
|---|---|
| 1 x 6 and 8 in. | $110.00 |
| 1 in., 8 in. and up wide | 130.00 |
| 1¼ and 1½ in. and up wide | 180.00 |
| 2 in. and up wide | 180.00 |

**Cuts and Better**

| | |
|---|---|
| 4/4 x 8 and up No. 1 and better | 125.00 |
| 5/4 and 6/4 and up No. 1 and better | 150.00 |
| 8/4 and 8 and up No. 1 and better | 150.00 |

**No. 1 Cuts**

| | |
|---|---|
| 1 in., 8 in. and up wide | 105.00 |
| 1¼ in., 8 in. and up wide | 125.00 |
| 1½ in., 8 in. and up wide | 125.00 |
| 2 in., 8 in. and up wide | 130.00 |
| 2½ in. and 3 in., 8 in. and up wide | 175.00 |
| 4 in., 8 in. and up wide | 185.00 |

**No. 1 Barn**

| | | |
|---|---|---|
| 1 in., 10 to 16 ft. long | $ 75.00 | $ 85.00 |
| 1¼, 1½ and 2 in., 10/16 ft. | 80.00 | 85.00 |
| 2½ to 3 in., 10/16 ft. | 85.00 | 100.00 |

**No. 2 Barn**

| | | |
|---|---|---|
| 1 in., 10 to 16 ft. long | 65.00 | 75.00 |
| 1¼, 1½ and 2 in., 10/16 ft. | | 66.00 |
| 2½, 1½ and 3 in. | | 85.00 |

**No. 3 Barn**

| | | |
|---|---|---|
| 1 in., 10 to 16 ft. long | 48.00 | 55.00 |
| 1¼, 1½ and 2 in., 10/16 ft. | 50.00 | 56.00 |

**Box**

| | | |
|---|---|---|
| 1 in., 1¼ and 1½ in., 10/16 ft. | 33.00 | 35.00 |

**Mill Culls**

| | |
|---|---|
| Mill Run Culls— | |
| 1 in., 4 in. and up wide, 6/16 ft. | 26.00 |
| 1¼, 1½ and 2 in. | 27.00 |

## WINNIPEG

**No. 1 Spruce**

| Dimension | S.1.S. and 1.E. 10 ft. | 12 ft. | 14 ft. | 16 ft. |
|---|---|---|---|---|
| 2 x 4 | $29 | $28 | $28 | $29 |
| 2 x 6 | 30 | 28 | 28 | 29 |
| 2 x 8 | 31 | 29 | 29 | 30 |
| 2 x 10 | 32 | 30 | 30 | 31 |
| 2 x 12 | 33 | 31 | 31 | 32 |

For 2 inches, rough, add 50 cents.
For S1E only, add 50 cents.
For S1S and 2E, S4S or D&M, add $3.00.
For timbers larger than 8 x 8, add 50c. for each additional 2 inches each way.
For lengths longer than 20 ft., add $1.00 for each additional two feet.
For selected common, add $5.00.
For No. 2 Dimension, $3.00 less than No. 1.
For 1 x 2 and 2 x 2, $2 more than 2 x 4 No. 1.
For Tamarac, open.

## BUFFALO and TONAWANDA

**White Pine**
Wholesale Selling Price

| | |
|---|---|
| Uppers, 4/4 | $225.00 |
| Uppers, 5/4 to 8/4 | 225.00 |
| Uppers, 10/4 to 12/4 | 250.00 |
| Selects, 4/4 | 200.00 |
| Selects, 5/4 to 8/4 | 200.00 |
| Selects, 10/4 to 12/4 | 225.00 |
| Fine Common, 4/4 | 155.00 |
| Fine Common, 5/4 | 160.00 |
| Fine Common, 6/4 | 160.00 |
| Fine Common, 8/4 | 160.00 |
| No. 1 Cuts, 4/4 | 115.00 |
| No. 1 Cuts, 5/4 | 130.00 |
| No. 1 Cuts, 6/4 | 135.00 |
| No. 1 Cuts, 8/4 | 140.00 |
| No. 2 Cuts, 4/4 | 70.00 |
| No. 2 Cuts, 5/4 | 100.00 |
| No. 2 Cuts, 6/4 | 105.00 |
| No. 2 Cuts, 8/4 | 110.00 |
| No. 3 Cuts, 5/4 | 60.00 |
| No. 3 Cuts, 6/4 | 65.00 |
| No. 3 Cuts, 8/4 | 67.00 |
| Dressing, 4/4 | 95.00 |
| Dressing 4/4 x 10 | 98.00 |
| Dressing, 4/4 x 12 | 110.00 |
| No. 1 Moulding, 5/4 | 150.00 |
| No. 1 Moulding, 6/4 | 150.00 |
| No. 1 Moulding, 8/4 | 155.00 |
| No. 2 Moulding, 5/4 | 125.00 |
| No. 2 Moulding, 6/4 | 125.00 |
| No. 2 Moulding, 8/4 | 130.00 |
| No. 1 Barn, 1 x 12 | 90.00 |
| No. 1 Barn, 1 x 6 and 8 | 76.00 |
| No. 1 Barn, 1 x 10 | 80.00 |
| No. 2 Barn, 1 x 6 and 8 | 62.00 |
| No. 2 Barn, 1 x 10 | 63.00 |
| No. 2 Barn, 1 x 12 | 75.00 |
| No. 3 Barn, 1 x 6 and 8 | 39.00 |
| No. 3 Barn, 1 x 10 | 39.00 |
| No. 3 Barn, 1 x 12 | 45.00 |
| No. 1 Box, 1 x 6 and 8 | 36.00 |
| No. 1 Box 1 x 10 | 37.00 |
| No. 1 Box, 1 x 12 | 38.00 |
| No. 1 Box, 1 x 13 and up | 39.00 |

## BUFFALO

The following quotations on hardwoods represent the jobber buying price at Buffalo and Tonawanda.

**Maple**

| | 1s & 2s | No. 1 Com. | No. 2 Com. |
|---|---|---|---|
| 1 in. | $ 75.00 | $ 45.00 | $ 28.00 |
| 5/4 to 8/4 | 80.00 | 50.00 | 28.00 |
| 10/4 to 4 in. | 86.00 | 56.00 | 28.00 |

**Sap Birch**

| | | | |
|---|---|---|---|
| 1 in. | 90.00 | 45.00 | 30.00 |
| 5/4 and up | 100.00 | 50.00 | 30.00 |

**Soft Elm**

| | | | |
|---|---|---|---|
| 1 in. | 70.00 | 45.00 | 30.00 |
| 5/4 to 2 in. | 75.00 | 50.00 | 30.00 |

**Red Birch**

| | | | |
|---|---|---|---|
| 1 in. | 120.00 | 75.00 | |
| 5/4 and up | 125.00 | 80.00 | |

**Basswood**

| | | | |
|---|---|---|---|
| 1 in. | 70.00 | 45.00 | 30.00 |
| 5/4 to 2 in. | 80.00 | 55.00 | 35.00 |

**Plain Oak**

| | | | |
|---|---|---|---|
| 1 in. | 95.00 | 55.00 | 35.00 |
| 5/4 to 2 in. | 105.00 | 65.00 | 40.00 |

**Ash**

| | | | |
|---|---|---|---|
| 1 in. | 80.00 | 48.00 | 30.00 |
| 5/4 to 2 in. | 85.00 | 52.00 | 30.00 |
| 10/4 and up | 100.00 | 65.00 | 30.00 |

## BOSTON

Quotations given below are for highest grades of Michigan and Canadian White Pine and Eastern Canadian Spruce as required in the New England market in car loads.

| | | |
|---|---|---|
| White Pine Uppers, 1 in. | | |
| White Pine Uppers, 1¼, 1½, 2 in. | | |
| White Pine Uppers, 2½, 3 in. | | |
| White Pine Uppers, 4 in. | | |
| Selects, 1 in. | | $190.00 |
| Selects, 1¼, 2 in. | | 200.00 |
| Selects, 2½, 3 in. | | |
| Selects, 4 in. | | |

Prices nominal

| | | |
|---|---|---|
| Fine Common, 1 in., 30%, 12 in. and up. | | 165.00 |
| Fine Common, 1 x 8 and up | | 165.00 |
| Fine Common, 1¼ to 2 in. | $165.00 | 170.00 |
| Fine Common, 2½ and 3 in. | | 180.00 |
| Fine Common, 4 in. | | 195.00 |
| 1 in. Shaky Clear | | 100.00 |
| 1¼ in. to 2 in. Shaky Clear | | 110.00 |
| 1 in. No. 2 Dressing | | 95.00 |
| 1¼ in. to 2 in. No. 2 Dressing | | 95.00 |
| No. 1 Cuts, 1 in. | | 110.00 |
| No. 1 Cuts, 1¼ to 2 in. | | 140.00 |
| No. 1 Cuts, 2½ to 3 in. | | 180.00 |
| No. 2 Cuts, 1 in. | | 80.00 |
| No. 2 Cuts, 1¼ to 2 in. | | 110.00 |
| Barn Boards, No. 1, 1 x 12 | | 95.00 |
| Barn Boards, No. 1, 1 x 10 | | 87.00 |
| Barn Boards, No. 1, 1 x 8 | | 83.00 |
| Barn Boards, No. 2, 1 x 12 | | 82.00 |
| Barn Boards, No. 2, 1 x 8 | | 69.00 |
| Barn Boards, No. 2, 1 x 10 | | 70.00 |
| Barn Boards, No. 3, 1 x 12 | | 48.00 |
| Barn Boards, No. 3, 1 x 10 | | 47.00 |
| Barn Boards, No. 3, 1 x 8 | | 47.00 |

**No. 1 Clear**

| | | |
|---|---|---|
| Can. Spruce, No. 1 and clear, 1 x 4 to 9" | | $ 78.00 |
| Can. Spruce, 1 x 10 in. | | 78.00 |
| Can. Spruce, No. 1, 1 x 4 to 7 in. | | 75.00 |
| Can. Spruce, No. 1, 1 x 8 and 9 in. | | 75.00 |
| Can. Spruce, No. 1, 1 x 10 in. | | 76.00 |
| Can. Spruce, No. 2, 1 x 4 and 5 in. | | 34.00 |
| Can. Spruce, No. 2, 1 x 6 and 7 in. | | 36.00 |
| Can. Spruce, No. 2, 1 x 8 and 9 in. | | 38.00 |
| Can. Spruce, No. 2, 1 x 10 in. | | 41.00 |
| Can. Spruce, No. 2, 1 x 12 in. | | 45.00 |
| Spruce, 12 in. dimension | | 44.00 |
| Spruce, 10 in. dimension | | 42.00 |
| Spruce, 9 in. dimension | | 41.00 |
| Spruce, 8 in. dimension | | 40.00 |
| 2 x 10 in. random lengths, 8 ft. and up | | 40.00 |
| 2 x 12 in., random lengths | | 43.00 |
| 2 x 3, 2 x 4, 2 x 5, 2 x 6, 2 x 7 | | 30.00 |
| 3 x 4 and 4 x 4 in. | | 31.00 |
| 2 x 9 | | 32.00 |
| All other random lengths, 7 in. and under, 8 ft. and up | 30.00 | 34.00 |
| 5 in. and up merchantable boards, 8 ft. and up, D 1s | 30.00 | 32.00 |
| 1 x 2 | 30.00 | 32.00 |
| 1 x 3 | | 30.00 |
| 1⅝ in. Spruce Lath | | 8.50 |
| 1½ in. Spruce Lath | 7.25 | 7.50 |

**New Brunswick Cedar Shingles**

| | | |
|---|---|---|
| Extras | 5.25 | 5.50 |
| Clears | 4.25 | 4.50 |
| Second Clear | 3.75 | 4.15 |
| Clear Whites | | 3.00 |

Second Hand Machinery & Equipment Wanted & For Sale

# Quick Action Section

Special Lots Of Lumber—Positions Wanted & Vacant

PUBLISHER'S NOTICE

Advertisements other than "Employment Wanted" or "Employees Wanted" will be inserted in this department at the rate of 25 cents per agate line (14 agate lines make one inch). $3.50 per inch, each insertion, payable in advance. Space measured from rule to rule. When four or more consecutive insertions of the same advertisement are ordered a discount of 25 per cent. will be allowed.

Advertisements of "Wanted Employment" will be inserted at the rate of one cent a word, net. Cash must accompany order. If Canada Lumberman box number is used, enclose ten cents extra for postage in forwarding replies. Minimum charge 25 cents.

Advertisements of "Wanted Employees" will be inserted at the rate of two cents a word, net. Cash must accompany the order. Minimum charge 50 cents.

Advertisements must be received not later than the 10th and 20th of each month to insure insertion in the subsequent issue.

## Lumber Wanted

### Wanted to Buy

Peeled spruce and balsam pulpwood. 50% cash, balance on arrival. Write P. O. Box 643, Montreal. 9-14

### Spruce Wanted

Parties having 4' peeled or 2' rossed Spruce for sale please communicate with Box 912, Canada Lumberman, Toronto. 11

### Oak Wanted

Canadian Plain Red Oak wanted. A few cars of 4/4 and 8/4 No. 2 Common and Better. Apply Box 866 Canada Lumberman, Toronto. 8-9

### We Will Buy

A block of Hemlock, Spruce, Red or White Pine that is sawn or will be sawn before the 15th of March. Box 770 Canada Lumberman, Toronto. 3 T.f.

### Wanted Lath

4' Nos. 1, 2 and 3, White Pine No. 1 No. 2 Spruce.
The George N. Comfort Lumber Co.,
11-14 1506 Kirby Bldg., Cleveland, O

### Lath for Sale

White Pine and Jack Pine. Write or wire for prices.
Brewster Loud Lumber Co.,
508 Lincoln Bldg.,
Detroit, Mich.
8-11

### Wanted

10 Cars No. 3 Jack Pine Lath also White Pine and Hemlock Lath in all grades.
Brewster Loud Lumber Co.,
508 Lincoln Bldg.,
Detroit, Mich.
8-11

### Wanted

Spruce Lath, 3/8 x 1½" x 4' also Spruce or Hemlock dimensions. State if you can saw long lengths in Spruce or Hemlock and quote prices.
BRIGHTON LUMBER CO.
11-14 Island Pond, Vt.

### Pulpwood Wanted

Wanted by old and reliabe firm in Northern Ontario a contract to represent either Canadian or American Paper Interests for the purchase of Pulpwood on a commission basis. We have Saw Mill and Retail Stores whereby we can supply jobbers throughout. For references apply, Royal Bank of Canada and Bradstreets.
PELLOW & McMEEKIN,
11-14 Hearst, Ont.

## Lumber For Sale

### For Sale

At Blind River, Ontario, Pine and Spruce Lath, also some Cedar and Hemlock Lath, Grades four foot mill run, 32" mill run, and four foot No. 3.
F. P. Potvin,
Blind River, Ont.
3-T.f.

### Sawdust

For sale, in car lots.
The London Box Mfg. &
9 T.f. Lumber Co., Limited.

### For Sale in Carload Lots

Telegraph Poles, Cedar and Hardwood Ties, Spruce Balsam and Poplar Pulpwood. Jas. Thos. Clair, Clair, N. B. 9-14

### Lumber for Sale

75 M 1½" Maple No 2 Common & Better 60 M 1" Soft Elm Log Run Dry Stock. A. J. McEwen, Box No. 204 Maxville, Ont. 8-11

### Standing Timber for Sale

15M. to 20M. feet straight clear white pine, situated Norfolk County 4 miles from Railroad Station. Would accept $500. Box 919 Canada Lumberman, Toronto. 11

### For Sale

1000 Cedar Poles 30' to 50' 75,000 feet square Cedar 3000 cords peeled spruce Pulpwood. Will sell cheap to prompt buyer. Box 904, Canada Lumberman, Toronto. 10-11

### Crating Spruce

About 100,000 ft., of ⅝" Common Sound Spruce, also 1, 2 & 3" Culls Spruce.
J. P. Abel-Fortin, Limited, 879 Desjardins Ave., Maisonneuve, Montreal, Quebec. 11

### For Sale

Chair Stock:
Bone Air Dried.
30 M. ft. 1" x 1" square 20" long.
20 M. ft. 1¼" x 1¼" square 20" long.
BIRCH—Clear Stock.
Apply P.O. Box 6, Victoriaville, Que.
11 T.f.

### Lumber for Sale

Maple and Soft Elm, 1" Thick Grades: No. 1, 2 and 3 Common. 1-inch Basswood No. 2 Common and Better. Must clear out to make room.
St. Mary's Wood Specialty Co. Ltd.,
11 St. Mary's, Ont.

## Sale of Timber to Close an Estate

South East Quarter of Township of PROUDFOOT containing twenty-three and a quarter square miles, and known as berth No. 2 Containing the following timber as cruised by one of the most reliable timber cruisers in Ontario.

Favorable terms can be arranged:—

| | |
|---|---|
| BIRCH | 10,950,000 ft. |
| MAPLE | 4,000,000 ft. |
| HEMLOCK | 2,000,000 ft. |
| ELM | 100,000 ft. |
| PINE | 100,000 ft. |
| CEDAR poles 25' up 50' | 5,000 |
| SPRUCE & BALSAM Cordwood | 5,000 cords |
| HARDWOOD CORDWOOD first-class | 90,000 cords |
| PRICE | $26,184.00 |

F. C. Clarkson, Assignee,
E. R. C. Clarkson & Son,
E.o.I. 5-11 TORONTO.

### For Sale Dry Lumber

1 car 8/4 Hard Maple, good widths.
1 C. & B. 50 1/1 1sts and 2nds.
3 cars 4/4 Beech 1 C. & B. allowing.
20 1/1 2 Common.
1 car Bass 4/4 Mill Run.
E. V. Wilson, Shanty Bay, Ontario. 11-12

### WHITE PINE LUMBER

### For Immediate Shipment—1920 Cut—Should Be Bone Dry

About 30,000 ft. 2 in.
" 18,000 ft. 1 in.
" 2,000 ft. 3 in.
Apply to J. A. Farnsworth, Cookshire, Quebec. 6-T.f.

## Machinery Wanted

### Wanted

Second hand independent feed works for saw carriage double friction from 30" to 36" face Drum for 2" line carriage to run 60 ft. Write us nearest size you have to offer. A. Hunter & Sons, Gooderham, Ont. 11

## Machinery For Sale

### Machine for Sale

1 new type C-3 Yates Moulder. For price and particulars regarding equipment apply Box 864 Canada Lumberman, Toronto. 8-11

### For Sale

1 E. Long Mfg. Co. Lath Mill with 11 saws.
1 Standard Machinery Co. 7 Saw Lath Bolter with 21 saws.
1 Diamond Iron Works 5 Ft. Horizontal Band Resaw, slat bed, with 3 saws.
1 28-Ton Lima Geared Locomotive, standard gauge.
Schroeder Mills & Timber Co., Pakesley, Ontario. Milwaukee, Wis. 9-12

### Engines, Boilers, etc., for Sale

One "Williams" Upright Engine 6" x 6"
One Upright Engine 5" x 6"
Six Return tubular boilers of following dimensions:-
One "Butterfield" 72" x 14' - 3½" tube - ½" shell.
One "Polson" 64" x 14' - 3½" tube - ½" shell
One "Doty" 60" x 15' - 4" tube - ½" shell
One "Doty" 60" x 14½' - 4" tube - ½" shell
One "Doty" 60" x 15' -4" tube - ½" shell
One "Inglis" 60" x 16' - 3" tube - ½" shell
One double acting "Northey" Fire pump, 6" suction, 5" discharge, 14" steam cylinder, 9" water cylinder, 12" stroke, Capacity 450 gallons per minute.
One "Northey" feed pump 6 x 4 x 7" stroke, Capacity 60 gallons per minute.
One brass Mill steam whistle.
For further particulars apply The Conger Lumber Co Limited., Parry Sound. Ontario. 24 T.f.

### Used Machinery

Boilers, Generator Sets, belted and direct drive, pumps, concrete mixers, pipe and sawmill machinery. Specialty Equipment Co., 66 Ottawa Street, Montreal 9-14-E.o.I.

### Corliss Engine for Sale

An E. Leonard & Sons 18" x 36" horizontal 175 H.P. Corliss Steam Engine, heavy duty girder frame and outbearing; 12' x 24" Band Wheel and Ball Governor; first class condition. Will sell at a bargain. Box 914 Canada Lumberman, Toronto. 11

### Wickes Gang

GANG: No. 12 Wickes Gang, 40" sash, 18" stroke, steam binder rolls, front and back in two sections, feed and oscillation combined, 1906 model, and has been in use for five years. We furnish with this gang 11 rolls for cants and stock, one filing machine, and 4 sets of saws.
THE PEMBROKE LUMBER CO.,
1t.f. Pembroke, Ont.

## Good Values

### Subject to Prior Sale

Band Resaw, Connell & Dengler, 54 and 60"
Band Rip Saw, Yates No. 281.
Circular Resaw, 44".
E. B. Hayes Dowell Gluer and Driver.
E. B. Hayes Standard Power Door Clamp.
Jointers, 16" and 24".
Matcher and Sizer, 30" x 12" American.
Matcher, 14" Woods.
Matcher, Hardwood American No. 229.
Matcher, 30" x 8" Connell & Dengler.
Moulder, Hermance 10" wide open side.
Moulder, Woods No. 2 light inside.
Moulder, Berlin 10" No. 118 inside.
Moulder, Woods 5 head, inside.
Planers, all sizes, single and double.
Sanders, 3-drum, 30, 42, 48 and 60".
Saws, circular, power feed, several makes.
Timber Sizers, Yates and American.
Woodworking Machinery Co., of Buffalo,
54 Mechanic Street,
Buffalo, N.Y.
9-e.o.I.-T.f.

## Situations Wanted

Circular sawyer, 10 years' experience right or left hand. Good references. Address Marshall Pettefer, Coe Hill, Ont. 11

Experienced trimmer or edger man. Good references. Address Harold O'Neil, Coe Hill, Ontario. 11

Wanted Position as Salesman—Would consider propositions on Commission basis for City. Experienced—references. Box 925 Canada Lumberman, Toronto. 11-13

Lath Maker wants position to run Lath or Picket Mill by the Day. 14 years' experience. References if required. Box No. 882 Canada Lumberman, Toronto. 9-11

Sash and Door Salesman—Young man with nine years' experience as Assistant Estimator and Order Clerk in factory making all kinds of millwork. Can work from plans and make details. Box 922, Canada Lumberman, Toronto. 11

Position wanted—As head shipper, have had over twenty years' experience in lumber trade, in different parts of Eastern Canada; have served in various capacities—Shipper and Yard Foreman, Salesman (both wholesale and retail) Scaler and Walking Boss. Hold Quebec Scaling License. Can furnish A1 references. Apply Box 920 Canada Lumberman, Toronto. 11

## Business Chances

### Carelessness with Matches

The habit of carrying "strike
anywhere" matches loose in the
pocket results in many serious
fires. In taking something out
of the pocket a match drops out
on the floor of barn or other
place, is stepped on and results
in a fire.—Deputy Fire Marshal
Lewis, Ontario.

### Trees Attract Birds

An interesting and unexpected
feature of tree planting· in the
Prairie Provinces is that in regard
to birds. Since considerable
planting has been done around
Regina, the Provincial Game
Guardian reports that several
species of birds that have never
been seen in that part of the
country before have taken up
their abode in Wascana park and
in the trees around the Parliament Buildings.

## The New Sales Tax on Lumber

According to a statement made by Hon. W. S. Fielding,
Minister of Finance, in his annual Budget speech at Ottawa,
the new sales tax situation on lumber is as follows:—

An increase of 50% on all sales taxes is now in effect,
starting on the morning of May 24th. Where the tax was
formerly 2%, it is now 3%, and where the tax was formerly
3%, (this applies to certain articles manufactured out of lumber, such as sash, doors, window frames, etc.,) it is now 4½%.

In connection with lumber, when the manufacturer sells
to the wholesaler, he collects the 3%, after which there is no
further tax upon re-sale; when the manufacturer sells direct
to the retailer, he also collects 3%.

## C. L. A. May Hold Summer Meeting

It is probable that a midsummer meeting of the Canadian Lumbermen's Association may be held either in July or August to discuss
trade conditions, production, the export situation and the general
outlook.

A. E. Clark, of Toronto, president of the C. L. A., has sent out
a questionnaire to the various directors and, in the great majority
of instances, the response favor a summer gathering, which would
be held at a week-end with a day or two of entertainment. The
question will be considered at the next meeting of the C. L. A.
Executive and a decision reached. If the directors endorse the proposition, a selection will be made of the time and place of assembly.

Hon. A. K. MacLean, chairman of the special parliamentary
committee on freight rates, has written the Canadian Lumbermen's
Association, asking that body if it would like to appear before the
members for a hearing. The C. L. A. officers have replied that they
would, and it is expected that a notification will be sent later of the
date when the lumbermen will be afforded an opportunity to
present their arguments.

## Valuable Eastern Timber Lands Change Hands

One of the largest timber deals on record in the Maritime
Provinces was concluded during the last few days and it is understood that $2,000,000. was involved in the turn-over.

The timberlands and licenses in New Brunswick of Chas. T.
White & Sons, Limited, Sussex, N. B., and the lands and licenses
in Nova Scotia of the Davison Lumber and Mfg. Co., Bridgewater,
N. S., were turned over to Hollingsworth & Whitney, Limited, who
recently secured a federal charter in Canada with a capital of $4,000,-
000, and headquarters in Halifax. This new company of Hollingsworth & Whitney Co. who are paper manufacturers, Boston, was
incorporated to take over Canadian properties.

Besides timber areas belonging to the White Company, which
aggregate nearly 50,000 acres in New Brunswick, the sale also included the transfer of licenses on 83 square miles of Crown Lands.
M. L. Madden vice-president and H. E. Fales, treasurer of the firm,
were in St. John recently.

The Davison Company, whose properties have been acquired,
have been in liquidation for some time. Their timberlands are located in
Lunenburg, King's, Annapolis and Queen's Counties in Nova Scotia,
while the White properties are situated in St. John, King's and Albert
Counties in New Brunswick, and Cumberland County in Nova Scotia.
Those in New Brunswick include lands at Little Salmon River, Alma,
West River and Point Wolfe. Three mills were included in the
purchase, including those at Alma and West River.

It is said that Hollingsworth & Whitney, Limited, intend erecting pulp mills in both Nova Scotia and New Brunswick.

A despatch from Campbellton, N. B. says there is no truth in
a report of amalgamation of lumber concerns there. The facts, the
despatch says, are that United States interests in two large concerns
are negotiating a loan to pull business out of a hole the recent slump
in lumber has placed it. A large trust company has had, for the last
week or two, cruisers going through the timber limits to ascertain
their value to secure this loan.

The city council of New Westminster, B. C., has leased a portion of the Indian Reserve on the North Arm to the Westminster
Paper Mills, at the head of which is J. J. Herb, who for many years
was superintendent of the Interlake Tissue Paper Company's mills
at Merritton, Ont. It is announced that the Westminster Paper Co.
are anxious to go ahead with the building of the mill as soon as possible. Several western capitalists have become interested in the
venture, which promises to be a success.

# Review of Current Trade Conditions

## Ontario Trade is Good in the Larger Cities

General business conditions in the lumber arena continue to improve slowly although in certain localities trade is yet being reported as spotty. The general trend, however, is upward, and in softwoods the volume is steadily increasing owing to the active building campaign which is going on, not only in the larger cities, but also manifesting itself in several smaller towns. Practically all the sawmills in Eastern Ontario have got off to a good start. Log driving conditions have, with few exceptions, been favorable, and there has been an abundance of labor which has in most cases accepted the decreased wages offered without any serious kick.

Throughout the lumber industry there is a better feeling prevailing than has been evident for some months, and while nothing like a boom is taking place, the outlook is steadily growing encouraging. There is a sane optimism among the majority of wholesalers and manufacturers, and even rural retailers are reporting that business is beginning to loosen up. If the crop prospects continue good, they say that the trade can look for a considerable demand from the agricultural districts which have not been consuming much lumber for some time. It is also stated that if this additional market is provided, the lumber business may become quite active this fall.

Hemlock is moving freely. There is a scarcity of 2 x 8, 2 x 10 and, in fact, other sizes. Retailers say that it is very difficult to get the assorted sizes required. White pine mill culls are moving rather slow but mill run is in good requisition across the line and locally as well.

In hardwoods some movement has been developed in the lower grades in thick stock, but as yet has not gained much impetus. Generally speaking, the demand for hardwoods in Canada is quiet but several firms report good sales across the border in thick birch, elm and maple. Prices in some instances particularly on the lower ends, are badly shot to get rid of stock. It is expected, however, that business in the hardwood line will pick up quite a bit within the next few weeks. One wholesaler recently said that in four weeks there would be no dry birch of five quarter and thicker in firsts and seconds and selects, on the market owing to the scarcity of the stock.

The export rate on lumber from Ontario points to the ports of Montreal and Quebec has been reduced by 1 to 2 cents per 100 lbs., plus terminal charges. The present export rate from Midland to Montreal is now 21 cents and from the same point to Quebec 23½ cents. The new rate became effective recently. Overseas business is beginning to brighten up.

Flooring manufacturers are enjoying an active business and are consuming considerable quantities of oak, maple and birch. In the better class of houses there is also quite a quantity of hardwoods being used for interior trim. Furniture factories are, however, rather quiet at present and are not factors in the market. On the whole the upper grades in hardwood remain quite strong with an upward tendency due to the stock scarcity and demand, particularly from across the border. Generally speaking, however, hardwoods are not yet as active or as strong as softwoods.

There are certain other features of the market which are arousing anxiety and one is the scarcity of shingles. From all over Ontario and the East come calls for quick shipments of B. C. red cedar shingles, which wholesalers are not able to supply. Deliveries are promised most any time within three to six weeks, but some representatives of B. C. mills are not accepting any orders for shingles. Retail lumber dealers report that due to the house-building activity in many centres there has been an unprecedentedly large call for shingles, and nearly all stocks are very low while some dealers have not a single bundle in their yards. The price is strengthening all the while.

White pine lath are rather scarce and firm in price. The supply of winter-cut lath is also about used up, and prices for them are stiffening. The lath department of many sawmills is now in operation but it will be about a month before the dry stock comes on the market. In the meantime a large quantity of spruce lath from Northern Ontario and New Brunswick is coming in and some jack pine lath, which are held at a firm figure. As to whether lath will maintain present quotations or not, remains to be seen, but the impression is that there will be a decrease in the figure asked along about the first of June.

In regard to the house-building boom, as the movement is gaining in momentum and volume each week, the query arises,—How long will it last? The general verdict is that it will continue until the shortage of dwellings is fully met or, in other words, until the supply adequately satisfies the call for homes and prices begin to sag. Those who have given the situation careful study, do not believe there is much of a possibility of over-production in the housing line for some time yet. The natural increase in population, the opening up of new sections, the desire of wage-earners to own and occupy better domicies and the anticipated resumption of industries in the near future should contribute to the stability and permanence of the housing situation. Then, too, owing to the ravages of time, a large number of formerly serviceable buildings have become dilapidated and unsanitary. Anything would answer during the war but that has passed. People were then willing to live in a shack and wear their old garments, but this state of affairs no longer obtains. Few can read the statistics of building permits issued in practically every city and town in Canada or view the work now under way in almost every centre without feeling that a building era is here at last and that the next few years are bound to see a steady demand for lumber and other materials that augurs well for the future and expansion of the forest products business.

## Halifax Reports Fair Demand With Low Prices

Since the opening of spring there has been no improvement in the price of Eastern lumber. Stocks of certain specifications are in good demand in the American market, and moving freely, but strange as it may seem, in the face of a fairly good demand, prices show a disposition to weaken.

While this may be mainly due to pauses whose explanation is in the realm of financial or trade exports, it is quite certain there are superficial reasons which have a strong bearing on the situation which are not far to seek. Many do not look for the return of good business until the British market returns to relieve the pressure on the American market. And in addition to this an entirely new source of supply has been opened up by the building of the Panama Canal. Western Stocks are being shipped in to the New England States from Washington and Oregon, and although they are not so well liked by the trade, they are a very formidable competitor against Eastern spruce and hemlock.

If reports reaching here are true, probably the worst feature of the situation is the fact that lumber is being carried by the steamship companies plying between the western coast and New England points as return cargos and consequently the rate of freight charged is not a matter of first importance.

It is reported that the regular rate has been fixed at $12.00 per M., but in many cases where no cargoes are offering the steamship companies buy cargos on the coast and sell them in New York or some other eastern port, at prices netting a freight as low as $5.00 and $6.00 per M.

When this rate is contrasted with a rate of $6.50 per M. on lumber from maritime ports to New York or Sound, and when it is remembered that the lower grades of western lumber enters into competition with Eastern spruce, it is not difficult to understand the very low prices offering at the present time. That this is merely a phase of present conditions, which will be adjusted as normal conditions return, there is little reason to doubt. This business must be a losing proposition both for the steamship companies and for the lumbermen on the coast, and as soon as his regular markets are able to absorb the output, he will naturally lose interest in the New England market.

Another feature of trade with the United States, which, while it is satisfactory from the stand-point of international trade in general, but which means considerable less return to the lumber-shipper is the return to normal currency value. Last year and the previous year, prices were based more or less on the premium obtained for New York funds. During the past five or six months the Canadian dollar has returned almost to par in the United States. In other words the United States currency has depreciated, relatively, without any compensating advance in the price of our lumber on the American market.

Freight rates, both water and rail, constitute a very serious problem to the Eastern shipper. Recently, owing to the strike in the United States coal-fields, there have been no return cargoes of coal offering to the coasters, and as a consequence, freights by vessel have

View of Mills in Sarnia.

# BUY THE BEST

Retailers and woodworking establishments who like to get A1 NORWAY and WHITE PINE LUMBER always buy their stocks from us because we can ship them on quick notice. It pays to have the goods, but it pays better to "deliver" them.

We also make a specialty of heavy timbers cut to order any length up to 60 feet from Pine or B. C. Fir.

*"Rush Orders Rushed"*

# Cleveland-Sarnia Sawmills Co., Limited
### SARNIA, ONTARIO

B. P. Bole, Pres.    F. H. Goff, Vice-Pres.    E. C. Barre, Gen. Mgr.    W. A. Saurwein, Ass't. Mgr.

gone from $6.00 to $6.50 per M., and at this figure the demand for vessels seems to be in excess of the supply.

So far as rail shipments to the United States or even to domestic points is concerned, the excessive freight rates still in effect places this method of transportation out of reach for all practical purposes. It is impossible to employ language too strong to express the ruinous effect the policy of the railways in maintaining the war-time tariff is having on the lumber industry in the maritime provinces in common with other industries. For the railways to urge the need of revenue as a sufficient reason for maintaining existing rates, is merely begging the question. The revival of shipping under a fair freight tariff, would more than make up for any loss that would be incurred by the lower rates. Many of the smaller operators have already been forced to quit, and others must inevitably suspend operations until the freight rates are reduced to a point where they can operate profitably. Recent press dispatches report that the rate on pulp-wood has been reduced by one third. The case for the lumber industry has been repeatedly and ably presented before the proper authorities, and any discrimination in favor of other classifications will not be tolerated.

The reduction recently made by the Steamship Companies covering liner shipments to Great Britain from 100s. to 85s. on softwood, and from 110s. to 95s. on hardwood has had very little effect in stimulating exports to the British market from the lower ports. While the cut is a move in the right direction, it is too small to be of any real benefit, as it does not place Canadian firms on a comparative basis with European countries where they have the advantage of a much lower rate.

Comparing the situation as it exists today with a year ago, the feeling on the whole is considerably more optimistic, and there seems to be considerable foundation for the belief that the balance of the year will see a steady improvement, and some advance in price. The winter cut was restricted by climatic conditions, and a very large proportion of what was manufactured has already been marketed. The summer cut is going to be very small, and with stocks on hand light, provided the demands holds out, the manufacturer feels that he should realize more satisfactory prices for his output.

## Montreal Reports Better Business and Outlook

A better tone characterises the Montreal market. Lumber, especially spruce, is still being sold at low prices, but the demand is growing to an extent that should strengthen values. Prices have been on a basis which has made it difficult for most wholesalers catering to the local trade to secure a profit, the retailers being disinclined to purchase unless the lumber was very cheap. The increase in building has a tendency to counterbalance this condition, for although there is a large quantity of lumber on offer, the demand is steadily expanding, and is likely to still further improve. Throughout Montreal district residences are being constructed in large numbers, and each week sees a gain in the permits issued. Several important projects are also going ahead, contractors stating that competition is very keen for this work.

"It looks to me," said one wholesaler. "As if we are on the eve of a distinctly better period. it is true that prices are not satisfactory for local business, but there are signs of a stronger market in which the manufacturer, wholesaler, and retailer will be able to make reasonable profits. Even now certain lines are commanding very fair prices. One great trouble is that Montreal will take such low class lumber, price being the main consideration."

Local wholesalers have been free buyers of the British Government stocks, a considerable quantity having been purchased within the past few days.

The hardwood market is a little better in tone and slightly more active for the best ends, but the low ends are still very difficult to dispose of.

There has been an advance of from 50 cents to $10.00, averaging $4.00, in B. C. forest products practically all on upper stocks. The mills are reported to be very busy—hence the advance. At the same time business has been booked here at prices, at least, $2.00 under the list.

Lath is a steady market. With the demand on a fair scale the mills are not inclined to shade prices.

The woodworking plants are busy, a portion of the orders being for outside points.

A considerable amount of lumber is being exported to the U. K. The season has opened in more promising fashion than last, when practically nothing was done during the first month. As in Quebec, representations have been made to the shipping companies in the direction of lower freights, but the response was not favorable, on the ground that the present rates are fair.

The British Government stocks are being rapidly disposed of.

considerable amounts having been sold within the last two weeks. The total in hand is not large. The stocks sold cover a wide territory so far as destination is concerned. The United Kingdom has taken substantial blocks, a considerable quantity has gone to Canadian firms. and United States buyers have also taken fair amounts. With regard to Canada, Montreal wholesalers have bought freely, while very extensive blocks have been disposed of to Maritime Province firms.

## Ottawa Witnesses Upward Trend in Demand

A further improvement in conditions marked the Ottawa lumber market during the closing period of May, when it was generally reported by the trade that stocks were beginning to move a little better. Prospects are, that the growth of the market was a sound one and would continue.

The increase in business while it was not as great as had been hoped for earlier in the year, was generally considered as being satisfactory. The principal demand came from the United States and was mostly for the mill run grades of pine. The movement of these stocks, exporters stated, indicated that increased building was being undertaken in the United States, which would mean an augmented demand.

In and around Ottawa the condition of the market was regarded as being fair and showing signs of improvement. Building permits for April were considerably greater than during the corresponding month a year ago, and the trade believed that the volume of building to be undertaken during June, would consume fairly large stocks.

Additional strength to the lumbermen's view regarding the expected increase in local building was reflected by the action of the civic authorities in continuing the work on the new civic hospital which will cost over three million dollars, and also of the Collegiate Board, to continue with new Collegiate Institute which will cost between a quarter and half a million dollars.

With the retailers, stocks for repairs and alterations moved more freely and it was reported that an increased demand for stocks suitable for new building was becoming evident. "The gain in trade while it has not been startling during the past two weeks is, it appears a healthy one and from now on; the market should continue to make headway and increase in firmness, was the opinion expressed by one of the large wholesalers and exporters to the United States."

It was also intimated that the Eastern stocks had begun to move more freely and Ottawa dealers pointed out that as soon as these were out of the way that the movement in Ottawa Valley stocks would likely show a considerable increase.

The announcement of Mr. E. W. Beatty, president of the Canadian Pacific Railway, before the House Committee on May 19th, that a downward revision of freight rates on basic commodities was desirable, was received with considerable satisfaction on the part of the lumber trade. High freight rates, as has been repeatedly stated, have for a considerable time tended to slow up the market, and contributed towards the present "considered" high price of lumber.

The C.P.R., Mr. Beatty said, was willing to put the reduced rates into effect, on the approval of the Railway Commission. Several lumbermen were of the opinion that if the reduced changes were put into effect and applied to lumber shipments that it would mean a stimulus to the trade.

Conditions with the sawmills and woodworking factories did not show much change, though the latter reported that they were beginning to get busier, and looked for a general increase in trade from now on.

The log drive of the various companies in the valley was reported to be progressing favorably. There is plenty of water in sight to get the logs to the mill. During the last two weeks of May the sawmill of John R. Booth Ltd., was put in operation though it did not run to capacity.

Prices, though the volume of trading was not as great as during the pre-war years, continued to hold firm, and with several companies it was reported as being unlikely that any considerable drop in price would be made for some time.

Transportation and labor conditions did not show any change.

## Rates on Lumber to Come Down

Replying to questions from New Brunswick members, C. A. Hayes, vice-president of the Canadian National lines, recently at Ottawa informed the special house committee on railway transportation costs that the C.N. proposed a cut of 16 or 17 per cent. in the freight rates on lumber.

President Beatty, of the C.P.R., giving evidence a few days ago, suggested a cut of 11.70 per cent.

## Shipment of Deals Starts Early at Quebec

Shipment of timber and deals from the port of Quebec to fill the orders obtained by the representatives of the Quebec exporting firms commenced earlier this season of navigation. The steamer "Venusia" which sailed for London in the second week of April, was partly loaded with spruce deals, shipped by the firm of Goodday & Co., and W. & J. Sharples, and was followed by the sailing of the steamer "Vennonia" carrying oak timber and spruce deals shipped to London by the firm of W. & J. Sharples, the Louise Lumber Co., deals and birch planks shipped by John Burstall & Co. The "Canadian Trapper," of the Canadian Government Merchant Marine fleet, arrived at Quebec April 14th and will take on a part cargo of oak timber and deals for the port of Greenock, shipped by W. & J. Sharples, on which the rate of freight paid on all three shipments is 85 shillings.

Judging by advices being received from the Quebec export lumber firms from their United Kingdom agents, a new feeling of confidence is commencing to pervade the lumber purchasing powers in the United Kingdom; nevertheless a spirit of optimism is still lacking, owing to the keen competition from the continental European countries and the high rate of freight still prevailing on lumber carried in the liners from Canada to the British Isles. There is not the least doubt that if the steamship companies were to reduce their freight rates to 70 or 75 shillings, the Canadian trade through their agents abroad would be able to place orders for timber and deals in Canada which would enhance the prospects for the late midsummer and fall trade shipments.

The Canadian lumber interests are not a little exercised over the high freight rates in vogue on the railways which prevent the trade from participating in the lumber markets of the United States, in consequence of the unprecedented boom in the building trade in every centre of the United States from Maine to California and Texas. The Canadian eastern lumber interests are practically shut out of the business being carried on in the New England, New York, Pennsylvania and Middle States, while the Western Canada lumber interests must equally suffer for the same barriers to taking part in American lumber activities by the abnormal rates charged for freight which would permit them to gain by the opportunities offered in the Middle and Western States.

---

## Big Lumber Shipments to Various Points

During the month of March the Canadian Western Lumber Co., Fraser Mills, B. C., made some heavy shipments by water to Japan, Atlantic Seaboard, China, Australia and New York. The ships loaded at Fraser Mills and carried heavy cargoes as follows:—

Japanese—S. S. "Oregon Maru", Japan, 150,393 feet. American —S. S. "Delco", Atlantic Seaboard, 810,350 feet. Canadian—S. S. "Canadian Prospector", China, 564,266 feet. Japanese—S. S. "Erie Maru", Japan, 795,648 feet. Canadian—S. S. "Canadian Transporter", Australia, 917,222 feet. American—S. S. "Lehigh", New York, 1,004,809 feet. a total of 4,242,688 feet.

---

## Classes of Wood for Free Entry

In a previous issue the "Canada Lumberman" gave details of the proposed duties on lumber imported into the U. S. under the McCumber Bill. The sections of the bill showing the classes of wood on the free list are as folllows:—

Par. 1683. Wood: Logs; timber, round, unmanufactured, hewn, sided or squared otherwise than by sawing; round timber used for spars or in building wharves; firewood, handle bolts, shingle bolts; and gun blocks for gunstocks, rough hewn or sawed or planed on one side; sawed boards, planks, deals, and other lumber, not further manufactured than sawed, planed, and tongued and grooved; clapboards, laths, ship timber; all of the foregoing not specially provided for: Provided, That if there is imported into the United States any of the foregoing lumber, planed on one or more sides and tongued and grooved, manufactured in or exported from any country, dependency, province, or other subdivision of government which imposes a duty upon such lumber exported from the United States, the President may enter into negotiations with such country, dependency, province, or other subdivision of government to secure the removal of such duty, and if such duty is not removed he may by proclamation declare such failure of negotiations, and in such proclamation shall state the facts upon which his action is taken together with the rates imposed, and make declaration that like and equal rates shall be forthwith imposed as hereinafter provided; whereupon, until such duty is removed, there shall be levied, collected, and paid upon such lumber, when imported directly or indirectly from such country, dependency, province, or other subdivision of government, a duty equal to the duty imposed by such country, dependency, province, or other subdivision of government upon such lumber imported from the United States.

Par. 1683a. Woods: Cedar, lignum-vitae, lancewood, ebony,

---

---

box, granadilla, mahogany, rosewood, satinwood, Japanese white oak, Japanese maple, and all forms of cabinet woods, in the log, rough or hewn only.

Par. 1684. Woods: Sticks of partridge, hair wood, pimento, orange, myrtle, bamboo, rattan, india malacca joints, and other woods not specially provided for, in the rough, or not further advanced than cut into lengths suitable for sticks for umbrellas, parasols, sunshades, whips, fishing rods, or walking canes.

Mechanical groundwood pulp and newsprint are on the free list, while chemical pulp is subject to a duty of 5%, but in each case there is a penalty clause in case any country should forbid the export of printing paper, pulp or pulpwood, or should impose an export fee. The object of the penalty clause is to force Canada to lift the embargo on pulpwood cut from Crown lands.

---

## Eastern Firm Says Fir Will Stay

A recent market letter sent by Simpson, Clapp & Co., New York, says in part: Although there has been no change in the market of importance enough to warrant a market letter in the middle of the month, we are writing to correct an impression which seems to be growing among the mills and the lumber trade journals. In other words, we saw recently in the "Canada Lumberman" the statement from one of their correspondents that in a few months fir would cease to come into Atlantic Coast markets and then the price of spruce would rise. Let us assure you that Douglas fir is in these markets to stay, and that the supply is inexhaustible for our lifetime at least. Furthermore, the chances are very good that ocean freight levels will gradually go lower. The steamers which are engaged in this intercoastal trade will not be taken off this trade, as they were in most cases especially designed for it, and are not suitable for offshore trade in competition with world tonnage. We would regret to have the mills fool themselves into thinking fir would disappear as a competitor as this would only hurt themselves and lead them to false plans.

Douglas fir is here for good and because of its quality and the fact that it is manufactured of even lengths and widths, fir is going to be from now on the determining factor in the price levels of merchantable lumber.

Of course spruce, particularly from the East will always be in demand at proportionate value, but it will have to be manufactured to suit the market, not the log, to get best results. The mills who will continue to manufacture random will continue to receive sacrifice prices, as there is no necessity or inducement for the yards buying undesirable widths or lengths in spruce, when they can buy anything they want in fir at around $27.00 to $29.00. This is just plain common sense.

There is also an impression down East that the price of spruce lath can be manipulated upward by maintaining a small production.

# EDGINGS

Queen Charlotte Timber Holding Co., Ltd., has been incorporated with a capital of $750,000.

The shingle mill of Skinner & Cole, North Keppel, Ont., which was recently destroyed by fire, is being rebuilt.

The planing mill of James Hill, Ottawa, recently suffered a slight fire loss which was covered by insurance.

The sawmill of Leger Giguere, at Weedon, Wolfe County, Que., was recently destroyed by fire. The loss is $17,000.

The New Westminster plant of the Dominion Shingle Company has been purchased by J. A. McKercher of Vancouver.

The Wm. Shirton Co., of Dunnville, Ont., are completing a handsome and commodious storage shed for dressed lumber. The shed will be one of the finest in Western Ontario.

The McDonagh Lumber Co., Toronto, have removed from 203 Confederation Life Bldg., to 226 in the same building where they have much larger and more commodious quarters.

The Lakefield Lumber Co., of Lakfield, Ont., with which the late John Duignan, of Peterboro, was associated, is not operating this season but the stock of lumber on hand is being sold off.

C. Kleanza Co. is completing the erection of a new sawmill at Usk, B. C., which will have a sawing capacity of 50,000 feet a day. There are 2,000,000 feet of logs at this point ready for cutting.

The biggest shipment of shingles ever made from Vancouver, B. C. went forward recently by the steamer Melville Dollar for New York. The consignment consisted of about 20,000,000 shingles.

Joseph Gauthier and Joseph Colbern, of Prince George, B. C., are erecting a shingle mill near Usk, B. C. They have secured the cedar rights from the timber limits of the Hayward Lumber Co.

The C. A. Larkin Co. are now occupying their new offices, 229 Confederation Life Bldg., Toronto, having removed from the sixth floor in the same building. Their new quarters are large, bright and airy.

At the annual meeting of Price Bros. & Co., held recently in Quebec, owing to the absence of Sir William Price in Europe, only routine business was discussed. The officials of the company were all re-elected.

A recent report from New Westminster, B. C., says that lumbermen report that the demand for lumber for the overseas markets is such that they contemplate putting on an extra shift in the mills, providing transportation difficulties can be adjusted.

The city council of New Westminster, B. C. granted a lease of a portion of the Indian Reserve on the North Arm some time ago to the United Shingle Co., which took over the shingle mill from the Dominion Shingle & Cedar Co., which was defunct.

The Spruce Falls Co., of Neenah, Wis., recently suffered a loss of pulpwood logs owing to the breakage of a boom on the Kapuskasing River. The logs were all carried down stream. Trouble is also reported from Faulkier, where Matt. Boivin lost 30,000 logs when a boom broke.

A charter has been granted to the M. Martin Lumber Co., Limited, to carry on a general lumber business and to deal in timber, logs, piling, poles, posts, wood and other products of the forest. The capital stock of the company is $50,000. and the head office is in Huntsville, Ont.

J. B. Mackenzie, of Georgetown, who in addition to many other lines turned out by him, started the manufacture of incubators and brooders, has worked up a nice business in this line. The firm sold more than they expected and are planning to go into the venture on a much larger scale next year.

In the Black Bay District near Port Arthur 10,000 cords of pulpwood were cut during the past season by Donald Clark. This wood was recently shipped to Muskegon, Mich., being towed to Port Arthur in rafts and there loaded into a tow barge and ship by means of an automatic pulpwood loader.

A lath mill at South Tetegouche, owned by George S. Kerr of Campbellton, N. B., which has been in operation all winter caught fire a few days ago and was totally destroyed. Time after time piles of finished lumber nearby caught fire as well as cedar logs yarded close to the mill. The loss is a heavy one.

At the recent meeting of the directors of the Canadian Forestry Association at the Chateau Frontenac, Quebec City, it was decided to institute a national essay competition for school children with

twenty seven prizes, to promote juvenile interest in forest protection, tree planting, care of the farm wood and allied topics.

Standard Lumber & Supplies, Limited, with headquarters in Windsor, Ont., and a capital stock of $40,000, has been granted a provincial charter to carry on the business of lumbering, logging, etc., and to deal in wood products of all kinds. Among the incorporators are James Kerby and Edwin J. Kerby, of Detroit, Mich.

The Union Lumber Co., Winnipeg, Man., recently made arrangements with the Starr Lumber Co., Chicago whereby they will represent the Union concern in that territory. W. E. Allen, who is head of the Starr Lumber Co., was formerly sales manager for the Finger Lumber Co., Winnipeg, manufacturers of Saskatchewan spruce.

The recent rains which visited New Brunswick have relieved a tense situation for the loggers, many of whom had their drives held up on small tributaries, but which are now in their retaining ponds at the mills. The sawmills at St. John which have been idle for nearly a year are expected to start up shortly in the face of a growing demand for lumber.

The two forestry survey parties of the Crown Land Department which have been employed in Restigouche county since the latter part of January, have completed their work and returned to Fredericton, N. B. One of these parties was employed on the headwaters of the Charlo River and the other on the Upsalquith River. These are the only parties which have been out this year.

The Grant Lumber Co., Ltd., Tilley, N. B., have been incorporated with a capital of $24,000 to conduct a general lumber business manufacturing and dealing in all kinds of timber products. H. Coleman Grant, Drummond, N. B., Warren Dexter, Doaktown, N. B. and Frank E. Whitman of Winthrop, Mass. are among the incorporators.

The International Paper Co., of Three Rivers, P. Q., has been making some shipments of newsprint by water down the St. Lawrence on the Atlantic Coast to New England. This has been carried out owing to the high freight rates and also to demonstrate the feasibility of water carriage. The mill itself turns out between 45 and 50 tons a day with a present capacity of about 70 to 75 tons.

Hon. T. D. Pattullo, Minister of Lands for British Columbia, informed a deputation from Prince George, B. C., that eastern interests would not erect a pulp mill as had been contemplated. Mr. Pattullo stated that while he was recently in Montreal he had conferred with the promoters, but negotiations had failed by reason of their insistence upon fixed royalties.

George W. Lee, of the Temiskaming & Northern Ontario Railway Commission, sees big business for this line which is owned by the Ontario Government and runs from North Bay to Cochrane, Ont. Mr. Lee says that there are 200,000 cords of pulpwood drying on sidings along the T. & N. O., and this, in addition to thousands of cords at present being cut, is expected to provide suitable business for the line this summer.

The Lake Ainslie Lumber Co., which was organized by some American capitalists, expects to begin operations at Lake Ainslie, C. B. One of the principal promoters of the organization is Donald McDonald of Catalone, N. S. Considerable sawmill equipment is being shipped in to Cape Breton and the plant will cut about 30,000 feet of hardwood daily. A furniture factory will also be erected as well as drying kilns, etc.

At the request of Hon. J. L. Perron, Minister of Highways for Quebec, Hon. Honore Mercier, Minister of Lands, has given authority to use plants from the Berthierville Government Nursery for the embellishment of the Quebec-Montreal and other Provincial Highways. It is understood that special arrangements will be made shortly by which residents on those roads will be supplied free with plants, which they can plant on the roadside.

According to John M. Imrie, of Edmonton, there is a rich and large tract of spruce timber within one hundred and twenty-five miles of Edmonton, in what is known as the Lower Athabasca Valley, which is untapped, and there is in ten years great pulp and paper enterprises will spring up there. In the region there is an abundant supply of water power and also natural gas which would permit of the cooking of the sulphite pulp at a very low cost.

A raft owned by the River Valley Lumber Co. at Oromocto, N. B., was considerably broken up when the company's tug endeavored to get through the draw of the C.N.R. bridge with a raft and tow of logs at the mouth of the Nashwaak River. Rafting operations by the Nashwaak Pulp and Paper Co., of St. John, N. B., have been going on at a rapid rate. More than 3,000,000 feet of logs have been rafted by the electric rafting machine which was installed last year, and the first consignment was delivered in St. John some time ago, thereby establishing what is believed to be a record for the early handling of logs in the St. John River.

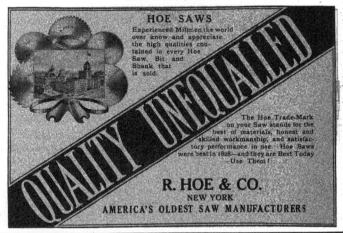

Linn Logging Tractor Hauling Approximately 9000 ft. of Hardwood—Doyle's Rule

# THE LINN LOGGING TRACTOR

The Linn Logging Tractor designed exclusively for Winter Log Hauling in the North Country. Was developed and perfected in actual logging operations in the north Woods.

The best Hardwood is each year becoming further distant from Mill or railroad and is consequently greatly increasing in cost.

In many cases very valuable wood cannot be touched, because horses cannot haul it the necessary distance.

At best, and under very easy conditions, a good team cannot haul more than 1,000 ft. —and a good team will seldom walk faster than two miles an hour.

The Linn Logging Tractor solves this difficulty. Travelling, as it does, at six miles an hour—operating without difficulty down steep sandhills and up stiff grades—and over river and lake ice—hauling such loads as above pictured.

By its use the operator is enabled to place his logs at the Mill for very low cost.

*—Logging Department—*

## MUSSENS LIMITED

Dubrule Building                                        MONTREAL

## ALPHABETICAL INDEX TO ADVERTISERS

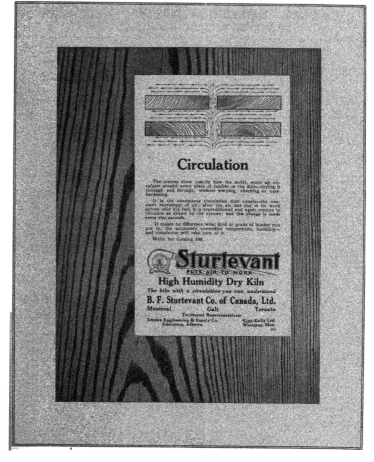

## Circulation

The arrows show exactly how the moist, warm air circulates around every piece of lumber in the Kiln—drying it through and through, without warping, checking or case-hardening.

It is the continuous circulation that counts—the constant movement of air; after the air has put in its work across only 3½ feet, it is reconditioned and again returns to circulate as shown by the arrows; and this change is made every nine seconds.

It makes no difference what kind or grade of lumber you put in; the accurately controlled temperature, humidity—and circulation will take care of it.

Write for Catalog 248.

## Sturtevant
### PUTS AIR TO WORK

### High Humidity Dry Kiln
*The kiln with a circulation you can understand*

### B. F. Sturtevant Co. of Canada, Ltd.
Montreal          Galt          Toronto

Territorial Representatives:
Empire Engineering & Supply Co.          Kipp-Kelly Ltd.
Edmonton, Alberta.          Winnipeg, Man.

# CANADA LUMBERMAN BUYERS' DIRECTORY

The following regulations apply to all advertisers:—Eighth page, every issue, three headings;
quarter page, six headings; half page, twelve headings; full page, twenty-four headings

**ALLIGATORS**
Payette Company, P.
West, Peachy & Sons

**BABBITT METAL**
Canada Metal Co.
General Supply Co., of Canada, Ltd.

**BALE TIES**
Canada Metal Co.
Laidlaw Bale Tie Company

**BAND MILLS**
Hamilton Company, William
Waterous Engine Works Company
Yates Machine Company, P. B.

**BAND SAW BLADES**
Simonds Mfg. Co.

**BAND RESAWS**
Mershon & Company, W. B..
Yates Machine Co., P.B.

**BARKERS**
Bertrand, F. X., La Compagnie
Manufacouriere.
Smith Foundry & Machine Co.

**BEARING METAL**
Canada Metal Co.
Beveridge Supply Co., Ltd.

**BEDSTEADS (STEEL)**
Simmons Limited

**BELT DRESSING**
Dominion Belting Co.
General Supply of Canada, Ltd.

**BELTING**
Canadian Consolidated Rubber Co.
Dominion Belting Co. . . . . . . . . .
General Supply Company
Goodhue & Co., J. L.
Gutta Percha & Rubber Company
D. K. McLaren, Limited
York Belting Co.

**BLOWERS**
Reed & Co., Geo. W.
B. F. Sturtevant Co., of Canada, Ltd.
Toronto Blower Company

**BOILERS**
Engineering & Machine Works of
Canada
Hamilton Company, William
Waterous Engine Works Company

**BOILER PRESERVATIVE**
Beveridge Supply Company
Shell-Bar, Boico Supply Co., Ltd.

**BOX MACHINERY**
Yates Machine Company, P. B.

**CABLE CONVEYORS**
Engineering & Machine Works of
Canada.
Hamilton Company, William
Waterous Engine Works Company

**CAMP SUPPLIES**
Davies Company, William
Dr. Bell Veterinary Wonder Co.
Johnson, A. H.
Turner & Sons, J. J.
Woods Manufacturing Co., Ltd.

**CANT HOOKS**
General Supply Co., of Canada, Ltd.
Pink & Company, Thomas

**CEDAR**
Bury & Co., Robt.
Cameron Lumber Co.
Canadian Western Lumber Co.
Chesbro, R. G.
Dry Wood Lumber Co.
Fesserton Timber Company
Fesserton Timber Company
McElroy Lumber Co., Ltd.
Muir & Kirkpatrick
Rose, McLaurin, Limited
Terry & Gordon
Thurston- Flavelle Lumber Co.
Vancouver Lumber Company.
Victoria Lumber & Mfg. Co.

**CHAINS**
Canadian Link-Belt Company, Ltd.
General Supply Co., of Canada, Ltd.
Engineering & Machine Works of
Canada
Hamilton Company, William
Pink & Company, Thomas
Waterous Engine Works Company

**CLOTHING**
Woods Mfg. Company

**CONVEYOR MACHINERY**
Canadian Link-Belt Company, Ltd.
General Supply Co., of Canada, Ltd.
Hamilton Company, William
Hopkins & Co., Ltd., F. H.
Waterous Engine Works Company

**CORDWOOD**
McClung, McLellan & Berry

**COUPLING (Shaft)**
Engineering & Machine Works of
Canada

**CRANES**
Hopkins & Co., Ltd., F. H.
Canadian Link-Belt Company, Ltd.

**CUTTER HEADS**
Shimer Cutter Head Company
Yates Machine Co., P.B.

**CYPRESS**
Maus Lumber Co., Chas. O.
Wistar, Underhill & Nixon

**DERRICKS AND DERRICK
FITTINGS**
Hopkins & Co., Ltd., F. H.

**DOORS**
Canadian Western Lumber Co.
Gardiner, P. W. & Son
Mason, Gordon & Co.
Terry & Gordon

**DRAG SAWS**
Gerlach Company, Peter
Hamilton Company, William

**DRYERS**
Coe Manufacturing Company
B. F. Sturtevant Co., of Canada, Ltd.

**DUST COLLECTORS**
Reed & Co., Geo. W.
B. F. Sturtevant Co. of Canada, Ltd.
Toronto Blower Company

**EDGERS**
Hamilton Company, Ltd., William
Green Company, G. Walter
Long Mfg. Company, E.
Payette Company, P.
Waterous Engine Works Company
Yates Machine Co., P.B.

**ELEVATING AND CONVEYING
MACHINERY**
Canadian Link-Belt Company, Ltd.
Engineering & Machine Works of
Canada
Hamilton Company, William
Waterous Engine Works Company

**ENGINES**
Engineering & Machine Works of
Canada
Hamilton Company, William
Payette Company, P.
Waterous Engine Works Company

**EXCELSIOR MACHINERY**
Elmira Machinery & Transmission
Company

**EXHAUST FANS**
B. F. Sturtevant Co. of Canada, Ltd.
Toronto Blower Company

**EXHAUST SYSTEMS**
Reed & Co., Geo. W.
B. F. Sturtevant Co. of Canada, Ltd.
Toronto Blower Company

**FIBRE BOARD**
Manley Chew

**FILES**
Disston & Sons, Henry
Simonds Canada Saw Company

**FIR**
Apex Lumber Co.
Associated Mills, Limited
Bainbridge Lumber Company
Cameron Lumber Co.
Canadian Western Lumber CO.
Canfield, P. L.
Chesbro, R. G.
Dry Wood Lumber Co.
Fesserton Timber Co.
Grier & Sons, Ltd., G. A.
Heeney. Percy E.
Knox Brothers
Mason, Gordon & Co.
McElroy Lumber Co.
Robertson & Hackett Sawmills
Rose, McLaurin, Limited
Terry & Gordon
Timberland Lumber Company
Timms, Phillips & Co.
Underhill Lumber Co.
Vancouver Lumber Company
Vanderhoof Lumber Company
Victoria Lumber & Mfg. Company

**FIRE BRICK**
Beveridge Supply Co., Limited
Elk Fire Brick Company of Canada
Shell-Bar, Boico Supply Co., Ltd.

**FIRE FIGHTING APPARATUS**
Waterous Engine Works Company

**FITTINGS**
Crane Limited

**FLOORING**
Cameron Lumber Co.
Chesbro, R. G.
Long-Bell Lumber Company

**GEARS (Cut)**
Smart-Turner Machine Company

**GUARDS (Machinery and Window)**
Canada Wire & Iron Goods Co.

**HARDWOODS**
Anderson Lumber Company, C. G.
Anderson, Shreiner & Mawson
Atlantic Lumber Company
Barrett, Wm.
Black Rock Lumber Co.
Bury & Co., Robt.
Cameron & Company
Edwards & Co., W. C.
Fassett Lumber Company, Limited
Fesserton Timber Co.
Gillespie, James
Gloucester Lumber & Trading Co.
Grier & Sons, Ltd., G. A.
Hart, Hamilton & Jackson
Heeney, Percy E.
Knox Brothers
Kinnon Lumber Co.
Mason & Company, Geo.
Maus Lumber Co., Chas. O.
McDonagh Lumber Company
McLennan Lumber Company
McLung, McLellan & Berry
Pedwell Hardwood Lumber Co.
W. & J. Sharples
Spencer, Limited, C. A.
Strong, G. M.
Summers, James R.

**HARDWOOD FLOORING**
Grier & Sons, Ltd., G. A.

**HARNESS**
Beal Leather Company, R. M.

**HEMLOCK**
Anderson Lumber Company, C. G.
Anderson, Shreiner & Mawson
Bartram & Ball
Beck Lumber Company
Bourgouin, H.
Canadian General Lumber Company
Edwards & Co., W. C.
Fesserton Timber Co.
Grier & Sons, Ltd., G. A.
Hart, Hamilton & Jackson
Hocken Lumber Company
Mason, Gordon & Company
McCormack Lumber Company
McDonagh Lumber Company
McElroy Lumber Co., Ltd.
Robertson & Hackett Sawmills
Spencer, Limited, C. A.
Stalker, Douglas A..
Terry & Gordon.
Vancouver Lumber Company
Vanderhoof Lumber Company

**HOISTING AND HAULING
ENGINES**
General Supply Co., of Canada, Ltd.

Hopkins & Co., Ltd., F. H.

**HOSE**
General Supply Co., of Canada, Ltd.
Gutta Percha & Rubber Company

**INSURANCE**
Barton & Ellis Company
Burns Underwriting Company
Hardy & Company, E. D.
Rankin Benedict Underwriting Co.

**INTERIOR FINISH**
Cameron Lumber Company
Canadian Western Lumber Co.
Canfield, P. L.
Eagle Lumber Company
Mason, Gordon & Co.
Rose, McLaurin, Limited
Terry & Gordon

**KILN DRIED LUMBER**
Bury & Co., Robt.

**KNIVES**
Disston & Sons, Henry
Simonds Canada Saw Company
Waterous Engine Works Company

**LARCH**
Otis Staples Lumber Company

**LATH**
Anderson, Shreiner & Mawson
Apex Lumber Company
Austin & Nicholson
Beck Lumber Company
Brennen & Sons, F. W.
Cameron Lumber Company
Canadian General Lumber Company
Carew Lumber Company, John
Chaleurs Bay Mills

Dadson, A. T.
Eagle Lumber Company
Fassett Lumber Company, Limited
Foley Lumber Company
Fraser Bryson Lumber Co., Ltd.
Gloucester Lumber & Trading Co.
Grier & Sons, Ltd., G. A.
Harris Tie & Timber Company, Ltd.
Larkin Company, C. A.
Mason & Company, Geo.
McLennan Lumber Company
Miller, W. H. Company
New Ontario Colonization Company
Otis Staples Lumber Company
Power Lumber Company
Price Bros. & Company
Shevlin-Clarke Company
Spencer, Limited, C. A.
Terry & Gordon
U. G. G. Sawmills, Limited
Union Lumber Company
Victoria Harbor Lumber Company

**LATH BOLTERS**
General Supply Co. of Canada, Ltd.
Hamilton Company, William
Payette & Company, P.

**LOCOMOTIVES**
Engineering & Machine Works of
Canada
General Supply Co. of Canada, Ltd.
Hopkins & Co., Ltd., F. H.
Climax Manufacturing Company
Montreal Locomotive Works

**LINK-BELT**
Canadian Link-Belt Company
Hamilton Company, William

**LOCOMOTIVE CRANES**
Canadian Link-Belt Company
Hopkins & Co., Ltd., F. H.

**LOGGING ENGINES**
Engineering & Machine Works of
Canada

Hopkins & Co., Ltd., F. H.
Mussens Limited

**LOG HAULER**
Engineering & Machine Works of
Canada
Green Company, G. Walter
Holt Manufacturing Company
Hopkins & Co., Ltd., F. H.
Payette & Company, P.

**LOGGING MACHINERY AND
EQUIPMENT**
General Supply Co. of Canada, Ltd.
Hamilton Company, William
Holt Manufacturing Company
Hopkins & Co., Ltd., F. H.
Payette & Company, P.
Waterous Engine Works Company
West, Peachey & Sons
Mussens Limited

**LUMBER EXPORTS**
Fletcher Corporation

**LUMBER TRUCKS**
Hamilton Company, William
Waterous Engine Works Company

**LUMBERMEN'S BOATS**
Adams Engine Company
Gidley Boat Company
West, Peachey & Sons

**LUMBERMEN'S CLOTHING**
Kitchen Overall & Shirt Company

**MATTRESSES**
Simmons Limited

**METAL REFINERS**
Canada Metal Company

**NAILING MACHINES**
Yates Machine Co., P.B.

**OAK**
Long-Bell Lumber Company
Maus Lumber Co., Chas. O.

**PACKING**
Beveridge Supply Company
Gutta Percha & Rubber Company

**PANELS**
Bury & Company, Robt.

**PAPER**
Beveridge Supply Company
Price Bros. & Company

**PINE**
Anderson Lumber Company, C. G.
Anderson, Shreiner & Mawson
Atlantic Lumber Company
Austin & Nicholson
Barratt, William
Beck Lumber Company
Black Rock Lumber Co.
Cameron & Company
Cameron Lumber Company
Canadian General Lumber Company
Canadian Western Lumber Co.
Canfield, P. L.
Chesbro, R. G.
Cleveland-Sarnia Sawmills Company
Cox, Long & Company
Dadson, A. T.
Dudley, Arthur N.
Eagle Lumber Company
Edwards & Co., W. C.
Excelsior Lumber Company
Fesserton Timber Co.
Fraser Bryson Lumber Co., Ltd.
Gillies Bros. Limited
Gloucester Lumber & Trading Co.
Gordon & Company, George
Goodday & Company, H. R.
Grier & Sons, Ltd., G. A.
Harris Tie & Timber Company, Ltd.
Hart, Hamilton & Jackson
Hettler Lumber Co., Herman H.
Hocken Lumber Company
Julien, Roch
Keewatin Lumber Co.
Lay & Haight
Lloyd, W. Y.
Loggie Company, W. S.
Long-Bell Lumber Company
Mason, Gordon & Co.
Mason & Company, Geo.

*Packard
Trucks
Save
Money*

It is perfectly plain that the Packard Truck never could have attained outstanding leadership were it not a sound, saving investment, from every viewpoint of truck operation.

*The comparatively low purchase price of Packard Trucks—generally lower than prices of other trucks of comparable quality—adds great emphasis to Packard value.*

The seasoned and stable organization building the Packard Truck will continue to advance and fortify still further its leadership and its reputation for lower-cost haulage.

**Packard Service**

In 585 cities and towns throughout the United States, Packard Truck Service Stations give owners highly skilled service at a reasonable cost. Packard Truck costs, always low because sound, Packard construction minimises need of repair, are held still lower by this expert, broadcast service.

*Packard Trucks range in capacity from 2 tons, to 7½ tons; and in price from $3,100 to $4,500*

PACKARD MOTOR CAR COMPANY, DETROIT

# PACKARD TRUCKS

McCormack Lumber Company
McFadden & Malloy
McLennan Lumber Company
Montreal Lumber Company
Muir & Kirkpatrick
Northern Lumber Mills
Otis Staples Lumber Company
Parry Sound Lumber Company
Rolland Lumber Company
W. & J. Sharples
Shevlin-Clarke Company
Spencer, Limited, C. A.
Stalker, Douglas A.
Strong, G. M.
Summers, James R.
Terry & Gordon
Union Lumber Company
Victoria Harbor Lumber Company
Watson & Todd, Limited

**PLANING MILL EXHAUSTERS**
Toronto Blower Company

**PLANING MILL MACHINERY**
Mershon & Company, W. B.
B. F. Sturtevant Co. of Canada, Ltd.
Toronto Blower Company
Yates Machine Company, P. B.

**POPLAR**
Keewatin Lumber Co.

**POST GRINDERS**
Smith Foundry Company

**POSTS AND POLES**
Anderson, Shreiner & Mawson
Canadian Tie & Lumber Co.
Dupuis, Limited, J. P.
Eagle Lumber Company
Harris Tie & Timber Company, Ltd.
Long-Bell Lumber Company
Mason, Gordon & Co.
McLennan Lumber Company
Terry & Gordon

**PULLEYS AND SHAFTING**
Canadian Link-Belt Company
General Supply Co. of Canada, Ltd.
Green Company, G. Walter
Engineering & Machine Works of
   Canada
Hamilton Company, William

**PULP MILL MACHINERY**
Canadian Link-Belt Company
Engineering & Machine Works of
   Canada
Hamilton Company, William
Payette & Company, P.
Waterous Engine Works Company

**PULPWOOD**
British & Foreign Agencies
D'Auteuil Lumber Company
Price Bros. & Company
Scott, Draper & Company

**PUMPS**
General Supply Co. of Canada, Ltd.
Engineering & Machine Works of
   Canada
Hamilton Company, William
Hopkins & Co., Ltd., F. H.
Smart-Turner Machine Company
Waterous Engine Works Company

**RAILS**
Gartshore, John J.
Hopkins & Co., Ltd., F. H.

**ROOFINGS**
(Rubber, Plastic and Liquid)
Beveridge Supply Company
Reed & Co., Geo. W.

**RUBBER GOODS**
Dunlop Tire & Rubber Goods Co.
Gutta Percha & Rubber Company

**SASH**
Midland Woodworkers

**SAWS**
Atkins & Company, E. C.
Disston & Sons, Henry
General Supply Co. of Canada, Ltd.
Gerlach Company, Peter

Green Company, G. Walter
Hoe & Company, R.
Radcliff Saw Mfg. Company
Shurly Lumber Co., Ltd., T. F.
Shurly-Dietrich Company
Simonds Canada Saw Company

**SAW GRINDERS**
Smith Foundry Company

**SAW MILL LINK-BELT**
Canadian Link-Belt Company

**SAW MILL MACHINERY**
Canadian Link-Belt Company
General Supply Co. of Canada, Ltd.
G. Walter Green Company, Ltd.
Hamilton Company, William
La Compagnie Manufacture, F. X.
   Bertrand
Long Mfg. Company, E.
Mershon & Company, W. B.
Parry Sound Lumber Company
Payette & Company, P.
Waterous Engine Works Company
Yates Machine Company, P. B.

**SAW SHARPENERS**
Hamilton Company, William
Waterous Engine Works Company

**SAW SLASHERS**
Hamilton Company, William
Payette & Company, P.
Waterous Engine Works Company

**SHINGLES**
Apex Lumber Company
Associated Mills, Limited
Brennen & Sons, P. W.
Cameron Lumber Company
Campbell-MacLaurin Lumber Co.
Canadian Western Lumber CO.
Carew Lumber Company, John
Chaleurs Bay Mills
Chesbro, R. G.
D'Auteuil Lumber Company
Dry Wood Lumber Co.
Eagle Lumber Company
Fraser, Companies Limited
Gillespie, James
Gloucester Lumber & Trading Co.
Grier & Sons, Ltd., G. A.
Harris Tie & Timber Co., Ltd.
Heaps & Sons
Heeney, Percy E.
Mason, Gordon & Co.
McLennan Lumber Company
Miller Company, Ltd., W. H.
Rose, McLaurin, Limited
Stalker, Douglas A.
Terry & Gordon
Timms, Phillips & Company
Vancouver Lumber Company
Vanderhoof Lumber Company

**SHINGLE & LATH MACHINERY**
Green Company, C. Walter
Hamilton Company, William
Long Manufacturing Company, E.
Payette & Company, P.
Smith Foundry Company

**SILENT CHAIN DRIVES**
Canadian Link-Belt Company

**SLEEPING EQUIPMENT**
Simmons Limited

**SLEEPING ROBES**
Woods Mfg. Company, Ltd.

**SMOKESTACKS**
Hamilton Company, William
Reed & Co., Geo. W.
Waterous Engine Works Company

**SNOW PLOWS**
Pink & Company, Thomas

**SOLDERS**
Canada Metal Company

**SPARK ARRESTORS**
Reed & Company, Geo. W.
Waterous Engine Works Company

**SPRUCE**
Anderson, Shreiner & Mawson
Barrett, Wm.
Cameron Lumber Company
Campbell, McLaurin Lumber Co.
Canadian Western Lumber Co.
Chesbro, R. G.
Cox, Long & Company
Dadson, A. T.
Dudley Arthur N.
Passett Lumber Company, Ltd.
Fraser, Companies Limited
Fraser Bryson Lumber Co., Ltd.
Gillies Brothers
Gloucester Lumber & Trading Co.
Goodday & Company, H. R.
Grier & Sons, Ltd. G. A.
Harris Lumber Co., Frank H.
Hart, Hamilton & Jackson
Hocken Lumber Company
Julien, Roch
Keewatin Lumber Co.
Larkin Co., C. A.
Lay & Haight
Lloyd, W. Y.
Loggie Co. W. S
Mason, Gordon & Co.
McCormack Lumber Co.
McDonagh Lumber Co.
McElroy Lumber Co.
McLennan Lumber Company
Muir & Kirkpatrick
New Ontario Colonization Co.
Northern Lumber Mills
Power Lumber Co.
Price Bros. & Company
Rolland Lumber Co.
Rose, McLaurin, Limited
W. & J. Sharples
Spencer, Limited, C. A.
Strong, G. M.
Terry & Gordon
U. G. G. Sawmills, Limited
Vanderhoof Lumber Company

**STEAM SHOVELS**
Hopkins & Co., Ltd., F. H.

**STEEL CHAIN**
Canadian Link-Belt Company
Hopkins & Co., Ltd., F. H.
Waterous Engine Works Company

**STEAM PLANT ACCESSORIES**
Waterous Engine Works Company

**STEEL BARRELS**
Smart-Turner Machine Company

**STEEL DRUMS**
Smart-Turner Machine Company

**TARPAULINS**
Turner & Sons, J. J.
Woods Manufacturing Company Ltd.

**TANKS**
Hopkins & Co., Ltd., F. H.

**TENTS**
Turner & Sons, J. J.
Woods Mfg. Company

**TIES**
Austin & Nicholson
Carew Lumber Co., John
Canadian Tie & Lumber Co.
Chaleurs Bay Mills
D'Auteuil Lumber Co.
Gloucester Lumber & Trading Co.
Harris Tie & Timber Company Ltd.
McLennan Lumber Company
Miller, W. H. Co.
Price Bros. & Company
Scott, Draper & Co.
Terry & Gordon

**TIMBER BROKERS**
Bradley, R. R.
Cant & Kemp
Farnworth & Jardine
Wright, Graham & Co.

**TIMBER CRUISERS AND
ESTIMATORS**
Savage & Bartlett
Sewell, James W.

**TIMBER LANDS**
Department of Lands & Forests, Ont.

**TOWING MACHINES**
Payette & Company, P.
West, Peachey & Sons

**TRACTORS**
Holt Manufacturing Company
Hopkins & Co., Ltd., F. H.
Mussens Limited

**TRANSMISSION MACHINERY**
Canadian Link-Belt Company
Engineering & Machine Works of
   Canada
General Supply Co. of Canada, Ltd.
Grand Rapids Vapor Kiln
Hamilton Company, William
Waterous Engine Works Co.

**TRUCKS**
Tudhope Anderson Co.

**TURBINES**
Engineering & Machine Works of
   Canada
Hamilton Company, William
B. F. Sturtevant Co. of Canada, Ltd.

**VALVES**
Crane, Limited

**VAPOR KILNS**
Grand Rapids Vapor Kiln
B. F. Sturtevant Co. of Canada. Ltd.

**VENEERS**
Bury & Co. Robt.

**VENEER DRYERS**
Coe Manufacturing Company
Sturtevant Co., B. F. of Canada Ltd.

**VENEER MACHINERY**
Coe Manufacturing Company

**VETERINARY REMEDIES**
Dr. Bell Vetinerary Wonder Co.
Johnson, A. H.

**WARPING TUGS**
West, Peachey & Sons

**WATER WHEELS**
Engineering & Machine Works of
   Canada
Hamilton Company, William

**WIRE**
Canada Metal Co.
Laidlaw Bale Tie Company
Canada Wire & Iron Goods Co.

**WIRE CLOTH**
Canada Wire & Iron Goods Co.

**WIRE ROPE**
Canada Wire & Iron Goods Co.
Hopkins & Co., Ltd., F. H.
Dominion Wire Rope Co.
Greening Wire Co., B.

**WOODWORKING MACHINERY**
General Supply Co. of Canada, Ltd.
Long Manufacturing Company, E.
Mershon & Company, W. B.
Waterous Engine Works Co.
Yates Machine Company, P. B.

**WOOD PRESERVATIVES**
Beveridge Supply Company
Austin & Nicholson
New Ontario Colonization Company
Power Lumber Co.

**WOOD PULP**
Austin & Nicholson
New Ontario Colonization Co.
Power Lumber Co.

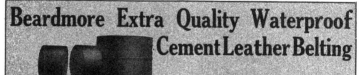

# Increase Your Profits! *YOU can do it by installing*
## the "Long" Heavy Duty Band Mill—the most economical means of manufacturing lumber

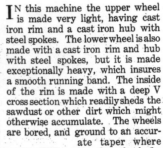

IN this machine the upper wheel is made very light, having cast iron rim and a cast iron hub with steel spokes. The lower wheel is also made with a cast iron rim and hub with steel spokes, but it is made exceptionally heavy, which insures a smooth running band. The inside of the rim is made with a deep V cross section which readily sheds the sawdust or other dirt which might otherwise accumulate. The wheels are bored, and ground to an accurate taper where they fit on the shafts to which they are keyed and held in place by large nuts.

In fact from end to end this machine is built with one object in view—the most economical means of manufacturing lumber, which in other words simply means greater profits for you.

### Write us for details.

# The E. Long Manufacturing Co., Limited
## Orillia                                    Canada

Robt. Hamilton & Co., Vancouver
Gormans, Limited,
    Calgary & Edmonton

A. R. Williams Machinery Co.,
of Canada, Ltd.
Williams & Wilson Ltd., Montreal

# Not Sufficient Refuse
## to Keep Burner Going

The above is not a record of a few days or a few weeks but is the usual state in a mill cutting 250,000 ft. per day with logs averaging about 18 inches diameter.

The remarkable condition is due to the marvelous efficiency of the **Waterous Super Resaw** which is handling **all** the slabs and half logs in this mill.

The Waterous super resaw handles one slab at a time at high speed, consequently the sawyer is changing gauge continuously and each slab is subjected to quick analysis.

The feed is speeded faster than the man can get the slabs into the machine, leaving a space of about 18 inches between the ends of the slabs and permitting the setter to change the size instantly so that every available, inch of good lumber is obtained from each slab.

In the Waterous super resaw the slab and the board separate instantly by gravity, the slab falling on the slasher chains and the board going to the edger.

Why not investigate the wonderful possibilities of this machine?

# Waterous
### BRANTFORD, ONTARIO, CANADA

Molson's Bank Building, Vancouver                    Winnipeg, Man.

# Would You Allow Your Scaler to work without his "stick"

YOU scale your lumber; of course, you do. Now, why? So that you will be sure of the lumber measurements.

Now, what about the time records, the time of your employees. Is it not just as important, if not more so, that you have a correct unchangeable record of the number of hours each employee puts in?

Does your time-keeper hand you time sheets made out in pencil, with possibly numerous changes? What assurance have you that these are correct, and yet your purchase of time annually is possibly one of your largest? Have you ever figured what three or ten minutes a day loss per man would mean to you annually? Well, it would mean a very serious loss.

International Time Recorders and Job Time Recorders will eliminate any loss by giving you an absolute record of the time each man enters or leaves his place of work. The employee recognizes that these records are unchangeable and he realizes that you do also and that it eliminates unpleasant discussions over time shortages.

Is it not worth while finding out if an INTERNATIONAL TIME RECORDER will save money for you? It will cost you nothing but it may save you many dollars.

Many, many of our lumber industries are fully equipped with International Time Recorders and they recommend them in no uncertain terms.

## International Business Machines
### Company, Limited

F. E. MUTTON, Vice-President and General Manager

**Head Office and Factory: 300-350 Campbell Avenue, Toronto**

HALIFAX, 44 Granville St. ST. JOHN, 59 Dock St. QUEBEC, 601 Merger Bldg.
MONTREAL... ... ... OTTAWA 58... ... LONDON, 50 ...
WATERVILLE, 44 Lincoln St. WINNIPEG, 327 McDermott Ave. VANCOUVER,
209 Cambie St. SASKATOON, 204 Third Ave. S.

Also manufacturers of International Dayton Scales and International
Electric Tabulators

# Canada Lumberman
*Founded 1880*

# "HAMILTON" PRODUCTS

"Hamilton" Machinery is built in a plant that has been specializing in **High Grade Dependable Saw Mill, Pulp Mill and Hydraulic Turbine Equipment** for over sixty years. We guarantee our products in material, design and workmanship to be the equal of any on the market, and to give perfect satisfaction wherever used.

No. 2 Jack Works

## "Quality First" Our Motto

### SAW MILL

Boom Chains
Warping Anchors
Capstans for Warping
Log Jacks
Log Deck Equipment
Band Mills
Log Carriages
Set Works (steam & hand)
Edgers
Husk Frames
Live Rolls and Drives
Slashers
Trimmers
Cut-off Saws
Lath Mill Machinery
Shingle Mill Machinery
Filing Room Machinery
Resaws (circular)
Hogs
Drag Saws
Gang Circulars
Twin Circulars
Steam Feeds
Friction Feeds
Transmission Machinery
Haul-up and Transfer
Chains
Refuse Burners
Conveyors

### SAW MILL—Cont'd.

Engines (slide and piston valve)
Boilers
Feed Water Heaters

### PULP MILL

Log Haul-Ups
Pulp Wood Slashers
Pulp Wood Conveyors
Barking Drums
Centrifugal Pulp Screens
   (horizontal and vertical)
Pulp Grinders
Centrifugal Stuff Pumps
   Simplex, Duplex and
      Triplex)
Stuff Pumps
Jordan Engines
Beating Engines
Slusher Tanks
Chippers
Chip Crushers
Chip Screens
   (rotary and flat)
Digester Fittings
Push Fans
Agitator Drives
Refuse Burners
Transmission machinery

### HYDRAULIC POWER PLANT

Water Wheels
Water Wheel Governors
Head Gate Hoists
Stop Log Winches
Trash Racks
Butterfly Valves
Power Transmission
Hand Power Travelling
   Cranes
Steel Feeder Pipes
Surge Tanks

### GENERAL

Gray Iron Castings
Brass Castings
Special Machines built to
   order
Patterns
Structural Steel Work
Transmission Machinery
Steel Plate Work
Tanks
Standpipes
Smoke Stacks
Boiler Breechings
Steel Pipe
Steel Bins and Hoppers

Horizontal Twin Turbine in Open Flume

# William Hamilton Co., Limited

Agents: J.L. Neilson & Co., Winnipeg, Man.    Peterboro, Ontario

# White Pine
# Red Pine
# Jack Pine
# Spruce
# Lumber
# and Lath

**UNION LUMBER COMPANY LIMITED**
701 DOMINION BANK BUILDING
TORONTO          CANADA

# Take a Tip From the Business Barometer

### It Says

## "NOW IS THE TIME TO STOCK UP"

"Is this a good time for lumbermen to stock up" is a question commanding universal attention. The answer is found in a survey of existing conditions in the building trade.

### Now is the Time to Buy Lumber Because

All sections of the country appear to be sharing to a greater or lesser degree in the general revival of business. Building reports show a surprising increase. There is a big demand all along the line for building materials. You can only meet this demand by having a thoroughly complete stock on hand.

### And Because

According to every indication there will be no further decline in lumber prices. To take full advantage of favorable prices means placing your orders now.

### And Finally Because

Procrastination is the thief of time—and profits. Carefulness is a virtue but confidence is better. You know your own local conditions—your good judgment tells you there is no time like the present to act.

In placing your orders remember our reputation for quality and service. We can make immediate shipments from Ontario, Quebec or British Columbia. Write us to-day for quotations.

# TERRY AND GORDON

### LIMITED

## CANADIAN FOREST PRODUCTS

HEAD OFFICE

### TORONTO

BRANCH
MONTREAL

EUROPEAN AGENTS

BRANCH
VANCOUVER

SPENCER LOCK & Co., LONDON, ENG.

Ontario Representatives for
THE BRITISH COLUMBIA MILLS TIMBER AND TRADING CO., VANCOUVER, B. C.

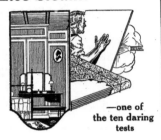

# BUY
## BRITISH COLUMBIA
# Red Cedar Shingles

The life of a British Columbia Red Cedar Shingle Roof can almost be gauged by the life of the nail with which the shingle is nailed in place. Judging from available data, the average life of the ordinary steel wire nail, which has been in such common use, is only from seven to twelve years. Some wire nails will last longer, depending upon the condition of exposure, climate and similar features, but considering our climate as a whole, at the end of from seven to twelve years a large percentage of wire nails will have rusted either completely through or so extensively that the first strong wind will complete the work. The shingles that have been held in position by such nails are then free to work down, permitting rains or melting snows to leak through and damage the interior of the structure. Examination will disclose that the fibre of the shingle itself is still in perfect condition, and a leaky roof, in the majority of occasions is due entirely to the use of faulty nails, but the average home owner, placed at such inconvenience, will not stop to reason this out and the poor wooden shingle comes in for more unjust abuse.

There are several kinds of nails which experience has proven will give lasting satisfaction, and the wise dealer will advise his customers of these satisfactory nails. A pure zinc shingle nail meets all the demands of durability required. Its principal drawback is its high cost and a slight tendency to bend under careless driving. Galvanized wire nails theoretically are rust proof, and if the galvanized coating is properly applied, and of sufficient thickness, such a nail will last as long as the shingle it holds in place. The life of this shingle roof, properly applied with these nails then is from 40 to 50 years. Pure iron nails, or the old cut or wrought nails are ideal but difficult to secure. Copper nails also constitute a perfect shingle nail.

# THE GREAT NATIONAL LUMBER JOURNAL

Pioneer and Leader
in the Industry

Canada Lumberman
/ounded 1880

Recognized Authority
for Forty Years

Vol. 42            Toronto, June 15, 1922            No.12

# Forward Movement of Nova Scotia Lumbermen

## How Producers and Distributors of Forest Products Down by the Sounding Sea Have Formed Aggressive Association—Bright Prospects for Organization

The Nova Scotia Lumbermen's Association was organized a few months ago and is making good progress. It has a live board of directors and capable, aggressive officers. During the past few weeks an active campaign for membership has been conducted with gratifying results. There are some four hundred lumbermen in Nova Scotia, large and small, and it is the intention of the directors to keep after these producers of forest products until they all come in to the Association.

In this issue the "Canada Lumberman" presents a group portrait of the newly-elected officers and directors. The picture gallery

R. B. Dickie, Stewiacke, N.S.
President of the Association

is complete with few exceptions, and readers of the "Canada Lumberman" will notice that no brighter or more pleasant- looking company of gentlemen have had their features illustrated in these columns. The "Nova Scotia boys" are, certainly, a lively-looking crowd, and are determined to make things hum. They realize that the lumbermen of every province in Canada have got together and formed an organization. The Acadians are determined not to be behind their brethren in other parts of the Dominion, and have got off to a satisfactory start. Every great association has had a small beginning, but as time went on such guilds or federations expanded in numbers and influence. This bids fair to be the history of the Nova Scotia organization.

There are many local problems to be taken up, domestic issues which affect only the men in the trade in the Bluenose province, and the Nova Scotia Lumbermen's Association is bound to create a better feeling, wider acquaintance, a more intimate touch and keener appreciation of the interests of the other fellow. Thus will the members be bound together in unity and fraternity and be able to reach an understanding on problems which individually they could not solve or take care of successfully. The members of the Executive

have been selected from various parts of Nova Scotia so that every part of the province is given adequate representation.

The officers and directors of the Nova Scotia Lumbermen's Association are,—

President, Rufus E. Dickie, Stewiacke.
Vice. Pres., I. J. Soy, (Maple Leaf Lumber Co.,) Amherst.
Sec. Treas. pro tem, E. A. Saunders, Halifax.

Executive:—M. R. Chappell, (Chappell's, Ltd.) Sydney; Chas. Hill, (Black Brook Lumber Co.,) Truro; C. A. Fownes, Sydney; A. S. McMillan, Antigonish; C. H. Read, Amherst; Fred. Campbell, Clarkesville; Colin C. Tyrer, (Colin C. Tyrer, Limited) Halifax; E. M. Curry, (Brooklyn Lumber Co.,) Brooklyn; F. C. Whitman, Annapolis; Peter G. Boutilier, (Cedar Lake Lumber Co., Ltd.) Tusket; George M. Goding, (Maitland Lumber Co.) Liverpool; F. H. Chambers, (Nova Scotia Steel & Coal Co.,) New.Glasgow; J. R. Gordon, (Milton Pulp & Paper Co.) Milton; Louis W. Logan, (F. J. Logan & Son) Musquodoboit Harbor; Percy L. Spicer, (Newville Lumber Co.) Parrsboro; G. T. MacNutt, (Standard Construction Co.) Halifax.

In a recent letter to the "Canada Lumberman" President Dickie sums up the whole situation comprehensively when he says,—"I have felt all along that Nova Scotia needed an organization, such as

I. J. Soy, Amherst, N.S.
Vice-President of the Association

we have now under way. Heretofore the lumbermen have not been able to get a permanent body going. In past years there have been one or two started. The Western Association was perhaps, the most successful and another one in another part of Nova Scotia, but through lack of interest and the firms represented going out of business, these organizations died out. We have started again and believe this time that we can keep things going. We have certainly got away to a good start, and if we can keep our members interested, we can ac-

complish something worth while. So far everyone is enthusiastic about our organization, and we are indebted to the "Canada Lumberman" for the full reports it has given us and its expressions of good wishes."

The lumber industry of Nova Scotia, while it is not the foremost activity of the province, still holds a high place in its industrial life. The past season was by no means an active one, trade being dull in the Maritime Provinces, the same as in other parts of the Canadian commonwealth. A competent authority has estimated that the production of long lumber in Nova Scotia for export and sale to local yards, in 1919-20, was 350,000,000 feet, b. m., valued at $10,500,-000, and in 1920-21, 175,000,000 feet valued at $3,500,000. The average value in the first year is put down at $30. per M., and the latter at $20. per M. these figures indicating approximately the difference in price in the two seasons.

These figures represent only a part of the forest products of Nova Scotia. There are besides,—pulp, cordwood, railway ties, barrel staves, pit props, ship timber, lath, shingles and other miscellaneous items of importance. The total value of the forest products of the province for 1921 is estimated at over $10,000,000.

Last year Nova Scotia suffered a good deal from forest fires owing to the prolonged drought. The number of acres burned was estimated 77,000. The cost of fighting the fires was, according to reports at the Legislative Buildings, Halifax, $40,000., while the estimated damage reached three times this amount.

In a recent issue of the "Canada Lumberman" one of the leading exponents of the industry in Nova Scotia made an interesting reference. His summing up shows what the lumbermen of the province have done without any central organization and now that they have one, the future should be much brighter. Here is a tribute.—"The lumber industry provides profitable employment for an important section of the population and at a season when other work could not easily be obtained. This applies not only to lumbering, as that term is usually employed, but to the gathering, manufacturing and utilization of all forest products. The importance of the lumber industry to Nova Scotia as a whole cannot be overstated. A considerable area of the province suitable for forest growth could not possibly be used for any other purpose."

### Forestry of the Province

In 1904 the Nova Scotia Government, in order to protect the forests from further damage by fire, passed an Act, entitled "The Forest Protection Act." which was consolidated in 1913, has reduced the annual fire loss to small proportions. In 1909 Dr. B. E. Fernow, of the University of Toronto, was engaged by the Provincial Government to make a reconnaissance survey of the forests of the province. Careful estimates in his report entitled "Forest Conditions of Nova Scotia" show that, in spite of the fact that an area of two million acres has at one time or another been so severely burned that it is now semi-barren of commercial trees, there were still, in 1912, 5,774,000 acres of coniferous saw timber on the mainland. The area, with the addition of that to be found on Cape Breton island, should yield ten billion feet of merchantable saw timber for Nova Scotia as a whole.

The reserve of pulpwood figured out at 24 million cords, viz.: 12,000,000 cords in the pulpwood and mine-prop forest of Victoria and Inverness counties, 2,000,000 in the other parts of Cape Breton island, and 10,000,000 cords on the mainland. The pure hardwood area of Nova Scotia amounted to 526,824 acres.

Timber conditions in Nova Scotia are related to the geological formation. The granite area, while seldom affording good farming land and showing a proportion of swamp and of natural or burned over barrens, has good forest soils, the thinner soil on the ridges for fir, that of the steeper slopes for mixed growth, that on the gentler slopes and on the bases for spruce and hemlock. The quartzite area, composed of rock less easily disintegrated than that of the granite they enclose, show more frequent barrens. It is the slate formations that occur in these areas and the better of the glacial deposits in the valleys that provide good farm lands and show a finer forest growth.

The spruce of Nova Scotia is not specially strong or durable but is much used for joists and light structural work, for inside and outside finish and for a variety of manufactured articles. The use of red pine for construction work has been replaced by Douglas fir or southern pine, but it is still used for masts, spars, piling and deck plank, and especially for car construction. It is considered the best eastern wood for paving blocks and for water tanks.

Hemlock is especially suitable for underwater construction and for joists, rafters, concrete forms, etc.

Birch maple and beech are used mainly for hardwood flooring, car construction and furniture.

Balsam fir is used for pulp, boxes and cooperages.

### Importance of the Industry

Poplar is the wood for excelsior and berry boxes.

Tamarack (hackmatack or larch) is used for ship-knees and treenails.

Apart from the fact that now most large manufactories save material and gain profit by using up their short pieces in the manufacture of smaller articles, it may be noted that shavings are sold for bedding, packing and for drying wet land, and small waste pieces as a substitute for gravel in cement work; that hardwood sawdust is good for smoking meat, and that sawdust besides its use for screw cleaning can be manufactured into valuable briquettes for fuel, and when combined with crushed marble is used as building material. Maple, birch and beech are the hardwoods mostly used for the extraction of acetic acid and methyl alcohol both of which are on the list of important Canadian exports. In Ontario and Quebec there are eleven such industries; there are none at present in Nova Scotia.

### Trying to Lift Embargo on Pulpwood

An examination of the clauses of the McCumber Bill relating to pulp and newsprint shows that another attempt is being made to force Canada to lift the embargo on the export of pulpwood cut from Crown Lands. A previous attempt by a Senate Committee was unsuccessful, and the authors of the McCumber Bill are trying to attain the same end by another method.

While the main object of the measure is to restrict general imports by the imposition of higher tariffs, the reverse is the case in respect to pulpwood. United States mills are very anxious to secure access to Canadian raw material in order to supplement their diminishing supplies, and the bill seeks to compel the Dominion to meet the needs of the American mills by imposing certain penalties on pulp and newsprint. The embargo has proved of great value to this country in that it has built up a large pulp and paper industry, in the place of Canada sending her pulpwood across the border to be manufactured into the finished products. It has also enabled Canada to compete in the markets of the world with newsprint in particular.

The McCumber Bill first allows the free admission of newsprint and groundwood, subjects chemical pulp to a duty of 5%—it is now free—and printing paper not otherwise provided for to a duty of ¼ cent per pound and 10% ad valorem. Then, in certain events, penalties are imposed which nullify the free admission and imposes higher duties on the other products referred to. The clause defining the penalties is in these terms:

"Mechanically ground wood pulp, including pulpboard in rolls, for use in the manufacture of wallboard: Provided, That whenever the President shall ascertain as a fact that any country, dependency, province, or other subdivision of government forbids or restricts in any way (whether by law, order, regulation, contractual relation, or otherwise, directly or indirectly) the exportation of, or imposes any export duty, export license fee, or other export charge of any kind whatever, either directly or indirectly (whether in the form of additional charge or license fee, or otherwise,) upon printing paper, mechanically ground wood pulp, or wood for use in the manufacture of wood pulp, he may, by proclamation declare such ascertainment setting forth the facts; whereupon, and until said proclamation shall be revoked, there shall be levied, collected, and paid upon mechanically ground wood pulp, when imported either directly or indirectly from such country, dependency, province, or other subdivision of government, a duty of 10 per centum ad valorem, and in addition thereto, an amount equal to the highest export duty or other export charge imposed by such country, dependency, province, or other subdivision of government, upon either an equal amount of mechanically ground wood pulp or an amount of wood necessary to manufacture such wood pulp, or an amount of printing paper ordinarily manufactured from such wood pulp."

The same penalties are attached to newsprint, chemical pulp, and printing paper. It will be noted that the penalties will apply to Canada in the case of all the four items named, as the Dominion comes under the clause by reason of the embargo on the export of pulpwood from Crown Lands. The object clearly is to compel the revocation of the embargo and thus avoid the penalties referred to, which, if carried into effect, would seriously affect Canada's export of newsprint, groundwood and chemical pulp to the United States. The bill is, in fact, an attempt to coerce Canada to open her forests for the benefit of American mills.

Pellow & McMeekin, lumber and general merchants, of Hearst, Ont., have recently installed a new set of E. Long trimmers and a new Cowan No. 232 knife grinder. They say conditions at Hearst are none too lively at the present time and very little lumber has been moving. The prospects for this summer and fall, they say, do not look very bright owing to the low price the settler in the district has to take for his pulpwood which leaves him little or nothing for branching out either in the way of new buildings or agricultural expenditure.

Colin C. Tyrer, Halifax, N.S.

M. R. Chappell, Sydney, N.S.

F. H. Chambers, New Glasgow, N.S

Chas. Hill, Truro, N.S.

E. M. Curry, Brooklyn, N.S.

P. L. Spicer, Parrsboro, N.S.

G. T. MacNutt, Halifax, N.S.

G. M. Goding, Liverpool, N.S.

A. S. McMillan, Antigonish, N.S.

J. R. Gordon, Liverpool, N.S.

F. C. Whitman, Annapolis Royal, N.S.

Fred. Campbell, Clarksville, N.S.

**Representative Eastern Lumbermen** who were recently elected members of the Executive of the newly organized Nova Scotia Lumbermen's Association

# How New Brunswick Safeguards Its Forests

### Recent Regulations Which Enjoin Upon All Classes the Necessity for Care, Precaution and Co-operation—"Be Careful of Fire" is Effective Slogan

The first fire in New Brunswick reported last year to the department of lands and mines was on May 7. This year there is only a few days difference but the fires appear to be more numerous and burning over larger areas. In April 1921 rain precipitation was recorded at 3.51 inches and this April 2.17 inches. The department of lands and mines in Fredericton, N. B. has issued a warning that the season is now here when danger from forest fires is imminent and New Brunswick must be prepared for a hazardous fire-season. Recent legislation makes municipal councillors responsible as fire wardens, except in the county of Westmoreland, which had its own special act passed. Councillors number 320 throughout the province. This added duty as fire fighters is not relished by the councillors, but each county has the remedy of putting into effect at any meeting of its county the same legislation which is in effect in Westmoreland. Under the act in effect in Westmoreland the municipal council can appoint a chief county fire warden and deputy wardens on recommendation of a majority of owners of forest lands in the county, and also can fix the rate of pay. Owners of fifty acres or more of forest lands and crown land licenses must contribute pro rata, to a protection fund which will be used for general fire fighting unless fire was caused by the owner or licensee or through his neglect. The department of lands and mines is now responsible for the fighting of fires on crown lands. The heavy cost of fighting fires on private owned lands in 1921 at Westreiff and other places made it necessary that a change be made. Now the owners or occupants of granted lands are responsible. If there is failure in that quarter the municipal councillor is the fire warden and can summon all males between the ages of sixteen and fifty years with certain exceptions. Services are to be given without pay and there is a maximum penalty of a fine of fifty dollars or thirty days in jail for failure or refusal.

The existing regulations require permits for the setting of fires after April 15. Wardens and councillors may issue them. The permit for such fires expired May 10, but special permits may be issued after this date, depending on weather conditions.

Any forest area can be set aside by the Minister of Lands and Mines as a reservation upon which no person shall enter for camping, fishing, hunting, picnicing or similiar purposes without a "travel permit."

According to present regulations each drive on a stream or river must appoint a foreman of the drive or foreman of the various sections of the drive, who will have the power to act as fire wardens and fight any fire in the vicinity.

The rate of wages on for fire fighting on crown lands when authorized by the department of lands and mines is considerably reduced. The rate is now by the calender day with board. Workmen get one dollar, foremen, time keepers and cooks $1.75 Rates for single and double teams and motor trucks also have been reduced.

The fire regulations also contain some interesting minor provisions. Indian chiefs are wardens on Indian reservations. Co-operative fire wardens work for private owners or firms and have powers extending only to the lands on which they operate and at the expense of the owners for whom they work.

The fire hazard in the Province of New Brunswick was emphasized in an editorial appearing recently in the St. John Times. The article was as follows:—"The unusually early outbreak and spread of brush fires in some parts of the province comes as very unpleasant news. If the rain of the last twenty-four hours is general it will do great good, but there will be need of the utmost vigilance throughout the next two months. The crown lands department has issued a pamphlet giving extracts from the forest fire laws as amended this year and if these were universally observed there would be much less danger. Not only can we not afford the loss of timber areas, but there is great danger to isolated houses and even to villages in portions of the wooded areas of the province. The loss through fires in the province recently is estimated at a quarter of a million dollars. Of course, this includes fires in towns and villages and the mills and houses of the Fraser Companies at Baker Brook; but whether in town or rural area the loss is complete and ought under proper conditions to be very largely avoidable. The people in general are too careless. Too many families are left homeless and too much property is destroyed because somebody neglected to take mere ordinary precautions against the spread of fire. We are approaching the season when campers and sportmen will be in the wilderness in large numbers and if they fail to realize their responsibilities heavy loss to the province as well as to individuals may result. Many people had a bitter experience in New Brunswick last year. It is a depressing fact that scarcely has the spring opened this year when reports of serious damages by fire in many parts of the province come to hand. More attention should be paid to this subject in the schools so that the rising generations may be taught to be more careful of our resources than are the citizens of today."

### Success in Prairie Tree Planting

There has been issued by the Forestry Branch of the Department of the Interior a bulletin (No. 72) entitled "Success in Prairie Tree Planting."

The object of the bulletin is to set forth the possibilities of tree-planting in general on the prairies, and more particularly to reveal the development of the co-operative tree-planting system inaugurated some twenty years ago by the Dominion Forestry Branch, the extent to which settlers have availed themselves of the plan and the general success of the plantations. Conclusions based on the experience obtained during the last score years regarding the best methods to follow in planting, cultivating and caring for the plantations generally, are given.

Prairie tree-planting has assisted agriculturists of the West in protecting their farm buildings and gardens by sheltered belts of those kinds of trees which tests have proved suitable. The stopping of sand-drifting by wind-breaks is also dealt with.

Copies of the bulletin are sent free to those interested upon application to R. H. Campbell, Director of Forestry, Ottawa. In this new publication an estimate is made of the cash value of the sixty million trees which have been sent out from the Dominion Government nursery stations, but the greater value is found in the increased comfort and homelike surroundings of prairie homesteads since the plan was inaugurated. In the pamphlet forty farmers scattered over the plains from Winnipeg to Calgary, tell of their success under the plan. While the free distribution of trees under this system is confined to the prairie provinces the work affects the whole of the Dominion both because improved conditions in one part must benefit all Canada, and because it shows that if trees of valuable kinds can be got to grow in what was once considered a treeless region a great opportunity exists for improving forest conditions and in growing timber in all parts of Canada.

---

#### Valuable Figures for Lumber Exporters

The National Lumber Bulletin, published by the National Lumber Manufacturers Association, published the following interesting information:

A standard equals 165 cubic feet or 1980 board feet of lumber about 1,650 board feet of squared timber; 1,320 board feet of logs.

A cubic meter equals 424 board feet of lumber; 353 board feet of hewn timber; 283 board feet of logs.

A metric ton equals 1,000 kilos or 2,204.6 pounds
It is equivalent to 735 board feet of softwood lumber; 551 board feet of hardwood lumber; 490 board feet of logs (Softwoods); 367 board feet of logs (hardwoods); 612 board feet of squared timber (softwoods); 459 board feet of squared timber (hardwoods).

A hectare equals 2,471 acres.

F. O. B. means "free on board;" that is with freight not pre-paid from point named.

F. O. W. means "first open water," applied particularly to deliveries on cargoes in northern countries.

C. I. F. means "cost, insurance and freight;" all three items being included in the quotation, to point named.

F. A. S. means "free alongside ship."

L. C. L. means "less than carload lot."

# Scattergood Baines Baits a Hook

## A Story of Lumber, Love and Finance

—By *Clarence Budington Kelland—

Lookin' kind of sour fer a young feller that's goin' to marry and live happy ever after in less'n a week," said Scattergood Baines.

Young Martin Waters bit his lip and turned away his face. "Hain't goin' to be married," he said gruffly.

"What ails ye? Eh? Hain't fit with Gracie, have ye? Hain't been cuttin' up no capers?"

"I jest can't git married," said Martin; "and I've come from tellin' her so."

"Um. Don't look like you enjoyed the job special. How's Gracie enjoy it?"

"She's cryin'," said Martin briefly.

"Wa-al, young fellers will change their minds," said Scattergood.

"Hain't changed my mind. Hain't that kind of a feller."

"Hain't been and got into no scrape? Hain't gone off and married somebody else kind of absent-minded, have ye?"

"Only times I been out of the woods since fall was to call on Gracie. Hain't seen no other woman— not to notice her. J—jes found out las' night that I hain't able to support no wife."

"Eh? dreamt it, didn't ye? Last I knowed you owned a half interest into a likely sawmill and as good a piece of timber as there is in this here section of the country. What's become of it?"

"I dunno." Martin scratched his head as one who is baffled by an inexplicable fact. "Figgered we was makin' money. Even went so fur's to git all axed up for a weddin' trip to Niagry Falls. Was going to git my tickets to-day; but las' night when I went to Watts to git him to draw the money fer me, he let on the' wa'n't none. Said we didn't have a cent in the bank, and creditors was goin' to put us into bankruptcy, or suthin' or other."

"Um. Be'n gittin' out plenty timber, hain't ye?"

Martin nodded dejectedly. "I was lookin' forward to us makin' ten thousand dollars betwixt us this year."

"Then why hain't ye?"

"Watts he says as how costs has et it all up. He says the woods costs has been suthin' to make you holler, says he. Kind of lays it onto me."

"Allus figgered you was a competent, economical woods boss, Martin. Bein' in love make you wasteful?"

"Mr. Baines," said Martin, "seems as though I cut every corner and squeezed every penny. Worked special hard on account of gittin' married. But he says my costs ruined us."

"Um. Jest tell ye, did he? Never make no complaints durin' the winter when you was runnin' up all this here expense?"

"Nary complaint. Says he thought I knowed my business, and then, when things commenced to go wrong, he kind of couldn't bear to tell me till he had to."

"You run the woods, and he run the mill and kept the books. That's the way of it, hain't it?"

"That's how we done it."

"Hain't much on bookkeepin', be ye?"

"Don't know nothin' about such matters. Cuttin' timber's my business."

"The showin' makes it look different," said Scattergood. "Um. Put the whole ten thousand your father left you into this deal, didn't ye?"

"Yes."

"And Watts put in ten thousand?"

"Yes."

"Drawed out much money yourself?"

"Hain't drawed a cent, hardly. Let everythin' lay figgerin', we'd buy that there Tubbs timber, layin' next to our'n."

*In the "American Magazine"

"What you calc'late on doin' now?"

"Nothin' fer me but to take my axe and turkey and go back to lumberjackin'."

Scattergood puffed out his fat cheeks.

"How much you folks go in the hole?"

"Watts says we owe so much there won't be a cent left after this here bankruptcy."

"Martin," said Scattergood, "you jest stay right here in Coldriver a couple days. Kind of aim to look into this here for you. Don't look jest pleasin' to the eye."

Scattergood sat squinting up the street, heavy with the mud of melted snow and spring rains; he grunted two or three times and then eased himself out of his reinforced arm chair and ambled across the bridge to the bank—of which he was one of the Finance Committee. Young Ovid Nixon looked up as he entered.

"Mornin', Ovid," said Scattergood. "Hain't wearin' them new pants to work, be you? Sh'u'dn't think your wife 'ud allow it. Um. Dressiest cashier we ever had, seems as though. Um. . . . How's Newman and Waters's balance?"

"Hain't got none, so to speak," said Ovid.

"How about Watts Newman?"

"Don't keep no account here. Hain't fer six months. Had me draw a New York draft fer all he had one day. Didn't say what he wanted with the money, but I calc'lae he was figgerin' to buy suthin'."

"Mebby so... Hear tell of his bankin' down to the city?"

Ovid concentrated. "Does seem like a check with his name onto it come through a spell back. Now, lemme see, what was that there bank. I got a pretty good mem'ry fer sich things. Seems like it was the Merchants'."

"Uh-huh. And, say, Ovid, when you git time, kind of gimme a statement of Newman Waters's account fer the past six months."

"Jest as soon as I kin git it," said Ovid.

From the bank Scattergood went to the station of his railroad, which ran twenty-odd miles down Coldriver valley, and sent a telegram to the Merchants' Bank, where he was well known and where a request for information would be promptly answered. Within an hour he knew how much Watts Newman had on deposit in that institution, and, in addition, the interesting fact that the young man rented a safety deposit box.

Before time for the noonday meal he found time to drop in at the Brooks home, where he found Gracie in the kitchen

"Mornin', Gracie," he said.

"M-mornin', M-mister Baines," she said tremulously.

"Eyes lookin' sort of red, Gracie." She made no reply.

"I seen Martin this mornin'," he said. "Looks like he's been kind of unfortnit."

"He's—goin' away, and—he' ain't—goin' to marry me."

"Um. Do tell! Now, Gracie, you listen here to me : Martin, he ain't goin' nowheres. Watts Newman been callin' on you off and on this winter, hain't he?"

"Said he was droppin' in to give me news of Martin, bein' his partner."

"To be sure. Worked around gradual to givin' you news of himself, didn't he?"

Gracie maintained a discreet silence.

"Kind of sweet on you, hain't he?"

"He—he—sort of hinted."

"Hintin' kind, Watts. Ruther have him than Martin?" She flashed out at him angrily.

"Martin, he was my man, and I don't want to have nobody else. If I can't have him, I don't want no livin' man at all."

"Figgered you'd be stanch. Now, Gracie. if you was to have a chanct to do suthin' fer Martin, d'you guess you could do it?"

"I'd do anythin' in the world fer him."

"Even go so fur's to act hospitable, and what you might call willin', toward Watts?"

"Scattergood Baines," she said sharply, "what be you up to?"

"I aim," said Scattergood, with a directness which was not characteristic, "to see Martin git what's fairly his'n."

"Then," said Gracie, "I'll do anythin' you tell me."

After his dinner—and by dinner must be understood a meal served promptly at twelve o'clock noon—Scatterfood resumed his seat on the piazza of his store, and there he reflected. Pliny Pickett, one-time stage driver, but now important in the uniform of conductor on the one train which operated over Scattergood's railway, stopped, as was his custom.

"Howdy, Pliny," said Scattered.

"Howdy, Mr. Baines."

"Consid'able, when I git spare time."

"What kind of bait you recommend."

"There's fish that likes worms, and fish that like bugs, and then there's them fish that won't eat nothin' but one another."

"I calc'late that's my kind of fish, Pliny.... And, say, Pliny, wanted to ask ye suthin'. Ever give away anythin' I tell ye in confidence?"

Pliny puffed up with righteous anger, and Scattergood's eyes twinkled. "I aim to keep a tight jaw," said Pliny.

"But," said Scattergood, "your habit of silence hain't sich that you couldn't spring a leak, is it? Eh? If it was necessary, Pliny, you could git discursive about my secrets, couldn't ye?"

Pliny hesitated, studied Scattergood in the light of twenty years' experience, and nodded. "I could," he said.

"Um." Scattergood then changed the subject with characteristic abruptness.

"Friendly with Watts Newman?"

"Could be, said Pliny.

"Beginnin' when?"

"Right off."

Um.... After you was real friendly with him, say, till a week come Sattidy, and I should let on to you I was thinkin' of buildin' the railroad on to Hampton, thutty more mile, and the road was goin' to run alongside of certain proppity, what would you do? Eh?"

"Study," said Pliny.

"Study hard, Pliny. Study hard'... Um. G'-by, Pliny."

"G'-by, Mr. Baines."

Scattergood blew out his cheeks, and peered at the bridge, and looked very solemn.

Martin Waters was sitting dejecedly in front of the livery stable uo the street: Scattergood called to him and they had a brief chat. Then Scattergood went back into his hardware store to study an atlas of the county which showed in detail the towns of timber, their owners, and, in cross hatchings of red ink, the land which had come into Scattervood's possession. There was much red ink. With a pencil he traced a line from Coldriver to Hampton. He traced two lines, over different routes through the mountains. One line was some miles shorter than the other, and passed through a narrow cleft in the hills known as the Notch. Here Scattergood set down a sturdy cross mark.

The map disclosed that the Notch lay in the middle of an irregular tract embracing some ten thousand acres of hillside and valley. The tract was ingrest from north to south ad Scattergood's line traversed its greatest length. On the atlas the land was set down to the ownership of one Silas P. Girty, and apparently Silas had cleared a small acreage and built himself a house upon it.

That evening, when Pliny came past after bringing in the train safely, he stopped to report.

"Um. Lent you a sight of things one time and another. Pliny, but don't recall ever lendin' you an atlas. Kind of round out our acquaintance, like, if I was to loan ye this here one."

"Don't call to mind no special use for no atlas."

"Don't, eh? Pliny, you hain't no idee the pleasure to be got from an atlas. Better'n a picture book. Yes, siree. Come in handy for you—entertainin' friends. Come a long evenin' with you settin' thinkin' of suthin' to say to your friend Watts Newman, and nothin' int'restin' occurrin' to you, why, you jest haul out the atlas and study her up together. Uh-huh. Lots of things to talk over in a atlas.... Specially one b'longin' to me with pencil marks into it. Give rise to theories and conjectures, Pliny."

"Gimme it, then," said Pliny.

"Look here, Pliny, at this here county map. See them pencil lines? What d'ye s'pose I drawed 'em fer?"

"No idee."

"Might be a line of a railroad from here to Hampton."

"Might be," said Pliny.

"What do you think?"

"Think the shortest one was a good line fer a railroad."

"You and me think alike, Pliny. 'Taint s'prisin', though, the years we done business together....See that cross in the Notch, Pliny. Mighty important cross, that. Guess its meaning?"

"That there cross," said Scattergood, "might mean that if the feller buildin' the railroad couldn't git to own the

You got to buy, I've got you by the short hairs

Notch, why, it wouldn't be possible for him to do no buildin' a-tall."

Pliny said nothing.

"Int'restin' fact that," said Scattergood. "A feller that wanted to take advantage; like, of anybody buildin'- this railroad, could sneak in and buy the Notch. Uh-huh. And then skin the eye teeth out of the man that had to have it."

"Sh'dn't be s'prised," said Pliny.

'It's a secret," said Scattergood, "and don't never let go no secrets, do you, Pliny?"

"Um...." said that gentleman.

"G'-by, Pliny."

"G'-by, Mr. Baines."

It was that day that Scattergood hired half a dozen men to begin grading a hundred feet of road bed just to the north of the station. Instantly Coldriver became excited.

"Folks say you're commencin' to run the road through to Hampton," said Deacon Pettybone.

"Hain't ree-sponsible for what folks says, Deacon."

That night he waited for Gracie Brooks to pass his store on her way to prayer meeting. When she was opposite him he cleared his throat. "Evenin', Gracie," he said. "Seen Mart?"

"Ketched a glimpse of him mopin' around," she said.

"Feels perty bad, I Calc'late. Um. Watts allus comes to town Friday nights, don't he? Eh?"

"Yes."

"Figger he'll come to set with you?"

"He might."

"Be sociable, Gracie. Be sociable.... Um. Never stretch your ear to hear folks talkin' private, do ye?.... 'Course not. Might 'a' knowed it. Uh-huh. But you could Any woman could....Comin' down-town to-morrow mornin', Gracie?"

"At mail time."

"Be suthin' you want in the hardware line, won't the'? To be sure the' will. Butcher knife, mebbe. Find 'em in the last show case but one on the right. Uh-huh....If the' wa'n't nobody in sight you'd stand and wait, most likely, eh?"

Why, I s'pose so."

"And if you heard two folks' talkin' private you wouldn't run off?"

"Not if you wanted me to stay."

"Huh. Figgered you had brains....And if what you overheard sounded like it might be int'restin' to Watts Newman, you might repeat it to him, mebbe?"

"I might."

"Um....Best time to buy knives is half-past eleven, sharp. G'-by, Gracie."

Shortly after eleven o'clock next morning, Johnny Bones, Scattergood's lawyer, entered the hardware store and sought his client in the space used as an office, just behind the stoves and refrigerators. This bulky merchandise concealed them from the front of the store. Presently Gracie Brooks came in and stood before the knife show case as Sattergood began talking.

"I'm goin' to build that there railroad through to Hampton, Johnny."

"But the right of way, Scattergood."

"Got it all, exceptin' a mile or two through the Notch. No worry about that."

"I'd worry about it a heap," said Johnny. "Most important stretch in the whole line."

"Mebbe so. But I kin git it."

"What if the news of the road gets out? Old Silas Girty would hold you up till you bled."

"'Twon't git out. Folks think I'm jest buildin' a freight yard....Say, Johnny, I kin buy that ten thousand acres of Silas fer around eight dollar an acre. It'll be wuth double that with the railroad through. Lays twenty mile from a railroad now.... Profit on that piece of timber'll dum nigh pay the cost of buildin' the road."

"It won't if somebody found out and went to Silas and got in ahead of you."

'Nobody's going to. It'll take forty-forty thousand to swing a deal with Silas. Nobody around here's got that much layin' idle."

When Johnny Bones went through the store, it was empty.

At almost that identical hour Mr. Watts Newman, although in the beholding eye he seemed frantic with alarm, was filled with an inward glow of satisfaction. The office of the mill which he owned in equal parts with Mart Waters was in flames, and it was evident it would burn to the ground with all its contents. The office contained all the written records of the company.

He drove into Coldriver that afternoon and stopped before the livery. There, before the door, sat Pliny Pickett.

"Howdy, Watts," said Pliny. "How you find yourself?"

'Finer'n frog's hair," said Watts.

"Um. Eatin' to the ho-tel? Calc'late to eat to the hotel?"

"Uh-huh," said Watts.

"Dunno but I'll eat with you," said Pliny, and he picked up a big book and crossed the street with Mr. Newman. "Feelin' kind of lonely, b'jing! Glad you dropped into town. Let's set here on the piazzy till supper."

"What you got there?" Watts asked.

"Atlas. Huh. Ever study the country atlas much? In-'trestin'. Mighty int'restin'. Shows every house and fence and cow pastur'.... Now, look at this here map. Everybody's proppity set down."

"Huh....Somebody's marked it all up."

"Oh, Scattergood Baines, he done that. B'longs to him. He lemme take it 'cause I got int'rested into it."

"What's all the red ink fer?" he asked.

"Baines's holdin's."

"Got a heap of timber land, hain't he? Say, that there pencil line to Hampton what's that?"

"Dunno. Looks like the tracin's of a road or suthin'. Um. Hold on, mebbe it's the railroad the's been talk of him runnin' through. Heard talk of it. Doin' some diggin' up to the depot now for suthin'."

"Let's see where she runs," Watts said, studying the map. "Owns most of the right of way, don't he."

"There's a chunk by the Notch he don't own, seems as though. Kind of funny, too. If I was aimin' to build a railroad seems like I'd git the Notch fust of all. Got to go through the Notch, hain't it? No Notch, no railroad."

Toward eight o'clock Newman extricated himself from Pliny's clinging companionship, and walked out to call upon Gracie Brooks. What Gracie said or did is not of record but Pliny Pickett waiting in the shadows, can testify that Watts left the house hastily.

Watts did not go back to the mill the following morning. Instead, he rode to the city. All the way his thoughts centered around the Notch and the ten-thousand-acre tract belonging to Silas Girty.

While in the city, Watts visited the Merchants' Bank and opened his safety deposit box.

The next day was Sunday, and no business could be transacted. Watts knew better than to approach old Silas P. Girty with any proposition on the Sabbath, but early on Monday morning he hired a rig at the livery.

"Goin' fur?" asked the liveryman.

"Mebbe won't git back till to-morrow," said Watts. 'Goin' east a ways."

"Huh. Everybody's hirin' rigs for the day—goin' east. Scattergood Baines and Johnny Bones they jest started off that way fifteen minutes ago."

Scattergood Baines and Johnny Bones! Going east! That could mean only one thing—Silas P. Girty! And they had fifteen minutes' start of him. Watts leaped into the buggy and drove off furiously. It was a race, though, he told himself. Scattergood did not know it was a race. Five miles out of town he came up with Scattergood and Johnny standing beside their buggy, which was tilted over the ditch, with one rear wheel standing against a tree.

"Hey!" said Scattergood. "Where you goin', Watts?"

"Over east a ways."

"So'm I," said Scattergood. Buggy's busted. Got some important business that way. Got to git there. You got room. Give me and Johnny a lift."

Watts grinned to himself. "Wisht I could," he said; "but the's reasons. I'm in a awful hurry." Whereupon he drove on.

"Um." Scattergood peered at Johnny. "When you fishin' for pike you want to make your bait look nat'ral. The more nat'ral you git it, the bigger fish you ketch. Let's git the wheel back on, Johnny."

His heart aglow with the satisfaction of success, Watts Newman drove on in more leisurely fashion, and reached Silas Girty's just after the midday meal. Mr. Girty, in shirt sleeves and stocking feet, was enjoying a half-hour of leisure on the sofa. He arose as Watts was shown into the oom and grunted a parsimonious greeting.

"Silas," said Watts, "I heard this timber of your'n was fer sale, and kind of dropped in to inquire if 'twas."

"'Tis and 'tain't, said Silas shortly. "'Tis if you mean business and got money; 'tain't if you're jest makin' talk."

"Hain't hirin' a rig and drivin' eighteen-nineteen mile jest to chin nobody. Got some money, and kin get more. Figgered I might's well put it into timber if I kin git it reasonable."

"You'n' me might not git the same idee what reasonable is," said Silas.

"Last timber sold around here ftched eight dollars an acre," said watts.

"It didn't do a sight of fetchin'," said Silas shortly, and it

didn't include the Notch, young feller, and the' wa'n't strong talk of railroad."

"Shucks,' said Watts, concerned that rumors had reached the old man. "Never be no road through here.'

"Mebbe not, mebbe so. Can't tell. Wuth considerin' of Calculate to want fifteen dollar an acre."

For two hours they labored with each other, the one raising his offer by a quarter an acre the other descending by twenty-five cents until they arrived jointly at a figure of eleven dollars and a half.

"Cash down," said Silas.

"Good's cash," said Watts. "I kin give ye thutty-five thousand cash money, and a sixty-day mortgage for the rest."

"Suits me," said Silas.

Watts stayed overnight at the farm-house, and next morning drove to Coldriver in company with Silas, where the deal was consummated and the money paid over. Without delay Watts registered deed and mortgage, and next day called on Scattergood Baines.

"Howdy, Watts," said Scattergood. "Hope you got where you was gittin' in sich a hurry t'other day. Johnny and me managed to fix our rig so's to git home."

"I got there all right," said Watts. "I was goin' out to see Silas Girty."

"See him? Find him home?"

"That's what I done, and that's why I come to see you. I bought that timber of Girty's"

"Um. Thought you 'n' Mart Waters was busted."

"Oh, I got money I didn't put into that deal."

"Um. Had bad luck. Burned your books, I hear tell."

"Suthin' set fire to the office. But what I come fer was to offer to sell you that Girty tract."

"Who? Me? Hain't in the market for no timber, Watts. Got more'n I need."

"But you hain't got the Notch."

"Um. What about the Notch?"

"Your railroad'll have to go through it."

"Twould—if I aimed to build one." Watts laughed.

Scattergood stood up. "G'-by, Watts. Busy. If you want to talk more about the Notch, drop around this evenin'."

At eight o'clock Watts presented himself at the hardware store again; but, to his surprise, he found there not only Scattergood but Mart Waters and Gracie Brooks.

"Come right in, Watts. Friends of yourn' dropped in. Go right ahead with business. Nothin' they needn't to listen to. Calc'lated to sell me timber, didn't ye?"

Watts stood uncertain and scowling.

"Um....'Fore we come to that, lemme talk a mite about suthin' else. You and Mart, f'r instance. D'ye know, if I'd opened that mill, and cut and sold the lumber you done, I'd

.'a' made a clost to twenty thousand dollars, instid bf goin' bankrupt. Uh-huh. And I wouldn't of burned my books, nor had no safety deposit box in the Merchants' Bank.... And I wouldn't be plannin' to buy in the proppity at sheriff's sale, like you be. Uh-huh. Don't figger you've acted jest square with Mart. Somehow, don't seem so to me."

"Nobody kin prove nothin'," said Watts.

"Hain't nobody goin' to try. Everybody's satisfied. Guess Mart'll come out full better'n he hoped. Uh-huh. Him and me's had a little deal all by ourselves....Lemme see. You paid Silas Girty thutty-five thousand down on your timber deal. And you promised to pay the balance in sixty days. Where you goin' to git the balance?"

"Off of you," Watts said savagely. "You got to buy. I've got you by the short hairs."

"Goin' to gouge me some, eh? Don't seem like I'd enjoy bein' gouged, Watts, so we'll kind of forgit that part. You been dependin' on me wantin' to build a railroad, hain't ye? And needin' the Notch. Waal, Watts, I hain't goin' to build no railroad. Not any a-tall....And suthin' eles, Watts; I owned this here Girty tract these ten years. Kep' it in his name fer reasons of my own. Dunno how you come to want to buy it, but I'm satisfied, seems as though. Cost me six dollars an acre. Uh-huh. Git eleven and a half out of you—that is, me 'n' Mart will. He's int'rested, too. He's cleared up thutty-five thousand fer his share—the money you paid down."

"But—but—"

"Jest you listen. Here's what's goin' to happen; I hain't goin' to buy that proppity off of you, havin' jest sold it to you. What Mart and me is goin' to do is jest wait—sixty days. Then we foreclose, and the proppity's sold. We bid it in fer the face of the mortgage, and we're thutty-five thousand ahead, seems as though. Hain't no other way out of it. Nobody else wants it. No bank'll lend you enough to carry it. Nope....Sixty days, Watts, and Mart gits back all you stole and hid out of the mill, and he bids in the mill and owns it himself, like you kind of planned to do....Seems like everythin's worked out sort of favorable for Mart, don't it?....Guess that's all the talkin' we got to do, Watts," G'-by. And .if I was you, I'd git out of this caounty. We hain't got much use fer fellers like you in Coldriver."

That night, as Scattergood ambled home he whistled a tuneless whistle. At his gate he stopped and looked backward at the town.

"Huh," he said, "if 'twan't for the honest folks in the world 'twouldn't be so easy for honest folks to make a decent livin'. Sometimes," he finished, "it seems like the Almighty created thieves to be kind of fodder for the righteous."

# What Canada's Forests Really Represent

The Canadian Forestry Association has declared many times that every acre of standing timber in Canada "represents potential pay envelopes, new population, new towns, new public revenues to lighten taxation," and that every forest fire is a 'job killer.'

Forest fires in Canada are destroying from five to ten times the amount of timber that is annually turned to commercial use. Most of such fires are human-set. Last year the big cause of fire loss was camping parties, fishermen, and other travellers in the woods.

The procession of United States paper mills over the Canadian border has already set in and must continue. This distinct industrial gain for Canada is due to one fact and one only: Canada holds large areas of spruce, coupled with convenient and dependable water powers: Spruce forests, therefore, are the magnet to pulp and paper industrial growth for this Dominion. With the drastic depletion of Eastern United States forests which is driving hard to a crisis for scores of U.S. mills, Canada faces the fact that free-running forest fires are undermining the superb advantages of forest possessions which their country at present holds. Timber areas in Canada (mostly owned by our Governments) are for the reasons given enjoying a rising market and five years from today will almost certainly command prices much in excess of those now established. Such being the case, the toleration of human-set forest fires year by year is one of the surprises to which the visiting foreigner can never quite accustom himself.

Commenting upon the rapid reduction of United States forests

and the certainty of great industrial growth for Canada, Mr. C. Price Green, chief commissioner of natural resources for the Canadian National Railways, Toronto, recently said:

"How important this conservation is to the country can be judged by present consumption. Today the United States is using one-half of the whole world's supply of white paper, representing 5,500,000 cords of wood yearly, or the equivalent of a pile of pulp, four feet wide and eight feet high, 4,500 miles long, or greater than the distance across the continent.

"Let us briefly review the situation in Canada, which has about half the forest resources of the United States or about 260,000,000 acres of commercial forest. About half her forest areas have been burned over in the past 100 years, some several times. British Columbia alone has lost over 600,000,000 feet from fire.

At the present rate of consumption, about 14,000,000,000 feet a year, we have lost by fire the equivalent of 450 years' supply. On the basis of tax of 50 cents per 1,000 feet board measure, the lowest in effect, it means that the people from this cause have lost $1,000,-000,000.

"The United States cannot look to Canada for any alleviation of her situation with respect to sawn lumber; in fact, it has been estimated that if Canada were called upon to supply the total demand of the United States, the supply would not last much longer than 15 years.

"It may be thought that the picture I have drawn is one of blue ruin, but it is simply a presentation of facts that must be faced."

# Lumber Standardization Off to Good Start

### Important Gathering Held Recently in Washington Makes Progress—Various Proposals are Outlined and Co-operation of Many Interests Assured

The National Wholesale Lumber Dealers' Association, was represented at the Standardization Conference under the auspices of the Department of Commerce, Washington, May 22-26, by a Committee on Lumber Standardization. The conference plans provided for the first two days being devoted to discussions by producers, retailers participating the third day, wholesalers and consumers the fourth day, and railroad and other consumers the fifth day. Secretary of Commerce Hoover attended several sessions and outlined the desirability of standardization in the lumber industry.

At the first conference of producers, and because of the peculiar conditions affecting their industry, hardwood representatives endeavored to obtain separate consideration for hardwoods on the theory, briefly stated, that softwood producers should not legislate for hardwoods, nor should hardwoods legislate for softwoods. This request was outvoted; thereupon the delegation from the National Hardwood Lumber Association recorded its dissensions and reasons for non-participation on the conference committees, but remained in the conference, and expressed their sincere desire to fully co-operate with the Department of Commerce and the lumber industry in any constructive standardization plan.

At the first session, committees were appointed on (1) Simplification of Grades; (2) Guarantees of Grade and Quality; and (3) Standardization of Sizes.

#### The Subdivisions of the Grades

The first committee recommended that the grade of all lumber be divided into three great subdivisions, namely:

A—representing the Best qualities.
B—representing the Intermediate qualities.
C—representing the Common qualities.

The second Committee recommended the following program:

1st. A. That all grading will be done by properly supervised and qualified graders or inspectors.

B. That in case of complaint on account of the grade or tally of any shipment, Official Association reinspection will be available.

C. That where buyers demand, and will pay the cost, a certificate made by a Certified Association inspector will be furnished with each shipment so arranged for.

2nd. To arrange for the placing in each car at the mill of a card giving grade and contents of car.

3rd. If found practicable, to place an association grade mark on a sufficient portion of each shipment to protect the consumers or re-manufacturers from substitution. Said grade mark to identify the members mill by number, the Association it belongs to by letter or other copyrighted insignia, and the grade in plain nomenclature or easily understandable abbreviations thereof.

The North Carolina Pine Association, The Northern Pine Association, and The Western Pine Manufacturers' Association dissented on the matter of grade marking at this time.

The third Committee, on Standard Sizes, submitted a majority report showing agreement on some sizes, but a minority report was filed by one member of the committee strongly disagreeing with the views of the majority. The minority report insisted that lumber when dry ready for commercial purposes should be full size in the rough and that there should be allowed for dressing only enough to dress smoothly on sides and edges. The delegation from the National Retail Lumber Dealers' Association endorsed the minority report.

These recommendations from the producers were submitted to the joint conference with retailers on Wednesday, when retail representatives were added to the committee, the intention being for these joint committees to report to the conference on Thursday morning, in which the wholesale delegation would participate. Generally speaking, the reports of the first two committees were well received by the retailers, and although there was agreement on some sizes, no definite conclusions were reached on standard sizes.

#### Conference of Preliminary Nature

Wholesalers participated in the Thursday morning session, President W. H. Schuette responding. Secretary Hoover addressed this joint conference stating that it should be possible for the lumber industry to effectuate a National Inspection Service not a Federal Inspection Bureau operated by the government, but an Inspection Service maintained by the lumber industry and available

to all, possibly one set of rules for softwoods with another for hardwoods.

It was recognized that this conference was to be of a preliminary nature only, and that any recommendations could not be binding upon the industry or any of the Associations represented, but it was hoped the conclusions would lead to an eventual and acceptable standardization plan. At one session the discussion centered largely on the method of necessary investigation among producers, distributors, consumers, the forest service, etc., to be reported and acted upon later, the result being the adoption of a plan for further conferences which will be attended by representatives from producers, wholesalers, retailers, and all consumers.

Secretary Hoover was unable to attend the concluding session, and W. A. Durgin, Chief of Division of Simplified Practice, Department of Commerce, addressed the conference to the effect that Mr. Hoover was well pleased with the progress made; that it was not expected any definite conclusions could now be reached, but that further conferences would be necessary when it was expected there would be a representative attendance. Mr. Durgin reiterated Secretary Hoover's opinion that a National Lumber Inspection Service was the solution for standardization in lumber industry and that "Mr. Hoover was not yet satisfied that hardwoods could not be included in a plan for a national inspection to cover both softwoods and hardwoods."

Secretary Hoover has been assured of the co-operation of this Association in the effort to reach an acceptable standardization plan and that representatives from the N. W. L. D. Association will participate in future conferences.

## Cross-Cut Saw which is One Man Tool

Sawing a log by hand is usually a two-man job, one man at each end of the saw, but with a saw invented by R. W. Graves of Elizabeth, N. J., it becomes an easy task for one man.

Mr. Grave's saw, which is already in use in several collieries, is attached to a frame with springs in it which keeps it always in line and helps its downward movement. It makes sawing mine timbers,

Operating Cross-cut saw single handed

felling trees, cutting logs in shipyards, cutting branches off trees at any angle and such jobs as these possible without assistance.

Tests made by Messrs. Sparhawk and Tillotson of the Forest Service, United States Department of Agriculture, proved that one man using this machine saw could cut an eleven-inch chestnut log with seventy strokes, while two men using a cross-cut saw needed ninety-two strokes to cut the same log. On a nine-inch poplar log the figures were thirty and forty-four strokes, and on a nine-inch white oak log they were ninety-six and one hundred and nine strokes, in each case in favor of the one-man saw.

The Ontario Handle Mfg. Co., recently took over the Plant of the Canada Handle Co., at Weston, Ont. Considerable new equipment has been added and several new lines will be turned out.

## Last Call for the Big Lake Outing

Preparations are now practically complete for the annual outing of the Ontario Retail Lumber Dealers' Association, which will be held from June 23rd to 27th. The cruise up the lake on the "Huronic" of the Northern Navigation Co., is sure to be an enjoyable one, and many wholesalers, travelling salesmen and others will, with their wives and families, accompany the retailers.

The itinerary has been published so frequently in these columns that it is not necessary to refer to it again except to say that the "Huronic" will leave Windsor at 5 P.M. on Friday June 23rd and Sarnia at 11 P.M. on the same evening, and returning from Killarney, Sault Ste Marie and Mackinac, will reach Sarnia at noon on Tuesday June 27th and arrive at Windsor at 5 P. M. the same evening.

A number of retail lumber dealers from Ohio, who had planned a similar trip a little earlier than that of the Ontario dealers' outing, have decided to join in with the latter instead of running one "off their own bat." F. M. Torrance, of Xenia, Ohio, secretary of the Ohio Retail Lumber Dealers' Association, has been communicating with L. H. Richards, of Sarnia, chairman of the Outing Committee, and all arrangements have now been concluded.

The excursion will be of an international character as there will be representatives from Michigan as well as Ohio. There will be plenty of entertainment on the boat and automobile rides and receptions by the Chambers of Commerce at Owen Sound, Sault Ste Marie and Sarnia.

Many dealers are interested in a house plan service and it is likely that a representative of a large firm will be on board to discuss with the members the possibility of the Ontario Association making use of the service.

Everything is now in ship-shape for the cruise up the lakes, and any retailer who has not already made arrangements to take a holiday and enjoy a respite from work for a few days to mingle with his brethren and broaden out, should do so at once. The time is short and action is the watchword.

Douglas Malloch, of Chicago, will be with "the boys" and give them a rollicking night on June 26th when he will speak on "Husbands and Wives." It might be in order for members of the Retail Lumber Dealers' Association to come along for this alone and get a few pointers.

## Wide Powers Proposed on Wage Question

A bill was recently introduced in the Ontario Legislature to amend the Minimum Wage Act. This measure confers considerable power on the Workmen's Compensation Board, and among other things says that "this Board shall have authority to conduct such investigations as may be necessary for the purpose of ascertaining the wages, hours and conditions prevailing in any class of employment, and for this purpose shall possess all the powers that may be conferred upon a commissioner under the Public Inquiries Act."

Power is also granted by the Board to establish a minimum wage, and the new bill says that, after due inquiry, the maximum hours for employees in any trade occupation or calling may be set forth, but a wage lower than the minimum wage may also be established by the Board of Employees, classified as "Handicapped" or "Part Time Employees" or as "Apprentices."

Another important clause is that when the maximum hours established by the Board for a trade occupation or calling in Ontario is lower than that permitted by the Factory, Shop and Office Building Act, the order of the Board shall prevail.

The last clause in the new bill relates to penalties, and is as follows:—

(1) Every employer who contravenes an order of the board by the payment of wages of less amount than that fixed by the board or by permitting any employee to work for any time in excess of the maximum working hours fixed by the board shall be guilty of an offence and shall incur a penalty not exceeding $500 and not less than $50 for each employee affected, and in addition thereto shall upon conviction be ordered to pay to such employees the difference between the wages actually received and the minimum wage fixed by the board.

## Death of Edward Loren Thornton

Many friends in the lumber industry will regret to learn of the death of Edward Loren Thornton, of Chicago, who passed away recently as the result of the accidental discharge of an old gun that he was cleaning at his home, 2244 Lincoln Parkway West.

The late Mr. Thornton was born in St. Lawrence County, New York, in 1864 and of recent years owned a little sawmill which his father owned fifty years ago, and was running it as a customs mill for that neighborhood. As a boy during vacation time Mr. Thornton laid the foundation of his career in the old-fashioned sawmill. It was

in 1892 that E. L. Thornton took over his father's business which consists of a sawmill and woodworking plant at Heuvelton, N. Y.

Mr. Thornton who is survived by his wife, one son and two daughters, came to Chicago in 1887 and secured a position in a retail yard and later became manager of it. The following year he joined Mr. Russell in taking hold of the business. He remained with Mr. Russell for three years when he established relations with the George E. Plum Lumber Co., which business was later merged into the Superior Lumber Co. Mr. Thornton was made secretary-treasurer and general-manager of the Superior Lumber Co. in 1891, remaining with that organization until 1900. Then he bought an interest in the John E. Burns Lumber Co. and was made vice-president. He stayed with this concern until 1906 when he sold his holdings and organized the Thornton-Claney Lumber Co., of which he was president and general-manager until 1920 when he resigned his various positions.

## Schroeder Company Open Office in Toronto

The Schroeder Mills & Timber Co., of Milwaukee, Wis., whose mills in Ontario, under the management of James Ludgate, are located at Pakesley, have opened up an Ontario sales office at 305 Stair Building, corner of Bay & Adelaide Sts., Toronto. F. J. Archibald is in charge of the new office and his associate is H. T. Whaley, of Toronto.

Mr. Archibald is well-known in the lumber arena with which he has been associated in a practical way for thirty years. He was for a long period engaged in the selling and inspecting end in the Parry Sound district and for the past six years has been in the sales and manufacturing departments of the Schroeder Mills & Timber Co., spending part of the time in Pakesley and the remainder in Florida.

Mr. Archibald states that the company's plant at Pakesley is now in full operation and is sawing red and white pine. He says the company have a large stock of dry lumber on hand, and reports that the trade outlook is getting better all the while.

## Hocken Lumber Company Lose Planing Mill

The planing mill of the Hocken Lumber Co. Limited, at West River, Ont., was recently destroyed by fire which broke out from some unknown cause while the plant was in operation. The mill was well equipped and the loss will be about $15,000, which is partly covered by insurance. A strong wind was blowing at the time but, fortunately, the excellent work of the men and the efficiency of the fire protection system of the company saved the adjoining lumber piles and the sawmill, which is about three hundred yards away. The Hocken Lumber Co. will rebuild their planing mill in the near future.

## Wholesale Lumbermen Talk Over Sales Tax

A meeting of the members of the Wholesale Lumber Dealers' Association, Inc., was held recently at the Board of Trade Rooms, Toronto, to discuss the sales tax Situation.

In connection with the sales tax of 3%, which the manufacturer levies and collects from the wholesaler, it was suggested that an effort should be made to have this tax divided on a fifty fifty basis, or, in otherwords, that the wholesaler should pay the manufacturer 1½% and the wholesaler should collect 1½% from the retailer. Various other proposals were presented,—that the whole amount should be passed on to the retailer, that the manufacturer should be made to pay the tax direct, etc. The project was discussed from many angles and various views were presented. Several were in favor of leaving the following clause as it at present reads.

In addition to any duty or tax that may be payable under this section or any other statute or law, there shall be imposed, levied and collected an excise tax of two and one-quarter per cent. on sales and deliveries by Canadian manufacturers or producers, and wholesalers or jobbers, and a tax of three and three quarters per cent. on the duty paid value of goods imported, but in respect of sales by manufacturers or producers to retailers or consumers, the excise tax payable shall be four and one-half per cent, and on goods imported by retailers or consumers the excise tax payable shall be six per cent. on the duty paid value.

Provided that in respect of lumber an excise tax of three per cent. shall be imposed, levied and collected on sales and deliveries by the Canadian manufacturer and of four and one-half per cent. on importations, and that no further excise tax shall be payable on re-sale.

The matter was finally referred to the Legislative Committee, composed of Messrs. Manbert, Eckardt and Gall, to watch the situation and report, if necessary.

The factory of The Elmira Planing Mill Co., Elmira, showing new office on the right

# How Live Elmira Firm Forged to the Front

### Well-equipped Woodworking Plant has Branched Out in Many Directions—Getting After Business of Farmer—Publicity Policy of Company Brings Results

One of the most enterprising and progressive concerns in the retail lumber and planing mill line is the Elmira Planing Mill Co., Limited, of Elmira, Ont. This organization, of which W. J. Letson is the president and N. M. Bearinger is the manager, covers a wide range of activities. The factory building is of concrete construction and in dimensions, 70 x 90 feet, and a new office was recently erected which affords every facility and convenience, and is most attractively laid out. It was formerly a brick edifice 20 x 30 feet, and was remodelled to harmonize with the other structures of the firm. The interior is finished in cherry done in mahogany.

The factory of the Elmira organization is equipped with all modern machinery for a planing mill and sash and door plant, and is operated by Niagara power. The company have a small dry kiln 20 x 32 feet and a lumber shed 20 x 180 feet built of galvanized iron. G. T. R. siding extends into the yard and the lumber is piled along the track.

The company's lines of merchandise include lumber, lath, shingles, frames, interior trim, lime, fibre board, cement, roofing, metal goods, etc. The company manufacture the "Elmira Silo," which has become well-known throughout the whole district, and are also in the contracting business, taking jobs to build houses, garages, etc.

The Elmira Planing Mill Co., in their building business, generally take charge of the work as general contractors and then sub-let the various branches excepting the concrete portion. The company, have a mixer and men to put up concrete walls and have laid all the Elmira sidewalks for the last three years.

The "Elmira Silo," is furnished in Norway pine staves, 2" x 6", tongued and grooved on the bevel. The firm supply all the material required for the erection of this silo and find a ready market in Waterloo and surrounding counties for the "Elmira."

In regard to deliveries, Mr. Bearinger says these are made in the town with horse and wagon. The company have a truck at their disposal for outside deliveries for which there are extra charges.

Mr. Bearinger, the manager of the Elmira Planing Mill Co., is a live wire and believes in going after business in an aggressive manner. and his concern has been doing some effective advertising. He believes in catching the attention of the people, and starts an announcement with something of a humorous character leading up to a reference to the lines handled or the service rendered by the company. At a recent meeting of the Stratford District of the Ontario Retail Lumber Dealers' Association, Mr. Bearinger declared that his advertisements were bringing splendid results and that he could trace many orders directly to the appearance of his productions from week to week in the local press. The regular advertisement is about 4 inches deep and set in double column width. It always appears in the same place in the paper, and Mr. Bearinger says that it is evidently perused by all classes who look forward to the advt. as one

of the regular departments of the weekly publication. Here are a few of recent date:—

#### Building Supplies

IT IS CLAIMED that a pessimist is a lucky man. He expects nothing and gets what he expects.

IN OUR BUSINESS we are not pessimists. We expect the building season to be a fairly brisk one and are making preparations to meet the requirements of our trade.

STAVE SILOS We can furnish a Red Pine stave silo 12x30 with roof at a very reasonable price. If interested order your silo early as the quantity of dry stock in this grade is limited.

B. C. STOCK Let us know your wants in long-length joists and rafters anything from 10 to 30 ft. Get our price on 3X and 5X Kirkpatrick Shingles.

OTHER LINES Tennessee Cedar Chests in a new design, at $15.00 each. Fibre Board, the latest substitute for laths and plaster, at $60.00 per M. Matched lumber in Spruce, Pine Fir and Hemlock in transit.

The Elmira Planing Mill Company Limited.

#### A Satisfactory Finish

A Scotchman once made a fortune by singing. He received fifty cents to begin and five dollars to quit.

OUR AIM is to satisfy our customers at the beginning and at the end. Our stock is all sized and matched lumber is quoted face measure. When you buy 1,000 ft. it will cover 1,000 ft.

BARN FLOOR A 2x8 matched Red Pine barn floor at a reasonable cost. Now is the time to repair the old floor.

BARN SIDING B. C. Hemlock 1 x 12 kiln dried from 12 to 18 ft. long. This makes excellent siding as it will not shrink.

SHINGLES 2 cars of Kirkpatrick shingles in transit. This is recognized as one of the best brands on the coast. Get our prices on Silos, Roofing and Fibre Board.

#### Efficiency

A citizen, whose wife has been away for a month, claims that he has reached the height of efficiency. He can now put on his socks from both ends.

WE CLAIM to have attained the standard of efficiency in serving the trade in the lumber line. Our dimension stock is sized and sorted before it leaves the mill and our dressed stock is all stored in sheds.

GET OUR PRICES on all kinds of sash, frames and doors made to order; sized, dressed and matched lumber

in Pine, Fir, Spruce and Hemlock; Shingles, Laths and Roofing.

A QUANTITY of Basswood and Hemlock still going at only $26.00 per M ft. planed.

Stave Silos or Cement for your cement silo, roofing and lime.

Office and Mill closed every Saturday afternoon.

### The Self-Starter

BUSINESS PLEASURES must be cranked up every now and then but business worries have a self-starter.

WE ARE CRANKING the lumber market in order to get the necessary stock demanded by our trade. Our Spring Stock will be low but will contain a good variety.

ON THE WAY. A car of spruce flooring and V Match pine flooring and V Match and 2 cars of Kirkpatrick shingles. Get our prices on this stock.

BARN MATERIAL. Red pine barn flooring 2x8 tongued and grooved. This makes a strong and durable barn floor. B. C. Hemlock barn siding 12 inch wide, 10 to 20 feet long, kiln dried. See this stock when it arrives.

STAVE SILOS. We are making preparations to handle stave silos on an extensive scale. Get our prices and compare them with others.

### Short in Cash

Sambo, nursing a bandaged head, claims that he would like to keep out of bad company but has not enough money to get a divorce.

IN RECENT YEARS people would have liked to built, but, owing to the high cost of materials, did not have the necessary cash. Times have changed. According to our estimates a house that would have cost $3,700.00 in 1920 can be built to-day for from $2,700 to $3,000.00. Our plans are nearing completion.

BARN FLOORING. A car containing red pine barn flooring has just arrived. This stock makes a substantial floor. Also a shipment of matched pine and spruce. Place your order now and get this material at the new prices.

CEDAR CHESTS. Our Tennessee Cedar Chests are now ready for delivery. These chests are moth proof and provide a splendid storing place for furs or woolens. Price $ 15.00.

### Permit System to Check Forest Fires

It is interesting to see the interest which is manifesting itself in forest fires and the plans that are being discussed for the elimination of this rapacious foe,—always more ferocious in a season of extremely warm dry weather. As a unit the press is endorsing the proposed permit system, and, in some cases, suggestions have gone farther and one is to have forest preserves for the season closed to sportsmen. Here is how one influential paper sums up the whole situation:—

"Last year, the New Brunswick government actually did close the woods, to prevent fires, and none of any consequence was reported. Is this to be the solution of the great problem? Why should Ontario, for instance, be put to heavy expense in patrolling forest areas by airplane, by ranging, or otherwise, to check fires started by careless tourists or camping parties? Hundreds of thousands of dollars may be the cost of permitting one party to roam the woods in the dry season. The theory of spontaneous combustion does not work well. Very seldom do the dryness and the heat combine to start a fire in dead leaves or brushwood. Usually there is a match, or a cigarette or cigar in the case. The penalties for criminal carelessness in this respect are heavy, but they are rarely enforceable. The offenders get away scot free because no one can prove that they were the guilty parties. In the vast stretches of timber and brushwood, the issue is between the camper and his conscience.

"The least that can be done, and a change that ought to be made, is the granting of permits to all persons going into public woods in defined areas. These permits should be issued only to responsible persons. As a rule, the permit system falls into a routine that makes it useless, but almost anything in the way of a check on wayfarers through our northern forests is better than none at all. The departments which have charge of forest protection should install a special radio system, covering all principal points, and thus increase, in an important direction, the effectiveness of the fire-ranging service."

### New Wholesale Firm Launched in Winnipeg

Adams River Lumber Company Ltd., of Chase, B. C., are now represented in Winnipeg by Lockhart-Wescott Lumber Co. Ltd., McIntyre Block, Winnipeg, and in Manitoba by D. E. McCarter, whose headquarters is at Winnipeg. They are handling pine, spruce, fir and cedar in mixed cars.

R. Lockhart, the senior member of the firm, who has just started in the wholesale lumber business in partnership with R. P. Westcott, under the name of the Lockhart-Westcott Lumber Co., was born in Holyrood, Bruce County, Ont., in 1875 and after, completing his education in London, started his career in his father's sawmill, staying their eight years. In 1908 he went to Emo in the Rainy River District, where in company with his father, they conducted a sawmill under the name of J. & R. Lockhart. Mr. Lockhart, Sr., soon after retired, and his son, with his associates, Dan. and John Mosher, built a mill at Rocky Inlet, which is located by the Rainy River Lake, which business is still being carried on under the name of R. L. Lockhart & Co., Limited, Mr. Lockhart being a stockholder and director of the concern. Mr. Lockhart went to Rocky Inlet in 1899, as manager of the company, and remained there until the beginning of the present year when he removed to Winnipeg.

R. P. Westcott, his partner in the newly-formed wholesale firm, which will give its attention chiefly to eastern pine, mountain and coast spruce, is a Hastings County boy. In his youth he first saw the light of day thirty six years ago. In his youth he removed to Kenora, and, after leaving school, started in the sawmill of the Rat Portage Lumber Co. at Rainy River. Leaving there after six years' service, he joined the staff of the Rainy River lumber Co., now doing business under the name of the Shevlin-Clarke Lumber Co., of Port Frances. He was associated with that firm for four years as its representative in the province of Manitoba.

Nine years ago Mr. Westcott moved to Calgary where he was salesman for the North Pacific Lumber Co. of Barnet, B. C., subsequently moving to Winnipeg where he joined the McDonald Lumber Co. He also had charge of the McDonald Lumber Yards, Limited.

### Mr. Clark Speaks on Lumber Freight Rates

That the Crow's Nest Pass agreement should be further suspended, that a specific list of rate reductions should be enacted by Parliament; and that the general structure of rates should be revised by the Railway Commission, were those recommendations made to the Special House Committee on Railway Costs recently by Alf. E. Clark, of Toronto, representing the Canadian Lumbermen's Association, of which he is President.

Mr. Clark stated in reply to W. A. Boys, M. P., that his application was based on the statement of the railways that a return to the Crow's Nest Pass agreement would prevent rate reductions on lumber.

"If these statements were incorrect, your representations would be amended?" asked Mr. Boys.

"Yes," replied Mr. Clark.

"Do you believe reductions in rates would increase business?" asked Hon. A. B. Hudson.

"We know that a good deal of business is holding back awaiting the decision of this committee," was the reply of Mr. Clark.

### New Hardwood Flooring Weston in Plant

W. T. Cole, who for the past ten years has been sales manager of Seaman, Kent Co., Limited, Toronto, has resigned his position and in company with W. C. Gardiner, Toronto, and others, will embark in the manufacture of hardwood flooring of all kinds.

The new organization which will be incorporated, has taken over the old K. & S. rubber plant on Oak St., Weston. The property covers some five acres. The latest equipment will be installed and the firm will produce oak, maple, birch and beech flooring exclusively. Both Mr. Cole and Mr. Gardiner are extensively known in the forest products arena, being well thought of and well spoken of. Many friends will wish them every success in their new enterprise.

### Western Lumber Company Had Good Year

The report of the Canadian Western Lumber Co. for 1921 states lumber sold at 85,679,969 feet was 18,800,265 feet less than for the previous year, and amount of lumber manufactured correspondingly less. In spite of reduced turnover and lower prices, interest on five per cent. first mortgage debenture stock for 1921 has been fully earned, and there remains a balance of $230,152 enabling payment towards arrears of 4 per cent., which were added to ordinary payment of 2½ per cent. on 1st June, reducing amount of arrears to approximately 16.4 per cent. This provision has been made after making adequate reserves for depreciation of plant, machinery, etc.

# Western Lumber Market Shows Some Revival

## Considerable Improvement in Sales and Distribution has Set in—Large Quantity of B. C. Forest Products Finding Way to the Atlantic Seaboard

### By HENRY C. COPELAND, Vancouver

Lumber markets in the Northwest are quite active. The last month has seen a considerable revival of demand, sales and price. This has been brought about by the realization that the Atlantic seaboard offered the best outlet for lumber from this section and a determined effort to secure a fair representation of the business going to that section. In 1921 British Columbia sent only two and one-half per cent of the lumber that went from Washington, Oregon and British Columbia to the eastern coast.

The long waited and hoped for building movement in the United States seems to be getting under way. Buyers from Puget Sound have already come into the B. C. market with inquiries and in many instances with substantial orders that they could not fill satisfactorily on that side. There is still a considerable distance to travel before there can be any assurance of the continued solidity of the movement. It will take but very little boom tendency to choke off this business. There are yet many lines of material that enter into buildings that have not reached an entirely satisfactory level. That means that there are lines of producing labor that are receiving relatively higher pay than in the lumber industry. The tendency for labor is to demand the adjustment upward and they are quick to take advantage of any excuse to do so.

In Washington and Oregon, the mill operators are in many cases putting on night shifts, figuring that they will thereby reduce their overhead. The result is that the men are claiming that if conditions warrant a double shift that they also warrant a higher scale than they are receiving. If the labor cost is increased the manufacturing cost is increased and on a slightly "sellers" market the price will advance and that can only mean that thousands, who are now on the verge of deciding whether or not to build, will be held off for an indefinite time.

### The Cost of Production

The result of "crowding" the market is the same whether an increase of the wage scale is granted or not. It isn't what a man is paid that tells the story but is the cost of what he produces.

As to the individual section that go to make up the British Columbia Lumber market, the local demand is exceptionally active. The building program seems to be crystalizing in good shape. The price condition is extremely competitive as local mills figure on getting rid of a considerable portion of their common without shipping. However, there seems to be developing a demand that may diametrically change the above condition. A very considerable quantity is being called for from the Atlantic in the water borne trade. This outlet for the lower grades may easily create a scarcity in the local market with an attendant stiffening in price.

The prairie market has been looked to as the source of the greater part of our lumber prosperity. It seems as if the long period of adverse conditions, there, had, at last, turned the greater part of the attention of the manufacturers and distributors into other fields. It would appear as if the greater part of the business going to the prairies in the future would be from the mountain districts.

A survey of the retail yards of the prairies show that they are carrying about 70% of their normal stocks. They are doing quite a little buying but 90% of that is only such as is necessary to keep up on sorts so that business can be done at all. The fact is that the yards are "in" as far as they can go until conditions are such that they can make collections. That means a crop assured before relief can come to any marked degree.

One of the most solid and best dealers in the prairies writes as follows. "As you are perhaps aware, many publications referring to the optimistic outlook in the building trade, suggest the usual blindness and stupidity of the over optimistic."

"It must be evident to everyone who gives the matter any thought that there are at least four outstanding obstacles to any great building program."

"First: The excessive and unreasonable demands of labor."
"Second: The excessive freight rates."
"Third: The impoverished condition of most of the farmers owing to the unprofitable prices obtained for their crop last year."

"Four: The general restrictions of credit as a result of the three above conditions."

"Until some, or all of these conditions are remedied any great building activity is impossible. To say that homes must be built is absolutely incorrect from the fact that people will put up with what they have until conditions improve and so long as people are determined to do with what they have, very little is absolutely required in the way of anything new."

With the above we can pass the prairie proposition. There is and will be some business in that field but no one should permit their hopes to become as actualities.

### How Export Field Shapes Up

In the export fields, Japan is through for a time, weather conditions, several financial disasters that were almost cataclysmic, added to a natural slackening at this season has stopped all buying for the present. Those "in the know" think that 60 to 90 days will see a gradual resumption of this business.

China was very active up to within the last month when the extreme heavy fighting stopped all matters in that field. It is expected that China will develop a strong and reliable market for B. C. timber products, as they get their internal troubles settled to some degree.

The trade to Australia and New Zealand is developing nicely and bids fair to be the best season yet to those countries. There is nothing doing with South Africa and as usual San Francisco is getting what little business there is along the west coast of South America. There is a fair amount to the United Kingdom in small parcels.

The conditions as referred to above are general conditions as they may be said to affect the entire industry. There are individual mills that have developed their own trade in certain fields and that go on without being affected by the general market condition without it undergoes some extremely unusual change.

As has been said before the real demand for lumber is from the United States. The only contingency to be feared is that a "run away" market will develop before the great building movement is well under way. Gray's Harbor mills are reported as cutting 500,000 feet per day in excess of the log supply. A number of mills have put on night shifts.

Prices quoted in a trade paper, frequently have but little real value. However, as showing the range about three weeks ago in Vancouver, the following may be of interest.

| | ASK | OFFER | SALES |
|---|---|---|---|
| Dimension | $12.00 to $14.00 | $10.50 to $12.00 | $11.00 to $13.00 |
| Timbers | 16.50 to 18.00 | 15.00 to 17.00 | 14.50 to 17.00 |
| Uppers | 3% off E list | 5% off E list | 3% off E list |

Another computation of averages would give as follows:

| | |
|---|---|
| Timbers (base) | 17.00 |
| Drop Siding | 27.00 |
| Edge grain Flooring | 53.00 |
| Flat grain Flooring and "V" Joint | 25.00 |
| Shiplap | 12.00 |
| Dimension (base) | $13.50 |

A further advance was looked for at the time of taking these prices, of up to $1.50 on the commons.

The British Columbia log market stands as follows:

| | No. 1 | No. 2 | No. 3 |
|---|---|---|---|
| Fir | $24.00 | $16.00 | $10.00 |
| Hemlock | 14.00 | 12.00 | 10.00 |
| Cedar (base) | $20.00 | | |

The market is strong at these prices. The only variance seems to be where the timber is small and of inferior quality. Cedar is unusually strong for shingle stock. No. 1 brings about $30.00 per thousand. Hemlock is not bringing the money it should but it is likely that as the eastern market becomes better acquainted with this timber that it will come into its own. Last month it was feared that so many logs would come into this market that it would be swamped, in view of the fact, however, that some 15 to 20 of the larger camps have agreed to shut down on one side, it is hardly likely that this will happen.

## Golden Wedding of Popular Lumberman

Henry Pedwell, Thornbury, Ont.

Henry Pedwell, who for over forty years has been connected with the lumber industry in Grey County, Ont., and resides in Thornbury, recently celebrated the 50th anniversary of his wedding. Both Mr. and Mrs. Pedwell are in good health and received the congratulations of numerous friends. They have nine children, living, five of whom are in the lumber line. Charlie at Mansfield, Ont. E. M., A. E., F. A. and A. W. all of Toronto.

Henry Pedwell, who is more familiarly known as "Harry," has filled many important public positions. He was elected reeve of Thornbury village for several years and has been in many municipal contests but always came out a victor with one exception and that was years ago.

Mr. Pedwell was born in Wales in the district in which Lloyd George, Premier of Great Britian was brought up. He came to America as a young man and had just 10 cents in his pocket when he landed but he was not long in securing a job. After spending some months in Uncle Sam's domain, he migrated to Collingwood where he took up the trade of machinist blacksmith. Later he removed to Thornbury which is fourteen miles from Collingwood and started in the blacksmithing and carriage shop industry which he later "swapped" for a sawmill which he conducted for many years. He also ran sawmills at Owen Sound and in Keppel Township, sawing considerable quantities of hardwoods.

Mr. Pedwell continued operating at Thornbury until the limits, which he owned, gave out and then the mill was dismantled. He has, however, continued in the retail lumber line and enjoys his association with the trade to-day.

As already stated, Mr. Pedwell has always been a public-spirited citizen and given liberally of his time and talent to the advancement of the community in which he resides. This was particularly in evidence during the war and fuel famine of a few years ago. To the first man who enlisted with the 148th (Grey County) Battalion he gave a present of $100, and to everyone who joined later he donated a $5.00 gold-piece. He also took an active part in the Victory bond and recruiting campaigns. Although over the three score and ten mark, Mr. Pedwell is remarkably agile for one of his years, and in winter takes delight in curling. He has long been interested in athletic events.

## How New Brunswick Arouses the Public

Hon. Wm. Pugsley, Lieutenant-governor of New Brunswick, recently issued a proclamation, proclaiming that the week beginning May 23rd was Forest Fire Prevention Week, and calling upon all citizens to observe it. His Honor also asked that there be spread broadcast a word of caution regarding forest fires. He requested clergymen, teachers, boards of trade and all public officials, societies and associations to exert themselves to the utmost to inform those with whom they come in contact of the transcendent importance of New Brunswick forests, and the need of their adequate protection from flame.

It is pointed out that the forests of New Brunswick constitute one of the greatest natural resources and are an asset of tremendous value and importance, essential to the prosperity and welfare of the province and its people. It is also stressed that fire is the greatest foe of the forest and that more earnest and conservative effort is imperative to safeguard the great natural heritage of woodlands.

Hon. C. W. Robinson, Minister of Lands and Forests, about the same time sent out an appeal to the school teachers and school children of New Brunswick for their active co-operation in forest fire prevention. Teachers were asked to lend their support to the salient work of safeguarding the timber of the province from flames by making this the subject of talks to pupils from time to time.

Hon. Mr. Robinson declared that it was not necessary to go into the details of the immense damage caused to the forests in the past. All would remember the fierce forest fires of last year, 90% of which were caused by mere carelessness. Residents of the province generally, and especially the younger generation, should be brought to realize the cost of carelessness and to become more careful of fire. It was expected many families may be reached through the school children in a more appealing manner than by any other route. Other organizations such as the clergy, Boy Scouts, the newspapers, etc., have been aiding, the propaganda of carefulness with fire throughout the provinces. All county councillors have been appointed fire wardens by law, and the government is doing everything possible to prevent the spread of any blaze.

## Arctic Regions Now Have Sawmill

The first sawmill for the Arctic Coast left Edmonton recently, being consigned to the Royal Canadian Mounted Police of Herschel Island by the waterways on the Mackenzie River. It will be used by the police for manufacturing lumber for various post buildings along the Arctic Coast. The equipment consists of a heavy portable saw mill and an 18 h.p. engine. The latter is of the two-cycle variety, is minus carburator or ignition, and can be run either on fish oil or crude oil from the Fort Norman well.

## Personal Paragraphs of Interest

A. Fenton of the Riordon Company, Limited, Montreal, spent a few days in Toronto last week.

A. Clermont has organized the Pointe Claire Lumber Company, Regd., to carry on a general lumber business at Pointe Claire, Que.

George Neilson, late of the Vancouver staff of Terry & Gordon, Limited, has taken a position in the Toronto office of the firm.

F. A. Kirkpatrick, of Muir & Kirkpatrick, Toronto, recently spent a few days in Montreal on his way from a buying trip in the East.

W. J. Merkel, vice-president of the Schroeder Mills & Timber Co., Milwaukee, Wis., was in Toronto recently on his way to visit the Ontario mills of the company at Pakesley.

J. A. Taylor, of the Brown Corporation, Quebec City, was among the Canadian representatives at the annual convention of the National Association of Purchasing Agents, held at Rochester, N. Y,

Crawford A. Govan has arrived in Canada form London, England, and will act as special representative of Cox, Long & Co Ltd., in connection with shipments of lumber to be made this summer from Eastern ports.

Col. R. M. Beckett, of Quebec, has resigned his position of advisor to the Eastern Canadian representative of the Timber Disposal Department of the Board of Trade, London, England. This is the department which is connected with the British Government lumber stocks in Canada.

J. D. McCormack, general manager of the Canadian Western Lumber Co., Fraser Mills, B. C., was in Toronto recently on business and called upon a number of friends in the lumber industry. Mr. McCormack is one of the outstanding lumber manufacturers of the West.

B. E. Hennessey, who was a widely-known lumberman throughout Northern Ontario, died recently in the Lady Minto Hospital in Cochrane. He was taken suddenly ill while at Lowbush. Mr. Hennessey was 56 years of age and had been engaged in lumbering in the Cobalt region for many years. He is survived by a widow three sons and a daughter.

In connection with the sale of the timber limits of Charles T. White & Sons, Limited, Sussex, N. B.; to Hollingsworth, Whitney & Co. Limited, Boston, it should be mentioned that the deal was negotiated by Messrs. G. N. Comeau and A. W. Barnhill, of Montreal, the financial arrangements being made by the Quebec Savings & Trust Company, Limited, Montreal. The approximate price was $1,500,000.

W. H. Kennedy, who was at one time a partner of the late Sir Douglas Cameron in the Rat Portage Lumber Co., died recently in Pasadena, California. Mr. Kennedy was born in Glengarry, Ont., and lived for many years in Kenora. His health became impaired and he had been a semi-invalid for many months. He is survived by his widow. The late Mr. Kennedy was well-known in lumber circles in the West.

George F. McCandless, of Toronto, president of the Canadian Tie & Lumber Co., accompanied by his wife, left recently on a holiday trip to Winnipeg, Edmonton, Calgary, Banff and many other points in the West. Mr. McCandless will not return until about the middle of next month. He has not been enjoying good health for some time and his many friends hope that the trip will result in restoring him to his former vigor.

G. O. Fleming, of the Central Canada Lumber Co., Toronto, is receiving the congratulations of his friends on his recent marriage to Miss Anna Jean Ross, daughter of Mrs. J. F. W. Ross, Dunvegan Road, Toronto. The ceremony took place in St. Paul's Anglican Church, Toronto. Mr. Fleming, who is a son of R. J. Fleming, is a popular young lumberman and many associates in the industry will wish him and his bride long life and abundant prosperity.

# Creosoted Fir Sleepers for the Indian Market

Creosoted pine sleepers from the Pacific Coast of North America first appeared in India in 1910, when a cargo of one hundred thousand was shipped from the United States. These were creosoted by a process now obsolete and apparently did not meet with any great degree of success, says H. A. Chisholm, Canadian Trade Commissioner, Calcutta. In 1914 and 1915, however, over 400,000 sleepers creosoted by the Rueping boiling process were shipped from the United States to the Indian railways. The war then interfered, and the shipments were not resumed until 1920. During the last two years Canada secured her first business with India, shipping over 300,000 sleepers and dividing the Indian business about equally with the United States. According to Government of India returns, the value of Canadian sleepers imported during the fiscal year 1920-21 amounted to over £200,000, while the American business amounted in value to about £150,000. Within the last few months Canadian exporters have secured two or three large orders in competition with the United States.

The importance of the Indian market may be gauged from the fact that over 40,000,000 sleepers are laid in the railways of India, and that the life of the average sleeper is between nine and twelve years. It is estimated that the Indian railways must replace from 3,000,000 to 4,000,000 of their sleepers per annum. Replacement has been held up during the war, and now that huge loans have been placed in London to be used for the rehabilitation of the railways, it is probable that for the next few years more than 4,000,000 new sleepers per annum will be laid.

What are Canada's chances of maintaining or increasing her share of this important trade? To determine this an examination must be made of India's possible sources of supply. The Indian railroad now have several possible sources of sleeper supplies.

It is probable that at present over 80 per cent of the sleeper contracts placed by the Indian railroads are for Indian hardwoods. Until about ten years ago the railways used native hardwoods almost exclusively, and it is only because these supplies have become more difficult to secure and more expensive that the railroads have been forced to go outside the country for a portion of their sleeper supplies.

Established connection means so much in India that the Canadian firms who introduce purely sleepers into the Indian market deserve much credit. American sleepers had been sold by firms in India enjoying the closest personal contract with the Indian railroads —firms who were in the front rank as far as dependability is concerned. Canadian sleepers were not known in India until 1920, but now at least 50 per cent of the sleepers shipped from the Pacific Coast to India are Canadian.

It is probable that in the near future Canada will get a greater percentage of this business, because there is an unwritten understanding that in the purchase of Indian Government supplies preference should be given to Empire products. The writer has ascertained that some railway officials were not aware of the fact that the Canadian sleepers were being sold in India in competition with American, due to an impression in certain quarters that the interests marketing American sleepers in India were also marketing Canadian. That misconception is now in progress of being corrected.

In order to hold this business, Canadian exporting interests will have to maintain the utmost care not only in the actual preparation of the sleepers but in shipping and in documents, so that any possibility of delay or confusion may be avoided. It is absolutely essential that shipments of creosoted sleepers ordered by the Indian railroads should arrive at the times specified. This time feature is the very essence of such contracts, because if the railroads thought that within such times they could procure sufficient supplies of Indian hardwoods, they would not place any orders for creosoted Douglas fir.

The following example of bad lumber export method has recently come to the notice of the writer. A certain well-known American export firm, who can usually be depended upon, made the mistake of routing a shipment via Colombo, where it had to be transhipped to India. This shipment received such rough treatment in transit that it was refused by the consignee. In addition, shipping documents were in mistake sent to the London house of the consignees instead of to Calcutta, the shipping documents arriving in India some time after the actual cargo, when there was a considerable slump in the market. The result is that the consignees referred to will not take the risk of doing business again with a firm who can make such serious mistakes.

# How New Sales and Other Taxes Are Being Applied

The Canadian Lumbermen's Association, whose headquarters are at Ottawa, recently sent out some interesting information in connection with the Budget Speech delivered by the Hon. W.S. Fielding, Minister of Finance. It is pointed out that the provisions outlined are now all effective except where otherwise mentioned. The data is as follows:—

**SALES TAX**—In the case of lumber, this has been increased from 2% to 3%, which will be charged by the manufacturer, and shown as a separate item on his invoice, the amount of the tax being 3% instead of 2% as formerly. On importations of lumber the tax will be 4½% to be paid by the importer, and there will be no further tax on re-sale, either on domestic or imported lumber.

**ABSORPTION OF ANY PORTION OF TAX**—There is no change from previous practice. The manufacturer may absorb portion of this 3% by billing his customer with not less than 2¼%, but will be required to pay the Government 3%.

**LICENSE**—The Minister may require every manufacturer to take out an annual license for the purpose aforesaid, and may prescribe a fee therefor, not exceeding two dollars, and the penalty for neglect or refusal shall be a sum not exceeding one thousand dollars.

**EXPORT**—There is no Sales Tax on goods exported and former regulations covering exports of lumber remain in force.

**SALES ON PRO FORMA**—Regulations in effect prior to May 24th, 1922, are continued. The new tax applies on domestic sales made on and after May 24th, 1922.

**LOGS AND UNMANUFACTURED TIMBER**—Former regulations still in effect.

**TIES, TELEGRAPH POLES, POSTS**—Former regulations, still in effect.

**INSURANCE**—Mutual companies are removed from the exempt class and all Insurance companies, mutuals, reciprocals, inter-insurers not registered with the Dominion Superintendent of Insurance, it is provided that every person using these facilities must make a return to the Superintendent of Insurance on or before the 31st day of December in each year, stating the total net cost to such person of all such insurance for the preceding calendar year, and pay to the Minister for the Consolidated Revenue Fund, in addition to any other tax payable under any existing law or statue, a tax of 5% of the total net cost, under a penalty of $50.00 for each and every day during which the default continues after the prescribed date, December 31st.

**CHEQUES**—The resolution provides for the attaching of revenue stamps to all cheques. The tax is 2 cents for each $50.00 or portion thereof. The effect of such a law will be to drive business firms to use cash instead of cheques. There will not be currency to satisfy necessities and the Banks will require to issue paper money far in excess of the safety point over the gold reserves. The tax is oppressive; serves no good purpose and will undoubtedly interfere with business transactions. For instance, a cheque for $5,000 will require to have $2.00 tax attached to it. This resolution is to become effective July 1st, 1922.

**TELEGRAPHS**—Instead of 1 cent tax as formerly, each and every telegram will now be charged 5 cents. This resolution to become effective July 1st, 1922.

**OLEOMARGARINE**—It will be noted that oleomargarine, margarine, butterine or other substitutes for butter; materials for use solely in the manufacture of oleomargarine or any substitutes of butter or lard, are all exempt from sales tax. This provision will not be of any value unless the Government, by a formal resolution, kills the bill which prohibits the manufacture and importation of oleomargarine into Canada. The above items are all under the Special War Revenue Act.

**TARIFF**—With regard to tariff, machinery for sawing lumber, etc., up to the point of planing, but not including this, the general tariff is reduced 2½%.

**BLANKETS**—The regulations are as follows: Blankets pure wool costing over 45 cents per lb., 22½%. Perferential; 30% Intermediate and 35% General. Blankets loose, not pure wool, 30% Preferential; 35% Intermediate and 35% General. This has now been changed to read: Blankets of any material—22½% Preferential; 30% Intermediate and 35% General.

**MARKING OF GOODS**—The Customs Tariff Amendment Act of 1921, provided for very onerous marking of goods to show the Country of Origin. This has now been changed to read:—

"The Governor in Council MAY from time to time, as he deems it expedient, order that goods, etc., etc. In other words it is now optional with the Governor in Council instead of being mandatory."

# Canada Lumberman

/ounded 1880

*The National Lumber Journal for Forty Years*

Issued on the 1st and 15th of every month by

**HUGH C. MACLEAN PUBLICATIONS, Limited**

THOS. S. YOUNG, Managing Director

HEAD OFFICE - - - - 347 Adelaide Street, West, TORONTO
Proprietors and Publishers also of Electrical News, Contract Record, Canadian Woodworker and Footwear in Canada.

VANCOUVER - - - - - - - Winch Building
MONTREAL - - - - - 119 Board of Trade Bldg.
WINNIPEG - - - - - - - 302 Travellers' Bldg.
NEW YORK - - - - - - - 296 Broadway
CHICAGO - - - - 14 West Washington Street
LONDON, ENG. - - - - - 16 Regent Street, S.W.

**TERMS OF SUBSCRIPTION**

Canada, United States and Great Britain, $3.00 per year, in advance; other foreign countries embraced in the General Postal Union, $4.00.
Single copies, 20 cents.

Authorized by the Postmaster-General for Canada, for transmission as second-class matter.

Vol. 42                Toronto, June 15, 1922                No. 12

## As Forests Burn Down Lumber Goes Up

The ordinary care-free individual who takes no thought of the morrow but like a butterfly is content to live day by day, would, possibly, give more heed to the all-important subject of the preservation and perpetuation of Canadian woodlands if certain basic facts were driven home.

The average Canadian should realize that the use of wood is constantly increasing rather than decreasing and that it is being put to new uses all the while in spite of the encroachment of competitive materials such as steel, concrete, aluminum, sheet metal, artificial stone, etc. Not only is the use of wood growing but the sources of supply are dwindling all the while, and it is most important that forests should be safeguarded to the fullest extent from fire.

A slogan that might well be heralded from one end of the land to the other is "as forests burn down, lumber goes up." Another companion cry might be "forest fires destroy in a few minutes what nature takes a century to build."

Now nearly every state and province holds a Fire Protection Week. The interest in this annual event against the despoilation of fire—the greatest enemy of the forest—is developing in every civilized community. It is pointed out that about 85% of forest fires is caused by human agencies that could have been prevented at the time by the exercise of a little care and forethought on the part of people who use the forests. If these qualities are not employed eternally, there will in a few years be no forests to afford the people places for camping, picnics, holiday haunts, hunting, strolling, etc.

Some irresponsible persons may say,—"Oh! This is a rather dismal picture to paint and such a state of affairs will not occur until long after we have passed away." In other words, the old cry is raised,—"Why should we do anything for posterity?" accompanied by the refrain,—"What has posterity done for us?" If such a narrow-gauged, short-sighted individual will sit down and dispassionately weigh matters, he will find that posterity has done a great deal for us, more than we think. Enjoying today many of the blessings, advantages and privileges, which have been handed down to us, why should not we of the present generation pass along something worth while to those who are to follow? No greater heritage can be transmitted than the forests.

There is very little use pointing out how much damage is done by forest fires as figures generally are not long remembered and constitutes a mental provender, rarely accepted and never digested or assimilated. One significant, however, is that in the United States alone during the last five years forest conflagrations have burned over an area equal almost to the combined area of New York and Massachusetts, and enough timber goes up in smoke annually to build a double row of frame houses from New York to Chicago.

It is declared that the Canadian citizen himself burns down by wilful carelessness each summer fully five times as much timber as is cut on all timber berths from ocean to ocean. It is asserted by the Canadian Forestry Association that 113 parties of fishermen did their best to burn up the forests of the Ottawa Valley during 1921, and that 308 camping parties left nothing undone that would have turned British Columbia last year, into a chambles. Much more might be said along the lines already indicated and the points of good citizenship further stressed. It should be remembered, however, that good citizenship demands being as careful with fire in the forest as with a fire in the home.

The following rules would assist materially in keeping down forest fires and solve this annually perplexing problem:—Put out your camp fire with water before leaving it. Be sure matches, cigarettes, cigars and pipe ashes are completely out before throwing them away—then step on them to make doubly sure. Build a small camp fire. Build it in the open, not against a tree or log. Scrape away all inflammable material around it. If you find a fire, try to put it out. If you can't, report it at once to the nearest Forest Ranger or Fire Warden. Keep in touch with the Forest Rangers.

## Injecting Common Sense Into Humans

The greatest foe of mankind is carelessness. This word is all-embracing and may mean thoughtlessness, callousness, selfishness, indifference or in common parlance,—"Don't give a cuss," or "Don't care a d—." Carelessness, in the ordinary acceptation of the term, has about as much effect and influence upon some as the attitude of a certain egotist who was asked why he was an optimist. His reply was ingenuous, if not ingenious, "I don't give a continental what happens so long as it don't happen to me."

This callousness or apathy, insensibility or whatever one may be disposed to denominate such a feeling, is, according to the best evidence that can be furnished, responsible for numerous forest fires which have recently broken out in many sections of the provinces of Ontario, Quebec, New Brunswick and British Columbia. Attempts have been made to lay the cause of these conflagrations at the door of the settler, the railway locomotive, spontaneous combustion, sawmill burners or freaks of lightning.

Inquiry, however, discourages all these theories, and the only alternative is that these fires have been started by campers, hunters, sportsmen or tourists who neglect to put out their camp fires or throw matches, cigar or cigarette butts, ashes of pipe, etc., away without making sure all trace of danger has been removed. 'One careless, devil-me-care individual, roaming the forest at large can start more blazes than one hundred rangers with all modern equipment in the way of flame-fighting appliances can put out.'

The whole situation resolves itself in the plain fact that where recent fires have taken place and the greatest loss was evidenced, the ordinary causes were not responsible and the conclusion is irresistibly forced upon the provincial and federal authorities that the conflagrations have been the work of careless people camping or passing through the woods.

Various systems and remedies have been proposed to eliminate this menace. Some have suggested that a license should be secured and that no one should be allowed to enter timberlands without presenting a duly-signed permit. Some will rise up and call such a proposal arbitrary and reactionary, but desperate diseases require desperate remedies. While it may be illogical and illiberal to declare that the end always justifies the means, still, in view of recent heavy losses in the forests, it would seem that such a course should prevail. Barriers, legal and otherwise, must be put up against the indiscriminate use of the forests by wandering wayfarers whose only thought is that of self and self alone. Too many do not care what happens so long as they are out of the way and have reached a place of safety.

Recent word received from Quebec states that the provincial authorities have considered the question of closing the forests for campers and others at this season of the year. The government are loath to adopt such a drastic measure, and, before doing so, will await the report of the losses sustained through the province as a result of the late outbreak. It is further shown that if the damage is excessive and demands the most stringent regulation, that the provincial legislature will take action along the lines mooted. Should the bars be applied to the forest lands of the province in the manner indicated, it is suggested that a system of permits should be instituted, whereby responsible people may still avail themselves of the opportunity of enjoying a vacation, stroll, hunt or picnic in the woods.

One gratifying feature emerging from the recent sombre situation is that no lives were lost in fighting the flames in the eastern provinces. This is regarded as rather remarkable in view of the serious nature of several of the outbreaks and the close proximity of some settlements to the scene.

The Forestry Department of New Brunswick is also looking into the advisability of the permit system, and one of the extracts of the forest fire laws, as amended during last season, says,—"The Minister

of Lands and Mines may set aside any forest area upon which no person shall enter for the purpose of camping, fishing, picnicing, etc., without a travel permit to do so."

This is the forerunner of what may in time become most effective and timely legislation not only in New Brunswick but in other provinces, and instead of waste areas being set aside at the option of the Minister of Lands and Forests, the departments may declare all Crown Lands closed to persons who have not the necessary license or permit to enter thereupon, and regard violators of this regulation as trespassers who, upon conviction, shall be summarily dealt with and heavily fined. Such a prophylactic measure would be a rather severe one, but the good often have to suffer for the evil owing to the wantoness, waywardness or waste of the few.

Another sensible regulation is that any adult in New Brunswick being aware of a forest fire must forthwith report it to a fire warden.

Other effective and far-seeing regulations have been passed by the various provincial governments, and in view of recent losses by forest fires at so early a period in the year, it would seem that legislation on many points, so far as controlling apparently irresponsible individuals is concerned, might proceed much further than it has. Public opinion will justify most any step that may be taken to protect and preserve Canada's most valuable asset.

## Why Lumber Can't be Sold by Sample

An interesting and forceful address was recently delivered before the lumber group of the National Association of Purchasing Agents in Rochester, N. Y., by Earl Palmer, of the National Hardwood Lumber Association, Chicago.

Mr. Palmer has for the past eighteen years served as an officer or as a director of the N. H. L. A., and took occasion to drive home some salient points which are seldom referred to at lumbermen's gatherings. He stated that while people were accustomed to refer to lumber as a manufactured product, it really comes to us as a product raw from nature's laboratory, changed in form but retaining most of the natural characteristics with which it was originally endowed. The sawmill can only reduce the log to certain dimensions, remove the bark and heart, rip out a defect here and trim off another there, leaving the inherent qualities of the final product absolutely unchanged from its natural condition. Nature deals in infinite variety. In a thousand leaves from a single tree no two can be found exactly alike. And so with the lumber produced from that tree, no two boards are duplicates. For that reason lumber cannot be sold by sample as is the case, with many other commodities, but each board must be judged and classified from its individual peculiarities, and this process of judging and classifying lumber is called grading, or inspecting.

In order that the process of grading may be possible standards of quality are demanded which set forth in detail the requirements of the various grades; and it is the duty of the lumber inspector to match the quality of each board handled by him with the particular requirements demanded by the grade to which it may be assigned. These standards are known as Inspection rules and are entirely arbitrary in nature. There is no reason for a specific inspection rule than there is for a specific freight rate. It is to be regretted that a complete set of hardwood inspection rules was not handed to Moses on Mount Sinai in connection with the Ten Commandments, but such was not the case; and those in existence today in no manner bear the stamp of divinity, nor are they inspirational in origin, but, instead, they are the product of finite intelligence, abetted in a degree by the process of evolutionary development.

The value of any standard does not depend so much upon the unit of quantity or of quality which it expresses as it does upon its uniformity and its stability. If a yard stick were two feet long instead of three feet, it would make no particular difference, if all yard sticks were always two feet long. But if there were other yard sticks three feet long, or if all yard sticks were sometimes two feet long and at other times three feet long, the situation would become confused. No one would be able to know what the length of a yard might be and the standard, as such, would be of no value. Such a situation prevailed in the hardwood lumber trade prior to the advent of the National Hardwood Lumber Association. There were a multiplicity of standards for the grading of hardwood lumber possessing about the same degree of stability as the mercury contained in the bulb of a thermometer during the month of April. Today there is but one standard of hardwood inspection which is expressed by the rules of the National Hardwood Lumber Association; and the stability of those rules, as they exist at the present time, is absolutely assured. In addition to the establishment of a permanent uniform system of inspection rules the National Hardwood Lumber Association has also developed and operates efficient machinery for the official application of those rules.

## Busy Huntsville Plant Swept by Fire

Fire recently destroyed the entire woodworking enterprises of the Muskoka Wood Mfg. Co., Limited, Huntsville, Ont. The blaze is believed to have originated from a smoker in an outhouse. A high wind was blowing at the time and the flames were not noticed until they had communicated with the dry kilns. The sawmill, woodworking factory, storage sheds, power plant and all other buildings were wiped out.

Fortunately the lumber escaped, and the company have in their yards at Huntsville several million feet. R. J. Hutcheson, president and managing-director, reports that the loss is very heavy as they have between 4,000,000 and 5,000,000 feet of logs at the mill yet unsawn, about half of the logs being hardwood.

The Muskoka Wood Mfg. Co. have not yet decided what they will do in the future, but owing to the assistance of friends in the trade, they are taking care of all flooring orders.

Sweep of the flames at Muskoka Wood Mfg. Co.

The insurance carried on the plant amounted to $162,500. The company have been successful financially, and if they decide to begin reconstruction, one of the most modern factories on the American continent will be carried out.

The plant had been running steadily during the winter months and was behind in shipments of flooring. "Red Deer" brand flooring was turned out by the company, and the product is well known from Coast to Coast.

The Muskoka Wood Mfg. Co., Limited, was organized in 1902 and erected a small sawmill and woodworking plant at Huntsville. During the first year thirty men were employed and at the time of the fire two hundred and fifty were on the pay-roll. The business has grown steadily. The company cut in the sawmill 6,000,000 feet and produced 3,000,000 to 5,000,000 feet of hardwood flooring each year. The Muskoka Wood Mfg. Co. also turned out lath and had a dry kiln capacity for about 250,000 feet at one time, and storage room for 1,000,000 feet of flooring.

The sawmill and factory were equipped with up-to-date machinery and a large dressing-in-transit business was done for a number of lumber firms. The power plant was of solid brick construction 40 x 40 with Waterous boilers carrying 115 lbs. of steam and developing more than 600 h.p. The boiler house was equipped with a Robb Armstrong and one each Waterous high speed and Filer & Stowell Corliss engines. The latter had been installed recently and would develop 750 h.p. It was the intention of the company to install further boiler capacity.

At the time of the fire the company were engaged in erecting an extension to their flooring plant, about 80 x 150 feet, and the walls of this building were up as high as 12 feet.

The Muskoka Wood Mfg. Co. had five kilns, two forced-draught and three natural-draught kilns. The plant covered about fifteen acres and there was a piling ground for 10,000,000 feet of lumber. There are eight railway spurs on the property which has splendid booming grounds, docks, etc.

R. J. Hutcheson is the president of the Muskoka Wood Mfg. Co. Many friends will extend their sympathy in the misfortune which has overtaken his organization and believe that his energy and aggressiveness will find expression in the reconstruction of even a larger industry than that which has just been obliterated. Mr. Hutcheson's sons are associated with him in the business, F. W. Hutcheson being vice-president and H. M. Hutcheson secretary-treasurer.

## Oliver Lumber Company Continued by Sons

The Oliver Lumber Co. Limited, of Toronto, which was organized in October 1897 by ex-mayor Joseph Oliver, who passed away in January last, is being continued by his sons, J. O. & W. F. Oliver, or as they are more familiarly known to their friends, as Ormsby and Frank. At a recent meeting of the company, Mrs. Elizabeth Oliver was elected president; W. F. Oliver, vice-president and J. O. Oliver, manager and secretary-treasurer. The company specializes in native

F. W. Oliver, Toronto

hardwoods, white pine and hemlock and has a wholesale sorting yard at the foot of Spadina Ave., Toronto. The firm has built up a large business in mixed carloads.

J. O. Oliver has been identified with the organization since its inception, and W. F. entered in 1904, having previously been with the Peterboro Lumber Co. and the Dickson Co. for a while. J. O. Oliver looks after the buying and executive end while W. F. devotes attention to the sales end and yards. Both Oliver boys are well-known in the wood products arena, W. F. being a former president of the Lake Shore Country Club, while J. O. is a member of the Scarboro Golf Club. They also belong to the National Club and other organizations, and many friends wish them continued success in the wholesale lumber business.

## Breezy Jottings from Far and Near

Fire recently swept the western portion of Prince Edward Island destroying several thousand dollars worth of lumber.

The saw and planing mill of Robinson, Wright & Co., Limited, Two Rivers, N. S., was recently destroyed by fire, entailing a loss of $20,000. This plant will be rebuilt at once.

J. McLaughlin, who has been in the lumber trade for several years, recently started a new lumber yard at Brampton, Ont., and is carrying a general line of stock. Mr. McLaughlin reports business very satisfactory at the present time.

The Pedwell Hardwood Lumber Co., Toronto, whose offices and yards have been at the foot of Spadina Ave., have leased a new site along the G.T.R. tracks and directly in line with the street, and will build a new office and lay out yards east of Spadina Ave.

Edward Walmsley has been appointed Crown Timber Agent for the district of New Westminster, B. C., succeeding E. W. Beckett resigned. Mr. Walmsley has been in the service of the department for fifteen years, having been appointed assistant to the agent in 1907.

The new plant of the Milverton Furniture Co., Milverton, Ont., is about complete. They are working now on their Sidman lumber curing kilns and expect to place their boilers in position shortly. This plant will be operated in connection with their associate company, the B. & N. Planing Mill Co.

The Three Rivers Pulp & Paper Co., of Montreal, of which N. A. Timmins is president, has been reorganized and will henceforth be known as the St. Lawrence Pulp & Paper Co. The shareholders in the old company will receive a like amount of stock in the new company. The capitalization of the new company is $1,000,000., 8%

cumulative, participating, preferred shares of no nominal par value. The new company are asking for tenders for a paper mill to cost $4,000,000.

The International Land & Lumber Co., of St. Felicien, Que., are at present shipping a large quantity of jack pine ties to the Canadian National Railways in accordance with the contract they received from them last fall. The company are also manufacturing a certain amount of lumber this season.

Myers Lumber & Mfg. Co., have moved their offices from 15 Toronto St., Toronto, to the new office building recently completed at their plant, corner of Spadina Road & Eglinton Ave. The new building provides a number of private offices and a large general office. The plant of this company has been completed and is in operation.

Richard C. Patterson, a New York capitalist, accompanied by several friends from the Metropolis, recently visited Vancouver Island to look over timber properties in the neighborhood of Renfrew, Port Alberni and Nootka. Mr. Patterson and his associates may invest in Island timber limits and may possibly establish sawmills and a pulp and paper plant on the Island.

W. H. Schuette, of Pittsburg, Pa., president of the National Wholesale Lumber Dealers' Association, has appointed standing committees of the Association to serve for the ensuing year. Dan. McLachlin, of Arnprior, Ont., has been appointed a member of the Executive Committee; W. C. Laidlaw, of Toronto, a member of the Fire Insurance Committee, and W. Gerard Power, of Quebec, has been named as a member of the Board of Managers of the Bureau of Information.

Hon. Beniah Bowman, Minister of Lands and Forests, recently introduced in the Ontario Legislature a bill which is of much interest to lumbermen, pulpwood owners and others. The measure is one respecting water-lots, and it was referred to a special committee to report on at the next session. The bill is for a revision of laws relating to rivers and streams and in it is a suggestion that a controller be appointed to direct and deal with all matters affecting the rights on waterways.

On Victoria Day, the Montreal office staff of the St. Maurice Paper Company, Limited, held a picnic at Cap de Madeleine, Three Rivers, Que., the outward journey being made by the company's own boat. The programme included the inspection of the company's lumber and paper mills and the principal points of interest in Three Rivers, a luncheon at the Cap de Madeleine mill, and dancing in the company's bungalow. The picnic was shared in by the employees at Cap de Madeleine and Three Rivers.

A charter has been granted to the Shackelton Forest Products, Limited, with a capital stock of $175,000.00 and headquarters in Toronto, to buy, sell and deal in wares of all kinds. Power is also given the company to erect, maintain and operate dry kilns and to buy, sell and lease timber and pulpwood limits as well as pulpwood, railway ties, lumber, etc. Among the incorporators of the company are: Andrew M. Moffat and John Bruce Hill, of Toronto, and Franklin E. Frantz, of Niagara Falls, Ont.

The Streetsville Lumber Co. Ltd., some time ago took over the plant of the Harris Wood Products Co., of Streetsville, Ont., and opened up a retail lumber yard in that place. The company, which is under the management of Thomas Wedgewood, has recently erected a two-storey frame building 40 x 108, in which doors, sash and other lines will be manufactured. The Streetsville Lumber Co., will make a specialty of turning out garage doors on a large scale. They also operate a planing mill and are carrying the usual lines of lumber, dimension, lath, shingles, posts, etc.

The National Wholesale Lumber Dealers' Association, whose headquarters are in New York City, have appointed membership committees that will cover each region during the coming year. The membership committee for Canada is composed of A. C. Manbert, Canadian General Lumber Co., Toronto, chairman; D. G. Gilmour, Gilmour & Co., Ottawa; J. B. Knox, Knox Bros., Limited, Montreal; Albert J. Smith, Albert J. Smith Lumber Co., Montreal; W. G. Power, Power Lumber Co., Quebec City; Angus McLean, The Bathurst Co., Limited, Bathurst, N. B., and H. J. Terry, Terry & Gordon, Limited, Toronto.

F. H. McLaughlin, who owns and operates the Commanda sawmill at Trout Creek, Ont., met with an accident recently which nearly cost him his life. He received several compound fractures and serious cuts and contusions. The signal for beginning the day's operations was given and Mr. McLaughlin was removing some debris from the basement wall when he slipped and fell backwards, striking the cuff of one of the shafts. A projecting belt and became entangled in his clothing and he was whirled around at the rate of many revolutions a minute, his body striking the sills and uprights on an adjacent pulley several times. He was finally thrown on a sawdust pile.

# PULPWOOD and PULP

## Pulpwood Business is not Very Brisk

A representative Eastern Canada firm who deal largely in pulpwood, say there does not seem to be any demand yet for wood, and add,—"If we had to depend upon this branch alone, we would have been out of business long ago, but we have recently been selling other forest products for which we find a larger requisition.

"So far as Quebec is concerned, we do not believe there is much wood being cut this year and there is no disposition on the part of any of our customers to contract or make a price. There is quite a large supply of local stock yet to be disposed of on the Quebec Central, a large amount of which has been sold and is awaiting delivery. Some of this was purchased at a rather high figure and may be thrown on the market on account of the contractor being unable to carry out his original agreement. There seems to be a disposition on the part of the mills to take only what is necessary for their immediate requirements, but should we get a reduction in freight rates and this matter be definitely settled, it may somewhat stimulate buying.

"Shippers are holding off for better prices," declared the head of this firm, "and our own view of the situation is that the mills will be well advised to take in any supplies of pulpwood that they can obtain at favorable prices as there is a likelihood of there being a much better demand in the fall and, perhaps, a shortage of cars for transportation.

"There was, no doubt, a big overproduction of pulpwood during the summer of 1920, purchased at very high cost. It is this supply that has to be cleaned up before business will be back on a normal basis. Under present conditions there is absolutely no encouragement to manufacture wood but our impression is that those who do manufacture peeled wood this summer, will find a good market for it next winter when they begin to haul it. The price of peeled wood to-day, delivered at Watertown, N. Y. is $18.00 to $19.00 and rossed $22.50 to $23.50.'

## Considerable Pulpwood on Railway Sidings

McGovern Bros. of LaSarre, Que., in writing the "Canada Lumberman" regarding the pulpwood situation in that district, say there are on a siding of the Canadian National Railway between LaReine and Nottaway, Que., nearly 100,000 cords of rough pulpwood, much of which was taken out during the season of 1920-21. This wood will, of course, deteriorate considerably if not moved this summer.

From LaReine east to O'Brien there are rossers operating at every siding and the wood is gradually being shipped out. East of O'Brien, however, conditions are not so satisfactory and scarcely any wood is being shipped. High freight rates place this district at a decided disadvantage in the marketing of the wood.

## Pulpwood Loss Was not so Heavy

The Spruce Falls Co., of Neenah, Wis., whose pulp mills are at Kapuskasing, Ont., say they have not yet been able to determine their loss accurately through the breaking of their booms, and consequent escape of some of their pulpwood caused by the spring freshets on the Kapuskasing River. As nearly as the firm can estimate, the loss will not be much over $100,000. The Spruce Falls Co. have resumed construction on their plant at Kapuskasing, but not with a very large crew. With the number of men they have, they feel confident they will be able to complete the plant in time to meet any improvement in the sulphite pulp market which, however, is as yet not showing much signs of a revival.

## Wood Pulp Silk is Not Yet Perfect

A jury before Supreme Court Justice Lydon in Montreal, gave a verdict recently for $19,257, for the Cohen Brothers Manufacturing Company, Inc., against the Edmund Wright-Ginsberg Company, and, after listening to evidence for ten days, decided that the manufacture of artificial silk from wood pulp has not yet reached the stage where perfect goods can be produced. The suit arose from the sale of 5,000 pounds of artificial silk cloth by the Cohen Company to William Heller, whose account was guaranteed by the defendant. After he had received and paid for $51,000 worth Heller refused to accept the final shipment amounting to $19,000 on the ground that the goods were not merchantable, and sued for the return of the $51,000 already paid. The seller sued for the $19,000, and that action was tried first.

Counsel for the plaintiff contended that the goods delivered were of as nearly perfect quality as can be made at present, and offered in evidence about 1,000 pounds of the cloth to prove it. It was alleged that the goods did not contain crossbars, as was testified by witnesses for the defendant, but that it was impossible to get uniform thread from wood pulp, and what appeared as crossbars was shading due to that fact. The jury found for the plaintiff on that point and also on the contention that holes in the cloth produced in court were caused by the buyer permitting the cloth to lie for two years in the neatsfoot oil in which it was made instead of having the cloth scoured at once. The oil contains germs which attack substances soaked in it and cause deterioration, the witnesses said.

## Pulp Business Great Factor on Coast

Pulp and paper activities have become a great factor in the timber industry of British Columbia. The business now represents an investment of $42,000,000, and requires one-fifth of the entire cut of timber. The present production of pulp and paper is about 800 tons a day. Several mills are projected at the present time, among them being the Harrison Lake Lumber & Pulp Co., of Harrison Lake. B. C.; the Kootenay Pulp & Paper Co., Limited, Nelson, B. C.; Prince George Pulp Co., Limited, Prince George, B. C.; and the Prince Rupert Pulp & Paper Co., Prince Rupert, B. C.

The most recent venture in this line is the projected plant to be built on North Arm near New Westminster, for the manufacture of tissue paper. The Westminster Paper Co., has been incorporated with a capital stock of $250,000, and will erect a plant costing about $100,000. The promoters of the plant are from Wisconsin and some time ago entered into negotiations with the New Westminster council for a lease of certain lands. It is understood that the mill, work on which is to begin shortly, will specialize in tissue paper.

## Timber Tests Data on Native Woods

Mr. C. Chaplin, supervisor of the timber tests, Forest Products Laboratories of Canada, Montreal, in a recent letter to the "Canada Lumberman," regarding the important and timely subject of shrinkage of lumber, says,—The Division of Timber Tests has in hand quantities of our various native woods which we are testing for shrinkage, radial, tangential, and volumetric, the measurements being taken in the green or saturated condition and then both in the oven dry and air dry conditions.

From the results we have obtained in drying from the green to air dry condition we find that white spruce shrinks in the radial direction about 1.8% and tangentially 5.0%. Balsam fir shrinks radially 2.2% and tangentially 5.6%.

The wood in the green condition as you know is saturated and would be in the condition referred to in the first paragraph of your letter. If this wood were sawn into planks 2x6 flat grain the white spruce would shrink about 0.04" in thickness and 0.30" in width and would measure after three years air drying about 1.97" x 5.70".

If this white spruce plank were sawn edge grain it would measure about 1.90" x 5.89" after the same period.

Two planks of balsam fir under the same conditions would measure about 1.96" x 5.66" (flat grain) and 1.89" x 5.87" (edge grain.)

If it is necessary to saw saturated material and have full dimensioned planks after drying it is necessary to add the following percentages to the dimensions taking into account the direction of grain:

| Direction of grain | Edge (radial) | Flat (tangential) |
|---|---|---|
| White Spruce | 1.8% | 5.2% |
| Balsam Fir | 2.2% | 5.9% |

We have at hand many results obtained from our tests which are available for those interested and which we are preparing to publish in the form of a bulletin in the near future.

# CURRENT LUMBER PRICES—WHOLESALE

## TORONTO

(In Car Load Lots, F.O.B. cars Toronto)

### White Pine

| | | |
|---|---|---|
| 1 x 4/7 Good Strips | $100.00 | $110.00 |
| 1¼ & 1½ x 4/7 Good Strips | 120.00 | 125.00 |
| 1 x 8 and up Good Sides | 150.00 | 160.00 |
| 2 x 4/7 Good Strips | 130.00 | 140.00 |
| 1¼ & 1½ x 8 and wider Good Sides | 185.00 | 190.00 |
| 2 x 8 and wider Good Sides | 190.00 | 200.00 |
| 5/4 and 6/4 No. 1, 2 and 3 Cuts | 90.00 | 95.00 |
| 2 in No. 1, 2 and 3 cuts | 100.00 | 105.00 |
| 1 x 4 and 5 Mill Run | 50.00 | 51.00 |
| 1 x 6 Mill Run | 51.00 | 52.00 |
| 1 x 7, 9 and 11 Mill Run | 52.00 | 53.00 |
| 1 x 8 Mill Run | 53.00 | 55.00 |
| 1 x 10 Mill Run | 55.00 | 58.00 |
| 1 x 12 Mill Run | 60.00 | 65.00 |
| 5/4 and 6/4 x 5 and up Mill Run | 58.00 | 60.00 |
| 2 x 4 Mill Run | 52.00 | 53.00 |
| 2 x 6 Mill Run | 53.00 | 56.00 |
| 2 x 8 Mill Run | 55.00 | 58.00 |
| 2 x 10 Mill Run | 58.00 | 60.00 |
| 2 x 12 Mill Run | 63.00 | 65.00 |
| 1 in. Mill Run Shorts | 35.00 | 40.00 |
| 1 x 4 and up 6/16 No. 1 Mill Culls | 30.00 | 32.00 |
| 1 x 10 and up 6/16 No. 1 Mill Culls | 34.00 | 36.00 |
| 1 x 12 and up 6/16 No. 1 Mill Culls | 34.00 | 36.00 |
| 1 x 4 and up 6/16 No. 2 Mill Culls | 23.00 | 25.00 |
| 1 x 10 x 12 6/16 No. 2 Mill Culls | 26.00 | 28.00 |
| 1 x 4 and up 6/16 No. 3 Mill Culls | 17.00 | 18.00 |

### Red Pine

(In Car Load Lots, F.O.B. Toronto)

| | | |
|---|---|---|
| 1 x 4 and 5 Mill Run | $34.00 | $35.00 |
| 1 x 6 Mill Run | 35.00 | 36.00 |
| 1 x 8 Mill Run | 37.00 | 38.00 |
| 1 x 10 Mill Run | 42.00 | 44.00 |
| 2 x 4 Mill Run | 37.00 | 38.00 |
| 2 x 6 Mill Run | 37.00 | 38.00 |
| 2 x 8 Mill Run | 38.00 | 39.00 |
| 2 x 10 Mill Run | 41.00 | 42.00 |
| 2 x 12 Mill Run | 46.00 | 47.00 |
| 1 in. Clear and Clear Face | 70.00 | 72.00 |
| 2 in. Clear and Clear Face | 70.00 | 72.00 |

### Spruce

| | | |
|---|---|---|
| 1 x 4 Mill Run | 34.00 | 35.00 |
| 1 x 6 Mill Run | 35.00 | 36.00 |
| 1 x 8 Mill Run | 37.00 | 38.00 |
| 1 x 10 Mill Run | 45.00 | 47.00 |
| 1 x 12 Mill Run Spruce | 48.00 | 50.00 |
| Mill Culls | 25.00 | 27.00 |

### Hemlock (M R)

(In Car Load Lots, F.O.B. Toronto)

| | | |
|---|---|---|
| 1 x 4 and 5 in. x 9 to 16 ft | $26.00 | $27.00 |
| 1 x 6 in. x 9 to 16 ft | 32.00 | 33.00 |
| 1 x 8 in. x 9 to 16 ft | 33.00 | 34.00 |
| 1 x 10 and 12 in. x 9 to 16 ft | 35.00 | 37.00 |
| 1 x 7, 9 and 11 in. x 9 to 16 ft | 32.00 | 33.00 |
| 2 x 4 to 12 in. 10/16 ft | 32.00 | 33.00 |
| 2 x 4 to 12 in., 18 ft | 37.00 | 39.00 |
| 2 x 4 to 12 in., 20 ft | 40.00 | 42.00 |
| 1 in. No. 2, 6 ft. to 16 ft | 23.00 | 25.00 |

### Fir Flooring

(In Car Load Lots, F.O.B. Toronto)

| | |
|---|---|
| Fir flooring, 1 x 3 and 4", No. 1 and 2 Edge Grain | $77.00 |
| Fir flooring, 1 x 3 and 4", No. 1 and 2 Flat Grain | 54.00 |
| 1 x 4 to 12 No. 1 and 2 Clear Fir Rough | 81.50 |
| 1¼ x 4 to 12 No. 1 and 2 Clear Fir, Rough | 85.50 |
| 2 x 4 to 12 No. 1 and 2 Clear Fir, Rough | 81.50 |
| 3 & 4 x 4 to 12 No. 1 & 2 Clear Fir Rough | 89.50 |
| 1 x 4, 5 and 6 in Fir Casing | 82.00 |
| 1 x 8 and 10 Fir Base | 87.00 |
| 1¼ and 1½ 8, 10 and 12 in. E.G. Stepping | 95.00 |
| 1¼ and 1½ 8, 10 and 12 in. F.G. Stepping | 85.00 |
| 1 x 4 to 12 Clear Fir, D4S | 78.00 |
| 1¼ and 1½ x 4 to 12 Clear Fir, D4S | 82.00 |
| XX Shingles, 6 butts to 2", per M | 3.35 |
| XXX Shingles, 6 butts to 2", per M. | 5.75 |
| XXXXX Shingles, 5 butts to 2", per M. | 6.40 |

### Lath

(F.O.B. Mill)

| | |
|---|---|
| No. 1 White Pine | $11.00 |
| No. 2 White Pine | 10.00 |
| No. 3 White Pine | 8.00 |
| Mill Run White Pine, 32 in. | 3.50 |
| Merchantable Spruce Lath, 4 ft. | 6.50 |

## TORONTO HARDWOOD PRICES

The prices given below are for car loads f.o.b. Toronto, from wholesalers to retailers, and are based on a good percentage of long lengths and good widths, without any wide stock having been sorted out.

The prices quoted on imported woods are payable in U. S. funds.

### Ash, White

(Dry weight 3800 lbs. per M. ft.)

| | 1s & 2s | No. 1 Com. | No. 2 Com. |
|---|---|---|---|
| 1" | $105.00 | $ 55.00 | $ 35.00 |
| 1¼ and 1½" | 110.00 | 65.00 | 40.00 |
| 2" | 120.00 | 70.00 | 40.00 |
| 2½ and 3" | 140.00 | 90.00 | 50.00 |
| 4" | 155.00 | 110.00 | 60.00 |

### Ash, Brown

| | | | |
|---|---|---|---|
| 1" | $110.00 | $ 50.00 | 30.00 |
| 1¼ and 1½" | 120.00 | 55.00 | 35.00 |
| 2" | 140.00 | 60.00 | 45.00 |
| 2½ and 3" | 150.00 | 75.00 | 45.00 |
| 4" | 165.00 | 85.00 | 50.00 |

### Birch

(Dry weight 4000 lbs. per M. ft.)

| | 1s & 2s | Sels. | No. 1 Com. | No. 2 Com. |
|---|---|---|---|---|
| 4/4 | $105.00 | $ 75.00 | $ 45.00 | $ 27.00 |
| 5/4 | 110.00 | 80.00 | 50.00 | 30.00 |
| 6/4 | 110.00 | 85.00 | 55.00 | 33.00 |
| 8/4 | 115.00 | 95.00 | 60.00 | 37.00 |
| 12/4 | 120.00 | 100.00 | 65.00 | 45.00 |
| 16/4 | 125.00 | 105.00 | 75.00 | 50.00 |

### Basswood

(Dry weight 2500 lbs. per M. ft.)

| | 1s & 2s | No. 1 Com. | No. 2 Com. |
|---|---|---|---|
| 4/4 | $ 75.00 | $ 45.00 | $ 35.00 |
| 5/4 and 6/4 | 80.00 | 55.00 | 25.00 |
| 8/4 | 85.00 | 60.00 | 30.00 |

### Chestnut

(Dry weight 2800 lbs. per M. ft.)

| | 1s & 2s | No. 1 Com. | Sound Wormy |
|---|---|---|---|
| 1" | $140.00 | $ 85.00 | $ 40.00 |
| 1¼ to 1½" | 145.00 | 93.00 | 40.00 |
| 2" | 158.00 | 103.00 | 42.00 |

### Maple, Hard

(Dry weight 4200 lbs. per M. ft.)

| | F.A.S. | Sels. | No. 1 Com. | No. 2 Com. |
|---|---|---|---|---|
| 4/4 | $ 90.00 | $ 65.00 | $ 50.00 | $ 33.00 |
| 5/4 | $ 90.00 | 65.00 | 50.00 | 38.00 |
| 6/4 | $ 90.00 | 70.00 | 55.00 | 45.00 |
| 8/4 | 95.00 | 70.00 | 55.00 | 45.00 |
| 12/4 | 100.00 | 70.00 | 60.00 | 55.00 |
| 16/4 | 120.00 | 95.00 | 65.00 | 60.00 |

### Elm, Soft

(Dry weight 3100 lbs. per M. ft.)

| | 1s & 2s | No. 1 Com. | No. 2 Com. |
|---|---|---|---|
| 4/4 | $ 75.00 | $ 50.00 | $ 30.00 |
| 4/4 | $ 85.00 | 60.00 | 35.00 |
| 12/4 | 100.00 | 70.00 | 40.00 |

### Gum, Red

(Dry weight 3300 lbs. per M. ft.)

| | —Plain— | | —Quartered— | |
|---|---|---|---|---|
| | 1s & 2s | No. 1 Com. | 1s & 2s | No. 1 Com. |
| 1" | $125.00 | $ 80.00 | $135.00 | $ 95.00 |
| 1¼" | 130.00 | 80.00 | 140.00 | 95.00 |
| 1½" | 130.00 | 85.00 | 140.00 | 100.00 |
| 2" | 130.00 | 90.00 | 150.00 | 105.00 |

Figured Gum, $30 per M. extra in both plain and quartered.

### Gum, Sap

| | 1s&2s | No. 1 Com. |
|---|---|---|
| 1" | 60.00 | $ 40.00 |
| 1¼ and 1½" | 60.00 | 45.00 |
| 2" | 65.00 | 50.00 |

### Hickory

(Dry weight 4500 lbs. per M. ft.

| | 1s&2s | No. 1 Com. |
|---|---|---|
| 1" | $125.00 | $ 70.00 |
| 1¼" | 145.00 | 70.00 |
| 1½" | 145.00 | 75.00 |
| 2" | 150.00 | 80.00 |

### Quarter Cut Red Oak

| | 1s&2s | No. 1 Com. |
|---|---|---|
| 4/4 | $145.00 | $ 80.00 |
| 5/4 and 6/4 | 160.00 | 90.00 |
| 8/4 | 165.00 | 95.00 |

### Plain White and Red Oak

(Plain sawed. Dry weight 4000 lbs. per M. ft.)

| | 1s&2s | No. 1 Com. |
|---|---|---|
| 4/4 | $130.00 | $ 75.00 |
| 5/4 and 6/4 | 135.00 | 80.00 |
| 8/4 | 140.00 | 85.00 |
| 10/4 | 145.00 | 95.00 |
| 12/4 | 145.00 | 100.00 |
| 16/4 | 150.00 | 105.00 |

### White Oak, Quarter Cut

(Dry weight 4000 lbs. per M. ft.)

| | 1s&2s | No. 1 Com. |
|---|---|---|
| 4/4 | $165.00 | $ 95.00 |
| 5/4 and 6/4 | 175.00 | 100.00 |
| 8/4 | 190.00 | 105.00 |

## OTTAWA

Manufacturers' Prices

### Pine

| | | |
|---|---|---|
| **Good sidings:** | | |
| 1 in. x 7 in. and up | | $140.00 |
| 1¼ in. and 1½ in., 8 in. and up. | | 165.00 |
| 2 in. x 7 in. and up | | 165.00 |
| No. 2 cuts 2 x 8 in. and up | | 80.00 |
| **Good strips:** | | |
| 1 in. | $100.00 | $105.00 |
| 1¼ in. and 1½ in. | | 120.00 |
| 2 in. | | 125.00 |
| **Good shorts:** | | |
| 1 in. x 7 in .and up | | 110.00 |
| 1 in. 4 in. to 6 in. | 85.00 | 90.00 |
| 1¼ in. and 1½ in. | | 110.00 |
| 2 in. | | 125.00 |
| 7 in. to 9 in. A sidings | 54.00 | 56.00 |
| No. 1 dressing sidings | 70.00 | 74.00 |
| No. 1 dressing strips | | 62.00 |
| No. 1 dressing shorts | 50.00 | 53.00 |
| 1 in. x 4 in. s.c. strips | | 48.00 |
| 1 in. x 5 in. s.c. strips | | 48.00 |
| 1 in. x 6 in. s.c. strips | | 50.00 |
| 1 in. x 7 in. s.c. strips | 51.00 | 64.00 |
| 1 in. x 8 in. s.c. strips, 12 to 16 ft. | | 54.00 |
| 1 in. x 10 in. M.R. | | 58.00 |
| S.C. sidings, 1½ and 2 in. | 58.00 | 60.00 |
| S.C. strips, 1 in. | | 45.00 |
| 1¼, 1½ and 2 in. | 50.00 | 55.00 |
| S.C. shorts, 1 x 4 to 6 in. | 34.00 | 36.00 |
| S.C. and bet., shorts, 1 x 5 | | 36.00 |
| S.C. and bet., shorts, 1 x 6 | | 42.00 |
| S.C. shorts, 6-11 ft., 1 x 10 in. | | 48.00 |
| **Box boards:** | | |
| 1 in. x 4 in. and up, 6 ft.-11 ft. | | 34.00 |
| 1 in. x 3 in. and up, 12 ft.-16 ft. | 35.00 | 37.00 |
| Mill cull shorts, 1 in. x 4 in. and x 4 in. and up, 12 ft. and up | 24.00 | 26.00 |
| Mill culls, strips and sidings, 1 in. up, 6 ft. to 11 ft. | | 22.00 |
| O. culls r and w p | 18.00 | 20.00 |

### Red Pine, Log Run

| | | |
|---|---|---|
| Mill culls out, 1 in. | 32.00 | 34.00 |
| Mill culls out, 1¼ in. | 32.00 | 34.00 |
| Mill culls out, 1½ in. | 32.00 | 34.00 |
| Mill culls out, 2 in. | 32.00 | 34.00 |
| Mill Culls, white pine, 1 in. x 7 in. and up | | 20.00 |

### Mill Run Spruce

| | | |
|---|---|---|
| 1 in. x 4 in. and up, 6 ft.-11 ft. | | 28.00 |
| 1 in. x 4 in. and up, 12 ft.-16 ft. | 30.00 | 32.00 |
| 1" x 9"-10" and up, 12 ft.-16 ft. | | 35.00 |
| 1¼" x 7, 8 and 9" up, 12 ft.-16 ft. | | 35.00 |
| 1¼ x 10 and up, 12 ft.-16 ft. | 38.00 | 42.00 |
| 1½" x 12" x 12" and up, 12'-16'. | | 42.00 |
| Spruce, 1 in. clear fine dressing and B | | 55.00 |
| Hemlock, 1 in. cull | | 20.00 |
| Hemlock, 1 in. log run | 24.00 | 26.00 |
| Hemlock, 2 x 4, 6, 8, 10 12/16 ft. | | 28.00 |
| Tamarac | 25.00 | 28.00 |
| Basswood, log run, dead culls out | 45.00 | 50.00 |
| Basswood, log run, mill culls out. | 50.00 | 54.00 |
| Birch, log run | 45.00 | 50.00 |
| Soft Elm, common and better, 1, 1½, 2 in. | 58.00 | 68.00 |
| Ash, black, log run | 62.00 | 65.00 |
| 1 x 10 No. 1 barn | 57.00 | 62.00 |
| 1 x 10 No. 2 barn | 51.00 | 56.00 |
| 1 x 8 and 9 No. 2 barn | 47.00 | 52.00 |

# CURRENT LUMBER PRICES—WHOLESALE

**Lath per M.:**

| | | |
|---|---|---|
| No. 1 White Pine, 1¼ in. x 4 ft. | | 8.00 |
| No. 2 White Pine | | 6.00 |
| Mill run White Pine | | 7.00 |
| Spruce, mill run, 1½ in. | | 6.00 |
| Red Pine, mill run | | 6.00 |
| Hemlock, mill run | | 5.50 |

**White Cedar Shingles**

| | | |
|---|---|---|
| XXXX, 18 in. | 9.00 | 10.00 |
| Clear butt, 18 in. | 6.00 | 7.00 |
| 18 in. XX | | 5.00 |

## QUEBEC

**White Pine**
(At Quebec)

| | Cts. Per Cubic Ft. | |
|---|---|---|
| First class Ottawa waney, 18 in. average according to lineal | 100 | 110 |
| 19 in. and up average | 110 | 120 |

**Spruce Deals**
(At Mill)

| | | |
|---|---|---|
| 3 in. unsorted, Quebec, 4 in. to 6 in. wide | $ 20.00 | $ 25.00 |
| 3 in. unsorted, Quebec, 7 in. to 8 in. wide | 26.00 | 28.00 |
| 3 in. unsorted, Quebec, 9 in. wide | 30.00 | 35.00 |

**Oak**
(At Quebec)

| | Cts. Per Cubic Ft. | |
|---|---|---|
| According to average and quality, 55 ft. cube | 125 | 130 |

**Elm**
(At Quebec)

| | | |
|---|---|---|
| According to average and quality, 40 to 45 ft. cube | 100 | 120 |
| According to average and quality, 30 to 35 ft. | 90 | 100 |

**Export Birch Planks**
(At Mill)

| | | |
|---|---|---|
| 1 to 4 in. thick, per M. ft. | $ 30.00 | $ 35.00 |

## ST. JOHN, N.B.

(From Yards and Mills—Retail)

**Rough Lumber**

| | | |
|---|---|---|
| 2x3, 2x4, 3x3, 3x4. Rgh Merch Spr. | $28.00 | |
| 2x3, 2x4, 3x3, 3x4, Dressed 1 edge | 30.00 | |
| 2x3, 2x4, 3x3, 3x4, Dressed 4 sides | 31.00 | |
| 2x6, 2x7, 3x5, 4x4, 4x6, all rough. | 28.00 | |
| 2x6, 2x7, 3x5, 4x4, 4x6, all rough. | 30.00 | |
| 2x8, 3x7, 5x5, 6x6 | 35.00 | $40.00 |
| 2x9, 3x8, 6x8, 7x7 | 37.00 | $40.00 |
| 2x10, 3x9 | 40.00 | |
| 2x12, 3x10, 3x12, 8x8 and up | 42.00 | |
| Merch. Spr. Bds. Rough, 1x3-4 & 5 | 28.00 | |
| Merch. Spr. Bds., Rough, 1x7 & up | 35.00 | |
| Refuse Bds., Deals and Setgs. | 18.00 | 20.00 |

Above random lengths up to 18-0 long.
Lengths 19-0 and up $5.00 extra per M.
For planing Merch. and Refuse Bds. add $2.00 per M. to above prices.
Laths, $7.00.

**Shingles**

| | Per M. |
|---|---|
| Cedar, Extras | $6.00 |
| Cedar, Clears | 5.00 |
| Cedar, 2nd Clears | 4.00 |
| Cedar, Extra No. 1 | 2.50 |
| Spruce | 3.50 |

## SARNIA, ONT.

**White Pine—Fine, Com. and Better**

| | |
|---|---|
| 1 x 6 and 8 in. | $110.00 |
| 1 in., 8 in. and up wide | 130.00 |
| 1¼ and 1½ in. and up wide | 180.00 |
| 2 in. and up wide | 180.00 |

**Cuts and Better**

| | |
|---|---|
| 4/4 x 8 and up No. 1 and better | 125.00 |
| 5/4 and 6/4 and up No. 1 and better | 150.00 |
| 8/4 and 8 and up No. 1 and better | 150.00 |

**No. 1 Cuts**

| | |
|---|---|
| 1 in., 8 in. and up wide | 105.00 |
| 1¼ in., 8 in. and up wide | 125.00 |
| 1½ in., 8 in. and up wide | 125.00 |
| 2 in., 8 in. and up wide | 130.00 |
| 2½ in. and 3 in., 8 in. and up wide | 175.00 |
| 4 in., 8 in. and up wide | 185.00 |

**No. 1 Barn**

| | | |
|---|---|---|
| 1 in., 10 to 16 ft. long | $ 75.00 | $ 85.00 |
| 1¼, 1½ and 2 in., 10/16 ft. | 80.00 | 85.00 |
| 2½ to 3 in., 10/16 ft. | 85.00 | 100.00 |

**No. 2 Barn**

| | | |
|---|---|---|
| 1 in., 10 to 16 ft. long | 65.00 | 75.00 |
| 1¼, 1½ and 2 in., 10/16 ft. | | 66.00 |
| 2½, 1½ and 3 in. | | 85.00 |

**No. 3 Barn**

| | | |
|---|---|---|
| 1 in., 10 to 16 ft. long | 48.00 | 55.00 |
| 1¼, 1½ and 2 in., 10/16 ft. | 50.00 | 56.00 |

**Box**

| | | |
|---|---|---|
| 1 in., 1¼ and 1½ in., 10/16 ft. | 33.00 | 35.00 |

**Mill Culls**

Mill Run Culls—

| | |
|---|---|
| 1 in., 4 in. and up wide, 6/16 ft. | 26.00 |
| 1¼, 1½ and 2 in. | 27.00 |

## WINNIPEG

**No. 1 Spruce**

| Dimension | S.1.S. and 1.E. 10 ft. | 12 ft. | 14 ft. | 16 ft. |
|---|---|---|---|---|
| 2 x 4 | $31 | $30 | $30 | $31 |
| 2 x 6 | 32 | 30 | 30 | 31 |
| 2 x 8 | 33 | 31 | 31 | 32 |
| 2 x 10 | 34 | 32 | 32 | 33 |
| 2 x 12 | 35 | 33 | 33 | 34 |

For 2 inches, rough, add 50 cents.
For S1E only, add 50 cents.
For S1S and 2E, S4S or D&M, add $3.00.
For timbers larger than 8 x 8, add 50c. for each additional 2 inches each way.
For lengths longer than 20 ft., add $1.00 for each additional two feet.
For selected common, add $5.00.
For No. 2 Dimension, $3.00 less than No. 1.
For 1 x 2 and 2 x 2, $2 more than 2 x 4 No. 1.
For Tamarac, open.

## BUFFALO and TONAWANDA

**White Pine**
Wholesale Selling Price

| | |
|---|---|
| Uppers, 4/4 | $225.00 |
| Uppers, 5/4 to 8/4 | 225.00 |
| Uppers, 10/4 to 12/4 | 250.00 |
| Selects, 4/4 | 200.00 |
| Selects, 5/4 to 8/4 | 200.00 |
| Selects, 10/4 to 12/4 | 225.00 |
| Fine Common, 4/4 | 155.00 |
| Fine Common, 5/4 | 160.00 |
| Fine Common, 6/4 | 160.00 |
| Fine Common, 8/4 | 160.00 |
| No. 1 Cuts, 4/4 | 115.00 |
| No. 1 Cuts, 5/4 | 130.00 |
| No. 1 Cuts, 6/4 | 135.00 |
| No. 1 Cuts, 8/4 | 140.00 |
| No. 2 Cuts, 4/4 | 70.00 |
| No. 2 Cuts, 5/4 | 100.00 |
| No. 2 Cuts, 6/4 | 105.00 |
| No. 2 Cuts, 8/4 | 110.00 |
| No. 3 Cuts, 5/4 | 60.00 |
| No. 3 Cuts, 6/4 | 65.00 |
| No. 3 Cuts, 8/4 | 67.00 |
| Dressing, 4/4 | 95.00 |
| Dressing 4/4 x 10 | 98.00 |
| Dressing, 4/4 x 12 | 110.00 |
| No. 1 Moulding, 5/4 | 150.00 |
| No. 1 Moulding, 6/4 | 150.00 |
| No. 1 Moulding, 8/4 | 155.00 |
| No. 2 Moulding, 5/4 | 125.00 |
| No. 2 Moulding, 6/4 | 125.00 |
| No. 2 Moulding, 8/4 | 130.00 |
| No. 1 Barn, 1 x 12 | 90.00 |
| No. 1 Barn, 1 x 6 and 8 | 76.00 |
| No. 1 Barn, 1 x 10 | 80.00 |
| No. 2 Barn, 1 x 6 and 8 | 62.00 |
| No. 2 Barn, 1 x 10 | 63.00 |
| No. 2 Barn, 1 x 12 | 75.00 |
| No. 3 Barn, 1 x 6 and 8 | 41.00 |
| No. 3 Barn, 1 x 10 | 43.00 |
| No. 3 Barn 1 x 12 | 46.00 |
| No. 1 Box, 1 x 6 and 8 | 36.00 |
| No. 1 Box 1 x 10 | 38.00 |
| No. 1 Box 1 x 12 | 39.00 |
| No. 1 Box, 1 x 13 and up | 39.00 |

## BUFFALO

The following quotations on hardwoods represent the jobber buying price at Buffalo and Tonawanda.

**Maple**

| | 1s & 2s | No. 1 Com. | No. 2 Com. |
|---|---|---|---|
| 1 in. | $ 75.00 | $ 45.00 | $ 28.00 |
| 5/4 to 8/4 | 80.00 | 50.00 | 28.00 |
| 10/4 to 4 in. | 85.00 | 55.00 | 28.00 |

**Sap Birch**

| | | | |
|---|---|---|---|
| 1 in. | 90.00 | 45.00 | 30.00 |
| 5/4 and up | 100.00 | 50.00 | 30.00 |

**Soft Elm**

| | | | |
|---|---|---|---|
| 1 in. | 70.00 | 45.00 | 30.00 |
| 5/4 to 2 in. | 75.00 | 50.00 | 30.00 |

**Red Birch**

| | | | |
|---|---|---|---|
| 1 in. | 120.00 | 75.00 | |
| 5/4 and up | 125.00 | 80.00 | |

**Basswood**

| | | | |
|---|---|---|---|
| 1 in. | 70.00 | 45.00 | 30.00 |
| 5/4 to 2 in. | 80.00 | 55.00 | 35.00 |

**Plain Oak**

| | | | |
|---|---|---|---|
| 1 in. | 95.00 | 55.00 | 35.00 |
| 5/4 to 2 in. | 105.00 | 65.00 | 40.00 |

**Ash**

| | | | |
|---|---|---|---|
| 1 in. | 80.00 | 48.00 | 30.00 |
| 5/4 to 2 in. | 85.00 | 52.00 | 30.00 |
| 10/4 and up | 100.00 | 65.00 | 30.00 |

## BOSTON

Quotations given below are for highest grades of Michigan and Canadian White Pine and Eastern Canadian Spruce as required in the New England market in car loads.

| | | |
|---|---|---|
| White Pine Uppers, 1 in. | | |
| White Pine Uppers, 1¼, 1½, 2 in. | | |
| White Pine Uppers, 2½, 3 in. | | |
| White Pine Uppers, 4 in. | | |
| Selects, 1 in. | | $190.00 |
| Selects, 1¼, 2 in. | | 200.00 |
| Selects, 2½, 3 in. | | |
| Selects, 4 in. | | |

Prices nominal

| | | |
|---|---|---|
| Fine Common, 1 in., 30%, 12 in. and up. | | 165.00 |
| Fine Common, 1 x 8 and up | | 165.00 |
| Fine Common, 1¼ to 2 in. | $165.00 | 170.00 |
| Fine Common, 2½ and 3 in. | | 180.00 |
| Fine Common, 4 in. | | 195.00 |
| 1 in. Shaky Clear | | 100.00 |
| 1¼ in. to 2 in. Shaky Clear | | 110.00 |
| 1 in. No. 2 Dressing | | 95.00 |
| 1¼ in. to 2 in. No. 2 Dressing | | 95.00 |
| No. 1 Cuts, 1 in. | | 110.00 |
| No. 1 Cuts, 1¼ to 2 in. | | 140.00 |
| No. 1 Cuts, 2½ to 3 in. | | 180.00 |
| No. 2 Cuts, 1 in. | | 80.00 |
| No. 2 Cuts, 1¼ to 2 in. | | 110.00 |
| Barn Boards, No. 1, 1 x 12 | | 95.00 |
| Barn Boards, No. 1, 1 x 10 | | 87.00 |
| Barn Boards, No. 1, 1 x 8 | | 83.00 |
| Barn Boards, No. 2, 1 x 12 | | 82.00 |
| Barn Boards, No. 2, 1 x 8 | | 69.00 |
| Barn Boards, No. 2, 1 x 10 | | 70.00 |
| Barn Boards, No. 3, 1 x 12 | | 48.00 |
| Barn Boards, No. 3, 1 x 10 | | 47.00 |
| Barn Boards, No. 3, 1 x 8 | | 47.00 |

**No. 1 Clear**

| | | | |
|---|---|---|---|
| Can. Spruce, No. 1 and clear, 1 x 4 to 9" | | | $ 78.00 |
| Can. Spruce, 1 x 10 in. | | | 78.00 |
| Can. Spruce, No. 1, 1 x 4 to 7 in. | | | 75.00 |
| Can. Spruce, No. 1, 1 x 8 and 9 in. | | | 75.00 |
| Can. Spruce, No. 1, 1 x 10 in. | | | 76.00 |
| Can. Spruce, No. 2, 1 x 4 and 5 in. | | | 34.00 |
| Can. Spruce, No. 2, 1 x 6 and 7 in. | | | 36.00 |
| Can. Spruce, No. 2, 1 x 8 and 9 in. | | | 38.00 |
| Can. Spruce, No. 2, 1 x 10 in. | | | 41.00 |
| Can. Spruce, No. 2, 1 x 12 in. | | | 45.00 |
| Spruce, 12 in. dimension | | | 46.00 |
| Spruce, 10 in. dimension | | | 44.00 |
| Spruce 9 in. dimension | | | 43.00 |
| Spruce, 8 in. dimension | | | 42.00 |
| 2 x 10 in. random lengths, 8 ft. and up | | | 41.00 |
| 2 x 12 in., random lengths | | | 43.00 |
| 2 x 3, 2 x 4, 2 x 5, 2 x 6, 2 x 7 | 31.00 | 32.00 | 30.00 |
| 2 x 9 | | | 38.00 |
| All other random lengths, 7 in. and under, 8 ft. and up | 30.00 | | 34.00 |
| 5 in. and up merchantable boards, 8 ft. and up, D 1s | 30.00 | | 32.00 |
| 1 x 2 | | | 32.00 |
| 1 x 3 | | | 31.00 |
| 1⅝ in. Spruce Lath | | | 9.00 |
| 1½ in. Spruce Lath | 7.75 | | 8.00 |

**New Brunswick Cedar Shingles**

| | | |
|---|---|---|
| Extras | | 5.75 |
| Clears | 4.25 | 4.50 |
| Second Clear | 3.75 | 4.15 |
| Clear Whites | | 3.00 |

Second Hand Machinery & Equipment Wanted & For Sale

# Quick Action Section

Special Lots Of Lumber—Positions Wanted & Vacant

## Lumber Wanted

### Wanted to Buy

Peeled spruce and balsam pulpwood. 50% cash, balance on arrival. Write P. O. Box 843, Montreal. 9-14

### Hemlock Wanted

Wanted a good sized block of Ontario Hemlock, also block of pine, spruce or Jack Pine. Box 985, Canada Lumberman, Toronto. 12

### We Will Buy

A block of Hemlock, Spruce, Red or White Pine that is sawn or will be sawn before the 15th of March. Box 770, Canada Lumberman, Toronto. 2 T.f.

### Wanted Lath

4' Nos. 1, 2 and 3, White Pine No. 1 No. 2 Spruce.

The George N. Comfort Lumber Co.,
11-14 1506 Kirby Bldg., Cleveland, O

### Wanted

Spruce Lath, ¼ x 1½" x 4' also Spruce or Hemlock dimensions. State if you can saw long lengths in Spruce or Hemlock and quote prices.

BRIGHTON LUMBER CO.
11-14 Island Pond, Vt.

### Pulpwood Wanted

Wanted by old and reliabe firm in Northern Ontario a contract to represent either Canadian or American Paper Interests for the purchase of Pulpwood on a commission basis. We have Saw Mill and Retail Stores whereby we can supply jobbers throughout. For references apply, Royal Bank of Canada and Bradstreets.

PELLOW & McMEEKIN,
11-14 Hearst, Ont.

## Lumber For Sale

### Sawdust

For sale, in car lots.
The London Box Mfg. & Lumber Co., Limited,
9 T.f.

### For Sale in Carload Lots

Telegraph Poles, Cedar and Hardwood Ties, Spruce Balsam and Poplar Pulpwood. Jas. Thos. Clair, Clair, N. B. 9-14

### For Sale

Chair Stock:
Bone Air Dried.
30 M. ft. 1" x 1" square 20" long.
20 M. ft. 1½" x 1½" square 20" long.
BIRCH—Clear Stock.
Apply P.O. Box 6, Victoriaville, Que
11 T.f.

### WHITE PINE LUMBER

#### For Immediate Shipment—1920 Cut—Should Be Bone Dry

About 30,000 ft. 2 in.
" 18,000 ft. 1 in.
" 2,000 ft. 3 in.
Apply to J. A. Farnsworth, Cookshire, Quebec. 6-T.f.

### PUBLISHER'S NOTICE

Advertisements other than "Employment Wanted" or "Employees Wanted" will be inserted in this department at the rate of 25 cents per agate line (14 agate lines make one inch). $3.50 per inch, each insertion, payable in advance. Space measured from rule to rule. When four or more consecutive insertions of the same advertisement are ordered a discount of 25 per cent. will be allowed.

Advertisements of "Wanted Employment" will be inserted at the rate of one cent a word, net. Cash must accompany order. If Canada Lumberman box number is used, enclose ten cents extra for postage in forwarding replies. Minimum charge 25 cents.

Advertisements of "Wanted Employees" will be inserted at the rate of two cents a word, net. Cash must accompany the order. Minimum charge 50 cents.

Advertisements must be received not later than the 10th and 20th of each month to insure insertion in the subsequent issue.

### For Sale

At Blind River, Ontario, Pine and Spruce Lath, also some Cedar and Hemlock Lath, Grades, four foot mill run, 32" mill run, and four foot No. 3.

F. P. Potvin,
2 T.f. Blind River, Ont.

### For Sale Dry Lumber

1 car 8/4 Hard Maple, good widths.
1 C. & B. 50 1/1 1sts and 2nds.
3 cars 4/4 Beech 1 C. & B. allowing.
20 1/1 2 Common.
1 car Bass 4/4 Mill Run.
E. V. Wilson, Shanty Bay, Ontario. 11-12

### For Sale

Ten cars mixed cordwood, one thousand railroad ties, and five cars of lumber.

1 car 2" Plain Oak.
2 cars 1" Elm.
1 car 1" Maple.
1 car 1" Basswood.

No reasonable offer refused. Apply to
Edgar Swick,
12 Canfield, Ont.

### Lumber for Sale

193 M. 8/4 and 86 M. 12/4 No. 2 Common & Better, Hard Maple.
301 M. 4/4 No. 2 & 3 Common Birch.

This is all well manufactured band sawn stock and dry.

Canada Wood Specialty Company, Ltd.,
12 Longford Mills, Ont.

## Machinery For Sale

### Engine for Sale

I only 15" x 34" Wheelock Engine 125 H. P. also 5' 6" x 15' H. R. T. Boiler—both in good condition for immediate delivery.

Apply the Steel Company of Canada Ltd., 1272 Notre Dame St. West, Montreal. 12

### For Sale

1 E Long Mfg. Co. Lath Mill with 11 saws.
1 Standard Machinery Co. 7 Saw Lath Bolter with 21 saws.
1 Diamond Iron Works 5 Ft. Horizontal Band Resaw, slat bed, with 3 saws.
1 28 Ton Lima Geared Locomotive, standard gauge.

Schroeder Mills & Timber Co., Pakesley, Ontario. Milwaukee, Wis. 9-12

### Wickes Gang

GANG: No. 12 Wickes Gang, 40" sash, 15" stroke, steam boiler rolls, front and back in two sections, feed and oscillation combined, 1908 model, and has been in use for five years. We furnish with this gang 11 rolls for cants and stock, one filing machine, and 4 sets of saws.

THE PEMBROOKE LUMBER CO.,
1 t. f. Pembrooke, Ont.

## Situations Wanted

Wanted Position as Salesman—Would consider propositions on Commission basis for City. Experienced—references. Box 925 Canada Lumberman, Toronto. 11-13

Experienced Accountant available immediately. Manufacturing costs, books, financing, banking, correspondence Excellent references Named. Apply Box 936, Canada Lumberman, Toronto. 12

Experienced Salesman open for responsible position with wholesale or retail lumber firm. First class experience in both outside selling and inside work. Apply Box 937, Canada Lumberman, Toronto. 12

Young married Scotchman, abstainer, wishes position as bookkeeper, stenographer in sawmill office, experience, six years banking, two years London, England, nine years sawmill office. Salary $100 with removal expenses up to $100, repayable in monthly instalments. Apply Box 983, Canada Lumberman, Toronto. 12

## Situations Vacant

WANTED—Experienced Yard Foreman for City of 16,000 Population in Western Ontario. Must be a hustler. Apply Box 927, Canada Lumberman, Toronto. 12

## Business Chances

### Sawmill for Sale

In Parry Sound. Near shipping point and plenty of timber for sale close. For particulars, write I. E. Brown, Box 34, Burk's Falls, Ontario. 12

### Wanted

BRITISH COLUMBIA TIMBER LIMITS for a client of mine. Send maps, estimates, price, terms and commission to Dwight J. Turner, Attorney at Law, 1937-9 Dime Bank Bldg., Detroit, Michigan. 10-13

### Timber Limit Wanted

We want a freehold timber limit near Sault Ste. Marie, Sudbury, and North Bay, accessible to a river, about one million cords of pulpwood, destination of that wood will be Niagara Falls, Michigan and Illinois. Full particulars will be appreciated. Apply to Quebec Lumber Co., 140 St. Peter St., Quebec. 12-13

### For Sale

DEBENTURE BONDS,—secured by agreement for sale of limits and plant on Nimpkish Lake and river, Vancouver Island. A small block of these Bonds are in my hands for sale at an attractive price. Re Payment in full provided for by October, 1925. PURCHASERS operating constantly, and are of unquestioned financial standing.

For all particulars apply to—

J. R. MACPHAIL, 525 Seymour St., Vancouver, B.C. 11-12

### For Sale

Hardwood limit on North Shore Georgian Bay, containing the finest Birch in the North country, large quantity of Maple, some Oak, a considerable quantity of Hemlock, Pine and Spruce, and a very large quantity of Ties. Can be bought on very reasonable terms and paid for largely in lumber. For reply address Box 928, Canada Lumberman, Toronto. 12-15

### Sawing Contract Wanted

for a term of years by a Company of expert sawmill men who are willing to go anywhere and understand manufacturing from ground floor up and who own a mill of 30-35 M. ft. daily capacity. Same can be viewed in operation until August, 1922, when our present contract will be completed. For full particulars and present location of plant, address Box 909, Canada Lumberman, Toronto. 10-15

### For Sale in Medora Township

½ million feet Birch and Maple, also some Hemlock and Softwoods, small portable saw mill, good camps, stables and full equipment, also teams, harness, sleighs, wagons and full camping equipment. This is ready for an energetic person to make money with siding on premises and only 120 miles from Toronto. Several million feet of hardwood all within two miles of this location. Half cash, balance terms to suit purchaser. Investigate address Box 908 Canada Lumberman, Toronto. 10-15

### Mills and Limits for Sale

145 sq. miles of standing spruce, close to railway.
Mill well equipped, capacity 75,000 to 100,000 ft.
Mill, well equipped, capacity 30,000 ft.
Phoenix Logging Engine.
Sleds and numerous other equipment.
Write for particulars.

The Saskatchewan Lumber Co. Limited,
Crooked River, Sask. 6-T.f

## Timber Limit for Sale

### Township of Gillmor

N. S. L. H. Berths Nos. 2, 3, and 4, area 27¼ square miles more or less. Rights to cut Red and White Pine Timber only. Any fair offer will be considered. For full information apply to A. C. Manbert, c/o Canadian General Lumber Company, Limited, Bank of Hamilton Building, Toronto. 12-13

## Timber Berth for Sale

NOTICE IS HEREBY GIVEN that Timber License Number 49, for the season 1922-1923 of Timber Berth Number Three, in the Township of Proudfoot, in the District of Nipissing, in the Province of Ontario, and comprising lots 1 to 20 inclusive in the ninth, tenth, eleventh, twelfth, thirteenth and fourteenth concessions of the said Township (except such lots as are excluded from said License) and containing an area of fifteen and one-quarter square miles more or less, will be offered for sale at public auction at the auction rooms of C. M. Henderson & Company, 128 King Street East, Toronto, on Wednesday the Twenty-first day of June 1922 at twelve o'clock noon.

For further particulars, terms and conditions of sale apply to The Seaman Kent Company, Limited, 268 Wallace Avenue, Toronto, or to

Ludwig & Ballantyne,
157 Bay Street, Toronto.
12 Solicitors for the Vendor.

## The Wanton Waste of Wooded Wealth

In an article recently published in the "World's Work" an alarming picture of the waste going on in the United States lumber industry is presented by Theodore M. Knappen, a former resident of Vancouver, B. C., who says that the incomparable white pine whose supply once seemed limitless in New England and the Great Lake States is all but gone, he says, virtually eradicated within 70 years. Southern pine, 650 million feet strong, called upon 30 years ago to fill the growing gaps in the white pine forces, now nears exhaustion itself. Cypress fights a hopeless battle in the Southern swamps.

The once great hardwood forests of the States have been slashed right and left, and the time is at hand when Ontario and Quebec hardwood, none too plentiful, will be called on to supply American needs. Upon the Western yellow pine and the redwoods, cedar, Douglas fir and spruce of the Pacific Coast, American and Canadian, devolves the task of making the last fight for the forest wealth of this continent—either the end of all timber or a winning fight that shall hold the fort till forestation or reforestation shall turn the tide.

Despite the 81,000,000 acres of eroded, fire-scarred useless desert which marks the path of the lumber hogs in the United States, and the 300,000,000 acres of scrub, where to the extinction of fire was not added, Knappen thinks he sees a ray of hope, and signs that this mad debauch is nearing an end, before it is too late. For from the very lumbermen who threatened to impeach Grover Cleveland for creating forest reserves, and who scoffed at conservation when Roosevelt barred the door to the last of the Federal forests, has come an outcry against the possibility of a resumption of the ancient policy of reckless use today, and forget tomorrow.

The consumption and destruction of saw timber in the States now proceeds at the rate of 56,000,000 feet board measure annually. These figures take no account of pulpwood, railroad ties, and firewood, of which the consumption far exceeds the growth, and for the first of which the States is helplessly dependent upon Canada. Seventy-nine percent. of American forest lands are privately owned. And much of the limits were bought for a song by the big lumbermen from American citizens whose easy homestead laws allowed an individual to purchase 160 acres of timber from Uncle Sam for $1.50 an acre. Needless to say much of the land thus acquired was unsuitable for farming, and bought with the deliberate intention of re-selling it to the lumbermen.

How is Uncle Sam going to bring back his vanished timber? Knappen cites Col. Greely as saying that while the saws cut five million acres of timber annually, fire eats up five million acres, and that if the 25,000 yearly fires were stopped 75 per cent. of the timber would come back naturally. Just how far tree planting would be carried out in any programme Knappen does not suggest, though he gives the opinion of other men that the administration of the forests should be left with the Department of Agriculture, who regard timber as a crop, and its care as a problem of agriculture.

## What Margin of Profit on Lumber?

There really isn't much choice.

It is impossible for any one to sell lumber below a certain point and stay in business. He cannot get business if he goes beyond a certain point.

This margin sector is not long.

Above it the average is too high. Below it he cannot make money.

There isn't much to worry about.

The logical thing, it would seem, would be to put his "Jag" trade price toward the top of this natural profit zone and his bill price near the bottom of it.

Then he will have but little to worry about. His price will be near enough to being correct all the time so that he will do a good volume of business and make a nominal profit on everything that he sells.

## Cheaper Woods Available for Fence Posts

It was stated recently at the Forests Products' Laboratories of Canada in Montreal that a series of experiments had just been successfully concluded with a view to demonstrating the possibility of using cheaper woods for fence posts instead of cedar, by a process of creosoting, similar to that used for preservation of railway ties. For years past, it was stated, the belief had been general that the only timber that would give a reasonable life for fence posts was cedar, which was becoming both scarce and expensive.

The experiments made with creosoting had shown that by a comparatively simple process it was possible to treat fence posts of certain hardwoods in such a way that they would have a life at least twice as long as ordinary cedar posts.

In carrying out these experiments fences were erected at the Forest Nursery at Indian Head in 1917, with posts of Russian poplar, both creosoted and untreated. The result of this experiment was that all the untreated posts had decayed and been removed, while the creosoted posts were all still in service, and apparently as sound as the day they were put in service.

In regard to the shrinkage of lumber air dried, which was discussed in the last issue of the "Canada Lumberman," a firm in the neighborhood of Espanola say,—"This is a somewhat difficult question to answer as lumber swells and shrinks under various weather conditions unless this is prevented by its being painted. In sawing lumber green we cut our 4 and 5-inch, 1/16 inch heavy; 6 inch, 1/8 inch; 8-inch, 3/16 inch, 10 and 12-inch, 1/4 inch over the respective widths, and in thickness 1/16 inch heavy to take care of shrinkage. When these rules are followed closely, there is no trouble with narrow or thin lumber."

# Review of Current Trade Conditions

## Conditions in Ontario are Getting Better

Market conditions continue to be quite extensive in volume but prices in most lines are as yet competitive. Considerable buying is going on and stocks of certain sizes of hemlock and white pine, such as No. 1, 2 and 3 cuts and good sides, are scarce. New 1922 cut stock, however, will be soon coming on the market to relieve the shortage.

While business has been developing steadily, prices on several lines are still weaker than the trade feel they should be in view of the cost of production. There is still a good demand for white pine lath and it is fully expected that the B. C. red shingle shortage will be taken care of.

Business in the rural community has not opened up yet as satisfactorily as some would like to see and there is a disposition on the part of certain buyers to hold back owing to. the anticipated reduction in freight rates. Just how soon this will eventuate, remains to be seen.

Generally speaking the softwood business, owing to the house building campaign, is in a more lively condition than the hardwood line, as the latter depends very much upon industrial aggressiveness and expansion and the erection or high-class residences and office buildings where hardwood trim is used exclusively, While there is a building boom at present, it is largely confined to dwellings of medium price which do not use any very large amount of hardwoods except chestnut and hardwood flooring.

It is not thought that the volume of business will grow any greater than it has during the past month, as generally July and August are comparatively quiet periods in the trade. Many wholesalers and retailers are looking forward with confidence to a strong demand this fall with the prediction that prices will stiffen and stocks will move more freely than they have for some time.

There is a fair business in both hardwoods and softwoods being done across the border and the export business is also looming up a little more promising. If ocean freight rates were brought down another 15 or 20%, it is believed that the volume of overseas trade in the forest products line would be considerably augmented.

A recent report from the West says that shipment of dimension boards to the Atlantic Coast is constantly increasing and the supply of this stock at the western mills was probably never less than it is at present time. Prices are higher than they were two months ago but even yet it is said the mills are not making any money on account of high manufacturing costs. With the increased requisitions, a firm market is looked forward to with a strong possibility of higher prices.

It is reported, that many Washington mills are now working night shifts and that there is likelihood of a reduced freight rate which while it may increase the demand, may result in correspondingly increased quotations.

A number of hardwood firms say that orders are increasing rapidly and considerable business is being done with the automobile concerns in Michigan, who are taking 2 and 3-inch birch and maple as well as some ash, in No. 1 common and better.

The export trade has also opened up and considerable white bass-wood and 2½ and 3-inch end-dried white maple are being sent overseas for use in the manufacture of pianofortes. Prices, however, offered are not very attractive, but as one local dealer expressed it "We have to keep our organization together and have to move some stock now and then even if we do not make any money."

Recently there was an increase in the price of doors owing to the advancement of various B. C. lines. All fir doors jumped in price about 10 per cent. and pine doors 5 per cent. Other lines are holding steady.

There have been several sales reported in the North. It is said that a big block of white pine changed hands recently on the basis of $43. for box and better. Some jack pine is also said to have sold en bloc at $26. with $18. for the culls. Spruce is getting a little stronger all the while and there have been advances of $3. to $6. in 1 x 6, 1 x 8 and other sizes. A number of mills in the Ontario hinterland are not running at the present time and it is declared by the owners that they will not start up until they can, at least, see their way clear of getting cost out of their lumber. A northern operator recently sold a large stock and when asked about it, replied,—"I did not sell it, I gave it away."

Hardwood flooring manufacturers say that they and the head of a progressive concern stated all their plants were running to capacity and that one was operating both night and day. The prices on all lines are well maintained and there had been a few upward revisions of late. The present house-building campaign had resulted in a strong demand for birch, maple and oak flooring. The requisitions for the latter still led, it being the most popular of the floorings for homes. A number of owners are, however, using birch and maple for upstairs and kitchen requirements. The speaker stated that several lines of hardwood would be very scarce within the next two or three months and he predicted that there would be a decided shortage of maple in all grades, while the better ends of birch would be none too plentiful. Some export business is being done in hardwood flooring but not to any great extent.

Building was very active in Toronto during the month of May when the items totalled $4,195,000 and broke all records. The nearest total for a single month previously was $3,900,000 and the cost of the new Union Station was included in that sum. A remarkable fact in connection with the activity of May is that $2,784,300 was invested in brick dwellings. The total value of building permits in Toronto issued during the first five months of 1922 is $13,501,754 as compared with $8,988,134 for the corresponding period of 1921. The permits issued last month included permits for 718 dwelling houses and 528 garages.

## Montreal Market Shows Some Improvement

So far as volume is concerned, the Montreal market continues to show improvement, accompanied by a better feeling. The requisitions have not been on a very satisfactory basis, but there appears to be a tendency for quotations to stiffen, due to the enlarged business. The weak spot is collections, which are slow, while there is also an inclination on the part of some wholesalers to curtail credits.

The increase in the demand is not confined to the Montreal district, some good orders having been received from outside points. An indication of the greater activity is the fact that one of the most extensive dressing mills in the province has a large amount of work in hand, and is unable to promise immediate delivery.

The building situation has a strong influence on the better buying. In April, the permits totalled $2,038,834 and in May, $2,831,490, the total for the year being $6,583,579 as against $4,921,019 in the corresponding period in 1921. The greater part is for residences, the cost now having come down to figures which will permit of construction on a profitable basis, so far as rents are concerned. A firm doing business in roofing paper reports that there is a brisk demand for its commodities and that these are practically all for small houses and flats. Contractors have again reduced wages, this time from 10 to 13 per cent.

The spruce lath market remains firm, with buying on a considerable scale. The mills are holding out for their quotations. B. C. forest products are not moving very fast, the recent advances in prices being calculated to divert orders for substitute woods. Another rise on common stock has gone into effect, due, it is stated, to the stronger buying for American account.

Exports to the United Kingdom are on a good scale, practically all the firms engaged in this department sending parcels of goods. The lumber includes spruce, red and white pine, birch logs and boards, bogwood and splints. The firms shipping are Watson and Todd, Limited, E. M. Nicholson, Cox, Long & Company, Limited, W. & J. Sharples and the Rolland Lumber Company. The steamship companies are curtailing their sailing lists on account of the small amount of general cargo offering.

British Government stocks are still finding a ready market. Cox, Long & Company, Limited, Montreal, have purchased about 20,000,-000 feet of Quebec, Nova Scotia and New Brunswick stock. Some additional sales have been made to firms in the Maritime Provinces.

Very little is doing in pulpwood, both the Canadian and American mills showing practically no interest in buying. Dealers are looking for a revival in the Fall, when the present stocks will be reduced. The exports in April were 49,076 cords, valued at $476,344., compared with 96,998 cords, of a value of $955,983 in March, and 73,071 cords, valued at $977,527 in April, 1921.

## Quebec Export of Deals Shows Increase

The export of timber and deals from the port of Quebec during the month of May and the first week of June has been almost double that of the season of navigation of 1921. The principal shippers have been the Quebec export firms of Price Bros., Limited, W. & J.

Sharples, R'gd., and John Burstall & Co., while the Louise Lumber Co. have also shipped quantities. The approximate quantity of wood thus far shipped is 2,795,782 feet. The firm of W. & J. Sharples, Limited, shipped 975,783 feet; Price Bros. & Co. Limited, 800,000 feet, and the balance was shipped by John Burstall & Co. and Louise Lumber Co. These shipments were made in part cargoes on the steamer "Venusia" for London; steamer "Venonis" also for London; C.G.M.M. "Canadian Trooper" for Greenock and Glasgow; "Bally-gally Head" for Belfast, etc. The average freight charges paid was 75 shillings, the big liners still adhering to 85 shillings. For the present tramp vessels are now offering freight rates of 72.6.

Advices from the United Kingdom indicate an increased demand for Canadian lumber, but speculating on ocean rates becoming lower, the British purchasers are lowering the prices at home, and offering to buy from Quebec export firms at figures too low for approval. The general opinion in Quebec is that the heft of the wood for the United Kingdom market will be shipped across by the end of June, and any more orders received will be small unless the freight rates go lower and reach the figure of 65 shillings. There is no sign, however, of these expectations being realized during this season of navigation, the steamship interests claiming that wages and general overhead charges will not permit the desired reduction.

The construction boom in the United States is having its effect in Quebec. The eastern mills are now kept busy manufacturing deals for shipment to the New England and Middle States, and the firms of Price Bros. Limited, and W. & J. Sharples, R'gd., as well as the Power Lumber Co's. mills at St. Pacome, situated on the South shore east of Quebec are doing a thriving trade. During the second week of May the Power Lumber Co. shipped seventy carloads of lumber to New York and the demand from the American Market still continues.

The reduction of ten per cent. on the American railways is in the main responsible for the shipments from the district of Quebec, and if the Canadian railways were to follow the example set, by a similar decrease in freight rates, business would be considerably increased.

Another element in connection with the demand from the United States for Canadian wood is the depletion of forest products in the markets of the United States, and the rise in price of the Pacific wood, which has caused the American purchasers to turn their attention to the Canadian lumber interests. It cannot be surmised just how long this demand will last but there is an indication that requisitions will continue well into the middle of the summer.

### Much Larger Demand in St. John District

While the prices of lumber show no change as yet, there is a much better demand in St. John, N. B. Buyers are frequently visiting in that section, and while not making any volume of purchases, still they are keeping in close touch, realizing as they travel among the trade that the day of further reductions has come to an end and, if they try to make any purchases of special sizes, they find both a shortage and a stiffening in price; for instance, 2 x 4 is growing more scarce, while 2 x 8 is very hard to find. During the last ten days, at least, a $2.00 per M advance took place in these two sizes, which would at the present time leave from $22.00 to $23.00 f.o.b., for 2 x 4 and $30.00 per M for 2 x 8. This, of course, applies to short random stocks. 2 x3 is also in demand, and 3 x 4 is now being sold to the American market at $30.00, delivered Boston, which will net the shipper $20.00 per M.

Certainly large quantities of lumber are being shipped from all over New Brunswick to the American market. From every siding the old stock is being sent and considerable quantities of old government stocks have been entirely cleaned up from all sections. It looks at the present as if this fall will find only a limited quantity held in New Brunswick; therefore should there be any demand, the price will, certainly, improve. Building in the New York and New England centres continues brisk and from day to day come information of further housing and building plans.

The British market is still inactive. A great deal of old British Government stocks is being shipped from all over New Brunswick, and will find its way into Great Britian, so until it is received and disposed of on the other side of the water, this market will show probably no change. Conditions on the other side are as yet unsettled, but more confidence is daily coming and exchange is gradually righting itself. If the Swedes hold on for prices, they are asking it will certainly have a good influence on this side of the water and have a steadying effect on spruce prices.

As there are no more sacrifice stocks for sale and mills running are well supplied with orders, the worst is over. While at St. John trade is not good, elsewhere throughout New Brunswick a goodly amount of building is going on and St. John factories are busy with an average number of men employed. Local prices at St. John for

house-building supplies are in no way uniform as a great lot of low-grade lumber is being offered much below quotations at which new stocks can be produced.

Only two mills are as yet in operation at St. John. Seemingly no others are planning to start. Rafting operations at the Federation booms are just starting. There are, probably, not over two million feet of logs in the booms but a considerable drive is yet to come in, some two to three million feet which may reach the booms this year should very high water prevail later in 1922.

Laths are in good demand with the mills at St. John and are all sold ahead for the season. Shingles are selling fairly well with prices unchanged.

### May Showed High Construction Total

The month of may was, with one exception, the biggest month for construction contracts Canada has known since 1914, according to statistics compiled by MacLean Building Reports. The total amount of reported contracts awarded was $34,827,300, as compared with $29,428,400 in April and $26,850,500 for May, 1921.

Residential building accounted for 45 per cent of the May total, and amounted to $15,623,300. Business building amounted to $11,516,000 or 33.1 per cent of the total. Industrial buildings amounted to $801,500 or 2.4 per cent; public works and utilities, $6,876,300 or 19.5 per cent.

The statistics for the different provinces are as follows: —

| | No. of Projects | Value. |
|---|---|---|
| Ontario | 2,048 | $20,012,900 |
| Quebec | 779 | 7,813,900 |
| British Columbia | 276 | 3,090,900 |
| Manitoba | 290 | 1,381,300 |
| Nova Scotia | 84 | 1,065,700 |
| Nova Scotia | 162 | 875,400 |
| New Brunswick | 94 | 818,400 |
| Saskatchewan | 136 | 668,500 |
| Prince Ed. Is. | 4 | 101,000 |
| Total for Dominion.. | 3873 | $34,827,300 |

### "Better Homes" Exposition at Hamilton

One of the most successful and attractive exhibits, known as "The Better Homes Show," has just been concluded in the new Armouries in Hamilton. The display, which drew a wide patronage and stirred up much interest, was arranged primarily as an exposition to encourage home-building and owning. Every detail of this angle was driven home through a series of exhibits which included all things from the financing of the house to suitably furnishing it. Every device that helped to reduce the amount of domestic work was also demonstrated. There were 165 booths in the exposition hall and practically every article used in the construction and furnishing of a domicile was on display. A large number of educational exhibits were also scattered throughout the hall. The lumbermen of Hamilton, building contractors and others joined whole-heartedly in the enterprise.

It was stated that at the exposition any visitor could do the following which affords some idea of the comprehensiveness of the display:—

Buy a lot—
Have plans for a home prepared—
Arrange for the excavation—
Make a selection of foundation materials, bricks and lumber—
Let the construction contract—
Select interior finish—
Arrange for modern, fire-proof roofing—
Buy the necessary eavetroughing and drain pipes—
Make a selection of electrical equipment—
Let the electrical contract—
Completely outfit the new home, from attic to cellar—
Personally test labor-saving devices—the modern inventions that have taken the drudgery out of housework—
Contract for the painting of the home—
Arrange for modern, sanitary plumbing—
Engage an expert landscape gardener—
Buy an automobile—
Place insurance upon everything that enters into the construction and equipment of the home—

During the progress of the "Better Homes Week" there were music, singing, radio demonstrations and many dollars' worth of free souvenirs.

Own Your Home, Limited, Toronto, has been incorporated with a capital of $40,000.00 to construct homes and build in all kinds of building materials.

# Sections of Great West are Heavily Wooded

## Prairie Provinces Have Substantial Resources of Pulpwood and Other Timber to Meet Growing Requirements—Ninety-eight Forest Reserves Beyond the Great Lakes

It seems a contradiction in terms to speak of timber or the lumber industry in regard to Manitoba, Saskatchewan and Alberta, that vast territory so widely known as the prairie provinces. But it is the term which is at fault, for the appellation is a misnomer and only the southern section of these provinces, that area first penetrated and settled, can strictly be called prairie, and, even so, this apparently treeless vast is relieved by general clumps of brush, by the wooded banks of river and stream, and by the density of forestation on its rocky eminences. When the northern boundary of this prairie expanse is passed, a fine luxuriant parkland is pierced with bush, at first light and scattered, but becoming thicker and denser as progress is made northwards. Finally, in the north, heavy woods and swamps are encountered containing much merchantable timber and pulpwood.

With the vast stands of merchantable timber in other provinces existing in close contiguity to the railroads and other transportation means, and with the comparatively recent settlement of the western provinces and the almost exclusive attention paid to agriculture and its many phases, not a great deal of attention has been paid to timber in the west, excluding, of course, British Columbia, where the industry is of prime importance. But in the light of the universal talk of conservation of forest wealth, the heavy toll put upon other Canadian forest areas by reason of the wasteful methods of other countries in the past in regard to their own forests, with the possibility of their depletion or indeed, exhaustion if the most rigorous methods of preservation are not extended, it will not be long before greater attention is paid to the more remote wooded areas of the prairie provinces and these areas be called upon to help out in the situation. A future awaits the prairie provinces at the hands of the lumberman and pulpman.

### Eight Million Acres of Forest

It has been estimated that there are about 500,000,000 acres of forest lands in Canada, about half of which is covered with merchantable timber, and the value of the forest products in 1918 was $279,-548,011. The prairie provinces contain about eight million acres of commercial timber lands, 5,400,000 acres of which are in Alberta, 1,920,000 acres in Manitoba and 750,000 acres in Saskatchewan. In addition to this, there are large resources of pulpwood upon which no really accurate estimate has been made.

Manitoba is about 70 per cent. wooded, and in this province the principal heavily timbered sections have been set aside as government forest reserves located west of the Red river, in the southern part of the province. On the upper plateau of this section are spruce, jack pine and tamarac; in the lower plateau are found poplar and white birch; in the coulees elm, oak, basswood and white pine. The principal trees in order of present importance are: White spruce, black spruce, jack pine, tamarac, balsam, fir, aspen, cedar, burr oak, paper or white birch, white elm, green ash, white oak, balsam, balm of Gilead, black ash, basswood, Manitoba maple, cotton-wood, red ash and mountain maple.

Whilst little extensive commercial use has been made of these woods from the lack of exploitation due to conditions already noted, they possess a potential worth commercially of some magnitude, and have already been extensively made use of locally. The province, it has been estimated, contains about 1,920,000 feet of saw timber or 4,000,000 feet B. M.

### Merchantable Forests of Saskatchewan

Alberta is estimated to contain about twenty-one billion board feet of saw timber, the principal species being spruce, lodgepole pine, Douglas fir, poplar, balsam, fir, white birch and tamarac. Fires have wrought destructive havoc in the forests of the province, much of which has been devastated and of the burnt-over areas the reproduction is mainly lodgepole pine, with areas of poplar and birch. Lumbering operations are principally confined to the Rocky mountains reserve, which contains all the lumber at present merchantable in Alberta. There are nearly eight hundred square miles at present under license or permits issued prior to the establishment of the reserve.

In Saskatchewan the area actually timbered with merchantable trees is about 750,000 acres, the country to the northeast being heav-

ily timbered with spruce, tamarac and jack pine. Prince Albert is the center of Saskatchewan's lumber industry.

Though the timber trade of the prairie provinces has not as yet made a startling record in Dominion figures, it is provincially of a high value and of great local importance, and the economic history of the great plains would have been very different but for their possession of the northern woods. Whilst little, if any, of the timber cut ever gets beyond the borders of its native province, there is a local market whose demands are increasing yearly. The prairie provinces are showing a steady expansion perhaps unprecedented in the history of new countries, and their cities and towns and, above all, their agricultural areas, have need of lumber in ever increasing quantities.

The lumber cut for the year 1918, the latest return available, for the prairie provinces, was, according to the Dominion bureau of statistics, 152,270 million feet B. M. valued at $3,836,053. This is divided among the three provinces as follows: Manitoba, 54,407 million feet, worth 1,240,052; Saskatchewan, 75,835 million feet, worth $2,-122,307, and Alberta, 22,388 million feet, worth $473,694. The total cut of the three provinces represents nearly three per cent. of the cut all over the Dominion.

### Controlled By Federal Authorities

In the provinces of Alberta, Saskatchewan and Manitoba, in common with the northwest territories and the railway belt in British Columbia, the forests are administered by the department of the interior of the Dominion government, from whom leases of timber or permits to cut upon forest reserves must be secured. There are 39 forest reserves in western Canada, 26 of which, with an aggregate area of nearly 32,500 square miles, are situated in the three prairie provinces.

Little has yet been noted of the pulpwood resources of these provinces, an important item at the present time in view of the heavy call being made upon the forests of the east and the commencement made upon those of British Columbia on the Pacific coast. Roughly, it may be stated that the prairie provinces have substantial resources of the raw material for the continent's paper mills which are delving into every corner of Canada's forests for supplies, and that these are practically untapped as yet.

### New Settlement Plan Interests Lumbermen

An innovation of great importance, which is to be put to trial by the Provincial Government was announced recently by Hon. J. E. Perreault, Minister of Colonization, when he stated that an order-in-council had been signed at his request, by which tenders will be asked for the clearing of 300 acres of timber on thirty lots in the Matapedia Valley and also for the building of a house and necessary buildings to establish a settler and his family. On those thirty lots provisions are made in the order-in-council to have the work done by lumber companies, which will be paid by timber which will be given to compensate for the expenses incurred. This is a new policy altogether and after the next session the Government will decide whether many colonization centres will be dealt with in this manner. The settlers will be supplied with those lots under special conditions.

### Seven Loggers Win Million Dollar Suit

A judgment in which liability is expected to exceed $1,000,000 was rendered recently in Vancouver by Mr. Justice Murphy against the Canada Timber & Lands, Limited, whose head office is in Toronto. The successful plaintiffs are seven loggers who entered into a contract with the company to purchase two hundred million feet of timber at Toba River, B. C. A portion of this had been logged when the company repudiated the contract.

According to the plaintiffs, the damages are the profits which they would have made from the contract, and they are calculated at $1,250,000.

The decision is to be appealed, and, in any event, it is said the case will be carried to the Privy Council in London. The plaintiffs are Julius Carlos Clausen and his associates.

The sawmill owned by Rouleau, Rocheleau & Dumontier, in the village of St. Barthelemi, Que., was destroyed by fire recently. The blaze spread to several dwellings nearby, which were consumed.

# EDGINGS

The shingle mill of Skinner & Cole, North Keppel, Ont., which was recently destroyed by fire will be rebuilt.

The sawmill of J. K. Eggenberger & Sons, High Prairie, Alta., was completely destroyed by fire recently.

The sawmill of Leger Giguere, Weedon, Quebec, was recently damaged by fire to the extent of $17,000. Some new equipment may be needed.

The owners of the Pacific Pulp Mills Co., Ocean Falls, B. C., are contemplating the construction of a diversion dam at Ocean Falls, which will cost $500,000.

Recently a fire started in the mill of the General Lumber & Mfg. Co., at Sherbrooke, P.Q. The blaze gave the firemen a hard battle and the damage done was estimated at $35,000.

The Hocken Lumber Co. are erecting a new office at their retail yard corner Van Horne St. & Dovercourt Road, Toronto. The interior of the building is finished in hardwood.

Montreal Hardwood Co. Ltd., Montreal, have been granted a federal charter to manufacture and market logs, pulpwood, lumber, including hard and softwoods. Capital $49,500.00.

The Schroeder Mills & Timber Co. of Milwaukee, Wis., whose mills are at Pakesley, Ont., have opened a sales office at 305 Stair Building, Toronto. F. J. Archibald being in charge.

The seaplane which is being used in the Ontario Government Service of Fire Rangers, is making its headquarters at Parry Sound during the summer. The limits in that district will be patrolled regularly.

M. Martin Lumber Co., Limited, Huntsville, Ont., have been incorporated with a capital of $50,000.00 to conduct a general lumber business dealing in all kinds of lumber, saw logs, fence posts and other forest products.

The Ruddy Mfg. Co. Limited, Brantford, Ont., who recently took over the business formerly conducted by Ham Bros., are installing a battery of three 11-car Sidman lumber curing kilns. These kilns will be of concrete construction.

The Canadian Match Co., Pembroke, Ont., recently placed notices in their factory that beginning July 1, the employees will get Saturday afternoons off and all legal holidays with full pay, provided the men work earnestly during the week.

Lincoln Mills, Limited, Montreal, have been incorporated with federal charter to operate sawmills in the manufacture of lumber and pulpwood. Capital $1,575,000. G. A. Campbell, K. C. and E. P. Harrain subsequently completely quenched the blaze.

Batchawana Timber & Improvement Co. Limited, Batchawana Bay, Ont., have been granted a provincial charter to conduct a general lumber and pulp wood business. Capital $30,000.00. B. W. Sippy and A. F. Sippy both of Chicago are two of the incorporators.

R. A. McInnis, manager of the Abitibi Power & Paper Co., Iroquois Falls, Ont., who for the past year and a half has been president of the Associated Boards of Trade of Northern Ontario, has resigned the latter position owing to pressure of private business.

St. Lawrence Paper Mills, Limited, Montreal, have recently been granted a federal charter to manufacture and market lumber, pulpwood and other forest products. Capital $1,200,000. Two of the incorporators are: J. G. Cartwright, office manager and Lawrence MacFarlane solicitor, both of Montreal.

The annual meeting of the shareholders of the Prince Rupert Pulp & Paper Co. was held recently in Vancouver. Interest on the first mortgage bonds, government licenses and fees, amounting to $300,000., are in arrears and will have to be met in a few months so the directors state.

Falls Machinery & Supplies, Limited, Niagara Falls, Ont., have been granted a provincial charter to manufacture and market engines, boilers and other machinery supplies for lumbermen. Capital $40,000.00. S. R. Frost and John C. Gardner, both of Niagara Falls are two of the incorporators.

The town of Chicoutimi, Que. and district which was recently threatened by the bush fires are now safe after several days of strenuous fire fighting. The recent heavy rains through the province of Quebec has saved many valuable tracts of timber and the fires are now all extinguished or under control.

The Fraser Companies, of Edmundston, N. B., state that they are working on plans to replace the mill at Baker Brook which was burned recently. They expect to have the new mill constructed and

in operation within the next few months. The new plant will be about the same capacity as the former one.

Writing to the "Canada Lumberman" a correspondent in Ottawa says,—"Everything is going very satisfactorily in the lumber industry, and we are pleased to report that local dealers find business very much improved. They all say that things are a great deal better than they have been for some time past."

Fire broke out recently in the lumber yard of O. P. Moxley, Dorchester, Ont., and for a time threatened the destruction of his sawmill and planing mill. The blaze was discovered shortly before noon and was extinguished through the effective service of a bucket brigade, supplemented by water from a power tank in the yards.

There is quite a demand just now for men in the northern camps. The cutting of pulpwood is progressing in the Temiskaming district and recently the T. S. Woollings Co., of Englehart, sent word to ago, thereby establishing what is believed to be a record for the Toronto that they required several men. the piece-work offered being at $2.50 per cord for poplar and $3.00 per cord for spruce cut and peeled.

"Dad" Denison, Clarkson, Ont., farmer, is a handy man with the broad axe. He built an attractive log bungalow of natural pine and cedar logs which recalls the days of pioneer life. Mr. Denison also erected two similar log cabins at Lorne Park for Ernest Thompson Seton when the noted author wrote his "Erindale Fox" and other sketches.

It is stated that the Riordon Co., Montreal, lately sold its standing pine on the Gatineau Limits in the province of Quebec at a price much ahead of expectations and that the first payment was made recently. The new financing plans of the company are also said to be completed. Some bank loans have either been wiped out or greatly reduced, while the mills are operating at a good profit.

Howard McFarlane, of the S. D. Warren Co., Westbrook, Maine, recently paid a visit to the company's holdings of pulpwood at Cabano, Que., where a system of carriers will be installed for taking the logs from the pond and conveying them to the pile from which they will be transferred to cars with the least amount of trouble. Mr. McFarlane says that the pulpwood industry is still very flat.

A charter has been granted to the Grant Lumber Co. Limited, of Tilley, N. B. The president of the new organization is H. C. Grant, of Tilley, N. B.; Vice-president, F. E. Whitman, Winthrop, Mass.; secretary-treasurer, Warren Dexter, Doaktown, N. B. The company is at present operating a portable mill and sawing long lumber but expects to branch out more extensively in the near future.

The sawmill of the Belgian Industrial Co. at Shawinigan Falls, Que., is not operating this year. The Riverside Mfg. Co., of Three Rivers, Que., are, however, putting in a new carriage, edger, steam nigger and loader, and have put in some improvements to the trimming and sorting tables. These have all been completed and the mill started operation on June 1st and expects to have a successful season.

Reports from Ottawa state that bush fires have been raging at different points along the G.T.R. Depot-Harbour-Ottawa line between Rock Lake and Algonquin Park. One fire extended for about four miles along the railway, though some distance back from it, west of Barry's Bay, and another for about five miles west to Rock Lake. Other fires are burning between the railway and Alyan Lake. However no valuable timber was in the path of the flames.

The Don Valley Paper Mills, Todmorden, which was recently damaged by fire to the approximate extent of $100,000 was an old landmark of the old Don Valley industrial district and was known as the Taylor Paper Mills years ago. The fire broke out in the paper storage room and was started by boys playing with matches. The Toronto fire department was called and succeeded in saving $250,. 000 worth of machinery, including a huge paper making machine,.

The sawmill of the Columbia River Lumber Co. started operations recently at Golden, B. C. The mill is the largest electrically-driven plant in the interior of British Columbia and has a capacity of 300,000 feet a day. The logs are being hauled from Donald, seventeen miles west of Golden, to a point five miles south of Golden where they are dumped into the Columbia River and floated down a boom to the mill. A special train is employed hauling these logs from the company's limits.

Forest fires raged recently in many parts of old Quebec and owing to the prolonged drought, threatened to do a great deal of damage. At Chicoutimi a fire, which has been smouldering for two weeks and has been looked upon as dangerous, was fanned to life by a heavy wind, 250 men fought the outbreak and all the available forest rangers and fire-fighting crews of the province were out to check the ravages of the flames at different points, but a heavy downpour of ris, advocate, both of Montreal are two of the incorporators.

## ALPHABETICAL INDEX TO ADVERTISERS

This Linn Logging Tractor, this past season, on a twelve mile haul— encountering en route steep down grades and long stiff up grades moved 2896 cords of mixed spruce and hemlock. The approximate equivalent in pine would be 1,425,000 feet Doyle's Rule.

# THE LINN LOGGING TRACTOR

The Canadian Lumberman of today is finding increasing difficult woods problems confronting him.

His Hauls are each season becoming longer, and the efficiency of the horse, as a haulage factor, is in the same ratio, decreasing.

The stream drive is expensive and troublesome.

Therefore—Reliable, Economical Mechanical haulage must be resorted to—and the only medium that will fulfill all the requirements of the Canadian Logger is the Linn Logging Tractor—designed and developed during the past eight years—exclusively for log hauling in the North Country.

During the past season, we had a very comprehensive motion picture taken—showing Linn Logging Tractors in operation over various limits.—If you have not already seen this film, we will gladly arrange to show it to you, in your own office—it is a revelation of logging methods—and not a set and arranged picture—it was taken over different operations, under ordinary working conditions.

And we also have a very comprehensive catalogue about to come from the printers. Your request for a copy will be immediately honored.

*—Logging Department—*

# MUSSENS LIMITED

**Dubrule Building**  **Philips Place**  **MONTREAL**

# CANADA LUMBERMAN BUYERS' DIRECTORY

The following regulations apply to all advertisers:—Eighth page, every issue, three headings;
quarter page, six headings; half page, twelve headings; full page, twenty-four headings

**ALLIGATORS**
Payette Company, P.
West, Peachy & Sons

**BABBITT METAL**
General Supply Co., of Canada. Ltd.

**BALE TIES**
Laidlaw Bale Tie Company

**BAND MILLS**
Hamilton Company, William
Waterous Engine Works Company
Yates Machine Company, P. B.

**BAND SAW BLADES**
Simonds Mfg., Co.

**BAND RESAWS**
Mershon & Company, W. B.
Yates Machine Co., P.B.

**BARKERS**
Bertrand, F. X., La Compagnie
Manufacturiere.
Smith Foundry & Machine Co.

**BEARING METAL**
Canada Metal Co.
Beveridge Supply Co., Ltd.

**BEDSTEADS (STEEL)**
Simmons Limited

**BELT DRESSING**
Dominion Belting Co.
General Supply of Canada. Ltd.
McLaren, D. K. Ltd.

**BELT FASTENERS**
McLaren, D. K. Ltd.

**BELTING**
Canadian Consolidated Rubber Co.
Dominion Belting Co. . . . . . . . . . . .
General Supply Company
Goodhue & Co., J. L.
Gutta Percha & Rubber Company
D. K. McLaren, Limited
York Belting Co.

**BLOWERS**
Reed & Co., Geo. W.
B. F. Sturtevant Co., of Canada. Ltd.
Toronto Blower Company

**BOILERS**
Engineering & Machine Works of
Canada.
Hamilton Company, William
Waterous Engine Works Company

**BOILER PRESERVATIVE**
Beveridge Supply Company
Shell-Bar, Boico Supply Co., Ltd.

**BOX MACHINERY**
Yates Machine Company, P. B.

**CABLE CONVEYORS**
Engineering & Machine Works of
Canada.
Hamilton Company, William
Waterous Engine Works Company

**CAMP SUPPLIES**
Davies Company, William
Dr. Bell Veterinary Wonder Co.
Johnson, A. H.
Turner & Sons, J. J.
Woods Manufacturing Co., Ltd.

**CANT HOOKS**
General Supply Co, of Canada, Ltd.
Pink & Company, Thomas

**CEDAR**
Bury & Co., Robt.
Cameron Lumber Co.
Canadian Western Lumber Co.
Chesbro, R. G.
Dry Wood Lumber Co.
Fesserton Timber Company
Fesserton Timber Company
McElroy Lumber Co., Ltd.
Muir & Kirkpatrick
Rose, McLaurin, Limited
Terry & Gordon
Thurston- Flavelle Lumber Co.
Vancouver Lumber Company.
Victoria Lumber & Mfg. Co.

**CHAINS**
Canadian Link-Belt Company, Ltd.
General Supply Co., of Canada. Ltd.
Engineering & Machine Works of
Canada .
Hamilton Company, William
Pink & Company, Thomas
Waterous Engine Works Company

**CLOTHING**
Woods Mfg. Company

**CONVEYOR MACHINERY**
Canadian Link-Belt Company, Ltd.
General Supply Co., of Canada, Ltd.
Hamilton Company, William
Hopkins & Co., Ltd., F. H.
Waterous Engine Works Company

**CORDWOOD**
McClung, McLellan & Berry

**COUPLING (Shaft)**
Engineering & Machine Works of
Canada

**CRANES**
Hopkins & Co., Ltd., F. H.
Canadian Link-Belt Company, Ltd.

**CUTTER HEADS**
Shimer Cutter Head Company
Yates Machine Co., P.B.

**CYPRESS**
Maus Lumber Co., Chas. O.
Wistar, Underhill & Nixon

**DERRICKS AND DERRICK
FITTINGS**
Hopkins & Co., Ltd., F. H.

**DOORS**
Canadian Western Lumber Co.
Gardiner, P. W. & Son
Mason, Gordon & Co.
Terry & Gordon

**DRAG SAWS**
Gerlach Company, Peter
Hamilton Company, William

**DRYERS**
Coe Manufacturing Company
B. F. Sturtevant Co. of Canada. Ltd.

**DUST COLLECTORS**
Reed & Co., Geo. W.
B. F. Sturtevant Co. of Canada. Ltd.
Toronto Blower Company

**EDGERS**
Hamilton Company, Ltd., William
Green Company, G. Walter
Long Mfg. Company, E.
Payette Company, P.
Waterous Engine Works Company
Yates Machine Co., P.B.

**ELEVATING AND CONVEYING
MACHINERY**
Canadian Link-Belt Comany, Ltd.
Engineering & Machine Works of
Canada
Hamilton Company, William
Waterous Engine Works Company

**ENGINES**
Engineering & Machine Works of
Canada
Hamilton Company, William
Payette Company, P.
Waterous Engine Works Company

**EXCELSIOR MACHINERY**
Elmira Machinery & Transmission
Company

**EXHAUST FANS**
B. F. Sturtevant Co. of Canada. Ltd.
Toronto Blower Company

**EXHAUST SYSTEMS**
Reed & Co., Geo. W.
B. F. Sturtevant Co. of Canada. Ltd.
Toronto Blower Company

**FIBRE BOARD**
Manley Chew

**FILES**
Diston & Sons, Henry
Simonds Canada Saw Company

**FIR**
Apex Lumber Co.
Associated Mjlls, Limited
Bainbridge Lumber Company
Cameron Lumber Co.
Canadian Western Lumber CO.
Canfield, P. L.
Chesbro, R. G.
Dry Wood Lumber Co.
Fesserton Timber Co.
Grier & Sons, Ltd., G. A.
Heeney, Percy E.
Knox Brothers
Mason, Gordon & Co.
McElroy Lumber Co., Ltd.
Robertson & Hackett Sawmills
Rose, McLaurin, Limited
Terry & Gordon
Timberland Lumber Company
Timms, Phillips & Co.
Underhill Lumber Co.
Vancouver Lumber Company
Vanderhoof Lumber Company
Victoria Lumber & Mfg. Company

**FIRE BRICK**
Beveridge Supply Co., Limited
Elk Fire Brick Company of Canada
Shell-Bar, Boico Supply Co., Ltd.

**FIRE FIGHTING APPARATUS**
Waterous Engine Works Company

**FITTINGS**
Crane Limited

**FLOORING**
Cameron Lumber Co.
Chesbro, R. G.
Long-Bell Lumber Company

**GEARS (Cut)**
Smart-Turner Machine Company

**GUARDS (Machinery and Window)**
Canada Wire & Iron Goods Co.

**HARDWOODS**
Anderson Lumber Company, C. G.
Anderson, Shreiner & Mawson
Atlantic Lumber Company
Barrett, Wm.
Black Rock Lumber Co.
Bury & Co., Robt.
Cameron & Company
Edwards & Co., W. C.
Fassett Lumber Company, Limited
Fesserton Timber Co.
Gillespie, James
Gloucester Lumber & Trading Co.
Grier & Sons, Ltd., G. A.
Hart, Hamilton & Jackson
Heeney, Percy E.
Knox Brothers
Kinnon Lumber Co.
Mason & Company, Geo.
Maus Lumber Co., Chas. O.
McDonagh Lumber Company
McLennan Lumber Company
McLung, McLellan & Berry
Pedwell Hardwood Lumber Co.
W. & J. Sharples
Spencer, Limited, C. A.
Strong, G. M.
Summers, James R.

**HARDWOOD FLOORING**
Grier & Sons, Ltd., G. A.

**HARNESS**
Beal Leather Company, R. M.

**HEMLOCK**
Anderson Lumber Company, C. G.
Anderson, Shreiner & Mawson
Bartram & Ball
Beck Lumber Company
Bourgouin, H.
Canadian General Lumber Company
Edwards & Co., W. C.
Fesserton Timber Co.
Grier & Sons, Ltd., G. A.
Hart, Hamilton & Jackson
Hocken Lumber Company
Mason, Gordon & Company
McCormack Lumber Company
McDonagh Lumber Company
McElroy Lumber Co., Ltd.
Robertson & Hackett Sawmills
Spencer, Limited, C. A.
Stalker, Douglas A.
Terry & Gordon
Vancouver Lumber Company
Vanderhoof Lumber Company

**HOISTING AND HAULING
ENGINES**
General Supply Co., of Canada, Ltd.

Installation at the Housing Corporation, Waltham, Mass.

# A Vacuum Cleaner at
# Every Cutting Head

That is exactly what a correctly designed collecting and conveying system means in your plant.

But the system must be installed so that the mill may be kept entirely free from refuse and waste, even when you are running at maximum speed and capacity. There are many other problems connected with your output which must also be taken into consideration.

And that is where the long, varied experience of our collecting and conveying specialists can be of inestimable value to you.

Our engineers will be glad to look over your plant—without the slightest obligation.

*Send for Catalogue No. 261*

## B. F. STURTEVANT COMPANY OF CANADA, LIMITED

TORONTO - - GALT - MONTREAL

—Territorial Representatives—

Empire Engineering & Supply Co., Edmonton, Alta.—Kipp Kelly Ltd., Winnipeg, Man.

Hopkins & Co., Ltd., F. H.

**HOSE**
General Supply Co., of Canada, Ltd.
Gutta Percha & Rubber Company

**INSURANCE**
Barton & Ellis Company
Burns Underwriting Company
Hardy & Company, E. D.
Rankin Benedict Underwriting Co.

**INTERIOR FINISH**
Cameron Lumber Company
Canadian Western Lumber Co.
Canfield, P. L.
Eagle Lumber Company
Mason, Gordon & Co.
Rose, McLaurin, Limited
Terry & Gordon

**KILN DRIED LUMBER**
Bury & Co., Robt.

**KNIVES**
Disston & Sons, Henry
Simonds Canada Saw Company
Waterous Engine Works Company

**LARCH**
Otis Staples Lumber Company

**LATH**
Anderson, Shreiner & Mawson
Apex Lumber Company
Austin & Nicholson
Beck Lumber Company
Cameron Lumber Company
Canadian General Lumber Company
Carew Lumber Company, John
Chaleurs Bay Mills

Dadson, A. T.
Eagle Lumber Company
Fassett Lumber Company, Limited
Foley Lumber Company
Fraser Bryson Lumber Co., Ltd.
Gloucester Lumber & Trading Co.
Grier & Sons, Ltd., G. A.
Harris Tie & Timber Company, Ltd.
Larkin Company, C. A.
Mason & Company, Geo.
McLennan Lumber Company
Miller, W. H. Company
New Ontario Colonization Company
Otis Staples Lumber Company
Power Lumber Company
Price Bros. & Company
Shevlin-Clarke Company
Spencer, Limited, C. A.
Terry & Gordon
U. G. G. Sawmills, Limited
Union Lumber Company
Victoria Harbor Lumber Company

**LATH BOLTERS**
General Supply Co. of Canada, Ltd.
Hamilton Company, William
Payette & Company, P.

**LOCOMOTIVES**
Engineering & Machine Works of Canada
General Supply Co. of Canada, Ltd.
Hopkins & Co., Ltd., F. H.
Climax Manufacturing Company
Montreal Locomotive Works

**LINK-BELT**
Canadian Link-Belt Company
Hamilton Company, William

**LOCOMOTIVE CRANES**
Canadian Link-Belt Company
Hopkins & Co., Ltd., F. H.

**LOGGING ENGINES**
Engineering & Machine Works of Canada

Hopkins & Co., Ltd., F. H.
Mussens Limited

**LOG HAULER**
Engineering & Machine Works of Canada
Green Company, G. Walter
Holt Manufacturing Company
Hopkins & Co., Ltd., F. H.
Payette & Company, P.

**LOGGING MACHINERY AND EQUIPMENT**
General Supply Co. of Canada, Ltd.
Hamilton Company, William
Holt Manufacturing Company
Hopkins & Co., Ltd., F. H.
Payette & Company, P.
Waterous Engine Works Company
West, Peachey & Sons
Mussens Limited

**LUMBER EXPORTS**
Fletcher Corporation

**LUMBER TRUCKS**
Hamilton Company, William
Waterous Engine Works Company

**LUMBERMEN'S BOATS**
Adams Engine Company
Gidley Boat Company
West, Peachey & Sons

**LUMBERMEN'S CLOTHING**
Kitchen Overall & Shirt Company

**MATTRESSES**
Simmons Limited

**METAL REFINERS**
Canada Metal Company

**NAILING MACHINES**
Yates Machine Co., P.B.

**OAK**
Long-Bell Lumber Company
Maus Lumber Co., Chas. O.

**PACKING**
Beveridge Supply Company
Gutta Percha & Rubber Company

**PANELS**
Bury & Company, Robt.

**PAPER**
Beveridge Supply Company
Price Bros. & Company

**PINE**
Anderson Lumber Company, C. G.
Anderson, Shreiner & Mawson
Atlantic Lumber Company
Austin & Nicholson
Barratt, William
Beck Lumber Company
Black Rock Lumber Co.
Cameron & Company
Cameron Lumber Company
Canadian General Lumber Company
Canadian Western Lumber Co.
Canfield, P. L.
Chesbro, R. G.
Cleveland-Sarnia Sawmills Company
Cox, Long & Company
Dadson, A. T.
Dudley, Arthur N.
Eagle Lumber Company
Edwards & Co., W. C.
Excelsior Lumber Company
Fesserton Timber Co.
Fraser Bryson Lumber Co., Ltd.
Gillies Bros. Limited
Gloucester Lumber & Trading Co.
Gordon & Company, George
Goodday & Company, H. R.
Grier & Sons, Ltd., G. A.
Harris Tie & Timber Company, Ltd.
Hart, Hamilton & Jackson
Hettler Lumber Co., Herman H.
Hocken Lumber Company
Julien, Roch
Keewatin Lumber Co.
Lay & Haight
Lloyd, W. Y.
Loggie Company, W. S.
Long-Bell Lumber Company
Mason, Gordon & Co.
Mason & Company, Geo.

# YATES

## Vertical Band Resaw

The V-5 is a Resaw for handling the heaviest work, and is used by the largest and best equipped mills in Canada to-day. One feature is a device which allows either set of rolls to be made rigid or yielding at the will of the operator.

*Our Circular gives you H.P. required, feeds, size of blade, etc. Send for your copy and obtain full information on this Resaw.*

### P. B. Yates Machine Co. Ltd.

**Hamilton          Canada**

Eastern Sales Office

**263 St. James St.                    Montreal, Que.**

McCormack Lumber Company
McFadden & Malloy
McLennan Lumber Company
Montreal Lumber Company
Muir & Kirkpatrick
Northern Lumber Company
Otis Staples Lumber Company
Parry Sound Lumber Company
Rolland Lumber Company
W. & J. Sharples
Shevlin-Clarke Company
Spencer, Limited, C. A.
Stalker, Douglas A.
Strong, G. M.
Summers, James R.
Terry & Gordon
Union Lumber Company
Victoria Harbor Lumber Company
Watson & Todd, Limited

**PLANING MILL EXHAUSTERS**
Toronto Blower Company

**PLANING MILL MACHINERY**
Mershon & Company, W. B.
B. F. Sturtevant Co. of Canada, Ltd.
Toronto Blower Company
Yates Machine Company, P. B.

**POPLAR**
Keewatin Lumber Co.

**POST GRINDERS**
Smith Foundry Company

**POSTS AND POLES**
Anderson, Shreiner & Mawson
Canadian Tie & Lumber Co.
Dupuis, Limited, J. P.
Eagle Lumber Company
Harris Tie & Timber Company, Ltd.
Long-Bell Lumber Company
Mason, Gordon & Co.
McLennan Lumber Company
Terry & Gordon

**PULLEYS AND SHAFTING**
Canadian Link-Belt Company
General Supply Co. of Canada, Ltd.
Green Company, G. Walter
Engineering & Machine Works of Canada
Hamilton Company, William
McLaren, D. K. Ltd.

**PULP MILL MACHINERY**
Canadian Link-Belt Company
Engineering & Machine Works of Canada
Hamilton Company, William
Payette & Company, P.
Waterous Engine Works Company

**PULPWOOD**
British & Foreign Agencies
D'Auteuil Lumber Company
Price Bros. & Company
Scott, Draper & Company

**PUMPS**
General Supply Co. of Canada, Ltd.
Engineering & Machine Works of Canada
Hamilton Company, William
Hopkins & Co., Ltd., F. H.
Smart-Turner Machine Company
Waterous Engine Works Company

**RAILS**
Gartshore, John J.
Hopkins & Co., Ltd., F. H.

**ROOFINGS**
(Rubber, Plastic and Liquid)
Beveridge Supply Company
Reed & Co., Geo. W.

**RUBBER GOODS**
Dunlop Tire & Rubber Goods Co.
Gutta Percha & Rubber Company

**SASH**
Midland Woodworkers

**SAWS**
Atkins & Company, E. C.
Disston & Sons, Henry
General Supply Co. of Canada, Ltd.
Gerlach Company, Peter

Green Company, G. Walter
Hoe & Company, R.
Radcliff Saw Mfg. Company
Shurly Company, Ltd., T. F.
Shurly-Dietrich Company
Simonds Canada Saw Company

**SAW GRINDERS**
Smith Foundry Company

**SAW MILL LINK-BELT**
Canadian Link-Belt Company

**SAW MILL MACHINERY**
Canadian Link-Belt Company
General Supply Co. of Canada, Ltd.
G. Walter Green Company, Ltd.
Hamilton Company, William
La Compagnie Manufacture, F. X. Bertrand
Long Mfg. Company, E.
Mershon & Company, W. B.
Parry Sound Lumber Company
Payette & Company, P.
Waterous Engine Works Company
Yates Machine Company, P. B.

**SAW SHARPENERS**
Hamilton Company, William
Waterous Engine Works Company

**SAW SLASHERS**
Hamilton Company, William
Payette & Company, P.
Waterous Engine Works Company

**SHINGLES**
Apex Lumber Company
Associated Mills, Limited
Brennen & Sons, F. W.
Cameron Lumber Company
Campbell-MacLaurin Lumber Co.
Canadian Western Lumber CO.
Carew Lumber Company, John
Chaleurs Bay Mills
Chesbro, R. G.
D'Auteuil Lumber Company
Dry Wood Lumber Co.
Eagle Lumber Company
Fraser, Companies Limited
Gillespie, James
Gloucester Lumber & Trading Co.
Grier & Sons, Ltd., G. A.
Harris Tie & Timber Co., Ltd.
Heaps & Sons
Heeney, Percy E.
Mason, Gordon & Co.
McLennan Lumber Company
Miller Company, Ltd., W. H.
Rose, McLaurin, Limited
Stalker, Douglas A.
Terry & Gordon
Timms, Phillips & Company
Vancouver Lumber Company
Vanderhoof Lumber Company

**SHINGLE & LATH MACHINERY**
Green Company, C. Walter
Hamilton Company, William
Long Manufacturing Company, E.
Payette & Company, P.
Smith Foundry Company

**SILENT CHAIN DRIVES**
Canadian Link-Belt Company

**SLEEPING EQUIPMENT**
Simmons Limited

**SLEEPING ROBES**
Woods Mfg. Company, Ltd.

**SMOKESTACKS**
Hamilton Company, William
Reed & Co., Geo. W.
Waterous Engine Works Company

**SNOW PLOWS**
Pink & Company, Thomas

**SOLDERS**
Canada Metal Company

**SPARK ARRESTORS**
Reed & Company, Geo. W.
Waterous Engine Works Company

**SPRUCE**
Anderson, Shreiner & Mawson
Barrett, Wm.
Cameron Lumber Company
Campbell, McLaurin Lumber Co.
Canadian Western Lumber Co.
Chesbro, R. G.
Cox, Long & Company
Dadson, A. T.
Dudley Arthur N.
Fassett Lumber Company, Ltd.
Fraser, Companies Limited
Fraser Bryson Lumber Co., Ltd.
Gillies Brothers
Gloucester Lumber & Trading-Co.
Goodday & Company, H. R.
Grier & Sons, Ltd G. A.
Harris Lumber Co., Frank H.
Hart, Hamilton & Jackson
Hocken Lumber Company
Julien, Roch
Keewatin Lumber Co.
Larkin Co., C. A.
Lay & Haight
Lloyd, W. Y.
Loggie Co., W. S.
Mason, Gordon & Co.
McCormack Lumber Co.
McDonagh Lumber Co.
McElroy Lumber Co., Ltd.
McLennan Lumber Company
Muir & Kirkpatrick
New Ontario Colonization Co.
Northern Lumber Mills
Power Lumber Co.
Price Bros. & Company
Rolland Lumber Co,
Rose, McLaurin, Limited
W. & J. Sharples
Spencer, Limited, C. A.
Strong, G. M.
Terry & Gordon
U. G. G. Sawmills, Limited
Vanderhoof Lumber Company

**STEAM SHOVELS**
Hopkins & Co., Ltd., F. H.

**STEEL CHAIN**
Canadian Link-Belt Company
Hopkins & Co., Ltd., F. H.
Waterous Engine Works Company

**STEAM PLANT ACCESSORIES**
Waterous Engine Works Company

**STEEL BARRELS**
Smart-Turner Machine Company

**STEEL DRUMS**
Smart-Turner Machine Company

**TARPAULINS**
Turner & Sons, J. J.
Woods Manufacturing Company Ltd.

**TANKS**
Hopkins & Co., Ltd., F. H.

**TENTS**
Turner & Sons, J. J.
Woods Mfg. Company

**TIES**
Austin & Nicholson
Carew Lumber Co., John
Canadian Tie & Lumber Co.
D'Auteuil Lumber Co.
Gloucester Lumber & Trading Co.
Harris Tie & Timber Company Ltd.
McLennan Lumber Company
Miller, W. H. Co.
Price Bros. & Company
Scott, Draper & Co.
Terry & Gordon

**TIMBER BROKERS**
Bradley, R. R.
Cant & Kemp
Farnworth & Jardine
Wright, Graham & Co.

**TIMBER CRUISERS AND ESTIMATORS**
Savage & Bartlett
Sewell, James W.

**TIMBER LANDS**
Department of Lands & Forests, Ont.

**TOWING MACHINES**
Payette & Company, P.
West, Peachey & Sons

**TRACTORS**
Holt Manufacturing Company
Hopkins & Co., Ltd., F. H.
Mussens Limited

**TRANSMISSION MACHINERY**
Canadian Link-Belt Company
Engineering & Machine Works of Canada
General Supply Co. of Canada, Ltd.,
Grand Rapids Vapor Kiln
Hamilton Company, William
Waterous Engine Works Co.

**TRUCKS**
Tudhope Anderson Co.

**TURBINES**
Engineering & Machine Works of Canada
Hamilton Company, William
B. F. Sturtevant Co. of Canada, Ltd.

**VALVES**
Crane, Limited

**VAPOR KILNS**
Grand Rapids Vapor Kiln
B. F. Sturtevant Co. of Canada, Ltd.

**VENEERS**
Bury & Co. Robt.

**VENEER DRYERS**
Coe Manufacturing Company
Sturtevant Co., B. F. of Canada Ltd.

**VENEER MACHINERY**
Coe Manufacturing Company

**VETERINARY REMEDIES**
Dr. Bell Vetinerary Wonder Co.
Johnson, A. H.

**WARPING TUGS**
West, Peachey & Sons

**WATER WHEELS**
Engineering & Machine Works of Canada
Hamilton Company, William

**WIRE**
Canada Metal Co.
Laidlaw Bale Tie Company
Canada Wire & Iron Goods Co.

**WIRE CLOTH**
Canada Wire & Iron Goods Co.

**WIRE ROPE**
Canada Wire & Iron Goods Co.
Hopkins & Co., Ltd., F. H.
Dominion Wire Rope Co.
Greening Wire Co., B.

**WOODWORKING MACHINERY**
General Supply Co. of Canada, Ltd.
Long Manufacturing Company, E.
Mershon & Company, W. B.
Waterous Engine Works Co.
Yates Machine Company, P. B.

**WOOD PRESERVATIVES**
Beveridge Supply Company
Austin & Nicholson
New Ontario Colonization Company
Power Lumber Co.

**WOOD PULP**
Austin & Nicholson
New Ontario Colonization Co.
Power Lumber Co.

Lightning Source UK Ltd.
Milton Keynes UK
UKHW010455060219
336804UK00008B/1058/P